BaseBall america®
2011 PROSPECT
HANDBOOK

BASEBALL AMERICA INC. · DURHAM, N.C.

FOR GREAT PROSPECTS COVERAGE
ALL YEAR, VISIT ...

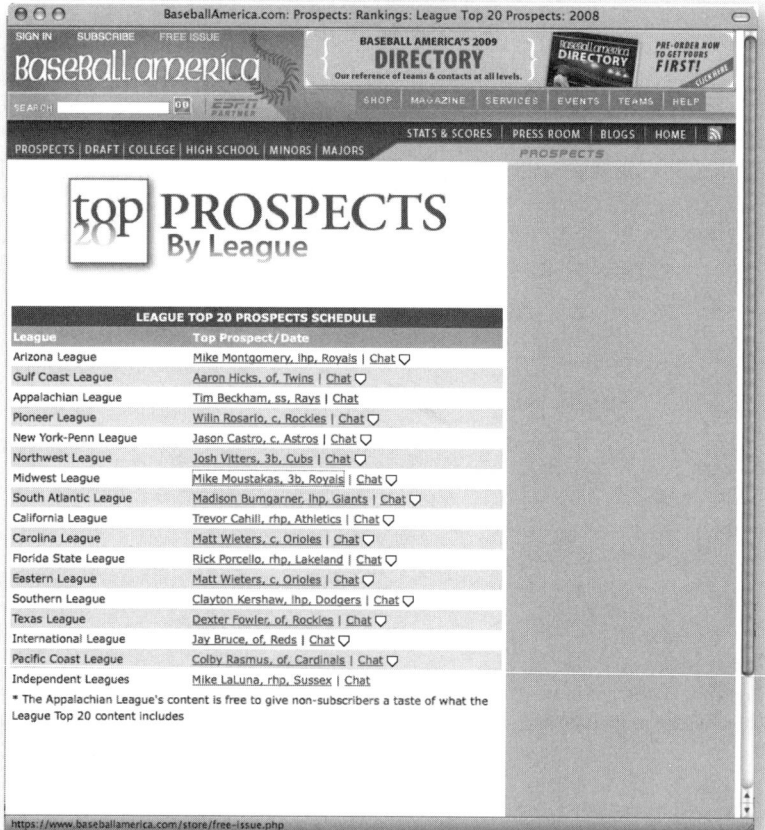

www.BaseballAmerica.com

BaseBall america
2011 PROSPECT
HANDBOOK

Editors
Jim Callis, Will Lingo, John Manuel

Assistant Editors
Ben Badler, J.J. Cooper, Matt Eddy, Aaron Fitt,
Conor Glassey, Josh Leventhal, Nathan Rode, Jim Shonerd

Database and Application Development
Brent Lewis

Contributing Writers
Andy Baggarly, James Bailey, Bill Ballew,
Matthew Forman, Derrick Goold, Tom Haudricourt,
Dejan Kovacevic, Bill Mitchell, Tracy Ringolsby, Phil Rogers

Photo Editor
Nathan Rode

Design & Production
Sara Hiatt McDaniel, Tiffany Schwarz, Linwood Webb

Cover Photo
Bryce Harper by Tom DiPace

BaseBall america

PRESIDENT/PUBLISHER: Lee Folger
EDITORS IN CHIEF: Will Lingo, John Manuel
EXECUTIVE EDITOR: Jim Callis
DESIGN & PRODUCTION DIRECTOR: Sara Hiatt McDaniel
TECHNOLOGY MANAGER: Brent Lewis

BaseballAmerica.com

EDITOR'S NOTE: Transactions for this book go through Dec. 13, so the last significant player transactions included here came out of the Rule 5 draft and the Cliff Lee signing with Philadelphia. As always, you can find players even if they have changed organizations by using the handy index in the back. We also have a scouting report for Japanese free agent Tsuyoshi Nishioka on Page 494. >> For the purposes of this book, a prospect is any player who has no more than 50 innings pitched, 30 relief appearances or 130 at-bats in the major leagues, regardless of service time. Finally, the grades you'll find for each team's drafts are based solely on the quality of the players signed, with no consideration for who players were traded for or how many picks a team might have lost.

TABLE OF CONTENTS

KEN BABBITT

302

The Yankees signed Venezuelan catcher Jesus Montero for $1.65 million in 2006, and he's been a fixture in the Prospect Handbook ever since. He repeats as New York's No. 1 prospect this year.

When I sit bolt upright in bed at 4 a.m., worried about how we're going to get all this done, that's when I know the Christmas season has arrived.

Welcome to the 10th anniversary of the Prospect Handbook, everyone! We had no idea what we were undertaking when we lit this candle back in 2000, but we're happy the book has proven so popular and has quickly grown into our signature publication.

The wives and children of the three editors you see on the title page almost certainly wish the book didn't have to go to press in mid-December, but it would be hard for us to do it much earlier, and if we did it much later you wouldn't have it in your greedy little hands before spring training. That means that while the world is cranking up for the holidays and winding down the business year, we're burning the midnight oil making sure DiDi Gregorius' scouting report is just right.

I realize this sounds like I'm complaining, and in the middle of it, when 15 teams are done and 15 teams are still stacked up in front of us, I do wonder if I should have gone into haberdashery. But then the teams get done, one by one, as they always have, and the beauty of the book starts to emerge.

Did I say beauty? Yes I did. This book is far from perfect, much as we try. But I defy you to find a book that has as much care put into its pages. If you've been reading these introductions over the years—we hope to collect them into their own volume eventually—you know I have tried in various ways to quantify the hours of work and thousands of words that are contained between these covers. This time around, let me just say simply that we never cut corners. When we're getting down toward deadline, I would love to tell Jim Callis to speed up his editing process so we can get the teams done more quickly. Then I remember how meticulously everything is reviewed, and how that comes through on every page.

After we finish the book each year, we go over ideas on how we can do the book better next time, reviewing not only what goes in the book but also the process of how we put it together. I would hate to say we have it down to a science, because if that were true then the aforementioned night terrors probably wouldn't be necessary. But we have polished the book and the process up pretty well, to the point that changes we make are more evolutionary than revolutionary.

The evolutionary steps this year are some changes in the statistics we provide for each player, as well as the addition of numerical scouting grades for the top prospect in each organization. The scouting grades are the result of feedback from readers, who love the specificity that a numerical grade provides. (For those of you unfamiliar with the grading scale scouts use, you can see more about it on the facing page.) Of course, some readers wanted us to provide grades for all 900 prospects, but while that isn't feasible, we thought this was a good start.

On the statistical front, we've added caught stealing numbers for hitters, and groundout/airout and WHIP (walks plus hits divided by innings) for pitchers. Caught stealing is a simple addition, and it gives you more information about how effective a player is in utilizing his speed. Groundout/airout (designated in the stat lines as G/A) and WHIP are two important rate stats that give you greater insight into a pitcher's style and effectiveness. To accommodate those numbers, we eliminated runs and earned runs from pitchers' stats. We figure ERA relays enough information on that front. For groundout/airout numbers, we used the best data available to us, which were raw groundout and airout numbers for the previous two seasons. We hope to add earlier years in future editions of the book and have a more robust calculation, but the numbers do get the point across about whether a pitcher generates a lot of ground balls. Thanks to technology manager Brent Lewis for his diligence in incoporating these statistical improvements, and in making the data in the book all run so smoothly.

As always, thanks are due to the talented writers who provide all the information in this book. We're fortunate to have much of this talent in-house at Baseball America, and 10 freelancers who round out our dream team of prospect writers.

Thanks also to our fabulous design and production staff, led by director Sara Hiatt McDaniel and assisted by Linwood Webb and Tiffany Schwarz. It's Sara and I that actually sit at her computer and give the pages one last look-see before sending them off to the printer, and Lord only knows how many things she has cleaned up for us before the final product comes out.

And of course, thank you for buying the book and making it so much fun to do every year. Sure it's a daunting project, but it's also the culmination of everything we do at Baseball America and probably our most satisfying labor as well.

WILL LINGO
EDITOR IN CHIEF
BASEBALL AMERICA

Among all the scouting lingo you'll come across in this book, perhaps no terms are more telling and prevalent than "profile" and "projection."

When scouts evaluate a player, their main objective is to identify—or project—what the player's future role will be in the major leagues. Each organization has its own philosophy when it comes to grading players, so we talked to scouts from several teams to provide general guidelines.

The first thing to know is what scouts are looking for. In short, tools. These refer to the physical skills a player needs to be successful in the major leagues. For a position player, the five basic tools are hitting, hitting for power, fielding, arm strength and speed. For a pitcher, the tools are based on the pitches he throws. Each pitch is graded, as well as a pitcher's control, delivery and durability.

The profiling system continues to evolve. Baseball is coming out of an era of historic offensive proportions, and in the first three years of the post-Mitchell Report era, Toronto's Jose Bautista became the only American Leaguer to top 40 home runs, with 54 last season. While the emphasis in recent years has tilted profiles more and more towards offense, speed and defense have begun to creep higher up the list of priorities.

While more emphasis has been placed on hitting—which also covers getting on base—fielding and speed remain at a premium up the middle. As teams have sacrificed defense at the corner outfield slots, they continue to seek speedy center fielders to make up ground in the alleys. Most scouts prefer at least a 55 runner (on the 20-80 scouting scale; see chart) at short and center field, but as power increases at those two positions, running comes down.

Shortstops need range and at least average arm strength, and second basemen need to be quick on the pivot. Teams are more willing to put up with an immobile corner infielder if he can mash.

Arm strength is the one tool moving way down preference lists. For a catcher, it was always the No. 1 tool, though in today's game, scouts are looking for more offensive production from the position. Receiving skills, including game-calling, blocking pitches and release times, can make up for the lack of a plus arm.

On the mound, it doesn't just come down to pure stuff. While a true No. 1 starter on a first-division team should have a couple of 70 or 80 pitches in his repertoire, such as Felix Hernandez and Tim

SCOUTING SCALE

When grading a player's tools, scouts use a standard 20-80 scale. When you read that a pitcher throws an above-average slider, it can be interpreted as a 60 pitch, or a plus pitch. Plus-plus is 70, or well-above-average, and so on. Scouts don't throw 80s around very freely. Here's what each grade means:

80	OUTSTANDING
70	WELL-ABOVE-AVERAGE
60	ABOVE-AVERAGE
50	MAJOR LEAGUE AVERAGE
40	BELOW-AVERAGE
30	WELL-BELOW-AVERAGE
20	POOR

Lincecum, they also need to produce 200-plus innings, 30 starts and consistent quality starts.

A player's overall future potential is also graded on the 20-80 scale, though some teams use a letter grade. This number is not just the sum of his tools, but rather a profiling system and a scout's ultimate opinion of the player.

70-80 (A): This category is reserved for the elite players in baseball. This player will be a perennial all-star, the best player at his position, one of the top five starters in the game or a frontline closer. Josh Hamilton, Felix Hernandez and Albert Pujols reside here.

60-69 (B): You'll find all-star-caliber players here: No. 2 starters on a championship club and first-division players. See Matt Cain, Brian McCann and Jayson Werth.

55-59 (C+): The majority of first-division starters are found in this range, including quality No. 2 and 3 starters, frontline set-up men and second-tier closers.

50-54 (C): Solid-average everyday major leaguers. Most are not first-division regulars. This group also includes No. 4 and 5 starters.

45-49 (D+): Fringe everyday players, backups, some No. 5 starters, middle relievers, pinch-hitters and one-tool players.

40-44 (D): Up-and-down roster fillers, situational relievers and 25th players.

38-39 (O): Organizational players who provide depth for the minor leagues but are not considered future major leaguers.

20-37 (NP): Not a prospect.

An Overview

Another feature of the Prospect Handbook is a depth chart of every organization's minor league talent. This shows you at a glance what kind of talent a system has and provides even more prospects beyond the Top 30.

Players are usually listed on the depth charts where we think they'll ultimately end up. To help you better understand why players are slotted at particular positions, we show you here what scouts look for in the ideal candidate at each spot, with individual tools ranked in descending order.

LF
Power
Hitting
Fielding
Arm Strength
Speed

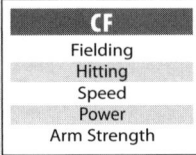

CF
Fielding
Hitting
Speed
Power
Arm Strength

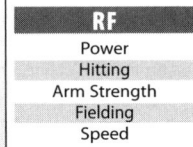

RF
Power
Hitting
Arm Strength
Fielding
Speed

3B
Power
Hitting
Fielding
Arm Strength
Speed

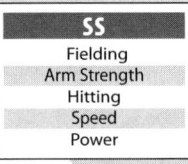

SS
Fielding
Arm Strength
Hitting
Speed
Power

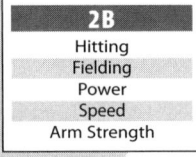

2B
Hitting
Fielding
Power
Speed
Arm Strength

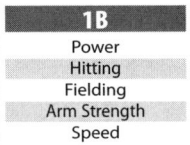

1B
Power
Hitting
Fielding
Arm Strength
Speed

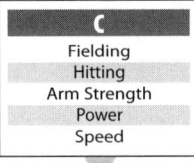

C
Fielding
Hitting
Arm Strength
Power
Speed

STARTING PITCHERS

No. 1 starter	No. 2 starter	No. 3 starter	No. 4-5 starters
• Two plus pitches	• Two plus pitches	• One plus pitch	• Command of two major league pitches
• Average third pitch	• Average third pitch	• Two average pitches	• Average velocity
• Plus-plus command	• Average command	• Average command	• Consistent breaking ball
• Plus makeup	• Average makeup	• Average makeup	• Decent changeup

CLOSER
• One dominant pitch
• Second plus pitch
• Plus command
• Plus-plus makeup

TOP 50 PROSPECTS

When Baseball America ranks prospects, there's almost always a byline attributing who finally put the players in order, who decided, "OK, this guy's 6 and this guy's 7." But all our rankings are more than one person's opinion. They are most often a reflection of the consensus of sources on the subject—managers, coaches, scouts, front-office personnel, the whole spectrum.

Except here, really. In this section of the Handbook, we get personal. Sifting through all the information we've gathered to this point, three of our editors give their own personal takes on the game's top 50 prospects. This helps form the basis of the arguments that shape Baseball America's Top 100 Prospects. That list comes out during spring training, and we consider it the definitive guide to the best talent in the minor leagues.

The rules for these lists are the same for any prospect who appears in the Handbook: no more than 130 at-bats, 50 innings or 30 relief appearances in the major leagues. We do not consider service time in our eligibility requirements.

As with any prospect list, these rankings represent how each person regarded the top minor league talent in the game at a moment in time. Ask us again in a few months—or even tomorrow—how these prospects stack up, and you'll get a different answer.

JIM CALLIS

1. Mike Trout, of, Angels
2. Bryce Harper, of, Nationals
3. Jesus Montero, c, Yankees
4. Julio Teheran, rhp, Braves
5. Aroldis Chapman, lhp, Reds
6. Jeremy Hellickson, rhp, Rays
7. Mike Moustakas, 3b, Royals
8. Jameson Taillon, rhp, Pirates
9. Manny Machado, ss, Orioles
10. Wil Myers, c, Royals
11. Eric Hosmer, 1b, Royals
12. Domonic Brown, of, Phillies
13. Dustin Ackley, 2b, Mariners
14. Michael Pineda, rhp, Mariners
15. Shelby Miller, rhp, Cardinals
16. Jacob Turner, rhp, Tigers
17. Zach Britton, lhp, Orioles
18. Matt Moore, lhp, Rays
19. Desmond Jennings, of, Rays
20. Freddie Freeman, 1b, Braves
21. John Lamb, lhp, Royals
22. Jarrod Parker, rhp, Diamondbacks
23. Chris Sale, lhp, White Sox
24. Lonnie Chisenhall, 3b, Indians
25. Mike Montgomery, lhp, Royals
26. Kyle Drabek, rhp, Blue Jays
27. Tyler Matzek, lhp, Rockies
28. Dee Gordon, ss, Dodgers
29. Wilin Rosario, c, Rockies
30. Randall Delgado, rhp, Braves
31. Kyle Gibson, rhp, Twins
32. Casey Kelly, rhp, Padres
33. Martin Perez, lhp, Rangers
34. Aaron Hicks, of, Twins
35. Chris Archer, rhp, Cubs
36. Alex White, rhp, Indians
37. Brett Jackson, of, Cubs
38. Zack Cox, 3b, Cardinals
39. Brett Lawrie, 2b, Blue Jays
40. Brandon Belt, 1b/of, Giants
41. Drew Pomeranz, lhp, Indians
42. Mike Minor, lhp, Braves
43. Jose Iglesias, ss, Red Sox
44. Anthony Ranaudo, rhp, Red Sox
45. Trey McNutt, rhp, Cubs
46. Travis d'Arnaud, c, Blue Jays
47. Gary Sanchez, c, Yankees
48. Jason Kipnis, 2b, Indians
49. Billy Hamilton, 2b/ss, Reds
50. Jonathan Singleton, 1b/of, Phillies

Scrawny ChiSox lefty Chris Sale went from the first round to the big leagues in 2010

Two of our three editors rank Julio Teheran as the top pitching prospect in the minors

WILL LINGO

1. Bryce Harper, of, Nationals
2. Mike Trout, of, Angels
3. Mike Moustakas, 3b, Royals
4. Jesus Montero, c, Yankees
5. Julio Teheran, rhp, Braves
6. Domonic Brown, of, Phillies
7. Jeremy Hellickson, rhp, Rays
8. Shelby Miller, rhp, Cardinals
9. Freddie Freeman, 1b, Braves
10. Eric Hosmer, 1b, Royals
11. Aroldis Chapman, lhp, Reds
12. Chris Sale, lhp, White Sox
13. Kyle Drabek, rhp, Blue Jays
14. Wil Myers, c, Royals
15. Dustin Ackley, 2b, Mariners
16. Jameson Taillon, rhp, Pirates
17. Manny Machado, ss, Orioles
18. Zach Britton, lhp, Orioles
19. Lonnie Chisenhall, 3b, Indians
20. Matt Moore, lhp, Rays
21. Michael Pineda, rhp, Mariners
22. Brandon Belt, 1b/of, Giants
23. Casey Kelly, rhp, Padres
24. Mike Montgomery, lhp, Royals
25. Jacob Turner, rhp, Tigers
26. John Lamb, lhp, Royals
27. Desmond Jennings, of, Rays
28. Martin Perez, lhp, Rangers
29. Gary Sanchez, c, Yankees
30. Dee Gordon, ss, Dodgers
31. Jenrry Mejia, rhp, Mets
32. Jonathan Singleton, 1b/of, Phillies
33. Simon Castro, rhp, Padres
34. Kyle Gibson, rhp, Twins
35. Brett Lawrie, 2b, Blue Jays
36. Chris Archer, rhp, Cubs
37. Travis d'Arnaud, c, Blue Jays
38. Grant Green, ss, Athletics
39. Alex White, rhp, Indians
40. Tyler Matzek, lhp, Rockies
41. Brett Jackson, of, Cubs
42. Jarrod Parker, rhp, Diamondbacks
43. Randall Delgado, rhp, Braves
44. Wilin Rosario, c, Rockies
45. Tony Sanchez, c, Pirates
46. Jordan Lyles, rhp, Astros
47. Mike Minor, lhp, Braves
48. Matt Dominguez, 3b, Marlins
49. Derek Norris, c, Nationals
50. Chris Carter, 1b, Athletics

Domonic Brown spends his third year atop the Phillies' Top 30 prospects list

Mike Trout's physicality and speed shocked scouts in 2010, his first full pro season

JOHN MANUEL

1. Bryce Harper, of, Nationals
2. Mike Trout, of, Angels
3. Jesus Montero, c, Yankees
4. Domonic Brown, of, Phillies
5. Jeremy Hellickson, rhp, Rays
6. Julio Teheran, rhp, Braves
7. Eric Hosmer, 1b, Royals
8. Dustin Ackley, 2b, Mariners
9. Shelby Miller, rhp, Cardinals
10. Matt Moore, lhp, Rays
11. Wil Myers, c, Royals
12. Mike Moustakas, 3b, Royals
13. Aroldis Chapman, lhp, Reds
14. Michael Pineda, rhp, Mariners
15. Martin Perez, lhp, Rangers
16. Freddie Freeman, 1b, Braves
17. Gary Sanchez, c, Yankees
18. Dellin Betances, rhp, Yankees
19. Jameson Taillon, rhp, Pirates
20. Manny Banuelos, lhp, Yankees
21. Manny Machado, ss, Orioles
22. Dee Gordon, ss, Dodgers
23. Zach Britton, lhp, Orioles
24. Kyle Drabek, rhp, Blue Jays
25. Mike Montgomery, lhp, Royals

26. Brandon Belt, 1b/of, Giants
27. Lonnie Chisenhall, 3b, Indians
28. Kyle Gibson, rhp, Twins
29. Chris Sale, lhp, White Sox
30. John Lamb, lhp, Royals
31. Alex White, rhp, Indians
32. Casey Kelly, rhp, Padres
33. Travis d'Arnaud, c, Blue Jays
34. Aaron Hicks, of, Twins
35. Brett Lawrie, 2b, Blue Jays
36. Desmond Jennings, of, Rays
37. Jonathan Singleton, 1b/of, Phillies
38. Randall Delgado, rhp, Braves
39. Chris Archer, rhp, Cubs
40. Jason Kipnis, 2b, Indians
41. Brett Jackson, of, Cubs
42. Tyler Matzek, lhp, Rockies
43. Jacob Turner, rhp, Tigers
44. Derek Norris, c, Nationals
45. Jordan Lyles, rhp, Astros
46. Wilmer Flores, ss, Mets
47. Mike Minor, lhp, Braves
48. Wilin Rosario, c, Rockies
49. Tony Sanchez, c, Pirates
50. Cesar Puello, of, Mets

	2010	2009	2008	2007	2006
1 Kansas City Royals	16	11	24	11	23

The Royals have proved they can't win at the big league level, with one winning season since 1994. General manager Dayton Moore has taken his team all-in on the draft and international markets, and most of their top talents had big years in 2010. Watch out, American League, in 2013.

	2010	2009	2008	2007	2006
2 Atlanta Braves	9	6	8	15	7

The faces in the front office and even scouting and player development change, but the Braves' focus remains the same. In 2010, Atlanta won at the big league level while simultaneously developing the industry's hardest-throwing, deepest pool of pitching prospects.

	2010	2009	2008	2007	2006
3 Tampa Bay Rays	1	4	1	1	10

As good as the Braves are, Tampa Bay is the gold standard for player development. The Rays are working on a Bobby Bowden-type streak of five straight seasons in the top four. Good thing, too, as Carl Crawford may be just the start of a group of stars who grow up Rays but leave St. Pete for free-agent riches.

	2010	2009	2008	2007	2006
4 Toronto Blue Jays	19	19	25	26	25

General manager Alex Anthopoulos had to trade Roy Halladay but got better talent back for him than any of the three Cliff Lee trades in the last two years. The Jays own the largest scouting department in the industry and got strong early returns from their large 2010 draft crop.

	2010	2009	2008	2007	2006
5 New York Yankees	22	15	5	5	17

Most of the Yankees' top prospects had strong 2010 seasons, including jumbo-sized pitchers Dellin Betances and Andrew Brackman. Cliff Lee's signing in Philadelphia instead of New York may mean those Yankees arms get tested in the Bronx, rather than being used as trade fodder.

	2010	2009	2008	2007	2006
6 Cincinnati Reds	17	14	3	12	30

The Reds have turned a nifty trick by getting better in the big leagues and in the minors at the same time. They have excellent depth of Triple-A talent ready to step in as needed in Cincinnati, plus the top-of-the-scale talent of Aroldis Chapman to front the farm system.

	2010	2009	2008	2007	2006
7 Cleveland Indians	3	7	19	10	9

Usually, teams that rank in this top 10 in three straight years get going in the right direction at the major league level. The Tribe may not have one signature player like Chapman gives the Reds, but they have plenty of options at several positions, such as second base and on the mound.

	2010	2009	2008	2007	2006
8 Chicago Cubs	14	27	18	18	15

The Cubs have significant major league contract commitments tied up in a handful of players, so their impressive minor league depth will come in handy, providing cheaper players to follow Starlin Castro into the lineup around the older, more expensive core.

	2010	2009	2008	2007	2006
9 San Diego Padres	20	29	13	29	29

Trading established big leaguers for prospects is a sure way to move up the talent rankings. The Padres' haul from the Red Sox for Adrian Gonzalez helped push them into the top 10 for the first time since 2002. Their inability to sign first-round pick Karsten Whitson didn't help matters, though.

	2010	2009	2008	2007	2006
10 Colorado Rockies	10	20	7	2	11

Colorado holds steady with its fifth top-10 mark in the last seven years. That success stems from a solid draft track record and a relatively unheralded international pipeline that keeps producing prospects such as catcher Wilin Rosario and righthander Juan Nicasio.

	2010	2009	2008	2007	2006
11 Philadelphia Phillies	18	12	22	21	22

Despite general manager Ruben Amaro Jr.'s best efforts to trade away talent, the Phillies still have an impressive stockpile. Of course, Amaro's trades have netted Roy Halladay and Roy Oswalt for the rotation—which means all those power arms the Phils have in A-ball may go on the block.

	2010	2009	2008	2007	2006
12 Los Angeles Dodgers	21	23	6	6	2

After a few leaner years in the system, brought on by tight budgets and the graduation of impact talent, Los Angeles turned the corner in 2010. Prospects such as Dee Gordon, Rubby de la Rosa and Jerry Sands continued to emerge, while the team gave first-rounder Zach Lee $5.25 million.

	2010	2009	2008	2007	2006
13 Minnesota Twins	6	22	15	8	6

The Twins keep winning in the majors, and despite poor win-loss records at their two top affiliates, they have plenty of prospects down below as well. Minnesota has subtly shifted its focus, though, with a greater focus on Latin America than it had in the previous decade.

	2010	2009	2008	2007	2006
14 Washington Nationals	24	21	10	30	24

Last year, the Nationals system consisted of Stephen Strasburg, Ian Desmond and a few other contributors. This year's system is Bryce Harper, Derek Norris, Danny Espinosa and the 2010 draft class, but the top is heavy enough to put the Nats in the first half of the rankings.

	2010	2009	2008	2007	2006
15 Texas Rangers	2	1	4	28	16

Executive of the Year Jon Daniels will trade the Rangers falling out of the top 10 for the first time in four seasons for a pennant. It would surprise no one if the Rangers, with a very young system, jump back in the top 10 if prospects like Jurickson Profar have success in their introduction to full-season ball.

	2010	2009	2008	2007	2006
16 Los Angeles Angels	26	25	11	4	4

Scouting director Eddie Bane was just starting to turn this system around with consecutive draft classes burgeoning with extra picks when his contract was not renewed in September. His parting gift to the franchise, top prospect Mike Trout, will keep giving for years.

	2010	2009	2008	2007	2006
17 Boston Red Sox	5	13	2	9	8

Trading prospects for a player like Adrian Gonzalez is a sure way to fall down the talent rankings. Boston still has depth—as it should, considering how much it spends internationally and on over-slot draft bonuses—but it no longer has a keynote prospect after trading Casey Kelly.

	2010	2009	2008	2007	2006
18 Seattle Mariners	12	24	12	24	27

A disastrous big league season in Seattle stretched down to the minors in some ways (the Josh Lueke controversy springs to mind). But the Mariners also had good news, from Dustin Ackley reaching Triple-A in his first season to Nick Franklin's surprise Midwest League home run title.

	2010	2009	2008	2007	2006
19 Pittsburgh Pirates	15	18	26	19	19

The Pirates have never ranked in the top 10 in these talent rankings in the 10-year history of the Prospect Handbook. They also haven't won more than 75 games in the majors in that span. This chapter of the rebuilding plan is centered on young, high-upside power arms.

	2010	2009	2008	2007	2006
20 New York Mets	25	17	28	13	28

The Omar Minaya Era ended in New York, a period marked in player-development terms by successes internationally (the top three current prospects are all 2007 signees from the Dominican Republic and Venezuela) and a tight-fisted approach to the draft. A top-heavy but thin system is what remains.

	2010	2009	2008	2007	2006
21 Baltimore Orioles	8	9	14	17	12

Not only is Baltimore the fifth-best big league roster in the American League East, but it also now has the division's weakest farm system. The graduations in recent years of Matt Wieters, Brian Matusz and Chris Tillman has left precious little behind beyond Manny Machado and Zach Britton.

	2010	2009	2008	2007	2006
22 Arizona Diamondbacks	28	26	20	3	1

Extra draft picks in 2009 started the Diamondbacks moving the talent meter in the right direction. Trading Dan Haren brought in more prospects in 2010, and the system could get another boost with two of the first seven picks in 2011 after the Barret Loux first-round debacle in last year's draft.

	2010	2009	2008	2007	2006
23 San Francisco Giants	4	5	23	20	18

First-round success stories such as Tim Lincecum, Madison Bumgarner and Buster Posey first led the Giants storming up our talent rankings, then to a World Series championship. Losing MadBum and Buster thinned the Giants' ranks, but the tradeoff was well worth it.

	2010	2009	2008	2007	2006
24 St. Louis Cardinals	29	8	16	23	21

St. Louis moved up the rankings a couple of years ago as its fruitful 2005 draft class matured. Now that Mitchell Boggs, Jaime Garcia and Colby Rasmus are established big leaguers, though, the Cardinals are left with an intriguing group of fireballers led by Shelby Miller and little else.

	2010	2009	2008	2007	2006
25 Detroit Tigers	27	28	27	14	13

The Tigers aren't afraid to spend in the draft for impact talent, with more than $8 million in bonuses tied up in their top two prospects, Jacob Turner and Nick Castellanos. This system also has power arms in abundance but it lacks hitters, particularly up the middle.

	2010	2009	2008	2007	2006
26 Houston Astros	30	30	29	22	20

Back-to-back No. 30 finishes are now a thing of the past for the Astros. All it took was three drafts, including the 2010 edition with three of the first 33 selections, and trading franchise cornerstones Lance Berkman and Roy Oswalt for prospects. Houston still has a ways to go, though.

	2010	2009	2008	2007	2006
27 Chicago White Sox	23	16	30	25	14

Chicago scored a coup when it signed 2010 first-rounder Chris Sale for a slot bonus, and his debut season gives the White Sox plenty of reason to be excited. The rest of the farm system, though, remains plagued by poor performances and has been thinned out by trades.

	2010	2009	2008	2007	2006
28 Oakland Athletics	11	3	9	27	26

Just about everything that could have gone wrong did for A's prospects last year. Grant Desme's retirement to enter the priesthood and Michael Ynoa's elbow surgery were lowlights in a year when most of Oakland's top prospects took a step (if not two) backward.

	2010	2009	2008	2007	2006
29 Florida Marlins	7	2	17	16	3

Mike Stanton, Gaby Sanchez and Logan Morrison already have walked through the door to the big leagues, leaving the Fish fairly flailing in the minors. It's not a good sign when power-armed relievers are the best source of depth in a farm system.

	2010	2009	2008	2007	2006
30 Milwaukee Brewers	13	10	21	7	5

The trade to Toronto of Brett Lawrie—who would have been the Brewers' top prospect—proves Milwaukee is going all-in in 2011. Losing first-round pick Dylan Covey, whose diabetes diagnosis led him to choose college over pro ball, was bad luck and bad timing for a system in need of help.

Arizona Diamondbacks

BY BILL MITCHELL

After a disastrous 2009 season, the Diamondbacks were looking forward to better times. Buoyed by free-agent acquisitions Kelly Johnson and Adam LaRoche, trade pickups Edwin Jackson and Ian Kennedy and the expected return of Conor Jackson and Brandon Webb from injury, Arizona hoped to bounce back from 70-92.

Instead, things got worse. The offense continued to set strikeout records, and the bullpen was the worst in baseball. Conor Jackson was ineffective before being traded to the Athletics at midseason, and Webb never made it back to the mound.

The controversial move of A.J. Hinch from farm director to manager in 2009 ended up costing both general manager Josh Byrnes and Hinch their jobs, despite long-term contracts for each. With a 31-48 record, owner Ken Kendrick and president Derek Hall pulled the plug. They installed director of player personnel Jerry DiPoto as interim GM and bench coach Kirk Gibson as manager. The Diamondbacks still finished 65-97, third-worst in baseball.

DiPoto undertook a major reduction in payroll and added depth to a thin farm system by trading Jackson, Dan Haren, Chad Qualls and Chris Snyder. The team gained further payroll relief after the season with the conclusion of the bloated $30 million contract of Eric Byrnes, who had been released in January.

More changes came in the offseason, highlighted by the hiring of Kevin Towers as GM, a position he held with the Padres for 14 years. Towers persuaded DiPoto to stay to oversee scouting and player development.

Farm director Mike Berger was reassigned to a pro scouting position and initially replaced by Double-A Mobile manager Rico Brogna. When Brogna resigned after one month, Arizona turned to minor league field coordinator Mike Bell. Scouting director Tom Allison was replaced by Ray Montgomery, who like Allison had been a Brewers crosschecker. Gibson had his "interim" tag removed at the end of the season.

The farm system benefited from DiPoto's trades. Daniel Hudson went 7-1, 1.69 after coming over from the White Sox in the Edwin Jackson deal, which also yielded young lefthander David Holmberg. The Diamondbacks picked up two more southpaws in Tyler Skaggs and Patrick Corbin when they sent Haren to the Angels. The system's biggest boost will be the return of top prospect Jarrod Parker, who sat out 2010 recuperating from Tommy John surgery.

After focusing on position prospects in the 2009

After 14 years with the Padres, Kevin Towers took over as Arizona's general manager

TOP 30 PROSPECTS

1. Jarrod Parker, rhp	16. Ryan Wheeler, 3b
2. Tyler Skaggs, lhp	17. Kam Mickolio, rhp
3. Matt Davidson, 3b	18. Collin Cowgill, of
4. Chris Owings, ss	19. Wagner Mateo, of
5. Marc Krauss, of	20. Tyler Green, rhp
6. A.J. Pollock, of	21. Robby Rowland, rhp
7. Bobby Borchering, 3b	22. David Holmberg, lhp
8. Wade Miley, lhp	23. J.R. Bradley, rhp
9. Pat Corbin, lhp	24. Charles Brewer, rhp
10. Keon Broxton, of	25. Raul Navarro, ss
11. Paul Goldschmidt, 1b	26. Chase Anderson, rhp
12. Ty Linton, of	27. Bryan Shaw, rhp
13. Kevin Munson, rhp	28. Ronny Mejias, ss
14. Eric Smith, rhp	29. Zach Walters, ss
15. Mike Belfiore, lhp	30. Adam Eaton, of

draft, Arizona went for pitchers with its first eight choices last June. The 2010 draft delivered the final snafu of the Byrnes regime when the team drafted righthander Barret Loux sixth overall, in large part because he accepted a below-slot deal for $2 million.

When Loux failed a postdraft physical due to concerns over his shoulder and elbow, the Diamondbacks withdrew their offer. In an unprecedented move, MLB declared Loux a free agent and he ultimately signed with the Rangers. Arizona receives the No. 7 overall pick in the 2011 draft for failing to sign Loux, along with the No. 3 pick it earned with its poor play.

ORGANIZATION OVERVIEW

General Manager: Kevin Towers. **Farm Director:** Mike Bell. **Scouting Director:** Ray Montgomery.

Class	Team	League	W	L	PCT	Finish*	Manager
Majors	Arizona Diamondbacks	National	65	97	.401	15th (16)	A.J. Hinch/Kirk Gibson
Triple-A	Reno Aces	Pacific Coast	69	74	.483	11th (16)	Brett Butler
Double-A	Mobile BayBears	Southern	75	62	.547	3rd (10)	Rico Brogna
High A	Visalia Rawhide	California	72	68	.514	7th (10)	Audo Vicente
Low A	South Bend Silver Hawks	Midwest	59	78	.431	13th (16)	Mark Haley
Short-season	Yakima Bears	Northwest	43	33	.566	t-2nd (8)	Bob Didier
Rookie	Missoula Osprey	Pioneer	28	47	.373	7th (8)	Hector de la Cruz
Overall 2010 Minor League Record			346	362	.489	22nd (30)	

*Finish in overall standings (No. of teams in league). †League champion.

LAST YEAR'S TOP 30

Player, Pos.		Status
1.	Jarrod Parker, rhp	No. 1
2.	Bobby Borchering, 3b	No. 7
3.	A.J. Pollock, of	No. 6
4.	Brandon Allen, 1b	Majors
5.	Chris Owings, ss	No. 4
6.	Mike Belfiore, lhp	No. 15
7.	Marc Krauss, of	No. 5
8.	Ryan Wheeler, 1b	No. 16
9.	Collin Cowgill, of	No. 18
10.	Matt Davidson, 3b	No. 3
11.	Bryan Augenstein, rhp	(Cardinals)
12.	Reynaldo Navarro, ss	(Royals)
13.	Paul Goldschmidt, 1b	No. 11
14.	Eric Smith, rhp	No. 14
15.	Wade Miley, lhp	No. 8
16.	Cole Gillespie, of	Dropped out
17.	Keon Broxton, of	No. 10
18.	Kevin Eichhorn, rhp	Dropped out
19.	David Nick, 2b	Dropped out
20.	Matt Helm, 1b/3b	Dropped out
21.	Patrick Schuster, lhp	Dropped out
22.	Rossmel Perez, c	Dropped out
23.	Josh Collmenter, rhp	Dropped out
24.	Enrique Burgos, rhp	Dropped out
25.	John Hester, c	Dropped out
26.	Leyson Septimo, lhp	Dropped out
27.	Pedro Ciriaco, ss/2b	(Pirates)
28.	Roque Mercedes, rhp	Dropped out
29.	Jordan Norberto, lhp	Majors
30.	Zach Kroenke, lhp	Dropped out

BEST TOOLS

Best Hitter for Average	A.J. Pollock
Best Power Hitter	Bobby Borchering
Best Strike-Zone Discipline	Jake Elmore
Fastest Baserunner	Westley Moss
Best Athlete	Ty Linton
Best Fastball	Jarrod Parker
Best Curveball	Tyler Skaggs
Best Slider	Jarrod Parker
Best Changeup	Chase Anderson
Best Control	Chase Anderson
Best Defensive Catcher	Rossmel Perez
Best Defensive Infielder	Chris Owings
Best Infield Arm	Raul Navarro
Best Defensive Outfielder	A.J. Pollock
Best Outfield Arm	Collin Cowgill

PROJECTED 2014 LINEUP

Catcher	Miguel Montero
First Base	Bobby Borchering
Second Base	Chris Owings
Third Base	Matt Davidson
Shortstop	Stephen Drew
Left Field	Marc Krauss
Center Field	Chris Young
Right Field	Justin Upton
No. 1 Starter	Jarrod Parker
No. 2 Starter	Tyler Skaggs
No. 3 Starter	Daniel Hudson
No. 4 Starter	Ian Kennedy
No. 5 Starter	Wade Miley
Closer	Kevin Munson

TOP PROSPECTS OF THE DECADE

Year	Player, Pos.	2010 Org.
2001	Alex Cintron, ss	Mets
2002	Luis Terrero, of	Reds
2003	Scott Hairston, 2b	Padres
2004	Scott Hairston, 2b	Padres
2005	Carlos Quentin, of	White Sox
2006	Stephen Drew, ss	Diamondbacks
2007	Justin Upton, of	Diamondbacks
2008	Carlos Gonzalez, of	Rockies
2009	Jarrod Parker, rhp	Diamondbacks
2010	Jarrod Parker, rhp	Diamondbacks

TOP DRAFT PICKS OF THE DECADE

Year	Player, Pos.	2010 Org.
2001	Jason Bulger, rhp	Angels
2002	Sergio Santos, ss	White Sox
2003	Conor Jackson, of	Athletics
2004	Stephen Drew, ss	Diamondbacks
2005	Justin Upton, of	Diamondbacks
2006	Max Scherzer, rhp	Tigers
2007	Jarrod Parker, rhp	Diamondbacks
2008	Daniel Schlereth, lhp	Tigers
2009	Bobby Borchering, 3b	Diamondbacks
2010	*Barret Loux, rhp	Rangers

*Did not sign.

LARGEST BONUSES IN CLUB HISTORY

Travis Lee, 1996	$10,000,000
Justin Upton, 2005	$6,100,000
John Patterson, 1996	$6,075,000
Stephen Drew, 2004	$4,000,000
Max Scherzer, 2006	$3,000,000

ARIZONA DIAMONDBACKS

TOP 2011 ROOKIE: Jarrod Parker, rhp. Fully recovered from Tommy John surgery, he should crack the big league rotation by midseason at the latest.

BREAKOUT PROSPECT: Wagner Mateo, of. If his vision problems truly are a thing of the past, he could show why the Cardinals were willing to pay him $3.1 million.

SLEEPER: Yonata Ortega, rhp. He made major strides in 2010 and could become closer material with better command and consistency.

SOURCE OF TOP 30 TALENT			
Homegrown	26	Acquired	4
College	14	Trades	4
Junior college	1	Rule 5 draft	0
High school	8	Independent leagues	0
Draft-and-follow	0	Free agents/waivers	0
Nondrafted free agents	0		
International	3		

LF
Marc Krauss (5)
Ty Linton (12)
Cole Gillespie
Socrates Brito

CF
A.J. Pollock (6)
Keon Broxton (10)
Adam Eaton (30)
Evan Frey
Yorman Garcia
Westley Moss

RF
Collin Cowgill (18)
Wagner Mateo (19)
David Winfree
Roberto Rodriguez
Alfredo Marte

3B
Matt Davidson (3)
Ryan Wheeler (16)
Matt Helm
Kyle Greene

SS
Chris Owings (4)
Raul Navarro (25)
Ronny Mejias (28)
Zach Walters (29)

2B
David Nick
Mike Freeman
Mark Hallberg
Jake Elmore

1B
Bobby Borchering (7)
Paul Goldschmidt (11)
Juan Miranda
Yazy Arbelo
Bryan Byrne
Bobby Stone

C
Konrad Schmidt
Rossmel Perez
John Hester
Jae Yun Kim

RHP

RHSP	RHRP
Jarrod Parker (1)	Kevin Munson (13)
Eric Smith (14)	Kam Mickolio (17)
Tyler Green (20)	Bryan Shaw (27)
Robby Rowland (21)	Yonata Ortega
J.R. Bradley (23)	Matt Gorgen
Charles Brewer (24)	Jeff Shields
Chase Anderson (26)	Rafael Rodriguez
Kevin Eichhorn	Daniel Stange
Blake Perry	Bradin Hagens
Enrique Burgos	Bryan Woodall
Kevin Mulvey	Jeremy Erben
Josh Collmenter	Mike Bolsinger
Juan Jaime	

LHP

LHSP	LHRP
Tyler Skaggs (2)	Zach Kroenke
Wade Miley (8)	Joe Paterson
Pat Corbin (9)	Leyson Septimo
Mike Belfiore (15)	Ryan Robowski
David Holmberg (22)	Eury de la Rosa
Cody Wheeler	
Patrick Schuster	

BEST PURE HITTER: Arizona was pleasantly surprised by 5-foot-9 OF Adam Eaton (19), who showed multiple tools. He's short to the ball, has a polished approach and has on-base skills.

BEST POWER HITTER: OF Ty Linton (14) has huge raw power and got a $1.25 million bonus to buy him out of a North Carolina football scholarship. He has a natural power stroke with a high finish and good swing path.

FASTEST RUNNER: Reed-thin OF Westley Moss (16) has work to do but is a 70 runner who occasionally puts up 80 times on the 20-80 scouting scale.

BEST DEFENSIVE PLAYER: Moss' speed gives him excellent range in center field, and he has solid instincts and a playable arm.

BEST FASTBALL: The Diamondbacks focused on projectable high school power arms, though RHP Kevin Munson (4), a college product, has the best consistent velocity at 92-94 mph. RHP Tyler Green (8) flashes a mid-90s fastball and the competitive streak to bring it when most necessary. RHP J.R. Bradley (2) could surpass him with a fluid, easy arm stroke and athletic, projectable body at 6-foot-4, 185 pounds. He has touched 93 mph but lost velocity as the year went on.

BEST SECONDARY PITCH: Munson's slider is a plus pitch that misses bats.

BEST PRO DEBUT: Eaton hit .385/.500/.575 with 20 steals in 28 attempts and led the Rookie-level Pioneer League in batting and OBP. 1B Yazy Arbelo (26) hit .285/.374/.517 and topped the short-season Northwest league with 55 RBIs while ranking second with 14 homers.

BEST ATHLETE: Area scout George Swain stayed on Linton, and Arizona gave him a 14th-round record bonus, because of his combination of plus speed, wiry strength, bat speed and explosiveness.

MOST INTRIGUING BACKGROUND: RHP Robby Rowland (3), whose father Rich caught in the big leagues for six years, formed a battery at Rookie-level Missoula with his brother Richie, who signed as a nondrafted college junior. Unsigned RHP Tad Barton's (49) dad Shawn also played in the majors. Unsigned RHP Kenny Sigman's (48) father Lee scouts for the Yankees and has signed several Mexican big leaguers, most notably Ted Higuera. Arbelo, RHP Victor Lara (34) and 3B/2B Eric Groff (44) all played together at NCAA Division II Keystone (Pa.).

CLOSEST TO THE MAJORS: Munson, the team's closer of the future.

BEST LATE-ROUND PICK: In the big-money category, Linton. In terms of a standard bonus, Eaton.

THE ONE WHO GOT AWAY: The Diamondbacks drafted RHP Barret Loux (1) sixth overall, largely because he was willing to sign for a below-slot $2 million. But Loux failed his physical and Arizona moved on. In an unprecedented move, MLB declared him a free agent, and he signed with the Rangers for $312,000 in November. The Diamondbacks hoped to make up for not signing Loux by landing LHP Kevin Ziomek (13), but couldn't sway him from his Vanderbilt commitment.

ASSESSMENT: It's hard to have a good draft without signing a top-10 pick. Arizona hopes to surmount that obstacle with its bevy of projectable pitchers and Linton's athleticism.

2009
BONUSES: $9.3 MILLION

The Diamondbacks had seven picks before the third round and found 10 of their top 16 prospects in this draft. They focused on position players, with 3B Matt Davidson (1s), SS Chris Owings (1s) and OF Marc Krauss (2) delivering the best early returns.

GRADE: B

2008
BONUSES: $4.5 MILLION

LHP Daniel Schlereth (1) reached the big leagues 10 months after turning pro, then was included in a three-team deal that sent Edwin Jackson and Ian Kennedy to Arizona. LHP Wade Miley's (1s) stuff picked back up in 2010 after slipping the year before.

GRADE: C

2007
BONUSES: $5.1 MILLION

RHP Jarrod Parker (1) remains the system's best prospect despite missing last season. RHP Barry Enright (2) won six games as a rookie last summer. LHP Scott Maine (6) and RHP Bryan Augenstein (7) also have appeared in the majors, though Maine blossomed after being traded and Augenstein was waived.

GRADE: B

2006
BONUSES: $6.6 MILLION

The Diamondbacks grabbed RHP Max Scherzer (1) and LHP Brett Anderson (2), but shipped them out in deals for Jackson/Kennedy and Dan Haren. They also found four other big leaguers in RHPs Hector Ambriz (5) and Daniel Stange (7), C John Hester (13) and LHP Clay Zavada (30).

GRADE: A

Draft analysis by John Manuel (2010) and Jim Callis (2006-09). Numbers in parentheses indicate draft rounds.

JARROD PARKER, RHP

Born: Nov. 24, 1988. **Bats:** R. **Throws:** R.
Height: 6-1. **Weight:** 180. **Drafted:** HS—
Norwell, Ind., 2007 (1st round). **Signed by:**
Mike Daughtry.

PROSPECT 1

Parker has ranked No. 1 on this list for three straight years, but he almost didn't become a Diamondback. If the Royals had taken Josh Vitters with the second overall pick in the 2007 draft, the Cubs would have followed by selecting Parker. But Kansas City switched to Mike Moustakas on the day of the draft, Chicago went for Vitters and Arizona landed Parker with the ninth choice. He signed for $2.1 million at the Aug. 15 deadline, too late to make his pro debut, and then jumped on the fast track. He began his pro career at low Class A South Bend in 2008 and reached Double-A Mobile by May of the following year. Parker had no trouble handling Double-A hitters as a 20-year old and ranked as the Southern League's top pitching prospect. Elbow tightness forced him to the sidelines in late July, however. After skipping planned stints with Team USA and in Arizona Fall League in an attempt to recover with rest, he had Tommy John surgery in October 2009 and sat out the entire 2010 season. After rehabbing at the Diamondbacks' Tucson complex early in the year, Parker spent the second half with Mobile, throwing side sessions and simulated games. He didn't pitch in a real game until instructional league.

Parker appeared to be back to full strength during instructional league, with more confidence and better mechanics than he had before he blew out his elbow. His delivery was smooth before he got hurt, however, and wasn't blamed for his injury. Parker has a quick arm that easily generates above-average velocity. During instructional league, his fastball sat at 94-95 mph and touched 97. His streamlined mechanics give him good fastball command as well. Despite the quality of his fastball, his slider is his best pitch. He throws it in the low 80s with nice tilt and two-plane depth, making it a true swing-and-miss pitch. Parker also throws an 80-83 mph changeup that was on its way to becoming a plus pitch before he got hurt. He also has an effective mid-70s curveball he uses mostly as a show-me pitch.

SCOUTING GRADES

Fastball: 65. **Command/**
Slider: 70. **Control:** 60.
Changeup: 60. **Delivery:** 60.

Based on 20-80 scouting scale, where 50 represents major league average, and future projection rather than present tools.

Parker has the stuff to become an ace. The track record for pitchers coming back from Tommy John is encouraging, and from all indications, he'll return as strong as before. Arizona hasn't ruled out the possibility that he could break camp in the big league rotation with an impressive spring training, and scouts who saw him in instructional league say he's ready to pitch in the majors. It's more likely that the Diamondbacks will be more cautious, having him start 2011 in Double-A and limiting him to 130-140 innings in his first year back. Regardless, Parker soon will be a key cog at the front of their rotation.

Year	Club (League)	Class	W	L	ERA	G	GS	CG	SV	IP	H	HR	BB	SO	G/A	WHIP	AVG
2008	South Bend (MWL)	LoA	12	5	3.44	24	24	0	0	118	113	8	33	117	—	1.24	.251
2009	Visalia (CAL)	HiA	1	0	0.95	4	4	0	0	19	12	0	4	21	1.77	0.84	.179
	Mobile (SL)	AA	4	6	3.68	16	16	0	0	78	82	2	34	74	1.56	1.48	.272
2010	Did Not Play—Injured																
Minor League Totals			17	11	3.31	44	44	0	0	215	207	10	71	212	1.60	1.29	.253

2 TYLER SKAGGS, LHP.

Born: July 13, 1991. **B-T:** L-L. **Ht.:** 6-4. **Wt.:** 195. **Drafted:** HS—Santa Monica, Calif., 2009 (1st round supplemental). **Signed by:** Bobby DeJardin (Angels).

The Diamondbacks hoped to take Skaggs with the 41st overall pick in 2009, but the Angels took him one choice earlier and signed him for $1 million. Arizona got him in the Dan Haren trade last July, with Skaggs the key player in a four-pitcher package that also included Joe Saunders and prospects Pat Corbin and Rafael Rodriguez. Skaggs has a long, lean athletic body with plenty of projection. His primary weapon is his above-average curveball, which he throws in the low 70s and locates where he wants. His curve ranks as the best in the system. He also commands his 88-92 mph fastball, and could add more velocity as he fills out his lanky frame. He's refining a changeup that could give him a third plus pitch down the road. Scouts note his aggressiveness and confidence on the mound, and they like how he goes about his business. Skaggs profiles as a solid No. 3 starter right now, and he can become a frontline starter if his fastball and changeup develop as hoped. He's still just 19 and has just 108 innings of pro experience, so the Diamondbacks won't rush him. He'll likely move through the minors one level at a time, which put him on schedule to begin 2011 at high Class A Visalia.

Year	Club (League)	Class	W	L	ERA	G	GS	CG	SV	IP	H	HR	BB	SO	G/A	WHIP	AVG
2009	Angels (AZL)	R	0	0	0.00	3	2	0	0	6	4	0	1	7	2.67	0.83	.182
	Orem (PIO)	R	0	0	4.50	2	0	0	0	4	5	0	1	6	—	1.50	.278
2010	Cedar Rapids (MWL)	LoA	8	4	3.61	19	14	0	0	82	78	6	21	82	1.87	1.20	.252
	South Bend (MWL)	LoA	1	1	1.69	4	4	0	0	16	13	1	4	20	1.89	1.06	.224
Minor League Totals			9	5	3.16	28	20	0	0	108	100	7	27	115	2.00	1.17	.246

3 MATT DAVIDSON, 3B

Born: March 26, 1991. **B-T:** R-R. **Ht.:** 6-3. **Wt.:** 225. **Drafted:** HS—Yucaipa, Calif., 2009 (1st round supplemental). **Signed by:** Jeff Mousser.

The first of three Diamondbacks supplemental first-round picks in 2009, Davidson signed for $900,000. Arizona has pushed him aggressively, sending him to short-season Yakima for his pro debut and promoting him to high Class A at age 19 last August. He looked overmatched at those stops, but in between he earned all-star honors playing against competition closer to his age in the low Class A Midwest League. One Diamondbacks scout proclaimed Davidson as the "crown jewel of the system," and MWL observers clearly preferred him to fellow South Bend third baseman Bobby Borchering, a 2009 first-rounder. Thanks to his quick hands, Davidson has above-average power to all fields. He's not afraid to let balls travel deep and should hit for a solid average as well. With below-average speed and fringy range, he won't be more than adequate at third base, but he's better than Borchering defensively. Arizona thinks Davidson can stay at the hot corner. With his strong arm, he could move to an outfield corner if necessary. A potential cleanup hitter in the majors, Davidson will return to Visalia, where he'll once again team up with many of the system's top prospects. The downside is that he'll have to share third base with Borchering again rather than getting daily reps at the hot corner.

Year	Club (League)	Class	AVG	G	AB	R	H	2B	3B	HR	RBI	BB	SO	SB	CS	OBP	SLG
2009	Yakima (NWL)	SS	.241	72	270	29	65	15	0	2	28	21	75	0	2	.312	.319
2010	South Bend (MWL)	LoA	.289	113	415	58	120	35	3	16	79	43	109	0	2	.371	.504
	Visalia (CAL)	HiA	.169	21	71	6	12	1	0	2	11	12	25	0	0	.298	.268
Minor League Totals			.261	206	756	93	197	51	3	20	118	76	209	0	4	.343	.415

4 CHRIS OWINGS, SS

Born: Aug. 12, 1991. **B-T:** R-R. **Ht.:** 5-11. **Wt.:** 175. **Drafted:** HS—Gilbert, S.C., 2009 (1st round supplemental). **Signed by:** George Swain.

Another 2009 sandwich pick, Owings signed just before the Aug. 15 deadline for $950,000. He has batted .300/.344/.421 in two pro seasons, but didn't play after appearing in the Midwest League all-star game last June because he came down with plantar fasciitis, an inflammation on the bottom of the foot. He did return for instructional league. When he was drafted, there were questions about whether Owings could stay at shortstop or would need to move to second base. Scouts now believe he has a future as a solid big league shortstop, with solid quickness and agility, dependable range and a strong arm. Owings has very quick hands at the plate and could develop 12-15 home run power. He needs to address his plate discipline, but his short swing and willingness to use the whole field could translate into a .280 average in the majors. He's a slightly above-average runner with good instincts on the bases. He has the work ethic to continue to improve his game. Ticketed for high Class A in 2011, Owings may not quite be ready when Stephen

Drew will be eligible for free agency after the 2012 season. If Drew stays in Arizona, Owings could move to second base, and he has the bat to profile at either middle-infield position.

Year	Club (League)	Class	AVG	G	AB	R	H	2B	3B	HR	RBI	BB	SO	SB	CS	OBP	SLG
2009	Missoula (PIO)	R	.306	24	108	20	33	5	1	2	10	3	25	3	0	.324	.426
2010	South Bend (MWL)	LoA	.298	62	255	39	76	19	2	5	28	9	50	1	3	.323	.447
Minor League Totals			.300	86	363	59	109	24	3	7	38	12	75	4	3	.324	.441

5 MARC KRAUSS, OF

Born: Oct. 5, 1987. **B-T:** L-R. **Ht.:** 6-3. **Wt.:** 235. **Drafted:** Ohio, 2009 (2nd round). **Signed by:** Frankie Thon Jr.

Krauss was advanced enough offensively that the Diamondbacks sent him straight to low Class A after signing him as a second-rounder in 2009. His pro debut was cut short by an ankle injury, yet Arizona was aggressive again and assigned him to high Class A last year. He hit at both stops, as well as in the Arizona Fall League after the 2010 season. Krauss can rake and he'll have to, because that's his only route to the big leagues. He's a patient hitter with a clean swing, though he doesn't have blazing bat speed and his stroke can get long at times. He uses the whole field and developed more pull-side power last season, continuing that trend in the AFL. He hits southpaws as well as he hits righthanders, so he won't get pigeonholed as a platoon player. With below-average speed and athleticism to go with a fringy arm, Krauss is limited to left field. He does take good routes to the ball. Scouts question whether he could handle a move to first base. Krauss will open 2011 in Double-A and could see Triple-A Reno before season's end. The Diamondbacks need outfielders and power bats, so he'll move quickly if he continues to hit. He's a good bet to be the first member of Arizona's 2009 draft class to reach the majors.

Year	Club (League)	Class	AVG	G	AB	R	H	2B	3B	HR	RBI	BB	SO	SB	CS	OBP	SLG
2009	South Bend (MWL)	LoA	.304	32	115	14	35	12	1	2	17	14	21	0	1	.377	.478
2010	Visalia (CAL)	HiA	.302	138	530	107	160	27	4	25	87	57	141	1	3	.371	.509
Minor League Totals			.302	170	645	121	195	39	5	27	104	71	162	1	4	.372	.504

6 A.J. POLLOCK, OF

Born: Dec. 5, 1987. **B-T:** R-R. **Ht.:** 6-2. **Wt.:** 200. **Drafted:** Notre Dame, 2009 (1st round). **Signed by:** Mike Daughtry.

Pollock parlayed Cape Cod League MVP honors in the summer of 2008 into becoming the 17th overall pick in 2009, signing for $1.4 million. After a solid pro debut at South Bend, where he starred collegiately at Notre Dame, he missed all of 2010 after a freak injury during a spring-training fielding drill left him needing surgery to repair a fractured growth plate in his right elbow. He spent his downtime working on conditioning, especially strengthening his lower half, before returning to play in instructional league and the Arizona Fall League. Other than his bat, Pollock may not have a plus tool, but he has well-rounded skills and instincts that let him play above his physical ability. He uses his quick hands to stroke line drives from gap to gap. He won't have big-time power but could develop into a 15-homer threat. His speed is slightly above average and he runs the bases well. Pollock reads balls well and covers a lot of ground in center field, and he had an average arm before he hurt his elbow. Pollock projects as a solid big league regular or at least a quality fourth outfielder on a contender. He was on the fast track prior to his injury, so he could jump to Double-A to begin 2011.

Year	Club (League)	Class	AVG	G	AB	R	H	2B	3B	HR	RBI	BB	SO	SB	CS	OBP	SLG
2009	South Bend (MWL)	LoA	.271	63	255	36	69	12	3	3	22	16	36	10	4	.319	.376
2010	Did Not Play—Injured																
Minor League Totals			.271	63	255	36	69	12	3	3	22	16	36	10	4	.319	.376

7 BOBBY BORCHERING, 3B

Born: Oct. 25, 1990. **B-T:** B-R. **Ht.:** 6-3. **Wt.:** 200. **Drafted:** HS—Fort Myers, Fla., 2009 (1st round). **Signed by:** Ray Blanco.

One of the top high school hitters in the 2009 draft, Borchering went 16th overall as the first of five Arizona picks before the second round. Signed for $1.8 million, he joined many others from his deep draft class last year at South Bend, where he split time at third base with Matt Davidson and also DHed. A switch-hitter, Borchering has all-star caliber raw power from both sides of the plate, but he struggled with his swing and approach in his first full pro season. He started using the whole field more later in the season, which was reflected in his .305/.385/.532 numbers in the final month. He'll have to continue adjusting to make more consistent contact and hit for average against more advanced pitching. He's a better hitter from the right side, as he tends to get out in front and a little jumpy batting lefthanded. Borchering has little chance of remaining at third base, because he lacks quick feet and has slightly below-average arm strength. He has below-average speed, so his only potential destinations are first base and left field. Borchering is still far from reaching his potential. He'll likely move one level at a time and figures to spend 2011 in high Class A, once again in a third-base timeshare with Davidson.

Year	Club (League)	Class	AVG	G	AB	R	H	2B	3B	HR	RBI	BB	SO	SB	CS	OBP	SLG
2009	Missoula (PIO)	R	.241	22	87	10	21	8	1	2	11	5	27	0	0	.290	.425
2010	South Bend (MWL)	LoA	.270	135	523	74	141	31	2	15	74	54	128	1	1	.341	.423
Minor League Totals			.266	157	610	84	162	39	3	17	85	59	155	1	1	.334	.423

8 WADE MILEY, LHP

Born: Nov. 13, 1986. **B-T:** L-L. **Ht.:** 6-2. **Wt.:** 190. **Drafted:** Southeastern Louisiana, 2008 (1st round supplemental). **Signed by:** Trip Couch.

No Diamondbacks farmhand improved as much in 2010 as Miley, a supplemental first-round pick two years earlier who signed for $887,000. After his stuff and prospect status began to slip in 2009, he hired a trainer for the offseason. The improvement in his conditioning and confidence showed as he took his game to another level after a midseason promotion to Double-A, and Arizona considered him for a big league promotion. Miley's fastball dipped to 87-88 mph at times in 2009, but he pitched at 92-93 last year and spiked as high as 96. He uses his 79-83 mph slider as a strikeout pitch, though it gets a little slurvy at times. His changeup flirts with being a plus pitch, improving as he threw it more and with better arm speed. Miley also throws a curveball, which is basically a softer version of his slider, and a cutter. He's still working to improve his command but showed more ability to pitch deep into starts in 2010. He's athletic and fields his position well. If Miley can prove that the strides he made at Mobile were for real, he could get his first big league callup in 2011. Arizona needs pitching, and he'll be just one level away in Triple-A.

Year	Club (League)	Class	W	L	ERA	G	GS	CG	SV	IP	H	HR	BB	SO	G/A	WHIP	AVG
2008	Yakima (NWL)	SS	1	1	4.91	7	0	0	0	11	11	0	5	11	—	1.45	.250
2009	South Bend (MWL)	LoA	5	9	4.12	21	21	0	0	114	127	8	29	91	1.73	1.37	.287
	Visalia (CAL)	HiA	1	1	4.80	3	3	0	0	15	18	0	4	11	1.46	1.47	.295
2010	Visalia (CAL)	HiA	4	5	3.25	14	14	0	0	80	81	1	37	50	3.37	1.47	.266
	Mobile (SL)	AA	5	2	1.98	13	13	1	0	73	60	5	28	63	3.50	1.21	.232
Minor League Totals			16	18	3.41	58	51	1	0	293	297	14	103	226	2.41	1.37	.267

9 PAT CORBIN, LHP

Born: July 19, 1989. **B-T:** L-L. **Ht.:** 6-3. **Wt.:** 165. **Drafted:** Chipola (Fla.) JC, 2009 (2nd round). **Signed by:** Tom Kotchman (Angels).

While Tyler Skaggs was the centerpiece of the Dan Haren trade from the Diamondbacks' perspective, Corbin could give them a second lefty starter out of the deal. He began his college career playing baseball and basketball at Mohawk Valley (N.Y.) CC in 2008 before transferring to Chipola (Fla.) JC and going in the second round the following year. Because Corbin already had pitched 118 innings at the time of the trade, Arizona limited him to three innings per start afterward. Corbin's fastball ranges from 88-92 mph with very good movement. He has the ability to throw nothing but fastballs for long periods because it tails and sinks and is never straight. Both of his secondary pitches have the potential to become at least solid if not more, and his slider currently rates ahead of his changeup. Corbin commands all three of his pitches, has an athletic delivery and possesses a feel for his craft. He has a projectable body, though there are questions about whether his slight build will allow him to hold up over a full season in the rotation. Corbin is ready for Double-A. He projects as a No. 3 or 4 starter and could get his first chance in the big leagues in 2012.

Year	Club (League)	Class	W	L	ERA	G	GS	CG	SV	IP	H	HR	BB	SO	G/A	WHIP	AVG
2009	Orem (PIO)	R	4	2	5.05	13	12	0	0	46	59	6	11	46	1.32	1.51	.291
2010	Cedar Rapids (MWL)	LoA	8	0	3.86	9	9	0	0	58	52	2	10	42	1.35	1.06	.245
	R. Cucamonga (CAL)	HiA	5	3	3.88	11	11	0	0	60	57	7	18	64	1.70	1.24	.247
	Visalia (CAL)	HiA	0	1	1.38	8	8	0	0	26	17	1	9	30	1.29	1.00	.189
Minor League Totals			17	6	3.82	41	40	0	0	191	185	16	48	182	1.43	1.22	.251

10 KEON BROXTON, OF

Born: May 7, 1990. **B-T:** R-R. **Ht.:** 6-3. **Wt.:** 190. **Drafted:** Santa Fe (Fla.) CC, 2009 (3rd round). **Signed by:** Luke Wrenn.

Broxton had a football scholarship to play wide receiver at Florida Atlantic, but he decided to focus on baseball and attend Santa Fe (Fla.) CC after the Phillies drafted him in the 29th round out of high school in 2008. He went 26 rounds higher a year later, adding athleticism to a system sorely in need of toolsy up-the-middle talent. Broxton is a classic high-risk, high-reward player. For all his tools, he lacks baseball instincts and the ability to make consistent contact. He has a sound swing and a quick bat, but he struggles to recognize pitches and handle offspeed stuff. He's a free swinger who doesn't have much usable power, accumulating most of his extra-base hits with his above-average speed. Broxton has the raw ability to be a plus defender in center field, though he needs to upgrade his jumps and routes. He has arm strength but needs more accuracy on throws. Broxton has one of the highest ceilings in the system and a lot of adjustments to make to get there. The Diamondbacks will be patient with him, as he's still only 20 and may need close to a full season at every minor league level. He figures to advance to high Class A in 2011.

Year	Club (League)	Class	AVG	G	AB	R	H	2B	3B	HR	RBI	BB	SO	SB	CS	OBP	SLG
2009	Missoula (PIO)	R	.246	72	272	38	67	11	9	11	37	19	93	6	1	.302	.474
2010	South Bend (MWL)	LoA	.228	133	531	74	121	17	19	5	32	65	172	21	13	.316	.360
Minor League Totals			.234	205	803	112	188	28	28	16	69	84	265	27	14	.311	.399

11 PAUL GOLDSCHMIDT, 1B

Born: Sept. 10, 1987. **B-T:** R-R. **Ht.:** 6-4. **Wt.:** 220 **Drafted:** Texas State, 2009 (8th round). **Signed by:** Trip Couch.

Goldschmidt has a proven track record as a power hitter. He set a school record with 36 career home runs at Texas State, after first coming to scouts' attention in 2006, when he and Kyle Drabek (now the Blue Jays' top prospect) led The Woodlands (Texas) High to the national championship. He led the Rookie-level Pioneer League in homers (18) and slugging percentage (.638) in his debut season, then jumped two levels to high Class A and topped the California League in doubles (42), home runs (35) and slugging (.606) en route to winning the MVP award. He also struck out 161 times, which some scouts see as an indication that he may struggle against better pitching as he moves higher in the system. There's no denying Goldschmidt's legitimate power to all fields, and his supporters believe he has a swing path that will allow him to improve as a hitter. He was especially dangerous against lefthanders last year, batting .413/.453/.860 with 16 homers in just 143 at-bats, so even those who don't believe in him as a regular in the big leagues believe he can at least have a solid career as a platoon player. His defense right now is adequate, and he has the potential to be an average major league first baseman because he's rangy for his size. His speed is well below-average, so he'll have to make it as a first baseman or DH. Goldschmidt will move up to Double A, where he'll be tested by better pitching.

Year	Club (League)	Class	AVG	G	AB	R	H	2B	3B	HR	RBI	BB	SO	SB	CS	OBP	SLG
2009	Missoula (PIO)	R	.334	74	287	51	96	27	3	18	62	36	74	4	3	.408	.638
2010	Visalia (CAL)	HiA	.314	138	525	102	165	42	3	35	108	57	161	5	1	.384	.606
Minor League Totals			.321	212	812	153	261	69	6	53	170	93	235	9	4	.392	.617

12 TY LINTON, OF

Born: Jan. 17, 1991. **B-T:** R-R. **Ht.:** 6-3. **Wt.:** 195. **Drafted:** HS—Charlotte, N.C., 2010 (14th round). **Signed by:** George Swain.

After the Diamondbacks withdrew their offer to first-round pick Barret Loux last summer due to concerns with his shoulder and elbow, they pursued two later picks with the extra money. They were unsuccessful in steering lefthander Kevin Ziomek away from Vanderbilt but signed Linton for $1.25 million at the Aug. 16 deadline, after he had already started football practice at North Carolina. He's extremely athletic and is an above-average runner, with plus bat speed and raw power. He draws Matt Holliday comparisons for his physicality. The Diamondbacks still aren't sure exactly what kind of player they're getting because, as a two-sport athlete, Linton never dedicated himself completely to baseball. It was obvious in instructional league that he was still in football shape. The big question mark with Linton is his swing, as some scouts saw him as a front-foot hitter in high school. During instructional league, coaches worked with him to improve the rhythm of this swing in order to get the lower half and the upper half working together. His arm strength has already improved, from below-average when he signed to average in instructional league. He profiles as a corner outfielder and is learning the nuances of defensive play as well. Linton will start the year in extended spring training before heading to one of the Diamondbacks' short-season teams for his official pro debut.

Year	Club (League)	Class	AVG	G	AB	R	H	2B	3B	HR	RBI	BB	SO	SB	CS	OBP	SLG
2010	Did Not Play—Signed Late																

13 KEVIN MUNSON, RHP

Born: Jan. 3, 1989. **B-T:** R-R. **Ht.:** 6-2. **Wt.:** 200. **Drafted:** James Madison, 2010 (4th round). **Signed by:** Shawn Barton.

After picking projectable, high-risk pitchers with their second- and third-round choices in 2010, the Diamondbacks went with a safer choice in Munson, who served as closer for James Madison. He went straight to South Bend after signing for $243,000 and pitched well there before ending the season with Visalia. Munson is a sinker/slider pitcher with deception to his delivery. His fastball sits comfortably at 92-94 mph with good life, sink and run. His hard slider, a legitimate above-average offering, is a swing-and-miss pitch that he can throw in any count. He has a curveball but it's not functional right now, and he may not need it out of the bullpen. He's a gamer with great makeup. Munson spent part of his time at James Madison as a catcher, so his arm is relatively fresh. He relies on his slider too much at times and will have to sharpen his command. He never started a game in college, so the Diamondbacks will keep him in the role he's comfortable with. He projects as a solid reliever but probably not a closer. New GM Kevin Towers is noted for his bullpen construction, so Munson's development will be watched closely. In all likelihood, he'll be the first player from Arizona's 2010 draft class to make the big leagues, but it may not be until 2012.

Year	Club (League)	Class	W	L	ERA	G	GS	CG	SV	IP	H	HR	BB	SO	G/A	WHIP	AVG
2010	South Bend (MWL)	LoA	2	0	1.10	12	0	0	3	16	8	1	5	17	1.31	0.80	.143
	Visalia (CAL)	HiA	0	0	13.50	1	0	0	0	1	1	0	2	0	1.00	4.50	.333
Minor League Totals			2	0	1.59	13	0	0	3	17	9	1	7	17	1.29	0.94	.153

14 ERIC SMITH, RHP

Born: Oct. 15, 1988. **B-T:** R-R. **Ht.:** 6-3. **Wt.:** 220. **Drafted:** Rhode Island, 2009 (2nd round). **Signed by:** Matt Merullo.

The Diamondbacks made Smith the highest-drafted player in University of Rhode Island history when they took him in the second round of the 2009 draft and signed him for $605,700. He split his first season between Rookie-level Missoula and South Bend, returning to low Class A to open his first full season and earning a promotion to Visalia for his last 10 starts. Smith throws three pitches for strikes and has the ability to pitch deep into his starts. He has a good frame and played basketball in high school. His fastball ranges from 88-93 mph with good movement and plus sink. His slider is an average offering, and his changeup has good dive. Smith throws with a three-quarters, short-arm delivery, hides the ball well and works quickly. He pitches to both sides of the plate and keeps the ball down. He needs to use his lower half more in his delivery and continue to improve his command. He has also worked on a curveball, which would give him a fourth legitimate pitch. Smith may return to high Class A or move up to Double-A with a strong spring training. He could be a middle-of-the-rotation starter, and his tendency to pound the bottom of the zone is well suited for hitter-friendly Chase Field.

Year	Club (League)	Class	W	L	ERA	G	GS	CG	SV	IP	H	HR	BB	SO	G/A	WHIP	AVG
2009	Missoula (PIO)	R	0	3	4.21	9	7	0	0	26	22	1	16	21	2.60	1.48	.232
	South Bend (MWL)	LoA	0	0	2.76	3	3	0	0	16	16	2	6	10	1.47	1.35	.250
2010	South Bend (MWL)	LoA	5	5	3.53	16	16	1	0	87	85	4	32	65	2.38	1.35	.257
	Visalia (CAL)	HiA	4	4	4.97	10	10	0	0	51	56	4	30	36	2.88	1.70	.284
Minor League Totals			9	12	3.96	38	36	1	0	179	179	11	84	132	2.40	1.47	.261

15 MIKE BELFIORE, LHP

Born: Oct. 3, 1988. **B-T:** R-L. **Ht.:** 6-2. **Wt.:** 220. **Drafted:** Boston College, 2009 (1st round supplemental). **Signed by:** Matt Merullo.

Belfiore was a closer during his college career, but the Diamondbacks moved him into the rotation after signing him for $725,000 as a sandwich pick in 2009. He had proven himself suited for the role with 9⅔ innings of scoreless relief in Boston College's epic NCAA regional game against Texas, which it finally lost 3-2 in 25 innings. He made a strong first impression by dominating Rookie-level hitters after signing, but he wasn't as effective in low Class A in 2010. Belfiore is still learning how to be a starting pitcher, and showed some positive signs in the second half of the season when his velocity increased a few ticks to 92-93 mph. He throws a slider and a changeup in the low 80s. His major league-average changeup is regarded as his best pitch and could get better since he really didn't start using it until he joined the pro ranks. He throws with an easy arm action, and his average command could grade as plus in the future, but he doesn't have swing-and-miss stuff. Belfiore has a No. 4 starter's upside, but he does look like he'll have the stuff and stamina to remain in the rotation. One scout sees him as a late bloomer who will come on later in his career, similar to former big leaguer Jeff Fassero.

Year	Club (League)	Class	W	L	ERA	G	GS	CG	SV	IP	H	HR	BB	SO	G/A	WHIP	AVG
2009	Missoula (PIO)	R	2	2	2.17	14	11	0	0	58	59	2	13	55	1.85	1.24	.259
2010	South Bend (MWL)	LoA	3	10	3.99	25	25	0	0	126	139	6	42	105	1.27	1.43	.277
Minor League Totals			5	12	3.42	39	36	0	0	184	198	8	55	160	1.43	1.37	.272

16 RYAN WHEELER, 3B

Born: July 10, 1988. **B-T:** L-R. **Ht.:** 6-4. **Wt.:** 220. **Drafted:** Loyola Marymount, 2009 (5th round). **Signed by:** Hal Kurtzman.

The Diamondbacks continued their run on corner infielders in the 2009 draft by selecting Wheeler, whose stock had fallen after a disappointing junior season at Loyola Marymount. He returned to form after signing, however, batting .361/.462/.540 between Yakima and South Bend and earning the organization's minor league player of the year award in just half a season. Because he's not viewed as a true masher, Wheeler moved across the infield to third base last spring and spent most of 2010 playing there, though he also played a little first base and left field. Wheeler is a bat-first player who stands right on top of the plate and uses the whole field. He shows the ability to drive the ball out to the big part of the park at times. He has a good approach and has worked hard to improve. Wheeler is a fringy defensive player at third base with limited range and footwork, but he did improve as the season went on. He has an average arm and some scouts think he can be an average defender at third, in spite of well below-average speed. He'll need to make that happen or show consistent power to all fields to avoid becoming a tweener, with not enough bat for first base and not enough defense for third. He'll return to Double-A to open 2011

Year	Club (League)	Class	AVG	G	AB	R	H	2B	3B	HR	RBI	BB	SO	SB	CS	OBP	SLG
2009	Yakima (NWL)	SS	.363	64	234	44	85	20	3	5	36	37	28	7	4	.461	.538
	South Bend (MWL)	LoA	.345	8	29	4	10	1	1	1	5	5	4	0	1	.472	.552
2010	Visalia (CAL)	HiA	.284	113	465	62	132	25	2	9	57	35	98	3	1	.340	.404
	Mobile (SL)	AA	.254	19	67	8	17	3	0	3	10	5	16	0	0	.315	.433
Minor League Totals			.307	204	795	118	244	49	6	18	108	82	146	10	6	.381	.452

17 KAM MICKOLIO, RHP

Born: May 10, 1984. **B-T:** R-R. **Ht.:** 6-9. **Wt.:** 240. **Drafted:** Utah Valley State, 2006 (18th round). **Signed by:** Phil Geisler (Mariners).

New GM Kevin Towers wasted no time in beginning his makeover of the Arizona bullpen, sending Mark Reynolds to the Orioles for David Hernandez and Mickolio. The Mickolio scouting report is starting to sound like a broken record, but when you can throw a fastball at 95-96 mph and touch 98 with nasty life in the zone, you'll get every possible chance to succeed. Mickolio was one of the players the Orioles got from the Mariners in the Erik Bedard trade before the 2008 season, and he has received big league looks in each of the last three seasons. He won a quick promotion to Baltimore last April, but he didn't throw enough strikes and got lit up in the big leagues, going back down after just three appearances. He was shut down for about six weeks in June and July with a shoulder strain. The dominant Mickolio reappeared in the Arizona Fall League, as he posted a 0.75 ERA with 18 strikeouts and two walks in 12 innings, including a scoreless inning in the league championship game. When he's on, Mickolio can pile up the scoreless innings, unleashing power fastballs and hard sliders from an intimidating 6-foot-9 frame and unorthodox crossfire delivery. He uses his changeup on occasion, though it's a below-average pitch and not an essential part of his arsenal. His ultimate success depends on his ability to repeat his delivery and establish better command. He shows it in flashes but so far has not done it consistently in the majors. The Diamondbacks are counting on him to contribute right away.

Year	Club (League)	Class	W	L	ERA	G	GS	CG	SV	IP	H	HR	BB	SO	G/A	WHIP	AVG
2006	Everett (NWL)	SS	1	0	2.78	21	0	0	4	32	34	1	7	26	—	1.27	.264
2007	West Tenn (SL)	AA	3	1	1.82	18	0	0	2	30	24	0	12	27	—	1.21	.224
	Tacoma (PCL)	AAA	3	3	3.75	14	0	0	1	24	19	3	10	28	—	1.21	.213
2008	Bowie (EL)	AA	2	1	4.70	28	0	0	1	38	39	2	22	40	—	1.59	.262
	Norfolk (IL)	AAA	1	0	1.80	17	0	0	2	20	13	0	9	23	—	1.10	.173
	Baltimore (AL)	MAJ	0	0	5.87	9	0	0	0	8	8	0	4	8	—	1.57	.267
2009	Norfolk (IL)	AAA	3	3	3.50	35	0	0	44	32	4	16	52	0.54	1.10	.203
	Baltimore (AL)	MAJ	0	2	2.63	11	0	0	0	14	11	0	7	14	1.08	1.32	.220
2010	Norfolk (IL)	AAA	4	3	6.37	30	0	0	0	35	44	4	17	48	2.86	1.73	.297
	Baltimore (AL)	MAJ	0	0	7.36	3	0	0	0	4	5	1	3	4	0.17	2.18	.313
	Aberdeen (NYP)	SS	1	0	1.80	4	0	0	0	5	1	1	1	7	1.00	0.40	.063
Major League Totals			0	3	4.32	23	0	0	0	25	24	1	14	26	0.79	1.52	.250
Minor League Totals			18	11	3.67	167	0	0	10	228	206	15	94	251	1.04	1.31	.237

18 COLLIN COWGILL, OF

Born: May 22, 1986. **B-T:** R-L. **Ht.:** 5-9. **Wt.:** 195. **Drafted:** Kentucky, 2008 (5th round). **Signed by:** Matthew Haas.

Arizona has few legitimate prospects who have significant playing time above the high Class A level, but Cowgill performed well for Mobile in his third professional season. He's a versatile outfielder who can play all three positions with average defense. Cowgill sports the best outfield arm in the system, combining strength with accuracy. It's his top tool and grades at 60 or better on the 20-80 scouting scale. Cowgill also is a slightly above-average runner and an instinctive basestealer. He made great strides in his approach at the plate this year, becoming more selective and working on his swing mechanics. He wraps his bat almost like Gary Sheffield and has a high finish, and he sometimes struggles against good fastball velocity. Cowgill's intangibles are off the charts. He's competitive and has a great work ethic, and scouts frequently observed him working out before games. He probably won't have enough bat for an outfield corner or enough speed to play center field every day, so Cowgill profiles better as a versatile fourth outfielder, but he's a good bet to have a major league career. He is sometimes compared to Cody Ross, primarily for the grinder mentality and the fact that both players bat right and throw left. He'll head to Triple-A this year with the chance for a callup when the need arises.

Year	Club (League)	Class	AVG	G	AB	R	H	2B	3B	HR	RBI	BB	SO	SB	CS	OBP	SLG
2008	Yakima (NWL)	SS	.304	20	79	21	24	3	1	11	28	12	17	5	0	.415	.785
	South Bend (MWL)	LoA	.249	50	201	31	50	13	3	1	17	25	61	1	0	.346	.358
2009	Visalia (CAL)	HiA	.277	61	220	39	61	9	5	6	36	29	49	11	4	.373	.445
2010	Mobile (SL)	AA	.285	131	502	89	143	34	4	16	83	57	73	25	9	.360	.464
Minor League Totals			.277	262	1002	180	278	59	13	34	164	123	200	42	13	.365	.464

19 WAGNER MATEO, OF

Born: March 30, 1993. **B-T:** L-L. **Ht.:** 6-2. **Wt.:** 190. **Drafted:** Dominican Republic, 2010. **Signed by:** Junior Noboa.

Mateo was one of the most heavily recruited Latin players during the 2009 international signing period, signing with the Cardinals on July 2 for a $3.1 million bonus. The Cardinals later voided the deal when their doctors found problems with Mateo's vision. He tried out for various teams during spring training 2010 and eventually came to terms with the Diamondbacks in May for $512,000. He made his pro debut in the Dominican Summer League before coming to the United States for instructional league in the fall. Mateo has a strong, athletic body and has a chance to be a major league corner outfielder. He has a good swing path, and the ball screams off his bat. His power is better to left-center. To become more consistent, he'll need to stop trying to yank everything and trust his natural power. He would benefit from better control of the strike zone after ranking second in the DSL with 83 strikeouts. Mateo has well-above-average arm strength, but his throws aren't very accurate and he's still a raw defender in the outfield. His speed is average right now, and he'll probably slow down as he gets bigger. As for his eyesight, the Diamondbacks believe Mateo's problems in 2009 resulted from using hard contact lenses without the proper solution. The true test will be when he plays for one of the Diamondbacks short-season affiliates in his first season in the States.

Year	Club (League)	Class	AVG	G	AB	R	H	2B	3B	HR	RBI	BB	SO	SB	CS	OBP	SLG
2010	Diamondbacks (DSL)	R	.257	67	237	45	61	14	4	4	45	35	83	16	10	.359	.401
Minor League Totals			.257	67	237	45	61	14	4	4	45	35	83	16	10	.359	.401

20 TYLER GREEN, RHP

Born: Nov. 24, 1991. **B-T:** R-R. **Ht.:** 6-1. **Wt.:** 175. **Drafted:** HS—Clute, Texas, 2010 (8th round). **Signed by:** Trip Couch.

Green was one of the better two-way players in the Texas high school ranks in 2010, but he fell in the draft due to signability concerns related to his commitment to Texas Christian. Arizona signed him for an above-slot bonus of $750,000 just before the Aug. 16 signing deadline. He was better known as a hitter during his high school career, and would have been a two-way player in college, but professional scouts focused on his fastball. His first action with the Diamondbacks was in instructional league, and he opened a lot of eyes by flashing a mid-90s fastball and displaying a bulldog mentality on the mound. He also throws a hard overhand curveball that has plus potential. Green's delivery will need of a lot of work. Though he has no problems throwing strikes, he doesn't do anything easy. With his 6-foot-1 frame and the effort in his delivery, he projects better as a relief pitcher, but the Diamondbacks will use him as a starter at the outset to get him plenty of innings. One scout who saw Green in instructional league called him a poor man's Brian Wilson. Because he's inexperienced as a pitcher, Green will start the year in extended spring training before launching his pro career with one of the Diamondbacks' short-season teams.

Year	Club (League)	Class	W	L	ERA	G	GS	CG	SV	IP	H	HR	BB	SO	G/A	WHIP	AVG
2010	Did Not Play—Signed Late																

21 ROBBY ROWLAND, RHP

Born: Dec. 15, 1991. **B-T:** B-R. **Ht.:** 6-6. **Wt.:** 205. **Drafted:** HS—Cloverdale, Calif., 2010 (3rd round). **Signed by:** Darold Brown.

The son of former major league catcher Rich Rowland, Robby could have gone to Oregon on a baseball scholarship or pursued a basketball offer, but instead he signed with the Diamondbacks for $395,000 after being taken in the third round. His older brother Richie joined him on the Missoula roster as a nondrafted free agent catcher. Rowland has a tall, strong body with room to fill out. He carries himself with confidence and has an outgoing personality. His 87-91 mph fastball has late run, and he offers projection with possibility of an increase in velocity as he fills out. His curveball, which he throws at 69-75 mph, has good spin and has 12-to-6 potential. His slider is slightly better than the curve, and he also throws a forkball, his swing and miss pitch, in the low 80s with diving action. He has a clean, over-the-top delivery and commands all of his pitches. Rowland projects as a back-of-the-rotation starter at present, but he could become more than that if the fastball becomes a plus pitch. He could move up to low Class A to start the 2011 season, but more likely will stay in extended spring training before reporting to Yakima in June.

Year	Club (League)	Class	W	L	ERA	G	GS	CG	SV	IP	H	HR	BB	SO	G/A	WHIP	AVG
2010	Missoula (PIO)	R	4	6	5.67	14	14	0	0	54	62	7	21	40	1.63	1.54	.291
Minor League Totals			4	6	5.67	14	14	0	0	54	62	7	21	40	1.63	1.54	.291

22 DAVID HOLMBERG, LHP

Born: July 19, 1991. **B-T:** R-L. **Ht.:** 6-4. **Wt.:** 220. **Drafted:** HS—Port Charlotte, Fla., 2009 (2nd round). **Signed by:** Joe Siers (White Sox).

The White Sox signed Holmberg away from a Florida scholarship in 2009, giving him $514,000 as the fourth of four picks they had before the third round that year. He opened the 2010 season in the Rookie-level Pioneer League before being included in a trade to the Diamondbacks (along with Daniel Hudson) for Edwin Jackson. Holmberg moved from Great Falls to Missoula and pitched his first two games with his new organization against his old Voyagers teammates. Holmberg is a typical strike-throwing lefty with three pitches (fastball, curveball, changeup), and he is also working on a slider that he previously threw in high school. Despite his big body, Holmberg rarely gets his fastball over 90 mph. His curveball has a tendency to get loopy, but later in the season he was becoming more aggressive in trying to finish the pitch. His above-average changeup is a better pitch. Holmberg's mechanics are smooth, and he has a better idea of pitching to the glove side than other southpaws. He's mature for his age and stays within himself on the mound. Holmberg may offer a little bit of projection, but realistically looks like a back-of-the-rotation workhorse. He'll get his first full-season assignment in 2011 with South Bend.

Year	Club (League)	Class	W	L	ERA	G	GS	CG	SV	IP	H	HR	BB	SO	G/A	WHIP	AVG
2009	Bristol (APP)	R	2	2	4.72	14	7	0	0	40	40	5	18	37	1.60	1.45	.256
2010	Great Falls (PIO)	R	1	1	4.46	8	8	0	0	40	52	2	9	29	2.36	1.51	.315
	Missoula (PIO)	R	1	4	3.86	7	7	0	0	37	47	2	7	47	1.73	1.45	.294
Minor League Totals			4	7	4.36	29	22	0	0	118	139	9	34	113	1.88	1.47	.289

23 J.R. BRADLEY, RHP

Born: June 9, 1992. **B-T:** R-R. **Ht.:** 6-4. **Wt.:** 185. **Drafted:** HS—Nitro, W.Va., 2010 (2nd round). **Signed by:** Shawn Barton.

The Diamondbacks stocked up on projectable righthanders early in the 2010 draft, starting with Bradley. He passed on a scholarship to North Carolina State and signed for a $643,500 bonus. Bradley's debut with Missoula was uneven, and his velocity fell off as the season progressed. His two-seam fastball sits at 92-93 mph when he's at his best, and he throws it with a fluid, easy delivery. He projects to gain velocity as he adds weight to his tall, slender frame. His secondary pitches are only rudimentary right now, and he lacks much feel for pitching, though he shows a knack for throwing strikes. At times he relied too much on his curveball and slider instead of working on his fastball and changeup. Bradley will be a bit of a project, but he's a hard worker who enjoys playing the game and wants to succeed. He likely won't be ready for a full season assignment in 2011 and will start the year in extended spring training.

Year	Club (League)	Class	W	L	ERA	G	GS	CG	SV	IP	H	HR	BB	SO	G/A	WHIP	AVG
2010	Missoula (PIO)	R	1	7	5.93	14	14	0	0	55	66	7	24	40	1.35	1.65	.301
Minor League Totals			1	7	5.93	14	14	0	0	55	66	7	24	40	1.35	1.65	.301

24 CHARLES BREWER, RHP

Born: June 4, 1988. **B-T:** R-R. **Ht.:** 6-4. **Wt.:** 205. **Drafted:** UCLA, 2009 (12th round). **Signed by:** Hal Kurtzman.

Brewer played his high school ball in the Phoenix area and was drafted by the Angels in the 18th round in 2006, but instead he headed to UCLA for three years. The Diamondbacks took him in the 12th round in 2009 and he started his career with a nice season in Missoula. He built on it in 2010 and turned out to be one of the more pleasant surprises in the system, splitting the year with good performances at both of Arizona's Class A affiliates. Brewer has a prototypical pitcher's body and throws with good arm action. He throws all three of his pitches (fastball, curveball, changeup) for strikes. His fastball ranges from 89-93 mph but is straight and doesn't offer a lot of deception. The changeup improved this year to an average pitch and is now his best offering. Brewer has the ability to locate his pitches in the strike zone from side to side and works up in the zone. Scouts are skeptical about how well his repertoire will work at higher levels, so a move to Double-A at some point in 2011 will be a good test for Brewer.

Year	Club (League)	Class	W	L	ERA	G	GS	CG	SV	IP	H	HR	BB	SO	G/A	WHIP	AVG
2009	Missoula (PIO)	R	7	2	2.47	17	7	0	0	55	43	4	15	61	1.62	1.06	.216
2010	South Bend (MWL)	LoA	4	5	1.83	13	13	0	0	69	55	3	20	78	1.36	1.09	.216
	Visalia (CAL)	HiA	7	3	2.98	14	14	0	0	82	74	5	15	75	1.64	1.09	.239
Minor League Totals			18	10	2.45	44	34	0	0	205	172	12	50	214	1.54	1.08	.225

25 RAUL NAVARRO, SS

Born: Feb. 5, 1992. **B-T:** R-R. **Ht.:** 5-11. **Wt.:** 160. **Drafted:** Dominican Republic, 2009. **Signed by:** Junior Noboa.

Navarro made his stateside debut with Missoula in the same season when his older brother, Yamaico, reached the big leagues with the Red Sox. Both Navarros are shortstops, not surprising since they hail from San Pedro de Macoris, long regarded as "the cradle of shortstops." They come by their abilities naturally, as their mother was a star softball player with the Dominican national team. Raul had a strong season in Missoula, and while projections on how he'll hit at higher levels vary, the Diamondbacks believe he can be an above-average hitter with gap-to-gap power. He has a good feel for hitting and is short to the ball. Navarro's strong arm is regarded as the best infield arm in the system. He has average range and his glove-to-hand speed is good, but he needs to improve his preparedness on defense in order to take advantage of his tools. The Diamondbacks believe Navarro turned a corner with regular instruction during the season and in instructional league. With older shortstops ahead of him in the lower levels of the system, Navarro will likely spend another year in short-season ball with an assignment to Yakima.

Year	Club (League)	Class	AVG	G	AB	R	H	2B	3B	HR	RBI	BB	SO	SB	CS	OBP	SLG
2009	Diamondbacks (DSL)	R	.280	67	271	43	76	12	1	1	11	35	42	12	8	.371	.343
2010	Missoula (PIO)	R	.305	63	243	39	74	11	5	2	28	18	41	2	3	.357	.416
Minor League Totals			.292	130	514	82	150	23	6	3	39	53	83	14	11	.365	.377

26 CHASE ANDERSON, RHP

Born: Nov. 30, 1987. **B-T:** R-R. **Ht.:** 6-1. **Wt.:** 175. **Drafted:** Oklahoma, 2009 (9th round). **Signed by:** Jason Karegeannes.

Anderson is another college righthander who pleasantly surprised the organization with his progress in his first full season. The Twins used late-round picks on Anderson out of high school and junior college in Texas in 2006 and 2007, but he headed to Oklahoma instead. He jumped to Visalia after just seven starts at South Bend last season. Anderson was a reliever in college, but the Diamondbacks believe he can be a starter and will continue to work him into a rotation to get him more innings. Anderson's best pitch is his changeup, a legitimate plus pitch that he will throw in any situation. It's considered the best in the organization. His fastball arrives at 89-92 mph with good sink, and he throws a slider and curveball as well. He has a clean delivery and above-average command. Anderson is not big or overpowering, but he mixes his pitches well and keeps hitters off balance. Anderson will move up to Double-A in 2011. If he can't make it as a starter long-term, he's expected to have a future as a middle reliever.

Year	Club (League)	Class	W	L	ERA	G	GS	CG	SV	IP	H	HR	BB	SO	G/A	WHIP	AVG
2009	Missoula (PIO)	R	3	1	2.38	18	4	0	0	45	35	1	13	48	1.43	1.06	.206
2010	South Bend (MWL)	LoA	2	4	2.82	7	7	1	0	38	36	1	9	31	1.00	1.17	.238
	Visalia (CAL)	HiA	5	3	3.60	19	4	0	3	70	58	7	16	83	0.80	1.06	.227
Minor League Totals			10	8	3.05	44	15	1	3	154	129	9	38	162	1.02	1.09	.224

27 BRYAN SHAW, RHP

Born: Nov. 8, 1987. **B-T:** B-R. **Ht.:** 6-1. **Wt.:** 210. **Drafted:** Long Beach State, 2008 (2nd round). **Signed by:** Jim Dedrick.

The Diamondbacks drafted Shaw in the second round in 2008 based on his impressive work as the closer at Long Beach State. He has bounced between the bullpen and rotation in this three years as a pro and pitched exclusively out of the bullpen in the Arizona Fall League following the 2010 season. While Arizona would have been delighted if he had blossomed as a starter, Shaw primarily has been in rotations to get innings. He profiles better as a reliever. His velocity is more consistent coming out of the bullpen, and he feels more comfortable there. Shaw has a four-pitch mix, and all are at least average offerings. His 90-94 mph fastball has plus movement and sink. His curveball has the potential to be a plus pitch, and he throws a good slider with cut action. Shaw will move to Triple-A in 2011 and could get a call to the big leagues when a reliever is needed.

Year	Club (League)	Class	W	L	ERA	G	GS	CG	SV	IP	H	HR	BB	SO	G/A	WHIP	AVG
2008	Missoula (PIO)	R	0	1	6.75	10	0	0	2	17	24	2	7	17	—	1.79	.316
	South Bend (MWL)	LoA	0	1	4.03	11	0	0	0	22	18	0	6	16	—	1.07	.217
2009	Visalia (CAL)	HiA	3	7	4.70	30	19	0	0	107	96	7	40	95	1.96	1.27	.236
2010	Mobile (SL)	AA	4	9	4.26	33	13	0	2	101	102	4	43	75	2.18	1.43	.266
Minor League Totals			7	18	4.60	84	32	0	4	248	240	13	96	203	2.06	1.35	.253

28 RONNY MEJIAS, SS

Born: May 9, 1994. **B-T:** B-R. **Ht.:** 6-1. **Wt.:** 175. **Signed:** Venezuela, 2010. **Signed by:** Marlon Urdaneta.

The Diamondbacks made two big acquisitions from Venezuela during the 2010 international signing period, signing outfielder Yorman Garcia for $200,000 and Mejias for $320,000. Mejias, a switch-hitting shortstop from Zulia who pitched and played shortstop in the Little League World Series in 2007, had one of the best swings in the Latin American class. He has projectable power from both sides of the plate, and a swing that allows the bat head to stay in the zone a long time. His lefthanded stroke is more advanced than his righthanded swing. He has above-average speed and was timed at 6.8 seconds in the 60-yard dash during workouts last summer. It's questionable whether Mejias will be able to stay at shortstop as he grows stronger, but he has the skills to play there now and the Diamondbacks will not move him off the position to start his career. His bat is projected to play at any position, and his average arm would allow him to handle third base or left field. Mejias will likely start his pro career in the Dominican Summer League, but could make it to the United States with the Diamondbacks' new affiliate in the Rookie-level Arizona League.

Year	Club (League)	Class	AVG	G	AB	R	H	2B	3B	HR	RBI	BB	SO	SB	CS	OBP	SLG
2010	Did Not Play—Signed 2011 Contract																

29 ZACH WALTERS, SS

Born: Sept. 5, 1989. **B-T:** B-R. **Ht.:** 6-3. **Wt.:** 193. **Drafted:** San Diego, 2010 (9th round). **Signed by:** Jeffrey Mousser.

Walters was the first position player drafted by the Diamondbacks after they selected eight straight pitchers to start the 2010 draft. He missed part of his junior season with a dislocated thumb but returned to help San Diego advance to NCAA regional play. Signed for $97,500, Walters was a favorite of short-season Northwest League managers in his pro debut. He's a smart, physical player whose aptitude for the game will probably outweigh his tools. He showed surprising pop from both sides of the plate, with the ability to hit for average. He's a good runner who shows instincts on the bases. He has a loose body with good actions on the field and the ability to slow the game down. He's a good, accurate thrower with good hands, but some scouts question whether he'll have the arm and range to play shortstop in the big leagues. Walters projects more as a utility player who can play all infield positions, drawing one comparison to major league veteran Geoff Blum, who coincidentally signed with Arizona for the 2011 season. Walters will move on to low Class A for his first full season.

Year	Club (League)	Class	AVG	G	AB	R	H	2B	3B	HR	RBI	BB	SO	SB	CS	OBP	SLG
2010	Yakima (NWL)	SS	.302	69	275	44	83	18	4	4	43	16	59	14	4	.338	.440
Minor League Totals			.302	69	275	44	83	18	4	4	43	16	59	14	4	.338	.440

30 ADAM EATON, OF

Born: Dec. 6, 1988. **B-T:** L-L. **Ht.:** 5-9. **Wt.:** 180. **Drafted:** Miami (Ohio), 2010 (19th round). **Signed by:** Frankie Thon Jr.

Arizona's biggest surprise of the 2010 draft came in a small package. Selected in the 19th round and signed for $35,000, Eaton turned out to be the best pure hitter in the Diamondbacks' draft class. He led the Pioneer League in hitting (.385) and on-base percentage (.500) in his pro debut. Eaton may be undersized at 5-foot-9 and 180 pounds, but he has a strong, developed body. With a short stroke and an all-fields approach, he puts the bat on the ball and makes consistent hard contact. He has surprising pop, though most of his power is to the gaps rather than over the fence. Eaton has solid speed that plays up on the bases and in center field due to his instincts. His arm strength is average. It would be simple to look at his size and write Eaton off as a fourth outfielder, but some scouts believe he could develop into a starter in the big leagues. Arizona will have a better idea of what it has in Eaton once it sees him in full-season ball in 2011, and he may start the year by jumping to high Class A.

Year	Club (League)	Class	AVG	G	AB	R	H	2B	3B	HR	RBI	BB	SO	SB	CS	OBP	SLG
2010	Missoula (PIO)	R	.385	68	226	48	87	14	4	7	37	35	44	20	8	.500	.575
Minor League Totals			.385	68	226	48	87	14	4	7	37	35	44	20	8	.500	.575

Atlanta Braves

BY BILL BALLEW

It may have seemed like forever to their fans, but it was just in 2005 that the Braves' run of National League East titles had ended.

Atlanta fell short of a division title in 2010 but did hold on for the wild card after four seasons out of the playoffs. The Braves succumbed to the Giants in the NL Division Series, but still provided a positive send-off for Bobby Cox, who retired after spending the last 21 seasons as manager.

Cox built the foundation for the run of division titles that began in 1991, coming to Atlanta as general manager in October 1985 and moving into the dugout after the 1990 season, when John Schuerholz came on board as GM. Now Cox has stepped down, three years after Schuerholz moved up to team president, but current GM Frank Wren and the rest of the Braves front office believe they're positioned for another run of success.

Reaching the postseason after the injuries that hit the roster in the second half was an achievement in itself. The most notable came when franchise cornerstone Chipper Jones tore the ACL in his left knee on Aug. 10. In fact, the only position players who were in the lineup on Opening Day and Game One of the playoffs were Brian McCann and Jason Heyward.

Heyward came into the season as one of the top prospects in the game and lived up to his billing, batting .277/.393/.456 with 18 home runs, playing a solid right field and winning Baseball America's Rookie of the Year award. Atlanta got contributions from several other rookies as well, including bullpen stalwart Jonny Venters, who made 79 appearances with a 1.95 ERA. Brandon Beachy, Craig Kimbrel and Mike Minor plugged holes on the pitching staff, while Brooks Conrad was a useful utility player.

Youth will be served again in 2011, with first baseman Freddie Freeman and a handful of pitchers ready to contribute. With those new arrivals and the hiring of manager Fredi Gonzalez, the Braves hope to continue contending while making over the organization from top to bottom.

Last year's Braves prospect list was heavy on pitching and light on position players, so Atlanta used the draft and international signings to bolster its stable of hitters. In his first draft as Braves scouting director, Tony DeMacio took hitters with his first four selections, starting with Texas high school shortstop Matt Lipka in the supplemental first round. Lipka notwithstanding, DeMacio also broke with the organization's recent tradition and focused on four-year college play-

From Opening Day through the playoffs, Jason Heyward lived up to expectations

TONY FARLOW

TOP 30 PROSPECTS

1. Julio Teheran, rhp
2. Freddie Freeman, 1b
3. Randall Delgado, rhp
4. Mike Minor, lhp
5. Craig Kimbrel, rhp
6. Matt Lipka, ss
7. Arodys Vizcaino, rhp
8. Brandon Beachy, rhp
9. Brett Oberholtzer, lhp
10. J.J. Hoover, rhp
11. Carlos Perez, lhp
12. Christian Bethancourt, c
13. Erik Cordier, rhp
14. Tyler Pastornicky, ss
15. Andrelton Simmons, ss
16. Edward Salcedo, ss
17. David Hale, rhp
18. Dimasther Delgado, lhp
19. Mycal Jones, 2b/ss
20. Todd Cunningham, of
21. Elmer Reyes, 2b
22. Adam Milligan, of
23. Joe Leonard, 3b
24. David Filak, rhp
25. Phil Gosselin, 2b
26. Paul Clemens, rhp
27. Juan Abreu, rhp
28. Brett Butts, rhp
29. Cory Harrilchak, of
30. Richard Sullivan, lhp

ers in the first 10 rounds.

International scouting director Johnny Almaraz signed Dominican shortstop Edward Salcedo for $1.6 million, the largest bonus the organization has ever given to an international free agent. The Braves have put focus on Latin America while boosting their presence in Europe via a facility in the Canary Islands.

Atlanta even became aggressive signing independent league players. The Braves acquired outfielder Beau Torbert, Baseball America's 2010 Independent League Player of the Year, and righthander Wes Alsup and first baseman Christian Garcia, BA's second- and third-ranked indy prospects last season.

General Manager: Frank Wren. **Farm Director:** Kurt Kemp. **Scouting Director:** Tony DeMacio.

Class	Team	League	W	L	PCT	Finish*	Manager
Majors	Atlanta Braves	National	91	71	.562	t-3rd (16)	Bobby Cox
Triple-A	Gwinnett Braves	International	72	71	.503	7th (14)	Dave Brundage
Double-A	Mississippi Braves	Southern	63	74	.460	8th (10)	Phillip Wellman
High A	Myrtle Beach Pelicans	Carolina	58	82	.414	8th (8)	Rocket Wheeler
Low A	Rome Braves	South Atlantic	59	80	.424	13th (14)	Randy Ingle
Rookie	Danville Braves	Appalachian	34	34	.500	t-4th (10)	Paul Runge
Rookie	GCL Braves	Gulf Coast	27	31	.466	11th (15)	Luis Ortiz
Overall 2010 Minor League Record			313	372	.457	28th (30)	

*Finish in overall standings (No. of teams in league). †League champion.
High Class A affiliate changes to Lynchburg (Carolina) in 2011.

LAST YEAR'S TOP 30

Player, Pos.		Status
1.	Jason Heyward, of	Majors
2.	Freddie Freeman, 1b	No. 2
3.	Julio Teheran, rhp	No. 1
4.	Mike Minor, lhp	No. 4
5.	Craig Kimbrel, rhp	No. 5
6.	Christian Bethancourt, c	No. 12
7.	Randall Delgado, rhp	No. 3
8.	Zeke Spruill, lhp	Dropped out
9.	Cody Johnson, of	(Yankees)
10.	Adam Milligan, of	No. 22
11.	J.J. Hoover, rhp	No. 10
12.	Dimasther Delgado, lhp	No. 18
13.	Brett Oberholtzer, lhp	No. 9
14.	David Hale, rhp	No. 17
15.	Tyler Stovall, lhp	Dropped out
16.	Robinson Lopez, rhp	(Cubs)
17.	Mycal Jones, ss	No. 19
18.	Brandon Hicks, ss	Dropped out
19.	Brett DeVall, lhp	Dropped out
20.	Juan Abreu, rhp	No. 27
21.	Caleb Brewer, rhp	Dropped out
22.	Richard Sullivan, lhp	No. 30
23.	Cole Rohrbough, lhp	Dropped out
24.	Kyle Cofield, rhp	(White Sox)
25.	Jose Ortegano, lhp	Dropped out
26.	Scott Diamond, lhp	(Twins)
27.	Jesus Sucre, c	Dropped out
28.	Paul Clemens, rhp	No. 26
29.	Riaan Spanjer-Furstenburg, 1b	Dropped out
30.	Jonny Venters, lhp	Majors

BEST TOOLS

Best Hitter for Average	Freddie Freeman
Best Power Hitter	Freddie Freeman
Best Strike-Zone Discipline	Cory Harrilchak
Fastest Baserunner	Matt Lipka
Best Athlete	Matt Lipka
Best Fastball	Julio Teheran
Best Curveball	Arodys Vizcaino
Best Slider	David Hale
Best Changeup	Mike Minor
Best Control	Brandon Beachy
Best Defensive Catcher	Jesus Sucre
Best Defensive Infielder	Andrelton Simmons
Best Infield Arm	Andrelton Simmons
Best Defensive Outfielder	Cory Harrilchak
Best Outfield Arm	Cory Harrilchak

PROJECTED 2014 LINEUP

Catcher	Brian McCann
First Base	Freddie Freeman
Second Base	Dan Uggla
Third Base	Martin Prado
Shortstop	Tyler Pastornicky
Left Field	Nate McLouth
Center Field	Matt Lipka
Right Field	Jason Heyward
No. 1 Starter	Tommy Hanson
No. 2 Starter	Julio Teheran
No. 3 Starter	Randall Delgado
No. 4 Starter	Mike Minor
No. 5 Starter	Jair Jurrjens
Closer	Craig Kimbrel

TOP PROSPECTS OF THE DECADE

Year	Player, Pos.	2010 Org.
2001	Wilson Betemit, ss	Royals
2002	Wilson Betemit, ss	Royals
2003	Adam Wainwright, rhp	Cardinals
2004	Andy Marte, 3b	Indians
2005	Jeff Francoeur, of	Rangers
2006	Jarrod Saltalamacchia, c	Red Sox
2007	Jarrod Saltalamacchia, c	Red Sox
2008	Jordan Schafer, of	Braves
2009	Tommy Hanson, rhp	Braves
2010	Jason Heyward, of	Braves

TOP DRAFT PICKS OF THE DECADE

Year	Player, Pos.	2010 Org.
2001	Macay McBride, lhp	Lancaster (Atlantic)
2002	Jeff Francoeur, of	Rangers
2003	Luis Atiliano, rhp (1st round supp.)	Nationals
2004	Eric Campbell, 3b (2nd round)	Mets
2005	Joey Devine, rhp	Athletics
2006	Cody Johnson, of	Braves
2007	Jason Heyward, of	Braves
2008	Brett DeVall (1st round supp.)	Braves
2009	Mike Minor, lhp	Braves
2010	Matt Lipka, ss	Braves

LARGEST BONUSES IN CLUB HISTORY

Mike Minor, 2009	$2,420,000
Jeff Francoeur, 2002	$2,200,000
Matt Belisle, 1998	$1,750,000
Jason Heyward, 2007	$1,700,000
Edward Salcedo, 2010	$1,600,000

ATLANTA BRAVES

TOP 2011 ROOKIE: Freddie Freeman, 1b. Freeman will reunite with Jason Heyward in Atlanta to from the young nucleus of the big league lineup.

BREAKOUT PROSPECT: Erik Cordier, rhp. Finally healthy the last two seasons, he's operating in the mid-90s with his fastball.

SLEEPER: Lee Hyde, lhp. Having recovered from Tommy John surgery in 2007, the former Georgia Tech star could return to Atlanta as a big league reliever in 2011.

SOURCE OF TOP 30 TALENT			
Homegrown	26	Acquired	4
College	9	Trades	3
Junior college	7	Rule 5 draft	0
High school	2	Independent leagues	0
Draft-and-follow	0	Free agents/waivers	1
Nondrafted free agents	1		
International	7		

LF	CF	RF
Todd Cunningham (20)	Cory Harrilchak (29)	David Rohm
Adam Milligan (22)	Jose Costanzo	
Matt Young	Kurt Fleming	
Robby Hefflinger	Cole Miles	
Beau Torbert	Kyle Rose	

3B	SS	2B	1B
Edward Salcedo (16)	Matt Lipka (6)	Mycal Jones (19)	Freddie Freeman (2)
Joe Leonard (23)	Tyler Pastornicky (14)	Elmer Reyes (21)	Barbaro Canizares
Shawn Bowman	Andrelton Simmons (15)	Phil Gosselin (25)	Mauro Gomez
Ed Lucas	Brandon Hicks		Riann Spanjer-Furstenburg
Joey Terdoslavich			Edison Sanchez

C
Christian Bethancourt (12)
Wilkin Castillo
Jesus Sucre
Matt Kennelly
Braeden Schlehuber
Carlos Sanchez

RHP		LHP	
RHSP	**RHRP**	**LHSP**	**LHRP**
Julio Teheran (1)	Craig Kimbrel (5)	Mike Minor (4)	Richard Sullivan (30)
Randall Delgado (3)	David Hale (17)	Brett Oberholtzer (9)	Lee Hyde
Arodys Vizcaino (7)	Paul Clemens (26)	Carlos Perez (11)	Luis Avilan
Brandon Beachy (8)	Juan Abreu (27)	Dimasther Delgado (18)	Tyler Stovall
J.J. Hoover (10)	Brett Butts (28)	Scott Diamond	Chase Shreve
Erik Cordier (13)	Michael Broadway	Brett DeVall	
David Filak (24)	Stephen Marek	Chris Masters	
Zeke Spruill	Thomas Berryhill	Cole Rohrbough	
Caleb Brewer	Cory Gearrin	Jose Ortegano	
Todd Redmond	Jay Sborz		
Tim Gustafson	Jaye Chapman		
Willie Kempf	Benino Pruneda		
Cory Rasmus	Angelo Paulino		
	Matt Suschak		
	Matt Lewis		

2010
BONUSES: $3.9 MILLION

BEST PURE HITTER: OF Todd Cunningham (2) has a track record of hitting with wood, winning batting titles in the summer college Texas Collegiate and Cape Cod leagues. He's a switch-hitter who stays inside the ball and has on-base skills, as evidenced by his 14 HBPs in his debut. OF David Rohm (9) matches him with a polished approach.

BEST POWER HITTER: 3B Joe Leonard (3) has a rangy body that evokes Troy Glaus. He has average present power with leverage in his swing, and he should add more as he gets stronger.

FASTEST RUNNER: SS Matt Lipka (1s) is a well-above-average runner and already has basestealing skills. He'll be an even greater threat as he polishes his ability to get jumps and read pitchers.

BEST DEFENSIVE PLAYER: SS Andrelton Simmons (2) was the draft's best defensive player. Though he hit 98 mph as a junior college pitcher, he wants to play shortstop, and his actions, arm strength and solid range will allow him to stay there if he can hit.

BEST FASTBALL: If he pitched, it would be Simmons. RHP Dave Filak (4) has reached 95 mph in the past but had elbow stiffness in the spring and hasn't quite shown that velocity as a pro. RHP Matt Lewis (10) hits a lot of 93s and 94s out of a relief role.

BEST SECONDARY PITCH: Filak led NCAA Division III in strikeouts per nine innings in each of the last two seasons, thanks mostly to a power curveball that falls off the table. He's raw but has a fresh arm and has the highest ceiling of any Braves pitching draftee this year.

BEST PRO DEBUT: Atlanta pushed several draftees to low Class A Rome, where 2B Phil Gosselin (5) was the team's player of the year. He earned a promotion to high Class A and batted .279/.353/.379 overall. RHP Willie Kempf (27) went 8-2, 1.70 with 71 strikeouts in 74 innings between three teams.

BEST ATHLETE: Lipka does a lot of things easily, and he edges out Simmons thanks to his speed.

MOST INTRIGUING BACKGROUND: LHP Matt Fouch (34) pitched at Army and pitched in six games before getting called to military duty. The Braves hope to get him back but don't know when that will happen. Unsigned RHP James Mahler's (48) father Rick spent 11 of his 13 big league seasons pitching in Atlanta. Unsigned OF/C Steven Sabol (16) is a cousin of NFL star Troy Polamalu. Lipka was a two-time Texas all-state wide receiver in high school, catching 22 touchdown passes last fall from Dodgers first-rounder Zach Lee. Simmons hails from Curacao but was drafted out of Western Oklahoma JC.

CLOSEST TO THE MAJORS: Cunningham and Gosselin.

BEST LATE-ROUND PICK: Kempf, a sinker/slider guy with command. His fastball sat at 88-90 mph as a starter, but he pushed 93 mph at Baylor in shorter stints.

THE ONE WHO GOT AWAY: The Braves were one of two teams that didn't exceed MLB slot recommendations with any draftee in 2010. They tried to with Sabol, who couldn't be swayed from his commitment to Oregon.

ASSESSMENT: With a pitcher-heavy system, Atlanta targeted athletic position players. Lipka, Simmons, Cunningham and Leonard immediately pushed toward the front of the organization's position-prospect pool.

2009
BONUSES: $4.4 MILLION

Atlanta drafted LHP Mike Minor (1) in part because he'd sign easily, but he repaid them by reaching the majors last August. RHP David Hale (3) and 2B/SS Mycal Jones (4) show some promise.

GRADE: B

2008
BONUSES: $5.1 MILLION

The Braves lacked a first-rounder and their top pick, LHP Brett DeVall (1s), has stalled. But RHP Craig Kimbrel (3) could take over as closer in 2011. LHP Brett Oberholtzer (8) and RHP J.J. Hoover (10), juco products like Kimbrel, rank among the system's best arms. Unsigned 3B Anthony Rendon (27) is the favorite to go No. 1 overall in 2011.

GRADE: C+

2007
BONUSES: $4.9 MILLION

OF Jason Heyward (1) alone makes this a special draft, and 1B Freddie Freeman (2) also should be a vital part of Atlanta's offense for years to come. SS Brandon Hicks (3) also has reached the majors.

GRADE: A

2006
BONUSES: $8.1 MILLION

With six picks in the first two rounds, the Braves came away with only one keeper: LHP Jeff Locke (2), whom they sent to the Pirates in a trade for Nate McLouth. RHP Kris Medlen (10) has been solid in multiple big league roles the last two years.

GRADE: C+

Draft analysis by John Manuel (2010) and Jim Callis (2006-09). Numbers in parentheses indicate draft rounds.

JULIO TEHERAN, RHP

Born: Jan. 27, 1991. **Bats:** R. **Throws:** R.
Height: 6-2. **Weight:** 170. **Signed:** Colombia,
2007. **Signed by:** Miguel Teheran/Carlos
Garcia.

ROBERT GURGANUS

The Braves signed Teheran out of Colombia in 2007 for $850,000, the largest bonus for a pitcher on the international market that year. His cousin Miguel was one of the scouts who signed him, and that relationship contributed to Julio's decision to turn down a higher offer from the Yankees. It took some time to start living up to his projections, as his 2008 pro debut lasted just 15 innings due to shoulder tendinitis. He returned to Rookie-level Danville in 2009 and ranked as the Appalachian League's top prospect before earning a late-season promotion to low Class A Rome. Atlanta turned Teheran loose last season, when he advanced three levels while ranking second in the system in ERA (2.59) and strikeouts (159 in 142 innings). He overpowered the low Class A South Atlantic League in April and May before jumping to high Class A Myrtle Beach, where he ranked as the No. 1 prospect in the Carolina League, then earned a promotion to Double-A Mississippi in late July. Teheran also stood out at the Futures Game, where he didn't throw a fastball under 95 mph.

Teheran has an electric arm, the ability to throw all of his pitches for strikes and the knowledge of how to exploit batters' weaknesses. His fastball clocks consistently in the 94-96 mph range, and he maintains his velocity throughout a game. He has a pair of above-average secondary pitches, with his changeup grading slightly better than his curveball. His changeup shows nice fade and he's willing to throw it in any count. His curve resides in the low 80s with hard bite and depth. Teheran's command is impressive, though he struggled a little with his precision shortly after being promoted to Double-A. He works both sides of the plate, usually keeping all of his offerings at the knees and below. Teheran needs to get stronger, but that will come naturally as his body matures. Some scouts say his delivery has a little bit of violence and worry about the long-term wear and tear on the elbow and shoulder, while others believe he throws easy gas and aren't worried about his mechanics. Comparisons to a young Pedro Martinez are commonplace, and Teheran's biggest backers think he's more advanced at the same stage of his career.

The Braves thought Teheran could jump on the fast track, and he exceeded their expectations, advancing to Double-A as a teenager. He may split 2011 between Mississippi and Triple-A Gwinnett, with a late-season cup of coffee in Atlanta a possibility. Chances are his first opportunity for a job in the big league rotation won't come until 2012. He has front-of-the-rotation talent and will challenge Tommy Hanson for the role as the Braves' No. 1 starter by the middle of the decade.

SCOUTING GRADES

Fastball: 65. **Command/**
Curveball: 60. **Control:** 65.
Changeup: 65. **Delivery:** 55.

Based on 20-80 scouting scale, where 50 represents major league average, and future projection rather than present tools.

Year	Club (League)	Class	W	L	ERA	G	GS	CG	SV	IP	H	HR	BB	SO	G/A	WHIP	AVG
2008	Danville (APP)	R	1	2	6.60	6	6	0	0	15	18	2	4	17	—	1.47	.305
2009	Danville (APP)	R	2	1	2.68	7	7	0	0	44	36	2	7	39	2.36	0.98	.229
	Rome (SAL)	LoA	1	3	4.78	7	7	0	0	38	42	2	11	28	1.11	1.41	.288
2010	Rome (SAL)	LoA	2	2	1.14	7	7	0	0	39	23	1	10	45	1.20	0.84	.168
	Myrtle Beach (CAR)	HiA	4	4	2.98	10	10	0	0	63	56	6	13	76	1.04	1.09	.233
	Mississippi (SL)	AA	3	2	3.38	7	7	0	0	40	29	2	17	38	0.94	1.15	.204
Minor League Totals			13	14	3.20	44	44	0	0	239	204	15	62	243	1.24	1.11	.232

2 FREDDIE FREEMAN, 1B

Born: Sept. 12, 1989. **B-T:** L-R. **Ht.:** 6-5. **Wt.:** 220. **Drafted:** HS—Orange, Calif., 2007 (2nd round). **Signed by:** Tom Battista.

The 78th overall pick in the 2007 draft, Freeman has been among the youngest players in every league he has played. He was the second-youngest starter in the Triple-A International League in 2010, when he was tabbed the circuit's rookie of the year. He led the IL in hits (147) and total bases (240), and managers rated him the loop's best defensive first baseman. Freeman has a smooth, aggressive swing from the left side. He possesses raw power that should generate 20-plus homers annually in the major leagues. He has good plate coverage with a patient approach that leads to consistent contact. He thrives in RBI situations and wants the bat in his hand with the game on the line. Defensively, Freeman has quick feet and above-average range at first base. He does all the little things well around the bag and he even has a cannon for an arm. Though not a blazer, he runs well for his size and shows outstanding instincts on the basepaths. Though his success was limited during his September callup, Freeman swatted his first big league homer against Roy Halladay. He may have an up-and-down 2011 season at the plate, but that roller-coaster ride should come as Atlanta's starting first baseman at age 21.

Year	Club (League)	Class	AVG	G	AB	R	H	2B	3B	HR	RBI	BB	SO	SB	CS	OBP	SLG
2007	Braves (GCL)	R	.268	59	224	24	60	7	0	6	30	7	33	1	2	.295	.379
2008	Rome (SAL)	LoA	.316	130	491	70	155	33	7	18	95	46	84	5	5	.378	.521
2009	Myrtle Beach (CAR)	HiA	.302	70	255	43	77	19	0	6	34	26	41	1	4	.394	.447
	Mississippi (SL)	AA	.248	41	149	15	37	8	0	2	24	11	19	0	0	.308	.342
2010	Gwinnett (IL)	AAA	.319	124	461	73	147	35	2	18	87	43	84	6	2	.378	.521
	Atlanta (NL)	MAJ	.167	20	24	3	4	1	0	1	1	0	8	0	0	.167	.333
Major League Totals			.167	20	24	3	4	1	0	1	1	0	8	0	0	.167	.333
Minor League Totals			.301	424	1580	225	476	102	9	50	270	133	261	13	13	.363	.472

3 RANDALL DELGADO, RHP

Born: Feb. 9, 1990. **B-T:** R-R. **Ht.:** 6-3. **Wt.:** 180. **Signed:** Panama, 2006. **Signed by:** Luis Ortiz.

Signed as an unheralded 16-year-old from Panama, Delgado has moved rapidly due to his maturity and repertoire. He led the Carolina League in strikeouts (120) last year despite getting promoted in mid-July, and he topped the system with 162 whiffs overall. He's similar to Julio Teheran in that he's a slender fireballer who reached Double-A well ahead of schedule. Delgado pounds the strike zone and challenges hitters. His fastball resides at 92-96 mph, and he mixes it well with a plus curveball and solid changeup. His curve has good downward bite, and his changeup shows impressive deception. Delgado struggled with his control in 2009 until altering his mechanics and mindset in July, leading to an impressive second half. When he got to Mississippi last summer, he had some problems leaving pitches thigh-high. He again adapted, improving his ability to throw his fastball down in the zone and on both sides of the plate. If not for Teheran's presence, Delgado would receive more hype. By making significant adjustments the past two seasons, he has shown he could pitch in the front half of a major league rotation. Added to the 40-man roster in November, he'll open 2011 in Double-A with the chance to advance quickly to Triple-A if he continues his rapid progress.

Year	Club (League)	Class	W	L	ERA	G	GS	CG	SV	IP	H	HR	BB	SO	G/A	WHIP	AVG
2007	Braves (DSL)	R	1	2	2.00	11	10	0	0	45	34	2	12	50	—	1.02	.213
2008	Danville (APP)	R	3	8	3.13	14	14	0	0	69	63	5	30	81	—	1.35	.249
2009	Rome (SAL)	LoA	5	10	4.35	25	25	1	0	124	123	9	49	141	1.52	1.39	.256
2010	Myrtle Beach (CAR)	HiA	4	7	2.76	20	20	0	0	117	89	7	32	120	1.46	1.03	.210
	Mississippi (SL)	AA	3	5	4.74	8	8	0	0	44	36	2	20	42	1.13	1.28	.222
Minor League Totals			16	32	3.45	78	77	1	0	399	345	25	143	434	1.42	1.22	.233

4 MIKE MINOR, LHP

Born: Dec. 26, 1987. **B-T:** R-L. **Ht.:** 6-3. **Wt.:** 200. **Drafted:** Vanderbilt, 2009 (1st round). **Signed by:** Brian Bridges.

Atlanta signed Minor to a $2.42 million bonus in 2009, the biggest in franchise history and the largest ever given to the seventh overall pick in the draft. His pure stuff was better than expected last year, when he reached the major leagues three days after his one-year anniversary of turning pro. He tied a Braves franchise rookie record with 12 strikeouts in a start against the Cubs but tired in September. Minor mixes three pitches with impressive command and acumen. His best offering is his changeup, which could become a plus-plus pitch as he gains experience. After throwing his fastball in the upper 80s in late 2009, he added velocity and worked at 91-94 mph in the early innings of his starts last season. His heater has significant movement, as does his slurvy curveball, which dives with three-quarters tilt. Minor can add and subtract with his pitches to keep hitters off-balance. He has a great pickoff move and fields his position well. In addition to needing more strength, he'll have to challenge hitters more often instead of being so fine in the strike zone. Minor should open 2011 as Atlanta's fifth starter. He has a ceiling as a No. 2 starter, though he may not serve in that role with Tommy Hanson, Julio Teheran and Randall Delgado all part of the Braves' future.

Year	Club (League)	Class	W	L	ERA	G	GS	CG	SV	IP	H	HR	BB	SO	G/A	WHIP	AVG
2009	Rome (SAL)	LoA	0	1	0.64	4	4	0	0	14	10	0	0	17	0.83	0.71	.208
2010	Mississippi (SL)	AA	2	6	4.03	15	15	0	0	87	74	8	34	109	1.23	1.24	.233
	Gwinnett (IL)	AAA	4	1	1.89	6	6	0	0	33	19	1	12	37	1.42	0.93	.171
	Atlanta (NL)	MAJ	3	2	5.98	9	8	0	0	41	53	6	11	43	0.80	1.57	.314
Major League Totals			3	2	5.98	9	8	0	0	41	53	6	11	43	0.80	1.57	.314
Minor League Totals			6	8	3.15	25	25	0	0	134	103	9	46	163	0.80	1.11	.216

5 CRAIG KIMBREL, RHP

Born: May 28, 1988. **B-T:** R-R. **Ht.:** 5-11. **Wt.:** 200. **Drafted:** Wallace State (Ala.) CC, 2008 (3rd round). **Signed by:** Brian Bridges.

The Braves selected 10 junior college players in the first 15 rounds of the 2008 draft, starting with Kimbrel in the third round. He signed for $391,000 after turning down $125,000 from Atlanta as a 33rd-round pick a year earlier. He ranked third in the International League with 23 saves and reached the big leagues in his second full pro season. He was dynamic during the pennant race, finishing the year with 12 scoreless big league outings while striking out 23 in 12 innings. Kimbrel has averaged 14.8 strikeouts per nine innings as a pro, thanks to his heavy fastball, which sits at 93-96 mph with excellent sink. His slurvy curveball gives him a second plus pitch to complement his heater. After rarely throwing a changeup in 2009, he worked on the pitch prior to last season and mixed it in on occasion. While moving faster than anticipated, Kimbrel has made significant strides with his command and his ability to pitch inside. Reminiscent of a righthanded Billy Wagner, he has the stuff and makeup to finish games. The Braves tried to expose Kimbrel to the job of a major league closer and Wagner's expertise without rushing him in 2010. He responded well, putting himself in position to take over as Atlanta's closer in 2011 following Wagner's retirement.

Year	Club (League)	Class	W	L	ERA	G	GS	CG	SV	IP	H	HR	BB	SO	G/A	WHIP	AVG
2008	Danville (APP)	R	1	2	0.47	12	0	0	6	19	5	0	10	27	—	0.79	.076
	Rome (SAL)	LoA	2	0	0.71	10	0	0	4	13	6	0	4	26	—	0.79	.140
	Myrtle Beach (CAR)	HiA	0	0	0.00	2	0	0	0	4	5	0	1	3	—	1.64	.385
2009	Rome (SAL)	LoA	0	0	0.90	16	0	0	10	20	9	0	6	38	1.20	0.75	.132
	Myrtle Beach (CAR)	HiA	2	2	5.47	19	0	0	2	26	18	2	28	45	2.56	1.75	.200
	Mississippi (SL)	AA	2	1	0.77	12	0	0	6	12	3	0	7	17	0.80	0.86	.083
	Gwinnett (IL)	AAA	0	0	0.00	2	0	0	0	2	0	0	4	3	2.00	2.00	.000
2010	Gwinnett (IL)	AAA	3	2	1.62	48	0	0	23	56	28	3	35	83	2.26	1.13	.148
	Atlanta (NL)	MAJ	4	0	0.44	21	0	0	1	21	9	0	16	40	0.25	1.21	.125
Major League Totals			4	0	0.44	21	0	0	1	21	9	0	16	40	0.25	1.21	.125
Minor League Totals			8	7	1.85	121	0	0	51	151	74	5	95	242	1.83	1.12	.145

6 MATT LIPKA, SS

Born: April 15, 1992. **B-T:** R-R. **Ht.:** 6-1. **Wt.:** 188. **Drafted:** HS—McKinney, Texas, 2010 (1st round supplemental). **Signed by:** Gerald Turner.

Lipka was a two-time all-state 4-A wide receiver at McKinney (Texas) High, where his quarterback was Dodgers 2010 first-round choice Zach Lee. Lipka went seven picks after Lee, 35th overall as Atlanta's top selection last June, and turned down an Alabama baseball scholarship to sign for $800,000. He earned Rookie-level Gulf Coast League all-star honors in his pro debut. A quick-twitch athlete and high-energy performer, Lipka is a throwback player with plus-plus speed. His quickness puts pressure on infielders when he hits routine groundballs, and he's a basestealing threat who runs the bases as well as anyone in the system. He has a line-drive stroke and an advanced feel for hitting the ball where it's pitched. Stronger than most speedsters, he has a quick bat and the chance to have average power. The Braves envisioned Lipka as a center fielder upon drafting him, but they believe he has the arm, actions and instincts to remain at shortstop for the foreseeable future. His hands are his biggest question as an infielder. Atlanta's coaches rave about his approach and obvious love for the game. Lipka has the potential to be an impact up-the-middle player who hits at the top of the lineup. He'll start his first full pro season as the everyday shortstop at Rome.

Year	Club (League)	Class	AVG	G	AB	R	H	2B	3B	HR	RBI	BB	SO	SB	CS	OBP	SLG
2010	Braves (GCL)	R	.302	48	192	33	58	8	4	1	24	14	22	20	3	.357	.401
	Danville (APP)	R	.125	4	16	1	2	0	0	0	1	1	2	1	0	.176	.125
Minor League Totals			.288	52	208	34	60	8	4	1	25	15	24	21	3	.344	.380

7 ARODYS VIZCAINO, RHP

Born: Nov. 13, 1990. **B-T:** R-R. **Ht.:** 6-0. **Wt.:** 189. **Signed:** Dominican Republic, 2007. **Signed by:** Alfredo Dominguez (Yankees).

Vizcaino ranked with Julio Teheran and Martin Perez (Rangers) as the best international amateur pitching prospects in 2007, when he signed with the Yankees for $800,000. New York traded him along with Melky Cabrera and Mike Dunn to obtain Javier Vazquez and Boone Logan from the Braves in December 2009. Vizcaino dominated low Class A hitters in 2010 but missed two months with a partially torn ligament shortly after a promotion in June. Vizcaino's fastball has good life while residing at 92-94 mph and touching 96. His best pitch, however, is a hammer curveball that he commands with precision. He made improvements with his changeup last year and is on the verge of having three plus pitches. In addition to his stuff, Atlanta was impressed with how he learned to pitch and work hard in 2010, rather than just trying to throw the ball past hitters. While he avoided surgery and returned before the end of season, he still has to answer questions about his durability. He never has pitched more than 85 innings in a season, and he also missed time in 2009 with a strained back muscle. Though Vizcaino must prove he can stay healthy, his high ceiling is undeniable. He'll open the year in high Class A at age 20, with a midseason promotion a possibility.

Year	Club (League)	Class	W	L	ERA	G	GS	CG	SV	IP	H	HR	BB	SO	G/A	WHIP	AVG
2008	Yankees (GCL)	R	3	2	3.68	12	6	0	0	44	38	5	13	48	—	1.16	.222
2009	Staten Island (NYP)	SS	2	4	2.13	10	10	0	0	42	34	2	15	52	1.34	1.16	.211
2010	Myrtle Beach (CAR)	HiA	0	0	4.61	3	3	0	0	14	16	1	3	11	2.14	1.39	.296
	Rome (SAL)	LoA	9	4	2.39	14	14	0	0	72	63	1	9	68	0.84	1.00	.229
Minor League Totals			14	10	2.83	39	33	0	0	172	151	9	40	179	1.06	1.11	.228

8 BRANDON BEACHY, RHP

Born: Sept. 3, 1986. **B-T:** R-R. **Ht.:** 6-3. **Wt.:** 215. **Signed:** Indiana Wesleyan, NDFA 2008. **Signed by:** Gene Kerns.

Beachy was a third baseman who moonlighted as a closer when he went undrafted following his junior season at Indiana Wesleyan in 2008. After starring as a pitcher in the collegiate Valley League that summer, he signed with the Braves for $20,000 as a free agent. He had a breakthrough season in 2010, leading the minors with a 1.73 ERA and making three solid starts for Atlanta in September. Beachy has a live, fresh arm with good overall command of three pitches. He gets ahead of hitters by establishing his 90-94 mph fastball with plus life, throwing it on a nice downhill plane and to both sides of the plate. His hard, sharp-breaking curveball has quality depth. After beginning last season in Mississippi's bullpen, he began using his effective changeup more often as a starter. Hitters rarely barreled Beachy's pitches last season, even when he reached the big leagues. His confidence has improved considerably, though he's still honing the mental aspects of pitching at the game's highest levels. He may not have a long track record of success on the mound, but Beachy's repertoire and feel for pitching bode well for the long term. He succeeded as both a reliever and a starter in 2010, enhancing his chances of making the Atlanta pitching staff this spring. His ceiling is as a No. 3 starter.

Year	Club (League)	Class	W	L	ERA	G	GS	CG	SV	IP	H	HR	BB	SO	G/A	WHIP	AVG
2008	Danville (APP)	R	2	0	2.25	6	0	0	0	12	12	1	2	16	—	1.17	.261
2009	Rome (SAL)	LoA	0	0	5.60	12	0	0	0	18	20	0	4	17	0.68	1.36	.290
	Mississippi (SL)	AA	0	0	0.00	1	0	0	0	1	1	0	0	0	2.00	1.00	.250
	Myrtle Beach (CAR)	HiA	4	3	3.41	22	8	0	1	58	59	2	15	47	1.18	1.28	.267
2010	Mississippi (SL)	AA	3	1	1.47	27	6	0	1	74	53	3	22	100	0.98	1.02	.200
	Gwinnett (IL)	AAA	2	0	2.17	8	7	0	1	46	40	2	6	48	1.24	1.01	.229
	Atlanta (NL)	MAJ	0	2	3.00	3	3	0	0	15	16	0	7	15	0.79	1.53	.267
Major League Totals			0	2	3.00	3	3	0	0	15	16	0	7	15	0.79	1.53	.267
Minor League Totals			11	4	2.55	76	21	0	3	208	185	8	49	228	1.08	1.13	.237

9 BRETT OBERHOLTZER, LHP

Born: July 1, 1989. **B-T:** L-L. **Ht.:** 6-2. **Wt.:** 220. **Drafted:** Seminole (Fla.) CC, 2008 (8th round). **Signed by:** Gregg Kilby.

Part of the Braves' influx of junior college talent in the 2008 draft, Oberholtzer didn't reach full-season ball until his third pro season. He needed just four starts to earn a promotion from Rome to Myrtle Beach, where he pitched well despite battling blister problems that cost him three weeks in June. He struck out 12 in his final start of the year, then turned in a strong showing in instructional league. Oberholtzer has plus command of three pitches. His fastball sits at 88-92 mph and touches 94 with good, late tailing life. He uses his solid average changeup to his advantage by mixing it in at any time in the count. His curveball is also a fringy above-average pitch. His herky-jerky mechanics create deception, and his aggressiveness and ability to work both sides of the plate enhance his stuff. An excellent athlete, particularly for a big lefthander, Oberholtzer fields his position well. He needs to improve his ability to hold runners after giving up 18 steals in 22 attempts last year. Oberholtzer has impressed Atlanta with the progress he has made in the last two seasons. A potential third or fourth starter in the big leagues, he's slated to spend 2011 in the Mississippi rotation.

Year	Club (League)	Class	W	L	ERA	G	GS	CG	SV	IP	H	HR	BB	SO	G/A	WHIP	AVG
2008	Braves (GCL)	R	4	1	2.89	10	0	0	0	37	34	1	10	32	—	1.18	.241
2009	Danville (APP)	R	6	2	2.01	12	12	1	0	67	46	1	6	56	1.21	0.78	.191
2010	Rome (SAL)	LoA	0	2	1.96	4	4	0	0	23	22	1	5	19	1.53	1.17	.262
	Myrtle Beach (CAR)	HiA	6	6	4.15	22	18	0	2	113	123	7	18	107	1.33	1.25	.279
Minor League Totals			16	11	3.15	48	34	1	2	240	225	10	39	214	1.31	1.10	.248

10 J.J. HOOVER, RHP

Born: Aug. 13, 1987. **B-T:** R-R. **Ht.:** 6-3. **Wt.:** 230. **Signed:** Calhoun (Ala.) CC, 2008 (10th round). **Signed by:** Brian Bridges.

Hoover joins Brett Oberholtzer as a junior college starter who has outshined more-heralded high school arms Brett DeVall, Tyler Stovall and Zeke Spruill from Atlanta's 2008 draft class. Hoover built on a strong developmental year in 2009 by leading the system with 14 wins last season while reaching Double-A. After making a mechanical adjustment with how he held his hands in his delivery in May, he finished on a tear, going 10-2, 2.17 with 93 strikeouts in 75 innings over the final two months. Hoover is a classic workhorse, possessing a strong body with thick thighs and a resilient arm. He pitches on a good downhill plane, generating a low-90s fastball with decent movement. He also throws an average curveball, slider and changeup—his curve may be his best secondary pitch—and commands all of his offerings well. The key for Hoover is staying on top of his pitches, because they flatten out and become hittable when he doesn't. Hoover projects as a potential No. 3 starter, but he has the mentality to work in relief if the Braves need bullpen help. He'll open 2011 back in the Mississippi rotation, with a promotion to Triple-A a strong possibility during the summer. His big league ETA is 2012.

Year	Club (League)	Class	W	L	ERA	G	GS	CG	SV	IP	H	HR	BB	SO	G/A	WHIP	AVG
2008	Danville (APP)	R	1	0	0.00	2	0	0	0	5	4	0	1	6	—	1.07	.235
2009	Myrtle Beach (CAR)	HiA	0	0	9.00	1	1	0	0	3	3	1	5	2	0.40	2.67	.250
	Rome (SAL)	LoA	7	6	3.35	25	18	0	1	134	135	9	25	148	1.06	1.19	.259
2010	Myrtle Beach (CAR)	HiA	11	6	3.26	24	24	0	0	133	126	7	35	118	0.76	1.21	.245
	Mississippi (SL)	AA	3	1	3.48	4	4	0	0	21	15	1	15	34	0.59	1.45	.203
Minor League Totals			22	13	3.32	56	47	0	1	295	283	18	81	308	0.87	1.23	.248

11 CARLOS PEREZ, LHP

Born: Nov. 20, 1991. **B-T:** L-L. **Ht.:** 6-2. **Wt.:** 205. **Signed:** Dominican Republic, 2008. **Signed by:** Roberto Aquino.

Perez signed in 2008 out of the Dominican Republic for $600,000, which could prove to be a steal considering the rapid progress he has shown. He overpowered the Appalachian League last year, earning recognition as the circuit's top prospect, then made two starts in low Class A before a right rib fracture sidelined him. Perez combines everything scouts want to see in a young pitcher, including stuff, poise and intelligence. His fastball sits in the low 90s and touches 94 mph. He works both sides of the plate, as well as the top and bottom of the strike zone. He tightened the spin on his breaking ball last year, inducing batters to chase it out of the strike zone. When he had feel for his changeup, he pitched with more confidence and hitters got few good swings against him. He still needs to improve the consistency of his secondary pitches. Perez is a hard worker who wants to be the best. He does an excellent job of holding runners with his quick delivery and above-average pickoff move. Scheduled to return to Rome to open 2011, he could move quickly.

Year	Club (League)	Class	W	L	ERA	G	GS	CG	SV	IP	H	HR	BB	SO	G/A	WHIP	AVG
2009	Braves (GCL)	R	1	2	5.28	10	5	0	0	31	35	2	13	23	1.10	1.57	.292
2010	Danville (APP)	R	2	0	1.13	6	6	0	0	32	20	0	14	27	2.21	1.06	.185
	Rome (SAL)	LoA	0	1	3.86	2	2	0	0	7	8	1	3	4	2.20	1.57	.267
Minor League Totals			3	3	3.23	18	13	0	0	70	63	3	30	54	1.60	1.33	.244

12 CHRISTIAN BETHANCOURT, C

Born: Sept. 2, 1991. **B-T:** R-R. **Ht.:** 6-2. **Wt.:** 195. **Signed:** Panama, 2008. **Signed by:** Luis Ortiz.

There's no doubt that Bethancourt has tools, but scouts are split on whether he'll be able to put them to use and become a major league catcher. He has everything a young catcher could want, including soft hands, a quick release and plus arm strength. His pop times average close to 1.8 seconds and he threw out 39 percent of basestealers last year. He also has an ideal frame and good athleticism behind the plate. He sets up high, and while he has good lateral movement, he needs to do a better job of blocking balls in the dirt. A free swinger, Bethancourt is a streaky hitter who needs to improve his command of the strike zone. He's capable of driving the ball and could develop at least average power as his body continues to mature. He's a below-average runner but not bad for a catcher. For all his physical ability, Bethancourt has plenty of questions to answer about his his approach to the game. He shows bad body language and a questionable work ethic. Scouts have concerns about his lack of energy behind the plate. Some say he doesn't give his pitchers enough support when they get into jams. Bethancourt will play the entire 2011 season at age 19, so there's plenty of time for him to grow up. He has the ability to become a special player once he matures. The next step in his development will come in high Class A.

Year	Club (League)	Class	AVG	G	AB	R	H	2B	3B	HR	RBI	BB	SO	SB	CS	OBP	SLG
2008	Braves (DSL)	R	.267	34	116	12	31	6	3	0	17	11	25	1	0	.328	.371
2009	Braves (GCL)	R	.284	32	116	22	33	9	1	2	19	11	22	7	0	.344	.431
	Danville (APP)	R	.260	14	50	10	13	5	0	2	8	6	16	1	1	.339	.480
2010	Rome (SAL)	LoA	.251	108	399	31	100	19	2	3	34	14	62	11	3	.276	.331
Minor League Totals			.260	188	681	75	177	39	6	7	78	42	125	20	4	.302	.366

13 ERIK CORDIER, RHP

Born: Feb. 25, 1986. **B-T:** R-R. **Ht.:** 6-4. **Wt.:** 230. **Drafted:** HS—Green Bay, Wis., 2004 (2nd round). **Signed by:** Phil Huttmann (Royals).

Acquired from the Royals for shortstop T.J. Pena near the end of spring training in 2007, Cordier finally has proven he can stay healthy and earned a spot on the Braves' 40-man roster this offseason. He missed all of 2005 with a knee injury and all of 2007 following Tommy John surgery, but he has worked 265 innings during the last two years. He made mechanical adjustments in mid-2010, improving his fastball command and pitching as well as at any time in his career during the second half. Cordier's fastball velocity returned in a big way last season. He now sits at 94-97 mph with his heater and has improved the consistency of his slider, which often gives him a second plus pitch. His changeup remains his weakest link, but he has shown a decent feel for it and should be able to develop it into an average offering. Cordier's makeup is off the charts, and his resilience could play a big role in allowing him to reach the big leagues. After a September promotion to Triple-A, for example, he gave up five earned runs in two-thirds of an inning in his first start, then bounced back with 7⅓ shutout innings in his second outing. Cordier should be a key member of the Gwinnett rotation in 2011, readying himself for the big leagues should an opportunity arise.

Year	Club (League)	Class	W	L	ERA	G	GS	CG	SV	IP	H	HR	BB	SO	G/A	WHIP	AVG
2004	Royals (AZL)	R	2	4	5.19	11	11	0	0	35	38	1	21	22	—	1.70	.279
2005	Did Not Play—Injured																
2006	Idaho Falls (PIO)	R	1	0	3.38	3	3	0	0	16	11	0	3	19	—	0.88	.186
	Burlington (MWL)	LoA	3	1	2.70	7	7	0	0	37	27	3	14	23	—	1.12	.203
2007	Did Not Play—Injured																
2008	Braves (GCL)	R	0	0	0.00	3	2	0	0	5	4	0	1	5	—	1.00	.211
	Rome (SAL)	LoA	1	2	5.18	9	9	0	0	40	51	3	21	31	—	1.80	.317
2009	Myrtle Beach (CAR)	HiA	7	8	3.87	25	25	1	0	121	115	13	74	88	1.22	1.56	.257
2010	Mississippi (SL)	AA	11	7	3.71	25	21	0	0	136	116	3	69	113	1.73	1.36	.236
	Gwinnett (IL)	AAA	1	1	5.63	2	2	0	0	8	7	0	7	4	1.38	1.75	.233
Minor League Totals			26	23	3.92	85	80	1	0	397	369	23	210	305	1.44	1.46	.250

14 TYLER PASTORNICKY, SS

Born: Dec. 13, 1989. **B-T:** R-R. **Ht.:** 5-11. **Wt.:** 170. **Drafted:** HS—Bradenton, Fla., 2008 (5th round). **Signed by:** Joel Grampietro (Blue Jays).

When the Braves shipped Yunel Escobar and Jo-Jo Reyes to Toronto last July, they got their shortstops of the present (Alex Gonzalez) and possibly the future (Pastornicky), as well as minor league lefthander Tim Collins. The son of Cliff Pastornicky, who played briefly for the Royals and now scouts for the Blue Jays, Tyler moved to Double-A after the trade. He impressed Atlanta officials with his all-around skills before a hamstring injury hampered him late in the season. A solid athlete who's fundamentally sound, Pastornicky has a smooth line-drive stroke and makes consistent contact. He has minimal power but can drive the ball into the gaps and should produce his share of doubles and triples while batting near the top of the lineup. He has above-average speed that he uses to his advantage by stealing bases and taking the extra base when the situation presents itself. Pastornicky is surehanded at shortstop and moves his feet well. His range and instincts are above-average, and his arm is strong enough to remain at short. The Braves have rebuilt their depth at the position, and Pastornicky is their most advanced shortstop prospect. He'll get a look as a potential long-term answer there, and if he doesn't pan out as a starter, he could be a good utility player. After playing in the Arizona Fall League, Pastornicky could make the jump to Triple-A in 2011.

Year	Club (League)	Class	AVG	G	AB	R	H	2B	3B	HR	RBI	BB	SO	SB	CS	OBP	SLG
2008	Blue Jays (GCL)	R	.263	50	160	32	42	6	3	1	17	21	21	27	5	.349	.356
2009	Lansing (MWL)	LoA	.269	109	413	63	111	11	9	1	31	39	50	51	15	.336	.346
	Dunedin (FSL)	HiA	.270	15	63	9	17	3	0	0	3	3	7	6	3	.303	.317
2010	Dunedin (FSL)	HiA	.258	77	287	50	74	16	0	6	35	39	49	24	7	.348	.376
	Mississippi (SL)	AA	.254	38	134	22	34	5	2	2	15	16	22	11	2	.333	.366
Minor League Totals			.263	289	1057	176	278	41	14	10	101	118	149	119	32	.339	.357

15 ANDRELTON SIMMONS, SS

Born: Sept. 4, 1989. **B-T:** R-R. **Ht.:** 6-2. **Wt.:** 170. **Drafted:** Western Oklahoma State JC, 2010 (2nd round). **Signed by:** Gerald Turner.

Simmons turned down several small offers from pro teams when he was 16 and growing up in Curacao, and it appeared his days on the diamond were numbered until Western Oklahoma State JC head coach Kurt Russell saw him during a Caribbean scouting trip. As a 20-year-old freshman in 2010, Simmons generated immediate scouting buzz despite missing a month with a broken toe. In 38 games, he hit a team-high .472 with seven homers, 40 RBIs and 15 stolen bases, and he also pitched 20 innings to help the Pioneers to third place in the Division II Junior College World Series. The best defensive player available in the 2010 draft, Simmons went in the second round and signed for $522,000. He has athletic actions, excellent range, soft and quick hands and an incredible feel for the position. His best tool is his arm, which has delivered fastballs clocked as high as 98 mph. While the Braves considered putting him on the mound, he wants to play shortstop and they fell in love with his defense after watching him in his pro debut. The question mark is Simmons' bat. He has some pop and is able to drive the ball, but his swing is long and he'll have to work on his approach to succeed against more advanced pitching. He runs well and has good instincts on the basepaths. Simmons will remain an everyday player for the time being. Given his age and experience, he could open 2011 with Atlanta's new high Class A Lynchburg affiliate.

Year	Club (League)	Class	AVG	G	AB	R	H	2B	3B	HR	RBI	BB	SO	SB	CS	OBP	SLG
2010	Danville (APP)	R	.276	62	239	36	66	11	1	2	26	16	14	18	4	.340	.356
Minor League Totals			.276	62	239	36	66	11	1	2	26	16	14	18	4	.340	.356

16 EDWARD SALCEDO, SS

Born: July 30, 1991. **B-T:** R-R. **Ht.:** 6-3. **Wt.:** 205. **Signed:** Dominican Republic, 2010. **Signed by:** Roberto Aquino.

Salcedo emerged as one of the hottest prospects on the international market in the summer of 2007, but he didn't sign until last February because of an extended investigation into his age by Major League Baseball. The Braves signed him for $1.6 million, the largest they've ever given to a foreign amateur. Having lost its 2010 first-round pick as compensation for signing free agent Billy Wagner, Atlanta regarded Salcedo as a fine substitute. He made a positive impression in spring training and during the early portion of the Rookie-level Dominican Summer League season before making a big jump to low Class A. Physically advanced for his age, Salcedo generates excellent bat speed and can put the barrel on the ball, though he had difficulty against pitchers who were skilled at setting up hitters. He has above-average speed and the potential to develop above-average power. Salcedo has a strong arm, but his defense needs more polish than some expected, due in part to his lack of playing time over the previous two years. His hands aren't particularly soft, and while his range is good, he tries to force too many plays. Add in his big frame, and Salcedo may have to move to third base eventually. His raw tools, especially on offense, make him an intriguing prospect. He should return to Rome to open 2011, with an in-season promotion to Lynchburg a possibility.

Year	Club (League)	Class	AVG	G	AB	R	H	2B	3B	HR	RBI	BB	SO	SB	CS	OBP	SLG
2010	Braves (DSL)	R	.297	23	74	16	22	5	1	1	11	18	19	8	1	.453	.432
	Rome (SAL)	LoA	.197	54	193	23	38	5	4	2	16	11	56	6	5	.239	.295
Minor League Totals			.225	77	267	39	60	10	5	3	27	29	75	14	6	.307	.333

17 DAVID HALE, RHP

Born: Sept. 27, 1987. **B-T:** R-R. **Ht.:** 6-2. **Wt.:** 205. **Drafted:** Princeton, 2009 (3rd round). **Signed by:** Kevin Barry.

The 87th overall pick in the 2009 draft, Hale was a two-way player at Princeton who spent most of his time in center field. The Braves preferred his lightning-quick arm and liked what they saw on the mound. After a promising pro debut, he struggled early last season in low Class A, going 0-4, 7.99 through six starts. He moved to the bullpen in mid-May and went 5-3, 2.16 with five saves in six opportunities as a reliever. Hale tended to lose focus as a starter and enjoyed working in relief because it more closely resembled the daily routine of an everyday player. He has two potential pitches: a 93-94 mph fastball that touches 96, and a hard slider at 84-86 mph. He has struggled to find consistency with his changeup, though it's effective on occasion. The quality of Hale's two primary pitches and his feel for pitching improved significantly last year as he focused solely on moundwork for the first time in his career. He still needs to improve his command and get ahead in the count more often. Those upgrades, combined with a deeper understanding of how to get pro hitters out, should allow Hale to move quickly as a reliever. A promotion to high Class A is next on his agenda.

Year	Club (League)	Class	W	L	ERA	G	GS	CG	SV	IP	H	HR	BB	SO	G/A	WHIP	AVG
2009	Danville (APP)	R	2	1	1.13	7	1	0	1	16	7	0	5	12	2.27	0.75	.130
2010	Rome (SAL)	LoA	5	8	4.13	28	7	0	5	94	97	1	44	69	1.98	1.51	.268
Minor League Totals			7	9	3.69	35	8	0	6	110	104	1	49	81	2.03	1.40	.250

18 DIMASTHER DELGADO, LHP

Born: March 9, 1989. **B-T:** L-L. **Ht.:** 6-2. **Wt.:** 180. **Signed:** Panama, 2007. **Signed by:** Luis Ortiz.

Delgado had an impressive full-season debut in 2009 and was slated to be part of a prospect-laden Myrtle Beach rotation last year. Instead, he was involved in a bad traffic accident in his native Panama in February that left him with a broken left hand just above his wrist, a broken femur in his right leg and a torn ligament in his right knee. He missed the entire season, though he was able to pitch during the final three weeks of instructional league. Delgado frustrates hitters by mixing a low-90s fastball and a plus changeup. He shows an advanced feel for pitching by commanding his fastball to both sides of the plate, hitting his spots and coming inside to both lefthanders and righthanders. His changeup has outstanding depth and fade, making it among the best in the organization. He has made steady improvements with his slow curveball, which still needs more definitive break. He's an above-average athlete and fielder, though he needs to improve at holding runners. A potential No. 3 starter, Delgado should be at full strength in 2011, when he'll finally make it to high Class A.

Year	Club (League)	Class	W	L	ERA	G	GS	CG	SV	IP	H	HR	BB	SO	G/A	WHIP	AVG
2007	Braves (DSL)	R	3	3	2.43	13	12	0	0	59	49	1	12	86	—	1.03	.217
2008	Braves (GCL)	R	5	1	4.31	11	3	0	0	40	51	2	9	39	—	1.51	.297
2009	Rome (SAL)	LoA	5	7	3.61	17	17	0	0	100	89	4	26	104	1.15	1.15	.237
2010	Did Not Play—Injured																
Minor League Totals			13	11	3.40	41	32	0	0	199	189	7	47	229	1.15	1.19	.245

19 MYCAL JONES, 2B/SS

Born: May 30, 1987. **B-T:** R-R. **Ht.:** 5-10. **Wt.:** 180. **Drafted:** Miami-Dade CC, 2009 (4th round). **Signed by:** Buddy Hernandez.

Jones started his college career with two years at North Florida before transferring to Miami-Dade CC, so he's older than the average junior college draft pick. He's making up for lost time, however, turning in a solid pro debut in 2009 and playing at three levels last season. He got off to a .125/.157/.188 start at Rome last April, because he had an uppercut that slowed his bat and made his swing long. He didn't hang his head, corrected the flaw and rebounded to hit .352/.398/.523 in May, leading to a promotion to Myrtle Beach in June and a late-season callup to Mississippi. Jones has some power and ranked fifth in the system with 15 homers last year, but he's much more effective when spraying line drives from pole to pole. He needs to tighten his strike zone and adopt a more disciplined approach so he can get on base and take advantage of his plus speed. A shortstop in his first two pro seasons, Jones moved to second base during instructional league and looked much more comfortable there. He has impressive quick-twitch athleticism and actions in the middle of the infield, giving him above-average range. His arm, which was fringy for shortstop, also plays much better at the keystone sack. Jones has plus makeup and a strong desire to succeed. He'll open 2011 as the starting second baseman at Mississippi.

Year	Club (League)	Class	AVG	G	AB	R	H	2B	3B	HR	RBI	BB	SO	SB	CS	OBP	SLG
2009	Danville (APP)	R	.258	64	244	50	63	18	6	4	27	26	55	19	4	.337	.430
2010	Rome (SAL)	LoA	.261	53	199	27	52	12	0	6	34	11	48	6	3	.301	.412
	Myrtle Beach (CAR)	HiA	.269	69	275	51	74	19	1	7	22	31	66	15	4	.354	.422
	Mississippi (SL)	AA	.200	7	30	5	6	0	1	2	5	1	9	1	0	.226	.467
Minor League Totals			.261	193	748	133	195	49	8	19	88	69	178	41	11	.330	.424

20 TODD CUNNINGHAM, OF

Born: March 20, 1989. **B-T:** B-R. **Ht.:** 6-0. **Wt.:** 200. **Drafted:** Jacksonville State, 2010 (2nd round). **Signed by:** Brian Bridges.

Braves scouting director Tony DeMacio put it simply enough when he said last June that Cunningham was drafted for his bat. He won a pair of summer league batting titles, hitting .310 in the Texas Collegiate League in 2008 and .378 in the Cape Cod League in 2009. After he batted .359 as a junior last spring, the Braves drafted him in the second round and signed him for $674,100. A switch-hitter, Cunningham stays inside the ball and drives pitches to the gaps from both sides of the plate. He has an outstanding approach, good patience and solid speed, allowing him to profile as a potential leadoff hitter. Atlanta believes he'll develop close to average power as he physically matures. Cunningham spent most of his time in center field last year, both in college and pro ball, and the Braves believe he can play almost anywhere in the infield or outfield. He has good hands and moves well, with his arm his lone tool that rates as below-average. His performance in spring training and whether Atlanta decides to try him as an infielder will determine whether he opens his first full pro season at Rome or Lynchburg.

Year	Club (League)	Class	AVG	G	AB	R	H	2B	3B	HR	RBI	BB	SO	SB	CS	OBP	SLG
2010	Rome (SAL)	LoA	.260	65	231	32	60	9	3	1	20	14	30	7	4	.341	.338
Minor League Totals			.260	65	231	32	60	9	3	1	20	14	30	7	4	.341	.338

21 ELMER REYES, 2B

Born: Nov. 26, 1990. **B-T:** R-R. **Ht.:** 5-11. **Wt.:** 150. **Signed:** Nicaragua, 2009. **Signed by:** Marvin Throneberry.

The Braves' improved depth at shortstop led them to shift Reyes to second base last season, his first in the United States. Signed as an 18-year-old out of Nicaragua, he played for both of Atlanta's Rookie-level affiliates last season and displayed excellent instincts in the field. He's a smooth defender who has the arm strength to play shortstop, along with a quick release. He has a quick first step with soft hands and consistently makes plays. At the plate, Reyes has surprising power for his size, with a good approach and the ability to put the barrel on the ball. To maximize his potential, he needs to get stronger, show more patience at the plate and make some changes to his stance. He tends to wrap his bat so far that it's nearly pointing at the pitcher. He loads and uncoils well, but he has a long path to the ball and scouts say his swing will make it hard to succeed at higher levels. He also must shorten his stroke with two strikes. Reyes isn't a burner, but he runs well once he gets going. He remains a work in progress, but the Braves like the early returns. He'll spend 2011 in low Class A.

Year	Club (League)	Class	AVG	G	AB	R	H	2B	3B	HR	RBI	BB	SO	SB	CS	OBP	SLG
2009	Braves (DSL)	R	.275	37	109	18	30	5	2	0	17	12	16	3	1	.367	.358
2010	Braves (GCL)	R	.364	6	22	8	8	0	0	1	5	2	5	3	0	.481	.500
	Danville (APP)	R	.294	53	194	27	57	15	2	5	24	7	36	2	3	.347	.469
Minor League Totals			.292	96	325	53	95	20	4	6	46	21	57	8	4	.364	.434

22 ADAM MILLIGAN, OF

Born: March 14, 1988. **B-T:** L-R. **Ht.:** 6-3. **Wt.:** 210. **Drafted:** Walters State (Tenn.) CC, 2008 (6th round). **Signed by:** Brian Bridges.

Milligan originally committed to play football at Austin Peay State before spending two years playing baseball at Walters State (Tenn.) CC, and the Braves drafted him three times before signing him as an eighth-rounder in 2008. He missed his first pro summer with a knee injury, and he missed most of 2010 with a shoulder injury that turned out to be a torn rotator cuff and required surgery in June. In between, he slugged .592 and reached high Class A during an impressive 2009 pro debut. When healthy, Milligan is an offensive-oriented player who can drive the ball to all fields. He showed above-average power in 2009 and Atlanta believes he can hit 20-25 homers annually at higher levels. He also should hit for average, possibly in the .275-.290 range, with his ability to make hard contact while going with pitches instead of trying to pull them. He's aggressive, so he may never walk much. Though not fleet of foot, Milligan doesn't clog the bases and displays good instincts in the outfield. He is a fringe-average defender who may be best suited for left field, but he has the arm strength as well as the carry on his throws to play in right. Milligan participated in the final week of instructional league and is expected to be healthy for spring training. He should open the season back in high Class A, but if he can regain his 2009 form, he could reach Double-A at some point during the year.

Year	Club (League)	Class	AVG	G	AB	R	H	2B	3B	HR	RBI	BB	SO	SB	CS	OBP	SLG
2009	Danville (APP)	R	.439	9	41	9	18	5	1	2	10	3	7	0	0	.500	.756
	Rome (SAL)	LoA	.345	52	197	28	68	14	2	10	33	12	43	4	5	.393	.589
	Myrtle Beach (CAR)	HiA	.167	6	24	2	4	1	0	1	6	0	8	0	0	.200	.333
2010	Myrtle Beach (CAR)	HiA	.200	21	85	13	17	3	0	4	8	9	35	2	0	.277	.376
Minor League Totals			.308	88	347	52	107	23	3	17	57	24	93	6	5	.364	.539

23 JOE LEONARD, 3B

Born: Aug. 26, 1988. **B-T:** R-R. **Ht.:** 6-5. **Wt.:** 215. **Drafted:** Pittsburgh, 2010 (3rd round). **Signed by:** Gene Kerns.

Leonard played a major role in one of the best seasons in Pittsburgh baseball history in 2010. The Panthers had a school-record 11-game winning streak and appeared in Baseball America's Top 25 poll for the first time in the program's history, while Leonard batted .436/.492/.678, saved a school-record eight games and was the Big East Conference player of the year. When the Braves picked him in the third round, it was the highest a Pitt player had been drafted since 1985. His father John was a righthander drafted six times from 1979-82. Signed for $324,900, Leonard has solid all-around skills. While his swing tends to get long, he has good bat speed and puts the barrel on the ball with consistency. He's adept at hitting to the opposite field. Atlanta believes he'll hit for at least average power as he learns to pull pitches and add loft to his flat swing. Though he's a below-average runner, Leonard's feet work well at third base. He has good instincts and a plus arm that delivered low-90s fastballs off the mound. He struggled with a sore elbow late in his pro debut and during instructional league, but he should be fine next spring. Leonard likely will open his first full pro season in high Class A.

Year	Club (League)	Class	AVG	G	AB	R	H	2B	3B	HR	RBI	BB	SO	SB	CS	OBP	SLG
2010	Danville (APP)	R	.278	10	36	6	10	2	0	1	5	3	7	0	0	.333	.417
	Rome (SAL)	LoA	.268	29	112	11	30	7	2	3	19	6	22	0	0	.303	.446
Minor League Totals			.270	39	148	17	40	9	2	4	24	9	29	0	0	.310	.439

24 DAVID FILAK, RHP

Born: Nov. 24, 1989. **B-T:** R-R. **Ht.:** 6-4. **Wt.:** 220. **Drafted:** Oneonta State (N.Y.), 2010 (4th round). **Signed by:** Kevin Barry.

The Braves scout the Northeast as heavily as any team, and Filak is a result of those efforts. They were delighted to get him with a fourth-round pick and a $204,300 bonus last June. He walked on as a catcher at Oneonta State (N.Y.) and quickly moved to the mound. He led NCAA Division III in strikeouts per nine innings in each of the last two seasons, with 14.9 in 2009 and 13.9 despite battling elbow stiffness in 2010. A big, physical pitcher, Filak has a low-90s fastball that touches 95 and bores in on righthanders. His low-80s spike curveball gives him a second plus pitch. He started throwing a changeup in 2009 and has made strides with the pitch. Filak is athletic and has a fresh arm, and he might add more velocity if he uses his legs more in his delivery and lengthens his stride. He possibly could have three legitimate major league pitches, and his fastball/curveball combination alone could make him an effective late-inning reliever. He'll begin his first full pro season in low Class A.

Year	Club (League)	Class	W	L	ERA	G	GS	CG	SV	IP	H	HR	BB	SO	G/A	WHIP	AVG
2010	Danville (APP)	R	0	2	2.42	10	8	0	0	26	18	1	11	27	1.53	1.12	.198
Minor League Totals			0	2	2.42	10	8	0	0	26	18	1	11	27	1.53	1.12	.198

25 PHIL GOSSELIN, 2B

Born: Oct. 3, 1988. **B-T:** R-R. **Ht.:** 6-1. **Wt.:** 190. **Drafted:** Virginia, 2010 (5th round). **Signed by:** Billy Best.

Gosselin played a key role in Virginia's run to the College World Series in 2009, including hitting a home run off San Diego State's Stephen Strasburg in the NCAA regionals. He became an offensive catalyst for a Cavaliers team that was ranked No. 1 in the nation for much of last spring, batting .382 and leading the club with 22 doubles and 11 home runs. That performance got him drafted in the fifth round last spring and earned him a $150,300 bonus. Gosselin is a good athlete who batted leadoff at Rome during his pro debut and is capable of hitting in a variety of slots in the lineup. He has plus bat speed and barrels up balls with consistency. He has gap power and average speed that plays up thanks to his baserunning savvy. Gosselin played several positions in college but stayed at second base after signing and exceeded the Braves' expectations. He showed nice footwork and instincts, and he turned the double play well. His range is fringy but his arm is average. Several club officials regard Gosselin as the steal of Atlanta's 2010 draft, and they think his blue-collar approach will take him to the big leagues. He'll probably open 2011 in high Class A and could reach Double-A by midseason.

Year	Club (League)	Class	AVG	G	AB	R	H	2B	3B	HR	RBI	BB	SO	SB	CS	OBP	SLG
2010	Rome (SAL)	LoA	.294	57	214	26	63	9	3	2	24	25	51	7	3	.374	.393
	Myrtle Beach (CAR)	HiA	.154	6	26	2	4	1	1	0	0	0	7	0	0	.154	.269
Minor League Totals			.279	63	240	28	67	10	4	2	24	25	58	7	3	.353	.379

26 PAUL CLEMENS, RHP

Born: Feb. 14, 1988. **B-T:** R-R. **Ht.:** 6-4. **Wt.:** 180. **Drafted:** Louisburg (N.C.) JC, 2008 (7th round). **Signed by:** Billy Best.

Clemens has as much raw ability as any pitcher in the organization. He just hasn't been able to put everything together on a consistent basis, a problem that dates back to his college days, when he pitched his way out of the Louisburg (N.C.) JC rotation as a sophomore. In 2010, he was overpowering during the first five weeks at Rome, only to walk four batters in two-thirds of an inning in his debut with Myrtle Beach. He finished strong, however, and posted a better ERA as a starter (2.95) than as a reliever (4.64) in high Class A. On his best days, Clemens hits 97 mph with his fastball and mixes it with an above-average curveball. On others, he tops out at 92 mph and is unable to find the strike zone. He has an ideal pitcher's frame and solid athleticism that should allow him to be a middle-of-the-rotation starter or a useful reliever. Clemens' future role will be determined by his ability to develop a changeup. He also has to improve his feel for pitching and his command, which have proven to be major hurdles in his development. The Braves still love his live arm and potential, however. They've worked with Clemens to help him harness his energy and maintain more of an even keel on the mound. He should reach Double-A at some point in 2011.

Year	Club (League)	Class	W	L	ERA	G	GS	CG	SV	IP	H	HR	BB	SO	G/A	WHIP	AVG
2008	Braves (GCL)	R	1	0	0.00	1	0	0	0	3	1	0	0	2	—	0.33	.111
	Danville (APP)	R	3	3	3.39	12	8	0	1	58	57	6	18	57	—	1.29	.252
	Rome (SAL)	LoA	0	1	9.00	1	1	0	0	4	7	0	2	0	—	2.25	.412
2009	Rome (SAL)	LoA	6	5	5.91	26	11	0	3	85	105	7	49	64	1.24	1.80	.296
2010	Rome (SAL)	LoA	2	0	1.42	8	0	0	1	19	11	1	8	16	0.73	1.00	.164
	Myrtle Beach (CAR)	HiA	0	4	3.69	27	8	0	2	76	83	5	28	65	1.16	1.47	.275
Minor League Totals			12	13	4.26	75	28	0	7	245	264	19	105	204	1.14	1.50	.270

27 JUAN ABREU, RHP

Born: April 8, 1985. **B-T:** R-R. **Ht.:** 6-0. **Wt.:** 170. **Signed:** Dominican Republic, 2003. **Signed by:** Pedro Silverio (Royals).

Abreu had one of the best fastballs in the Royals system, which prompted Kansas City to agree to a deal to re-sign him as a minor league free agent after he reached Double-A in 2009. A contract snafu allowed him to hit the open market, however, and the Braves landed him by giving him a big league contract. Atlanta removed him from the 40-man roster at the end of last March, but added him again in November. He got knocked around in high Class A to start last season, but pitched much better after a May promotion and became Mississippi's closer during the second half. Employing a whip-like arm action, Abreu sits at 95-96 mph with his sinking fastball and was clocked as high as 99 mph last summer. He also has a 78-80 mph curveball that could be a plus pitch. He lacks feel for his changeup and abandoned the pitch at times last season. Abreu gets into trouble when he overthrows, causing him to leave his pitches up in the strike zone and making him susceptible to the longball. He needs to throw more strikes after averaging 4.5 walks per nine innings in 2010, and he also must do a better job of commanding his pitches in the strike zone. When he hits 96 mph on the inner half of the plate, few hitters can do much against him. A potential set-up man and a spot closer if it all comes together, Abreu should move up to Triple-A in 2011.

Year	Club (League)	Class	W	L	ERA	G	GS	CG	SV	IP	H	HR	BB	SO	G/A	WHIP	AVG
2003	Royals (DSL)	R	0	2	2.25	5	2	0	0	16	16	0	7	10	—	1.44	.242
2004	Royals (DSL)	R	2	1	4.06	9	7	0	0	31	22	0	20	33	—	1.35	.198
2005	Royals (AZL)	R	2	5	6.88	14	13	0	0	52	72	4	27	52	—	1.89	.327
2006	Idaho Falls (PIO)	R	4	2	5.76	20	0	0	2	50	39	4	35	57	—	1.48	.223
2007	Did Not Play—Injured																
2008	Burlington (MWL)	LoA	4	4	3.66	22	4	0	7	76	59	6	42	104	—	1.32	.214
2009	Wilmington (CAR)	HiA	3	2	1.69	20	0	0	12	21	8	1	14	28	0.64	1.03	.114
	NW Arkansas (TL)	AA	2	2	5.75	16	0	0	4	20	19	3	22	25	1.06	2.02	.247
2010	Myrtle Beach (CAR)	HiA	0	0	8.22	8	0	0	1	15	14	5	8	15	0.87	1.43	.241
	Mississippi (SL)	AA	4	2	3.02	39	0	0	11	45	41	2	22	47	0.52	1.41	.243
Minor League Totals			21	20	4.59	153	26	0	37	327	290	25	197	371	0.68	1.49	.237

28 BRETT BUTTS, RHP

Born: April 24, 1986. **B-T:** R-R. **Ht.:** 6-1. **Wt.:** 205. **Drafted:** Auburn, 2007 (19th round). **Signed by:** Al Goetz.

The Braves kept things in the family when they drafted Butts in the 19th round out of Auburn in 2007. His uncle Alan Butts is the major league club's baseball systems operator as well as its longtime bullpen catcher. While growing up south of Atlanta, Brett attended Braves games on a regular basis. He became a reliever midway through his college career and has stayed in that role in pro ball. He made steady progress in the minors, pitching well in Double-A the last two years before injuring his elbow last May and having Tommy John surgery in July. Before he got hurt, Butts' fastball was sitting at 90-94 mph with plus movement. He also had good command of an above-average changeup, which has been his out pitch since college, and a 12-to-6 curveball that's a solid-average offering with good downward break. He attacks hitters, throwing strikes and mixing his pitches to keep them off-balance. Butts was on the verge of being promoted to Triple-A at the time of his injury. His recovery has progressed as hoped, but he's not expected to pitch before July 1 at the earliest. He has a chance to make an impact in the major league bullpen in 2012.

Year	Club (League)	Class	W	L	ERA	G	GS	CG	SV	IP	H	HR	BB	SO	G/A	WHIP	AVG
2007	Danville (APP)	R	2	0	0.73	5	0	0	0	12	8	1	3	12	—	0.89	.178
	Rome (SAL)	LoA	1	1	3.47	9	0	0	1	23	21	2	5	17	—	1.11	.244
	Myrtle Beach (CAR)	HiA	0	1	3.18	2	0	0	0	6	7	0	1	1	—	1.41	.318
2008	Myrtle Beach (CAR)	HiA	3	4	4.16	36	2	0	10	76	62	9	24	66	—	1.14	.220
2009	Mississippi (SL)	AA	7	3	2.58	53	0	0	5	73	63	5	36	68	1.14	1.35	.233
2010	Mississippi (SL)	AA	0	1	1.52	15	0	0	3	24	18	0	6	28	2.33	1.01	.212
Minor League Totals			13	10	3.03	120	2	0	19	214	179	17	75	192	1.32	1.19	.227

29 CORY HARRILCHAK, OF

Born: Oct. 27, 1987. **B-T:** L-L. **Ht.:** 6-0. **Wt.:** 185. **Drafted:** Elon, 2009 (14th round). **Signed by:** Billy Best.

Though he had played just a half-year at high Class A, Harrilchak went to the Arizona Fall League after the 2010 season and hit .333/.432/.520 in 75 at-bats. His performance was a testament to the progress he made in his first two years of pro ball after signing for $1,000 as an unheralded 14th-round senior sign from Elon. Harrilchak is a grinder who can hit and get on base. He battles every time he steps in the batter's box and his swing produces line drives from gap to gap. He has below-average power but average speed and the baserunning instincts to steal 15-20 bases per year. Harrilchak is the best defensive outfielder in the system. He gets good jumps and covers both gaps in center field, and he has the solid arm strength and carry on his throws to play right field. He gets the most out of his abilities, though his tools fit more of a fourth-outfielder profile than that of a regular. A promotion to Double-A is on Harrilchak's immediate horizon.

Year	Club (League)	Class	AVG	G	AB	R	H	2B	3B	HR	RBI	BB	SO	SB	CS	OBP	SLG
2009	Danville (APP)	R	.324	60	222	43	72	10	5	2	41	22	19	2	.401	.441	
2010	Rome (SAL)	LoA	.306	60	219	31	67	10	3	1	22	24	24	18	11	.380	.393
	Myrtle Beach (CAR)	HiA	.269	58	234	29	63	16	5	2	25	21	45	4	4	.329	.406
Minor League Totals			.299	178	675	103	202	36	13	5	88	72	91	41	17	.370	.413

30 RICHARD SULLIVAN, LHP

Born: April 14, 1987. **B-T:** L-L. **Ht.:** 6-3. **Wt.:** 230. **Drafted:** Savannah College of Art and Design (Ga.), 2008 (11th round). **Signed by:** Brian Bridges.

When the Braves selected Sullivan in the 11th round in 2008, he became just the second player ever drafted from the Savannah College of Art and Design, an NAIA school. A two-way player in college, he became a full-time pitcher in pro ball and reached Double-A briefly in his first full season in the system. When he returned to Mississippi in 2010, he struggled with his command as a starter, going 1-7, 7.17 and allowing opponents to bat .346 against him. Atlanta moved him to the bullpen at midseason and he took to that role, posting 2.72 ERA and limiting the opposition to a .230 average. Sullivan thrives when he pitches down in the strike zone with his heavy two-seam fastball. He adds and subtracts from it, ranging from 87-93 mph and inducing groundball. His second pitch is a hard three-quarters breaking ball that at times has true tilt and is a plus slider. He also has a decent changeup. Sullivan has made rapid adjustments while moving quickly through the minors but still is fine-tuning his ability to set up hitters. He's also susceptible to the running game, especially for a lefthander. He improved his conditioning in 2010 but still doesn't stick out in terms of athleticism or fielding his position. Sullivan's future is as a set-up man or middle reliever. With a strong spring training, he could open 2011 in Triple-A.

Year	Club (League)	Class	W	L	ERA	G	GS	CG	SV	IP	H	HR	BB	SO	G/A	WHIP	AVG
2008	Danville (APP)	R	2	0	1.40	4	4	0	0	19	10	1	0	22	—	0.52	.149
	Rome (SAL)	LoA	2	2	2.80	8	8	0	0	35	40	0	4	27	—	1.25	.282
2009	Rome (SAL)	LoA	4	1	3.72	5	5	1	0	29	37	2	5	27	3.67	1.45	.306
	Myrtle Beach (CAR)	HiA	2	12	4.25	19	19	1	0	112	115	5	39	80	2.30	1.37	.266
	Mississippi (SL)	AA	0	1	9.45	3	3	0	0	13	21	0	10	8	3.00	2.32	.389
2010	Mississippi (SL)	AA	4	11	5.09	36	13	0	2	120	140	10	40	91	2.40	1.50	.294
Minor League Totals			14	27	4.40	75	52	2	2	330	363	18	98	255	2.47	1.40	.281

Baltimore Orioles

BY WILL LINGO

Replacing their manager got all the attention, but the Orioles are making modifications throughout the organization to try to reverse a 13-year run of losing seasons.

Dumping Dave Trembley became an obvious move after Baltimore got off to a 15-39 start in 2010, and interim replacement Juan Samuel was little better at 17-34. Hiring Buck Showalter at the end of July  brought the team instant credibility, however, and he won more games in two months, 34, than Trembley and Samuel had in four. Showalter also got credit for bringing a more professional approach, discipline and confidence to the major league club, and the Orioles' young players responded. Rookie lefthander Brian Matusz, for example, went 3-11, 5.46 before Showalter was hired, then went 7-1, 2.18 the rest of the way.

The changes went deeper. Baltimore reassigned farm director David Stockstill at the end of spring training, essentially having him switch jobs with his brother John, who had been director of international scouting. John Stockstill wants to oversee a return to The Oriole Way, the uniform instruction of fundamentals at every level of the system that became the foundation of the organization in the 1950s and carried the team through the rest of the century.

The Orioles will have fewer roving minor league instructors, choosing instead to have an extra coach at each level in hopes of bringing greater consistency to the daily instruction players receive. Stockstill himself will focus more directly on personnel than farm directors traditionally do, working with players in the majors as well as the minors.

To that end, Baltimore moved longtime batting coach Terry Crowley into a new system-wide hitting evaluation job, and Showalter hired Jim Presley as the new hitting coach, part of significant changes in the major and minor league coaching staffs.

The Orioles dropped their longtime affiliation with Bluefield after sending players there for 53 seasons. The organization decided its resources were spread too thin with seven affiliations and went with one Rookie-level club in the Gulf Coast League instead.

The GCL team will play in new digs in 2011, as a $33 million renovation project nears completion in Sarasota, Fla. Baltimore moved its big league spring-training operation back to Sarasota in 2010, putting their major and minor league complexes in the same city for the first time since 1995.

Young players such as Brian Matusz put up better results with Buck Showalter managing

TOP 30 PROSPECTS

1. Manny Machado, ss	**16.** Trent Mummey, of
2. Zach Britton, lhp	**17.** Connor Narron, ss/3b
3. Xavier Avery, of	**18.** Tyler Townsend, 1b
4. L.J. Hoes, 2b	**19.** Ronnie Welty, of
5. Dan Klein, rhp	**20.** Brandon Snyder, 1b
6. Wynn Pelzer, rhp	**21.** Luis Lebron, rhp
7. Mychal Givens, ss	**22.** Tyler Henson, of
8. Ryan Adams, 2b/3b	**23.** Brandon Waring, 3b/1b
9. Ryan Berry, rhp	**24.** Chorye Spoone, rhp
10. Jonathan Schoop, ss	**25.** Eddie Gamboa, rhp
11. Joe Mahoney, 1b/of	**26.** Greg Miclat, ss
12. Parker Bridwell, rhp	**27.** Brandon Erbe, rhp
13. Matt Angle, of	**28.** Caleb Joseph, c
14. Bobby Bundy, rhp	**29.** Pedro Florimon, ss
15. Matt Hobgood, rhp	**30.** Adrian Rosario, rhp

Because of the renovations, the team could not hold a traditional instructional league program in the fall, so it brought 15 of its top position players to Camden Yards for 10 days of focused instruction.

Still, the Orioles face an uphill battle to compete in the American League East. The farm system has thinned out despite the addition of first-rounder Manny Machado, with numerous graduations in the last couple of seasons as well as an inordinate number of injuries to top prospects in 2010.

General Manager: Andy MacPhail. **Farm Director:** John Stockstill. **Scouting Director:** Joe Jordan.

Class	Team	League	W	L	PCT	Finish*	Manager
Majors	Baltimore Orioles	American	66	96	.407	13th (14)	D.Trembley/J.Samuel/B.Showalter
Triple-A	Norfolk Tides	International	67	77	.465	t-10th (14)	Gary Allenson/Bobby Dickerson
Double-A	Bowie Baysox	Eastern	75	67	.528	5th (12)	Brad Komminsk
High A	Frederick Keys	Carolina	72	68	.514	4th (8)	Orlando Gomez
Low A	Delmarva Shorebirds	South Atlantic	59	81	.421	14th (14)	Ryan Minor
Short-season	Aberdeen Ironbirds	New York-Penn	34	40	.459	t-10th (14)	Gary Kendall
Rookie	Bluefield Orioles	Appalachian	23	45	.338	10th (10)	Einar Diaz
Rookie	GCL Orioles	Gulf Coast	25	34	.424	14th (15)	Ramon Sambo

Overall 2010 Minor League Record 355 412 .463 27th (30)
*Finish in overall standings (No. of teams in league). †League champion.
Orioles will drop Bluefield affiliate in 2011.

LAST YEAR'S TOP 30

Player, Pos.		Status
1.	Brian Matusz, lhp	Majors
2.	Josh Bell, 3b	Majors
3.	Zach Britton, lhp	No. 2
4.	Jake Arrieta, rhp	Majors
5.	Matt Hobgood, rhp	No. 15
6.	Brandon Snyder, 1b	No. 20
7.	Brandon Erbe, rhp	No. 27
8.	Kam Mickolio, rhp	(Diamondbacks)
9.	Mychal Givens, ss	No. 7
10.	Caleb Joseph, c	No. 28
11.	Luis Lebron, rhp	No. 21
12.	Pedro Florimon, ss	No. 29
13.	Xavier Avery, of	No. 3
14.	Troy Patton, lhp	Dropped out
15.	Michael Ohlman, c	Dropped out
16.	Brett Jacobson, rhp	(Twins)
17.	Brandon Cooney, rhp	Dropped out
18.	Brandon Waring, 1b/3b	No. 23
19.	Cameron Coffey, lhp	Dropped out
20.	Kyle Hudson, of	Dropped out
21.	L.J. Hoes, 2b	No. 4
22.	Oliver Drake, rhp	Dropped out
23.	Jake Cowan, rhp	Dropped out
24.	Ryan Berry, rhp	No. 9
25.	Matt Angle, of	No. 13
26.	Ryan Adams, 2b	No. 8
27.	Garabez Rosa, ss	Dropped out
28.	Chorye Spoone, rhp	No. 24
29.	Eddie Gamboa, rhp	No. 25
30.	Billy Rowell, of	Dropped out

BEST TOOLS

Best Hitter for Average	Manny Machado
Best Power Hitter	Brandon Waring
Best Strike-Zone Discipline	Brian Conley
Fastest Baserunner	Glynn Davis
Best Athlete	Xavier Avery
Best Fastball	Zach Britton
Best Curveball	Dan Klein
Best Slider	Zach Britton
Best Changeup	Dan Klein
Best Control	Ryan Berry
Best Defensive Catcher	Caleb Joseph
Best Defensive Infielder	Manny Machado
Best Infield Arm	Billy Rowell
Best Defensive Outfielder	Matt Angle
Best Outfield Arm	Matt Angle

PROJECTED 2014 LINEUP

Catcher	Matt Wieters
First Base	Joe Mahoney
Second Base	L.J. Hoes
Third Base	Mark Reynolds
Shortstop	Manny Machado
Left Field	Xavier Avery
Center Field	Adam Jones
Right Field	Nick Markakis
Designated Hitter	Luke Scott
No. 1 Starter	Brian Matusz
No. 2 Starter	Zach Britton
No. 3 Starter	Jake Arrieta
No. 4 Starter	Chris Tillman
No. 5 Starter	Jeremy Guthrie
Closer	Wynn Pelzer

TOP PROSPECTS OF THE DECADE

Year	Player, Pos.	2010 Org.
2001	Keith Reed, of	Out of baseball
2002	Richard Stahl, lhp	Out of baseball
2003	Erik Bedard, lhp	Mariners
2004	Adam Loewen, lhp	Blue Jays
2005	Nick Markakis, of	Orioles
2006	Nick Markakis, of	Orioles
2007	Billy Rowell, 3b	Orioles
2008	Matt Wieters, c	Orioles
2009	Matt Wieters, c	Orioles
2010	Brian Matusz, lhp	Orioles

TOP DRAFT PICKS OF THE DECADE

Year	Player, Pos.	2010 Org.
2001	Chris Smith, lhp	Out of baseball
2002	Adam Loewen, lhp	Blue Jays
2003	Nick Markakis, of	Orioles
2004	*Wade Townsend, rhp	Laredo (United)
2005	Brandon Snyder, c	Orioles
2006	Billy Rowell, 3b	Orioles
2007	Matt Wieters, c	Orioles
2008	Brian Matusz, lhp	Orioles
2009	Matt Hobgood, rhp	Orioles
2010	Manny Machado, ss	Orioles

*Did not sign.

LARGEST BONUSES IN CLUB HISTORY

Matt Wieters, 2007	$6,000,000
Manny Machado, 2010	$5,250,000
Adam Loewen, 2002	$3,200,000
Brian Matusz, 2008	$3,200,000
Matt Hobgood, 2009	$2,422,000

BALTIMORE ORIOLES

TOP 2011 ROOKIE: Zach Britton, lhp. A strong performance in Triple-A could allow him to break through quickly—if he doesn't win a job in spring training.

BREAKOUT PROSPECT: Parker Bridwell, rhp. Some scouts thought he was better suited for college ball, but the Orioles couldn't resist his strong frame and athleticism.

SLEEPER: Cameron Coffey, lhp. He's still overcoming Tommy John surgery from his senior year of high school but had a 92-95 mph fastball before he got hurt.

SOURCE OF TOP 30 TALENT			
Homegrown	27	Acquired	3
College	9	Trades	2
Junior college	2	Rule 5 draft	1
High school	13	Independent leagues	0
Draft-and-follow	0	Free agents/waivers	0
Nondrafted free agents	0		
International	3		

LF
Tyler Henson (22)
Brenden Webb

CF
Xavier Avery (3)
Matt Angle (13)
Trent Mummey (16)
Kyle Hudson
Glynn Davis
Steven Bumbry

RF
Ronnie Welty (19)
Rhyne Hughes

3B
Ryan Adams (8)
Connor Narron (17)
Brandon Waring (23)
Billy Rowell

SS
Manny Machado (1)
Mychal Givens (7)
Jonathan Schoop (10)
Greg Miclat (26)
Pedro Florimon (29)
Garabez Rosa

2B
L.J. Hoes (4)
Carlos Rojas

1B
Joe Mahoney (11)
Tyler Townsend (18)
Brandon Snyder (20)
Jacob Julius
Robbie Widlansky

C
Caleb Joseph (28)
Michael Ohlman
Wynston Sawyer
Justin Dalles
Ryan Hornback
Brian Ward

RHP

RHSP	RHRP
Dan Klein (5)	Wynn Pelzer (6)
Ryan Berry (9)	Luis Lebron (21)
Parker Bridwell (12)	Chorye Spoone (24)
Bobby Bundy (14)	Brandon Erbe (27)
Matt Hobgood (15)	Adrian Rosario (30)
Eddie Gamboa (25)	Clay Schrader
Oliver Drake	Brandon Cooney
Jake Cowan	Raul Rivero
Steve Johnson	Steven Mazur
Mitch Atkins	
Jaime Esquivel	
Ryan O'Shea	
Sebastian Vader	

LHP

LHSP	LHRP
Zach Britton (2)	Pedro Viola
Cameron Coffey	Nathan Moreau
Troy Patton	Brett Bordes
Matt Bywater	Cole McCurry
Aaron Wirsch	
Rick Zagone	
Jarret Martin	

2010   BONUSES: $9.2 MILLION

BEST PURE HITTER: SS Manny Machado (1) went No. 3 overall because of his five-tool ability and all-around polish. He had no trouble adjusting to wood, hitting .306 and striking out just three times in 36 late-August at-bats.

BEST POWER HITTER: The A-Rod comparisons are a bit much, but Machado's solid-average power is the best among Orioles draftees. Baltimore focused more on athletes than mashers.

FASTEST RUNNER: OFs Trent Mummey (4) and Jeremy Shelby (38) have plus speed. OF Glynn Davis, a nondrafted free agent from CC of Baltimore County-Catonsville (Md.), has true 80 speed on the 20-80 scouting scale.

BEST DEFENSIVE PLAYER: Connor Narron (5) has the feet, hands and arm to be a standout at third base. Baltimore also likes the defensive ability of Machado, Mummey and C Wynston Sawyer (8).

BEST FASTBALL: RHP Clay Schrader (10) has some effort to his delivery, but it's hard to argue with his 91-96 mph fastball. RHP Parker Bridwell (9) currently tops out at 94 mph, but he does it easier and is more projectable than Schrader and should pass him in time.

BEST SECONDARY PITCH: RHP Dan Klein's (3) curveball. Used as a closer on a talented UCLA staff, Klein has enough ammunition to be a starter with a 91-93 mph fastball and a good changeup. Schrader throws a power slider in the mid-80s.

BEST PRO DEBUT: The Orioles signed several players for over-slot money close to the deadline, so many of their top picks didn't get a chance to play much. RHP Steven Mazur (33), who has an average fastball and a solid slider, had a 1.20 ERA, six saves and 38 strikeouts in 30 innings between two teams.

BEST ATHLETE: Machado's worst tool, his speed, is average.

MOST INTRIGUING BACKGROUND: Shelby's father John was part of Baltimore's 1983 World Series championship team and is the club's first-base coach. Narron's father Jerry played and managed in the majors, and his great-uncle and cousin (both named Sam Narron) played in the big leagues as well. Unsigned SS Coty Blanchard (41) punted and served as the No. 2 quarterback for Jacksonville State as a freshman this fall.

CLOSEST TO THE MAJORS: Machado should reach the big leagues quicker than most high schoolers. Klein could be the first player from this group to join the Orioles if they make him a reliever. Schrader, who will stay in the bullpen, is another candidate.

BEST LATE-ROUND PICK: RHP Jaime Esquivel (28) has the body of a young Matt Garza and a fastball that reaches 93 mph. Baltimore likes C Riley Hornback's (12) line-drive bat and his defense.

THE ONE WHO GOT AWAY: The Orioles never got close to a deal with RHP Dixon Anderson (6), who took his mid-90s fastball back to California for his senior season. They would have made a bigger play for Blanchard if they hadn't already loaded up on middle infielders.

ASSESSMENT: Picking third guaranteed the Orioles one of the three elite talents in the draft, and they're thrilled with Machado. They also went over slot for Klein, Narron, LHP Matt Bywater (7), Sawyer, Bridwell, Schrader and Esquivel.

2009   BONUSES: $8.7 MILLION

None of Baltimore's big-money investments—RHP Matt Hobgood (1), C Michael Ohlman (11), LHP Cameron Coffey (22)—did much in 2010, though Coffey had Tommy John surgery before he signed. SS Mychal Givens (2) and RHP Ryan Berry (9) have some promise.

GRADE: C

2008   BONUSES: $8.0 MILLION

LHP Brian Matusz (1) already has become the Orioles' best big league starter. OF Xavier Avery (2) and 2B L.J. Hoes (3) are two of the system's top position prospects.

GRADE: A

2007   BONUSES: $6.9 MILLION

C Matt Wieters' (1) path to superstardom has been slower than expected, but he's still young. Baltimore made up for not having second- and third-round picks by spending $1.1 million on RHP Jake Arrieta (5), and it has hopes for 1B/OF Joe Mahoney (6) and OF Matt Angle (7).

GRADE: B+

2006   BONUSES: $5.4 MILLION

3B Billy Rowell (1) and RHP Pedro Beato (1s) are shells of what the Orioles hoped they would become, but LHP Zach Britton (3) has made up for those disappointments. 2B/3B Ryan Adams (2) has hit when healthy, while RHP Jason Berken (6) was an effective big league reliever in 2010.

GRADE: B

Draft analysis by Jim Callis. Numbers in parentheses indicate draft rounds.

MANNY MACHADO, SS

Born: July 6, 1992. **Bats:** R. **Throws:** R. **Height:** 6-3. **Weight:** 185. **Drafted:** HS—Hialeah, Fla., 2010 (1st round). **Signed by:** John Martin.

RODGER WOOD

The Orioles have leaned toward pitching at the top of recent drafts and hadn't selected a shortstop in the first round since taking Rich Dauer out of Southern California in 1974, but Machado's talent was too much to pass up. The scouting consensus was that the top three players in the 2010 draft—Bryce Harper, Jameson Taillon and Machado—were a cut above everyone else, so the Orioles were happy to grab their shortstop of the future with the No. 3 overall choice after the Nationals picked Harper and the Pirates selected Taillon. Machado laid the groundwork for going near the top of the draft with his standout showcase performances in 2009, with the highlight coming when he batted .367 to help the U.S. 18-and-under team win the Pan American Junior Championship. He earned BA High School All-America honors as a senior, batting .639 with 12 homers and 17 steals for Brito Miami Private High. Machado gave up a scholarship from Florida International to sign at the Aug. 16 deadline, netting a $5.25 million bonus that's the sixth-highest ever for a high schooler and the second-highest in franchise history, trailing only Matt Wieters' $6 million bonus in the 2007 draft. The Orioles let him get his feet wet with brief assignments in the Rookie-level Gulf Coast League and at short-season Aberdeen, then brought him to their abbreviated instructional camp in Baltimore in September.

The Orioles brought in J.J. Hardy to fill their gaping hole at shortstop, but long-term they had no one in the system to take over the position until signing Machado, who has legitimate five-tool ability. He has a good swing and bat speed. He makes consistent hard contact—he struck out just three times in 36 pro at-bats—and repeatedly puts the barrel on the ball. The ball already carries well off his bat, and he has the room to add muscle to his wiry 6-foot-3 frame. Baltimore believes he can become a .300 hitter with 20 homers a season as he matures. Machado also has the arm, build and strength to be a major league shortstop. He shows advanced defensive skills, with solid range, soft hands

SCOUTING GRADES

Batting: 70.   **Defense:** 60.
Power: 50.   **Arm:** 60.
Speed: 45.

Based on 20-80 scouting scale, where 50 represents major league average, and future projection rather than present tools.

and a plus arm. His weakest tool is his speed, but even that rates as fringe average. In addition to his physical ability, Machado has made a quick impression with his makeup, showing a great work ethic and receptiveness to instruction. When working on nuances of shortstop with Orioles instructor Mike Bordick in the fall, such as the footwork on his feeds from shortstop on the double play, he quickly made adjustments and never reverted to his previous habits. He would execute the new skill within two or three ground balls.

Machado has all the tools and just needs to play. Because of his build, Dominican bloodlines and hype as a high school shortstop coming out of South Florida, he earns obvious Alex Rodriguez comparisons. He's not as physically mature as Rodriguez was when he came into pro ball, and his ceiling isn't as lofty, but Machado still has the look of a perennial all-star. He'll open his first full season at low Class A Delmarva, and should move quickly through the system if he hits as expected. He could be ready for Baltimore at some point in 2013.

Year	Club (League)	Class	AVG	G	AB	R	H	2B	3B	HR	RBI	BB	SO	SB	CS	OBP	SLG
2010	Orioles (GCL)	R	.143	2	7	1	1	0	0	1	2	0	1	0	0	.143	.571
	Aberdeen (NYP)	SS	.345	7	29	2	10	1	1	0	3	3	2	0	0	.406	.448
Minor League Totals			.306	9	36	3	11	1	1	1	5	3	3	0	0	.359	.472

2 ZACH BRITTON, LHP

RODGER WOOD

Born: Dec. 22, 1987. **B-T:** L-L. **Ht.:** 6-3. **Wt.:** 195. **Drafted:** HS—Weatherford, Texas, 2006 (3rd round). **Signed by:** Jim Richardson.

Britton has boosted his stock every year since getting drafted in 2006 and now ranks as one of the best pitching prospects in the minors. In 2010, he aced his Double-A debut, pitched in the Futures Game and finished strong in Triple-A, getting added to the 40-man roster after the season. He led Orioles farmhands in ERA (2.70) while ranking second in wins (10) and strikeouts (124). Britton has the best sinker in the minor leagues and generated a 2.8 groundout/airout ratio last season. Showing more than just good action, his fastball sits in the low 90s and peaks at 94 mph. His slider is also a plus pitch, though at he times throws it too hard while trying to get more break out of it. His changeup has developed to the point where he's willing to throw it behind in the count and use it to get quick outs rather than strikeouts. Britton showed his best stuff more consistently in 2010. He does a good job of spotting all of his pitches within the strike zone. The Orioles liked how Britton refined his arsenal and came after hitters with a plan rather than just overpowering them with his sinker. He'll probably return to Triple-A Norfolk at the start out of 2011, but it's not out of question that he could pitch his way into the big league rotation.

Year	Club (League)	Class	W	L	ERA	G	GS	CG	SV	IP	H	HR	BB	SO	G/A	WHIP	AVG
2006	Bluefield (APP)	R	0	4	5.29	11	11	0	0	34	35	4	20	21	—	1.62	.271
2007	Aberdeen (NYP)	SS	6	4	3.68	15	15	0	0	64	64	1	22	45	—	1.35	.256
2008	Delmarva (SAL)	LoA	12	7	3.12	27	27	1	0	147	118	9	49	114	—	1.13	.219
2009	Frederick (CAR)	HiA	9	6	2.70	25	24	0	0	140	123	6	55	131	3.38	1.27	.232
2010	Bowie (EL)	AA	7	3	2.48	15	14	0	0	87	76	4	28	68	3.60	1.20	.231
	Norfolk (IL)	AAA	3	4	2.98	12	12	0	0	66	63	3	23	56	3.33	1.30	.245
Minor League Totals			37	28	3.09	105	103	1	0	538	479	27	197	435	3.44	1.26	.235

3 XAVIER AVERY, OF

Born: Jan. 1, 1990. **B-T:** L-L. **Ht.:** 6-0. **Wt.:** 188. **Drafted:** HS—Ellenwood, Ga., 2008 (2nd round). **Signed by:** Dave Jennings.

The Orioles knew Avery was a development project when they signed him away from a Georgia football scholarship for $900,000 in 2008. He started to translate his tools into performance in 2010, reaching Double-A as a 20-year-old. A premium athlete, Avery stands out most with his well above-average speed. It already translates into plus defense in center field even though he's polishing his routes and instincts. He's learning the nuances of basestealing as well, and went 10-for-10 stealing bases at Double-A Bowie. Avery batted leadoff all season and knows his game is to put the ball in play and put pressure on the defense. He showed better plate discipline and pitch recognition in 2010. He still struggles against breaking stuff, however, and particularly against lefthanders, batting .193 against them. He's strong enough to sting the ball on occasion but will never be a power hitter. His arm has improved, though it still rates as fringe-average. He gets by on his pure tools more often than not, but he has a thirst for instruction and is making up his deficiencies in baseball polish. Avery has made progress but still has refinements to make to become a consistent hitter. He'll return to Double-A to open 2011.

Year	Club (League)	Class	AVG	G	AB	R	H	2B	3B	HR	RBI	BB	SO	SB	CS	OBP	SLG
2008	Orioles (GCL)	R	.280	47	175	27	49	8	1	0	7	10	51	13	3	.333	.337
2009	Delmarva (SAL)	LoA	.262	129	473	55	124	15	8	2	36	27	111	30	10	.306	.340
2010	Frederick (CAR)	HiA	.280	109	447	73	125	25	6	4	48	42	96	28	14	.349	.389
	Bowie (EL)	AA	.234	27	107	10	25	6	0	3	18	7	34	10	0	.288	.374
Minor League Totals			.269	312	1202	165	323	54	15	9	109	86	292	81	27	.325	.361

4 L.J. HOES, 2B

Born: March 5, 1990. **B-T:** R-R. **Ht.:** 6-1. **Wt.:** 190. **Drafted:** HS—Washington D.C., 2008 (3rd round). **Signed by:** Dean Albany.

Hoes was in the midst of a breakout season at high Class A Frederick, batting .310/.435/.416 in mid-May, when he developed a case of mononucleosis that knocked him out for more than a month. He didn't hit with the same authority when he returned to action at the end of June, as the mono seemed to sap his strength for the rest of the season. With great balance at the plate and good command of the strike zone, Hoes is going to hit. He has quick hands and uses the middle of the field, projecting as a .300

hitter with gap power and average speed. A pitcher and outfielder in high school, he's still working on the nuances of playing second base. He has average actions and defensive tools, and he improved his fielding percentage from .939 in 2009 to .967 last season. Third base and left field are other possibilities, though his bat wouldn't profile nearly as well there. The Orioles are pleased with Hoes' progress and think he could be poised to consider his breakout in 2011. He'll probably spend the season in Double-A after finishing 2010 there.

Year	Club (League)	Class	AVG	G	AB	R	H	2B	3B	HR	RBI	BB	SO	SB	CS	OBP	SLG
2008	Orioles (GCL)	R	.308	48	159	36	49	4	3	1	18	30	22	10	0	.416	.390
2009	Delmarva (SAL)	LoA	.260	119	431	42	112	19	0	2	47	23	80	20	5	.299	.318
2010	Aberdeen (NYP)	SS	.464	8	28	8	13	5	1	1	5	2	1	1	1	.531	.821
	Bowie (EL)	AA	.222	3	9	1	2	0	0	0	1	0	1	0	0	.222	.222
	Frederick (CAR)	HiA	.278	97	353	52	98	19	2	3	44	53	70	10	8	.375	.368
Minor League Totals			.280	275	980	139	274	47	6	7	115	108	174	41	14	.354	.361

5 DAN KLEIN, RHP

Born: July 27, 1988. **B-T:** R-R. **Ht.:** 6-3. **Wt.:** 190. **Drafted:** UCLA, 2010 (3rd round). **Signed by:** Mark Ralston.

The Orioles took Klein, who was also a standout quarterback in high school in southern California, in the 24th round of the 2007 draft. He also had football scholarship options, but he opted to attend UCLA to play baseball instead. He missed the 2009 season after shoulder surgery but returned to be the closer for the Bruins' College World Series runners-up last spring. He signed for a slightly over-slot $499,900 as a third-round pick. Though Klein worked as a closer at UCLA and in his pro debut, Baltimore likes his big, strong frame and ability to throw four pitches for strikes, so they will try to develop him as a starter. He isn't overpowering but has an easy delivery and consistently throws his fastball at 91-93 mph with good life. His changeup is his second-best pitch, and it and his curveball already rate as the best in the system. He also uses a slider as another breaking pitch option. Klein throws strikes and commands his pitches well within the strike zone. Because of Klein's limited college workload, the Orioles will use him carefully in 2011. He's advanced enough to handle a jump to high Class A. His ceiling is as a No. 3 starter, and it also could be tempting to move him quickly to the big leagues as a set-up man.

Year	Club (League)	Class	W	L	ERA	G	GS	CG	SV	IP	H	HR	BB	SO	G/A	WHIP	AVG
2010	Aberdeen (NYP)	SS	1	0	0.00	5	0	0	1	6	1	0	1	10	0.50	0.32	.048
Minor League Totals			1	0	0.00	5	0	0	1	6	1	0	1	10	0.50	0.32	.048

6 WYNN PELZER, RHP

Born: June 23, 1986. **B-T:** R-R. **Ht.:** 6-1. **Wt.:** 205. **Drafted:** South Carolina, 2007 (9th round). **Signed by:** Pete DeYoung (Padres).

Miguel Tejada certainly didn't figure into the Orioles' future, and they got a solid return for him at the trade deadline by sending him to the Padres for Pelzer. Pelzer had spent his pro career as a starter until San Diego moved him to the bullpen two weeks before the deal. He continued in that role at Bowie. Pelzer offers a potent fastball/slider combination, but he never dominated as a starter because he couldn't find a consistent third pitch and his delivery didn't allow him to establish reliable command. He throws both two-seam and four-seam fastballs, sitting at 91-94 mph and touching 97 with good life. His slider is at least major league average and shows flashes of becoming a true plus pitch. He has used both a changeup and splitter but never has embraced either. His delivery can get out of sync, causing him to miss up in the strike zone. The Orioles are still open to trying Pelzer as a starter, but focusing on his two best pitches will give him the opportunity to pitch at the back of a bullpen. While his landing spot out of spring training will depend on his performance as well as his role, he should reach Triple-A at some point during 2011.

Year	Club (League)	Class	W	L	ERA	G	GS	CG	SV	IP	H	HR	BB	SO	G/A	WHIP	AVG
2008	Fort Wayne (MWL)	LoA	9	6	3.19	29	23	0	0	118	114	9	32	100	—	1.23	.248
	Lake Elsinore (CAL)	HiA	0	0	27.00	1	0	0	0	1	3	0	1	0	—	4.00	.500
2009	Lake Elsinore (CAL)	HiA	11	8	3.94	27	27	0	0	151	134	6	59	147	2.00	1.28	.244
2010	San Antonio (TL)	AA	6	9	4.20	22	18	0	0	94	102	9	56	83	1.54	1.67	.277
	Bowie (EL)	AA	1	0	4.50	10	1	0	0	20	24	2	7	20	1.25	1.55	.296
Minor League Totals			27	23	3.86	89	69	0	0	384	377	26	155	350	1.75	1.38	.258

7 MYCHAL GIVENS, SS

Born: May 13, 1990. **B-T:** R-R. **Ht.:** 6-1. **Wt.:** 190. **Drafted:** HS—Tampa, 2009 (2nd round). **Signed by:** John Martin.

Givens signed too late to play in his first summer, so he stayed in extended spring training before reporting to Delmarva at the end of May. Just seven games into his season, he ruptured a tendon in his left thumb sliding into first base, essentially turning 2010 into a lost year. Givens has a quiet approach at the plate, and his bat takes a short path to the ball and generates sharp contact. He should offer gap power, with the ability to hit 15 homers annually, though he'll need a lot of at-bats to refine his swing. He has middle-infield skills with solid-average range, a plus arm and good hands. Some clubs liked him more as a pitcher after clocking him up to 97 mph in high school. He has solid speed but won't be a big basestealing threat. Givens' injury cost him a year of development and created a jumble in the organization's middle-infield depth chart. The Orioles want Manny Machado to play shortstop at Delmarva, but it may be a reach to send Givens to Frederick given his limited experience. He could end up playing second base across from Machado.

Year	Club (League)	Class	AVG	G	AB	R	H	2B	3B	HR	RBI	BB	SO	SB	CS	OBP	SLG
2010	Delmarva (SAL)	LoA	.222	7	18	2	4	0	0	0	4	5	4	1	1	.444	.222
	Orioles (GCL)	R	.207	7	29	2	6	2	0	0	2	0	4	0	0	.207	.276
	Aberdeen (NYP)	SS	.364	8	33	8	12	3	0	3	5	6	2	2	1	.488	.727
	Frederick (CAR)	HiA	.500	1	4	2	2	0	0	0	1	0	0	0	1	.600	.500
Minor League Totals			.286	23	84	14	24	5	0	3	12	11	10	3	3	.402	.452

8 RYAN ADAMS, 2B/3B

Born: April 21, 1987. **B-T:** R-R. **Ht.:** 6-0. **Wt.:** 195. **Drafted:** HS—New Orleans, 2006 (2nd round). **Signed by:** Mike Tullier.

Adams has had an up-and-down ride through the organization, balancing his offensive potential with injuries and questions about his approach. He hit a low point in 2009, missing two months with a groin injury and then getting suspended for disciplinary reasons for the final two weeks. He turned things around in 2010, making the Eastern League all-star team and leading the circuit in hits (158), doubles (43) and extra-base hits (58). Adams squares the ball up more consistently than any other hitter in the system, but he still hasn't found a position where he's serviceable. While he doesn't have great bat speed, he has a compact swing and gap power. He has improved his flexibility after bulking up too much when he entered pro ball, but he's still a below-average runner. He has a quick first step and decent defensive tools, but he's erratic at both second and third base. Some club officials think the faster action at the hot corner keeps him more focused. Adams is blocked by Brian Roberts at second base and Mark Reynolds and Josh Bell at third base. He'll go to spring training looking to win a job in Triple-A.

Year	Club (League)	Class	AVG	G	AB	R	H	2B	3B	HR	RBI	BB	SO	SB	CS	OBP	SLG
2006	Bluefield (APP)	R	.256	34	133	24	34	8	1	2	7	19	32	2	2	.361	.376
	Aberdeen (NYP)	SS	.316	6	19	2	6	3	0	1	5	4	7	0	0	.458	.632
2007	Aberdeen (NYP)	SS	.236	67	246	29	58	10	2	3	22	18	63	8	3	.296	.329
2008	Delmarva (SAL)	LoA	.308	119	448	68	138	26	5	11	57	36	109	12	5	.367	.462
2009	Frederick (CAR)	HiA	.288	59	215	27	62	14	0	2	25	19	41	2	4	.349	.381
2010	Bowie (EL)	AA	.298	134	530	81	158	43	0	15	68	47	121	2	3	.365	.464
Minor League Totals			.287	419	1591	231	456	104	8	34	184	143	373	26	17	.354	.426

9 RYAN BERRY, RHP

Born: Oct. 1, 1991. **B-T:** R-R. **Ht.:** 6-1. **Wt.:** 195. **Drafted:** Rice, 2009 (9th round). **Signed by:** Rich Morales.

Berry was pitching himself into first-round consideration for the 2009 draft before straining his shoulder that spring at Rice. He fell to the ninth round and signed late in the summer for $417,600, though he didn't see his first pro action until 2010. He looked strong all season, quickly reaching high Class A, and the Orioles put him in the bullpen in late July to keep his innings down. Berry works quickly and throws strikes, coming after hitters with four pitches. His fastball, which usually ranges from 87-90 mph, plays above its below-average velocity because it has good life. His best pitch is a knuckle-curve with 12-to-6 break, and he also throws a more slurvy breaking ball. His changeup should be an average pitch. Berry gets in trouble when his fastball loses its sink. Because he lacks a putaway pitch, he has to be sharp with his command. His herky-jerky delivery gives him deception without detracting from his ability to find the strike zone. He'll have to prove himself at every level because he lacks overpowering stuff. He profiles as a back-of-the-rotation option who could be a useful bullpen arm if starting doesn't work out. He'll move up to Double-A to open 2011.

Year	Club (League)	Class	W	L	ERA	G	GS	CG	SV	IP	H	HR	BB	SO	G/A	WHIP	AVG
2010	Delmarva (SAL)	LoA	0	3	3.50	8	8	0	0	46	49	4	11	43	1.58	1.29	.268
	Frederick (CAR)	HiA	2	2	3.04	17	12	0	2	71	57	5	25	63	2.00	1.15	.218
Minor League Totals			2	5	3.22	25	20	0	2	117	106	9	36	106	1.82	1.21	.238

10 JONATHAN SCHOOP, SS

Born: Oct. 6, 1991. **B-T:** R-R. **Ht.:** 6-2. **Wt.:** 187. **Signed:** Curacao, 2008. **Signed by:** Ernst Meyer.

After Schoop made his pro debut in 2009, he came Stateside and worked with Gulf Coast League hitting coach Milt May in extended spring training to refine his swing and approach. He earned a quick promotion from the GCL and hit the last homer in Bluefield Orioles history. Schoop was the most improved player in the system in 2010. He improved his bat speed and showed an ability to hit for average and spray the ball around the field, though he still has holes and is seeking his ideal swing mechanics. His gangly frame has started to fill out, and he could develop average home run power as he gets stronger. Schoop has good defensive instincts at shortstop, with agility, soft hands and a strong arm. His speed also got a boost as he improved his body control, though he'll be just an average runner. He's ready for full-season ball, though he may not have a spot to play at Delmarva if the Orioles send Manny Machado and Mychal Givens there. Schoop is built similarly to Machado but projects to be bigger and stronger, which could mean a move to third base or the outfield.

Year	Club (League)	Class	AVG	G	AB	R	H	2B	3B	HR	RBI	BB	SO	SB	CS	OBP	SLG
2009	Orioles (DSL)	R	.239	68	247	28	59	7	3	0	35	24	39	11	3	.320	.291
2010	Orioles (GCL)	R	.250	17	60	11	15	4	0	3	16	7	7	0	0	.329	.467
	Bluefield (APP)	R	.316	39	133	16	42	11	1	2	16	12	14	1	1	.372	.459
	Frederick (CAR)	HiA	.238	6	21	5	5	3	0	0	3	1	4	0	0	.273	.381
Minor League Totals			.262	130	461	60	121	25	4	5	70	44	64	12	4	.334	.367

11 JOE MAHONEY, 1B/OF

Born: Feb. 1, 1987. **B-T:** L-L. **Ht.:** 6-6. **Wt.:** 240. **Drafted:** Richmond, 2007 (6th round). **Signed by:** Dean Albany.

Mahoney seemingly came out of nowhere in 2010, earning honors as the Orioles' minor league player of the year, but in reality his emergence had been years in the making. He showed good power in college at Richmond but remade his swing in pro ball, improving his balance, getting his hands in better position and becoming less stiff. Since the 2008 season, when he endured a torn quadriceps, he has lost more than 40 pounds and now shows fringe-average speed. Mahoney is a contact-oriented hitter with good command of the strike zone. He shows raw power in batting practice and is working to tap into it in games. Some scouts think his stroke remains too stiff to succeed against major league pitching. Mahoney has become a solid defender at first base and will get more time in the outfield this season to increase his versatility. He has an average arm. He left winter ball in Venezuela after one game with a sprained right wrist, and then doctors found a meniscus tear in his right knee, requiring arthroscopic surgery in October. He may return to Bowie to open the season and will have to prove 2010 year wasn't a fluke, but Baltimore showed it believes in him by adding him to the 40-man roster.

Year	Club (League)	Class	AVG	G	AB	R	H	2B	3B	HR	RBI	BB	SO	SB	CS	OBP	SLG
2007	Aberdeen (NYP)	SS	.269	65	242	31	65	10	2	9	44	19	57	1	1	.330	.438
2008	Delmarva (SAL)	LoA	.222	95	352	37	78	22	1	7	61	24	96	2	0	.275	.349
2009	Delmarva (SAL)	LoA	.278	108	395	61	110	16	7	7	53	30	93	29	1	.331	.408
	Frederick (CAR)	HiA	.267	7	30	2	8	4	0	1	5	0	10	0	1	.258	.500
2010	Frederick (CAR)	HiA	.299	72	271	37	81	18	0	9	49	22	56	5	3	.358	.465
	Bowie (EL)	AA	.319	52	191	30	61	12	2	9	29	17	39	8	1	.378	.545
Minor League Totals			.272	399	1481	198	403	82	12	42	241	112	351	45	7	.327	.429

12 PARKER BRIDWELL, RHP

Born: Aug. 2, 1991. **B-T:** R-R. **Ht.:** 6-4. **Wt.:** 190. **Drafted:** HS—Hereford, Texas, 2010 (9th round). **Signed by:** Ernest Jacobs.

Though he was known better as a football prospect coming out of high school in Texas, Bridwell's lifelong dream had been to play professional baseball. He was a quarterback in high school (and played basketball as well), throwing for 4,789 yards and 36 touchdowns in his career, with 10 rushing TDs. He drew football recruiting interest before accepting a baseball scholarship from Texas Tech, but then Baltimore took him in the ninth round and signed him for an above-slot $625,000 bonus. Bridwell has an ideal pitcher's frame with a lanky, athletic build that offers lots of room for projection. He already can dial his fastball into the low 90s, touching 94. The ball jumps out of his hand and his pitches all show good life. He throws both a curveball and slider. He's developing a changeup, which he rarely threw in high school. His command will need polish, and he'll require lots of innings because of his limited baseball experience. He'll try to win a spot in the low Class A rotation this year.

Year	Club (League)	Class	W	L	ERA	G	GS	CG	SV	IP	H	HR	BB	SO	G/A	WHIP	AVG
2010	Orioles (GCL)	R	0	0	5.40	2	2	0	0	2	1	0	3	4	—	2.40	.167
	Aberdeen (NYP)	SS	0	0	0.00	2	0	0	0	4	3	0	1	2	2.33	1.00	.214
Minor League Totals			0	0	1.59	4	2	0	0	6	4	0	4	6	2.33	1.41	.200

13 MATT ANGLE, OF

Born: Sept. 10, 1985. **B-T:** L-R. **Ht.:** 5-10. **Wt.:** 175. **Drafted:** Ohio State, 2007 (7th round). **Signed by:** Rich Morales.

In his last at-bat of spring training last year, Angle broke the hamate bone in his right hand. He had the bone removed and reported to Double-A in mid-May, hitting just as well as he had the year before and earning a promotion to Triple-A. Angle is a gamer whose biggest asset is his defense. He's an above-average center fielder, with legitimate speed for the position and an above-average arm. His speed plays on the bases as well. Angle is a solid hitter who is fundamentally sound at the plate and can lay down a bunt when needed. He shows good feel for the strike zone and makes consistent contact with a line-drive stroke. He has virtually no power, so he has to accentuate the other aspects of his game. Because he doesn't have a truly standout tool, most scouts see Angle as a fourth or fifth outfielder, but he's the kind of player managers love to have at their disposal. Added to the 40-man roster in November, he'll open 2011 back at Norfolk and could find a spot in the big leagues if he continues to hit.

Year	Club (League)	Class	AVG	G	AB	R	H	2B	3B	HR	RBI	BB	SO	SB	CS	OBP	SLG
2007	Aberdeen (NYP)	SS	.301	66	236	60	71	4	4	0	14	47	40	34	4	.421	.352
2008	Delmarva (SAL)	LoA	.287	126	478	82	137	22	5	4	35	71	86	37	11	.385	.379
2009	Frederick (CAR)	HiA	.289	123	478	78	138	17	4	1	32	59	72	40	12	.370	.347
	Bowie (EL)	AA	.357	8	28	6	10	1	0	0	1	4	5	2	0	.438	.393
2010	Bowie (EL)	AA	.383	14	60	11	23	2	0	1	9	6	5	5	2	.433	.467
	Norfolk (IL)	AAA	.260	87	350	55	91	4	4	1	24	41	54	24	4	.338	.303
Minor League Totals			.288	424	1630	292	470	50	17	7	115	228	262	142	33	.379	.353

14 BOBBY BUNDY, RHP

Born: Jan. 13, 1990. **B-T:** R-R. **Ht.:** 6-2. **Wt.:** 218. **Drafted:** HS—Sperry, Okla., 2008 (8th round). **Signed by:** Jim Richardson.

Bundy rewrote the record book at Sperry (Okla.) High, and now his brother Dylan is one of the top high school pitchers in the 2011 draft class—though he now attends Oklahoma powerhouse Owasso High. The two played together in Bobby's senior year in 2008, though Bobby missed part of the season with a knee injury sustained during basketball season. Signed for $600,000 after falling to the eighth round, he got off to a slow start in pro ball because he got out of shape after his knee injury. The Orioles moved him to bullpen to open 2010, but he pitched himself into the Delmarva rotation in May. Bundy is built to eat innings, with a strong, sturdy frame and a fastball that he can dial up to the mid-90s. He more frequently pitches at 88-92 mph with good sink. He throws both a curveball and slider, using the latter more frequently in 2010, but both pitches need to be tightened up. His changeup shows promise, flashing above-average potential. Bundy has a long arm action and will have to clean up his delivery, and he doesn't throw enough quality strikes. He'll open the 2011 season at age 21 in the Frederick rotation.

Year	Club (League)	Class	W	L	ERA	G	GS	CG	SV	IP	H	HR	BB	SO	G/A	WHIP	AVG
2008	Orioles (GCL)	R	0	0	9.00	2	0	0	0	2	5	1	0	4	—	2.50	.455
2009	Bluefield (APP)	R	2	7	5.10	12	12	1	0	55	47	6	19	38	1.58	1.21	.229
2010	Delmarva (SAL)	LoA	4	6	3.65	28	18	1	0	116	100	12	42	91	1.48	1.22	.238
Minor League Totals			6	13	4.17	42	30	2	0	173	152	19	61	133	1.52	1.23	.239

15 MATT HOBGOOD, RHP

Born: Aug. 3, 1990. **B-T:** R-R. **Ht.:** 6-4. **Wt.:** 250. **Drafted:** HS—Norco, Calif., 2009 (1st round). **Signed by:** Mark Ralston.

It would be harder to have a less auspicious full-season debut than Hobgood had, after the Orioles made him the No. 5 overall pick and the first high school pitcher selected in the 2009 draft. He signed for a slightly below-slot bonus of $2.422 million. Hobgood came to spring training last year out of shape and never showed the stuff he had the previous spring, when he dominated prep competition with a mid-90s fastball with sink. At times his fastball sat at 87-89 mph, and he showed a slurvy breaking ball and poor command. He was overweight and had mild tendinitis in his shoulder, so the Orioles shut him down for a few weeks in June and again in August as a precaution. At his best, Hobgood will have a low-90s fastball and an above-average curveball with tight break. His changeup is a work in progress, as he slows his arm when he throws it, but he does throw it for strikes. He needs to work on his command and establish his fastball first. Baltimore doesn't question Hobgood's work ethic and just thinks he needs to learn how to take better care of himself. To that end, they sent him to Athletes' Performance in California to get in better shape. Hobgood will get a do-over for 2010, but it will be important for him to come out of the gates strong from the beginning of spring training this year.

Year	Club (League)	Class	W	L	ERA	G	GS	CG	SV	IP	H	HR	BB	SO	G/A	WHIP	AVG
2009	Bluefield (APP)	R	1	2	4.72	8	8	0	0	27	32	0	8	16	1.65	1.50	.305
2010	Delmarva (SAL)	LoA	3	7	4.40	21	21	0	0	94	90	6	38	59	2.53	1.36	.257
Minor League Totals			4	9	4.48	29	29	0	0	121	122	6	46	75	2.27	1.39	.268

16 TRENT MUMMEY, OF

Born: Jan. 5, 1989. **B-T:** L-L. **Ht.:** 5-10. **Wt.:** 185. **Drafted:** Auburn, 2010 (4th round). **Signed by:** Dave Jennings.

Auburn was counting on Mummey in the middle of its lineup in 2010, but he sustained a high ankle sprain in an intrasquad workout and missed the first half of the regular season. He swung a hot bat when he returned, batting .366 with 17 home runs in 153 at-bats, and the Tigers made it to the NCAA playoffs for the first time since 2005. The Orioles signed him for $252,000 in the fourth round and compare him to Matt Angle as an athletic gamer who can hold down center field. Mummey has more power than Angle, though his best pure tool is his plus speed, which allows him to steal bases and should make him a quality defender as well. He also has a strong arm. Mummey has a simple swing and should be an average hitter, though he'll need to improve his pitch recognition. The intrigue comes with how much power he'll develop. He's not going to be a masher, but if he has average power to go with his defense and speed he could develop into a poor man's Lenny Dykstra. Mummey showed power and speed with wood bats in the Cape Cod League in 2009, so Baltimore hopes to see a similar package in his first full pro season. He should open 2011 in low Class A.

Year	Club (League)	Class	AVG	G	AB	R	H	2B	3B	HR	RBI	BB	SO	SB	CS	OBP	SLG
2010	Aberdeen (NYP)	SS	.266	49	207	30	55	16	2	3	24	23	28	6	2	.342	.406
	Delmarva (SAL)	LoA	.167	13	54	7	9	0	3	0	5	3	8	2	2	.224	.278
Minor League Totals			.245	62	261	37	64	16	5	3	29	26	36	8	4	.318	.379

17 CONNOR NARRON, SS/3B

Born: Nov. 12, 1991. **B-T:** B-R. **Ht.:** 6-3. **Wt.:** 195. **Drafted:** HS—Pikeville, N.C., 2010 (5th round). **Signed by:** Dominic Viola.

Narron has deep baseball bloodlines. His father Jerry is the best-known member of the family, having played and managed in the major leagues, but his uncle Johnny is also a longtime minor league player and coach who's currently a special-assignment coach with the Rangers. His great-uncle Sam was a big league catcher with the Cardinals; Sam's son Rooster was a minor league catcher; and Rooster's son Sam is a lefthander who spent 2010 in the Brewers system and has reached the majors. So it probably shouldn't have been a surprise that Narron took the Orioles' $650,000 bonus offer as a fifth-round pick in 2010, passing up a scholarship to North Carolina. His father's time in major league dugouts gave Narron ample exposure to the professional game, including serving as a batboy, and he was a four-year starter in high school, leading Aycock High (Pikeville, N.C.) to a state champi-onship in 2007. Narron's best tool is his bat, as he's a switch-hitter with pop from both sides of the plate. Some scouts like his swing better from the right side, though he may have better bat speed lefthanded. He's lean and lanky and played shortstop in high school, but third base will be his position as a pro. He started the move there toward the end of his pro debut. He has good hands and arm strength, as well as average speed. Some amateur scouts thought Narron showed a big league attitude in high school, but Baltimore has seen none of that and likes his work ethic. He'll get an opportunity to break camp with Delmarva as a teenager in his first full pro season.

Year	Club (League)	Class	AVG	G	AB	R	H	2B	3B	HR	RBI	BB	SO	SB	CS	OBP	SLG
2010	Orioles (GCL)	R	.206	11	34	0	7	0	0	0	4	2	11	1	0	.282	.206
	Aberdeen (NYP)	SS	.121	8	33	1	4	1	0	0	0	3	13	0	0	.216	.152
Minor League Totals			.164	19	67	1	11	1	0	0	4	5	24	1	0	.250	.179

18 TYLER TOWNSEND, 1B

Born: May 14, 1988. **B-T:** L-R. **Ht.:** 6-3. **Wt.:** 205. **Drafted:** Florida International, 2009 (3rd round). **Signed by:** John Martin.

The Orioles love what they have seen of Townsend. The problem is that they just haven't seen enough. Townsend had a left wrist injury that limited him after he signed as a third-round pick, and then he pulled his hamstring in spring training in 2010. The hamstring injury bothered him all season, so the Orioles sent him to the Arizona Fall League—and he had to leave after one game to have a cyst removed from his hand. Townsend shot up draft boards with an MVP performance in the Shenandoah Valley League in the summer of 2008, followed by a .434/.512/.858 performance with 24 home runs at Florida International. He has shown the same smooth, lefthanded stroke as a professional, with a swing and set-up that have drawn comparisons to Mark Grace. He should have more power than Grace did. Townsend played mostly in the outfield in college, but because he's a below-average runner with an average arm, Baltimore moved him to first base. He should be an average defender in time. Townsend may return to high Class A to start 2011, but the Orioles believe he'll move quickly if he can stay healthy.

Year	Club (League)	Class	AVG	G	AB	R	H	2B	3B	HR	RBI	BB	SO	SB	CS	OBP	SLG
2009	Aberdeen (NYP)	SS	.143	31	119	11	17	7	0	4	16	10	39	1	1	.226	.303
2010	Orioles (GCL)	R	.385	3	13	3	5	4	0	0	5	1	2	0	0	.429	.692
	Delmarva (SAL)	LoA	.342	30	117	16	40	12	2	3	26	9	18	0	1	.398	.556
	Frederick (CAR)	HiA	.284	19	67	6	19	5	2	3	14	10	15	1	0	.385	.552
Minor League Totals			.256	83	316	36	81	28	4	10	61	30	74	2	2	.331	.465

19 RONNIE WELTY, OF

Born: Jan. 19, 1988. **B-T:** R-R. **Ht.:** 6-4. **Wt.:** 210. **Drafted:** Chandler-Gilbert (Ariz.) CC, 2008 (20th round). **Signed by:** John Gillette.

Welty has made the postseason league all-star teams in each of his three seasons, but it was only when he added power in 2010 that more scouts started to take notice. Welty has added 30 pounds to his gangly frame since high school in Arizona and tapped into his power potential. He's aggressive and confident at the plate and can handle just about any fastball. He has good leverage in his swing and uses the middle of the field. He generates far too many swings and misses, however, particularly against breaking balls and pitches on the outer half, and he has a tendency to expand his strike zone. Welty has improved as a right fielder and rates as a solid-average defender with enough arm for the position. He's a slightly below-average runner. Before 2010 Welty looked like a tweener outfielder, but if his power continues to grow he could be more. The key will be maintaining his power without striking out so much, which will be a big challenge against Double-A pitching this year.

Year	Club (League)	Class	AVG	G	AB	R	H	2B	3B	HR	RBI	BB	SO	SB	CS	OBP	SLG
2008	Bluefield (APP)	R	.314	55	207	26	65	13	2	3	34	9	49	6	3	.362	.440
2009	Delmarva (SAL)	LoA	.290	121	431	60	125	24	2	10	67	46	120	13	5	.373	.425
2010	Frederick (CAR)	HiA	.282	130	504	86	142	32	3	18	82	47	159	11	4	.349	.464
Minor League Totals			.291	306	1142	172	332	69	7	31	183	102	328	30	12	.360	.445

20 BRANDON SNYDER, 1B

Born: Nov. 23, 1986. **B-T:** R-R. **Ht.:** 6-2. **Wt.:** 215. **Drafted:** HS—Centreville, Va., 2005 (1st round). **Signed by:** Ty Brown.

The Orioles hoped Snyder would seize their first-base job in 2010, but injuries and poor performance kept that from happening. The son of former big leaguer Brian Snyder, Brandon signed for $1.7 million in 2005 and made his major league debut as a September callup last season. He missed five weeks with a back injury and pressed when he did play, causing him to slump. At his best, Snyder shows a smooth swing with good hands that allow him to take the ball to all fields, which should allow him to be a .300 hitter. He doesn't have prototypical power for first base but should be able to hit 15-20 homers a season. He got himself in trouble last year by getting too aggressive and putting himself in bad counts. Snyder has significantly improved at first base since moving from behind the plate and now is an average defender, with plenty of arm for the position. He's a slightly below-average runner. The Orioles will make Snyder earn his spot in the big leagues, so he will return to Triple-A to open 2011.

Year	Club (League)	Class	AVG	G	AB	R	H	2B	3B	HR	RBI	BB	SO	SB	CS	OBP	SLG
2005	Bluefield (APP)	R	.271	44	144	26	39	8	0	8	35	28	36	7	2	.380	.493
	Aberdeen (NYP)	SS	.393	8	28	4	11	2	0	0	6	2	7	0	0	.419	.464
2006	Delmarva (SAL)	LoA	.194	38	144	12	28	12	0	3	20	9	55	0	0	.237	.340
	Aberdeen (NYP)	SS	.234	34	124	14	29	8	1	1	11	5	43	2	1	.267	.339
2007	Delmarva (SAL)	LoA	.283	118	448	63	127	23	3	11	58	44	107	0	2	.354	.422
2008	Frederick (CAR)	HiA	.315	116	435	70	137	33	2	13	80	29	83	3	2	.358	.490

2009	Bowie (EL)	AA	.343	58	201	24	69	19	1	10	45	27	45	0	1	.421	.597
	Norfolk (IL)	AAA	.248	73	262	36	65	18	2	2	43	24	64	3	1	.316	.355
2010	Aberdeen (NYP)	SS	.231	3	13	2	3	1	0	1	4	0	2	0	0	.231	.538
	Norfolk (IL)	AAA	.257	98	339	36	87	22	1	9	43	28	101	4	1	.324	.407
	Baltimore (AL)	MAJ	.300	10	20	1	6	2	0	0	3	0	3	0	1	.300	.400
Major League Totals			.300	10	20	1	6	2	0	0	3	0	3	0	1	.300	.400
Minor League Totals			.278	590	2138	287	595	146	10	58	345	196	543	19	10	.342	.437

21 LUIS LEBRON, RHP

Born: March 13, 1985. **B-T:** R-R. **Ht.:** 6-1. **Wt.:** 180. Signed: Dominican Republic, 2004. **Signed by:** Carlos Bernhardt.

Lebron had positioned himself for a spot in the major league bullpen last season, but he felt elbow discomfort late in spring training, was shut down for a few weeks and had to cut short a bullpen session in early May. He had Tommy John surgery and missed the entire year. When healthy, he's a legitimate power arm out of the bullpen, pairing a fastball that sits in the mid-90s and touches 97 with a plus slider. He gained confidence in his changeup in the last couple of seasons, making it a useful third option. Lebron has legitimate swing-and-miss stuff, though he can still tighten up his command. The Orioles hope he can follow the path of Alfredo Simon, who had Tommy John surgery in May 2009 and was closing games by April 2010. Lebron will come to spring training just looking to work himself back into pitching shape, and he'll move as quickly as his arm will allow.

Year	Club (League)	Class	W	L	ERA	G	GS	CG	SV	IP	H	HR	BB	SO	G/A	WHIP	AVG
2004	Orioles (DSL)	R	0	2	4.76	14	0	0	1	17	19	0	21	22	—	2.35	.271
2005	Bluefield (APP)	R	2	4	11.16	14	7	0	0	25	34	2	22	45	0.81	2.24	.318
2006	Delmarva (SAL)	LoA	1	0	27.00	2	0	0	0	1	3	1	1	1	0.00	3.00	.500
	Aberdeen (NYP)	SS	0	2	1.17	32	0	0	20	31	17	2	16	46	0.52	1.03	.163
2007	Delmarva (SAL)	LoA	1	2	5.04	46	0	0	5	55	48	1	55	86	0.64	1.87	.233
	Bowie (EL)	AA	0	0	3.86	2	0	0	0	2	1	0	1	4	0.50	1.00	.125
2008	Orioles (GCL)	R	0	1	14.40	11	0	0	2	10	20	0	15	6	0.47	3.50	.426
	Aberdeen (NYP)	SS	0	0	6.52	10	0	0	0	10	11	0	12	11	0.89	2.30	.314
2009	Frederick (CAR)	HiA	2	3	3.00	28	0	0	11	33	20	2	20	52	0.70	1.21	.168
	Bowie (EL)	AA	1	0	1.98	24	0	0	9	27	8	3	13	39	0.68	0.78	.093
2010	Did Not Play—Injured																
Minor League Totals			7	14	5.10	183	7	0	48	212	181	11	175	312	0.64	1.68	.226

22 TYLER HENSON, OF

Born: Dec. 15, 1987. **B-T:** R-R. **Ht.:** 6-1. **Wt.:** 205. **Drafted:** HS—Tuttle, Okla., 2006 (5th round). **Signed by:** Jim Richardson.

A standout three-sport athlete as an Oklahoma high schooler, Henson gave shortstop and third base a shot in his first four years in the organization, then moved to left field last year and held his own against Double-A pitching. Henson remains athletic and has gotten bigger and stronger since he was drafted, but he's more steady than flashy. He has good bat speed and seldom gets beat in the strike zone, showing the ability to hit to all fields. He should have average power but tries to pull the ball too much. He'll have to cut down on his strikeouts to advance, and he's susceptible to chasing breaking balls out of the zone. Henson should be at least an average defender in left field, with solid-average speed and arm strength. He takes good routes and gets good jumps on balls. Unless he adds more power he isn't an ideal corner outfield profile, but his versatility still could win him a major league bench role. He'll have a big opportunity to prove himself in Triple-A.

Year	Club (League)	Class	AVG	G	AB	R	H	2B	3B	HR	RBI	BB	SO	SB	CS	OBP	SLG
2006	Bluefield (APP)	R	.230	43	148	21	34	5	2	0	13	18	49	1	1	.314	.291
2007	Aberdeen (NYP)	SS	.289	67	256	44	74	18	4	5	31	22	68	20	2	.353	.449
	Frederick (CAR)	HiA	.059	6	17	0	1	0	0	0	1	1	8	0	0	.105	.059
2008	Delmarva (SAL)	LoA	.265	127	502	71	133	25	3	11	62	25	121	20	3	.310	.392
2009	Frederick (CAR)	HiA	.267	125	460	68	123	31	2	8	71	38	125	18	6	.329	.396
	Bowie (EL)	AA	.250	7	20	3	5	0	0	1	3	3	5	0	0	.333	.400
2010	Bowie (EL)	AA	.278	124	486	69	135	37	3	12	60	38	156	7	5	.329	.440
Minor League Totals			.267	499	1889	276	505	116	14	37	241	145	532	66	17	.324	.402

23 BRANDON WARING, 3B/1B

Born: Jan. 2, 1986. **B-T:** R-R. **Ht.:** 6-3. **Wt.:** 215. **Drafted:** Wofford, 2007 (7th round). **Signed by:** Steve Kring (Reds).

Waring has hit 49 homers in two seasons since coming over from the Reds (along with Justin Turner and

Ryan Freel) in a trade for Ramon Hernandez in December 2008. Waring's calling card is his above-average power, and he has the ability to drive the ball to all fields as well as the strength to drive it deep. He's confident and aggressive at the plate, but he doesn't adjust his approach to hit for average. He continues to work on pitch selection, though he'll always pile up large strikeout numbers. The bigger impediment toward Waring claiming a big league role is finding him a defensive home. He split time between third base, first base, left field and DH in 2010, seeing most of his action at the hot corner. He has an average arm and surprising quickness and agility for his size, but most scouts don't think he can hold down third base on an everyday basis. He's a below-average runner. Waring should get an opportunity to play every day in Triple-A this season, though his long-term role is most likely as a power bat off the bench.

Year	Club (League)	Class	AVG	G	AB	R	H	2B	3B	HR	RBI	BB	SO	SB	CS	OBP	SLG
2007	Billings (PIO)	R	.311	68	267	63	83	17	2	20	61	21	83	1	0	.369	.614
	Dayton (MWL)	LoA	1.000	1	1	0	1	0	0	0	0	2	0	0	0	1.000	1.000
2008	Dayton (MWL)	LoA	.270	119	441	63	119	23	2	20	71	43	156	1	0	.346	.467
2009	Frederick (CAR)	HiA	.273	128	473	70	129	35	2	26	90	51	121	5	3	.354	.520
	Bowie (EL)	AA	.292	8	24	4	7	3	0	1	6	3	9	0	0	.414	.542
2010	Bowie (EL)	AA	.242	129	472	70	114	32	2	22	70	59	179	0	1	.338	.458
Minor League Totals			.270	453	1678	270	453	110	8	89	300	177	548	7	4	.351	.504

24 CHORYE SPOONE, RHP

Born: Sept. 16, 1985. **B-T:** R-R. **Ht.:** 6-1. **Wt.:** 210. **Drafted:** Catonsville (Md.) CC, 2005 (8th round). **Signed by:** Ty Brown.

Spoone went down with a shoulder injury and had surgery to repair a small tear in his labrum after the 2008 season and pitched sparingly in 2009 as he worked his arm back into shape. He pitched 132 innings last year, finding his mechanics and getting comfortable with his pitches again, though he had an eight-start stretch in the middle of the season when he allowed just nine earned runs in 49 innings. At his best, Spoone has a fastball that ranges from 88-92 mph with life and touches a few ticks higher. At times, his power curveball is his most effective pitch. His changeup has improved and shows good sink, and he's comfortable throwing it in any count. His command is still coming back, though it never was his strong suit. Spoone had electric stuff when he first emerged as a prospect but he didn't show it very often last year, so some scouts think he'd be better off as a reliever. Baltimore will keep him as a starter for now, and he'll try to win a rotation spot in Triple-A during spring training.

Year	Club (League)	Class	W	L	ERA	G	GS	CG	SV	IP	H	HR	BB	SO	G/A	WHIP	AVG
2005	Bluefield (APP)	R	2	5	8.03	15	3	0	0	25	27	3	13	27	—	1.62	.273
2006	Delmarva (SAL)	LoA	7	9	3.56	26	25	0	0	129	118	5	80	90	—	1.53	.241
2007	Frederick (CAR)	HiA	10	9	3.26	26	25	3	0	152	108	8	67	133	—	1.15	.200
2008	Bowie (EL)	AA	3	3	4.57	9	9	0	0	41	40	4	27	32	—	1.62	.252
2009	Orioles (GCL)	R	0	1	4.38	5	5	0	0	12	9	1	2	11	4.00	0.89	.200
	Aberdeen (NYP)	SS	0	0	0.00	1	1	0	0	3	1	0	3	3	5.00	1.33	.100
	Frederick (CAR)	HiA	0	2	9.42	4	4	0	0	14	17	3	14	12	1.31	2.16	.298
2010	Bowie (EL)	AA	7	6	4.02	24	24	0	0	132	132	12	79	88	2.02	1.60	.267
Minor League Totals			29	35	4.05	110	96	3	0	509	452	36	285	396	2.05	1.45	.239

25 EDDIE GAMBOA, RHP

Born: Dec. 21, 1984. **B-T:** R-R. **Ht.:** 6-2. **Wt.:** 210. **Drafted:** UC Davis, 2008 (21st round). **Signed by:** James Keller.

Gamboa has grown accustomed to being overlooked. He played basketball and soccer in high school before focusing on baseball, and UC Davis was his only Division I scholarship offer. Gamboa had Tommy John surgery in 2006 and entered pro ball as a fifth-year senior who signed for $1,000 in 2008. He was so effective working out of the bullpen in Double-A in 2010 that he got a chance in the rotation in the second half, going 4-1, 3.98 in 11 starts. He attacks hitters with a fastball, cutter and changeup, and he gives them different looks by varying his arm angle. His fastball ranges from 88-91 mph with good sink, generating a lot of groundballs. His cutter is probably his second-best pitch, and his changeup also shows good sink. He throws a slider on occasion, but he lacks confidence in it. Gamboa throws strikes and is working on his command in the zone, as he has a tendency to nibble. He's a good athlete and should be able to handle a starter's workload. Gamboa's arsenal doesn't leave a lot of margin for error, but he has been effective with it and will compete for a spot in the Norfolk rotation this year.

Year	Club (League)	Class	W	L	ERA	G	GS	CG	SV	IP	H	HR	BB	SO	G/A	WHIP	AVG
2008	Bluefield (APP)	R	1	7	3.63	12	12	1	0	62	64	6	14	41	—	1.26	.264
2009	Delmarva (SAL)	LoA	6	0	1.86	18	0	0	1	39	30	5	3	35	2.17	0.85	.219
	Frederick (CAR)	HiA	4	0	0.55	14	0	0	1	33	27	0	7	29	1.34	1.03	.227

Bowie (EL)		AA	1	0	0.00	7	0	0	1	12	7	0	7	11	1.00	1.17	.167
2010	Bowie (EL)	AA	7	5	3.75	36	11	0	2	98	97	10	27	83	1.97	1.26	.261
Minor League Totals			19	12	2.80	87	23	1	5	244	225	21	58	199	1.77	1.16	.247

26 GREG MICLAT, SS

Born: July 23, 1987. **B-T:** B-R. **Ht.:** 5-9. **Wt.:** 180. **Drafted:** Virginia, 2008 (5th round). **Signed by:** Dean Albany.

Miclat signed for an over-slot bonus of $225,000 in 2008 even though he had battled shoulder and arm injuries in his last two seasons at Virginia. Overcoming a broken nose in April and a sprained foot in May, he ranked fourth in the high Class A Carolina League last season in on-base percentage (.403) when he earned a promotion to Bowie. He struggled against Double-A pitching, but finished the year on a high note with a .308/.390/.385 performance in the Arizona Fall League. Defense remains Miclat's calling card, as he makes all the routine plays even though he doesn't have pure shortstop actions. He's an above-average runner with good range, and he uses his speed well on the bases. His arm is average now and may be a bit short for plays deep in the hole, with most of his errors being a result of errant throws. Miclat is a slap hitter who uses the whole field, and his offensive success is predicated on plate discipline. In Double-A, he looked overmatched at times and piled up too many strikeouts. His power is well below-average. The Orioles have worked Miclat out at second base, and he profiles as a utilityman who can play both middle-infield positions. He'll go back to Double-A to open the season.

Year	Club (League)	Class	AVG	G	AB	R	H	2B	3B	HR	RBI	BB	SO	SB	CS	OBP	SLG
2008	Orioles (GCL)	R	.500	1	4	1	2	1	0	0	1	0	2	0	0	.500	.750
	Aberdeen (NYP)	SS	.291	16	55	9	16	2	0	0	6	8	13	3	2	.391	.327
2009	Delmarva (SAL)	LoA	.228	111	400	49	91	14	2	0	22	42	79	25	6	.299	.273
	Frederick (CAR)	HiA	.208	6	24	4	5	1	0	0	1	3	4	1	0	.296	.250
2010	Frederick (CAR)	HiA	.311	48	164	30	51	12	0	1	19	20	27	8	2	.403	.402
	Bowie (EL)	AA	.246	62	228	35	56	9	2	1	16	24	52	4	6	.317	.316
Minor League Totals			.253	244	875	128	221	39	4	2	65	97	177	41	16	.331	.313

27 BRANDON ERBE, RHP

Born: Dec. 25, 1987. **B-T:** R-R. **Ht.:** 6-4. **Wt.:** 195. **Drafted:** HS—Baltimore, 2005 (3rd round). **Signed by:** Ty Brown.

The Orioles were counting on Erbe to be part of the wave of young pitching that has surged into Baltimore, but he had a disastrous 2010 season. He went 0-10, 5.74 before the Orioles shut him down, and then had surgery in August to repair a torn labrum. Before his injury, Erbe had been held back by his inability to develop an effective secondary pitch to complement his fastball. He works in the low 90s, touching 94 mph with good life. But advanced hitters have teed off on his below-average slider. His changeup is a fringy pitch as well. Erbe battled his mechanics, leading to inconsistent command and ultimately his injury. The hope is that he'll come out of his rehab with a cleaner delivery. He started a throwing program in December, and the Orioles are optimistic he will bounce back like Chorye Spoone and Jim Hoey have after similar procedures. The optimistic view is that he'll be ready by spring training, but he probably won't return to game action until May or June.

Year	Club (League)	Class	W	L	ERA	G	GS	CG	SV	IP	H	HR	BB	SO	G/A	WHIP	AVG
2005	Bluefield (APP)	R	1	1	3.09	11	3	0	1	23	8	1	10	48	—	0.77	.103
	Aberdeen (NYP)	SS	1	1	7.71	3	1	0	0	7	6	0	4	9	—	1.43	.261
2006	Delmarva (SAL)	LoA	5	9	3.22	28	27	0	0	115	88	2	47	133	—	1.18	.217
2007	Frederick (CAR)	HiA	6	8	6.26	25	25	0	0	119	127	14	62	111	—	1.58	.273
2008	Frederick (CAR)	HiA	10	12	4.30	28	28	2	0	151	120	21	50	151	—	1.13	.216
2009	Aberdeen (NYP)	SS	0	1	4.61	4	4	0	0	14	13	3	2	11	0.93	1.10	.245
	Bowie (EL)	AA	5	3	2.34	14	14	2	0	73	44	5	35	62	0.90	1.08	.170
2010	Norfolk (IL)	AAA	0	10	5.73	14	14	0	0	71	86	11	22	50	0.83	1.53	.294
	Aberdeen (NYP)	SS	0	0	6.00	1	1	0	0	3	1	0	2	1	7.00	1.00	.111
Minor League Totals			28	45	4.43	128	117	4	1	575	493	57	234	576	0.91	1.26	.230

28 CALEB JOSEPH, C

Born: June 18, 1986. **B-T:** R-R. **Ht.:** 6-3. **Wt.:** 180. **Drafted:** Lipscomb, 2008 (7th round). **Signed by:** Rich Morales.

Joseph emerged in 2009 with a solid year in high Class A, but he gave that progress back in Double-A last year. He struggled both at the plate and behind it, and his problems were exacerbated when he injured his shoulder in late July in a home-plate collision with 225-pound Giants outfielder Thomas Neal. The Orioles sent him to the Arizona Fall League, where he went 16-for-41 (.390), but as a taxi squad member his emphasis was on instruction. At the plate, he worked on letting the ball travel deeper and hitting to right field more consistently. Behind the plate, he focused on his footwork and getting a wider base in order to improve his throwing and blocking skills. Joseph's defense grades higher than his offense anyway, and the adjustments should solidify him as an average defender with a solid-average arm. He threw out 26 percent of basestealers in 2010. Joseph's bat will determine whether he can be more than a backup. He's a bit lean for a catcher, and his lack of strength hurts him offensively. He has below-average power, so he'll have to hit for better average. He's a below-average runner but not bad for a catcher. Joseph has played a few games at first base and in the outfield, but Baltimore still sees him as a catcher. He'll go back to Double-A to try to get himself back on track this season.

Year	Club (League)	Class	AVG	G	AB	R	H	2B	3B	HR	RBI	BB	SO	SB	CS	OBP	SLG
2008	Aberdeen (NYP)	SS	.261	63	238	34	62	19	0	8	34	15	56	2	0	.303	.441
2009	Frederick (CAR)	HiA	.284	104	380	50	108	23	2	12	60	26	64	2	1	.337	.450
2010	Bowie (EL)	AA	.235	106	378	43	89	15	1	11	51	33	63	1	6	.301	.368
Minor League Totals			.260	273	996	127	259	57	3	31	145	74	183	5	7	.315	.417

29 PEDRO FLORIMON, SS

Born: Dec. 10, 1986. **B-T:** B-R. **Ht.:** 6-2. **Wt.:** 180. **Signed:** Dominican Republic, 2004. **Signed by:** Carlos Bernhardt.

Florimon played his way on to the 40-man roster in 2009, but couldn't build on his progress with the bat, hitting .183 in two months at Bowie before a strained left oblique knocked him out of action for a month. After a rehab stint at Aberdeen, Florimon got himself back on track at Frederick. A switch-hitter, he has learned to use the whole field and improved his two-strike approach late in the season. He has a little bit of pop, particularly from the right side. He has an aggressive approach, leading him to strike out too much for a player with his offensive profile. He makes better contact from the left side. He's a solid-average runner but not a huge basesteal-ing threat. Tall and athletic, Florimon has flashy defensive skills, showing soft hands, good range and a strong arm. His arm can be erratic and he still has a tendency to botch routine plays, piling up 27 errors in 103 games at short last year. The question is whether Florimon can hit advanced pitching, and so far he hasn't. He remains on the 40-man roster, however, and will give Double-A another shot in 2011.

Year	Club (League)	Class	AVG	G	AB	R	H	2B	3B	HR	RBI	BB	SO	SB	CS	OBP	SLG
2004	Orioles (DSL)	R	.204	52	167	33	34	5	5	0	19	34	59	17	5	.351	.293
2005	Orioles (DSL)	R	.200	63	170	35	34	4	2	0	8	41	55	19	4	.387	.247
2006	Bluefield (APP)	R	.333	33	120	23	40	6	1	1	8	28	29	7	6	.456	.425
	Aberdeen (NYP)	SS	.248	26	105	13	26	4	1	0	5	13	26	0	0	.336	.305
2007	Delmarva (SAL)	LoA	.197	111	371	50	73	14	1	4	34	28	107	16	6	.257	.272
2008	Delmarva (SAL)	LoA	.223	81	269	28	60	18	1	0	19	27	97	13	2	.298	.297
2009	Frederick (CAR)	HiA	.267	115	430	76	115	32	5	9	68	42	107	26	9	.336	.428
	Bowie (EL)	AA	.091	7	22	0	2	0	0	0	1	1	9	0	0	.130	.091
2010	Bowie (EL)	AA	.183	37	120	16	22	3	0	1	12	11	31	4	1	.250	.233
	Aberdeen (NYP)	SS	.158	5	19	1	3	0	0	0	0	1	6	0	1	.200	.158
	Frederick (CAR)	HiA	.288	62	222	32	64	10	4	4	33	20	52	8	5	.361	.423
Minor League Totals			.235	592	2015	307	473	96	20	19	207	246	578	110	39	.326	.331

30 ADRIAN ROSARIO, RHP

Born: Sept. 30, 1989. **B-T:** R-R. **Ht.:** 6-4. **Wt.:** 180. **Signed:** Dominican Republic, 2006. **Signed by:** Fernando Arango/Fausto Sosa Pena (Brewers).

The Orioles lost two relievers in the 2010 major league Rule 5 draft—Pat Egan and Pedro Beato—but think they found a pitcher with more upside when they took Rosario from the Brewers. He hasn't played above low Class A, so it will be a challenge for him to stick in the big leagues. Rosario has a low-90s fastball and backs it up with a plus changeup that falls off the table. That's what gets scouts interested, but it's also about all he has at this point. He lacks a reliable breaking ball and struggles with the command of all of his pitches. He needs to become more confident and aggressive on the mound. At some point he could become a major league set-up man, but not this year. The Orioles will have to stash Rosario as the 25th man on their roster and use him sparingly. If they can't keep him on the major league roster, he'll have to clear waivers and be offered back to Milwaukee.

Year	Club (League)	Class	W	L	ERA	G	GS	CG	SV	IP	H	HR	BB	SO	G/A	WHIP	AVG
2007	Brewers (AZL)	R	3	3	6.75	14	2	0	0	37	50	2	32	23	—	2.20	.313
2008	Brewers (AZL)	R	1	3	4.20	11	5	0	0	41	47	1	13	28	—	1.48	.292
2009	Helena (PIO)	R	3	7	5.06	15	8	0	1	59	78	4	14	45	1.65	1.57	.322
2010	Helena (PIO)	R	1	0	1.26	5	0	0	1	14	11	0	3	15	7.33	0.98	.224
	Wisconsin (MWL)	LoA	4	0	4.50	14	0	0	2	32	28	0	15	44	1.45	1.34	.230
Minor League Totals			12	13	4.82	59	15	0	4	183	214	7	77	155	1.84	1.59	.292

Boston Red Sox

BY JIM CALLIS

L ittle went as planned for the Red Sox in 2010. Before the season started, general manager Theo Epstein referred to it as a "bridge period," meaning the team would try to balance contending with building for the future. Boston focused on upgrading via run prevention, spending $120.5 million on free agents Adrian Beltre, Mike Cameron, John Lackey and Marco Scutaro to bolster its defense and rotation.

Nevertheless, the Red Sox dropped from third in the American League in runs allowed in 2009 to 11th last season. The defense was erratic, as was the pitching. Lackey, Josh Beckett and Daisuke Matsuzaka combined for 29 wins at a cost of $38 million, and the middle-relief corps set more fires than it put out.

Boston's offense was considered its potential weak link, yet ranked second in the majors in scoring despite injuries that sidelined Cameron and Jacoby Ellsbury for most of the year, and Dustin Pedroia and Kevin Youkilis for much of the second half. Despite a franchise-record Opening Day payroll of $168.1 million—second-highest in baseball—Boston missed out on the postseason for the second time in eight years.

For all the things that went wrong, though, the Red Sox still won 89 games while playing in baseball's toughest division. Then they pulled off two blockbuster moves in a three-day span at the Winter Meetings, solidifying the core of their lineup for years to come.

On the day the meetings began, Boston sent its No. 1 prospect (righthander Casey Kelly), best offensive prospect (first baseman Anthony Rizzo) and most athletic prospect (Reymond Fuentes), as well as utilityman Eric Patterson, to the Padres for Adrian Gonzalez, whom the Red Sox long had coveted. The fallout from that trade had barely subsided when Boston followed up by signing free agent outfielder Carl Crawford away from fellow AL East contender Tampa Bay for seven years and $142 million.

Though the Gonzalez deal skimmed much of the cream off the top, Boston's farm system is far from barren. Shortstop Jose Iglesias and lefthander Felix Doubront may be the only prospects who figure to make much of a major league impact in the next two years, but the Red Sox have depth in the lower levels and the luxury of having the time to let those youngsters develop.

Boston spent a club-record $10.7 million on draft bonuses in 2010, the fourth-highest total in baseball history, including seven-figure deals for righthander

MICHEAL IVINS — BOSTON RED SOX

Bringing in Adrian Gonzalez cost lots of prospects but should solidify the lineup

TOP 30 PROSPECTS

1. Jose Iglesias, ss	**16.** Ryan Lavarnway, c
2. Anthony Ranaudo, rhp	**17.** Bryce Brentz, of
3. Drake Britton, lhp	**18.** Brandon Workman, rhp
4. Josh Reddick, of	**19.** Alex Wilson, rhp
5. Felix Doubront, lhp	**20.** Kyle Weiland, rhp
6. Stolmy Pimentel, rhp	**21.** Tim Federowicz, c
7. Garin Cecchini, 3b	**22.** Jeremy Hazelbaker, of
8. Lars Anderson, 1b	**23.** Junichi Tazawa, rhp
9. Kolbrin Vitek, 3b	**24.** Madison Younginer, rhp
10. Oscar Tejeda, 2b	**25.** Che-Hsuan Lin, of
11. Will Middlebrooks, 3b	**26.** Chris Balcom-Miller, rhp
12. Yamaico Navarro, ss/3b	**27.** Brandon Jacobs, of
13. Sean Coyle, 2b	**28.** Juan Carlos Linares, of
14. Xander Bogaerts, ss	**29.** Miguel Celestino, rhp
15. Derrik Gibson, ss	**30.** Ryan Westmoreland, of

Anthony Ranaudo, third basemen Kolbrin Vitek and Garin Cecchini, and second baseman Sean Coyle. The Red Sox lead all teams with $41.7 million in bonuses paid in the last five drafts, which have produced closer-in-waiting Daniel Bard, six other big leaguers and trade bait used to acquire Gonzalez and Victor Martinez.

As frustrating as 2010 may have been, Boston's future looks as bright as ever. The last time the Red Sox missed the playoffs, in an injury-riddled 2006, they came back and won the World Series the following year.

General Manager: Theo Epstein. **Farm Director:** Mike Hazen. **Scouting Director:** Amiel Sawdaye.

Class	Team	League	W	L	PCT	Finish*	Manager
Majors	Boston Red Sox	American	89	73	.549	5th (14)	Terry Francona
Triple-A	Pawtucket Red Sox	International	66	78	.458	12th (14)	Torey Lovullo
Double-A	Portland Sea Dogs	Eastern	70	71	.496	7th (12)	Arnie Beyeler
High A	Salem Red Sox	Carolina	73	65	.529	3rd (8)	Kevin Boles
Low A	Greenville Drive	South Atlantic	77	62	.554	3rd (14)	Billy McMillon
Short-season	Lowell Spinners	New York-Penn	24	50	.324	14th (14)	Bruce Crabbe
Rookie	GCL Red Sox	Gulf Coast	31	28	.525	t-5th (15)	Dave Tomlin

Overall 2010 Minor League Record   341   354   .491   19th (30)
*Finish in overall standings (No. of teams in league). †League champion.

LAST YEAR'S TOP 30

Player, Pos.	Status
1. Ryan Westmoreland, of	No. 30
2. Casey Kelly, rhp	(Padres)
3. Josh Reddick, of	No. 4
4. Lars Anderson, 1b	No. 8
5. Ryan Kalish, of	Majors
6. Junichi Tazawa, rhp	No. 23
7. Reymond Fuentes, of	(Padres)
8. Anthony Rizzo, of	(Padres)
9. Jose Iglesias, ss	No. 1
10. Derrik Gibson, ss/2b	No. 15
11. Stolmy Pimentel, rhp	No. 6
12. Yamaico Navarro, ss	No. 12
13. Michael Bowden, rhp	Dropped out
14. David Renfroe, ss	Dropped out
15. Drake Britton, lhp	No. 3
16. Madison Younginer, rhp	No. 24
17. Stephen Fife, rhp	Dropped out
18. Felix Doubront, lhp	No. 5
19. Will Middlebrooks, 3b	No. 11
20. Che-Hsuan Lin, of	No. 25
21. Alex Wilson, rhp	No. 19
22. Tim Federowicz, c	No. 21
23. Roman Mendez, rhp	(Rangers)
24. Luis Exposito, c	Dropped out
25. Mark Wagner, c	Dropped out
26. Kyle Weiland, rhp	No. 20
27. Dustin Richardson, lhp	Dropped out
28. Ryan Dent, 2b/ss	Dropped out
29. Jose Vinicio, ss	Dropped out
30. Brandon Jacobs, of	No. 27

BEST TOOLS

Best Hitter for Average	Garin Cecchini
Best Power Hitter	Ryan Lavarnway
Best Strike-Zone Discipline	Che-Hsuan Lin
Fastest Baserunner	Felix Sanchez
Best Athlete	Derrik Gibson
Best Fastball	Drake Britton
Best Curveball	Drake Britton
Best Slider	Alex Wilson
Best Changeup	Stolmy Pimentel
Best Control	Chris Balcom-Miller
Best Defensive Catcher	Tim Federowicz
Best Defensive Infielder	Jose Iglesias
Best Infield Arm	Will Middlebrooks
Best Defensive Outfielder	Che-Hsuan Lin
Best Outfield Arm	Che-Hsuan Lin

PROJECTED 2014 LINEUP

Catcher	Ryan Lavarnway
First Base	Adrian Gonzalez
Second Base	Dustin Pedroia
Third Base	Garin Cecchini
Shortstop	Jose Iglesias
Left Field	Carl Crawford
Center Field	Jacoby Ellsbury
Right Field	Ryan Kalish
Designated Hitter	Kevin Youkilis
No. 1 Starter	Jon Lester
No. 2 Starter	Clay Buchholz
No. 3 Starter	Josh Beckett
No. 4 Starter	Anthony Ranaudo
No. 5 Starter	Drake Britton
Closer	Jonathan Papelbon

TOP PROSPECTS OF THE DECADE

Year	Player, Pos.	2010 Org.
2001	Dernell Stenson, of/1b	Deceased
2002	Seung Song, rhp	Lotte (Korea)
2003	Hanley Ramirez, ss	Marlins
2004	Hanley Ramirez, ss	Marlins
2005	Hanley Ramirez, ss	Marlins
2006	Andy Marte, 3b	Indians
2007	Daisuke Matsuzaka, rhp	Red Sox
2008	Clay Buchholz, rhp	Red Sox
2009	Lars Anderson, 1b	Red Sox
2010	Ryan Westmoreland, of	Red Sox

TOP DRAFT PICKS OF THE DECADE

Year	Player, Pos.	2010 Org.
2001	Kelly Shoppach, c (2nd round)	Rays
2002	Jon Lester, lhp (2nd round)	Red Sox
2003	David Murphy, of	Rangers
2004	Dustin Pedroia, ss (2nd round)	Red Sox
2005	Jacoby Ellsbury, of	Red Sox
2006	Jason Place, of	Red Sox
2007	Nick Hagadone, lhp (1st round supp.)	Indians
2008	Casey Kelly, rhp/ss	Red Sox
2009	Reymond Fuentes, of	Red Sox
2010	Kolbrin Vitek, 3b	Red Sox

LARGEST BONUSES IN CLUB HISTORY

Jose Iglesias, 2009	$6,250,000
Casey Kelly, 2008	$3,000,000
Anthony Ranaudo, 2010	$2,550,000
Daisuke Matsuzaka, 2006	$2,000,000
Ryan Westmoreland, 2008	$2,000,000

BOSTON RED SOX

TOP 2011 ROOKIE: Felix Doubront, lhp. He offers the versatility to be the Red Sox's top lefty reliever or contribute in the rotation.

BREAKOUT PROSPECT: Xander Bogaerts, ss. His bat, power and athleticism make him Boston's most exciting Dominican Summer League prospect since Hanley Ramirez.

SLEEPER: Henry Ramos, of. A 2010 fifth-round pick out of Puerto Rico, he flashes all five tools and is more advanced at the plate than expected.

SOURCE OF TOP 30 TALENT

Homegrown	28	Acquired	2
College	9	Trades	2
Junior college	1	Rule 5 draft	0
High school	9	Independent leagues	0
Draft-and-follow	0	Free agents/waivers	0
Nondrafted free agents	0		
International	9		

LF
Brandon Jacobs (27)
Ronald Bermudez

CF
Jeremy Hazelbaker (22)
Che-Hsuan Lin (25)
Juan Carlos Linares (28)
Ryan Westmoreland (30)
Pete Hissey
Keury de la Cruz
Felix Sanchez

RF
Josh Reddick (4)
Bryce Brentz (17)
Henry Ramos
Kendrick Perkins
Alex Hassan
Jordan Parraz
Lucas LeBlanc
Mitch Dening

3B
Garin Cecchini (7)
Kolbrin Vitek (9)
Will Middlebrooks (11)
Xander Bogaerts (14)
Michael Almanzar
David Renfroe

SS
Jose Iglesias (1)
Derrik Gibson (15)
Jose Vinicio
Brent Dlugach
Ryan Dent

2B
Oscar Tejeda (10)
Yamaico Navarro (12)
Sean Coyle (13)
Nate Spears

1B
Lars Anderson (8)
Miles Head

C
Ryan Lavarnway (16)
Tim Federowicz (21)
Luis Exposito
Mark Wagner
Adalberto Ibarra
Dan Butler
Christian Vazquez

RHP

RHSP
Anthony Ranaudo (2)
Stolmy Pimentel (6)
Brandon Workman (18)
Junichi Tazawa (23)
Chris Balcom-Miller (26)
Miguel Celestino (29)
Stephen Fife
Ryan Pressly
Mathew Price
Sergio Gomez
Kendal Volz
Juan Rodriguez
Raul Alcantara
Jacob Dahlstrand
Jason Garcia

RHRP
Alex Wilson (19)
Kyle Weiland (20)
Madison Younginer (24)
Michael Bowden
Robert Coello
Matt Fox
Jason Rice
Eammon Portice
Seth Garrison
Pete Ruiz
Mitch Herold
Michael Lee
Keith Couch

LHP

LHSP
Drake Britton (3)
Felix Doubront (5)
Manuel Rivera

LHRP
Chris Hernandez

2010 BONUSES: $10.7 MILLION

BEST PURE HITTER: The Red Sox landed three high-average hitters in 3B Kolbrin Vitek (1), 2B Sean Coyle (3) and 3B Garin Cecchini (4)—at a combined cost of $4 million. Cecchini is the best pure hitter in the system, while Coyle has an advanced all-fields approach and uncanny hand-eye coordination.

BEST POWER HITTER: OF Bryce Brentz (1s) led NCAA Division I with 28 homers as a sophomore in 2009. He has explosive bat speed but is working to quiet his approach after a .198/.259/.340 debut.

FASTEST RUNNER: OF Lucas LeBlanc (11) has 60-65 speed on the 20-80 scouting scale. Coyle is a half-step behind him.

BEST DEFENSIVE PLAYER: Brentz could be an above-average defender in right field. He moves well and played some center field in college, where he also pitched and showed a low-90s fastball. A high school shortstop, Coyle has the quickness, range and arm to be an asset at second base.

BEST FASTBALL: RHPs Anthony Ranaudo (1s) and Brandon Workman (2) work at 91-94 mph and peak at 96. Workman's late life makes his heater more of a swing-and-miss pitch, while Ranaudo uses his 6-foot-7 frame to throw his on a tough angle and induce weak contact. RHP Mathew Price (8) has similar velocity and more projectability, though he's not as consistent.

BEST SECONDARY PITCH: LHP Chris Hernandez's (7) 87-89 cutter will break a lot of bats. Ranaudo's curveball is the best breaking pitch in this crop, and Price has a nifty changeup.

BEST PRO DEBUT: Given that baseball was OF Henry Ramos' (5) third sport and he didn't face quality pitching in Puerto Rico, the Red Sox were delighted to see him hit .309/.370/.449 with 12 steals in the Rookie-level Gulf Coast League.

BEST ATHLETE: Ramos, a member of Puerto Rico's junior national soccer and tennis teams, has solid all-around tools. OF Kendrick Perkins (6) ran for 3,454 yards and 47 touchdowns in his last two seasons as a high school running back and drew interest from college football programs.

MOST INTRIGUING BACKGROUND: C Zach Kapstein's (44) father Jeremy is a Red Sox senior adviser who was formerly an agent and Padres club president. Unsigned C Shane Rowland's (36) dad Donnie is the Yankees' director of international scouting.

CLOSEST TO THE MAJORS: Ranaudo, who overcame elbow trouble in the spring to dominate in the Cape Cod League before signing for $2.55 million, will start in high Class A. Hernandez could beat him

to Boston as a lefty reliever.

BEST LATE-ROUND PICK: Signed at the deadline for $500,000, LeBlanc has solid tools across the board.

THE ONE WHO GOT AWAY: SS Steve Wilkerson (15) is a slick fielder who opted to attend Clemson. RHPs Adam Duke (16) and Eric Jaffe (19), who both flash 95-mph fastballs, are now Pacific-10 Conference rivals at Oregon State and California.

ASSESSMENT: The Red Sox didn't change their approach in Amiel Sawdaye's first year as scouting director. They looked at talent rather than price tags and aggressively signed their share of prospects.

2009 BONUSES: $7.1 MILLION

None of the Red Sox's picks has torn up pro ball, though Reymond Fuentes (1) and Jeremy Hazelbaker (5) are toolsy center fielders and RHPs Alex Wilson (2) and Madison Younginer (7) could be electric bullpen arms. Fuentes was part of the Adrian Gonzalez trade.

GRADE: C

2008 BONUSES: $10.5 MILLION

RHP Casey Kelly (1) was the key to the Gonzalez deal. OF Ryan Westmoreland (5) was the system's best prospect before missing 2010 after he had brain surgery. Boston used RHP Bryan Price (1s) in a trade for Victor Martinez and may find its catcher of the future in either Ryan Lavarnway (6) or Tim Federowicz (7).

GRADE: B

2007 BONUSES: $4.8 MILLION

1B Anthony Rizzo (6) beat cancer, hit 25 home runs last year and now will try to replace Gonzalez in San Diego. LHP Drake Britton (23) has bounced back from Tommy John surgery, as did LHP Nick Hagadone (1s), who was part of the Martinez deal.

GRADE: C+

2006 BONUSES: $8.6 MILLION

The Red Sox scored with only one of their four picks before the second round, but they scored big with closer-in-waiting Daniel Bard (1). RHP Justin Masterson (2), another piece of the Martinez deal, and OF Ryan Kalish (9) have had their moments in the big leagues. Four other draftees have made it to the majors, including OF Josh Reddick (17) and 1B Lars Anderson (18).

GRADE: B+

Draft analysis by Jim Callis. Numbers in parentheses indicate draft rounds.

JOSE IGLESIAS, SS

Born: Jan. 5, 1990. **Bats:** R. **Throws:** R.
Height: 5-11. **Weight:** 180. **Signed:** Cuba,
2009. **Signed by:** Craig Shipley/Johnny
DiPuglia.

KEN BABBITT

Iglesias was skilled enough to not only crack the Serie Nacional, Cuba's top league, as a 17-year-old, but also to bat .322. He also played on Cuban national teams with Blue Jays shortstop prospect Adeiny Hechavarria, with Iglesias shifting over to second base. Iglesias defected along with Royals lefthander Noel Arguelles while at the World Junior Championships in Edmonton in July 2008, then established residency in the Dominican Republic. In September 2009, Iglesias signed a four-year, $8.25 million major league contract with the Red Sox that included a franchise-record $6.25 million bonus. His first exposure to pro ball came in the Arizona Fall League, where he hit .275/.324/.420 despite his long layoff and left scouts raving about his defensive ability. Boston sent him to Double-A Portland for his pro debut last April, and Iglesias was batting .306 as the youngest regular in the Eastern League before an errant pitch broke his right middle finger in late May. He missed two months and didn't swing the bat quite as well when he returned to Portland and then the AFL, but the Red Sox were pleased with the overall results from his first pro season.

Iglesias is an exceptional defender who could challenge for a Gold Glove in the big leagues right now. He plays low to the ground, using his quick feet, lightning-fast hands and strong arm to make all the plays. His instincts and body control also stand out, and he made just seven errors in 57 games at short last season. He's fearless in the field, almost to the point of overconfidence, but he makes more web gems than mistakes. When he had to play some third base in the AFL, he handled hot smashes so easily he looked like he had been at the hot corner for years. Iglesias will provide some offense as well. With good bat speed and hand-eye coordination to go with a line-drive stroke, Iglesias should hit for average. He may not be a double-digit home run threat, but he can sting some balls and should have some gap power once he adds more strength. He's aggressive at the plate, attacking pitches early in the counts and sometimes getting overly concerned with trying to crush balls,

SCOUTING GRADES

Batting: 55. **Defense:** 70.
Power: 40. **Arm:** 60.
Speed: 50.

Based on 20-80 scouting scale, where 50 represents major league average, and future projection rather than present tools.

an approach that won't lead to many walks. If he develops some patience, it's possible that he could fit in the No. 2 slot in a big league batting order. More quick than fast, he's an average runner out of the batter's box and slightly better on the bases. Iglesias also has quickly adapted to life in the U.S. He quickly picked up English and communicates well with teammates.

After going through six shortstops in seven seasons since trading Nomar Garciaparra, the Red Sox believe Iglesias can bring some stability to the position. When they signed Marco Scutaro as a free agent, they gave him a two-year contract with a mutual option for 2012, forecasting that Iglesias would be ready by then. He's developing according to plan and will spend 2011 at Triple-A Pawtucket. He might be ready by midseason.

Year	Club (League)	Class	AVG	G	AB	R	H	2B	3B	HR	RBI	BB	SO	SB	CS	OBP	SLG
2010	Lowell (NYP)	SS	.350	13	40	8	14	2	2	0	7	7	8	2	1	.458	.500
	Portland (EL)	AA	.285	57	221	29	63	10	3	0	13	8	49	5	2	.315	.357
Minor League Totals			.295	70	261	37	77	12	5	0	20	15	57	7	3	.339	.379

2 ANTHONY RANAUDO, RHP

Born: Sept. 9, 1989. **B-T:** R-R. **Ht.:** 6-7. **Wt.:** 230. **Drafted:** Louisiana State, 2010 (1st round supplemental). **Signed by:** Matt Dorey.

Ranaudo entered 2010 as the draft's top pitching prospect, but he came down with a stress reaction in his elbow after his first start, missed a month and battled his mechanics and command when he returned. He posted a 7.32 ERA for Louisiana State before returning to form in the Cape Cod League, where he didn't allow an earned run in 30 innings. He signed for $2.55 million at the Aug. 16 deadline. Ranaudo uses his 6-foot-7 frame to leverage his 91-96 mph fastball down in the zone, generating strikeouts and weak contact. He also can throw his heater to both sides of the plate, and he complements it with a plus curveball and solid changeup. When he's on top of his game, he commands all three pitches well. Ranaudo never lost velocity when he struggled at LSU, but his delivery fell out of sync and his pitches flattened out. Though the Red Sox aren't concerned about his health, he also had elbow tendinitis that limited him to 12 innings as a freshman. Assuming Ranaudo's elbow problems are behind him, Boston may have stolen a frontline starter with the 39th overall pick. He'll make his pro debut at high Class A Salem and could reach the majors by the end of 2012.

Year	Club (League)	Class	W	L	ERA	G	GS	CG	SV	IP	H	HR	BB	SO	G/A	WHIP	AVG
2010	Did Not Play—Signed Late																

3 DRAKE BRITTON, LHP

Born: May 22, 1989. **B-T:** L-L. **Ht.:** 6-2. **Wt.:** 200. **Drafted:** HS—Tomball, Texas, 2007 (23rd round). **Signed by:** Jim Robinson.

Britton flashed early-round potential as a high school senior in 2007, but inconsistent velocity and a Texas A&M scholarship caused him to slide to the 23rd round. When he showed a low-90s fastball in summer ball, the Red Sox signed him at the Aug. 15 deadline for $700,000. He blew out his elbow at the end of his 2008 pro debut, but returned to hit 97 mph in instructional league at the end of 2009. Britton has bounced back from Tommy John surgery to now have the best fastball in the system, sitting at 92-94 mph with sink. He has regained his big-breaking curveball that he can throw for strikes, and he also has the makings of an effective changeup. Because he has pitched just 121 pro innings, he needs more time to repeat his high three-quarters delivery and refine his control and command. He's a hard worker who got leaner and stronger during his rehab. After playing it safe last season, limiting Britton's pitch counts and keeping him on the disabled list for six weeks as a precaution with an early-season biceps strain, the Red Sox will turn him loose in high Class A. He has all the ingredients to become a No. 3 starter or a late-inning bullpen weapon.

Year	Club (League)	Class	W	L	ERA	G	GS	CG	SV	IP	H	HR	BB	SO	G/A	WHIP	AVG
2008	Lowell (NYP)	SS	1	2	4.28	8	7	0	0	34	30	3	16	26	—	1.37	.234
2009	Red Sox (GCL)	R	0	0	0.00	4	4	0	0	7	2	0	4	11	1.00	0.86	.080
	Lowell (NYP)	SS	0	0	1.93	3	3	0	0	5	4	0	3	8	0.50	1.50	.235
2010	Greenville (SAL)	LoA	2	3	2.97	21	21	0	0	76	69	5	23	78	1.38	1.22	.240
Minor League Totals			3	5	3.12	36	35	0	0	121	105	8	46	123	1.29	1.25	.229

4 JOSH REDDICK, OF

Born: Feb. 19, 1987. **B-T:** L-R. **Ht.:** 6-2. **Wt.:** 180. **Drafted:** Middle Georgia JC, 2006 (17th round). **Signed by:** Rob English.

Injuries created several openings in Boston's outfield in 2010, but Reddick couldn't seize the opportunity. After batting .390 in big league camp but losing an Opening Day roster spot to Jeremy Hermida, Reddick didn't hit in April and June callups. He also endured his most extended slump in four minor league seasons, not getting going until he hit .351/.372/.627 in the second half in Triple-A. While Reddick doesn't have a below-average tool, he'll need to develop more patience and put less pressure on himself to make it in the majors. Though he has good bat speed and repeatedly barrels balls, he too often gets himself out by putting pitches in play that he should let go by. Reddick has solid power and speed, and he has improved defensively to the point where he can man center field. He fits best in right field, where his combination of arm strength, quick release and uncanny accuracy make him an assists machine. The Red Sox haven't given up on Reddick by any means, but Ryan Kalish has passed him and they signed Carl Crawford as a free agent. Boston doesn't appear to have an opening for Reddick on its 2011 roster, so he'll try to tone down his approach and make himself attractive to other clubs when he returns to Pawtucket.

BOSTON RED SOX

Year	Club (League)	Class	AVG	G	AB	R	H	2B	3B	HR	RBI	BB	SO	SB	CS	OBP	SLG
2007	Greenville (SAL)	LoA	.306	94	369	60	113	17	6	18	72	26	51	8	5	.352	.531
	Portland (EL)	AA	.000	1	1	0	0	0	0	0	0	0	0	0	0	.000	.000
2008	Greenville (SAL)	LoA	.340	14	53	7	18	4	2	0	9	5	8	2	1	.397	.491
	Lancaster (CAL)	HiA	.343	76	312	60	107	11	8	17	57	17	49	9	1	.375	.593
	Portland (EL)	AA	.214	34	117	22	25	4	2	6	25	12	25	3	1	.290	.436
2009	Portland (EL)	AA	.277	63	256	47	71	17	3	13	29	30	62	5	5	.352	.520
	Pawtucket (IL)	AAA	.127	18	71	1	9	0	2	0	6	6	13	0	1	.190	.183
	Boston (AL)	MAJ	.169	27	59	5	10	4	0	2	4	2	17	0	0	.210	.339
2010	Pawtucket (IL)	AAA	.266	114	451	59	120	28	4	18	65	25	73	4	7	.301	.466
	Boston (AL)	MAJ	.194	29	62	5	12	3	1	1	5	1	15	1	0	.206	.323
Major League Totals			.182	56	121	10	22	7	1	3	9	3	32	1	0	.208	.331
Minor League Totals			.284	414	1630	256	463	81	27	72	263	121	281	31	21	.332	.499

5 FELIX DOUBRONT, LHP

Born: Oct. 23, 1987. **B-T:** L-L. **Ht.:** 6-2. **Wt.:** 190. **Signed:** Venezuela, 2004. **Signed by:** Miguel Garcia.

Signed for $150,000 out of Venezuela in 2004, Doubront became the first Latin American signee of GM Theo Epstein's regime to reach the majors when he beat the Dodgers in an emergency start in June. He made two more decent starts in July, then earned two saves in September. He also went 8-3, 2.81 in the minors to earn the organization's minor league pitcher of the year award. As a starter, Doubront works at 88-92 mph and touches 94 with his fastball, with good sink. As a reliever, he challenges hitters more often with a fastball that sits at 92-93. He uses a changeup and a cutter to keep righthanders at bay. He made major strides with his curveball in 2010. After minor league pitching coordinator Ralph Treuel helped him find a new grip, Doubront shocked the Red Sox by returning to the majors in July and showing a solid curve. He repeats his high three-quarters delivery well, but sometimes nibbles too much and loses the strike zone. The Red Sox lacked an effective southpaw reliever in 2010, and Doubront could fill that role while being more than just a left-on-left specialist. He's also ready to contribute if Boston needs a starter.

Year	Club (League)	Class	W	L	ERA	G	GS	CG	SV	IP	H	HR	BB	SO	G/A	WHIP	AVG
2005	Red Sox/Padres (VSL)	R	7	1	0.97	13	13	0	0	65	32	0	29	58	—	0.94	.152
2006	Red Sox (GCL)	R	2	3	2.52	11	11	0	0	54	41	6	13	36	—	1.01	.212
	Lowell (NYP)	SS	2	0	4.91	2	2	0	0	11	7	1	3	7	—	0.91	.179
2007	Greenville (SAL)	LoA	3	7	8.93	11	11	0	0	42	63	8	17	22	—	1.89	.337
	Lowell (NYP)	SS	1	3	5.66	8	8	0	0	35	41	2	11	25	—	1.49	.283
2008	Greenville (SAL)	LoA	12	8	3.67	23	23	0	0	115	115	9	24	118	—	1.21	.260
	Lancaster (CAL)	HiA	1	1	3.86	3	3	0	0	14	15	1	4	20	—	1.36	.278
2009	Portland (EL)	AA	8	6	3.35	26	26	1	0	121	119	8	52	101	1.10	1.41	.255
2010	Portland (EL)	AA	4	0	2.51	8	8	0	0	43	39	0	17	38	1.29	1.30	.250
	Pawtucket (IL)	AAA	4	3	3.16	9	8	0	0	37	36	1	16	34	1.73	1.41	.261
	Boston (AL)	MAJ	2	2	4.32	12	3	0	2	25	27	3	10	23	1.00	1.48	.270
Major League Totals			2	2	4.32	12	3	0	2	25	27	3	10	23	1.00	1.48	.270
Minor League Totals			44	32	3.60	114	113	1	0	537	508	36	186	459	1.23	1.29	.250

6 STOLMY PIMENTEL, RHP

Born: Feb. 1, 1990. **B-T:** R-R. **Ht.:** 6-4. **Wt.:** 220. **Signed:** Dominican Republic, 2006. **Signed by:** Luis Scheker.

Since signing for $25,000 out of the Dominican Republic in 2006, Pimentel has made steady progress in four years of pro ball. He represented the Red Sox at the 2010 Futures Game, where he retired the two batters he faced—the Marlins' Logan Morrison and the Nationals' Danny Espinosa, both of whom finished the year in the majors. Pimentel does an excellent job of commanding and pitching off his fastball for a youngster. As he has matured physically, his four-seamer has risen from 84-86 mph when he signed to 90-95. His fastball has good riding life and sets up his swing-and-miss changeup, a legitimate plus pitch. Pimentel's curveball can become a solid third offering. He still needs to stay on top of the pitch more consistently, but he has improved its break and velocity over the last two seasons. Pimentel has also done a better job of staying in good condition, which helps him maintain his fastball deeper into starts. He throws strikes, though his arm action is long and gives hitters a good look at his pitches. Pimentel has proven that he's ready for Double-A at age 21 and could get his first shot at the big leagues by the end of 2012. He has the stuff and feel to become a No. 3 starter.

Year	Club (League)	Class	W	L	ERA	G	GS	CG	SV	IP	H	HR	BB	SO	G/A	WHIP	AVG
2007	Red Sox (DSL)	R	3	1	2.90	14	13	0	0	62	44	2	22	60	—	1.06	.202
2008	Lowell (NYP)	SS	5	2	3.14	13	11	0	0	63	51	7	17	61	—	1.08	.224
2009	Greenville (SAL)	LoA	10	7	3.82	24	23	1	0	118	135	12	29	103	0.88	1.39	.290
2010	Salem (CAR)	HiA	9	11	4.06	26	26	0	0	129	120	11	42	102	1.27	1.26	.248
Minor League Totals			27	21	3.64	77	73	1	0	371	350	32	110	326	1.07	1.24	.251

7 GARIN CECCHINI, 3B

GAINES DUVALL

Born: April 20, 1991. **B-T:** L-R. **Ht.:** 6-3. **Wt.:** 195. **Drafted:** HS—Lake Charles, La., 2010 (4th round). **Signed by:** Matt Dorey.

One of the best high school hitters in the 2010 draft, Cecchini projected as a possible first-rounder until he tore the anterior cruciate ligament in his right knee and needed reconstructive surgery in mid-March. His reported $1.75 million price tag further scared teams off, so the Red Sox were able to grab him in the fourth round. He gave up a Louisiana State scholarship to sign for $1.31 million at the deadline. His brother Gavin is a top infield prospect for the 2012 draft. Cecchini's sweet lefthanded swing could end up being the best in the system. He's a pure hitter with outstanding hand-eye coordination, and he should have at least solid power once he learns to turn on more pitches. A shortstop in high school, he'll shift to third base as a pro and has the soft hands and strong arm to make the move work. His knee injury isn't a long-term concern because his fringe-average speed isn't a major part of his game. Cecchini was healthy enough to play at the end of instructional league, and he'll be 100 percent when he makes his pro debut in 2011. Boston may ease him into pro ball by sending him to short-season Lowell, but his bat may accelerate his timetable once he gets going.

Year	Club (League)	Class	AVG	G	AB	R	H	2B	3B	HR	RBI	BB	SO	SB	CS	OBP	SLG
2010	Did Not Play—Injured																

8 LARS ANDERSON, 1B

Born: Sept. 25, 1987. **B-T:** L-L. **Ht.:** 6-4. **Wt.:** 215. **Drafted:** HS—Carmichael, Calif., 2006 (18th round). **Signed by:** Blair Henry.

Anderson ranked No. 1 on this list following the 2008 season, then had the worst year of his pro career, batting .233/.328/.345 in Double-A in 2009. He returned to Portland and destroyed Eastern League pitching last April, only to struggle for two months after his initial promotion to Triple-A. He recovered to hit .286/.345/.484 in the second half and earn his first big league callup. Anderson has the bat speed, hand-eye coordination and strength to hit for average and power. When he spiraled downward in 2009, he tinkered too much with his swing and approach, but he didn't panic and battled through his slump last season. He has yet to unlock home run power because he doesn't have much loft in his swing. He has had little success against lefthanders the last two years, batting .226/.310/.302 against them, and his naysayers see him as a platoon player with questionable pop. The Red Sox still think he can become a big league regular. A fringy defender in the past, Anderson has worked hard to improve at first base, becoming competent enough that Boston used him as a defensive replacement in September. He's a below-average runner. The blockbuster trade for Adrian Gonzalez all but ended Anderson's chances of becoming the everyday first baseman for the Red Sox, though they'll eventually need a replacement at DH for David Ortiz. Anderson will spend most of 2011 in Triple-A.

Year	Club (League)	Class	AVG	G	AB	R	H	2B	3B	HR	RBI	BB	SO	SB	CS	OBP	SLG
2007	Greenville (SAL)	LoA	.288	124	458	69	132	35	3	10	69	71	112	2	4	.385	.443
	Lancaster (CAL)	HiA	.343	10	35	13	12	2	0	1	9	11	9	0	0	.489	.486
2008	Lancaster (CAL)	HiA	.317	77	306	58	97	19	1	13	50	46	64	0	0	.408	.513
	Portland (EL)	AA	.316	41	133	27	42	13	0	5	30	29	43	1	0	.436	.526
2009	Portland (EL)	AA	.233	119	447	50	104	23	0	9	51	63	114	2	0	.328	.345
2010	Portland (EL)	AA	.355	17	62	13	22	5	0	5	16	7	16	1	1	.408	.677
	Pawtucket (IL)	AAA	.262	113	409	49	107	32	3	10	53	44	109	2	2	.340	.428
	Boston (AL)	MAJ	.200	18	35	4	7	1	0	0	4	7	8	0	0	.326	.229
Major League Totals			.200	18	35	4	7	1	0	0	4	7	8	0	0	.326	.229
Minor League Totals			.279	501	1850	279	516	129	7	53	278	271	467	8	7	.372	.442

9 KOLBRIN VITEK, 3B

RODGER WOOD

Born: April 1, 1989. **B-T:** R-R. **Ht.:** 6-2. **Wt.:** 195. **Drafted:** Ball State, 2010 (1st round). **Signed by:** Sam Ray.

One of the best hitters available in the 2010 draft, Vitek went 20th overall and signed for $1.359 million. With his quick hands, sound approach and ability to recognize pitches, he should hit for a high average. He struck out more than expected in his pro debut, mainly because he needs to make some adjustments against breaking pitches, but he still showed a knack for barreling balls. He should have at least average power, if not more. Vitek is a slightly above-average runner out of the box and has plus speed once he gets going, making him a threat to take extra bases and swipe a few bags. The big question is where he'll play. Vitek played second base last spring at Ball State, in part to save his arm for pitching. With an 88-92 mph fastball and the ability to throw three pitches for strikes, he led the Missouri Valley Conference with a 3.28 ERA and was named MVC player of the year. He lacks soft hands and true middle-infield actions, so the Red Sox shifted him to third base, where he played as a sophomore. He has more than enough arm strength and athleticism for the hot corner, but he'll have to improve his hands and footwork after making 15 errors in 34 games. He had to share the position at both of his minor league stops, because both Lowell (David Renfroe) and Greenville (Michael Almanzar) had bonus babies at third base. Many clubs projected Vitek as an outfielder and he might have enough range to play in center field. If not, his bat and arm strength would allow him to profile well in right field. He'll stay at third base in 2011, when he has a chance to open the season in high Class A.

Year	Club (League)	Class	AVG	G	AB	R	H	2B	3B	HR	RBI	BB	SO	SB	CS	OBP	SLG
2010	Lowell (NYP)	SS	.270	56	204	30	55	13	3	4	30	26	61	13	2	.360	.422
	Greenville (SAL)	LoA	.275	12	40	7	11	3	1	0	3	7	13	4	1	.383	.400
Minor League Totals			.270	68	244	37	66	16	4	4	33	33	74	17	3	.364	.418

10 OSCAR TEJEDA, 2B

Born: Dec. 26, 1989. **B-T:** R-R. **Ht.:** 6-1. **Wt.:** 177. **Signed:** Dominican Republic, 2006. **Signed by:** Luis Scheker.

Tejeda struggled through two years as a teenager in low Class A, hitting .259/.306/.340 as he battled physical problems (including a recurring staph infection in his forearm), more experienced pitchers and defensive difficulties at shortstop. Healthier, stronger and more relaxed after a move to second base last season, he showed the talent that led an exuberant rival international scouting director to compare him to Alfonso Soriano when the Red Sox signed Tejeda for $525,000 in 2006. He set career highs across the board and earned all-star recognition in the Carolina League. Tejeda has well-above-average bat speed and more raw power than most middle infielders, projecting as a possible 15-20 home run threat. He has little trouble making sweet-spot contact and doesn't chase pitches off the plate, but he's an aggressive hitter who swings early in the count and doesn't draw many walks. If he doesn't refine his approach, upper-level pitchers will let him get himself out. Tejeda has only fringe-average speed, which gave him less-than-ideal range at shortstop. He covers enough ground at second base, where his quick hands and strong arm are assets. He's still learning his new position and led CL second basemen with 24 errors in 2010, and third base or right field could be his ultimate destination. Tejeda will be just 21 when he advances to Double-A this season. If he can duplicate the progress he made last year, a big league callup will be on the horizon.

Year	Club (League)	Class	AVG	G	AB	R	H	2B	3B	HR	RBI	BB	SO	SB	CS	OBP	SLG
2007	Red Sox (GCL)	R	.295	45	173	23	51	13	1	1	21	15	27	6	2	.344	.399
	Lowell (NYP)	SS	.298	22	94	14	28	5	2	0	12	6	26	4	1	.347	.394
2008	Greenville (SAL)	LoA	.261	97	372	44	97	18	1	4	38	20	76	11	5	.301	.347
2009	Greenville (SAL)	LoA	.257	99	370	50	95	13	3	3	50	30	89	3	5	.311	.332
2010	Salem (CAR)	HiA	.307	126	508	76	156	32	5	11	69	32	96	17	7	.344	.455
Minor League Totals			.281	389	1517	207	427	81	12	19	190	103	314	41	20	.325	.388

11 WILL MIDDLEBROOKS, 3B

Born: Sept. 9, 1988. **B-T:** R-R. **Ht.:** 6-4. **Wt.:** 200. **Drafted:** HS—Texarkana, Texas, 2007 (5th round). **Signed by:** Jim Robinson.

Middlebrooks made a postseason all-star team for the first time since signing for $925,000 in 2007, earning high Class A Carolina League honors last year while continuing to make steady progress. He looks exactly like scouts want a third baseman to look, and he's starting to translate his tools into skills. Middlebrooks has a quick bat and his 6-foot-4, 200-pound frame gives him the strength and leverage for significant raw power, though he needs to add more loft to his swing. He also must improve the load and timing with his stroke, because he's prone to swings and misses when he gets out of whack. He's still figuring out his swing path and approach at the plate, and he's still learning how to solve breaking balls. He also has made strides, especially with using the entire field. Middlebrooks had a low-90s fastball as a high school pitcher and has had the best infield arm in the system since he signed. Managers cited him as the best defensive third baseman and strongest infield arm in the Carolina League last season. He runs and moves well for his size, showing the athleticism that made him a potential NFL-caliber punter who drew interest from college football programs. While Middlebrooks has moved just one level per year, he'll spend 2011 in Double-A as a 22-year-old.

Year	Club (League)	Class	AVG	G	AB	R	H	2B	3B	HR	RBI	BB	SO	SB	CS	OBP	SLG
2008	Lowell (NYP)	SS	.254	59	209	21	53	17	2	1	21	12	73	10	0	.298	.368
2009	Greenville (SAL)	LoA	.265	103	374	53	99	25	3	7	57	48	123	7	4	.349	.404
2010	Salem (CAR)	HiA	.276	114	435	69	120	31	2	12	70	35	121	5	3	.331	.439
Minor League Totals			.267	276	1018	143	272	73	7	20	148	95	317	22	7	.331	.412

12 YAMAICO NAVARRO, SS/3B

Born: Oct. 31, 1987. **B-T:** R-R. **Ht.:** 5-11. **Wt.:** 190. **Signed:** Dominican Republic, 2005. **Signed by:** Pablo Lantigua.

Navarro is one of the best upper-level talents in the system and perhaps its most frustrating prospect as well. After his 2009 season was ruined when he broke the hamate bone in his left hand on Opening Day, he bounced back last year and played his way from Double-A to Boston. Navarro has as much bat speed as any Red Sox farmhand, giving him uncommon power for a middle infielder and the potential for 15-20 homers annually. He showed more plate discipline in 2010 than he had in the past, making consistent hard contact to all fields. Navarro has average speed and enough athleticism to play some shortstop at the big league level, though not as a regular. With his quickness, soft hands and strong arm, he could handle everyday duty at second or third base. At the least, he could be a quality utilityman. Navarro's future depends as much on his dedication as his talent. Though he has grown up some since signing as a 17-year-old, his maturity still remains in question. He doesn't keep his body in peak shape, at times resembling a slightly less rotund Juan Uribe, and doesn't always run hard. Some scouts have clocked him in times befitting a 20 runner on the 20-80 scouting scale. He also can get out of control at the plate and in the field, taking wild swings or trying to make impossible plays. Navarro has played just 16 games at the Triple-A level, so he'll probably begin 2011 in Pawtucket.

Year	Club (League)	Class	AVG	G	AB	R	H	2B	3B	HR	RBI	BB	SO	SB	CS	OBP	SLG
2006	Red Sox (DSL)	R	.279	53	201	29	56	13	5	3	37	21	29	5	3	.344	.438
2007	Lowell (NYP)	SS	.289	62	225	36	65	10	1	5	37	22	52	12	6	.357	.409
2008	Greenville (SAL)	LoA	.280	83	325	46	91	14	4	7	54	29	73	3	2	.341	.412
	Lancaster (CAL)	HiA	.348	42	181	33	63	13	2	4	23	12	30	3	2	.393	.508
2009	Lowell (NYP)	SS	.238	5	21	1	5	1	0	0	2	2	3	0	2	.304	.286
	Salem (CAR)	HiA	.319	23	94	10	30	9	0	4	17	6	12	2	2	.373	.543
	Portland (EL)	AA	.185	39	135	16	25	6	2	2	11	14	28	5	1	.270	.304
2010	Portland (EL)	AA	.274	88	329	49	90	19	3	8	55	42	53	16	5	.358	.422
	Pawtucket (IL)	AAA	.283	16	53	8	15	4	0	3	6	5	6	2	1	.339	.528
	Boston (AL)	MAJ	.143	20	42	4	6	0	0	0	5	2	17	0	0	.174	.143
Major League Totals			.143	20	42	4	6	0	0	0	5	2	17	0	0	.174	.143
Minor League Totals			.281	411	1564	228	440	89	17	36	242	153	286	48	24	.348	.429

13 SEAN COYLE, 2B

Born: Jan. 17, 1992. **B-T:** R-R. **Ht.:** 5-8. **Wt.:** 175. **Drafted:** HS—Fort Washington, Pa., 2010 (3rd round). **Signed by:** Chris Calciano.

The Red Sox already struck it rich with one diminutive second baseman in Dustin Pedroia, and they're hoping history repeats itself with Coyle. They drafted him in the third round last June and signed him away from a commitment to North Carolina, where his brother Tommy is the starting second baseman, for $1.3 million at the Aug. 16 deadline. He stands out with his offense, and his overall game resembles that of Brian Roberts more than Pedroia's. Coyle's compact stroke isn't a surprise given his size, but his power is. He has a strong lower half and uncanny hand-eye coordination, allowing him to barrel balls all over the field, and he should be a doubles machine who can reach double digits in homers annually. He's a plus runner with good instincts and an aggressive nature on the bases, though he could lose a step as he fills out. A shortstop in high school, Coyle played third base on the U.S. national team that won the gold medal at the Pan American Junior Championships in October 2009. He'll be a second baseman as a pro, and he has the quickness, range, hands and arm to be a plus defender there. Though he played just three pro games after signing late, Coyle is advanced enough at the plate to possibly start 2011 in low Class A.

Year	Club (League)	Class	AVG	G	AB	R	H	2B	3B	HR	RBI	BB	SO	SB	CS	OBP	SLG
2010	Red Sox (GCL)	R	.200	3	10	5	2	1	0	0	0	1	1	0	0	.333	.300
Minor League Totals			.200	3	10	5	2	1	0	0	0	1	1	0	0	.333	.300

14 XANDER BOGAERTS, SS

Born: Oct. 1, 1992. **B-T:** R-R. **Ht.:** 6-2. **Wt.:** 185. **Signed:** Aruba, 2009. **Signed by:** Mike Lord.

Bogaerts is the most intriguing prospect to play for the Red Sox' Rookie-level Dominican Summer League team since Hanley Ramirez in 2001. Boston signed him for $410,000 out of Aruba in 2009, and also landed his twin brother Jair, a catcher/first baseman, for $180,000. Xander was named the organization's 2010 Latin program player of the year after hitting .314/.396/.423 in the DSL in his pro debut. His performance was all the more impressive considering that the Red Sox had promised his mother that he could finish high school, so he had only two weeks to prepare for the DSL season. Bogaerts already has a sound approach and a good swing, and his strong hands and still-growing 6-foot-2, 185-pound frame portend above-average power in the future. He drives balls to the opposite field and will learn to turn on more pitches as he adds experience. Though Bogaerts is quick and athletic, he figures to slow down at least a little as he fills out, which likely will lead to a move from shortstop. He has plus arm strength, so he would profile well at third base. After his scintillating performance in the DSL and instructional league, the Red Sox are excited to see what Bogaerts will do when he comes Stateside and plays in the Rookie-level Gulf Coast League in 2011.

Year	Club (League)	Class	AVG	G	AB	R	H	2B	3B	HR	RBI	BB	SO	SB	CS	OBP	SLG
2010	Red Sox (DSL)	R	.314	63	239	39	75	7	5	3	42	30	37	4	5	.396	.423
Minor League Totals			.314	63	239	39	75	7	5	3	42	30	37	4	5	.396	.423

15 DERRIK GIBSON, SS

Born: Dec. 5, 1989. **B-T:** R-R. **Ht.:** 6-1. **Wt.:** 170. **Drafted:** HS—Seaford, Del., 2008 (2nd round). **Signed by:** Chris Calciano.

After two successful years at the Rookie and short-season levels, Gibson struggled for the first time in low Class A last year. He batted .230, 46 points below his previous career average, and hit just .168 in the final month. He didn't handle adversity well and got too hard on himself, which made it more difficult to snap out of his slump. Though Gibson didn't perform in 2010 like he had in his past, his swing remained quick and sound and he generally did a good job of controlling the strike zone. A late bloomer physically with broad shoulders and a lean frame, he'll be more effective at the plate once he adds some strength. He possibly could hit 10-15 homers on an annual basis. Gibson enhances his on-base ability with a knack for drawing walks, and his plus-plus speed makes him a huge stolen base threat. He didn't allow his hitting woes to affect his defense, leading South Atlantic League shortstops with a .960 fielding percentage in his first year playing the position full-time. He also saw action at second and third base in his first two pro seasons, but he has the range and arm strength for shortstop. Though he has a funky throwing motion, he has cleaned it up some since signing. Gibson has one of the highest ceilings in the system, with the potential to become a dynamic leadoff man and solid defender. He also could be valuable as a Chone Figgins-type utilityman. Despite his struggles, he'll move up to high Class A in 2011.

Year	Club (League)	Class	AVG	G	AB	R	H	2B	3B	HR	RBI	BB	SO	SB	CS	OBP	SLG
2008	Red Sox (GCL)	R	.309	27	94	15	29	6	1	0	9	14	18	14	0	.411	.394
	Lowell (NYP)	SS	.086	14	35	4	3	0	0	0	3	6	11	2	0	.233	.086
2009	Lowell (NYP)	SS	.290	67	255	54	74	15	4	0	25	39	42	28	5	.395	.380
2010	Greenville (SAL)	LoA	.230	122	487	77	112	22	3	2	40	61	101	39	7	.321	.300
Minor League Totals			.250	230	871	150	218	43	8	2	77	120	172	83	12	.349	.325

16 RYAN LAVARNWAY, C

Born: Aug. 7, 1987. **B-T:** R-R. **Ht.:** 6-4. **Wt.:** 225. **Drafted:** Yale, 2008 (6th round). **Signed by:** Ray Fagnant.

If the Red Sox could combine Lavarnway's bat with Tim Federowicz's defense, they'd have an easy solution behind the plate. Lavarnway set an Ivy League record with 33 homers in three years at Yale before signing for $325,000 as a sixth-round pick in 2008. He led Red Sox farmhands with 21 homers in 2009 and with 102 RBIs last season, when Boston named him its co-minor league offensive player of the year along with since-traded Anthony Rizzo. Lavarnway has above-average power to all fields and controls the strike zone well. His long arms give him some length to his swing and leave him with some holes on the inside part of the plate, but he makes consistent hard contact. Whether Lavarnway can make it behind the plate remains uncertain. Scouts gave him virtually no chance of catching when he first entered pro ball, and he has worked very hard to develop adequate catch-and-throw skills. He has an average arm but not quick feet, leading to fringy pop times in the 2.1-second range. He did throw out 33 percent of basestealers in 2010. He has a thick lower half and lacks flexibility, so he'll have to continue his diligence to have a shot as a catcher. He'll always be a well-below-average runner. Lavarnway kept on hitting in the Arizona Fall League, and he'll put himself in contention for a big league job in 2012 if he performs well in the upper levels of the minors this season. He and Federowicz will open the year sharing catching duties in Double-A.

Year	Club (League)	Class	AVG	G	AB	R	H	2B	3B	HR	RBI	BB	SO	SB	CS	OBP	SLG
2008	Lowell (NYP)	SS	.211	22	71	10	15	5	0	2	9	8	18	0	0	.317	.366
2009	Greenville (SAL)	LoA	.285	106	404	60	115	36	2	21	87	50	113	1	2	.367	.540
2010	Salem (CAR)	HiA	.289	82	304	66	88	18	0	14	63	44	62	1	0	.392	.487
	Portland (EL)	AA	.285	44	158	25	45	9	0	8	39	26	42	0	0	.395	.494
Minor League Totals			.281	254	937	161	263	68	2	45	198	128	235	2	2	.376	.502

17 BRYCE BRENTZ, OF

Born: Dec. 30, 1988. **B-T:** R-R. **Ht.:** 6-1. **Wt.:** 180. **Drafted:** Middle Tennessee State, 2010 (1st round supplemental). **Signed by:** Danny Watkins.

The Indians made Brentz a 30th-round pick out of high school in 2007 as a pitcher, but it quickly became clear his future was as a hitter. He led NCAA Division I in hitting (.465), homers (28) and slugging (.930) as a sophomore in 2009, then followed up by batting .366 with Team USA, laying the groundwork for going 36th overall in the 2010 draft. After he signed for $889,200, the Red Sox had him try contact lenses to improve his vision. He didn't take to the lenses and eventually ditched them toward the end of a lackluster pro debut. His all-or-nothing approach also created problems. Brentz has explosive bat speed and power, but Boston is trying to settle him down at the plate. He started to use the opposite field and shorten his swing with two strikes more often toward the end of the season and in instructional league. He'll always strike out some, but the Red Sox want to find a happy medium where makes more contact and hits for a decent average without sacrificing much power. Brentz has solid-average speed and plus arm strength that should make him a good defender in right field. He'll continue to work on making adjustments at the plate this year in Class A.

Year	Club (League)	Class	AVG	G	AB	R	H	2B	3B	HR	RBI	BB	SO	SB	CS	OBP	SLG
2010	Lowell (NYP)	SS	.198	69	262	28	52	14	4	5	39	21	76	5	4	.259	.340
Minor League Totals			.198	69	262	28	52	14	4	5	39	21	76	5	4	.259	.340

18 BRANDON WORKMAN, RHP

Born: Aug. 13, 1988. **B-T:** R-R. **Ht.:** 6-4. **Wt.:** 195. **Drafted:** Texas, 2010 (2nd round). **Signed by:** Jim Robinson.

The Phillies drafted Workman in the third round out of high school in 2007, but he wanted $350,000 and they wouldn't move past $275,000. Though he earned all-star honors in consecutive summers in the Cape Cod League, he didn't become a full-time starter at Texas until last spring, when he ranked fifth in NCAA Division I with 12 victories. Some teams considered him with their first-round pick before mild signability concerns dropped him to the Red Sox in the second round. He signed for $800,000 at the Aug. 16 deadline. Workman pitches off a 91-94 mph fastball that peaks at 96 and creates swings and misses with its late life. His curveball had been his best pitch for much of his college career, but it now takes a back seat to a high-80s cutter that he uses as a strikeout pitch against lefthanders. He improved his changeup as well as his command in 2010, learning that it doesn't pay to overthrow. If Workman performs well in spring training, he could begin his pro career in high Class A next April.

Year	Club (League)	Class	W	L	ERA	G	GS	CG	SV	IP	H	HR	BB	SO	G/A	WHIP	AVG
2010	Did Not Play—Signed Late																

19 ALEX WILSON, RHP

Born: Nov. 3, 1986. **B-T:** R-R. **Ht.:** 6-1. **Wt.:** 205. **Drafted:** Texas A&M, 2009 (2nd round). **Signed by:** Jim Robinson.

Few pitchers in the Red Sox system have a combination of pitches more devastating than Wilson's fastball and slider. While throwing 134 innings in his first full year as a pro in 2010, he sat at 92-93 mph and topped out at 95 with his fastball throughout the season. His low-80s, late-breaking slider can be unhittable. Though all 40 of Wilson's pro appearances have been as a starter, his future is as a reliever. There's some effort to his delivery—he had Tommy John surgery in 2007—and he overthrows at times, so his command can come and go. He doesn't have a reliable third pitch to help him turn over a lineup two or three times, which became apparent when Double-A hitters tattooed him to the tune of a 6.66 ERA. He'll flash an average changeup but it often lacks enough separation from his fastball, and his curveball is just a show-me pitch. Wilson has the makeup to work the late innings and the stuff to be a closer. There's no timetable for moving him to the bullpen, but Boston needs relief help and he might be able to contribute by the end of 2011. He'll return to Double-A to start the year.

Year	Club (League)	Class	W	L	ERA	G	GS	CG	SV	IP	H	HR	BB	SO	G/A	WHIP	AVG
2009	Lowell (NYP)	SS	0	1	0.50	13	13	0	0	36	10	0	7	33	1.09	0.47	.085
2010	Salem (CAR)	HiA	2	1	3.40	11	11	0	0	56	43	4	15	50	1.89	1.04	.212
	Portland (EL)	AA	4	5	6.66	16	16	0	0	78	95	15	34	56	0.93	1.65	.302
Minor League Totals			6	7	4.29	40	40	0	0	170	148	19	56	139	1.19	1.20	.233

20 KYLE WEILAND, RHP

Born: Sept. 12, 1986. **B-T:** L-R. **Ht.:** 6-4. **Wt.:** 195. **Drafted:** Notre Dame, 2008 (3rd round). **Signed by:** Chris Mears.

Like Alex Wilson, Weiland has worked as a starter in pro ball but could help cure Boston's bullpen woes in the near future. He has a better chance to start than Wilson does because he has more pitches and more command. Weiland's best pitch is a low-90s fastball that peaks at 95 mph but is most notable for its hard sink. He surrendered just 10 homers in his first 263 pro innings before tiring and pitching up in the zone more in the last two months of 2010, when he gave up eight more longballs. His breaking ball has improved since he turned pro, going from a slurve to a true curve that generates swings and misses against righthanders. He also has upgraded his feel for his changeup, though he needs to use it more often and do a better job of maintaining his arm speed when he throws it. Weiland relishes pitching inside, as evidenced by him leading the Carolina League and Eastern League in hit batters (16 both times) the last two seasons. He does a good job of controlling the running game, giving up just six steals in 17 attempts in 2010. He excelled as a closer at Notre Dame, setting school records for single-season (16) and career (25) saves. As with Wilson, the Red Sox haven't decided to make Weiland a reliever yet, though it could happen in 2011. He'll open the season in Triple-A.

Year	Club (League)	Class	W	L	ERA	G	GS	CG	SV	IP	H	HR	BB	SO	G/A	WHIP	AVG
2008	Lowell (NYP)	SS	3	3	1.50	15	10	0	0	60	36	1	10	68	—	0.77	.166
2009	Salem (CAR)	HiA	7	9	3.46	26	26	0	0	133	119	4	57	112	1.63	1.33	.240
2010	Portland (EL)	AA	5	9	4.42	25	25	0	0	128	112	13	49	120	1.51	1.25	.236
Minor League Totals			15	21	3.48	66	61	0	0	321	267	18	116	300	1.58	1.19	.225

21 TIM FEDEROWICZ, C

Born: Aug. 5, 1987. **B-T:** R-R. **Ht.:** 5-10. **Wt.:** 213. **Drafted:** North Carolina, 2008 (7th round). **Signed by:** Quincy Boyd.

Federowicz doesn't have Ryan Lavarnway's bat, but there aren't any questions as to whether he can remain behind the plate. He's the best defensive catcher in the system, with average arm strength that plays up because of his good footwork and quick transfer and release. He consistently produces 1.9-2.0 second pop times and threw out 33 percent of basestealers in 2010. He has improved his receiving since turning pro, and his intelligence and leadership are assets behind the plate. Federowicz opened eyes by batting .345/.393/.562 in low Class A to start 2009, but he has hit .254/.309/.377 in high Class A since. Though he has a decent idea of the strike zone and manages his at-bats well, his offensive ceiling is probably a .260 hitter with gap power. He runs well for a catcher but still has below-average speed. The Red Sox would like Federowicz to get a little quicker and in a little better shape. He and Lavarnway will share catching duties in Double-A to start the season.

Year	Club (League)	Class	AVG	G	AB	R	H	2B	3B	HR	RBI	BB	SO	SB	CS	OBP	SLG
2008	Lowell (NYP)	SS	.244	36	127	14	31	6	0	1	15	19	24	10	3	.338	.315
2009	Greenville (SAL)	LoA	.345	55	226	34	78	19	0	10	34	15	42	1	0	.393	.562
	Salem (CAR)	HiA	.257	51	187	18	48	13	0	4	24	5	22	1	0	.276	.390
2010	Salem (CAR)	HiA	.253	109	407	47	103	34	1	4	61	43	86	1	1	.324	.371
Minor League Totals			.275	251	947	113	260	72	1	19	134	82	174	13	4	.333	.413

22 JEREMY HAZELBAKER, OF

Born: Aug. 14, 1987. **B-T:** L-R. **Ht.:** 6-3. **Wt.:** 190. **Drafted:** Ball State, 2009 (4th round). **Signed by:** Chris Mears.

A teammate of Kolbrin Vitek at Ball State, Hazelbaker hit just .246 and made 31 errors at second base in his first two college seasons. Like Vitek, he used a strong summer performance in the Great Lakes League as a springboard to a standout junior season, ranking among the NCAA Division I leaders in hitting (.429), on-base percentage (.550) and steals (29) in 2009. A fourth-round pick that June, he had a dismal pro debut but started to turn things around in instructional league. In 2010, he made the South Atlantic League all-star team, led Red Sox farmhands with 63 steals (the most in the system since 1981) in 80 attempts and won the organization's minor league baserunner of the year award. Hazelbaker can go from the left side of the plate to first base in less than 4.0 seconds on a bunt and his speed rates a 70 on the 20-80 scouting scale. In addition to sheer quickness, he also possesses the best baserunning instincts in the system. More than just a speedster, Hazelbaker also has plus raw power to his pull side. He's willing to take walks, but his swing can get long at times and he needs to make more consistent contact so he can take advantage of his speed. Hazelbaker has the athleticism to handle center field, though he didn't get much of an opportunity to do so playing alongside superior defender Reymond Fuentes in low Class A last year. He played more in right field, where his fringy arm isn't a great fit, but should get a shot in center this year in high Class A, after Fuentes went to the Padres in the Adrian Gonzalez trade. Hazelbaker will be old for that level at 23, so Boston would like him to force his way to Double-A at some point during the season.

Year	Club (League)	Class	AVG	G	AB	R	H	2B	3B	HR	RBI	BB	SO	SB	CS	OBP	SLG
2009	Lowell (NYP)	SS	.125	3	8	0	1	0	0	0	0	4	3	0	0	.417	.125
	Greenville (SAL)	LoA	.167	45	150	16	25	5	1	1	9	23	58	11	2	.280	.233
2010	Greenville (SAL)	LoA	.267	116	442	78	118	29	9	12	62	59	135	63	17	.360	.455
Minor League Totals			.240	164	600	94	144	34	10	13	71	86	196	74	19	.341	.395

23 JUNICHI TAZAWA, RHP

Born: June 6, 1986. **B-T:** R-R. **Ht.:** 5-11. **Wt.:** 180. **Signed:** Japan, 2008. **Signed by:** Craig Shipley/Jon Deeble.

Tazawa starred in Japan's industrial leagues and created a furor when he asked Japanese major league teams to let him go undrafted so he could play in the United States. After signing a three-year, $3.3 million big league deal with the Red Sox in December 2008, he reached Boston eight months later. He didn't pitch at all in 2010, however, after injuring his elbow in big league camp and requiring Tommy John surgery in April. Before he got hurt, Tazawa went after hitters with four average pitches and plus control. His fastball command made his 88-92 heater his best pitch, and his slider and splitter were effective as well. He also threw a curveball to give hitters a different look. Tazawa isn't big and wore down at the end of 2009, getting in trouble against major league hitters when he left pitches up in the zone. His funky arm action gave him deception but also may have contributed to his elbow problems. Tazawa's ceiling is as a No. 4 starter or a seventh-inning reliever, and he'll find more opportunity with the Red Sox in the latter role. He'll be ready for spring training but Boston may wait until the weather warms up in May before turning him loose in Triple-A.

Year	Club (League)	Class	W	L	ERA	G	GS	CG	SV	IP	H	HR	BB	SO	G/A	WHIP	AVG
2009	Portland (EL)	AA	9	5	2.57	18	18	0	0	98	80	8	26	88	0.95	1.08	.222
	Pawtucket (IL)	AAA	0	2	2.38	2	2	0	0	11	7	0	1	6	1.45	0.70	.184
	Boston (AL)	MAJ	2	3	7.46	6	4	0	0	25	43	4	9	13	0.36	2.05	.374
2010	Did Not Play—Injured																
Major League Totals			2	3	7.46	6	4	0	0	25	43	4	9	13	0.36	2.05	.374
Minor League Totals			9	7	2.55	20	20	0	0	109	87	8	27	94	0.82	1.043	.219

24 MADISON YOUNGINER, RHP

Born: Nov. 3, 1990. **B-T:** R-R. **Ht.:** 6-4. **Wt.:** 195. **Drafted:** HS—Mauldin, S.C., 2009 (7th round). **Signed by:** Quincy Boyd.

When the Red Sox gave first-round money ($975,000) to seventh-rounder Younginer in 2009, they knew they were getting one of the most electric arms in the draft but also one that would need plenty of time to develop. He lived up to that reputation during his 2010 pro debut. Younginer consistently threw 92-94 mph fastballs and topped out at 96, but he didn't throw nearly enough quality strikes. His control and command are still works in progress, hampered by a stiff delivery that features hesitation and a long arm action. Boston is working to get him to consistently repeat his mechanics rather than trying to overhaul them. Younginer still is figuring out his secondary pitches as well. After showing a power 12-to-6 curveball in instructional league in 2009, he had a slower bender last summer. His changeup was better than the Red Sox anticipated but still has a ways to go. He also has to figure out how to combat the running game after leading the short-season New York-Penn League by giving up 27 steals in 62 innings. While Younginer looks more like a reliever than a starter in the long run, he does have closer potential. Boston will keep him in the rotation this year in low Class A in order to give him innings to work on his long to-do list.

Year	Club (League)	Class	W	L	ERA	G	GS	CG	SV	IP	H	HR	BB	SO	G/A	WHIP	AVG
2010	Lowell (NYP)	SS	3	7	4.79	14	14	0	0	62	56	2	31	40	1.32	1.40	.247
Minor League Totals			3	7	4.79	14	14	0	0	62	56	2	31	40	1.32	1.40	.247

25 CHE-HSUAN LIN, OF

Born: Sept. 21, 1988. **B-T:** R-R. **Ht.:** 6-0. **Wt.:** 180. **Signed:** Taiwan, 2007. **Signed by:** Jon Deeble/Louie Lin.

Lin controls the strike zone and plays center field better than anyone in the system, but it's still uncertain whether he can contribute enough with the bat to make an impact in the major leagues. Signed for $400,000 out of high school in Taiwan, where he was a national 100-meter and high-jump champion, he has continued to play for his nation at the 2008 Olympics and 2009 World Baseball Classic. The Red Sox named him their minor league defensive player of the year in 2010, when managers rated him the top outfield defender in the Eastern League. He has plus speed and tremendous instincts in center field, getting quick jumps and making good reads. Unlike most center fielders, he has a cannon for an arm and has recorded 33 assists during the last two seasons. He settled down defensively last year, making just three errors after trying to do too much at times and committing 11 in 2009. Though Lin is an extremely disciplined hitter who draws walks and rarely strikes out, his offensive contributions have been minimal. He has just fair bat speed and a flat swing, so he makes a lot of soft contact. He had just 23 extra-base hits in 2010 and owns a career .363 slugging percentage. He gets on base but isn't an efficient basestealer and makes mistakes on the basepaths. Until Lin starts driving the ball, it's difficult to project him as a big league regular. He'll advance to Triple-A at age 22.

Year	Club (League)	Class	AVG	G	AB	R	H	2B	3B	HR	RBI	BB	SO	SB	CS	OBP	SLG
2007	Red Sox (GCL)	R	.263	43	175	33	46	10	6	4	22	17	42	14	3	.330	.457
	Lowell (NYP)	SS	.163	11	43	7	7	2	0	0	3	5	10	3	2	.265	.209
2008	Greenville (SAL)	LoA	.249	91	362	60	90	13	6	5	37	43	62	33	7	.342	.359
2009	Salem (CAR)	HiA	.265	131	479	75	127	23	2	7	54	66	75	26	11	.355	.365
2010	Portland (EL)	AA	.275	119	458	88	126	17	4	2	34	72	63	26	12	.386	.343
Minor League Totals			.261	395	1517	263	396	65	18	18	150	203	252	102	35	.356	.363

26 CHRIS BALCOM-MILLER, RHP

Born: March 3, 1989. **B-T:** R-R. **Ht.:** 6-2. **Wt.:** 210. **Drafted:** West Valley (Calif.) JC, 2009 (6th round). **Signed by:** Gary Wilson (Rockies).

Mostly a shortstop in high school, Balcom-Miller opted to focus on pitching at West Valley (Calif.) JC. The Red Sox nearly drafted him in 2009, but the Rockies beat them to him in the sixth round. Boston finally landed him last August, getting him in a trade for Manny Delcarmen. Balcom-Miller has enjoyed success in his brief pro career, winning Rookie-level Pioneer League pitcher of the year honors in his debut and ranking third in the South Atlantic League in baserunners per nine innings (1.07) and strikeout-walk ratio (6.3) in 2010. He can't overpower hitters but he can put his pitches wherever he wants. He runs his fastball from 89-93 mph, and it's more notable for its sink and command than velocity. His slider and changeup are average complementary pitches, though he needs to use his changeup more often. His delivery is less than smooth, but it adds deception and doesn't stop him from filling the strike zone. While his ceiling is as a No. 4 or 5 starter, his advanced pitchability gives him a good chance to reach it. He'll move up the ladder to high Class A in 2011.

Year	Club (League)	Class	W	L	ERA	G	GS	CG	SV	IP	H	HR	BB	SO	G/A	WHIP	AVG
2009	Casper (PIO)	R	4	0	1.58	11	11	1	0	57	37	3	10	60	2.86	0.82	.181
2010	Asheville (SAL)	LoA	6	7	3.31	19	19	1	0	109	86	3	19	117	2.83	0.97	.214
	Greenville (SAL)	LoA	1	0	3.00	1	1	0	0	6	5	1	0	3	4.00	0.83	.217
Minor League Totals			11	7	2.73	31	31	2	0	172	128	7	29	180	2.89	0.91	.204

27 BRANDON JACOBS, OF

Born: Dec. 8, 1990. **B-T:** R-R. **Ht.:** 6-1. **Wt.:** 225. **Drafted:** HS—Lilburn, Ga., 2009 (10th round). **Signed by:** Tim Hyers.

Built like but unrelated to the New York Giants running back of the same name, Jacobs was a prime running-back recruit with a football scholarship from Auburn, where his football doppelganger played for one season. Boston was able to divert him from football by drafting him in the 10th round in 2009 and signing him for $750,000. He has one of the highest offensive ceilings in the system, drawing comparisons to former MVP Kevin Mitchell. Jacobs is still very raw in baseball, however, though he held his own as one of the few teenage regulars in the New York-Penn League last summer. Jacobs packs a lot of power in his muscular frame and led Lowell with 18 doubles and six homers. He has a very quick bat, though he needs to do a better job of controlling the strike zone and using the entire field. Despite his football background, Jacobs isn't an all-around athlete and his value comes almost entirely from his bat. He doesn't have a quick first step and has just fringy speed once he gets going. He's a work in progress as an outfield corner, and he'll eventually settle in left field because he has well-below-average arm strength and lacks accuracy on his throws. The Red Sox are set in left field with Carl Crawford for the foreseeable future, so they can afford to give Jacobs all the time he needs to develop. He'll make his full-season debut in Greenville this year.

Year	Club (League)	Class	AVG	G	AB	R	H	2B	3B	HR	RBI	BB	SO	SB	CS	OBP	SLG
2009	Red Sox (GCL)	R	.250	8	24	1	6	2	0	0	0	2	8	0	0	.333	.333
2010	Lowell (NYP)	SS	.242	64	236	30	57	18	2	6	31	21	59	4	1	.308	.411
Minor League Totals			.242	72	260	31	63	20	2	6	31	23	67	4	1	.310	.404

28 JUAN CARLOS LINARES, OF

Born: Sept. 7, 1984. **B-T:** R-R. **Ht.:** 5-11. **Wt.:** 190. **Signed:** Cuba, 2010. **Signed by:** Craig Shipley/Todd Claus.

The Red Sox signed a pair of Cuban defectors in July. Catcher Adalberto Ibarra initially drew more attention than Linares because he's three years younger, plays the position at which Boston is the weakest and originally agreed to a $3 million major league contract. But Ibarra failed his physical, signed a renegotiated deal for a $750,000 bonus and had labrum surgery on his throwing shoulder in November. By then, Linares had opened eyes with his play in the Arizona Fall League, where he finished second in the batting race at .397. He spent seven seasons in Cuba's Serie Nacional with the same La Habana club that top Red Sox prospect Jose Iglesias played for, with Linares leading the league with a .586 slugging percentage in 2006-07 and winning a pair of Cuban Gold Gloves. He defected in November 2009 after failing to make Cuba's World Cup team and signed with

Boston for $750,000. He didn't stand out during his brief pro debut in the Gulf Coast League and at Portland, but he looked like a different player in the Arizona Fall League. Linares has a quick, short swing and had a better approach in Arizona, using the whole field. He's a free swinger who can handle most fastballs, but he'll need more patience to hit major league pitching. He has average power and plus speed, and he's capable of playing all three outfield spots. He enhances his range by getting quick jumps and taking direct routes to balls, and he has solid arm strength. Linares is already 26 and may not be more than a fourth outfielder, but he's definitely intriguing. The Red Sox will know more about what they have in him after he spends 2011 in Triple-A.

Year	Club (League)	Class	AVG	G	AB	R	H	2B	3B	HR	RBI	BB	SO	SB	CS	OBP	SLG
2010	Red Sox (GCL)	R	.267	4	15	2	4	1	0	0	1	1	2	0	0	.313	.333
	Portland (EL)	AA	.239	13	46	3	11	4	0	1	4	0	13	1	1	.271	.391
Minor League Totals			.246	17	61	5	15	5	0	1	5	1	15	1	1	.281	.377

29 MIGUEL CELESTINO, RHP

Born: Oct. 10, 1989. **B-T:** R-R. **Ht.:** 6-6. **Wt.:** 205. **Signed:** Dominican Republic, 2006. **Signed by:** Patrick Guerrero/Bob Engle/Franklin Taveras (Mariners).

When the Red Sox traded Casey Kotchman to the Mariners for third baseman Bill Hall last January, the deal couldn't have been much more one-sided. Boston saved about $5 million in luxury-tax calculations after getting rid of Kotchman's salary and having Milwaukee and Seattle pick up most of Hall's. Hall had his best season since 2006, hitting 18 homers while playing seven different positions before becoming a free agent. The cherry on top is Celestino, who hadn't played above Rookie ball when he became the player to be named in the deal in March. Red Sox scout Matt Dorey had liked what he saw of Celestino in instructional league the previous fall, and Boston monitored his progress that winter in the Dominican League. Celestino pitched with a low-90s sinker during the 2010 season, then started popping some 95 mph fastballs during instructional league. With his tall body and long arms, he delivers balls at an angle that's tough on hitters. His fastball is by far his best pitch right now, though he does show some feel for a changeup. The key to his development will be his ability to refine his breaking ball, which is only rudimentary at this point. His control is fine but he'll need to improve his command. Celestino will make his full-season debut in 2011 when he starts the season at Greenville. He'll remain a starter for now but could be destined for the bullpen in the long run if his secondary pitches don't come around.

Year	Club (League)	Class	W	L	ERA	G	GS	CG	SV	IP	H	HR	BB	SO	G/A	WHIP	AVG
2007	Mariners (DSL)	R	4	2	3.38	14	1	0	0	29	25	1	17	14	—	1.43	.234
2008	Mariners (DSL)	R	5	1	2.48	15	12	0	0	58	45	0	15	47	—	1.03	.212
2009	Mariners (AZL)	R	5	3	4.72	13	12	0	0	67	76	5	23	48	1.98	1.49	.293
2010	Red Sox (GCL)	R	2	0	0.90	4	3	0	0	20	18	0	3	14	1.05	1.05	.228
	Lowell (NYP)	SS	2	2	2.62	9	9	0	0	45	39	0	17	28	1.51	1.25	.245
Minor League Totals			18	8	3.17	55	37	0	0	219	203	6	75	151	1.64	1.27	.249

30 RYAN WESTMORELAND, OF

Born: April 27, 1990. **B-T:** L-R. **Ht.:** 6-2. **Wt.:** 195. **Drafted:** HS—Portsmouth, R.I., 2008 (5th round). **Signed by:** Ray Fagnant.

The No. 1 prospect on this list a year ago, Westmoreland appeared poised to join the ranks of the game's elite prospects in 2010. That changed last March, when headaches and numbness led him to take a medical leave from minor league camp. Doctors detected a cavernous malformation (an abnormal cluster of blood vessels) in his brain, and he underwent five hours of surgery to repair it. It typically takes 12-18 months for full recovery from the procedure, and Westmoreland made encouraging progress in the first six months afterward. He was running, throwing and hitting off a tee by mid-August, and he took some light batting practice during instructional league. The Red Sox aren't putting any timetable on his return to the diamond. Before the shocking diagnosis, Westmoreland wowed scouts with his tools and skills. Signed away from a Vanderbilt commitment for $2 million as a fifth-round pick in 2008, he ranked as the New York-Penn League's top prospect during his 2009 pro debut. He displayed plus-plus speed, above-average power potential and center-field range and an average arm. He also had advanced hitting instincts, with a short stroke, an all-fields approach and good control of the strike zone.

Year	Club (League)	Class	AVG	G	AB	R	H	2B	3B	HR	RBI	BB	SO	SB	CS	OBP	SLG
2009	Lowell (NYP)	SS	.296	60	223	38	66	15	3	7	35	38	49	19	0	.401	.484
2010	Did Not Play—Injured																
Minor League Totals			.296	60	223	38	66	15	3	7	35	38	49	19	0	.401	.484

Chicago Cubs

BY JIM CALLIS

After the Ricketts family completed its $845 million purchase of the Cubs and related assets in October 2009, the team unveiled its marketing campaign for 2010: "Year One."

Unfortunately, Year One was a lot like the previous 101. Chicago still is seeking its first World Series championship since 1908 and first appearance since 1945, and the big league club is trending in the wrong direction.

The Cubs won 97 games and a second straight National League Central title in 2008, then dropped to 83 victories in 2009 and 75 a year ago. That's not exactly what the Ricketts family thought it was getting with a $146.6 million Opening Day payroll that trailed only the Yankees and Red Sox among major league teams.

Chicago still is paying the price for overaggressive spending, first when it was rebuilding following a 96-loss season in 2006, then when it was trying to get over the hump after getting swept out of the playoffs the next two years. General manager Jim Hendry signed Ryan Dempster, Kosuke Fukudome, Aramis Ramirez, Alfonso Soriano and Carlos Zambrano to long-term deals totaling $404.5 million during that period, and the Cubs owe those five players $77.5 million for 2011 alone.

There were some silver linings during a disappointing 2010 season. Chicago promoted several prospects to Wrigley Field, and they acquitted themselves well. Starlin Castro nearly made the team out of spring training and came up for good May 7. He became just the third shortstop age 20 or younger to hit .300 while qualifying for the batting title, joining Hall of Famer Arky Vaughan and Alex Rodriguez.

Andrew Cashner made tremendous progress as a starter in the minors before getting summoned to the big league bullpen at the end of May. He held his own with a mid-90s fastball and a mid-80s slider, and he'll move into the rotation for 2011. Casey Coleman, Tyler Colvin and Scott Maine also made successful debuts and claimed jobs for the upcoming season.

The Cubs responded well to an unanticipated managerial change, playing their best ball after Lou Piniella abruptly resigned Aug. 23 to take care of his ailing mother. They went 51-74 under Piniella and 24-13 under former third-base coach Mike Quade. Quade instilled a greater sense of accountability, including benching Castro for two games for concentration lapses, and had "interim" removed from his job title after the season.

Cubs GM Jim Hendry has five players who are owed $77.5 million for the 2011 season

TOP 30 PROSPECTS

1.	Chris Archer, rhp	16.	Robinson Chirinos, c
2.	Brett Jackson, of	17.	Welington Castillo, c
3.	Trey McNutt, rhp	18.	Marcus Mateo, rhp
4.	Hak-Ju Lee, ss	19.	Robinson Lopez, rhp
5.	Josh Vitters, 3b	20.	Kyle Smit, rhp
6.	Chris Carpenter, rhp	21.	Logan Watkins, 2b/of/ss
7.	Matt Szczur, of	22.	Ryan Flaherty, 2b/3b
8.	Hayden Simpson, rhp	23.	Reggie Golden, of
9.	Rafael Dolis, rhp	24.	Ben Wells, rhp
10.	Brandon Guyer, of	25.	Aaron Kurcz, rhp
11.	Alberto Cabrera, rhp	26.	Brooks Raley, lhp
12.	Darwin Barney, ss/2b	27.	Junior Lake, ss/3b
13.	D.J. LeMahieu, inf	28.	Jae-Hoon Ha, of
14.	Scott Maine, lhp	29.	Esmailin Caridad, rhp
15.	Jay Jackson, rhp	30.	Dae-Eun Rhee, rhp

Life was better down on the farm than it was at Wrigley Field. Righthanders Chris Archer and Trey McNutt went a combined 25-4, while outfielder Brett Jackson pounded Double-A pitching in his first full pro season, establishing themselves as the best prospects in the system. Triple-A Iowa and Double-A Tennessee had the best regular-season records in their leagues, and both Class A affiliates had winning marks, with legitimate talent driving all those victories. One pro scout who covered the Cubs opined that they had more future big leaguers than any other organization.

General Manager: Jim Hendry. **Farm Director:** Oneri Fleita. **Scouting Director:** Tim Wilken.

Class	Team	League	W	L	PCT	Finish*	Manager
Majors	Chicago Cubs	National	75	87	.463	13th (16)	Lou Piniella/Mike Quade
Triple-A	Iowa Cubs	Pacific Coast	82	62	.569	t-1st (16)	Ryne Sandberg
Double-A	Tennessee Smokies	Southern	86	53	.619	1st (10)	Bill Dancy
High A	Daytona Cubs	Florida State	75	64	.540	4th (12)	Buddy Bailey
Low A	Peoria Chiefs	Midwest	71	66	.518	8th (16)	Casey Kopitzke
Short-season	Boise Hawks	Northwest	34	42	.447	5th (8)	Jody Davis
Rookie	AZL Cubs	Arizona	26	29	.473	8th (12)	Juan Cabreja
Overall 2010 Minor League Record			374	316	.542	2nd (30)	

*Finish in overall standings (No. of teams in league). †League champion.

LAST YEAR'S TOP 30

Player, Pos.		Status
1.	Starlin Castro, ss	Majors
2.	Brett Jackson, of	No. 2
3.	Josh Vitters, 3b	No. 5
4.	Andrew Cashner, rhp	Majors
5.	Jay Jackson, rhp	No. 15
6.	Hak-Ju Lee, ss	No. 4
7.	Logan Watkins, 2b	No. 21
8.	Chris Carpenter, rhp	No. 6
9.	Ryan Flaherty, inf	No. 22
10.	D.J. LeMahieu, ss/2b	No. 13
11.	Kyler Burke, of	Dropped out
12.	Dae-Eun Rhee, rhp	No. 30
13.	Rafael Dolis, rhp	No. 9
14.	John Gaub, lhp	Dropped out
15.	Chris Archer, rhp	No. 1
16.	Trey McNutt, rhp	No. 3
17.	Tyler Colvin, of	Majors
18.	Darwin Barney, ss	No. 12
19.	Jeffry Antigua, lhp	Dropped out
20.	Blake Parker, rhp	Dropped out
21.	Brooks Raley, lhp	No. 26
22.	Esmailin Caridad, rhp	No. 29
23.	Sam Fuld, of	Majors
24.	Marcos Mateo, rhp	No. 18
25.	Casey Coleman, rhp	Majors
26.	Robinson Chirinos, c	No. 16
27.	Welington Castillo, c	No. 17
28.	David Cales, rhp	Dropped out
29.	Junior Lake, ss/2b	No. 27
30.	Jim Adduci, of	Dropped out

BEST TOOLS

Best Hitter for Average	D.J. LeMahieu
Best Power Hitter	Brett Jackson
Best Strike-Zone Discipline	Matt Cerda
Fastest Baserunner	Matt Szczur
Best Athlete	Matt Szczur
Best Fastball	Chris Archer
Best Curveball	Trey McNutt
Best Slider	Chris Archer
Best Changeup	Chris Rusin
Best Control	Chris Rusin
Best Defensive Catcher	Robinson Chirinos
Best Defensive Infielder	Darwin Barney
Best Infield Arm	Junior Lake
Best Defensive Outfielder	Brandon Guyer
Best Outfield Arm	Kyler Burke

PROJECTED 2014 LINEUP

Catcher	Geovany Soto
First Base	Tyler Colvin
Second Base	Starlin Castro
Third Base	Josh Vitters
Shortstop	Hak-Ju Lee
Left Field	Brandon Guyer
Center Field	Matt Szczur
Right Field	Brett Jackson
No. 1 Starter	Andrew Cashner
No. 2 Starter	Chris Archer
No. 3 Starter	Trey McNutt
No. 4 Starter	Carlos Zambrano
No. 5 Starter	Ryan Dempster
Closer	Carlos Marmol

TOP PROSPECTS OF THE DECADE

Year	Player, Pos.	2010 Org.
2001	Corey Patterson, of	Orioles
2002	Mark Prior, rhp	Rangers
2003	Hee Seop Choi, 1b	Kia (Korea)
2004	Angel Guzman, rhp	Cubs
2005	Brian Dopirak, 1b	Blue Jays
2006	Felix Pie, of	Orioles
2007	Felix Pie, of	Orioles
2008	Josh Vitters, 3b	Cubs
2009	Josh Vitters, 3b	Cubs
2010	Starlin Castro, ss	Cubs

TOP DRAFT PICKS OF THE DECADE

Year	Player, Pos.	2010 Org.
2001	Mark Prior, rhp	Rangers
2002	Bobby Brownlie, rhp	Out of baseball
2003	Ryan Harvey, of	Rockies
2004	Grant Johnson, rhp (2nd round)	Out of baseball
2005	Mark Pawelek, lhp	Gateway (Frontier)
2006	Tyler Colvin, of	Cubs
2007	Josh Vitters, 3b	Cubs
2008	Andrew Cashner, rhp	Cubs
2009	Brett Jackson, of	Cubs
2010	Hayden Simpson, rhp	Cubs

LARGEST BONUSES IN CLUB HISTORY

Mark Prior, 2001	$4,000,000
Kosuke Fukudome, 2007	$4,000,000
Corey Patterson, 1998	$3,700,000
Josh Vitters, 2007	$3,200,000
Luis Montanez, 2000	$2,750,000

CHiCAGO CUBS

TOP 2011 ROOKIE: Darwin Barney, ss/2b. The best middle-infield defender in the organization keeps overachieving and could steal playing time at second base.

BREAKOUT PROSPECT: Aaron Kurcz, rhp. With his 91-95 mph fastball and promising secondary pitches, he won't remain an anonymous 10th-round pick for much longer.

SLEEPER: Matt Cerda, 3b. He has unusual feel for hitting and strike-zone control for someone so young.

SOURCE OF TOP 30 TALENT			
Homegrown	25	**Acquired**	**5**
College	10	Trades	5
Junior college	2	Rule 5 draft	0
High school	4	Independent leagues	0
Draft-and-follow	9	Free agents/waivers	0
Nondrafted free agents	0		
International	0		

LF
Ty Wright

CF
Brett Jackson (2)
Matt Szczur (7)
Brandon Guyer (10)
Tony Campana
Jim Adduci
Evan Crawford
Oliver Zapata

RF
Reggie Golden (23)
Jae-Hoon Ha (28)
Brad Snyder
Kyler Burke
Alvaro Ramirez

3B
Josh Vitters (5)
D.J. LeMahieu (13)
Ryan Flaherty (22)
Junior Lake (27)
Matt Cerda
Marquez Smith
Wes Darvill
Dustin Geiger

SS
Hak-Ju Lee (4)
Darwin Barney (12)
Logan Watkins (21)
Marwin Gonzalez
Elliot Soto
Gioskar Amaya
Marco Hernandez

2B
Tony Thomas
Pierre LePage
Arismendy Alcantara

1B
Justin Bour

C
Robinson Chirinos (16)
Welington Castillo (17)
Micah Gibbs
Steve Clevenger
Michael Brenly

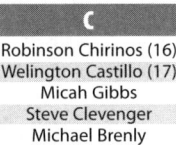

RHP

RHSP	RHRP
Chris Archer (1)	Marcus Mateo (18)
Trey McNutt (3)	Kyle Smit (20)
Chris Carpenter (6)	Aaron Kurcz (25)
Hayden Simpson (8)	Esmailin Caridad (29)
Rafael Dolis (9)	Brian Schlitter
Alberto Cabrera (11)	Jeff Stevens
Jay Jackson (15)	Blake Parker
Robinson Lopez (19)	David Cales
Ben Wells (24)	Kevin Rhoderick
Dae-Eun Rhee (30)	Ty'Relle Harris
Austin Reed	Charles Thomas
Robert Whitenack	Jordan Latham
Brett Wallach	Larry Suarez
Austin Bibens-Dirkx	Mike Perconte
Thomas Diamond	
Nick Struck	
Su-Min Jung	
Hung-Wen Chen	
Dallas Beeler	
Dustin Fitzgerald	
Ryan Hartman	
Colin Richardson	
Starling Peralta	
Amaury Paulino	

LHP

LHSP	LHRP
Brooks Raley (26)	Scott Maine (14)
Chris Rusin	John Gaub
Austin Kirk	Jeff Beliveau
Jeffry Antigua	
Cameron Greathouse	
Hunter Ackerman	
Eric Jokisch	
Casey Harman	

2010 BONUSES: $4.7 MILLION

BEST PURE HITTER: OF Matt Szczur (5) began his pro career with a 21-game hitting streak and batted .347/.414/.465 in his debut.

BEST POWER HITTER: With a short swing and an explosive bat, OF Reggie Golden (2) has close to plus-plus raw power.

FASTEST RUNNER: Szczur can get from the right side of the plate to first base in under four seconds. Villanova football coach Andy Talley says Szczur is the fastest player he's ever had, faster even than longtime NFL star Brian Westbrook.

BEST DEFENSIVE PLAYER: C Micah Gibbs (3) was the best receiver in the draft. SS Elliot Soto (15) has the range, hands and arm to make any play, though his bat remains a question.

BEST FASTBALL: RHP Hayden Simpson (1) missed the summer and instructional league because of mono, but Chicago saw him repeatedly hit 96-97 mph in an NCAA Division II playoff game. RHPs Ben Wells (7) and Aaron Kurcz (10) both can touch 95, and Wells may have more velocity to come.

BEST SECONDARY PITCH: Several Cubs draftees have good breaking balls, led by LHP Cam Greathouse's (8) curveball and Wells' slider. Simpson's curveball and slider both have promise. RHP Austin Reed (12) has an advanced changeup for a high schooler.

BEST PRO DEBUT: Szczur or Kurcz, who had a 1.98 ERA, nine saves and 48 strikeouts in 27 innings, mostly in the short-season Northwest League. 2B Pierre LePage (13) was an NWL all-star after hitting .345 and leading the league with 20 doubles.

BEST ATHLETE: Szczur is also a wide receiver who earned MVP honors as Villanova won the NCAA football championship subdivision title game in 2009. He signed for $100,000 and will get an additional $500,000 if he makes a written commitment to baseball before the 2011 NFL scouting combine. Golden has five-tool potential.

MOST INTRIGUING BACKGROUND: Szczur generated more headlines in May when he donated peripheral blood cells to a 1-year-old girl battling leukemia. Unsigned LHP Bryan Harper's (27) brother Bryce was the draft's No. 1 overall pick. Unsigned 1B Benito Santiago Jr.'s (31) father was a five-time all-star and three-time Gold Glove catcher. Unsigned RHP Trey Nielsen's (42) dad Scott also played in the big leagues.

CLOSEST TO THE MAJORS: Simpson or Kurcz.

BEST LATE-ROUND PICK: Kurcz, who got overlooked in high school and overshadowed by Bryce Harper and a talented pitching staff at the JC of Southern Nevada. Chicago is enthused by several late-round sleepers, including Reed, 3B Dustin Geiger (24) and RHP Dallas Beeler (41).

THE ONE WHO GOT AWAY: OF Ivan DeJesus (6), who has solid all-around tools, didn't come close to signing and headed to Alabama-Birmingham. RHP/OF Brooks Pinckard (18), a draft-eligible sophomore who returned to Baylor, has a fastball that reaches 95 mph but Chicago liked his plus-plus speed even more.

ASSESSMENT: The Cubs surprised draft observers by taking Simpson 16th overall, but they see a four-pitch righty with plus stuff who'll move quickly. Szczur and Wells could be steals, as could several players in double-digit rounds.

2009 BONUSES: $4.0 MILLION

OF Brett Jackson (1) and RHP Trey McNutt (34) are two of the system's three blue-chip prospects, while INF D.J. LeMahieu (2) is its best pure hitter.

GRADE: A

2008 BONUSES: $5.5 MILLION

RHPs Andrew Cashner (1) and Casey Coleman (15) reached the majors in their second full pro season, and Cashner could be Chicago's ace of the future. RHP Chris Carpenter (3) isn't far behind after hitting 100 mph in the Arizona Fall League.

GRADE: B+

2007 BONUSES: $6.1 MILLION

The Cubs still believe 3B Josh Vitters (1) has an impact bat, but scouts with other clubs are skeptical. SS/2B Darwin Barney (4) and LHP James Russell (14) are effective role players who have gotten to Chicago. OF Brandon Guyer (5) had a breakout 2010 season, while C Josh Donaldson (1s) was used in the Rich Harden trade.

GRADE: C

2006 BONUSES: $5.0 MILLION

OF Tyler Colvin (1) hit 20 homers as a rookie last year. But Chicago didn't have picks in the second through fourth rounds, then paid $10 million for RHP Jeff Samardzija (5), who may be a better wide receiver than pitcher.

GRADE: C+

Draft analysis by Jim Callis. Numbers in parentheses indicate draft rounds.

CHRIS ARCHER, RHP

Born: Sept. 26, 1988. **Bats:** R. **Throws:** R.
Height: 6-3. **Weight:** 180. **Drafted:** HS—
Clayton, N.C., 2006 (5th round). **Signed by:**
Bob Mayer (Indians).

TONY FARLOW

Archer was an afterthought in the class of 2006 high school pitching prospects until he earned a last-minute invitation to the East Coast Professional Showcase the summer before his senior year. He showed a high-80s fastball and an athletic, projectable frame, piquing scouts' interest, then displayed a low-90s heater and sharp slider the following spring. The Indians selected him in the fifth round and signed him away from a Miami commitment for $161,000. Archer struggled in his first few seasons, but he hasn't looked nearly as raw since coming to the Cubs along with relief prospects John Gaub and Jeff Stevens in the Mark DeRosa trade in December 2008. Archer made progress while repeating low Class A in 2009 and then took off last season, when he was Chicago's minor league pitcher of the year and led the system in wins (15), ERA (2.34) and strikeouts (149). Promoted to Double-A in July, he didn't allow an earned run in his first 31⅓ innings at Tennessee. He continued to star after the season, striking out 10 in six scoreless innings against Cuba in the Pan American Games qualifying tournament in October. He was a no-brainer addition to Chicago's 40-man roster a month later.

Now that Andrew Cashner has graduated to the big leagues, Archer has the best fastball and slider in the system. He operates from 92-95 mph and touches 97, and though he has an over-the-top delivery, his fastball has some run and sink to it. His slider sits in the mid-80s and peaks at 91 mph, giving him two plus-plus pitches when his command is at its best. His changeup has improved markedly since the trade, and while he throws it a bit hard at times, it should give him an effective third pitch. The Cubs love the way he competes, reaching back for extra velocity when he needs it and demonstrating an ability to win on days when he doesn't have his best stuff. Archer is athletic and has a fluid delivery, and all he has left to do is improve his consistency and command. Though he has cut his walk rate the last three years, he still gives up too many free passes. He works up in the strike zone too often, and his high arm slot doesn't afford him much deception, but his stuff is so good that he has surrendered just six homers in 251 innings as a Chicago farmhand.

Archer draws some Edwin Jackson comparisons, with scouts noting that Archer has better secondary pitches at the same age. He's ready for Triple-A Iowa at age 22 and not far off from the majors, especially if the Cubs wanted to promote him as a reliever like they did with Cashner last year. If Archer continues to progress as he has the last two years, he'll arrive in Wrigley Field around midseason. He projects as a frontline starter if he refines his command, and he easily has the stuff and poise to become a closer.

SCOUTING GRADES

Fastball: 70.   **Command/**
Slider: 65.   **Control:** 55.
Changeup: 50. **Delivery:** 65.

Based on 20-80 scouting scale, where 50 represents major league average, and future projection rather than present tools.

Year	Club (League)	Class	W	L	ERA	G	GS	CG	SV	IP	H	HR	BB	SO	G/A	WHIP	AVG
2006	Indians (GCL)	R	0	3	7.45	7	6	0	0	19	17	1	17	21	—	1.76	.224
	Burlington (APP)	R	0	0	10.80	1	0	0	0	2	2	1	1	1	—	1.80	.333
2007	Indians (GCL)	R	1	7	5.64	12	11	0	0	53	56	4	21	48	—	1.46	.271
	Lake County (SAL)	LoA	0	0	9.00	1	0	0	0	4	5	0	3	5	—	2.00	.333
2008	Lake County (SAL)	LoA	4	8	4.29	27	27	0	0	115	92	8	84	106	—	1.53	.220
2009	Peoria (MWL)	LoA	6	4	2.81	27	26	0	0	109	78	0	66	119	1.48	1.32	.202
2010	Daytona (FSL)	HiA	7	1	2.86	15	14	0	0	72	54	4	26	82	1.47	1.11	.202
	Tennessee (SL)	AA	8	2	1.80	13	13	0	0	70	48	2	39	67	1.80	1.24	.198
Minor League Totals			26	25	3.67	103	97	0	0	444	352	20	257	449	1.56	1.37	.218

2 BRETT JACKSON, OF

Born: Aug. 2, 1988. **B-T:** R-R. **Ht.:** 6-2. **Wt.:** 210. **Drafted:** California, 2009 (1st round). **Signed by:** John Bartsch.

The Cubs rated Jackson's bat speed as the best in the 2009 draft, and they got him with the 31st overall pick because many clubs worried about his ability to make consistent contact. That hasn't been an issue since he signed for $972,000, as he already has conquered Double-A. He has been bothered by minor injuries: a strained wrist cut short his pro debut, a bruised heel hampered him with Team USA last October, and a staph infection in his shin ended his time in the Arizona Fall League. Jackson's quick bat, loft in his swing and plus speed should make him an annual 20-20 threat in the majors. He could stand to cut down his strikeouts, but he doesn't swing and miss as much as some teams feared and should hit for power and average. He played all three outfield positions last year, showing enough range to get the job done in center and honing his instincts with the help of roving instructor Bobby Dernier. Jackson gets good reads and jumps, has average arm strength and makes accurate throws. His even-keeled demeanor suits him well. He's not a true five-tool player or a pure center fielder, but Jackson does a reasonable impression of both. He'll open 2011 in Triple-A, and the Cubs are counting on him to crack their lineup in 2012—if not sooner.

Year	Club (League)	Class	AVG	G	AB	R	H	2B	3B	HR	RBI	BB	SO	SB	CS	OBP	SLG
2009	Cubs (AZL)	R	.455	3	11	6	5	0	1	0	4	3	4	0	0	.533	.636
	Boise (NWL)	SS	.330	24	88	14	29	1	1	1	15	17	20	2	1	.443	.398
	Peoria (MWL)	LoA	.295	26	112	30	33	5	1	7	17	11	32	11	1	.383	.545
2010	Daytona (FSL)	HiA	.316	67	263	56	83	19	8	6	38	43	63	12	7	.420	.517
	Tennessee (SL)	AA	.276	61	228	47	63	13	6	6	28	30	63	18	4	.366	.465
Minor League Totals			.303	181	702	153	213	38	17	20	102	104	182	43	13	.402	.491

3 TREY McNUTT, RHP

Born: Aug. 2, 1989. **B-T:** R-R. **Ht.:** 6-4. **Wt.:** 205. **Drafted:** Shelton State (Ala.) CC, 2009 (32nd round). **Signed by:** Jim Crawford/Al Geddes.

When their Alabama area scout quit early in 2009, the Cubs decided not to replace him. So while other teams saw McNutt work in the high 80s at the start of Shelton State (Ala.) CC's season and backed off, Chicago didn't catch him until the Junior College World Series in June, when he showed a 90-93 mph fastball. After he turned down an eighth-round offer from the Twins, he slid all the way to 32nd round, where the Cubs signed him for $115,000. His stuff has continued to improve, propelling him to Double-A in his first full pro season. When he's going good, McNutt has two plus-plus pitches. Though his fastball comes in on a bit of a flat plane, he blows it by hitters at 92-98 mph. He can neutralize lefthanders by pitching to their back foot with his power breaking ball, which is more of a curveball than a slider. Once McNutt uses his changeup more, it should become an average third pitch. He's stingy with walks but sometimes lapses into overthrowing, costing him command. Ticketed for a return trip to Double-A, McNutt has a profile similar to that of Andrew Cashner and Chris Archer. All three have the stuff to pitch at the front of a rotation or close games.

Year	Club (League)	Class	W	L	ERA	G	GS	CG	SV	IP	H	HR	BB	SO	G/A	WHIP	AVG
2009	Cubs (AZL)	R	0	1	0.00	6	4	0	0	7	5	0	3	7	1.33	1.09	.167
	Boise (NWL)	SS	3	0	1.33	7	2	0	0	20	9	1	12	21	1.47	1.03	.132
2010	Peoria (MWL)	LoA	6	0	1.51	13	13	0	0	60	43	0	24	70	1.13	1.12	.202
	Daytona (FSL)	HiA	4	0	2.63	9	9	0	0	41	29	3	9	49	0.81	0.93	.191
	Tennessee (SL)	AA	0	1	5.74	3	3	0	0	16	21	2	4	13	3.29	1.60	.333
Minor League Totals			13	2	2.19	38	31	0	0	144	107	6	52	160	1.22	1.10	.203

4 HAK-JU LEE, SS

Born: Nov. 4, 1990. **B-T:** L-R. **Ht.:** 6-2. **Wt.:** 175. **Signed:** Korea, 2008. **Signed by:** Steve Wilson.

Few clubs scout the Far East as actively as the Cubs, whose biggest recent prize is Lee, signed for $725,000 out of Korea in 2008. He had Tommy John surgery before coming to the United States, but it hasn't held him back. He ranked as the short-season Northwest League's No. 1 prospect in his 2009 pro debut, and he and Brett Jackson represented Chicago at the Futures Game last July. A potential leadoff hitter, Lee controls the strike zone and has plus-plus speed. He has the bat speed and strength in his hands to hit for some power once he develops his upper body, though he can get overly aggressive and spin off some balls. Managers rated Lee the best defensive shortstop in the low Class A Midwest League in 2010. He has quick reactions, good range to both sides and a strong arm, though he needs to improve his reads and his focus after making 34 errors in 118 games last year. He also has to break a habit of flipping throws to first base. He picked up English quickly, helping him soak up instruction. Lee will play at high Class A Daytona at age 20. The Cubs have time before they'll have to decide where to play him and Starlin Castro on the same club. Lee is quicker and flashier, so he could push Castro to second base.

Year	Club (League)	Class	AVG	G	AB	R	H	2B	3B	HR	RBI	BB	SO	SB	CS	OBP	SLG
2008	Did Not Play—Injured																
2009	Boise (NWL)	SS	.330	68	264	56	87	14	2	2	33	31	50	25	8	.399	.420
2010	Peoria (MWL)	LoA	.282	122	485	85	137	22	4	1	40	49	86	32	7	.354	.351
Minor League Totals			.299	190	749	141	224	36	6	3	73	80	136	57	15	.370	.375

5 JOSH VITTERS, 3B

Born: Aug. 27, 1989. **B-T:** R-R. **Ht.:** 6-3. **Wt.:** 195. **Drafted:** HS—Cypress, Calif., 2007 (1st round). **Signed by:** Denny Henderson/Tim Wilken.

The No. 3 overall pick in the 2007 draft and recipient of a $3.2 million bonus, Vitters reached Double-A before he turned 21 but doesn't get a universal seal of approval from scouts. He hit .361 in his first 11 games at Tennessee last May, then just .194 in the next two months before a pitch broke his left hand in late July. He returned in the Arizona Fall League, where he continued to generate mixed opinions. In Chicago's view, Vitters has the compact stroke, bat speed, strength and hand-eye coordination to hit .280 with 25 homers a season. Club officials believe he's realizing he has to stop trying to pull everything and avoid putting tough pitches in play, though scouts outside the organization think his lack of patience will undermine his potential. He has worked hard on his quickness and body control, improving his speed and range to close to average. His detractors, however, wonder whether he has enough athleticism for the hot corner. His above-average arm is not in question. The Cubs noted a greater sense of urgency in Vitters this offseason and think he's poised to break out at Tennessee in 2011. They hoped he'd be ready in time for them to decline Aramis Ramirez's $16 million contract action for 2012, but that might be pushing it.

Year	Club (League)	Class	AVG	G	AB	R	H	2B	3B	HR	RBI	BB	SO	SB	CS	OBP	SLG
2007	Cubs (AZL)	R	.067	7	30	0	2	0	0	0	2	1	9	0	0	.094	.067
	Boise (NWL)	SS	.190	7	21	2	4	0	0	0	1	2	5	1	1	.261	.190
2008	Peoria (MWL)	LoA	.214	4	14	1	3	3	0	0	1	0	5	0	0	.214	.429
	Boise (NWL)	SS	.328	61	259	38	85	25	2	5	37	13	45	1	3	.365	.498
2009	Peoria (MWL)	LoA	.316	70	269	42	85	12	1	15	46	7	42	4	0	.351	.535
	Daytona (FSL)	HiA	.238	50	189	21	45	7	2	3	22	5	23	2	1	.260	.344
2010	Daytona (FSL)	HiA	.291	28	110	16	32	8	0	3	13	8	22	4	1	.350	.445
	Tennessee (SL)	AA	.223	63	206	28	46	12	0	7	26	13	41	2	0	.292	.383
Minor League Totals			.275	290	1098	148	302	67	5	33	148	49	192	14	6	.317	.435

6 CHRIS CARPENTER, RHP

Born: Dec. 26, 1985. **B-T:** R-R. **Ht.:** 6-4. **Wt.:** 215. **Drafted:** Kent State, 2008 (3rd round). **Signed by:** Lukas McKnight.

The highest-drafted high school pitcher in 2004 (seventh round, Tigers) who opted for college, Carpenter had Tommy John surgery as a Kent State freshman and a second elbow procedure the following year. Though his medical history dropped him to the third round of the 2008 draft, he hasn't missed a start as a pro. He opened eyes as a reliever in the Arizona Fall League after last season. Carpenter profiles as a No. 3 starter or set-up man. Pitching out of the rotation, he works at 91-96 mph with his fastball, which has good life for a four-seamer. In relief in the AFL, he pitched at 94-99 mph and touched 100 in the Rising Stars Game. His low-80s breaking ball is a solid slider with bite at times and more slurvy at others. His changeup has deception and fade but probably won't ever be more than his third pitch. Carpenter still is figuring out control and command, as he runs into problems with walks and gets hit more than someone with his fastball should. He needs to do a better job of controlling the running game after giving up 23 steals in 29 attempts last year. He works diligently to stay healthy. Carpenter hasn't dominated as a starter, so he may be in for a change of roles. It's possible he could begin 2011 in Iowa's rotation and finish the season in Chicago's bullpen.

Year	Club (League)	Class	W	L	ERA	G	GS	CG	SV	IP	H	HR	BB	SO	G/A	WHIP	AVG
2008	Cubs (AZL)	R	0	0	18.00	1	1	0	0	1	2	0	1	1	—	3.00	.500
	Boise (NWL)	SS	4	2	4.22	10	6	0	0	32	32	2	22	24	—	1.69	.258
2009	Peoria (MWL)	LoA	4	3	2.44	15	15	1	0	74	55	4	33	60	1.68	1.19	.210
	Daytona (FSL)	HiA	2	1	1.44	5	5	0	0	25	15	1	8	33	1.93	0.92	.163
	Tennessee (SL)	AA	0	3	4.78	7	7	0	0	32	30	0	11	25	1.76	1.28	.246
2010	Tennessee (SL)	AA	8	6	3.16	23	23	0	0	120	118	5	48	100	2.07	1.39	.262
	Iowa (PCL)	AAA	0	0	5.40	3	3	0	0	15	19	3	9	12	3.83	1.87	.317
Minor League Totals			18	15	3.29	64	60	1	0	298	271	15	132	255	1.95	1.35	.243

7 MATT SZCZUR, OF

Born: July 29, 1989. **B-T:** R-R. **Ht.:** 6-1. **Wt.:** 190. **Drafted:** Villanova, 2010 (5th round). **Signed by:** Tim Adkins.

Szczur led Villanova to the 2009 NCAA football championship subdivision title, winning MVP honors in the final game with 270 all-purpose yards and two touchdowns. He made more headlines last May, when he took time out of his baseball season to donate peripheral blood cells to a 1-year-old girl fighting leukemia. After missing three weeks, Szczur homered in his first at-bat back. The Cubs fell in love with his hitting ability, athleticism and makeup and drafted him in the fifth round. He signed for $100,000 and began his pro career with a 21-game hitting streak. Szczur returned to Villanova for his senior football season. Though he missed time with a high ankle sprain, he accounted for five touchdowns in an FCS quarterfinal game before the Wildcats were eliminated in the next round. Szczur's athletic ability is exciting enough, but it's his hitting skills that could make him a special player. Chicago marvels at his knack for barreling balls, and combined with his top-of-the-scale speed he should hit for high averages. He hits 400-foot bombs in batting practice, and once he gets more coaching and learns to finish through the ball better, he could have average or better power. He's refining his basestealing and baserunning, but his speed alone makes him a threat. Villanova football coach Andy Talley says Szczur is his fastest player ever, ahead of star NFL running back Brian Westbrook. In his short time in pro ball, Szczur's center-field play and his throwing made significant strides. He'll have plus-plus range once he improves his jumps, and his arm strength rated as average after he loosened up some of his football tightness. His competitiveness and work ethic are impeccable. He has more upside than any position player in the system, but Szczur also projects as a mid-round NFL draft pick as a slot receiver and kick returner. The Cubs would hate to lose him. If he makes a written commitment to them before the NFL scouting combine in February, his baseball contract calls for an additional $500,000 payment.

Year	Club (League)	Class	AVG	G	AB	R	H	2B	3B	HR	RBI	BB	SO	SB	CS	OBP	SLG
2010	Cubs (AZL)	R	.500	1	2	1	1	0	0	0	0	1	0	1	0	.750	.500
	Boise (NWL)	SS	.397	18	73	17	29	9	0	0	8	6	11	1	0	.439	.521
	Peoria (MWL)	LoA	.192	6	26	6	5	1	1	0	2	3	5	0	0	.300	.308
Minor League Totals			.347	25	101	24	35	10	1	0	10	10	16	2	0	.414	.465

8 HAYDEN SIMPSON, RHP

Born: May 20, 1989. **B-T:** R-R. **Ht.:** 6-0. **Wt.:** 175. **Drafted:** Southern Arkansas, 2010 (1st round). **Signed by:** Jim Crawford.

Chicago pulled the first huge surprise of the 2010 draft when it selected Simpson with the 16th overall pick. Considered as a fourth- to sixth-round talent by most clubs, he ranked second in NCAA Division II in wins (13) and strikeouts (131) last spring and went 35-2, 2.39 in three college seasons. A bad case of mononucleosis prevented him from pitching during the summer or instructional league, after he signed for a below-slot $1.06 million. Simpson uses a quick arm and a strong lower half to throw a low-90s fastball, and the Cubs saw him work at 94-97 in a Division II playoff game. They project him as a No. 2 or 3 starter with four average or better pitches, including a knee-buckling curveball, hard slider and effective changeup, not to mention plus control and command. Other teams don't rate his stuff quite as highly and think he'll have to add life to his fastball and work lower in the strike zone. They also wonder if he has the size to hold up as a starter, though Chicago thinks his athleticism will help in that regard. Simpson lost 15 pounds before heading to the Cubs' Arizona complex in November to regain strength. If he performs well in spring training, he could make his pro debut at high Class A Daytona.

Year	Club (League)	Class	W	L	ERA	G	GS	CG	SV	IP	H	HR	BB	SO	G/A	WHIP	AVG
2010	Did Not Play—Illness																

9 RAFAEL DOLIS, RHP

Born: Jan. 10, 1988. **B-T:** R-R. **Ht.:** 6-4. **Wt.:** 215. **Signed:** Dominican Republic, 2004. **Signed by:** Jose Serra/Marino Encarnacion.

The Cubs like to experiment with failed position players as pitchers, and they've turned former catchers into their closer (Carlos Marmol) and No. 4 starter (Randy Wells). They signed Dolis as a shortstop and moved him to the mound before he made his U.S. debut in 2006. He missed most of 2007 and all of 2008 with elbow issues that resulted in Tommy John surgery, then claimed a spot on the 40-man roster when he hit 101 mph in instructional league in 2009. Dolis' stuff kicked up a notch when current big league pitching coach Mark Riggins had him go to a full windup in the fall of 2009. Dolis pitched at 94-96 mph as a starter last season, holding his velocity deep into games, and if he moves to the bullpen he could work in the upper 90s. His mid-80s slider gives him a second potential plus pitch, and he also shows feel for a changeup. His command and control are still works in progress, understandable for a former infielder with less than 300 innings under his belt. Dolis has the power repertoire to close games, though it's too early to give up on him as a starter. At worst, the extra innings will give him some much-needed experience. After finishing 2010 in Double-A, he'll return there to start this season.

Year	Club (League)	Class	W	L	ERA	G	GS	CG	SV	IP	H	HR	BB	SO	G/A	WHIP	AVG
2005	Did Not Play																
2006	Cubs (AZL)	R	0	2	8.28	13	3	0	0	25	30	1	16	33	—	1.84	.294
2007	Peoria (MWL)	LoA	3	1	1.80	6	6	0	0	30	23	1	16	24	—	1.30	.223
2008	Did Not Play—Injured																
2009	Daytona (FSL)	HiA	3	9	3.79	27	25	0	0	100	78	4	53	75	1.64	1.31	.221
2010	Daytona (FSL)	HiA	4	5	2.92	14	13	0	0	71	63	3	30	48	2.62	1.31	.242
	Tennessee (SL)	AA	5	4	4.07	12	12	0	0	55	65	3	27	45	2.26	1.66	.295
Minor League Totals			15	21	3.81	72	59	0	0	281	259	12	142	225	2.04	1.43	.250

10 BRANDON GUYER, OF

Born: Jan. 26, 1986. **B-T:** R-R. **Ht.:** 6-1. **Wt.:** 210. **Drafted:** Virginia, 2007 (5th round). **Signed by:** Billy Swoope.

When the Cubs scouted Guyer at a 2007 NCAA playoff game, they saw him dislocate his left shoulder in a home-plate collision. The shoulder bothered him for his first two years in pro ball, and it led to another stint on the disabled list last May. That didn't stop him from leading the system in batting (.344) and the Double-A Southern League in slugging (.588) and OPS (.986), which earned him the organization's minor league player of the year award and a spot on the 40-man roster. An all-Virginia high school running back and linebacker who drew interest from college football programs, Guyer has solid power, plus speed and the best present outfield skills in the system. He's aggressive in all phases of the game, which hurts him at the plate because he makes contact so easily that he doesn't draw many walks. He knows how to use his quickness on the bases, swiping 30 bags in 33 tries last year. Guyer can play all three outfield positions, thanks to his speed and instincts. His arm has improved to where it's now average, and it's accurate as well. Scouts see Guyer as a lesser version of Brett Jackson or a stronger version of Reed Johnson. Guyer's encore this year in Triple-A will help determine whether he'll become a regular or a fourth outfielder.

Year	Club (League)	Class	AVG	G	AB	R	H	2B	3B	HR	RBI	BB	SO	SB	CS	OBP	SLG
2007	Cubs (AZL)	R	.222	17	72	10	16	4	1	1	5	5	16	6	2	.309	.347
	Boise (NWL)	SS	.268	19	71	9	19	1	0	0	14	6	9	5	0	.346	.282
2008	Peoria (MWL)	LoA	.269	88	327	55	88	27	3	14	38	19	63	22	7	.331	.498
2009	Daytona (FSL)	HiA	.347	73	265	40	92	16	3	2	32	24	34	23	2	.407	.453
	Tennessee (SL)	AA	.190	57	189	22	36	12	2	1	14	10	33	7	5	.236	.291
2010	Tennessee (SL)	AA	.344	102	369	76	127	39	6	13	58	27	51	30	3	.398	.588
Minor League Totals			.292	356	1293	212	378	99	15	31	161	91	206	93	19	.352	.464

11 ALBERTO CABRERA, RHP

Born: Oct. 25, 1988. **B-T:** R-R. **Ht.:** 6-4. **Wt.:** 210. **Signed:** Dominican Republic, 2005. **Signed by:** Jose Serra/Sandy Nin.

Cabrera spent his first two years in full-season leagues battling shoulder and elbow tenderness, but he finally stayed healthy in 2010 and showed enough to claim a spot on the 40-man roster. He has one of the best arms in the system, maintaining a 92-97 mph fastball as a starting pitcher. He carries that velocity deep into games, and his fastball has good tailing and running life. He has a pair of mid-80s secondary pitches that lack reliability but show promise. His slider can freeze hitters at times and his changeup features some fade. Cabrera took a more direct path to the plate and did a better job of repeating his delivery last year, but he still needs to replicate his mechanics more consistently. His long arm action gives hitters a good look at the ball and makes him more hittable, especially when he falls behind in the count. He made strides with his control in Daytona at the start of 2010, but battled the strike zone and got torched following a promotion to Tennessee in mid-May and returned to high Class A in July. Cabrera will take another crack at Double-A hitters this year. He ultimately may be best suited for relief, but the Cubs haven't given up on him as a starter.

Year	Club (League)	Class	W	L	ERA	G	GS	CG	SV	IP	H	HR	BB	SO	G/A	WHIP	AVG
2006	Cubs (DSL)	R	5	6	2.27	15	14	0	0	71	69	4	18	55	—	1.22	.257
2007	Boise (NWL)	SS	3	3	5.40	9	9	0	0	38	41	4	18	33	—	1.54	.287
2008	Peoria (MWL)	LoA	4	6	5.71	12	11	0	0	52	55	7	30	37	—	1.63	.281
2009	Peoria (MWL)	LoA	8	2	4.48	27	8	0	1	96	94	6	54	73	1.18	1.54	.256
2010	Daytona (FSL)	HiA	7	5	3.28	18	17	1	0	93	92	6	26	90	1.49	1.26	.253
	Tennessee (SL)	AA	0	4	6.33	10	9	0	0	43	57	1	24	35	1.65	1.90	.315
Minor League Totals			27	26	4.25	91	68	1	1	394	408	28	170	323	1.37	1.47	.269

12 DARWIN BARNEY, SS/2B

Born: Nov. 8, 1985. **B-T:** R-R. **Ht.:** 5-10. **Wt.:** 180. **Drafted:** Oregon State, 2007 (4th round). **Signed by:** John Bartsch.

Winning follows Barney. He led Oregon State to consecutive World Series championships in 2006-07, captured the Florida State League title with Daytona in his first full pro season in 2008, helped Tennessee to the Southern League finals in 2009 and was a major reason why Iowa had the best regular-season record in the Pacific Coast League last year. Along the way, Barney consistently has improved all facets of his game, which earned him his first big league callup last August. He isn't flashy but he's the best defensive infielder in the organization, including the majors. He has excellent instincts, solid range, soft hands and an average arm that he enhances with a quick release and uncanny accuracy. He led PCL shortstops with a .970 fielding percentage in 2010. Barney has grown as a hitter, shortening his stroke and learning to use the entire field. Scouts thought his bat was a little quicker last year than it had been in the past. He won't have much power, but he knows that and focuses on making contact. He has average speed but runs the bases well and can steal on occasion. Barney's hustle and reliability endear him to managers and likely will win him a utility role with the Cubs in 2011. He's good enough to be an everyday shortstop but is blocked by Starlin Castro in Chicago. Don't bet against him finding a way to beat out Blake DeWitt and Jeff Baker for the Cubs' second-base job.

Year	Club (League)	Class	AVG	G	AB	R	H	2B	3B	HR	RBI	BB	SO	SB	CS	OBP	SLG
2007	Cubs (AZL)	R	.444	5	18	6	8	3	0	0	2	4	0	0	0	.545	.611
	Peoria (MWL)	LoA	.273	44	176	27	48	9	3	2	21	11	22	5	2	.323	.392
2008	Daytona (FSL)	HiA	.262	123	409	46	107	22	4	3	51	38	58	8	3	.325	.357
2009	Tennessee (SL)	AA	.317	74	252	30	80	12	0	3	32	23	33	5	1	.368	.401
	Iowa (PCL)	AAA	.264	63	212	25	56	12	1	0	17	13	32	4	1	.304	.330
2010	Iowa (PCL)	AAA	.299	114	479	72	143	24	4	2	49	23	52	11	3	.333	.378
	Chicago (NL)	MAJ	.241	30	79	12	19	4	0	0	2	6	12	0	0	.294	.291
Major League Totals			.241	30	79	12	19	4	0	0	2	6	12	0	0	.294	.291
Minor League Totals			.286	423	1546	206	442	82	12	10	172	112	197	33	10	.334	.374

13 D.J. LeMAHIEU, INF

Born: July 13, 1988. **B-T:** R-R. **Ht.:** 6-3. **Wt.:** 215. **Drafted:** Louisiana State, 2009 (2nd round). **Signed by:** Steve Riha.

LeMahieu is the best pure hitter in the system, but his future will be determined by what else he can bring to the table. He led Louisiana State's 2009 College World Series championship team with a .350 average before signing for an above-slot $508,000 as a second-round pick. LeMahieu makes consistent sweet-spot contact, using an inside-out swing to lace balls to the opposite field. He makes good adjustments, as evidenced by him rallying from hitting .227 through mid-May to bat .344 in the second half of 2010. The problem is that his approach leads to few walks and little power. He can turn on pitches occasionally—as he showed when he hit a 390-foot blast off a 94-mph fastball from Phillies prospect Phillippe Aumont in September—but that represented half of his home run output for the year. LeMahieu has size and strength, and the Cubs believe he can hit 15 homers a season once he learns to recognize pitches he can drive. Skeptics aren't as optimistic and think more advanced pitchers will pound him relentlessly with inside fastballs. LeMahieu has played second base, third base and shortstop but isn't ideal at any of the three. His speed and quickness are fringy, which makes playing shortstop in the majors impossible and works against him as a second basemen. He has soft hands and a strong arm, so he could handle third, but he doesn't fit the power profile there. LeMahieu will see time at multiple positions again when he plays in Double-A this year, and he's probably facing a ceiling as a utilityman if he can't find more power.

Year	Club (League)	Class	AVG	G	AB	R	H	2B	3B	HR	RBI	BB	SO	SB	CS	OBP	SLG
2009	Cubs (AZL)	R	.417	3	12	2	5	0	1	0	4	1	3	1	0	.429	.583
	Peoria (MWL)	LoA	.316	38	152	19	48	4	2	0	30	12	22	2	2	.371	.368
2010	Daytona (FSL)	HiA	.314	135	554	63	174	24	5	2	73	29	61	15	7	.346	.386
Minor League Totals			.316	176	718	84	227	28	8	2	107	42	86	18	9	.353	.386

14 SCOTT MAINE, LHP

Born: Feb. 2, 1985. **B-T:** L-L. **Ht.:** 6-3. **Wt.:** 210. **Drafted:** Miami, 2007 (6th round). **Signed by:** Ray Blanco (Diamondbacks).

Maine projected as a potential sandwich pick in the 2003 draft but went unselected because he was strongly committed to Miami. He had Tommy John surgery, costing him the entire 2004 season, but that was minor compared to what happened to him in August 2005, when he lost control of his truck on the Florida Turnpike in an accident that left him hospitalized for three weeks. Despite spending two days in an induced coma and needing surgery to reduce swelling in his brain and place seven titanium screws in his skull, Maine returned in the spring of 2006 to win 12 games. He turned down the Rockies, who drafted him in the 23rd round that June, and signed a year later as a seventh-rounder with the Diamondbacks. He came to Chicago with first-base prospect Ryne White in a November 2009 trade for Aaron Heilman. The deal seemed like little more than a salary savings for the Cubs last April, when they released White and watched Maine throw 87-90 mph fastballs and ineffective slurves. Fast forward to September, and Maine was one of the big league club's best relievers, weathering a demotion to Double-A and watching his stuff take a huge step forward. His fastball shot up to 93-95 mph and touched 97, and his slider added velocity and bite. He throws from a low three-quarters arm slot while flying open in his delivery and spinning off toward third base, providing deception. It's not always easy to repeat those mechanics or stay on top of his pitches, so Maine has trouble throwing strikes and maintaining a reliable slider. He has an effective changeup but doesn't use it much. If Maine's improved stuff is for real, he'll have a major league job for a long time. He has all but locked up an Opening Day roster spot with the Cubs for 2011.

Year	Club (League)	Class	W	L	ERA	G	GS	CG	SV	IP	H	HR	BB	SO	G/A	WHIP	AVG
2007	Yakima (NWL)	SS	1	0	6.10	8	0	0	1	10	6	0	12	20	—	1.74	.154
2008	Visalia (CAL)	HiA	3	2	3.19	32	0	0	5	48	48	4	21	53	—	1.44	.262
2009	Mobile (SL)	AA	3	3	2.66	36	0	0	5	47	56	2	15	46	1.12	1.50	.298
	Reno (PCL)	AAA	1	2	3.68	12	0	0	2	15	13	0	7	15	1.42	1.36	.228
2010	Tennessee (SL)	AA	1	1	2.20	12	0	0	5	16	12	1	4	15	1.06	0.98	.200
	Iowa (PCL)	AAA	3	1	3.51	33	0	0	5	41	33	4	21	47	1.38	1.32	.213
	Chicago (NL)	MAJ	0	0	2.08	13	0	0	0	13	9	1	5	11	2.13	1.08	.188
Major League Totals			0	0	2.08	13	0	0	0	13	9	1	5	11	2.13	1.08	.187
Minor League Totals			12	9	3.24	133	0	0	23	178	168	11	80	196	1.22	1.40	.246

15 JAY JACKSON, RHP

Born: Oct. 27, 1987. **B-T:** R-R. **Ht.:** 6-1. **Wt.:** 195. **Drafted:** Furman, 2008 (9th round). **Signed by:** Antonio Grissom.

Jackson breezed through his first two pro seasons while zooming to Triple-A, but when Chicago promoted a dozen pitchers from Iowa in 2010, he wasn't one of them. The Cubs moved him to the bullpen in May to prepare him for a possible callup, but when he pitched well and didn't get promoted he went into a funk. His stuff regressed slightly, as did his command, and he posted a 5.70 ERA in his final 20 starts. Jackson works with two fastballs, a low-90s four-seamer that's straight and a high-80s two-seamer with more run than sink. He used to feature two distinct breaking balls, a mid-80s slider and high-70s curveball, but they morphed into a low-80s slurve for much of last year. His changeup lost effectiveness too. He pitched up in the strike zone too often and got tagged for 20 homers. While Jackson had a disappointing season, he still flashed three average or better pitches and threw strikes as a 22-year-old in Triple-A. He's motivated to catch up to the pitchers who passed him and he still has upside as a possible No. 3 or 4 starter. He'll return to Iowa in 2011, with a trip to Chicago on the horizon if he can improve his stuff and especially his command.

Year	Club (League)	Class	W	L	ERA	G	GS	CG	SV	IP	H	HR	BB	SO	G/A	WHIP	AVG
2008	Boise (NWL)	SS	0	0	5.00	3	1	0	0	9	7	1	1	14	—	0.89	.212
	Peoria (MWL)	LoA	2	2	3.00	6	1	0	0	24	22	3	5	37	—	1.13	.253
	Daytona (FSL)	HiA	2	0	1.59	4	3	0	0	17	11	0	7	21	—	1.06	.183
2009	Tennessee (SL)	AA	5	5	3.70	16	16	1	0	83	73	7	39	77	0.87	1.35	.236
	Daytona (FSL)	HiA	2	2	1.64	7	7	0	0	38	31	3	4	46	1.24	0.91	.218
	Iowa (PCL)	AAA	1	0	1.50	1	1	0	0	6	5	1	3	4	0.40	1.33	.227
2010	Iowa (PCL)	AAA	11	8	4.63	32	25	0	0	157	153	20	48	119	0.86	1.28	.256
Minor League Totals			23	17	3.74	69	54	1	0	334	302	35	107	318	0.88	1.22	.241

16 ROBINSON CHIRINOS, C

Born: June 5, 1984. **B-T:** R-R. **Ht.:** 6-1. **Wt.:** 195. **Signed:** Venezuela, 2000. **Signed by:** Hector Ortega.

Chirinos was stalling in Double-A when the Cubs decided to move him behind the plate, making him a viable prospect and even jump-starting his bat. Calling games has given him a better understanding of hitting, and he has batted .310/.416/.543 since donning the tools of ignorance. He earned Southern League all-star recognition in 2010 and hit .471 in the playoffs. Chirinos always had shown an ability to handle the bat and control the strike zone, and now he has developed average power to all fields. He projects as a possible .275 hitter with 15 homers a year. Even more surprising is how quickly he has taken to catching. Managers rated him the best defensive backstop in the SL. Chirinos receives the ball and calls games like he has been doing so for years. He has solid arm strength, though his release is long and drops his pop times into the 1.95-2.05 second range. He still threw out 32 percent of basestealers in 2010. He's working on framing pitches and other nuances of the position, and he has the soft hands and quick feet to make it happen. He has below-average speed but isn't a bad runner for a catcher. The Cubs don't need a starting catcher with Geovany Soto on hand, but Chirinos could be a quality backup as a useful righthanded bat who can fill in behind the plate and around the infield.

Year	Club (League)	Class	AVG	G	AB	R	H	2B	3B	HR	RBI	BB	SO	SB	CS	OBP	SLG
2001	Cubs (AZL)	R	.234	47	154	15	36	12	0	2	15	10	42	4	3	.292	.351
2002	Boise (NWL)	SS	.247	62	231	35	57	15	2	8	38	16	66	5	2	.311	.433
2003	Lansing (MWL)	LoA	.232	108	362	51	84	27	1	7	39	28	82	10	2	.298	.370
2004	Lansing (MWL)	LoA	.241	84	319	56	77	18	6	7	39	25	70	7	2	.313	.401

2005	Daytona (FSL)	HiA	.273	74	231	30	63	6	0	7	27	16	42	3	4	.325	.390
2006	Peoria (MWL)	LoA	.242	126	433	74	105	30	2	9	47	69	79	19	10	.360	.383
2007	Daytona (FSL)	HiA	.259	79	239	35	62	14	2	3	20	37	48	8	5	.385	.372
	Tennessee (SL)	AA	.220	42	127	11	28	4	2	2	16	13	31	1	1	.298	.331
2008	Tennessee (SL)	AA	.243	38	103	12	25	7	3	0	8	10	18	0	0	.304	.369
	Cubs (AZL)	R	.462	4	13	5	6	1	1	0	3	6	2	1	0	.632	.692
	Daytona (FSL)	HiA	.283	37	120	22	34	4	2	5	18	26	21	3	1	.431	.475
2009	Daytona (FSL)	HiA	.300	69	227	40	68	13	5	11	47	35	40	2	2	.400	.546
	Tennessee (SL)	AA	.257	12	35	4	9	3	0	0	5	7	4	0	1	.372	.343
2010	Tennessee (SL)	AA	.318	77	264	53	84	24	0	15	64	42	35	1	5	.412	.580
	Iowa (PCL)	AAA	.364	15	55	10	20	4	0	3	10	2	8	0	0	.435	.600
Minor League Totals			.260	874	2913	453	758	182	26	79	396	342	588	64	38	.350	.422

17 WELINGTON CASTILLO, C

Born: April 24, 1987. **B-T:** R-R. **Ht.:** 6-0. **Wt.:** 200. **Signed:** Dominican Republic, 2004. **Signed by:** Jose Serra.

There's debate within the organization whether Castillo or Robinson Chirinos is the system's best catching prospect. Castillo's proponents point out that he's three years younger, throws better and has proven himself in Triple-A. He even hit his first big league homer last September, capping a rebound from his worst year as a pro in 2009. Castillo matured last season and implemented suggestions from Cubs coaches. He stopped selling out for power at the plate and still slugged a career-high .498. He has average pop, though he lacks quality bat speed and gives away too many at-bats with his impatient approach, so he probably won't hit for much of an average. Defensively, Castillo improved his focus and cleaned up his receiving and game-calling, which still need further work. He has a stronger arm and quicker release than Chirinos, and he erased 39 percent of basestealers in 2010. He has little speed, though he was in better shape and played with more energy last year. It's easier to project Castillo developing into a regular than it is with Chirinos. Neither figures to displace Geovany Soto, and if Koyie Hill caddies for Soto again, then Castillo and Chirinos will share time in Iowa this year.

Year	Club (League)	Class	AVG	G	AB	R	H	2B	3B	HR	RBI	BB	SO	SB	CS	OBP	SLG
2005	Cubs (DSL)	R	.289	60	204	29	59	14	0	1	28	19	28	1	2	.370	.373
2006	Boise (NWL)	SS	.167	3	6	1	1	0	0	0	0	1	0	0	0	.286	.167
	Cubs (AZL)	R	.192	7	26	4	5	0	0	0	0	1	6	0	0	.250	.192
2007	Peoria (MWL)	LoA	.271	98	317	41	86	11	2	11	44	23	77	1	3	.334	.423
2008	Daytona (FSL)	HiA	.273	33	121	15	33	8	0	0	12	4	23	1	0	.299	.339
	Tennessee (SL)	AA	.298	57	198	25	59	11	0	4	24	14	50	0	0	.362	.414
	Iowa (PCL)	AAA	.200	1	5	0	1	0	0	0	1	0	1	0	0	.200	.200
2009	Tennessee (SL)	AA	.232	95	319	27	74	16	0	11	39	15	71	1	0	.275	.386
2010	Iowa (PCL)	AAA	.255	69	239	35	61	17	1	13	59	19	58	0	2	.317	.498
	Chicago (NL)	MAJ	.300	7	20	3	6	4	0	1	5	1	7	0	0	.333	.650
Major League Totals			.300	7	20	3	6	4	0	1	5	1	7	0	0	.333	.650
Minor League Totals			.264	423	1435	177	379	77	3	40	207	96	314	4	7	.323	.406

18 MARCUS MATEO, RHP

Born: April 18, 1984. **B-T:** R-R. **Ht.:** 6-1. **Wt.:** 160. **Signed:** Dominican Republic, 2004. **Signed by:** Johnny Almaraz (Reds).

Mateo became the second member of his family to pitch for the Cubs when he got the call last August, following in the footsteps of his cousin Juan Mateo. He posted a 10.32 ERA in his first 11 big league appearances, but he settled down to pitch scoreless ball in nine of his final 10 outings. Originally signed by the Reds, he came to Chicago in an August 2007 trade for Buck Coats and has flashed huge upside but not much consistency. Mateo settled down some when the Cubs made him a full-time reliever in mid-2009, and his stuff played up in shorter stints. He pushes triple digits with his fastball, usually working at 94-97. When it's on, his upper-80s slider might be the most unhittable pitch in the system. He has a mediocre changeup and doesn't trust it enough. While Chicago has helped him calm down his delivery to some degree, Mateo still throws with a lot of effort at the expense of his command. He slashed his walk rate to a career-low 1.8 per nine innings in the minors last year. It's probably unrealistic to expect Mateo to become reliable enough to close games at the big league level, but his power stuff could make him a set-up man one day. He performed well in the Dominican League this winter, which could help his cause when he competes for a job in the Cubs' bullpen in spring training.

Year	Club (League)	Class	W	L	ERA	G	GS	CG	SV	IP	H	HR	BB	SO	G/A	WHIP	AVG
2004	Reds (DSL)	R	4	2	2.61	15	8	1	0	69	62	2	17	57	—	1.14	.238
2005	Reds (GCL)	R	2	3	4.30	13	4	0	0	44	54	2	10	23	—	1.45	.309
2006	Billings (PIO)	R	5	1	3.20	18	0	0	1	45	43	2	20	30	—	1.40	.262
2007	Dayton (MWL)	LoA	2	4	3.50	41	0	0	6	72	68	2	24	63	—	1.28	.260
2008	Peoria (MWL)	LoA	1	0	1.20	8	0	0	1	15	4	1	7	20	—	0.73	.085
	Daytona (FSL)	HiA	4	3	3.57	25	16	0	0	88	87	6	29	65	—	1.31	.257
2009	Daytona (FSL)	HiA	0	0	0.00	3	3	0	0	9	4	0	2	7	1.86	0.67	.143
	Tennessee (SL)	AA	3	6	4.07	34	14	0	0	97	97	9	43	70	1.05	1.44	.258

2010	Cubs (AZL)	R	0	0	0.00	1	0	0	0	1	0	0	0	1	—	0.00	.000
	Tennessee (SL)	AA	0	0	2.18	17	1	0	4	21	23	2	3	29	1.23	1.26	.258
	Iowa (PCL)	AAA	0	1	4.97	8	0	0	0	13	12	0	4	15	1.56	1.26	.235
	Chicago (NL)	MAJ	0	1	5.82	21	0	0	0	22	20	6	9	26	1.19	1.34	.247
Major League Totals			0	1	5.82	21	0	0	0	22	20	6	9	26	1.19	1.34	.247
Minor League Totals			21	20	3.38	183	46	1	12	474	454	26	159	380	1.16	1.29	.253

19 ROBINSON LOPEZ, RHP

Born: March 2, 1991. **B-T:** R-R. **Ht.:** 6-2. **Wt.:** 200. **Signed:** Dominican Republic, 2008. **Signed by:** Roberto Aquino (Braves).

When the Cubs fell out of the National League Central race last summer, they moved to trade veterans for prospects, sending Derrek Lee to the Braves for minor league pitchers Lopez, Ty'Relle Harris and Jeff Lorick. Lopez was the key to deal from Chicago's perspective, as he held his own as a teenage starter in low Class A. He's far from a finished product, but his fastball touched 97 mph at times in 2010 while usually sitting at 88-93 mph. He'll cut his fastball at times, too. Lopez has an advanced changeup for his age, throwing it with sink and deception. He throws two breaking pitches, with his slider flashing depth and bite in the low 80s, giving it more promise than his curveball. He works from a high three-quarters delivery and like many young pitchers, he seeks more consistent control and command. Lopez has a ceiling of a No. 3 starter and may begin 2011 where he finished last season, at low Class A Peoria.

Year	Club (League)	Class	W	L	ERA	G	GS	CG	SV	IP	H	HR	BB	SO	G/A	WHIP	AVG
2009	Braves (GCL)	R	3	1	1.29	11	8	0	0	49	41	1	12	42	1.00	1.09	.229
2010	Rome (SAL)	LoA	3	8	4.37	24	16	0	0	93	84	5	43	70	1.10	1.37	.241
	Peoria (MWL)	LoA	1	0	2.61	4	2	0	0	10	10	1	9	6	1.50	1.84	.256
Minor League Totals			7	9	3.26	39	26	0	0	152	135	7	64	118	1.10	1.31	.238

20 KYLE SMIT, RHP

Born: Oct. 14, 1987. **B-T:** R-R. **Ht.:** 6-3. **Wt.:** 165. **Drafted:** HS—Sparks, Nev., 2006 (5th round). **Signed by:** Paul Fryer (Dodgers).

In another midsummer deal from 2010, the Cubs swapped Ted Lilly and Ryan Theriot to the Dodgers for Blake DeWitt and minor league righthanders Smit and Brett Wallach. DeWitt could start at second base for Chicago this year, and both pitchers are keepers. Wallach has one of the best curveballs in the system as well as big league bloodlines—his father Tim played in five All-Star Games and won three Gold Gloves as a third baseman. Smit became a full-time reliever last season and took quickly to his new role. His stuff improved in shorter stints, he threw more strikes and he claimed a spot on the Cubs' 40-man roster. Tall and wiry, he resembles a young Ryan Madson. Smit has a deceptive delivery, allowing his 92-97 mph fastball to get on hitters quickly. His tight slider gives him a second strikeout pitch, and he uses a splitter as a change of pace. He figures to open 2011 in Triple-A, and he could make his major league debut by season's end.

Year	Club (League)	Class	W	L	ERA	G	GS	CG	SV	IP	H	HR	BB	SO	G/A	WHIP	AVG
2006	Dodgers (GCL)	R	0	2	4.09	6	3	0	1	11	15	1	2	9	—	1.55	.319
2007	Dodgers (GCL)	R	4	0	2.82	8	6	1	0	38	31	2	13	40	—	1.15	.217
	Great Lakes (MWL)	LoA	0	5	8.34	5	5	0	0	23	26	2	12	26	—	1.68	.280
2008	Great Lakes (MWL)	LoA	1	4	6.55	16	12	0	0	58	68	6	36	44	—	1.80	.296
	Ogden (PIO)	R	0	1	6.55	7	6	0	0	22	29	2	15	18	—	2.00	.319
2009	Great Lakes (MWL)	LoA	1	3	5.36	21	2	0	0	47	55	5	18	43	0.78	1.55	.284
	Inland Empire (CAL)	HiA	0	4	7.84	5	5	0	0	21	23	2	10	18	1.80	1.60	.288
2010	Inland Empire (CAL)	HiA	5	3	2.49	34	1	0	6	51	51	4	10	46	2.13	1.20	.262
	Chattanooga (SL)	AA	0	0	0.00	3	0	0	0	3	1	0	0	1	2.00	0.33	.100
	Tennessee (SL)	AA	5	1	1.96	12	0	0	1	18	23	0	4	16	1.43	1.47	.311
Minor League Totals			16	23	4.94	117	40	1	8	291	322	24	120	261	1.39	1.52	.278

21 LOGAN WATKINS, 2B/OF/SS

Born: Aug. 29, 1989. **B-T:** L-R. **Ht.:** 5-11. **Wt.:** 175. **Drafted:** HS—Goddard, Kan., 2008 (21st round). **Signed by:** Brandon Mozley.

Watkins flew under the scouting radar as a Kansas high schooler, but the Cubs liked his athleticism and intensity enough to give him $500,000 to buy him away from a Wichita State commitment. After hitting .326 in his first two years as a pro, he found the going rougher in his introduction to full-season ball in 2010. He did make adjustments and started turning on more pitches and hitting the ball with more authority in the second half. Watkins has a quick bat, good hand-eye coordination and plus speed, so he should hit for a solid average if he can smooth out the movement in his set-up. He won't ever have much home run power, but he's stronger than he looks and can sting balls into the gaps. His game is more about getting on base, and he shows patience and bunting skills. He's learning to steal bases, having succeeded on just two-thirds of his pro attempts. An all-Kansas quarterback and defensive back, Watkins is a versatile defender with above-average range, soft hands and solid arm strength. He has spent most of his career at second base, where he turns the pivot well on the double play.

BaseballAmerica.com

Chicago had resolved to get him time at shortstop and center field, and when that finally happened in 2010, he looked like a natural at both positions. Watkins plays with an intensity that inspires his teammates, and double-play partner Hak-Ju Lee in particular. They'll move up to high Class A together in 2011.

Year	Club (League)	Class	AVG	G	AB	R	H	2B	3B	HR	RBI	BB	SO	SB	CS	OBP	SLG
2008	Cubs (AZL)	R	.325	27	80	15	26	3	0	0	14	20	19	2	0	.462	.363
2009	Boise (NWL)	SS	.326	72	279	48	91	14	2	0	29	27	31	14	7	.389	.391
2010	Peoria (MWL)	LoA	.261	118	440	69	115	15	8	1	30	58	97	19	10	.351	.339
Minor League Totals			.290	217	799	132	232	32	10	1	73	105	147	35	17	.376	.359

22 RYAN FLAHERTY, 2B/3B

Born: July 27, 1986. **B-T:** L-R. **Ht.:** 6-3. **Wt.:** 220. **Drafted:** Vanderbilt, 2008 (1st round supplemental). **Signed by:** Antonio Grissom.

Flaherty batted cleanup behind Pedro Alvarez at Vanderbilt before signing for $1.5 million as the 41st overall pick in the 2008 draft. He's the son of Ed Flaherty, who has won two NCAA Division III College World Series as the head coach at Southern Maine. The Cubs wanted to separate him and D.J. LeMahieu, but they spent the last four months of the season together at Daytona after Flaherty was demoted. The two have a lot in common as big-bodied former Southeastern Conference stars who are best suited for third base. LeMahieu is more athletic and a better pure hitter, while Flaherty bats lefthanded and has more power. With a quick bat and some loft in his swing, he has pop to all fields and 20-homer potential, Flaherty has good instincts and a solid arm, but he's still seeking a full-time position. The Cubs have played him at second base and shortstop, but he lacks middle-infield actions, quickness and range. He has been erratic at third base, committing 17 errors in 74 games there. He played some left field in the Arizona Fall League after the season, and his ticket to the big leagues might be as an offensive-minded utilityman. Flaherty will try to solve Double-A pitching in 2011, when he and LeMahieu will shuttle around Tennessee's infield.

Year	Club (League)	Class	AVG	G	AB	R	H	2B	3B	HR	RBI	BB	SO	SB	CS	OBP	SLG
2008	Boise (NWL)	SS	.297	56	219	39	65	19	2	8	26	24	51	4	2	.369	.511
2009	Peoria (MWL)	LoA	.276	131	485	81	134	24	5	20	81	50	98	7	6	.344	.470
2010	Tennessee (SL)	AA	.183	23	71	10	13	2	0	1	9	10	12	1	0	.286	.254
	Daytona (FSL)	HiA	.286	108	420	65	120	34	3	9	63	41	74	6	3	.348	.445
Minor League Totals			.278	318	1195	195	332	79	10	38	179	125	235	18	11	.346	.456

23 REGGIE GOLDEN, OF

Born: Oct. 10, 1991. **B-T:** R-R. **Ht.:** 5-10. **Wt.:** 220. **Drafted:** HS—Wetumpka, Ala., 2010 (2nd round). **Signed by:** Tom Clark.

Multiple scouts have compared Golden to a young Kevin Mitchell for his stocky build and well above-average raw power. He showed off his pop during instructional league, when he homered to the opposite field off a 94 mph fastball from the White Sox' Brian Omogrosso, seven years his senior. Golden gutted through a severe hamstring pull as a high school senior to go in the second round of the 2010 draft, turning down an Alabama scholarship to sign for an above-slot $720,000. The hamstring limited him to 15 at-bats in his pro debut. With his short swing, fast bat and sheer strength, Golden qualifies as one of the top power hitters in the system. If everything comes together, he could be a five-tool player. He has the tools to hit, though he'll have to develop better plate discipline. Golden has plus speed and a chance to play center field, but he figures to lose a step as he fills out and probably will end up in right field. His solid arm will fit anywhere. He didn't face tough competition as an Alabama high schooler, so Golden may need time to adjust if the Cubs send him to low Class A in 2011.

Year	Club (League)	Class	AVG	G	AB	R	H	2B	3B	HR	RBI	BB	SO	SB	CS	OBP	SLG
2010	Cubs (AZL)	R	.333	4	15	3	5	1	0	0	1	1	7	1	0	.412	.400
Minor League Totals			.333	4	15	3	5	1	0	0	1	1	7	1	0	.412	.400

24 BEN WELLS, RHP

Born: Sept. 10, 1992. **B-T:** R-R. **Ht.:** 6-3. **Wt.:** 230. **Drafted:** HS—Bryant, Ark., 2010 (7th round). **Signed by:** Jim Crawford.

Wells was a late bloomer, spending most of his high school career pitching at 84-87 mph. His fastball jumped to 90-95 mph with sink right before the draft, and he threw a five-inning perfect game in the state 7-A finals. A handful of teams quietly followed Wells, who might have gone in the first three rounds had he been thoroughly crosschecked. He signed at the Aug. 16 deadline for $530,000. Wells backs up his fastball with a hard slider that has a chance to be a plus pitch, and he throws a splitter as well. He quickly picked up a changeup after reporting to instructional league, so Chicago may scrap the splitter. He's athletic and repeats his delivery well, though he's going to have to work to make sure his 6-foot-3, 230-pound body doesn't go soft on him. Wells' performance in minor league camp will determine whether he makes his pro debut at Peoria or short-season Boise.

Year	Club (League)	Class	W	L	ERA	G	GS	CG	SV	IP	H	HR	BB	SO	G/A	WHIP	AVG
2010	Did Not Play—Signed Late																

25 AARON KURCZ, RHP

Born: Aug. 8, 1990. **B-T:** R-R. **Ht.:** 6-1. **Wt.:** 170. **Drafted:** JC of Southern Nevada, 2010 (10th round). **Signed by:** Steve McFarland.

Kurcz spent his college freshman year at the Air Force Academy in 2009 before deciding he wanted to pursue a career in baseball. He transferred to the JC of Southern Nevada, where he benefited from the exposure that came from playing with Bryce Harper, the No. 1 overall pick in the 2010 draft. The Cubs signed him away from an Oral Roberts commitment for $125,000 in the 10th round. Kurcz struck out 48 in 27 innings in his pro debut, thanks to a 91-95 mph fastball and a deceptive three-quarters breaking ball with good bite. He flashed a plus changeup in instructional league, leading Chicago to consider developing him as a starter. At worst, he'd get more innings to work on honing a more consistent delivery, which would lead to improved control. His small, wiry frame scared some clubs off, but his arm works well and he was durable enough to maintain his stuff last summer. If the Cubs keep him in the bullpen, Kurcz could be the first member of their 2010 draft class to reach Wrigley Field. He'll begin his first full pro season in Class A, possibly skipping a level and jumping to Daytona.

Year	Club (League)	Class	W	L	ERA	G	GS	CG	SV	IP	H	HR	BB	SO	G/A	WHIP	AVG
2010	Cubs (AZL)	R	0	0	0.00	1	0	0	0	1	0	0	0	2	0.00	0.00	.000
	Boise (NWL)	SS	2	1	2.05	25	0	0	9	26	15	2	11	46	0.60	0.99	.161
Minor League Totals			2	1	1.98	26	0	0	9	27	15	2	11	48	0.57	0.95	.156

26 BROOKS RALEY, LHP

Born: June 29, 1988. **B-T:** L-L. **Ht.:** 6-3. **Wt.:** 185. **Drafted:** Texas A&M, 2009 (6th round). **Signed by:** Trey Forkerway.

Raley was one of college baseball's top two-way players in 2009, when he leveraged his sophomore-eligible status into a $750,000 bonus as a sixth-round pick. Though he could have been drafted as a center fielder/leadoff hitter, teams preferred him on the mound. The biggest knock on Raley was his lack of an out pitch, but the Cubs believe he addressed that by improving his curveball during his first full pro season. Focusing solely on pitching for the first time also helped his sinker, which bumped up a tick or two to 88-92 mph last year. His changeup also got better as Chicago forced him to throw it more often. Raley is extremely athletic and repeats his delivery well, so he has no problem filling the strike zone. His command could stand some improvement, however. He loves to compete and challenges hitters on the inside corner, almost to a fault. Raley had no trouble handling high Class A in his first full pro season, and he'll spend 2011 in Double-A. He has a ceiling of a No. 4 starter.

Year	Club (League)	Class	W	L	ERA	G	GS	CG	SV	IP	H	HR	BB	SO	G/A	WHIP	AVG
2009	Cubs (AZL)	R	0	1	4.15	3	3	0	0	4	2	1	2	3	1.50	0.92	.125
	Boise (NWL)	SS	0	0	1.42	2	0	0	0	6	3	1	1	2	1.50	0.63	.150
2010	Daytona (FSL)	HiA	8	6	3.50	27	27	0	0	136	151	9	43	97	1.18	1.42	.284
Minor League Totals			8	7	3.43	32	30	0	0	147	156	11	46	102	1.21	1.37	.275

27 JUNIOR LAKE, SS/3B

Born: March 27, 1990. **B-T:** R-R. **Ht.:** 6-2. **Wt.:** 200. **Signed:** Dominican Republic, 2007. **Signed by:** Jose Serra.

Born three days after Dominican countryman Starlin Castro, Lake teamed with him in the Rookie-level Arizona League in 2008. While Castro sped to the majors less than two years later, Lake was in Class A. He still has an impressive package of raw tools and work to do to refine them. His size, strength and quick hands give him plus raw power, but he has holes in his swing and chases too many pitches out of the strike zone. He showed more patience in 2010, but his plate discipline still leaves a lot to be desired. His speed and skills on the bases took a step back, and he's now a below-average runner. Lake's signature tool is his cannon arm, which grades as an 80 on the 20-80 scouting scale. He doesn't always harness it, contributing to his 41 errors last year. His hands are an asset, but he lacks the range to stick at shortstop and needs to improve his overall defensive focus. If he doesn't make progress in 2011, it will become tempting to think of his arm on the mound. Lake probably will return to high Class A because he's best suited for third base, as are Double-A bound D.J. LeMahieu and Ryan Flaherty.

Year	Club (League)	Class	AVG	G	AB	R	H	2B	3B	HR	RBI	BB	SO	SB	CS	OBP	SLG
2007	Cubs (DSL)	R	.274	62	223	41	61	16	2	3	30	16	53	9	3	.341	.404
2008	Cubs (AZL)	R	.286	47	168	24	48	4	6	2	23	13	42	12	2	.335	.417
2009	Peoria (MWL)	LoA	.248	131	463	71	115	19	7	7	42	18	138	10	7	.277	.365
2010	Daytona (FSL)	HiA	.264	120	394	56	104	18	4	9	46	35	99	13	9	.333	.398
Minor League Totals			.263	360	1248	192	328	57	19	21	141	82	332	44	21	.315	.389

28 JAE-HOON HA, OF

Born: Oct. 29, 1990. **B-T:** R-R. **Ht.:** 6-1. **Wt.:** 185. **Signed:** Korea, 2008. **Signed by:** Steve Wilson/Aaron Tassano.

Though the Cubs signed Ha as a catcher out of Korea in 2008, he made his pro debut as an outfielder the following year at Boise. They worked him behind the plate in instructional league afterward, but he couldn't overcome a case of the yips on throws to second base. Ha returned to right field and had a strong 2010 season in low Class A at age 19, leading Peoria in batting (.317) and slugging (.468) after arriving from extended spring training in late May. He caught fire in the final month, when he hit .364/.370/.537, and one club official credited him with having the most competitive at-bats of any Chicago farmhand. Ha added some loft and backspin to his stroke last year, and he projects to have power to the gaps while maxing out at 15 homers per season. He could hit for a solid average as well, though a more disciplined approach would help. He has average speed and runs the bases well. Ha gets good breaks on balls from the outfield corners and he can fill in as a center fielder for short stints. With his strong, accurate arm, he fits best in right field. Whether Ha can develop into an everyday outfielder at the big league level remains to be seen, but he definitely has caught the Cubs' attention. He'll advance to high Class A in 2011.

Year	Club (League)	Class	AVG	G	AB	R	H	2B	3B	HR	RBI	BB	SO	SB	CS	OBP	SLG
2009	Boise (NWL)	SS	.242	65	248	31	60	15	0	2	37	6	31	5	5	.264	.327
2010	Peoria (MWL)	LoA	.317	77	293	36	93	15	4	7	46	10	45	9	4	.334	.468
Minor League Totals			.283	142	541	67	153	30	4	9	83	16	76	14	9	.302	.403

29 ESMAILIN CARIDAD, RHP

Born: Oct. 28, 1983. **B-T:** R-R. **Ht.:** 5-10. **Wt.:** 195. **Signed:** Dominican Republic, 2007. **Signed by:** Jose Serra.

Like Alfonso Soriano, Caridad is a Dominican who began his pro career with Japan's Hiroshima Carp and played briefly in the Japanese majors before using a technicality to become a free agent. The Cubs signed Caridad in December 2007 for $175,000 and an invitation to big league camp. He reached the big leagues at the end of his second U.S. season, earning manager Lou Piniella's trust by not allowing a run in 11 September outings. Caridad made Chicago's Opening Day roster last April, but made just four appearances before going on the disabled list with elbow problems. He avoided surgery, but Caridad wasted most of the year with two stints on the DL, pitching just 16 innings between the majors and rehab assignments. When healthy, he can reach 96 mph with his fastball, though he's more effective pitching in the low 90s with more sink. While he's undersized, he generates velocity with arm speed and smooth mechanics rather than an abundance of effort. He relies mainly on his fastball and his command, because his slurvy breaking ball is average at best and his changeup is fringy. If he can put his elbow problems behind him, Caridad will get another opportunity to make Chicago's bullpen in spring training.

Year	Club (League)	Class	W	L	ERA	G	GS	CG	SV	IP	H	HR	BB	SO	G/A	WHIP	AVG
2007	Hiroshima (CL)	JPN	0	0	0.00	2	0	0	0	1	2	0	1	0	—	4.50	—
	Hiroshima (WeL)	JPN	1	2	4.06	25	0	0	1	31	21	—	17	30	—	1.23	—
2008	Daytona (FSL)	HiA	6	4	4.41	14	13	0	0	69	64	3	17	38	—	1.17	.252
	Tennessee (SL)	AA	7	3	3.16	14	14	0	0	83	67	15	21	50	—	1.06	.218
2009	Iowa (PCL)	AAA	5	10	4.17	25	25	0	0	132	139	17	46	114	0.66	1.41	.271
	Chicago (NL)	MAJ	1	0	1.40	14	0	0	0	19	15	0	3	17	0.63	0.93	.221
2010	Iowa (PCL)	AAA	0	1	3.00	2	0	0	0	3	2	1	1	2	0.75	1.00	.182
	Chicago (NL)	MAJ	0	1	11.25	8	0	0	0	4	4	1	5	4	1.00	2.25	.235
	Cubs (AZL)	R	0	0	13.50	1	1	0	0	1	3	0	0	1	—	4.50	.600
	Tennessee (SL)	AA	0	1	5.19	7	0	0	1	9	12	1	3	8	0.55	1.73	.324
Major League Totals			1	1	3.09	22	0	0	0	23	19	1	8	21	0.68	1.16	.224
Minor League Totals			18	19	3.98	63	53	0	1	296	287	37	88	213	0.66	1.27	.255
Japanese League Totals			0	0	0.00	2	0	0	0	1	2	0	1	0	—	4.50	—

30 DAE-EUN RHEE, RHP

Born: March 23, 1989. **B-T:** L-R. **Ht.:** 6-2. **Wt.:** 190. **Signed:** Korea, 2007. **Signed by:** Steve Wilson.

Signed for $525,000 out of a Korean high school in 2007, Rhee was so advanced that the Cubs sent him to low Class A to make his pro debut the next spring. He allowed just one run in his first three starts while showing precocious feel for three average or better pitches. He hurt his elbow in his fourth outing, however, leading to Tommy John surgery that cost him most of the 2009 season. Rhee was able to make a full schedule of starts in 2010, though he was kept on tight pitch counts. His stuff isn't as crisp as it was before he got hurt but Chicago sees signs that it's coming back. He has regained most but not all of his velocity, working at 88-92 mph with his fastball last year. His formerly plus changeup is just an average pitch for the moment, but his curveball showed improvement late in the season. He's back to throwing strikes, though he leaves too many pitches up in the strike zone. The Cubs consider 2010 a recovery year for Rhee and may have him return to high Class A to begin 2011. He'll still be just 22, giving him plenty of time to reclaim his potential as frontline starter.

Year	Club (League)	Class	W	L	ERA	G	GS	CG	SV	IP	H	HR	BB	SO	G/A	WHIP	AVG
2008	Peoria (MWL)	LoA	4	1	1.80	10	10	0	0	40	28	0	16	33	—	1.10	.194
2009	Cubs (AZL)	R	0	0	7.71	3	2	0	0	5	4	0	5	3	9.00	1.93	.235
	Boise (NWL)	SS	0	1	11.25	2	2	0	0	4	8	2	1	4	7.00	2.25	.421
2010	Daytona (FSL)	HiA	5	13	5.27	26	25	0	0	114	125	11	40	70	1.75	1.44	.279
Minor League Totals			9	15	4.64	41	39	0	0	163	165	13	62	110	1.88	1.39	.263

Chicago White Sox

BY PHIL ROGERS

White Sox general manager Ken Williams basked in the glow of a 2005 World Series title, the only one on either side of Chicago in the last 83 years. His maneuvering in 2004 and '05 played a huge role for that team, as he added Jose Contreras, Jermaine Dye, Freddy Garcia and A.J. Pierzynski with money freed by discarding Carlos Lee and Magglio Ordonez.

But 2005 is a long time ago.

In 10 seasons as GM, Williams has gotten the White Sox into the playoffs twice. His 2010 team featured just two truly homegrown regulars, Mark Buehrle and Gordon Beckham. Buehrle and Paul Konerko, the franchise's two cornerstone players during Williams' decade at the helm, already were in the organization when he replaced Ron Schueler after a 95-win season in 2000.

An old-school type, Schueler believed in scouting and player development. When the White Sox made the White Flag trade in 1997 and then let Albert Belle and Robin Ventura leave after 1998, Schueler reinvested those salaries in amateur talent (an admirable strategy, even if Joe Borchard did get $5 million). By contrast, Williams has shown little patience, constantly borrowing from tomorrow for today.

As a result of Williams' willingness to trade away prospects and the team's bungled efforts in Latin America, Chicago has one of the weakest farm systems in baseball. While Williams has dealt away 53 players (and counting) who have been ranked on Baseball America's annual White Sox Top 30 Prospects lists, few have come back to bite him—though righthander Daniel Hudson did go 7-1, 1.69 in 11 starts after being shipped to Arizona for Edwin Jackson in July.

Owner Jerry Reinsdorf rarely lets his team exceed Major League Baseball's bonus recommendations in the draft, a philosophy that has hurt the farm system. The White Sox gave out just $3.9 million on bonuses in the 2010 draft, the fifth-lowest total in the majors, though first-round pick Chris Sale emerged as their closer by season's end. Chicago ranks last over the last five years with a total of $18.5 million in bonuses.

The one area in which Chicago has invested heavily is in Cuban players. The White Sox are happy with the return on the $4.75 million major league contract they gave Alexei Ramirez in December 2007, and still have high hopes for slugging prospect Dayan Viciedo.

Williams remains popular with much of the White Sox's fan base, as it's easy to buy into his attempts to win as many games as possible every season. Critiques

The White Sox signed Paul Konerko to a three-year contract after the 2010 season

TOP 30 PROSPECTS

1. Chris Sale, lhp	16. Thomas Royse, rhp
2. Brent Morel, 3b/ss	17. Tyler Flowers, c
3. Dayan Viciedo, 1b/3b	18. Jordan Danks, of
4. Jared Mitchell, of	19. Andy Wilkins, 3b
5. Eduardo Escobar, ss	20. Tyler Saladino, ss
6. Gregori Infante, rhp	21. Nate Jones, rhp
7. Jacob Petricka, rhp	22. Jhonny Nunez, rhp
8. Brandon Short, of	23. Kyle Cofield, rhp
9. Trayce Thompson, of	24. Miguel Gonzalez, c
10. Anthony Carter, rhp	25. Andre Rienzo, rhp
11. Charlie Leesman, lhp	26. Josh Phegley, c
12. Santos Rodriguez, lhp	27. Matt Heidenreich, rhp
13. Addison Reed, rhp	28. Jon Gilmore, 3b
14. Mike Blanke, c	29. Cameron Bayne, rhp
15. Lucas Harrell, rhp	30. Spencer Arroyo, lhp

generally focus on his tempestuous relationship with manager Ozzie Guillen, which flared up several times in 2010, most notably when the club waited until the 22nd round to draft Guillen's son Ozney.

With the farm system unable to provide internal options, Williams turned to the free-agent market to bolster the big league club for 2011. Chicago gave Adam Dunn a four-year, $56 million contract, then brought back Konerko and Pierzynski with deals totaling another $45.5 million.

General Manager: Ken Williams. **Farm Director:** Buddy Bell. **Scouting Director:** Doug Laumann.

Class	Team	League	W	L	PCT	Finish*	Manager
Majors	Chicago White Sox	American	88	74	.543	6th (14)	Ozzie Guillen
Triple-A	Charlotte Knights	International	67	77	.465	t-10th (14)	Chris Chambliss
Double-A	Birmingham Barons	Southern	53	87	.379	10th (10)	Ever Magallanes
High A	Winston-Salem Dash	Carolina	81	58	.583	1st (8)	Joe McEwing
Low A	Kannapolis Intimidators	South Atlantic	65	74	.468	t-9th (14)	Ernie Young
Rookie	Bristol White Sox	Appalachian	32	36	.471	7th (10)	Ryan Newman
Rookie	Great Falls Voyagers	Pioneer	47	28	.627	1st (8)	Chris Cron
Overall 2010 Minor League Record			345	360	.489	21st (30)	

*Finish in overall standings (No. of teams in league). †League champion.

LAST YEAR'S TOP 30

Player, Pos.		Status
1.	Jared Mitchell, of	No. 4
2.	Tyler Flowers, c	No. 17
3.	Dan Hudson, rhp	(Diamondbacks)
4.	Brent Morel, 3b	No. 2
5.	Jordan Danks, of	No. 18
6.	Trayce Thompson, of	No. 9
7.	Dayan Viciedo, 3b	No. 3
8.	David Holmberg, lhp	(Diamondbacks)
9.	Clevelan Santeliz, rhp	(Free agent)
10.	Miguel Gonzalez, c	No. 24
11.	Josh Phegley, c	No. 26
12.	John Ely, rhp	(Dodgers)
13.	Sergio Santos, rhp	Majors
14.	Stefan Gartrell, of	Dropped out
15.	C.J. Retherford, 2b	Dropped out
16.	Carlos Torres, rhp	(Yomiuri/Japan)
17.	Lucas Harrell, rhp	No. 15
18.	Santos Rodriguez, lhp	No. 12
19.	Eduardo Escobar, ss	No. 5
20.	Nevin Griffith, rhp	Dropped out
21.	Christian Marrero, of/1b	Dropped out
22.	Jhonny Nunez, rhp	No. 22
23.	Dan Remenowsky, rhp	Dropped out
24.	Kyle Bellamy, rhp	Dropped out
25.	John Shelby, of	Dropped out
26.	Nate Jones, rhp	No. 21
27.	Charlie Leesman, lhp	No. 11
28.	Jon Link, rhp	(Dodgers)
29.	Jose Martinez, of	Dropped out
30.	Justin Collup, rhp	Dropped out

BEST TOOLS

Best Hitter for Average	Brent Morel
Best Power Hitter	Dayan Viciedo
Best Strike-Zone Discipline	Jimmy Gallagher
Fastest Baserunner	Qualon Millender
Best Athlete	Jared Mitchell
Best Fastball	Chris Sale
Best Curveball	Nate Jones
Best Slider	Chris Sale
Best Changeup	Chris Sale
Best Control	Dylan Axelrod
Best Defensive Catcher	Miguel Gonzalez
Best Defensive Infielder	Eduardo Escobar
Best Infield Arm	Brent Morel
Best Defensive Outfielder	Jordan Danks
Best Outfield Arm	Jose Martinez

PROJECTED 2014 LINEUP

Catcher	Mike Blanke
First Base	Adam Dunn
Second Base	Gordon Beckham
Third Base	Brent Morel
Shortstop	Eduardo Escobar
Left Field	Jared Mitchell
Center Field	Alexei Ramirez
Right Field	Alex Rios
Designated Hitter	Carlos Quentin
No. 1 Starter	John Danks
No. 2 Starter	Chris Sale
No. 3 Starter	Jake Peavy
No. 4 Starter	Gavin Floyd
No. 5 Starter	Mark Buehrle
Closer	Sergio Santos

TOP PROSPECTS OF THE DECADE

Year	Player, Pos.	2010 Org.
2001	Jon Rauch, rhp	Twins
2002	Joe Borchard, of	Giants
2003	Joe Borchard, of	Giants
2004	Joe Borchard, of	Giants
2005	Brian Anderson, of	Royals
2006	Bobby Jenks, rhp	White Sox
2007	Ryan Sweeney, of	Athletics
2008	Aaron Poreda, lhp	Padres
2009	Gordon Beckham, ss	White Sox
2010	Jared Mitchell, of	White Sox

TOP DRAFT PICKS OF THE DECADE

Year	Player, Pos.	2010 Org.
2001	Kris Honel, rhp	Chico (Golden)
2002	Royce Ring, lhp	Yankees
2003	Brian Anderson, of	Royals
2004	Josh Fields, 3b	Royals
2005	Lance Broadway, rhp	Blue Jays
2006	Kyle McCulloch, rhp	White Sox
2007	Aaron Poreda, lhp	Padres
2008	Gordon Beckham, ss	White Sox
2009	Jared Mitchell, of	White Sox
2010	Chris Sale, lhp	White Sox

LARGEST BONUSES IN CLUB HISTORY

Joe Borchard, 2003	$5,300,000
Dayan Viciedo, 2008	$4,000,000
Gordon Beckham, 2008	$2,600,000
Jason Stumm, 1999	$1,750,000
Chris Sale, 2010	$1,656,000

CHICAGO WHITE SOX

TOP 2011 ROOKIE: Chris Sale, lhp. He went from a first-round pick last June to closing big league games three months later.

BREAKOUT PROSPECT: Mike Blanke, c. Another 2010 draftee, the 14th-round pick's all-around tools are better than the White Sox expected.

SLEEPER: Drew Lee, 2b/ss. Yet another 2010 draft pick, he's a switch-hitter with a potent bat.

SOURCE OF TOP 30 TALENT			
Homegrown	24	Acquired	6
College	13	Trades	5
Junior college	2	Rule 5 draft	0
High school	4	Independent leagues	0
Draft-and-follow	0	Free agents/waivers	1
Nondrafted free agents	0		
International	5		

LF
Brandon Short (8)
Tyler Kuhn
Brady Shoemaker
Kyle Colligan

CF
Jared Mitchell (4)
Trayce Thompson (9)
Jordan Danks (18)
Jose Martinez
John Shelby III
Justin Greene
Randall Thorpe

RF
Stefan Gartrell
Nick Ciolli

3B
Brent Morel (2)
Andy Wilkins (19)
Jon Gilmore (28)
Juan Silverio
Rangel Ravelo

SS
Eduardo Escobar (5)
Tyler Saladino (20)
Greg Paiml

2B
Drew Lee
Ross Wilson
C.J. Retherford
Daniel Wagner

1B
Dayan Viciedo (3)
Christian Marrero
Jimmy Gallagher
Jose Vargas

C
Mike Blanke (14)
Tyler Flowers (17)
Miguel Gonzalez (24)
Josh Phegley (26)
Jason Bour

RHP

RHSP	RHRP
Jacob Petricka (7)	Gregori Infante (6)
Addison Reed (13)	Anthony Carter (10)
Lucas Harrell (15)	Jhonny Nunez (22)
Thomas Royse (16)	Kyle Cofield
Nate Jones (21)	Kyle Bellamy
Andre Rienzo (25)	Brian Omogrosso
Matt Heidenreich (27)	Duente Heath
Cameron Bayne (29)	Henry Mabee
Justin Collop	Dan Remenowsky
Nevin Griffith	Kevin Moran
Ryan Buch	J.R. Ballinger
Jeff Marquez	Leroy Hunt
Brandon Hynick	
Dylan Axelrod	
Johnnie Lowe	
Terry Doyle	
Stephen Sauer	
Charlie Shirek	

LHP

LHSP	LHRP
Chris Sale (1)	Santos Rodriguez (12)
Charlie Leesman (11)	Hector Santiago
Spencer Arroyo (30)	
Justin Edwards	

2010

BEST PURE HITTER: 3B Andy Wilkins (5) struggled with wood bats with Team USA in 2009, and some teams questioned how well his swing would play against quality pitching, but he hit .307/.396/.463 at Rookie-level Great Falls.

BEST POWER HITTER: Wilkins, who hit 42 homers in three seasons at Arkansas.

FASTEST RUNNER: OF Randall Thorpe (18) has plus-plus speed but is still figuring out how to get the most out of it on the bases. The White Sox also drafted him in the 29th round out of high school two years ago.

BEST DEFENSIVE PLAYER: SS Tyler Saladino (7) is a flashy defender with above-average range and arm strength. C Mike Blanke's (14) catch-and-throw skills were better than Chicago realized.

BEST FASTBALL: RHP Jacob Petricka (2) touched 98 mph in college and 100 during his pro debut. He usually works at 92-96. LHP Chris Sale (1) worked at 90-95 mph with good life as a college starter, then averaged 96 mph as big league reliever, hitting 100 mph three times in a game against the Royals.

BEST SECONDARY PITCH: Sale had one of the best changeups in the draft, though he didn't use it much in the majors. His slider was devastating at times when he came out of the bullpen, and he and RHP Addison Reed (3) have the best sliders in the system.

BEST PRO DEBUT: Sale finished the season as Chicago's closer, posting a 1.93 ERA, four saves and 32 strikeouts in 23 big league innings. Wilkins and 2B/SS Drew Lee (12) were all-stars in Rookie leagues, with Lee batting .282 and topping the Appy League with 24 doubles.

BEST ATHLETE: OF Dusty Harvard (34) was recruited by Colorado State and Wyoming in football before he decided to play baseball at Oklahoma State.

MOST INTRIGUING BACKGROUND: Unsigned OF Ozney Guillen's (22) father Ozzie manages the White Sox, and the fact the team waited so long to draft Ozney was a bone of contention between Ozzie and general manager Ken Williams. Unsigned 2B Audry Santana's (48) dad Rafael oversees the club's Dominican operations. Both fathers also played in the majors. INF Ross Wilson (10) was featured on MTV's "Two-A-Days" reality show as a high school quarterback in Alabama. His brother John Parker is a backup QB on the NFL's Atlanta Falcons.

CLOSEST TO THE MAJORS: Sale was the first 2010 draftee to reach the majors, and the quickest draftee to get there since the Reds' Ryan Wagner in 2003. Next in line are Reed and Saladino, with the latter finishing the summer in low Class A.

BEST LATE-ROUND PICK: The White Sox may have their catcher of the future in Blanke, who also has plus power.

THE ONE WHO GOT AWAY: Chicago lost out on projectable RHP Matthew Grimes (4), who will attend Georgia Tech, and offensive-minded 2B Josef Terry (8), who transferred from Cerritos (Calif.) JC to Cal State Fullerton.

ASSESSMENT: Sale projected to go as high as No. 4 overall before his signability worried teams, yet the White Sox were able to land him for slot money ($1,656,000) at No. 13 and got an almost immediate return on their investment.

2009

The jury is still out on this group after OF Jared Mitchell (1) and C Josh Phegley (1s) barely played in 2010, and OF Trayce Thompson (2) looked overmatched in low Class A. LHP Dennis Holmberg (3) was part of the Edwin Jackson trade with the Diamondbacks.

GRADE: C

2008

The White Sox will build their lineup around 2B Gordon Beckham (1), and 3B/SS Brent Morel (3) will contribute as well. RHP Dan Hudson (5), who blossomed after Chicago sent him to Arizona in the Jackson deal, could be a solid No. 3 starter. LHP Charlie Leesman (11) is a nice sleeper.

GRADE: A

2007

LHP Aaron Poreda (1) and RHP John Ely (3) have reached the majors, but neither has high upside and the White Sox used them in trades for Jake Peavy and Juan Pierre. The best prospect from this crop still in this system is erratic RHP Nate Jones (5).

GRADE: D

2006

This draft may not produce a single player who ever plays for Chicago. They traded RHP Kanekoa Texeira (22), the only big league so far, and no member of this class appears on our White Sox Top 30.

GRADE: F

Draft analysis by Jim Callis. Numbers in parentheses indicate draft rounds.

CHRIS
SALE, LHP

Born: March 30, 1989. **Bats:** L. **Throws:** L.
Height: 6-6. **Weight:** 172. **Drafted:** Florida
Gulf Coast, 2010 (1st round). **Signed by:** Jose
Ortega.

RON VESELY

Sale not only became the first player from the 2010 draft to reach the big leagues, he also finished the season closing games for a contender. His quick rise couldn't have been forseen when he came out of Lakeland (Fla.) High. The Rockies selected him in the 21st round of the 2007 draft, but he failed to attract interest from Florida's college powers and wound up at Florida Gulf Coast, which started its program in 2003. He got off to a rough start, with an awful fall ball season where his only usable pitch was his changeup. He worked out of the bullpen as a freshman, then lowered his arm slot that summer and improved the velocity and life on his pitches. He exploded by ranking as the top talent in the summer Cape Cod League after his sophomore season, then went 11-0, 2.01 with 146 strikeouts in 103 innings last spring. Some clubs rated him as the best college pitching prospect in the 2010 draft, but teams also worried about his asking price, making him available to Chicago with the No. 13 overall pick. The White Sox signed Sale for the slot recommendation of $1.656 million—along with the promise that he'd get every opportunity to race through the minors. He made his big league debut on Aug. 6, faster than any draftee since the Reds' Ryan Wagner in 2003.

Sale has the stuff and lanky build to be a facsimile of future Hall of Famer Randy Johnson, throwing three plus pitches from a low three-quarters delivery. His fastball ranged from 90-95 mph with outstanding late life when he worked as a starter in college, and he averaged 96 mph out of the bullpen in the majors. He hit 100 mph three times in a game against the Royals. Chicago considered his changeup his best pitch when it drafted him—GM Ken Williams compares it to Mark Buehrle's—but he didn't use it much out of the bullpen. Sale used his slider more as a reliever, and it also played up, sitting in the high 80s and topping out at 90. That was important as his slider was questioned coming into the draft. His command is solid, though

SCOUTING GRADES

Fastball: 70.   **Command/**
Slider: 60.   **Control:** 55.
Changeup: 65. **Delivery:** 45.

*Based on 20-80 scouting scale, where
50 represents major league average, and
future projection rather than present tools.*

his arm angle leads to times when he doesn't stay on top of his pitches and leaves them up in the zone. Sale is unusually poised, capable of making adjustments and pitching out of trouble. Some scouts wonder how durable Sale will be because of his skinny frame, arm action and low slot. He has no history of arm problems, however.

Despite his immediate bullpen impact, the White Sox plan to develop Sale as a starter. He'll get the chance to make their rotation out of spring training, though it's more realistic to expect him to open the season at Triple-A Charlotte. If he stays healthy, he has the stuff to be a frontline starter or a closer.

Year	Club (League)	Class	W	L	ERA	G	GS	CG	SV	IP	H	HR	BB	SO	G/A	WHIP	AVG
2010	Winston-Salem (CAR)	HiA	0	0	2.25	4	0	0	0	4	3	0	2	4	2.00	1.25	.200
	Charlotte (IL)	AAA	0	0	2.84	7	0	0	0	6	3	2	4	15	3.00	1.11	.136
	Chicago (AL)	MAJ	2	1	1.93	21	0	0	4	23	15	2	10	32	1.83	1.07	.185
Major League Totals			2	1	1.93	21	0	0	4	23	15	2	10	32	1.83	1.07	.185
Minor League Totals			0	0	2.61	11	0	0	0	10	6	2	6	19	2.33	1.16	.162

2 BRENT MOREL, 3B/SS

Born: April 21, 1987. **B-T:** R-R. **Ht.:** 6-1. **Wt.:** 220. **Drafted:** Cal Poly, 2008 (3rd round). **Signed by:** Gary Woods/Derek Valenzuela.

A mature player who has handled every test in three pro seasons, Morel spent September as Chicago's third baseman. He hit .435 to win the Arizona Fall League batting title in 2009, then .322 last season. Morel has a compact, line-drive swing and does an excellent job recognizing pitches and adjusting to how pitchers are working against him. He covers the plate well and doesn't get overly anxious with two strikes, though he sometimes expands the strike zone, which limits his walk totals. He has shown more doubles than home run power, and some scouts question how much pop he'll have in the big leagues unless he adds more loft to his swing. Morel is an intelligent fielder with first-step quickness and a solid arm. He had strictly been a third baseman until moving to shortstop when Dayan Viciedo returned to Charlotte in August, and played errorless defense in 17 games there. He's a below-average runner. Morel has a shot at winning the White Sox's third-base job in 2011. Other options include Mark Teahen, Viciedo and Omar Vizquel, but Morel has more all-around upside than any of them.

Year	Club (League)	Class	AVG	G	AB	R	H	2B	3B	HR	RBI	BB	SO	SB	CS	OBP	SLG
2008	Great Falls (PIO)	R	.375	15	64	11	24	0	2	0	3	6	7	7	0	.437	.438
	Kannapolis (SAL)	LoA	.297	45	172	26	51	6	2	6	24	16	28	5	2	.359	.459
2009	Winston-Salem (CAR)	HiA	.281	128	481	82	135	33	1	16	79	38	66	25	9	.335	.453
2010	Birmingham (SL)	AA	.326	49	184	25	60	13	1	2	30	14	36	5	5	.376	.440
	Charlotte (IL)	AAA	.320	81	306	40	98	24	4	8	34	13	50	3	0	.348	.503
	Chicago (AL)	MAJ	.231	21	65	9	15	3	0	3	7	4	17	2	0	.271	.415
Major League Totals			.231	21	65	9	15	3	0	3	7	4	17	2	0	.271	.415
Minor League Totals			.305	318	1207	184	368	76	10	32	170	87	187	45	16	.354	.464

3 DAYAN VICIEDO, 1B/3B

Born: March 10, 1989. **B-T:** R-R. **Ht.:** 6-1. **Wt.:** 240. **Signed:** Cuba, 2008. **Signed by:** Doug Laumann/Jose Ortega.

An organizational favorite who has never let a $10 million big league contract affect his work ethic and interaction with teammates, Viciedo shook off a lackluster 2009 pro debut to hit 25 homers last season. That included five longballs in the majors during a midseason trial while Mark Teahen was on the disabled list. White Sox manager Ozzie Guillen nicknamed him "The Tank." Viciedo's strength, bat speed and hand-eye coordination give him game-changing power. But he rarely sees a pitch he doesn't like—he didn't draw a big league walk until his 83rd plate appearance—and pitchers can exploit his lack of patience. He has a strong arm and has worked hard on his defense at third base, but he's a well below-average athlete and runner who lacks quickness. He's not nearly as good a defender as Brent Morel and projects more as a first baseman or DH. He has done a good job with his conditioning since arriving overweight when he signed, but he could balloon if he loses focus. Given Viciedo's production as a rookie, not to mention Chicago's financial commitment, he could get a chance to earn a regular spot in the big league lineup in 2011, either at DH or on an infield corner. His lack of plate discipline could hold him back, however, and he could use some Triple-A time to work more on his defense.

Year	Club (League)	Class	AVG	G	AB	R	H	2B	3B	HR	RBI	BB	SO	SB	CS	OBP	SLG
2009	Birmingham (SL)	AA	.280	130	504	72	141	20	0	12	78	23	89	5	2	.317	.391
2010	Charlotte (IL)	AAA	.274	86	343	42	94	15	0	20	47	11	78	1	1	.308	.493
	Chicago (AL)	MAJ	.308	38	104	17	32	7	0	5	13	2	25	1	0	.321	.519
Major League Totals			.308	38	104	17	32	7	0	5	13	2	25	1	0	.321	.519
Minor League Totals			.277	216	847	114	235	35	0	32	125	34	167	6	3	.313	.432

4 JARED MITCHELL, OF

Born: Oct. 31, 1988. **B-T:** L-L. **Ht.:** 5-11. **Wt.:** 192. **Drafted:** Louisiana State, 2009 (1st round). **Signed by:** Warren Hughes.

Mitchell won national championships in football and baseball at Louisiana State, winning MVP honors at the College World Series shortly before signing for $1.2 million as the 23rd overall pick in the 2009 draft. He was the most electric player in the White Sox' big league camp early last spring, but tore a tendon in his left ankle after colliding with the outfield wall in a game against the Angels. The injury cost him the entire 2010 season. Mitchell is a tremendous athlete with good baseball aptitude despite his two-sport background, but he also has more learning to do. He's a promising hitter with an idea of the strike zone. He has some unnecessary movement in his approach, which Chicago has worked to smooth out. Before he got hurt, Mitchell showed the plus-plus speed to steal bases and cover the gaps in center field, though he's still honing his instincts in both areas. He doesn't have a lot of power, and it's possible that his below-average arm could relegate him to left field. The White Sox considered sending Mitchell to Double-A before he got hurt, and now they'll move him less aggressively. He returned to action in the Arizona Fall League but his speed hadn't fully returned, which is crucial to his game. Chicago believes he'll be back to 100 percent by spring training and ready to open 2011 at high Class A Winston-Salem.

Year	Club (League)	Class	AVG	G	AB	R	H	2B	3B	HR	RBI	BB	SO	SB	CS	OBP	SLG
2010	Did Not Play—Injured																

5 EDUARDO ESCOBAR, SS

Born: Jan. 5, 1989. **B-T:** B-R. **Ht.:** 5-10. **Wt.:** 150. **Signed:** Venezuela, 2006. **Signed by:** Amador Arias.

Escobar is a highly skilled fielder who could be the next in the long line of White Sox shortstops from Venezuela (Luis Aparicio, Ozzie Guillen, Omar Vizquel). He enjoyed his best season at the plate in 2010, driving the ball better than in the past and totaling 43 extra-base hits, one shy of his total in four previous pro seasons. He stung the ball in the Arizona Fall League, batting .300 with 13 extra-base hits in 28 games, and earned a spot on the 40-man roster. Escobar is a technically solid shortstop with plus range and a quick release that helps him get outs with an average arm. He sometimes tries to force plays, though he made just 25 errors in 136 games last season, a respectable amount for a 21-year-old shortstop. His bat remains a question mark, especially from the left side of the plate. He does have some strength that he has started to tap into, but power won't be a big part of his game and he needs to focus on doing a better job of controlling the strike zone. He has good speed but hasn't developed into a basestealing threat. The White Sox are pleased with Alexei Ramirez at shortstop, but Escobar could provide an alternative if he continues to make strides at the plate. He'll likely begin 2011 back at Double-A Birmingham but could earn big league consideration during the season.

Year	Club (League)	Class	AVG	G	AB	R	H	2B	3B	HR	RBI	BB	SO	SB	CS	OBP	SLG
2006	Orioles/White Sox (VSL)	R	.236	46	123	21	29	3	1	0	17	14	25	7	6	.317	.276
2007	White Sox2 (DSL)	R	.291	64	247	56	72	5	4	0	18	22	45	19	14	.359	.344
2008	Great Falls (PIO)	R	.417	6	24	6	10	2	1	1	4	2	3	1	1	.464	.708
	Kannapolis (SAL)	LoA	.267	60	243	37	65	6	1	0	22	13	65	4	3	.302	.300
2009	Kannapolis (SAL)	LoA	.256	128	464	64	119	10	7	3	41	29	91	20	6	.300	.328
2010	Winston-Salem (CAR)	HiA	.285	87	368	57	105	18	8	3	39	23	76	8	5	.327	.402
	Birmingham (SL)	AA	.262	49	202	22	53	8	3	3	22	9	35	3	0	.294	.376
Minor League Totals			.271	440	1671	263	453	52	25	10	163	112	340	62	35	.318	.350

6 GREGORI INFANTE, RHP

Born: July 10, 1987. **B-T:** R-R. **Ht.:** 6-2. **Wt.:** 185. **Signed:** Venezuela, 2006. **Signed by:** Amador Arias.

Nearly 19 when he signed in 2006, Infante was old for a Latin American prospect entering pro ball. In his first four pro seasons, primarily as a starter, Infante lacked consistency and developed blisters late in games. The White Sox decided to try him as a full-time reliever in 2010, and he shot from high Class A to the the big leagues. He didn't allow a run in five September appearances for Chicago. Infante can light up a radar gun as much as anyone in the system, working at 94-98 mph and capable of breaking triple digits, though he doesn't always know where his fastball is going. His secondary pitches need work, but he does have a power curveball that can buckle knees when it's on. He also has a mid-80s changeup, though he doesn't need it much in relief. He gets a lot of groundballs and didn't allow a home run in 2010. Infante could push to make the White Sox with a strong spring training. He has pitched just 31 innings above Class A and none in Triple-A, so he might be better off with some time in Charlotte. His raw power stuff gives him a ceiling as a closer, though his ultimate role will depend on how much command he develops.

Year	Club (League)	Class	W	L	ERA	G	GS	CG	SV	IP	H	HR	BB	SO	G/A	WHIP	AVG
2006	Orioles/White Sox (VSL)	R	0	0	8.61	10	2	0	0	23	25	2	26	17	—	2.22	.291
2007	Bristol (APP)	R	2	3	4.01	10	8	0	0	34	25	1	23	33	—	1.43	.207
2008	Kannapolis (SAL)	LoA	1	2	6.59	4	3	0	0	14	16	0	12	11	—	2.05	.286
	Bristol (APP)	R	4	3	2.66	13	12	0	0	74	63	4	19	57	—	1.10	.232
2009	Kannapolis (SAL)	LoA	3	5	3.26	15	15	0	0	88	76	4	37	75	1.54	1.28	.239
	Winston-Salem (CAR)	HiA	1	2	7.84	6	5	0	0	21	18	3	23	10	1.00	1.98	.243
2010	Winston-Salem (CAR)	HiA	1	2	3.48	31	0	0	9	34	32	0	15	35	2.56	1.40	.250
	Birmingham (SL)	AA	2	2	3.42	24	0	0	3	26	23	0	12	34	1.25	1.33	.235
	Chicago (AL)	MAJ	0	0	0.00	5	0	0	0	5	2	0	4	5	0.50	1.29	.133
Major League Totals			0	0	0.00	5	0	0	0	5	2	0	4	5	0.50	1.29	.133
Minor League Totals			14	19	4.07	113	45	0	12	314	278	14	167	272	0.50	1.42	.241

7 JACOB PETRICKA, RHP

Born: June 5, 1988. **B-T:** R-R. **Ht.:** 6-5. **Wt.:** 170. **Drafted:** Indiana State, 2010 (2nd round). **Signed by:** Mike Shirley.

The White Sox drafted Petricka in the 38th round out of a Minnesota high school in 2006, but had to wait four years to sign him. He had Tommy John surgery as a freshman at Iowa Western CC, and his velocity began to rise when he was a redshirt sophomore at Indiana State in 2009, when the Yankees drafted him in the 34th round. Petricka returned to the Sycamores, continued to add velocity and signed for $540,000 as a second-round pick in June. Petricka has a powerful, relatively low-mileage arm. He usually pitches at 92-96 mph with his fastball, and Chicago clocked him at 100 during his first pro summer. He holds his velocity deep into games. He has developed a solid breaking ball as his No. 2 pitch and he flashes a serviceable changeup. To keep his innings down, he moved to the bullpen after a promotion to low Class A Kannapolis. Relief may be his best role, because he has just one plus pitch and sometimes has difficulty repeating his delivery, which costs him command. The White Sox lack starting-pitching depth, so Petricka will remain in the rotation for now. He's still learning how to use his stuff and shouldn't be expected to move as quickly as recent Chicago draft picks Daniel Hudson and Chris Sale. Petricka should open 2011 in high Class A.

Year	Club (League)	Class	W	L	ERA	G	GS	CG	SV	IP	H	HR	BB	SO	G/A	WHIP	AVG
2010	Bristol (APP)	R	2	4	2.86	8	8	0	0	35	25	1	7	38	2.87	0.92	.197
	Kannapolis (SAL)	LoA	0	1	3.72	9	0	0	0	10	13	0	8	10	2.20	2.17	.295
Minor League Totals			2	5	3.05	17	8	0	0	44	38	1	15	48	2.70	1.20	.222

8 BRANDON SHORT, OF

Born: Sept. 9, 1988. **B-T:** R-R. **Ht.:** 6-1. **Wt.:** 175. **Drafted:** St. John's River (Fla.) Cc, 2008 (28th Round). **Signed by:** Joe Siers.

"Irrepressible" might be the word that best fits Short, who signed for $20,000 as a 28th-round pick in 2008. He made a positive impression on White Sox manager Ozzie Guillen when brought over to big league camp during spring training, then hit .352 in the first two months of the 2010 season before cooling off, a strong enough start to help him win the Carolina League batting title. He missed the final two weeks of the season with a strained oblique. Short has shown steady development as a hitter in each of his three pro seasons. His edge comes from unusually quick hands that allow him to let pitches get in deeper on him before he commits. He's able to fight off good pitches and punish hangers. He's learning to drive the ball more consistently. He likes to hack and seldom works walks. Short has average speed and a below-average arm and split time between right and center field in 2010. His baserunning instincts are a liability, and he hasn't learned to read pitchers. Short is on the same career path that John Shelby III was on a couple of years ago, and 2011 will show if he can avoid stalling in Double-A like Shelby did. He may be a tweener, lacking the range to be a regular center fielder and the true power to be an everyday player on an outfield corner in the big leagues.

Year	Club (League)	Class	AVG	G	AB	R	H	2B	3B	HR	RBI	BB	SO	SB	CS	OBP	SLG
2008	Bristol (APP)	R	.273	49	183	30	50	13	2	1	23	16	37	14	7	.357	.383
2009	Kannapolis (SAL)	LoA	.284	97	345	56	98	19	3	7	55	27	78	12	1	.342	.417
2010	Winston-Salem (CAR)	HiA	.316	116	491	77	155	31	5	15	79	28	107	7	10	.365	.491
Minor League Totals			.297	262	1019	163	303	63	10	23	157	71	222	33	18	.356	.447

9 TRAYCE THOMPSON, OF

Born: March 15, 1991. **B-T:** R-R. **Ht.:** 6-4. **Wt.:** 200. **Drafted:** HS—Santa Margarita, Calif., 2009 (2nd Round). **Signed by:** Mike Baker.

The son of former No. 1 overall NBA draft pick Mychal Thompson, Trayce is one of just three players to receive an over-slot bonus from the White Sox in the last five drafts, joining Gordon Beckham and outfield prospect Jordan Danks. Signed for $625,000 as a second-round pick in 2009, Thompson got off to a slow start in his first full pro season before a pitch shattered his right thumb in late May, sidelining him for nearly three months. As an athletic slugger from Southern California's high school ranks, Thompson drew some comparisons to Mike Stanton as an amateur. He's definitely a high-ceiling player with enormous power potential, but filling Stanton's spikes will be tough. He has hit just .218 as a pro, in large part because he chases breaking pitches out of the strike zone. He has a long swing that leads to high strike-out totals. He's young, however, and has shown an ability to make adjustments. He has solid range and speed to go with average arm strength, but needs to be more aggressive in the field and on the bases. Thompson will return to low Class A in 2011. He'll need time to develop, but few White Sox prospects can match his potential. He wants to stay in center field but seems destined for a corner spot.

Year	Club (League)	Class	AVG	G	AB	R	H	2B	3B	HR	RBI	BB	SO	SB	CS	OBP	SLG
2009	Bristol (APP)	R	.188	25	85	8	16	3	1	0	10	4	33	2	0	.247	.247
	Great Falls (PIO)	R	.238	7	21	2	5	0	0	0	0	3	8	1	0	.333	.238
2010	Kannapolis (SAL)	LoA	.229	58	210	28	48	13	3	8	31	21	69	6	4	.302	.433
Minor League Totals			.218	90	316	38	69	16	4	8	41	28	110	9	4	.290	.370

10 ANTHONY CARTER, RHP

Born: April 4, 1986. **B-T:** R-R. **Ht.:** 6-3. **Wt.:** 180. **Drafted:** Georgia Perimeter JC, 2005 (26th round). **Signed by:** John Tumminia/Alex Slattery.

Like Gregori Infante, Carter took off in 2010 after moving to the bullpen in his fifth pro season. He had instant success, tying for the Double-A Southern League lead with 22 saves. He followed that with a successful stint with Team USA in the fall, making four scoreless appearances and earning a save against highly-regarded Cuba in the Pan Am qualifying tournament in Puerto Rico, then was added to the White Sox's 40-man roster. Carter can get outs in the late innings with his fastball, which sits at 93-94 mph and spikes as high as 97, though he gets into trouble when he leaves it up in the strike zone. He complements his heater with an 80-84 mph slider that grades as a plus pitch at times. He also can fool hitters with a changeup on occasion. His high three-quarters delivery provides some natural deception. In order to succeed at higher levels, he'll need to be more consistent with his control and command. He handled lefthanders easily in 2010 (.154/.245/.264) but surprisingly struggled against righties (.282/.338/.479). Carter figures to open 2011 as Charlotte's closer, but the White Sox are revamping their bullpen and will give him a long look in spring training. He could make his big league debut later in the year. His realistic ceiling is as a set-up man.

Year	Club (League)	Class	W	L	ERA	G	GS	CG	SV	IP	H	HR	BB	SO	G/A	WHIP	AVG
2006	Bristol (APP)	R	2	8	7.67	13	13	0	0	63	88	7	21	35	—	1.72	.321
2007	Great Falls (PIO)	R	5	3	3.93	15	15	0	0	71	78	6	17	62	—	1.34	.280
2008	Kannapolis (SAL)	LoA	5	2	2.77	11	11	0	0	62	47	5	11	66	—	0.94	.213
	Winston-Salem (CAR)	HiA	6	5	4.90	17	16	0	0	83	91	11	30	41	—	1.46	.278
2009	Winston-Salem (CAR)	HiA	11	7	4.36	27	27	1	0	155	149	21	43	119	0.84	1.24	.256
2010	Birmingham (SL)	AA	1	4	3.92	46	2	0	22	57	47	6	22	58	0.81	1.20	.226
Minor League Totals			30	29	4.57	129	84	1	22	491	500	56	144	381	0.83	1.31	.264

11 CHARLIE LEESMAN, LHP

Born: March 10, 1987. **B-T:** L-L. **Ht.:** 6-4. **Wt.:** 210. **Drafted:** Xavier, 2008 (11th round). **Signed by:** Mike Shirley/Phil Gulley.

There's nothing flashy about Leesman, but he has advanced quickly by never backing down from a challenge. An unsigned 40th-round pick of the Twins out of high school, he won just six games in three years at Xavier and posted a 5.32 ERA as a junior. Drafted on the basis of his arm strength, he has found more success as a pro. He received a nonroster invitation to big league camp in 2010 before splitting the season between high Class A and Double-A—doing his best pitching after his promotion. Leesman has a good mix of pitches but pitches behind in the count too much. His bread and butter is an 88-92 mph fastball that has some natural sink. He has improved his slider and changeup and has learned to mix in a few cutters. The slider has late bite and could develop into his out pitch. He also throws a curveball that has loose rotation. Leesman is equally effective against lefthanders and righthanders, and the White Sox will keep developing him as a starter. His makeup is an asset but he'll have to improve his command to carve out a major league role. He got knocked around in the Arizona Fall League, compiling an 11.81 ERA in 11 relief innings, but still stands out as one of the few legitimate pitching prospects in the upper levels of the system.

Year	Club (League)	Class	W	L	ERA	G	GS	CG	SV	IP	H	HR	BB	SO	G/A	WHIP	AVG
2008	Bristol (APP)	R	0	0	0.00	2	0	0	1	5	5	0	1	6	—	1.13	.263
	Kannapolis (SAL)	LoA	0	0	0.00	1	1	0	0	5	3	0	2	5	—	1.07	.188
2009	Kannapolis (SAL)	LoA	13	5	3.08	27	27	1	0	158	165	4	58	117	1.80	1.41	.275
2010	Winston-Salem (CAR)	HiA	9	4	5.10	17	17	0	0	85	98	6	44	39	1.84	1.68	.294
	Birmingham (SL)	AA	5	2	2.69	11	11	0	0	64	47	1	20	51	1.82	1.05	.210
Minor League Totals			27	11	3.45	58	56	1	1	316	318	11	125	218	1.81	1.40	.267

12 SANTOS RODRIGUEZ, LHP

Born: Jan. 2, 1988. **B-T:** L-L. **Ht.:** 6-5. **Wt.:** 180. **Signed:** Dominican Republic, 2006. **Signed by:** Roberto Aquino (Braves).

Rodriguez profiles as a classic late bloomer—assuming he can develop the durability that has failed him thus far. Acquired along with Brent Lillibridge, Tyler Flowers and third-base prospect Jon Gilmore from the Braves in the Javier Vazquez trade after the 2008 season, Rodriguez has one of the best arms in the system but never has pitched more than 40 innings in a season. He didn't pitch after July 22 last year, as the White Sox cautiously shut him down with nagging arm problems that weren't major and didn't require surgery. Rodriguez had his usual impact when he pitched out of the Winston-Salem bullpen, striking out 13.2 batters per nine innings and completing his third straight season without allowing a home run. His fastball has tremendous velocity, running from 93-98 mph, but he gets it from a max-effort delivery that leaves him with little command. He struggles with the consistency of his secondary pitches, though he has made strides with his changeup and throws it with good arm speed. His slurvy breaking ball is a potential average pitch. If he can tone down his wild arm action and improve his command, Rodriguez could pitch in the back of a major league bullpen primarily on his fastball alone. Chicago expects him at full strength in spring training and may send him to Double-A this year.

Year	Club (League)	Class	W	L	ERA	G	GS	CG	SV	IP	H	HR	BB	SO	G/A	WHIP	AVG
2007	Braves (GCL)	R	0	1	6.67	12	2	0	2	28	29	3	21	35	—	1.76	.248
2008	Braves (GCL)	R	1	2	2.79	14	0	0	5	29	16	0	13	45	—	1.00	.155
2009	Bristol (APP)	R	2	0	1.33	19	0	0	4	27	18	0	17	42	1.06	1.30	.189
	Kannapolis (SAL)	LoA	0	0	0.00	3	0	0	0	4	3	0	1	8	0.33	1.00	.200
2010	Winston-Salem (CAR)	HiA	2	0	3.57	32	0	0	0	40	27	0	32	59	1.42	1.46	.193
Minor League Totals			5	3	3.50	80	2	0	11	129	93	3	84	189	1.02	1.38	.198

13 ADDISON REED, RHP

Born: Dec. 27, 1988. **B-T:** L-R. **Ht.:** 6-4. **Wt.:** 215. **Drafted:** San Diego State, 2010 (3rd round). **Signed by:** George Kachigian.

Did a little bit of Stephen Strasburg rub off on Reed? The White Sox sure hope so. Reed, whose younger brother Austin signed with the Cubs as a 12th-round pick last summer, closed out games for Strasburg at San Diego State in 2009, compiling 20 saves and a 0.65 ERA. After Strasburg went No. 1 overall in the 2009 draft, Reed moved into his spot as the Aztecs' Friday-night starter in 2010. He went 8-2, 2.50 in 79 innings to push himself into the third round of the 2010 draft and earn a $358,200 bonus. He looked polished in his pro debut, using his fastball/slider combination to dominate Rookie-level Pioneer League hitters. Reed pairs a 91-95 mph fastball with a slider that some scouts grade as a plus-plus pitch. Righthanders have trouble against him because his fastball runs in on them and his slider has late bite. He commands both of those pitches, pounding the strike zone when he's on. His changeup is a below-average offering, and his ability to improve it will determine whether his future is in the rotation or the bullpen. Reed has excellent makeup and a confident presence on the mound. He could move quickly as a reliever, but Chicago plans on keeping him as a starter for the time being. He could skip a level and open 2011 in high Class A.

Year	Club (League)	Class	W	L	ERA	G	GS	CG	SV	IP	H	HR	BB	SO	G/A	WHIP	AVG
2010	Great Falls (PIO)	R	1	0	1.80	13	2	0	1	30	17	1	6	44	0.61	0.77	.162
Minor League Totals			1	0	1.80	13	2	0	1	30	17	1	6	44	0.61	0.77	.162

14 MIKE BLANKE, C

Born: Oct. 17, 1988. **B-T:** R-R. **Ht.:** 6-4. **Wt.:** 220. **Drafted:** Tampa, 2010 (14th round). **Signed by:** Joe Siers.

Blanke traveled a crooked path to the 2010 draft, going from Seton Hall in 2008 to St. Petersburg (Fla.) JC in 2009 and NCAA Division II Tampa last year before landing with the White Sox as a 14th-round selection. He was born in Canada but raised in Florida, and his father, who played in the Quebec Major Junior Hockey League, taught him to play baseball with an aggressive hockey mentality. He grew from about 5-foot-9 as a high school junior to his present 6-foot-4 frame and is still filling out. Signed for $65,000, he looks like a steal. Blanke had a reputation as a bat-first catcher coming out of the draft, but he opened eyes with both his power and his catching skills after signing, making the Pioneer League all-star team. His plus arm was considered his best tool coming out of college, and he threw out a league-best 35 percent of basestealers and both runners who attempted to steal against him in the PL playoffs. He moves well behind the plate, and in the words of Great Falls manager Chris Cron, Blanke "folds up real nice" for his size. He was also one of the most dangerous hitters in the league, showing a good approach and an ability to use the whole field. He shows above-average power potential, even to the opposite field. He has played first and third base in the past, but there's no reason he can't stay behind the plate. He'll open his first full pro season in low Class A.

Year	Club (League)	Class	AVG	G	AB	R	H	2B	3B	HR	RBI	BB	SO	SB	CS	OBP	SLG
2010	Great Falls (PIO)	R	.329	62	240	35	79	20	1	7	43	23	33	0	0	.400	.508
Minor League Totals			.329	62	240	35	79	20	1	7	43	23	33	0	0	.400	.508

15 LUCAS HARRELL, RHP

Born: June 3, 1985. **B-T:** B-R. **Ht.:** 6-2. **Wt.:** 200. **Drafted:** HS—Ozark, Mo., 2004 (4th round). **Signed by:** Alex Slattery.

In his seventh year as a pro, Harrell finally reached the major leagues in 2010. Winning his big league debut was a huge accomplishment after a shoulder injury forced him to spend more time off the field than on it from 2006-08, including missing all of 2007 following capsule surgery. He now has put together back-to-back healthy seasons, making 29 starts between the big leagues and Triple-A last year while also showing the ability to pitch out of the bullpen. Harrell's best pitch is a two-seam fastball he throws at 88-92 mph. Its sink and tail makes it an above-average pitch. His four-seamer peaks at 93 mph, though he seemed reluctant to throw it in the big leagues. Harrell uses good fastball command to set up a slurvy slider and a changeup with good sink. He mixes his pitches well and has nice feel for pitching. He has a ceiling as a back-of-the-rotation starter and also could find his niche as a middle reliever. The White Sox are coping with rotation uncertainty and rebuilding their bullpen, so they'll give Harrell a long look in spring training.

Year	Club (League)	Class	W	L	ERA	G	GS	CG	SV	IP	H	HR	BB	SO	G/A	WHIP	AVG
2004	Bristol (APP)	R	3	5	5.59	13	9	0	0	48	53	5	32	33	—	1.76	.282
2005	Kannapolis (SAL)	LoA	7	11	3.64	26	26	0	0	133	128	8	71	85	—	1.49	.248
2006	Winston-Salem (CAR)	HiA	7	2	2.45	17	17	0	0	92	58	3	44	70	—	1.11	.182
	Birmingham (SL)	AA	0	2	10.24	3	3	0	0	10	12	1	14	4	—	2.69	.316
2007	Did Not Play—Injured																
2008	Bristol (APP)	R	0	0	3.00	1	1	0	0	3	3	0	1	5	—	1.33	.273
	Kannapolis (SAL)	LoA	1	1	5.91	3	3	0	0	11	13	0	4	7	—	1.59	.302
	Birmingham (SL)	AA	3	3	3.46	11	10	0	0	55	56	3	19	34	—	1.37	.272
2009	Birmingham (SL)	AA	8	3	3.25	14	14	0	0	80	78	4	32	51	2.60	1.37	.264
	Charlotte (IL)	AAA	4	1	3.29	11	11	0	0	66	58	3	37	42	1.98	1.45	.246
2010	Charlotte (IL)	AAA	10	10	4.58	26	26	0	0	138	141	11	61	84	2.18	1.47	.268
	Chicago (AL)	MAJ	1	0	4.88	8	3	0	0	24	34	2	17	15	2.92	2.13	.337
Major League Totals			1	0	4.88	8	3	0	0	24	34	2	17	15	2.92	2.13	.337
Minor League Totals			43	38	3.86	125	120	0	0	635	600	38	315	415	2.24	1.44	.252

16 THOMAS ROYSE, RHP

Born: Sept. 7, 1988. **B-T:** R-R. **Ht.:** 6-5. **Wt.:** 210. **Drafted:** Louisville, 2010 (3rd round supplemental). **Signed by:** Phil Gulley.

Selected with the compensation pick the White Sox received after failing to sign Tennessee lefthander Bryan Morgado as a third-round choice in 2009, Royse looks like a potential steal after signing for $263,500. One Pioneer League coach who saw him wondered how Royse lasted 114 picks in the draft. Teams shied away from him because he doesn't have front-of-the-rotation velocity and has had health issues, including a compression fracture in his lower back that cut short his sophomore college season. He pitched 104 innings as Louisville's ace in 2010, going 9-1, 2.85 with 99 strikeouts, but encountered mild elbow problems after getting off to a fast start for Great Falls. Royse's fastball, which sits at 88-90 mph and peaks at 93 is effective because of its downward angle and natural sink. His slider is a plus pitch at times, eliciting swings and misses at its best, and Chicago was encouraged by the early improvements he made with his changeup. He repeats his delivery well and pounds the strike zone. With a healthy 2011 season, Royse could vault his way up the organization's pitching depth chart. He'll likely begin the season in low Class A.

Year	Club (League)	Class	W	L	ERA	G	GS	CG	SV	IP	H	HR	BB	SO	G/A	WHIP	AVG
2010	Great Falls (PIO)	R	1	1	3.41	10	8	0	0	34	28	2	6	28	2.33	0.99	.217
Minor League Totals			1	1	3.41	10	8	0	0	34	28	2	6	28	2.33	0.99	.217

17 TYLER FLOWERS, C

Born: Jan. 24, 1986. **B-T:** R-R. **Ht.:** 6-4. **Wt.:** 220. **Drafted:** Chipola (Fla.) JC, D/F 2005 (33rd round). **Signed by:** Al Goetz (Braves).

When the White Sox got Flowers from the Braves in the Javier Vazquez trade before the 2009 season, his bat seemed to be a given. The question was whether he could handle a pitching staff well enough to become a full-time regular behind the plate. His power was his calling card and made him one of the organization's top prospects—until he floundered in Triple-A last year. Flowers looked lost at the plate early in the season and never really recovered. He still has size, strength and raw power but didn't take advantage of hitter-friendly Knights Stadium in Charlotte, slugging a career-low .434. His plate discipline and pitch recognition regressed, especially when he got breaking balls in fastball counts, and Triple-A pitchers exploited the holes in his max-effort swing. While Flowers has improved his receiving skills, his stiff body and limited athleticism still raise concerns. He has an average arm and threw out 26 percent of basestealers last season. He's a well below-average runner who's a liability on the bases. Flowers hasn't earned the confidence of manager Ozzie Guillen, who rarely played him during a September callup, even after Chicago was eliminated from playoff contention. The White Sox had hoped Flowers would be ready when A.J. Pierzynski's contract expired after the 2010 season, but they re-signed Pierzynski and plan to use Ramon Castro as his backup. Flowers' power is still intriguing, so he'll return to Triple-A and try to erase memories of 2010.

Year	Club (League)	Class	AVG	G	AB	R	H	2B	3B	HR	RBI	BB	SO	SB	CS	OBP	SLG
2006	Danville (APP)	R	.279	34	129	24	36	9	0	5	16	16	30	0	0	.373	.465
2007	Rome (SAL)	LoA	.298	106	389	65	116	34	2	12	70	49	74	3	4	.378	.488
2008	Myrtle Beach (CAR)	HiA	.288	122	413	72	119	32	1	17	88	98	102	8	7	.427	.494
2009	Birmingham (SL)	AA	.302	77	248	54	75	18	2	13	43	57	76	3	0	.445	.548
	Charlotte (IL)	AAA	.286	31	105	13	30	10	0	2	13	10	32	0	0	.364	.438
	Chicago (AL)	MAJ	.188	10	16	3	3	1	0	0	0	3	8	0	0	.350	.250
2010	Charlotte (IL)	AAA	.220	100	346	43	76	22	2	16	53	55	121	2	1	.334	.434
	Chicago (AL)	MAJ	.091	8	11	2	1	0	0	0	0	4	5	0	0	.333	.091
Major League Totals			.148	18	27	5	4	1	0	0	0	7	13	0	0	.343	.185
Minor League Totals			.277	470	1630	271	452	125	7	65	283	285	435	16	12	.391	.482

18 JORDAN DANKS, OF

Born: Aug. 7, 1986. **B-T:** L-R. **Ht.:** 6-4. **Wt.:** 210. **Drafted:** Texas, 2008 (7th round). **Signed by:** Keith Staab/Derek Valenzuela.

A rare over-slot signing for Chicago at $525,000 for a seventh-rounder, Danks moved quickly through the minors and briefly received consideration to make the 2010 big league club before the White Sox traded for Juan Pierre. Danks' younger brother John led Chicago with 15 wins last season, but Jordan won't join him at U.S. Cellular Field until he learns how to solve more advanced pitching. He has batted just .244/.322/.366 since getting promoted to Double-A in May 2009. Advancing him to Triple-A in 2010 looks like a dubious decision in retrospect. He struggled against breaking pitches throughout the year, making it hard to believe he had once been projected as a leadoff candidate. His used to spray the ball all over the field with occasional flashes of gap power, but now he mostly makes weak contact to the opposite field. He was projected as a big-time power hitter when he came out of high school but never has come close to delivering that kind of pop. Though he struggled at the plate, Danks continued to provide quality defense in center field and earned respect playing through a variety of minor injuries. He has plus speed and an average arm, allowing him to play all three outfield spots, though his quickness hasn't translated into big stolen-base numbers. Pierre is expected to return for one more year as the Sox' left fielder, leaving Danks to return to Charlotte.

Year	Club (League)	Class	AVG	G	AB	R	H	2B	3B	HR	RBI	BB	SO	SB	CS	OBP	SLG
2008	Kannapolis (SAL)	LoA	.325	10	40	10	13	4	1	2	7	4	14	1	0	.400	.625
2009	Winston-Salem (CAR)	HiA	.322	30	118	25	38	11	2	3	21	18	32	5	1	.409	.525
	Birmingham (SL)	AA	.243	73	284	50	69	12	1	6	20	37	73	7	3	.337	.356
2010	Charlotte (IL)	AAA	.245	119	445	62	109	27	3	8	42	41	151	15	6	.312	.373
Minor League Totals			.258	232	887	147	229	54	7	19	90	100	270	28	10	.338	.399

19 ANDY WILKINS, 3B

Born: Sept. 13, 1988. **B-T:** L-R. **Ht.:** 6-2. **Wt.:** 225. **Drafted:** Arkansas, 2010 (5th round). **Signed by:** Clay Overcash.

A middle-of-the-lineup bat for the Arkansas team that also featured 2010 draft picks Zack Cox (first round, Cardinals) and Brett Eibner (second round, Royals), Wilkins was overshadowed at times in college but hit 42 home runs in three seasons. After the White Sox drafted him in the fifth round and signed him for $195,000, he immediately became one of the best power prospects in the White Sox system. He hit so well at Great Falls that one scout compared his arrival to that of Giants first-base prospect Brandon Belt, who has performed much better as a pro than he did in college at Texas. Wilkins shows the ability to hit the ball to all fields and handle lefthanded pitching, with an advanced approach that produced more walks than strikeouts in his pro debut. His six homers allayed worries that his power wouldn't play with wood bats, which arose after he hit just two homers in the summer of 2009 with Team USA. The deep load in his swing does raise concerns about his ability to handle quality pitching, however. After playing mostly first base at Arkansas in deference to Cox, Wilkins moved to the hot corner in pro ball. He's a below-average runner—though he isn't afraid to steal a base—and will have to work to become an average defender. His makeup and work ethic remind some club officials of Jim Thome. The White Sox believe Wilkins could be a special hitter, and his advanced bat might allow him to skip to high Class A to open his first full season.

Year	Club (League)	Class	AVG	G	AB	R	H	2B	3B	HR	RBI	BB	SO	SB	CS	OBP	SLG
2010	Great Falls (PIO)	R	.307	53	218	37	67	14	1	6	40	33	31	7	2	.396	.463
Minor League Totals			.307	53	218	37	67	14	1	6	40	33	31	7	2	.396	.463

20 TYLER SALADINO, SS

Born: July 20, 1989. **B-T:** R-R. **Ht.:** 5-11. **Wt.:** 180. **Drafted:** Oral Roberts, 2010 (7th round). **Signed by:** Clay Overcash.

All Saladino does is hit. He was a conference player of the year in consecutive seasons, first when he batted .453 for Palomar (Calif.) JC in 2009, and again when he hit .381 with 17 home runs at Oral Roberts last spring. Undrafted out of high school, he turned down the Astros as a 36th-round pick in 2009 before signing for $115,000 as a seventh-rounder last June. Saladino's swing can get long, leading to strikeouts, but he has a quick bat that gives him surprising gap power for his build. He has plus speed and could fit as a No. 2 hitter if he makes more consistent contact. Saladino's first-step quickness allows him to get to a lot of balls at shortstop, and he has the plus arm get outs on tough chances deep in the hole. Some scouts believe his defense will allow him to climb the ladder even if he slows down as a hitter. He profiles as a big league middle infielder if he continues to hit, or a productive utility player if his bat doesn't quite measure up. He could start his first full pro season in high Class A after batting .309 at Kannapolis in his pro debut.

Year	Club (League)	Class	AVG	G	AB	R	H	2B	3B	HR	RBI	BB	SO	SB	CS	OBP	SLG
2010	Bristol (APP)	R	.292	13	48	7	14	3	0	1	6	5	12	1	2	.364	.417
	Kannapolis (SAL)	LoA	.309	47	165	40	51	14	1	2	18	22	44	4	2	.397	.442
Minor League Totals			.305	60	213	47	65	17	1	3	24	27	56	5	4	.390	.437

21 NATE JONES, RHP

Born: Jan. 28, 1986. **B-T:** R-R. **Ht.:** 6-5. **Wt.:** 190. **Drafted:** Northern Kentucky, 2007 (5th round). **Signed by:** Mike Shirley.

Long one of the organization's most intriguing prospects, Jones is growing into more than just a guy with a big arm and little idea how to use it. He has made major strides the last two seasons, becoming a full-time starter and earning a spot on the 40-man roster in 2010. He posted a 3.05 ERA in his final 10 starts, the best stretch ever for a guy who previously had earned comparisons to Bobby Jenks with his high-90s fastball and hammer curveball. Jones' heater sat at 91-95 mph after he moved to the rotation, and he did a much better job adding and subtracting velocity from it last year. His curveball also added depth, yet some scouts think his changeup might be the better secondary pitch, giving him a good weapon against lefthanders. Jones has shortened his delivery and does a better job of repeating it, and he seemed more willing to pitch to contact last season. He still has stiff arm action and throws across his body, though, costing him consistency and command. He gets hit harder than someone with his stuff should, primarily because he works up in the strike zone too often. Ticketed for Double-A to open 2011, he could reach Chicago quickly if he can improve the location of his pitches.

Year	Club (League)	Class	W	L	ERA	G	GS	CG	SV	IP	H	HR	BB	SO	G/A	WHIP	AVG
2007	Bristol (APP)	R	0	4	5.13	13	10	0	0	47	44	4	29	42	—	1.54	.250
2008	Bristol (APP)	R	1	0	1.35	4	1	0	0	7	6	0	2	12	—	1.20	.222
	Kannapolis (SAL)	LoA	1	7	6.83	18	10	1	0	57	63	8	35	71	—	1.73	.281
	Winston-Salem (CAR)	HiA	0	0	3.38	2	0	0	0	3	1	0	2	1	—	1.13	.111
2009	Kannapolis (SAL)	LoA	2	0	2.41	13	0	0	1	19	8	0	9	25	1.14	0.91	.129
	Winston-Salem (CAR)	HiA	2	1	3.65	32	0	0	0	49	44	4	13	43	1.04	1.16	.244
2010	Winston-Salem (CAR)	HiA	11	6	4.08	28	28	1	0	152	176	10	56	109	1.57	1.52	.296
Minor League Totals			17	18	4.48	110	49	2	1	334	342	26	146	303	1.40	1.46	.269

22 JHONNY NUNEZ, RHP

Born: Nov. 26, 1985. **B-T:** L-R. **Ht.:** 6-3. **Wt.:** 185. **Signed:** Dominican Republic, 2003. **Signed by:** Andres Lopez (Dodgers).

After reaching the big leagues in 2009, Nunez took a step backward last season. The White Sox got him in the deal that sent Nick Swisher to the Yankees after the 2008 season, and he previously had been traded by the Dodgers (for Marlon Anderson) and Nationals (for Alberto Gonzalez). Nunez worked mostly as a starter earlier in his career, but Chicago made him a full-time reliever in 2009. Last year, the White Sox sent him down to Double-A to work as a starter, and he bombed when promoted him to their Triple-A bullpen. Nunez works off a 90-94 mph fastball that touches 97, locating it to both sides of the plate. He failed to command his slider in Triple-A, getting hit hard when he left it up in the zone, but it gives him a second plus pitch when it's on. He showed an average changeup as a starter but didn't use it much as a reliever. Scouts were impressed with his ability to dial his stuff up and down and pitch to contact as a starter, feeling that he took charge of the game in that role. Nunez's most likely route to Chicago is working out of the bullpen, however, and his struggles in Triple-A were perplexing. After pitched well in relief in the Dominican Winter League, he could claim a big league role in spring training.

Year	Club (League)	Class	W	L	ERA	G	GS	CG	SV	IP	H	HR	BB	SO	G/A	WHIP	AVG
2004	Dodgers1 (DSL)	R	2	1	1.73	7	7	0	0	36	30	1	6	23	—	0.99	.229
	Dodgers2 (DSL)	R	2	0	4.60	4	3	0	0	16	17	0	4	12	—	1.34	.262
2005	Dodgers (DSL)	R	4	3	1.92	15	8	1	0	52	29	0	13	40	—	0.81	.153

Year	Club (League)	Class	W	L	ERA	G	GS	CG	SV	IP	H	HR	BB	SO	G/A	WHIP	AVG
2006	Dodgers (GCL)	R	6	0	1.58	10	7	0	0	57	35	0	19	56	—	0.95	.177
2007	Hagerstown (SAL)	LoA	4	6	4.05	23	22	0	0	107	97	10	48	86	—	1.36	.239
2008	Potomac (CAR)	HiA	2	8	5.22	21	17	0	0	81	88	11	21	82	—	1.35	.276
	Harrisburg (EL)	AA	0	0	1.13	5	0	0	0	8	9	0	6	8	—	1.88	.300
	Trenton (EL)	AA	1	0	1.86	8	0	0	0	19	16	2	6	26	—	1.14	.229
2009	Birmingham (SL)	AA	3	0	2.14	26	0	0	3	46	38	3	21	57	0.76	1.27	.229
	Charlotte (IL)	AAA	2	0	3.33	16	0	0	1	24	19	3	5	22	0.63	0.99	.221
	Chicago (AL)	MAJ	0	0	9.53	7	0	0	0	6	10	1	2	3	0.56	2.12	.370
2010	Birmingham (SL)	AA	1	4	3.71	10	10	0	0	51	53	3	17	38	0.96	1.37	.265
	Charlotte (IL)	AAA	5	2	5.48	32	0	0	1	44	46	6	19	45	0.76	1.47	.274
Major League Totals			0	0	9.53	7	0	0	0	6	10	1	2	3	0.56	2.12	.370
Minor League Totals			32	24	3.39	177	74	1	5	542	477	39	185	495	0.80	1.22	.235

23 KYLE COFIELD, RHP

Born: Jan. 23, 1987. **B-T:** R-R. **Ht.:** 6-5. **Wt.:** 220. **Drafted:** HS—Gadsden, Ala., 2005. **Signed by:** Al Goetz (Braves).

There are a lot of things to like about Cofield, yet he wasn't able to consistently harness his stuff in six years in the Braves system. The White Sox will try to help him get over the hump after acquiring him for Scott Linebrink in December. Cofield made strides in 2008 and 2009 before missing two months last years with an elbow injury. He has an ideal pitcher's frame, and when he's dialed in he has two potential plus pitches: a low-90s fastball that tops out at 95 with good movement, and a sharp curveball that buckles the knees of righthanders on occasion. Cofield struggles with his control, because he lacks feel for his pitches and nibbles too much. He needs to command his fastball and breaking ball better in the strike zone, and to add more depth and fade to his changeup. After spending the past two seasons in Double-A, Cofield should make the jump to Triple-A with his new organization. He projects as a reliever in the long run.

Year	Club (League)	Class	W	L	ERA	G	GS	CG	SV	IP	H	HR	BB	SO	G/A	WHIP	AVG
2005	Braves (GCL)	R	0	0	7.31	10	0	0	2	16	16	0	6	15	0.78	1.38	.254
2006	Danville (APP)	R	2	3	6.21	13	8	0	0	42	50	2	22	29	1.44	1.71	.289
2007	Rome (SAL)	LoA	4	8	3.86	25	16	0	1	112	96	7	56	90	1.58	1.36	.236
2008	Myrtle Beach (CAR)	HiA	8	6	3.26	24	22	0	0	116	113	2	66	80	1.50	1.54	.260
2009	Mississippi (SL)	AA	10	5	3.90	26	24	1	0	141	122	9	89	87	1.12	1.50	.236
2010	Braves (GCL)	R	0	1	6.00	2	2	0	0	3	4	0	1	3	1.50	1.67	.333
	Mississippi (SL)	AA	1	3	4.39	18	10	0	0	55	58	4	23	38	2.72	1.46	.264
Minor League Totals			25	26	4.12	118	82	1	3	485	459	24	263	342	1.42	1.49	.252

24 MIGUEL GONZALEZ, C

Born: Dec. 3, 1990. **B-T:** R-R. **Ht.:** 6-0. **Wt.:** 200. **Signed:** Venezuela, 2008. **Signed by:** Amador Arias.

Gonzalez fulfilled expectations shutting down the running game in 2010, but he often looked lost as a hitter during his first full-season assignment. He combines a strong arm with a quick release, reminiscent of Ivan Rodriguez, and he ranked second in the low Class A South Atlantic League by erasing 50 percent of basestealers last year. The only knock on his throwing is that he had a head snap in his mechanics that can affect his accuracy. Gonzalez's heavy body works against him behind the plate, and his footwork needs improvement. He remains a work in progress as a blocker and game-caller. His bat remains his biggest question. After hitting .302 and showing power in his 2009 U.S. debut, he had to rally to get above the Mendoza Line and generated little power last year. He chases a lot of pitches and tries to pull everything, and he particularly struggles against offspeed pitches. He's a major project for the organization's hitting coaches. He's a below-average runner, no surprise for a stocky catcher. The White Sox praise his mental toughness and hope his .270 August will be a springboard to a better 2011, but scouts outside the organization see him as a max-effort player with little projection. He'll move up to high Class A and try to get his bat going.

Year	Club (League)	Class	AVG	G	AB	R	H	2B	3B	HR	RBI	BB	SO	SB	CS	OBP	SLG
2008	White Sox 1 (DSL)	R	.500	2	2	0	1	1	0	0	0	0	0	0	0	.500	1.000
	White Sox 2 (DSL)	R	.291	43	141	25	41	9	1	0	23	16	18	8	1	.388	.369
2009	Bristol (APP)	R	.311	45	151	24	47	15	1	4	19	16	25	2	1	.385	.503
	Charlotte (IL)	AAA	.182	3	11	1	2	0	0	0	1	0	2	0	0	.182	.182
2010	Kannapolis (SAL)	LoA	.218	92	326	35	71	9	2	2	19	16	63	2	1	.260	.276
Minor League Totals			.257	185	631	85	162	34	4	6	62	48	108	12	3	.320	.352

25 ANDRE RIENZO, RHP

Born: June 5, 1988. **B-T:** R-R. **Ht.:** 6-3. **Wt.:** 160. **Signed:** Brazil, 2006. **Signed by:** Orlando Santana.

An organization lacking pitching depth found a young arm to fall in love with when Rienzo used his raw stuff to dominate low Class A hitters in the second half of 2010. He was especially locked in late in the season, holding opponents to two runs or fewer in each of his last 10 starts, including a 10-strikeout, no-walk game against Asheville. Rienzo throws his 88-92 mph fastball with good angle, and his curveball has sharp downward break when it's on. His changeup needs work but could become an average pitch. He's athletic but has a long arm action and rushes his delivery, which hurts his command and consistency. He does show a knack for throwing strikes. Because he started the 2010 season conditioned to be a reliever, the White Sox held down his innings. They hope to get him to about 150 innings in 2011, when he'll pitch in high Class A.

Year	Club (League)	Class	W	L	ERA	G	GS	CG	SV	IP	H	HR	BB	SO	G/A	WHIP	AVG
2007	White Sox2 (DSL)	R	1	1	7.63	7	3	0	0	15	16	1	11	22	—	1.76	.286
2008	White Sox 2 (DSL)	R	2	1	1.64	5	4	0	0	22	17	0	6	22	—	1.05	.218
	White Sox 1 (DSL)	R	3	0	0.96	3	3	0	0	19	15	0	3	22	—	0.96	.214
2009	Bristol (APP)	R	2	6	4.14	13	9	0	0	54	55	4	13	49	1.28	1.25	.263
2010	Kannapolis (SAL)	LoA	8	4	3.65	20	18	2	0	101	95	5	32	125	1.10	1.26	.242
Minor League Totals			16	12	3.62	48	37	2	0	211	198	10	65	240	1.17	1.24	.246

26 JOSH PHEGLEY, C

Born: Feb. 12, 1988. **B-T:** R-R. **Ht.:** 5-10. **Wt.:** 210. **Drafted:** Indiana, 2009 (1st round supplemental). **Signed by:** Mike Shirley.

The White Sox didn't see much production from Phegley in 2010, but that was the least of their concerns. He played in just 48 games because of a rare condition (idiopathic thrombocytopenic purpura in which his blood doesn't clot properly because of a low number of platelets. It can be a chronic condition, though it's not usually considered life-threatening. He held his own late in the season in Double-A, but wasn't able to make up for lost time in the Arizona Fall League because he wasn't medically cleared to play. He had his spleen removed in November after doctors determined his spleen may have been destroying platelets. An offensive-minded catcher, Phegley went 38th overall in the 2009 draft and signed for $858,600. He has the potential to hit for both average and power but needs to improve his pitch recognition to cut down on his strikeouts. He shows raw power to all fields, though he can get pull-conscious and some scouts question his bat speed. Phegley is rough behind the plate, with a thick body and below-average receiving skills. He does have an above-average arm and has thrown out 53 percent of pro basestealers, though his lack of athleticism slows his release at times. He's a below-average runner. Barring further setbacks, Phegley will return to Birmingham this year.

Year	Club (League)	Class	AVG	G	AB	R	H	2B	3B	HR	RBI	BB	SO	SB	CS	OBP	SLG
2009	Kannapolis (SAL)	LoA	.224	52	196	27	44	9	0	9	33	11	40	1	1	.277	.408
2010	Bristol (APP)	R	.200	5	15	1	3	1	0	0	1	2	4	0	0	.333	.267
	Winston-Salem (CAR)HiA	.292	25	89	16	26	3	0	3	12	7	22	0	0	.337	.427
	Birmingham (SL)	AA	.292	18	72	7	21	4	0	2	13	2	22	0	0	.316	.431
Minor League Totals			.253	100	372	51	94	17	0	14	59	22	88	1	1	.301	.411

27 MATT HEIDENREICH, RHP

Born: Jan. 17, 1991. **B-T:** L-R. **Ht.:** 6-5. **Wt.:** 190. **Drafted:** HS—Lake Elsinore, Calif., 2009 (4th round). **Signed by:** Mike Baker.

Heidenreich was in over his head when he entered pro ball as a fourth-round pick out of high school in 2009, but he was much better when he returned to Rookie-level Bristol last summer. He laid the groundwork for a strong season with his work in extended spring training, proving to be a quick learner with both his mechanics and approach. Heidenreich features a low-90s sinker with late movement, and his projectable 6-foot-5 frame suggests he may eventually complement it with a four-seamer in the mid-90s. He has improved his changeup, which should develop into an average pitch. His slider lags behind his other pitches, but he throws it for strikes. He fills the strike zone with all of his offerings, pitching to contact and getting groundouts. He'll spend 2011 in low Class A, and the White Sox hope he can continue to progress at the same rate he did last year.

Year	Club (League)	Class	W	L	ERA	G	GS	CG	SV	IP	H	HR	BB	SO	G/A	WHIP	AVG
2009	Bristol (APP)	R	0	1	4.50	16	0	0	0	22	22	1	12	12	1.79	1.55	.256
2010	Bristol (APP)	R	6	2	2.49	13	11	0	0	76	73	2	11	58	1.96	1.11	.253
	Kannapolis (SAL)	LoA	0	0	18.00	1	0	0	0	1	3	0	0	2	—	3.00	.600
Minor League Totals			6	3	3.09	30	11	0	0	99	98	3	23	72	1.93	1.22	.259

28 JON GILMORE, 3B

Born: Aug. 23, 1988. **B-T:** R-R. **Ht.:** 6-3. **Wt.:** 195. **Drafted:** HS—Iowa City, Iowa, 2007 (1st round supplemental). **Signed by:** Terry Tripp (Braves).

The Braves generally have a knack for trading away prospects who don't blossom elsewhere. While Gilmore still has a ways to go before becoming known as one who got away, he made a major move forward in 2010. One of four players the White Sox got in the Javier Vazquez trade after the 2008 season, he flashed a dangerous bat in high Class A Carolina League, finishing second to teammate Brandon Short in the league batting race (.312) and fourth in RBIs (80). His numbers were inflated by Winston-Salem's new BB&T Ballpark, where he hit .350/.386/.449. Interestingly, Chicago offered him to the Dodgers when acquired for Manny Ramirez in August, but Los Angeles preferred to let Ramirez go on a straight waiver claim rather than take Gilmore in exchange for picking up part of Ramirez' contract in a trade. The brother-in-law of Ben Zobrist, Gilmore made a big leap last year by destroying lefthanders (.396/.435/.490) and taking pitches from righthanders to the opposite field. He should be an above-average hitter but doesn't generate the power his 6-foot-3 frame suggests he should, in part because of his line-drive, gap-oriented approach. He makes consistent contact, though he doesn't walk much. Gilmore's bat will have to carry him because he's a substandard third baseman. He has hard hands, limited range and a below-average arm with a funky throwing motion. He has committed 78 errors over the last two seasons, and his below-average speed makes first base and DH his only other options. Gilmore has great makeup, and his bat gives him a chance to find a major league role. He'll likely get one more year at third base, this time in Double-A.

Year	Club (League)	Class	AVG	G	AB	R	H	2B	3B	HR	RBI	BB	SO	SB	CS	OBP	SLG
2007	Braves (GCL)	R	.284	43	162	11	46	5	1	1	29	4	28	0	0	.296	.346
2008	Danville (APP)	R	.337	67	258	27	87	23	0	4	31	13	41	0	3	.365	.473
	Rome (SAL)	LoA	.186	27	102	6	19	1	0	0	4	2	20	1	0	.202	.196
2009	Kannapolis (SAL)	LoA	.274	130	504	60	138	27	1	5	67	34	83	4	3	.322	.361
2010	Winston-Salem (CAR)	HiA	.312	135	568	79	177	24	4	5	80	34	89	1	3	.349	.394
Minor League Totals			.293	402	1594	183	467	80	6	15	211	87	261	6	9	.329	.379

29 CAMERON BAYNE, RHP

Born: Feb. 14, 1988. **B-T:** R-R. **Ht.:** 6-2. **Wt.:** 195. **Drafted:** Concordia (Calif.), 2009 (13th round). **Signed by:** Mike Baker.

Bayne is one of the best athletes in the system. He earned all-state honors in baseball, basketball and football at his Hawaii high school, and he was a two-way player in college at South Mountain (Ariz.) CC and Concordia (Calif.). He reminds some club officials of John Ely, whom the White Sox sent to the Dodgers in a trade for Juan Pierre after the 2009 season, though he doesn't have a pitch to match Ely's changeup. Bayne did little during his 2009 pro debut to get noticed, but he refined his delivery in instructional league. He threw so well in minor league camp that he landed a surprise spot in the Kannapolis rotation and held onto it all season. Bayne's four-seam fastball can reach the mid-90s, and he gets good sink on an 89-91 mph two-seamer. His velocity varies from game to game, in part because his feel for the two pitches fluctuates as well, and he's still learning how to use his fastball. Both of Bayne's secondary pitches need plenty of work. He flashes an average changeup but often slows his arm speed when he throws it. He hangs his curveball too often. Bayne goes after hitters with all three pitches and tries to work the bottom of the strike zone. His arm slot varies from high three-quarters to low three-quarters, and he still needs consistency with his mechanics and command. He's get another full season of starts in high Class A this year to address those concerns.

Year	Club (League)	Class	W	L	ERA	G	GS	CG	SV	IP	H	HR	BB	SO	G/A	WHIP	AVG
2009	Great Falls (PIO)	R	0	2	6.26	19	1	0	2	27	35	2	14	27	1.30	1.79	.318
2010	Kannapolis (SAL)	LoA	12	9	3.60	27	26	2	0	165	174	9	35	101	1.92	1.27	.269
Minor League Totals			12	11	3.98	46	27	2	2	192	209	11	49	128	1.59	1.34	.276

30 SPENCER ARROYO, LHP

Born: Aug. 9, 1988. **B-T:** L-L. **Ht.:** 6-2. **Wt.:** 170. **Drafted:** Modesto (Calif.) JC, 2008 (31st round). **Signed by:** Joey Davis (Phillies).

Arroyo got a $70,000 bonus from the Phillies as a 31st-round pick in 2008, but they released him at the end of spring training last year. The White Sox held him in extended spring training after signing him a few weeks later, then sent him to the Appalachian League. He was old for Rookie ball at 21, but he led the league in strikeouts (75) and ranked third in ERA (2.49). Arroyo's fastball sits in the high 80s, but he can throw it for strikes to both sides of the plate. He complements it with a plus changeup and a breaking ball that has gotten tighter since he has cleaned up his mechanics. He has a good understanding of pitching, challenging hitters, working quickly and holding runners on base. Arroyo will finally reach full-season ball in his fourth year as a pro. He could jump up to high Class A so Chicago can see if his fringy stuff will play against more advanced hitters.

Year	Club (League)	Class	W	L	ERA	G	GS	CG	SV	IP	H	HR	BB	SO	G/A	WHIP	AVG
2008	Williamsport (NYP)	SS	0	2	9.28	4	2	0	1	11	12	2	9	4	—	1.97	.261
	Phillies (GCL)	R	0	2	4.26	9	4	0	0	32	37	0	5	25	—	1.33	.296
2009	Williamsport (NYP)	SS	2	2	3.67	16	1	0	0	34	38	0	20	25	1.11	1.69	.281
2010	Bristol (APP)	R	7	2	2.49	13	13	1	0	76	57	7	14	75	1.55	0.93	.206
	Great Falls (PIO)	R	0	0	0.82	2	2	0	0	11	4	0	6	11	1.11	0.91	.121
Minor League Totals			9	8	3.41	44	22	1	1	164	148	9	54	140	0.89	1.23	.240

Cincinnati Reds

BY J.J. COOPER

The future finally arrived.

After nine years of losing records, the youth movement that had been building in Cincinnati paid off in 2010. Despite an Opening Day payroll of $71.8 million that put them near the bottom of baseball's middle class, the Reds returned to the playoffs by winning the National League Central. The Phillies swept them in the Division Series, but simply making the postseason was an accomplishment for a team that has made only three playoff trips since 1980.

Like the rest of baseball's middle class, Cincinnati's hopes rest on its ability to develop homegrown talent. Before the 2007 season, Homer Bailey, Jay Bruce, Joey Votto, Johnny Cueto, Drew Stubbs and Travis Wood occupied the first six spots on our Reds' prospect list. In 2010, Votto became the NL MVP; Bailey, Cueto and Wood all pitched in the major league rotation; and Bruce and Stubbs formed two-thirds of the starting outfield as the Reds won 91 games.

Now Cincinnati has to prove it can build on success. The team appears to be built to remain in playoff contention, and it goes into 2011 with a surplus of starting pitching, a lineup relatively set at six positions and plenty of candidates for the other two spots.

They Reds also will head into the upcoming season with Aroldis Chapman poised as a top rookie-of-the-year candidate, either as the hardest-throwing reliever in baseball or as a fireballing starter. Signed to a $30.25 million contract, the Cuban defector took the baseball world by storm when he made his major league debut last August. In September, he threw the fastest pitch ever recorded, at 105.1 mph.

Behind its stars, Cincinnati also has developed solid depth. Its Triple-A Louisville affiliate, for example, fielded solid prospects at most every position by the end of 2010. The newfound pitching depth is especially good news for an organization that went more than a decade without developing a reliable starter. The Reds got 97 starts from homegrown pitchers in 2010, and four of them—Bailey, Cueto, Wood and Mike Leake—were 24 or younger.

Cincinnati further added to its stock of prospects with a solid 2010 draft in which it was more aggressive than usual. The Reds gave catcher Yasmani Grandal, their first-round pick, a major league contract worth $3.2 million and also went over slot to sign high schoolers Drew Cisco and Kyle Waldrop.

NL MVP Joey Votto is the top example of the Reds' success developing homegrown talent

TOP 30 PROSPECTS

1. Aroldis Chapman, lhp	**16.** Ismael Guillon, lhp
2. Billy Hamilton, 2b/ss	**17.** Junior Arias, ss
3. Devin Mesoraco, c	**18.** Brad Boxberger, rhp
4. Yonder Alonso, 1b/of	**19.** DiDi Gregorius, ss
5. Yorman Rodriguez, of	**20.** Dave Sappelt, of
6. Yasmani Grandal, c	**21.** Kyle Waldrop, of
7. Juan Francisco, 3b	**22.** Ronald Torreyes, inf
8. Zack Cozart, ss	**23.** Henry Rodriguez, 2b
9. Todd Frazier, of/3b/1b	**24.** Neftali Soto, 1b
10. Kyle Lotzkar, rhp	**25.** Sam LeCure, rhp
11. Ryan LaMarre, of	**26.** Jonathan Correa, rhp
12. Drew Cisco, rhp	**27.** Daryl Thompson, rhp
13. Donnie Joseph, lhp	**28.** Juan Duran, of
14. Chris Valaika, 2b/ss	**29.** Philippe Valiquette, lhp
15. Daniel Corcino, rhp	**30.** Felix Perez, of

At the minor league level, not all the news was good. When the Myrtle Beach Pelicans swapped their high Class A affiliation, it led Lynchburg to shift from the Reds to the Braves. With no other options, Cincinnati was left with Bakersfield in the California League. Many teams try to avoid the Cal League because it's a difficult one for pitchers, and Eastern teams in particular prefer to be closer to their affiliates.

The Bakersfield situation is particularly bad. The stadium is considered by many to be the worst in the minors and doesn't meet Minor League Baseball's facility standards.

ORGANIZATION OVERVIEW

General Manager: Walt Jocketty. **Farm Director:** Terry Reynolds. **Scouting Director:** Chris Buckley.

Class	Team	League	W	L	PCT	Finish*	Manager
Majors	Cincinnati Reds	National	91	71	.562	t-3rd (16)	Dusty Baker
Triple-A	Louisville Bats	International	79	64	.552	3rd (14)	Rick Sweet
Double-A	Carolina Mudcats	Southern	58	79	.423	9th (10)	David Bell
High A	Lynchburg Hillcats	Carolina	61	77	.442	7th (8)	Pat Kelly
Low A	Dayton Dragons	Midwest	53	85	.384	15th (16)	Todd Benzinger
Rookie	Billings Mustangs	Pioneer	38	37	.507	5th (8)	Delino DeShields
Rookie	AZL Reds	Arizona	31	24	.564	t-3rd (12)	Julio Garcia
Overall 2010 Minor League Record			320	366	.466	26th (30)	

*Finish in overall standings (No. of teams in league). †League champion.
*High Class A affiliate changes to Bakersfield (California) in 2011.

LAST YEAR'S TOP 30

Player, Pos.	Status
1. Todd Frazier, of/2b/3b	No. 9
2. Yonder Alonso, 1b	No. 4
3. Mike Leake, rhp	Majors
4. Chris Heisey, of	Majors
5. Juan Francisco, 3b	No. 7
6. Yorman Rodriguez, of	No. 5
7. Travis Wood, lhp	Majors
8. Matt Maloney, lhp	Majors
9. Brad Boxberger, rhp	No. 18
10. Zack Cozart, ss	No. 8
11. Billy Hamilton, ss	No. 2
12. Chris Valaika, ss/2b	No. 14
13. Neftali Soto, 3b	No. 24
14. Logan Ondrusek, rhp	Majors
15. DiDi Gregorius, ss	No. 19
16. Jordan Smith, rhp	Majors
17. Miguel Rojas, ss	Dropped out
18. Juan Duran, of	No. 28
19. Enerio del Rosario, rhp	(Astros)
20. Kyle Lotzkar, rhp	No. 10
21. Donnie Joseph, lhp	No. 13
22. Pedro Viola, lhp	(Orioles)
23. Phillippe Valiquette, rhp	No. 29
24. Mark Serrano, rhp	Dropped out
25. J.C. Sulbaran, rhp	Dropped out
26. Josh Fellhauer, of	Dropped out
27. Daniel Tuttle, rhp	Dropped out
28. Cody Puckett, 2b/ss	Dropped out
29. Byron Wiley, of	(Diamondbacks)
30. Devin Mesoraco, c	No. 3

BEST TOOLS

Best Hitter for Average	Yonder Alonso
Best Power Hitter	Juan Francisco
Best Strike-Zone Discipline	Yonder Alonso
Fastest Baserunner	Billy Hamilton
Best Athlete	Billy Hamilton
Best Fastball	Aroldis Chapman
Best Curveball	Kyle Lotzkar
Best Slider	Aroldis Chapman
Best Changeup	Ismael Guillon
Best Control	Kyle Lotzkar
Best Defensive Catcher	Yasmani Grandal
Best Defensive Infielder	Miguel Rojas
Best Infield Arm	Juan Francisco
Best Defensive Outfielder	Ryan LaMarre
Best Outfield Arm	Yorman Rodriguez

PROJECTED 2014 LINEUP

Catcher	Devin Mesoraco
First Base	Joey Votto
Second Base	Billy Hamilton
Third Base	Juan Francisco
Shortstop	Zack Cozart
Left Field	Yorman Rodriguez
Center Field	Drew Stubbs
Right Field	Jay Bruce
No. 1 Starter	Johnny Cueto
No. 2 Starter	Edinson Volquez
No. 3 Starter	Homer Bailey
No. 4 Starter	Mike Leake
No. 5 Starter	Travis Wood
Closer	Aroldis Chapman

TOP PROSPECTS OF THE DECADE

Year	Player, Pos.	2010 Org.
2001	Austin Kearns, of	Yankees
2002	Austin Kearns, of	Yankees
2003	Chris Gruler, rhp	Out of baseball
2004	Ryan Wagner, rhp	Out of baseball
2005	Homer Bailey, rhp	Reds
2006	Homer Bailey, rhp	Reds
2007	Homer Bailey, rhp	Reds
2008	Jay Bruce, of	Reds
2009	Yonder Alonso, 1b	Reds
2010	Todd Frazier, 3b/of	Reds

TOP DRAFT PICKS OF THE DECADE

Year	Player, Pos.	2010 Org.
2001	*Jeremy Sowers, lhp	Indians
2002	Chris Gruler, rhp	Out of baseball
2003	Ryan Wagner, rhp	Out of baseball
2004	Homer Bailey, rhp	Reds
2005	Jay Bruce, of	Reds
2006	Drew Stubbs, of	Reds
2007	Devin Mesoraco, c	Reds
2008	Yonder Alonso, 1b	Reds
2009	Mike Leake, rhp	Reds
2010	Yasmani Grandal, c	Reds

*Did not sign.

LARGEST BONUSES IN CLUB HISTORY

Aroldis Chapman, 2010	$16,250,000
Chris Gruler, 2002	$2,500,000
Yorman Rodriguez, 2008	$2,500,000
Homer Bailey, 2004	$2,300,000
Mike Leake, 2009	$2,270,000

CINCINNATI REDS

TOP 2011 ROOKIE: Aroldis Chapman, lhp. Baseball's hardest thrower could be closing games by midseason.

BREAKOUT PROSPECT: Drew Cisco, rhp. He's a polished pitcher with exceptional command of three solid pitches.

SLEEPER: Daniel Tuttle, rhp. He can run his fastball into the mid-90s, though his immaturity has held him back.

SOURCE OF TOP 30 TALENT

Homegrown	29	Acquired	1
College	10	Trades	1
Junior college	0	Rule 5 draft	0
High school	7	Independent leagues	0
Draft-and-follow	0	Free agents/waivers	0
Nondrafted free agents	0		
International	12		

LF
Kyle Waldrop (21)
Danny Dorn
Jaren Matthews
David Cook
Theodis Bowe

CF
Ryan LaMarre (11)
Dave Sappelt (20)
Felix Perez (30)
Josh Fellhauer
Andrew Means

RF
Yorman Rodriguez (5)
Juan Duran (28)

3B
Juan Francisco (7)
Todd Frazier (9)
Junior Arias (17)
David Vidal

SS
Billy Hamilton (2)
Zack Cozart (8)
DiDi Gregorius (19)
Kris Negron
Miguel Rojas
Devin Lohman
Brandon Dailey

2B
Chris Valaika (14)
Ronald Torreyes (22)
Henry Rodriguez (23)
Brodie Greene
Cody Puckett

1B
Yonder Alonso (4)
Neftali Soto (24)

C
Devin Mesoraco (3)
Yasmani Grandal (6)
Tucker Barnhart
Mark Fleury

RHP

RHSP	RHRP
Kyle Lotzkar (10)	Brad Boxberger (18)
Drew Cisco (12)	Daniel Tuttle
Daniel Corcino (15)	Porfirio Martinez
Sam LeCure (25)	Mark Serrano
Jonathan Correa (26)	Brian Pearl
Darryl Thompson (27)	Pedro Villareal
Wes Mugarian	Justin Freeman
J.C. Sulbaran	Drew Hayes
Stalin Gerson	Kevin Arico
Josh Smith	Chad Rogers
Matt Klinker	Lucas O'Rear
Tony Amezcua	
Josh Ravin	
Clayton Shunick	
Dallas Buck	
Jacob Johnson	
Tim Crabbe	

LHP

LHSP	LHRP
Ismael Guillon (16)	Aroldis Chapman (1)
Matt Fairel	Donnie Joseph (13)
Tanner Robles	Philippe Valiquette (29)
	Jeremy Horst
	Blaine Howell

2010

BEST PURE HITTER: 3B David Vidal (8) is just 5-foot-10 and 180 pounds, but he swings the bat with balance and surprising power. He earns Placido Polanco comparisons for his swing and hitting ability.

BEST POWER HITTER: OF Kyle Waldrop (12) got a $500,000 bonus because of his athletic ability and plus raw power. He has excellent strength and a fast bat. C Yasmani Grandal (1) became more selective and less pull-conscious as a junior and hit for power more consistently. He could hit 20-25 homers annually.

FASTEST RUNNER: OF Ryan LaMarre (2) lasted longer than expected in the draft, thanks in part to breaking his left thumb. He's a well above-average runner, getting to first base in 4.05 seconds from the right side and earning comparisons to current Reds center fielder Drew Stubbs.

BEST DEFENSIVE PLAYER: LaMarre is the best defensive outfielder in the system. Grandal's release can get long, but he has the arm strength and receiving skills to be an average to plus defender. SS Brodie Greene (4) has the quickness, speed and arm strength to be solid at shortstop, second base and center field.

BEST FASTBALL: RHP Drew Cisco's (6) fastball has average velocity, but he can cut it, run it, sink it and command it. In those regards, he reminds the Cincinnati of 2009 first-rounder Mike Leake. RHPs Tony Amezcua (7) and Drew Hayes (11) throw harder, topping out around 94 mph, but no Reds draftee will threaten Aroldis Chapman anytime soon.

BEST SECONDARY PITCH: Cisco commands his curveball and changeup well and knows how to use his full repertoire. RHP Wes Mugarian (5) has a solid curveball that could develop into a plus pitch.

BEST PRO DEBUT: LHP Tanner Robles (9) went 3-3, 2.98 at Rookie-level Billings with 66 strikeouts in 60 innings while limiting batters to a .179 average. Vidal hit .297/.354/.538 in the Rookie-level Arizona League as a 20-year-old.

BEST ATHLETE: LaMarre has the best all-around baseball athleticism. A star safety and wide receiver, Waldrop committed to play football and baseball at South Florida. RHP Lucas O'Rear (13) played more college basketball than baseball at Northern Iowa, as the Panthers dropped baseball after the 2009 season.

MOST INTRIGUING BACKGROUND: Cisco's grandfather Galen pitched and coached in the majors, while his older brother Mike pitches in the Phillies system. Unsigned SS Jacob May's (39) grandfather Lee made three all-star teams as a first baseman and his father Lee Jr. was the Mets' first-round pick in 1986.

CLOSEST TO THE MAJORS: Grandal, who signed a major league contract worth $3.2 million. Greene's versatility will help him move quickly.

BEST LATE-ROUND PICK: Waldrop and 1B/OF Jaren Matthews (32), who struggled for much of his Rutgers career but adjusted his swing since signing. He's athletic and has a chance to hit for power.

THE ONE WHO GOT AWAY: Cincinnati likes OF Josh Alexander's (19) solid athleticism and bat speed but didn't buy him out of a commitment to Utah.

ASSESSMENT: Signing Grandal to a big league deal allowed the Reds to stretch their budget to add Cisco and Waldrop. They went heavy on hitters, going against the grain in a deep pitching draft.

2009

RHP Mike Leake (1), who was somewhat of a signability pick, went straight to the majors and won eight games as a rookie. 2B/SS Billy Hamilton (2) is Cincinnati's leadoff hitter of the future, while RHP Brad Boxberger (1s) and LHP Donnie Joseph (3) could provide bullpen help in short order.

GRADE: B+

2008

1B Yonder Alonso (1) is ready for a big league job but finds himself blocked by Joey Votto. RHP Zach Stewart (3) was the key player in the trade that brought Scott Rolen from the Blue Jays. OF Dave Sappelt (9) won he Double-A Southern League batting title (.361) last year.

GRADE: C+

2007

C Devin Mesoraco (1) finally started delivering on his potential last year, joining OF/3B/1B Todd Frazier (1s) and SS Zack Cozart (3) among the system's top position prospects. RHP Kyle Lotzkar (1s) has a lot of upside but needs to stay healthy.

GRADE: C+

2006

OF Drew Stubbs (1) had a 20-20 season for the Reds last year, and OF Chris Heisey (17) is a solid reserve. 2B/SS Chris Valaika (3), RHP Jordan Smith (6) and the since-traded INF Justin Turner (7) and RHP Josh Roenicke (10) have seen big league action. Roenicke was part of the Rolen deal.

GRADE: B

Draft analysis by John Manuel (2010) and Jim Callis (2006-09). Numbers in parentheses indicate draft rounds.

AROLDIS CHAPMAN, LHP

Born: February 28, 1988. **Bats:** L. **Throws:** L.
Height: 6-4. **Weight:** 185. **Signed:** Cuba, 2010.
Signed by: Chris Buckley / Tony Arias / Miguel Machado.

DIAMOND IMAGES

When Chapman was in Cuba, his talented left arm was coveted by major league scouts, even if he was off limits and never exhibited much consistency. He first tried to defect in 2008 but got caught and was left off Cuba's Olympic team as punishment. He rejoined the national team for the 2009 World Baseball Classic, where he sat in the mid-90s and touched 100 mph with his fastball. Chapman bolted from the team at the World Port Tournament in the Netherlands that July and became a free agent after establishing residency in Andorra. He signed with the Reds last January, received a six-year, $30.25 million major league contract that included a $16.25 million bonus. Chapman's adjustment to the United States wasn't always easy. He had to get used to a new culture and deal with the daily grind of pro ball. He was surprised to learn that MLB organizations practiced every day, and he never had done any video work. After spending his first two months at Triple-A Louisville as a starter, he took off after moving to the bullpen in mid-June. Cincinnati called him up in August, and he made history on Sept. 24 by throwing the fastest recorded fastball in big league history at 105.1 mph. He took the loss in Game Two of the Division Series when the Phillies roughed him up for three unearned runs.

Any discussion about Chapman begins with his fastball. It's a freak of nature, arguably the hottest heater ever seen. The 20-80 scouting scale fails to fully encapsulate the pitch, because at its best it's 7-8 mph harder than an 80 fastball. He sits at 99-100 mph and touches 103-105 as a reliever. Even as a starter, he can work at 95-96 mph and get to 101. Hitters can't try to sit on his fastball because Chapman has a plus-plus slider, a mid-80s dart with sharp break. He also throws a below-average changeup with too much velocity, though that pitch became less important when he moved out of the rotation. His fastball and slider are good enough to get both lefthanders and righthanders out. Chapman is a premium athlete, but he struggled with his tempo and with repeating his delivery as a starter. He likely never will have plus command, partly because his fastball has so much life at times that it runs out of the strike zone, though more consistent mechanics would help. He didn't have much of a grasp of the nuances of pitching—fielding his position, covering first base, holding runners—but improved over the course of the season.

The big question is whether Chapman will be a starter or reliever. Reds GM Walt Jocketty already has stated publicly that Chapman won't return to the minor leagues, making it more likely that he'll be a bullpen weapon. The needs of a contender often trump developmental concerns, and Chapman could supplant Francisco Cordero as the Reds' closer before the all-star break.

SCOUTING GRADES

Fastball: 80.   **Command/**
Slider: 70.   **Control:** 45.
Changeup: 40. **Delivery:** 50.

Based on 20-80 scouting scale, where 50 represents major league average, and future projection rather than present tools.

Year	Club (League)	Class	W	L	ERA	G	GS	CG	SV	IP	H	HR	BB	SO	G/A	WHIP	AVG
2010	Louisville (IL)	AAA	9	6	3.57	39	13	1	8	96	77	7	52	125	1.14	1.35	.218
	Cincinnati (NL)	MAJ	2	2	2.03	15	0	0	0	13	9	0	5	19	3.75	1.05	.196
Major League Totals			2	2	2.03	15	0	0	0	13	9	0	5	19	3.75	1.05	.196
Minor League Totals			9	6	3.57	39	13	1	8	96	77	7	52	125	1.14	1.35	.218

2 BILLY HAMILTON, 2B/SS

Born: Sept. 9, 1990. **B-T:** B-R. **Ht.:** 6-1. **Wt.:** 160. **Drafted:** HS—Taylorsville, Miss., 2009 (2nd round). **Signed by:** Tyler Jennings.

Hamilton's hometown of Taylorsville, Miss., has produced four NFL players despite a population of less than 2,000, but he's the town's first-ever baseball draftee. He was headed to Mississippi State as a wide receiver until the Reds signed him for $623,000 as a second-rounder in 2009. He led the Rookie-level Pioneer League with 48 steals and rated as the circuit's top prospect last summer. Hamilton's speed ranks among the best in the minors. A switch-hitter, he has been timed in 3.9 seconds to first base on a swing from the right side, and in 3.5 seconds on a bunt from the left. Like Ichiro Suzuki, he'll run into his swing, slapping the ball the other way while racing down the line. He's already a dangerous basestealer, reading pitchers well and getting good jumps. Hamilton has well below-average power, but his speed allows him to accumulate doubles and triples. He has solid strike-zone awareness for his age. His quickness gives him plenty of range for either middle-infield position, but his average arm strength and low arm slots have some scouts questioning whether he throws well enough at shortstop. He spent most of his time in 2010 playing second base. Hamilton again will play mostly second base when he heads to low Class A Dayton in 2011. He could be the leadoff hitter Cincinnati has sought for years.

Year	Club (League)	Class	AVG	G	AB	R	H	2B	3B	HR	RBI	BB	SO	SB	CS	OBP	SLG
2009	Reds (GCL)	R	.205	43	166	19	34	6	3	0	11	11	47	14	3	.253	.277
2010	Billings (PIO)	R	.318	69	283	61	90	13	10	2	24	28	56	48	9	.383	.456
Minor League Totals			.276	112	449	80	124	19	13	2	35	39	103	62	12	.336	.390

3 DEVIN MESORACO, C

Born: June 19, 1988. **B-T:** R-R. **Ht.:** 6-1. **Wt.:** 220. **Drafted:** HS—Punxsutawney, Pa., 2007 (1st round). **Signed by:** Lee Seras.

When the Reds made Mesoraco the 15th overall pick in the 2007 draft and signed him for $1.4 million, they thought he'd be a power-hitting catcher. They just didn't know it would take this long. After slugging a combined .368 while battling wrist and finger injuries in his first three years as a pro, he broke out in 2010 by batting .302/.377/.587 while climbing from high Class A Lynchburg to Louisville. Mesoraco's swing has some uppercut to it, but he has a good load and hits from a strong base. Add in his bat speed and hand-eye coordination, and he should hit for a solid average to go with his plus power. He's athletic for a catcher and has average speed. Reviews of Mesoraco's performance behind the plate are mixed. He has a strong arm with consistent 1.95-2.0 second pop times, and he threw out 41 percent of basestealers last year. But he struggles at times to handle velocity cleanly, a noticeable problem late last season after he hurt his left index finger. He allowed 10 passed balls in 18 Arizona Fall League games. Mesoraco ranks ahead of 2010 first-rounder Yasmani Grandal both athletically and developmentally. Ticketed for Triple-A this season, Mesoraco could take over in Cincinnati before long if he can stay healthy.

Year	Club (League)	Class	AVG	G	AB	R	H	2B	3B	HR	RBI	BB	SO	SB	CS	OBP	SLG
2007	Reds (GCL)	R	.219	40	137	16	30	4	0	1	8	15	26	2	0	.310	.270
2008	Dayton (MWL)	LoA	.261	83	306	29	80	13	1	9	42	20	64	2	3	.311	.399
2009	Sarasota (FSL)	HiA	.228	92	312	32	71	22	1	8	37	35	76	0	1	.311	.381
2010	Lynchburg (CAR)	HiA	.335	43	158	24	53	11	2	10	31	19	29	2	2	.414	.620
	Carolina (SL)	AA	.294	56	187	42	55	11	3	13	31	18	37	1	0	.363	.594
	Louisville (IL)	AAA	.231	14	52	5	12	3	0	3	13	6	14	0	1	.310	.462
Minor League Totals			.261	328	1152	148	301	64	7	44	162	113	246	7	7	.334	.444

RODGER WOOD

4 YONDER ALONSO, 1B/OF

Born: April 8, 1987. **B-T:** L-R. **Ht.:** 6-2. **Wt.:** 210. **Drafted:** Miami, 2008 (1st round). **Signed by:** Tony Arias.

The seventh overall pick in the 2008 draft, Alonso proved to be much more difficult to sign then expected, holding out until the Aug. 15 deadline for a $4.55 million major league contract. His bat has been as good as advertised, though he slumped early in 2010 while getting over his disappointment of starting the season at Double-A Carolina. He responded to a Triple-A promotion by hitting .335/.415/.561 in the second half to earn his first big league callup. Alonso's approach impresses scouts. He uses the entire field and has a good feel for the strike zone. He struggled early last season when fed a steady diet of offspeed pitches away, but he adapted. He also made good adjustments against lefthanders. He shows the potential to hit for average with plus power and on-base ability. With National League MVP Joey Votto at first base in the majors, Cincinnati has tried and failed to find Alonso another position. A spring-training trial at third base quickly proved futile, and his well below-average speed makes him a liability in left field. He's adequate at first base and has some arm strength. If Votto gets hurt, Alonso is ready to step in and play first base. Otherwise, he doesn't have a spot in Cincinnati. He'll head back to Triple-A for a second time to start the 2011 season.

Year	Club (League)	Class	AVG	G	AB	R	H	2B	3B	HR	RBI	BB	SO	SB	CS	OBP	SLG
2008	Sarasota (FSL)	HiA	.316	6	19	1	6	1	0	0	2	5	5	0	0	.440	.368
2009	Reds (GCL)	R	.133	6	15	0	2	0	0	0	0	3	1	0	0	.278	.133
	Sarasota (FSL)	HiA	.303	49	175	21	53	13	0	7	38	24	30	0	1	.383	.497
	Carolina (SL)	AA	.295	29	105	12	31	11	0	2	14	14	15	1	0	.372	.457
2010	Carolina (SL)	AA	.267	31	101	19	27	5	0	3	13	19	16	4	2	.388	.406
	Louisville (IL)	AAA	.296	101	406	50	120	31	2	12	56	37	76	9	1	.355	.470
	Cincinnati (NL)	MAJ	.207	22	29	2	6	2	0	0	3	0	10	0	0	.207	.276
Major League Totals			.207	22	29	2	6	2	0	0	3	0	10	0	0	.207	.276
Minor League Totals			.291	222	821	103	239	61	2	24	123	102	143	14	4	.368	.458

5 YORMAN RODRIGUEZ, OF

Born: Aug. 15, 1992. **B-T:** R-R. **Ht.:** 6-3. **Wt.:** 180. **Signed**: Venezuela, 2008. **Signed by:** Tony Arias.

Rodriguez signed for $2.5 million in 2008, setting a since-broken record for a Venezuelan amateur bonus and paving the way for a significant influx of Latin talent in the system. He has one of the highest upsides among Reds farmhands, and though he repeated Billings in 2010, he was still the Pioneer League's youngest regular at age 17. Rodriguez showed a more mature approach in his second stint at Billings. He did a better job of using the whole field and made more consistent contact. He still has a ways to go at recognizing breaking balls, and there's still more swing and miss in his swing than scouts would like. He has a quick bat and above-average raw power to all fields. If he tightens his strike zone as he matures, he should hit for a solid average. His plus speed makes him a threat to steal, though he'll likely slow down a little as he continues to get bigger. Mostly a center fielder in his pro debut, Rodriguez saw more action in right field last season. Because of his size, he profiles better in right, and he easily has enough arm strength for the position. The Reds initially viewed Rodriguez as a potential five-tool center fielder, but as he has filled out, he now looks more like a prototypical right fielder. He'll head to low Class A Dayton for his first taste of full-season ball.

Year	Club (League)	Class	AVG	G	AB	R	H	2B	3B	HR	RBI	BB	SO	SB	CS	OBP	SLG
2009	Reds (GCL)	R	.274	22	84	9	23	2	1	0	2	10	23	5	0	.347	.321
	Billings (PIO)	R	.219	46	183	21	40	10	2	3	17	9	61	5	2	.259	.344
2010	Billings (PIO)	R	.339	43	171	25	58	8	3	2	39	8	30	12	2	.361	.456
Minor League Totals			.276	111	438	55	121	20	6	5	58	27	114	22	4	.316	.384

6 YASMANI GRANDAL, C

Born: Nov. 8, 1988. **B-T:** B-R. **Ht.:** 6-2. **Wt.:** 215. **Drafted:** Miami, 2010 (1st round). **Signed by:**Miguel Machado

Much like Alonso, Grandal was born in Cuba but emigrated to Florida and played collegiately at Miami. He was one of the top high school catchers available in the 2007 draft, but his $1 million asking price dropped him to the Red Sox in the 27th round. He more than tripled that when he went 12th overall last June and signed a $3.2 million big league contract with a $2 million bonus at the Aug. 16 deadline. His scouting report is similar to Devin Mesoraco's. Grandal has a little less pop, arm strength and athleticism, but he's more polished and a better overall defender. A switch-hitter, Grandal uses the whole field and has good plate discipline. He projects as a plus hitter with perhaps 20-25 homers per season. He's a solid receiver, though his long release takes away from his average arm strength and results in pop times as slow as 2.1 seconds. Like most catchers, he doesn't run well and will slow down further as he piles up games behind the plate. He's relatively advanced for a player fresh out of the draft, but Mesoraco's development means the Reds have no reason to rush Grandal. He'll spend his first full pro season at Cincinnati's new high Class A Bakersfield affiliate.

Year	Club (League)	Class	AVG	G	AB	R	H	2B	3B	HR	RBI	BB	SO	SB	CS	OBP	SLG
2010	Reds (AZL)	R	.286	8	28	4	8	1	0	0	1	4	4	0	1	.394	.321
Minor League Totals			.286	8	28	4	8	1	0	0	1	4	4	0	1	.394	.321

7 JUAN FRANCISCO, 3B

Born: June 24, 1987. **B-T:** L-R. **Ht.:** 6-2. **Wt.:** 210. **Signed**: Dominican Republic, 2004. **Signed by:** Juan Peralta.

Francisco was a surprise addition to the Reds' Opening Day roster in 2010. His stay lasted only a week and he missed two months in Triple-A following an appendectomy, but he spent much of the final two months of the season in Cincinnati and made the postseason roster. Francisco has the best raw power in the system and destroys balls when he squares them up. He'll never be selective at the plate, but he gradually has improved his approach and now works counts. His swing has several moving parts, with a waggle and a toe-tap timing mechanism, but he has shortened his stroke. He has struggled throughout his career to hit lefties, who limited him to a .216 average last year. Francisco has 30-plus homer potential but needs to find a defensive home. He has below-average range at third base, though his plus-plus arm makes up for some of his deficiencies. First base isn't an option because of Joey Votto and Yonder Alonso, and Francisco's well below-average speed doesn't play well in left field. Francisco needs to stay in shape to continue to be an option at third base, where he's currently blocked by Scott Rolen. He may need a trade to get regular big league playing time in the near future.

Year	Club (League)	Class	AVG	G	AB	R	H	2B	3B	HR	RBI	BB	SO	SB	CS	OBP	SLG
2005	Reds (DSL)	R	.228	49	158	7	36	10	1	4	10	14	26	2	5	.293	.380
2006	Reds (GCL)	R	.280	45	182	24	51	14	0	3	30	6	35	2	0	.305	.407
	Billings (PIO)	R	.333	9	36	6	12	3	0	0	2	0	8	2	1	.333	.417
2007	Dayton (MWL)	LoA	.268	135	534	69	143	21	4	25	90	23	161	12	6	.301	.463
2008	Sarasota (FSL)	HiA	.277	127	516	71	143	34	5	23	92	19	123	1	2	.303	.496
2009	Carolina (SL)	AA	.281	109	437	64	123	26	2	22	74	20	91	6	2	.317	.501
	Louisville (IL)	AAA	.359	22	92	17	33	5	1	5	19	4	24	0	0	.384	.598
	Cincinnati (NL)	MAJ	.429	14	21	4	9	1	0	1	7	3	7	0	0	.520	.619
2010	Louisville (IL)	AAA	.286	77	308	46	88	24	4	18	59	16	81	1	0	.325	.565
	Cincinnati (NL)	MAJ	.273	36	55	3	15	3	0	1	7	4	20	0	1	.322	.382
Major League Totals			.316	50	76	7	24	4	0	2	14	7	27	0	1	.381	.447
Minor League Totals			.278	573	2263	304	629	137	17	100	376	102	549	26	16	.311	.486

8 ZACK COZART, SS

Born: Aug. 12, 1985. **B-T:** R-R. **Ht.:** 6-0. **Wt.:** 195. **Drafted:** Mississippi, 2007 (2nd round). **Signed by:** Jerry Flowers.

When Cozart starred at Mississippi and with Team USA, scouts liked his glove but wondered if he'd hit enough with wood bats. The Reds believed in his offensive potential because they thought he could make adjustments, and he has exceeded expectations at the plate while continuing to provide steady defense and reaching Triple-A. Cozart has tweaked his swing as a pro to get his legs more involved. The result is surprising pop for a shortstop, as he has reached double figures in home runs in each of his three full pro seasons, including a career-high 17 last year. He does strike out some, so he might not hit for a high average or post a gaudy on-base percentage. An average runner, he stole 30 bases in 34 attempts in 2010 thanks to his ability to read pitchers. Cozart projects as a useful offensive player who makes all the routine plays at shortstop. He has quick feet, soft hands and a solid, accurate arm. He led International League shortstops with a .977 fielding percentage last year. Newly added to the 40-man roster, Cozart will head to spring training with a chance to wrest the Cincinnati's starting shortstop job from Paul Janish. Cozart offers more offensive upside and similar defensive ability, though Janish has a better arm.

Year	Club (League)	Class	AVG	G	AB	R	H	2B	3B	HR	RBI	BB	SO	SB	CS	OBP	SLG
2007	Dayton (MWL)	LoA	.239	53	184	28	44	7	2	2	18	11	36	3	1	.288	.332
2008	Dayton (MWL)	LoA	.280	109	418	57	117	20	6	14	49	24	77	3	3	.330	.457
2009	Carolina (SL)	AA	.262	131	462	72	121	29	2	10	59	63	87	10	2	.360	.398
2010	Louisville (IL)	AAA	.255	136	553	91	141	30	4	17	67	40	107	30	4	.310	.416
Minor League Totals			.262	429	1617	248	423	86	14	43	193	138	307	46	10	.327	.412

CINCINNATI REDS

9 TODD FRAZIER, OF/3B/1B

Born: Feb. 12, 1986. **B-T:** R-R. **Ht.:** 6-3. **Wt.:** 220. **Drafted:** Rutgers, 2007 (1st round supplemental). **Signed by:** Lee Seras.

The star of the Toms River (N.J.) team that won the 1998 Little League World Series, Frazier followed his brothers Charles and Jeff into pro ball when the Reds signed him for $875,000 as the 34th overall pick in the 2007 draft. No. 1 on this list a year ago, he experienced the worst slump of his career when he batted .197/.274/.369 in the first two months of last season. He recovered to hit a more typical .288/.362/.486 the rest of the way. Frazier's aggressive approach did him no favors when Triple-A pitchers gave him offspeed pitches on the outer half of the plate. He eventually adjusted, standing taller and using the opposite field more, and still showed plus power even while slumping. Some scouts question whether he'll hit enough to profile as a regular left fielder, however. Frazier has average speed, range and arm strength. He's a better defender than Juan Francisco at third base, but Francisco's lack of other options has limited Frazier's time there. He has seen action at all four infield positions. The best-case scenario is that Frasier ends up as a Ben Zobrist type who hits for power and decent average while playing multiple positions. Placed on the 40-man roster in November, he appears blocked from playing anything more than a utility role in Cincinnati, which could mean a third stint in Triple-A.

Year	Club (League)	Class	AVG	G	AB	R	H	2B	3B	HR	RBI	BB	SO	SB	CS	OBP	SLG
2007	Billings (PIO)	R	.319	41	160	29	51	6	5	5	25	18	22	3	3	.409	.513
	Dayton (MWL)	LoA	.318	6	22	4	7	3	0	2	5	2	4	0	0	.375	.727
2008	Dayton (MWL)	LoA	.321	30	112	25	36	10	0	7	20	15	28	4	2	.402	.598
	Sarasota (FSL)	HiA	.281	100	366	62	103	20	3	12	54	41	84	8	4	.357	.451
2009	Carolina (SL)	AA	.290	119	451	59	131	40	2	14	68	42	67	7	8	.350	.481
	Louisville (IL)	AAA	.302	16	63	9	19	5	0	2	9	6	12	2	0	.362	.476
2010	Louisville (IL)	AAA	.258	130	480	71	124	32	4	17	66	45	127	14	4	.333	.448
Minor League Totals			.285	442	1654	259	471	116	14	59	247	169	344	38	21	.357	.479

10 KYLE LOTZKAR, RHP

Born: Oct. 24, 1989. **B-T:** L-R. **Ht.:** 6-4. **Wt.:** 200. **Drafted:** HS—Delta, B.C., 2007 (1st round supplemental). **Signed by:** Bill Byckowski.

The Reds have had to be very patient with Lotzkar. A sandwich pick in 2007, he went down with a stress fracture in his elbow in 2008 and required Tommy John surgery when he tore an elbow ligament the following year. He missed all of 2009 before returning last June and showing the same stuff he had before the injuries. Lotzkar features a 90-94 mph fastball with good life. He has a hard curveball that he can bury for strikeouts as well as a slower curve that he uses as a get-me-over pitch, and his breaking stuff seemed better after his layoff. His changeup shows promise, as does his cutter. He showed improved feel for pitching in his return to action and now does a better job of working both sides of the plate. Lotzkar used to pitch with a high elbow in his delivery, which many suspected led to his injuries. He since has toned down his mechanics and lowered his elbow by breaking his hands quicker in his windup. If Lotzkar can stay healthy, he has the biggest upside of any pitcher in the system other than Aroldis Chapman. Still relatively young at age 21, he'll try to prove he can make a full season's worth of starts at Dayton in 2011.

Year	Club (League)	Class	W	L	ERA	G	GS	CG	SV	IP	H	HR	BB	SO	G/A	WHIP	AVG
2007	Reds (GCL)	R	0	2	3.86	7	7	0	0	21	21	2	7	24	—	1.33	.263
	Billings (PIO)	R	0	0	1.13	2	2	0	0	8	1	1	3	12	—	0.50	.040
2008	Dayton (MWL)	LoA	2	3	3.58	10	10	0	0	38	29	2	24	50	—	1.41	.215
2009	Did Not Play—Injured																
2010	Reds (AZL)	R	1	1	3.33	8	6	0	0	24	20	1	12	27	1.67	1.32	.230
	Billings (PIO)	R	2	0	0.45	4	4	0	0	20	8	1	2	33	1.08	0.50	.119
Minor League Totals			5	6	2.84	31	29	0	0	111	79	7	48	146	1.41	1.14	.201

11 RYAN LAMARRE, OF

Born: Nov. 21, 1988. **B-T:** R-L. **Ht.:** 6-2. **Wt.:** 185. **Drafted:** Michigan, 2010 (2nd round). **Signed by:** Brad Meador.

LaMarre's junior season at Michigan got off to an awful start, as he broke his thumb while diving to make a catch in the outfield. He ended up missing 20 games, but showed few problems upon his return as he led Michigan in batting, on-base percentage and slugging percentage. He was considered quite signable, which he proved by signing for $587,700 almost immediately after the draft. LaMarre is an excellent athlete. He was the leading tackler on back-to-back state championship football teams in high school and was an all-star hockey player. His best tool is his speed, and he's a well above-average runner who has been timed at 4.05 seconds from home to first. He also showed a knack for stealing bases in low Class A—something he hadn't been asked to do much at Michigan. LaMarre should hit for average because of a smooth stroke and plenty of bat speed. He has average power as well. He profiles as an average center fielder defensively, and his arm is a tick above-average, easily enough for center. He struggled at times with his reads off the bat in center. LaMarre isn't particularly polished for a college draftee, but he has more power and hitting ability than most center fielders. He'll head to high Class A in 2011.

Year	Club (League)	Class	AVG	G	AB	R	H	2B	3B	HR	RBI	BB	SO	SB	CS	OBP	SLG
2010	Dayton (MWL)	LoA	.282	60	227	44	64	11	0	5	29	21	53	18	7	.370	.396
	Lynchburg (CAR)	HiA	.222	8	27	2	6	2	0	1	3	2	4	1	1	.276	.407
Minor League Totals			.276	68	254	46	70	13	0	6	32	23	57	19	8	.361	.398

12 DREW CISCO, RHP

Born: July 29, 1991. **B-T:** R-R. **Ht.:** 6-0. **Wt.:** 205. **Drafted:** HS—Mt. Pleasant, S.C., 2010 (6th round). **Signed by:** Perry Smith.

When the Reds worked out a major league deal with 2010 first-round pick Yasmani Grandal that kept his initial bonus relatively low, it freed up money in the draft budget to work out deals with Cisco and outfielder Kyle Waldrop. Cisco passed on a commitment to Georgia to sign for $975,000. Even though he's a high school pitcher, Cisco already is regarded as one of the more polished arms in the system. His grandfather Galen was a major league pitching coach, and his brother Mike is a pitcher in the Phillies system, so pitching runs in the family. Cisco has a solid, mature body. He works with an 89-91 mph fastball that has good life, and he has an ability to manipulate the ball to make it run or cut. He also has an advanced curveball for his age and an effective changeup. All three pitches project as at least average. Cisco should move quickly for a high school pitcher, but he's pitching on a razor's edge. Because his frame is so mature, he is not expected to gain velocity, and if his stuff takes a step back once he gets into the routine of working every fifth day, he'll be trying to succeed with average stuff. Cisco signed too late to pitch in 2010 and will start his pro career in low Class A. He could be in Double-A before long thanks to his polish.

Year	Club (League)	Class	W	L	ERA	G	GS	CG	SV	IP	H	HR	BB	SO	G/A	WHIP	AVG
2010	Did Not Play—Signed Late																

13 DONNIE JOSEPH, LHP

Born: Nov. 1, 1987. **B-T:** L-L. **Ht.:** 6-3. **Wt.:** 190. **Drafted:** Houston, 2009 (3rd round). **Signed by:** Jerry Flowers.

The Reds drafted Joseph after he had an up-and-down career at Houston that didn't really take off until he moved into the bullpen as a junior. Cincinnati knew what it was getting and believed Joseph would move quickly if he stuck to a bullpen role, and so far he has lived up to every expectation. When Joseph is pitching with tempo, hitters have trouble handling him. He throws a plus-plus slider that proved unhittable at three different levels last year, and hitters sometimes flailed at pitches that would almost hit them. Joseph's fastball is a solid pitch in its own right, sitting at 90-93 mph. He's working on a changeup but has rarely used it and is unlikely to need it unless he slides into a long relief role. Joseph's delivery isn't particularly clean and it has plenty of effort, and he has a tendency to open up too soon in his delivery, but he somewhat tamed that in 2010. Joseph has yet to hit a speed bump on his climb through the minors. He should open the year in Triple-A, but a promotion to Cincinnati at some point seems likely.

Year	Club (League)	Class	W	L	ERA	G	GS	CG	SV	IP	H	HR	BB	SO	G/A	WHIP	AVG
2009	Billings (PIO)	R	2	1	0.77	8	0	0	0	12	6	0	4	11	1.56	0.86	.146
	Dayton (MWL)	LoA	2	2	4.35	16	0	0	4	21	13	0	10	31	0.88	1.11	.176
2010	Dayton (MWL)	LoA	2	1	0.78	19	0	0	6	23	13	0	7	40	1.70	0.87	.160
	Lynchburg (CAR)	HiA	0	4	2.31	31	0	0	17	35	23	2	16	56	1.56	1.11	.181
	Carolina (SL)	AA	1	0	5.14	7	0	0	1	7	7	0	2	7	6.00	1.29	.250
Minor League Totals			7	8	2.40	81	0	0	28	97	62	2	39	145	1.54	1.04	.177

14 CHRIS VALAIKA, 2B/SS

Born: Aug. 14, 1985. **B-T:** R-R. **Ht.:** 6-0. **Wt.:** 215. **Drafted:** UC Santa Barbara, 2006 (3rd round). **Signed by:** Rex de la Nuez.

As an offense-first second baseman, Valaika's rise to the big leagues took a big detour when he hit .235 in his first taste of Triple-A in 2009 and missed time after punching a water cooler, breaking his hand. He bounced back in 2010, topping .300 for the third time in his five-year career. A shortstop in college, Valaika has shown steady improvement at his new position. He led International League second basemen with a .984 fielding percentage last year and has become comfortable turning double plays. His range is still below-average, but he generally scoops up whatever he gets to, and his arm is strong enough for second base. He's a slightly below-average runner. At the plate, Valaika hits plenty of line drives and is sometimes too aggressive. He doesn't walk much at all, which leads to low on-base percentages. His slightly below-average power plays fine at second base. Some scouts see Valaika as a second-division regular with enough bat to make up for his defensive deficiencies, while others see him as an offense-first utility type who can play third base and even shortstop in a pinch. His chances of making the big league roster as a backup this season will depend on how the battle between Paul Janish and Zack Cozart shakes out at shortstop.

Year	Club (League)	Class	AVG	G	AB	R	H	2B	3B	HR	RBI	BB	SO	SB	CS	OBP	SLG
2006	Billings (PIO)	R	.324	70	275	58	89	22	4	8	60	24	61	2	2	.387	.520
2007	Dayton (MWL)	LoA	.307	79	300	38	92	20	3	10	56	17	72	1	4	.353	.493
	Sarasota (FSL)	HiA	.253	57	217	26	55	9	1	2	23	13	42	0	3	.310	.332
2008	Sarasota (FSL)	HiA	.363	32	135	20	49	9	0	7	31	7	28	2	0	.393	.585
	Chattanooga (SL)	AA	.301	97	379	58	114	19	1	11	50	28	74	7	4	.352	.443
2009	Louisville (IL)	AAA	.235	95	366	32	86	20	1	6	36	16	76	1	0	.271	.344
2010	Louisville (IL)	AAA	.304	118	424	49	129	28	2	4	53	19	72	3	3	.330	.408
	Cincinnati (NL)	MAJ	.263	19	38	3	10	1	0	1	2	1	9	0	0	.282	.368
Major League Totals			.263	19	38	3	10	1	0	1	2	1	9	0	0	.282	.368
Minor League Totals			.293	548	2096	281	614	127	12	48	309	124	425	16	16	.337	.434

15 DANIEL CORCINO, RHP

Born: Aug. 26, 1990. **B-T:** R-R. **Ht.:** 5-11. **Wt.:** 165. **Signed**: Dominican Republic, 2008. **Signed by:** Richard Jimenez.

When watching Corcino pitch, scouts have a hard time avoiding Johnny Cueto comparisons. Like Cueto, Corcino is a short Dominican righthander with a thick body, tree-trunk legs and a plus fastball. He also uses a similar fast delivery that ends with a pronounced spin off his lead leg. Corcino even bears a facial resemblance to Cueto. Like the Reds rotation stalwart, Corcino has plenty of upside. He showcases a 92-94 mph fastball that touches 97 at its best, and pairs it with a potentially plus 75-78 mph slider. His changeup is a little firm right now, and he needs to develop more separation between it and his fastball. Corcino's stuff tailed off a little after his promotion to low Class A last year, and he needs to improve his command, but his combination of plus stuff and competitive makeup makes him one of the best young pitching prospects in the system. He'll help anchor the Dayton rotation in 2011.

Year	Club (League)	Class	W	L	ERA	G	GS	CG	SV	IP	H	HR	BB	SO	G/A	WHIP	AVG
2008	Reds (DSL)	R	6	2	5.29	23	0	0	0	34	37	2	14	26	—	1.50	.280
2009	Reds (GCL)	R	0	1	0.00	2	0	0	0	3	5	0	1	2	2.00	2.25	.455
	Billings (PIO)	R	1	4	4.91	20	0	0	3	26	23	2	15	30	0.91	1.48	.245
2010	Billings (PIO)	R	1	3	3.40	9	9	0	0	40	38	2	17	31	1.52	1.39	.255
	Dayton (MWL)	LoA	1	1	4.31	6	6	0	0	31	31	1	15	29	1.70	1.47	.254
Minor League Totals			9	11	4.32	60	15	0	3	133	134	7	62	118	1.41	1.47	.264

16 ISMAEL GUILLON, LHP

Born: Feb. 13, 1992. **B-T:** L-L. **Ht.:** 6-3. **Wt.:** 185. **Signed**: Venezuela, 2008. **Signed by:** Tony Arias.

Guillon was another significant international signing during the Reds' spending spree in 2008. Not long after the Reds signed him for $220,000, however, they found that he had a torn elbow ligament. His original contract was voided, and he signed for a significantly lower amount. The Reds then waited until 2010 to see him get back on the mound. Because he signed a second contract with his original team, Guillon will be eligible for the Rule 5 draft every year until he's added to the 40-man roster; he wasn't taken in the 2010 Rule 5 draft. When he did get back on the hill, he showed much of what the Reds liked before his injury. Guillon is advanced for a young pitcher, with a live 90-92 mph fastball, but his out pitch is a plus changeup that overmatched hitters in the Rookie-level Arizona League. He didn't use his fringy breaking ball much last year because he was coming back from injury, so that will be a focus for him this year. Guillon has cleaned up his delivery, reducing a wrap, and he shows good feel for setting up hitters. He'll battle for a full-season spot with Dayton but may open the season in extended spring training.

Year	Club (League)	Class	W	L	ERA	G	GS	CG	SV	IP	H	HR	BB	SO	G/A	WHIP	AVG
2010	Reds (AZL)	R	3	3	3.32	12	10	0	0	57	39	1	23	73	0.76	1.09	.193
Minor League Totals			3	3	3.32	12	10	0	0	57	39	1	23	73	0.76	1.09	.193

17 JUNIOR ARIAS, SS

Born: Jan. 9, 1992. **B-T:** R-R. **Ht.:** 6-2. **Wt.:** 178. **Signed**: Dominican Republic, 2008. **Signed by:** Richard Jimenez.

In the scouting leading up to the 2008 international signing period, Arias became one of the Reds' top targets. They learned he had an elbow problem that needed surgery, but when other teams backed off they decided to sign him anyway, giving him a $330,000 bonus. Because of the elbow problems, it took Arias two more years to get to the U.S., and he still shows some effects—his arm isn't as loose as it was before the surgery—but the Reds think the injury has given them a quality prospect at a bargain rate. Unlike other Latin shortstops in the system,

Arias is more of a hitter than a glove man. His hits show plenty of carry when he squares up the ball, and he does it with a nice, short stroke and simple bat path. He shows plenty of opposite-field power. Like many young players, he's too aggressive and willing to chase pitches out of the zone. He has slightly above-average speed, but his long limbs and solid frame make it likely he'll end up as an average runner at best after he fills out. He'll probably outgrow shortstop as well. He played some third base in instructional league, and his average arm should play there. Arias should have enough bat for the position as well, and his bat may even play as a corner outfielder if he can't stick at third base. He should make his full-season debut at Dayton this spring.

Year	Club (League)	Class	AVG	G	AB	R	H	2B	3B	HR	RBI	BB	SO	SB	CS	OBP	SLG
2009	Reds (DSL)	R	.231	55	208	33	48	11	2	6	27	19	66	10	6	.304	.389
2010	Reds (AZL)	R	.287	47	195	44	56	10	5	6	25	12	58	4	3	.336	.482
Minor League Totals			.258	102	403	77	104	21	7	12	52	31	124	14	9	.320	.434

18 BRAD BOXBERGER, RHP

Born: May 27, 1988. **B-T:** R-R. **Ht.:** 6-2. **Wt.:** 185. **Drafted:** Southern California, 2009 (1st round supplemental). **Signed by:** Rex de la Nuez.

When the Reds drafted Boxberger out of Southern California, they planned on using the same approach they had mapped out for Zach Stewart in his first professional season—half the season in the rotation, then to the bullpen to limit his innings. It worked out with Stewart, who was traded to the Blue Jays in the Scott Rolen deal, but didn't go nearly as well with Boxberger. The son of 1978 College World Series MVP Rod Boxberger, Brad showed excellent stuff in the first half of the season in high Class A. He used a 91-93 mph fastball, an average slider and an improving changeup to rank among the Carolina League's ERA leaders at the time of his promotion. At that point, his season fell apart. When he moved up and into the pen, Boxberger tried too much to blow his fastball past hitters. He lost the feel for his slider and changeup, dropped his release point and struggled to throw strikes. He allowed at least one earned run in his first 10 Double-A appearances. Boxberger started to regain his stuff in the final weeks of the season and looked better in instructional league, but he has to prove that he can maintain his stuff over a full season. He'll return to Carolina, this time in the rotation.

Year	Club (League)	Class	W	L	ERA	G	GS	CG	SV	IP	H	HR	BB	SO	G/A	WHIP	AVG
2010	Lynchburg (CAR)	HiA	4	6	3.19	14	13	0	0	62	57	3	20	70	1.91	1.24	.249
	Carolina (SL)	AA	1	4	8.49	22	0	0	0	30	35	4	22	40	1.35	1.92	.289
Minor League Totals			5	10	4.91	36	13	0	0	92	92	7	42	110	1.73	1.46	.263

19 DIDI GREGORIUS, SS

Born: Feb. 18, 1990. **B-T:** L-R. **Ht.:** 6-1. **Wt.:** 183. **Signed**: Netherlands Antilles, 2007. **Signed by:** Jim Stoeckel.

Gregorius' father played in the top professional league in the Netherlands, and he is eligible to play for both the Netherlands Antilles and Dutch teams in international play because he was born in Amsterdam. He played for the Dutch team in the 2009 World Cup. A mature 20-year-old, Gregorius' best work comes in the field. He has a 65 arm on the 20-to-80 scouting scale that allows him to make any throw, often without needing to set his feet. His above-average speed and quick feet give him good range as well, though his hands are still somewhat erratic. Many of his errors come from a lack of focus and a tendency to rush plays, and that should improve as he matures. His excellent body control and fluidity prompt scouts to project him as an above-average defensive shortstop. At the plate, he has more work to do. He is relatively helpless against lefties, but he knows how to bunt, has a relatively direct stroke and has added strength to his wiry frame. He doesn't yet read pitchers well and isn't particularly aggressive on the basepaths. Gregorius will get another taste of high Class A in 2011.

Year	Club (League)	Class	AVG	G	AB	R	H	2B	3B	HR	RBI	BB	SO	SB	CS	OBP	SLG
2008	Reds (GCL)	R	.155	31	97	6	15	0	0	0	9	10	10	2	1	.241	.155
2009	Sarasota (FSL)	HiA	.254	22	71	8	18	4	0	0	2	1	9	0	0	.274	.310
	Billings (PIO)	R	.314	50	204	28	64	10	1	1	16	12	27	8	6	.363	.387
2010	Dayton (MWL)	LoA	.273	120	501	65	137	16	11	5	41	33	62	16	7	.327	.379
	Lynchburg (CAR)	HiA	.240	7	25	4	6	0	0	0	0	2	6	0	0	.321	.240
Minor League Totals			.267	230	898	111	240	30	12	6	68	58	114	26	14	.321	.347

20 DAVE SAPPELT, OF

Born: Jan. 2, 1987. **B-T:** R-R. **Ht.:** 5-9. **Wt.:** 193. **Drafted:** Coastal Carolina, 2008 (9th round). **Signed by:** Steve Kring.

Sappelt has proven detractors wrong every step up the way, and he has continued to be a productive hitter despite his short stature. After an excellent career at Coastal Carolina, where his college teammates nicknamed him Gary Coleman, Sappelt slipped to the ninth round because scouts had a hard time profiling him, and he signed for $75,000. He has continued to hit, culminating in a Double-A Southern League batting title in 2010 and a late-season promotion to Triple-A. Sappelt has excellent hand-eye coordination and an ability to turn pitches off the plate into line drives. He's especially tough on lefties (batting .411 against them in 2010) and is an above-average hitter with below-average power. Some scouts see him as a fourth outfielder. Sappelt is a tick above average in center field and has enough arm to play right field. He's an above-average runner. Sappelt may not profile as an everyday player, and being a righthanded hitter limits his platoon potential, but like Chris Heisey, another late-round Reds find, he has a knack for surprising people. Sappelt will get his first extended taste of Triple-A in 2011.

Year	Club (League)	Class	AVG	G	AB	R	H	2B	3B	HR	RBI	BB	SO	SB	CS	OBP	SLG
2008	Billings (PIO)	R	.299	62	254	47	76	19	5	7	35	21	45	6	3	.354	.496
2009	Dayton (MWL)	LoA	.269	74	301	44	81	14	7	3	25	23	46	26	11	.322	.392
	Sarasota (FSL)	HiA	.295	62	251	27	74	10	3	4	21	13	29	21	11	.333	.406
2010	Lynchburg (CAR)	HiA	.282	19	71	7	20	5	0	0	4	5	15	6	4	.338	.352
	Carolina (SL)	AA	.361	89	330	53	119	19	8	9	62	31	46	15	13	.416	.548
	Louisville (IL)	AAA	.324	25	108	12	35	8	3	1	8	6	13	4	1	.365	.481
Minor League Totals			.308	331	1315	190	405	75	26	24	155	99	194	78	43	.359	.459

21 KYLE WALDROP, OF

Born: Nov. 26, 1991 **B-T:** L-L. **Ht.:** 6-3 **Wt.:** 190. **Drafted:** HS—Fort Myers, Fla., 2010 (12th round). **Signed by:** Greg Zunino.

It took Waldrop until his senior high school season to get a chance to fully show what he can do on the baseball diamond. He missed part of his sophomore baseball season with a broken hand, and part of his junior year with a broken leg. He made more noise on the football field, where he was a standout safety and wide receiver, and he committed to South Florida to play both sports. The Reds were able to put an end to his football career with a $500,000 bonus that they spread over multiple years under draft provisions for two-sport athletes. Waldrop has plenty of strength in his swing and he should provide good lefthanded power. He's quite raw right now, with a pull-heavy approach that leaves him vulnerable to anything on the outer half of the plate. Once he develops a more advanced approach, his bat speed should allow him to hit for average as well. Waldrop is a slightly above-average runner, though he doesn't cover enough ground to be a center fielder. As with many football players, his arm is below average, but as he stretches it out and gets used to throwing, it may improve enough to let him play right field. Waldrop is still relatively raw and may not be ready for full-season ball yet, so a trip to the Arizona League or Billings seems likely.

Year	Club (League)	Class	AVG	G	AB	R	H	2B	3B	HR	RBI	BB	SO	SB	CS	OBP	SLG
2010	Reds (AZL)	R	.214	7	28	1	6	1	0	0	1	1	9	0	0	.241	.250
Minor League Totals			.214	7	28	1	6	1	0	0	1	1	9	0	0	.241	.250

22 RONALD TORREYES, INF

Born: Sept. 2, 1992. **B-T:** R-R. **Ht.:** 5-7. **Wt.:** 150. **Signed**: Venezuela, 2010. **Signed by:** Jose Fuentes.

As a 17-year-old in the Rookie-level Venezuelan Summer League last year, Torreyes led the league in batting, doubles, triples, slugging percentage and runs. So it might be surprising to hear that what the Reds really like is his defense at second base. Torreyes is a wizard with the glove, capable of making the highlight play ranging into the outfield or behind the bag, and he also knows how to position himself to make a tough play look easy. He has also played shortstop and third base, but his lack of arm strength makes second base a much better fit. At the plate, Torreyes has surprising pop for his size, and he profiles as a top-of-the-order hitter who is a good bunter with a solid batting eye. Though the Reds list him at 5-foot-10, he's probably three inches shorter, so some scouts worry about his projection. His ability to handle the bat and his impressive instincts make him worth watching, and he should be ready for the Pioneer League as an 18-year-old.

Year	Club (League)	Class	AVG	G	AB	R	H	2B	3B	HR	RBI	BB	SO	SB	CS	OBP	SLG
2010	Reds (VSL)	R	.390	67	241	56	94	20	10	4	33	23	11	23	15	.468	.606
	Reds (AZL)	R	.349	18	83	13	29	7	1	1	11	1	5	2	2	.379	.494
	Dayton (MWL)	LoA	.240	6	25	3	6	2	1	0	2	0	3	0	0	.240	.400
Minor League Totals			.370	91	349	72	129	29	12	5	46	24	19	25	17	.434	.564

23 HENRY RODRIGUEZ, 2B

Born: Feb. 9, 1990. **B-T:** B-R. **Ht.:** 5-10. **Wt.:** 150. **Signed**: Venezuela, 2007. **Signed by:** Tony Arias.

Dayton was one of the worst teams in minor league baseball in 2010, and at one point the Dragons lost 24 straight home games. On a team with plenty of disappointing players, Rodriguez was one of the few bright spots. At the plate, he's a switch-hitter who shows power from both sides. He has a conventional set-up from the right side, while lefthanded he has to bring the bat a long way to the zone from a rather noisy, high-handed stance. He chases a lot of balls out of the zone, but his hand-eye coordination allows him to get away with it more than most. Rodriguez is an average runner. He needs to hit because he's a tick below average defensively, with limited range. His arm works at second base and is short for shortstop and possibly third base. Rodriguez has a ways to go when it comes to mastering the more intricate aspects of the game. He forgets to cover bases at times and makes a variety of other mental mistakes, including failing to run out balls. Rodriguez is somewhat similar to Chris Valaiaka, as an offense-first second baseman. He'll advance to high Class A this year.

Year	Club (League)	Class	AVG	G	AB	R	H	2B	3B	HR	RBI	BB	SO	SB	CS	OBP	SLG
2007	Devil Rays/Reds (VSL)	R	.267	54	206	30	55	14	5	3	25	28	29	4	2	.361	.427
	Reds (DSL)	R	.235	7	17	3	4	0	0	0	4	1	1	1	0	.263	.235
2008	Reds (DSL)	R	.240	13	50	5	12	1	0	0	3	7	9	5	1	.328	.260
	D'backs/Reds (DSL)	R	.337	46	181	25	61	8	3	1	18	20	14	16	6	.405	.431
2009	Reds (GCL)	R	.322	42	152	24	49	10	1	1	19	7	18	9	0	.354	.421
2010	Dayton (MWL)	LoA	.307	124	514	76	158	37	3	14	78	22	70	33	13	.337	.473
	Lynchburg (CAR)	HiA	.250	6	24	2	6	0	0	0	4	0	4	0	0	.250	.250
Minor League Totals			.302	292	1144	165	345	70	12	19	151	85	145	68	22	.352	.434

24 NEFTALI SOTO, 1B

Born: Feb. 28, 1989 **B-T:** R-R. **Ht.:** 6-2. **Wt.:** 200. **Drafted:** HS—Manati, P.R., 2008 (3rd round). **Signed by:** Tony Arias.

It has taken him several position swaps, but Soto finally found a home on defense. Unfortunately for him, that position will also make it harder for him to reach the big leagues with Cincinnati. Drafted as a shortstop, Soto moved to third base in his first full pro season. Because of his lack of range and strong arm, the Reds tried him as a catcher in 2010. He didn't stay there long, partly because the Reds now have Devin Mesoraco and Yasmani Grandal, and he ended up moving to first base during the 2010 season. Soto showed potential behind the plate, and he has the hands to be a solid first baseman, though his best defensive attribute, a plus arm, is wasted at first. Offensively, Soto has some of the best power in the organization, especially when he gets to extend his arms. His swing is relatively uncomplicated and easy to maintain, but it's also a long stroke, and scouts have concerns that he'll struggle to catch up with good fastballs. He's a below-average runner who figures to get slower as he matures. After two years in high Class A, Soto will head to Carolina in 2011.

Year	Club (League)	Class	AVG	G	AB	R	H	2B	3B	HR	RBI	BB	SO	SB	CS	OBP	SLG
2007	Reds (GCL)	R	.303	40	152	18	46	7	5	2	28	11	31	2	0	.355	.454
2008	Billings (PIO)	R	.388	15	67	12	26	10	1	4	11	4	10	1	0	.423	.746
	Dayton (MWL)	LoA	.326	52	218	26	71	15	1	7	36	7	36	1	1	.343	.500
2009	Sarasota (FSL)	HiA	.248	131	505	53	125	21	2	11	57	23	95	1	3	.282	.362
2010	Lynchburg (CAR)	HiA	.268	134	522	73	140	33	2	21	73	32	105	0	0	.319	.460
Minor League Totals			.279	372	1464	182	408	86	11	45	205	77	277	5	4	.318	.445

25 SAM LECURE, RHP

Born: May 4, 1984. **B-T:** R-R. **Ht.:** 6-1. **Wt.:** 205. **Drafted:** Texas, 2005 (4th round). **Signed by:** Brian Wilson.

After 600 minor league innings, LeCure finally got the call to the big leagues in 2010. His reward was the opportunity to face Chris Carpenter, Matt Cain, Zack Greinke and Felix Hernandez in four of his first five starts. He didn't buckle under the pressure, but that's not surprising. At Texas, LeCure won elimination games in the Big 12 Conference tournament and College World Series as a freshman. He missed his junior season after being declared academically inelibgle, and the Reds drafted him in the fourth round. LeCure's scouting report hasn't changed much since the Reds drafted him. He's a righthander without a plus pitch, but with enough savvy and command to survive. He has a wrap in his delivery, but it doesn't seem to affect his command and he's been durable, making at least 20 starts in every full pro season. His fastball sits around 88-90 mph, touching 92 at its best. He also throws an average slider and changeup. LeCure's command allows him to have success with three average pitches. His upside is that of a fifth starter, and he faces an uphill battle to fill that role with the Reds' deep pitching staff. He's major league ready and will be waiting in Triple-A if injuries strike in Cincinnati.

Year	Club (League)	Class	W	L	ERA	G	GS	CG	SV	IP	H	HR	BB	SO	G/A	WHIP	AVG
2005	Billings (PIO)	R	5	1	3.27	13	6	0	0	41	43	2	15	44	—	1.40	.272
2006	Sarasota (FSL)	HiA	7	12	3.43	27	27	0	0	142	130	12	46	115	—	1.24	.243
2007	Sarasota (FSL)	HiA	1	0	1.80	1	1	0	0	5	2	0	0	8	—	0.40	.125
	Chattanooga (SL)	AA	7	5	4.17	21	21	0	0	110	119	12	46	104	—	1.50	.281
2008	Chattanooga (SL)	AA	9	7	3.42	27	27	0	0	155	147	12	58	128	—	1.32	.251
2009	Louisville (IL)	AAA	10	8	4.46	25	25	0	0	143	143	17	44	125	0.83	1.30	.264
2010	Louisville (IL)	AAA	8	3	3.67	15	15	1	0	98	98	8	23	87	2.24	1.23	.262
	Cincinnati (NL)	MAJ	2	5	4.50	15	6	0	0	48	50	6	25	37	1.45	1.56	.272
Major League Totals			2	5	4.50	15	6	0	0	48	50	6	25	37	1.45	1.56	.272
Minor League Totals			47	36	3.77	129	122	1	0	695	682	63	232	611	1.20	1.32	.259

26 JONATHAN CORREA, RHP

Born: Sept. 13, 1990. **B-T:** R-R. **Ht.:** 6-1. **Wt.:** 168. **Signed**: Dominican Republic, 2008. **Signed by:** Richard Jimenez.

It has been a long path to the United States for Correa. Signed in 2008, he was suspended for 50 games at the end of the 2008 season when he tested positive for performance-enhancing drugs. At the same time, he was diagnosed with a torn elbow ligament that required Tommy John surgery. The suspension and rehab wiped out almost all of his 2009 season, and he showed few ill effects last year as he pitched his way out of the Arizona League to the Pioneer League. Correa's fastball sits at 90-92 mph, touching 94, and shows good life. He also throws a slurvy but effective curveball. His changeup is raw at this point, and he hasn't needed it much yet. Correa has a clean, three-quarters delivery that the Reds have tried to make more over-the-top. Reds officials have been impressed with his work ethic and his receptiveness to instruction. Correa's spring will help determine if he makes the jump to low Class A or heads back to Billings.

Year	Club (League)	Class	W	L	ERA	G	GS	CG	SV	IP	H	HR	BB	SO	G/A	WHIP	AVG
2008	Reds (DSL)	R	2	1	1.19	4	4	0	0	23	17	0	8	20	—	1.10	.215
2009	Reds (DSL)	R	0	1	0.68	6	6	0	0	13	8	0	8	14	1.33	1.20	.170
2010	Reds (AZL)	R	4	2	2.06	8	8	0	0	39	36	1	9	49	1.00	1.14	.243
	Billings (PIO)	R	2	2	5.00	6	6	0	0	27	25	3	10	34	1.17	1.30	.248
Minor League Totals			8	6	2.46	24	24	0	0	102	86	4	35	117	1.11	1.18	.229

27 DARYL THOMPSON, RHP

Born: Nov. 2, 1985. **B-T:** R-R. **Ht.:** 6-0. **Wt.:** 205. **Drafted:** HS—La Plata, Md., 2003 (8th round). **Signed by:** Alex Smith (Expos).

When the Reds dealt Austin Kearns and Felipe Lopez to the Nationals in an ill-fated playoff push in 2006, the deal quickly fell flat. Gary Majewski and Bill Bray, the two relievers brought in to bolster the Reds' bullpen, proved to be duds, while Royce Clayton and Brendan Harris were soon playing elsewhere. Thompson, a low Class A pitcher at the time, may still bring the Reds some return on their investment. When he has been healthy he has shown major league stuff, but injury problems have slowed his development, causing him to miss time in each of the past two seasons. He was shut down in 2009 with elbow problems, then had surgery to clean up his labrum after the season and was taken off the 40-man roster. His stuff bounced back last year, and he was showing a 92-94 mph fastball, a usable, slow curveball and an average changeup, but he missed time with mononucleosis. Thompson's skinny frame and injury history lead to lingering concerns about his durability and may eventually cause him to move to the bullpen. Cincinnati was impressed enough with his showing in the Arizona Fall League to add him back to the 40-man roster.

Year	Club (League)	Class	W	L	ERA	G	GS	CG	SV	IP	H	HR	BB	SO	G/A	WHIP	AVG
2003	Expos (GCL)	R	1	2	2.15	12	10	0	0	46	49	1	11	18	—	1.30	.288
2004	Savannah (SAL)	LoA	4	9	5.08	25	21	0	0	103	117	13	30	79	—	1.43	.296
2005	Savannah (SAL)	LoA	2	3	3.35	11	11	0	0	54	46	3	24	48	—	1.30	.232
2006	Vermont (NYP)	SS	0	1	6.75	4	4	0	0	7	5	0	5	8	—	1.50	.200
	Reds (GCL)	R	0	0	2.57	5	4	0	0	14	10	1	4	16	—	1.00	.222
2007	Dayton (MWL)	LoA	5	0	0.96	5	5	0	0	28	16	1	2	24	—	0.64	.165
	Sarasota (FSL)	HiA	9	5	3.77	22	22	0	0	105	106	19	31	97	—	1.30	.262
2008	Chattanooga (SL)	AA	3	2	1.76	10	10	0	0	61	44	2	14	56	—	0.95	.208
	Cincinnati (NL)	MAJ	0	2	6.91	3	3	0	0	14	20	3	7	6	—	1.88	.328
	Reds (GCL)	R	0	0	0.00	1	0	0	0	4	2	0	0	3	—	0.50	.133
	Sarasota (FSL)	HiA	0	2	6.89	3	3	0	0	16	20	2	7	7	—	1.72	.339
	Louisville (IL)	AAA	5	0	2.76	7	7	0	0	46	39	4	9	33	—	1.05	.232
2009	Louisville (IL)	AAA	1	2	6.59	8	6	0	0	29	34	3	7	8	0.77	1.43	.288
	Reds (GCL)	R	0	0	27.00	1	1	0	0	1	2	0	2	1	0.00	6.00	.500
2010	Reds (AZL)	R	0	0	2.45	3	3	0	0	11	10	1	2	17	0.75	1.09	.238
	Carolina (SL)	AA	0	5	3.71	12	12	0	0	51	38	3	11	52	0.54	0.96	.211
Major League Totals			0	2	6.91	3	3	0	0	14	20	3	7	6	—	1.88	.328
Minor League Totals			31	31	3.61	129	119	0	0	574	538	53	159	467	0.64	1.21	.252

28 JUAN DURAN, OF

Born: Sept. 2, 1991. **B-T:** R-R. **Ht.:** 6-7. **Wt.:** 204. Signed: Dominican Republic, 2008. **Signed by:** Tony Arias.

Aside from Juan Francisco, there may not be a Reds prospect who has better raw power than Duran. The Reds signed him in 2008 for $2 million, when assistant general manager Bob Miller noticed a loophole that allowed him to sign before the traditional July 2 signing date. Since then Duran has grown three inches, which has resulted in growth plate problems that have caused elbow and knee injuries. He was healthier in 2010, though he missed instructional league after injuring his ankle making a diving catch. Like Francisco, Duran can put on a show during batting practice. Unfortunately for the massive outfielder, BP doesn't count on the scoreboard.

When the game begins and pitchers aren't throwing everything down the middle, Duran has significant problems making contact, largely because his pitch recognition is poor. With his large strike zone and long levers, Duran projects more as a slugger than someone who will hit for average. He is still relatively lanky and is an average runner. Defensively, Duran has problems reading line drives off the bat and takes poor routes. He does have an above-average arm. Duran still has loads of potential, and he will play the entire season as a 20-year-old, but he'll find low Class A to be a tough assignment unless his approach comes along.

Year	Club (League)	Class	AVG	G	AB	R	H	2B	3B	HR	RBI	BB	SO	SB	CS	OBP	SLG
2008	Reds (DSL)	R	.215	41	135	15	29	3	4	1	14	24	47	8	5	.340	.319
2009	Reds (GCL)	R	.177	45	164	15	29	7	4	0	17	8	52	0	0	.218	.268
2010	Billings (PIO)	R	.244	54	201	23	49	10	1	6	25	19	71	2	3	.309	.393
Minor League Totals			.214	140	500	53	107	20	9	7	56	51	170	10	8	.290	.332

29 PHILIPPE VALIQUETTE, LHP

Born: Feb. 14, 1987 **B-T:** L-L. **Ht.:** 6-1. **Wt.:** 205. **Drafted:** HS—Montreal, 2004 (7th round). **Signed by:** Jason Baker.

Valiquette's scouting report for the past six years has been numbingly consistent: great arm, needs to develop a feel for a second pitch. That was true when he signed with the Reds in 2004, and it's still true nearly seven years later. Valiquette will play the entire 2011 season at 24, and he'll get plenty more chances because it's hard to find a lefty who can run it up to 97-98 mph. At the same time, he still has little feel for pitching and shows wavering command that often forces him to take something off his fastball to get it over the plate. He will sometimes shake off calls for his slider, though it's a usable pitch with average potential. With his fastball, that would be plenty to make it effective. His changeup is a show-me pitch at best. Valiquette's delivery has plenty of effort and he doesn't always get all the pieces to work together, which affects his command. The Reds may eventually run out of patience, but Valiquette's stuff is good enough that he will get plenty of time to figure out how to be a big league reliever—he still has less than 400 pro innings. He'll head to Triple-A for another try at mastering his slider, and if he does that he has the stuff to work late in games.

Year	Club (League)	Class	W	L	ERA	G	GS	CG	SV	IP	H	HR	BB	SO	G/A	WHIP	AVG
2005	Dayton (MWL)	LoA	2	5	6.30	19	16	0	0	64	81	3	44	42	—	1.94	.315
	Billings (PIO)	R	2	1	6.43	7	3	0	0	21	23	1	10	18	—	1.57	.291
2006	Dayton (MWL)	LoA	2	4	7.54	12	9	0	0	37	52	5	21	24	—	1.97	.327
2007	Billings (PIO)	R	3	1	1.77	11	0	0	3	41	31	0	11	29	—	1.03	.214
	Dayton (MWL)	LoA	1	2	6.75	7	0	0	0	11	17	1	2	8	—	1.78	.347
2008	Dayton (MWL)	LoA	0	1	3.12	16	0	0	1	26	25	2	10	32	—	1.35	.250
	Sarasota (FSL)	HiA	2	2	3.92	31	0	0	2	39	45	4	18	33	—	1.62	.294
2009	Sarasota (FSL)	HiA	1	1	2.29	17	0	0	6	20	11	2	9	19	1.44	1.02	.175
	Carolina (SL)	AA	1	1	2.76	27	0	0	3	33	25	2	20	27	1.34	1.38	.217
2010	Carolina (SL)	AA	2	0	3.99	25	0	0	4	29	34	0	16	21	2.73	1.70	.309
	Louisville (IL)	AAA	2	1	4.29	29	0	0	1	36	34	2	14	31	3.06	1.35	.250
Minor League Totals			18	19	4.50	201	28	0	20	356	378	22	175	284	2.01	1.55	.277

30 FELIX PEREZ, OF

Born: Nov. 14, 1984. **B-T:** L-L. **Ht.:** 6-2. **Wt.:** 190. **Signed**: Cuba, 2010. **Signed by:** Richard Jimenez.

Perez was considered one of the top Cuban defectors in recent years when he went to the Dominican in 2008. Just before he wrapped up a $3.5 million deal with the Yankees, Major League Baseball suspended him for a year after discovering that he lied about his age—he had claimed to be 20 when he was actually 25. The discrepancy cost Perez millions, and he ended up signing with Cincinnati for $550,000. At 26, Perez has little projection remaining, but he is already a useful outfielder. He missed time with a shoulder injury after running into an outfield wall at Carolina to make a spectacular catch in a late July game. Upon his return, it took him a while to start swinging free and easy again. Perez is an above-average center fielder who can play right field. He's an average runner with below-average power, so his potential as a big leaguer rests with his ability to hit for average. Perez points the bat at the pitcher in his stance, with his hands well away from his body. That forces his hands to come a long way to a hitting position and leaves him vulnerable to being busted in with power stuff. Perez could play in the big leagues right now defensively, and his bat isn't far away either, but he has little upside and profiles as a big league backup.

Year	Club (League)	Class	AVG	G	AB	R	H	2B	3B	HR	RBI	BB	SO	SB	CS	OBP	SLG
2010	Reds (DSL)	R	.429	16	63	11	27	5	1	1	14	7	8	2	3	.486	.587
	Lynchburg (CAR)	HiA	.338	16	65	8	22	4	2	0	9	4	10	1	1	.397	.462
	Carolina (SL)	AA	.266	35	139	11	37	5	1	2	11	5	31	8	4	.325	.360
Minor League Totals			.322	67	267	30	86	14	4	3	34	16	49	11	8	.381	.438

Cleveland Indians

BY BEN BADLER

The highlight of the Indians' 2010 season came when top prospect Carlos Santana made his major league debut on June 11. The 24-year-old catcher hit .260/.401/.467 before his season ended on Aug. 2 in a gruesome home-plate collision, leading to surgery on his left knee.

The Indians finished 69-93 on the heels of going 65-97 in 2009, their worst back-to-back years since 1914-15. The losing on the field has coincided with a decline in attendance, and the 1.39 million fans who came out in 2010 were the fewest since 1992.

After the season, general manager Mark Shapiro moved up to team president and assistant GM Chris Antonetti took over for Shapiro, a move the club had announced in February. Major changes in how the club operates aren't expected, as Antonetti already was heavily involved in the team's decision-making process and the rest of the front office remained largely in place.

Cleveland had difficulty creating and preventing runs in 2010, ranking 26th in runs scored and 24th in runs allowed while getting few contributions from truly homegrown players. Fausto Carmona led the pitching staff, but he was signed back in 2000 out of the Dominican Republic. Tony Sipp, a 45th-round draft-and-follow from 2004, was an effective set-up man. Trevor Crowe, a 2005 first-rounder, had the lowest OPS (.634) among regular American League outfielders. David Huff, the team's top pick (sandwich round) in 2006, had a 6.21 ERA in 15 starts.

The Indians have had more success trading for young players than signing and developing them. Chris Perez emerged as a somewhat wild but effective closer, and Carlos Carrasco came up in September and showed the potential to be a mid-rotation starter.

Based on the on-field success of recent top picks, Cleveland's draft drought could end soon. Lonnie Chisenhall, the club's 2008 first-round pick, has become one of the game's best third-base prospects. The Indians' picks from the first three rounds in 2009—righthander Alex White, second baseman Jason Kipnis and righthander Joe Gardner—all dominated in their first full seasons.

Though many of their premium choices in 2010 signed too late to play much, Baseball America rated the crop headlined by lefthander Drew Pomeranz and outfielder LeVon Washington as the best draft in the game. Cleveland spent $9.4 million on bonuses, more than all but four other teams.

Carlos Santana's brief big league stint was the highlight of the year for the Indians

TOP 30 PROSPECTS

1. Lonnie Chisenhall, 3b	16. Jordan Henry, of
2. Alex White, rhp	17. Zach Putnam, rhp
3. Jason Kipnis, 2b	18. Bryce Stowell, rhp
4. Drew Pomeranz, lhp	19. Josh Judy, rhp
5. Nick Weglarz, of	20. Cord Phelps, 2b
6. Jason Knapp, rhp	21. Chen Lee, rhp
7. LeVon Washington, of	22. Chun Chen, c
8. Tony Wolters, ss	23. Matt Packer, lhp
9. Joe Gardner, rhp	24. Kelvin de la Cruz, lhp
10. Nick Hagadone, lhp	25. Luigi Rodriguez, of
11. Kyle Blair, rhp	26. Corey Kluber, rhp
12. Alex Lavisky, c	27. Jess Todd, rhp
13. Felix Sterling, rhp	28. Tyler Holt, of
14. T.J. House, lhp	29. Rob Bryson, rhp
15. Hector Rondon, rhp	30. Giovanny Urshela, 3b

The development of several other starters hit some speed bumps. Promising righthanders Alexander Perez and Hector Rondon had Tommy John surgery. Kelvin de la Cruz and Nick Hagadone, who missed significant time in the past with arm injuries, battled their deliveries and struggled to take the next step forward.

Their return to contention might still be a few years away, but the Indians hope the ability to develop their own draft picks will give them a more stable pipeline of talent for the big league club. That's preferable to relying on getting young talent by trading away their best big leaguers as they've had to in recent years.

General Manager: Chris Antonetti. **Farm Director:** Ross Atkins. **Scouting Director:** Brad Grant.

Class	Team	League	W	L	PCT	Finish*	Manager
Majors	Cleveland Indians	American	69	93	.426	11th (14)	Manny Acta
Triple-A	Columbus Clippers	International	79	65	.549	†4th (14)	Mike Sarbaugh
Double-A	Akron Aeros	Eastern	71	71	.500	6th (12)	Joel Skinner
High A	Kinston Indians	Carolina	73	67	.521	2nd (8)	Aaron Holbert
Low A	Lake County Captains	Midwest	77	62	.554	†4th (16)	Ted Kubiak
Short-season	Mahoning Valley Scrappers	New York-Penn	30	46	.395	13th (14)	Travis Fryman
Rookie	AZL Indians	Arizona	21	35	.375	10th (12)	Chris Tremie
Overall 2010 Minor League Record			351	346	.504	15th (30)	

*Finish in overall standings (No. of teams in league). †League champion.

LAST YEAR'S TOP 30

Player, Pos.		Status
1.	Carlos Santana, c	Majors
2.	Lonnie Chisenhall, 3b	No. 1
3.	Nick Hagadone, lhp	No. 10
4.	Jason Knapp, rhp	No. 6
5.	Michael Brantley, of	Majors
6.	Nick Weglarz, of	No. 5
7.	Hector Rondon, rhp	No. 15
8.	Carlos Carrasco, rhp	Majors
9.	Alex White, rhp	No. 2
10.	Jason Kipnis, of/2b	No. 3
11.	Lou Marson, c	Majors
12.	T.J. House, lhp	No. 14
13.	Kelvin de la Cruz, lhp	No. 24
14.	Jordan Brown, 1b	Dropped out
15.	Jason Donald, ss	Majors
16.	Zach Putnam, rhp	No. 17
17.	Carlos Rivero, ss	(Phillies)
18.	Jess Todd, rhp	No. 27
19.	Josh Judy, rhp	No. 19
20.	Alexander Perez, rhp	Dropped out
21.	Jeanmar Gomez, rhp	Majors
22.	Chen-Chang Lee, rhp	No. 21
23.	Abner Abreu, of	Dropped out
24.	Beau Mills, 1b	Dropped out
25.	Jesus Brito, 3b	Dropped out
26.	Connor Graham, rhp	Dropped out
27.	Wes Hodges, 3b	Dropped out
28.	Bryan Price, rhp	Dropped out
29.	Scott Barnes, lhp	Dropped out
30.	Eric Berger, lhp	Dropped out

BEST TOOLS

Best Hitter for Average	Lonnie Chisenhall
Best Power Hitter	Nick Weglarz
Best Strike-Zone Discipline	Jordan Henry
Fastest Baserunner	Delvi Cid
Best Athlete	LeVon Washington
Best Fastball	Jason Knapp
Best Curveball	Drew Pomeranz
Best Slider	Josh Judy
Best Changeup	T.J. House
Best Control	Matt Packer
Best Defensive Catcher	Roberto Perez
Best Defensive Infielder	Kyle Bellows
Best Infield Arm	Giovanny Urshela
Best Defensive Outfielder	Ezequiel Carrera
Best Outfield Arm	Abner Abreu

PROJECTED 2014 LINEUP

Catcher	Carlos Santana
First Base	Matt LaPorta
Second Base	Jason Kipnis
Third Base	Lonnie Chisenhall
Shortstop	Asdrubal Cabrera
Left Field	LeVon Washington
Center Field	Grady Sizemore
Right Field	Shin-Soo Choo
Designated Hitter	Nick Weglarz
No. 1 Starter	Alex White
No. 2 Starter	Drew Pomeranz
No. 3 Starter	Carlos Carrasco
No. 4 Starter	Fausto Carmona
No. 5 Starter	Jason Knapp
Closer	Chris Perez

TOP PROSPECTS OF THE DECADE

Year	Player, Pos.	2010 Org.
2001	C.C. Sabathia, lhp	Yankees
2002	Corey Smith, 3b	Dodgers
2003	Brandon Phillips, ss/2b	Reds
2004	Grady Sizemore, cf	Indians
2005	Adam Miller, rhp	Indians
2006	Adam Miller, rhp	Indians
2007	Adam Miller, rhp	Indians
2008	Adam Miller, rhp	Indians
2009	Carlos Santana, c	Indians
2010	Carlos Santana, c	Indians

TOP DRAFT PICKS OF THE DECADE

Year	Player, Pos.	2010 Org.
2001	Dan Denham, rhp	Angels
2002	Jeremy Guthrie, rhp	Orioles
2003	Michael Aubrey, 1b	Orioles
2004	Jeremy Sowers, lhp	Indians
2005	Trevor Crowe, of	Indians
2006	David Huff, lhp (1st round supp.)	Indians
2007	Beau Mills, 3b/1b	Indians
2008	Lonnie Chisenhall, 3b	Indians
2009	Alex White, rhp	Indians
2010	Drew Pomeranz, lhp	Indians

LARGEST BONUSES IN CLUB HISTORY

Danys Baez, 1999	$4,500,000
Jeremy Guthrie, 2002	$3,000,000
Drew Pomeranz, 2010	$2,650,000
Jeremy Sowers, 2004	$2,475,000
Alex White, 2009	$2,250,000

CLEVELAND INDIANS

TOP 2011 ROOKIE: Zach Putnam, rhp. Among Cleveland's several relievers nearly ready in the upper minors, he has the best combination of polish and upside.

BREAKOUT PROSPECT: Luigi Rodriguez, of. He has plus-plus speed and an advanced approach at the plate, making him a potentially dynamic leadoff man.

SLEEPER: Austin Adams, rhp. A converted shortstop still learning the finer points of pitching, he has a mid-90s fastball.

SOURCE OF TOP 30 TALENT

Homegrown	25	**Acquired**	**5**
College	12	Trades	5
Junior college	2	Rule 5 draft	0
High school	4	Independent leagues	0
Draft-and-follow	0	Free agents/waivers	0
Nondrafted free agents	0		
International	7		

LF
Nick Weglarz (5)
Bo Greenwell
John Drennen
Tim Fedroff

CF
LeVon Washington (7)
Jordan Henry (16)
Luigi Rodriguez (25)
Tyler Holt (28)
Ezequiel Carrera
Delvi Cid
Mark Brown
Marcus Bradley
Henry Dunn

RF
Abner Abreu

3B
Lonnie Chisenhall (1)
Giovanny Urshela (30)
Jared Goedert
Kyle Bellows
Juan Romero
Hunter Jones

SS
Casey Frawley
Jorge Martinez
Ronny Rodriguez
Jairo Kelly
Nick Bartolone

2B
Jason Kipnis (3)
Tony Wolters (8)
Cord Phelps (20)

1B
Jordan Brown
Matt McBride
Beau Mills
Chase Burnette

C
Alex Lavisky (12)
Chun Chen (22)
Alex Monsalve
Roberto Perez

RHP

RHSP	RHRP
Alex White (2)	Zach Putnam (17)
Jason Knapp (6)	Bryce Stowell (18)
Joe Gardner (9)	Josh Judy (19)
Kyle Blair (11)	Chen Lee (21)
Felix Sterling (13)	Jess Todd (27)
Hector Rondon (15)	Rob Bryson (29)
Corey Kluber (26)	Austin Adams
Zach McAllister	Bryan Price
Alexander Perez	Vinnie Pestano
Tony Dischler	Corey Burns
Michael Goodnight	Omar Aguilar
Trey Haley	Connor Graham
Marty Popham	Tyler Sturdevant
Manuel Carmona	Preston Guilmet
Brett Brach	Adam Miller
Robbie Aviles	
Jordan Cooper	
Luis Encarnacion	

LHP

LHSP	LHRP
Drew Pomeranz (4)	Nick Hagadone (10)
T.J. House (14)	Eric Berger
Matt Packer (23)	Vidal Nuno
Kelvin de la Cruz (24)	
Scott Barnes	
Giovanni Soto	
T.J. McFarland	
Elvis Araujo	
Cole Cook	

2010   BONUSES: $9.4 MILLION

BEST PURE HITTER: OF LeVon Washington's (2) speed attracts the most attention, but his bat may wind up being his best tool. He has drawn comparisons to Carl Crawford, and he's a more advanced hitter than Crawford was at the same stage of his career.

BEST POWER HITTER: 1B/OF Chase Burnette (18), who hit nine regular-season homers and two more in the low Class A Midwest League playoffs, has the most present power. C Alex Lavisky (8), who signed for $1 million, may have as much raw power.

FASTEST RUNNER: Washington has plus-plus speed, but he's not the 80 runner he was on the 20-80 scouting scale when the Rays made him a first-round pick in 2009. His game speed also plays down another notch, too. OF Henry Dunn (50) is also a well above-average runner.

BEST DEFENSIVE PLAYER: SS/3B Nick Bartolone (6) has good range, hands and arm strength. SS Tony Wolters (3), Lavisky and OF Tyler Holt (10) are up-the-middle defenders with fine instincts.

BEST FASTBALL: LHP Drew Pomeranz (1) has a 90-95 mph fastball, and it's not even his best pitch. RHP Tony Dischler (23), the ace of Louisiana State-Eunice's Divison II national juco champions, also can pop a 95. So could RHP Robbie Aviles (7), before he injured his elbow on the eve of the draft and required Tommy John surgery.

BEST SECONDARY PITCH: Pomeranz's curveball has hard 12-to-6 break and is a strikeout pitch.

BEST PRO DEBUT: Burnette was Lake County's best postseason hitter, leading the Captains to the MWL title.

BEST ATHLETE: Washington. The Indians targeted athletes and got several other intriguing ones, including 3B Hunter Jones (11) and OFs Mark Brown (19), Marcus Bradley (49) and Dunn.

MOST INTRIGUING BACKGROUND: RHP Cole Cook's (5) father Peter MacKenzie has acted in dozens of movies and television shows, including "It's Complicated" with Meryl Streep. Jones (Tracy), 2B Logan Thompson (33, Robbie) and 2B Aaron Fields (42, Bruce) are all sons of former big leaguers.

CLOSEST TO THE MAJORS: Pomeranz will follow the same path as Cleveland 2009 first-rounder Alex White, beginning his pro career in high Class A with the opportunity to move quickly to Double-A.

BEST LATE-ROUND PICK: Dischler had the talent to go in the first five rounds, and he was a relatively

easy over-slot sign, agreeing to a $255,000 bonus. RHP Michael Goodnight (13) is inconsistent, but at his best he has a plus fastball and slider.

THE ONE WHO GOT AWAY: The Indians signed their first 14 choices but would have liked to get RHP Burch Smith (20), whom they also drafted in the 49th round in 2009. Smith, who has a 90-93 mph fastball and a potential plus slider, transferred from Howard (Texas) JC to Oklahoma.

ASSESSMENT: Based on early returns, the rebuilding Indians had baseball's best draft. They nearly doubled their bonus spending from 2009, handing seven-figure bonuses to Pomeranz, Washington, Wolters and Lavisky and giving over-slot deals to six other players.

2009   BONUSES: $4.9 MILLION

RHPs Alex White (1) and Joe Gardner (3) and 2B Jason Kipnis (2) all had strong first full pro seasons and could make their presence felt in Cleveland as early as 2011.

GRADE: B+

2008   BONUSES: $7.0 MILLION

3B Lonnie Chisenhall (1) is the system's best prospect and one of the top pure hitters in the minors. He, 2B Cord Phelps (2) and RHPs Zach Putnam (5) and Bryce Stowell (22) all are on the fast track to the big leagues.

GRADE: B

2007   BONUSES: $3.6 MILLION

The Indians took 1B Beau Mills (1), whom they didn't bother to protect this offseason, one pick ahead of Jason Heyward. They didn't have second- or third-round picks, and RHP Josh Judy (34) is the best this crop has to offer.

GRADE: F

2006   BONUSES: $6.5 MILLION

RHP Chris Archer (5) was a steal, but Cleveland sent him to the Cubs in a trade for Mark DeRosa. The Tribe didn't have a first-round pick but found three big league pitchers in LHP David Huff (1s) and RHPs Josh Tomlin (19) and Vinnie Pestano (20).

GRADE: B

Draft analysis by Jim Callis. Numbers in parentheses indicate draft rounds.

LONNIE CHISENHALL, 3B

Born: Oct. 4, 1988. **Bats:** L. **Throws:** R.
Height: 6-1. **Weight:** 200. **Drafted:** Pitt (N.C.)
CC, 2008 (1st round). **Signed by:** Bob Mayer.

MIKE JANES

After turning down the Pirates as an 11th-round pick out of high school, Chisenhall entered the 2007 season as Baseball America's top-ranked freshman in college baseball. But he didn't last long at South Carolina. That March, he and teammate Nick Fuller stole computer and television equipment from a dorm room and $3,100 in cash from an assistant coach's locker. The Gamecocks dismissed both players from the program, and in February 2008, Chisenhall received six months of probation after pleading guilty to misdemeanor charges of burglary and larceny. By that point, he was attending Pitt (N.C.) CC. He batted .410 and struck out just eight times in 219 plate appearances that spring, establishing himself as one of the top hitters available in the 2008 draft. The Indians drafted him 29th overall and signed him for $1.1 million. They may have had more insight into his makeup than most teams, as assistant general manager John Mirabelli was a former roommate and pitching coach for Ray Tanner, Chisenhall's coach at South Carolina. A shortstop in college, Chisenhall stayed there in his first pro summer but slid over to third base in 2009. He struggled while playing through a right shoulder strain early last season at Akron, then went on the disabled list on May 12. He returned two weeks later, then hit .284/.359/.493 with 17 homers in his final 90 games.

Chisenhall is one of the best pure hitters in the minors. He has a simple lefthanded swing that's easy for him to repeat and allows him to stay inside the baseball. He has good bat speed, routinely makes sweet-spot contact and can drive the ball to all fields. He's a balanced hitter with good rhythm, and his bat path creates a nice swing plane, so there aren't many holes in his stroke. Chisenhall also has solid power and projects to hit 20-25 homers per season. While it wasn't a weakness in the past, he made strides improving his strike-zone discipline in 2010. Chisenhall isn't a standout defender but scouts don't seem to have much concern about his ability to remain at third base. He's an average fielder who has the hands and footwork to handle the position. Though he's a below-average runner, his range and agility are solid. He's still refining the consistency and accuracy of his throws but has solid-average arm strength. He's also still learning some of the nuances of third base, such as improving his pre-pitch setup to be able to react to the ball better off the bat.

Chisenhall will open 2011 in Triple-A Columbus, where he should be one of the International League's better hitters. He projects as an above-average regular in the majors and should take over the starting job in Cleveland by the start of 2012. The Indians entered the offseason with Jayson Nix as their best option at the hot corner, so they could summon Chisenhall before the end of 2011.

SCOUTING GRADES

Batting: 70.   **Defense:** 50.
Power: 55.   **Arm:** 55.
Speed: 40.

Based on 20-80 scouting scale, where 50 represents major league average, and future projection rather than present tools.

Year	Club (League)	Class	AVG	G	AB	R	H	2B	3B	HR	RBI	BB	SO	SB	CS	OBP	SLG
2008	Mahoning Valley (NYP)	SS	.290	68	276	38	80	20	3	5	45	24	32	7	2	.355	.438
2009	Kinston (CAR)	HiA	.276	99	388	59	107	26	2	18	79	37	80	2	1	.346	.492
	Akron (EL)	AA	.183	24	93	13	17	5	1	4	13	7	16	1	0	.238	.387
2010	Akron (EL)	AA	.278	117	460	81	128	22	3	17	84	46	77	3	0	.351	.450
Minor League Totals			.273	308	1217	191	332	73	9	44	221	114	205	13	3	.342	.456

2 ALEX WHITE, RHP

Born: Aug. 29, 1988. **B-T:** R-R. **Ht.:** 6-3. **Wt.:** 200. **Drafted:** North Carolina, 2009 (1st round). **Signed by:** Bob Mayer.

The 15th overall pick in the 2009 draft, White signed with the Indians for a slightly over-slot $2.25 million. He made his pro debut in 2010 at high Class A Kinston, near his hometown of Greenville, N.C., and quickly progressed to Double-A. White's velocity fluctuated throughout his first pro season, but he generally sat at 87-92 mph with his two-seam fastball and topped out at 95 mph. His two-seamer has plus sink and he throws it for strikes. When White gets to a two-strike count, he uses his plus splitter to put away both lefties and righties. His main point of emphasis in 2010 was his slider, which showed promise in high school and early in his college career. He'll flash a solid-average slider and is working on mechanical adjustments to stay on top of the pitch and repeat his release more consistently. He's a quality athlete. When the Indians drafted White, they thought he might be a future reliever, but the plan now is to continue to develop him as a starter. The hope is that he can become at least a No. 3 starter, and he has the potential to be more than that. He should begin 2011 in Triple-A and could push for a big league promotion in the second half.

Year	Club (League)	Class	W	L	ERA	G	GS	CG	SV	IP	H	HR	BB	SO	G/A	WHIP	AVG
2010	Kinston (CAR)	HiA	2	3	2.86	8	8	0	0	44	32	4	19	41	1.86	1.16	.204
	Akron (EL)	AA	8	7	2.28	18	17	0	0	107	91	8	27	76	2.58	1.11	.226
Minor League Totals			10	10	2.45	26	25	0	0	151	123	12	46	117	2.35	1.12	.220

3 JASON KIPNIS, 2B

Born: April 3, 1987. **B-T:** L-R. **Ht.:** 5-10. **Wt.:** 180. **Drafted:** Arizona State, 2009 (2nd round). **Signed by:** Byron Ewing.

Kipnis was named Pacific-10 Conference player of the year and signed for $575,000 as a second-round pick in 2009. He had a strong pro debut as an outfielder, then moved to second base in instructional league. He made the transition surprisingly smoothly, tearing through two levels and joining Columbus for the playoffs. Kipnis is an advanced, aggressive hitter who takes advantage of mistakes with a simple, balanced stroke. His swing can get big, but he usually stays inside the ball, employs the whole field and hangs in well against lefties. Despite his size, he generates average power with strong hands and forearms. He's an average runner with good baserunning instincts. Though he's still learning how to play second, Kipnis doesn't look like a converted outfielder. He's athletic, has good range and reads ground balls well. He has a fringy arm and lacks classic infield actions, but his feet are quick and his hands are solid. His lack of experience still shows with his double-play pivots and positioning on relays. The Indians have youngsters Luis Valbuena and Jason Donald at second base in the majors, but neither has Kipnis' offensive potential. He'll likely return to Triple-A to start 2011 but could end the season in Cleveland.

Year	Club (League)	Class	AVG	G	AB	R	H	2B	3B	HR	RBI	BB	SO	SB	CS	OBP	SLG
2009	Mahoning Valley (NYP)	SS	.306	29	111	19	34	8	3	1	19	15	18	3	3	.388	.459
2010	Kinston (CAR)	HiA	.300	54	203	33	61	12	3	6	31	24	46	2	3	.387	.478
	Akron (EL)	AA	.311	79	315	63	98	20	5	10	43	31	61	7	1	.385	.502
Minor League Totals			.307	162	629	115	193	40	11	17	93	70	125	12	7	.386	.486

4 DREW POMERANZ, LHP

Born: Nov. 22, 1988. **B-T:** R-L. **Ht.:** 6-5. **Wt.:** 230. **Drafted:** Mississippi, 2010 (1st round). **Signed by:** Chuck Bartlett.

The younger brother of Cardinals 2003 third-round pick Stu Pomeranz, Drew almost signed with the Rangers out of high school as a 12th-rounder in 2007. He set the career strikeout record at Mississippi and was the 2010 Southeastern Conference pitcher of the year despite having to deal with a mild pectoral strain in May. He recovered to become the first college pitcher drafted in 2010, going No. 5 overall and signing for $2.65 million at the Aug. 16 deadline. Pomeranz has two plus pitches in his fastball and curveball. His fastball sits in the low 90s and touches 95 mph. It has good life and the deception in his delivery makes it tough to track the ball out of his hand. His breaking ball is even more devastating, a knuckle-curve with hard 12-to-6 action. Pomeranz dominated college lineups when he threw his curve for strikes, though he still must to corral his control after walking 4.4 batters per nine innings as a junior. He has flashed a solid-average changeup at times and will need to use it more as a pro. Pomeranz could follow the path of 2009 first-rounder Alex White, debuting in high Class A with the chance for a quick promotion to Double-A. He could be in Cleveland by 2012, profiling as a frontline starter if he improves his changeup, control and command.

Year	Club (League)	Class	W	L	ERA	G	GS	CG	SV	IP	H	HR	BB	SO	G/A	WHIP	AVG
2010	Did Not Play—Signed Late																

5 NICK WEGLARZ, OF

Born: Dec. 16, 1987. **B-T:** L-L. **Ht.:** 6-3. **Wt.:** 240. **Drafted:** HS—Stevensville, Ont., 2005 (3rd round). **Signed by:** Les Pajari.

After devoting part of 2008 to the Olympics and part of 2009 to the World Baseball Classic, Weglarz committed the entire 2010 season to the Indians. He reached Triple-A in late May, but in July a sprained right thumb ended his season. Weglarz is a very patient hitter with outstanding pitch recognition. He's still learning to be aggressive against pitches in the zone in order to better tap into his above-average raw power. There's some effort to his swing but he doesn't chase pitches out of the zone. Weglarz's bat will have to carry him, as his defense in left field is adequate at best. He's a well below-average runner with a fringy arm and substandard range. Staying healthy has been a problem for Weglarz, who missed time with a broken hand (2006) and a stress fracture in his left shin (2009). Weglarz has the potential to slot into the middle of the order and produce a high OBP with power, though he'll have to work on his defense to make sure he doesn't give back too many runs in the field. He'll report to major league spring training but will likely end up starting the year in Columbus, though he should make his big league debut at some point in 2011.

Year	Club (League)	Class	AVG	G	AB	R	H	2B	3B	HR	RBI	BB	SO	SB	CS	OBP	SLG
2005	Burlington (APP)	R	.231	41	147	22	34	11	0	2	13	17	42	2	1	.313	.347
2006	Indians (GCL)	R	.000	1	2	0	0	0	0	0	0	0	2	0	0	.000	.000
2007	Lake County (SAL)	LoA	.276	125	439	75	121	28	0	23	82	82	129	1	1	.395	.497
	Kinston (CAR)	HiA	.143	2	7	1	1	0	0	1	1	1	2	0	0	.250	.571
2008	Kinston (CAR)	HiA	.272	106	375	68	102	20	5	10	41	71	78	9	5	.396	.432
2009	Akron (EL)	AA	.227	105	339	69	77	17	2	16	65	75	78	2	3	.377	.431
2010	Akron (EL)	AA	.285	37	137	21	39	10	0	7	27	22	26	1	0	.387	.511
	Columbus (IL)	AAA	.286	50	175	30	50	17	1	6	20	28	43	2	2	.392	.497
Minor League Totals			.262	467	1621	286	424	103	8	65	249	296	400	17	12	.383	.455

6 JASON KNAPP, RHP

Born: Aug. 31, 1990. **B-T:** R-R. **Ht.:** 6-5. **Wt.:** 235. **Drafted:** HS—Annandale, N.J., 2008 (2nd round). **Signed by:** Gene Schall (Phillies).

The Phillies drafted Knapp in the second round in 2008, then sent him to the Indians with three other prospects to acquire Cliff Lee in 2009. While the other players in the deal—Carlos Carrasco, Jason Donald and Lou Marson—already have reached Cleveland, Knapp offers the greatest upside. He also comes with considerable risk, as he had arthroscopic surgery to remove loose bodies in his shoulder after the 2009 season and missed much of 2010. When healthy, Knapp has a knockout fastball that can sit in the mid-90s and reach 98. If his curveball is working, he's extremely difficult to hit. His curve can be a swing-and-miss pitch, though at times he overthrows it and doesn't stay on top of it. His changeup needs further development as well. Though Knapp has made strides with his mechanics since high school, he still is learning to repeat his delivery and keep his massive frame back over the rubber. He has effort in his high three-quarters delivery. Knapp probably will start 2011 in high Class A, with the Indians monitoring his innings to try to keep him healthy. If he proves to be more durable, Knapp could pitch in the front of a big league rotation. If not, his power repertoire could make him a closer.

Year	Club (League)	Class	W	L	ERA	G	GS	CG	SV	IP	H	HR	BB	SO	G/A	WHIP	AVG
2008	Phillies (GCL)	R	3	1	2.61	7	6	0	0	31	26	1	12	38	—	1.23	.228
2009	Lakewood (SAL)	LoA	2	7	4.01	17	17	0	0	85	63	3	39	111	0.97	1.20	.208
	Lake County (SAL)	LoA	0	0	5.40	4	4	0	0	12	10	0	8	12	0.44	1.54	.238
2010	Indians (AZL)	R	0	2	1.46	5	5	0	0	12	5	0	4	18	0.89	0.73	.119
	Lake County (SAL)	LoA	1	0	3.94	4	4	0	0	16	12	0	8	29	1.25	1.25	.207
Minor League Totals			6	10	3.63	37	36	0	0	156	116	4	71	208	0.90	1.20	.208

7 LEVON WASHINGTON, OF

Born: July 26, 1991. **B-T:** L-R. **Ht.:** 5-11. **Wt.:** 170. **Drafted:** Chipola (Fla.) JC, 2010 (2nd round). **Signed by:** Chuck Bartlett.

One of the fastest runners and best athletes in the 2009 high school draft class, Washington went 30th overall to the Rays. He didn't sign and failed to qualify academically at Florida, ending up at Chipola (Fla.) JC. Many scouts still didn't know what to make of Washington, but the Indians drafted him 55th overall and gave him $1.2 million. Washington has everything he needs to hit for a high average. He sees the ball well, recognizes spin and has a good idea of the strike zone. He has quick hands and good bat speed, routinely barreling balls. He could hit 15-20 homers per season once he's physically mature, though some scouts question his power. The Indians consider Washington a 70 runner on the 20-80 scale, but he seems to have lost a step since 2009 and his game speed seems slower than his stopwatch times. While he has the raw speed to play center field, he needs to improve his reads and has a well below-average arm. The Indians went after athletes in the 2010 draft, none with more upside than Washington. He has drawn Carl Crawford comparisons and might have the highest ceiling of anyone in the organization, though he's far from reaching it. He could spend his first full season at low Class A Lake County.

Year	Club (League)	Class	AVG	G	AB	R	H	2B	3B	HR	RBI	BB	SO	SB	CS	OBP	SLG
2010	Indians (AZL)	R	.444	3	9	0	4	0	0	0	3	3	1	1	0	.583	.444
Minor League Totals			.444	3	9	0	4	0	0	0	3	3	1	1	0	.583	.444

8 TONY WOLTERS, SS

Born: June 9, 1992. **B-T:** L-R. **Ht.:** 5-10. **Wt.:** 165. **Drafted:** HS—Vista, Calif., 2010 (3rd round). **Signed by:** Jason Smith.

Wolters had an accomplished amateur career, winning MVP honors at the 2009 Aflac All-American Game as a Southern California high school standout. He lasted 87 picks in the 2010 draft, then turned down a San Diego commitment to sign in August for $1.35 million, the highest bonus of any third-round pick. Wolters has an intriguing combination of athleticism and feel for the game. He's an instinctive player on both sides of the ball, showing a polished approach at the plate with the patience to work counts. He has an unusual hitting style, using a wide stance and holding his hands low before launching an uppercut swing, at times releasing his top hand too quickly. He has the offensive upside to hit at the top of the order, spraying liners to all fields with the potential for 10-15 homers per season. A fringe-average runner, Wolters has the tools to play up the middle. Though he's fluid in the field and has quick hands and a strong arm, some scouts believe his range might be better suited for second. Ticketed to open 2011 in low Class A, Wolters is advanced for a high school player but still years away from Cleveland. The Indians have no plans to move him off shortstop and believe he can remain there in the long run.

Year	Club (League)	Class	AVG	G	AB	R	H	2B	3B	HR	RBI	BB	SO	SB	CS	OBP	SLG
2010	Indians (AZL)	R	.211	5	19	2	4	0	0	0	3	2	5	2	0	.286	.211
Minor League Totals			.211	5	19	2	4	0	0	0	3	2	5	2	0	.286	.211

9 JOE GARDNER, RHP

Born: Mary 18, 1988. **B-T:** R-R. **Ht.:** 6-4. **Wt.:** 220. **Drafted:** UC Santa Barbara, 2009 (3rd round). **Signed by:** Vince Sagisi.

The co-MVP of the Alaskan Baseball League in 2008, Gardner transferred from Ohlone (Calif.) JC to UC Santa Barbara for his junior season. He signed quickly for $363,000 as a third-round pick in 2009, but a ribcage injury prevented him from making his pro debut until 2010. Though he's not quite as tall, Gardner draws some comparisons to Justin Masterson, Cleveland's No. 2 starter. Both are loose, long-levered righthanders who attack hitters with quality sinkers from a low three-quarters arm slot. Gardner's sinker sits at 89-92 mph and touches 94, allowing him to post an exemplary groundout/airout ratio last season. He leans heavily on his two-seamer, which has so much life that he has problems locating it at times. Though he can dominate a lineup with his fastball, Gardner needs to improve his secondary pitches. His low arm slot makes it tough to maintain a consistent slider, which is average at its best. He needs a better changeup to combat lefthanders. Gardner has the potential to be a mid-rotation starter if he can develop a reliable slider and changeup. If not, his ability to get groundout would have value out of the bullpen. He should open 2011 in Double-A.

Year	Club (League)	Class	W	L	ERA	G	GS	CG	SV	IP	H	HR	BB	SO	G/A	WHIP	AVG
2009	Did not play—Signed late																
2010	Lake County (SAL)	LoA	1	0	3.24	6	6	0	0	25	17	2	11	38	6.40	1.12	.185
	Kinston (CAR)	HiA	12	6	2.65	22	22	0	0	122	85	4	51	104	3.65	1.11	.199
Minor League Totals			13	6	2.75	28	28	0	0	147	102	6	62	142	3.89	1.11	.197

10 NICK HAGADONE, LHP

Born: Jan. 1, 1986. **B-T:** L-L. **Ht.:** 6-5. **Wt.:** 230. **Drafted:** Washington, 2007 (1st round supplemental). **Signed by:** John Booher (Red Sox).

Hagadone flashed electric stuff for the Red Sox but missed almost the entire 2008 season after Tommy John surgery. He returned in 2009, then went to Cleveland in the midseason trade for Victor Martinez. Hagadone missed two weeks in 2010 with a shoulder strain and moved to the bullpen in late July, a move the Indians had planned prior to the season to manage his workload. Hagadone's fastball touched 98 mph in 2009, but his stuff wasn't quite as nasty last season. His fastball sat in the low 90s and topped out at 96. His slider is inconsistent but can be a putaway pitch. He also shows some feel for a changeup but operated from behind in the count so frequently in 2010 that he didn't use it often. Hagadone struggled to repeat his mechanics and averaged 6.6 walks per nine innings. While he's a good athlete, his arm action and the effort in his delivery concern some scouts. He went as many as five innings in just three of his starts, so he still has to prove his durability. The Indians added Hagadone to the 40-man roster and still plan to send him back to the rotation in 2011, possibly in Double-A. It wouldn't be a surprise to see him quickly transitioned to the bullpen, a role most scouts believe best suits him.

Year	Club (League)	Class	W	L	ERA	G	GS	CG	SV	IP	H	HR	BB	SO	G/A	WHIP	AVG
2007	Lowell (NYP)	SS	0	1	1.85	10	10	0	0	24	14	1	8	33	—	0.90	.163
2008	Greenville (SAL)	LoA	1	1	0.00	3	3	0	0	10	5	0	6	12	—	1.10	.135
2009	Greenville (SAL)	LoA	0	2	2.52	10	10	0	0	25	13	0	14	32	2.42	1.08	.149
	Lake County (SAL)	LoA	0	1	2.45	5	5	0	0	15	8	0	5	21	1.50	0.89	.163
	Kinston (CAR)	HiA	0	0	5.06	2	2	0	0	5	5	0	5	6	8.00	1.88	.250
2010	Kinston (CAR)	HiA	1	3	2.39	10	10	0	0	38	28	2	29	45	1.42	1.51	.206
	Akron (EL)	AA	2	2	4.50	19	7	0	1	48	44	5	34	44	1.02	1.63	.242
Minor League Totals			4	10	2.89	59	47	0	1	165	117	8	101	193	1.43	1.32	.196

11 KYLE BLAIR, RHP

Born: Sept. 27, 1988. **B-T:** R-R. **Ht.:** 6-4. **Wt.:** 200. **Drafted:** San Diego, 2010 (4th round). **Signed by:** Jason Smith.

One of the top high school pitchers in the 2007 draft, Blair dropped to the Dodgers in the fifth round because of signability questions and opted instead to attend San Diego. After two solid college seasons, he earned West Coast Conference pitcher of the year honors as a junior last spring. The Indians drafted him in the fourth round and signed him for an above-slot $580,000 bonus. Blair attacks hitters with a low-90s fastball that reaches 95 mph and bores in on righthanders. He has made strides with his mechanics and doesn't overthrow as much as he used to, but he still needs to do a better job of locating his fastball. He throws a slider that isn't a power pitch but can give him a second above-average offering, while also mixing in an overhand curve and a firm changeup. He's a good athlete with a strong frame who has improved his conditioning since missing six weeks in 2009 with shoulder inflammation. He's also a free thinker who traveled the world as a teenager, climbing Mount Kilimanjaro on an African safari and building houses with Habitat For Humanity in Honduras. Blair didn't pitch after signing, so he'll make his pro debut with one of Cleveland's Class A affiliates in 2011. If everything comes together, he has the potential to be a mid-rotation starter.

Year	Club (League)	Class	W	L	ERA	G	GS	CG	SV	IP	H	HR	BB	SO	G/A	WHIP	AVG
2010	Did Not Play—Signed Late																

12 ALEX LAVISKY, C

Born: Jan. 13, 1991. **B-T:** R-R. **Ht.:** 6-1. **Wt.:** 200. **Drafted:** HS—Lakewood, Ohio, 2010 (8th round). **Signed by:** Junie Melendez.

The Indians didn't have to go far to scout Lavisky, who went to high school five miles from Progressive Field. He won a 2010 Ohio Division I championship at St. Edward High (Lakewood, Ohio), where his teammates included Pirates second-round pick Stetson Allie and Tommy Mirabelli, whose father John is Cleveland's vice president of scouting operations. Some teams considered Lavisky a sandwich-round talent, but his seven-figure asking price allowed him to slide to the Indians in the eighth round. He signed for $1 million and has the potential to be a solid all-around catcher. Handling Allie's high-90s (and sometimes erratic) fastballs in high school prepared Lavisky well for pro ball. He's athletic and a good receiver. He has a solid-average, accurate arm, though his release can get long. Lavisky's best offensive tool is his above-average raw power. He's strong and has quick wrists, but he's not a pure hitter. His swing can get long and can create timing problems, leading to strikeouts. Like most catchers, he's a below-average runner. Lavisky draws great reviews for his leadership and intangibles behind the plate, showing advanced maturity for his age. He should open 2011 at Lake County, 25 miles from his hometown.

Year	Club (League)	Class	AVG	G	AB	R	H	2B	3B	HR	RBI	BB	SO	SB	CS	OBP	SLG
2010	Indians (AZL)	R	.200	5	15	0	3	0	0	0	0	0	7	0	0	.200	.200
Minor League Totals			.200	5	15	0	3	0	0	0	0	0	7	0	0	.200	.200

13 FELIX STERLING, RHP

Born: March 15, 1993. **B-T:** R-R. **Ht.:** 6-3. **Wt.:** 200. **Signed:** Dominican Republic, 2009. **Signed by:** Ramon Pena.

The Indians had a few interesting Latin American teenagers on their Rookie-level Arizona League team in 2010, including shortstop Jorge Martinez and Alex Monsalve, with Sterling having the most upside. He already sits in the low 90s with his fastball and runs it up to 94 mph. Though he already has a strong lower half and his body is relatively filled out for his age, he still has some projection in his frame and could add another tick or two to his fastball. His No. 2 pitch is a slider that has short, tight break and could be at least an average pitch. Sterling is primarily a fastball/slider pitcher at this point, because he hasn't had to use his changeup much in games yet. He's still refining his control but it's solid for a teenager. Sterling has a durable frame and projects as a starter, though he's far from reaching his potential as a mid-rotation arm. He could go to short-season Mahoning Valley and has a chance to pitch in low Class A this year.

Year	Club (League)	Class	W	L	ERA	G	GS	CG	SV	IP	H	HR	BB	SO	G/A	WHIP	AVG
2010	Indians (AZL)	R	2	3	3.16	12	11	0	0	51	40	2	20	57	0.79	1.17	.222
Minor League Totals			2	3	3.16	12	11	0	0	51	40	2	20	57	0.79	1.17	.222

14 T.J. HOUSE, LHP

Born: Sept. 29, 1989. **B-T:** R-L. **Ht.:** 6-2. **Wt.:** 215. **Drafted:** HS—Picayune, Miss., 2008 (16th round). **Signed by:** Chuck Bartlett.

In the 2008 draft, the Indians went well over slot to sign a pair of high school pitchers. Though Trey Haley went in the second round and got $1.25 million, compared to the 16th round and $750,000 for House, the latter has performed better and become the better prospect. Though he doesn't have a true plus pitch, House has been solid across the board and extremely durable, making 26 starts in each of his first two pro seasons. A good athlete, he has a solid delivery that he's able to repeat and throws strikes from a three-quarters arm slot. His fastball isn't overpowering, operating at 87-91 mph and touching 93, but he succeeds with it when he locates it where he wants. At times, though, he'll leave it up in the strike zone. His best pitch is his changeup, which took a step forward in 2010. It's now the best in the system and could become a plus offering, generating swings and misses at times. House threw a slurvy breaking ball in high school that has turned into a slider, but it's still a below-average pitch that lacks consistency. He doesn't project as a future star, but his stuff, feel for pitching and durability could make him a solid back-of-the-rotation starter. He should make the jump this year to Double-A, where at 21 he would be one of the Eastern League's youngest pitchers.

Year	Club (League)	Class	W	L	ERA	G	GS	CG	SV	IP	H	HR	BB	SO	G/A	WHIP	AVG
2009	Lake County (SAL)	LoA	6	11	3.15	26	26	0	0	134	127	8	49	109	1.31	1.31	.250
2010	Kinston (CAR)	HiA	6	10	3.91	27	26	0	0	136	135	7	61	106	1.41	1.44	.264
Minor League Totals			12	21	3.53	53	52	0	0	270	262	15	110	215	1.36	1.38	.257

15 HECTOR RONDON, RHP

Born: Feb. 26, 1988. **B-T:** R-R. **Ht.:** 6-3. **Wt.:** 180. **Signed:** Venezuela, 2004. **Signed by:** Stewart Ruiz.

Rondon has emerged as one of the Indians' most promising Latin American pitching prospects, but his development took a step backwards in 2010. He posted an 8.53 ERA in seven Triple-A starts, the last of which came on May 12, when he went on the disabled list with a right elbow injury. After attempting to rehab his elbow, he eventually had Tommy John surgery after the season, which likely will cost him all of 2011. When healthy, Rondon pitched off a lively low-90s fastball that peaked at 96 mph. He had yet to develop another offering that would qualify as an out pitch. His second-best weapon was his changeup, an average pitch at times. His slider was fringy and inconsistent. Rondon is a good athlete who repeats his delivery and fields his position well. Missing nearly two full seasons hurts, because he needs more time to refine his secondary pitches. He'll be 24 when he returns to the mound in 2012.

Year	Club (League)	Class	W	L	ERA	G	GS	CG	SV	IP	H	HR	BB	SO	G/A	WHIP	AVG
2005	Indians1 (DSL)	R	3	3	1.65	15	12	1	1	65	60	2	8	55	—	1.04	.230
2006	Indians (GCL)	R	3	4	5.13	11	11	0	0	53	62	6	3	32	—	1.23	.286
2007	Lake County (SAL)	LoA	7	10	4.37	27	27	0	0	136	143	13	27	113	—	1.25	.269
2008	Kinston (CAR)	HiA	11	6	3.60	27	27	0	0	145	130	12	42	145	—	1.19	.239
2009	Akron (EL)	AA	7	5	2.75	15	13	1	0	72	60	3	16	73	0.79	1.06	.227
	Columbus (IL)	AAA	4	5	4.00	12	12	0	0	74	83	8	13	64	0.72	1.29	.282
2010	Columbus (IL)	AAA	1	3	8.53	7	7	0	0	32	48	12	10	33	1.04	1.83	.343
Minor League Totals			36	36	3.92	114	109	2	1	577	586	56	119	515	0.79	1.22	.260

16 JORDAN HENRY, OF

Born: June 13, 1988. **B-T:** L-R. **Ht.:** 6-3. **Wt.:** 175. **Drafted:** Mississippi, 2009 (7th round). **Signed by:** Chuck Bartlett.

Henry's older brother Justin is a Triple-A second baseman in the Tigers system, and the two were college teammates at Mississippi. More athletic than his brother, Jordan has a game built around plus-plus speed and outstanding strike zone awareness. He gets on base at a high clip because he hits for average and doesn't chase many pitches out of the strike zone. He enhances his quickness with good baserunning instincts, and he has stolen 51 bases in 58 tries in two pro seasons. He became better at doing the little things like bunting this season. Despite his 6-foot-3 frame, Henry has a contact-oriented swing with little leverage and power that grades as a 20 on the 20-80 scouting scale. He has just 28 extra-base hits in 186 pro games, many of which can be attributed to his speed. More advanced pitchers may pick him apart unless he gets stronger and learns to pull the ball with more authority. Henry is a fine defender in center field, playing shallow while able to go get balls hit over his head. He has an average, accurate arm. With the Indians' outfield depth, Henry could start 2011 back in Double-A, where he batted .300 in the second half last season.

Year	Club (League)	Class	AVG	G	AB	R	H	2B	3B	HR	RBI	BB	SO	SB	CS	OBP	SLG
2009	Mahoning Valley (NYP)	SS	.286	67	248	48	71	12	0	0	23	49	37	22	1	.408	.335
2010	Kinston (CAR)	HiA	.333	42	162	32	54	4	0	0	13	30	27	14	2	.438	.358
	Akron (EL)	AA	.300	74	287	45	86	8	4	0	16	46	59	15	4	.396	.355
Minor League Totals			.303	183	697	125	211	24	4	0	52	125	123	51	7	.410	.349

17 ZACH PUTNAM, RHP

Born: July 3, 1987. **B-T:** R-R. **Ht.:** 6-2. **Wt.:** 225. **Drafted:** Michigan, 2008 (5th round). **Signed by:** Derrick Ross.

Putnam was a two-way player at Michigan, but scouts always considered him a better prospect as a pitcher. The Indians signed him to an above-slot $600,000 bonus in the fifth round in 2008 and he began his career as a starter, but he has been mostly a reliever since advancing to Double-A in May 2009. His stuff has played up a notch since he moved to the bullpen, with his fastball sitting in the low to mid-90s and touching 96 mph with plus sink and occasional cutting action. Putnam can keep the ball on the ground with his fastball and his plus splitter, another pitch with big sink. His splitter is his best weapon, and it became more of a swing-and-miss pitch with late tumble when he became a reliver. Putnam also throws a straight changeup and a slider, though the latter is mostly just a spinner. He throws from a three-quarters arm slot and has a herky-jerky delivery, but he's able to throw all of his pitches for strikes and attacks hitters aggressively. He's on the verge of helping the big league club and should be in Cleveland's bullpen at some point in 2011.

Year	Club (League)	Class	W	L	ERA	G	GS	CG	SV	IP	H	HR	BB	SO	G/A	WHIP	AVG
2008	Mahoning Valley (NYP)	SS	0	1	3.72	3	3	0	0	10	7	0	5	8	—	1.24	.206
2009	Kinston (CAR)	HiA	2	0	4.13	5	5	0	0	24	22	1	5	23	1.40	1.13	.247
	Akron (EL)	AA	4	2	4.13	33	0	0	2	57	59	2	18	57	2.06	1.36	.261
2010	Akron (EL)	AA	4	1	3.86	20	7	0	3	51	58	2	9	41	1.31	1.31	.286
	Columbus (IL)	AAA	0	1	3.33	17	0	0	0	24	20	2	7	24	1.53	1.11	.222
Minor League Totals			10	5	3.90	78	15	0	5	166	166	7	44	153	1.58	1.27	.259

18 BRYCE STOWELL, RHP

Born: Sept. 23, 1986. **B-T:** R-R. **Ht.:** 6-2. **Wt.:** 205. **Drafted:** UC Irvine, 2008 (22nd round). **Signed by:** Jason Smith.

Another Indians over-slot signing from the 2008 draft, Stowell received a $725,000 bonus as a draft-eligible sophomore taken in the 22nd round. When he turned pro, he was a starter with a low-90s fastball that peaked at 95 mph. Moved to the bullpen in 2010, he saw his velocity skyrocket and operated in the mid-90s and touching 98 with solid life. He used his suddenly overpowering fastball to go from high Class A to Triple-A, tailing off in Columbus and coming down with an elbow strain that didn't require surgery. Stowell also throws a hard slider that lacks consistency, and he can mix in a changeup on occasion. He also missed the first six weeks of the 2009 season with biceps tendinitis, so he still has to prove he can stay healthy for a full season. He also must learn to command his fastball better. The Indians expect Stowell to be 100 percent again by spring training, and he'll likely open the season back in Triple-A. He'll be in Cleveland once he learns to harness his newfound heat.

Year	Club (League)	Class	W	L	ERA	G	GS	CG	SV	IP	H	HR	BB	SO	G/A	WHIP	AVG
2009	Lake County (SAL)	LoA	0	0	1.00	3	1	0	0	9	4	1	3	15	1.00	0.78	.133
	Kinston (CAR)	HiA	4	6	5.31	19	6	0	0	61	64	6	34	62	0.65	1.61	.270
2010	Kinston (CAR)	HiA	1	0	1.42	11	0	0	0	25	16	2	8	41	1.67	0.95	.186
	Akron (EL)	AA	1	0	0.00	14	1	0	7	22	15	0	11	33	1.33	1.16	.192
	Columbus (IL)	AAA	1	1	5.49	17	0	0	0	20	11	2	17	28	0.71	1.42	.167
Minor League Totals			7	7	3.47	64	8	0	7	137	110	11	73	179	0.85	1.33	.221

19 JOSH JUDY, RHP

Born: Feb. 9, 1986. **B-T:** R-R. **Ht.:** 6-4. **Wt.:** 200. **Drafted:** Indiana Tech, 2007 (34th round). **Signed by:** Derrick Ross.

After throwing well in big league camp, Judy began the 2010 season on the disabled list with an elbow injury before returning in mid-May and spending most of the year in Triple-A. He struggled in his first two weeks back, then was one of the most dominant relievers in the International League before finishing his year with a strong showing in the Dominican League. While Judy doesn't have the arm strength of fellow Columbus relievers Zach Putnam and Bryce Stowell, he does have good command of a low-90s fastball that reaches 94 mph. His delivery has a lot of moving parts, but it helps him hide the ball and makes his fastball seem quicker. His slider is a swing-and-miss pitch with late, two-plane break that puts hitters away. Without an adequate changeup, Judy struggles to retire lefthanders. He could break camp in the big league bullpen or return to Triple-A for additional polish at the start of 2011.

Year	Club (League)	Class	W	L	ERA	G	GS	CG	SV	IP	H	HR	BB	SO	G/A	WHIP	AVG
2007	Indians (GCL)	R	1	2	0.63	9	0	0	0	14	11	0	8	14	—	1.33	.204
	Mahoning Valley (NYP)	SS	0	0	0.00	4	1	0	1	11	7	0	3	7	—	0.91	.194
2008	Lake County (SAL)	LoA	12	1	3.51	35	0	0	1	74	60	6	25	80	—	1.14	.223
	Kinston (CAR)	HiA	0	0	1.93	7	0	0	0	14	12	0	1	17	—	0.93	.226
2009	Kinston (CAR)	HiA	0	0	0.00	5	0	0	3	5	4	0	0	7	6.00	0.86	.235
	Akron (EL)	AA	4	3	3.10	36	1	0	11	49	35	2	18	63	1.68	1.07	.198
2010	Akron (EL)	AA	0	0	9.00	2	0	0	0	2	6	0	0	2	—	3.00	.545
	Columbus (IL)	AAA	3	0	2.68	38	0	0	2	47	48	5	14	55	0.59	1.32	.262
Minor League Totals			20	6	2.74	136	2	0	18	217	183	13	69	245	1.13	1.16	.229

20 CORD PHELPS, 2B

Born: Jan. 23, 1987. **B-T:** B-R. **Ht.:** 6-2. **Wt.:** 200. **Drafted:** Stanford, 2008 (3rd round). **Signed by:** Don Lyle.

After ranking seventh in the minors in walks with 93 walks in 2009, Phelps continued to work counts but more aggressively attacked pitches last season. He batted .308/.368/.457 between Double-A and Triple-A, improved his production after he got to Columbus and continue to hit in the Arizona Fall League. Phelps doesn't have a standout tool, but he's a smart hitter with a tremendous approach and the ability to make in-game adjustments. He sets up from a deep crouch and keeps his hands in a low trigger position, but he has a smooth swing and doesn't strike out often. He's a spray hitter with a contact-oriented swing and good instincts at the plate, but he's not a threat to hit for power. A below-average runner, he's a serviceable defender with an average arm. He made eight errors in a brief trial at third base in the Arizona Fall League. Where Phelps will fit with Cleveland remains a question. The Indians' two best hitting prospects, Lonnie Chisenhall and Jason Kipnis, play both of his positions. They're both likely to open 2011 in Triple-A, which is likely Phelps' destination as well. He could fill in on the big league roster before Chisenhall and Kipnis are ready.

Year	Club (League)	Class	AVG	G	AB	R	H	2B	3B	HR	RBI	BB	SO	SB	CS	OBP	SLG
2008	Indians (GCL)	R	.000	1	3	0	0	0	0	0	1	0	2	0	0	.000	.000
	Mahoning Valley (NYP)	SS	.312	35	141	24	44	10	2	2	21	15	22	4	3	.376	.454
2009	Kinston (CAR)	HiA	.261	130	479	72	125	27	5	4	53	93	97	17	14	.386	.363
2010	Akron (EL)	AA	.296	53	199	25	59	8	3	2	23	15	29	1	4	.346	.397
	Columbus (IL)	AAA	.317	66	243	41	77	20	4	6	31	24	39	3	2	.386	.506
Minor League Totals			.286	285	1065	162	305	65	14	14	129	147	189	25	23	.376	.413

21 CHEN LEE, RHP

Born: Oct. 21, 1986. **B-T:** R-R. **Ht.:** 5-11. **Wt.:** 175. **Signed:** Taiwan, 2008. **Signed by:** Jason Lee.

The Indians tried to sign Lee out a Taiwanese high school, but he turned them down to go to college. The Indians continued scouting him and signed him for $400,000 in September 2008. He pitched in the Olympics in 2008 and in the World Baseball Classic in 2009. Lee has been a prolific strikeout pitcher in two pro seasons, averaging 10.3 whiffs per nine innings in his career. From a low three-quarters arm slot, he goes after hitters with a lively 92-93 mph fastball that tops out at 96. He can vary the shape of his solid slider, giving it late tilt at times and longer, slurvy break at others. With his low arm slot, he has to work to stay on top of his slider. Lee's changeup needs improvement, but that didn't stop him from limiting lefthanders to a .479 OPS in 2010. He finished the season strong, with a 0.57 ERA in the final two months, and should open this year in a crowded Columbus bullpen. He could make his big league debut in the second half of the season.

Year	Club (League)	Class	W	L	ERA	G	GS	CG	SV	IP	H	HR	BB	SO	G/A	WHIP	AVG
2009	Kinston (CAR)	HiA	4	6	3.35	45	0	0	2	83	67	5	28	97	1.14	1.14	.220
2010	Akron (EL)	AA	5	4	3.22	44	0	0	0	73	59	6	22	82	1.74	1.11	.219
Minor League Totals			9	10	3.29	89	0	0	2	156	126	11	50	179	1.38	1.13	.220

22 CHUN CHEN, C

Born: Nov. 1, 1988. **B-T:** R-R. **Ht.:** 6-1. **Wt.:** 200. **Signed:** Taiwan, 2007. **Signed by:** Jason Lee.

Cleveland signed Chen out of Taiwan as an 18-year-old in September 2007. Known in his amateur days as an offensive-oriented catcher, he hit just .215/.328/.308 at Mahoning Valley in 2009. When he arrived at spring training last year, he worked with Indians coaches to remove the big leg kick in his swing, an adjustment that allowed him to see the ball earlier and maintain better balance. The change helped Chen take off as one of Cleveland's biggest breakthrough prospects in 2010, and he even earned a Futures Game berth. He has a natural feel for hitting, gap power and good control of the strike zone. Though he posted a .315/.404/.521 season at two Class A stops, some scouts have concerns about his bat speed playing at higher levels. He also can become too pull-conscious at times. Chen's biggest need, however, is to improve his receiving. He had 18 passed balls in just 60 games last year, splitting his time between catcher and DH. He struggles with balls in the dirt and looks stiff behind the plate at times. He does have a solid arm and threw out 37 percent of basestealers in 2010. He's a well below-average runner. The Indians could push Chen to Double-A in 2011, though they also could send him to Kinston to focus on his defense.

Year	Club (League)	Class	AVG	G	AB	R	H	2B	3B	HR	RBI	BB	SO	SB	CS	OBP	SLG
2008	Indians (GCL)	R	.261	38	115	11	30	4	2	3	15	13	29	1	1	.336	.409
2009	Mahoning Valley (NYP)	SS	.215	59	195	24	42	15	0	1	19	31	42	9	2	.328	.308
2010	Lake County (SAL)	LoA	.312	58	218	27	68	21	3	6	39	17	38	1	1	.368	.518
	Kinston (CAR)	HiA	.320	52	172	31	55	17	0	6	30	38	36	4	1	.442	.523
Minor League Totals			.279	207	700	93	195	57	5	16	103	99	145	15	5	.371	.443

23 MATT PACKER, LHP

Born: Aug. 28, 1987. **B-T:** L-L. **Ht.:** 6-0. **Wt.:** 200. **Drafted:** Virginia, 2009 (32nd round). **Signed by:** Bob Mayer.

Packer led NCAA Division I baseball with a 1.14 ERA as a Virginia sophomore in 2008. His ERA swelled to 4.13 in his draft year in 2009, and he lasted until the 32nd round and signed for $50,000. He turned into one of the biggest surprises in the system last year, overwhelming low Class A hitters before jumping to Double-A in August. Packer gets hitters out by pounding the strike zone and keeping the ball on the ground, posting a strong groundout/airout ratio in 2010. Throwing from a three-quarters slot, he gets quality sink on an 88-91 mph fastball that tops out at 93. He has an above-average changeup with armside tail and sink. He throws both a slider and a curveball, but his breaking pitches are still works in progress. With his athleticism, he's able to repeat his delivery and throw all of his pitches for strikes. Packer likely will return to Akron to begin 2011 and ultimately profiles as a No. 4 or 5 starter.

Year	Club (League)	Class	W	L	ERA	G	GS	CG	SV	IP	H	HR	BB	SO	G/A	WHIP	AVG
2009	Mahoning Valley (NYP)	SS	0	0	2.38	5	0	0	1	11	8	1	1	13	2.67	0.79	.186
2010	Lake County (SAL)	LoA	8	5	1.60	24	13	1	1	96	77	4	13	92	3.50	0.94	.218
	Akron (EL)	AA	1	2	3.16	6	5	0	0	37	35	3	9	31	3.63	1.19	.267
Minor League Totals			9	7	2.06	35	18	1	2	144	120	8	23	136	3.45	0.99	.227

24 KELVIN DE LA CRUZ, LHP

Born: Jan. 8, 1988. **B-T:** L-L. **Ht.:** 6-5. **Wt.:** 190. **Signed:** Dominican Republic, 2004. **Signed by:** Johnny Martinez.

De la Cruz ranked No. 7 on this list, Cleveland's second-best pitching prospect, after the 2008 season. He struck out 19 over 12 innings in his first two starts in 2009, but a strained elbow ligament subsequently shut him down for most of the year. He was healthy again last season but his pitches weren't as crisp as they had been in the past. His fastball sat at 87-91 mph and rarely touched 94 like it had previously. His hard curveball was a plus pitch at times but slurvy at others. De la Cruz mixes in a changeup that has its moments, but he got behind in the count so frequently last year that he didn't use it often. Many of his struggles stemmed from his inability to repeat his mechanics, which led to an average of 5.1 walks per nine innings. He throws across his body, has trouble maintaining his high three-quarters arm slot and spins off his front leg. With his first post-injury season behind him, 2011 will be a crucial year for de la Cruz, who will return to Double-A to begin the season.

Year	Club (League)	Class	W	L	ERA	G	GS	CG	SV	IP	H	HR	BB	SO	G/A	WHIP	AVG
2005	Indians1 (DSL)	R	3	3	2.36	13	12	0	1	53	49	3	16	39	—	1.22	.234
2006	Indians (GCL)	R	1	2	10.98	9	4	0	0	20	32	2	13	15	—	2.29	.360
2007	Indians (GCL)	R	3	0	0.50	3	3	0	0	18	7	1	2	20	—	0.50	.117
	Mahoning Valley (NYP)	SS	2	4	3.98	12	12	0	0	54	41	5	34	53	—	1.38	.216
2008	Akron (EL)	AA	1	0	7.20	1	1	0	0	5	4	1	3	4	—	1.40	.222
	Lake County (SAL)	LoA	8	4	1.69	18	18	1	0	96	71	2	34	96	—	1.10	.207
	Kinston (CAR)	HiA	3	2	6.44	8	8	0	0	29	35	1	25	36	—	2.05	.292
2009	Kinston (CAR)	HiA	2	0	1.50	2	2	0	0	12	6	1	2	19	0.89	0.67	.146
	Indians (AZL)	R	0	2	9.39	3	3	0	0	8	10	1	5	5	0.45	1.96	.323
2010	Kinston (CAR)	HiA	2	2	2.91	6	6	0	0	34	22	3	8	28	1.68	0.88	.183
	Akron (EL)	AA	5	6	5.77	20	20	0	0	94	98	12	64	77	0.95	1.73	.274
Minor League Totals			30	25	3.98	95	89	1	1	423	375	32	206	392	1.05	1.37	.237

25 LUIGI RODRIGUEZ, OF/2B

Born: Nov. 13, 1992. **B-T:** B-R. **Ht.:** 5-11. **Wt.:** 160. **Signed:** Dominican Republic, 2009. **Signed by:** Lino Diaz.

The Indians scaled back their high-scale spending in Latin America since 2008, when they gave $715,000 to Venezuelan catcher Alex Monsalve and $575,000 to Dominican shortstop Jose Ozoria. Monsalve hasn't hit as hoped and Ozoria turned out to be named Wuali Bryan and three years old than expected. Cleveland released Bryan after the 2010 season. Rodriguez wasn't a big-ticket signing out of the Dominican Republic in 2009, and he may deliver a much better return. He offers a promising package of tools and performance. Though he lacks projectable size, he's a good athlete with plus-plus speed. Rodriguez has nice feel for hitting with an advanced idea of the strike zone for his age. His swing path is short and direct to the ball, and his quick, contact-oriented stroke helps him stay inside the ball. Though he doesn't have much power, his approach helps him get on base at a high clip. Signed as a second baseman, Rodriguez spent his first month in the Rookie-level Dominican Summer League at the position before moving to center field, where his speed makes him a better fit. He went to instructional league after the season and should make his U.S. debut in 2011, likely in the Arizona League.

Year	Club (League)	Class	AVG	G	AB	R	H	2B	3B	HR	RBI	BB	SO	SB	CS	OBP	SLG
2010	Indians (DSL)	R	.301	63	206	43	62	7	10	2	27	36	35	31	9	.403	.461
Minor League Totals			.301	63	206	43	62	7	10	2	27	36	35	31	9	.403	.461

26 COREY KLUBER, RHP

Born: April 10, 1986. **B-T:** R-R. **Ht.:** 6-4. **Wt.:** 215. **Drafted:** Stetson, 2007 (4th round). **Signed by:** Joe Bochy (Padres).

The Indians, Cardinals and Padres pulled off a three-way deal at the July 31 trade deadline, with Cleveland sending Jake Westbrook to St. Louis and getting Kluber from San Diego in return. He led the Double-A Texas League with 136 strikeouts despite leaving the circuit after the trade. He racks up whiffs more with his deceptive short-arm delivery than with pure stuff. Kluber does have a solid arsenal of pitches, working mainly off his 88-92 mph fastball and average slider. He also flashes an average changeup and throws strikes. He still needs to refine his command, because he's around the strike zone almost too much and is fairly hittable. He'd durable, having made 82 starts and worked 455 innings in his three full pro seasons. Kluber doesn't have high upside, but he has good feel for pitching and could be a back-of-the-rotation starter. He'll open 2011 in the Columbus rotation after finishing last season with two starts there.

Year	Club (League)	Class	W	L	ERA	G	GS	CG	SV	IP	H	HR	BB	SO	G/A	WHIP	AVG
2007	Eugene (NWL)	SS	1	1	3.51	10	7	0	0	33	28	1	15	33	—	1.29	.230
2008	Lake Elsinore (CAL)	HiA	2	5	6.01	19	16	0	0	85	93	9	34	75	—	1.49	.280
	Fort Wayne (MWL)	LoA	4	3	3.21	10	10	0	0	56	49	8	13	72	—	1.11	.229
2009	Lake Elsinore (CAL)	HiA	7	9	4.54	19	19	0	0	109	110	9	36	124	1.27	1.34	.261
	San Antonio (TL)	AA	2	4	4.60	9	9	0	0	45	45	5	34	35	0.58	1.76	.266
2010	San Antonio (TL)	AA	6	6	3.45	22	21	0	0	123	121	7	40	136	0.91	1.31	.259
	Akron (EL)	AA	2	2	3.76	5	5	0	0	26	38	0	10	21	1.30	1.82	.345
	Columbus (IL)	AAA	1	1	3.27	2	2	0	0	11	10	1	6	8	0.82	1.45	.263
Minor League Totals			25	31	4.24	96	89	0	0	489	494	40	188	504	0.97	1.40	.264

27 JESS TODD, RHP

Born: April 20, 1986. **B-T:** R-R. **Ht.:** 5-11. **Wt.:** 210. **Drafted:** Arkansas, 2007 (2nd round). **Signed by:** Roger Smith (Cardinals).

Todd signed with the Cardinals as a second-round pick in 2007, then vaulted to Triple-A as a starting pitcher by the end of his first full pro season. The Cardinals moved Todd to the bullpen in 2009 before shipping him and Chris Perez to the Indians for Mark DeRosa that June. Perez has emerged as one of the game's most promising young closers, and Todd could start setting him up in the future. Todd's basic scouting report largely has remained the same since his college days at Arkansas. He attacks hitters from a three-quarters arm slot with a solid fastball/slider combination. His fastball reaches the low 90s and his slider is a plus pitch that misses bats. He doesn't have a reliable third offering, yet he still has been effective against lefthanders. He missed two weeks in August with shoulder soreness but should be 100 percent in spring training. After pitching briefly in Cleveland in each of the last two years, he'll get the opportunity to stick full-time in 2011.

Year	Club (League)	Class	W	L	ERA	G	GS	CG	SV	IP	H	HR	BB	SO	G/A	WHIP	AVG
2007	Batavia (NYP)	SS	4	1	2.78	16	7	0	0	58	48	2	14	69	—	1.06	.223
2008	Palm Beach (FSL)	HiA	3	0	1.65	7	4	0	1	27	18	0	7	35	—	0.91	.184
	Springfield, MO (TL)	AA	4	5	2.97	17	16	0	0	103	79	12	24	81	—	1.00	.216
	Memphis (PCL)	AAA	1	1	3.97	4	4	0	0	23	19	4	11	20	—	1.32	.232
2009	St. Louis (NL)	MAJ	0	0	10.80	1	0	0	0	2	3	1	2	2	2.00	3.00	.375
	Memphis (PCL)	AAA	4	2	2.20	41	0	0	24	49	39	3	13	59	0.85	1.06	.214
	Columbus (IL)	AAA	0	0	0.00	3	0	0	1	4	1	0	0	7	1.50	0.25	.077
	Cleveland (AL)	MAJ	0	1	7.40	19	0	0	0	21	31	3	7	18	0.72	1.84	.356
2010	Cleveland (AL)	MAJ	0	0	7.50	5	0	0	0	6	9	0	3	9	0.60	2.00	.333
	Columbus (IL)	AAA	4	2	3.31	44	0	0	4	49	46	6	18	53	1.35	1.31	.241
Major League Totals			0	1	7.62	25	0	0	0	28	43	4	12	29	1.35	1.94	.352
Minor League Totals			20	11	2.79	132	31	0	30	313	250	27	87	324	1.35	1.08	.218

28 TYLER HOLT, OF

Born: March 10, 1989. **B-T:** R-R. **Ht.:** 5-11. **Wt.:** 190. **Drafted:** Florida State, 2010 (10th round). **Signed by:** Brad Tyler.

Holt put up gaudy numbers at Florida State, where he hit .355/.471/.629 as a junior and walked more than he struck out in each of his three seasons. His asking price dropped him to the 10th round of the 2010 draft, and he signed for an over-slot $500,000 before continuing his strong hitting in low Class A. While Holt's performance thus far has been outstanding, scouts debate whether his skills will translate at higher levels. He doesn't have standout physical tools, but his instincts and aggressiveness help him get the most out of his abilities. He's an extremely disciplined hitter who works counts, doesn't chase many pitches, sprays the ball to all fields and gets on base at a high rate. Though Holt hit 13 homers as a Seminoles junior after totaling eight in his first two college seasons, scouts still project his power as below average. He employs an open stance and deep crouch that don't get him into a good position to load his hands and drive the ball. Holt has plus speed that plays better than that, as he's a smart baserunner and efficient basestealer. He'll have to maintain his quickness to stay in center field, where he shows good instincts and has a fringy arm. Holt is advanced enough to begin his first full pro season in high Class A.

Year	Club (League)	Class	AVG	G	AB	R	H	2B	3B	HR	RBI	BB	SO	SB	CS	OBP	SLG
2010	Lake County (SAL)	LoA	.286	22	70	12	20	8	2	0	8	15	12	5	3	.409	.457
Minor League Totals			.286	22	70	12	20	8	2	0	8	15	12	5	3	.409	.457

29 ROB BRYSON, RHP

Born: Dec. 11, 1987. **B-T:** R-R. **Ht.:** 6-1. **Wt.:** 200. **Drafted:** Seminole (Fla.) JC, D/F 2006 (31st round). **Signed by:** Charlie Aliano (Brewers).

Bryson signed with the Brewers in 2007 for $300,000 as a draft-and-follow in the final year before Major League Baseball eliminated the rule. He pitched well in the Milwaukee system before the Brewers packaged him along with Matt LaPorta, Michael Brantley and Zach Jackson to acquire C.C. Sabathia from the Indians in July 2008. Bryson made just seven more appearances that season before injuring his shoulder and requiring surgery to repair a torn labrum and rotator cuff. That type of shoulder surgery is usually the kiss of death for a pitcher, but he bounced back strong last year after missing nearly the entire 2009 season. Bryson's low-90s fastball tops out at 95 mph and is a swing-and-miss pitch with good deception. Both of his secondary pitches need work. Though he flashes an average slider at times, it has long, slow break. He has worked on his changeup, but still uses it only occasionally and it's a below-average pitch. He throws strikes but still is honing his command after losing so much time to injury. He may return to Double-A to begin 2011.

Year	Club (League)	Class	W	L	ERA	G	GS	CG	SV	IP	H	HR	BB	SO	G/A	WHIP	AVG
2007	Helena (PIO)	R	3	0	2.67	18	4	0	8	54	49	2	12	70	—	1.13	.245
2008	West Virginia (SAL)	LoA	3	2	4.25	22	5	0	5	55	43	3	20	73	—	1.15	.209
	Lake County (SAL)	LoA	0	1	2.19	7	0	0	0	12	6	1	6	11	—	0.97	.140
2009	Indians (AZL)	R	0	0	12.00	3	3	0	0	3	4	2	2	5	0.50	2.00	.308
2010	Lake County (SAL)	LoA	4	0	4.05	8	0	0	0	13	13	2	2	21	0.88	1.13	.236
	Kinston (CAR)	HiA	2	1	2.25	13	0	0	1	20	7	2	8	38	1.57	0.75	.108
	Akron (EL)	AA	1	1	1.80	12	3	0	0	20	11	1	11	21	0.68	1.10	.162
Minor League Totals			13	5	3.24	83	15	0	14	178	133	13	61	239	0.87	1.09	.205

30 GIOVANNY URSHELA, 3B

Born: October 11, 1991. **B-T:** R-R. **Ht.:** 6-0. **Wt.:** 185. **Signed:** Colombia, 2008. **Signed by:** Jose Quintero.

Urshela was one of Colombia's top prospects in 2008, when he signed with the Indians for $300,000. He has developed into an outstanding defensive third baseman with legitimate Gold Glove potential, making difficult plays seem routine. He has excellent defensive instincts and shows good actions, range to both sides and a plus-plus arm. He's not an outstanding athlete but has good footwork and advanced feel for the position considering his age. Urshela's bat isn't quite as advanced as his glove, but he has a projectable frame and makes consistent contact. His swing does get long, however, and he would benefit from a more patient approach. The Indians hope he'll develop some home run power as he fills out, but he doesn't project as a slugger. Speed won't be a big part of his game either. Urshela will make his full-season debut in low Class A this year at age 19.

Year	Club (League)	Class	AVG	G	AB	R	H	2B	3B	HR	RBI	BB	SO	SB	CS	OBP	SLG
2009	Indians (DSL)	R	.269	27	108	10	29	8	1	1	24	7	14	2	2	.316	.389
	Indians (AZL)	R	.257	32	105	10	27	2	0	0	11	10	12	3	0	.322	.276
2010	Mahoning Valley (NYP)SS		.290	58	221	22	64	8	0	3	35	12	32	5	3	.326	.367
Minor League Totals			.276	117	434	42	120	18	1	4	70	29	58	10	5	.323	.350

Colorado Rockies

BY TRACY RINGOLSBY

The Rockies were Baseball America's Organization of the Year and advanced to the World Series in 2007, then returned to the playoffs in 2009. They fell short of the postseason in 2010, but still won 83 games and look positioned to continue contending in the National League West.

The constant in Colorado's recent success has been an emphasis on scouting and player development. The team has homegrown players throughout its roster, from franchise icon Todd Helton to ace Ubaldo Jimenez—who threw the first no-hitter in franchise history last April—to cornerstone Troy Tulowitzki,

who signed a $158 million extension in November that will keep him under contract through at least 2020. Six of the eight hitters in the projected 2011 lineup and three of the five starters in the rotation were signed and developed by the Rockies.

And yet they weren't satisfied with the quality of players they were getting in recent drafts. So in 2009 the Rockies took lefthander Tyler Matzek in the first round and signed him for a club-record $3.9 million. Last June, they selected Clemson quarterback/outfielder Kyle Parker in the first round and eventually signed him for $1.4 million, agreeing to allow him to play football last fall before focusing on baseball.

Colorado had a reputation for adhering to the bonus guidelines prescribed by the commissioner's office and for not gambling with its early picks. That has changed, as the organization realized it was putting itself at a disadvantage compared to others that routinely ignored MLB's informal slotting system.

"We just got fed up," general manager Dan O'Dowd said. "We just started taking the best player available. We felt we would make the effort to get them signed, and if it got to the point where we had to walk away, we would walk away and take the compensation pick for the next year."

The wakeup call came for the Rockies after they spent three consecutive first-round picks on pitchers Greg Reynolds, Casey Weathers and Christian Friedrich in 2006-08. Reynolds, taken No. 2 overall instead of Evan Longoria because Colorado had selected infielders with its previous three first-rounders, has been healthy enough to make 20 starts just once in four full pro seasons. Weathers, taken ahead of Jason Heyward, has pitched just 29 innings since having Tommy John surgery following the 2008 season. Friedrich has been limited to 155 innings in three

TONY FARLOW

Shortstop Troy Tulowitzki is one of many homegrown Rockies big league cornerstones

TOP 30 PROSPECTS

1. Tyler Matzek, lhp	16. Will Swanner, c
2. Wilin Rosario, c	17. Chris Nelson, inf
3. Nolan Arenado, 3b	18. Jordan Pacheco, c
4. Christian Friedrich, lhp	19. Russell Wilson, 2b
5. Peter Tago, rhp	20. Matt Reynolds, lhp
6. Kyle Parker, of	21. Tim Wheeler, of
7. Rex Brothers, lhp	22. Cole Garner, of
8. Juan Nicasio, rhp	23. Samuel Deduno, rhp
9. Chad Bettis, rhp	24. Parker Frazier, rhp
10. Hector Gomez, ss	25. Cory Riordan, rhp
11. Charlie Blackmon, of	26. Corey Dickerson, of
12. Rosell Herrera, ss	27. Edgmer Escalona, rhp
13. Albert Campos, rhp	28. Ben Paulsen, 1b
14. Casey Weathers, rhp	29. Thomas Field, ss
15. Rob Scahill, rhp	30. Edwar Cabrera, lhp

years as a pro because of shoulder ailments.

The residual effect is that the Rockies do have a gap in their farm system. They don't have any top rookie candidates for 2011 or an abundance of prospects in Triple-A, but they have done a good job of restocking their supply prospects and feel comfortable with a coming wave of talent at the Double-A level on down. Matzek and Parker are still a few years away, but catcher Wilin Rosario, lefty reliever Rex Brothers, righty Juan Nicasio and outfielder Charlie Blackmon may be able to make some big league contributions in the near future.

ORGANIZATION OVERVIEW

General Manager: Dan O'Dowd. **Farm Director:** Marc Gustafson. **Scouting Director:** Bill Schmidt.

Class	Team	League	W	L	PCT	Finish*	Manager
Majors	Colorado Rockies	National	83	79	.512	7th (16)	Jim Tracy
Triple-A	Colorado Springs Sky Sox	Pacific Coast	64	79	.448	14th (16)	Stu Cole
Double-A	Tulsa Drillers	Texas	69	70	.496	5th (8)	Ron Gideon
High A	Modesto Nuts	California	73	67	.521	6th (10)	Jerry Weinstein
Low A	Asheville Tourists	South Atlantic	69	70	.496	7th (14)	Joe Mikulik
Short-season	Tri-City Dust Devils	Northwest	30	46	.395	8th (8)	Fred Ocasio
Rookie	Casper Ghosts	Pioneer	37	39	.487	6th (8)	Tony Diaz
Overall 2010 Minor League Record			342	371	.480	25th (30)	

*Finish in overall standings (No. of teams in league). †League champion.

LAST YEAR'S TOP 30

Player, Pos.		Status
1.	Tyler Matzek, lhp	No. 1
2.	Christian Friederich, lhp	No. 4
3.	Wilin Rosario, c	No. 2
4.	Jhouyls Chacin, rhp	Majors
5.	Hector Gomez, ss	No. 10
6.	Eric Young Jr., 2b/of	Majors
7.	Tim Wheeler, of	No. 21
8.	Rex Brothers, lhp	No. 7
9.	Esmil Rogers, rhp	Majors
10.	Nolan Arenado, 3b	No. 3
11.	Samuel Deduno, rhp	No. 23
12.	Charlie Blackmon, of	No. 11
13.	Michael McKenry, c	Dropped out
14.	Casey Weathers, rhp	No. 14
15.	Juan Nicasio, rhp	No. 8
16.	Chris Balcom-Miller, rhp	(Red Sox)
17.	Delta Cleary, of	Dropped out
18.	Jordan Pacheco, c	No. 18
19.	Kent Matthes, of	Dropped out
20.	Al Albuquerque, rhp	(Tigers)
21.	Parker Frazier, rhp	No. 24
22.	Craig Baker, rhp	Dropped out
23.	Shane Lindsay, rhp	(Indians)
24.	Chaz Roe, rhp	(Mariners)
25.	Matt Reynolds, lhp	No. 20
26.	Jonathan Vargas, lhp	Dropped out
27.	Edgmer Escolona, rhp	No. 27
28.	Tyler Massey, of	Dropped out
29.	Chris Nelson, ss	No. 17
30.	Kiel Roling, 1b	Dropped out

BEST TOOLS

Best Hitter for Average	Nolan Arenado
Best Power Hitter	Kyle Parker
Best Strike-Zone Discipline	Jordan Pacheco
Fastest Baserunner	Russell Wilson
Best Athlete	Russell Wilson
Best Fastball	Tyler Matzek
Best Curveball	Christian Friedrich
Best Slider	Rex Brothers
Best Changeup	Edwar Cabrera
Best Control	Parker Frazier
Best Defensive Catcher	Wilin Rosario
Best Defensive Infielder	Thomas Field
Best Infield Arm	Nolan Arenado
Best Defensive Outfielder	Eliezer Mesa
Best Outfield Arm	Tim Wheeler

PROJECTED 2014 LINEUP

Catcher	Wilin Rosario
First Base	Nolan Arenado
Second Base	Hector Gomez
Third Base	Ian Stewart
Shortstop	Troy Tulowitzki
Left Field	Kyle Parker
Center Field	Dexter Fowler
Right Field	Carlos Gonzalez
No. 1 Starter	Ubaldo Jimenez
No. 2 Starter	Tyler Matzek
No. 3 Starter	Jhouyls Chacin
No. 4 Starter	Peter Tago
No. 5 Starter	Christian Freidrich
Closer	Rex Brothers

TOP PROSPECTS OF THE DECADE

Year	Player, Pos.	2010 Org.
2001	Chin-Hui Tsao, rhp	Out of baseball
2002	Chin-Hui Tsao, rhp	Out of baseball
2003	Aaron Cook, rhp	Rockies
2004	Chin-Hui Tsao, rhp	Out of baseball
2005	Ian Stewart, 3b	Rockies
2006	Ian Stewart, 3b	Rockies
2007	Troy Tulowitzki, ss	Rockies
2008	Franklin Morales, lhp	Rockies
2009	Dexter Fowler, of	Rockies
2010	Tyler Matzek, lhp	Rockies

TOP DRAFT PICKS OF THE DECADE

Year	Player, Pos.	2010 Org.
2001	Jayson Nix, 2b (1st round supp.)	Indians
2002	Jeff Francis. lhp	Rockies
2003	Ian Stewart, 3b	Rockies
2004	Chris Nelson, ss	Rockies
2005	Troy Tulowitzki, ss	Rockies
2006	Greg Reynolds, rhp	Rockies
2007	Casey Weathers, rhp	Rockies
2008	Christian Friedrick. Lhp	Rockies
2009	Tyler Matzek, lhp	Rockies
2010	Kyle Parker, of	Rockies

LARGEST BONUSES IN CLUB HISTORY

Tyler Matzek, 2009	$3,900,000
Greg Reynolds, 2006	$3,250,000
Jason Young, 2000	$2,750,000
Troy Tulowitzki, 2005	$2,300,000
Chin-Hui Tsao, 1999	$2,200,000

COLORADO ROCKIES

TOP 2011 ROOKIE: Rex Brothers, lhp. He's drawing Billy Wagner comparisons after hitting 97 mph in the Arizona Fall League.

BREAKOUT PROSPECT: Rosell Herrera, ss. He was impressive in the Rookie-level Dominican Summer League that he was added to instructional league roster.

SLEEPER: Josh Rutledge, ss. The third-round pick was one of the best middle-infield defenders available in the 2010 draft.

SOURCE OF TOP 30 TALENT			
Homegrown	30	Acquired	0
College	14	Trades	0
Junior college	1	Rule 5 draft	0
High school	7	Independent leagues	0
Draft-and-follow	0	Free agents/waivers	0
Nondrafted free agents	0		
International	8		

LF
Corey Dickerson (26)
Jared Simon

CF
Charlie Blackmon (11)
Delta Cleary
Eliezer Mesa
Rafael Ortega

RF
Kyle Parker (6)
Tim Wheeler (21)
Cole Garner (22)
Kent Matthes
Juan Crousset

3B
Brett Tanos

SS
Hector Gomez (10)
Rosell Herrera (12)
Thomas Field (29)
Josh Rutledge
Cristhian Adames

2B
Chris Nelson (17)
Russell Wilson (19)
Angelys Nina
Jimmy Cesario

1B
Nolan Arenado (3)
Ben Paulsen (28)
Jared Clark

C
Wilin Rosario (2)
Will Swanner (16)
Jordan Pacheco (18)
Michael McKenry
Ryan Casteel

RHP

RHSP	RHRP
Peter Tago (5)	Casey Weathers (14)
Juan Nicasio (8)	Edgmer Escalona (27)
Chad Bettis (9)	Adam Jorgenson
Albert Campos (13)	Juan Gonzalez
Rob Scahill (15)	Vianney Mayo
Samuel Deduno (23)	
Parker Frazier (24)	
Cory Riordan (25)	
Bruce Billings	
Josh Slaats	
Erik Stavert	
Ethan Hollingsworth	
Nick Schnaitmann	
Geoff Parker	
Rafael Suarez	

LHP

LHSP	LHRP
Tyler Matzek (1)	Rex Brothers (7)
Christian Friedrich (4)	Matt Reynolds (20)
Edwar Cabrera (30)	
Keith Weiser	
Kraig Sitton	
Jonathan Vargas	

2010

BEST PURE HITTER: OF Corey Dickerson (8) is a bat-first player with a left-field profile. He's strong and got off to a tremendous start at Rookie-level Casper, hitting .348/.412/.634.

BEST POWER HITTER: OF Kyle Parker (1) has pole-to-pole power and projects to hit 30 homers annually. A quarterback at Clemson, he should be even better once he focuses 100 percent on baseball.

FASTEST RUNNER: Another Atlantic Coast Conference quarterback, North Carolina State 2B Russell Wilson (4), is a well above-average runner who impressed the Rockies last summer by running better than he did as an amateur. He consistently gets from the right side of the plate to first base in 4.1 seconds or less.

BEST DEFENSIVE PLAYER: SS Josh Rutledge (3) has an average arm and strong infield actions. He can be a solid defender at shortstop or above average at second base.

BEST FASTBALL: RHP Chad Bettis (2) has the best present velocity, running his fastball up to 98 mph at times and pitching comfortably at 93-94 as a starter. Prep RHP Peter Tago (1s) also touched 98 in a predraft workout and has a projectable, athletic build and loose arm, which should allow him to grow into more consistent elite velocity.

BEST SECONDARY PITCH: Bettis and RHP Josh Slaats (5) both flashed plus sliders after signing.

BEST PRO DEBUT: Dickerson destroyed Pioneer League pitching, leading the Rookie-level circuit with 61 RBIs and 175 total bases. Bettis, who finished with three starts in low Class A, went 6-1, 1.07 with 56 strikeouts in 67 innings. He learned to be pitch-efficient, going seven innings in one start despite a pitch limit of 75. Slaats had a 1.95 ERA with 42 strikeouts in 32 innings.

BEST ATHLETE: Wilson stands out for his athleticism and aptitude. No one really knows how good he can be at baseball, as he got just 241 at-bats in three college seasons. He hopes to play both baseball and football professionally, a la Deion Sanders and Bo Jackson.

MOST INTRIGUING BACKGROUND: Parker became the first player in NCAA Division I history to hit 20 homers and throw 20 touchdown passes in one school year. His father Carl is a former NFL wide receiver. 1B Mark Tracy's (22) dad Jim manages the Rockies and played in the majors, as did unsigned SS Logan Davis' (38) father Mark—a former Cy Young Award winner—and unsigned SS Mike Benjamin's (45) dad, also named Mike.

CLOSEST TO THE MAJORS: Bettis could fly to the big league bullpen.

BEST LATE-ROUND PICK: C Will Swanner (15), an over-slot signee for $490,000, has good raw power and catch-and-throw tools.

THE ONE WHO GOT AWAY: The Rockies wanted to follow RHP Ryan Eades (19) over the summer, but he didn't pitch because he was coming off shoulder surgery. He wound up at Louisiana State and is regarded as one of the school's top recruits.

ASSESSMENT: Even with power arms such as Bettis and Tago, much of this draft class is riding on its pair of quarterbacks. Parker and Wilson both have significant upside.

2009

LHP Tyler Matzek (1) could be a steal as the No. 11 overall pick, and the Rockies also have high expectations for LHP Rex Brothers (1s) and 3B Nolan Arenado (2).

GRADE: A

2008

LHP Christian Friedrich (1) is on the verge of helping the big league rotation if he can just stay healthy. OF Charlie Blackmon (12) also could see some time in Colorado this season.

GRADE: C+

2007

This draft class has been slow to produce, in part because RHPs Casey Weathers (1) and Parker Frazier (8) had Tommy John surgery. C Jordan Pacheco (9) and LHP Matt Reynolds (20) are nice late-round finds.

GRADE: C

2006

RHP Greg Reynolds (1) has had repeated injuries since the Rockies drafted him second overall—ahead of Evan Longoria. Colorada drafted four big leaguers in Reynolds, C Michael McKenry (7), RHP Andrew Cashner (18) and LHP Scott Maine (23) but didn't sign the best two, Cashner and Maine.

GRADE: D

Draft analysis by John Manuel (2010) and Jim Callis (2006-09). Numbers in parentheses indicate draft rounds.

TYLER MATZEK, LHP

Born: Oct. 19, 1990. **Bats:** L. **Throws:** L.
Height: 6-3. **Weight:** 213. **Drafted:** HS—
Capistrano Valley, Calif., 2009 (1st round).
Signed by: Jon Lukens.

TONY FARLOW

PROSPECT 1

Matzek emerged as the top high school pitcher and top lefthander in the 2009 draft class, but his reported bonus demands and Oregon commitment drove him down many draft boards. The Rockies had a reputation for being conservative in the draft, but in their first major deviation from their previous draft philosophy, they took Matzek 11th overall. Though he had told teams he was looking for "unprecedented money," Colorado was able to land him for a club-record $3.9 million at the Aug. 17 deadline. He signed too late to make his pro debut, though he did make a strong impression in instructional league. The Rockies kept him in extended spring training for the first six weeks of the 2010 season, in an attempt to keep his innings down in his first pro season. Matzek didn't make his first start at low Class A Asheville until May 24, and even in August he worked with an 85-pitch limit. He also was slowed by biceps tendinitis at season's end, though he still ranked as the No. 3 prospect (and top pitching prospect) in the South Atlantic League.

Matzek has a legitimate four-pitch assortment, with strong present stuff and plenty of room for improvement. His fastball sits at 88-92 mph and touches 96. He throws his fastball with good angle, and it jumps on hitters with late life. He pitched in the mid-90s more frequently toward the end of the season, and he flashed upper-90s heat leading up to the 2009 draft. At 20, he should get stronger as he fills out. Matzek is still developing feel for and consistency with his secondary pitches. He presently has more feel for his decent curveball, but his slider should develop into his more reliable breaking ball, a potential plus offering and perhaps a legitimate out pitch. His changeup shows promise in bullpen sessions, but he doesn't use it enough in games. Eventually he'll learn that he needs the changeup to combat righthanders, though for now he noticeably slows his arm when he throws it. Matzek has good arm action and a nice release, but he opens up too soon in his delivery and lands on a stiff front leg, which is why he has been so inconsistent with his command. He averaged 6.2 walks per nine innings in his pro debut, which makes his 2.92 ERA a testament to his ability to dominate hitters. A quality athlete, Matzek fields his position well. His biggest challenge has nothing to do with his physical ability, as he must do a better job of not showing his emotions on the mound. Having never dealt with failure, he got frustrated at times last season. He also got himself in trouble by being too analytical. He's meticulous in his approach, but Colorado would like him to simplify things and not outthink himself.

Matzek has all the stuff to pitch at the top of a rotation, but he also has a lot to learn. If his control and command come together, he could move more quickly than a typical Rockies high school draft pick. He'll start 2011 at high Class A Modesto, with a midseason move up to Double-A Tulsa and a big league ETA of late 2012 not out of the question.

SCOUTING GRADES

Fastball: 70. **Command/**
Slider: 60. **Control:** 55.
Changeup: 55. **Delivery:** 55.

Based on 20-80 scouting scale, where 50 represents major league average, and future projection rather than present tools.

Year	Club (League)	Class	W	L	ERA	G	GS	CG	SV	IP	H	HR	BB	SO	G/AWHIP	AVG
2010	Asheville (SAL)	LoA	5	1	2.92	18	18	0	0	89	62	6	62	88	1.01 1.39	.204
Minor League Totals			5	1	2.92	18	18	0	0	89	62	6	62	88	1.01 1.39	.204

2 WILIN ROSARIO, C

Born: Feb. 23, 1989. **B-T:** R-R. **Ht.:** 5-11. **Wt.:** 195. **Signed:** Dominican Republic, 2006. **Signed by:** Rolando Fernandez/Felix Feliz.

Rosario was in the midst of a breakout year when he tore the anterior cruciate ligament in his right knee during a rundown in early August. He had just played in the Futures Game and won the Double-A Texas League's player-of-the-month award for July when knee surgery ended his season. Colorado added him to its 40-man roster in November. Rosario is a rare catcher with an impact bat. He has a compact swing and can turn on any fastball, and he showed improvement handling breaking balls last year. He has power to all fields and could hit 20-30 homers a year if he taps into his strength, though he'll need to improve his strike-zone discipline. While he's a well below-average runner, Rosario has the athleticism to be a quality defensive catcher. He moves well behind the plate and blocks and receives balls well. He has a strong arm and threw out 44 percent of basestealers in 2010. He's refining his game-calling and working on keeping up his energy behind the plate even when he has a bad game at bat. The Rockies hoped Rosario could reach the major leagues sometime in 2011, but the knee injury probably pushes that timetable back a year. His rehabilitation was progressing well, and he could be able to participate in spring training. When he's ready for action, he'll head to Triple-A Colorado Springs.

Year	Club (League)	Class	AVG	G	AB	R	H	2B	3B	HR	RBI	BB	SO	SB	CS	OBP	SLG
2006	Rockies (DSL)	R	.249	62	213	28	53	7	0	3	25	16	56	5	2	.309	.324
2007	Casper (PIO)	R	.209	34	115	11	24	4	0	2	9	11	38	2	2	.283	.296
2008	Casper (PIO)	R	.316	66	263	48	83	15	3	12	49	24	57	4	3	.371	.532
2009	Modesto (CAL)	HiA	.266	58	203	17	54	12	2	4	33	10	55	2	1	.297	.404
2010	Tulsa (TL)	AA	.285	73	270	42	77	13	1	19	52	21	57	1	0	.342	.552
Minor League Totals			.273	293	1064	146	291	51	6	40	168	82	263	14	8	.328	.445

3 NOLAN ARENADO, 3B

Born: April 16, 1991. **B-T:** R-R. **Ht.:** 6-1. **Wt.:** 223. **Drafted:** HS—El Toro, Calif., 2009 (2nd round). **Signed by:** Jon Lukens.

The Rockies drafted Arenado 56th overall and signed him for $625,000 because of his bat. He hit .529 as a high school senior and then .300 in his pro debut, when he was the second-youngest everyday player in the Rookie-level Pioneer League. He got off to a slow start in 2010 because of a groin injury, reporting to Asheville on May 21, but still batted .308 and finished second in the South Atlantic League with 41 doubles. Arenado is strong and makes consistent, hard contact, so he should have above-average power. His inside-out stroke serves him well in two-strike situations, though there's some stiffness in his swing. He has a situational approach that allows him to turn on fastballs thrown on the inner portion of the plate. A middle-of-the-lineup hitter, he admits he has to draw more walks. A shortstop in high school, Arenado has moved to third base as a pro and has a strong, accurate arm. He needs to work on his first-step quickness to develop better range, and he could end up at first base. He's not athletic and has below-average speed. Arenado will move up to high Class A to open the 2011 season, but if he hits he could earn a second-half promotion. He'll stay at third base for now, but he profiles as the eventual heir to Todd Helton at first base.

Year	Club (League)	Class	AVG	G	AB	R	H	2B	3B	HR	RBI	BB	SO	SB	CS	OBP	SLG
2009	Casper (PIO)	R	.300	54	203	28	61	15	0	2	22	16	18	5	2	.351	.404
2010	Asheville (SAL)	LoA	.308	92	373	45	115	41	1	12	65	19	52	1	3	.338	.520
Minor League Totals			.306	146	576	73	176	56	1	14	87	35	70	6	5	.342	.479

4 CHRISTIAN FRIEDRICH, LHP

Born: July 8, 1987. **B-T:** L-L. **Ht.:** 6-4. **Wt.:** 215. **Drafted:** Eastern Kentucky, 2008 (1st round). **Signed by:** Scott Corman.

Undrafted out of a suburban Chicago high school, Friedrich went 25th overall in the 2008 draft and signed for $1.35 million after three years at Eastern Kentucky. He ranked second in the minors with 12.0 strikeouts per nine innings in his first full season, but he has missed a month in each of the last two years with elbow inflammation. His 2010 season ended on Aug. 19 because of a strained lat muscle. Friedrich offers a pair of plus pitches and mixes his entire arsenal well. His fastball ranges from 89-93 mph, touching 95, and he loves to challenge hitters with it. His curveball has big bite when he finishes it but needs to get more consistent. He shows feel for a changeup and locates it well, and he has worked on a slider to give hitters a different look. Tulsa pitching coach Bryan Harvey worked with Friedrich to get him to stay back longer in his delivery, allowing him to create a better downhill plane on his pitches. His main challenge is to stay healthy. Provided he's durable enough, Friedrich can be a No. 3 starter, and he's nearly ready for the big leagues. He'll open 2011 in Triple-A and figures to reach Colorado before the season ends.

Year	Club (League)	Class	W	L	ERA	G	GS	CG	SV	IP	H	HR	BB	SO	G/A	WHIP	AVG
2008	Tri-City (NWL)	SS	2	1	3.25	8	8	0	0	36	31	2	8	50	—	1.08	.228
	Asheville (SAL)	LoA	0	1	7.50	3	3	0	0	12	14	2	7	15	—	1.75	.269
2009	Asheville (SAL)	LoA	3	3	2.18	8	8	0	0	45	35	2	15	66	1.71	1.10	.215
	Modesto (CAL)	HiA	3	2	2.54	14	14	0	0	74	59	3	28	93	0.77	1.17	.215
2010	Tulsa (TL)	AA	3	6	5.05	18	18	0	0	87	100	10	35	78	1.20	1.55	.293
Minor League Totals			11	13	3.67	51	51	0	0	255	239	19	93	302	1.09	1.30	.247

5 PETER TAGO, RHP

Born: July 5, 1992. **B-T:** R-R. **Ht.:** 6-3. **Wt.:** 190. **Drafted:** HS—Dana Hills, Calif., 2010 (1st round supplemental). **Signed by:** Jon Lukens.

Jason Marquis won 15 games and made the all-star team in his lone season with Colorado, but his legacy well could turn out to be Tago, selected 47th overall in the 2010 draft with a compensation choice the Rockies received for losing Marquis to free agency. Of Samoan descent, Tago initially committed to UCLA and looked headed to Cal State Fullerton until he signed for $982,500 hours before the Aug. 16 deadline. Tago has the size and stuff to be a frontline starter. He first caught the attention of scouts when he hit 90 mph with his fastball at age 14. He now works at 91-93 mph, with a frame and arm action that portend more velocity, and he hit 98 in predraft workouts. His curveball has promise but needs tighter spin, and he's working on a changeup after not using it much as an amateur. Tago has a smooth, relaxed motion, but he needs to do a better job of incorporating his lower half in his delivery. He throws strikes and has a good demeanor on the mound. Tago got his first taste of pro ball in instructional league and spent a month at the team's facility in the Dominican Republic. The Rockies don't rush young arms, but he could force his way into the Asheville rotation in 2011.

Year	Club (League)	Class	W	L	ERA	G	GS	CG	SV	IP	H	HR	BB	SO	G/A	WHIP	AVG
2010	Did Not Play—Signed Late																

6 KYLE PARKER, OF

Born: Sept. 30, 1989. **B-T:** R-R. **Ht.:** 6-1. **Wt.:** 200. **Drafted:** Clemson, 2010 (1st round). **Signed by:** Jay Matthews.

In 2009-10, Parker became the first player in NCAA Division I history to throw 20 touchdown passes and hit 20 homers in the same school year. The 26th overall pick in the 2010 baseball draft, he declined a $2.2 million offer from the Rockies in mid-July that would have required him to immediately give up playing quarterback at Clemson. He signed for $1.4 million at the Aug. 16 deadline with the agreement that he would play one more season of college football before focusing on baseball—he was already participating in fall practice with the Tigers at the time. Parker's final football season was a disappointment. He threw 12 touchdowns and 10 interceptions for a 6-6 Tigers team. His disappointing fall reaffirmed his decision to focus on baseball starting this spring. His father Carl is a former NFL wide receiver. Parker hit 46 homers in three seasons at Clemson and has tremendous bat speed to go with strength, so scouts think his power is legitimate. He shows a great feel for the game and improved his discipline last spring, giving him the ability to hit for a solid average as well. He's a good athlete but not an overwhelming one. He has average speed, range and arm strength and will fit on an outfield corner. The leadership he showed at quarterback translates into a no-nonsense mentality on the baseball field. Parker's experience playing at the highest level of college baseball should allow him to hit the ground running in full-season ball, and he'll probably make his debut at Asheville. Colorado will fast-track him if he can handle it.

Year	Club (League)	Class	AVG	G	AB	R	H	2B	3B	HR	RBI	BB	SO	SB	CS	OBP	SLG
2010	Did Not Play—Signed Late																

7 REX BROTHERS, LHP

Born: Dec. 18, 1987. **B-T:** L-L. **Ht.:** 6-0. **Wt.:** 212. **Drafted:** Lipscomb, 2009 (1st round supplemental). **Signed by:** Scott Corman.

The 34th player taken in the 2009 draft, Brothers has moved quickly since signing for $969,000. Converted to a reliever after turning pro, he reached Double-A in July of his first full pro season, struggling initially but finishing with a 1.50 ERA and 18 strikeouts in his final 12 innings. He continued to perform well in the Arizona Fall League, where he appeared in the Rising Stars Game. Brothers has just two pitches, but they're both nasty and he goes right after hitters with them. His fastball touches 97 and sits comfortably in the low to mid-90s with running movement. His mid-80s slider has dramatic late tilt, allowing him to use it as an out pitch against both lefthanders and righthanders. Command and control are all that stand between him and a big league promotion. Tulsa pitching coach Bryan Harvey helped smooth out Brothers' mechanics, getting him to eliminate a shoulder rotation that caused his pitches to stay up in the zone. Harvey draws compares Brothers to Billy Wagner. The Rockies will give Brothers a long look in big league camp after nearly promoting him to the majors last September. The team's closer of the future, he'll probably open 2011 in Triple-A and reach Colorado during the season.

Year	Club (League)	Class	W	L	ERA	G	GS	CG	SV	IP	H	HR	BB	SO	G/AWHIP	AVG
2009	Tri-City (NWL)	SS	2	0	3.38	8	0	0	0	11	10	0	5	18	1.80 1.41	.256
	Asheville (SAL)	LoA	0	0	3.38	9	0	0	0	11	6	1	3	10	2.50 0.84	.171
2010	Modesto (CAL)	HiA	0	2	2.68	33	0	0	3	37	20	0	19	43	2.05 1.05	.165
	Tulsa (TL)	AA	2	1	3.91	24	0	0	4	23	14	2	18	27	1.67 1.39	.177
Minor League Totals			4	3	3.21	74	0	0	7	81	50	3	45	98	1.96 1.17	.182

8 JUAN NICASIO, RHP

Born: Aug. 31, 1986. **B-T:** R-R. **Ht.:** 6-3. **Wt.:** 234. **Signed:** Dominican Republic, 2006. **Signed by:** Rolando Fernandez/Felix Feliz.

Nicasio is a late bloomer, signing out of the Dominican Republic at age 19 and making his full-season debut three years later. He took a major step forward in 2010, leading the high Class A California League in wins (12), innings (177) and strikeouts (171). Despite blowing away his previous career high of 112 innings, he finished with a flourish, going 4-1, 2.30 ERA with just four walks in 43 innings over his final six starts. Nicasio has the stuff and size to pitch near the front of a big league rotation, and one Cal League scout compared him to a young Ubaldo Jimenez. Nicasio has an 89-94 mph fastball and the ability to reach back and hit 97. He throws two versions of a breaking ball, a true curveball and a slurvier version that some scouts call a slider. He's developing a changeup that elicits swings and misses at times. Nicasio posted a 5.5 K-BB ratio last year, and at times he's around the strike zone too much. He had more success one he adjusted and began pitching inside more, moving hitters off the plate. Nicasio will take his four-pitch mix to Double-A in 2011. If all goes well, he could challenge for a job in Colorado's rotation by mid-2012.

Year	Club (League)	Class	W	L	ERA	G	GS	CG	SV	IP	H	HR	BB	SO	G/AWHIP	AVG
2006	Rockies (DSL)	R	2	1	2.89	8	5	0	0	28	27	1	8	24	— 1.25	.250
2007	Casper (PIO)	R	0	3	4.36	13	8	0	0	43	48	3	13	33	— 1.41	.276
2008	Tri-City (NWL)	SS	2	4	4.50	12	12	0	0	54	46	1	19	61	— 1.20	.229
2009	Asheville (SAL)	LoA	9	3	2.41	18	18	1	0	112	110	6	23	115	1.37 1.19	.252
2010	Modesto (CAL)	HiA	12	10	3.91	28	28	1	0	177	186	14	31	171	1.33 1.22	.266
Minor League Totals			25	21	3.56	79	71	2	0	415	417	25	94	404	1.34 1.23	.258

9 CHAD BETTIS, RHP

Born: April 26, 1989. **B-T:** R-R. **Ht.:** 6-1. **Wt.:** 210. **Drafted:** Texas Tech, 2010 (2nd round). **Signed by:** Dar Cox.

An eighth-round draft choice coming out of high school in 2007, Bettis was among seven Astros picks in the first 15 rounds that year who did not sign. He showed versatility at Texas Tech, working as a starter as a freshman, reliever as a sophomore and in both roles last spring. He also starred in the bullpen for Team USA in the summer of 2009, and signed for $477,000 as the 76th overall pick last June. An excellent competitor, Bettis has the fluid delivery and quick arm to allow him to look effortless while generating velocity and movement. He usually pitches at 92-94 mph with his fastball, and he has hit 98 out of the bullpen. His slider is a plus pitch at times, but it lacks consistency and he tends to overthrow it. He has a developing changeup that he uses against lefthanders. Bettis relies too heavily on his secondary pitches and needs to use his fastball more. He throws strikes and works down in the zone, giving up just one homer in 67 pro innings. Bettis could open his first full pro season in high Class A and pitch his way to Double-A by mid-season. While he has the stuff and resilience to thrive as a reliever, the Rockies will develop him as a potential middle-of-the-rotation starter.

Year	Club (League)	Class	W	L	ERA	G	GS	CG	SV	IP	H	HR	BB	SO	G/AWHIP	AVG
2010	Tri-City (NWL)	SS	4	1	1.12	10	9	0	0	48	44	0	10	39	2.16 1.12	.227
	Asheville (SAL)	LoA	2	0	0.96	3	3	0	0	19	14	1	3	17	0.94 0.91	.209
Minor League Totals			6	1	1.07	13	12	0	0	67	58	1	13	56	1.73 1.06	.222

10 HECTOR GOMEZ, SS

Born: March 5, 1988. **B-T:** R-R. **Ht.:** 6-2. **Wt.:** 180. **Signed:** Dominican Republic, 2004. **Signed by:** Rolando Fernandez/Felix Feliz/Frank Roa.

Injuries have slowed Gomez the last three years, but he had a much more significant obstacle to overcome last year. His first son, Hector Jr., died shortly after his birth in late June. Gomez also dealt with a stress fracture in his right leg, sustained in the second game of 2010. He fouled a ball off his left leg in the first game of 2008, then blew out his elbow while rehabbing a stress fracture and required Tommy John surgery. In 2009, he missed a month with a groin strain. Gomez has the prototypical tools of a modern shortstop. He has tremendous arm strength, soft hands and quick feet, which allow him to cover ground and make off-balance plays. His focus tends to wander on routine grounders, however. At the plate, Gomez can turn on any fastball and shows at least 15-homer potential. He's impatient and vulnerable to breaking pitches, which dents his average. He has plus speed but is still learning as a basestealer. The Rockies believe most of his deficiencies can be alleviated with playing time. The two things holding Gomez back are his health and his position. With Troy Tulowitzki entrenched at Coors Field, Gomez will have to move to second base if he stays with Colorado. First on his agenda is getting in a full season of at-bats in Double-A.

Year	Club (League)	Class	AVG	G	AB	R	H	2B	3B	HR	RBI	BB	SO	SB	CS	OBP	SLG
2005	Rockies (DSL)	R	.335	67	242	49	81	16	1	6	43	24	38	15	12	.423	.483
2006	Casper (PIO)	R	.327	50	202	24	66	9	4	5	35	11	26	5	3	.364	.485
	Tri-City (NWL)	SS	.244	12	45	4	11	3	0	0	6	0	14	0	1	.255	.311
2007	Asheville (SAL)	LoA	.266	124	534	89	142	34	8	11	61	29	120	20	10	.309	.421
2008	Modesto (CAL)	HiA	.333	1	3	0	1	0	0	0	0	0	0	0	0	.333	.333
2009	Modesto (CAL)	HiA	.275	83	338	39	93	21	4	7	46	15	68	10	4	.310	.423
2010	Tri-City (NWL)	SS	.246	18	69	8	17	2	1	2	7	5	15	0	3	.293	.391
	Tulsa (TL)	AA	.314	9	35	6	11	4	0	0	3	0	8	0	0	.314	.429
Minor League Totals			.287	364	1468	219	422	89	18	31	201	84	289	50	33	.335	.436

11 CHARLIE BLACKMON, OF

Born: July 1, 1986. **B-T:** L-L. **Ht.:** 6-3. **Wt.:** 200. **Drafted:** Georgia Tech, 2008 (2nd round). **Signed by:** Alan Matthews.

Drafted twice as a pitcher (by the Marlins out of high school and Red Sox out of junior college), Blackmon moved to the outfield while playing in a summer league after the 2007 college season, and wound up as the Rockies' second-round draft choice the next June. He had a setback out of spring training last year, suffering a strained hamstring that sidelined him the first two months—the result of an ill-advised attempt at bulking up in the offseason—but finished strong in Double-A and then played in the Arizona Fall League. Blackmon's compact stroke and ability to drive the ball into the gaps keeps him from extended slumps. His contact approach serves him well against lefthanders. His above-average speed returned as his hamstring healed, and he has stolen 62 bases in the minor leagues while being caught 27 times. He is working on getting better jumps in center field and needs to streamline his throwing mechanics. He has a tendency to wind up. Blackmon will make the move to Triple-A this year and figures to see time in the big leagues by September, if not sooner.

Year	Club (League)	Class	AVG	G	AB	R	H	2B	3B	HR	RBI	BB	SO	SB	CS	OBP	SLG
2008	Tri-City (NWL)	SS	.338	68	290	42	98	21	5	2	33	16	37	13	7	.390	.466
2009	Modesto (CAL)	HiA	.307	133	550	87	169	34	7	7	69	39	83	30	13	.370	.433
2010	Tulsa (TL)	AA	.297	86	337	53	100	22	4	11	55	32	43	19	7	.360	.484
Minor League Totals			.312	287	1177	182	367	77	16	20	157	87	163	62	27	.372	.455

12 ROSELL HERRERA, SS

Born: Oct. 16, 1992. **B-T:** B-R. **Ht.:** 6-3. **Wt.:** 180. **Signed:** Dominican Republic, 2009. **Signed by:** Rolando Fernandez/Jhonathan Leyba.

Herrera is the latest find for the Rockies' Latin American scouting department, signing for $800,000 in the summer of 2009. After making his debut in the Rookie-level Dominican Summer League in 2010, he was invited to instructional league in the fall, which underscores how the organization feels about his future. His numbers aren't eye-popping, but Herrera shows great enthusiasm to play, regardless of his struggles on the field. A switch-hitter who projects to have power as his lean body fills out, Herrera showed surprising plate discipline, averaging more than nine at-bats per strikeout. He has pull power from both sides of the plate and shows the ability to drive the ball into the gaps. Colorado has smoothed out Herrera's throwing motion, and he already has a solid arm, and plus range. His hands are average but figure to soften as he gains playing experience. If he outgrows shortstop his skills should fit in center field. Herrera will make his domestic debut with Rookie-level Casper in 2011. Given his youth and lack of experience, the Rockies will take a cautious approach for a couple of years. Given his size and focus, he already has drawn comparisons to Troy Tulowitzki.

Year	Club (League)	Class	AVG	G	AB	R	H	2B	3B	HR	RBI	BB	SO	SB	CS	OBP	SLG
2010	Rockies (DSL)	R	.237	67	232	27	55	6	1	1	26	24	24	17	8	.323	.284
Minor League Totals			.237	67	232	27	55	6	1	1	26	24	24	17	8	.323	.284

13 ALBERT CAMPOS, RHP

Born: Feb. 4, 1991. **B-T:** R-R. **Ht.:** 6-4. **Wt.:** 232. **Signed:** Venezuela, 2007. **Signed by:** Rolando Fernandez/Francisco Cartaya.

After two years in the Dominican Summer League, Campos earned Pioneer League pitcher of the year honors in 2010. He never issued more than two walks in any of his 15 starts, and he finished strong, working at least six innings in each of his final seven starts. He has a physical frame with long, strong legs and room to fill out in his upper body. Despite his inexperience, Campos has a quality three-pitch mix. His fastball sits anywhere from 88-93 mph, averaging 90-91, and he gets a good downhill plane from his high three-quarters arm slot. His curveball is an out pitch with good bite and arm speed, and he throws it with some power, in the upper 70s. During the 2010 season at Casper he developed a changeup with good fade action that he can use against lefties. Campos needs to use his lower body more to ease strain on shoulder. He's a solid athlete who controls the running game with consistently quick times to the plate. Campos may just need innings to learn how good he can become, and could have a breakout year at Asheville in 2011.

Year	Club (League)	Class	W	L	ERA	G	GS	CG	SV	IP	H	HR	BB	SO	G/A	WHIP	AVG
2008	Rockies (DSL)	R	0	1	1.56	15	4	0	0	35	28	0	12	27	—	1.15	.219
2009	Rockies (DSL)	R	2	6	4.11	25	5	0	5	50	50	2	14	31	1.31	1.27	.259
2010	Casper (PIO)	R	4	4	2.05	15	15	1	0	88	80	5	17	68	1.36	1.10	.244
Minor League Totals			6	11	2.55	55	24	1	5	173	158	7	43	126	1.34	1.16	.243

14 CASEY WEATHERS, RHP

Born: June 10, 1985. **B-T:** R-R. **Ht.:** 6-1. **Wt.:** 216. **Drafted:** Vanderbilt, 2007 (1st round). **Signed by:** Damon Iannelli.

Weathers did not begin pitching until his second year in junior college, having been an outfielder prior to that. Drafted by Detroit in the 25th round after his junior year at Vanderbilt, Weathers made the decision to return to college for another year to develop as a pitcher. Initially projected to be in the big leagues by sometime in the 2009 season, if not sooner, Weathers' development has been slowed by Tommy John surgery. His operation was on Oct. 21, 2008, and he is still working his way back. After missing the entire 2009 season, he began the 2010 season in extended spring training, reworking his mechanics. He has a power fastball that will sit at 95 mph and touch 99, and he complements it with a hard slider. Weathers gets himself in trouble by losing his balance on his back side. The Rockies are working to lower his leg kick to alleviate that. Colorado thought enough of Weathers' comeback to add him to the 40-man roster this offseason for the first time, protecting him from the Rule 5 draft.

Year	Club (League)	Class	W	L	ERA	G	GS	CG	SV	IP	H	HR	BB	SO	G/A	WHIP	AVG
2007	Asheville (SAL)	LoA	0	1	4.61	13	0	0	2	14	6	2	7	19	—	0.95	.130
	Modesto (CAL)	HiA	0	0	0.00	1	0	0	0	1	0	0	2	2	—	2.00	.000
2008	Tulsa (TL)	AA	2	1	3.05	44	0	0	2	44	34	1	28	54	—	1.40	.210
2009	Did Not Play—Injured																
2010	Tri-City (NWL)	SS	0	0	0.00	10	0	0	0	12	2	0	5	21	3.33	0.60	.056
	Modesto (CAL)	HiA	0	1	6.75	20	0	0	4	19	18	2	17	25	1.42	1.87	.250
Minor League Totals			2	3	3.63	88	0	0	8	89	60	5	59	121	1.80	1.33	.188

15 ROB SCAHILL, RHP

Born: Feb. 15, 1987. **B-T:** L-R. **Ht.:** 6-2. **Wt.:** 219. **Drafted:** Bradley, 2009 (8th round). **Signed by:** Mark Germann.

Spending 2010 in Modesto meant Scahill had a chance to watch the Giants on television, and he should benefit from that. Watching a slow-motion video of how Tim Lincecum held his changeup, Scahill adopted a similar style late in the season and then went to the Arizona Fall League to perfect the pitch, which he had thrown too hard with his previous grip. Scahill jumped over low Class A and had his struggles in the first half with Modesto, but he rebounded in his final 14 starts to go 7-3, 3.41, and he followed it up with a five-hit, 11-strikeout, no-walk effort against Stockton in the playoffs. The key for Scahill, besides an improved changeup, was a refinement of mechanics that gave him better command of his fastball and hard-breaking slider. He has a power arm, with an easy delivery that produces a 90-94 mph fastball that touches 96. His slider has real power, with reports of it hitting 88 mph. He also benefitted from the development of a slow curveball. The curve is significantly behind the slider, but it has the potential to be a fringe-average pitch as well. Scalhill generally has life down in the strike zone and gets his share of groundballs while keeping the ball in the ballpark. Scahill is a breakout candidate if he maintains his second-half improvements, and he'll report to the Tulsa rotation.

Year	Club (League)	Class	W	L	ERA	G	GS	CG	SV	IP	H	HR	BB	SO	G/AWHIP	AVG
2009	Tri-City (NWL)	SS	1	4	3.14	15	15	0	0	63	58	2	20	58	2.38 1.24	.245
2010	Modesto (CAL)	HiA	10	7	4.73	27	27	1	0	156	173	9	59	140	1.68 1.49	.284
Minor League Totals			11	11	4.27	42	42	1	0	219	231	11	79	198	1.86 1.42	.273

16 WILL SWANNER, C

Born: Sept. 10, 1991. **B-T:** R-R. **Ht.:** 6-2. **Wt.:** 182. **Drafted:** HS—Carlsbad, Calif., 2010 (15th round). **Signed by:** John Lukens.

Each year Rockies scouting director Bill Schmidt looks for a player who slipped in the draft, with the idea that he can make a late push for the player if the budget allows. Swanner was the focus in 2010, and shortly before he was supposed to head to Pepperdine the Rockies signed him for $490,000, roughly third-round money. Swanner has raw power, and with guidance from personal hitting coach Deron Johnson Jr., son of the 1965 National League RBI leader, he has developed the ability to use all fields. He has good bat speed, but will get in a hurry and collapse his back side. He wasn't terribly selective in his debut and will have to control the strike zone against better-quality pitching for his raw power to play in games. Swanner has a good frame, shows legitimate catching actions and has arm strength. His throwing motion is long, and he struggled with the faster pace of the pro game, failing to throw out a basestealer in seven tries and committing four passed balls in eight games. Swanner has exciting tools, but like most catchers he may need time to develop, so it's not a lock that he'll report to low Class A in 2011.

Year	Club (League)	Class	AVG	G	AB	R	H	2B	3B	HR	RBI	BB	SO	SB	CS	OBP	SLG
2010	Casper (PIO)	R	.303	18	76	14	23	4	0	7	13	0	33	0	1	.321	.632
Minor League Totals			.303	18	76	14	23	4	0	7	13	0	33	0	1	.321	.632

17 CHRIS NELSON, INF

Born: Sept. 3, 1985. **B-T:** R-R. **Ht.:** 5-11. **Wt.:** 190. **Drafted:** HS—Decatur, Ga., 2004 (1st round). **Signed by:** Damon Inannelli

A summer teammate of Dexter Fowler during their high school days in Georgia, Nelson actually was clocked at 99 mph with his fastball while pitching in the Connie Mack World Series after his junior year. The debate over infield or pitching, however, ended when he tore the ligament in the elbow during the Connie Mack event that year. Injuries have slowed Nelson's pro career, too. After a breakthrough season at high Class A in 2007, Nelson broke his left hamate bone in 2008, tore a ligament in his right wrist in 2009, and tore his left oblique at the end of last spring, costing him a shot at a big league promotion early in the season. He made it up for a week in the majors in June, and another trip to Colorado as a September callup. He provided one of the Rockies' highlights of the season by stealing home to beat the Reds on Sept. 9. Nelson has Gary Sheffield bat speed and can hit any fastball. He is still adjusting to offspeed and breaking pitches, but for a middle infielder he he has good power. Nelson has a tremendous arm and soft hands but has to keep his focus. With Troy Tulowitzki at short for the long term, the Rockies have given Nelson exposure at second and third. The trade of Clint Barmes to the Astros opens second base for competition between Nelson, Jonathan Herrera, Eric Young Jr., and perhaps Jose Lopez. Nelson will need to have a huge spring, because he has an option left. If he doesn't win the everyday job, he likely will return to Triple-A so he can continue to work on his game.

Year	Club (League)	Class	AVG	G	AB	R	H	2B	3B	HR	RBI	BB	SO	SB	CS	OBP	SLG
2004	Casper (PIO)	R	.347	38	147	36	51	6	3	4	20	20	42	6	5	.432	.510
2005	Asheville (SAL)	LoA	.241	79	315	51	76	13	3	3	38	25	88	7	4	.304	.330
2006	Asheville (SAL)	LoA	.260	118	466	69	121	38	1	11	76	32	101	14	2	.313	.416
2007	Modesto (CAL)	HiA	.289	133	529	97	153	42	7	19	99	55	92	27	5	.358	.503
2008	Modesto (CAL)	HiA	.167	8	30	2	5	1	0	1	5	2	8	0	2	.219	.300
	Tulsa (TL)	AA	.237	73	283	38	67	18	2	3	42	35	69	6	1	.324	.346
2009	Tulsa (TL)	AA	.280	29	107	21	30	5	2	4	17	12	21	5	2	.355	.477
2010	Colo. Springs (PCL)	AAA	.313	85	319	60	100	15	3	12	55	29	53	7	3	.376	.492
	Colorado (NL)	MAJ	.280	17	25	7	7	1	0	0	0	1	4	1	0	.308	.320
Major League Totals			.280	17	25	7	7	1	0	0	0	1	4	1	0	.308	.320
Minor League Totals			.275	563	2196	374	603	138	21	57	352	210	474	72	24	.342	.434

18 JORDAN PACHECO, C

Born: Jan. 30, 1986. **B-T:** R-R. **Ht.:** 6-1. **Wt.:** 195. **Drafted:** New Mexico, 2007 (9th round). **Signed by:** Mike Ericson.

Pacheco was the Mountain West Conference player of the year in 2007 for New Mexico, when he was a second baseman. He stayed in the infield his first year in pro ball, but in 2008 made the move behind the plate. Pacheco is an accomplished hitter, though he doesn't have a great deal of power. He has a game plan at the plate and works counts, controls the strike zone and uses the whole field. A career .310 hitter in pro ball, he opened last year in high Class A but moved to Double-A when Wilin Rosario injured his knee and was lost for the season.

He finished with a turn in the Arizona Fall League and earned a 40-man roster spot. The debate is over whether he can refine his catching game enough to be a regular at the position. He is still learning his footwork and has made adjustments in his throwing mechanics, helping him throw out 34 of the 100 basestealers who tested him in 2010. Scouts like his soft hands and consistent 2.0-second pop times, and he should be the regular at Tulsa in 2011. Looking long-term, however, right now he projects to be a super-utility player in the big leagues because of his background in the middle infield.

Year	Club (League)	Class	AVG	G	AB	R	H	2B	3B	HR	RBI	BB	SO	SB	CS	OBP	SLG
2007	Casper (PIO)	R	.292	55	192	27	56	10	2	3	29	21	36	3	1	.380	.411
	Tri-City (NWL)	SS	.258	8	31	5	8	2	0	0	3	1	6	0	0	.324	.323
2008	Tri-City (NWL)	SS	.280	54	214	25	60	8	3	1	35	26	20	3	3	.368	.360
2009	Asheville (SAL)	LoA	.322	117	451	67	145	30	4	13	79	38	44	12	2	.379	.492
2010	Modesto (CAL)	HiA	.321	104	390	59	125	27	3	5	70	54	36	5	6	.407	.444
	Tulsa (TL)	AA	.333	21	78	11	26	5	0	1	19	6	6	1	1	.396	.436
Minor League Totals			.310	359	1356	194	420	82	12	23	235	146	148	24	13	.386	.439

19 RUSSELL WILSON, 2B

Born: Nov. 29, 1988. **B-T:** R-R. **Ht.:** 6-0. **Wt.:** 200. **Drafted:** North Carolina State, 2010 (4th round). **Signed by:** Jay Matthews.

Wilson has been a living contradiction at North Carolina State. He has been a three-year starting quarterback and an all-Atlantic Coast Conference choice in football and a platoon player in baseball, even though he is going to play baseball professionally. He passed for 3,288 yards and 26 touchdowns in the 2010 regular season as N.C. State went 8-4. On the diamond last spring, however, he made just 25 starts at second base and the outfield, playing almost exclusively against lefthanders. Wilson was drafted by the Orioles out of high school in the 41st round in 2007, when he turned down six-figure overtures from other clubs. He signed as a fourth-round pick for $200,000 last summer, with the Rockies allowing him to return to quarterback N.C. State. He has the athleticism and aptitude that gave scouts reason to believe he could be a quality infielder. He has game-changing speed but has to learn the subtleties that will allow him to turn it into an asset. He understands the offensive game, hitting the ball the other way and incorporating the bunt into his game, and scouts have long liked his fairly compact swing. Wilson shows plus range with good hands and a solid arm but needs reps in the infield and will have to adjust to the speed of the game. He did get into 32 games at short-season Tri-City last summer before returning to college and will play in low Class A this year. While the Rockies are counting on 2010 being his final football season—and N.C. State honored him on its senior day, even though he is a junior in football eligibility—it remains possible that he could return for another season of football. He has expressed a desire to reach the major leagues in both sports.

Year	Club (League)	Class	AVG	G	AB	R	H	2B	3B	HR	RBI	BB	SO	SB	CS	OBP	SLG
2010	Tri-City (NWL)	SS	.230	32	122	18	28	4	4	2	11	16	36	4	6	.336	.377
Minor League Totals			.230	32	122	18	28	4	4	2	11	16	36	4	6	.336	.377

20 MATT REYNOLDS, LHP

Born: Oct. 2, 1984. **B-T:** L-L. **Ht.:** 6-5. **Wt.:** 240. **Drafted:** Austin Peay State, 2007 (20th round). **Signed by:** Scott Corman.

He may have been a 20th-round draft pick, but Reynolds was the first member of the Rockies' 2007 draft class to get to the big leagues, earning a mid-August callup last year when Colorado needed bullpen help down the stretch. He exceeded expectations in his 20 appearances, allowing 10 hits and five walks in 18 innings. Reynolds doesn't overpower hitters, but he has a live fastball that's a deceiving 90 mph, at times hitting 92. He uses his height to get the downward action on his pitches. He has a usable breaking ball, alternately described as a slider or curve, but it is his split-fingered pitch that gives him a weapon against righthanders. A starter in college, Reynolds has the resilient arm and full-speed-ahead mentality that have allowed him to fit into a relief role in pro ball. His late-season audition was a success and Reynolds earned a big league job for 2011.

Year	Club (League)	Class	W	L	ERA	G	GS	CG	SV	IP	H	HR	BB	SO	G/AWHIP	AVG
2007	Tri-City (NWL)	SS	1	4	3.60	20	0	0	0	35	37	4	4	27	— 1.17	.264
2008	Asheville (SAL)	LoA	6	2	2.53	42	0	0	2	57	49	4	14	53	— 1.11	.226
2009	Modesto (CAL)	HiA	5	3	1.29	39	0	0	3	49	32	2	8	58	1.31 0.82	.190
	Tulsa (TL)	AA	1	2	4.21	21	0	0	1	26	23	3	9	29	0.92 1.25	.237
2010	Colorado Springs (PCL)	AAA	1	3	2.62	50	0	0	7	55	49	2	16	67	1.90 1.18	.236
	Colorado (NL)	MAJ	1	0	2.00	21	0	0	0	18	10	2	5	17	1.21 0.83	.164
Major League Totals			1	0	2.00	21	0	0	0	18	10	2	5	17	1.21 0.83	.164
Minor League Totals			14	14	2.64	172	0	0	13	222	190	15	51	234	1.40 1.09	.229

21 TIM WHEELER, OF

Born: Jan. 21, 1988. **B-T:** L-R. **Ht.:** 6-4. **Wt.:** 200. **Drafted:** Sacramento State, 2009 (1st round). **Signed by:** Gary Wilson.

Wheeler was challenged in his first full pro season, skipping a level and going to high Class A. His production wasn't impressive, but the Rockies were encouraged as the season went along, and he got what he needed most: playing time. Wheeler was a pure pull hitter when the season started, trying to get to his plus raw power, but hitting coach Duane Espy worked to get him away from hanging over the plate and taught him to drive the ball to the bigger part of the ballpark, particularly against lefthanders. Wheeler's biggest challenge at the plate is learning to recognize breaking pitches from southpaws. He hit .206 with 43 strikeouts in 141 at-bats against lefties at Modesto, compared to hitting .266 with 71 strikeouts in 369 at-bats against righthanders. Wheeler has a solid major league arm and could remain in center field, although given the wide-open spaces at Coors Field it is more likely he will wind up in a corner spot. With his solid-average arm, right field is a possibility. He does need to work on his first step and must streamline his routes. He's a plus runner who should continue to steal bases as he moves up the ladder. A willing worker who addresses his shortcomings, Wheeler most likely will move to Double-A for 2011.

Year	Club (League)	Class	AVG	G	AB	R	H	2B	3B	HR	RBI	BB	SO	SB	CS	OBP	SLG
2009	Tri-City (NWL)	SS	.256	68	273	44	70	13	3	5	35	29	60	10	4	.332	.381
2010	Modesto (CAL)	HiA	.249	129	510	88	127	21	6	12	63	60	114	22	8	.341	.384
Minor League Totals			.252	197	783	132	197	34	9	17	98	89	174	32	12	.338	.383

22 COLE GARNER, OF

Born: Dec. 15, 1984. **B-T:** R-R. **Ht.:** 6-2. **Wt.:** 210. **Drafted:** HS—Westminster, Calif., 2003 (26th round). **Signed by:** Todd Blyleven.

Best known as a high school teammate of Ian Stewart and Ian Kennedy, Garner has battled his way to the point that he's on the verge of joining them in the big leagues. He was one of three position players—along with catchers Wilin Rosario and Jordan Pacheco—added to Colorado's 40-man roster in the offseason. Garner signed as a 26th-rounder in 2003, and his career initially was slowed by shoulder surgery, resulting in his pro debut being delayed until 2005. He then had an ill-fated experiment with switch-hitting. A power bat, Garner has never had problems hitting fastballs or hanging breaking balls, but has shown a propensity to chase breaking pitches out of the zone. With the help of veteran Jay Payton and Colorado Springs hitting coach Rene Lachemann, he finally showed an ability to adjust during at-bats. He also became more consistent in driving the ball the other way. He could become more than an extra outfielder but will need to get better jumps and read the ball off the bat better, and he tends to shy away from walls. Garner will get a shot as a righthanded backup in the corner positions in the big leagues this year.

Year	Club (League)	Class	AVG	G	AB	R	H	2B	3B	HR	RBI	BB	SO	SB	CS	OBP	SLG
2004	Did Not Play—Injured																
2005	Casper (PIO)	R	.260	66	265	34	69	21	1	10	48	9	105	2	8	.303	.460
2006	Asheville (SAL)	LoA	.302	120	464	100	140	40	2	19	88	25	127	35	13	.353	.519
2007	Modesto (CAL)	HiA	.213	96	319	39	68	18	4	8	33	20	115	7	5	.274	.370
2008	Modesto (CAL)	HiA	.318	50	192	27	61	14	2	2	17	9	51	7	5	.361	.443
2009	Tulsa (TL)	AA	.288	112	396	65	114	25	4	16	64	23	78	13	5	.342	.492
2010	Colo. Springs (PCL)	AAA	.304	111	415	81	126	31	10	13	61	39	89	8	5	.374	.520
Minor League Totals			.282	555	2051	346	578	149	23	68	311	125	565	72	41	.337	.476

23 SAMUEL DEDUNO, RHP

Born: July 2, 1983. **B-T:** R-R. **Ht.:** 6-3. **Wt.:** 190. **Signed:** Dominican Republic, 2003. **Signed by:** Rolando Fernandez/Felix Feliz/Frank Roa.

Deduno hit another speed bump in his development during the 2010 season, suffering a stress fracture in his right elbow that forced him to sit out three months. He did work his way back to earn a promotion to the big leagues in August. He had also missed the entire 2008 season following Tommy John surgery. Deduno worked out of the bullpen with the Rockies, which is his most likely destination in the big leagues. He has a fastball that will sit at 88-93 mph and a hard curveball, but he's still working on the changeup he needs to get lefthanders out. Deduno, who won the pitching triple crown in the Double-A Texas League in 2009, can dominate hitters when he throws strikes, but he still doesn't throw consistent quality strikes. Basic control has been an issue throughout his career, and at 27, Deduno may be best suited as a long reliever or set-up man.

Year	Club (League)	Class	W	L	ERA	G	GS	CG	SV	IP	H	HR	BB	SO	G/A	WHIP	AVG
2003	Rockies (DSL)	R	3	4	2.47	12	12	0	0	69	53	1	26	61	—	1.14	.202
2004	Casper (PIO)	R	6	4	3.18	15	15	0	0	76	62	3	32	118	—	1.23	.219
2005	Asheville (SAL)	LoA	8	8	5.62	20	20	1	0	90	82	9	65	110	—	1.64	.248
2006	Modesto (CAL)	HiA	5	8	4.80	27	26	0	0	146	121	3	92	167	—	1.46	.222
2007	Modesto (CAL)	HiA	1	1	6.55	2	2	0	0	11	9	1	7	8	—	1.45	.214
	Tulsa (TL)	AA	5	8	5.44	21	21	1	0	124	120	13	66	121	—	1.50	.251
2008	Did Not Play—Injured																
2009	Tulsa (TL)	AA	12	4	2.57	24	24	1	0	133	94	3	72	123	2.10	1.25	.202
	Colorado Springs (PCL)	AAA	0	1	6.35	1	1	0	0	6	5	0	4	8	1.25	1.59	.250
2010	Colorado Springs (PCL)	AAA	3	1	2.93	6	6	0	0	31	20	3	18	29	3.36	1.24	.190
	Tri-City (NWL)	SS	0	2	5.51	4	4	0	0	16	18	0	5	20	4.20	1.41	.290
	Colorado (NL)	MAJ	0	0	3.38	4	0	0	0	3	3	1	1	3	1.00	1.50	.273
Major League Totals			0	0	3.38	4	0	0	0	3	3	1	1	3	1.00	1.50	.273
Minor League Totals			43	41	4.16	132	131	3	0	702	584	36	387	765	2.33	1.38	.228

24 PARKER FRAZIER, RHP

Born: Nov. 11, 1988. **B-T:** R-R. **Ht.:** 6-5. **Wt.:** 185. **Drafted:** HS—Tulsa, 2007 (8th round). **Signed by:** Dar Cox.

Frazier's 2010 season was all about him getting back on the mound and showing that he is healthy. Frazier was back pitching nine months after having Tommy John surgery. The son of former big league reliever and current Rockies television analyst George Frazier, Parker is a strike thrower, which is why he figures to benefit from reaching higher levels in the minors, as he gets more consistent umpires. He did fairly well anyway after he settled in against high Class A hitters, throwing strikes and getting the movement he needs on his fastball. He yielded only one homer in 46 innings in the hitter-friendly California League. Frazier features a hard, heavy sinker that sits in the low 90s when he's at his best and induces plenty of ground balls. He uses a hard slider as his best secondary pitch but needs to refine his changeup if he's going to stay in the rotation. While Frazier rushed back from elbow surgery, Colorado won't rush him in 2011, and he'll likely open the season back at Modesto.

Year	Club (League)	Class	W	L	ERA	G	GS	CG	SV	IP	H	HR	BB	SO	G/A	WHIP	AVG
2007	Casper (PIO)	R	3	5	10.07	16	10	0	0	45	78	8	18	22	—	2.15	.386
2008	Tri-City (NWL)	SS	5	5	3.83	15	15	0	0	87	94	3	20	47	—	1.31	.281
2009	Asheville (SAL)	LoA	10	7	4.48	23	23	1	0	131	158	7	33	98	1.88	1.46	.303
2010	Tri-City (NWL)	SS	1	3	7.52	5	5	0	0	20	28	1	8	15	1.50	1.77	.318
	Modesto (CAL)	HiA	2	2	4.70	9	9	0	0	46	49	1	11	38	1.31	1.30	.269
Minor League Totals			21	22	5.28	68	62	1	0	329	407	20	90	220	1.69	1.51	.307

25 CORY RIORDAN, RHP

Born: May 25, 1986. **B-T:** R-R. **Ht.:** 6-4. **Wt.:** 200. **Drafted:** Fordham, 2007 (6th round). **Signed by:** Mike Garlatti.

Riordan had a successful college career at Fordham, becoming the first Rams pitcher with 100 strikeouts in a season since 1939. He has a four-pitch mix and primarily has started in pro ball. He has proven to be a workhorse, throwing 500 innings the last three seasons, and his work in 2010 earned him a spot on the 40-man roster. None of Riordan's pitches stands out from the pack, but he throws strikes with his 87-93 mph fastball, often cruising in the upper 80s with sink on his two-seamer, then reaching back for the 93 with his four-seamer when he needs it. He uses his curveball and slider well, with scouts generally preferring the curve, and he's more effective against righthanders. His changeup is usable but more of a fringy pitch than a true weapon against lefties. Riordan works with a quick tempo but sometimes loses focus and can get homer-prone. He's set to help anchor the Colorado Springs rotation in 2011 and profiles as a back-of-the-rotation starter or long reliever.

Year	Club (League)	Class	W	L	ERA	G	GS	CG	SV	IP	H	HR	BB	SO	G/A	WHIP	AVG
2007	Tri-City (NWL)	SS	2	3	4.25	14	11	0	1	66	69	5	17	65	—	1.31	.265
2008	Asheville (SAL)	LoA	8	9	3.65	26	25	2	0	168	185	18	29	160	—	1.28	.274
2009	Modesto (CAL)	HiA	12	7	3.93	28	27	2	0	170	185	11	48	134	0.85	1.37	.274
2010	Tulsa (TL)	AA	8	5	4.01	27	24	0	0	162	168	20	38	135	0.94	1.27	.270
Minor League Totals			30	24	3.90	95	87	4	1	565	607	54	132	494	0.89	1.31	.272

26 COREY DICKERSON, OF

Born: May 22, 1989. **B-T:** L-R. **Ht.:** 6-1. **Wt.:** 199. **Drafted:** Meridian (Miss.) CC, 2010 (8th round). **Signed by:** Damon Iannelli.

The Rockies obviously liked what they saw in Dickerson. After drafting him in the 29th round in 2009 and failing to sign him, they drafted Dickerson again last June and this time signed him away from a Mississippi State commitment for $125,000. Coming off a junior college all-America season for Meridian (Miss.) CC, in which he hit .459 with 21 home runs and 71 RBIs, Dickerson made an impact in his pro debut, hitting .348 and leading the Pioneer League with 61 RBIs and 175 total bases. Dickerson has quick hands and big-time bat speed. His offense is what will carry him to the big leagues. He profiles as a left fielder with fringy speed and a below-average arm that has yet to rebound from 2007 surgery for a torn right labrum. Given his age, he could play his way onto the Modesto roster in the spring.

Year	Club (League)	Class	AVG	G	AB	R	H	2B	3B	HR	RBI	BB	SO	SB	CS	OBP	SLG
2010	Casper (PIO)	R	.348	69	276	54	96	22	9	13	61	28	51	12	6	.412	.634
Minor League Totals			.348	69	276	54	96	22	9	13	61	28	51	12	6	.412	.634

27 EDGMER ESCALONA, RHP

Born: Oct. 6, 1986. **B-T:** R-R. **Ht.:** 6-4. **Wt.:** 215. **Signed:** Venezuela, 2004. **Signed by:** Rolando Fernandez/Francisco Cartaya.

Escalona is strictly a reliever, and he has yet to start a game in six minor league seasons, covering 212 appearances. He can dominate hitters with a heavy, sinking fastball that runs between 92-96 mph. His slider is a decent No. 2 pitch at times but no more than average. His inability to command a splitter denies him the offspeed pitch he needs to be effective against lefthanders. He has the size to be durable. The biggest problem for Escalona has been his inability to become consistent with his delivery, and his poor arm action makes it hard for him to find a consistent release point. After two years of showing marked improvement in command, Escalona took a step backward in 2010, giving up 32 walks and an alarming 17 homers in 69 innings in Triple-A. He did get a late-season call to the big leagues and kept his 40-man roster spot this offseason. He's projected to return to Colorado Springs unless his control improves in the spring.

Year	Club (League)	Class	W	L	ERA	G	GS	CG	SV	IP	H	HR	BB	SO	G/AWHIP	AVG
2005	Rockies (DSL)	R	2	2	1.64	20	0	0	2	38	28	1	9	13	— 0.97	.204
2006	Rockies (DSL)	R	0	2	7.11	14	0	0	0	19	22	1	11	17	— 1.74	.297
2007	Casper (PIO)	R	1	1	4.05	18	0	0	1	27	22	1	13	20	— 1.31	.212
2008	Asheville (SAL)	LoA	6	2	3.22	44	0	0	1	78	71	9	18	79	— 1.14	.242
2009	Modesto (CAL)	HiA	2	0	2.48	28	0	0	0	33	25	3	7	34	0.80 0.98	.207
	Tulsa (TL)	AA	1	2	2.45	31	0	0	4	37	33	5	11	32	0.71 1.20	.232
2010	Colorado Springs (PCL)	AAA	3	5	6.00	57	0	0	1	69	66	17	32	74	0.98 1.42	.253
	Colorado (NL)	MAJ	0	0	1.50	5	0	0	0	6	4	0	4	2	0.36 1.33	.190
Major League Totals			0	0	1.50	5	0	0	0	6	4	0	4	2	0.36 1.33	.190
Minor League Totals			15	14	3.80	212	0	0	9	301	267	37	101	269	0.85 1.22	.236

28 BEN PAULSEN, 1B

Born: Oct. 27, 1987. **B-T:** L-R. **Ht.:** 6-4. **Wt.:** 200. **Drafted:** Clemson, 2009 (3rd round). **Signed by:** Jay Matthews.

At Clemson, Paulsen played for his father, assistant coach Tom Riginos, who since has become the head coach at Winthrop. Paulsen's pure hitting ability prompted the Rockies to jump him to high Class A for his first full pro season, and he handled it well. He led the team with 83 RBIs and hit .311. Paulsen has big-time power potential, although he has only 13 home runs in pro ball, thanks to his hand-eye coordination and a textbook swing. He already understands the value of using all fields, and is strong enough to hit the ball out of any spot in a ballpark. He'll have to be more selective for his power to play more often. He's a below-average runner. He shows range and agility, particularly for his size, but his footwork around first base needs work, and he has to be more aggressive in throwing. After spending his first two pro seasons with teams with pitcher-friendly parks, Paulsen could get a chance to show some power at Tulsa in 2011.

Year	Club (League)	Class	AVG	G	AB	R	H	2B	3B	HR	RBI	BB	SO	SB	CS	OBP	SLG
2009	Tri-City (NWL)	SS	.280	44	175	28	49	10	2	1	25	12	32	2	1	.325	.377
2010	Modesto (CAL)	HiA	.311	130	498	65	155	29	8	12	83	33	113	5	4	.353	.474
Minor League Totals			.303	174	673	93	204	39	10	13	108	45	145	7	5	.346	.449

29 THOMAS FIELD, SS

Born: Feb. 22, 1987. **B-T:** R-R. **Ht.:** 5-9. **Wt.:** 181. **Drafted:** Texas State, 2008 (24th round). **Signed by:** Chris Forbes.

Field is the old-fashioned baseball player. He's not going to overwhelm observers, but he gets the job done. He profiles as a utility infielder in the Jamey Carroll mold, capable of playing second, third and shortstop at the big league level. Field got to show off his glove in the Arizona Fall League, making a dazzling play to squelch a ninth-inning threat in the championship game for Scottsdale. Field only got to go to the AFL due to a back injury that sidelined Hector Gomez. He shows some pull power and led Modesto with 15 homers in 2010. Given his limited size, he does need to develop a better two-strike approach and make more consistent contact. Field is considered a plus runner under way but takes such a big swing that he's below-average out of the box. He has been too tentative on the bases to be a basestealing threat. He does have an average arm, and decent range thanks to his feel for the game. Field will move to Double-A in 2011.

Year	Club (League)	Class	AVG	G	AB	R	H	2B	3B	HR	RBI	BB	SO	SB	CS	OBP	SLG
2008	Tri-City (NWL)	SS	.247	56	182	34	45	8	2	5	32	42	34	10	6	.403	.396
2009	Asheville (SAL)	LoA	.257	89	304	42	78	17	0	2	32	26	58	8	3	.335	.332
2010	Modesto (CAL)	HiA	.284	124	440	84	125	21	7	15	72	66	114	16	5	.397	.466
Minor League Totals			.268	269	926	160	248	46	9	22	136	134	206	34	14	.379	.408

30 EDWAR CABRERA, LHP

Born: Oct. 10, 1987. **B-T:** L-L. **Ht.:** 6-0. **Wt.:** 184. **Signed:** Dominican Republic, 2008. **Signed by:** Rolando Fernandez/Jhonathan Leyba/Martin Cabrera.

An older Latin American signee—he was a few months shy of 21 when the Rockies signed him in 2008—Cabrera pitched his way to the United States in his first professional season. After back-to-back seasons spent in Rookie ball, Cabrera made the move to Tri-City in 2010 and led the short-season Northwest League in strikeouts (87) and strikeouts per nine innings (10.7). He has a solid fastball that sits at 91-92 mph, and his out pitch is a changeup he can throw in any count. He understands how to set up the changeup, and has been able to replicate his fastball delivery when throwing the pitch. Cabrera is still working to refine and focus on a breaking pitch he is going to need to be a starter at higher levels, but he has flashed some ability to spin the ball. Cabrera is projected to move to low Class A in 2011.

Year	Club (League)	Class	W	L	ERA	G	GS	CG	SV	IP	H	HR	BB	SO	G/A	WHIP	AVG
2008	Rockies (DSL)	R	5	1	0.92	8	8	0	0	49	26	1	18	75	—	0.90	.158
	Casper (PIO)	R	0	4	7.80	9	5	0	0	30	38	7	15	38	—	1.77	.304
2009	Rockies (DSL)	R	1	0	1.16	7	3	0	0	31	16	0	10	50	0.59	0.84	.145
	Casper (PIO)	R	0	0	3.38	9	1	0	0	21	19	2	12	28	0.84	1.45	.235
2010	Tri-City (NWL)	SS	1	8	3.07	14	14	0	0	73	71	2	24	87	2.14	1.30	.251
Minor League Totals			7	13	3.00	47	31	0	0	204	170	12	79	278	1.34	1.22	.223

Detroit Tigers

BY CONOR GLASSEY

After their 2009 season ended in heartbreaking fashion—with a 12th-inning loss to the Twins in a one-game playoff for the American League Central title—the Tigers switched gears as they headed into 2010. At the Winter Meetings, general manager Dave Dombrowski sent Curtis Granderson to the Yankees and Edwin Jackson to the Diamondbacks in a three-way trade that brought back outfield prospect Austin Jackson and lefthander Phil Coke from New York and righthander Max Scherzer and lefthander Daniel Schlereth from Arizona.

Granderson was beloved in Detroit, but all four players the Tigers received in the trade performed well their first year in Motown. Jackson had big shoes to fill in center field, but hit .293 with 27 steals and played excellent defense. Scherzer went 12-11, 3.50 and ranked sixth in the AL with 8.5 strikeouts per nine innings. Coke was solid out of the bullpen and Schlereth showed the potential to be Detroit's closer of the future.

Though the trade accomplished two goals for the Tigers, making them both younger and cheaper, it couldn't put them over the top in the American League Central. They went 48-38 and stood just a half-game out of first place in the first half, but lost their first six games after the all-star break and never recovered. Detroit finished 81-81 and in third place, 13 games behind the Twins.

The Tigers had plenty of money to play with in the offseason after a combined $64 million in salaries for Jeremy Bonderman, Johnny Damon, Gerald Laird, Magglio Ordonez, Nate Robertson and Dontrelle Willis came off the books. They quickly re-signed Brandon Inge and Jhonny Peralta for a combined $22.75 million, then added Joaquin Benoit for $16.5 million, Victor Martinez for $50 million and brought back Ordonez for $10 million.

Detroit is in good shape on the mound with a rotation led by Justin Verlander and Scherzer and a strong bullpen fronted by Jose Valverde, but the team needs to find some help for Miguel Cabrera in its lineup. Though Brennan Boesch and Will Rhymes had their moments as rookies in 2010, both are complementary players. The farm system will offer no immediate help, so the Tigers had to pay dearly for Martinez. Their best hope for an impact bat is third baseman Nick Castellanos, who signed for $3.45 million in August.

The Tigers' front office has gone through as much turnover as their roster. The team fired farm director

After supplanting Curtis Granderson, Austin Jackson was one of the league's best rookies

TOP 30 PROSPECTS

1. Jacob Turner, rhp	16. Matt Hoffman, lhp
2. Nick Castellanos, 3b	17. Lester Oliveros, rhp
3. Andy Oliver, lhp	18. Brayan Villarreal, rhp
4. Francisco Martinez, 3b	19. Casper Wells, of
5. Daniel Fields, of	20. Bryan Holaday, c
6. Casey Crosby, lhp	21. Rob Brantly, c
7. Chance Ruffin, rhp	22. Cale Iorg, ss
8. Drew Smyly, lhp	23. Gustavo Nunez, ss
9. Avisail Garcia, of	24. Danry Vasquez, of
10. Jose Ortega, rhp	25. Wade Gaynor, 3b
11. Andy Dirks, of	26. Charlie Furbush, lhp
12. Robbie Weinhardt, rhp	27. Adam Wilk, lhp
13. Bruce Rondon, rhp	28. Dixon Machado, ss
14. Ryan Strieby, of/1b	29. Kyle Ryan, lhp
15. Duane Below, lhp	30. Cole Nelson, lhp

Glenn Ezell in June and replaced him with field coordinator Mike Rojas. Detroit also promoted scouting director David Chadd to vice president for amateur scouting and special assistant to Dombrowski, giving him additional responsibilities with major and minor league evaluation. Chadd will continue to help make the decision on the team's early draft picks, along with new scouting director Scott Pleis, who moved up from national crosschecker. The Tigers also added two former scouting directors after the season ended, hiring Tim Hallgren (Dodgers) to fill Pleis' old role and Eddie Bane (Angels) as a pro scout.

General Manager: Dave Dombrowski. **Farm Director:** Mike Rojas. **Scouting Director:** David Chadd.

Class	Team	League	W	L	PCT	Finish*	Manager
Majors	Detroit Tigers	American	81	81	.500	t-8th (14)	Jim Leyland
Triple-A	Toledo Mud Hens	International	70	73	.490	9th (14)	Larry Parrish
Double-A	Erie SeaWolves	Eastern	66	76	.465	t-10th (12)	Phil Nevin
High A	Lakeland Flying Tigers	Florida State	71	67	.514	7th (12)	Andy Barkett
Low A	West Michigan Whitecaps	Midwest	62	79	.440	11th (16)	Joe DePastino
Short-season	Connecticut Tigers	New York-Penn	38	37	.507	7th (14)	Howie Bushong
Rookie	GCL Tigers	Gulf Coast	30	28	.517	7th (15)	Basilio Cabrera
Overall 2010 Minor League Record			337	358	.485	t-23rd (30)	

*Finish in overall standings (No. of teams in league). †League champion.

LAST YEAR'S TOP 30

Player, Pos. Status

1.	Jacob Turner, rhp	No. 1
2.	Casey Crosby, lhp	No. 6
3.	Austin Jackson, of	Majors
4.	Andy Oliver, lhp	No. 3
5.	Daniel Schlereth, lhp	Majors
6.	Alex Avila, c	Majors
7.	Gustavo Nunez, ss	No. 23
8.	Wilkin Ramirez, of	(Braves)
9.	Daniel Fields, ss	No. 5
10.	Scott Sizemore, 2b	Majors
11.	Ryan Strieby, 1b/of	No. 14
12.	Robbie Weinhardt, rhp	No. 12
13.	Cale Iorg, ss	No. 22
14.	Cody Satterwhite, rhp	Dropped out
15.	Alfredo Figaro, rhp	Orix (Japan)
16.	Casper Wells, of	No. 19
17.	Avisail Garcia, of	No. 9
18.	Brayan Villarreal, rhp	No. 18
19.	Jared Gayhart, rhp	Dropped out
20.	Luke Putkonen, rhp	Dropped out
21.	Jay Sborz, rhp	(Braves)
22.	Tyler Stohr, rhp	Dropped out
23.	Melvin Mercedes, rhp	Dropped out
24.	Wade Gaynor, 3b	No. 25
25.	Brennan Boesch, of	Majors
26.	Dusty Ryan, c	(Padres)
27.	Casey Fien, rhp	(Astros)
28.	Scott Green, rhp	Dropped out
29.	James Robbins, 1b	Dropped out
30.	Edwin Gomez, ss	Dropped out

BEST TOOLS

Best Hitter for Average	Nick Castellanos
Best Power Hitter	Nick Castellanos
Best Strike-Zone Discipline	Jamie Johnson
Fastest Baserunner	Gustavo Nunez
Best Athlete	Daniel Fields
Best Fastball	Jose Ortega
Best Curveball	Jacob Turner
Best Slider	Chance Ruffin
Best Changeup	Jacob Turner
Best Control	Adam Wilk
Best Defensive Catcher	Bryan Holaday
Best Defensive Infielder	Cale Iorg
Best Infield Arm	Nick Castellanos
Best Defensive Outfielder	Andy Dirks
Best Outfield Arm	Casper Wells

PROJECTED 2014 LINEUP

Catcher	Alex Avila
First Base	Miguel Cabrera
Second Base	Scott Sizemore
Third Base	Nick Castellanos
Shortstop	Jhonny Peralta
Left Field	Francisco Martinez
Center Field	Austin Jackson
Right Field	Daniel Fields
Designated Hitter	Victor Martinez
No. 1 Starter	Justin Verlander
No. 2 Starter	Jacob Turner
No. 3 Starter	Max Scherzer
No. 4 Starter	Rick Porcello
No. 5 Starter	Andy Oliver
Closer	Ryan Perry

TOP PROSPECTS OF THE DECADE

Year	Player, Pos.	2010 Org.
2001	Brandon Inge, c	Tigers
2002	Nate Cornejo, rhp	Out of baseball
2003	Jeremy Bonderman, rhp	Tigers
2004	Kyle Sleeth, rhp	Out of baseball
2005	Curtis Granderson, of	Yankees
2006	Justin Verlander, rhp	Tigers
2007	Cameron Maybin, of	Marlins
2008	Rick Porcello, rhp	Tigers
2009	Rick Porcello, rhp	Tigers
2010	Jacob Turner, rhp	Tigers

TOP DRAFT PICKS OF THE DECADE

Year	Player, Pos.	2010 Org.
2001	Kenny Baugh, rhp	Out of baseball
2002	Scott Moore, ss	Orioles
2003	Kyle Sleeth, rhp	Out of baseball
2004	Justin Verlander, rhp	Tigers
2005	Cameron Maybin, of	Marlins
2006	Andrew Miller, lhp	Marlins
2007	Rick Porcello, rhp	Tigers
2008	Ryan Perry, rhp	Tigers
2009	Jacob Turner, rhp	Tigers
2010	Nick Castellanos, 3b (1st round supp.)	Tigers

LARGEST BONUSES IN CLUB HISTORY

Jacob Turner, 2009	$4,700,000
Rick Porcello, 2007	$3,580,000
Andrew Miller, 2006	$3,550,000
Eric Munson, 1999	$3,500,000
Nick Castellanos, 2010	$3,450,000

DETROIT TIGERS

TOP 2011 ROOKIE: Andy Oliver, lhp. He reached Detroit ahead of schedule in 2010, and with a little more polish, he could help solidify Detroit's rotation.

BREAKOUT PROSPECT: Bruce Rondon, rhp. With a fastball that gets up to 98 mph, he could soar through the system.

SLEEPER: Javier Azcona, ss. He's still very raw, but he has exciting tools and can play anywhere in the infield.

SOURCE OF TOP 30 TALENT			
Homegrown	30	Acquired	0
College	14	Trades	0
Junior college	1	Rule 5 draft	0
High school	6	Independent leagues	0
Draft-and-follow	0	Free agents/waivers	0
Nondrafted free agents	0		
International	9		

LF
Andy Dirks (11)
Edwin Gomez
P.J. Polk
Jeff Rowland

CF
Daniel Fields (5)
Jamie Johnson
Ben Guez

RF
Avisail Garcia (9)
Casper Wells (19)
Danry Vasquez (24)
Steven Moya

3B
Nick Castellanos (2)
Francisco Martinez (4)
Wade Gaynor (25)
Edgar Corcino
Audy Ciriaco
Bryan Pounds

SS
Cale Iorg (22)
Gustavo Nunez (23)
Dixon Machado (28)
Javier Azcona
Danny Worth
Hernan Perez

2B
Corey Jones
Brandon Douglas
Alden Carrithers
Alexander Nunez

1B
Ryan Strieby (14)
James Robbins
Tony Plagman
Michael Bertram
Rawley Bishop
Jordan Lennerton

C
Bryan Holaday (20)
Rob Brantly (21)
John Murrian
Patrick Leyland
Julio Rodriguez
Gabriel Purroy

RHP

RHSP	RHRP
Jacob Turner (1)	Chance Ruffin (7)
Luke Putkonen	Jose Ortega (10)
Thad Weber	Robbie Weinhardt (12)
Josue Carreno	Bruce Rondon (13)
Wilsen Palacios	Lester Oliveros (17)
Jeff Ferrell	Brayan Villarreal (18)
Patrick Cooper	Al Albuquerque
L.J. Gagnier	Ramon Lebron
Brooks Brown	Cory Hamilton
Mark Sorensen	Cody Satterwhite
	Brendan Wise
	Jared Gayhart
	Tyler Stohr
	Jordan Pratt
	Michael Torrealba
	Melvin Mercedes
	Matt Little
	Tyler White
	Scott Green
	Tyler Clark
	Zach Simons
	Michael Morrison

LHP

LHSP	LHRP
Andy Oliver (3)	Matt Hoffman (16)
Casey Crosby (6)	Cole Nelson (30)
Drew Smyly (8)	Austin Wood
Duane Below (15)	Antonio Cruz
Charlie Furbush (26)	Kenny Faulk
Adam Wilk (27)	Jay Voss
Kyle Ryan (29)	
Alex Burgos	
Jared Wesson	
Shawn Teufel	
Jade Todd	

2010
BONUSES: $7.3 MILLION

BEST PURE HITTER: 3B Nick Castellanos' (1s) rumored $6 million price tag scared clubs off, and the Tigers were elated to get a player near the top of their draft board with the No. 44 choice. He cost them a supplemental round-record $3.45 million, but they love his swing and track record with wood bats. 2B Corey Jones (6) hit .360/.450/.460 in 48 games in low Class A.

BEST POWER HITTER: The natural extension and loft in Castellanos' stroke should enable him to hit 20-25 homers a year in the majors.

FASTEST RUNNER: OF P.J. Polk (13), who stole 29 bases in 64 pro games, has plus speed and good instincts.

BEST DEFENSIVE PLAYER: C Bryan Holaday's (6) catch-and-throw skills are so advanced that the Tigers sent him right to high Class A. Castellanos has the athleticism and arm strength to be an asset at the hot corner.

BEST FASTBALL: For sheer velocity, it's LHP Cole Nelson (10), whose fastball began sitting at 94-95 mph after the Tigers lengthened his stride and raised his arm slot. But the best fastball belongs to RHP Chance Ruffin (1s), who operates at 90-93 mph and maxes out at 95 with tremendous life and command.

BEST SECONDARY PITCH: Ruffin's slider or LHP's Alex Burgos' (5) curveball. LHP Drew Smyly (2) has a nice cutter.

BEST PRO DEBUT: Jones, who jumped to low Class A after three games in the Rookie-level Gulf Coast League, or Nelson, who had a 0.66 ERA and 36 strikeouts in 27 innings. He limited high Class A Florida State League hitters to one hit in 12 frames.

BEST ATHLETE: Castellanos isn't a classic athlete, but his worst tool is his average speed.

MOST INTRIGUING BACKGROUND: The Tigers signed the sons of manager Jim Leyland (C Patrick Leyland, 8) and batting coach Lloyd McClendon (OF Bo McClendon, 39), and also selected the son of pitching coach Rick Knapp (RHP Ricky Knapp, 44) and the brother of ace Justin Verlander (RHP Ben Verlander, 46). Ruffin's father Bruce and LHP Shawn Teufel's (25) dad Tim played in the majors, as did McClendon.

CLOSEST TO THE MAJORS: Detroit sent Ruffin to the Arizona Fall League and will start his pro career in Double-A, just like it did with Andy Oliver from the 2009 draft.

BEST LATE-ROUND PICK: LHP Kyle Ryan (12), who throws 88-92 mph from a low three-quarters arm slot. He comes from the same area of Florida as White

Sox first-rounder Chris Sale, and looks a lot like Sale did coming out of high school.

THE ONE WHO GOT AWAY: Finesse RHP Cole Green (4) is the highest-drafted four-year college pitcher from the 2010 draft to return to school. He went back to Texas. SS Dominic Ficociello (23) has the power potential to become a prominent pick in the 2013 draft after three years at Arkansas.

ASSESSMENT: The Tigers were the last team to make a pick in 2010, but still came away with a player they coveted (Castellanos), a nearly big league-ready reliever (Ruffin) and several intriguing lefthanders (Smyly, Burgos, Nelson, Ryan).

2009
BONUSES: $9.4 MILLION

RHP Jacob Turner (1) looks worthy of his $5.5 million big league contract, LHP Andy Oliver (2) is a second potential impact starter and OF Daniel Fields (6) is the best athlete in the system. Oliver reached the majors 10 months after signing, while Turner and Fields handled high Class A as teenagers.

GRADE: A

2008
BONUSES: $3.7 MILLION

RHPs Ryan Perry (1) and Robbie Weinhardt (10) and C Alex Avila (5) graduated quickly to the big leagues. Perry could be Detroit's closer of the future.

GRADE: C+

2007
BONUSES: $8.0 MILLION

RHP Rick Porcello (1) matched a high school record with a $7 million contract and already has delivered 24 big league wins in return, though he slumped in 2010. LHP Casey Crosby (5) has similar upside but can't stay healthy, while $1.5 million SS Cale Iorg (6) just hasn't hit. SS/2B Danny Worth (2) spent two months in the majors last year.

GRADE: B

2006
BONUSES: $6.0 MILLION

LHP Andrew Miller (1) hasn't lived up to his $5.45 million contact, but the Tigers used him to trade for Miguel Cabrera. OF Brennan Boesch (3) was baseball's most productive rookie in the first half of 2010 before dropping off after the all-star break. 2B Scott Sizemore (5) and RHP Casey Fien (20) also have seen time in Detroit.

GRADE: C

Draft analysis by Jim Callis. Numbers in parentheses indicate draft rounds.

JACOB TURNER, RHP

Born: May 21, 1991. **Bats:** R. **Throws:** R. **Height:** 6-5.
Weight: 210. **Drafted:** HS—St. Louis, 2009 (1st round). **Signed By:** Marty Miller.

PROSPECT 1

CHRIS PROCTOR

Turner rated as the top righthander in a standout class of high school arms in the 2009 draft. He dominated on the showcase circuit the previous summer, highlighted by five straight strikeouts at the Aflac All-America Game, then added some polish as a senior at Westminster Christian Academy in St. Louis. His pitching coach was former all-star closer Todd Worrell, and ex-big leaguers Andy Benes and Mike Matheny also had sons on the team. To their credit, the Tigers never let a lecture from Bud Selig scare them away from getting the top player on their draft board, so they took Turner with the No. 9 overall pick and signed him away from a commitment to North Carolina with a $5.5 million big league contract. The deal included a $4.7 million bonus, setting a since-broken record for a high school pitcher. Turner signed too late to pitch in the minors in 2009, and he made just one appearance in instructional league before developing shoulder stiffness and getting shut down as a precaution. Turner made his pro debut in April but made just two starts at low Class A West Michigan before getting sidelined again with minor elbow stiffness. He returned three weeks later and made 21 more starts without incident, earning a promotion to high Class A Lakeland in June.

Turner has the ideal frame for a power pitcher. He throws both two- and four-seam fastballs, sitting at 92-94 mph and peaking at 96. In addition to its easily above-average velocity, Turner's fastball also has heavy sink. While Turner was polished for a prep pitcher, he was able to carve up high school lineups by simply blowing his heater by hitters, so he entered pro ball with secondary pitches that needed refinement. He made strides with both his curveball and changeup in 2010. He throws a 12-6 curve that can get a little short but also shows glimpses of being an upper-70s hammer. His changeup should become at least a solid third pitch, with a chance to be better. Turner throws strikes but will need to sharpen his command within the strike zone as he climbs the ladder. Doing so shouldn't be a problem because he's a good athlete with a strong work ethic and relatively clean mechan-

ics, though his delivery could use a little more fluidity. Turner shows terrific savvy and mound presence for his age, mixing his pitches well and rarely gets rattled. He has the swagger scouts want to see in a pitcher projected for the front of a major league rotation. He still has to add the strength to take the ball every fifth day and work deeper into games. He averaged fewer than five innings per start in 2010 and has never pitched in the 7th inning.

Turner likely will start 2011 where he finished 2010, in Lakeland. But the Tigers are not shy about promoting their prospects, so he could make the jump to Double-A Erie by the beginning of June. If he continues to progress like he did last season, he could make it to Detroit before the end of 2012. Turner won't reach the big leagues as quickly as Rick Porcello, who went from a high school first-rounder to the big leagues in 22 months, but he has a higher ceiling.

SCOUTING GRADES

Fastball: 70. **Command/**
Curveball: 65. **Control:** 60.
Changeup: 60. **Delivery:** 55.

Based on 20-80 scouting scale, where 50 represents major league average, and future projection rather than present tools.

Year	Club (League)	Class	W	L	ERA	G	GS	CG	SV	IP	H	HR	BB	SO	G/A	WHIP	AVG
2010	West Michigan (MWL)	LoA	2	3	3.67	11	10	0	0	54	53	4	9	51	1.14	1.15	.245
	Lakeland (FSL)	HiA	4	2	2.93	13	13	0	0	61	53	3	14	51	1.09	1.09	.231
Minor League Totals			6	5	3.28	24	23	0	0	115	106	7	23	102	1.11	1.12	.238

2 NICK CASTELLANOS, 3B

Born: March 4, 1992. **B-T:** R-R. **Ht.:** 6-4. **Wt.:** 195. **Drafted:** HS—Southwest Ranches, Fla., 2010 (1st round supplemental). **Signed by:** Rolando Casanova.

Castellanos put himself on the map by winning the 2009 Under Armour All-American Game home run derby and then going 4-for-4 with four doubles in the showcase. He rose near the top of the Tigers' 2010 draft board, and they were thrilled to land him with their first pick, No. 44 overall. He signed two minutes before the Aug. 16 deadline for a supplemental first-round record $3.45 million bonus. Castellanos generates exciting loft and leverage, and he has the power to hit the ball out to any part of the park. He could hit 20-25 homers annually as he learns to turn on more pitches. Detroit also likes his swing and envisions him as a potential .300 hitter. Others don't think he'll make enough contact to hit for that high of an average. As with many tall, young hitters, his long arms leave him exposed against hard stuff on the inner half of the plate. A shortstop in high school, Castellanos immediately moved to third base as a pro. He made the transition seamlessly and projects as an average defender with an arm a tick above average. He's a solid runner. Castellanos got a brief taste of pro ball after signing and likely will begin 2011 in low Class A. He's probably at least three years away from Detroit.

Year	Club (League)	Class	AVG	G	AB	R	H	2B	3B	HR	RBI	BB	SO	SB	CS	OBP	SLG
2010	Tigers (GCL)	R	.333	7	24	5	8	2	0	0	3	4	5	0	1	.414	.417
Minor League Totals			.333	7	24	5	8	2	0	0	3	4	5	0	1	.414	.417

3 ANDY OLIVER, LHP

Born: Dec. 3, 1987. **B-T:** L-L. **Ht.:** 6-3. **Wt.:** 210. **Drafted:** Oklahoma State, 2009 (2nd round). **Signed by:** Chris Wimmer.

The NCAA sued Oliver in 2008 for having an adviser during 2006 negotiations with the Twins, when they drafted him out of high school. Reinstated after receiving a $750,000 settlement, he went in the second round of the 2009 draft and signed for $1.495 million. Oliver made his major league debut 10 months after signing, but returned to the minors after five starts. Oliver has a loose arm that produces an electric 93-94 mph fastball that tops out at 96. While he threw mostly fastballs during his junior year at Oklahoma State, he worked hard to regain confidence in his secondary offerings. His changeup ranks ahead of his slider at this point, though both still need more consistency. His 81-85 mph slider has more vertical break than tilt. Oliver needs to sharpen his command and focus on keeping balls in the lower half of the strike zone. He cleaned up his delivery this year, keeping his hips closed longer and no longer landing on his heel. Oliver still needs more time in the minors. The Tigers want him to begin in Triple-A Toledo's rotation in 2011 and project him as an impact starter.

Year	Club (League)	Class	W	L	ERA	G	GS	CG	SV	IP	H	HR	BB	SO	G/A	WHIP	AVG
2010	Erie (EL)	AA	6	4	3.61	14	14	0	0	77	74	7	25	70	0.96	1.28	.253
	Toledo (IL)	AAA	3	4	3.23	9	9	0	0	53	43	6	25	49	0.90	1.28	.226
	Detroit (AL)	MAJ	0	4	7.36	5	5	0	0	22	26	3	13	18	1.47	1.77	.310
Major League Totals			0	4	7.36	5	5	0	0	22	26	3	13	18	1.47	1.77	.310
Minor League Totals			9	8	3.45	23	23	0	0	130	117	13	50	119	0.93	1.28	.242

4 FRANCISCO MARTINEZ, 3B

Born: Sept. 1, 1990. **B-T:** R-R. **Ht.:** 6-1. **Wt.:** 180. **Signed:** Venezuela, 2007. **Signed by:** Alejandro Rodriguez/Pedro Chavez.

Though he previously hadn't played higher than the Rookie-level Gulf Coast League, Martinez spent the last week of 2009 in high Class A and returned there last May at age 19. He has played against older competition since he was a child, so the Tigers figured he could handle the assignment. He survived and Detroit continued to challenge him by sending him to the Arizona Fall League. Martinez has a good frame with present strength and projection remaining. He has all the raw tools of a prototypical third baseman, with the added bonus of above-average speed. With a quick bat and a flat swing path, he produces a lot of hard groundballs and line drives. While he hit just three homers in 2010, he should have solid over-the-fence power as he continues to physically mature and learns to deal with more experienced pitchers. Martinez has soft hands and a strong arm at third base, but he needs to clean up his footwork and cut down on mental mistakes. He made 17 errors in 86 games last season. Martinez should get his first taste of Double-A in 2011 and could be ready to take over third base for the Tigers when Brandon Inge's contract expires after the 2012 season. If Nick Castellanos is as good as advertised, Martinez may have to move to the outfield.

DETROIT TIGERS

Year	Club (League)	Class	AVG	G	AB	R	H	2B	3B	HR	RBI	BB	SO	SB	CS	OBP	SLG
2008	Tigers (VSL)	R	.321	68	249	32	80	4	0	1	23	28	28	20	10	.394	.349
2009	Tigers (GCL)	R	.222	43	153	21	34	9	0	2	23	5	38	11	1	.256	.320
	Lakeland (FSL)	HiA	.167	6	18	1	3	0	0	0	2	0	3	1	0	.167	.167
2010	Lakeland (FSL)	HiA	.271	89	340	47	92	17	1	3	29	28	71	12	5	.330	.353
Minor League Totals			.275	206	760	101	209	30	1	6	77	61	140	44	16	.333	.341

5 DANIEL FIELDS, OF

Born: Jan. 23, 1991. **B-T:** L-R. **Ht.:** 6-2. **Wt.:** 200. **Drafted:** HS—Detroit, 2009 (6th round). **Signed by:** Tom Osowski.

His father Bruce won three minor league batting titles and played briefly in the majors, allowing Daniel to grow up around the game. He homered in batting practice at Comerica Park as a 12-year-old in 2003, when Bruce was the Tigers' batting coach. Detroit signed Fields away from a Michigan commitment with a $1.625 million bonus as a sixth-round pick in 2009, then made him the youngest regular in the high Class A Florida State League in his 2010 pro debut. The system's best athlete, Fields has above-average speed and power potential. He showed maturity while jumping from Michigan high school baseball to high Class A, remaining patient at the plate and holding his own. He's still learning how to recognize pitches and deal with quality lefthanders. The Tigers would like to see him put his speed to better use on the basepaths. Drafted as a shortstop, Fields moved to center field and adjusted well, though he's still learning to throw from a higher arm slot to give his throws more carry. Fields will almost certainly repeat in Lakeland. That shouldn't be taken as a slight, but the Tigers are in a tough spot with Fields—they can't send him down after a respectable year, but he's definitely not ready for Double-A yet.

Year	Club (League)	Class	AVG	G	AB	R	H	2B	3B	HR	RBI	BB	SO	SB	CS	OBP	SLG
2010	Lakeland (FSL)	HiA	.240	109	375	33	90	13	6	8	47	55	119	8	9	.343	.371
Minor League Totals			.240	109	375	33	90	13	6	8	47	55	119	8	9	.343	.371

6 CASEY CROSBY, LHP

Born: Sept. 17, 1988. **B-T:** R-L. **Ht.:** 6-5. **Wt.:** 200. **Drafted:** HS—Maple Park, Ill., 2007 (5th round). **Signed by:** Marty Miller.

After signing for $748,500 as a fifth-round pick in 2007, Crosby hurt his elbow in the instructional league that fall and required Tommy John surgery. He spent 2008 rehabbing and came back strong the following year, but 2010 was a lost season. A talented wide receiver in high school, Crosby has a football mentality and may have pushed too hard to make a quick recovery, which cost him most of the 2010 season. He made just three starts because he wasn't able to pitch without pain, though doctors didn't find any structural damage in his elbow and he did not require surgery. When Crosby is right, his stuff is undeniable. He has well above-average velocity for a lefthander, sitting at 92-95 mph and getting as high as 98 with late life on his fastball while using his height to get good plane on the pitch. He mixes in a true curveball that shows potential to be an above-average pitch with tight rotation and late break. He also shows some feel for a changeup. He needs to work on the consistency and command of all of his pitches—no surprise, considering he has just 122 innings of pro experience. If healthy, Crosby will start the 2011 season in high Class A, but the Tigers still have to see how he feels and looks during spring training. As talented as he is, there are serious questions about whether he'll be able to handle a starter's workload.

Year	Club (League)	Class	W	L	ERA	G	GS	CG	SV	IP	H	HR	BB	SO	G/A	WHIP	AVG
2008	Tigers (GCL)	R	0	0	0.00	3	3	0	0	5	4	0	3	2	—	1.50	.211
2009	West Michigan (MWL)	LoA	10	4	2.41	24	24	0	0	105	70	3	48	117	1.39	1.13	.195
2010	Tigers (GCL)	R	0	1	8.76	3	3	0	0	12	21	1	4	10	11.00	2.03	.382
Minor League Totals			10	5	2.96	30	30	0	0	122	95	4	55	129	1.64	1.23	.219

7 CHANCE RUFFIN, RHP

Born: Sept. 8, 1988. **B-T:** R-R. **Ht.:** 6-0. **Wt.:** 185. **Drafted:** Texas, 2010 (1st round supplemental). **Signed by:** Tim Grieve.

The son of lefthander Bruce Ruffin, who pitched 12 seasons in the majors, Chance followed in his father's footsteps by attending Texas. He moved to the Longhorns bullpen as a junior last spring and led NCAA Division I in strikeouts per nine innings (13.5) while ranking second in ERA (1.11) and third in saves (14). He signed at the deadline for $1.15 million as a sandwich pick. Because of his size, stuff, makeup and alma mater, Ruffin draws comparisons to former Longhorns closer Huston Street. Ruffin's fastball sat at 89-91 mph when he was a starter, and it has jumped to 90-93 mph and gotten as high as 95 since he became a reliever. His fastball also has tremendous life, but his 78-82 mph wipeout slider is easily his best pitch—and the best slider in the Tigers system. He'll also mix in a curveball against lefthanders and an occasional changeup, though he'll likely scrap the latter pitch as a reliever. While some scouts believed Ruffin could succeed as a starter, the Tigers intend to put him on the fast track as a reliever. They sent him to the Arizona Fall League for his first exposure to pro ball. He'll likely start 2011 in Double-A, but his polished repertoire and no-nonsense mentality on the mound give him a chance to appear in Detroit later in the season.

Year	Club (League)	Class	W	L	ERA	G	GS	CG	SV	IP	H	HR	BB	SO	G/A	WHIP	AVG
2010	Did not play—Signed late																

8 DREW SMYLY, LHP

Born: June 13, 1989. **B-T:** L-L. **Ht.:** 6-3. **Wt.:** 190. **Drafted:** Arkansas, 2010 (2nd round). **Signed by:** Chris Wimmer.

Smyly had back problems as a high school senior and redshirted his first season at Arkansas with a stress fracture in his elbow. He struck out 12 while beating Oklahoma in a regional championship game in 2009, setting the stage for becoming the Razorbacks' ace last spring. A draft-eligible sophomore, he signed for $1.1 million as a second-rounder. Smyly throws a lot of strikes and has an exceptional feel for pitching. He knows what it's like to pitch in big situations and he did well under the Friday night lights in the Southeastern Conference. His best pitches are an 89-92 mph fastball with some sink and armside run, and a low- to mid-80s cutter. He still needs to refine his curveball, which occasionally shows good depth, and his changeup, which he throws too hard at 84-86 mph. He has a few things to clean up in his delivery—he has a little wrist wrap and his front side can be a little stiff—but the Tigers are impressed with how easily the ball comes out of his hand. He gets good downhill plane on his fastball. Projecting as a mid-rotation starter, Smyly probably will make his pro debut in high Class A. Given his polish and Detroit's propensity to put pitchers on the fast track, he could reach the big leagues toward the end of 2012.

Year	Club (League)	Class	W	L	ERA	G	GS	CG	SV	IP	H	HR	BB	SO	G/A	WHIP	AVG
2010	Did not play—Signed late																

9 AVISAIL GARCIA, OF

Born: June 12, 1991. **B-T:** R-R. **Ht.:** 6-4. **Wt.:** 232. **Signed:** Venezuela, 2007. **Signed by:** Alejandro Rodriguez/Pedro Chavez.

Garcia signed out of Venezuela as a 16-year-old for $200,000. He made his U.S. debut as the youngest regular in the low Class A Midwest League in 2009, and the Tigers decided to have Garcia return to West Michigan last season because of his youth. Still one of the youngest players in the MWL, he improved his numbers across the board and cemented his reputation as one of the toolsiest players in Detroit's system. Garcia passes the eye test at 6-foot-4 and 232 pounds, and he has the tools to match his impressive frame. He's an above-average runner with long, graceful strides and covers a lot of ground in right field. He has the bat speed and strength to be an average hitter with at least average power. Because he's so young, Garcia still has a lot of learning to do. He's a free swinger who needs to improve his pitch recognition and discipline. He has difficulty pulling his hands in on pitches on the inner half of the plate. He makes youthful mistakes with his solid arm and on the basepaths. Garcia will move up to high Class A in 2011, starting the season as one of the Florida State League's few teenagers. He may require a year at each level, but that still would put him in Detroit at age 22.

Year	Club (League)	Class	AVG	G	AB	R	H	2B	3B	HR	RBI	BB	SO	SB	CS	OBP	SLG
2008	Tigers (VSL)	R	.298	63	245	33	73	12	2	7	34	15	39	7	5	.342	.449
2009	Lakeland (FSL)	HiA	.250	3	8	1	2	0	0	0	0	0	2	0	0	.250	.250
	West Michigan (MWL)	LoA	.264	81	299	36	79	11	2	1	31	8	70	8	7	.289	.324
2010	West Michigan (MWL)	LoA	.281	125	494	58	139	17	4	4	63	20	113	20	4	.313	.356
Minor League Totals			.280	272	1046	128	293	40	8	12	128	43	224	35	16	.313	.368

10 JOSE ORTEGA, RHP

Born: Oct. 11, 1988. **B-T:** R-R. **Ht.:** 5-11. **Wt.:** 187. **Signed:** Venezuela, 2006. **Signed by:** German Robles.

Signed out of Venezuela in 2006, Ortega didn't reach full-season ball until his fourth year as a pro. Once he did, he pitched at three levels and vaulted all the way to Double-A in 2010. Ortega has a small frame and he's wiry strong and has a quick arm that generates blistering 94-95 mph fastballs that get as high as 98. He has a short arm action and a high three-quarters arm slot, so his fastball is fairly flat and straight. He tends to fall in love with his heater, and the Tigers would like him to mix his pitches more efficiently. His 81-85 mph slider can get slurvy, but it also shows flashes of being an above-average pitch. His changeup is below average and just for show. Ortega throws with some effort in his delivery. His front side can be a little stiff and he lands upright with a head whack, leading to command problems. Ortega has the power fastball succeed as a late-inning reliever. He'll likely begin 2011 back in Double-A, working to smooth out his delivery and mix up his sequencing. If he can do that, he could be in Detroit's high octane bullpen by the end of the season.

Year	Club (League)	Class	W	L	ERA	G	GS	CG	SV	IP	H	HR	BB	SO	G/A	WHIP	AVG
2007	Tigers (VSL)	R	0	0	2.45	10	0	0	0	11	9	1	3	11	—	1.09	.209
2008	Tigers (VSL)	R	1	1	2.20	23	0	0	5	45	43	5	15	27	—	1.29	.256
2009	Oneonta (NYP)	SS	2	2	3.97	25	0	0	1	34	28	2	23	32	0.94	1.50	.220
2010	West Michigan (MWL)	LoA	0	3	4.56	18	0	0	1	26	28	1	17	22	1.27	1.75	.275
	Lakeland (FSL)	HiA	2	1	0.95	10	0	0	0	19	14	0	7	20	1.31	1.11	.212
	Erie (EL)	AA	1	0	3.04	15	1	0	0	24	22	2	7	19	1.35	1.23	.242
Minor League Totals			6	7	2.96	101	1	0	7	158	144	11	72	131	1.17	1.36	.241

11 ANDY DIRKS, OF

Born: Jan. 24, 1986. **B-T:** L-L. **Ht.:** 6-0. **Wt.:** 195. **Drafted:** Wichita State, 2008 (8th round). **Signed by:** Chris Wimmer.

After Blake Tekotte and Jason Kipnis went off the board in the third and fourth round to the Padres in the 2008 draft, Tigers scouting director David Chadd had Dirks as a gut-feel sleeper he liked nearly as much. He flew under the radar as a senior at Wichita State that spring, even after hitting .388/.498/.632. Dirks has a contact-oriented approach and sprays the ball to all fields with a balanced, compact swing. Though he hit 15 homers last season, he profiles more as a gap-power guy who might hit 8-12 longballs per year. Scouts say he drifts to his front side too much in his swing and has to cheat to hit good fastballs. This causes him to commit his hands early, so he's often out in front against good breaking balls. He put up impressive numbers en route to being named Detroit's 2010 minor league player of the year, though he batted just .248/.290/.303 against lefthanders. Dirks is a solid-average runner who gets good enough jumps in the outfield to get the job done in center, though his fringy arm plays better in left. He doesn't have standout tools, but he grows on managers because he plays the game the right way and always gives 100 percent. If it all works out, he could be a David Dellucci-type regular, and he should at least have value as a fourth outfielder. Dirks figures to open 2011 in Triple-A, where he hit well last August.

Year	Club (League)	Class	AVG	G	AB	R	H	2B	3B	HR	RBI	BB	SO	SB	CS	OBP	SLG
2008	West Michigan (MWL)	LoA	.100	3	10	0	1	0	0	0	2	1	2	0	0	.182	.100
	Tigers (GCL)	R	.412	10	34	10	14	3	2	0	7	3	6	2	0	.447	.618
2009	Lakeland (FSL)	HiA	.330	27	103	11	34	5	0	0	18	13	11	10	2	.410	.379
	Erie (EL)	AA	.255	98	361	46	92	14	1	6	44	36	61	11	5	.323	.349
2010	Erie (EL)	AA	.278	98	388	64	108	20	2	11	46	35	59	19	4	.342	.425
	Toledo (IL)	AAA	.375	22	88	14	33	10	1	4	17	3	12	3	0	.398	.648
Minor League Totals			.287	258	984	145	282	52	6	21	134	91	151	45	11	.349	.416

12 ROBBIE WEINHARDT, RHP

Born: Dec. 8, 1985. **B-T:** R-R. **Ht.:** 6-2. **Wt.:** 205. **Drafted:** Oklahoma State, 2008 (10th round). **Signed by:** Chris Wimmer.

After posting a 1.64 ERA in his first two pro seasons since signing for $15,000 as a 10th-round college senior, Weinhardt picked up where he left off last year. He made it to the big leagues in July, 11 days behind Andy Oliver, his former Oklahoma State roommate. Weinhardt may have made his major league debut sooner if not for a shoulder strain that sidelined him for a month. He uses a low, almost sidearm slinging arm action that makes it difficult for hitter to pick up his pitches. His fastball sits at 90-93 mph with good sink, generating a lot of groundballs. His fastball straightens out when he leaves it up in the zone, and he quickly learned that he doesn't have the gas to just blow it by big league hitters. To combat that problem, he's working to create a little more downward angle to the plate. Weinhardt also throws an 81-84 mph slider that can get a little sweepy. He occasionally mixes in a changeup but is mostly a two-pitch guy. He pitched well enough to lay claim to a middle-relief spot on Detroit's Opening Day roster in 2011.

Year	Club (League)	Class	W	L	ERA	G	GS	CG	SV	IP	H	HR	BB	SO	G/A	WHIP	AVG
2008	Tigers (GCL)	R	0	0	0.00	3	0	0	0	6	6	0	2	4	—	1.41	.261
	Lakeland (FSL)	HiA	3	1	2.04	21	0	0	4	35	19	1	11	44	—	0.85	.162
2009	Lakeland (FSL)	HiA	1	1	0.85	22	0	0	3	32	24	2	10	40	1.39	1.07	.200
	Erie (EL)	AA	0	1	2.30	20	0	0	2	31	28	0	16	32	1.07	1.40	.233
2010	Connecticut (NYP)	SS	1	0	2.25	3	0	0	0	4	2	0	2	5	—	1.00	.133
	Toledo (IL)	AAA	1	1	1.57	24	0	0	1	34	26	0	7	25	2.40	0.96	.211
	Detroit (AL)	MAJ	2	2	6.14	28	0	0	0	29	40	2	8	21	2.73	1.64	.328
Major League Totals			2	2	6.14	28	0	0	0	29	40	2	8	21	2.73	1.64	.328
Minor League Totals			6	4	1.64	93	0	0	10	142	105	3	48	150	1.64	1.07	.203

13 BRUCE RONDON, RHP

Born: Dec. 9, 1990. **B-T:** R-R. **Ht.:** 6-1. **Wt.:** 250. **Signed:** Venezuela, 2007. **Signed by:** German Robles/Pedro Chavez/Miguel Garcia.

In 2010, his first full season in the United States, Rondon led the Gulf Coast League in saves (15) and opponent average by a reliever (.133). He wasn't comfortable with the over-the-top arm slot he opened the year with, so the Tigers dropped him down to angle slightly below three-quarters at midseason, and he really took off. Rondon sits at 92-94 mph with his heavy, sinking fastball and dials it up as high as 98. He also throws a slider in the mid-80s that shows flashes of being a plus pitch, but it's inconsistent and flattens out when he gets under it from his new arm slot. Despite thighs the size of tree trunks, Rondon doesn't really utilize his lower half in his delivery. Perhaps because of his new arm slot, some inconsistencies in his mechanics or just his youth, Rondon can struggle with his command. He'll need to improve the location of his pitches and the reliability of his slider, but he has the weapons to help the big league bullpen in a few years. He finished 2010 in high Class A and could return there this season.

Year	Club (League)	Class	W	L	ERA	G	GS	CG	SV	IP	H	HR	BB	SO	G/A	WHIP	AVG
2008	Tigers (VSL)	R	2	6	3.58	13	13	1	0	55	48	0	20	34	—	1.23	.225
2009	Tigers (GCL)	R	0	1	4.76	3	3	0	0	11	12	0	8	15	2.60	1.76	.267
	Tigers (VSL)	R	0	0	13.50	3	0	0	0	4	5	0	7	4	6.00	3.00	.313
2010	Tigers (GCL)	R	0	0	0.70	24	0	0	15	26	11	1	14	26	1.87	0.97	.133
	Lakeland (FSL)	HiA	0	0	1.35	4	0	0	2	7	2	1	2	7	1.00	0.60	.095
Minor League Totals			2	7	3.23	47	16	1	17	103	78	2	51	86	2.00	1.25	.206

14 RYAN STRIEBY, OF/1B

Born: Aug. 9, 1985. **B-T:** R-R. **Ht.:** 6-5. **Wt.:** 235. **Drafted:** Kentucky, 2006 (4th round). **Signed by:** Harold Zonder.

Since breaking Lakeland's franchise record with 29 homers in 2008, Strieby has struggled to stay healthy. He broke the hamate bone in his left wrist that August and has spent five different stints on the disabled list with related problems, playing a total of just 162 games the last two seasons. Both years, the Tigers had to nix plans to send Strieby to the Arizona Fall League. When he's healthy, Strieby has above-average power. The hulking slugger projects as an average hitter, with the ability to stay inside the ball well and good bat speed that allows him to catch up to quality fastballs. He's still working on pitch identification, which isn't surprising considering all the time he's missed. He also has a tendency to get out on his front foot too soon and he's susceptible to chasing pitches up in the strike zone. Because the Tigers have Miguel Cabrera at first base, they had Strieby play mostly in left field last season. While he showed improvement compared to 2009, he still wasn't pretty as an outfielder. He's a well below-average runner with average arm strength. Health and defensive limitations likely will make Strieby more of an impact bat off the bench rather than an everyday contributor. He still needs more Triple-A at-bats before he's ready for the majors.

Year	Club (League)	Class	AVG	G	AB	R	H	2B	3B	HR	RBI	BB	SO	SB	CS	OBP	SLG
2006	Oneonta (NYP)	SS	.241	61	224	26	54	9	0	4	25	25	58	1	1	.319	.335
2007	West Michigan (MWL)	LoA	.253	123	443	65	112	23	2	16	76	63	78	6	5	.347	.422
2008	Lakeland (FSL)	HiA	.278	112	421	65	117	19	7	29	94	46	101	0	1	.352	.563
2009	Erie (EL)	AA	.303	86	294	64	89	18	1	19	58	57	80	2	0	.427	.565
2010	Toledo (IL)	AAA	.245	76	290	29	71	15	0	10	49	33	85	1	1	.323	.400
Minor League Totals			.265	458	1672	249	443	84	10	78	302	224	402	10	8	.355	.467

15 DUANE BELOW, LHP

Born: Nov. 15, 1985. **B-T:** L-L. **Ht.:** 6-2. **Wt.:** 205. **Drafted:** Lake Michigan CC, 2006 (19th round). **Signed by:** Tom Osowski.

Below missed most of 2009 after having Tommy John surgery, but he's been very effective when healthy. He was the Tigers' minor league pitcher of the year and led the Midwest League with 160 strikeouts in 2007. A year later, he topped the Florida State League with 126 whiffs. Below made a quick recovery from elbow reconstruction and paced the Double-A Eastern League with 28 starts in 2010. Detroit was cautious with him, generally limiting him to 85 pitches per start. Though Below has an effortless delivery and looks like he's just playing catch, his fastball sits at 90-94 mph. He can vary the speed on his curveball, which can be a swing-and-miss pitch at times. He also mixes in a slurvy slider and a changeup with some sink. Command is often the last thing to come back following Tommy John surgery, but Below actually located his pitches better last year than he did before he got hurt. Added to the 40-man roster in November, he could fit into the back of the Tigers' rotation as early as the second half of 2011.

Year	Club (League)	Class	W	L	ERA	G	GS	CG	SV	IP	H	HR	BB	SO	G/A	WHIP	AVG
2006	Tigers (GCL)	R	2	0	1.60	15	4	0	0	34	27	1	10	30	—	1.10	.216
	Oneonta (NYP)	SS	0	0	3.86	2	2	0	0	9	11	0	5	8	—	1.71	.282
2007	West Michigan (MWL)	LoA	13	5	2.97	26	26	0	0	146	128	6	58	160	—	1.28	.236
2008	Lakeland (FSL)	HiA	8	7	4.46	27	26	0	0	133	144	10	70	126	—	1.61	.280
2009	Lakeland (FSL)	HiA	1	4	3.14	6	6	0	0	29	22	4	14	38	1.18	1.26	.208
	Erie (EL)	AA	1	0	1.59	2	2	0	0	11	7	1	6	7	1.00	1.15	.175
2010	Erie (EL)	AA	7	12	4.93	28	28	0	0	126	137	17	37	103	1.24	1.38	.275
Minor League Totals			32	28	3.78	106	94	0	0	488	476	39	200	472	1.21	1.39	.255

16 MATT HOFFMAN, LHP

Born: Nov. 18, 1988. **B-T:** L-L. **Ht.:** 6-2. **Wt.:** 195. **Drafted:** HS—Owasso, Okla., 2007 (26th round). **Signed by:** Steve Taylor.

Hoffman got plenty of exposure at Oklahoma powerhouse Owasso High in 2007, when he played alongside Cardinals first-round pick Pete Kozma. Hoffman entered his senior year as a center fielder but showed good arm strength on the mound, getting up to 91-92 mph. Many teams worried about his strong commitment to Oklahoma, but the Tigers nabbed him with a 26th-round pick and a $175,000 bonus. The athletic Hoffman continues to develop as a pitcher, making that investment look worth while. He became a full-time reliever in 2010 after splitting time between the rotation and bullpen in his first two pro seasons. His velocity took off when he worked shorter stints, as Hoffman now sits at 93-95 mph with his fastball and can reach back to hit 97. He also has done a nice job of tightening his 82-85 mph slider, which has good tilt. He'll flash an occasional 85-mph changeup with some sink and fade, but it's mostly just a pitch to give hitters something else to think about. He clearly prefers his fastball-slider combination. Hoffman's body is a little soft, but he has an easy delivery and works fast. His control disintegrated and he got pounded after a promotion to Double-A last year, so he'll try again to solve that level in 2011.

Year	Club (League)	Class	W	L	ERA	G	GS	CG	SV	IP	H	HR	BB	SO	G/A	WHIP	AVG
2008	West Michigan (MWL)	LoA	0	2	4.60	5	2	0	0	16	19	1	14	20	—	2.11	.284
	Oneonta (NYP)	SS	3	5	3.05	12	10	0	0	56	49	1	24	44	—	1.30	.237
2009	West Michigan (MWL)	LoA	5	0	1.12	7	3	0	1	40	24	1	8	33	1.69	0.79	.169
	Lakeland (FSL)	HiA	3	7	6.79	16	10	1	0	62	79	9	21	32	1.13	1.60	.309
2010	Lakeland (FSL)	HiA	0	1	1.59	16	0	0	3	23	17	1	2	18	3.60	0.84	.215
	Toledo (IL)	AAA	0	0	10.38	3	0	0	0	4	9	1	4	4	1.00	3.00	.474
	Erie (EL)	AA	1	2	7.43	26	0	0	0	27	36	3	20	22	2.18	2.10	.308
Minor League Totals			12	17	4.34	85	25	1	4	228	233	17	93	173	1.58	1.43	.263

17 LESTER OLIVEROS, RHP

Born: May 28, 1988. **B-T:** R-R. **Ht.:** 6-0. **Wt.:** 185. **Signed:** Venezuela, 2005. **Signed by:** Ramon Pena.

The Tigers aren't generally big spenders in Latin America, but they still get a good bang for their buck. Signing Oliveros for $8,500 out of Venezuela in 2005 is a case in point. He had his best season since coming to the United States in 2010, dominating high Class A hitters and finishing strong in Double-A to earn a spot on the 40-man roster. Oliveros profiles as a middle reliever and works mostly off his fastballs, using a 91-92 mph two-seamer with sink and a 94-96 mph four-seamer with good run. He doesn't quite hold his velocity when used in consecutive games, topping out at 93 on the second day. His best secondary pitch is a changeup that could be a solid-average offering. His 80-83 mph slider has lazy, slurvy action and gets hit hard, so he rarely throws it. Despite his clean delivery and easy arm action, Oliveros still is seeking consistent control and command. Though he had trouble finding the strike zone in Double-A, he'll advance to Triple-A to start 2011.

Year	Club (League)	Class	W	L	ERA	G	GS	CG	SV	IP	H	HR	BB	SO	G/A	WHIP	AVG
2006	Tigers/Marlins (VSL)	R	1	3	2.72	20	2	0	4	40	29	2	20	46	—	1.24	.193
2007	Tigers (VSL)	R	2	0	1.41	27	0	0	19	38	25	0	13	59	—	0.99	.181
2008	Oneonta (NYP)	SS	1	2	1.74	15	0	0	4	21	15	1	6	34	—	1.02	.197
	Lakeland (FSL)	HiA	1	1	4.22	5	0	0	0	11	12	0	9	3	—	1.97	.293
2009	Lakeland (FSL)	HiA	4	2	4.17	34	0	0	2	54	53	5	16	58	1.00	1.28	.249
	Toledo (IL)	AAA	0	0	0.00	1	0	0	0	2	2	0	1	3	0.50	1.50	.250
2010	Lakeland (FSL)	HiA	0	1	1.89	20	0	0	9	19	13	0	6	24	1.14	1.00	.194
	Erie (EL)	AA	1	2	4.97	24	0	0	14	25	20	3	21	36	1.25	1.62	.217
Minor League Totals			10	11	3.00	146	2	0	52	210	169	11	92	263	1.06	1.24	.215

18 BRAYAN VILLARREAL, RHP

Born: Oct. 5, 1987. **B-T:** R-R. **Ht.:** 6-0. **Wt.:** 170. **Signed:** Venezuela, 2005. **Signed by:** Ramon Pena.

Villarreal became a full-time starter in 2011 and put together a strong season, pitching well throughout and finishing in Double-A. He has bounced back from Tommy John surgery in 2007 and claimed a spot on Detroit's 40-man roster in November. Villarreal isn't big, but he has wiry strength to his frame and good arm speed. While he didn't reach the mid-90s as often as he did in 2009, he pitched at 90-94 mph with his fastball last season. His fastball is mostly straight, so he can get hit when he doesn't keep it down in the strike zone. His slider shows flashes of becoming an above-average offering but often breaks too early, making it easy for the hitters to see out of his hand. He gained more confidence in his changeup in 2010, but it too can be simple to spot. Villarreal pitches with good tempo and shows strong mound presence. The Tigers want him to trust his defenders more instead of trying to strike everyone out. Detroit will continue to start Villarreal so he can get innings to sharpen his secondary pitches but his future role is likely in the bullpen. He'll probably open 2011 back in Erie.

Year	Club (League)	Class	W	L	ERA	G	GS	CG	SV	IP	H	HR	BB	SO	G/A	WHIP	AVG
2006	Tigers/Marlins (VSL)	R	0	2	3.48	14	5	0	0	41	35	3	20	23	—	1.33	.233
2007	Tigers (GCL)	R	0	0	6.23	1	1	0	0	4	4	0	3	5	—	1.62	.235
2008	Tigers (GCL)	R	1	5	3.65	11	6	1	0	37	26	0	11	37	—	1.00	.197
	West Michigan (MWL)	LoA	0	1	16.20	1	1	0	0	3	7	1	1	0	—	2.40	.438
2009	West Michigan (MWL)	LoA	5	5	2.87	26	16	0	2	103	85	5	34	118	0.93	1.15	.231
2010	Lakeland (FSL)	HiA	7	4	3.47	16	16	1	0	86	73	8	23	90	0.90	1.12	.232
	Erie (EL)	AA	0	4	3.71	8	8	0	0	44	37	6	16	46	0.81	1.21	.231
Minor League Totals			13	21	3.50	77	53	2	2	319	267	23	108	319	0.81	1.18	.231

19 CASPER WELLS, OF

Born: Nov. 23, 1984. **B-T:** R-R. **Ht.:** 6-2. **Wt.:** 210. **Drafted:** Towson, 2005 (14th round). **Signed by:** Bill Buck.

Wells was one of just two minor leaguers to hit 25 homers and steal 25 bases in 2008, but he missed half of the following season when he broke the hamate bone in his left hand in April. Healthy again in 2010, he made his major league debut in May and played well when he got regular time in September. Scouts still wonder about his long-term ability with the bat, because there are a lot of moving parts to Wells' swing. He has some raw power, but he struggles to hit quality fastballs, especially up in the zone, and has trouble recognizing breaking balls. He may never make enough consistent contact or hit for a high average. Wells has solid speed but has succeeded in just 15 of 32 basestealing attempts since his breakout 2008 season. He's a respectable center fielder who fits best in right field. He has the best outfield arm in the system, with above-average strength and accuracy. Wells' holes at the plate will limit him to being a role player in the big leagues, but he could be useful with his power, speed and ability to play all three outfield spots.

Year	Club (League)	Class	AVG	G	AB	R	H	2B	3B	HR	RBI	BB	SO	SB	CS	OBP	SLG
2005	Tigers (GCL)	R	.220	45	141	25	31	9	5	5	20	18	59	6	0	.341	.461
2006	Lakeland (FSL)	HiA	.152	11	33	4	5	1	0	1	4	4	9	1	0	.300	.273
	Oneonta (NYP)	SS	.229	35	105	19	24	8	0	1	14	9	27	1	1	.305	.333
2007	Lakeland (FSL)	HiA	.500	2	2	0	1	1	0	0	0	0	1	0	0	.500	1.000
	Oneonta (NYP)	SS	.265	67	260	46	69	18	11	9	47	18	64	8	7	.323	.523
2008	West Michigan (MWL)	LoA	.240	50	179	30	43	7	0	10	26	22	39	17	5	.351	.447
	Erie (EL)	AA	.289	75	270	60	78	18	6	17	53	30	66	8	3	.376	.589
2009	Erie (EL)	AA	.260	86	311	52	81	18	4	15	41	43	103	8	8	.369	.489
2010	Toledo (IL)	AAA	.233	103	387	56	90	22	6	21	46	34	111	7	8	.309	.483
	Detroit (AL)	MAJ	.323	36	93	14	30	6	1	4	17	6	19	0	1	.364	.538
Major League Totals			.323	36	93	14	30	6	1	4	17	6	19	0	1	.364	.538
Minor League Totals			.250	474	1688	292	422	102	32	79	251	178	479	56	32	.340	.489

20 BRYAN HOLADAY, C

Born: Nov. 19, 1987. **B-T:** R-R. **Ht.:** 6-0. **Wt.:** 205. **Drafted:** Texas Christian, 2010 (6th round). **Signed by:** Tim Grieve.

Though Holaday has more of a reputation as a defensive standout, he finished his amateur career by tying a College World Series with four homers in one tournament. As a junior in 2009, he was one of just four college players to hit a homer off Stephen Strasburg. A sixth-round pick last June, Holaday signed for $115,000 and ran out of gas after reporting directly to high Class A. While his stroke is unorthodox, he consistently puts the barrel on the ball. He does have some strength, but his power is more suited to drive the ball to the gaps rather than over the fence. Like most catchers, he's a below-average runner. Holaday's best tools are his strong arm and his receiving ability, and he's also a hard-nosed leader who calls a good game. He sometimes gets too quick on his throws, costing him accuracy. He threw out just 21 percent of basestealers in his pro debut. Holaday figures to begin 2011 back in Lakeland and could move quickly.

Year	Club (League)	Class	AVG	G	AB	R	H	2B	3B	HR	RBI	BB	SO	SB	CS	OBP	SLG
2010	Lakeland (FSL)	HiA	.220	44	159	14	35	8	0	3	12	21	43	0	0	.335	.327
Minor League Totals			.220	44	159	14	35	8	0	3	12	21	43	0	0	.335	.327

21 ROB BRANTLY, C

Born: July 14, 1989. **B-T:** L-R. **Ht.:** 6-2. **Wt.:** 188. **Drafted:** UC Riverside, 2010 (3rd round). **Signed by:** Steve Pack.

A 46th-round pick by the Nationals out of high school, Brantly headed to UC Riverside rather than turn pro. He ranked as the Northwoods League's top prospect in the summer of 2009, then followed up with a strong season last spring that got him drafted in the third round as a sophomore-eligible. Signed for $330,300, he's a consistent defensive catcher with a patient approach at the plate. Brantly projects as an average hitter who sprays line drives to all fields and has a good idea of the strike zone. His present power grades as below average, but the Tigers see strength in his swing and believe he could develop into a 15-homer hitter. To tap into that power, he'll need to incorporate more of a load into his swing. He's more athletic and runs better than most catchers. Brantly also moves well behind the plate and has a strong, accurate throwing arm with a quick release. Despite his defensive reputation, Brantly looked a little stiff and mechanical behind the plate in his pro debut, and he threw out just 23 percent of basestealers. He did look more fluid later in the summer, so he may have just developed some rust after the college season ended. Brantly could begin his first full pro season in high Class A, though that might mean splitting time at catcher with fellow 2010 draftee Bryan Holaday.

Year	Club (League)	Class	AVG	G	AB	R	H	2B	3B	HR	RBI	BB	SO	SB	CS	OBP	SLG
2010	West Michigan (MWL)	LoA	.255	52	188	26	48	10	1	1	21	23	22	2	2	.352	.335
Minor League Totals			.255	52	188	26	48	10	1	1	21	23	22	2	2	.352	.335

22 CALE IORG, SS

Born: Sept. 6, 1985. **B-T:** R-R. **Ht.:** 6-2. **Wt.:** 180. **Drafted:** Alabama, 2007 (6th round). **Signed by:** David Chadd.

After a solid freshman season at Alabama, Iorg spent two years in Portugal on a Mormon mission. The Tigers believed enough in his talent to pay him $1.5 million as a sixth-round pick after he finished his assignment in 2007, diverting him from transferring to Arizona State. Detroit made the investment in part because of Iorg's bloodlines, as his father Garth and uncle Dane both played in the big leagues. However, hitting is tough enough without a two-year layoff, and Iorg has struggled mightily as a pro. He's career .228/.283/.358 hitter whose production has declined in each of his three full pro season. Iorg is a gifted athlete with a sound stroke, bat speed and some raw power, but his pitch recognition is poor and he regularly swings through offspeed pitches. He's overly aggressive and scouts question how well he can see the ball. He doesn't make adjustments at the plate and often loads too late to get his hands going in time against good velocity. Despite his offensive shortcomings, Iorg may still get a shot as a major league regular because of his prowess with the glove. He's a special defender with extraordinary range and hands. His arm is also an asset, though it wasn't on full display last year, when he experienced some shoulder stiffness late in the season. Though Detroit added Iorg to the 40-man roster in November, it also re-signed Jhonny Peralta to a two-year contract. That likely limits Iorg to a reserve role with the Tigers, though he'll have to improve offensively before he gets that opportunity.

Year	Club (League)	Class	AVG	G	AB	R	H	2B	3B	HR	RBI	BB	SO	SB	CS	OBP	SLG
2007	Tigers (GCL)	R	.182	3	11	1	2	0	0	0	0	1	6	0	0	.308	.182
	Lakeland (FSL)	HiA	.278	5	18	0	5	2	0	0	5	1	5	0	0	.316	.389
2008	Lakeland (FSL)	HiA	.251	99	383	61	96	15	7	10	47	35	111	22	11	.329	.405
2009	Erie (EL)	AA	.222	129	491	57	109	17	3	11	41	32	149	13	7	.274	.336
2010	Erie (EL)	AA	.211	110	427	50	90	22	1	10	33	17	139	12	5	.248	.337
	Toledo (IL)	AAA	.242	16	66	7	16	6	1	1	9	2	20	0	1	.271	.409
Minor League Totals			.228	362	1396	176	318	62	12	32	135	88	430	47	24	.283	.358

23 GUSTAVO NUNEZ, SS

Born: Feb. 8, 1988. **B-T:** B-R. **Ht.:** 5-10. **Wt.:** 168. **Signed:** Dominican Republic, 2007. **Signed by:** Julian German/Ramon Perez.

Nunez's stock soared when he hit .315/.360/.425 in low Class A in 2009. His bat came back to earth last season, but his glove remained his calling card. Managers rated him the best defensive shortstop in the Florida State League in 2010. He has fluid actions, terrific footwork and one of the strongest arms in the system. He cam make routine and flashy plays alike, and can throw out runners from deep in the hole. Nunez has 65 speed on the 20-80 scouting scale, with his quickness giving him plus range at shortstop and also making him a basestealing threat. He was more efficient with his speed last year, improving his basestealing success rate to 80 percent, up from 66 percent in 2009. After his rough 2010 season at the plate, Nunez will have to prove he can hit enough to be a big league regular. He has a slender frame that lacks strength, so he utilizes a slap-and-slash approach. He has little power and is too impatient at the plate, striking out too much and rarely drawing walks. He'll need to repeat high Class A, which isn't a good sign for a 23-year-old.

Year	Club (League)	Class	AVG	G	AB	R	H	2B	3B	HR	RBI	BB	SO	SB	CS	OBP	SLG
2007	Tigers (DSL)	R	.284	64	243	50	69	10	3	0	42	32	45	9	7	.370	.350
2008	Tigers (GCL)	R	.200	13	40	5	8	3	0	0	5	2	6	1	1	.233	.275
	Lakeland (FSL)	HiA	.245	45	147	14	36	4	0	0	15	11	29	1	3	.304	.272
2009	Tigers (GCL)	R	.190	6	21	5	4	0	0	1	4	1	5	3	0	.261	.333
	West Michigan (MWL)	LoA	.315	112	464	82	146	16	10	5	40	25	62	45	25	.360	.425
2010	Lakeland (FSL)	HiA	.222	128	523	66	116	13	6	2	33	21	93	33	8	.263	.281
Minor League Totals			.264	368	1438	222	379	46	19	8	139	92	240	92	44	.317	.339

24 DANRY VASQUEZ, OF

Born: Jan. 8, 1994. **B-T:** L-R. **Ht.:** 6-2. **Wt.:** 168. **Signed:** Venezuela, 2010. **Signed by:** Oscar Garcia/Pedro Chavez.

Vasquez represents a rare exception to the Tigers' usually thrifty approach in Latin America, as they paid $1.2 million to sign him out of Venezuela in July. He had been on the team's radar since he was 14, which made Detroit more comfortable giving him the largest international signing bonus in team history. With broad shoulders and a high waist on his 6-foot-2, 170-pound frame, Vasquez has room to add muscle and projects to be a physical player in four or five years. There are a lot of moving parts to his swing right now and he was over-matched against the competition in instructional league, but his raw tools are exciting. He has above-average bat speed and good barrel control. He uses the whole field and should grow into home run power as he gets stronger. Vasquez has played some center field, but his average speed and plus arm have him destined for right field. He'll make his pro debut in Rookie ball this year, probably in the Venezuelan Summer League.

Year	Club (League)	Class	AVG	G	AB	R	H	2B	3B	HR	RBI	BB	SO	SB	CS	OBP	SLG
2010	Did not play—Signed 2011 contract																

25 WADE GAYNOR, 3B

Born: April 19, 1988. **B-T:** R-R. **Ht.:** 6-2. **Wt.:** 210. **Drafted:** Western Kentucky, 2009 (3rd round). **Signed by:** Harold Zonder.

The last big league position player to come out of Western Kentucky was catcher Chris Turner, an Angels 1991 seventh-round pick. Gaynor went four rounds higher in 2009 after turning in a 20-20 season, leading the Hilltoppers to the NCAA regional finals and impressing Tigers scouts with his power at a predraft workout at Comerica Park. He's big and strong and has a quick bat, so it's no surprise that his most obvious tool is his raw power. He won't be able to tap into it or hit for a decent average, however, if he can't lay off breaking balls on the outer half of the plate and make more consistent contact. His swing can get long and he struggles to pull his hands in against inside fastballs. Gaynor is surprisingly athletic for his size and used his average speed to steal 11 bases in 2010. His athleticism doesn't translate well at third base, however. He has slow reactions and limited range. His arm is average, but his funky throwing motion makes it difficult for him to throw from different slots. He is a hard worker with good makeup, but he faces an uphill battle with Nick Castellanos and Francisco Martinez ahead of him on the organization's third-base depth chart. Gaynor will spend 2011 in high Class A.

Year	Club (League)	Class	AVG	G	AB	R	H	2B	3B	HR	RBI	BB	SO	SB	CS	OBP	SLG
2009	Oneonta (NYP)	SS	.192	67	234	37	45	10	1	3	23	21	52	8	3	.281	.282
2010	West Michigan (MWL)	LoA	.286	131	514	91	147	39	4	10	80	46	111	13	5	.354	.436
Minor League Totals			.257	198	748	128	192	49	5	13	103	67	163	21	8	.331	.388

26 CHARLIE FURBUSH, LHP

Born: April 11, 1986. **B-T:** L-L. **Ht.:** 6-5. **Wt.:** 217. **Drafted:** Louisiana State, 2007 (4th round). **Signed by:** Jim Rough.

Just seven players born in Maine have appeared in the big leagues, and Furbush is on the verge of making it eight after shooting three levels to Triple-A and ranking second in the minors with 183 strikeouts in 2010. His path has been circuitous, as he started his college career at NCAA Division III St. Joseph's (Maine) before starring in the Cape Cod League and transferring to Louisiana State. After the Tigers made him a fourth-round pick in 2007, he missed his first full pro season after having Tommy John surgery. Despite his strikeouts, Furbush doesn't have overpowering stuff. In fact, he doesn't have a true plus pitch, relying more on the deception in his funky delivery to generate swings and misses. He pitches with a high elbow and falls off the mound, which makes it difficult for him to maintain a consistent release point and leads to command difficulties at times. Furbush works with an 89-91 mph fastball, a loopy curveball and a straight changeup. His curve has tighter spin when he pitches from the stretch, which could mean his future is in relief. After grabbing a 40-man roster spot in November, he'll probably open 2011 in Toledo.

Year	Club (League)	Class	W	L	ERA	G	GS	CG	SV	IP	H	HR	BB	SO	G/A	WHIP	AVG
2007	Tigers (GCL)	R	2	0	2.81	4	3	0	0	16	11	2	3	23	—	0.88	.186
	West Michigan (MWL)	LoA	4	1	2.17	8	7	0	0	46	40	2	11	46	—	1.12	.237
2008	Did not play—Injured																
2009	Lakeland (FSL)	HiA	6	7	3.96	24	23	0	0	111	111	10	32	93	0.89	1.28	.257
2010	Lakeland (FSL)	HiA	4	5	3.39	13	13	0	0	77	68	7	14	109	1.04	1.06	.229
	Erie (EL)	AA	1	0	3.24	5	5	0	0	33	31	5	10	37	1.00	1.23	.248
	Toledo (IL)	AAA	3	4	6.29	9	9	0	0	49	59	9	16	37	1.42	1.54	.311
Minor League Totals			20	17	3.80	63	60	0	0	332	320	35	86	345	1.02	1.22	.252

27 ADAM WILK, LHP

Born: Dec. 9, 1987. **B-T:** L-L. **Ht.:** 6-2. **Wt.:** 175. **Drafted:** Long Beach State, 2009 (11th round). **Signed by:** Phil Huttmann.

Wilk went from an 11th-round pick in 2009 to the Tigers' minor league pitcher of the year in 2010. He led Detroit farmhands with a 2.74 ERA and topped the Florida State League in fewest walks per nine innings (1.2). While many of the Tigers' best pitching prospects have big-time velocity, Wilk gets by more with command and control, a four-pitch mix and guile. His fastball sits at 86-89 mph, reaching 92 on occasion. He locates his fastball to all four quadrants of the strike zone, and he changes speeds to keep hitters off balance. He has good feel for an average curveball and a cutter/slider. His best pitch is a 77-80 mph changeup that he throws with the same arm speed as his fastball. Wilk has some funk to his delivery, which adds to his deception. He helps his cause with his attention to detail, including meticulous preparation between starts. He projects as a back-of-the-rotation starter. Wilk finished his first full pro season in Double-A and should return there in 2011.

Year	Club (League)	Class	W	L	ERA	G	GS	CG	SV	IP	H	HR	BB	SO	G/A	WHIP	AVG
2009	Oneonta (NYP)	SS	2	0	1.45	7	7	1	0	37	23	0	5	34	0.69	0.75	.173
	West Michigan (MWL)	LoA	2	1	1.49	7	7	0	0	36	30	2	2	33	0.97	0.88	.222
2010	Lakeland (FSL)	HiA	9	5	3.01	24	24	1	0	144	139	8	19	100	0.78	1.10	.250
	Erie (EL)	AA	2	0	1.14	3	3	0	0	24	10	1	5	14	0.66	0.63	.128
Minor League Totals			15	6	2.35	41	41	2	0	241	202	11	31	181	0.78	0.97	.224

28 DIXON MACHADO, SS

Born: Feb. 22, 1992. **B-T:** R-R. **Ht.:** 6-0. **Wt.:** 169. **Signed:** Venezuela, 2008. **Signed by:** German Robles.

The Tigers are one of the few teams that still has an academy in Venezuela, and it's no coincidence that seven Venezuelans made this Top 30 Prospects list. Machado gives Detroit another slick-fielding shortstop in the system, though like Cale Iorg and Gustavo Nunez he has yet to prove he can be a factor at the plate. In his U.S. debut in 2010, Machado stood out as the top shortstop in the Gulf Coast League. He's an acrobatic defender with fantastic range, smooth hands and a strong arm. At the plate, Machado has a short swing and a contact-oriented approach. He lacks power and knows his limitations, but could have some pop as his wiry frame fills out. He's a slightly above-average runner who should steal a few bases. He'll likely start 2011 in extended spring training before heading to short-season Connecticut in June.

Year	Club (League)	Class	AVG	G	AB	R	H	2B	3B	HR	RBI	BB	SO	SB	CS	OBP	SLG
2009	Tigers (VSL)	R	.205	63	234	41	48	6	1	3	26	32	32	27	6	.310	.278
2010	Tigers (GCL)	R	.261	43	165	22	43	4	3	0	11	14	27	12	3	.315	.321
	Connecticut (NYP)	SS	.292	7	24	4	7	1	0	0	1	3	5	1	2	.393	.333
Minor League Totals			.232	113	423	67	98	11	4	3	38	49	64	40	11	.317	.298

29 KYLE RYAN, LHP

Born: Sept. 25, 1991. **B-T:** L-L. **Ht.:** 6-4. **Wt.:** 193. **Drafted:** HS—Auburndale, Fla., 2010 (12th round). **Signed by:** Jim Rough.

Detroit knew Ryan better than any team. Auburndale (Fla.) High, his alma mater, is located just 10 miles from the Tigers' complex in Lakeland, and he pitched for their team in the East Coast Professional Showcase in the summer of 2009. That fall, he pitched for the U.S. 18-and-under team that won a gold medal at the Pan Am Championships in Venezuela. When Ryan came out throwing 84-86 mph in his first start last spring, several scouts backed off of him, figuring he'd be better off following through on his commitment to South Florida. Detroit continued to monitor him and saw his fastball rise to 89-92 mph late in his senior season, which was enough for the club to invest a 12th-round pick and $100,000 bonus. A lanky lefthander with a low three-quarters arm angle, Ryan resembles White Sox first-rounder Chris Sale when Sale was coming out of high school in the same part of Florida three years earlier. Though Ryan shows the potential for a good slider, it's still inconsistent and he sometimes tips it off by dropping his arm slot a little. His changeup occasionally has some drop, but it still needs a lot of work. Ryan has enough stuff and maturity to handle a low Class A assignment as a teenager this year. The Tigers are intrigued by his projectability.

Year	Club (League)	Class	W	L	ERA	G	GS	CG	SV	IP	H	HR	BB	SO	G/A	WHIP	AVG
2010	Tigers (GCL)	R	2	4	4.17	12	12	0	0	54	58	2	13	46	2.16	1.31	.267
Minor League Totals			2	4	4.17	12	12	0	0	54	58	2	13	46	2.16	1.31	.267

30 COLE NELSON, LHP

Born: July 14, 1989. **B-T:** L-L. **Ht.:** 6-7. **Wt.:** 240. **Drafted:** Auburn, 2010 (10th round). **Signed by:** Bryson Barber.

Nelson went from a Minnesota high school to Des Moines Area CC, where he turned down the Rays as a 45th-round pick in 2009, to Auburn. He had an inconsistent junior season at Auburn, going 6-3, 5.64 as a starter, but shaved nearly five runs off his ERA in his pro debut after signing for $90,000 as a 10th-round pick. Detroit lengthened Nelson's stride and raised his arm slot, boosting his fastball from 89-92 mph to 94-95. His heater has some sink and tailing action, and it gets on hitters quick because his size allows him to release the ball closer to the plate than most pitchers. His breaking ball is a slurve that breaks down more than laterally. He also mixes in a low-80s changeup, but it's a below-average pitch that he needs to use more to gain feel for it. Nelson has an extra-large frame but below-average athleticism, and his stiffness makes it more difficult for him to repeat his delivery and throw strikes. He finished his first pro summer by allowing one hit in two starts in high Class A, and he may return to Lakeland to begin 2011. He'll have to improve his secondary pitches to make it as a starter, but his newfound velocity alone could be nearly enough for him to have a big league career as a lefthanded reliever.

Year	Club (League)	Class	W	L	ERA	G	GS	CG	SV	IP	H	HR	BB	SO	G/A	WHIP	AVG
2010	Tigers (GCL)	R	1	0	0.59	7	1	0	1	15	11	0	7	27	0.70	1.17	.186
	Lakeland (FSL)	HiA	0	0	0.75	2	2	0	0	12	1	0	6	9	2.13	0.58	.028
Minor League Totals			1	0	0.66	9	3	0	1	27	12	0	13	36	1.33	0.91	.126

Florida Marlins

BY JAMES BAILEY

Though his team headed into the 2010 season with the National League's third-lowest payroll, Marlins owner Jeffrey Loria expressed high hopes during spring training. "I expect us to make the playoffs," Loria said. "We've got all the ammunition we need."

That optimism proved to be misplaced, as little went right in South Florida. In mid-May, Hanley Ramirez wound up in the doghouse for lollygagging after a booted popup—and initially refusing to apolo-

gize to his teammates. Twelve days later, Roy Halladay threw a perfect game against Florida.

On June 23, with the team sitting at 34-36, Loria dumped manager Fredi Gonzalez and replaced him with Triple-A New Orleans skipper Edwin Rodriguez on an interim basis. The Marlins dallied with Bobby Valentine before negotiations fell apart, and Rodriguez kept the job after the team went 46-46 with him at the helm.

Then came the injuries. Chris Coghlan, the 2009 NL rookie of the year, tore the meniscus in his left knee while jamming a shaving-cream pie in Wes Helms' face. Ricky Nolasco tore the meniscus in his right knee when he took off a shoe. All told, a team-record 57 players rotated through the clubhouse.

The bad news continued after the season ended, with the Marlins getting rid of Cameron Maybin and Andrew Miller in separate deals for three relievers. Once the centerpieces of the blockbuster trade that sent Miguel Cabrera and Dontrelle Willis to the Tigers in December 2007, Maybin and Miller failed to establish themselves in Florida. The franchise also continued its tradition of trading away cornerstone players as they get expensive, shipping Dan Uggla to the Braves in November for Omar Infante and Mike Dunn.

There were some positives, however. Mike Stanton opened the year with 21 home runs in 192 at-bats in Double-A Jacksonville and smacked another 22 longballs after his promotion to the big leagues. Logan Morrison and Gaby Sanchez also claimed regular spots in the lineup. By season's end, the Marlins often were running out a lineup composed of mostly rookies, leading the majors by using 21 in total.

Several more farmhands should add to the youth movement in 2011. The system's top prospect, Matt Dominguez should take over third base at some point. Scott Cousins, who hit .297 during a September call-up, will get a shot at the center-field job in spring

Mike Stanton showed his power with 43 home runs between the minors and majors

TOP 30 PROSPECTS

1. Matt Dominguez, 3b	**16.** Dan Jennings, lhp
2. Chad James, lhp	**17.** Isaac Galloway, of
3. Christian Yelich, of	**18.** Bryan Petersen, of
4. Jhan Marinez, rhp	**19.** Steve Cishek, rhp
5. Osvaldo Martinez, ss	**20.** Arquimedes Caminero, rhp
6. Brad Hand, lhp	**21.** Sandy Rosario, rhp
7. Scott Cousins, of	**22.** Edgar Olmos, lhp
8. Kyle Skipworth, c	**23.** Omar Poveda, rhp
9. Marcell Ozuna, of	**24.** Jake Smolinski, 3b/of
10. Rob Rasmussen, lhp	**25.** Kevin Cravey, rhp
11. Mike Dunn, lhp	**26.** Noah Perio, ss/2b
12. Jose Ceda, rhp	**27.** Ramon Benjamin, lhp
13. Tom Koehler, rhp	**28.** Robert Morey, rhp
14. Elih Villanueva, rhp	**29.** Brett Hayes, c
15. J.T. Realmuto, c	**30.** Joey O'Gara, rhp

training. Lefties Dunn and Dan Jennings and righties Jhan Marinez, Jose Ceda and Steve Cishek all will factor into the bullpen mix.

Overall, though, the farm system is down in the wake of Florida graduating so many prospects to the big leagues in the last couple of years while taking a conservative approach in recent drafts. Relievers are the strength of the system, which is rarely a good sign. Marinez, Ceda, Arquimedes Caminero, Sandy Rosario, Ramon Benjamin and Josh Hodges all can touch the upper 90s, with Caminero clocked at 101 mph in low Class A last year.

General Manager: Larry Beinfest. Farm **Director:** Brian Chattin. **Scouting Director:** Stan Meek.

Class	Team	League	W	L	PCT	Finish*	Manager
Majors	Florida Marlins	National	80	82	.494	t-8th (16)	Fredi Gonzalez/Edwin Rodriguez
Triple-A	New Orleans Zephyrs	Pacific Coast	66	77	.462	13th (16)	Edwin Rodriguez/Greg Norton
Double-A	Jacksonville Suns	Southern	81	59	.579	†2nd (10)	Tim Leiper
High A	Jupiter Hammerheads	Florida State	46	92	.333	12th (12)	Ron Hassey
Low A	Greensboro Grasshoppers	South Atlantic	66	74	.471	8th (14)	Andy Haines
Short-season	Jamestown Jammers	New York-Penn	43	32	.573	3rd (14)	Dave Berg
Rookie	GCL Marlins	Gulf Coast	37	19	.661	1st (15)	Jorge Hernandez
Overall 2010 Minor League Record			339	353	.490	20th (30)	

*Finish in overall standings (No. of teams in league). †League champion.

LAST YEAR'S TOP 30

Player, Pos.	Status
1. Mike Stanton, of	Majors
2. Logan Morrison, 1b	Majors
3. Chad James, lhp	No. 2
4. Matt Dominguez, 3b	No. 1
5. Gaby Sanchez, 1b/3b	Majors
6. Ryan Tucker, rhp	(Rangers)
7. Kyle Skipworth, c	No. 8
8. Isaac Galloway, of	No. 17
9. Scott Cousins, of	No. 7
10. Jhan Marinez, rhp	No. 4
11. Bryan Petersen, of	No. 18
12. Marcell Ozuna, of	No. 9
13. Dan Jennings, lhp	No. 16
14. Jose Ceda, rhp	No. 12
15. Edgar Olmos, lhp	No. 16
16. Jake Smolinski, 3b	No. 24
17. Brad Hand, lhp	No. 6
18. Chris Leroux, rhp	(Pirates)
19. Bryan Berglund, rhp	Dropped out
20. Tim Wood, rhp	Majors
21. Jorge Jimenez, 3b	(Red Sox)
22. Graham Johnson, rhp	Dropped out
23. Jay Voss, lhp	(Tigers)
24. Brett Sinkbeil, rhp	Dropped out
25. Kris Harvey, rhp	Dropped out
26. Brett Hayes, c	No. 29
27. Curtis Petersen, rhp	Dropped out
28. Jai Miller, of	(Royals)
29. Greg Burns, of	(Free agent)
30. Osvaldo Martinez, ss	No. 5

BEST TOOLS

Best Hitter for Average	Christian Yelich
Best Power Hitter	Marcell Ozuna
Best Strike-Zone Discipline	Osvaldo Martinez
Fastest Baserunner	Kevin Mattison
Best Athlete	Scott Cousins
Best Fastball	Jhan Marinez
Best Curveball	Brad Hand
Best Slider	Dan Jennings
Best Changeup	Jose Alvarez
Best Control	Elih Villanueva
Best Defensive Catcher	Chris Hatcher
Best Defensive Infielder	Matt Dominguez
Best Infield Arm	Osvaldo Martinez
Best Defensive Outfielder	Scott Cousins
Best Outfield Arm	Bryan Petersen

PROJECTED 2014 LINEUP

Catcher	Kyle Skipworth
First Base	Logan Morrison
Second Base	Chris Coghlan
Third Base	Matt Dominguez
Shortstop	Hanley Ramirez
Left Field	Christian Yelich
Center Field	Scott Cousins
Right Field	Mike Stanton
No. 1 Starter	Josh Johnson
No. 2 Starter	Chad James
No. 3 Starter	Ricky Nolasco
No. 4 Starter	Anibal Sanchez
No. 5 Starter	Brad Hand
Closer	Jhan Marinez

TOP PROSPECTS OF THE DECADE

Year	Player, Pos.	2010 Org.
2001	Josh Beckett, rhp	Red Sox
2002	Josh Beckett, rhp	Red Sox
2003	Miguel Cabrera, 3b	Tigers
2004	Jeremy Hermida, of	Athletics
2005	Jeremy Hermida, of	Athletics
2006	Jeremy Hermida, of	Athletics
2007	Chris Volstad, rhp	Marlins
2008	Cameron Maybin, of	Marlins
2009	Cameron Maybin, of	Marlins
2010	Mike Stanton, of	Marlins

TOP DRAFT PICKS OF THE DECADE

Year	Player, Pos.	2010 Org.
2001	Garrett Berger, rhp (2nd round)	Out of baseball
2002	Jeremy Hermida, of	Athletics
2003	Jeff Allison, rhp	Marlins
2004	Taylor Tankersley, rhp	Marlins
2005	Chris Volstad, rhp	Marlins
2006	Brett Sinkbeil, rhp	Marlins
2007	Matt Dominguez, 3b	Marlins
2008	Kyle Skipworth, c	Marlins
2009	Chad James, lhp	Marlins
2010	Christian Yelich, of	Marlins

LARGEST BONUSES IN CLUB HISTORY

Josh Beckett, 1999	$3,625,000
Adrian Gonzalez, 2000	$3,000,000
Livan Hernandez, 1996	$2,500,000
Kyle Skipworth, 2008	$2,300,000
Jason Stokes, 2000	$2,027,000

FLORIDA MARLINS

TOP 2011 ROOKIE: Matt Dominguez, 3b. While his bat is streaky, Dominguez's glove is ready for a close-up, and the position is wide open.

BREAKOUT PROSPECT: Arquimedes Caminero, rhp. He tightened his slider in fall minicamp, giving him a second weapon to complement his 101-mph heat.

SLEEPER: Jheyson Manzueta, rhp. He pairs a lively mid-90s fastball with a potential plus changeup.

SOURCE OF TOP 30 TALENT

Homegrown	26	Acquired	4
College	10	Trades	4
Junior college	1	Rule 5 draft	0
High school	9	Independent leagues	0
Draft-and-follow	0	Free agents/waivers	0
Nondrafted free agents	1		
International	5		

LF
Christian Yelich (3)
Brandon Tripp
Brent Keys
Mark Canha

CF
Scott Cousins (7)
Isaac Galloway (17)
Kevin Mattison
Marquise Cooper
Rand Smith

RF
Marcell Ozuna (9)
Bryan Petersen (18)
Tom Hickman
Kyle Jensen
Nestor Castillo

3B
Matt Dominguez (1)
Jake Smolinski (24)
Chase Austin
Ryan Fisher

SS
Osvaldo Martinez (5)
Jose Torres
Pedro Mendoza
Yefri Perez

2B
Noah Perio (26)
Ryan Curry
Tim Torres
Danny Black
Danny Pertusati
Paul Gran

1B
Vinny Rottino
Aaron Senne
Jaime Ortiz

C
Kyle Skipworth (8)
J.T. Realmuto (15)
Brett Hayes (29)
Brad Davis
Chris Hatcher
Jobduan Morales

RHP

RHSP	RHRP
Tom Koehler (13)	Jhan Marinez (4)
Elih Villanueva (14)	Jose Ceda (12)
Omar Poveda (23)	Steve Cishek (19)
Kevin Cravey (25)	Arquimedes Caminero (20)
Robert Morey (28)	Sandy Rosario (21)
Joey O'Gara (30)	Brett Sinkbeil
Jheyson Manzueta	Pete Andrelczyk
Josh Hodges	Jay Buente
Adalberto Mendez	Corey Madden
Rett Varner	Evan Reed
Bryan Berglund	Zach Dials
Jose Rosario	Garrett Parcell
Graham Johnson	Kris Harvey
Matt Montgomery	Dan Mahoney
Alan Oaks	Todd Doolittle
Kyle Kaminska	Alvaro Estevez
Curtis Petersen	
Jared Rogers	
Austin Brice	
Jared Rogers	

LHP

LHSP	LHRP
Chad James (2)	Mike Dunn (11)
Brad Hand (6)	Dan Jennings (16)
Rob Rasmussen (10)	Ramon Benjamin (27)
Edgar Olmos (22)	Dustin Richardson
Jose Alvarez	Andy Loomis
Beau Wright	Stephen Richards

2010

BEST PURE HITTER: The Marlins drafted OF Christian Yelich (1) 23rd overall because of his bat and compare him favorably at a similar stage to 2002 first-rounder Jeremy Hermida. He has a pure, easy swing, hangs in well against lefthanders and went 17-for-47 (.362) in his debut.

BEST POWER HITTER: Righthanded-hitting OF Mark Canha (7) has power to all fields, with his best pop to right field. He hit four homers in his first 14 games at short-season Jamestown.

FASTEST RUNNER: Raw OF Kentrell Dewitt (13) has well above-average speed, covering 60 yards in 6.5 seconds. He has contact issues to work on, though, after hitting .183 with 32 strikeouts in 93 pro at-bats.

BEST DEFENSIVE PLAYER: Right now, it's 1B Aaron Senne (10), who has arm strength and good actions. Down the line, it should be C J.T. Realmuto (3), a prep shortstop who is moving behind the plate. Scouting director Stan Meek saw a rare catching appearance by Realmuto in high school and saw soft hands, a 1.87-second pop time and natural footwork.

BEST FASTBALL: None of the Marlins' draftees has a jaw-dropping fastball, but there are plenty of above-average ones, led by prep RHP Austin Brice (9) and college RHPs Robert Morey (5), Rett Varner (6) and Alan Oaks (8). Morey and Varner have touched 95, while Oaks and the projectable Brice have hit 94.

BEST SECONDARY PITCH: LHP Rob Rasmussen (2) helped get UCLA to the College World Series with two breaking balls, a plus curveball in the mid-70s and a hard slider that can reach the mid-80s. RHP Mike Ojala (25) also has a nifty curve.

BEST PRO DEBUT: Yelich reached low Class A Greensboro and held his own. Jamestown's 3B/OF Ryan Fisher (15) wasn't an everyday player at UC Irvine, but he led the short-season New York-Penn League in extra-base hits (41) and doubles (24). Jamestown teammate Varner went 4-1, 2.14. RHP Jared Rogers (36) went 6-1, 1.21 in the Rookie-level Gulf Coast League, though he's a 22-year-old collegian.

BEST ATHLETE: Realmuto, a middle-of-the-diamond athlete and a former quarterback. 2B Danny Black (13) has wiry strength and athletic ability in his lean 6-foot-3, 170-pound frame.

MOST INTRIGUING BACKGROUND: Realmuto's uncle John Smith has won five NCAA championships as Oklahoma State's wrestling coach and two Olympic gold medals himself as a wrestler. Unsigned OF Andrew Toles (4) is the son of former NFL linebacker Alvin Toles.

CLOSEST TO THE MAJORS: Rasmussen. The Marlins want him to start, but he'll move even quicker as a lefty specialist thanks to his feel for spinning the ball.

BEST LATE-ROUND PICK: The Marlins love Fisher's bat and have to find a position for him. He's probably ticketed for an outfield corner.

THE ONE WHO GOT AWAY: Toles was the most athletic player the Marlins picked, but they couldn't keep him away from Tennessee. The Marlins also made a run at RHP Randy LeBlanc (16), who took his low-90s fastball to Tulane.

ASSESSMENT: The Marlins once again mined two areas where they've been productive, southern California (Yelich, Rasmussen) and Oklahoma (Realmuto). They went more for college arms than high schoolers, with the exception of Brice.

2009

LHP Chad James (1) had a so-so first full pro season, but he still has frontline-starter potential. RHP Bryan Berglund (2) needed shoulder surgery and has yet to pitch since signing.

GRADE: C

2008

C Kyle Skipworth (1), who was supposed to be an offensive force, has hit .226/.285/.381 as a pro. LHP Brad Hand (2) has passed him as a prospect, and the Marlins scored in the late rounds with RHPs Tom Koehler (18) and Elih Villanueva (27).

GRADE: C

2007

OF Mike Stanton (2) hit 22 homers as a 20-year-old rookie last season. 3B Matt Dominguez (1) is the system's top prospect.

GRADE: A

2006

OF Chris Coghlan (1s) was the 2009 National League rookie of the year. RHP Brett Sinkbeil (1) hasn't panned out as hoped, but he has made it to the big leagues, as have OFs Scott Cousins (3) and John Raynor (9), C Chris Hatcher (5), LHP Graham Taylor (10), SS Osvaldo Martinez (11) and RHPs Jay Buente (14) and Alex Sanabia (32).

GRADE: B

Draft analysis by John Manuel (2010) and Jim Callis (2006-09).
Numbers in parentheses indicate draft rounds.

MATT DOMINGUEZ, 3B

Born: Aug. 28, 1989. **Bats:** R. **Throws:** R.
Height: 6-1. **Weight:** 205. **Drafted:** HS—
Chatsworth, Calif., 2007 (1st round). **Signed
by:** Tim McDonnell.

JERRY HALE

Chatsworth (Calif.) High landed two infielders in the first dozen picks of the 2007 draft, with Mike Moustakas going second overall to the Royals and Dominguez 10 picks later to the Marlins. Florida signed Dominguez away from a Cal State Fullerton scholarship with a $1.8 million bonus. While his high school teammate has grabbled more headlines with his prolific power—Moustakas shared the minor league home run crown in 2010—Dominguez hasn't given the Marlins any reason to regret their selection. He earned MVP honors in the Double-A Southern League all-star game last summer, setting the stage for a strong finish. He batted .301 with 34 RBIs in his final 35 regular-season contests, then his .296 with three homers and eight RBIs in the playoffs to lead Jacksonville to its second consecutive title.

Dominguez stands out most with his Gold Glove ability at the hot corner. Managers have rated him his league's best defensive third baseman in each of the last two years, and he's big league-ready with the glove already. He anticipates well and gets himself in the right position to make plays with quick feet. He scoops the ball with smooth hands, then gets rid of it with strong, accurate throws. Dominguez hasn't been nearly as consistent with the bat. He has struggled throughout his career with breaking pitches and good inside fastballs, but the Marlins noted significant improvement after they made some adjustments to his swing last summer. They dropped his hands from up around his shoulders to a couple of inches lower, and also eliminated a top-hand hiccup that created a hole on the inner half of the plate. The changes gave Dominguez a clearer path to the ball, allowing him to make more consistent contact and drive the ball better. He also showed a more disciplined approach, something Florida has sought from him for years, though he still has room for further improvement. Though he has yet to top the 18 homers he produced at hitter-friendly Greensboro in 2008, Dominguez projects to have average major league power. He drives balls from the left-field line to right-center. A quiet kid who never seems to panic, he avoids emotional ups and downs even as he endures slumps or catches fire. Despite his quickness in the field, Dominguez's speed is well below average and he has tallied just one stolen base in four pro seasons. The third-base job is wide open in Florida, with the likes of Emilio Bonifacio, Ruben Gotay and Wes Helms competing with Dominguez on the depth chart. He still has to prove he can handle upper-level pitching and will get at least a couple of months at Triple-A New Orleans to do so. Often compared to former Marlins all-star and Gold Glover Mike Lowell, Dominguez eventually should end the revolving door Florida has had at the hot corner since trading Miguel Cabrera after the 2007 season.

SCOUTING GRADES

Batting: 50. **Defense:** 70.
Power: 50. **Arm:** 60.
Speed: 30.

Based on 20-80 scouting scale, where 50 represents major league average, and future projection rather than present tools.

Year	Club (League)	Class	AVG	G	AB	R	H	2B	3B	HR	RBI	BB	SO	SB	CS	OBP	SLG
2007	Marlins (GCL)	R	.100	5	20	0	2	0	0	0	2	1	2	0	0	.136	.100
	Jamestown (NYP)	SS	.189	10	37	3	7	2	0	1	4	1	12	0	0	.211	.324
2008	Greensboro (SAL)	LoA	.296	88	345	59	102	16	0	18	70	28	68	0	1	.354	.499
2009	Jupiter (FSL)	HiA	.262	103	381	49	100	25	1	11	53	38	68	1	0	.333	.420
	Jacksonville (SL)	AA	.186	31	97	10	18	7	0	2	9	14	24	0	0	.292	.320
2010	Jacksonville (SL)	AA	.252	138	504	61	127	34	2	14	81	56	96	0	2	.333	.411
Minor League Totals			.257	375	1384	182	356	84	3	46	219	138	270	1	3	.330	.422

2 CHAD JAMES, LHP

Born: Jan. 23, 1991. **B-T:** L-L. **Ht.:** 6-3. **Wt.:** 185. **Drafted:** HS—Yukon, Okla., 2009 (1st round). **Signed by:** Ryan Wardinsky.

James has been the Marlins' top-rated pitching prospect since signing for $1.7 million as the 18th overall pick in the 2009 draft. He made his pro debut in low Class A last year, struggling at times but also showing plenty of upside. His brother Justin is a righthander in the Brewers system. Lefthanders with plus fastballs are always intriguing, and James throws his at 91-95 mph. But what makes him special is his power breaking ball, which comes in with slider velocity and breaks down and hard like a curveball. He also flashes a plus changeup, though it's inconsistent and needs to be utilized more frequently. While James got himself into trouble with walks in 2010, his problems came more from nibbling and not trusting his stuff rather than a true lack of control. He pitched behind in the count too often, allowing hitters to sit on his fastball. His mechanics sometimes go awry, with him clearing his lead arm too quickly or landing too upright. He's slow to the plate and needs to learn a slide step after giving up 33 steals in 24 starts. His arsenal makes him a potential No. 2 starter, but it will be a couple of years before Florida can pencil James in behind Josh Johnson. He should open 2011 at high Class A Jupiter and could move quickly if he starts challenging hitters.

Year	Club (League)	Class	W	L	ERA	G	GS	CG	SV	IP	H	HR	BB	SO	G/A	WHIP	AVG
2010	Greensboro (SAL)	LoA	5	10	5.12	24	24	0	0	114	116	3	65	105	1.42	1.58	.269
Minor League Totals			5	10	5.12	24	24	0	0	114	116	3	65	105	1.42	1.58	.269

3 CHRISTIAN YELICH, OF

BRIAN FLEMING

Born: Dec. 5, 1991. **B-T:** L-R. **Ht.:** 6-4. **Wt.:** 189. **Drafted:** HS—Westlake Village, Calif., 2010 (1st round). **Signed by:** Tim McDonnell.

Yelich comes from the same Westlake High (Westlake Village, Calif.) program that produced big leaguers Matt Franco, Mike Lieberthal and John Snyder, as well as fellow Marlins farmhand Graham Johnson. Yelich produced against top competition in high school and on the showcase circuit, propelling him to the No. 23 overall pick in the 2010 draft. He signed an above-slot $1.7 million deal at the Aug. 16 signing deadline and reached low Class A in his brief pro debut. Yelich has an advanced approach for a high school hitter, with smooth swing mechanics that have elicited comparisons to Will Clark's. He reads pitches well and projects as a high-average hitter with average power. Lefthanders don't bother him. Though Yelich played first base at Westlake, he has slightly above-average speed and moved to left field in pro ball. The Marlins will try him in center field in 2011, though he'll likely settle on a corner. His arm was a question going into the draft, but Florida tweaked his mechanics and believes his throwing can become at least close to average. Yelich will return to Greensboro to begin his first full season. After witnessing how seamlessly he transitioned to pro ball last year, the Marlins won't be afraid to move him should his bat warrant another jump. He should arrive in Florida by 2013.

Year	Club (League)	Class	AVG	G	AB	R	H	2B	3B	HR	RBI	BB	SO	SB	CS	OBP	SLG
2010	Marlins (GCL)	R	.375	6	24	3	9	1	1	0	3	2	7	1	0	.423	.500
	Greensboro (SAL)	LoA	.348	6	23	2	8	2	0	0	2	1	6	0	0	.375	.435
Minor League Totals			.362	12	47	5	17	3	1	0	5	3	13	1	0	.400	.468

4 JHAN MARINEZ, RHP

Born: Aug. 12, 1988. **B-T:** R-R. **Ht.:** 6-1. **Wt.:** 165. **Signed:** Dominican Republic, 2006. **Signed by:** Sandy Nin.

Marinez long has teased the Marlins with a frustrating combination of great stuff and immaturity. He finally reached full-season ball in 2009, his fourth pro season, and continued his ascent last year by making four big league appearances in July before going on the disabled list with an elbow strain. Armed with an explosive four-seam fastball that sits at 92-95 mph and reaches 98, Marinez has the stuff to close games. He exhibits an easy arm action that belies his incredible velocity. He also can mix in a two-seamer with good sink. The key to his success will be the continued development of his slider, which he throws at 88-89 mph. While it took a step forward last year, the slider lacks consistent action. Marinez loses the zone at times and didn't throw strikes in the big leagues like he did in Double-A. He has to prove he can stay healthy, because he has pitched just 168 innings in five seasons and his 45 last year were a career high. He had been resistant to coaching earlier in his career, but was much more willing to listen last year. Marinez was throwing without pain in Florida's minor league minicamp in September. He should be a candidate for ninth-inning duties in the not-too-distant future, though he may open 2011 in Triple-A.

Year	Club (League)	Class	W	L	ERA	G	GS	CG	SV	IP	H	HR	BB	SO	G/A	WHIP	AVG
2006	Marlins (DSL)	R	2	1	7.00	20	2	0	1	36	44	0	26	22	—	1.94	.324

2007	Marlins (GCL)	R	0	0	10.80	3	0	0	0	3	5	0	4	4	—	2.70	.357
	Marlins (DSL)	R	2	3	4.70	5	5	0	0	23	14	1	19	25	—	1.43	.163
2008	Marlins (GCL)	R	1	1	6.11	12	1	0	1	18	21	0	14	18	—	1.98	.296
2009	Jupiter (FSL)	HiA	1	1	3.14	29	0	0	1	43	28	4	20	42	0.69	1.12	.185
2010	Florida (NL)	MAJ	1	1	6.75	4	0	0	0	3	3	1	3	3	0.67	2.25	.273
	Jupiter (FSL)	HiA	0	1	1.42	21	1	0	4	25	12	1	14	44	0.65	1.03	.148
	Jacksonville (SL)	AA	1	0	2.16	15	0	0	6	17	9	1	7	20	0.87	0.96	.164
Major League Totals			1	1	6.75	4	0	0	0	3	3	1	3	3	0.87	2.25	.273
Minor League Totals			7	7	4.31	105	9	0	13	165	133	7	104	175	0.72	1.44	.224

5 OSVALDO MARTINEZ, SS

Born: May 7, 1988. **B-T:** R-R. **Ht.:** 5-10. **Wt.:** 190. **Drafted:** Porterville (Calif.) JC, 2006 (11th round). **Signed by:** Carlos Berroa.

Martinez got a new perspective on life after taking three bullets in a September 2009 drive-by shooting in his native Puerto Rico. After representing the Marlins in the Futures Game last July, he helped Jacksonville capture the Southern League title and earned his first big league callup. He batted .326 in September, with his first hit coming off Chris Carpenter. Martinez sprays line drives from gap to gap with a level swing. He won't hit a lot of home runs, though he does have the strong hands to collect his share of doubles. He profiles as a solid No. 2 hitter because he has excellent hand-eye coordination and controls the strike zone well. More quick than fast, he's was caught nine times in 22 steal attempts last year. At shortstop, Martinez's best asset is his strong arm. He anticipates well and shows good instincts and soft hands. Florida loves his all-around game and the way he doesn't let anything intimidate him. Hanley Ramirez is blocking his path at shortstop, which could push Martinez to second base. At worst, he should be a quality utilityman capable of playing almost anywhere on the diamond. He figures to spend much of 2011 in Triple-A, getting time at other positions to enhance his versatility.

Year	Club (League)	Class	AVG	G	AB	R	H	2B	3B	HR	RBI	BB	SO	SB	CS	OBP	SLG
2006	Marlins (GCL)	R	.263	49	171	21	45	4	1	1	21	19	21	7	4	.335	.316
2007	Jupiter (FSL)	HiA	—	1	0	0	0	0	0	0	0	1	0	0	0	1.000	—
	Jamestown (NYP)	SS	.184	38	114	8	21	5	0	0	6	11	25	8	2	.262	.228
2008	Greensboro (SAL)	LoA	.296	85	304	44	90	11	3	6	29	13	46	5	5	.331	.411
2009	Jupiter (FSL)	HiA	.254	130	433	54	110	16	5	1	45	41	51	16	4	.323	.321
2010	Jacksonville (SL)	AA	.302	130	516	90	156	28	4	5	54	49	64	13	9	.372	.401
	Florida (NL)	MAJ	.326	14	43	8	14	4	1	0	2	4	6	1	0	.383	.465
Major League Totals			.326	14	43	8	14	4	1	0	2	4	6	1	0	.383	.465
Minor League Totals			.274	433	1538	217	422	64	13	13	155	134	207	49	24	.338	.358

6 BRAD HAND, LHP

Born: March 20, 1990. **B-T:** L-L. **Ht.:** 6-2. **Wt.:** 185. **Drafted:** HS—Chaska, Minn., 2008 (2nd round). **Signed by:** Bob Oldis.

A quality athlete who also played football and hockey in high school, Hand became the highest-drafted Minnesota prepster since Joe Mauer when the Marlins made him a second-round pick in 2008. He made steady progress at Jupiter last year, getting promoted to Jacksonville in time for the postseason. He spun 13 scoreless frames in the Southern League playoffs, including a seven-inning, three-hit gem in the finals. All three of Hand's pitches have plus potential, with his hard curveball the most advanced. He delivers it in the upper 70s with 11-to-4 break. The pitch bites away from lefties and he also can back-door it for strikes against righties. He has improved his command of his 91-94 mph fastball, though he needs to utilize it more frequently instead of relying too much on his curve. Florida is working to lengthen Hand's stride, which should add a little velocity to his fastball. He also needs to use his fringy changeup more often and do a better job of holding runners. The Marlins love his moxie and presence on the mound. He needs to learn to hold runners better. Hand will be one of the youngest starters in the Southern League this year at age 21. A potential No. 3 starter, he'll show Florida he's ready when he masters pitch sequences and learns how to set hitters up.

Year	Club (League)	Class	W	L	ERA	G	GS	CG	SV	IP	H	HR	BB	SO	G/A	WHIP	AVG
2008	Marlins (GCL)	R	2	0	2.48	9	7	0	0	33	25	0	11	34	—	1.10	.212
	Jamestown (NYP)	SS	1	2	3.00	3	3	0	0	15	11	0	10	12	—	1.40	.208
2009	Greensboro (SAL)	LoA	7	13	4.86	26	26	0	0	128	130	12	66	122	1.22	1.54	.264
2010	Jupiter (FSL)	HiA	8	8	3.33	26	26	2	0	141	153	10	49	134	1.37	1.44	.278
	Jacksonville (SL)	AA	1	0	3.00	1	1	0	0	6	3	0	3	4	0.44	1.00	.143
Minor League Totals			19	23	3.83	65	63	2	0	322	322	22	139	306	1.26	1.43	.261

7 SCOTT COUSINS, OF

Born: Jan. 22, 1985. **B-T:** L-L. **Ht.:** 6-1. **Wt.:** 195. **Drafted:** San Francisco, 2006 (3rd round). **Signed by:** John Hughes.

A two-way star in college at San Francisco, Cousins has played at every level during his five-year march through the system. He got off to a slow start in 2010 by hitting .210 in April and separating his shoulder when he ran into an outfield wall in May. He rebounded to bat .335/.386/.544 in the second half of the minor league season and performed well during a September callup. Cousins owns average to plus tools across the board. He projects as a .280 hitter with 15-20 homer potential. A streaky hitter, he gets in trouble when he chases pitches outside the zone. He also tends to overthink instead of trusting his natural ability. He credited a tip from veteran Doug Mientkiewicz with helping him solve lefties, against whom he batted .319 last year. Cousins has the speed to steal 20 bases a year and to cover enough ground to play center field. He has plus range and arm strength and the outfield instincts to match. Cameron Maybin's failure to secure Florida's center-field job and his subsequent trade leave the door open for Cousins, though the Marlins say they will try Chris Coghlan there first. He'll have to make more consistent contact to win it. He may have to put some time in as a fourth outfielder first, but he has the tools to be a productive everyday player.

Year	Club (League)	Class	AVG	G	AB	R	H	2B	3B	HR	RBI	BB	SO	SB	CS	OBP	SLG
2006	Jamestown (NYP)	SS	.211	21	90	11	19	1	0	1	6	4	17	3	1	.253	.256
2007	Greensboro (SAL)	LoA	.292	110	421	69	123	25	0	18	74	38	92	16	7	.358	.480
2008	Marlins (GCL)	R	.000	2	6	0	0	0	0	0	0	0	5	0	0	.000	.000
	Jupiter (FSL)	HiA	.304	49	191	35	58	9	2	9	29	20	47	11	3	.370	.513
	Carolina (SL)	AA	.264	27	91	15	24	7	1	1	9	10	28	4	1	.350	.396
2009	Jacksonville (SL)	AA	.263	130	482	60	127	31	11	12	74	42	107	27	9	.323	.448
2010	New Orleans (PCL)	AAA	.285	118	410	74	117	20	5	14	49	32	78	12	4	.336	.461
	Florida (NL)	MAJ	.297	27	37	2	11	2	2	0	2	1	13	0	0	.316	.459
Major League Totals			.297	27	37	2	11	2	2	0	2	1	13	0	0	.316	.459
Minor League Totals			.277	457	1691	264	468	93	19	55	241	146	374	73	25	.337	.452

8 KYLE SKIPWORTH, C

Born: March 1, 1990. **B-T:** L-R. **Ht.:** 6-4. **Wt.:** 205. **Drafted:** HS—Rubidoux, Calif., 2008 (1st round). **Signed by:** Robby Corsaro.

After setting a California high school record with hits in 18 consecutive at-bats, Skipworth landed a $2.3 million deal as the sixth overall pick in the 2008 draft. That offensive prowess was missing until he reeled off a 15-game hitting streak last May while repeating low Class A. He capped a strong first half by homering in the South Atlantic League all-star game but tailed off afterward. The above-average power Skipworth had shown during batting practice finally surfaced during games in 2010, though he continued to strike out in a third of his at-bats. An all-or-nothing hitter, he's tempted too frequently by low breaking balls and high fastballs. His swing is mechanically sound and has good leverage, and he punishes pitches left over the plate. Skipworth has improved behind the dish and he was up to the challenge of handling a staff of high-velocity hurlers at Greensboro. After throwing out only 20 percent of basestealers in 2009, he caught 35 percent last year. His arm is plenty strong and his footwork has gotten better. He does a good job blocking pitches, though he has occasional lapses. He's a below-average runner but not terrible for a catcher. Lefthanded-hitting catchers with plus power are a rarity, so the Marlins will be patient with Skipworth. He'll open the year in high Class A.

Year	Club (League)	Class	AVG	G	AB	R	H	2B	3B	HR	RBI	BB	SO	SB	CS	OBP	SLG
2008	Marlins (GCL)	R	.208	43	159	22	33	6	0	5	21	13	46	2	2	.263	.340
2009	Greensboro (SAL)	LoA	.208	70	264	28	55	14	1	7	37	18	91	1	2	.263	.348
2010	Greensboro (SAL)	LoA	.249	107	397	55	99	17	1	17	59	32	132	1	2	.312	.426
	Jacksonville (SL)	AA	.000	2	7	1	0	0	0	0	0	1	3	0	0	.125	.000
Minor League Totals			.226	222	827	106	187	37	2	29	117	64	272	4	6	.285	.381

9 MARCELL OZUNA, OF

Born: Nov. 12, 1990. **B-T:** R-R. **Ht.:** 6-2. **Wt.:** 190. **Signed:** Dominican Republic, 2008. **Signed by:** Sandy Nin.

A cousin of former Marlins infielder Pablo Ozuna, Marcell opened the 2010 season in Greensboro but lasted only a week before breaking a bone in his left wrist on a play in the outfield. When he healed, he headed to short-season Jamestown, where he set franchise records and led the New York-Penn League with 21 homers and 60 RBIs. Ozuna possesses legitimate corner-outfield power. He can drive a fastball out of the park on a rope and can fight off inside pitches to the opposite field. The problem for him is making contact, as he also topped the NY-P with 94 whiffs. He's starting to understand the strike zone better, but he still has a long ways to go. He'll show patience on some days and swing at anything on others. Ozuna runs well, though as his body fills out he may have just average speed. He's still learning how to steal bases. While he has seen time in center field, his future lies in right, where he should be adequate. He has a plus arm, though it's not always accurate. Ozuna will return to Greensboro and take another shot at full-season ball in 2011. As he advances, he'll see fewer and fewer strikes until he demonstrates a more disciplined approach.

Year	Club (League)	Class	AVG	G	AB	R	H	2B	3B	HR	RBI	BB	SO	SB	CS	OBP	SLG
2008	Marlins (DSL)	R	.279	63	233	33	65	14	0	6	43	23	61	8	1	.335	.416
2009	Marlins (GCL)	R	.313	55	214	32	67	22	0	5	39	22	52	4	2	.377	.486
2010	Greensboro (SAL)	LoA	.160	6	25	3	4	0	0	1	2	2	10	0	0	.222	.280
	Jamestown (NYP)	SS	.267	68	270	53	72	11	2	21	60	17	94	3	1	.314	.556
Minor League Totals			.280	192	742	121	208	47	2	33	144	64	217	15	4	.336	.482

10 ROB RASMUSSEN, LHP

Born: April 2, 1989. **B-T:** R-L. **Ht.:** 5-11. **Wt.:** 170. **Drafted:** UCLA, 2010 (2nd round). **Signed by:** Tim McDonnell.

Rasmussen struggled his first two seasons at UCLA before breaking out in the Cape Cod League in the summer of 2009. Last spring, he helped steer the Bruins to a runner-up finish at the College World Series, where he tossed six shutout innings in the finale. By the time he signed for $499,500 as a second-round pick, he had a tired arm, so the Marlins limited his pro debut to seven innings. Rasmussen won't wow anyone with his 5-foot-11 build, but he has the four-pitch arsenal and dogged determination to succeed. His fastball sits at 90-93 mph, though it takes a backseat to his breaking stuff. He has an above-average slider in the mid-80s, and he also has a cutter that looks similar but doesn't dive as deeply. His over-the-top, mid-70s curveball has two-plane break. He also throws a changeup. Rasmussen has a loose arm and the ball comes out of his hand easily, though he rushes his delivery at times. He improved his command last spring, but it still wavers when his mechanics get out of alignment. Florida has yet to determine Rasmussen's long-term role. His array of pitches serve him well as a starter, but he could move faster as a reliever who could shut down lefties with his breaking balls. He'll likely open his first full pro season in high Class A.

Year	Club (League)	Class	W	L	ERA	G	GS	CG	SV	IP	H	HR	BB	SO	G/A	WHIP	AVG
2010	Greensboro (SAL)	LoA	0	0	1.35	5	0	0	0	7	6	0	2	4	2.50	1.20	.240
Minor League Totals			0	0	1.35	5	0	0	0	7	6	0	2	4	2.50	1.20	.240

11 MIKE DUNN, LHP

Born: May 23, 1985. **B-T:** L-L. **Ht.:** 6-1. **Wt.:** 195. **Drafted:** JC of Southern Nevada, D/F 2004 (33rd round). **Signed by:** Jeff Patterson (Yankees).

Dunn has been traded twice in the last two years. First, he went to the Braves with Melky Cabrera and Arodys Vizcaino in a December 2009 deal that sent Javier Vazquez and Boone Logan to the Yankees. Eleven months later, Atlanta paired him with Omar Infante to get Dan Uggla from the Marlins. Dunn spent most of 2010 in Triple-A while pitching well down the stretch with the Braves and earning a spot on their postseason roster. He's very athletic for a pitcher, not surprising because he spent his first pro season and part of his second as an outfielder in the Yankees system. He became a full-time reliever in 2009 and has produced consistent 91-94 mph heat ever since, peaking at 97. The depth of his hard slider became more consistent last year, giving him a solid second pitch. Dunn's biggest challenge comes in maintaining a consistent delivery and release point. While his athleticism allows him to make corrections, his command deserts him when he gets out of sync. The Marlins always have job openings, and Dunn should fill one as a lefty in their big league bullpen this year.

Year	Club (League)	Class	AVG	G	AB	R	H	2B	3B	HR	RBI	BB	SO	SB	CS	OBP	SLG
2005	Yankees (GCL)	R	.194	24	62	4	12	2	2	0	9	8	16	0	1	.284	.290
	Tampa (FSL)	HiA	.167	28	90	8	15	5	0	0	6	11	28	2	2	.265	.222
2006	Charleston, SC (SAL)	LoA	.086	14	35	7	3	2	0	0	2	8	13	1	1	.256	.143
2010	Gwinnett (IL)	AAA	.000	10	2	0	0	0	0	0	0	0	1	0	0	.000	.000
	Atlanta (NL)	MAJ	.000	25	2	1	0	0	0	0	0	0	1	0	0	.000	.000
Major League Totals			.000	25	2	1	0	0	0	0	0	0	1	0	0	.000	.000
Minor League Totals			.159	76	189	19	30	9	2	0	17	27	58	3	4	.267	.228

Year	Club (League)	Class	W	L	ERA	G	GS	CG	SV	IP	H	HR	BB	SO	G/A	WHIP	AVG
2006	Yankees (GCL)	R	3	0	0.73	11	0	0	4	25	13	0	9	26	—	0.89	.155
	Staten Island (NYP)	SS	0	0	5.68	3	0	0	0	6	3	0	7	7	—	1.58	.125
2007	Charleston, SC (SAL)	LoA	12	5	3.42	27	27	0	0	145	136	14	45	138	—	1.25	.253
2008	Tampa (FSL)	HiA	4	7	4.55	30	22	0	1	125	124	10	58	118	—	1.46	.266
	Trenton (EL)	AA	1	0	0.00	1	0	0	0	2	1	0	1	2	—	1.20	.167
2009	Trenton (EL)	AA	3	3	3.71	26	0	0	2	53	41	3	32	76	1.02	1.37	.211
	Scranton/W-B (IL)	AAA	1	0	2.25	12	0	0	0	20	17	1	14	23	0.95	1.55	.230
	New York (AL)	MAJ	0	0	6.75	4	0	0	0	4	3	1	5	5	0.75	2.00	.200

			W	L	ERA	G	GS	CG	SV	IP	H	HR	BB	SO	G/A	WHIP	AVG
2010	Gwinnett (IL)	AAA	2	0	1.52	38	0	0	7	47	31	1	25	64	1.09	1.18	.183
	Atlanta (NL)	MAJ	2	0	1.89	25	0	0	0	19	15	1	17	27	1.33	1.68	.211
Major League Totals			2	0	2.74	29	0	0	0	23	18	2	22	32	1.33	1.74	.209
Minor League Totals			26	15	3.39	148	49	0	14	423	366	29	191	454	1.03	1.32	.235

12 JOSE CEDA, RHP

Born: Jan. 28, 1987. **B-T:** R-R. **Ht.:** 6-4. **Wt.:** 275. **Signed:** Dominican Republic, 2004. **Signed by:** Felix Francisco/Randy Smith (Padres).

Originally signed by the Padres out of the Dominican Republic in 2004, Ceda moved to the Cubs two years later in a deal for Todd Walker, then came to Florida in a 2008 trade for Kevin Gregg. He sat out the 2009 season while rehabbing from shoulder surgery and threw his first official pitch as Marlins property last June. Though Ceda's fastball scraped 100 mph in the Cubs system, his peak with Florida has been 97 and he usually settles in at 95-96. He complements his heat with a solid-average slider that has good, late break when it's working. He needs to be more consistent with it, however. Ceda also began working on a splitter while rehabbing, though it's not effective yet. Control has been his nemesis, and it really got away from him following his brief big league callup last year. A big-bodied man, he showed more dedication to conditioning in 2010, but his flexibility always will be a concern. Opportunity abounds in the Marlins' bullpen, and Ceda will get every opportunity to win a job this spring. He must prove he can throw his slider for strikes, because his fastball alone isn't enough when big league hitters can sit on it.

Year	Club (League)	Class	W	L	ERA	G	GS	CG	SV	IP	H	HR	BB	SO	G/A	WHIP	AVG
2005	Padres (DSL)	R	4	2	1.50	13	9	2	2	60	38	2	29	83	—	1.12	.174
2006	Padres (AZL)	R	2	0	5.09	8	4	0	0	23	20	1	13	31	—	1.43	.235
	Cubs (AZL)	R	0	0	0.75	5	3	0	0	12	6	0	7	21	—	1.08	.154
	Boise (NWL)	SS	1	0	3.27	3	3	0	0	11	5	1	2	11	—	0.64	.139
2007	Cubs (AZL)	R	0	0	2.45	2	1	0	0	4	2	0	3	3	—	1.36	.182
	Peoria (MWL)	LoA	2	2	3.11	21	6	0	0	46	14	1	31	66	—	0.97	.093
2008	Daytona (FSL)	HiA	2	2	4.80	15	12	0	0	54	41	4	28	53	—	1.27	.212
	Tennessee (SL)	AA	2	1	2.08	22	0	0	9	30	26	2	14	42	—	1.32	.234
2009	Did Not Play—Injured																
2010	Greensboro (SAL)	LoA	0	0	4.50	7	0	0	0	8	7	2	1	5	1.43	1.00	.226
	Jacksonville (SL)	AA	4	1	1.39	27	0	0	6	32	18	2	20	45	0.91	1.18	.168
	Florida (NL)	MAJ	0	0	5.19	8	0	0	0	9	8	1	11	9	0.42	2.19	.242
Major League Totals			0	0	5.19	8	0	0	0	9	8	1	11	9	0.42	2.19	.242
Minor League Totals			17	8	2.88	123	38	2	17	281	177	15	148	360	1.03	1.16	.180

13 TOM KOEHLER, RHP

Born: June 29, 1986. **B-T:** R-R. **Ht.:** 6-3. **Wt.:** 235. **Drafted:** Stony Brook, 2008 (18th round). **Signed by:** Steve Payne.

The fiercely competitive Koehler has turned himself into a prospect since signing for $1,000 as an 18th-rounder out of Stony Brook in 2008. He went 16-2, 2.61 for Jacksonville last season, tying for the minor league lead in victories while being named the Southern League's most outstanding pitcher. He also finished second to Jacksonville teammate Elih Villanueva in the SL ERA race. Though the two prompt natural comparisons because they had similar seasons in Double-A, they differ in style. Koehler has better pure stuff, starting with a fastball that operates at 91-94 mph. It tends to run too true at times, and he needs to command it better down in the zone. The Marlins took away his slider last season and had him throw a cutter instead, and it came on nicely as the year progressed. Koehler also throws a hard spike curveball. His changeup is a work in progress, though it shows flashes of being a plus pitch. Koehler is a workhorse who projects as a back-of-the-rotation starter or long reliever. He should move to Triple-A in 2011, where he'll continue to refine his command and his changeup.

Year	Club (League)	Class	W	L	ERA	G	GS	CG	SV	IP	H	HR	BB	SO	G/A	WHIP	AVG
2008	Jamestown (NYP)	SS	5	5	3.68	15	13	0	0	66	66	0	29	58	—	1.44	.261
2009	Greensboro (SAL)	LoA	5	5	3.20	18	18	0	0	98	88	9	39	82	1.24	1.29	.238
	Jupiter (FSL)	HiA	4	1	3.38	6	6	0	0	35	35	0	9	25	1.11	1.27	.271
2010	Jacksonville (SL)	AA	16	2	2.61	28	28	0	0	159	140	11	46	145	1.03	1.17	.241
Minor League Totals			30	13	3.04	67	65	0	0	358	329	20	123	310	1.11	1.26	.247

14 ELIH VILLANUEVA, RHP

Born: July 26, 1986. **B-T:** R-R. **Ht.:** 6-2. **Wt.:** 235. **Drafted:** Florida State, 2008 (27th round). **Signed by:** Carmen Carcone.

Villanueva battled fellow 2008 late-round steal Tom Koehler on the Southern League pitching leaderboards last year, finishing first in ERA (2.26), innings (179), WHIP (0.96), complete games (four) and shutouts (three). He tied for the minor league lead in the latter two categories, and threw a rain-shortened, five-inning no-hitter against Carolina in mid-August. Villanueva is greater than the sum of his pitches, which play up because he mixes them so well and hits his spots. He attacks hitters with an 88-92 mph fastball that he can locate wherever he wants. Villanueva utilizes two different breaking balls. His 12-to-6 curveball could become an average pitch. He also throws a hard slider, which he can spot in the zone or throw outside of it to induce swings and misses. He gets good action on his changeup, which he keeps down. He's also working on a cutter. The Marlins love Villanueva's fearlessness and winning attitude. He's a dependable strike-thrower, averaging just 1.5 walks per nine innings as a pro, and he has a great feel for pitching. A deceptive wrist wrap in his delivery helps him hide the ball. The caveat is that Villanueva doesn't have a plus pitch, so his ceiling appears to be as a back-of-the-rotation starter or swingman. He already has defied expectations and should open 2011 in Triple-A.

Year	Club (League)	Class	W	L	ERA	G	GS	CG	SV	IP	H	HR	BB	SO	G/A	WHIP	AVG
2008	Marlins (GCL)	R	0	0	3.00	2	1	0	0	6	4	0	0	9	—	0.67	.200
	Jamestown (NYP)	SS	2	1	1.89	5	1	0	0	19	15	2	5	20	—	1.05	.205
	Jupiter (FSL)	HiA	1	0	0.77	4	2	0	0	12	7	0	4	12	—	0.94	.167
2009	Jupiter (FSL)	HiA	9	12	3.47	26	25	2	0	158	159	10	18	110	0.85	1.12	.259
	Jacksonville (SL)	AA	0	1	4.50	2	2	0	0	10	12	0	3	5	1.27	1.50	.293
2010	Jacksonville (SL)	AA	14	4	2.26	28	28	4	0	179	137	15	34	115	0.77	0.96	.212
Minor League Totals			26	18	2.77	67	59	6	0	384	334	27	64	271	0.82	1.04	.232

15 J.T. REALMUTO, C

Born: March 18, 1991. **B-T:** R-R. **Ht.:** 6-1. **Wt.:** 190. **Drafted:** HS—Midwest City, Okla., 2010 (3rd round). **Signed by:** Steve Taylor.

A three-sport standout at Albert High in Midwest City, Okla., Realmuto quarterbacked his football team to the 5-A state championship title in the fall of his senior year, then set national high school records with 88 hits and 119 RBIs last spring. He batted .595 with 28 homers in 42 games. While Realmuto spent most of his prep career at shortstop, the Marlins believe he has the athleticism and leadership to thrive as a catcher. They took him in the third round and signed him for an above-slot $600,000. Realmuto has an unorthodox batting style, crouching deeper than most hitters and holding his bat parallel to the ground. Florida tinkered with him slightly, getting him to start earlier and calming the loading of his hands, but won't overhaul what has worked for him unless he struggles against pro pitching. He projects as a solid-average hitter who should provide at least average power. Defensively, his quick feet and soft hands will serve him well at catcher, as will his strong arm. He's a plus runner and won't be a typical baseclogging catcher. Realmuto has a track record of winning, and his makeup and intelligence should allow him to make a successful transition to catching. The Marlins will use spring training to determine if he's ready for a full-season assignment or should head to Jamestown.

Year	Club (League)	Class	AVG	G	AB	R	H	2B	3B	HR	RBI	BB	SO	SB	CS	OBP	SLG
2010	Marlins (GCL)	R	.175	12	40	2	7	0	0	0	4	7	11	0	1	.298	.175
Minor League Totals			.175	12	40	2	7	0	0	0	4	7	11	0	1	.298	.175

16 DAN JENNINGS, LHP

Born: April 17, 1987. **B-T:** L-L. **Ht.:** 6-3. **Wt.:** 190. **Drafted:** Nebraska, 2008 (9th round). **Signed by:** Bob Oldis.

No relation to the Marlins assistant GM of the same name, Jennings shot to Double-A in his first full pro season in 2009 after moving to the bullpen. He struggled at the outset of last season, pitching too cautiously and issuing 13 walks in his first seven appearances. Once he stopped trying to minimize mistakes and attacked hitters again, he got on a roll that ended when he tested positive for a banned substance in late July and was suspended for 50 games. He blamed an over-the-counter stimulant. Jennings succeeds by mixing a 90-93 mph fastball with a solid slider. He gets a nice, wide angle on his fastball, and he pitches low in the zone with life. He has allowed just three homers in 176 pro innings. He disguises his slider well and gives it different looks for lefties and righties, though he relies on it too much at times. Jennings has been effective against righthanders, allowing him to profile as a possible set-up man and not just a lefty specialist. He has to serve the final 11 games of his suspension at the start of the 2011 season, but could move quickly once he returns.

Year	Club (League)	Class	W	L	ERA	G	GS	CG	SV	IP	H	HR	BB	SO	G/A	WHIP	AVG
2008	Jamestown (NYP)	SS	1	4	3.53	13	13	0	0	59	79	2	18	62	—	1.65	.321
2009	Greensboro (SAL)	LoA	1	2	2.74	34	0	0	0	49	42	1	21	54	2.48	1.28	.237
	Jupiter (FSL)	HiA	0	0	0.00	8	0	0	6	12	5	0	4	13	1.63	0.77	.132
	Jacksonville (SL)	AA	0	0	0.00	3	0	0	0	2	2	0	1	2	2.00	1.80	.286
2010	Jacksonville (SL)	AA	4	2	2.56	37	0	0	0	53	49	0	26	44	2.71	1.42	.257
Minor League Totals			6	8	2.74	95	13	0	6	174	177	3	70	175	2.47	1.42	.269

17 ISAAC GALLOWAY, OF

Born: Oct. 10, 1989. **B-T:** R-R. **Ht.:** 6-2. **Wt.:** 190. **Drafted:** HS—Rancho Cucamonga, Calif., 2008 (8th round). **Signed by:** Robby Corsaro.

The Marlins were excited when Galloway fell to them in the eighth round in 2008, and they signed him to an above-slot $245,000 deal. He hasn't provided much return on the investment so far because he can't stay on the field. A sprained left wrist helped limit him to 83 games in 2009, and last year he got in 100 at-bats before an outfield collision damaged his kidneys and ended his season. Galloway has plenty of raw talent and all of his tools eventually could rate as average or better. His best attribute is his speed, as he's a plus runner who can cover a lot of ground with his long strides. Toss in an average arm and he's built for center field, though he needs more experience to polish up his routes. Galloway has the bat speed to hit for average, but he needs a lot more at-bats to work through his poor strike-zone discipline. He frequently gets himself out by chasing pitches. As he fills out and gets stronger he may have average power, though he hasn't shown it yet. Galloway should be fully healthy in spring training and will return to high Class A in 2011. He's still young at age 21, but he has lost a lot of development time.

Year	Club (League)	Class	AVG	G	AB	R	H	2B	3B	HR	RBI	BB	SO	SB	CS	OBP	SLG
2008	Marlins (GCL)	R	.286	48	199	29	57	13	5	1	23	4	33	4	2	.303	.417
2009	Greensboro (SAL)	LoA	.268	83	340	44	91	24	3	3	30	12	89	15	9	.293	.382
2010	Jupiter (FSL)	HiA	.200	30	100	9	20	3	3	0	6	5	21	4	3	.259	.290
Minor League Totals			.263	161	639	82	168	40	11	4	59	21	143	23	14	.291	.379

18 BRYAN PETERSEN, OF

Born: April 9, 1986. **B-T:** L-R. **Ht.:** 6-0. **Wt.:** 205. **Drafted:** UC Irvine, 2007 (4th round). **Signed by:** Tim McDonnell.

On the heels of a strong Double-A showing in 2009, Petersen went to the Arizona Fall League and finished fourth in the league in batting at .379. He was hitting .290 at New Orleans last May when he earned his first major league callup, but he struggled off the bench in a couple of stints with Florida. His troubles followed him back to Triple-A, as he lost his short, line-drive stroke and became a bit pull-happy. When it's right, it's one of the lowest-maintenance swings in the system, straight to the ball without a lot of wasted movement. A table-setting leadoff man in 2009, Petersen bounced around the order last year. He won't be a big power producer, though he could hit 10-15 homers per season. Despite above-average speed, he has been a poor basestealer, getting nabbed in 16 of 34 attempts the past two years. He can play all three outfield spots, providing above-average range on the corners, and his plus arm is one of the best in the system. Petersen is smart and plays with a lot of intensity. At worst, he should make a fine fourth outfielder. If his swing returns to form, he may become more than that. He'll try to win a job in Florida's outfield in spring training.

Year	Club (League)	Class	AVG	G	AB	R	H	2B	3B	HR	RBI	BB	SO	SB	CS	OBP	SLG
2007	Jamestown (NYP)	SS	.250	57	216	27	54	13	1	5	24	18	53	11	2	.318	.389
2008	Greensboro (SAL)	LoA	.301	79	296	60	89	10	2	19	58	38	74	15	6	.381	.541
	Jupiter (FSL)	HiA	.265	40	155	23	41	5	0	3	12	15	29	7	1	.339	.355
	Carolina (SL)	AA	.351	12	37	5	13	2	0	1	10	5	6	1	2	.409	.486
2009	Jacksonville (SL)	AA	.297	121	431	64	128	15	7	7	49	50	66	13	12	.368	.413
2010	New Orleans (PCL)	AAA	.255	91	322	47	82	13	2	5	27	34	63	5	4	.332	.354
	Florida (NL)	MAJ	.083	23	24	1	2	0	0	0	2	1	6	0	0	.120	.083
Major League Totals			.083	23	24	1	2	0	0	0	2	1	6	0	0	.120	.083
Minor League Totals			.279	400	1457	226	407	58	12	40	180	160	291	52	27	.354	.418

19 STEVE CISHEK, RHP

Born: June 18, 1986. **B-T:** R-R. **Ht.:** 6-6. **Wt.:** 200. **Drafted:** Carson-Newman (Tenn.), 2007 (5th round). **Signed by:** Brian Bridges.

When the Marlins summoned him late last September, Cishek became the first player from Carson-Newman (Tenn.) to reach the majors since Clyde Wright in 1966. Cishek made a good impression with three scoreless outings, retiring 13 of the 15 big leaguers he faced. He throws a 91-94 mph fastball with a lot of sink to induce groundouts. He also can climb the ladder and dial up his velocity with a four-seamer. Tall and gangly, he utilizes a low arm slot that makes him especially tough on righthanders. Cishek's sweeping slider improved significantly last year, developing into a pitch he can use to finish hitters. His fading changeup can become an asset as well, and he needs to use it more often to keep lefthanders honest and be more than just a right-on-right specialist. He's not terribly wild but he needs to throw more strikes to have success against major league hitters. Cishek posted a 4.05 ERA while getting in a little extra work in the Arizona Fall League after the season, laying more groundwork to make Florida's bullpen in 2011.

Year	Club (League)	Class	W	L	ERA	G	GS	CG	SV	IP	H	HR	BB	SO	G/A	WHIP	AVG
2007	Jamestown (NYP)	SS	1	2	1.95	25	0	0	9	32	20	1	19	30	—	1.21	.175
2008	Greensboro (SAL)	LoA	3	5	4.66	50	0	0	2	75	69	8	34	75	—	1.37	.246
2009	Jupiter (FSL)	HiA	3	4	2.84	37	0	0	2	57	36	2	16	45	1.98	0.91	.182
2010	Jupiter (FSL)	HiA	0	6	2.83	26	0	0	4	35	29	0	19	28	1.25	1.37	.223
	Jacksonville (SL)	AA	3	1	4.31	22	0	0	2	31	30	0	10	34	1.17	1.28	.250
	Florida (NL)	MAJ	0	0	0.00	3	0	0	0	4	1	0	1	3	1.25	0.46	.071
Major League Totals			0	0	0.00	3	0	0	0	4	1	0	1	3	1.25	0.46	.071
Minor League Totals			10	18	3.51	160	0	0	19	231	184	11	98	212	1.54	1.22	.219

FLORIDA MARLINS

20 ARQUIMEDES CAMINERO, RHP

Born: June 16, 1987. **B-T:** R-R. **Ht.:** 6-4. **Wt.:** 185. **Signed:** Dominican Republic, 2005. **Signed by:** Fred Ferreira/Marc DelPiano/Enrique Constante.

Caminero was a hot name leading up to the 2009 major league Rule 5 draft, as the Marlins loved his arm but didn't protect him on the 40-man roster. They gambled successfully that he was too raw to stick with a major league club, but they didn't try their luck twice, adding him to the 40-man roster in November. After years of lighting up radar guns, Caminero has started to post results to back up his velocity. Premium arm strength allows him to dial his fastball up to 101 mph, and he typically sits at 95-98 mph. He loves to attack hitters with his fastball, but he needs to develop a consistently effective second pitch. His slider tends to get too big and sweepy or flatten out. He focused on his slider during Florida's minor league minicamp in September and was able to tighten it. Caminero began throwing a splitter in late 2009 to try to combat lefthanders. Command is his biggest problem, because he doesn't repeat his delivery and his arm drops under the ball too frequently. He has trouble maintaining his velocity when he pitches from the stretch. He added a slide step last year to vary his looks with runners on base. The Marlins envision Caminero as a set-up man, and he'd have closer stuff if he could develop a second weapon. After taking six years to graduate from low Class A, he should move faster from this point.

Year	Club (League)	Class	W	L	ERA	G	GS	CG	SV	IP	H	HR	BB	SO	G/A	WHIP	AVG
2005	Marlins (DSL)	R	1	2	5.54	17	0	0	0	26	32	1	23	12	—	2.12	.299
2006	Marlins (DSL)	R	0	1	7.36	18	0	0	2	22	28	0	14	20	—	1.91	.322
2007	Marlins (DSL)	R	2	3	2.83	16	4	0	1	48	36	0	24	48	—	1.26	.209
2008	Marlins (GCL)	R	0	1	1.56	14	0	0	3	17	9	0	11	20	—	1.15	.158
	Jamestown (NYP)	SS	1	0	4.91	6	0	0	0	7	8	0	3	8	—	1.50	.276
	Greensboro (SAL)	LoA	0	0	3.00	1	0	0	0	3	2	1	0	3	—	0.67	.182
2009	Jupiter (FSL)	HiA	0	0	30.86	2	0	0	0	2	7	3	2	2	0.25	3.86	.500
	Jamestown (NYP)	SS	3	1	3.00	15	0	0	0	24	19	1	16	42	0.35	1.46	.218
	Greensboro (SAL)	LoA	0	0	5.65	10	0	0	0	14	16	1	8	17	0.92	1.67	.276
2010	Greensboro (SAL)	LoA	5	2	3.01	48	0	0	3	75	55	4	34	97	1.11	1.19	.200
Minor League Totals			12	10	4.03	147	4	0	9	239	212	11	135	269	0.88	1.45	.236

21 SANDY ROSARIO, RHP

Born: Aug. 22, 1985. **B-T:** R-R. **Ht.:** 6-1. **Wt.:** 170. **Signed:** Dominican Republic, 2004. **Signed by:** Fred Ferreira/Enrique Constante.

Rosario missed most of the 2007 and 2008 seasons with an elbow injury, but he has made up for lost time since. He led minor league full-time relievers with 125 strikeouts in 92 innings last year, when he began the season in low Class A and ended it in Florida. Two of his first three major league pitches left the yard, and he served up hits to the first five Brewers he faced before recording an out. In his next outing he surrendered four hits and a walk before getting hooked. Still, the progress he made was unmistakable. For someone with a 96-97 mph fastball, Rosario throws a ton of strikes—maybe too many. His 125-17 K-BB ratio was exceptional, but he needs to command his fastball better within the strike zone. Someone with his heat shouldn't give up more than a hit per inning. He also flashes a plus slider that reaches 90 mph, but it's inconsistent. It flattens out when he doesn't stay on top of the ball. He'll show a changeup occasionally, but shies away from it because his other pitches are better. While he pitched in a variety of roles last year, even closing for Jacksonville in the Southern League playoffs, Rosario is best suited for the seventh or eighth inning in the big leagues. He should return to Double-A to open 2011.

Year	Club (League)	Class	W	L	ERA	G	GS	CG	SV	IP	H	HR	BB	SO	G/A	WHIP	AVG
2004	Marlins (DSL)	R	3	1	2.89	10	4	0	0	37	34	1	9	32	—	1.15	.239
2005	Marlins (DSL)	R	6	3	1.03	14	4	1	0	44	28	0	10	52	—	0.87	.178
2006	Marlins (GCL)	R	3	2	2.25	10	6	0	0	40	41	0	10	27	—	1.27	.256
2007	Greensboro (SAL)	LoA	0	1	9.82	2	2	0	0	7	11	1	2	7	—	1.77	.355
2008	Greensboro (SAL)	LoA	0	0	13.50	1	1	0	0	2	3	0	3	4	—	3.00	.375
2009	Jamestown (NYP)	SS	4	2	1.70	9	9	0	0	42	48	1	8	41	1.16	1.32	.277
	Greensboro (SAL)	LoA	3	2	5.13	7	7	0	0	40	57	4	6	36	1.28	1.56	.322
2010	Greensboro (SAL)	LoA	7	2	3.60	43	0	0	3	90	92	9	17	122	1.74	1.21	.263
	Jacksonville (SL)	AA	1	0	0.00	1	0	0	0	2	0	0	0	3	—	0.00	.000
	Florida (NL)	MAJ	0	0	54.00	2	0	0	0	1	9	2	1	0	—	10.00	.818
Major League Totals			0	0	54.00	2	0	0	0	1	9	2	1	0	—	10.00	.818
Minor League Totals			27	13	3.10	97	33	1	3	305	314	16	65	324	1.45	1.24	.261

22 EDGAR OLMOS, LHP

Born: April 12, 1990. **B-T:** L-L. **Ht.:** 6-5. **Wt.:** 180. **Drafted:** HS—Van Nuys, Calif., 2008 (3rd round). **Signed by:** Tim McDonnell.

Shoulder problems limited Olmos to four starts in his first two seasons after he signed for $478,000 as a third-round pick in 2008. Finally healthy last year, he made his full-season debut and got in 25 starts at Greensboro, though he averaged less than five innings per outing. A lean, projectable lefty with a loose arm, Olmos throws a lively 89-92 mph fastball. He has thrown two breaking balls in the past, but last year he scrapped his curveball and went with his slider, which can become average if he tightens it up. His changeup is another potential average offering. He relied on it too heavily early in 2010, which cost him some overall arm speed. Olmos' pitches can flatten out when his arm slot wanders, and that usually happens when he slows his tempo down. When he pitches more quickly, he's more likely to keep his arm and get a good downhill plane on his pitches. He must repeat his delivery more consistently, keeping his arm and body working together. Profiling as a No. 4 or 5 starter, Olmos will advance to high Class A this year and work on commanding his fastball so he can pitch deeper into starts.

Year	Club (League)	Class	W	L	ERA	G	GS	CG	SV	IP	H	HR	BB	SO	G/A	WHIP	AVG
2008	Marlins (GCL)	R	0	0	0.00	1	1	0	0	2	2	0	0	5	—	1.20	.250
2009	Marlins (GCL)	R	0	0	0.00	2	2	0	0	5	1	0	2	5	1.67	0.60	.077
	Jamestown (NYP)	SS	0	0	2.25	1	1	0	0	4	3	0	2	4	1.00	1.25	.214
2010	Greensboro (SAL)	LoA	3	9	4.37	25	25	0	0	117	122	9	59	108	1.44	1.54	.271
Minor League Totals			3	9	4.08	29	29	0	0	128	128	9	63	122	1.43	1.49	.263

23 OMAR POVEDA, RHP

Born: Sept. 28, 1987. **B-T:** R-R. **Ht.:** 6-4. **Wt.:** 215. **Signed:** Venezuela, 2004. **Signed by:** Andres Espinosa/Manny Batista (Rangers).

Poveda blew out his elbow in February and had Tommy John surgery during spring training, sidelining him for the entire 2010 season. The Marlins had good scouting reports from the past on Poveda, and figured they were buying low when they got him and relief prospect Evan Reed from the Rangers in a July trade for Jorge Cantu. Prior to his injury, Poveda threw an 88-92 mph fastball, mixing a two-seamer into his repertoire to give him a little more movement. His best pitch is an above-average changeup that he's comfortable throwing to both lefties and righties. He also uses an average downer curveball. Despite striking out better than a hitter per inning in Class A ball in 2007-08, he never has been an overpowering pitcher. His game is throwing strikes and letting his defense work. Poveda impressed the Marlins with his rehab effort following the trade. He was progressing a little ahead of schedule, though he likely won't be ready for the beginning of the 2011 season. He'll return to Double-A when he's back to full strength and projects as a command-oriented No. 4 or 5 starter.

Year	Club (League)	Class	W	L	ERA	G	GS	CG	SV	IP	H	HR	BB	SO	G/A	WHIP	AVG
2005	Rangers (AZL)	R	2	6	5.71	14	9	0	0	52	64	1	12	56	1.50	1.46	.305
2006	Clinton (MWL)	LoA	4	13	4.88	26	26	0	0	149	167	12	37	133	0.84	1.37	.286
	Frisco (TL)	AA	0	1	1.80	1	1	0	0	5	4	0	5	1	1.17	1.80	.222
2007	Clinton (MWL)	LoA	11	4	2.79	21	21	0	0	126	94	10	32	120	0.81	1.00	.208
	Bakersfield (CAL)	HiA	1	2	5.14	5	5	0	0	28	27	4	13	33	0.88	1.43	.250
2008	Bakersfield (CAL)	HiA	4	4	4.47	17	17	0	0	91	82	10	40	97	1.05	1.35	.241
2009	Frisco (TL)	AA	11	5	4.14	22	22	2	0	130	133	11	48	73	1.22	1.39	.263
	Rangers (AZL)	R	0	0	0.00	1	1	0	0	3	2	0	0	2	2.50	0.67	.182
	Oklahoma City (PCL)	AAA	0	1	5.14	1	1	0	0	7	5	0	4	3	0.70	1.29	.208
2010	Did Not Play—Injured																
Minor League Totals			33	36	4.25	108	103	2	0	591	578	48	191	518	1.00	1.30	.257

24 JAKE SMOLINSKI, 3B/OF

Born: Feb. 9, 1989. **B-T:** R-R. **Ht.:** 5-11. **Wt.:** 185. **Drafted:** HS—Rockford, Ill., 2007 (2nd round). **Signed by:** Steve Arnieri (Nationals).

When the Marlins sent Scott Olsen and Josh Willingham to the Nationals in November 2008, they received Emilio Bonifacio, pitching prospect P.J. Dean and Smolinski in return. Smolinski had reconstructive surgery on his left knee just before the trade, so he really wasn't 100 percent until 2010. Florida loves Smolinski's mental and physical toughness, as well as his bat. He has a simple line-drive stroke, though he tends to cut it off, making contact at the expense of power. If he can correct that flaw, he has the strength to hit 15 homers per season. Smolinski's plate discipline took a step back early last year, when he got a little too aggressive and had trouble recognizing breaking pitches. He was much better in the second half, drawing 17 walks and striking out just 21 times in 196 at-bats. Smolinski played left field and second base in the Washington system, but he has spent the bulk of his time at third base with the Marlins. It hasn't been pretty at the hot corner—he has trouble reading balls off the bat and gets eaten up by in-between hops. He has an average arm and average reaction. A move back to left field may be coming soon, and some club officials would like to try him behind the plate. Smolinski's bat will have to carry him, because he has been a liability in the field. He'll move up to Double-A this year.

Year	Club (League)	Class	AVG	G	AB	R	H	2B	3B	HR	RBI	BB	SO	SB	CS	OBP	SLG
2007	Nationals (GCL)	R	.305	28	105	18	32	8	0	1	16	13	24	7	2	.387	.410
2008	Hagerstown (SAL)	LoA	.261	50	184	28	48	12	1	4	22	19	33	1	2	.338	.402
	Nationals (GCL)	R	.111	3	9	0	1	0	0	0	2	1	0	0	0	.200	.111
	Vermont (NYP)	SS	.306	24	98	17	30	8	1	0	9	9	17	4	0	.370	.408
2009	Greensboro (SAL)	LoA	.283	77	279	50	79	25	0	7	31	38	45	2	5	.379	.448
2010	Jupiter (FSL)	HiA	.264	109	405	45	107	27	3	5	51	31	62	8	5	.318	.383
Minor League Totals			.275	291	1080	158	297	80	5	17	131	111	182	22	14	.348	.406

25 KEVIN CRAVEY, RHP

Born: Aug. 15, 1987. **B-T:** R-R. **Ht.:** 6-1. **Wt.:** 180. **Signed:** Texas A&M, NDFA 2010. **Signed by:** Steve Taylor.

Cravey sat out his first season at Texas A&M in 2007 with elbow tendinitis, which finally was resolved by surgery to remove bone spurs. He threw just 12 innings the next spring and lost his scholarship. Instead of transferring, he stayed at A&M to pursue his degree. Cravey spent three months working with pitching guru Ron Wolforth last spring, then drew interest at a Major League Scouting Bureau tryout camp in June by striking out all six hitters he faced. The Marlins signed him as a nondrafted free agent for $1,000, and his stuff makes that investment look like a bargain. Cravey throws a 92-93 mph fastball, touching 95 on occasion. He has experimented with a four-seam fastball, but after walking four batters in his first six pro innings, he switched back to his two-seamer and didn't issue another free pass during the rest of his debut. Cravey's out pitch is a plus curveball with which he can vary the break from 1-to-7 or 2-to-8. He can throw his curve for strikes against lefthanders or bend it out of the zone as a chase pitch against righties. His changeup lags well behind his two main pitches. Though Cravey throws with a somewhat stiff delivery, the ball comes out of his hand easily. He'll likely work as a starter this year to get innings and make up for lost time, but he could move quickly as a reliever.

Year	Club (League)	Class	W	L	ERA	G	GS	CG	SV	IP	H	HR	BB	SO	G/A	WHIP	AVG
2010	Marlins (GCL)	R	3	2	0.76	11	6	0	0	36	30	0	4	35	3.40	0.95	.222
	Jamestown (NYP)	SS	1	0	0.00	3	0	0	0	7	2	0	0	3	6.50	0.29	.087
Minor League Totals			4	2	0.63	14	6	0	0	43	32	0	4	38	3.76	0.84	.203

26 NOAH PERIO, SS/2B

Born: Nov. 14, 1991. **B-T:** L-R. **Ht.:** 6-0 **Wt.:** 170. **Drafted:** HS—Concord, Calif., 2009 (39th round). **Signed by:** John Hughes.

A two-sport star in high school, Perio received more attention for his work as a wide receiver and defensive back in football than for his baseball prowess. Because of his football background and commitment to Texas, he fell in the draft and was leaning toward joining the Longhorns. The Marlins made a late run at him and inked him to a $150,000 deal. The athletic Perio has a solid line-drive stroke to all fields. While he needs to add strength, he has flashed enough raw power to make Florida believe some of his drives will eventually clear the fence. He also has demonstrated good knowledge of the strike zone, and lefthanders don't seem to bother him. Perio has plus speed and went 7-for-7 stealing bases last season. He has the instincts, quickness and soft hands to play shortstop, but his below-average arm may necessitate a move to second base. Perio is ready for full-season ball and should see time at both middle-infield spots at Greensboro in 2011.

Year	Club (League)	Class	AVG	G	AB	R	H	2B	3B	HR	RBI	BB	SO	SB	CS	OBP	SLG
2009	Marlins (GCL)	R	.429	4	14	2	6	1	1	0	5	0	0	1	0	.429	.643
2010	Jamestown (NYP)	SS	.258	59	225	30	58	10	0	0	31	17	25	7	0	.313	.302
Minor League Totals			.268	63	239	32	64	11	1	0	36	17	25	8	0	.319	.322

27 RAMON BENJAMIN, LHP

Born: June 14, 1987. **B-T:** R-L. **Ht.:** 6-2. **Wt.:** 180. **Signed:** Dominican Republic, 2006. **Signed by:** Sandy Nin.

Benjamin missed the 2008 season following shoulder surgery, but he came back with raw stuff that most lefthanders only can dream of. He works at 92-94 mph with his fastball and can reach 95. His hard slider could develop into a plus pitch. It's effective against both lefties and righties, and he shows the ability to put it on the back foot of the latter. Early in his career, Benjamin got by on pure arm strength and often had no idea where the ball was going. His location improved dramatically last year, especially in the second half, as he cleaned up his mechanics. He still has a little violence in his delivery, though, with his head clearing off to the third-base side as he throws. When he gets out of sync, his command suffers. Benjamin is strong and athletic. He's doing a better job of controlling his emotions, though he still doesn't always maintain an even keel. His ceiling is more as a set-up man than a closer, though he definitely has the arsenal to be more than a lefty specialist. He'll turn 24 in 2011, and the Marlins will try to get him to Double-A before the end of the year.

Year	Club (League)	Class	W	L	ERA	G	GS	CG	SV	IP	H	HR	BB	SO	G/A	WHIP	AVG
2006	Marlins (DSL)	R	2	4	5.75	13	7	0	0	41	53	1	17	30	—	1.72	.323
2007	Marlins (GCL)	R	4	3	2.82	16	2	0	0	38	25	0	20	32	—	1.17	.187
2008	Did Not Play—Injured																
2009	Jamestown (NYP)	SS	1	1	3.77	18	0	0	0	29	25	1	11	31	1.27	1.26	.243
	Greensboro (SAL)	LoA	1	0	1.00	6	0	0	0	9	5	0	7	11	0.42	1.33	.147
2010	Greensboro (SAL)	LoA	3	3	3.46	43	0	0	1	68	57	6	34	71	1.12	1.34	.218
Minor League Totals			11	11	3.76	96	9	0	1	184	165	8	89	175	1.07	1.38	.237

28 ROBERT MOREY, RHP

Born: Nov. 27, 1988. **B-T:** R-R. **Ht.:** 6-1. **Wt.:** 185. **Drafted:** Virginia, 2010 (5th round). **Signed by:** Joel Matthews.

A 29th-round pick by the Rays out of high school in 2007, Morey chose to attend Virginia instead. As a sophomore, he handed Stephen Strasburg his only loss of 2009 by striking out nine over six shutout innings in an NCAA regional matchup. A fifth-round pick last June, he signed for $150,000. Morey works with four solid pitches. He gets good downhill plane on his fastball, which runs up to 95 mph but sits more in the low 90s. His sharp mid-80s slider is his best secondary pitch, and he also throws an over-the-top curveball and a promising changeup. His delivery reminds some of Jack Morris because Morey sits down a little and arches his back. His lead arm has a tendency to come up too high. He approached pitching coordinator Wayne Rosenthal about making adjustments after the season, and tweaked his mechanics to keep his shoulders more level. That eagerness exemplifies Morey's makeup and hard-working attitude. He's a good athlete but probably won't add much to his stuff because his smallish frame lacks projection. He should start 2011 in high Class A.

Year	Club (League)	Class	W	L	ERA	G	GS	CG	SV	IP	H	HR	BB	SO	G/A	WHIP	AVG
2010	Greensboro (SAL)	LoA	1	3	3.65	12	12	0	0	44	45	6	12	41	1.35	1.29	.257
Minor League Totals			1	3	3.65	12	12	0	0	44	45	6	12	41	1.35	1.29	.257

29 BRETT HAYES, C

Born: Feb. 13, 1984. **B-T:** R-R. **Ht.:** 6-1. **Wt.:** 205. **Drafted:** Nevada, 2005 (2nd round supplemental). **Signed by:** John Hughes.

Baseball runs in Hayes' blood. His grandfather Tim played in the minor leagues, and his father (also named Tim) was a Royals fourth-round pick in the January 1975 draft, though he never played pro ball. Brett has received cups of coffee in Florida the last two seasons, and he got national attention last August when Nyjer Morgan steamrolled him at the plate, setting off a brawl. Hayes held onto the ball for the out, but he separated his shoulder, ending his season. Defense is his strength and should carve him a niche as a backup catcher. He nabbed 32 percent of basestealers in his big league trial and has a strong, accurate arm. His footwork has improved over the past couple of seasons, and he does a solid job of blocking balls in the dirt. His hitting ability, power and speed are all below average, though he has made strides with his pitch recognition. With John Baker on the mend from Tommy John surgery, Hayes once again will be in the Marlins' catching mix in 2011.

Year	Club (League)	Class	AVG	G	AB	R	H	2B	3B	HR	RBI	BB	SO	SB	CS	OBP	SLG
2005	Marlins (GCL)	R	.417	3	12	2	5	1	0	0	2	0	2	0	1	.417	.500
	Jamestown (NYP)	SS	.239	36	117	11	28	6	1	1	12	12	21	3	3	.313	.333
2006	Greensboro (SAL)	LoA	.245	82	278	39	68	13	1	9	38	29	61	4	3	.321	.396
2007	Jupiter (FSL)	HiA	.338	17	65	10	22	3	1	1	11	9	10	2	3	.413	.462
	Carolina (SL)	AA	.234	74	273	22	64	16	0	3	31	18	51	2	0	.280	.326
2008	Carolina (SL)	AA	.232	54	181	19	42	8	0	6	18	10	43	1	4	.275	.376
	Albuquerque (PCL)	AAA	.293	37	116	21	34	3	1	5	17	4	23	1	1	.331	.466
2009	New Orleans (PCL)	AAA	.240	90	321	27	77	15	0	4	37	20	66	2	0	.281	.324
	Florida (NL)	MAJ	.273	14	11	5	3	1	0	1	2	0	4	0	0	.333	.636
2010	New Orleans (PCL)	AAA	.220	16	59	7	13	3	0	1	5	2	9	0	0	.254	.322
	Jupiter (FSL)	HiA	.217	7	23	6	5	1	0	2	7	4	7	0	0	.333	.522
	Florida (NL)	MAJ	.208	26	77	6	16	6	1	2	6	6	26	0	0	.265	.390
Major League Totals			.216	40	88	11	19	7	1	3	8	6	30	0	0	.274	.420
Minor League Totals			.248	416	1445	164	358	69	4	32	178	108	293	15	15	.302	.367

30 JOEY O'GARA, RHP

Born: April 20, 1988. **B-T:** R-R. **Ht.:** 6-7. **Wt.:** 205. **Drafted:** Indiana, 2009 (31st round). **Signed by:** Kevin Ibach.

The sixth of seven Indiana players drafted in 2009, O'Gara has come on much faster than expected. Signed for $60,000 as a 31st-round pick, he had a rough pro debut and opened 2010 in extended spring training. The Marlins turned to him when they needed an arm in Jupiter in late May, and O'Gara tossed five shutout innings in his first start. What was supposed to be a short-term assignment turned into a permanent job. His fastball has improved from 87-89 mph in college to 90-92 now, with tremendous sink that induces a lot of groundouts. He's working to add a four-seamer to give hitters something else to think about. His slider can become an average pitch, though it tends to flatten out when he doesn't stay on top of it. He telegraphs his changeup at times by slowing down his arm. Many tall pitchers have trouble repeating their delivery, and the 6-foot-7 O'Gara is no exception. An intelligent pitcher and dedicated worker, he has a rubber arm that lends itself to either starting or relieving. He'll remain in the rotation this year in Double-A.

Year	Club (League)	Class	W	L	ERA	G	GS	CG	SV	IP	H	HR	BB	SO	G/A	WHIP	AVG
2009	Jamestown (NYP)	SS	3	4	6.46	15	3	0	0	39	53	4	14	28	1.83	1.72	.338
2010	Jupiter (FSL)	HiA	7	6	3.84	18	16	1	0	96	113	3	19	42	2.30	1.38	.301
Minor League Totals			10	10	4.60	33	19	1	0	135	166	7	33	70	2.16	1.47	.311

Houston Astros

BY JOHN MANUEL

Houston started rebuilding for real in 2010, giving players like Chris Johnson playing time

History will look back at 2010 as a year when the Astros switched directions. Houston began to retool at the major league level and re-emphasized scouting and player development. Most significantly, owner Drayton McLane put the team on the market after the season.

Franchise stalwarts Lance Berkman and Roy Oswalt were the two biggest remaining links to the franchise's lone pennant, won in 2005. But as the Astros got off to a 0-8 start and sat at 17-34 in mid-May under first-year manager Brad Mills, it was the clear the team had no chance to contend. General manager Ed Wade finally was able to convince McLane that it was time to rebuild, and Houston traded both Berkman and Oswalt in July.

Oswalt went first, going to the Phillies for J.A. Happ and two prospects, outfielder Anthony Gose and shortstop Jonathan Villar. Houston immediately spun Gose to the Blue Jays for Brett Wallace. Two days later, Berkman joined the Yankees in exchange for Mark Melancon and minor league infielder Jimmy Paredes. Happ and Melancon bolstered the Astros' pitching staff, Wallace took over at first base for Berkman and Villar and Paredes immediately became two of the system's best prospects.

The trades brought in some much-needed talent to a system slowly climbing out of the hole it dug with a run of poor drafts and a fallow period in Latin America. Combined with the Astros' narrow focus on competing at the major league level and not investing in their future, those factors conspired to drain the system.

While Houston hasn't hit the jackpot yet in three drafts under assistant GM/scouting director Bobby Heck, those drafts have given the system a boost. Jason Castro, Heck's first first-rounder, graduated to the majors in 2010 and has a chance to have an A.J. Pierzynski career. His second selection, righthander Jordan Lyles, has blossomed from a surprise supplemental first-round pick in 2008 to a No. 1 prospect.

Houston had extra picks and emphasized athletes in the 2010 draft. Heck hasn't been afraid to buck the industry consensus, and he did it again by taking outfielder/second baseman Delino DeShields Jr. with the eighth overall pick. DeShields signed for $2.15 million, a club record for a draft pick. The club also gave out its largest amateur bonus ever, landing Dominican outfielder Ariel Ovando for $2.6 million.

The Astros still have much more work to do with their farm system and the major league club, which

TOP 30 PROSPECTS

1.	Jordan Lyles, rhp	16.	Fernando Abad, lhp
2.	Delino DeShields Jr., of/2b	17.	Ross Seaton, rhp
3.	Jonathan Villar, ss	18.	J.B. Shuck, of
4.	Mike Foltynewicz, rhp	19.	Jay Austin, of
5.	Jio Mier, ss	20.	Jorge DeLeon, rhp
6.	J.D. Martinez, of	21.	Ben Heath, c
7.	Jimmy Paredes, inf	22.	Henry Villar, rhp
8.	Tanner Bushue, rhp	23.	Dallas Keuchel, lhp
9.	Austin Wates, of	24.	Kyle Greenwalt, rhp
10.	Ariel Ovando, of	25.	David Carpenter, rhp
11.	Aneury Rodriguez, rhp	26.	Chia-Jen Lo, rhp
12.	Vince Velasquez, rhp	27.	Brian Bogusevic, of/1b
13.	Telvin Nash, of	28.	Jose Altuve, 2b
14.	Mike Kvasnicka, of/3b	29.	Lance Pendleton, rhp
15.	R.J. Alaniz, rhp	30.	Zachary Grimmett, rhp

has had three losing seasons in the last four years. A rotation built around veterans Brett Myers and Wandy Rodriguez and younger arms Happ and Bud Norris holds promise, but the bullpen needs help and the offense ranked 28th in the majors in scoring. Houston wants more production from Castro and Wallace, and hopes third baseman Chris Johnson can build on an impressive half-season big league debut.

Mills showed some managerial acumen; the Astros went 40-33 in the second half and played with more energy than they had under Cecil Cooper, his predecessor. Now Mills needs more young talent to work with.

General Manager: Ed Wade. **Farm Director:** Fred Nelson. **Scouting Director:** Bobby Heck.

Class	Team	League	W	L	PCT	Finish*	Manager
Majors	Houston Astros	National	76	86	.469	12th (16)	Brad Mills
Triple-A	Round Rock Express	Pacific Coast	57	87	.396	16th (16)	Marc Bombard
Double-A	Corpus Christi Hooks	Texas	63	77	.450	7th (8)	Wes Clements
High A	Lancaster JetHawks	California	54	86	.386	9th (10)	Tom Lawless
Low A	Lexington Legends	South Atlantic	71	68	.511	6th (14)	Rodney Linares
Short-season	Tri-City Dust Devils	New York-Penn	38	36	.514	†6th (14)	Jim Pankovits
Rookie	Greeneville Astros	Appalachian	31	35	.470	8th (10)	Ed Romero
Rookie	GCL Astros	Gulf Coast	20	36	.357	15th (15)	Omar Lopez
Overall 2010 Minor League Record			334	432	.436	29th (30)	

*Finish in overall standings (No. of teams in league). †League champion.
Triple-A affiliate changes to Oklahoma City (Pacific Coast) in 2011.

LAST YEAR'S TOP 30

Player, Pos.		Status
1.	Jason Castro, c	Majors
2.	Jiovanni Mier, ss	No. 5
3.	Jordan Lyles, rhp	No. 1
4.	Sammy Gervacio, rhp	Majors
5.	Chia-Jen Lo, rhp	No. 26
6.	Ross Seaton, rhp	No. 17
7.	Tanner Bushue, rhp	No. 8
8.	Jay Austin, of	No. 19
9.	Jon Gaston, of	Dropped out
10.	T.J. Steele, of	Dropped out
11.	Tommy Manzella, ss	Majors
12.	Danny Meszaros, rhp	Dropped out
13.	J.B. Shuck, of	No. 18
14.	Fernando Abad, lhp	No. 16
15.	Matt Nevarez, rhp	Dropped out
16.	Chris Johnson, 3b	Majors
17.	Telvin Nash, of	No. 13
18.	Jonathan Meyer, 3b	Dropped out
19.	Arcenio Leon, rhp	Dropped out
20.	Koby Clemens, c/of	Dropped out
21.	Brian Bogusevic, of	No. 27
22.	Wilton Lopez, rhp	Majors
23.	Evan Englebrook, rhp	(Free agent)
24.	Dallas Keuchel, lhp	No. 23
25.	Collin DeLome, of	Dropped out
26.	Polin Trinidad, lhp	(Cubs)
27.	Henry Villar, rhp	No. 22
28.	Ashton Mowdy, rhp	Dropped out
29.	Brad Dydalewicz, lhp	Dropped out
30.	Kyle Greenwalt, rhp	No. 24

BEST TOOLS

Best Hitter for Average	J.D. Martinez
Best Power Hitter	Telvin Nash
Best Strike-Zone Discipline	J.B. Shuck
Fastest Baserunner	Delino DeShields Jr.
Best Athlete	Delino DeShields Jr.
Best Fastball	Mike Foltynewicz
Best Curveball	R.J. Alaniz
Best Slider	Jordan Lyles
Best Changeup	Jordan Lyles
Best Control	Jordan Lyles
Best Defensive Catcher	Roberto Pena
Best Defensive Infielder	Jonathan Villar
Best Infield Arm	Jonathan Villar
Best Defensive Outfielder	Jon Gaston
Best Outfield Arm	Jon Gaston

PROJECTED 2014 LINEUP

Catcher	Jason Castro
First Base	Brett Wallace
Second Base	Delino DeShields Jr.
Third Base	Chris Johnson
Shortstop	Jonathan Villar
Left Field	J.D. Martinez
Center Field	Michael Bourn
Right Field	Hunter Pence
No. 1 Starter	Jordan Lyles
No. 2 Starter	Wandy Rodriguez
No. 3 Starter	Mike Foltynewicz
No. 4 Starter	Brett Myers
No. 5 Starter	J.A. Happ
Closer	Bud Norris

TOP PROSPECTS OF THE DECADE

Year	Player, Pos.	2010 Org.
2001	Roy Oswalt, rhp	Phillies
2002	Carlos Hernandez, lhp	Rays
2003	John Buck, c	Blue Jays
2004	Taylor Buchholz, rhp	Blue Jays
2005	Chris Burke, 2b	Reds
2006	Jason Hirsh, rhp	Yankees
2007	Hunter Pence, of	Astros
2008	J.R. Towles, c	Astros
2009	Jason Castro, c	Astros
2010	Jason Castro, c	Astros

TOP DRAFT PICKS OF THE DECADE

Year	Player, Pos.	2010 Org.
2001	Chris Burke, 2b	Reds
2002	Derick Grigsby, rhp	Out of baseball
2003	Jason Hirsh, rhp (2nd round)	Yankees
2004	Hunter Pence, of (2nd round)	Astros
2005	Brian Bogusevic, lhp	Astros
2006	Max Sapp, c	Out of baseball
2007	*Derek Dietrich, 3b (3rd round)	Rays
2008	Jason Castro, c	Astros
2009	Jiovanni Mier, ss	Astros
2010	Delino DeShields Jr., 2b/of	Astros

*Did not sign.

LARGEST BONUSES IN CLUB HISTORY

Ariel Ovando, 2010	$2,600,000
Delino DeShields, Jr., 2010	$2,150,000
Chris Burke, 2001	$2,125,000
Jason Castro, 2008	$2,070,000
Max Sapp, 2006	$1,400,000

MINOR LEAGUE DEPTH CHART

HOUSTON ASTROS

TOP 2011 ROOKIE: Aneury Rodriguez, rhp. The Rule 5 pickup could win Houston's No. 5 starter job after taking a step forward in winter ball.

BREAKOUT PROSPECT: Telvin Nash, of. He has the raw power to mash 20-plus homers when he makes his full-season debut at Lexington.

SLEEPER: Jose Perdomo, rhp. He used good command of an 86-92 mph fastball and a four-pitch mix to post a 1.67 ERA in the Rookie-level Gulf Coast League last year.

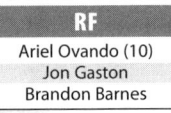

SOURCE OF TOP 30 TALENT			
Homegrown	25	**Acquired**	**5**
College	7	Trades	3
Junior college	0	Rule 5 draft	2
High school	11	Independent leagues	0
Draft-and-follow	0	Free agents/waivers	0
Nondrafted free agents	1		
International	6		

LF
J.D. Martinez (6)
Telvin Nash (13)
J.B. Shuck (18)
Brian Bogusevic (27)
Collin DeLome
Jake Goebbert
Bryce Lane
Jordan Scott

CF
Austin Wates (9)
Jay Austin (19)
T.J. Steele
Daniel Adamson

RF
Ariel Ovando (10)
Jon Gaston
Brandon Barnes

3B
Jimmy Paredes (7)
Mike Kvasnicka (14)
Jonathan Meyer
Yonathan Mejia

SS
Jonathan Villar (3)
Jiovanni Mier (5)
Ben Orloff

2B
Delino DeShields Jr. (2)
Jose Altuve (28)
Josh Magee

1B
Koby Clemens

C
Ben Heath (21)
Federico Hernandez
Roberto Pena
Chris Wallace

RHP

RHSP	RHRP
Jordan Lyles (1)	Jorge DeLeon (20)
Mike Foltynewicz (4)	Henry Villar (22)
Tanner Bushue (8)	David Carpenter (25)
Aneury Rodriguez (11)	Chia-Jen Lo (26)
Vince Velasquez (12)	Lance Pendleton (29)
R.J. Alaniz (15)	Arcenio Leon
Ross Seaton (17)	Enerio del Rosario
Kyle Greenwalt (24)	Danny Meszaros
Zachary Grimmett (30)	Matt Nevarez
Jose Perdomo	Rodney Quintero
Cesar Carrillo	Andrew Robinson
Bobby Doran	
Carlos Quevedo	
Juan Minaya	
Jake Buchanan	

LHP

LHSP	LHRP
Dallas Keuchel (23)	Fernando Abad (16)
Luis Cruz	Pat Urckfitz
Tommy Shirley	
Evan Grills	
Brad Dydalewicz	
Alex Sogard	

2010
BONUSES: $7.3 MILLION

BEST PURE HITTER: The Astros are strong believers in OF/2B Delino DeShields Jr. (1). He has quick hands, lets the ball travel deep and doesn't get out on his front foot. He has shown the ability to catch up to premium fastballs with excellent bat speed. OF Austin Wates (3) has an unorthodox swing but has good timing and barrel awareness.

BEST POWER HITTER: C Ben Heath (5) has above-average raw power and hit 19 home runs this spring to set Penn State's single-season record. He then hit 10 in 210 pro at-bats.

FASTEST RUNNER: DeShields is a true burner and top-of-the-scale runner, getting to first base in less than 4.0 seconds from the right side and turning in 6.3-second 60-yard-dash times.

BEST DEFENSIVE PLAYER: C Roberto Pena (7) shows flashes of plus-plus arm strength and threw out 44 percent of basestealers in his pro debut. He's also intelligent and bilingual, and he has a feel for game-calling.

BEST FASTBALL: RHP Mike Foltynewicz (1) is projectable and touched 96 mph regularly in instructional league. RHP Rodney Quintero (25) reaches 94-95 mph more consistently as a reliever.

BEST SECONDARY PITCH: RHP Vince Velasquez (2) showed a plus changeup before requiring Tommy John surgery after the season. LHP Alex Sogard (26), who has shoulder surgery in his past, has a power curveball with depth.

BEST PRO DEBUT: Heath batted .276/.387/.495 between three stops, including a taste of Double-A Corpus Christi, where he had a pair of three-hit games. LHP Tommy Shirley (9) didn't allow an earned run and struck out 28 in 17 innings at short-season Tri-City before he was shut down with a bone bruise in his right knee. Shirley's fastball reaches 93 mph.

BEST ATHLETE: DeShields, whom Houston intends to move to second base. If he can't handle the infield, he has a chance to be a premium center fielder.

MOST INTRIGUING BACKGROUND: DeShields' father Delino Sr. stole 463 bases in a 13-season major league career and was traded for Pedro Martinez. Pena's dad Bert and 2B Josh Magee's (18) father Wendell were bit players in the majors. Quintero is a Cuban refugee who gained asylum in Chile and became a naturalized U.S. citizen. He played a year of semipro ball in Miami before attending Chipola (Fla.) JC.

CLOSEST TO THE MAJORS: Wates and Heath stand out in a high school-flavored draft.

BEST LATE-ROUND PICK: While scouting Braves second-rounder Todd Cunningham at Jacksonville State, the Astros took a liking to his teammate, 23-year-old OF Daniel Adamson (20). He has present strength, runs well enough to play center field and has plus raw power. If he makes more consistent contact, he'll be a well-rounded player.

THE ONE WHO GOT AWAY: RHP Adam Plutko (6) flashes a plus fastball and curveball, and could blossom at UCLA.

ASSESSMENT: The Astros strayed again from the herd on picks such as DeShields, Foltynewicz and OF/3B Mike Kvasnicka (1s). Velasquez's injury doesn't help in the short term for a youthful class that will need time to pan out.

2009
BONUSES: $4.2 MILLION

SS Jio Mier (1) and RHP Tanner Bushue (2) show promise but will need time to develop. OF J.D. Martinez (20) has been a revelation, winning two batting titles in two pro seasons.

GRADE: C

2008
BONUSES: $6.5 MILLION

C Jason Castro (1) is starting in Houston and showing all-around aptitude. RHP Jordan Lyles (1s) has gone from surprise pick to the system's best prospect, reaching Triple-A at age 19.

GRADE: B+

2007
BONUSES: $1.6 MILLION

An utter disaster. The Astros didn't have picks in the first two rounds and failed to sign SS Derek Dietrich (3), RHP/OF Brett Eibner (4) and RHP Chad Bettis (8), all of whom went in the top two rounds in 2010. OF Collin DeLome (5), the top signee, has stalled, and only RHP Kyle Greenwalt (20) is much of a prospect.

GRADE: F

2006
BONUSES: $3.6 MILLION

Houston found two big league regulars in RHP Bud Norris (4) and 3B Chris Johnson (6). C Max Sapp (1) hit just .224 in three seasons, came down with viral meningitis and was released last spring.

GRADE: C+

Draft analysis by John Manuel (2010) and Jim Callis (2006-09). Numbers in parentheses indicate draft rounds.

JORDAN LYLES, RHP

Born: Oct. 19, 1990. **Bats:** R. **Throws:** R.
Height: 6-4. **Weight:** 185. **Drafted:**
HS—Hartsville, S.C., 2008 (1st round supplemental). **Signed by:** J.D. Alleva/Clarence Johns.

CORPUS CHRISTI HOOKS

Lyles starred in three sports at Hartsville (S.C.) High. While he used his 6-foot-4 frame to start in basketball, Lyles stood out more in baseball and football. As a prep senior, he was an all-state wide receiver who had 81 catches for 1,568 yards and 23 touchdowns. His three-sport background kept him off the baseball showcase circuit, but he entered the spring of 2008 as the top prep prospect in Palmetto State and committed to South Carolina. Coached by 1994 Braves first-round pick Jacob Shumate at Hartsville, Lyles came out of basketball season throwing just 86-88 mph. Astros area scout J.D. Alleva and crosschecker Clarence Johns stayed on him all spring, and Lyles' velocity became more consistent as he got into baseball mode. He clinched Houston's interest with a strong workout at Minute Maid Park, where he hit 90 mph and commanded his fastball well. The Astros drafted him 38th overall and signed him for $930,000. Considered an overdraft at the time, Lyles has made Houston look smart. He has breezed through the minors and was the only teenager to play in the Triple-A Pacific Coast League in 2010.

Lyles has mound presence and a knack for pitching that are beyond his years. He throws four average to plus pitches, and his athleticism, clean arm action and textbook delivery help him throw quality strikes with all of them. His fastball sits at 88-93 mph with average life. He commands it well down in the strike zone and to both sides of the plate. While his fastball grades out as a tick above-average thanks to his command, his slider and changeup are true plus pitches. Scouts prefer his changeup, which he throws with good arm speed and has some depth. At times, it's a 70 pitch on the 20-80 scouting scale. His changeup helped him neutralize lefthanders at Double-A Corpus Christi, though he was hit harder at Triple-A Round Rock. Lyles throws a low-80s slider with depth and also a cutter that reaches as high as 87

mph. He's able to pitch inside well with the fastball and cutter, which helps him saw off hitters and sets up his changeup on the outside corner. Lyles has great body control, allowing him to repeat his delivery and pound the strike zone. He has been durable as a pro, never missing a start and pitching a career-high 159 innings last year.

He may gain a little more fastball velocity as he matures physically, but Lyles doesn't overpower hitters and won't be a power pitcher. He profiles as a No. 3 starter on a major league contender. Manager Brad Mills says Lyles is a leading candidate for the fifth spot in Houston's rotation, competing with journeyman Nelson Figueroa, free-agent signee Ryan Rowland-Smith and Rule 5 draft picks Aneury Rodriguez and Lance Pendleton. Lyles could use some time to solve Triple-A hitters, but he'll pitch in the big leagues in 2011, whether it's in April or later.

SCOUTING GRADES

Fastball: 55. **Command/**
Slider: 60. **Control:** 65.
Changeup: 70. **Delivery:** 70.

Based on 20-80 scouting scale, where 50 represents major league average, and future projection rather than present tools.

Year	Club (League)	Class	W	L	ERA	G	GS	CG	SV	IP	H	HR	BB	SO	G/A	WHIP	AVG
2008	Greeneville (APP)	R	3	3	3.99	13	13	0	0	50	44	4	10	64	—	1.09	.228
	Tri-City (NYP)	SS	0	0	6.35	2	2	0	0	6	7	2	7	4	—	2.47	.292
2009	Lexington (SAL)	LoA	7	11	3.24	26	26	0	0	145	134	5	38	167	1.02	1.19	.247
2010	Corpus Christi (TL)	AA	7	9	3.12	21	20	1	0	127	133	10	35	115	1.27	1.32	.267
	Round Rock (PCL)	AAA	0	3	5.40	6	6	1	0	32	48	2	11	22	1.96	1.86	.348
Minor League Totals			17	26	3.54	68	67	2	0	359	366	23	101	372	1.21	1.30	.262

2 DELINO DESHIELDS JR., OF/2B

MIKE JANES

Born: Aug. 16, 1992. **B-T:** R-R. **Ht.:** 5-9. **Wt.:** 188. **Drafted:** HS—Norcross, Ga., 2010 (1st round). **Signed by:** Lincoln Martin.

Rated by Baseball America's as the top 12-year-old prospect in 2005, DeShields has worn the spotlight that comes with that notoriety and his name for years. His father Delino Sr. played 13 seasons in the majors and was traded straight up for Pedro Martinez in 1993. The son went eighth overall in the 2010 draft—four spots higher than his old man went in 1987—and signed for $2.125 million, a franchise draft record. Few 2010 draftees can match DeShields' athleticism, top-of-the-line speed and sheer explosiveness. He's an 80 runner and should be even more of a basestealing threat than his dad, who swiped 463 bases in the big leagues. His bat speed helps him catch up to the best of fastballs, and he has the strength to project to hit for average power. His swing is fairly low-maintenance and compact. The Astros started DeShields in the center field and intended to move him to second base in instructional league until elbow soreness kept him from throwing. He has a below-average arm, but it's fine for second or center. While his low-energy body language put off some scouts, Houston believes in his makeup. The Astros expect DeShields to be healthy enough to give second base a try in 2011 at low Class A Lexington. His bat will play anywhere. He projects as a leadoff man or possibly a No. 3 hitter.

Year	Club (League)	Class	AVG	G	AB	R	H	2B	3B	HR	RBI	BB	SO	SB	CS	OBP	SLG
2010	Astros (GCL)	R	.111	2	9	3	1	0	0	0	0	1	2	0	0	.200	.111
	Greeneville (APP)	R	.313	16	67	11	21	6	1	0	8	5	18	5	1	.356	.433
Minor League Totals			.289	18	76	14	22	6	1	0	8	6	20	5	1	.337	.395

3 JONATHAN VILLAR, SS

Born: May 2, 1991. **B-T:** B-R. **Ht.:** 6-1. **Wt.:** 180. **Signed:** Dominican Republic, 2008. **Signed by:** Sal Agostinelli (Phillies).

Signed out of the Dominican Republic for $105,000, Villar began blowing up as a prospect when he made his full-season debut last year. The Astros targeted him in the Roy Oswalt trade, securing him as the key piece after general manager Ed Wade saw him play in person. They immediately pushed Villar to high Class A Lancaster after acquiring him. He has impressive raw tools, with his speed, arm and defense all rating ahead of his bat at this point. That's not a huge shock considering he has plus-plus speed and arm strength, and some scouts think his shortstop play will be just as good once he develops. He has excellent range, especially to his left. The game still gets too quick for him at times, which contributed to his 56 errors in 130 games last year. Villar is overly aggressive at the plate, and his swing (especially from the left side) can get long. He has a hitch in his lefthanded stroke and will have to shorten up to make more consistent contact. He doesn't have much power, though it's not an important part of his game. He needs to polish his skills, but Villar has huge upside as a switch-hitting, top-of-the-order disruptor and potential Gold Glove shortstop. With 2009 first-round pick Jio Mier pushing him from behind, he could spend 2011 in Double-A.

Year	Club (League)	Class	AVG	G	AB	R	H	2B	3B	HR	RBI	BB	SO	SB	CS	OBP	SLG
2008	Phillies (DSL)	R	.271	62	214	37	58	6	3	1	21	30	56	27	8	.367	.341
2009	Phillies (GCL)	R	.277	31	94	14	26	7	1	0	14	13	24	11	2	.364	.372
	Williamsport (NYP)	SS	.231	11	39	6	9	1	1	0	5	4	14	6	0	.302	.308
2010	Lakewood (SAL)	LoA	.272	100	371	61	101	18	4	2	36	26	103	38	13	.332	.358
	Lancaster (CAL)	HiA	.225	32	129	18	29	6	2	3	19	12	50	7	2	.294	.372
Minor League Totals			.263	236	847	136	223	38	11	6	95	85	247	89	25	.338	.355

4 MIKE FOLTYNEWICZ, RHP

Born: Oct. 7, 1991. **B-T:** R-R. **Ht.:** 6-4. **Wt.:** 200. **Drafted:** HS—Minooka, Ill., 2010 (1st round). **Signed by:** Troy Hoerner.

Foltynewicz gave up a three-run homer in the afternoon on draft day last June, but got a lift that evening when the Astros made him the first Illinois high school pitcher drafted in the first round since Kris Honel in 2001. They bought him out of a Texas scholarship with a $1.305 million bonus, the second-largest Houston ever has given to a pitcher. While Jordan Lyles is a better overall prospect, Foltynewicz has the best raw arm in the system and flashes three plus pitches. His fastball hit 96 in the spring and sat at 93-96 mph in instructional league, though it dipped into the upper 80s at times during his debut. He has good life on his fastball and pitches aggressively with it. His changeup was his best pitch in his debut, featuring heavy late sink and good arm speed, and it comes out looking like his fastball. Houston tightened up his slurvy breaking ball in instructional league, and if the changes take he'll have a true curveball in the upper 70s. His delivery is fairly clean and his arm works well. Ticketed for low Class A in 2011, Foltynewicz has a high ceiling and just needs innings to improve his feel and command. If he maintains his top-end velocity and improved breaking ball, he could be a future front-of-the-rotation starter.

Year	Club (League)	Class	W	L	ERA	G	GS	CG	SV	IP	H	HR	BB	SO	G/A	WHIP	AVG
2010	Greeneville (APP)	R	0	3	4.03	12	12	0	0	45	46	3	15	39	2.32	1.37	.272
Minor League Totals			0	3	4.03	12	12	0	0	45	46	3	15	39	2.32	1.37	.272

5 JIO MIER, SS

Born: Aug. 26, 1990. **B-T:** R-R. **Ht.:** 6-2. **Wt.:** 175. **Drafted:** HS—Bonita, Calif., 2009 (1st round). **Signed by:** Doug Deutsch.

The first prep shortstop drafted in 2009, Mier signed for $1.358 million, then ranked as the top position prospect in the Rookie-level Appalachian League after hitting .276/.380/.484. His first full pro season was rougher, as he was hitting .199 as late as June 17. He grinded his way through the season, however, batting .260 in the second half and ranking sixth in the low Class A South Atlantic League with 63 walks. Mier draws J.J. Hardy comparisons as a solid athlete with smooth actions and sound fundamental skills at shortstop. He's fairly consistent and projects as a possible plus defender with soft hands and a slightly above-average arm. He controls the strike zone and has average raw power. He has a frame capable of carrying more weight and will have to eat better and get stronger after losing 15 pounds during last season. While Mier has a quick bat when he's right, his slow start led to pressing and a stiff, robotic stroke as he worried about his swing mechanics. He struggled at times with his first serious bout of adversity. He has average speed. The acquisition of Jonathan Villar pushed Mier down the organization's depth chart. Villar is younger but has played at a higher level, and the Astros will separate them in 2011. Mier figures to start the season in high Class A

Year	Club (League)	Class	AVG	G	AB	R	H	2B	3B	HR	RBI	BB	SO	SB	CS	OBP	SLG
2009	Greeneville (APP)	R	.276	51	192	32	53	7	6	7	32	30	45	10	5	.380	.484
2010	Lexington (SAL)	LoA	.235	131	493	83	116	31	1	2	53	63	107	15	7	.323	.314
Minor League Totals			.247	182	685	115	169	38	7	9	85	93	152	25	12	.339	.362

6 J.D. MARTINEZ, OF

Born: Aug. 21, 1987. **B-T:** R-R. **Ht.:** 6-3. **Wt.:** 195. **Drafted:** Nova Southeastern (Fla.), 2009 (20th round). **Signed by:** Greg Brown.

Nova Southeastern had four players drafted in 2009. The Astros had a strong report on Martinez thanks to area scout Greg Brown, who since has become the Fort Lauderdale-based NAIA school's head coach. Martinez signed for $30,000 as a 20th-round pick, then won the short-season New York-Penn League batting title (.326) in his pro debut. He won the South Atlantic League MVP award after leading the league in hitting (.362), on-base percentage (.433) and slugging (.598), and he ranked second overall in the minors in hits (183) while reaching Double-A. A late bloomer physically, Martinez has added 20 pounds since signing, gaining strength for his unorthodox swing. He gets his front foot down early, lays the bat back and then unloads with good natural timing. Despite the front-foot approach, he recognizes pitches, stays back on breaking balls and squares up good pitches. His flat swing path means much of his power is to the gaps, and he projects to hit 35-40 doubles and 15-20 homers annually. He's capable in right field and has an accurate arm but profiles better in left because he has below-average speed and fringy arm strength. Martinez already has moved quickly and will start 2011 back in Double-A. If Houston finds a taker for Carlos Lee's albatross contract, Martinez could provide a high-energy, low-cost replacement. He profiles as a second-division regular.

Year	Club (League)	Class	AVG	G	AB	R	H	2B	3B	HR	RBI	BB	SO	SB	CS	OBP	SLG
2009	Greeneville (APP)	R	.403	19	77	17	31	9	1	5	23	5	14	0	0	.446	.740
	Tri-City (NYP)	SS	.326	53	187	25	61	15	2	7	33	15	30	1	0	.380	.540
2010	Lexington (SAL)	LoA	.362	88	348	83	126	31	3	15	64	33	55	3	0	.433	.598
	Corpus Christi (TL)	AA	.302	50	189	24	57	9	1	3	25	15	42	2	2	.357	.407
Minor League Totals			.343	210	801	149	275	64	7	30	145	68	141	6	2	.404	.553

7 JIMMY PAREDES, INF

Born: Nov. 25, 1988. **B-T:** B-R. **Ht.:** 6-1. **Wt.:** 178. **Signed:** Dominican Republic, 2006. **Signed by:** Victor Mata (Yankees).

Paredes advanced slowly through the Yankees system, in part because of 2008 shoulder surgery that pushed him to the right side of the infield. He showed enough tools in his 2010 full-season debut to be the key prospect the Astros got from New York in the Lance Berkman trade. Paredes ranked second in the South Atlantic League in hits (158) and third in steals (50). Houston has targeted athletes and speed while rebuilding its farm system, and Paredes fits the mold. He's both quick and fast, with an explosive first step and easy plus speed. He already has a feel for stealing bases, getting caught just 11 times last year. A switch-hitter, he has more power and a better swing from the right side. As a lefty, he has a contact-oriented approach and needs to incorporate his lower half more in his swing. Paredes' arm strength has returned to average, and he has decent hands and infield actions. Footwork was a problem for him at second base, and most scouts discount his ability to stay in the middle infield. Some see him as a better fit in center field or as an offensive-minded utilityman. The Astros moved Paredes to third base in instructional league and were pleased with the results, adding him to the 40-man roster. He'll play the hot corner in high Class A this year.

Year	Club (League)	Class	AVG	G	AB	R	H	2B	3B	HR	RBI	BB	SO	SB	CS	OBP	SLG
2007	Yankees1 (DSL)	R	.259	64	266	31	69	14	4	2	42	6	44	5	4	.287	.365
2008	Yankees (GCL)	R	.280	47	161	23	45	9	2	1	15	8	20	6	0	.328	.379
2009	Staten Island (NYP)	SS	.302	54	205	36	62	8	4	2	17	10	30	23	9	.336	.410
2010	Charleston, SC (SAL)	LoA	.282	99	404	59	114	24	6	5	48	18	82	36	10	.312	.408
	Lexington (SAL)	LoA	.299	34	147	24	44	10	1	3	17	7	25	14	1	.331	.442
Minor League Totals			.282	298	1183	173	334	65	17	13	139	49	201	84	24	.315	.399

8 TANNER BUSHUE, RHP

Born: June 20, 1991. **B-T:** R-R. **Ht.:** 6-4. **Wt.:** 180. **Drafted:** HS—Farina, Ill., 2009 (2nd round). **Signed by:** Troy Hoerner.

Bushue split time between baseball and basketball in high school, and his athleticism attracted the Astros. He wasn't expected to be a second-round pick in 2009, but his late helium, projectable frame and flashes of 93-mph heat prompted Houston to jump up and draft him there. Lexington's youngest player for much of 2010, he missed two weeks with a toe injury that required postseason surgery but still led the Legends with 134 innings—and the South Atlantic League with 18 homers allowed. The owner of the system's best curveball, Bushue uses a high arm slot to throw it with plenty of depth. He commands the curve well and misses bats with it. His velocity backed up in his first full season, with his fastball usually sitting at 86-88 mph and his curve operating at 69-73. He'll need to add strength and improve his finish in his delivery to get to the low-90s fastball the Astros and most scouts who saw him as an amateur projected him to have. Bushue has decent feel for his developing changeup. His delivery is fluid and he throws with ease, giving him good control. Houston hopes Bushue's experience, full health and some added strength will lead to improved velocity in 2011. He'll need it as he heads to Lancaster's launching pad.

Year	Club (League)	Class	W	L	ERA	G	GS	CG	SV	IP	H	HR	BB	SO	G/A	WHIP	AVG
2009	Astros (GCL)	R	1	0	2.42	5	5	0	0	22	18	2	5	19	0.96	1.03	.220
2010	Lexington (SAL)	LoA	7	8	4.11	25	25	0	0	134	129	18	48	114	0.83	1.32	.256
Minor League Totals			8	8	3.87	30	30	0	0	156	147	20	53	133	0.85	1.28	.251

9 AUSTIN WATES, OF

Born: Sept. 2, 1988. **B-T:** R-R. **Ht.:** 6-1. **Wt.:** 179. **Drafted:** Virginia Tech, 2010 (3rd round). **Signed by:** Everett Stull.

Wates was an NCAA Division I recruit in soccer as well as baseball, hinting at his athletic ability. He established himself as a prospect by hitting .312 with wood bats in the summer Cape Cod League in 2009. He hit .367 as a three-year starter at Virginia Tech, where he was one of a school-record eight Hokies drafted in 2010, signing for $550,000 as the 90th overall pick. While he played first base and the outfield corners in college, Wates profiles best in center field thanks to his above-average speed and athleticism. His below-average arm is playable in center, and his bat fits better there. Wates has an unorthodox swing that's short but a bit loopy. While he has a knack for barreling balls and uses the entire field, his swing path lends itself to average power at best. He has a polished approach, having developed better patience and improved pitch recognition as he's gained experience. He also has good instincts on the bases. An athlete who can hit, Wates has a chance to be a Shannon Stewart type of offensive player with center-field ability as a bonus. His polish gives him the chance to move quickly, and he could start his first full pro season in high Class A.

Year	Club (League)	Class	AVG	G	AB	R	H	2B	3B	HR	RBI	BB	SO	SB	CS	OBP	SLG
2010	Astros (GCL)	R	.000	1	3	1	0	0	0	0	0	0	2	0	0	.250	.000
	Tri-City (NYP)	SS	.316	12	38	11	12	2	1	1	6	8	6	9	0	.447	.500
Minor League Totals			.293	13	41	12	12	2	1	1	6	8	8	9	0	.431	.463

10 ARIEL OVANDO, OF

Born: Sept. 15, 1993. **B-T:** L-R. **Ht.:** 6-4. **Wt.:** 180. **Signed:** Dominican Republic, 2010. **Signed by:** Felix Francisco.

Houston once owned a virtual monopoly on top Venezuelan talent, but that pipeline dried up when scout Andres Reiner moved on to the Rays. Now the Astros are trying to re-establish themselves in Latin America, which led to signing Ovando for a franchise-record $2.6 million last July. They announced the signing with a lengthy press release comparing him physically to players such as Cliff Floyd, Jason Heyward and Darryl Strawberry. Big money in Latin America often goes to players who show present hitting ability and power, and that describes Ovando. The Astros like his feel for hitting and solid pitch-recognition skills for his age, which make them confident he'll get to his plus raw power. His swing has a lot of movement in it, but Houston believes he can tone that down while maintaining his natural rhythm. His long, lean frame leads to some length and holes in his swing. The Astros project Ovando as a future right fielder, though he has inconsistent throwing mechanics and grades on his arm strength range from below- to above-average. He's a fringe-average runner who should slow down as his body thickens. Ovando had a solid instructional league while facing the best pitching he's ever seen, an encouraging start. He'll begin 2011 in extended spring training before making his pro debut with one of the organization's two Rookie-level teams.

Year	Club (League)	Class	W	L	ERA	G	GS	CG	SV	IP	H	HR	BB	SO	G/A	WHIP	AVG
2010	Did Not Play—Signed 2011 Contract																

11 ANEURY RODRIGUEZ, RHP

Born: Dec. 13, 1987. **B-T:** R-R. **Ht.:** 6-3. **Wt.:** 180. **Signed:** Dominican Republic, 2005. **Signed by:** Felix Feliz (Rockies).

Looking for competition for their No. 5 starter spot, the Astros double-dipped in the major league Rule 5 draft pool, starting with Rodriguez (and followed by Yankees farmhand Lance Pendleton in the second round). He's a good fit for the back of the rotation with a track record for durability. Originally signed by the Rockies, Rodriguez went to the Rays in the spring of 2009 in a trade for Jason Hammel. Rodriguez was once considered a projection righthander but has never filled out physically or added significant velocity. He tends to cut off his delivery and doesn't get enough extension out front. He has become a reliable starter, with four pitches that peak at average and often are fringy. His fastball sat at 88-92 mph last season, but he threw harder in the winter Dominican League, working at 90-91 and touching 93. He throws both a slurvy curveball in the upper 70s, and a mid-80s cutter-type slider. When it's on, the slider stands out as his best secondary pitch, with late tilt. His changeup remains fringy, and he's a flyball pitcher. Rodriguez will compete with Jordan Lyles, almost three years his junior, and veteran Nelson Figueroa for the fifth starter spot. If he doesn't win it, he'll likely be placed on waivers and offered back to the Rays rather than shifted to the bullpen.

Year	Club (League)	Class	W	L	ERA	G	GS	CG	SV	IP	H	HR	BB	SO	G/A	WHIP	AVG
2005	Casper (PIO)	R	3	4	7.55	15	15	0	0	62	77	7	26	47	—	1.66	.309
2006	Tri-City (NWL)	SS	4	4	4.14	15	15	1	0	76	78	2	30	69	—	1.42	.261
2007	Asheville (SAL)	LoA	9	9	5.15	28	28	1	0	152	182	19	48	160	—	1.51	.298
2008	Modesto (CAL)	HiA	9	10	3.74	27	27	2	0	156	148	12	40	139	—	1.20	.251
2009	Montgomery (SL)	AA	9	11	4.50	27	27	1	0	142	122	17	59	111	0.66	1.27	.231
2010	Montgomery (SL)	AA	1	0	2.70	2	2	0	0	10	9	0	2	6	0.91	1.10	.243
	Durham (IL)	AAA	6	5	3.80	27	17	0	0	114	104	10	49	94	0.65	1.35	.240
Minor League Totals			41	43	4.56	141	131	5	0	712	720	67	254	626	0.66	1.37	.262

12 VINCE VELASQUEZ, RHP

Born: June 7, 1992. **B-T:** B-R. **Ht.:** 6-3. **Wt.:** 185. **Drafted:** HS—Garey, Calif., 2010 (2nd round). **Signed by:** Tim Costic/Bobby Heck.

Velasquez would rank in our Astros Top 10 if not for postseason Tommy John surgery, and he's not expected to pitch until instructional league in 2011. While the track record for players recovering from that procedure is strong, Velasquez still has a long rehabilitation road ahead of him. In his brief pro debut, he showed athleticism, a projectable body and good present stuff. A two-way recruit who would have played shortstop and pitched had he made it to Cal State Fullerton, Velasquez signed for $655,830 as a second-round pick last June. He has a fluid delivery and good arm strength, showing average present fastball velocity with more to come. He sat at 88-93 mph after signing, and his curveball has some power as well. He showed an aggressive approach and willingness to attack hitters inside with his fastball. His changeup is advanced for a high school pitcher, especially one with his limited experience, and some scouts grade it as a future plus pitch. He missed much of his junior season with a stress fracture and ligament strain, though he still played shortstop and outfield and even tried throwing lefthanded. Now he'll miss another year of development.

Year	Club (League)	Class	W	L	ERA	G	GS	CG	SV	IP	H	HR	BB	SO	G/A	WHIP	AVG
2010	Greeneville (APP)	R	2	2	3.07	8	6	0	0	29	24	4	5	25	1.11	0.99	.216
Minor League Totals			2	2	3.07	8	6	0	0	29	24	4	5	25	1.11	0.99	.216

13 TELVIN NASH, OF

Born: Feb. 20, 1991. **B-T:** R-R. **Ht.:** 6-2. **Wt.:** 222. **Drafted:** HS—Griffin, Ga., 2009 (3rd round). **Signed by:** Lincoln Martin.

Nash has the best raw power in the organization, and with righthanded power getting harder to find, he has definite value. The 100th overall pick in the 2009 draft, he played with 2008 No. 1 overall pick Tim Beckham at Griffin (Ga.) High and has moved from first base to left field as a pro. He's a below-average runner and has solid arm strength, and he's a fair athlete who played tight end and defensive end in high school football. The Astros plan to keep him in left field as long as possible, and he'll have to commit to himself more to defense for the move to take. His strength plays best at the plate, where he generates good bat speed and has plenty of leverage. Some scouts gave his raw power well above-average grades when he was an amateur, and he ranked fourth in the Rookie-level Appalachian League in home runs. He has some feel for hitting despite his high strikeout totals, and the Astros see him developing into a .250-.260 hitter with 30-homer power. Nash is strong enough to drive the ball to the opposite field but is raw at the plate due to his football focus in high school. He responded well to instruction, especially from outfield and baserunning coordinator Eric Young, who has left the organization to become Arizona's first-base coach. Nash figures to hit in the middle of the order for Lexington in 2011 and may need 2,000 pro at-bats to get it all figured out.

Year	Club (League)	Class	AVG	G	AB	R	H	2B	3B	HR	RBI	BB	SO	SB	CS	OBP	SLG
2009	Astros (GCL)	R	.218	40	142	15	31	10	1	1	20	12	45	1	2	.280	.324
2010	Greeneville (APP)	R	.265	57	200	30	53	12	1	12	39	25	64	1	1	.348	.515
	Tri-City (NYP)	SS	.308	4	13	2	4	1	1	1	1	0	7	0	1	.308	.769
Minor League Totals			.248	101	355	47	88	23	3	14	60	37	116	2	4	.320	.448

14 MIKE KVASNICKA, 3B/OF

Born: Dec. 7, 1988. **B-T:** B-R. **Ht.:** 6-2. **Wt.:** 200. **Drafted:** Minnesota, 2010 (1st round supplemental). **Signed by:** Troy Hoerner.

Kvasnicka was a second-generation Minnesota player and is now a second-generation pro. His father Jay played for the Gophers, was a Twins eighth-round pick in 1988 and topped out in Triple-A. Mike was drafted by the Twins out of high school but went to college instead and became a three-year starter at Minnesota, leading the Big Ten Conference in doubles as a junior. Kvasnicka was an all-conference choice as an outfielder his last two seasons, but as a junior he attracted draft interest at catcher. The Astros drafted him in the supplemental first round and signed him for $936,000 last June. They liked his power potential, athleticism and defensive versatility. He split most of his pro debut between right field and the hot corner, and he also spent five games behind the plate. He's physical and has the strength and bat potential to fit a corner spot. He switch-hits with a sound swing and power from both sides. Kvasnicka started convincing skeptical Astros coaches that he could handle third base in instructional league, as his baseball savvy and work ethic helped him make rapid improvements. His hands and feet work well enough that he should become an average defender, and he has a solid, accurate arm. He has fringy speed but moves well for his size. Kvasnicka profiles well if he can handle third base, so the Astros will watch his defense closely when he makes his full-season debut in low Class A.

Year	Club (League)	Class	AVG	G	AB	R	H	2B	3B	HR	RBI	BB	SO	SB	CS	OBP	SLG
2010	Tri-City (NYP)	SS	.234	68	261	31	61	10	1	5	36	27	48	2	1	.305	.337
Minor League Totals			.234	68	261	31	61	10	1	5	36	27	48	2	1	.305	.337

15 R.J. ALANIZ, RHP

Born: June 14, 1991. **B-T:** R-R. **Ht.:** 6-4. **Wt.:** 175. **Signed:** HS—La Joya, Texas, NDFA 2009. **Signed by:** Rusty Pendergrass.

It's understandable how Alaniz slipped through the cracks of the draft. The tall, projectable righty was injured midway through the 2008 high school season, then a swine flu outbreak in the Rio Grande Valley canceled his 2009 high school baseball season. Alaniz already had made an impression on area scout Rusty Pendergrass, who followed him during the summer as Alaniz tried to make up for lost time by pitching in summer league games at Atlanta's East Cobb complex and various tryouts. He touched 95 mph in the Astros workout Pendergrass set up, and Houston won his services with a $150,000 bonus. Alaniz led Rookie-level Greeneville in wins in his debut and generally dominated with the exception of three awful starts, when he yielded 21 of his 32 runs in eight innings. He showed good life on his fastball, which reached 94 mph after signing and sat at 90-91, and impressed with his ability to locate it. His curveball ranks as the best in a system populated more by sliders than curves. It's an average pitch with depth when he stays on top of it, and it can get better because he has a nice ability to spin it. His changeup has good sink and gives him a third potential average to plus pitch. Alaniz has to be more consistent with his mechanics and release point, but his upside is intriguing. He's set to join the Lexington rotation in 2011.

Year	Club (League)	Class	W	L	ERA	G	GS	CG	SV	IP	H	HR	BB	SO	G/A	WHIP	AVG
2010	Greeneville (APP)	R	6	4	4.21	12	12	0	0	58	65	5	10	42	1.15	1.30	.280
Minor League Totals			6	4	4.21	12	12	0	0	58	65	5	10	42	1.15	1.30	.280

16 FERNANDO ABAD, LHP

Born: Dec. 17, 1985. **B-T:** L-L. **Ht.:** 6-2. **Wt.:** 205. **Signed:** Dominican Republic, 2002. **Signed by:** Julio Linares/Adriano Rodriguez.

Abad is one of the Astros' biggest success stories. It took him seven seasons to get past A-ball, and in 2009 he made three Double-A starts and earned a 40-man roster spot. He followed that up by jumping from Corpus Christi to the major leagues in 2010—despite missing six weeks with a shoulder strain—and finishing the year in the big league bullpen after a brief return to Triple-A. Abad has the fastball command and solid changeup to start, though he's had a hard time staying healthy as a starter. His fastball can touch 93-94 mph and usually operates at 88-91. He has natural deception in his delivery and has maintained looseness in his arm while adding 35 pounds since signing. He has average fastball command and excellent control, with a career walk rate of 1.4 per nine innings in the minors. Abad varies the speed on his slurvy breaking ball, which has inconsistent shape and varies from below average to fringy. He impressed manager Brad Mills in his big league callup, and while he could get a shot at the fifth starter competition, he'll more likely fill a lefty reliever role in Houston.

Year	Club (League)	Class	W	L	ERA	G	GS	CG	SV	IP	H	HR	BB	SO	G/A	WHIP	AVG
2003	Astros (DSL)	R	6	2	1.61	14	14	0	0	78	55	0	7	87	—	0.79	.190
2004	Astros (DSL)	R	4	1	1.29	8	8	0	0	42	24	0	7	39	—	0.74	.155
2005	Astros (DSL)	R	0	0	3.00	1	1	0	0	3	4	0	0	2	—	1.33	.308
2006	Astros (DSL)	R	5	2	1.32	15	11	0	1	61	50	1	7	64	—	0.93	.221
2007	Greeneville (APP)	R	6	4	4.14	17	4	0	1	50	47	6	12	54	—	1.18	.246
	Tri-City (NYP)	SS	0	0	6.00	2	0	0	0	3	2	0	2	5	—	1.33	.182
2008	Lexington (SAL)	LoA	2	7	3.30	45	0	0	3	76	78	9	13	94	—	1.19	.259
2009	Lancaster (CAL)	HiA	4	6	4.14	41	0	0	6	83	78	8	8	79	0.62	1.04	.252
	Corpus Christi (TL)	AA	0	1	3.21	3	3	0	0	14	12	1	3	13	1.08	1.07	.222
2010	Corpus Christi (TL)	AA	4	3	2.50	14	4	0	0	40	48	3	6	33	1.11	1.36	.306
	Round Rock (PCL)	AAA	0	0	1.42	5	0	0	0	6	5	1	2	9	0.67	1.11	.208
	Houston (NL)	MAJ	0	1	2.84	22	0	0	0	19	14	3	5	12	0.50	1.00	.200
Major League Totals			0	1	2.84	22	0	0	0	19	14	3	5	12	0.50	1.00	.200
Minor League Totals			31	26	2.72	165	45	0	11	457	403	29	67	479	0.77	1.03	.233

17 ROSS SEATON, RHP

Born: Sept. 18, 1989. **B-T:** L-R. **Ht.:** 6-4. **Wt.:** 212. **Drafted:** HS—Houston, 2008 (3rd round supplemental). **Signed by:** Rusty Pendergrass/Mike Burns.

Signed for an over-slot $700,000 bonus as a supplemental third-rounder in 2008, Seaton had the unenviable task last season of being the workhorse pitcher for Lancaster, where the wind howls out past the outfield fences and the dry infield is one of the minors' fastest. He had some of the worst numbers in the minor leagues, ranking fourth-worst in ERA and seventh in hits allowed. The Astros admit it's difficult to evaluate players at Lancaster, and Seaton is a fine example. At home, he posted a 9.16 ERA and gave up 16 home runs in 56 innings, with a .387 opponent average. On the road, he allowed six homers in 90 innings and a .283 average. Seaton's stuff was better in 2010 than in his first full season, as his velocity returned to prep levels. His two-seam fastball sat at 90-91 mph, and he ran his four-seamer back to 94. He also maintained his velocity throughout the season, and took every turn for the second straight year. Seaton can spin a breaking ball, and at times his slider has two-plane break, giving him a strikeout pitch. His firm changeup has its moments. Seaton doesn't get a ton of movement on his fastball, and leaves it up in the zone when he doesn't finish off his delivery. He doesn't locate well when he's behind in the count. His delivery got more out of whack out of the stretch, though his numbers were better with runners on base. Seaton is a hard worker and student of the game, and the Astros are encouraged by his velocity. He'd likely return to the high Class A if not for Lancaster's unforgiving environment, but a promotion to Corpus Christi is likely.

Year	Club (League)	Class	W	L	ERA	G	GS	CG	SV	IP	H	HR	BB	SO	G/A	WHIP	AVG
2008	Greeneville (APP)	R	0	0	13.50	3	3	0	0	4	8	1	2	4	—	2.50	.381
2009	Lexington (SAL)	LoA	8	10	3.29	24	24	1	0	137	137	11	39	88	0.90	1.29	.261
2010	Lancaster (CAL)	HiA	6	13	6.64	28	28	0	0	146	198	22	45	85	1.14	1.66	.327
Minor League Totals			14	23	5.14	55	55	1	0	287	343	34	86	177	1.01	1.49	.298

18 J.B. SHUCK, OF

Born: June 18, 1987. **B-T:** L-L. **Ht.:** 5-11. **Wt.:** 197. **Drafted:** Ohio State, 2008 (6th round). **Signed by:** Nick Venuto.

Shuck had a 3.87 ERA in 223 innings at Ohio State and slugged .409 with metal bats as a two-way player, with 34 stolen bases and one home run. His best tool always was his above-average speed, and the Astros drafted him as an outfielder. He has already reached Triple-A and was off to a hot start in the Arizona Fall League (7-for-20) before a knee strain shut him down. Shuck has good bat control and a slashing approach. He has excellent plate coverage and isn't afraid of hitting with two strikes. He has walked more than he has struck out in the minors and has the best strike-zone discipline in the system. He's an above-average runner who has posted sub-4.0 seconds times to first base. Shuck remains an inefficient baserunner who needs to become more aggressive and smarter as a basestealer. His arm is below-average but playable in left or center field. He fits better in left, and the Astros would like to see Shuck work harder on his defense, so they can see if he could handle center long-term. One club official compared his game to that of Dave Roberts, who moved much slower through the minors than Shuck and was a good fourth outfielder on championship-caliber clubs in Cleveland and Boston. Shuck figures to start 2011 back in Triple-A at the Astros' new Oklahoma City affiliate. He should earn a 40-man roster spot after the season, unless he secures one with a big league callup first.

Year	Club (League)	Class	AVG	G	AB	R	H	2B	3B	HR	RBI	BB	SO	SB	CS	OBP	SLG
2008	Tri-City (NYP)	SS	.300	65	263	51	79	12	5	4	24	35	34	8	6	.385	.430
2009	Lancaster (CAL)	HiA	.315	133	556	98	175	30	11	1	36	64	55	18	9	.389	.414
2010	Corpus Christi (TL)	AA	.298	101	389	52	116	14	2	2	28	46	56	9	9	.372	.360
	Round Rock (PCL)	AAA	.273	36	139	15	38	2	2	0	7	16	15	7	3	.348	.317
Minor League Totals			.303	335	1347	216	408	58	20	7	95	161	160	42	27	.380	.391

19 JAY AUSTIN, OF

Born: Aug. 10, 1990. **B-T:** L-L. **Ht.:** 5-11. **Wt.:** 187. **Drafted:** HS—Atlanta, 2008 (2nd round). **Signed by:** Lincoln Martin/Clarence Johns.

Inside and outside the organization, scouts were stunned at the lack of athleticism in Houston's farm system when Bobby Heck took over as scouting director. Starting with his first draft in 2008, Heck has emphasized athleticism, often over instincts, and Austin is perhaps the greatest example of this. Houston signed him away from a Southern California scholarship for a $715,000 bonus, and he remains one of the system's best athletes. However, he has put in two full seasons and remains green, raw and unskilled. His bat has lagged behind as he struggles in many aspects. He remains both undisciplined and poor at pitch recognition. He hasn't picked up bunting yet, nor has he become the student of the game he needs to be. His pure talent has gotten him this far, as he slaps pitches the other way and uses his well above-average speed to beat out hits and steal bases. He led the high Class A California League with 54 steals last season (though he was caught 20 times) and plays a strong center field, with good range that could become better with improved jumps and routes. Austin's arm has backed up as a pro, and is merely fringy though he once hit 90 mph off the mound as an amateur. He's young and his numbers weren't stunning for Lancaster, so he could return there to begin 2011.

Year	Club (League)	Class	AVG	G	AB	R	H	2B	3B	HR	RBI	BB	SO	SB	CS	OBP	SLG
2008	Greeneville (APP)	R	.198	55	212	31	42	4	2	0	14	19	69	14	6	.277	.236
2009	Lexington (SAL)	LoA	.267	101	397	49	106	22	6	1	33	31	78	23	13	.320	.360
2010	Lancaster (CAL)	HiA	.261	131	532	83	139	25	13	10	59	39	126	54	20	.314	.414
Minor League Totals			.252	287	1141	163	287	51	21	11	106	89	273	91	39	.309	.362

20 JORGE DELEON, RHP

Born: Aug. 15, 1987. **B-T:** R-R. **Ht.:** 6-0. **Wt.:** 176. **Signed:** Dominican Republic, 2006. **Signed by:** Sergio Beltre/Julio Linares.

DeLeon was converted to pitching in 2010 and finished the season on the 40-man roster. A shortstop for his first four pro seasons, he hit .213 with just six home runs and 173 strikeouts in 653 at-bats. He showed the biggest arm in the system this year, running his fastball up as high as 98 mph and sitting at 94-96 out of the bullpen. DeLeon dominated the New York-Penn League essentially with one pitch, though he showed more confidence in his short, show-me slider as the season wore on. The Astros stretched DeLeon out late in the season, as he threw 8⅔ innings in his final four outings, including a save in Tri-City's NY-P championship run. There's nothing subtle about DeLeon, who has a quick arm and lets it fly. He's athletic enough to project him to have average control down the line, but his lack of experience could be more exposed as he heads to full-season ball as a pitcher. He could begin the year in low Class A with a chance to skip a level to Corpus Christi if he gets off to a strong start.

Year	Club (League)	Class	AVG	G	AB	R	H	2B	3B	HR	RBI	BB	SO	SB	CS	OBP	SLG
2006	Astros (DSL)	R	.230	56	183	21	42	8	3	3	19	15	57	5	7	.297	.355
2007	Astros (DSL)	R	.190	52	179	23	34	9	3	2	17	15	41	3	3	.298	.307
2008	Greeneville (APP)	R	.235	32	102	16	24	6	2	1	14	6	24	1	2	.297	.363
2009	Lexington (SAL)	LoA	.187	43	123	14	23	5	1	0	9	3	38	2	2	.219	.244
	Tri-City (NYP)	SS	.242	23	66	7	16	4	2	0	7	4	13	1	0	.296	.364
Minor League Totals			.213	206	653	81	139	32	11	6	66	43	173	12	14	.283	.323

Year	Club (League)	Class	W	L	ERA	G	GS	CG	SV	IP	H	HR	BB	SO	G/A	WHIP	AVG
2010	Tri-City (NYP)	SS	2	1	0.64	23	0	0	6	28	26	0	12	29	1.29	1.36	.248
Minor League Totals			2	1	0.64	23	0	0	6	28	26	0	12	29	1.29	1.36	.248

21 BEN HEATH, C

Born: Oct. 7, 1988. **B-T:** R-R. **Ht.:** 6-2. **Wt.:** 220. **Drafted:** Penn State, 2010 (5th round). **Signed by:** Everett Stull.

Heath had hit just three home runs in his first two seasons at Penn State, but he hit 29 in 2010 between college and pro ball. He set a new Penn State single-season record with 19 in the spring, then slammed 10 more in his pro debut after signing for $160,000 as a fifth-round pick. Heath has more raw power than any 2010 Astros draftee despite a fairly unorthodox swing. Even though he's good-sized, he squats (though not quite as low as Jeff Bagwell) and has a lot of pre-swing movement. He has quick, strong hands and the classic high finish most power hitters have, and while he won't hit for a high average, he should get to his power consistently enough to hit 20-25 homers annually. The question is whether he'll be able to stay behind the plate. He doesn't do much pretty back there and has just average arm strength. He threw out 24 percent of basestealers in his first pro summer. His hands and footwork have to improve for him to be an average receiver down the line. He has to learn to call a game and handle a pro pitching staff, and he got a crash course in doing that in his debut. He runs like a typical catcher. Injuries and the Astros' lack of catching depth allowed Heath to finish the season in Double-A. He's likely to head back a step to Class A in 2011, and he could post amazing numbers if he stays at Lancaster for a while.

Year	Club (League)	Class	AVG	G	AB	R	H	2B	3B	HR	RBI	BB	SO	SB	CS	OBP	SLG
2010	Tri-City (NYP)	SS	.248	37	129	20	32	9	0	6	21	20	36	1	0	.365	.457
	Lexington (SAL)	LoA	.290	20	69	9	20	2	2	4	13	11	17	0	1	.405	.551
	Corpus Christi (TL)	AA	.500	4	12	0	6	1	0	0	4	1	3	0	0	.538	.583
Minor League Totals			.276	61	210	29	58	12	2	10	38	32	56	1	1	.387	.495

22 HENRY VILLAR, RHP

Born: May 24, 1987. **B-T:** R-R. **Ht.:** 5-11. **Wt.:** 170. **Signed:** Dominican Republic, 2005. **Signed by:** Julio Linares/Ricardo Aponte.

The 2009 season was Villar's first full season in the United States, and he earned a spot on the 40-man roster in spite of peaking at low Class A. The Astros sped up his development in 2010, opening him in the Corpus Christi bullpen. He moved into the rotation in July after serving as the Hooks' part-time closer, and he finished the season in the big league bullpen. Villar's best pitch is his changeup, which has depth and fade and at times gets mistaken for a splitter. His changeup and solid command of his 86-92 mph sinking fastball help him neutralize lefthanders, who posted a .677 OPS against him in Double-A. At his best, Villar's slider gives him a third average pitch, but it's more of a groundball pitch than a swing-and-miss offering. Righthanders had a .770 OPS against him. The Astros intend to give Villar a shot to start in spring training, and he's a longshot candidate for their fifth starter's job. Considering he's had more success as a reliever than as a starter, it's more likely that he'll earn a bullpen spot in Houston in 2011.

Year	Club (League)	Class	W	L	ERA	G	GS	CG	SV	IP	H	HR	BB	SO	G/A	WHIP	AVG
2006	Astros (DSL)	R	1	1	2.16	13	7	0	0	42	33	1	9	32	—	1.01	.217
2007	Astros (DSL)	R	4	4	2.45	13	13	0	0	73	64	4	12	69	—	1.04	.233
2008	Greeneville (APP)	R	3	6	4.41	13	13	0	0	65	69	6	12	65	—	1.24	.272
2009	Lexington (SAL)	LoA	3	4	2.60	43	3	0	5	90	80	6	18	109	1.41	1.09	.235
2010	Corpus Christi (TL)	AA	4	7	4.15	36	11	0	5	102	95	11	42	68	1.39	1.34	.242
	Houston (NL)	MAJ	0	0	4.50	8	0	0	0	6	5	0	3	3	1.00	1.33	.227
Major League Totals			0	0	4.50	8	0	0	0	6	5	0	3	3	1.00	1.33	.227
Minor League Totals			15	22	3.26	118	47	0	10	372	341	28	93	343	1.40	1.17	.241

23 DALLAS KEUCHEL, LHP

Born: Jan. 1, 1988. **B-T:** L-L. **Ht.:** 6-3. **Wt.:** 200. **Drafted:** Arkansas, 2009 (7th round). **Signed by:** Jim Stevenson.

Keuchel's pedigree suggests he would rank much higher on this list. He was a Friday starter in the Southeastern Conference at Arkansas, and enough of an athlete to be recruited as a quarterback by his hometown college, Tulsa. But he doesn't have the pure stuff to rate as a premium prospect. Keuchel had a successful 2010 season, leading the organization with 174 innings and reaching Double-A. He generates impressive sink on his fastball and changeup, and he gave up just 10 home runs in the hitter-friendly California League—with eight in 58 innings at Lancaster's unforgiving park. His 1.9 walks per nine innings ratio adds to his appeal. The problem is that his fastball has lost velocity since college. He sat at 86-91 mph and touched 93 for the Razorbacks, but his delivery has become stiffer and more mechanical since signing, and he worked at 83-86 in 2010. Keuchel's curveball has been a swing-and-miss pitch at lower levels because he locates it well, but scouts consider it fringy because it breaks early. If he regains velocity and arm speed by improving his tempo and delivery, he should fit at the back of a big league rotation. It's hard to see him continuing to have success otherwise, so the Astros hope his velo bounces back when he returns to Corpus Christi to start 2011.

Year	Club (League)	Class	W	L	ERA	G	GS	CG	SV	IP	H	HR	BB	SO	G/A	WHIP	AVG
2009	Tri-City (NYP)	SS	2	3	2.70	11	10	0	0	57	52	2	9	44	1.60	1.08	.240
2010	Lancaster (CAL)	HiA	5	8	3.36	19	18	3	0	121	129	10	25	97	3.32	1.28	.273
	Corpus Christi (TL)	AA	2	6	4.70	9	9	0	0	54	59	2	11	36	2.76	1.30	.285
Minor League Totals			9	17	3.51	39	37	3	0	231	240	14	45	177	2.59	1.23	.268

24 KYLE GREENWALT, RHP

Born: Sept. 29, 1988. **B-T:** R-R. **Ht.:** 6-0. **Wt.:** 208. **Drafted:** HS—Souderton, Pa., 2007 (20th round). **Signed by:** Ed Edwards.

Greenwalt committed to South Carolina in 2007, part of a recruiting class that helped the Gamecocks win the College World Series in 2010, but he signed with the Astros instead for a $120,000 bonus. He's the only viable member of the Astros' historically thin 2007 draft class, when they lacked a first- or second-round pick and failed to sign their third-, fourth- and eighth-round picks. Greenwalt has never had great success, but he's becoming a durable bulldog on the mound with a back-of-the-rotation ceiling. He threw well in the Arizona Fall League and didn't give up a home run in 15 innings. His fastball will never be a plus pitch, as it sits at 88-91 mph and maxes out at 93, but he gets solid sink on it. His slider and changeup, though, are both plus pitches at times. He has depth to his slider, which helps him get groundballs as well, and sink on his changeup, which most scouts consider his best pitch. He's consistent with his secondary pitches, with decent command of both. His fastball command suffers due to his short arm action and stiff delivery. Greenwalt will report to Double-A and hope to build off his AFL success.

Year	Club (League)	Class	W	L	ERA	G	GS	CG	SV	IP	H	HR	BB	SO	G/A	WHIP	AVG
2007	Greeneville (APP)	R	0	7	7.53	12	8	0	0	35	55	1	12	28	—	1.93	.353
2008	Greeneville (APP)	R	6	4	3.14	13	13	0	0	72	77	2	14	53	—	1.27	.274
	Tri-City (NYP)	SS	1	0	1.50	2	1	0	0	6	3	0	2	5	—	0.83	.143
2009	Lexington (SAL)	LoA	8	13	4.20	25	25	0	0	139	154	7	28	90	1.38	1.31	.278
2010	Lancaster (CAL)	HiA	8	7	5.93	27	27	1	0	137	191	14	42	90	2.15	1.70	.332
Minor League Totals			23	31	4.87	79	74	1	0	388	480	24	98	266	1.70	1.49	.302

25 DAVID CARPENTER, RHP

Born: July 15, 1985. **B-T:** R-R. **Ht.:** 6-2. **Wt.:** 200. **Drafted:** West Virginia, 2006 (12th round). **Signed by:** Brian Hopkins (Cardinals).

Carpenter was a catcher at West Virginia and in his first two years in the minor leagues with the Cardinals. St. Louis shifted him to the mound in the middle of 2008, putting him back in Rookie ball as he learned his new craft. Carpenter has credited Cardinals ace Chris Carpenter (no relation) as well as another catcher-to-pitcher conversion, Jason Motte, with helping him adjust to the mound. He took to pitching quickly, racking up 32 saves in his first two full seasons before St. Louis traded him to Houston for Pedro Feliz last year. Carpenter showed similar stuff after the trade as he had before, with a good fastball and feel for throwing strikes. His fastball and raw arm strength are his biggest weapons, as he reaches 95 mph and sits in the low 90s. Carpenter's breaking ball is a slurvy slider with some power, reaching 81-82 mph at its best. He goes after hitters but lacks command at this point, and he rushes through his delivery. Added to the 40-man roster, he could work into Houston's sixth- or seventh-inning mix by late 2011.

Year	Club (League)	Class	AVG	G	AB	R	H	2B	3B	HR	RBI	BB	SO	SB	CS	OBP	SLG
2006	State College (NYP)	SS	.189	37	111	6	21	4	0	0	9	11	38	1	1	.278	.225
2007	Cardinals (GCL)	R	.000	2	1	0	0	0	0	0	0	0	1	0	0	.000	.000
	Batavia (NYP)	SS	.221	38	131	11	29	9	0	1	8	5	32	1	0	.250	.313
2008	Quad Cities (MWL)	LoA	.280	8	25	3	7	1	1	0	5	5	6	0	0	.400	.400
	Palm Beach (FSL)	HiA	.175	12	40	4	7	3	0	1	3	1	12	0	0	.190	.325
Minor League Totals			.208	97	308	24	64	17	1	2	25	22	89	2	1	.266	.289

Year	Club (League)	Class	W	L	ERA	G	GS	CG	SV	IP	H	HR	BB	SO	G/A	WHIP	AVG
2008	Cardinals (GCL)	R	0	0	1.04	9	0	0	3	9	9	0	6	9	—	1.73	.281
	Johnson City (APP)	R	0	0	3.00	6	0	0	0	6	7	1	1	8	—	1.33	.280
2009	Quad Cities (MWL)	LoA	5	3	4.28	52	0	0	12	67	61	2	36	77	0.75	1.44	.244
2010	Palm Beach (FSL)	HiA	5	3	2.36	49	0	0	20	53	45	3	15	50	1.04	1.13	.227
	Lancaster (CAL)	HiA	1	1	3.52	6	0	0	0	8	8	0	4	8	0.88	1.57	.267
Minor League Totals			11	7	3.27	122	0	0	35	143	130	6	62	152	0.87	1.34	.243

26 CHIA-JEN LO, RHP

Born: April 7, 1986. **B-T:** R-R. **Ht.:** 5-11. **Wt.:** 181. **Signed:** Taiwan, 2008. **Signed by:** Glen Barker.

The Astros know they still have a long way to go to rebuild the farm system and have cast a wide net to find talent. They signed Lo at age 22 out of Taiwan in 2008 for $250,000, after he put together a distinguished career on Taiwan's national teams, including the 2008 Olympic squad and World Baseball Classic roster in 2009. Lo has worked in relief exclusively since signing but missed almost all of the 2010 season with a partial tear of the ulnar collateral ligament in his elbow. He threw his last pitch that counts on April 30. Lo tried to get back on the field with rehabilitation and rest but wasn't ready to let it fly. Astros officials say he'll be ready by spring training, and he never had surgery. When he was healthy, Lo reached 96 mph with his fastball, though it was fairly straight from a high three-quarters arm slot. He had more movement when his fastball ranged from 88-93 mph, and he had plenty of confidence in his heater. He made progress in spring training using his hard, upper 70s curveball more, and it has potential to be an average or better big league pitch. Lo's changeup is more for show than anything, and he's strictly a relief option. Houston's bullpen is wide open, and if healthy Lo could work into that equation with a strong start.

Year	Club (League)	Class	W	L	ERA	G	GS	CG	SV	IP	H	HR	BB	SO	G/A	WHIP	AVG
2009	Lancaster (CAL)	HiA	1	0	1.78	12	0	0	1	25	10	1	13	36	1.24	0.91	.120
	Corpus Christi (TL)	AA	0	2	2.31	30	0	0	2	39	30	1	20	39	1.03	1.28	.213
2010	Corpus Christi (TL)	AA	0	1	1.80	7	0	0	0	15	9	0	10	13	0.55	1.27	.176
Minor League Totals			1	3	2.04	49	0	0	3	79	49	2	43	88	0.95	1.16	.178

27 BRIAN BOGUSEVIC, OF/1B

Born: Feb. 18, 1984. **B-T:** L-L. **Ht.:** 6-3. **Wt.:** 210. **Drafted:** Tulane, 2005 (1st round). **Signed by:** Mike Rosamond.

Bogusevic completed the journey from first-round pitcher to big league hitter in 2010, reaching Houston in a September callup. He'll never have a conventional first-round pick's ceiling, but he has a chance to become a useful big league reserve along the lines of John Mabry. A star for Tulane's top-ranked 2005 team as a two-way player, Bogusevic returned to first base in 2010 and should be an average defender there. His average speed and plus arm, a natural carryover from his pitching days, leave him capable in all three outfield spots, ideal for a fourth outfielder. Now he just has to hit his way there. Bogusevic has a quick bat but doesn't have enough strength or loft in his swing to hit for more than below-average power. He has a contact approach yet still strikes out too much, in part because he's willing to work deep counts. His instincts are good for a conversion project, and he's an efficient basestealer and handles lefthanders well (.851 OPS, vs. .752 against righthanders). The total package should allow Bogusevic to carve out a career as a useful reserve in Houston, starting in 2011.

Year	Club (League)	Class	W	L	ERA	G	GS	CG	SV	IP	H	HR	BB	SO	G/A	WHIP	AVG
2005	Tri-City (NYP)	SS	0	2	7.59	13	0	0	3	21	30	2	9	17	—	1.83	.316
2006	Tri-City (NYP)	SS	0	0	4.09	3	3	0	0	11	10	1	5	6	—	1.36	.233
	Lexington (SAL)	LoA	2	5	4.73	17	17	0	0	70	76	6	24	60	—	1.42	.274
2007	Salem (CAR)	HiA	9	7	4.01	21	21	1	0	114	133	7	39	91	—	1.50	.296
	Corpus Christi (TL)	AA	1	1	7.40	6	6	0	0	24	29	1	14	17	—	1.77	.296
2008	Corpus Christi (TL)	AA	2	6	5.50	17	17	0	0	88	94	15	32	34	—	1.43	.275
Minor League Totals			14	21	5.05	77	64	1	3	330	372	32	123	225	—	1.50	.285

Year	Club (League)	Class	AVG	G	AB	R	H	2B	3B	HR	RBI	BB	SO	SB	CS	OBP	SLG
2007	Corpus Christi (TL)	AA	.500	2	2	0	1	0	0	0	0	0	0	0	0	.500	.500
2008	Salem (CAR)	HiA	.217	8	23	4	5	2	0	1	6	4	1	1	0	.357	.435
	Corpus Christi (TL)	AA	.371	42	124	21	46	10	2	3	20	16	24	8	1	.447	.556
2009	Round Rock (PCL)	AAA	.271	138	520	68	141	25	3	6	53	53	118	22	3	.342	.365
2010	Round Rock (PCL)	AAA	.277	131	502	91	139	26	2	13	57	67	108	23	1	.364	.414
	Houston (NL)	MAJ	.179	19	28	5	5	3	0	0	3	3	12	1	1	.258	.286
Major League Totals			.179	19	28	5	5	3	0	0	3	3	12	1	1	.258	.286
Minor League Totals			.284	321	1171	184	332	63	7	23	136	140	251	54	5	.363	.408

28 JOSE ALTUVE, 2B

Born: May 6, 1990. **B-T:** R-R. **Ht.:** 5-7. **Wt.:** 166. **Signed:** Venezuela, 2006. **Signed by:** Pablo Torrealba/ Wolfgang Ramos.

Altuve fits no standard profile. He doesn't lack tools, but he's difficult to compare to other players. He has a unique build, compared by some scouts to a fire hydrant, and some say he is two inches shorter than his listed height. At the end of last season, he may have been 10 pounds lighter as well. But he has baseball skills and enough tools to make things interesting. Defense is his best attribute. He has quick, strong hands that work well at the plate and in the field. He's agile and at times a dazzling second baseman, with arm strength to turn the double play well. He has developed a good rapport with shortstop Jio Mier, whom he has played with the last two seasons, and has gotten in time at third base as well. Offensively, Altuve shows enough power to punish mistakes but mostly plays a No. 2 hitter's game. He uses the whole field, has excellent baserunning skills that augment his average speed and shows the bat control to move runners. Altuve plays with energy that makes him a team leader and keeps winning people over. He may put up big numbers at Lancaster this season but will have to keep proving himself at higher levels to scouts who remain skeptical of a player with such a small body.

Year	Club (League)	Class	AVG	G	AB	R	H	2B	3B	HR	RBI	BB	SO	SB	CS	OBP	SLG
2007	Astros (VSL)	R	.343	64	204	40	70	12	4	0	36	28	16	15	5	.429	.441
2008	Greeneville (APP)	R	.284	40	141	26	40	9	3	2	21	8	26	8	2	.320	.433
2009	Greeneville (APP)	R	.324	45	179	45	58	20	2	3	18	26	16	21	4	.408	.508
	Tri-City (NYP)	SS	.250	21	76	13	19	5	0	0	7	8	10	7	2	.337	.316
2010	Lexington (SAL)	LoA	.308	94	393	75	121	15	3	11	45	33	49	39	14	.364	.445
	Lancaster (CAL)	HiA	.276	31	116	18	32	5	2	4	22	9	17	3	4	.333	.457
Minor League Totals			.307	295	1109	217	340	66	14	20	149	112	134	93	31	.373	.445

29 LANCE PENDLETON, RHP

Born: Sept. 10, 1983. **B-T:** L-R. **Ht.:** 6-3. **Wt.:** 205 **Drafted:** Rice, 2005 (4th round). **Signed by:** Steve Boros (Yankees).

Pendleton has flown under the radar since his college days at Rice. He was a reliever on the 2003 national championship team but got more playing time as a hitter, with 20 homers in three seasons. The Yankees drafted him as a pitcher in 2005 and nursed him back from Tommy John surgery in his first full pro season. Pendleton has proven his durability since then, tossing 430 innings over the last three seasons and reaching Triple-A in 2010. The Astros plucked him in the second round of the major league Rule 5 draft in December, and Pendleton immediately began working out at Minute Maid Park preparing for 2011. Pendleton throws strikes with an average fastball at 89-93 mph and three fringy secondary pitches: curveball, slider and changeup. His fastball command stands out more than any particular pitch, as he works on a downhill plane and keeps the ball down to both sides of the plate. Some scouts identify Pendleton's sinking changeup as his best pitch, but he was more effective with his fringy downer curveball, holding righthanders to a .189 average last year. If Pendleton doesn't snag one of the Astros' 25-man roster spots, he'll have to clear waivers and be offered back to the Yankees before he can be sent to the minors. He has a chance to stick, either as the fifth starter or more likely in relief.

Year	Club (League)	Class	W	L	ERA	G	GS	CG	SV	IP	H	HR	BB	SO	G/A	WHIP	AVG
2005	Staten Island (NYP)	SS	1	0	2.33	9	6	0	0	27	27	1	13	23	—	1.48	.248
2006	Did Not Play—Injured																
2007	Yankees (GCL)	R	0	0	4.61	8	6	0	0	14	14	1	6	16	—	1.46	.255
2008	Charleston, SC (SAL)	LoA	7	9	3.52	28	23	0	0	128	136	3	46	119	—	1.42	.270
2009	Tampa (FSL)	HiA	11	5	2.58	20	18	0	0	105	101	1	31	87	0.69	1.26	.256
	Trenton (EL)	AA	1	3	4.47	8	8	0	0	44	40	4	15	43	0.78	1.24	.241
2010	Trenton (EL)	AA	10	4	3.43	23	22	0	0	121	95	9	45	111	0.89	1.16	.215
	Scranton/W-B (IL)	AAA	2	1	4.24	6	5	0	0	34	29	6	12	22	0.88	1.21	.225
Minor League Totals			32	22	3.39	102	88	0	0	472	442	25	168	421	0.80	1.29	.246

30 ZACHARY GRIMMETT, RHP

Born: Feb. 5, 1990. **B-T:** R-R. **Ht.:** 6-3. **Wt.:** 199. **Drafted:** HS—Beggs, Okla., 2008 (28th round). **Signed by:** Jim Stevenson.

The Astros have focused on high school pitchers in the last three drafts, and Dallas Keuchel and Lance Pendleton are the only college pitchers in the Top 30. While Jordan Lyles, Mike Foltynewicz and Tanner Bushue exemplify what the Astros are looking for—lean, athletic, projectable prep arms—Grimmett is in the next tier. He made a strong move in 2010, dominating in the first half as a reliever in low Class A before some uneven performances in eight starts down the stretch. Grimmett was headed to Connors State (Okla.) JC with his twin brother Nick, who has since moved on to Arkansas-Little Rock, when the Astros signed him away for a $100,000 bonus. Grimmett's fastball sits at 90-92 mph when he starts and bumps 93-94 repeatedly when he relieves. He throws both a curveball and a slider. His curve is soft, and some scouts consider his slider his best pitch. He throws it with tight rotation and power in the low 80s, has a knack for throwing it for strikes and uses it to neutralize righthanders. Grimmett's changeup has shown flashes but lags behind, and he needs a weapon to give lefthanders something to worry about. His overall command is below average, and he hasn't refined his mechanics enough to earn the label "strike-thrower" yet. If his change comes around, he'll return to a starting role in high Class A this year. He had a strong instructional league in longer three- and four-inning stints, so the Astros are optimistic he can hold down a rotation spot for at least another year.

Year	Club (League)	Class	W	L	ERA	G	GS	CG	SV	IP	H	HR	BB	SO	G/A	WHIP	AVG
2008	Greeneville (APP)	R	1	2	5.40	13	0	0	0	32	41	3	6	18	—	1.48	.318
2009	Tri-City (NYP)	SS	0	7	7.34	12	12	0	0	42	63	5	16	28	1.02	1.90	.362
2010	Lexington (SAL)	LoA	5	3	4.61	29	9	0	2	98	89	11	32	84	0.98	1.24	.243
Minor League Totals			6	12	5.42	54	21	0	2	171	193	19	54	130	0.99	1.44	.288

Kansas City Royals

BY J.J. COOPER

When Dayton Moore took over as Royals general manager in mid-2006, one of the first things he said he wanted to do was figure out a way to develop pitching. "If you have 20 pitching prospects," he said, "you might get four or five to the big leagues."

Now he has his pitching prospects, and plenty of position prospects as well. Thanks to a willingness to spend large amounts of money in the draft and a solid player-development system, the Royals now have the deepest farm system in baseball. If Moore is going to be a success in Kansas City, it will depend on the young talent coming up through the organization.

That focus on the future is good news for Moore, because little has gone right for him at the big league level. The Royals have been just as disastrous under Moore as they were under previous GM Allard Baird. Kansas City has topped 70 wins only once in Moore's four-plus years running the franchise, and only twice in the last decade.

And it's hard to say that the 2010 Royals were any better than the group Moore inherited four years earlier. Kansas City continues to rank near the bottom of the American League in most significant batting, pitching and fielding stats. Many of the cornerstones of the current team—Billy Butler, David DeJesus, Zack Greinke—already were in the big leagues or nearly ready when Moore took over.

With a farm system bereft of talent when he arrived, Moore ended up signing a revolving cast of low-level free agents and veteran trade acquisitions to fill holes at the big league level. Few of them turned out to be finds, and most were soon headed elsewhere. That steady stream of mercenaries should start to slow down in 2011, thanks to a system almost ready to start producing contributors.

Third baseman Mike Moustakas should filter into the lineup at some point during the season, and first baseman Eric Hosmer could join him before the end of 2011. All five of the Royals' top pitching prospects—John Lamb, Mike Montgomery, Danny Duffy, Chris Dwyer, Aaron Crow—will open the year in the Double-A Northwest Arkansas rotation, and some of them could bolster the big league staff later in the year. It will be 2012 before the majority of their best prospects reach Kansas City for good.

By devoting resources to player development, the Royals have found a possible path to success. They

Zack Greinke's production dipped slightly as he fell short of his 2009 Cy Young campaign

CLIFF WELCH

TOP 30 PROSPECTS

1. Eric Hosmer, 1b	16. Robinson Yambati, rhp
2. Wil Myers, c	17. Salvador Perez, c
3. Mike Moustakas, 3b	18. Johnny Giavotella, 2b
4. John Lamb, lhp	19. Louis Coleman, rhp
5. Mike Montgomery, lhp	20. Jarrod Dyson, of
6. Christian Colon, ss	21. Jeff Bianchi, ss
7. Danny Duffy, lhp	22. Patrick Keating, rhp
8. Chris Dwyer, lhp	23. Humberto Arteaga, ss
9. Aaron Crow, rhp	24. Orlando Calixte, ss
10. Brett Eibner, of	25. David Lough, of
11. Jason Adam, rhp	26. Derrick Robinson, of
12. Yordano Ventura, rhp	27. Henry Barrera, rhp
13. Tim Collins, lhp	28. Clint Robinson, 1b
14. Tim Melville, rhp	29. Elisaul Pimentel, rhp
15. Cheslor Cuthbert, 3b	30. Kelvin Herrera, rhp

rank fifth in draft spending over the last five years at $37.8 million. They've also done well internationally, finding such talents as Dominican righthanders Yordano Ventura and Robinson Yambati and Nicaraguan third baseman Cheslor Cuthbert.

But just as their investments are starting to pay off, the Royals may have to plan a different approach. There has been much talk about a mandated slotting system for the draft beginning in 2012, which would cost Kansas City one of the few competitive advantages a small-revenue team can have—a willingness to sign over-slot players.

General Manager: Dayton Moore. **Farm Director:** J.J. Picollo. **Scouting Director:** Lonnie Goldberg.

Class	Team	League	W	L	PCT	Finish*	Manager
Majors	Kansas City Royals	American	67	95	.414	12th (14)	Trey Hillman/Ned Yost
Triple-A	Omaha Royals	Pacific Coast	81	63	.563	3rd (16)	Mike Jirschele
Double-A	Northwest Arkansas Naturals	Texas	86	54	.614	†1st (8)	Brian Poldberg
High A	Wilmington Blue Rocks	Carolina	68	70	.493	6th (8)	Brian Rupp
Low A	Burlington Bees	Midwest	46	90	.338	16th (16)	Jim Gabella
Rookie	Idaho Falls Chukars	Pioneer	27	49	.355	8th (8)	Brian Buchanan
Rookie	Burlington Royals	Appalachian	34	34	.500	t-4th (10)	Nelson Liriano
Rookie	AZL Royals	Arizona	31	25	.554	5th (12)	Darryl Kennedy
Overall 2010 Minor League Record			373	385	.492	18th (30)	

*Finish in overall standings (No. of teams in league). †League champion.
Low Class A affiliate changes to Kane County (Midwest) in 2011.

LAST YEAR'S TOP 30

Player, Pos.		Status
1.	Mike Montgomery, lhp	No. 5
2.	Aaron Crow, rhp	No. 9
3.	Wil Myers, c	No. 2
4.	Mike Moustakas, 3b	No. 3
5.	Eric Hosmer, 1b	No. 1
6.	Tim Melville, rhp	No. 14
7.	John Lamb, lhp	No. 4
8.	Danny Duffy, lhp	No. 7
9.	Chris Dwyer, lhp	No. 8
10.	David Lough, of	No. 25
11.	Jeff Bianchi, ss	No. 21
12.	Louis Coleman, rhp	No. 19
13.	Carlos Rosa, rhp	(Diamondbacks)
14.	Tyler Sample, rhp	Dropped out
15.	Kila Ka'aihue, 1b	Majors
16.	Johnny Giavotella, 2b	No. 18
17.	Cheslor Cuthbert, 3b	No. 15
18.	Kelvin Herrera, rhp	No. 30
19.	Jordan Parraz, of	(Red Sox)
20.	Salvador Perez, c	No. 17
21.	Jose Bonilla, c	Dropped out
22.	Derrick Robinson, of	No. 26
23.	Keaton Hayenga, rhp	Dropped out
24.	Blake Wood, rhp	Majors
25.	Patrick Keating, rhp	No. 22
26.	Crawford Simmons, lhp	Dropped out
27.	Edgar Osuna, lhp	Dropped out
28.	Matt Mitchell, rhp	Dropped out
29.	Cole White, rhp	Dropped out
30.	Hilton Richardson, of	Dropped out

BEST TOOLS

Best Hitter for Average	Eric Hosmer
Best Power Hitter	Mike Moustakas
Best Strike-Zone Discipline	Wil Myers
Fastest Baserunner	Jarrod Dyson
Best Athlete	Derrick Robinson
Best Fastball	Yordano Ventura
Best Curveball	Chris Dwyer
Best Slider	Aaron Crow
Best Changeup	John Lamb
Best Control	John Lamb
Best Defensive Catcher	Salvador Perez
Best Defensive Infielder	Humberto Arteaga
Best Infield Arm	Mike Moustakas
Best Defensive Outfielder	Jarrod Dyson
Best Outfield Arm	Brett Eibner

PROJECTED 2014 LINEUP

Catcher	Salvador Perez
First Base	Eric Hosmer
Second Base	Mike Aviles
Third Base	Mike Moustakas
Shortstop	Christian Colon
Left Field	Alex Gordon
Center Field	Brett Eibner
Right Field	Wil Myers
Designated Hitter	Billy Butler
No. 1 Starter	Zack Greinke
No. 2 Starter	John Lamb
No. 3 Starter	Mike Montgomery
No. 4 Starter	Danny Duffy
No. 5 Starter	Chris Dwyer
Closer	Joakim Soria

TOP PROSPECTS OF THE DECADE

Year	Player, Pos.	2010 Org.
2001	Chris George, lhp	Orioles
2002	Angel Berroa, ss	Giants
2003	Zack Greinke, rhp	Royals
2004	Zack Greinke, rhp	Royals
2005	Billy Butler, of	Royals
2006	Alex Gordon, 3b	Royals
2007	Alex Gordon, 3b	Royals
2008	Mike Moustakas, ss	Royals
2009	Mike Moustakas, 3b	Royals
2010	Mike Mongtomery, lhp	Royals

TOP DRAFT PICKS OF THE DECADE

Year	Player, Pos.	2010 Org.
2001	Colt Griffin, rhp	Out of baseball
2002	Zack Greinke, rhp	Royals
2003	Chris Lubanski, of	Blue Jays
2004	Billy Butler, of	Royals
2005	Alex Gordon, 3b	Royals
2006	Luke Hochevar, rhp	Royals
2007	Mike Moustakas, ss	Royals
2008	Eric Hosmer, 1b	Royals
2009	Aaron Crow, rhp	Royals
2010	Christian Colon, ss	Royals

LARGEST BONUSES IN CLUB HISTORY

Eric Hosmer, 2008	$6,000,000
Alex Gordon, 2005	$4,000,000
Mike Moustakas, 2007	$4,000,000
Luke Hochevar, 2006	$3,500,000
Noel Arguelles, 2010	$3,400,000

MINOR LEAGUE DEPTH CHART

KANSAS CITY ROYALS

TOP 2011 ROOKIE: Mike Moustakas, 3b. The 2010 minor league home run leader could be the hot-corner star the Royals hoped Alex Gordon would become.

BREAKOUT PROSPECT: Yordano Ventura, rhp. He's only 5-foot-11, but he has the best pure arm strength in the system.

SLEEPER: Kevin Chapman, lhp. His fastball/slider combination give him a chance to develop into a closer.

SOURCE OF TOP 30 TALENT

Homegrown	28	Acquired	2
College	8	Trades	2
Junior college	1	Rule 5 draft	0
High school	11	Independent leagues	0
Independent/drafted	1	Free agents/waivers	0
Nondrafted free agents	0		
International	7		

LF
David Lough (25)
Tim Smith
Brian Fletcher
Carlo Testa

CF
Brett Eibner (10)
Jarrod Dyson (20)
Derrick Robinson (26)
Tim Ferguson
Darian Sandford
Pat White

RF
Wil Myers (2)
Geuilin Beltre
Lane Adams
Whit Merrifield

3B
Mike Moustakas (3)
Cheslor Cuthbert (15)
Mike Antonio

SS
Christian Colon (6)
Jeff Bianchi (21)
Humberto Arteaga (23)
Orlando Carlixte (24)
Yowill Espinal
Lance Zawadzki
Alex McClure
Justin Trapp

2B
Johnny Giavotella (18)
Kurt Mertins
Rey Navarro

1B
Eric Hosmer (1)
Clint Robinson (28)
Jake Kuebler
Henry Moreno
Murray Watts

C
Salvador Perez (17)
Lucas May
Manny Pina
Jose Bonilla
Kevin David
Ben Theriot
Jin-Ho Shin

RHP

RHSP	RHRP
Aaron Crow (9)	Louis Coleman (19)
Jason Adam (11)	Patrick Keating (22)
Yordano Ventura (12)	Henry Barrera (27)
Tim Melville (14)	Kelvin Herrera (30)
Robinson Yambati (16)	Greg Holland
Elisaul Pimentel (29)	Michael Mariot
Nathan Adcock	Mike Giovenco
Tyler Sample	Eric Cantrell
Leonel Santiago	Nick Rogers
Keaton Hayenga	
Kevin Pucetas	

LHP

LHSP	LHRP
John Lamb (4)	Tim Collins (13)
Mike Montgomery (5)	Buddy Baumann
Danny Duffy (7)	Kevin Chapman
Chris Dwyer (8)	Blaine Hardy
Everett Teaford	Brandon Sisk
Justin Marks	
Noel Arguelles	
Crawford Simmons	
Will Smith	
Scott Alexander	

2010   BONUSES: $6.7 MILLION

BEST PURE HITTER: One of the best hitters available in the draft, SS Christian Colon (1) has a quick bat and the ability to consistently barrel balls. The Royals sent him to high Class A, where he more than held his own.

BEST POWER HITTER: OF/RHP Brett Eibner (2) had borderline first-round talent as both a position player and a pitcher, and both he and Kansas City want him to be an everyday player. He hit 42 homers in three years at Arkansas and should tap into his power more now that he'll be fully focused on hitting.

FASTEST RUNNER: OF Darian Sandford (47) can flat-out fly. He can run the 60-yard dash in 6.2 seconds and get from the left side of the plate to first base in 3.65 seconds on a jailbreak swing. He led the Rookie-level Arizona League with 30 steals in 38 games.

BEST DEFENSIVE PLAYER: SS Alex McClure (11) gets the nod over Colon because of his superior arm strength. Both have good hands, footwork and instincts. Some scouts think Colon is destined for second base.

BEST FASTBALL: RHP Jason Adam (5) reached 98 mph during instructional league and has more projection in his 6-foot-4, 225-pound frame. Eibner can throw 97 mph, but he's done pitching. Nondrafted free agent RHP Nick Rogers, a two-way player at North Carolina A&T, can hit 96. LHP Kevin Chapman (4) and RHP Mike Giovenco (14) peak at 95.

BEST SECONDARY PITCH: Chapman's slider is his out pitch and gives him closer potential. Adam has the best curveball in this group, though it's inconsistent.

BEST PRO DEBUT: Colon had no problems competing in high Class A, batting .278/.326/.380 with three home runs in 60 games. 1B Murray Watts (28), a 6-foot-7, 270-pound hulk, hit .279 with 14 homers to make the Rookie-level Pioneer League all-star team.

BEST ATHLETE: Eibner's raw power and arm strength are borderline plus-plus tools, and he also has slightly above-average speed.

MOST INTRIGUING BACKGROUND: Unsigned C Joe Jackson (50) is the great-great nephew of Shoeless Joe Jackson of Black Sox infamy. Unsigned RHP Mark Blackmar's (34) dad Phil is a pro golfer who won three times on the PGA Tour and most recently on the Champions Tour in 2009. OF Brian Fletcher's (18) father Scott played 15 years in the majors and is a roving infield instructor for the Royals.

CLOSEST TO THE MAJORS: Colon and Chapman both debuted in high Class A and will open 2011 in Double-A. As a lefty reliever, Chapman could move a little quicker.

BEST LATE-ROUND PICK: C Kevin David (19) has power potential and arm strength. Watts' power bears watching as well.

THE ONE WHO GOT AWAY: Kansas City signed 21 of its first 22 picks. The lone exception was RHP Jon Gray (13), who has a heavy 88-93 mph fastball and a hard slider. He's attending Oklahoma.

ASSESSMENT: There was no slam-dunk pick at No. 4, and the Royals went with Colon, the safest bet to be a big league regular in the entire draft. Kansas City continued to spend in later rounds, paying $1.25 million for Eibner and $800,000 for Adam.

2009   BONUSES: $6.7 MILLION

Initial returns on a $2 million investment in C Wil Myers (3) and a $1.45 million outlay for LHP Chris Dwyer (4) are extremely positive. RHP Aaron Crow (1) has quality stuff, while RHP Louis Coleman (5) could pitch in Kansas City's bullpen in 2011.

GRADE: A

2008   BONUSES: $11.1 MILLION

1B Eric Hosmer (1) showed why he went No. 3 overall with a breakout 2010 season. Mike Montgomery (1s) and John Lamb (5) are two of the best LHP prospects in baseball.

GRADE: A

2007   BONUSES: $6.6 MILLION

3B Mike Moustakas (1) led the minors in homers last year and is ready for a starting job with the Royals. LHP Danny Duffy (3) adds to their southpaw depth, while RHP Greg Holland (10) rode his mid-90s fastball to the big league bullpen.

GRADE: A

2006   BONUSES: $6.7 MILLION

RHP Luke Hochevar (1), the No. 1 overall pick, has been a total bust. Getting RHP Blake Wood (3) and OF Jarrod Dyson (50) to the majors doesn't salvage this draft.

GRADE: D

Draft analysis by Jim Callis. Numbers in parentheses indicate draft rounds.

ERIC HOSMER, 1B

Born: Oct. 24, 1989. **Bats:** L. **Throws:** L.
Height: 6-4. **Weight:** 215. **Drafted:** HS—
Plantation, Fla., 2008 (1st round). **Signed by:**
Alex Mesa.

ROBERT GURGANUS

At its simplest, hitting has been described as "see the ball, hit the ball." Hosmer showed in 2010 how important it is to see the ball. After signing for $6 million at the Aug. 15 deadline as the No. 3 overall pick in 2008, he initially struggled to live up to his reputation as the best high school bat in his draft class. During his first full season in pro ball, he batted .241/.334/.361 between two Class A stops and was diagnosed with astigmatism. He had his vision corrected with LASIK surgery, and he looked like a totally different hitter last season. Recovering from a broken knuckle on his right hand in 2009 and improving his conditioning also helped. Hosmer led the high Class A Carolina League in batting (.354) and on-base percentage (.545) and showed increased power after a promotion to Double-A Northwest Arkansas, which he helped lead to the Texas League title. He rated as the No. 2 prospect in both leagues. After the season, he led Team USA by hitting .389 at the Pan Am qualifier before heading to the Arizona Fall League for some more seasoning.

Hosmer's approach is very advanced for his age, and one scout likened it to Joey Votto's. He already likes to use the opposite field and has the strength to drive the ball out of the park while going the other way. Pitchers who nibble on the outside corner to stay away from his power are doing just what he prefers. The Royals would like to see Hosmer become a little more pull-conscious, as they believe his home run numbers will jump once he turns on inside fastballs more often. He has shown the ability to do so and he has enough bat speed to pull good fastballs, but at times he seems reluctant to abandon the opposite field. He projects as well-above -average as a hitter and power hitter, with a swing that has drawn comparisons to Will Clark's with the same kind of high finish. While fellow Royals prospect Mike Moustakas gets his power from a big rip, Hosmer prefers an easier, if less powerful, stroke.

After struggling against lefties in 2009, he showed no problems in 2010, batting .360/.409/.566 against southpaws. Defensively, Hosmer showed increased agility and good range at first base last season. The Royals believe he has Gold Glove ability down the road. He was clocked up to 97 mph as a high school pitcher, though his plus arm strength rarely comes into play at first base. He shags balls in the outfield regularly and is good enough to play occasionally out there if the Royals want to get his and Billy Butler's bats in the lineup in interleague games. Though he's a below-average runner, he knows how to pick his spots to run.

Hosmer should start 2011 in Northwest Arkansas. A midseason promotion to Triple-A Omaha is likely, and he could make it to K.C. late in the year. He projects as the team's long-term three-hole hitter.

SCOUTING GRADES

Batting: 70. **Defense:** 55.
Power: 65. **Arm:** 65.
Speed: 35.

Based on 20-80 scouting scale, where 50 represents major league average, and future projection rather than present tools.

Year	Club (League)	Class	AVG	G	AB	R	H	2B	3B	HR	RBI	BB	SO	SB	CS	OBP	SLG
2008	Idaho Falls (PIO)	R	.364	3	11	2	4	2	0	0	2	3	2	0	0	.533	.545
2009	Burlington (MWL)	LoA	.254	79	280	31	71	17	2	5	49	44	68	3	2	.352	.382
	Wilmington (CAR)	HiA	.206	27	97	9	20	2	2	1	10	9	22	0	0	.280	.299
2010	Wilmington (CAR)	HiA	.354	87	325	48	115	29	6	7	51	44	39	11	1	.429	.545
	NW Arkansas (TL)	AA	.313	50	195	39	61	14	3	13	35	15	27	3	1	.365	.615
Minor League Totals			.298	246	908	129	271	64	13	26	147	115	158	17	4	.378	.483

2 WIL MYERS, C

Born: Dec. 10, 1990. **B-T:** R-R. **Ht.:** 6-3. **Wt.:** 190. **Drafted:** HS—High Point, N.C., 2009 (3rd round). **Signed by:** Steve Connelly.

The Royals thought about drafting Myers 12th overall in 2009, but gambled success-fully that his $2 million price tag would drop him to their next choice in the third round. Now that he has hit .324/.429/.533 in two pro seasons, plenty of teams wish they had met his price. Myers' success at the plate comes in large part from excellent pitch recognition. He often stops loading his swing just as a pitcher releases the ball—because he quickly determines whether it's a pitch he wants to hit. He's a pull hitter who works deep counts and projects to have easy above-average power down the road. The big question is whether he'll be able to catch in the big leagues. Though he threw out 32 percent of basestealers in 2010 and has plus arm strength, he stands too tall and drops his elbow, costing him accuracy. His long arms and legs make it hard for him to receive and block balls. He's more athletic and a better runner than most catchers, and should be able to handle a move to an outfield corner if needed. While the Royals believe Myers can stay behind the plate, they also know they can get him to the majors quicker and get more offensive production out of him if they move him to the outfield. He'll spend 2011 in Double-A, with his position still to be determined.

Year	Club (League)	Class	AVG	G	AB	R	H	2B	3B	HR	RBI	BB	SO	SB	CS	OBP	SLG
2009	Burlington (APP)	R	.125	4	16	1	2	0	1	1	4	0	3	0	0	.125	.438
	Idaho Falls (PIO)	R	.426	18	68	18	29	7	1	4	14	9	15	2	0	.488	.735
2010	Burlington (MWL)	LoA	.289	68	242	42	70	19	1	10	45	48	55	10	3	.408	.500
	Wilmington (CAR)	HiA	.346	58	205	28	71	18	2	4	38	37	39	2	3	.453	.512
Minor League Totals			.324	148	531	89	172	44	5	19	101	94	112	14	6	.429	.533

3 MIKE MOUSTAKAS, 3B

Born: Sept. 11, 1988. **B-T:** L-R. **Ht.:** 5-11. **Wt.:** 230. **Drafted:** HS—Chatsworth, Calif., 2007 (1st round). **Signed by:** John Ramey.

The No. 2 overall pick in the 2007 draft and the recipient of a $4 million bonus, Moustakas led the low Class A Midwest League with 22 homers in his first full pro season. After a poor 2009 encore, he bounced back to earn Texas League MVP honors and tie for the minor league lead with 36 homers. Moustakas' swing isn't that different than what it was in 2009, but a better approach led to better results. He started laying off pitches that he couldn't do much damage to, leading to more favorable counts and more opportunities to unleash his plus-plus power. With his excellent bat speed, he can drive the ball out of the park to any field. He may never walk a lot, but he also has an uncanny ability to make contact. Scouts worry about Moustakas' ability to stay at third base. He's a below-average runner who likely will continue to get slower, and his footwork and mechanics lack consistency. He does have some assets at the hot corner, with a strong arm and average first-step quickness and hands. Moustakas probably will spend a couple of months in Triple-A to open 2011, but he should be the first of the much-anticipated wave of prospects to arrive in Kansas City. He should hit in the middle of the Royals' lineup for years.

Year	Club (League)	Class	AVG	G	AB	R	H	2B	3B	HR	RBI	BB	SO	SB	CS	OBP	SLG
2007	Idaho Falls (PIO)	R	.293	11	41	6	12	4	1	0	10	4	8	0	0	.383	.439
2008	Burlington (MWL)	LoA	.272	126	496	77	135	25	3	22	71	43	86	8	4	.337	.468
2009	Wilmington (CAR)	HiA	.250	129	492	66	123	32	2	16	86	32	90	10	6	.297	.421
2010	NW Arkansas (TL)	AA	.347	66	259	58	90	25	0	21	76	26	42	0	1	.413	.687
	Omaha (PCL)	AAA	.293	52	225	36	66	16	0	15	48	8	25	2	0	.314	.564
Minor League Totals			.282	384	1513	243	426	102	6	74	291	113	251	20	11	.336	.504

4 JOHN LAMB, LHP

Born: July 10, 1990. **B-T:** L-L. **Ht.:** 6-3. **Wt.:** 195. **Drafted:** HS—Laguna Hills, Calif., 2008 (5th round). **Signed by:** Gary Johnson/John Ramey.

Lamb lasted five rounds in the 2008 draft because he missed his high school senior season after fracturing his elbow in a car accident. The Royals were able to sign a premium talent for $165,000, and he has shown no ill effects since. He led Kansas City farmhands with a 2.38 ERA and 159 strikeouts while reaching Double-A at age 20 in 2010. Few lefthanders can match Lamb's combination of three possible plus pitches and exquisite command. He paints the outside corner with his fastball, which usually ranges from 90-95 mph, and works down and away with a quality changeup. He also throws a curveball that isn't as consistent as his other two offerings. While Lamb's stuff is a tick below Mike Montgomery's, his ability to succeed without his best stuff could make him the better pitcher. He already has shown he can win on nights when his fastball sits at 89-90 mph and he doesn't have feel for his curve. He keeps the ball down in the zone, allowing just five homers in 148 innings last season. Lamb is expected to be part of an all-prospect Northwest

Arkansas rotation with Montgomery, Danny Duffy, Chris Dwyer and Aaron Crow to start the 2011 season. If he makes as much progress as he did in 2010, he could end the year in Kansas City.

Year	Club (League)	Class	W	L	ERA	G	GS	CG	SV	IP	H	HR	BB	SO	G/A	WHIP	AVG
2009	Burlington (APP)	R	2	2	3.95	6	6	0	0	27	24	4	9	25	0.93	1.21	.238
	Idaho Falls (PIO)	R	3	1	3.70	8	8	0	0	41	33	4	11	46	1.15	1.06	.217
2010	Burlington (MWL)	LoA	2	3	1.58	8	8	0	0	40	26	2	17	43	0.82	1.08	.188
	Wilmington (CAR)	HiA	6	3	1.45	13	13	0	0	75	59	1	15	90	1.51	0.99	.219
	NW Arkansas (TL)	AA	2	1	5.45	7	7	0	0	33	37	2	13	26	0.68	1.52	.280
Minor League Totals			15	10	2.83	42	42	0	0	216	179	13	65	230	1.05	1.13	.226

5 MIKE MONTGOMERY, LHP

Born: July 1, 1989. **B-T:** L-L. **Ht.:** 6-5. **Wt.:** 180. **Drafted:** HS—Newhall, Calif., 2008 (1st round supplemental). **Signed by:** Dan Ontiveros.

Signed for $988,000 as the 36th overall pick in the 2008 draft, Montgomery ranked No. 1 on this list a year ago. He missed nearly two months with a strained forearm in 2010, but he returned in mid-July and was healthy down the stretch, pitching with Team USA (he won two starts in the Pan Am qualifier) and in the Arizona Fall League where he started in the Rising Stars Game. On his best nights, Montgomery features a plus-plus fastball to go with an above-average curveball and changeup. He generates excellent angle with his fastball while running it up to 95-96 mph, more often sitting at 91-93. He has junked his high school palmball/curve and developed a more traditional, big-breaking 74-76 mph bender. He's still learning how to locate his curve for strikes. His changeup has some late fade, and his ability to throw it with excellent arm speed and keep it down in the zone makes it a plus pitch. His mechanics are solid, so his health isn't a major concern going forward. The forearm injury slowed Montgomery's ascent, but he's still not far away from Kansas City. He'll return to Double-A to start 2011, but he's yet another blue-chip prospect who could debut with the Royals later in the year.

Year	Club (League)	Class	W	L	ERA	G	GS	CG	SV	IP	H	HR	BB	SO	G/A	WHIP	AVG
2008	Royals (AZL)	R	2	1	1.69	12	9	0	0	43	31	2	12	34	—	1.01	.211
2009	Burlington (MWL)	LoA	2	3	2.17	12	12	0	0	58	42	1	24	52	1.92	1.14	.206
	Wilmington (CAR)	HiA	4	1	2.25	9	9	0	0	52	38	0	12	46	0.83	0.96	.196
2010	Wilmington (CAR)	HiA	2	0	1.09	4	4	0	0	25	14	0	4	33	2.00	0.73	.165
	Royals (AZL)	R	0	1	1.04	3	3	0	0	9	6	0	1	7	0.80	0.81	.207
	NW Arkansas (TL)	AA	5	4	3.47	13	13	0	0	60	56	4	26	48	1.52	1.37	.255
Minor League Totals			15	10	2.27	53	50	0	0	246	187	7	79	220	1.36	1.08	.213

6 CHRISTIAN COLON, SS

Born: May, 14, 1989 **B-T:** R-R. **Ht.:** 6-1. **Wt.:** 180. **Drafted:** Cal State Fullerton, 2010 (1st round). **Signed by:** Scott Groot.

Though there was no clear-cut No. 4 overall pick in the 2010 draft, the Royals were pleased to get the highly skilled Colon. Baseball America's 2009 Summer Player of the Year, he led the Big West Conference with 17 homers last spring. He signed quickly for MLB's slot recommendation of $2.75 million, enabling him to play 60 games in high Class A. Outside of his bat, Colon's tools grade mostly as average, but his consistency and feel for the game let him play well above his pure physical ability. His best attribute is his ability to make solid contact, which allows him to hit for average and project as a No. 2 hitter. He has a quick bat and his hands work well, allowing him to drive the ball to the opposite field even when he gets caught out on his front foot. His average power will really stand out if he can remain at shortstop, which is in question because he has fringy speed and limited quickness. He doesn't have outstanding range, but he can make all the routine plays with his solid hands and average arm. At worst, he should be an offensive second baseman. By signing quickly, Colon put himself in position to move to Double-A in 2011. When the Royals' youth movement really takes hold the following year, he could be their starting shortstop.

Year	Club (League)	Class	AVG	G	AB	R	H	2B	3B	HR	RBI	BB	SO	SB	CS	OBP	SLG
2010	Wilmington (CAR)	HiA	.278	60	245	38	68	12	2	3	30	13	33	2	4	.326	.380
Minor League Totals			.278	60	245	38	68	12	2	3	30	13	33	2	4	.326	.380

7 DANNY DUFFY, LHP

Born: Dec. 21, 1988. **B-T:** L-L. **Ht.:** 6-3. **Wt.:** 195. **Drafted:** HS—Lompoc, Calif., 2007 (3rd round). **Signed by:** Rick Schroeder.

After posting a 2.49 ERA in three pro seasons and pitching in the Futures Game in 2009, Duffy surprisingly walked away from the game during spring training in 2010. He had a minor elbow injury that would have sidelined him in April, but he says that wasn't an issue. He returned in June and looked as good as ever, touching 95-97 mph regularly throughout the summer. Duffy often paces himself in the early innings, sitting at 90-92 mph before reaching the mid-90s later in games. His velocity jump sometimes comes with a propensity to overthrow. He generally commands his fastball well and creates deception with a crossfire delivery, though he has gotten better about staying online to the plate. His best secondary pitch is a changeup that's slightly above-average at times, but his feel for it wavers. His slow curveball has plenty of depth, but he'll probably switch to a slider that will be a better fit for his three-quarters arm slot. He has a relatively advanced feel for setting up hitters. Though Duffy has made just seven starts above Class A, he's not that far away from the big leagues. He'll return to Double-A to open 2011 and could reach Kansas City by September.

Year	Club (League)	Class	W	L	ERA	G	GS	CG	SV	IP	H	HR	BB	SO	G/A	WHIP	AVG
2007	Royals (AZL)	R	2	3	1.45	11	9	0	0	37	24	0	17	63	—	1.10	.178
2008	Burlington (MWL)	LoA	8	4	2.20	17	17	0	0	82	56	4	25	102	—	0.99	.193
2009	Wilmington (CAR)	HiA	9	3	2.98	24	24	1	0	127	108	6	41	125	0.96	1.18	.230
2010	Royals (AZL)	R	0	0	3.38	2	2	0	0	3	2	0	1	4	2.00	1.13	.222
	Idaho Falls (PIO)	R	0	1	1.50	2	2	0	0	6	4	0	0	6	9.00	0.67	.182
	Wilmington (CAR)	HiA	0	0	2.57	3	3	0	0	14	8	2	7	18	1.38	1.07	.170
	NW Arkansas (TL)	AA	5	2	2.95	7	7	1	0	40	38	3	9	41	1.16	1.18	.255
Minor League Totals			24	13	2.54	66	64	2	0	308	240	15	100	359	1.07	1.10	.214

8 CHRIS DWYER, LHP

Born: April 10, 1988. **B-T:** L-L. **Ht.:** 6-3. **Wt.:** 210. **Drafted:** Clemson, 2009 (4th round). **Signed by:** Steve Connelly.

Because he was held back in elementary school and attended prep school, Dwyer was a rare draft-eligible freshman because he was 21 after his only year at Clemson. His seven-figure asking price and extra leverage scared teams off, but the Royals gave him mid-first-round money ($1.45 million) as a fourth-rounder and now consider him the equal of any college lefthander in the 2009 draft. He was shut down at the end of July with a back injury, but the Royals do not believe it will be a long-term problem. Dwyer's sharp, 12-to-6 curveball is the best in the system and rates as a 60-65 on the 20-80 scouting scale. Unlike most young pitchers, he can locate his curve start after start. He sets it up with a 91-92 mph fastball that touches 95. He's not afraid to bust hitters inside with his fastball, and improved his command of it during the season. He also made strides with his straight changeup. When he struggles, it's often because Dwyer starts to throw across his body, causing him to leave his fastball up in the zone. Because he's an excellent athlete, he's able to make quick adjustments. Dwyer could have returned to action in late August and should be fully recovered from his back problems by spring training. He'll be part of the minors' best rotation at Northwest Arkansas in 2011.

Year	Club (League)	Class	W	L	ERA	G	GS	CG	SV	IP	H	HR	BB	SO	G/A	WHIP	AVG
2009	Idaho Falls (PIO)	R	0	0	4.15	4	4	0	0	9	12	1	8	15	0.43	2.31	.324
2010	Wilmington (CAR)	HiA	6	3	2.99	15	15	1	0	84	79	3	33	93	0.83	1.33	.246
	NW Arkansas (TL)	AA	2	1	3.06	4	4	0	0	18	11	2	10	20	0.73	1.19	.175
Minor League Totals			8	4	3.09	23	23	1	0	111	102	6	51	128	0.78	1.38	.242

9 AARON CROW, RHP

Born: Nov. 11, 1986. **B-T:** R-R. **Ht.:** 6-3. **Wt.:** 195. **Drafted:** Fort Worth (American Association), 2009 (1st round). **Signed by:** Scott Melvin.

The top college righthander in the 2008 draft, Crow turned down a $3.5 million bonus offer from the Nationals as the No. 9 overall pick. He took a detour to the independent Fort Worth Cats (American Association) before the Royals drafted him 12th overall in 2009 and signed him that September to a $3 million big league contract. He struggled throughout 2010, earning a demotion to high Class A in August. Crow's problems were largely mechanical, as he sped up the start of his delivery and opened up too quickly. As a result, hitters saw the ball early, his fastball flattened out and his command slipped. He also has a wrist wrap that Kansas City is willing to live with. There's nothing wrong with his stuff. His fastball often sits at 95-96 mph and touched 98, but he may be better sitting at 92-94 with natural sink. Crow's 84-87 mph slider is still a plus pitch with good bite, but his command issues gave him few chances to use it. His upper-

80s changeup is too hard, so he began throwing a low-80s knuckle-curve as an offspeed pitch late in the season. Crow will return to Double-A after flunking his first trial there in 2010. If he can't figure out his delivery and command, he has the stuff to be a late-inning reliever.

Year	Club (League)	Class	W	L	ERA	G	GS	CG	SV	IP	H	HR	BB	SO	G/A	WHIP	AVG
2010	NW Arkansas (TL)	AA	7	7	5.66	22	22	0	0	119	130	13	59	90	2.97	1.58	.279
	Wilmington (CAR)	HiA	2	3	5.93	7	7	0	0	44	51	6	6	53	1.85	1.30	.290
Minor League Totals			9	10	5.73	29	29	0	0	163	181	19	65	143	2.63	1.51	.282

10 BRETT EIBNER, OF

Born: Dec. 2, 1988. **B-T:** R-R. **Ht.:** 6-4. **Wt.:** 210. **Drafted:** Arkansas, 2010 (2nd round). **Signed by:** Lloyd Simmons.

The Astros made Eibner a fourth-round pick as a high school pitcher in 2007, but he turned down their $180,000 slot offer to attend Arkansas as a two-way player. That move paid off handsomely, as the Royals signed him for $1.25 million as a second-round pick three years later. Though he can hit 97 mph on the mound, Kansas City drafted Eibner to hit, his preference. Eibner's raw power is just as impressive as his fastball. His swing can get sweepy and long at times, but he can drive the ball out of any part of any ballpark. He doesn't always make consistent contact, but he improved during his college career and should be at least an average hitter now that he's focusing on it full-time—he showed significant improvement as a college junior. He's a slightly above-average runner who gets good enough jumps to stay in center field, but he projects better in right field, where his plus arm strength will be quite useful. He always could fall back on being a pitcher, as he also flashed a plus slider and showed feel for a changeup. Eibner signed late and is still a relatively raw hitter for a college product, so he could begin his pro career at the Royals' new low Class A Kane County affiliate. By 2013, he could be another powerful bat in the middle of Kansas City's lineup.

Year	Club (League)	Class	AVG	G	AB	R	H	2B	3B	HR	RBI	BB	SO	SB	CS	OBP	SLG
2010	Did Not Play—Signed Late																

11 JASON ADAM, RHP

Born: Aug. 4, 1991. **B-T:** R-R. **Ht.:** 6-4. **Wt.:** 225. **Drafted:** HS—Overland Park, Kan., 2010 (5th round). **Signed by:** Steve Gossett.

After they watched Kansas City product Shawn Marcum pitch in the big leagues against them, the Royals intensified their efforts to ensure that they scouted local players more comprehensively than anyone else. That work paid off with Adam, a member of the Royals' elite team that practiced regularly and played occasionally at Kauffman Stadium. Kansas City also scouted every one of his starts for Blue Valley Northwest High in Overland Park, Kan., which wasn't hard considering the school sits 22 miles from the Kauffman Stadium. Despite his solid commitment to Missouri, the Royals took him in the fifth round last June and signed him at the Aug. 16 deadline for a well-above-slot $800,000. Adam signed too late to play in an official game, but he made an impression by consistently sitting at 94-95 mph and touching 98 with his fastball during instructional league. He also has a potential plus curveball that he commands well for a high school draftee. As with most hard-throwing young pitchers, his changeup is more of an idea than a useable pitch at this point. Kansas City tweaked his mechanics slightly, eliminating a Derek Lowesque side step to get Adam more over the rubber at the beginning of his windup. They Royals usually hold their young pitchers in extended spring training during April, but he could move quicker because he's used to cold weather. He's advanced enough to make his pro debut in low Class A.

Year	Club (League)	Class	W	L	ERA	G	GS	CG	SV	IP	H	HR	BB	SO	G/A	WHIP	AVG
2010	Did Not Play—Signed Late																

12 YORDANO VENTURA, RHP

Born: June 3, 1991. **B-T:** R-R. **Ht.:** 5-11. **Wt.:** 160. **Signed:** Dominican Republic, 2008. **Signed by:** Pedro Silverio.

There are a lot of impressive pitching prospects in the Royals system, and none of them throws as hard as consistently as Ventura, the top pitching prospect in the Rookie-level Arizona League last summer. Signed for only $28,000 in 2008 as a 17-year-old who threw 87-89 mph, he has significantly boosted his velocity as he has gained 20 pounds and refined his delivery. He has touched 100 mph on several occasions, hits 98 almost every time out and sits at 94-97 mph. What's most surprising is that he generates that heat from such a small frame, a tribute to his excellent arm speed. His stuff, size and arm slots have prompted comparisons to Neftali Feliz and even the patron saint of small righthanders: Pedro Martinez. Ventura's curveball was very erratic during his U.S. debut in 2010, but after some further instruction during instructional league, he showed improved feel for it. Some scouts project it as a plus pitch, and his promising changeup could develop into at least an average offering. Ventura's delivery is relatively clean and conventional. He hasn't made it past the AZL yet, so he has a lot of development remaining.

Year	Club (League)	Class	W	L	ERA	G	GS	CG	SV	IP	H	HR	BB	SO	G/A	WHIP	AVG
2009	Royals (DSL)	R	0	1	2.78	10	5	0	3	23	28	0	5	11	0.96	1.46	.304
2010	Royals (DSL)	R	0	1	2.31	3	3	0	0	12	9	0	1	13	1.86	0.86	.209
	Royals (AZL)	R	4	2	3.25	14	6	0	0	53	49	3	17	58	1.70	1.25	.236
Minor League Totals			4	4	3.00	27	14	0	3	87	86	3	23	82	1.42	1.25	.251

13 TIM COLLINS, LHP

Born: Aug. 29, 1989. **B-T:** L-L. **Ht.:** 5-7. **Wt.:** 155. **Signed:** HS—Worcester, Mass., NDFA, 2007. **Signed by:** J.P. Ricciardi (Blue Jays).

When he was with Toronto, where former GM J.P. Ricciardi signed him as a nondrafted free agent, Collins' nickname was Tim LinceCollins. Like the two-time Cy Young Award winner, Collins is an undersized pitcher with outsized stuff. He was traded twice last summer, going to the Braves as part of a package for Yunel Escobar in June and then to the Royals as part of a deal for Rick Ankiel and Kyle Farnsworth a month later. Collins' next stop likely will be the Kansas City bullpen. Listed at 5-foot-7, he's closer to 5-foot-5 in reality, but he manages to generate a 90-93 mph fastball that touches 95 and backs it up with two solid secondary pitches. That arsenal has allowed him to average 13.3 strikeouts per nine innings as a pro. Not only does he have good velocity on his fastball, but he also can sink or cut it as needed. His 12-to-6 curveball gives him a second plus pitch at times. He began throwing his slightly above-average changeup more in 2010, and it has nice late fade. Collins attacks hitters and generates excellent deception from a high leg kick, a high set position and a rock and turn that presents his back to the hitter as he begins his delivery. Equally capable of retiring lefties or righties, he projects as a set-up man with the upside as the majors' most physically unimposing closer.

Year	Club (League)	Class	W	L	ERA	G	GS	CG	SV	IP	H	HR	BB	SO	G/A	WHIP	AVG
2007	Blue Jays (GCL)	R	0	0	4.50	7	0	0	0	6	6	0	2	7	—	1.33	.273
2008	Lansing (MWL)	LoA	4	2	1.58	39	0	0	14	68	36	3	32	98	—	1.00	.156
2009	Dunedin (FSL)	HiA	7	4	2.37	40	0	0	3	65	47	2	28	99	1.00	1.16	.199
	New Hampshire (EL)	AA	2	3	5.68	9	0	0	0	13	12	1	7	17	0.54	1.50	.255
2010	New Hampshire (EL)	AA	1	0	2.51	35	0	0	9	43	27	4	16	73	0.89	1.00	.174
	Mississippi (SL)	AA	0	0	1.13	6	0	0	2	8	4	1	3	14	0.80	0.88	.154
	Omaha (PCL)	AAA	2	1	1.33	15	0	0	4	20	9	0	8	21	0.81	0.84	.127
Minor League Totals			16	10	2.26	151	0	0	32	223	141	11	96	329	0.88	1.06	.179

14 TIM MELVILLE, RHP

Born: Oct. 9, 1989. **B-T:** R-R. **Ht.:** 6-5. **Wt.:** 210. **Drafted:** HS—Wentzville, Mo., 2008 (4th round). **Signed by:** Phil Huttman.

Melville was one of the few prominent Royals prospects who took a step backwards in 2010. He showed flashes of dominance with a one-hitter in April and a two-hitter in June, but command issues usually left him struggling to make it out of the fifth inning. His problems are partly related to his mechanics. He has difficulty maintaining a consistent tempo, and when his delivery slows down, it's a good sign he's going to be in trouble. When he's on, Melville has a 91-93 mph fastball that tops out at 96 with good downhill plane. But he doesn't pitch aggressively with his heater, instead working away from hitters and nibbling at the corners. That adds to his trouble in falling behind in the count. Melville also throws a slow 12-to-6 curveball that can be a plus pitch and an improving changeup. However, his curve often isn't as tight as it needs to be, and he leaves his changeup up in the zone when his mechanics get out of whack. Instead he often tries to work away from hitters, nibbling at the corners. Melville's stuff and excellent frame still give him the potential to develop into a solid middle-of-the-rotation starter, but he must sharpen his feel for pitching and his awareness of his delivery. He'll try to do that when he repeats high Class A in 2011.

Year	Club (League)	Class	W	L	ERA	G	GS	CG	SV	IP	H	HR	BB	SO	G/A	WHIP	AVG
2009	Burlington (MWL)	LoA	7	7	3.79	21	21	0	0	97	89	10	43	96	0.89	1.36	.245
2010	Royals (AZL)	R	0	1	3.86	2	2	0	0	5	4	0	2	6	1.67	1.29	.222
	Wilmington (CAR)	HiA	2	12	4.97	22	22	0	0	112	101	10	54	90	0.91	1.38	.240
Minor League Totals			9	20	4.41	45	45	0	0	214	194	20	99	192	0.91	1.37	.242

15 CHESLOR CUTHBERT, 3B

Born: Nov. 16, 1992. **B-T:** R-R. **Ht.:** 6-1. **Wt.:** 190. **Signed:** Nicaragua, 2009. **Signed by:** Orlando Esteves/Juan Lopez.

Cuthbert's father Luis, an amateur catcher, always dreamed of having a son to whom he could teach the game. He and his wife had three daughters first, but the birth of Cheslor in 1992 finally granted his wish. Living on tiny Big Corn Island with a population of 7,000, Luis Cuthbert built a field and formed a youth baseball league to ensure his son would be able to play. It paid off as Cuthbert quickly became one of the best young players in Nicaragua and earned him a national-record $1.35 million bonus in 2009. With the exception of his speed, he has solid tools across the board and stands out most with his bat. Cuthbert has an advanced approach for his age, using the whole field and drives balls to both gaps. He projects to have plus home run power as he matures. Though he's a below-average runner, he moves well enough to become a slightly above-average defender with an average arm at third base. Cuthbert will be 18 this season, so he could see more action in Rookie ball. The Royals also like his makeup—the use of English in the Corn Islands has speeded his transition to life in the United States—so they could challenge him with an assignment to low Class A at some point in 2011.

Year	Club (League)	Class	AVG	G	AB	R	H	2B	3B	HR	RBI	BB	SO	SB	CS	OBP	SLG
2010	Royals (AZL)	R	.265	18	68	14	18	3	2	1	5	6	19	1	1	.342	.412
	Idaho Falls (PIO)	R	.233	14	60	10	14	4	1	2	10	3	16	1	0	.281	.433
Minor League Totals			.250	32	128	24	32	7	3	3	15	9	35	2	1	.314	.422

16 ROBINSON YAMBATI, RHP

Born: Jan. 15, 1991. **B-T:** R-R. **Ht.:** 6-3. **Wt.:** 185. **Signed:** Dominican Republic, 2008. **Signed by:** Edis Perez.

The owner of an ugly 8.89 ERA in his U.S. debut in 2009, Yambati was much better in his return to the Arizona League last year. He ranked right behind teammate Yordano Ventura as the circuit's best pitching prospect. Yambati was more comfortable and his stuff picked up after dipping the previous season. He resolved some mechanical problems and did a better job of repeating his delivery, resulting in improved velocity and command. Yambati's fastball sits between 90-93 mph and peaks at 96. He also throws a hard slurve in the low 80s and a changeup that clearly ranks as his third-best pitch right now. He's actually a little taller than his listed 6-foot-3 height, though his three-quarters release point means he doesn't have the steep downward plane of an over-the-top pitcher. He'll compete for a spot in the Kane County rotation as a teenager this season.

Year	Club (League)	Class	W	L	ERA	G	GS	CG	SV	IP	H	HR	BB	SO	G/A	WHIP	AVG
2008	Royals (DSL)	R	4	1	3.09	14	8	0	0	55	49	0	16	40	—	1.17	.236
2009	Royals (DSL)	R	2	0	0.77	5	5	0	0	23	16	1	9	16	1.55	1.07	.198
	Royals (AZL)	R	2	3	8.89	12	1	0	1	27	41	3	14	18	2.37	2.01	.333
2010	Royals (AZL)	R	8	2	2.71	14	6	0	0	66	65	0	12	64	2.74	1.16	.252
Minor League Totals			16	6	3.55	45	20	0	1	172	171	4	51	138	2.32	1.29	.255

17 SALVADOR PEREZ, C

Born: May 10, 1990. **B-T:** R-R. **Ht.:** 6-3. **Wt.:** 175. **Signed:** Venezuela, 2006. **Signed by:** Juan Indiago.

After serving as Wilmington's starting catcher during the first half of last season, Perez shared the job with Wil Myers in the second half. The reduced workload paid off as Perez hit .318/.343/.432 after the all-star break. He already was the best defensive catcher in the system, and he now shows as much offensive potential as any Royals backstop prospect besides Myers. Perez has slightly above-average arm strength and threw out 42 percent of basestealers in 2010. He does a good job of framing pitches, handling velocity and calling a game. He makes consistent contact and has some gap power, though he rarely draws a walk. The biggest concern with Perez is his lack of speed. He grades as a 25 runner on the 20-80 scouting scale right now, and he already has a thick lower half at age 20. If he continues to gain wait, he'll enter the Molina Zone and his mobility as a catcher could be affected. If Myers continues to catch in 2011, Perez either will split time with him again in Double-A or return to Wilmington to get more action behind the plate. If Myers does move to the outfield, Perez becomes Kansas City's catcher of the future.

Year	Club (League)	Class	AVG	G	AB	R	H	2B	3B	HR	RBI	BB	SO	SB	CS	OBP	SLG
2007	Royals (AZL)	R	.244	30	86	10	21	3	0	0	10	5	10	1	1	.320	.279
2008	Burlington (APP)	R	.325	13	40	4	13	0	1	0	10	5	5	0	0	.404	.375
	Idaho Falls (PIO)	R	.395	12	43	7	17	3	1	1	6	2	5	0	1	.413	.581
2009	Burlington (MWL)	LoA	.189	36	127	10	24	6	0	0	7	6	15	0	1	.230	.236
	Idaho Falls (PIO)	R	.309	59	233	35	72	14	3	2	38	19	25	0	1	.357	.421
2010	Wilmington (CAR)	HiA	.290	99	365	35	106	21	1	7	53	18	38	1	1	.322	.411
Minor League Totals			.283	249	894	101	253	47	6	10	124	55	98	2	5	.326	.383

18 JOHNNY GIAVOTELLA. 2B

Born: July 10, 1987. **B-T:** R-R. **Ht.:** 5-8. **Wt.:** 185. **Drafted:** New Orleans, 2008 (2nd round). **Signed by:** Scott Nichols.

An offensive second baseman, Giavotella has proven he can turn on just about any fastball. He has very good awareness of the strike zone, and his ability to draw walks is enhanced by his pronounced crouch in his stance. He has gap power, though he takes aggressive swings like a power hitter. While he has slightly below-average speed, he does run the bases well. Giavotella's long-term future depends on his glove. After he had a disappointing 2009 season, the Royals challenged him to become a better defender. While he didn't turn into a Gold Glove candidate, Giavotella's work to improve his agility did pay off. He's now adequate rather than below-average at second base. His range still leaves something to be desired, especially on balls up the middle. His arm is good for his position, and he has improved at turning double plays. If Giavotella can't cut it at second base, he doesn't have enough bat to move to the outfield and lacks the versatility to fill a utility role. But if he can handle second base, his bat would make him a useful regular. He'll continue to polish his defense this year in Triple-A.

Year	Club (League)	Class	AVG	G	AB	R	H	2B	3B	HR	RBI	BB	SO	SB	CS	OBP	SLG
2008	Burlington (MWL)	LoA	.299	68	278	50	83	18	2	4	26	25	34	10	7	.355	.421
2009	Wilmington (CAR)	HiA	.258	133	476	84	123	24	8	6	52	66	54	26	9	.351	.380
2010	NW Arkansas (TL)	AA	.322	134	522	92	168	35	5	9	65	61	67	13	7	.395	.460
Minor League Totals			.293	335	1276	226	374	77	15	19	143	152	155	49	23	.370	.422

19 LOUIS COLEMAN, RHP

Born: April 4, 1986. **B-T:** R-R. **Ht.:** 6-4. **Wt.:** 195. **Drafted:** Louisiana State, 2009 (5th round). **Signed by:** Scott Nichols.

After stocking the system with high-ceiling high school talents, the Royals started filling in gaps in 2009 by signing college players who could move quickly. Coleman, who helped lead Louisiana State to the 2009 College World Series championship, is a prime example. He shot to Triple-A in his first full pro season and has a chance to pitch in Kansas City's bullpen in his second. Coleman's slinging crossfire delivery is both a long-term health concern and a huge part of his success. It helps his 91-93 mph fastball run in on righthanders and makes his average slider harder for them to pick up. He limited righties to a .146 average in 2010 but needs to improve his below-average changeup to better handle lefties, who get a better look at this stuff. Coleman is able to throw strikes from his low three-quarters arm slot and repeat his mechanics. His performance in spring training will determine whether he opens the season in Omaha or in the big leagues. He may not be more than a seventh-inning reliever, but he has the resilient arm and competitive nature to be an asset in that role.

Year	Club (League)	Class	W	L	ERA	G	GS	CG	SV	IP	H	HR	BB	SO	G/A	WHIP	AVG
2009	Burlington (MWL)	LoA	1	0	2.45	4	0	0	1	7	2	0	1	6	1.29	0.41	.091
	Wilmington (CAR)	HiA	3	1	1.26	10	0	0	1	14	8	0	3	16	0.93	0.77	.157
2010	NW Arkansas (TL)	AA	2	1	2.09	21	1	0	6	52	31	5	14	55	0.88	0.87	.171
	Omaha (PCL)	AAA	5	2	2.23	21	0	0	1	40	31	2	11	48	0.79	1.04	.215
Minor League Totals			11	4	2.06	56	1	0	9	114	72	7	29	125	0.88	0.89	.181

20 JARROD DYSON, OF

Born: Aug. 15, 1984. **B-T:** L-R. **Ht.:** 5-9. **Wt.:** 161. **Drafted:** Southwest Mississippi CC, 2006 (50th round). **Signed by:** Brian Rhees.

Dyson is proof that even the latest late-round picks can turn out. A 50th-rounder in 2006, he was the 1,475th player taken that year and signed for $5,000. Because of his late-round pedigree, Dyson has had a slow climb and often was viewed as the fourth outfielder on his minor league teams. His development also was delayed by a 50-game suspension in 2009 for amphetamine use, and he missed nearly two months in 2010 with a torn lat muscle and a high ankle sprain. Dyson is one of the fastest runners in baseball, with an explosive first step that serves him well on the bases and in center field. He stole nine bases in 10 attempts during his September callup with the Royals. A potential Gold Glove defender, he had 10 putouts in his eighth big league start, tying the franchise record held by Amos Otis and Carlos Beltran. And unlike many small, speedy outfielders, Dyson has solid arm strength. However, there are legitimate questions about his bat. He's prone to chase pitches up and out of the zone, and he walks less than desired for a leadoff hitter. He also offers no power at all, so he has to focus entirely on getting on base. There are a lot of reasons to be concerned about Dyson's long term potential, as he's already 26, he never has played 100 games in a season and his profile is very similar to failed prospect Joey Gathright. But the Royals are excited by Dyson's electric speed and believe he's a late bloomer. He'll head to spring training with a chance to win their center-field job.

Year	Club (League)	Class	AVG	G	AB	R	H	2B	3B	HR	RBI	BB	SO	SB	CS	OBP	SLG
2006	Royals (AZL)	R	.273	51	161	40	44	4	6	0	19	18	30	19	4	.358	.373
2007	Burlington (MWL)	LoA	.270	10	37	6	10	1	0	0	0	2	12	3	1	.308	.297
2008	Wilmington (CAR)	HiA	.260	93	288	40	75	8	0	0	24	32	60	39	9	.337	.288
2009	Burlington (MWL)	LoA	.343	17	67	14	23	2	1	0	5	5	14	9	4	.397	.403
	NW Arkansas (TL)	AA	.258	63	248	38	64	7	4	0	14	27	54	37	6	.331	.319
2010	Royals (AZL)	R	.520	6	25	4	13	1	1	0	6	0	3	3	1	.520	.640
	Wilmington (CAR)	HiA	.327	12	49	7	16	6	2	0	9	1	9	5	1	.327	.531
	NW Arkansas (TL)	AA	.240	7	25	6	6	0	0	0	6	5	2	3	3	.375	.240
	Omaha (PCL)	AAA	.272	46	195	33	53	10	1	1	19	16	32	13	3	.327	.349
	Kansas City (AL)	MAJ	.211	18	57	11	12	4	2	1	5	6	16	9	1	.286	.404
Major League Totals			.211	18	57	11	12	4	2	1	5	6	16	9	1	.286	.404
Minor League Totals			.278	305	1095	188	304	39	15	1	102	106	216	131	32	.344	.343

21 JEFF BIANCHI, SS

Born: Oct. 5, 1986. **B-T:** R-R. **Ht.:** 6-0. **Wt.:** 175. **Drafted:** HS—Lampeter, Pa., 2005 (2nd round). **Signed by:** Sean Rooney.

If it wasn't for injuries, Bianchi likely would be starting for the Royals, but he has had one completely healthy season in six years of pro ball. His outstanding pro debut in 2005 was cut short by a back injury. A torn labrum in his shoulder caused him to miss almost all of 2006 and part of 2007 before a groin injury sidelined him for part of 2008. He finally got a chance to play a full season in 2009, but tore an elbow ligament in spring training and missed all of 2010. Bianchi's short swing gives him a chance to be a solid hitter, though he won't for much power and never has walked much. Like Christian Colon, he doesn't have exceptional range, but he has excellent fundamentals that allow him to be an average shortstop and he makes few errors. Bianchi's arm was slightly above average before his latest injury. He's following in Mike Aviles' footsteps in returning from Tommy John surgery, which suggests it may be midway through this season before Bianchi fully feels comfortable at the plate and in the field. He'll head to Triple-A and hope to stay healthy.

Year	Club (League)	Class	AVG	G	AB	R	H	2B	3B	HR	RBI	BB	SO	SB	CS	OBP	SLG
2005	Royals (AZL)	R	.408	28	98	29	40	7	4	6	30	16	22	5	2	.484	.745
2006	Royals (AZL)	R	.429	12	42	13	18	4	0	2	6	9	3	1	1	.537	.667
2007	Burlington (MWL)	LoA	.247	99	368	43	91	19	0	2	36	25	72	15	4	.296	.315
2008	Wilmington (CAR)	HiA	.255	104	396	57	101	34	5	10	61	20	95	13	4	.290	.442
2009	Wilmington (CAR)	HiA	.300	60	220	32	66	12	2	4	28	20	47	12	2	.360	.427
	NW Arkansas (TL)	AA	.315	68	270	42	85	17	1	5	42	19	58	10	4	.356	.441
2010	Did Not Play—Injured																
Minor League Totals			.288	371	1394	216	401	93	12	29	203	109	297	56	17	.339	.434

22 PATRICK KEATING, RHP

Born: June 9, 1987. **B-T:** R-R. **Ht.:** 6-2. **Wt.:** 215. **Drafted:** Florida, 2009 (20th round). **Signed by:** Colin Gonzalez.

Keating posted a 5.01 ERA in four seasons at Florida and pitched his way out of the Gators' rotation as a senior, which is why he was available for a 20th-round pick and $1,000 bonus in 2009. He has thrived as a full-time reliever in pro ball, shooting to Double-A in his first full pro season. He has focused on throwing his four-seam fastball and curveball in shorter stints, enabling his stuff to take a significant step forward. Keating now sits at 91-94 mph with his fastball, and he makes it tougher to hit by hiding the ball well with his delivery. His curve has become a solid-average pitch. He also has a show-me changeup, but he's doing hitters a favor if he throws it more than once or twice an outing. Keating's fastball can sometimes straighten out and he'll never have plus command, but his two-pitch assortment is good enough to get him to a big league bullpen as a sixth- or seventh-inning option. He'll probably open 2011 in Triple-A and could reach Kansas City later in the year.

Year	Club (League)	Class	W	L	ERA	G	GS	CG	SV	IP	H	HR	BB	SO	G/A	WHIP	AVG
2009	Idaho Falls (PIO)	R	5	1	1.78	22	0	0	8	30	20	1	10	46	1.80	0.99	.187
	Wilmington (CAR)	HiA	1	0	0.00	2	0	0	1	3	1	0	0	1	1.00	0.38	.125
2010	Wilmington (CAR)	HiA	2	0	1.19	13	0	0	5	30	18	2	10	41	0.88	0.92	.171
	NW Arkansas (TL)	AA	1	1	3.10	27	0	0	10	41	33	3	19	60	1.75	1.28	.221
Minor League Totals			9	2	2.08	64	0	0	24	104	72	6	39	148	1.39	1.07	.195

23 HUMBERTO ARTEAGA, SS

Born: Jan. 3, 1994 **B-T:** B-R. **Ht.:** 6-1. **Wt.:** 160. **Signed:** Venezuela, 2010. **Signed by:** Orlando Estevez/ Richard Castro.

One of the few obvious weaknesses in baseball's deepest farm system is a lack of plus defenders at shortstop. The Royals have tried to address that, first by signing Yowill Espinal in 2008. Last year, they handed out seven-figure bonuses to Arteaga ($1.1 million) and Orlando Calixte ($1 million). A smooth-fielding Venezuelan, Arteaga had one of the best gloves on the international market in 2010 and immediately became the best defensive infielder in Kansas City's system. He has soft hands and a strong arm, and he also has a knack for positioning himself well. At the plate, Arteaga has a simple direct swing path but is limited right now by his lack of power. Some scouts wonder about his ability to become an average hitter, but the Royals believe he'll improve as he adds strength. He's an average runner. Artega displays impressive maturity for his age, and one of his first purchases with his bonus was the Rosetta Stone language tutorials so he could start learning English. He doesn't figure to make his U.S. debut until 2012 at the earliest.

Year	Club (League)	Class	AVG	G	AB	R	H	2B	3B	HR	RBI	BB	SO	SB	CS	OBP	SLG
2010	Did Not Play—Signed 2011 Contract																

24 ORLANDO CALIXTE, SS

Born: Feb. 3, 1992. **B-T:** R-R. **Ht.:** 5-11. **Wt.:** 160. **Signed:** Dominican Republic, 2010. **Signed by:** Alvin Cuevas/Hector Pineda.

Calixte was a mystery man for much of the past two years. He was considered one of the better prospects in the 2008 international crop and was expected to sign a seven-figure deal before questions about his name and age cropped up. He apparently had swapped identities with his brother. The Royals, who had been watching him for three years, stepped in and worked out a deal in 2010. It took several months for his identity questions to be worked out, as Paul Carlixte turned out to be Orlando Caxito and then Orlando Calixte. At one point MLB asked the Royals to pull Calixte from the Rookie-level Dominican Summer League until the matter was resolved. With some time and a $1 million bonus, the Royals added their second high-ceiling Latin shortstop signing of the summer when Calixte officially signed in August. Calixte has more hitting and power potential than Humberto Arteaga, but he's also two years older as he starts out his career. Calixte is only an average runner, though he moves pretty well once under way and should be able to stick at shortstop. He has quick actions, good hands and feet and a plus arm. Calixte has his visa and made it to the United States for instructional league. He'll make his U.S. debut in Rookie ball, either at Idaho Falls or in the Arizona League this summer.

Year	Club (League)	Class	AVG	G	AB	R	H	2B	3B	HR	RBI	BB	SO	SB	CS	OBP	SLG
2010	Royals (DSL)	R	.227	20	66	10	15	6	0	0	12	13	13	3	1	.350	.318
Minor League Totals			.227	20	66	10	15	6	0	0	12	13	13	3	1	.350	.318

25 DAVID LOUGH, OF

Born: Jan. 20, 1986. **B-T:** L-L. **Ht.:** 6-0. **Wt.:** 180. **Drafted:** Mercyhurst (Pa.), 2007 (11th round). **Signed by:** Jason Bryan.

The Royals not only have had success drafting players with signability concerns, but they've also found their share of bargains as well. A former baseball walk-on who was also a wide receiver at NCAA Division II Mercyhurst (Pa.), Lough cost them only an 11th-round pick and $49,500. Thought to be a somewhat raw athlete with above-average speed, he quickly proved to be a more advanced hitter than expected. Lough has a short, quick stroke that allows him to hit for average with doubles power and solid on-base ability. He traditionally has struggled to hit lefthanders, but he did do a better job of staying in against them in 2010. His above-average speed helps make up for his so-so reads of the ball off the bat, but he's only an average center fielder at best and his below-average arm plays better in left field. Lough isn't far away from the big leagues but profiles as a reserve rather than as a regular. Added to the 40-man roster in November, he'll have to beat out Mitch Maier for a spot as a fourth outfielder in 2011.

Year	Club (League)	Class	AVG	G	AB	R	H	2B	3B	HR	RBI	BB	SO	SB	CS	OBP	SLG
2007	Burlington (APP)	R	.337	24	86	15	29	6	0	2	12	4	13	6	1	.380	.477
2008	Burlington (MWL)	LoA	.268	126	488	76	131	21	11	16	62	35	70	12	11	.329	.455
2009	Wilmington (CAR)	HiA	.320	65	222	28	71	15	2	5	30	12	34	6	4	.370	.473
	NW Arkansas (TL)	AA	.331	61	236	41	78	13	2	9	31	12	30	13	4	.371	.517
2010	Omaha (PCL)	AAA	.280	120	460	65	129	15	12	11	58	40	72	14	5	.346	.437
Minor League Totals			.294	396	1492	225	438	70	27	43	193	103	219	51	25	.350	.463

26 DERRICK ROBINSON, OF

Born: Sept. 28, 1987. **B-T:** B-L. **Ht.:** 5-11. **Wt.:** 170. **Drafted:** HS—Gainesville, Fla., 2006 (4th round). **Signed by:** Cliff Pastornicky.

Robinson accepted a football scholarship to play cornerback at Florida, but the Royals bought him away from that commitment for $850,000 after drafting him in the fourth round in 2006. At the time, he represented a rare over-slot signing for Kansas City outside of the first round. The Royals have had to be patient with him, but he came on in the second half of 2009 and had his best pro season in 2010. Robinson had good timing, because the club decided to protect him on the 40-man roster rather than risk losing him in the Rule 5 draft. He has 70-75 speed on the 20-80 scale, and since shortening his stride in mid-2009, he has hit lefthanders well for the first time in his career. But even with the progress he has made, Robinson still has a long ways to go. He continues to strike out too much and walk too infrequently, he has very little power and he gets thrown out more than someone with his speed should. He's a plus defender in center field, but his poor jumps at times keep him from running down as many balls as fellow center fielder Jarrod Dyson. Robinson's arm is below average. He'll move up to Triple-A this year, and he'll have to keep getting better to be productive enough to become a big league regular.

Year	Club (League)	Class	AVG	G	AB	R	H	2B	3B	HR	RBI	BB	SO	SB	CS	OBP	SLG
2006	Royals (AZL)	R	.233	54	176	25	41	6	3	1	24	24	55	20	14	.335	.318
2007	Burlington (MWL)	LoA	.243	102	407	42	99	11	3	2	26	32	100	34	7	.299	.300
	Wilmington (CAR)	HiA	.385	3	13	1	5	1	0	0	0	1	0	1	0	.429	.462
2008	Wilmington (CAR)	HiA	.245	124	497	69	122	22	8	0	34	51	97	62	17	.316	.322
2009	Wilmington (CAR)	HiA	.239	128	522	72	125	19	5	5	47	35	90	69	23	.290	.324
2010	NW Arkansas (TL)	AA	.286	127	511	74	146	26	8	2	48	45	86	50	17	.345	.380
Minor League Totals			.253	538	2126	283	538	85	27	10	179	188	428	236	78	.316	.333

27 HENRY BARRERA, RHP

Born: Nov. 25, 1985. **B-T:** R-R. **Ht.:** 6-0. **Wt.:** 205. **Drafted:** HS—Rosemead, Calif., 2004 (5th round). **Signed by:** Luis Cordoba.

Since signing as a fifth-round pick in 2004, Barrera has had one of the best arms in the system, as well as its worst delivery. His poor mechanics came back to haunt him in 2009, when he broke down and needed Tommy John surgery. Since returning last June, he has cleaned up his delivery some but it still has some effort. He has a whippy arm action, collapses on the back side and finishes out of alignment with the plate. His less-than-smooth mechanics do add deception, making his overpowering fastball that much more difficult to hit. Barrera sits at 93-94 mph on his bad nights and can hit 97-98 regularly when he's going good. His hard slider gives him a potential second plus pitch, though he seems reluctant to snap it off as hard as he did before his elbow reconstruction. In his first year back from the surgery, the Royals took away his hard splitter that actually had more cut than drop. He exhibited better command than he had in the past, though it's still just average. Barrera has a ceiling as a late-inning reliever and could move quickly if he feels more comfortable letting loose in his second year after the surgery. He could open 2011 in Triple-A.

Year	Club (League)	Class	W	L	ERA	G	GS	CG	SV	IP	H	HR	BB	SO	G/A	WHIP	AVG
2005	Royals (AZL)	R	1	1	4.72	19	0	0	6	27	33	1	9	23	—	1.58	.289
2006	Royals (AZL)	R	0	1	5.48	16	0	0	2	23	20	0	17	30	—	1.61	.225
2007	Burlington (MWL)	LoA	2	2	4.35	30	0	0	4	52	53	4	15	53	—	1.32	.261
2008	Wilmington (CAR)	HiA	0	3	2.81	42	0	0	4	58	47	2	24	78	—	1.23	.224
2009	Burlington (MWL)	LoA	0	0	12.27	4	0	0	0	4	2	0	5	5	1.00	1.91	.154
2010	Wilmington (CAR)	HiA	0	0	4.50	6	0	0	1	8	9	0	3	10	0.56	1.50	.281
	NW Arkansas (TL)	AA	3	1	1.80	16	0	0	1	25	17	1	7	25	1.35	0.96	.193
Minor League Totals			6	8	3.91	133	0	0	18	196	181	8	80	224	1.09	1.33	.242

28 CLINT ROBINSON, 1B

Born: Feb. 16, 1985. **B-T:** L-L. **Ht.:** 6-5. **Wt.:** 225. **Drafted:** Troy, 2007 (25th round). **Signed by:** Max Semler.

Robinson didn't get taken seriously as a prospect until he won the Texas League triple crown in 2010. Despite solid numbers at Troy, Robinson went undrafted as a college junior, then lasted to the 25th round and signed for just $1,000 in 2007. Even after he hit .336 and led the Rookie-level Pioneer League with 66 RBIs in his pro debut, he still didn't draw many positive reviews because of his lack of athleticism and defensive ability. Robinson is starting to show that he can do more than just hit for power. He uses the whole field and covers the plate well, which allows him to hit for a solid average despite his well-below-average speed. He is a liability in the field, as he doesn't move well at first base and can't play anywhere else on the diamond. Many scouts still project Robinson as a player who will spend more time in Triple-A than in the majors, but he has exceeded expectations since he was drafted. A November addition to the 40-man roster, he heads to Omaha for the first time, one step away from his ultimate goal.

Year	Club (League)	Class	AVG	G	AB	R	H	2B	3B	HR	RBI	BB	SO	SB	CS	OBP	SLG
2007	Idaho Falls (PIO)	R	.336	67	253	39	85	18	1	15	66	19	42	2	0	.388	.593
2008	Burlington (MWL)	LoA	.264	106	379	53	100	22	3	17	64	37	67	0	3	.333	.472
2009	Wilmington (CAR)	HiA	.298	124	436	65	130	31	1	13	57	35	79	4	3	.356	.463
2010	NW Arkansas (TL)	AA	.335	129	477	90	160	41	5	29	98	58	86	4	3	.410	.625
Minor League Totals			.307	426	1545	247	475	112	10	74	285	149	274	10	9	.373	.537

29 ELISAUL PIMENTEL, RHP

Born: July 10, 1988. **B-T:** R-R. **Ht.:** 6-2. **Wt.:** 170. **Signed:** Dominican Republic, 2006. **Signed by:** Victor Baez (Dodgers).

Kansas City's signing of outfielder Scott Podsednik to a one-year, $1.75 million deal last offseason paid off handsomely. Podsednik had a strong first half for the Royals before they traded him to the Dodgers last July for Pimentel and Lucas May, who may be their backup catcher in 2011. Pimentel is a relatively late bloomer who didn't sign out of the Dominican Republic until he was 18. He spent three years in Rookie ball before reaching low Class A last year, where he showed the stuff to project as a back-of-the-rotation starter or a power reliever. Pimentel uses an easy delivery to let loose 90-93 mph fastballs and has more projection remaining in his skinny frame. He complements his fastball with a hard, tight slider that's a potential plus pitch. He's more effective against lefthanders than righthanders because of his ability to run his slider in on lefties. He maintains his arm speed on his changeup, though it's still a below-average pitch. Pimentel's arsenal is intriguing, but he'll have to learn to control it better. That will be one of his goals this year in high Class A.

Year	Club (League)	Class	W	L	ERA	G	GS	CG	SV	IP	H	HR	BB	SO	G/A	WHIP	AVG
2007	Dodgers (DSL)	R	0	1	4.23	8	3	0	0	28	26	3	10	24	—	1.30	.241
2008	Dodgers (GCL)	R	3	6	2.41	11	10	2	0	56	43	0	13	43	—	1.00	.212
	Ogden (PIO)	R	0	1	6.75	2	0	0	0	4	5	0	2	2	—	1.75	.357
2009	Ogden (PIO)	R	4	4	4.73	13	12	0	0	59	71	4	15	48	1.95	1.46	.300
2010	Great Lakes (MWL)	LoA	9	3	3.49	17	16	0	0	90	71	6	35	97	1.01	1.17	.215
	Burlington (MWL)	LoA	1	3	5.76	5	5	0	0	25	29	1	16	19	0.86	1.80	.299
Minor League Totals			17	18	3.88	56	46	2	0	262	245	14	91	233	1.24	1.28	.247

30 KELVIN HERRERA, RHP

Born: Dec. 31, 1989. **B-T:** R-R. **Ht.:** 5-10. **Wt.:** 170. **Signed:** Dominican Republic, 2006. **Signed by:** Daurys Nin/Rafael Vasquez.

Herrera once ranked among the Royals' best pitching prospects, but he has made just nine starts in the last two years with repeated elbow problems that haven't required surgery. His elbow issues may be related to changes in his mechanics. He had been putting stress on his arm by landing on his heel, and Kansas City tried to get him to land on the ball of his foot. He overcompensated and shortened his stride, which still resulted in a jarring delivery. Herrera did return during instructional league last fall, showing the same stuff he had before his elbow started bothering him. He throws a low-90s fastball and touches 95. His best secondary pitch is a potential plus changeup, and he also throws a fringe-average slurve. Herrera's small frame leads to further questions about his durability, which could have him destined for the bullpen, where his fastball could play up even more. His immediate goal is to stay healthy in 2011, when he could return to low Class A for the fourth straight season.

Year	Club (League)	Class	W	L	ERA	G	GS	CG	SV	IP	H	HR	BB	SO	G/A	WHIP	AVG
2007	Royals (DSL)	R	4	1	0.84	11	5	0	1	43	30	1	15	50	—	1.05	.197
2008	Burlington (APP)	R	2	2	1.42	11	8	0	0	51	48	0	5	45	—	1.05	.254
	Burlington (MWL)	LoA	2	0	2.13	3	1	0	0	13	13	0	2	7	—	1.18	.265
2009	Burlington (MWL)	LoA	1	0	0.00	1	1	0	0	5	3	0	0	1	2.25	0.60	.176
2010	Burlington (MWL)	LoA	2	3	4.35	8	8	0	0	41	38	2	15	40	1.59	1.28	.253
Minor League Totals			11	6	2.07	34	23	0	1	152	132	3	37	143	1.68	1.11	.237

Los Angeles Angels

BY MATT EDDY

The 2007 Angels won 94 regular-season games, captured the American League West by six games and had no shortage of optimism for the future.

The organization's young, homegrown core had arrived. John Lackey won 19 games and led the American League with a 3.01 ERA, first-round phenom Jered Weaver completed his first full season and 25-year-old closer Francisco Rodriguez saved 40 games. Howie Kendrick and Casey Kotchman had terrific seasons after claiming starting jobs in their early 20s, and Chone Figgins batted .330 and stole 41 bases.

On the farm, shortstop Brandon Wood and righthander Nick Adenhart stood as the two brightest prospects. They seemed about a half-season away from making major contributions in Los Angeles.

Fast-forward three short years, and only Weaver, now the staff ace, and Kendrick, coming off his worst year, remain in the picture. In the course of two years, the Angels lost Figgins, Lackey and Rodriguez as free agents. They traded Kotchman to the Braves to rent Mark Teixeira for three months.

Los Angeles acted prudently in letting the free agents walk, in light of the dollars involved or the players' subsequent diminished production. But the farm system has struggled to fill in the gaps.

Despite recently graduating quality regulars such as Erick Aybar, Kevin Jepsen and Kendry Morales, the Angels simply didn't have the talent on hand, homegrown or imported, to contend in 2010. Los Angeles went 80-82, its first losing record in seven seasons, and finished third in the AL West.

The Angels' offense never recovered from the loss of Morales—who broke his leg celebrating a walkoff homer May 29—or the departure of Figgins and lesser years by Aybar and Kendrick. The club scored 202 fewer runs than it did in 2009, plummeting from an exemplary 5.5 runs per game to a below-average 4.2.

Wood's failure to develop has hurt the offense. In parts of four seasons with the Angels, he has hit .169, the second-lowest average in major league history for a player with as many as 479 plate appearances.

The loss of Adenhart, killed by a drunk driver in April 2009, also continues to hurt. Los Angeles surrendered standout Double-A lefty Alex Torres to acquire Scott Kazmir from the Rays in August 2009. It made a similar move last July, sending four pitchers, most notably athletic lefties Tyler Skaggs and Pat

The Angels' offense never recovered from losing Kendry Morales to a broken leg

TOP 30 PROSPECTS

1. Mike Trout, of
2. Tyler Chatwood, rhp
3. Jean Segura, 2b
4. Hank Conger, c
5. Jordan Walden, rhp
6. Kaleb Cowart, 3b
7. Garrett Richards, rhp
8. Fabio Martinez, rhp
9. Mark Trumbo, 1b/of
10. Cam Bedrosian, rhp
11. Trevor Reckling, lhp
12. Randal Grichuk, of
13. Chevez Clarke, of
14. Daniel Tillman, rhp
15. Michael Kohn, rhp
16. Jeremy Moore, of
17. Andrew Romine, ss
18. Alexi Amarista, 2b
19. Taylor Lindsey, 2b
20. Orangel Arenas, rhp
21. Travis Witherspoon, of
22. Luis Jimenez, 3b
23. Johnny Hellweg, rhp
24. Bobby Cassevah, rhp
25. Donn Roach, rhp
26. Ryan Bolden, of
27. Ysmael Carmona, rhp
28. Drew Taylor, lhp
29. Drew Heid, of
30. Loek Van Mil, rhp

Corbin, to get Dan Haren from the Diamondbacks.

After going without a true first-round pick three times in four years from 2005-08, the Angels had six picks among the top 100 in each of the past two drafts. Those choices included dynamic center fielder Mike Trout as well as Skaggs and Corbin.

Los Angeles opted not to renew scouting director Eddie Bane's contract at the end of the season. His seven drafts with the club yielded Weaver and promising 2010 rookies Peter Bourjos, Hank Conger and Jordan Walden. The Angels promoted national crosschecker Ric Wilson to take over as scouting director.

General Manager: Tony Reagins. **Farm Director:** Abe Flores. **Scouting Director:** Ric Wilson.

Class	Team	League	W	L	PCT	Finish*	Manager
Majors	Los Angeles Angels	American	80	82	.494	10th (14)	Mike Scioscia
Triple-A	Salt Lake Bees	Pacific Coast	73	71	.507	9th (16)	Bobby Mitchell
Double-A	Arkansas Travelers	Texas	55	85	.393	8th (8)	Bobby Magallanes
High A	Rancho Cucamonga Quakes	California	78	62	.557	2nd (10)	Keith Johnson
Low A	Cedar Rapids Kernels	Midwest	82	56	.594	3rd (16)	Bill Mosiello
Rookie	Orem Owlz	Pioneer	39	36	.520	4th (8)	Tom Kotchman
Rookie	AZL Angels	Arizona	24	31	.436	9th (12)	Tyrone Boykin
Overall 2010 Minor League Record			351	341	.507	13th (30)	

*Finish in overall standings (No. of teams in league). †League champion.
High Class A affiliate changes to Inland Empire (California) in 2011.

LAST YEAR'S TOP 30

Player, Pos.		Status
1.	Hank Conger, c	No. 4
2.	Peter Bourjos, of	Majors
3.	Mike Trout, of	No. 1
4.	Trevor Reckling, lhp	No. 11
5.	Garrett Richards, rhp	No. 7
6.	Fabio Martinez, rhp	No. 8
7.	Randal Grichuk, of	No. 12
8.	Tyler Skaggs, lhp	(Diamondbacks)
9.	Jordan Walden, rhp	No. 5
10.	Trevor Bell, rhp	Majors
11.	Mark Trumbo, 1b/of	No. 9
12.	Pat Corbin, lhp	(Diamondbacks)
13.	Jean Segura, 2b	No. 3
14.	Tyler Chatwood, rhp	No. 2
15.	Will Smith, lhp	(Royals)
16.	Chris Pettit, of	Dropped out
17.	Alexi Amarista, 2b	No. 18
18.	Tyler Kehrer, lhp	Dropped out
19.	Jon Bachanov, rhp	Dropped out
20.	Carlos Ramirez, c	Dropped out
21.	Ryan Chaffee, rhp	Dropped out
22.	Rafael Rodriguez, rhp	(Diamondbacks)
23.	Bobby Mosebach, rhp	(Free agent)
24.	Mason Tobin, rhp	(Rangers)
25.	Rolando Gomez, ss	Dropped out
26.	Bobby Wilson, c	Dropped out
27.	Andrew Romine, ss	No. 17
28.	Ryan Mount, 2b	Dropped out
29.	Clay Fuller, of	Dropped out
30.	Michael Kohn, rhp	No. 15

BEST TOOLS

Best Hitter for Average	Mike Trout
Best Power Hitter	Mark Trumbo
Best Strike-Zone Discipline	Hank Conger
Fastest Baserunner	Mike Trout
Best Athlete	Mike Trout
Best Fastball	Jordan Walden
Best Curveball	Tyler Chatwood
Best Slider	Fabio Martinez
Best Changeup	Trevor Reckling
Best Control	Tim Kiely
Best Defensive Catcher	Alberto Rosario
Best Defensive Infielder	Andrew Romine
Best Infield Arm	Kaleb Cowart
Best Defensive Outfielder	Mike Trout
Best Outfield Arm	Angel Castillo

PROJECTED 2014 LINEUP

Catcher	Hank Conger
First Base	Kendry Morales
Second Base	Jean Segura
Third Base	Kaleb Cowart
Shortstop	Erick Aybar
Left Field	Mike Trout
Center Field	Peter Bourjos
Right Field	Torii Hunter
Designated Hitter	Mark Trumbo
No. 1 Starter	Jered Weaver
No. 2 Starter	Dan Haren
No. 3 Starter	Ervin Santana
No. 4 Starter	Tyler Chatwood
No. 5 Starter	Garrett Richards
Closer	Jordan Walden

TOP PROSPECTS OF THE DECADE

Year	Player, Pos.	2010 Org.
2001	Joe Torres, lhp	White Sox
2002	Casey Kotchman, 1b	Mariners
2003	Francisco Rodriguez, rhp	Mets
2004	Casey Kotchman, 1b	Mariners
2005	Casey Kotchman, 1b	Mariners
2006	Brandon Wood, ss	Angels
2007	Brandon Wood, ss	Angels
2008	Brandon Wood, ss	Angels
2009	Nick Adenhart, rhp	Deceased
2010	Hank Conger, c	Angels

TOP DRAFT PICKS OF THE DECADE

Year	Player, Pos.	2010 Org.
2001	Casey Kotchman, 1b	Mariners
2002	Joe Saunders, lhp	Diamondbacks
2003	Brandon Wood, ss	Angels
2004	Jered Weaver, rhp	Angels
2005	Trevor Bell, rhp (1st round supp.)	Angels
2006	Hank Conger, c	Angels
2007	Jon Bachanov, rhp (1st round supp.)	Angels
2008	Tyler Chatwood, rhp (2nd round)	Angels
2009	Randal Grichuk, of	Angels
2010	Kaleb Cowart, 3b	Angels

LARGEST BONUSES IN CLUB HISTORY

Jered Weaver, 2004	$4,000,000
Kendry Morales, 2004	$3,000,000
Kaleb Cowart, 2010	$2,300,000
Troy Glaus, 1997	$2,250,000
Joe Torres, 2000	$2,080,000

LOS ANGELES ANGELS

TOP 2011 ROOKIE: Jordan Walden, rhp. A flamethrower, he's poised to close games if Fernando Rodney falters.

BREAKOUT PROSPECT: Daniel Tillman, rhp. An aggressive strike-thrower with two plus pitchrs could reach Double-A by the end of 2011.

SLEEPER: Jeremy Cruz, of/3b/1b. Repeated injuries have limited him to 69 games in two pro seasons, but he has hit the ball with authority when healthy.

SOURCE OF TOP 30 TALENT			
Homegrown	29	Acquired	1
College	6	Trades	1
Junior college	3	Rule 5 draft	0
High school	13	Independent leagues	0
Draft-and-follow	1	Free agents/waivers	0
Nondrafted free agents	0		
International	6		

LF
Drew Heid (29)
Chris Pettit
Matt Long
Kole Calhoun

CF
Mike Trout (1)
Chevez Clarke (13)
Jeremy Moore (16)
Travis Witherspoon (21)
Tyson Auer

RF
Randal Grichuk (12)
Ryan Bolden (26)
Angel Castillo
Clay Fuller

3B
Kaleb Cowart (6)
Luis Jimenez (22)
Jeremy Cruz
Freddy Sandoval
Dillon Baird

SS
Andrew Romine (17)
Rolando Gomez
Wendell Soto
Darwin Perez
Kevin Moesquit

2B
Jean Segura (3)
Alexi Amarista (18)
Taylor Lindsey (19)
Wes Hatton

1B
Mark Trumbo (9)
Brandon Decker
Casey Haerther
Gabe Jacobo

C
Hank Conger (4)
Bobby Wilson
Alberto Rosario
Roberto Lopez
Carlos Ramirez
Anel de los Santos

RHP

RHSP	RHRP
Tyler Chatwood (2)	Jordan Walden (5)
Garrett Richards (7)	Fabio Martinez (8)
Cam Bedrosian (10)	Daniel Tillman (14)
Orangel Arenas (20)	Michael Kohn (15)
Donn Roach (25)	Johnny Hellweg (23)
Anthony Ortega	Bobby Cassevah (24)
	Ysmael Carmona (26)
	Loek Van Mil (30)
	Justin LaTempa
	Jon Bachanov
	Ryan Chaffee
	Ryan Brasier
	Bryant George
	David Carpenter
	Jose Perez
	Ariel Pena
	Matt Oye
	Brian Diemer
	A.J. Schugel
	Eddie McKiernan
	Danny Reynolds

LHP

LHSP	LHRP
Trevor Reckling (11)	Drew Taylor (28)
Max Russell	Tyler Kehrer
Aaron Meade	Barret Browning

2010   BONUSES: $8.1 MILLION

BEST PURE HITTER: Most clubs didn't rate 2B Taylor Lindsey (1s) as a sandwich pick, but the Angels believed in his bat. He hit .592 and .557 in his last two high school seasons, then .284/.325/.407 in his pro debut in the Rookie-level Arizona League.

BEST POWER HITTER: 3B/RHP Kaleb Cowart (1) and OF Ryan Bolden (1s) have above-average raw power. Several teams liked Cowart better as a pitcher, but he and the Angels prefer that he plays every day.

FASTEST RUNNER: Bolden has 70 speed on the 20-80 scouting scale, with OF Chevez Clarke (1) a step behind him.

BEST DEFENSIVE PLAYER: SS Wendell Soto (3) is a quality defender who needs to add strength to hold his own at the plate. Cowart and Clarke had two of the strongest arms among position players in the entire draft.

BEST FASTBALL: RHP Daniel Tillman (2) pitched at 91-96 mph in his pro debut. RHPs Cam Bedrosian (1), Donn Roach (3s) and Justin LaTempa (12) top out at 95.

BEST SECONDARY PITCH: Bedrosian's hard slider is his best pitch. Tillman's slider gives him a second weapon for late-inning relief.

BEST PRO DEBUT: Tillman, OF Drew Heid (9) and OF Brandon Decker (27) all stood out at Rookie-level Orem. Tillman had a 1.95 ERA, 10 saves and 50 strikeouts in 32 innings, while Heid batted .362/.435/.505 and led the Pioneer League with 104 hits and Decker batted .341/.429/.653 with 13 home runs.

BEST ATHLETE: Bolden offers power and speed in a center-field package, and his only substandard tool is his fringy arm. Clarke has average or better tools across the board.

MOST INTRIGUING BACKGROUND: In part because he spent four years in the military, RHP Chance Mistric (42) was one of the oldest draftees ever at age 26. Mistric, who won the championship game of the Division II Junior College World Series for Louisiana State-Eunice, throws a heavy sinker in the low 90s. Bedrosian's father Steve won the National League Cy Young Award in 1987. RHP A.J. Schugel (25), who showed a 92-93 mph fastball after converting from third base, is the son of Angels big league scout Jeff. Clarke is related to the Hairston clan, which has produced five big leaguers. 2B Mike Sodders' (31) father Mike was the 11th overall pick in the June 1981 draft.

CLOSEST TO THE MAJORS: As a reliever with two plus pitches, Tillman could shoot through the minors.

BEST LATE-ROUND PICK: Decker.

THE ONE WHO GOT AWAY: LHP Josh Osich (7) peaked at 99 mph and had a sharp curveball before blowing out his elbow and missing the 2009 season following Tommy John surgery. The Angels made a run at him, but he returned to Oregon State. They also failed to sign projectable RHP Jesus Valdez (5), who's attending Arizona.

ASSESSMENT: The Angels had three first-round picks and spent them all on Georgia high school products. Los Angeles fired scouting director Eddie Bane in September, reportedly because of tension between him and GM Tony Reagins.

2009   BONUSES: $6.8 MILLION

A year later, it's hard to fathom how OF Mike Trout (1) lasted 25 picks. The Angels had five other picks in the top two rounds: OF Randal Grichuk (1) and RHP Garrett Richards (1s) are developing nicely; LHPs Tyler Skaggs (1s) and Pat Corbin (2) were keys to the Dan Haren trade; and only LHP Tyler Kehrer (1s) has been a disappointment.

GRADE: A

2008   BONUSES: $2.7 MILLION

Los Angeles didn't have a first-round choice, but its top pick, RHP Tyler Chatwood (2), has become the system's best mound prospect. Signed for $5,000, funky RHP Michael Kohn (13) reached the majors last July.

GRADE: C

2007   BONUSES: $1.8 MILLION

The Angels had no first- or second-rounders, and RHP Jon Bachanov (1s), their top choice, had Tommy John surgery soon after signing. The best player they drafted, RHP Matt Harvey (3), didn't sign and went seventh overall in 2010. SS Andrew Romine (5) made a big league cameo last year, while this crop's best prospect, LHP Trevor Reckling (8), went backward.

GRADE: D

2006   BONUSES: $4.0 MILLION

C Hank Conger (1) and draft-and-follow RHP Jordan Walden (12) could be the team's catcher and closer of the near future. RHP David Herndon (5), lost in the Rule 5 draft, and OF Chris Pettit (19) have played in the majors. 3B Matt Sweeney (8) helped land Scott Kazmir in a 2009 trade.

GRADE: C+

Draft analysis by Jim Callis. Numbers in parentheses indicate draft rounds.

MIKE TROUT, OF

Born: Aug. 7, 1991. **Bats:** R. **Throws:** R.
Height: 6-1. **Weight:** 200. **Drafted:** HS—
Millville, N.J., 2009 (1st round). **Signed by:**
Greg Morhardt.

LARRY GOREN

Trout lived a charmed life in 2009. After going 25th overall to the Angels and signing for $1.215 million, he ranked as the No. 1 prospect in the Rookie-level Arizona League. Not bad for a player who some feel got somewhat underrated in the draft because he hails from the Northeast. Incredibly, Trout was even more spectacular in his full-season followup in 2010. He began the year by hitting .362 at low Class A Cedar Rapids, winning the Midwest League's batting and on-base (.454) titles and MVP award despite getting promoted in mid-July. Managers rated him the best hitter, best and fastest runner, best defensive outfielder and most exciting player in the MWL. After going 2-for-4 with a double and a steal in the Futures Game in Anaheim, Trout headed to high Class A Rancho Cucamonga at the tender age of 18. He erased a rough start by hitting .338 over his final 34 games and then .367 with three homers in the California League playoffs. All told, he batted .341/.428/.490 with 10 home runs and a 73-to-85 walk-to-strikeout ratio. He ranked fifth in the minors in steals (56 in 71 attempts) and sixth in runs (106) and OBP. Trout ranked as the No. 1 prospect in both the Midwest and California leagues, giving observers little to dislike.

Built like a football defensive back, Trout is a rare five-tool talent who can really hit, a product of his strong, compact stroke and impressive batting eye. He shows no fear of hitting with two strikes, an unusual trait in a teenager. He scores well above-average marks for his running speed—a present and future 80 on the 20-80 scouting scale—and center-field range. One scout saw him hit a 400-foot homer in one at-bat, then get to first base in 3.65 seconds on a bunt his next time up. Trout's weakest present tools, his power and throwing arm, still grade as future average. His physicality and bat speed hint at more power down the road. He handles inside pitches well but has yet to demonstrate that he can pull or loft the ball with consistency. If and when he does, he has the potential to hit 20 or more homers annually. He compensates for fringy arm strength with above-average accuracy. His maturity, drive and instincts further separate him from other prospects his age.

During a four-year pro career in the Twins system, Trout's father Jeff first reached Double-A at age 23. Mike ought to get to Double-A by July at the latest—four years ahead of Jeff's pace. Like the Braves' Jason Heyward and the Marlins' Mike Stanton in 2010, Trout could be ready to produce in the majors as a 20-year-old come 2012. The presence of Peter Bourjos, an elite defensive center fielder, in Anaheim clouds Trout's future somewhat. If Bourjos hits enough to stay in the lineup, then Trout may move to an outfield corner, probably left field because of his arm. Even in that scenario he profiles as a top-third-of-the-order hitter with a wide array of offensive skills and Gold Glove potential on defense.

SCOUTING GRADES

Batting: 70.   **Defense:** 70.
Power: 55.   **Arm:** 50.
Speed: 80.

Based on 20-80 scouting scale, where 50 represents major league average, and future projection rather than present tools.

Year	Club (League)	Class	AVG	G	AB	R	H	2B	3B	HR	RBI	BB	SO	SB	CS	OBP	SLG
2009	Angels (AZL)	R	.360	39	164	29	59	7	7	1	25	18	28	13	2	.418	.506
	Cedar Rapids (MWL)	LoA	.267	5	15	1	4	0	0	0	0	4	6	0	0	.421	.267
2010	Cedar Rapids (MWL)	LoA	.362	81	312	76	113	19	7	6	39	46	52	45	9	.454	.526
	R. Cucamonga (CAL)	HiA	.306	50	196	30	60	9	2	4	19	27	33	11	6	.388	.434
Minor League Totals			.344	175	687	136	236	35	16	11	83	95	119	69	17	.426	.489

2 TYLER CHATWOOD, RHP

Born: Dec. 16, 1989. **B-T:** R-R. **Ht.:** 6-0. **Wt.:** 185. **Drafted:** HS—Redlands, Calif., 2008 (2nd round). **Signed by:** Tim Corcoran.

The Angels lost their first-round pick in the 2008 draft after signing free agent Torii Hunter, but they made up for the deficit by selecting Chatwood in the second round and buying him out of a UCLA commitment for $547,000. Acute wildness was a problem early in his career, but he has cut his walk rate at each stop of the minors—though his strikeout rate also plummeted once he got to Double-A Arkansas in late June. At his best, Chatwood works with a mid-90s four-seam fastball and a mid-70s, knee-buckling curve. His heater runs in on the hands of righthanders, and when he keeps the ball down he generates plenty of groundouts. He started working in more low-90s two-seamers in 2010. He also made big strides with his changeup, which now rates as at least average. Chatwood toned down the stabbing action on the backswing in his delivery, reaping tangible gains in control. However, he still showed below-average command of his fastball and curve, too often missing up in the zone. Chatwood's plus stuff and aggressive style—"There's no quit in anything he does," one California League manager said—speak louder than his smallish stature. If he commands his pitches better, he profiles as a front-end starter. If not, he could thrive in a bullpen role.

Year	Club (League)	Class	W	L	ERA	G	GS	CG	SV	IP	H	HR	BB	SO	G/A	WHIP	AVG
2008	Angels (AZL)	R	1	2	3.08	11	11	0	0	38	25	1	36	48	—	1.61	.195
2009	Cedar Rapids (MWL)	LoA	8	7	4.02	24	24	0	0	116	99	3	66	106	1.52	1.42	.237
2010	R. Cucamonga (CAL)	HiA	8	3	1.77	14	13	0	0	81	70	6	36	70	3.42	1.32	.241
	Arkansas (TL)	AA	4	6	3.82	12	12	1	0	68	72	3	27	36	1.88	1.45	.273
	Salt Lake (PCL)	AAA	1	0	6.35	1	1	0	0	6	9	1	0	3	2.33	1.59	.346
Minor League Totals			22	18	3.31	62	61	1	0	310	276	14	165	263	2.02	1.42	.244

3 JEAN SEGURA, 2B

Born: March 17, 1990. **B-T:** R-R. **Ht.:** 5-10. **Wt.:** 185. **Signed:** Dominican Republic, 2007. **Signed by:** Leo Perez.

Though the Angels signed Segura with little fanfare in January 2007, he quickly has developed into one of the organization's most dynamic prospects. A broken ankle in 2008 and a broken finger in 2009 truncated his first two seasons in the United States, but he stayed healthy and ranked third in the Midwest League in batting (.313) and steals (50) last season. An aggressive hitter, Segura makes frequent contact and hits the ball to all fields. Stocky, strong and athletic, he generates the bat speed to hit for average power down the road, especially to his pull side. He takes his share of walks and steals bases with plus running speed. Though managers rated him the MWL's best defensive second baseman, Segura suffers from occasional concentration lapses. His arm strength is plus and his hands are clean, but he flubs routine plays on occasion. Some scouts are concerned that his thick lower half could eventually lead to diminished range and quickness. The Angels played Segura at shortstop during instructional league and plan to try him there when he moves up to high Class A in 2011. It's a no-lose proposition: If he can't handle shortstop defensively, he has more than enough bat to develop into a quality regular at second.

Year	Club (League)	Class	AVG	G	AB	R	H	2B	3B	HR	RBI	BB	SO	SB	CS	OBP	SLG
2007	Angels (DSL)	R	.324	61	219	39	71	5	2	2	31	22	28	22	6	.392	.393
2008	Angels (AZL)	R	.250	11	36	13	9	0	0	0	4	6	5	1	0	.372	.250
2009	Salt Lake (PCL)	AAA	.421	7	19	2	8	2	0	0	2	0	4	0	0	.421	.526
	Orem (PIO)	R	.346	36	162	33	56	10	4	3	21	11	11	11	3	.392	.512
2010	Cedar Rapids (MWL)	LoA	.313	130	515	89	161	24	12	10	79	45	72	50	10	.365	.464
Minor League Totals			.321	245	951	176	305	41	18	15	137	84	120	84	19	.377	.449

4 HANK CONGER, C

Born: Jan. 29, 1988. **B-T:** B-R. **Ht.:** 6-1. **Wt.:** 220. **Drafted:** HS—Huntington Beach, Calif., 2006 (1st round). **Signed by:** Bobby DeJardin.

The top power hitter in the 2006 high school ranks, Conger signed for $1.35 million as the 25th overall pick. He hit for power from the outset, but hand, back, hamstring and shoulder injuries prevented him from logging many innings behind the plate until he reached Double-A in 2009. He belted a three-run homer to win MVP honors at the 2010 Futures Game in Anaheim and made his big league debut in September. A switch-hitter, Conger can put a charge into the ball from the left side, where his bat is noticeably quicker. He's geared more for gap power, however, with his line-drive stroke. He makes steady contact and gets on base consistently from both sides. Observers aren't as sold on Conger's defense. He receives and blocks well, but his footwork on throws gets out of whack on any pitch he doesn't handle cleanly, detracting from his average arm strength. He's an easily below-average runner who will have to stay in shape to remain behind the plate. Even his detractors concede Conger is a safe bet to hit between .270-.280 with 15-20 homers at his peak. But that presents the Angels with a tough profile if he has to move to first base or DH. He'll work on refining his defense at Triple-A Salt Lake to start 2011.

Year	Club (League)	Class	AVG	G	AB	R	H	2B	3B	HR	RBI	BB	SO	SB	CS	OBP	SLG
2006	Angels (AZL)	R	.319	19	69	11	22	3	4	1	11	7	11	1	0	.382	.522
2007	Angels (AZL)	R	.267	3	15	2	4	1	0	0	3	0	3	0	0	.267	.333
	Cedar Rapids (MWL)	LoA	.290	84	290	33	84	20	0	11	48	21	48	9	4	.336	.472
2008	R. Cucamonga (CAL)	HiA	.303	73	294	47	89	20	2	13	75	14	55	2	1	.333	.517
2009	Arkansas (TL)	AA	.295	123	458	61	135	20	3	11	68	55	68	4	2	.369	.424
2010	Salt Lake (PCL)	AAA	.300	108	387	56	116	26	2	11	49	55	58	0	2	.385	.463
	Los Angeles (AL)	MAJ	.172	13	29	2	5	1	1	0	5	5	9	0	0	.294	.276
Major League Totals			.172	13	29	2	5	1	1	0	5	5	9	0	0	.294	.276
Minor League Totals			.297	410	1513	210	450	90	11	47	254	152	243	16	9	.360	.465

5 JORDAN WALDEN, RHP

Born: Nov. 16, 1987. **B-T:** R-R. **Ht.:** 6-5. **Wt.:** 240. **Drafted:** Grayson County (Texas) CC, D/F 2006 (12th round). **Signed by:** Arnold Brathwaite.

Much as he rebounded from a poor senior season in high school to land a $1 million draft-and-follow bonus from the Angels, Walden bounced back from a 2009 season marred by a strained elbow ligament to reach the big leagues. Los Angeles converted him to the bullpen during spring training and he finished the year as its top set-up man. Walden hit triple digits on the radar gun multiple times in the big leagues and sat consistently at 94-97 mph. He throws mostly riding four-seamers, but the pitch features sinking, two-seam action when he pitches to his arm side. Opposing batters struggle to lift pitches against Walden, who has permitted just 17 home runs in 346 pro innings—and only one in his big league debut. His low-80s slider is average at best and serves mostly to keep batters off his fastball. His control remains below-average and his changeup is unrefined, so he's in the bullpen to stay. Relieving suits Walden's personality and inconsistent delivery, and it's a role in which he can excel. If Angels closer Fernando Rodney falters, Walden could pick up save opportunities with an eye toward assuming that role full-time in 2012.

Year	Club (League)	Class	W	L	ERA	G	GS	CG	SV	IP	H	HR	BB	SO	G/A	WHIP	AVG
2007	Orem (PIO)	R	1	1	3.08	15	15	0	0	64	49	3	17	63	—	1.03	.209
2008	Cedar Rapids (MWL)	LoA	4	6	2.18	18	18	1	0	107	80	3	32	91	—	1.04	.207
	R. Cucamonga (CAL)	HiA	5	2	4.04	9	9	0	0	49	42	4	24	50	—	1.35	.226
2009	Arkansas (TL)	AA	1	5	5.25	13	13	0	0	60	72	4	29	57	0.98	1.68	.301
2010	Arkansas (TL)	AA	1	1	3.35	38	0	0	8	43	44	2	22	38	1.79	1.53	.277
	Salt Lake (PCL)	AAA	0	0	4.05	6	0	0	0	7	8	0	2	3	0.60	1.50	.296
	Los Angeles (AL)	MAJ	0	1	2.35	16	0	0	1	15	13	1	7	23	3.60	1.30	.224
Major League Totals			0	1	2.35	16	0	0	1	15	13	1	7	23	3.60	1.30	.224
Minor League Totals			12	15	3.38	99	55	1	8	330	295	16	126	302	1.18	1.27	.239

6 KALEB COWART, 3B

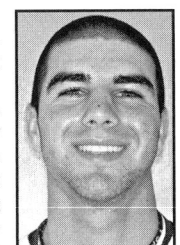

Born: June 2, 1992. **B-T:** B-R. **Ht.:** 6-3. **Wt.:** 190. **Drafted:** HS—Adel, Ga., 2010 (1st round). **Signed by:** Chris McAlpin.

The first of three successive Angels 2010 first-round picks from Georgia high schools, Cowart went 18th overall and signed for $2.3 million at the signing deadline. A two-way standout, he batted .654 with 11 home runs and went 10-1, 1.05 on the mound to win BA's High School Player of the Year award. Most clubs preferred the Florida State recruit as a pitcher, but he wanted to hit and Los Angeles liked his potential as a switch-hitting third baseman. Cowart has undeniable power potential, but he swings with more authority from the right side and must improve his efficiency and pitch recognition while batting lefthanded. He's strong and has an excess of bat speed, though the Angels would like to see him shorten his swing and keep his bat in the zone longer. A below-average runner, Cowart makes routine plays at third base but projects as an average defender at best. His hands are fine and he has plus arm strength. His fastball sat in the low 90s with sink in high school. The Angels recognized Cowart as most improved player in Angels instructional league. Because of his background as a two-way player and the need to iron out his lefthanded swing, he'll need time to develop. He'll probably begin 2011 in low Class A.

Year	Club (League)	Class	AVG	G	AB	R	H	2B	3B	HR	RBI	BB	SO	SB	CS	OBP	SLG
2010	Angels (AZL)	R	.143	6	21	0	3	0	0	0	4	0	6	0	0	.136	.143
	Orem (PIO)	R	.400	1	5	1	2	0	0	1	3	1	2	0	0	.500	1.000
Minor League Totals			.192	7	26	1	5	0	0	1	7	1	8	0	0	.214	.308

7 GARRETT RICHARDS, RHP

Born: May 27, 1988. **B-T:** R-R. **Ht.:** 6-3. **Wt.:** 210. **Drafted:** Oklahoma, 2009 (1st round supplemental). **Signed by:** Arnold Brathwaite.

Richards posted a 6.57 ERA in three years at Oklahoma, but his live arm and strong finish in 2009 made him the 42nd overall pick that June. He has had little trouble since signing for $802,000, succeeding in high Class A at the end of his first full season. All four of Richards' pitches have a chance to be at least average, and his plus fastball and slider are weapons. He touches 96 mph at times and sits comfortably at 92-93 with sink and occasional cutting action. His low- to mid-80s slider is his go-to secondary pitch, and he also throws a big-breaking 12-to-6 curveball. He mixes in an occasional changeup that flashes average. Richards throws so far across his body that it adds deception—but it also places extra strain on his shoulder. When he stays down and through the ball, he creates good angle to the plate from his three-quarters arm slot, but his stuff flattens out when he gets under his pitches. He'll need to improve his pitch efficiency to work later into games. The Angels moved Richards conservatively in 2010, but he's ready for Double-A. Depending on how they assess his delivery and attendant command concerns, observers peg him as everything from a mid-rotation starter to a power reliever.

Year	Club (League)	Class	W	L	ERA	G	GS	CG	SV	IP	H	HR	BB	SO	G/A	WHIP	AVG
2009	Orem (PIO)	R	3	1	1.53	8	8	0	0	35	37	0	4	30	1.59	1.16	.278
2010	Cedar Rapids (MWL)	LoA	8	4	3.41	19	19	2	0	108	92	6	34	108	2.45	1.16	.229
	R. Cucamonga (CAL)	HiA	4	1	3.89	7	7	0	0	35	38	4	9	41	1.95	1.36	.281
Minor League Totals			15	6	3.13	34	34	2	0	178	167	10	47	179	2.13	1.20	.249

8 FABIO MARTINEZ, RHP

Born: Oct. 29, 1989. **B-T:** R-R. **Ht.:** 6-3. **Wt.:** 190. **Signed:** Dominican Republic, 2007. **Signed by:** Leo Perez.

Martinez and Jean Segura have distinguished themselves as the system's top two international talents since signing out of the Dominican Republic in early 2007. Martinez burst on the U.S. scene in 2009 by leading the Arizona League in strikeouts (92). He was on pace to repeat the feat in the Midwest League last season, but he missed the final month of the season with shoulder tendinitis. The scouting consensus on Martinez boils down to: great stuff with marginal pitchability. He obsesses over radar-gun readings, seeking to overpower the opposition. His fastball sits at 90-96 mph, with a few 98s thrown in, though his arm slot is so high that his heater tends to be straight. Because he overthrows, he doesn't locate his fastball well, often missing up in the zone and running into trouble with walks. Martinez's low-80s slider can be devastating, featuring so much tilt at times that it resembles a splitter. He gained more confidence in his circle changeup last season, but it's still below-average. Martinez's love for lighting up the radar gun, poor command and busy, hard-to-repeat delivery point to a future in the bullpen. His two plus pitches are up to the task. He returned to the mound in instructional league, and he'll head to the Angels' new high Class A Inland Empire affiliate in 2011.

Year	Club (League)	Class	W	L	ERA	G	GS	CG	SV	IP	H	HR	BB	SO	G/A	WHIP	AVG
2007	Angels (DSL)	R	1	2	6.75	13	3	0	1	25	27	0	26	30	—	2.09	.270
2008	Angels (DSL)	R	6	1	1.53	13	13	1	0	76	55	1	32	93	—	1.14	.202
2009	Angels (AZL)	R	3	2	3.26	14	13	0	0	61	45	1	36	92	1.13	1.34	.197
	Orem (PIO)	R	1	0	3.86	2	2	0	0	7	5	2	2	10	0.38	1.00	.192
2010	Cedar Rapids (MWL)	LoA	7	3	3.92	20	19	0	0	103	80	6	76	141	1.61	1.51	.216
Minor League Totals			18	8	3.37	62	50	1	1	273	212	10	172	366	1.33	1.41	.213

9 MARK TRUMBO, 1B/OF

Born: Jan. 16, 1986. **B-T:** R-R. **Ht.:** 6-4. **Wt.:** 220. **Drafted:** HS—Villa Park, Calif., 2004 (18th round). **Signed by:** Tim Corcoran.

Signed for an 18th-round record $1.425 million in 2004, Trumbo spent two years in low Class A and didn't reach Double-A until late 2008. Moving from a pitcher-friendly park in Double-A in 2009 to a launching pad in Triple-A last season, Trumbo boosted his home run output from 15 to 36 and tied the Royals' Mike Moustakas for the minor league lead. Trumbo has plus power and could produce 25 homers annually in the big leagues if he improves his feel for the strike zone. He maintains good balance and doesn't have glaring holes in his swing, though he's still a little too tempted by high fastballs. He doesn't chase offspeed stuff away like he once did, but he swings and misses too much to hit for a high average. Detractors question whether he has the bat speed to hit the very best fastballs. Trumbo rates as an adequate defender at first base. A standout pitcher in high school, he possesses plus arm strength and isn't afraid to make tough throws on the infield. He has dabbled in right field but has below-average speed and range. Trumbo didn't hit much in a September callup, but his power could earn him a supporting role with the Angels in 2011. He also serves as insurance in case Kendry Morales stumbles in his comeback from a broken leg.

Year	Club (League)	Class	AVG	G	AB	R	H	2B	3B	HR	RBI	BB	SO	SB	CS	OBP	SLG
2005	Orem (PIO)	R	.274	71	299	45	82	23	1	10	45	21	67	2	2	.322	.458
2006	Cedar Rapids (MWL)	LoA	.220	118	428	43	94	19	0	13	59	44	99	5	5	.293	.355
2007	Cedar Rapids (MWL)	LoA	.272	128	471	57	128	27	2	14	76	34	98	10	8	.326	.427
2008	R. Cucamonga (CAL)	HiA	.283	103	407	70	115	28	2	26	68	26	67	7	3	.329	.553
	Arkansas (TL)	AA	.276	32	123	13	34	7	1	6	25	7	29	1	2	.311	.496
2009	Arkansas (TL)	AA	.291	137	533	54	155	35	3	15	88	37	100	6	3	.333	.452
2010	Salt Lake (PCL)	AAA	.301	139	532	103	160	29	5	36	122	58	126	3	4	.368	.577
	Los Angeles (AL)	MAJ	.067	8	15	2	1	0	0	0	2	1	8	0	0	.125	.067
Major League Totals			.067	8	15	2	1	0	0	0	2	1	8	0	0	.125	.067
Minor League Totals			.275	728	2793	385	768	168	14	120	483	227	586	34	27	.330	.474

10 CAM BEDROSIAN, RHP

Born: Oct. 2, 1991. **B-T:** R-R. **Ht.:** 6-0. **Wt.:** 204. **Drafted:** HS—Sharpsburg, Ga., 2010 (1st round). **Signed by:** Chris McAlpin.

Bedrosian's father Steve pitched 14 seasons in the major leagues and won the 1987 National League Cy Young Award. Cam's middle name, Rock, serves as homage to Steve's nickname, Bedrock. The Angels used the 29th pick in the draft to select Bedrosian, signing him away from a Louisiana State commitment for $1.116 million. He didn't pitch after Aug. 5, not even in instructional league, after they shut him down for precautionary reasons with a sore elbow. Bedrosian has such a strong lower half that most scouts are willing to overlook the fact that at 6 feet, he's shorter than the prototypical righty starter. His fastball tops out at 96 mph and sits comfortably at 92-94. Like his father, he features a plus power slider that gives righthanders fits. Bedrosian also throws a fringe-average changeup and curveball, both of which will require additional refinement if he's to remain a starter. He repeats his delivery well, but it's not without effort, leading to some concerns about his future command. While Bedrosian's power repertoire could allow him to move quickly in a relief role, he has the chance to have at least three solid pitches and average command, so Los Angeles will develop him as a starter. Expected to be 100 percent healthy by spring training, he'll probably open 2011 in low Class A.

Year	Club (League)	Class	W	L	ERA	G	GS	CG	SV	IP	H	HR	BB	SO	G/A	WHIP	AVG
2010	Angels (AZL)	R	0	2	4.50	5	4	0	0	12	13	0	7	10	2.50	1.67	.283
Minor League Totals			0	2	4.50	5	4	0	0	12	13	0	7	10	2.50	1.67	.283

11 TREVOR RECKLING, LHP

Born: May 22, 1989. **B-T:** L-L. **Ht.:** 6-2. **Wt.:** 205. **Drafted:** HS—Newark, N.J., 2007 (8th round). **Signed by:** Greg Morhardt.

The organization's pitcher of the year in 2009, Reckling raced to Double-A as a 19-year-old and showed flashes of dominance while ranking fourth in the Texas League in ERA (2.93) and strikeouts per nine innings (7.0). Pushed a step further to Triple-A in 2010, he responded with his worst performance as a pro, going 4-7, 8.53 with more walks (50) than strikeouts (46) before getting demoted to Arkansas in late June. Reckling lost a few ticks on his fastball last season, dropping to 88-90 mph, and the Angels concede that his entire repertoire went backwards. They asked him to deemphasize his plus changeup in order to concentrate on locating his fastball, especially when behind in the count. He paid the price for his poor fastball command in the Pacific Coast League, where anything left up and over the plate is in danger of being hit a long way. Reckling also threw two versions of a breaking ball: a sweepy mid-70s slider to lefthanders and a harder low-80s offering with tilt to righties. Los Angeles wants him to focus on mastering the hard breaker. Reckling's herky-jerky delivery—he tends to rush his arm and get offline to the plate because he doesn't get over his front side—makes him deceptive but also can make throwing strikes a challenge. After his demotion, Reckling re-established his strikeout rate and showed improved control, providing a silver lining to an otherwise dismal season. Energetic, competitive and with the potential for three average or better pitches, Reckling will take another shot at Triple-A in 2011.

Year	Club (League)	Class	W	L	ERA	G	GS	CG	SV	IP	H	HR	BB	SO	G/A	WHIP	AVG
2007	Angels (AZL)	R	3	1	2.75	9	5	0	2	36	33	2	7	55	—	1.11	.236
2008	Cedar Rapids (MWL)	LoA	10	7	3.37	26	26	1	0	152	137	8	59	128	—	1.29	.246
2009	R. Cucamonga (CAL)	HiA	1	2	0.95	3	3	0	0	19	9	2	3	16	1.60	0.63	.138
	Arkansas (TL)	AA	8	7	2.93	23	23	1	0	135	118	4	75	106	1.49	1.43	.244
2010	Salt Lake (PCL)	AAA	4	7	8.53	14	14	0	0	70	99	11	50	46	1.14	2.14	.339
	Arkansas (TL)	AA	3	6	4.56	14	14	1	0	79	74	4	35	62	1.13	1.38	.254
Minor League Totals			29	30	4.03	89	85	3	2	491	470	31	229	413	1.31	1.42	.257

12 RANDAL GRICHUK, OF

Born: Aug. 13, 1991. **B-T:** R-R. **Ht.:** 6-1. **Wt.:** 195. **Drafted:** HS—Rosenberg, Texas, 2009 (1st round). **Signed by:** Kevin Ham.

Taken with back-to-back picks in the first-round of the 2009 draft, Grichuk and Mike Trout teamed in the Arizona League in their pro debuts. Signed for $1.242 million, Grichuk led the AZL in hits (76) and ranked second in extra-base hits (30), while Trout batted .360. But while Trout ascended to the ranks of the game's elite prospects in 2010, Grichuk got off to a slow start and then tore a ligament in his right thumb in early May while diving back into third base, forcing him to miss nearly two months. He hit much better after returning from the disabled list in August, batting .366/.385/.645 in 93 at-bats. Both before and after the thumb injury, though, Grichuk showed the same undisciplined hitting approach. He did improve at identifying and making contact with offspeed pitches after missing them by a foot at times in 2009 and the start of 2010. Scouts like his bat speed but wonder if the lack of contact and the handsiness of his swing will allow him to hit for high averages. Grichuk's raw power is well above-average, and he appeared more multidimensional last season. His throwing and baserunning had improved to average, though he'll need more work to become average in right field. Grichuk lost further development time right before the Midwest League playoffs when he broke a bone in his left wrist while bracing his hand against the outfield wall to make a defensive play. Wrist injuries are always a concern for power hitters, and Grichuk's future value is predicated on hitting for power—and lots of it. After he played in just 52 games at low Class A, a promotion to begin 2011 is far from a given.

Year	Club (League)	Class	AVG	G	AB	R	H	2B	3B	HR	RBI	BB	SO	SB	CS	OBP	SLG
2009	Angels (AZL)	R	.322	53	236	47	76	13	10	7	53	9	64	6	4	.352	.551
2010	Angels (AZL)	R	.327	12	49	7	16	3	2	4	10	3	9	0	0	.365	.714
	Cedar Rapids (MWL)	LoA	.292	52	202	41	59	19	4	7	36	9	50	4	0	.327	.530
Minor League Totals			.310	117	487	95	151	35	16	18	99	21	123	10	4	.343	.559

13 CHEVEZ CLARKE, OF

Born: Jan. 9, 1992. **B-T:** B-R. **Ht.:** 5-11. **Wt.:** 185. **Drafted:** HS—Marietta, Ga., 2010 (1st round). **Signed by:** Chris McAlpin.

Five Georgia high school players went in the 2010 draft's first round, with the Angels responsible for three of them. They tabbed Kaleb Cowart (18th overall) and Cam Bedrosian (29th) with compensation picks and used their own choice at No. 30 to select Clarke, a potential five-tool player whom they signed for $1.089 million. He's related to the Hairston family, which has produced five big leaguers, including his cousins Jerry Jr. and Scott Hairston. A switch-hitter since age 13, Clarke has unquestionable bat speed from both sides of the plate, yet he didn't dominate amateur competition. At his best, he shows average power from both sides, but he'll need to add more finish to his swing and keep his bat in the zone longer to unlock that potential. He struck out 55 times in 38 games during his pro debut, highlighting the need for enhanced pitch recognition. Clarke boasts above-average speed and arm strength and rates as at least an average defender in center field. He's far from a finished product, but in Clarke the Angels can see the outline of an all-around regular in its nascent stages. He'll spend his first full pro season in low Class A.

Year	Club (League)	Class	AVG	G	AB	R	H	2B	3B	HR	RBI	BB	SO	SB	CS	OBP	SLG
2010	Angels (AZL)	R	.216	38	162	26	35	5	7	3	16	14	55	9	2	.294	.389
Minor League Totals			.216	38	162	26	35	5	7	3	16	14	55	9	2	.294	.389

14 DANIEL TILLMAN, RHP

Born: March 14, 1989. **B-T:** R-R. **Ht.:** 6-1. **Wt.:** 195. **Drafted:** Florida Southern, 2010 (2nd round). **Signed by:** Tom Kotchman.

A standout closer at NCAA Division II power Florida Southern, Tillman enhanced his draft profile considerably with a dominating performance in the Cape Cod League in the summer of 2009. He didn't allow an earned run in 16 appearances for Cotuit, while striking out 31 in 22 innings. Signed for $443,700 as a second-round pick last June, Tillman overmatched Pioneer League competition in his debut. He led the league's relievers in strikeouts per nine innings (13.9) and opponent average (.195), while racking up five times as many strikeouts (50) as walks (10). Tillman's quick arm unleashes a consistent 90-95 mph fastball that touches 97 with plus sinking life. He improved the quality of his low-80s slider from below average to a tick above by toying with his grip on the pitch all season. His arm action is surprisingly clean for such a hard-throwing reliever, and he also shows an occasional average changeup. Though he has enough stuff and command to possibly make it as a starter, the Angels plan to keep him in the bullpen, a role in which he could move quickly. Evaluators value his competitive makeup and ultimately see him as a potential set-up man or possible closer. He's equipped to start his first full pro season in high Class A.

Year	Club (League)	Class	W	L	ERA	G	GS	CG	SV	IP	H	HR	BB	SO	G/A	WHIP	AVG
2010	Orem (PIO)	R	2	2	1.95	22	0	0	10	32	23	0	10	50	0.82	1.02	.195
Minor League Totals			2	2	1.95	22	0	0	10	32	23	0	10	50	0.82	1.02	.195

15 MICHAEL KOHN, RHP

Born: June 26, 1986. **B-T:** R-R. **Ht.:** 6-0. **Wt.:** 200. **Drafted:** College of Charleston, 2008 (13th round). **Signed by:** Chris McAlpin.

Kohn (pronounced Kahn) advanced so quickly through the minors that one would be forgiven for mistaking him for a premium draft pick. In reality, he's a 13th-round senior sign for $5,000 who converted from power-hitting first baseman to the mound during his draft year at the College of Charleston. What's more, the Angels stumbled on him only because scout Tom Kotchman's daughter played softball at the same school. Kohn averaged 13.6 strikeouts per nine innings and allowed just five homers in 135 minor league innings. He made his big league debut on July 26, becoming the first player from the club's 2008 draft to make it to Anaheim. While he finished his big league debut with a shiny 2.11 ERA in 24 appearances, his 16 walks suggest that trouble was often just a batter away. Kohn has plus velocity—his fastball sits at 90-93 mph and touches 96—but it's his delivery that makes him so effective. His severely short arm swing in back adds maximum deception. By the time the batter picks up the ball, it's often already past him. Whenever he suspects batters have timed his fastball, Kohn uses a slurvy break-ing ball in the low 80s to keep them honest. Unless he dramatically improves his control or the shape of his slider, Kohn's best role would seem to be low-leverage relief. He's positioned to begin 2011 in the big league bullpen.

Year	Club (League)	Class	W	L	ERA	G	GS	CG	SV	IP	H	HR	BB	SO	G/A	WHIP	AVG
2008	Orem (PIO)	R	2	0	1.93	16	0	0	0	23	11	1	11	44	—	0.94	.134
2009	Cedar Rapids (MWL)	LoA	4	1	2.19	28	0	0	6	37	20	1	12	60	0.74	0.86	.161
	R. Cucamonga (CAL)	HiA	2	0	0.94	22	0	0	3	29	13	0	14	43	0.50	0.94	.141
2010	Arkansas (TL)	AA	2	2	2.45	15	0	0	3	18	12	0	8	25	1.09	1.09	.194
	Salt Lake (PCL)	AAA	2	1	1.95	26	0	0	8	28	16	3	17	32	0.69	1.19	.170
	Los Angeles (AL)	MAJ	2	0	2.11	24	0	0	1	21	17	0	16	20	0.70	1.55	.227
Major League Totals			2	0	2.11	24	0	0	1	21	17	0	16	20	0.70	1.55	.227
Minor League Totals			13	5	1.87	107	0	0	20	135	72	5	62	204	0.73	0.99	.159

16 JEREMY MOORE, OF

Born: June 29, 1987. **B-T:** L-R. **Ht.:** 6-1. **Wt.:** 190. **Drafted:** HS—Vivian, La., 2005 (6th round). **Signed by:** Chad MacDonald.

Moore divided his time in high school between four sports: baseball, football, basketball and track. His athleti-cism and above-average speed convinced the Angels to sign him for $100,000 as a sixth-round pick in 2005, with the expectation that he'd refine his feel for hitting through repetition. He showed signs of breaking through in 2009, his fifth pro season, by hitting .281, though he still struck out 151 times. Moore's simple, consistent and quick stroke from the left side gives him a chance to hit .280 in the big leagues, and as evidence, he topped .300 for the first time during his first extended trial in Double-A last season. In the process, he erased a mediocre first half with Arkansas to hit .336/.382/.531 in 211 at-bats in the second half, and his hitting exploits continued in the Arizona Fall League. Moore's power and speed have been evident from the start. He had 17 homers and 28 steals in low Class A in 2007, and scouts see the potential for average power if he continues to refine his approach. Moore plays all three outfield spots and has the instincts and closing speed to hold down center on a daily basis. His below-average arm makes him a mismatch for right. The improvement Moore showed this season led the Angels to place him on their 40-man roster after leaving him unprotected the previous winter. Through patience and persistence, they've developed a near-perfect reserve outfielder or, if everything breaks right, a solid-average regular in center field. He'll advance to Triple-A this year.

Year	Club (League)	Class	AVG	G	AB	R	H	2B	3B	HR	RBI	BB	SO	SB	CS	OBP	SLG
2005	Angels (AZL)	R	.227	34	110	15	25	3	1	0	11	11	46	12	6	.303	.273
2006	Angels (AZL)	R	.254	41	142	25	36	7	2	3	19	18	37	4	8	.348	.394
2007	Orem (PIO)	R	.272	68	254	50	69	13	6	14	54	19	68	17	5	.329	.535
2008	Cedar Rapids (MWL)	LoA	.240	96	362	47	87	11	12	17	48	21	125	28	10	.284	.478
2009	Arkansas (TL)	AA	.333	7	21	5	7	0	1	2	10	3	7	1	1	.423	.714
	R. Cucamonga (CAL)	HiA	.279	124	470	61	131	20	12	11	58	34	144	17	13	.330	.443
2010	Arkansas (TL)	AA	.303	128	456	72	138	14	10	13	61	39	122	24	10	.358	.463
Minor League Totals			.272	498	1815	275	493	68	44	60	261	145	549	103	53	.329	.457

17 ANDREW ROMINE, SS

Born: Dec. 24, 1985. **B-T:** B-R. **Ht.:** 6-1. **Wt.:** 190. **Drafted:** Arizona State, 2007 (5th round). **Signed by:** John Gracio.

When Erick Aybar, Alberto Callaspo and Maicer Izturis all went down with injuries in late September, the Angels called on Romine, who had been readying to travel to Puerto Rico to play in the Pan Am qualifying tournament with Team USA. In getting the call to the big leagues, he arrived before his younger brother Austin, a promising catching prospect in the Yankees system who, like Andrew, was drafted in 2007 and spent 2010 in Double-A. Their father Kevin spent seven seasons in the majors with the Red Sox. The Angels don't expect miracles from Romine's bat—his career minor league slugging percentage (.361) barely edges his on-base percent-age (.352)—but he switch-hits, makes contact, works the count, can bunt and is an excellent baserunner with solid speed. The Angels emphasized a shorter path to the ball this season, but even still he's strictly No. 9 hitter material until he proves he can handle being pounded inside with fastballs. It's Romine's defensive ability that will keep him in the picture. He's a potential Gold Glove shortstop because of his plus athleticism, hands and instincts. His throws are accurate and strong. He led TL shortstops with a .974 fielding percentage last year, and managers rated him the league's best defender at the position. Romine is ticketed for Triple-A this season.

Year	Club (League)	Class	AVG	G	AB	R	H	2B	3B	HR	RBI	BB	SO	SB	CS	OBP	SLG
2007	Orem (PIO)	R	.286	56	231	38	66	6	6	5	35	16	38	12	4	.337	.429
2008	Cedar Rapids (MWL)	LoA	.260	126	461	79	120	21	4	2	34	55	76	62	18	.347	.336
2009	R. Cucamonga (CAL)	HiA	.278	131	479	68	133	13	9	1	36	51	83	26	11	.351	.349
2010	Arkansas (TL)	AA	.282	106	383	55	108	15	4	3	34	50	66	21	9	.370	.366
	Los Angeles (AL)	MAJ	.091	5	11	0	1	0	0	0	0	0	4	0	0	.091	.091
Major League Totals			.091	5	11	0	1	0	0	0	0	0	4	0	0	.091	.091
Minor League Totals			.275	419	1554	240	427	55	23	11	139	172	263	121	42	.352	.361

18 ALEXI AMARISTA, 2B

Born: April 6, 1989. **B-T:** L-R. **Ht.:** 5-8. **Wt.:** 150. **Signed:** Venezuela, 2007. **Signed by:** Denny Suarez.

Generously listed at 5-foot-8, Amarista was easy to overlook when he played mostly outfield in the Arizona League in 2008. Back then, he hit .332 with 22 stolen bases, and he hasn't stopped hitting or running since. Evaluators really took notice when Amarista moved back to his natural position of second base in 2009, and one year later managers in both the California and Texas leagues rated him their circuit's best defender at the position. He's more average than exemplary, however. While his arm is light for shortstop, it's adequate at second base. Because he's undersized, Amarista understands the value of constant hustle and motion. A lefty hitter, Amarista takes an aggressive swing and gives away too many at-bats, but he also does a lot of things right at the plate. He's short to the ball and can produce occasional gap power. He runs and bunts well, though he'll need to improve his stolen-base efficiency, which has hovered at 66 percent the last two years. Few prospects have extensive winter-ball resumes to match that of Amarista, who played for Caribes in the Venezuelan League in each of the past three offseasons. He brings a well-rounded game to the table—everything but power—and as a result will continue to earn chances in the system. He finished 2010 in Triple-A at age 21 and should return there at some point this season, perhaps on Opening Day.

Year	Club (League)	Class	AVG	G	AB	R	H	2B	3B	HR	RBI	BB	SO	SB	CS	OBP	SLG
2007	Angels (DSL)	R	.340	65	241	52	82	14	4	5	39	25	23	16	6	.408	.494
2008	Angels (AZL)	R	.332	51	202	46	67	6	4	2	21	29	20	22	14	.416	.431
	Cedar Rapids (MWL)	LoA	.000	1	2	0	0	0	0	0	0	0	1	0	0	.000	.000
2009	Cedar Rapids (MWL)	LoA	.319	125	477	84	152	39	10	4	49	50	61	38	20	.390	.468
2010	R. Cucamonga (CAL)	HiA	.303	72	297	39	90	19	6	4	39	19	42	17	10	.349	.448
	Arkansas (TL)	AA	.288	48	191	25	55	2	1	1	20	13	15	4	1	.332	.325
	Salt Lake (PCL)	AAA	.400	15	65	13	26	6	3	0	9	1	4	4	2	.412	.585
Minor League Totals			.320	377	1475	259	472	86	28	16	177	137	166	101	53	.382	.449

19 TAYLOR LINDSEY, 2B

Born: Dec. 2, 1991. **B-T:** L-R. **Ht.:** 6-0. **Wt.:** 195. **Drafted:** HS—Scottsdale, Ariz., 2010 (1st round supplemental). **Signed by:** John Gracio.

Few teams valued Lindsey as highly as the Angels, who selected him with the 37th overall pick last June and paid out an $873,000 bonus to keep him away from Arizona State. As a shortstop at Desert Mountain High (Scottsdale, Ariz.), he hit .592 and .557 in his final two amateur seasons, though some scouts worried that his metal-bat swing wouldn't translate to wood. Lindsey didn't light up the Arizona League after signing, but he made solid contact and went 19-for-52 (.356) in his final 13 games to finish at .284. He has a sweet lefthanded swing but below-average power, though that doesn't stop him from looking to pull almost exclusively. A below-average runner, Lindsey moved to second base as a pro where he showed just playable range and a below-average arm. Some scouts think his future lies in the outfield. Lindsey can hit, but if he doesn't improve his defensive play or grow into more power he may struggle to find a natural position. He'll move up to low Class A this year.

Year	Club (League)	Class	AVG	G	AB	R	H	2B	3B	HR	RBI	BB	SO	SB	CS	OBP	SLG
2010	Angels (AZL)	R	.284	45	194	26	55	12	6	0	18	12	33	8	3	.325	.407
Minor League Totals			.284	45	194	26	55	12	6	0	18	12	33	8	3	.325	.407

20 ORANGEL ARENAS, RHP

Born: March 31, 1989. **B-T:** R-R. **Ht.:** 6-0. **Wt.:** 165. **Signed:** Venezuela, 2007. **Signed by:** Denny Suarez.

The No. 6 starter option on a deep Cedar Rapids pitching staff when 2010 began, Arenas shot past three first-round or sandwich picks and flamethrower Fabio Martinez to earn a promotion to high Class A in late May. His maturation helped cover the Angels in a season in which they parted with five young pitchers to acquire

Dan Haren and Alberto Callaspo. Arenas enhanced his standing in the organization with a strong full-season debut, more than doubling his previous high for innings. He induces plenty of groundballs, relying on a low-90s two-seam fastball that features plus sink and movement. He can dial his four-seamer up to 95 mph but it's fairly straight. His fastball gets on batters quickly because of his easy motion. Los Angeles was impressed by Arenas' improved fastball command in 2010, as they were with the consistency of his average slider. His changeup lags behind his other pitches, and he doesn't shown a whole lot of confidence in it. Arenas could be in line for a promotion to Double-A for 2011, and further progress suggests future back-of-the-rotation or relief possibilities.

Year	Club (League)	Class	W	L	ERA	G	GS	CG	SV	IP	H	HR	BB	SO	G/A	WHIP	AVG
2007	Angels (DSL)	R	1	3	2.45	10	4	0	1	33	31	1	6	21	—	1.12	.250
2008	Angels (DSL)	R	8	1	1.36	13	13	1	0	86	52	2	25	71	—	0.90	.173
2009	Orem (PIO)	R	4	3	4.65	15	15	0	0	70	76	7	18	48	2.10	1.35	.281
2010	Cedar Rapids (MWL)	LoA	4	5	2.01	9	9	0	0	54	41	2	15	36	3.00	1.04	.212
	R. Cucamonga (CAL)	HiA	7	3	4.55	17	17	0	0	97	93	9	45	71	2.36	1.42	.255
Minor League Totals			24	15	3.16	64	58	1	1	339	293	21	109	247	2.40	1.18	.234

21 TRAVIS WITHERSPOON, OF

Born: April 16, 1989. **B-T:** R-R. **Ht.:** 6-2. **Wt.:** 190. **Drafted:** Spartanburg Methodist (S.C.) JC, 2009 (12th round). **Signed by:** Chris McAlpin.

Prior to the 2009 draft, Angels scout Chris McAlpin turned in a report on Witherspoon as a premium defensive player with a below-average bat, the type of hitter who would require much work to develop. He signed for $100,000 as a 12th-round pick out of the same Spartanburg Methodist (S.C.) JC program that produced Reggie Sanders and Orlando Hudson. The live-bodied center fielder showed remarkable progress and a diligent work ethic while repeating the Pioneer League in 2010, exciting Los Angeles about his future growth potential. Witherspoon already had plus bat speed and the strength to hit for power, and last season he better identified breaking balls and put himself in position to make more contact. He hit three of his 10 homers for Orem to the opposite field, abandoning 2009's pull-happy approach and affording himself better plate coverage. Witherspoon went a perfect 20-for-20 in stolen base attempts, showing plus speed and impressive instincts. He runs excellent routes in center field, and the organization regards his range as being on par with Mike Trout's and just a step behind Peter Bourjos'. Witherspoon brings a solid-average arm to the table, meaning that if he hits he has five-tool potential. If he settles in south of .260, he still could provide value as a slick-fielding center fielder with contributions in the power and speed departments. He'll get his first full-season assignment in 2011, advancing to Cedar Rapids.

Year	Club (League)	Class	AVG	G	AB	R	H	2B	3B	HR	RBI	BB	SO	SB	CS	OBP	SLG
2009	Angels (AZL)	R	.231	5	13	2	3	1	0	0	0	1	3	0	0	.286	.308
	Orem (PIO)	R	.227	58	194	37	44	3	6	6	26	10	61	10	1	.281	.397
2010	Orem (PIO)	R	.309	71	288	57	89	11	3	10	45	24	73	20	0	.365	.472
Minor League Totals			.275	134	495	96	136	15	9	16	71	35	137	30	1	.330	.438

22 LUIS JIMENEZ, 3B

Born: Jan. 18, 1988. **B-T:** R-R. **Ht.:** 6-0. **Wt.:** 170. **Signed:** Dominican Republic, 2005. **Signed by:** Leo Perez.

Jimenez led the Pioneer League with 15 home runs in 2008, when he also batted .331/.361/.630 for Orem in the thin Utah air. The PL is an extreme hitter's league, but he did rank among its youngest regulars at age 20. He didn't get a chance to build on his success, however, because he tore the labrum in his right shoulder and missed the entire 2009 season. While Jimenez returned to the field in 2010, he split time between third base and DH, never playing more than four consecutive games at the hot corner. If Jimenez makes the big leagues, it will be on the strength of his bat. He can hit fastballs and breaking balls, perhaps a bit too well, because he's convinced he can hit any pitch in any location. As a result he puts a lot of pitcher's pitches in play early in counts, and his bat doesn't play up quite as well as it could. He has average power if not overwhelming bat speed, and he could knock out 15-20 homers in a good year. Jimenez is an average defender with a solid arm, as well as a fringe-average runner with good instincts on the bases. He tweaked his arm toward the end of the season and didn't get in any defensive reps during instructional league. Given another two years to develop, he could become a high-contact, .280ish hitter with double-digit power and a solid glove at third. He should reach Double-A at some point in 2011.

Year	Club (League)	Class	AVG	G	AB	R	H	2B	3B	HR	RBI	BB	SO	SB	CS	OBP	SLG
2006	Angels (DSL)	R	.284	25	74	12	21	9	1	1	10	7	9	4	0	.341	.473
2007	Angels (DSL)	R	.313	67	256	49	80	19	2	11	55	10	27	16	4	.347	.531
2008	Orem (PIO)	R	.331	66	284	57	94	28	6	15	65	11	45	6	2	.361	.630
2009	Did not play—Injured																
2010	Cedar Rapids (MWL)	LoA	.292	43	168	32	49	15	5	2	38	11	27	6	2	.332	.476
	R. Cucamonga (CAL)	HiA	.286	81	318	52	91	31	4	12	43	13	43	15	8	.324	.522
Minor League Totals			.305	282	1100	202	335	102	18	41	211	52	151	47	16	.341	.542

23 JOHNNY HELLWEG, RHP

Born: Oct. 29, 1988. **B-T:** R-R. **Ht.:** 6-7. **Wt.:** 200. **Drafted:** Florida CC, 2008 (16th round). **Signed by:** Tom Kotchman.

The Marlins took a 46th-round flier on Hellweg in 2007, even though he had missed his senior year at St. Dominic High (O'Fallon, Mo.) after having a bone spur shaved down in his pitching elbow. He decided to attend Florida CC in Jacksonville, where he spent one season before signing with the Angels for $150,000 as a 16th-round pick in 2008. To say Hellweg has been wild as a pro would be an understatement. He walked 45 batters in 44 relief innings in low Class A last season, and his career rate of 9.2 walks per nine innings is obviously not tenable. On the flip side, Hellweg fanned 13.6 batters per nine with Cedar Rapids, a better rate than all but two other MWL pitchers with at least 40 innings. In fact, 57 percent of batters to oppose him didn't put the ball in play—they walked, struck out or were hit by a pitch. The ball jumps out of his hand, and Hellweg's fastball sits at 94-98 mph with sink. His low-80s slider gives him a second potential plus pitch, though it's extremely inconsistent. Hellweg's lack of control, which grades generously at 35 on the 20-80 scouting scale, stems from his delivery. He loses his direction to plate and often throws against his body. But if Los Angeles can find a way to iron out Hellweg's mechanics, he could be a potential high-leverage reliever—possibly a Kyle Farnsworth type. Just don't expect that to happen overnight. He'll move up to high Class A this year.

Year	Club (League)	Class	W	L	ERA	G	GS	CG	SV	IP	H	HR	BB	SO	G/A	WHIP	AVG
2008	Angels (AZL)	R	1	0	4.98	14	3	0	0	22	19	1	38	25	—	2.63	.224
2009	Angels (AZL)	R	2	1	2.96	18	0	0	6	24	16	0	8	25	1.24	0.99	.186
	Cedar Rapids (MWL)	LoA	0	0	1.35	5	0	0	2	7	4	0	7	7	0.86	1.65	.160
2010	Cedar Rapids (MWL)	LoA	2	4	4.33	41	0	0	16	44	20	2	45	66	1.32	1.49	.133
Minor League Totals			5	5	3.92	78	3	0	24	96	59	3	98	123	1.23	1.63	.171

24 BOBBY CASSEVAH, RHP

Born: Sept. 11, 1985. **B-T:** R-R. **Ht.:** 6-3. **Wt.:** 195. **Drafted:** HS—Pace, Fla., 2004 (34th round). **Signed by:** Tom Kotchman.

The Angels had a total of six relievers selected in the 2008 through 2010 major league Rule 5 drafts. Darren O'Day (Rangers by way of Mets) and David Herndon (Phillies) stuck with their drafting teams, while Bobby Mosebach (Phillies) and Cassevah (Athletics) ultimately returned to Los Angeles. The Rangers and Yankees have until April to decide what to do with 2010 picks Mason Tobin and Robert Fish. Cassevah may be the most extreme groundball pitcher in the minors. From a three-quarters arm slot, Cassevah throws strikes with a plus 90-91 mph sinker and a mid-80s slider. However, he doesn't miss many bats and got hit harder than ever before in a full-season league last year. The Angels believe the remedy could be his splitter, which has swing-and-miss potential, but he hasn't mastered his arm speed on the pitch. Cassevah joined several rookie relievers in the Los Angeles bullpen after the all-star break last year and proved useful in a limited role, holding righthanders to six hits in 39 at-bats (.154). Lefties tagged him for a .386 average, so he'll need to master his splitter to be more than a situational option.

Year	Club (League)	Class	W	L	ERA	G	GS	CG	SV	IP	H	HR	BB	SO	G/A	WHIP	AVG
2005	Angels (AZL)	R	2	5	5.40	15	4	0	0	45	57	2	14	27	—	1.58	.318
2006	Orem (PIO)	R	2	5	6.80	16	10	0	0	41	57	1	38	32	—	2.32	.337
2007	Orem (PIO)	R	0	0	4.32	6	0	0	0	8	9	0	5	9	—	1.68	.290
	Cedar Rapids (MWL)	LoA	2	1	2.32	18	0	0	1	31	25	0	13	25	—	1.23	.227
2008	R. Cucamonga (CAL)	HiA	2	3	3.79	44	0	0	1	71	67	1	40	52	—	1.50	.250
2009	Arkansas (TL)	AA	3	7	3.68	57	0	0	4	73	64	2	37	45	4.03	1.38	.236
2010	Salt Lake (PCL)	AAA	3	4	4.27	45	0	0	5	59	69	7	25	38	6.17	1.59	.290
	Los Angeles (AL)	MAJ	1	2	3.15	16	0	0	0	20	23	0	8	8	3.27	1.55	.277
Major League Totals			1	2	3.15	16	0	0	0	20	23	0	8	8	3.27	1.55	.277
Minor League Totals			14	25	4.32	201	14	0	11	329	348	13	172	228	4.77	1.58	.275

25 DONN ROACH, RHP

Born: Dec. 14, 1989. **B-T:** R-R. **Ht.:** 6-2. **Wt.:** 190. **Drafted:** JC of Southern Nevada, 2010 (3rd round supplemental). **Signed by:** Jeff Scholzen.

For a junior college team, Southern Nevada received unprecedented scouting exposure in 2010 because of the presence of eventual No. 1 overall pick Bryce Harper. Eight more Coyotes followed Harper off the draft board, including four in the top 10 rounds. The quick-armed Roach was the highest regarded of the non-Harper faction. He signed for $261,000 as the 115th overall pick, a compensation choice after the third round awarded to the Angels for their failure to sign third-rounder Josh Spence a year earlier. Roach won three state championships at Bishop Gorman High in Las Vegas and attended Arizona as a freshman. He transferred to Southern Nevada as a sophomore, following brothers Bryce and Bryan Harper, whom he has known since he was 10 years old. Roach throws a power sinker that sits at 91-93 mph and touches 95, as well as a hard high-70s slider that rates as solid-average. Both pitches are geared toward keeping the ball on the ground. He uses a splitter for a change of pace but it's fringy at best, and Los Angeles wants him to emphasize his fastball anyway. Roach logged 103 innings during the college season and came to the Angels gassed. They placed him in the bullpen for three weeks, using the time to streamline his max-effort delivery by softening his landing and improving his direction to the plate. He returned with a vengeance for the Pioneer League playoffs, striking out nine in 5⅓ innings. Roach has back-of-the-rotation potential if his command improves with a cleaner delivery. He'll pitch in low Class A during his first full pro season.

Year	Club (League)	Class	W	L	ERA	G	GS	CG	SV	IP	H	HR	BB	SO	G/A	WHIP	AVG
2010	Orem (PIO)	R	4	1	6.04	16	10	0	0	54	64	6	16	59	7.00	1.49	.294
Minor League Totals			4	1	6.04	16	10	0	0	54	64	6	16	59	7.00	1.49	.294

26 RYAN BOLDEN, OF

Born: Sept. 17, 1991. **B-T:** R-L. **Ht.:** 6-2. **Wt.:** 195. **Drafted:** HS—Madison, Miss., 2010 (1st round supplemental). **Signed by:** Jim Bryant.

Bolden will try to make good where other Mississippi high school products thrust into pro ball have faltered. He has explosive raw power and speed, just like Brewers 1998 sixth-rounder Bill Hall, a Nettleton, Miss., prep product made good. Hall needed six years in the minors to develop into a major league talent, however, and Bolden is so raw that he'll need plenty of time as well. That didn't stop the Angels from selecting him with the 40th overall pick last June and paying him out of a Mississippi commitment for $829,800. True to form, Bolden struck out in 45 percent of his at-bats in the Arizona League, though he did begin taking better swings at the end of the season. Scouts question his pitch recognition and ability to hit breaking balls. A rare righty hitter/lefty thrower, he probably won't make enough contact to hit for much average. He has plus raw power, but to unlock it he'll have to better implement his lower half and not rotate his upper body so dramatically. Bolden also is unrefined in the outfield, despite his plus-plus speed, and will need to improve his reads to stick in center field. His fringy arm probably will make him a left fielder if he can't handle center. Bolden pulled his hamstring during instructional league and took just a handful of at-bats. Even without that setback, he would have been a strong candidate to begin 2011 in extended spring training.

Year	Club (League)	Class	AVG	G	AB	R	H	2B	3B	HR	RBI	BB	SO	SB	CS	OBP	SLG
2010	Angels (AZL)	R	.187	44	150	17	28	1	5	0	16	14	68	11	7	.278	.260
Minor League Totals			.187	44	150	17	28	1	5	0	16	14	68	11	7	.278	.260

27 YSMAEL CARMONA, RHP

Born: Feb. 12, 1985. **B-T:** R-R. **Ht.:** 6-1. **Wt.:** 190. **Signed:** Dominican Republic, 2003. **Signed by:** Leo Perez.

Carmona began 2010 in the same Arkansas bullpen as Jordan Walden and Michael Kohn. While Carmona didn't receive a callup during the season like they did, he received the next best thing: a spot on the 40-man roster in November. The move was aimed at shielding him from minor league free agency as well as selection in the Rule 5 draft, which he passed through untaken the previous two winters. Signed as an outfielder, Carmona hit an empty .127 in the Dominican Summer League in 2004 and never got a chance to redeem himself as a position player. The Angels shifted his top-shelf arm strength to the mound, where he sits comfortably at 92-94 mph and touches 96. Carmona's two-seamer sinks dramatically and his four-seamer has armside run. The life on his fastball, coupled with his low three-quarters arm slot, leads to all problems finding the strike zone. He has averaged 6.7 walks per nine innings in pro ball. Carmona's average 81-84 mph slider with short, late bite makes him particularly tough for righthanders to hit, but he struggles to come in on lefties, in part because his low arm angle gives them such a long look at the ball. In an organization brimming with power arms, Carmona ranks among the hardest throwers. At age 26 this season, it's time for him to put up results to match his raw stuff.

Year	Club (League)	Class	W	L	ERA	G	GS	CG	SV	IP	H	HR	BB	SO	G/A	WHIP	AVG
2005	Angels (DSL)	R	1	0	2.91	14	1	0	1	22	16	0	12	21	—	1.29	.195
2006	Angels (AZL)	R	0	0	13.09	10	1	0	0	11	19	1	16	10	—	3.18	.373
2007	Did not play—Injured																
2008	Cedar Rapids (MWL)	LoA	2	4	5.37	44	0	0	2	54	51	3	47	47	—	1.83	.244
2009	R. Cucamonga (CAL)	HiA	0	8	5.74	42	0	0	20	42	45	5	26	55	1.34	1.68	.274
2010	Arkansas (TL)	AA	4	2	2.60	38	0	0	12	55	35	2	34	52	1.97	1.25	.188
	Salt Lake (PCL)	AAA	1	1	3.18	6	0	0	0	6	5	0	6	7	2.33	1.94	.227
Minor League Totals			8	15	4.75	154	2	0	35	190	171	11	141	192	1.71	1.64	.239

28 DREW TAYLOR, LHP

Born: Aug. 18, 1986. **B-T:** R-L. **Ht.:** 6-2. **Wt.:** 190. **Drafted:** North Carolina State, 2008 (34th round). **Signed by:** Chris McAlpin.

Taylor made only one start in three years at North Carolina State, but after signing for $45,000 as a 34th-round pick in 2008, he showed potential as a three-pitch lefty. Intrigued, the Angels gave him a brief spin in the

Rookie-level Orem rotation during his pro debut, but he imploded in that role. After successfully climbing three levels to Double-A as a reliever, Taylor asked the Angels if he could try starting again. He made four abbreviated starts at the end of the 2010 season, going 1-1, 4.05 but with 13 strikeouts and 10 walks in 20 innings. Taylor throws a firm 91-94 mph fastball with nice run and two promising secondary pitches: a low-80s changeup and a short, late-breaking mid-80s slider. He's death on lefthanders with his fastball and slider—they went 29-for-181 (.160) against him in the past two seasons—and he keeps righties in check with his fading changeup. Taylor's herky-jerky, head-snapping delivery provides camouflage for his pitches. He didn't trust his fastball in college but has learned to pitch off the heater as a pro. With better command, Taylor would profile as a mid-rotation starter, but it remains to be seen if he'll develop the feel for pitching to avoid life as a situational reliever. He'll see Triple-A for the first time in 2011.

Year	Club (League)	Class	W	L	ERA	G	GS	CG	SV	IP	H	HR	BB	SO	G/A	WHIP	AVG
2008	Orem (PIO)	R	2	1	4.37	21	3	0	5	35	33	4	13	39	—	1.31	.248
2009	R. Cucamonga (CAL)	HiA	1	0	9.53	5	0	0	0	6	8	2	8	8	2.00	2.82	.320
	Cedar Rapids (MWL)	LoA	3	0	1.23	40	0	0	8	51	29	0	19	83	0.76	0.94	.166
2010	R. Cucamonga (CAL)	HiA	4	1	2.06	20	0	0	0	35	24	1	14	39	1.68	1.09	.186
	Arkansas (TL)	AA	1	3	4.70	15	4	0	0	38	38	2	18	21	1.36	1.46	.264
Minor League Totals			11	5	3.16	101	7	0	13	165	132	9	72	190	1.22	1.23	.218

29 DREW HEID, OF

Born: Dec. 14, 1987. **B-T:** L-R. **Ht.:** 5-10. **Wt.:** 175. **Drafted:** Gonzaga, 2010 (9th round). **Signed by:** Casey Harvie.

As a senior last spring, Heid broke a 33-year-old Gonzaga record for hits in a season with 92. He produced with wood bats in summer college leagues, too, hitting .403 (West Coast Collegiate) and .427 (Alaska) in successive years. Undrafted in 2009 because he wanted to complete his degree, Heid provided incredible value to the Angels as a ninth-round senior sign for $20,000 a year later. In his pro debut, he led the Pioneer League in hits (104), while ranking second in on-base percentage (.435), third in batting (.362) and fifth in plate appearances per strikeout (8.3). Heid is a manager's favorite as a scrappy, undersized player who can hit for average, draw walks and play all three outfield spots. He's an average runner but good enough to profile as a pesky leadoff type, which is fortunate seeing as he has below-average power. He smacked nine homers in his pro debut, so he's not exactly a slap hitter. Heid is an average defender on a corner, and one PL manager described him as a blue-collar center fielder. He used his strong, accurate arm to rack up 12 assists while playing mostly left field. If he continues to perform, Heid has reserve big league outfielder written all over him. With his hitting ability and age (23), he could reach high Class A during his first full pro season.

Year	Club (League)	Class	AVG	G	AB	R	H	2B	3B	HR	RBI	BB	SO	SB	CS	OBP	SLG
2010	Orem (PIO)	R	.362	68	287	62	104	12	1	9	34	35	40	9	6	.435	.505
Minor League Totals			.362	68	287	62	104	12	1	9	34	35	40	9	6	.435	.505

30 LOEK VAN MIL, RHP

Born: Sept. 15, 1984. **B-T:** R-R. **Ht.:** 7-1. **Wt.:** 222. **Signed:** Netherlands, 2005. **Signed by:** Howard Norsetter (Twins).

If the 7-foot-1 Van Mil makes it to Anaheim, he'll expunge the 6-foot-11 Jon Rauch from the record books as tallest big leaguer ever. He missed the last six weeks of the 2008 season with an elbow injury and consequently passed through that winter's Rule 5 draft. The Twins added the hard-throwing Dutchman to their 40-man roster following the 2009 season, but he pitched so poorly in Double-A last season that they designated him for assignment in late August. Again, 29 other teams passed on Van Mil and he cleared waivers before the Angels selected him as the player to be named in the Brian Fuentes trade. Scouts long have admired Van Mil's stuff, but given his spotty performance record at Double-A, he often seems more novelty than prospect. In 32 appearances at that level, he has a 5.45 ERA, a 2.00 WHIP and more walks (29) than strikeouts (26). Van Mil couples 93-96 mph velocity with impressive angle to the plate to give him a fastball that's a plus-plus pitch at his best. His best high-80s sliders register as plus offerings. Even his changeup has average potential. Van Mil has very good body control for a pitcher of his size, but he remains too wild—in and out of the strike zone. He never has exceeded 45 innings in a season, so staying free from nagging injuries will be a top priority for Van Mil as he gives Double-A another go.

Year	Club (League)	Class	W	L	ERA	G	GS	CG	SV	IP	H	HR	BB	SO	G/A	WHIP	AVG
2006	Twins (GCL)	R	1	2	3.30	10	8	0	0	44	51	3	17	24	—	1.56	.290
2007	Elizabethton (APP)	R	2	2	2.63	13	0	0	0	24	14	0	17	23	—	1.29	.171
2008	Beloit (MWL)	LoA	2	2	3.22	28	0	0	3	45	36	5	25	42	—	1.37	.221
2009	Fort Myers (FSL)	HiA	0	0	2.86	25	0	0	5	35	29	3	17	23	0.80	1.33	.236
	New Britain (EL)	AA	1	0	2.45	8	0	0	1	7	7	0	6	5	2.40	1.77	.269
2010	Fort Myers (FSL)	HiA	0	1	4.50	3	0	0	0	4	4	0	0	6	5.00	1.00	.267
	New Britain (EL)	AA	1	2	6.37	23	0	0	0	30	40	1	22	21	1.87	2.09	.315
	Arkansas (TL)	AA	0	0	0.00	1	0	0	0	1	0	0	1	0	—	1.00	.000
Minor League Totals			7	10	3.57	111	8	0	9	189	181	12	105	144	1.33	1.51	.253

Los Angeles Dodgers

BY JIM SHONERD

After back-to-back National League West titles and NL Championship Series appearances in 2008-09, the Dodgers fell to fourth place last year. As if its first losing record since 2005 wasn't bad enough, Los Angeles also suffered the ignominy of their owners' divorce proceedings.

Frank and Jamie McCourt were once the first couple of Dodgers baseball, but their relationship disintegrated and the franchise took center stage in their divorce. The McCourts' feud hung over everything the club did in 2010. Frank attempted to take sole control of the franchise through a marital property agreement, but in December a Los Angeles Superior Court judge ruled it invalid and reinstated Jamie as co-owner. That decision promises to drag the dispute well into 2011.

More than the mechanics of who gets control of the Dodgers, however, documents filed in the divorce case revealed that the McCourts used the franchise as their personal piggybank. At the same time, the front office continually has had to pinch pennies on the big league roster, often sending premium prospects away in trades in order to get other teams to pick up salaries for the veterans they obtain. The most notable example was the 2008 deal that sent Carlos Santana to the Indians for Casey Blake, with Santana subsequently blossoming into one of the game's best young catchers and Los Angeles in need of help behind the plate.

The Dodgers started out well enough in 2010 and were tied for first place in the NL West as late as June 17. A six-game losing streak coming out of the all-star break started a fast fade, however. Los Angeles ended with an 80-82 record, a distant 12 games behind the rival Giants, who went on to win their first World Series since the franchises moved to California.

The Manny Ramirez experiment ended ingloriously, when the slugger was waived and picked up by the White Sox at the end of August. General manager Ned Colletti tried to keep hope alive with several midseason trades, sending away a total of seven young big leaguers or prospects, including Andrew Lambo and James McDonald, the top two players on this list two years ago.

The team will have a new manager in 2011, after Joe Torre retired at the end of the season. Former hitting coach Don Mattingly, who had also coached under Torre with the Yankees and followed him to Los Angeles in 2008, will take over despite having no real managerial experience. The Dodgers also ousted team

The divorce of co-owners Frank and Jamie McCourt loomed over the Dodgers' season

TOP 30 PROSPECTS

1. Dee Gordon, ss	16. Josh Lindblom, rhp
2. Zach Lee, rhp	17. Nate Eovaldi, rhp
3. Rubby de la Rosa, rhp	18. Garrett Gould, rhp
4. Chris Withrow, rhp	19. Brian Cavazos-Galvez, of
5. Allen Webster, rhp	20. Ralston Cash, rhp
6. Jerry Sands, of/1b	21. Jonathan Garcia, of
7. Scott Elbert, lhp	22. Pedro Baez, 3b
8. Kenley Jansen, rhp	23. Scott Schebler, of
9. Ethan Martin, rhp	24. Jake Lemmerman, ss
10. Trayvon Robinson, of	25. Joc Pederson, of
11. Leon Landry, of	26. Javy Guerra, rhp
12. James Baldwin, of	27. Blake Smith, of
13. Aaron Miller, lhp	28. Angelo Songco, of
14. Ivan DeJesus Jr., 2b/ss	29. Derek Cone, rhp
15. Kyle Russell, of	30. Luis Vasquez, rhp

president Dennis Mannion after the season, clearing the way for Frank McCourt to take on a larger role in the team's day-to-day operations again.

The Dodgers did make waves in the 2010 draft. When they used their first-round pick on high school righthander Zach Lee, who had a scholarship to play quarterback at Louisiana State, the consensus was that they had no chance of meeting his asking price. Instead, Los Angeles gave Lee more in one bonus-- $5.25 million, spread over five years in a backloaded deal—than it handed out to any of its previous three draft classes as a whole.

ORGANIZATION OVERVIEW

General Manager: Ned Colletti. **Farm Director:** DeJon Watson. **Scouting Director:** Logan White.

Class	Team	League	W	L	PCT	Finish*	Manager
Majors	Los Angeles Dodgers	National	80	82	.494	t-8th (16)	Joe Torre
Triple-A	Albuquerque Isotopes	Pacific Coast	72	71	.503	10th (16)	Tim Wallach
Double-A	Chattanooga Lookouts	Southern	65	74	.468	7th (10)	Carlos Subero
High A	Inland Empire 66ers	California	50	90	.357	10th (10)	Jeff Carter
Low A	Great Lakes Loons	Midwest	90	49	.647	1st (16)	Juan Bustabad
Rookie	Ogden Raptors	Pioneer	44	31	.587	2nd (8)	Damon Berryhill
Rookie	AZL Dodgers	Arizona	30	25	.545	7th (12)	Lorenzo Bundy
Overall 2010 Minor League Record			351	340	.508	11th (30)	

*Finish in overall standings (No. of teams in league). †League champion.
High Class A affiliate changes to Rancho Cucamonga (California) in 2011.

LAST YEAR'S TOP 30

Player, Pos.		Status
1.	Dee Gordon, ss	No. 1
2.	Chris Withrow, rhp	No. 4
3.	Aaron Miller, lhp	No. 13
4.	Ethan Martin, rhp	No. 9
5.	Josh Lindblom, rhp	No. 16
6.	Scott Elbert, lhp	No. 7
7.	Andrew Lambo, of	(Pirates)
8.	Ivan DeJesus Jr., ss	No. 14
9.	Trayvon Robinson, of	No. 10
10.	Allen Webster, rhp	No. 5
11.	Garrett Gould, rhp	No. 18
12.	Kyle Russell, of	No. 15
13.	Nate Eovaldi, rhp	No. 17
14.	Kenley Jansen, rhp	No. 8
15.	Pedro Baez, 3b	No. 22
16.	Javy Guerra, rhp	No. 26
17.	Lucas May, c	(Royals)
18.	Alfredo Silverio, of	Dropped out
19.	Scott Van Slyke, of	Dropped out
20.	Brett Wallach, rhp	(Cubs)
21.	Austin Gallagher, 1b/3b	Dropped out
22.	Blake Smith, of	No. 27
23.	Xavier Paul, of	Majors
24.	Jonathan Garcia, of	No. 21
25.	Jerry Sands, of/1b	No. 6
26.	Brian Cavazos-Galvez, of	No. 19
27.	Daigoro Rondon, rhp	Dropped out
28.	Tommy Giles, of	(Released)
29.	Danny Danielson, rhp	(Retired)
30.	Gorman Erickson, c	Dropped out

BEST TOOLS

Best Hitter for Average	Dee Gordon
Best Power Hitter	Jerry Sands
Best Strike-Zone Discipline	Justin Sellers
Fastest Baserunner	Dee Gordon
Best Athlete	Dee Gordon
Best Fastball	Kenley Jansen
Best Curveball	Chris Withrow
Best Slider	Scott Elbert
Best Changeup	Allen Webster
Best Control	Zach Lee
Best Defensive Catcher	Gorman Erickson
Best Defensive Infielder	Dee Gordon
Best Infield Arm	Pedro Baez
Best Defensive Outfielder	James Baldwin
Best Outfield Arm	Blake Smith

PROJECTED 2014 LINEUP

Catcher	Dioner Navarro
First Base	James Loney
Second Base	Ivan DeJesus Jr.
Third Base	Pedro Baez
Shortstop	Dee Gordon
Left Field	Jerry Sands
Center Field	Matt Kemp
Right Field	Andre Ethier
No. 1 Starter	Clayton Kershaw
No. 2 Starter	Zach Lee
No. 3 Starter	Chad Billingsley
No. 4 Starter	Rubby de la Rosa
No. 5 Starter	Chris Withrow
Closer	Jonathan Broxton

TOP PROSPECTS OF THE DECADE

Year	Player, Pos.	2010 Org.
2001	Ben Diggins, rhp	Out of baseball
2002	Ricardo Rodriguez, rhp	Out of baseball
2003	James Loney, 1b	Dodgers
2004	Edwin Jackson, rhp	White Sox
2005	Joel Guzman, ss/of	Orioles
2006	Chad Billingsley, rhp	Dodgers
2007	Andy LaRoche, 3b	Pirates
2008	Clayton Kershaw, lhp	Dodgers
2009	Andrew Lambo, of	Pirates
2010	Dee Gordon, ss	Dodgers

TOP DRAFT PICKS OF THE DECADE

Year	Player, Pos.	2010 Org.
2001	Brian Pilkington, rhp (2nd round)	Out of baseball
2002	James Loney, 1b	Dodgers
2003	Chad Billingsley, rhp	Dodgers
2004	Scott Elbert, lhp	Dodgers
2005	*Luke Hochevar, rhp (1st round supp.)	Royals
2006	Clayton Kershaw, lhp	Dodgers
2007	Chris Withrow, rhp	Dodgers
2008	Ethan Martin, rhp	Dodgers
2009	Aaron Miller, lhp (1st round supp.)	Dodgers
2010	Zach Lee, rhp	Dodgers

*Did not sign.

LARGEST BONUSES IN CLUB HISTORY

Hiroki Kuroda, 2007	$7,300,000
Zach Lee, 2010	$5,250,000
Clayton Kershaw, 2006	$2,300,000
Joel Guzman, 2001	$2,255,000
Ben Diggins, 2000	$2,200,000

LOS ANGELES DODGERS

TOP 2011 ROOKIE: Kenley Jansen, rhp. The flamethrowing former catcher was sensational in the Dodgers' bullpen last year and will be counted upon in a set-up role in 2011.

BREAKOUT PROSPECT: Scott Schebler, rhp. One of the Dodgers' over-slot signings from the 2010 draft, he offers power and speed among his mix of tools.

SLEEPER: Shawn Tolleson, rhp. A 30th-round steal in last year's draft, he has a low-90s fastball and a crisp slider.

SOURCE OF TOP 30 TALENT

Homegrown	30	Acquired	0
College	9	Trades	0
Junior college	3	Rule 5 draft	0
High school	14	Independent leagues	0
Draft-and-follow	0	Free agents/waivers	0
Nondrafted free agents	0		
International	4		

LF
Jerry Sands (6)
Angelo Songco (28)
Nick Akins
Elian Herrera

CF
Trayvon Robinson (10)
Leon Landry (11)
James Baldwin (12)
Scott Schebler (23)
Jamie Hoffmann
Noel Cuevas

RF
Kyle Russell (15)
Brian Cavazos-Galvez (19)
Jonathan Garcia (21)
Joc Pederson (25)
Blake Smith (27)
Scott Van Slyke
Alfredo Silverio
Bobby Coyle

3B
Pedro Baez (22)
Russ Mitchell
Matt Kirkland
Jeff Hunt

SS
Dee Gordon (1)
Jake Lemmerman (24)
Justin Sellers

2B
Ivan DeJesus Jr. (14)
Jaime Pedroza

1B
Austin Gallagher
Blake Dean

C
Tony Delmonico
Gorman Erickson
A.J. Ellis
Hector Gimenez
J.T. Wise
Steve Domecus

RHP

RHSP	RHRP
Zach Lee (2)	Kenley Jansen (8)
Rubby de la Rosa (3)	Josh Lindblom (16)
Chris Withrow (4)	Javy Guerra (26)
Allen Webster (5)	Luis Vasquez (30)
Ethan Martin (9)	Shawn Tolleson
Nate Eovaldi (17)	Javier Solano
Garrett Gould (18)	Justin Miller
Ralston Cash (20)	Travis Schlichting
Derek Cone (29)	Jon Link
Carlos Frias	Eric Krebs
Matt Magill	Steven Ames
Gustavo Gomez	
Josh Wall	
Jon Michael Redding	

LHP

LHSP	LHRP
Aaron Miller (13)	Scott Elbert (7)
Ryan Christenson	Andrew Suiter
Greg Wilborn	Brent Leach
	James Adkins
	Wilkin de la Rosa
	Geison Aguasviva
	Cole St. Clair

DRAFT ANALYSIS

2010

BEST PURE HITTER: OF Leon Landry (4) has proven his prowess with wood bats, hitting .364 in the Cape Cod League last summer and .349/.399/.510 at Rookie-level Ogden in his pro debut. OFs Joc Pederson (11) and Scott Schebler (26) also have upside with the bat.

BEST POWER HITTER: OF Noel Cuevas (21) has the most raw power but also a lot of holes in his swing. OF Blake Dean (8), who hit 56 homers in four seasons at Louisiana State, has the most present power.

FASTEST RUNNER: OF James Baldwin (4), who has plus-plus speed, stole 17 bases in 20 pro attempts.

BEST DEFENSIVE PLAYER: Baldwin has Gold Glove potential in center field. Landry, another legitimate center fielder, is more refined at this point.

BEST FASTBALL: RHP Zach Lee (1) has a 90-93 mph fastball that peaks at 95, with plenty of running, boring action and exquisite command. RHP Ralston Cash (2) throws 91-94 mph but isn't as polished.

BEST SECONDARY PITCH: RHP Derek Cone's (31) plus curveball is a strikeout pitch. Lee has a hard curveball.

BEST PRO DEBUT: SS Jake Lemmerman (5) won MVP honors in the Pioneer League after hitting .363/.434/.610 at Ogden with league highs in runs (69) and doubles (24). RHPs Red Patterson (29) and Shawn Tolleson (30) joined him on the Pioneer League all-star team. Patterson went 6-1, 3.33 with 66 strikeouts in 68 innings. Tolleson, who battled injuries and inconsistency during four years at Baylor, conquered both in pro ball and had a 0.63 ERA, 17 saves and a 39-5 K-BB ratio in 29 innings. Both throw in the low 90s and have a solid second pitch.

BEST ATHLETE: Baldwin is rangy and projectable, reminding the Dodgers of Garret Anderson with more speed and athleticism. Lee was one of the top quarterback recruits in the nation and attended summer football camp at Louisiana State before signing.

MOST INTRIGUING BACKGROUND: Los Angeles drafted seven players with big league connections. OF Devon Ethier's (32) brother Andre is an all-star outfielder for the Dodgers. Baldwin (James), LHP Ryan Christenson (7, Gary), Pederson (Stu), unsigned RHP Chad Wallach (43, Tim) and unsigned 2B Anthony Garcia (48, Leo) all have fathers who played in the majors, and the senior Wallach and Garcia managed and coached in the Los Angeles system in 2010. 1B Beau Brett (35) is the nephew of Hall of Famer George Brett and former all-star Ken Brett. Unsigned 1B Cody Martin's (47) brother Ethan was the Dodgers' 2008

first-rounder, and they're cousins of Cash.

CLOSEST TO THE MAJORS: Landry or Tolleson, but don't rule out Lee.

BEST LATE-ROUND PICK: Pederson and Schebler, with Tolleson and Cone as deeper sleepers.

THE ONE WHO GOT AWAY: RHP Kevin Gausman (6) flashed first-round ability, but his $4 million price tag sent him to Louisiana State.

ASSESSMENT: Critics said the Dodgers drafted Lee so they could save money by not signing him, but they got the deal done with a backloaded $5.25 million contract. They made their draft on deadline day by landing Lee, Pederson and Schebler.

2009

The Dodgers didn't have a first-round pick, and this group has yet to produce a breakout player. The top picks—LHP Aaron Miller (1s), RHP Garrett Gould (2) and OF Blake Smith (2)—are making steady progress, and RHP Brett Wallach (3) yielded Ted Lilly in a trade last summer.

GRADE: C+

2008

SS Dee Gordon (4), the system's top prospect, RHP Allen Webster (18) and OF/1B Jerry Sands (25) all qualify as major steals. RHPs Ethan Martin (1) and Nate Eovaldi (11) have electric arms but need more polish. Unsigned 3B Zack Cox (20) was a first-round pick and the best pure hitter available in the 2010 draft.

GRADE: B+

2007

RHP Chris Withrow (1) is another mid-90s arm who's figuring things out. OF Andrew Lambo (4) was one of the best hitters in the system until he failed a drug test last May and was part of the Octavio Dotel trade two months later.

GRADE: C

2006

LHP Clayton Kershaw (1) quickly became Los Angeles' No. 1 starter. RHP Bryan Morris (1), part of the Jason Bay/Manny Ramirez blockbuster, is now one of the Pirates' best prospects. OF Preston Mattingly (1s), whose father Don is the Dodgers' new manager, is a classic draft bust.

GRADE: A

Draft analysis by Jim Callis. Numbers in parentheses indicate draft rounds.

DEE GORDON, SS

Born: April 22, 1988. **Bats:** L. **Throws:** R.
Height: 5-11. **Weight:** 150. **Drafted:** Seminole
(Fla.) CC, 2008 (4th round). **Signed by:** Scott
Hennessey.

PROSPECT 1

DANNY PARKER

Gordon's father Tom pitched 22 seasons in the majors, winning 138 games and saving 158 in a career that ended in 2009, but Dee didn't take up baseball until his senior year of high school. A basketball player up to that point, he quickly took to the diamond. Gordon went undrafted out of high school in 2006 and landed at Southeastern (Fla.), where he hit .378 in his one season at the NAIA school. He planned to transfer to Seminole (Fla.) CC for his sophomore season, but a problem with his high school transcript nixed that plan. That's when his father's connections came in handy. The elder Gordon roomed with Dodgers farm director DeJon Watson in the minors when Dee was born, and he tipped Watson off about his son. After working him out, Los Angeles took Gordon in the fourth round of the 2008 draft and signed him for $250,000. He batted .331 in Rookie-level Ogden in his pro debut, won MVP honors in the low Class A Midwest League in his first full season and started at shortstop for the U.S. team in the Futures Game last summer. The Dodgers jumped him two levels to Double-A Chattanooga in 2010, and he responded by leading the Southern League with 53 steals. Managers voted him the league's most exciting player.

Gordon's athleticism is off the charts, giving him the potential for four plus tools. He has a short, compact swing that's geared to let him take advantage of his well above-average speed. He did a better job of taking balls back up the middle last season, and he has a knack for barreling up balls and spraying line drives from gap to gap. He has plus bat speed and while he's primarily a fastball hitter, he has shown he can adjust to breaking pitches. Though he hits balls hard consistently, Gordon lacks power and his approach isn't designed for it, so he'll likely max out at 10 homers per year. He did a better job of incorporating the bunt into his game last year, and he has the skills to be an effective top-of-the-order hitter. He comes to the plate with an aggressive mentality, however, and needs to learn to see more pitches. He carries that

SCOUTING GRADES

Batting: 60. **Defense:** 70.
Power: 35. **Arm:** 65.
Speed: 70.

Based on 20-80 scouting scale, where 50 represents major league average, and future projection rather than present tools.

same aggressiveness with him on the bases and in the field as well. Along with leading the SL in steals, he also ranked first by getting caught stealing 20 times, the second consecutive season he's topped his league in both categories. He has blazing speed but still has to learn to pick his spots. Gordon is a flashy defender whose range allows him to reach balls few can, and he has an above-average arm. However, he can get a bit out of control on defense and led SL shortstops with 37 errors in 133 games. He rushes plays at times and makes some ill-advised, off-balance throws.

Most of Gordon's deficiencies should be correctable with experience, and all the tools are there for him to be an above-average major league shortstop and leadoff hitter. He followed up his strong season with an outstanding turn with Carolina in the Puerto Rican League. He'll move up to Triple-A Albuquerque in 2011 and should be ready to make his big league debut by September, if not sooner.

Year	Club (League)	Class	AVG	G	AB	R	H	2B	3B	HR	RBI	BB	SO	SB	CS	OBP	SLG
2008	Ogden (PIO)	R	.331	60	251	45	83	13	3	2	27	16	29	18	5	.371	.430
2009	Great Lakes (MWL)	LoA	.301	131	538	96	162	17	12	3	35	43	90	73	25	.362	.394
2010	Chattanooga (SL)	AA	.277	133	555	86	154	17	10	2	39	40	89	53	20	.332	.355
Minor League Totals			.297	324	1344	227	399	47	25	7	101	99	208	144	50	.351	.385

2 ZACH LEE, RHP

Born: Sept. 13, 1991. **B-T:** R-R. **Ht.:** 6-3. **Wt.:** 190. **Drafted:** HS—McKinney, Texas, 2010 (1st round). **Signed by:** Calvin Jones.

A highly rated quarterback recruit headed to Louisiana State, Lee was considered the 2010 draft's most unsignable player. When the Dodgers took him 28th overall, there was speculation they did so to save money by not signing him. Lee went to LSU's campus to take summer classes and participate in football workouts before Los Angeles shocked the industry by signing him at the Aug. 16 deadline for $5.25 million, the largest draft bonus in franchise history. Lee has a chance to have three plus pitches. His lively fastball sits in the low 90s and was hitting 95 mph during instructional league. He also attacks hitters with a power curveball that gets slurvy at times but has above-average potential, and he has a changeup that's advanced for his age. Despite his two-sport background, Lee is very polished for a high school pitcher. He has a smooth delivery with no real flaws, and he's beyond his years in terms of command and pitchability. Lee has the makings of a true frontline starter. One of the Dodgers' selling points in getting him to sign was their recent success in developing young pitchers, and he could move quickly for a high school player. He'll make his pro debut at low Class A Great Lakes.

Year	Club (League)	Class	W	L	ERA	G	GS	CG	SV	IP	H	HR	BB	SO	G/A	WHIP	AVG
2010	Did Not Play—Signed Late																

3 RUBBY DE LA ROSA, RHP

Born: March 4, 1989. **B-T:** R-R. **Ht.:** 6-1. **Wt.:** 170. **Signed:** Dominican Republic, 2007. **Signed by:** Ezequiel Sepulveda.

De la Rosa's U.S. debut in 2009 didn't go auspiciously, as he posted a 6.06 ERA in five games before getting sent home to the Dominican Republic for disciplinary reasons. One year later, he was the Dodgers' minor league pitcher of the year after going 7-2, 2.37 and reaching Double-A. De la Rosa weighed 130 pounds and threw 89-91 mph when he signed as an 18-year-old. Since getting on a proper diet, he has added 40 pounds of quality weight and fueled his breakout with a fastball that lights up radar guns. He pitches at 95-96 mph and registered as high as 102 mph at Great Lakes. He's capable of holding that velocity deep into games and finding an extra gear when he needs it. De la Rosa has two promising secondary pitches in his changeup and slider. His changeup is the more consistent of the two, with late fade at 85-89 mph. The slider has sharp, late break when he stays on top of it. His command has improved but still needs work, as he has some effort in his delivery and loses his arm slot at times. De la Rosa has the potential to be a No. 2 starter or a closer. He'll begin 2011 back in Chattanooga and could contribute in Los Angeles by the end of the season.

Year	Club (League)	Class	W	L	ERA	G	GS	CG	SV	IP	H	HR	BB	SO	G/A	WHIP	AVG
2007	Dodgers (DSL)	R	0	0	13.50	6	1	0	0	6	11	0	10	6	—	3.50	.393
2008	Dodgers (DSL)	R	1	4	1.71	12	12	0	0	47	34	0	21	51	—	1.16	.197
2009	Dodgers (AZL)	R	0	1	6.06	5	2	0	0	16	17	0	11	22	1.67	1.71	.266
2010	Great Lakes (MWL)	LoA	4	1	3.19	14	5	0	6	59	49	3	17	55	2.31	1.11	.223
	Chattanooga (SL)	AA	3	1	1.41	8	8	0	0	51	38	1	21	39	2.52	1.16	.215
Minor League Totals			8	7	2.90	45	28	0	6	180	149	4	80	173	2.31	1.27	.225

4 CHRIS WITHROW, RHP

Born: April 1, 1989. **B-T:** R-R. **Ht.:** 6-3. **Wt.:** 195. **Drafted:** HS—Midland, Texas, 2007 (1st round). **Signed by:** Calvin Jones.

Withrow would have been a two-way player at Baylor had his work on the mound not earned him a $1.35 million bonus as the 20th overall pick in 2007. His father Mike pitched in the White Sox system and was his high school pitching coach. Chris spent 2010 in Double-A at age 21, but he was rarely able to get into any kind of groove and led the Southern League in earned runs allowed (86). Despite of his numbers, Withrow still looked like a future frontline starter when at his best. He pitches in the mid-90s with his sinking fastball and tops out at 98 mph, though he doesn't command it well. His curveball is a legitimate strikeout pitch, featuring sharp, late break and plenty of depth. However, he has trouble staying on top of the ball at times, resulting in too many straight fastballs and inconsistent curves. His changeup is fringy, though his struggles with his other pitches forced him to develop a better feel for it. The Dodgers have tinkered with Withrow's mechanics a bit, trying to stop him from tilting his head toward third base and give him more balance over the rubber. Withrow still has a ceiling as a No. 2 starter, but he still needs to refine his pitches and learn to deal with adversity. He'll get another crack at Double-A in 2011.

Year	Club (League)	Class	W	L	ERA	G	GS	CG	SV	IP	H	HR	BB	SO	G/A	WHIP	AVG
2007	Dodgers (GCL)	R	0	0	5.00	6	4	0	0	9	5	0	4	13	—	1.00	.167

Year	Club (League)	Class	W	L	ERA	G	GS	CG	SV	IP	H	HR	BB	SO	G/A	WHIP	AVG
2008	Inland Empire (CAL)	HiA	0	0	4.50	4	0	0	0	4	2	0	6	1	—	2.00	.182
2009	Inland Empire (CAL)	HiA	6	6	4.69	19	16	0	0	86	80	3	45	105	1.33	1.45	.252
	Chattanooga (SL)	AA	2	2	3.95	6	6	0	0	27	24	2	12	26	0.76	1.32	.240
2010	Chattanooga (SL)	AA	4	9	5.97	27	27	1	0	130	146	13	69	120	1.07	1.66	.285
Minor League Totals			12	17	5.27	62	53	1	0	256	257	18	136	265	1.11	1.53	.265

5 ALLEN WEBSTER, RHP

Born: Feb. 10, 1990. **B-T:** R-R. **Ht.:** 6-2. **Wt.:** 170. **Drafted:** HS—Madison, N.C., 2008 (18th round). **Signed by:** Lon Joyce.

Webster was primarily a shortstop in high school and saw only limited action on the mound, but the Dodgers immediately converted him to pitching full-time after signing him for $20,000 as an 18th-rounder in 2008. He quickly developed into one of their best pitching prospects, and the Diamondbacks brought his name up in trade talks when he was in Rookie ball in 2009. Webster made his full-season debut last season, tying for the Midwest League lead in wins and topping the system in wins and ERA (2.88). Webster's fastball sat at 88-90 mph in his predraft workout with Los Angeles, and he has gotten bigger and added some more heat since then, now working in the low 90s and topping out at 95 with plus late sink. His best secondary pitch is an above-average changeup with fading action, and he's starting to trust it more. He also has a solid curveball with some bite. With his compact, natural delivery and easy arm action, he should develop into a dependable strike-thrower. Webster's biggest need at this point is experience. He could become a mid-rotation starter and possibly more if he tightens his curveball. He'll deal with the challenging pitching environment in the high Class A California League in 2011.

Year	Club (League)	Class	W	L	ERA	G	GS	CG	SV	IP	H	HR	BB	SO	G/A	WHIP	AVG
2008	Dodgers (GCL)	R	1	1	3.44	12	0	0	1	18	12	1	17	13	—	1.58	.197
2009	Dodgers (AZL)	R	2	1	2.08	12	8	0	0	48	35	0	14	56	2.11	1.03	.197
	Ogden (PIO)	R	2	0	3.00	4	3	0	0	21	23	1	4	21	1.05	1.29	.277
2010	Great Lakes (MWL)	LoA	12	9	2.88	26	23	0	0	131	119	6	53	114	1.45	1.31	.239
Minor League Totals			17	11	2.76	54	34	0	1	218	189	8	88	204	1.52	1.27	.231

6 JERRY SANDS, OF/1B

Born: Sept. 28, 1987. **B-T:** R-R. **Ht.:** 6-4. **Wt.:** 225. **Drafted:** Catawba (N.C.), 2008 (25th round). **Signed by:** Lon Joyce.

Sands set school records at NCAA Division II Catawba (N.C.) for career homers (61), walks (132) and slugging (.752), but that still only netted him a $5,000 bonus as a 25th-round pick in 2008. After spending most of his first two years in Rookie ball, he reached Double-A in 2010, earning the Dodgers' minor league player of the year award after tying for third in the minors with 35 homers. Sands' has plus power to all fields. He focused on shortening up his swing coming into last year, and he now has a sound stroke with some loft and above-average bat speed. While he has trouble laying off high fastballs at times, he shows an aptitude for handling breaking pitches, so he shouldn't just be a one-dimensional slugger. Sands split his time between the outfield and first base last season and was surprisingly effective on the outfield corners. Though he has below-average speed, his instincts compensate for it and make him an average defender. His arm strength is a tick below average but enough to get by. Sands has the power to profile as a solid everyday left fielder or first baseman, and he also might get a chance to play some third base. He'll return to Chattanooga to begin 2011, but a September callup isn't out of the question.

Year	Club (League)	Class	AVG	G	AB	R	H	2B	3B	HR	RBI	BB	SO	SB	CS	OBP	SLG
2008	Dodgers (GCL)	R	.205	46	146	29	30	4	0	10	33	29	43	5	0	.346	.438
2009	Ogden (PIO)	R	.350	41	163	41	57	9	2	14	39	22	28	0	1	.427	.687
	Great Lakes (MWL)	LoA	.260	32	104	22	27	7	2	5	19	15	32	1	0	.361	.510
2010	Great Lakes (MWL)	LoA	.333	69	243	48	81	16	3	18	46	40	61	14	2	.432	.646
	Chattanooga (SL)	AA	.270	68	259	54	70	12	2	17	47	33	62	4	0	.360	.529
Minor League Totals			.290	256	915	194	265	48	9	64	184	139	226	24	3	.388	.572

7 SCOTT ELBERT, LHP

Born: Aug. 13, 1985. **B-T:** L-L. **Ht.:** 6-1. **Wt.:** 215. **Drafted:** HS—Seneca, Mo., 2004 (1st round). **Signed by:** Mitch Webster.

Coming off a 2009 season in which he spent four separate stints in the majors and made the Dodgers' postseason roster, Elbert had a forgettable 2010. The 15th overall pick in the 2004 draft, he made a single appearance for Los Angeles on May 29 and left Albuquerque for personal reasons shortly after being sent back down. He made up for lost time with a strong showing in the Arizona Fall League, where he got a chance to audition for new Dodgers manager Don Mattingly, who piloted Elbert's AFL squad. Elbert has been a starter for most of his minor league career, but his big league future looks to be in the bullpen. He attacks hitters with riding fastballs that sit at 93-94 mph and can reach 96 mph. His 87-88 mph slider gives him a putaway pitch with tilt and depth. He also has a solid-average changeup, though he doesn't use it much. A star running back in high school, Elbert has a football mentality. His aggressiveness leads him to rush his delivery, causing his fastball to miss up in the zone and his slider to flatten out. Some club officials believe Elbert has the repertoire to be a starter, but he's expected to make the big league bullpen in 2011. With better command, he could emerge as a dominant two-pitch reliever.

Year	Club (League)	Class	W	L	ERA	G	GS	CG	SV	IP	H	HR	BB	SO	G/A	WHIP	AVG
2004	Ogden (PIO)	R	2	3	5.26	12	12	0	0	50	47	5	30	45	—	1.55	.270
2005	Columbus (SAL)	LoA	8	5	2.66	25	24	1	0	115	83	8	57	128	—	1.22	.200
2006	Vero Beach (FSL)	HiA	5	5	2.37	17	15	0	0	84	57	4	41	97	—	1.17	.193
	Jacksonville (SL)	AA	6	4	3.61	11	11	0	0	62	40	11	44	76	—	1.35	.187
2007	Jacksonville (SL)	AA	0	1	3.86	3	3	0	0	14	6	0	10	24	—	1.14	.128
2008	Jacksonville (SL)	AA	4	1	2.40	25	1	0	0	41	22	2	20	46	—	1.02	.157
	Los Angeles (NL)	MAJ	0	1	12.00	10	0	0	0	6	9	2	4	8	—	2.17	.346
2009	Chattanooga (SL)	AA	2	3	3.90	12	11	0	0	62	59	5	30	87	0.92	1.43	.248
	Albuquerque (PCL)	AAA	2	1	3.74	8	7	1	0	34	34	2	14	38	1.73	1.43	.262
	Los Angeles (NL)	MAJ	2	0	5.03	19	0	0	0	20	19	4	7	21	0.95	1.32	.253
2010	Los Angeles (NL)	MAJ	0	0	13.50	1	0	0	0	1	1	0	3	0	0.00	6.00	.333
	Albuquerque (PCL)	AAA	1	1	4.98	9	9	0	0	43	46	4	34	45	1.58	1.85	.277
Major League Totals			2	1	6.84	30	0	0	0	26	29	6	14	29	0.86	1.63	.279
Minor League Totals			30	24	3.42	122	93	2	0	505	394	41	280	586	1.30	1.33	.216

8 KENLEY JANSEN, RHP

Born: Sept. 30, 1987. **B-T:** B-R. **Ht.:** 6-6. **Wt.:** 220. **Signed:** Curacao, 2004. **Signed by:** Camilo Pascual/Rolando Chirino.

Jansen first gained some notoriety as a cannon-armed backstop for the Dutch squad that upset the Dominican Republic twice at the 2009 World Baseball Classic. However, he hit just .229/.310/.337 in five seasons as a catcher, and the Dodgers decided to try his arm on the mound in mid-2009. Less than a year after his first pro pitching appearance, he made his big league debut. Major leaguers had no answer for Jansen's power fastball. His heater sits in the mid-90s, reached triple digits at times and features some cutting action. He has a loose, easy delivery and the ball jumps out of his hand, making it that much more overpowering. Jansen's second pitch is a slurvy 82-84 mph slider that could become a plus pitch if he can tighten it up. He also has some feel for a changeup but rarely uses it. He does a good job of being around the strike zone considering his size and limited time on the mound. Though his command isn't pinpoint, he won't need it to be. Jansen might benefit from some Triple-A time to sharpen his slider, but after his dominant turn in Los Angeles last year, the Dodgers are counting on him for their big league bullpen. He'll be a set-up man for Jonathan Broxton for now and could emerge as a closer down the road if his slider develops.

Year	Club (League)	Class	AVG	G	AB	R	H	2B	3B	HR	RBI	BB	SO	SB	CS	OBP	SLG
2005	Dodgers (GCL)	R	.304	34	102	16	31	9	1	1	18	6	19	1	0	.339	.441
	Ogden (PIO)	R	.182	3	11	2	2	1	0	0	1	1	5	0	0	.250	.273
2006	Dodgers (GCL)	R	.248	35	117	14	29	2	1	1	10	19	32	1	0	.362	.308
2007	Great Lakes (MWL)	LoA	.102	20	59	5	6	1	0	1	2	6	18	0	1	.214	.169
	Ogden (PIO)	R	.240	53	183	26	44	5	1	2	22	28	50	0	0	.346	.311
2008	Great Lakes (MWL)	LoA	.227	79	247	31	56	15	0	9	27	23	72	3	0	.298	.397
2009	Albuquerque (PCL)	AAA	.185	8	27	1	5	0	0	0	2	1	7	0	0	.214	.185
	Inland Empire (CAL)	HiA	.202	26	89	7	18	6	0	1	11	7	21	0	1	.268	.303
2010	Chattanooga (SL)	AA	.200	16	5	1	1	1	0	0	0	0	2	1	0	.200	.400
	Los Angeles (NL)	MAJ	1.000	26	1	1	1	0	0	0	0	1	0	0	0	1.000	1.000
Major League Totals			1.000	26	1	1	1	0	0	0	0	1	0	0	0	1.000	1.000
Minor League Totals			.229	274	840	103	192	40	3	15	97	92	226	6	2	.310	.337

Year	Club (League)	Class	W	L	ERA	G	GS	CG	SV	IP	H	HR	BB	SO	G/A	WHIP	AVG
2009	Inland Empire (CAL)	HiA	0	0	4.63	12	0	0	0	12	14	1	11	19	0.67	2.14	.298
2010	Inland Empire (CAL)	HiA	1	1	1.50	11	0	0	0	18	15	0	6	28	1.18	1.17	.231
	Chattanooga (SL)	AA	4	0	1.67	22	0	0	8	27	14	0	17	50	0.63	1.15	.151
	Los Angeles (NL)	MAJ	1	0	0.67	25	0	0	4	27	12	0	15	41	0.68	1.00	.130
Major League Totals			1	0	0.67	25	0	0	4	27	12	0	15	41	0.68	1.00	.130
Minor League Totals			5	1	2.22	45	0	0	8	57	43	1	34	97	0.81	1.36	.210

9 ETHAN MARTIN, RHP

JON SOOHOO-LA DODGERS

Born: June 6, 1989. **B-T:** R-R. **Ht.:** 6-2. **Wt.:** 195. **Drafted:** HS—Toccoa, Ga., 2008 (1st round). **Signed by:** Lon Joyce.

Martin was a highly rated prospect in high school as both a pitcher and a power-hitting third baseman. He also could have been a college quarterback but opted to sign with the Dodgers for $1.73 million as the 15th overall pick in 2008. He had a rough 2010 at high Class A Inland Empire, losing seven consecutive starts to end his season. Martin is one of the best athletes in the system and has an effortless delivery with a loose arm. When he's at his best, his fastball sits at 94-95 mph and can reach as high as 98. He had trouble maintaining that velocity last year, dipping to the low 90s at season's end. When he throws it for strikes, Martin's curveball is a wipeout pitch. He also has a changeup with slight sinking action that's a work in progress at this point. His command held him back in 2010, when he led the California League with 81 walks. He'd fall prey to big innings when he'd struggle with his mechanics and start leaving his fastball up in the zone. Martin still has the ceiling of No. 2 starter if he can improve his command. He could end up starting 2011 back in high Class A, but could move quickly one he puts everything together.

Year	Club (League)	Class	W	L	ERA	G	GS	CG	SV	IP	H	HR	BB	SO	G/A	WHIP	AVG
2009	Great Lakes (MWL)	LoA	6	8	3.87	27	19	0	1	100	85	4	61	120	0.89	1.46	.232
2010	Inland Empire (CAL)	HiA	9	14	6.35	25	22	1	0	113	120	10	81	105	1.21	1.77	.279
Minor League Totals			15	22	5.19	52	41	1	1	213	205	14	142	225	1.05	1.63	.258

10 TRAYVON ROBINSON, OF

Born: Sept. 1, 1987. **B-T:** B-R. **Ht.:** 5-11. **Wt.:** 195. **Drafted:** HS—Los Angeles, 2005 (10th round). **Signed by:** Bobby Darwin.

A product of MLB's RBI program, Robinson played at Los Angeles' Crenshaw High, whose notable baseball alumni include former all-stars Chris Brown, Darryl Strawberry and Ellis Valentine. Robinson has made steady progress in the minors, improving his on-base percentage in each of his four years in full-season leagues. Placed on the 40-man roster after a breakout 2009 season, he ranked third in the Southern League in OBP (.404) and steals (38) last year. Robinson is loaded with athleticism and could have four average or better tools. A righthanded hitter when he signed, he's now a switch-hitter with bat speed, loft and average power from both sides of the plate. He should be able to hit for a solid average as well, thanks to his plus speed and improved approach. His strikeout totals remain high, however, as he usually takes aggressive hacks rather than settling for putting the ball in play. Robinson has improved his basestealing technique but still can make further gains. He has above-average range and a fringy arm in center field. If the Dodgers decide to trade Matt Kemp, Robinson could be his successor in center field. He needs a full season in Triple-A before he's ready for his big league debut.

Year	Club (League)	Class	AVG	G	AB	R	H	2B	3B	HR	RBI	BB	SO	SB	CS	OBP	SLG
2005	Dodgers (GCL)	R	.296	40	115	19	34	7	2	3	15	8	25	6	4	.357	.470
	Ogden (PIO)	R	.217	8	23	2	5	0	0	1	2	0	9	0	0	.217	.348
2006	Dodgers (GCL)	R	.254	39	134	24	34	7	2	2	20	16	48	5	1	.340	.381
	Vero Beach (FSL)	HiA	.400	3	5	1	2	0	0	0	1	0	2	1	0	.400	.400
2007	Great Lakes (MWL)	LoA	.253	110	396	50	100	9	4	2	31	32	119	22	9	.314	.311
2008	Inland Empire (CAL)	HiA	.276	112	439	67	121	20	8	4	42	33	104	22	12	.328	.385
2009	Inland Empire (CAL)	HiA	.306	117	470	82	144	28	9	15	54	50	125	43	18	.375	.500
	Chattanooga (SL)	AA	.246	19	57	8	14	1	2	2	10	10	18	4	2	.358	.439
2010	Chattanooga (SL)	AA	.300	120	434	80	130	23	5	9	57	73	125	38	15	.404	.438
Minor League Totals			.282	568	2073	333	584	95	32	38	232	222	575	141	61	.355	.413

11 LEON LANDRY, OF

Born: Sept. 20, 1989. **B-T:** L-R. **Ht.:** 5-11. **Wt.:** 185. **Drafted:** Louisiana State, 2010 (3rd round). **Signed by:** Matt Paul.

Landry lost his starting job during Louisiana State's run to the 2009 College World Series title but recovered to bat .364 in the Cape Cod League that summer and came back with a vengeance last spring. Landry hit .338 and stole 16 bases for the Tigers, the best numbers of his college career, and didn't slow down after signing for $284,400 as the Dodgers' third-round pick, finishing fifth in the Rookie-level Pioneer League in batting (.349). Landry could develop four average or better tools. His swing is short and compact and he should be able to hit for a solid average. He started controlling the strike zone better and became a much tougher out last year when he stopped selling out for power, which isn't his strength. He'll probably settle in around 8-12 home runs a year, but he can be a difference-maker in center field. Landry has outstanding instincts on defense, getting good reads and jumps on balls. He's able to range well in all directions and make highlight-reel plays, even though his straight-ahead speed is only a tick above-average. With the makings of a capable leadoff hitter and center fielder,

Landry should advance to low Class A to get his first look at full-season ball in 2011.

Year	Club (League)	Class	AVG	G	AB	R	H	2B	3B	HR	RBI	BB	SO	SB	CS	OBP	SLG
2010	Ogden (PIO)	R	.349	57	249	46	87	20	4	4	38	20	36	13	9	.399	.510
Minor League Totals			.349	57	249	46	87	20	4	4	38	20	36	13	9	.399	.510

12 JAMES BALDWIN, OF

Born: Oct. 10, 1991. **B-T:** L-R. **Ht.:** 6-3. **Wt.:** 187. **Drafted:** HS—Southern Pines, N.C., 2010 (4th round). **Signed by:** Lon Joyce.

Baldwin grew up around big league clubhouses, as his father James pitched 11 seasons in the majors and was an all-star in 2000. The younger Baldwin was a three-sport standout in high school, also excelling in basketball and football, and got a $180,000 bonus as a fourth-round pick last June to pass up a commitment to Elon. Baldwin is a tremendous athlete, with a frame that should allow him to get stronger as he matures. He can be a dynamic center fielder, getting good jumps on balls, and his speed rates a 70 on the 20-80 scouting scale. That's not to say he doesn't have offensive potential as well. Baldwin's swing has drawn comparisons to Garret Anderson's, and he worked on getting shorter to the ball after turning pro. He's able to keep the head of the bat in the zone for a long time and is willing to drive pitches the other way. He won't be a major power threat, but he could develop enough to hit 12-15 home runs a year as he gets stronger. He's still raw in other respects, such as picking up on how pitchers are attacking him and learning when to utilize his speed to steal bases. He's a few years away and could end up staying in extended spring training to start 2011 before taking an assignment to Ogden.

Year	Club (League)	Class	AVG	G	AB	R	H	2B	3B	HR	RBI	BB	SO	SB	CS	OBP	SLG
2010	Dodgers (AZL)	R	.274	46	179	25	49	6	2	2	22	9	60	17	3	.313	.363
Minor League Totals			.274	46	179	25	49	6	2	2	22	9	60	17	3	.313	.363

13 AARON MILLER, LHP

Born: Sept. 18, 1987. **B-T:** L-L. **Ht.:** 6-3. **Wt.:** 200. **Drafted:** Baylor, 2009 (1st round supplemental). **Signed by:** Chris Smith.

Though he was also a highly rated pitching prospect in high school, Miller was drafted as an outfielder by the Rockies in the 11th round in 2006 and played outfield almost exclusively during his first two years at Baylor. He became a two-way player as a junior and pitched his way into the sandwich round, earning an $889,200 bonus as the Dodgers' top 2009 pick. Miller would have won the California League ERA title last year if he had enough innings there to qualify, but he got a six-start trial at Double-A at midseason before being sent back to Inland Empire. Miller was able to hit 93-94 mph when he signed, but his velocity dipped into the 87-91 range last year. Los Angeles wasn't too surprised, given the rigors of his first full season after pitching so little in college. Miller shows good command of both his fastball and his above-average changeup. He has a slider that flashes above-average potential at times but is inconsistent, flattening out when he has trouble maintaining his arm slot. He has an easy delivery but can be too slow and deliberate at times. Miller handled his demotion with the right attitude, and while he's raw for his age, he is working hard to catch up. The Dodgers believe he can be a mid-rotation starter. After getting a taste of Double-A in 2010, he'll get another opportunity there to start 2011.

Year	Club (League)	Class	W	L	ERA	G	GS	CG	SV	IP	H	HR	BB	SO	G/A	WHIP	AVG
2009	Dodgers (AZL)	R	0	0	6.35	3	3	0	0	6	8	0	2	10	6.00	1.76	.320
	Great Lakes (MWL)	LoA	3	1	2.08	7	7	0	0	30	22	3	10	38	0.78	1.05	.208
2010	Inland Empire (CAL)	HiA	6	4	2.92	19	17	0	0	102	76	6	48	99	0.89	1.22	.207
	Chattanooga (SL)	AA	1	4	7.04	6	6	0	0	23	28	3	18	22	1.18	2.00	.304
Minor League Totals			10	9	3.47	35	33	0	0	161	134	12	78	169	0.94	1.32	.227

14 IVAN DEJESUS JR., 2B/SS

Born: May 1, 1987. **B-T:** R-R. **Ht.:** 5-11. **Wt.:** 190. **Drafted:** HS—Guaynabo, P.R., 2005 (2nd round). **Signed by:** Manny Estrada.

DeJesus lost his 2009 season when he broke the tibia in his right leg during spring training. Otherwise he would've been on track to make his big league debut last year. As it was, he spent all of 2010 in Triple-A, where he took some time to get going but hit .316/.351/.435 from June on. DeJesus could be a similar offensive player to his father Ivan Sr., who played 15 seasons in the majors and now works on the Cubs coaching staff. He has a short swing with solid-average bat speed. He'll never hit many home runs, but he has a solid up-the-middle approach and can drive balls into both gaps. Although DeJesus logged most of his time at second base last year, he has also played shortstop, and some in the organization think he could still end up there. He has the arm strength for short, but his first-step quickness still lags after his broken leg, and he has to improve his double-play pivot. He's only an average runner and isn't a major threat on the bases. The Dodgers believe DeJesus is ready for the majors from an offensive standpoint, but the signing of Juan Uribe means he's likely ticketed for Triple-A again until there's a need in the middle infield in Los Angeles.

Year	Club (League)	Class	AVG	G	AB	R	H	2B	3B	HR	RBI	BB	SO	SB	CS	OBP	SLG
2005	Dodgers (GCL)	R	.339	33	121	18	41	5	0	0	11	10	22	8	2	.389	.380
	Ogden (PIO)	R	.208	20	72	4	15	1	0	0	3	6	18	3	3	.296	.222
2006	Columbus (SAL)	LoA	.277	126	483	65	134	17	2	1	44	63	85	16	5	.361	.327
2007	Inland Empire (CAL)	HiA	.287	121	428	69	123	22	3	4	52	57	64	11	6	.371	.381
2008	Jacksonville (SL)	AA	.324	128	463	91	150	21	2	7	58	76	81	16	2	.419	.423
2009	Dodgers (AZL)	R	.200	4	10	1	2	1	0	0	3	1	6	0	0	.308	.300
2010	Albuquerque (PCL)	AAA	.296	130	533	89	158	33	2	7	70	32	81	6	1	.335	.405
Minor League Totals			.295	562	2110	337	623	100	9	19	241	245	357	60	19	.369	.378

15 KYLE RUSSELL, OF

Born: June 27, 1986. **B-T:** L-L. **Ht.:** 6-5. **Wt.:** 195. **Drafted:** Texas, 2008 (3rd round). **Signed by:** Chris Smith.

Russell set the University of Texas single-season home run record when he belted 28 as a draft-eligible sophomore in 2007, but he opted to return for his junior season rather than sign for a reported $800,000 as the Cardinals' fourth-round pick. He hit another 19 home runs as a junior in 2008, setting the program's career record at 57, but settled for $410,000 as the Dodgers' third-rounder. Russell has hit 52 home runs in his two full seasons in the minors, and there's little doubt what he's at the plate to do. Russell has an uppercut swing with outstanding bat speed, giving him plus raw power, and he swings for the downs almost every time. While he'll always be able to crush mistakes, Russell's swing is long and he struggles to recognize breaking pitches. His throwing arm is average to a tick above, but that looks like his only other potentially plus tool. He gets good reads and runs well enough to be solid corner outfielder who can play center field in a pinch. Russell could deliver 20-25 home runs a year in the majors if given a chance to play everyday, though he won't hit for much average against big league pitching. If nothing else, he should be able to carve out a career as lefthanded power threat off a big league bench. He still has to conquer Double-A, though, and he'll return to Chattanooga to start 2011.

Year	Club (League)	Class	AVG	G	AB	R	H	2B	3B	HR	RBI	BB	SO	SB	CS	OBP	SLG
2008	Ogden (PIO)	R	.279	61	219	46	61	13	5	11	46	27	82	4	0	.365	.534
2009	Great Lakes (MWL)	LoA	.272	133	481	90	131	39	7	26	102	72	180	20	2	.371	.545
2010	Inland Empire (CAL)	HiA	.354	53	198	42	70	11	4	16	53	32	64	8	3	.448	.692
	Chattanooga (SL)	AA	.245	76	273	36	67	23	3	10	28	29	113	3	2	.319	.462
Minor League Totals			.281	323	1171	214	329	86	19	63	229	160	439	35	7	.372	.548

16 JOSH LINDBLOM, RHP

Born: June 15, 1987. **B-T:** R-R. **Ht.:** 6-5. **Wt.:** 240. **Drafted:** Purdue, 2008 (2nd round). **Signed by:** Chet Sergo.

Lindblom blossomed as Purdue's closer in the spring of 2008, landing a $663,000 bonus as the Dodgers' second-round pick. Los Angeles believed he had the arsenal to be a starter, and he worked in that role for most of his first two pro seasons. He had shown 94-95 mph fastballs with sink in the past, but his velocity dropped as a starter last spring, sitting in the high 80s. After going 2-1, 7.06 in 10 starts, Lindblom moved back to the bullpen in late May. His velocity recovered in the shorter stints, and he was working in the low 90s by the end of the regular season and flashing 94-95 mph in instructional league. His changeup was his most consistent secondary pitch, featuring late downward action. He also has an average curveball, a slider that looked plus at times and a developing cutter. Lindblom has to tighten his command, but he has a good delivery and a clean arm action, which should help. He could still make for a back-of-the-rotation starter, but his future appears to be in relief. With his velocity back, he'll head to spring training with an outside chance to make the big league bullpen. Otherwise, he'll return to Triple-A.

Year	Club (League)	Class	W	L	ERA	G	GS	CG	SV	IP	H	HR	BB	SO	G/A	WHIP	AVG
2008	Great Lakes (MWL)	LoA	0	0	1.86	8	8	0	0	29	14	2	4	33	—	0.62	.137
	Jacksonville (SL)	AA	0	0	3.60	1	1	0	0	5	5	0	1	4	—	1.20	.263
2009	Chattanooga (SL)	AA	3	5	4.71	14	11	0	0	57	55	4	14	46	1.02	1.20	.250
	Albuquerque (PCL)	AAA	3	0	2.54	20	3	0	1	39	34	3	12	36	1.08	1.18	.236
2010	Albuquerque (PCL)	AAA	3	2	6.54	40	10	0	0	95	143	12	32	84	1.00	1.84	.340
Minor League Totals			9	7	4.71	83	33	0	1	225	251	21	63	203	1.02	1.39	.277

17 NATE EOVALDI, RHP

Born: Feb. 13, 1990. **B-T:** R-R. **Ht.:** 6-2. **Wt.:** 185. **Drafted:** HS—Alvin, Texas, 2008 (11th round). **Signed by:** Chris Smith.

Eovaldi had Tommy John surgery as a high school junior. That, along with his price tag and strong commitment to Texas A&M, caused him to drop to the 11th round of the 2008 draft. Sales pitches by Joe Torre, Chad Billingsley and Jonathan Broxton, to say nothing of a $250,000 bonus, swayed Eovaldi to sign that July. He was the only pitcher in the California League to throw two shutouts last year, but he was shut down in July with a strained lat muscle. Eovaldi owns a heavy fastball that comes at hitters in the low to mid-90s and tops out at 96 mph with occasional late life. He has a wrap in his arm action that causes inconsistency with his curveball. The curve shows above-average potential with tilt and depth when it's on, but it can get slurvy. He also has a fringy changeup that he developed a better feel for last season, and he has to command the strike zone more effectively. The Dodgers laud Eovaldi for his fearless nature on the mound as well as his maturity off it. He has the potential to be a mid-rotation starter, though he also could end up as a weapon out of the bullpen. Like Ethan Martin, he could find himself back in high Class A to start 2011 but should be on his way to Chattanooga at some point.

Year	Club (League)	Class	W	L	ERA	G	GS	CG	SV	IP	H	HR	BB	SO	G/A	WHIP	AVG
2008	Dodgers (GCL)	R	0	1	1.13	6	0	0	1	8	6	0	3	9	—	1.13	.207
	Ogden (PIO)	R	0	0	0.00	1	0	0	0	3	1	0	0	2	—	0.38	.125
2009	Great Lakes (MWL)	LoA	3	5	3.27	26	16	0	1	96	95	2	41	71	1.01	1.41	.265
2010	Inland Empire (CAL)	HiA	3	5	4.45	16	14	2	0	85	99	3	33	58	1.69	1.55	.302
	Dodgers (AZL)	R	0	1	4.32	3	3	0	0	8	6	0	4	10	—	1.20	.214
	Ogden (PIO)	R	1	0	1.80	1	1	0	0	5	3	0	0	4	3.50	0.60	.167
Minor League Totals			7	12	3.64	53	34	2	2	205	210	5	81	154	1.38	1.42	.273

18 GARRETT GOULD, RHP

Born: July 19, 1991. **B-T:** R-R. **Ht.:** 6-4. **Wt.:** 190. **Drafted:** HS—Maize, Kan., 2009 (2nd round). **Signed by:** Scott Little.

Gould broke out on the high school scouting showcase circuit in 2008, most notably by beating Shelby Miller in the World Wood Bat Association Championships and being named the event's MVP. He was an all-state quarterback as a high school junior, but gave up the gridiron as a senior to concentrate on baseball. He netted the largest bonus in Los Angeles' 2009 draft class, signing for $900,000. Gould's fastball velocity jumped into the low 90s in the spring of 2009, but he didn't show that same heat consistently last season. He pitched mostly at 88-91 mph, topping out at 93. With his physical frame, he could add velocity as he matures. His above-average curveball is his best weapon right now, featuring tight break and good depth. Gould's changeup is a work in progress but shows promising fading action. He lands on a bit of a stiff front leg, but his delivery is otherwise simple and repeatable with clean arm action. His command will have to be tightened as he moves up but it's at least average to a tick above for a pitcher his age. Gould profiles as a mid-rotation starter for now, and his ceiling goes higher if his velocity does pick up. He took his lumps in the Pioneer League last season but should find a more hospitable pitching environment in low Class A in 2011.

Year	Club (League)	Class	W	L	ERA	G	GS	CG	SV	IP	H	HR	BB	SO	G/A	WHIP	AVG
2009	Ogden (PIO)	R	0	1	10.13	3	3	0	0	3	4	1	2	4	0.50	2.25	.333
2010	Ogden (PIO)	R	1	4	4.06	13	13	0	0	58	68	4	20	52	2.00	1.53	.292
Minor League Totals			1	5	4.33	16	16	0	0	60	72	5	22	56	1.92	1.56	.294

19 BRIAN CAVAZOS-GALVEZ, OF

Born: May 17, 1987. **B-T:** R-R. **Ht.:** 6-0. **Wt.:** 225. **Drafted:** New Mexico, 2009 (12th round). **Signed by:** Calvin Jones.

Cavazos-Galvez's father, Balvino Galvez, made 10 appearances for the Dodgers in 1986 and spent 11 seasons pitching in the minor leagues, though the two haven't been in contact since Balvino left to go play in China in 1994. Cavazos-Galvez has hit everywhere he's played, batting .495 over two seasons at New Mexico JC before being a two-time all-Mountain West Conference selection at New Mexico. He hit .392 in the spring of 2009 for the Lobos, received a $15,000 bonus and then won Pioneer League MVP honors in his pro debut. He pressed early on in low Class A last year but caught fire in the second half, hitting .375/.386/.656. He had trouble with being too pull-conscious and flying open in his swing, and he had more success once Los Angeles got him focused on taking balls up the middle. Cavazos-Galvez has outstanding bat speed, allowing him to square up any fastball and have above-average power to all fields. As his low walk total from last year suggests, he has an overly aggressive approach at the plate, frequently swinging at the first pitch. A better runner than he looks, Cavazos-Galvez has a strong arm and has become a solid defender. He has seen time at all three outfield positions and fits best in right field. He's a candidate to move up to Double-A in 2011, where more advanced pitchers would offer a much stiffer test.

Year	Club (League)	Class	AVG	G	AB	R	H	2B	3B	HR	RBI	BB	SO	SB	CS	OBP	SLG
2009	Ogden (PIO)	R	.322	71	301	59	97	29	3	18	63	10	43	17	8	.353	.618
2010	Great Lakes (MWL)	LoA	.318	121	490	76	156	43	4	16	77	12	60	43	13	.343	.520
Minor League Totals			.320	192	791	135	253	72	7	34	140	22	103	60	21	.347	.558

20 RALSTON CASH, RHP

Born: Aug. 20, 1991. **B-T:** R-R. **Ht.:** 6-3. **Wt.:** 207. **Drafted:** HS—Cornelia, Ga., 2010 (2nd round). **Signed by:** Lon Joyce.

Cash, a cousin of fellow Dodgers pitching prospect Ethan Martin, has faced his share of adversity off the field. His mother died in a car accident when he was 3 years old, and Cash walked away from a violent accident of his own in November 2008. He had committed to Georgia before signing with Los Angeles for $463,500 as the 78th overall pick in last June's draft. Cash's velocity can fluctuate from one outing to the next, and some days his fastball sits in the upper 80s while on others it's in the low 90s. When he's fresh, Cash works at 91-92 mph and can touch 94 with running and sinking action. He has a good delivery and a clean arm action, along with the frame to add velocity as he matures. He flashes an effective curveball at times, though he sometimes gets caught between a curve or a slider. The Dodgers prefer the curveball. He also shows a feel for a changeup that could be average down the road. Cash also stands out for his strong character and work ethic. A potential No. 3 starter, he should advance to low Class A for his first full season.

Year	Club (League)	Class	W	L	ERA	G	GS	CG	SV	IP	H	HR	BB	SO	G/A	WHIP	AVG
2010	Dodgers (AZL)	R	2	2	3.60	9	8	0	0	30	29	0	11	25	1.77	1.33	.248
	Ogden (PIO)	R	0	0	12.00	2	2	0	0	6	11	2	3	5	1.60	2.33	.367
Minor League Totals			2	2	5.00	11	10	0	0	36	40	2	14	30	1.74	1.50	.272

21 JONATHAN GARCIA, OF

Born: Nov. 11, 1991. **B-T:** R-R. **Ht.:** 5-11. **Wt.:** 180. **Drafted:** HS—Yauco, P.R., 2009 (8th round). **Signed by:** Manny Estrada.

As a high schooler, Garcia developed a reputation as a player who looked great in workouts but struggled to hit in games. He hasn't had that problem as a pro. He was the youngest player on Ogden's roster last season but put up numbers on par with his older teammates. Garcia, who received a $120,000 bonus in 2009, shows the ability to consistently square balls up and has above-average bat speed. He should generate average to potentially above-average power as he moves along. He has good plate coverage and can hit balls in different parts of the strike zone. He's usually able to maintain a short, compact stroke, though his swing does have some moving parts. He's still raw in terms of selectivity, and breaking balls can give him problems. Ogden's everyday right fielder last season, Garcia has average arm strength, though he registered 12 outfield assists last season, tying him for the Pioneer League lead. He's an average runner and his range is good enough for now, but he'll have to watch his conditioning if he's going to stay in the outfield long term. Garcia will move up to low Class A for 2011.

Year	Club (League)	Class	AVG	G	AB	R	H	2B	3B	HR	RBI	BB	SO	SB	CS	OBP	SLG
2009	Dodgers (AZL)	R	.304	41	138	22	42	16	1	3	21	10	37	4	0	.362	.500
2010	Ogden (PIO)	R	.305	61	239	45	73	19	2	10	40	19	59	4	1	.365	.527
Minor League Totals			.305	102	377	67	115	35	3	13	61	29	96	8	1	.364	.517

22 PEDRO BAEZ, 3B

Born: March 11, 1988. **B-T:** R-R. **Ht.:** 6-2. **Wt.:** 195. **Signed:** Dominican Republic, 2007. **Signed by:** Elvio Jimenez.

Baez has been selected for the last two Futures Games, and he looked to be picking up steam in 2009 after a strong first half in high Class A, but his progress has slowed since. He injured his knee and required surgery shortly after returning from the 2009 Futures Game, ending his season. Returning to Inland Empire last season, he was never able to get his bat going and was bothered by the effects of dislocating his left shoulder early in the season. From a tools standpoint, Baez's upside remains impressive. He has plus raw power, but getting to it in games has been a problem. He is too pull-conscious, and his lack of pitch recognition holds him back. He expands his strike zone against breaking pitches, swinging at too many balls he can't drive. Baez can be an above-average defender at the hot corner. He's a below-average runner, but his hands and arm strength are both pluses. Problems arise because his focus can waver. If Baez can develop a consistent approach both at the plate and on defense, he has the tools to be a big league third baseman. He got his feet wet in Double-A at the end of last season and should be back there in 2011.

Year	Club (League)	Class	AVG	G	AB	R	H	2B	3B	HR	RBI	BB	SO	SB	CS	OBP	SLG
2007	Dodgers (GCL)	R	.274	53	201	35	55	14	2	3	39	17	40	3	1	.341	.408
2008	Great Lakes (MWL)	LoA	.178	59	185	23	33	10	1	1	16	17	45	3	1	.244	.259
	Ogden (PIO)	R	.267	61	247	37	66	20	1	12	50	18	69	2	2	.317	.502
2009	Inland Empire (CAL)	HiA	.286	79	308	48	88	17	1	10	61	16	84	5	1	.326	.445
2010	Inland Empire (CAL)	HiA	.259	75	309	41	80	10	0	6	42	17	68	4	1	.306	.350
	Dodgers (AZL)	R	.000	2	7	0	0	0	0	0	1	1	1	0	0	.111	.000
	Chattanooga (SL)	AA	.385	7	26	2	10	1	0	0	2	2	8	1	0	.448	.423
Minor League Totals			.259	336	1283	186	332	72	5	32	211	88	315	18	6	.311	.398

23 SCOTT SCHEBLER, OF

Born: Oct. 6, 1990. **B-T:** L-R. **Ht.:** 6-1. **Wt.:** 205. **Drafted:** Des Moines Area CC, 2010 (26th round). **Signed by:** Scott Little.

Schebler batted .446 with 20 home runs last spring for Des Moines Area CC. He was set to transfer to Wichita State for the 2011 season and would've been the Shockers' starting left fielder, but the Dodgers changed his mind with a $300,000 bonus at the Aug. 16 signing deadline. One of Los Angeles' goals with last year's draft was to inject speed and athleticism into the system, and Schebler is another piece of that puzzle along with Leon Landry and James Baldwin. Schebler has plus speed in the outfield and should have a chance to play center as he moves up. He shows promise at the plate as well. He has a sound swing that's short to the ball. He primarily has a line drive, gap-to-gap approach, with the strength and bat speed to hit for at least average power. While Schebler has plus speed, it doesn't translate into stolen bases yet. It does help him leg out more hits than an average runner, but he needs to getter better reads and jumps to be a more effective basestealer. His throwing arm is below-average and would dictate a move to left field if he isn't able to play in center. Schebler could find himself playing on a corner anyway if he's alongside Landry in low Class A in 2011.

Year	Club (League)	Class	AVG	G	AB	R	H	2B	3B	HR	RBI	BB	SO	SB	CS	OBP	SLG
2010	Dodgers (AZL)	R	.294	5	17	3	5	0	2	0	1	1	5	1	0	.333	.529
Minor League Totals			.294	5	17	3	5	0	2	0	1	1	5	1	0	.333	.529

24 JAKE LEMMERMAN, SS

Born: May 4, 1989. **B-T:** R-R. **Ht.:** 6-1. **Wt.:** 192. **Drafted:** Duke, 2010 (5th round). **Signed by:** Lon Joyce.

Lemmerman took over as Duke's everyday shortstop as a freshman and missed just two games in his three-year college career. After two productive seasons, he came on as a junior in 2010, leading the Blue Devils with a .335 average and 11 homers and earning a $139,500 bonus as Los Angeles' fifth-rounder. He kept right on hitting after turning pro, winning the Pioneer League MVP award after finishing second in the batting race and leading the league in doubles (24) and runs (69). Lemmerman's best tool may be his brain, as he's a heady player whose feel for the game stands out, but he's not lacking physical talent. He has a compact swing with surprising bat speed. He has a bit of a dead start swing but should still be able to hit for a solid average with an up-the-middle approach. An average runner with a strong arm, Lemmerman made an uncharacteristic 16 errors with Ogden. He made just three in the spring with Duke and is generally regarded with as a surehanded defender who can play either middle-infield position. Some in the Pioneer League compared Lemmerman to either Mark Loretta or Mark Grudzielanek as a heady player who has solid tools and gets the most out of what he has. After thriving in the Pioneer League's hitter-friendly environment, Lemmerman will move up to the more challenging Midwest League in 2011.

Year	Club (League)	Class	AVG	G	AB	R	H	2B	3B	HR	RBI	BB	SO	SB	CS	OBP	SLG
2010	Ogden (PIO)	R	.363	66	259	69	94	24	2	12	47	31	56	5	4	.434	.610
Minor League Totals			.363	66	259	69	94	24	2	12	47	31	56	5	4	.434	.610

25 JOC PEDERSON, OF

Born: April 21, 1992. **B-T:** L-L. **Ht.:** 6-1. **Wt.:** 185. **Drafted:** HS—Palo Alto, Calif., 2010 (11th round). **Signed by:** Orsino Hill.

In Los Angeles' 2010 draft class, only first-rounder Zach Lee received a larger bonus than Pederson. Los Angeles gave the 11th-rounder $600,000 at the Aug. 16 deadline to steer him away from a commitment to Southern California. Pederson's father Stu was an outfielder who played briefly for the Dodgers in 1985 and had a 12-year pro career. Joc, who was also a wide receiver in high school, doesn't have any dominant tools, but he has the potential to be average across the board and certainly would have gone higher in the draft if not for his price tag. He has a physical, athletic build and the potential to add strength as he matures. His pedigree shows through in his mechanically sound lefthanded swing and all-fields approach. He has a quick bat and average raw power. He'll have to do a better job of staying back, though, because he does have a tendency to get out on his front foot. He has an average arm and is a tick above-average runner, and his instincts help his speed play up and give him a chance to be a center fielder. Pederson may be advanced enough to handle an assignment to low Class A for his first full season.

Year	Club (League)	Class	AVG	G	AB	R	H	2B	3B	HR	RBI	BB	SO	SB	CS	OBP	SLG
2010	Dodgers (AZL)	R	.000	3	7	1	0	0	0	0	0	4	5	0	0	.417	.000
Minor League Totals			.000	3	7	1	0	0	0	0	0	4	5	0	0	.417	.000

26 JAVY GUERRA, RHP

Born: Oct. 31, 1985. **B-T:** R-R. **Ht.:** 6-0. **Wt.:** 205. **Drafted:** HS—Denton, Texas, 2004 (4th round). **Signed by:** Mike Leuzinger.

Because of injuries, the Dodgers have had to be patient with Guerra, whom they gave $275,000 in 2004, but his power arm could be worth waiting for. He had Tommy John surgery in 2005 and was bothered by shoulder inflammation and hamstring problems in 2010, but he was effective when healthy. His fastball touches as high as 98 mph and sits at 93-95. He throws it on a nice downhill plane despite his lack of size, but it takes some effort in his over-the-top delivery. He also used to hop off the mound on his back leg, making it hard for him to keep the ball down, but he has smoothed that out. His main secondary weapon is a hard slider at 86-88 mph with average movement. Guerra developed his changeup over the last few years and it has late sink. He can also mix in a solid-average curveball. Guerra will need better command if he's going to succeed against major league hitters, and the effort in his delivery makes that more of a challenge. He can be a major league set-up man if the command is there. Guerra should advance at least to Triple-A in 2011 and can put himself in position to join the big league bullpen during the season.

Year	Club (League)	Class	W	L	ERA	G	GS	CG	SV	IP	H	HR	BB	SO	G/A	WHIP	AVG
2004	Dodgers (GCL)	R	4	1	3.38	11	9	0	0	40	31	3	19	36	—	1.25	.214
2005	Columbus (SAL)	LoA	2	5	4.96	11	11	0	0	53	51	3	23	40	—	1.41	.249
2006	Dodgers (GCL)	R	0	1	4.15	4	4	0	0	9	10	0	4	11	—	1.62	.278
	Ogden (PIO)	R	1	3	4.82	7	7	0	0	28	37	1	20	22	—	2.04	.330
2007	Inland Empire (CAL)	HiA	6	9	6.27	27	24	0	1	118	139	10	80	121	—	1.86	.296
2008	Inland Empire (CAL)	HiA	5	4	4.07	31	3	0	2	66	68	0	44	63	—	1.69	.262
2009	Great Lakes (MWL)	LoA	3	1	1.54	28	0	0	16	41	23	1	15	55	0.86	0.93	.161
	Chattanooga (SL)	AA	3	1	4.13	23	0	0	0	28	32	2	16	29	1.13	1.69	.291
2010	Chattanooga (SL)	AA	2	0	2.33	28	0	0	5	27	24	1	22	27	2.20	1.70	.240
	Dodgers (AZL)	R	0	1	4.50	2	0	0	0	2	2	1	0	3	—	1.00	.250
Minor League Totals			26	26	4.44	172	58	0	24	412	417	22	243	407	1.25	1.60	.262

27 BLAKE SMITH, OF

Born: Dec. 9, 1987. **B-T:** L-R. **Ht.:** 6-2. **Wt.:** 225. **Drafted:** California, 2009 (2nd round). **Signed by:** Fred Costello.

Scouts were divided on Smith entering the 2009 draft. He showed promise as both a hitter and a pitcher during his time at California, and had an outstanding summer with USA Baseball's college national team in 2008. He had the tools for either role, but the Dodgers decided to make him an outfielder after signing him for $643,500. He rebounded from a difficult pro debut with a strong showing in low Class A last year, finishing fourth in the Midwest League in home runs. That power will drive Smith's career as a position player. He has the strength and bat speed to generate plus raw power, projecting as a potential 25-homer threat in the majors. Scouts question whether he'll hit enough, though. He struggles with plate discipline and tends pull off pitches. Smith threw 92-94 mph off the mound, giving him an easy plus arm as a right fielder. He's only a fringy runner, but he gets good reads and has enough range to be an average outfielder. Los Angeles hasn't abandoned the idea that Smith could make an intriguing pitching prospect, but they'll continue developing him as a hitter for now. With his power, he could be in for a big year as he moves up to the high Class A California League with the Dodgers' new Rancho Cucamonga affiliate.

Year	Club (League)	Class	AVG	G	AB	R	H	2B	3B	HR	RBI	BB	SO	SB	CS	OBP	SLG
2009	Dodgers (AZL)	R	.227	6	22	3	5	1	0	0	2	2	9	0	0	.346	.273
	Ogden (PIO)	R	.212	30	104	14	22	7	0	1	12	13	38	0	0	.311	.308
2010	Great Lakes (MWL)	LoA	.281	115	430	77	121	28	2	19	76	49	135	2	3	.363	.488
Minor League Totals			.266	151	556	94	148	36	2	20	90	64	182	2	3	.353	.446

28 ANGELO SONGCO, OF

Born: Sept. 9, 1988. **B-T:** L-R. **Ht.:** 6-0. **Wt.:** 190. **Drafted:** Loyola Marymount, 2009 (4th round). **Signed by:** Bobby Darwin.

Songco was a three-year starter for Loyola Marymount and his draft stock climbed as a junior, when he led the West Coast Conference in on-base percentage while hitting .360/.481/.678 with 15 homers. He received a $225,000 bonus in the fourth round. He earned a trip to the Midwest League all-star game in his first full season, batting .301/.358/.483 in the first half before tailing off as the year went on. Songco uses a slightly open stance and holds the bat up high. He has a fluid lefthanded stroke, though it's not without shortcomings. He can be long to the ball at times and swings with some uppercut. He has a chance for at least average raw power, though it's geared mostly to his pull side. He also has trouble squaring up lefthanders, and he had just five extra-base hits against southpaws in 2010. Songco is a capable defender but doesn't have any flashy tools, rating as an average runner with a fringy arm. He played right field in college but has already made the move to left as a pro, and that's where his arm dictates he should stay as he moves up to Rancho Cucamonga.

Year	Club (League)	Class	AVG	G	AB	R	H	2B	3B	HR	RBI	BB	SO	SB	CS	OBP	SLG
2009	Ogden (PIO)	R	.306	36	144	27	44	11	1	9	29	10	41	0	1	.361	.583
	Great Lakes (MWL)	LoA	.150	33	120	8	18	6	2	1	16	10	28	1	0	.226	.258
2010	Great Lakes (MWL)	LoA	.274	135	507	87	139	30	6	15	71	51	91	6	1	.344	.446
Minor League Totals			.261	204	771	122	201	47	9	25	116	71	160	7	2	.329	.442

29 DEREK CONE, RHP

Born: June 20, 1990. **B-T:** R-R. **Ht.:** 6-5. **Wt.:** 210. **Drafted:** Mesa (Ariz.) CC, 2010 (31st round). **Signed by:** Tom Thomas.

In Cone's final start for Mesa (Ariz.) CC in an NJCAA playoff game, he worked 11⅓ innings, including a span of 9⅔ no-hit innings, but ended up taking a 3-2 loss. Cone finished the college season with a 6-4, 1.93 record and was ready to transfer to Brigham Young for his junior year, but the Dodgers persuaded him to turn pro with a $150,000 bonus one day before the signing deadline. Cone has a lanky, projectable frame. He has average fastball velocity right now, usually pitching at 90-91 mph, but Los Angeles believes he'll have an above-average fastball once he fills out and gets stronger. Cone's promising 12-to-6 curveball is his best pitch, and he also has shown some feel for a changeup. He has a good, clean delivery and arm action, and he's already a solid strike-thrower. Cone didn't pitch extensively in high school, and the Dodgers feel he could be a late bloomer. He'll have a chance to move up to low Class A in 2011.

Year	Club (League)	Class	W	L	ERA	G	GS	CG	SV	IP	H	HR	BB	SO	G/A	WHIP	AVG
2010	Ogden (PIO)	R	0	0	0.00	3	0	0	0	4	4	0	1	1	3.00	1.15	.235
Minor League Totals			0	0	0.00	3	0	0	0	4	4	0	1	1	3.00	1.15	.235

30 LUIS VASQUEZ, RHP

Born: April 3, 1986. **B-T:** R-R. **Ht.:** 6-4. **Wt.:** 174. **Signed:** Dominican Republic, 2003. **Signed by:** Andres Lopez.

The Dodgers originally signed Vasquez as a shortstop in 2003, but he converted to pitching after only one season. His progress has been slowed by injuries, including missing the 2006 season after Tommy John surgery, but Los Angeles added him to its 40-man roster after last season to protect him from the Rule 5 draft, though he had never pitched above high Class A. When Vasquez gets on the mound, it doesn't take long to see why the Dodgers felt he needed protection. He runs his fastball up as high as 100 mph while sitting in the mid-90s. He gets boring action on the fastball as well, though his combination of velocity and movement can lead to poor command. Tall and skinny, Vasquez uses a high three-quarters delivery, but he tends to have trouble getting over his front side enough, which also contributes to his command problems. He has a couple of average secondary pitches in his slider and changeup, though in one-inning stints he relies on his fastball almost exclusively. Coming off his best season as a pro, Vasquez could climb the ladder quickly, a notion the Dodgers' move to put him on the 40-man backs up. He could be a candidate to move straight to Double-A in 2011, or he could get there quickly if he does have to open in high Class A.

Year	Club (League)	Class	AVG	G	AB	R	H	2B	3B	HR	RBI	BB	SO	SB	CS	OBP	SLG
2004	Dodgers 2 (DSL)	R	.188	36	117	14	22	3	0	0	5	4	31	3	3	.240	.214
Minor League Totals			.188	36	117	14	22	3	0	0	5	4	31	3	3	.240	.214

Year	Club (League)	Class	W	L	ERA	G	GS	CG	SV	IP	H	HR	BB	SO	G/A	WHIP	AVG
2005	Dodgers (DSL)	R	1	1	3.25	8	6	0	1	28	15	0	14	11	—	1.05	.158
2006	Did Not Play—Injured																
2007	Dodgers (GCL)	R	0	0	9.64	9	0	0	0	9	9	1	11	8	—	2.14	.250
2008	Ogden (PIO)	R	0	0	1.50	6	0	0	0	12	9	0	6	6	—	1.25	.220
	Inland Empire (CAL)	HiA	0	0	4.74	8	1	0	0	19	14	1	14	8	—	1.47	.219
2009	Inland Empire (CAL)	HiA	0	2	9.95	7	1	0	0	13	16	3	10	11	1.25	2.05	.291
	Ogden (PIO)	R	3	3	5.09	13	13	0	0	58	56	8	35	40	1.42	1.56	.258
2010	Great Lakes (MWL)	LoA	3	2	2.68	37	0	0	20	40	24	2	26	39	2.04	1.24	.173
Minor League Totals			7	8	4.57	88	21	0	21	179	143	15	116	123	1.57	1.44	.221

Milwaukee Brewers

BY TOM HAUDRICOURT

The Brewers reached the playoffs with a largely homegrown lineup in 2008, so it's no surprise they continue to try to bolster their roster with players coming through the farm system. Alcides Escobar, the organization's top prospect a year ago, was the 2010 Opening Day shortstop after pushing J.J. Hardy out the door. Escobar was just the beginning.

With future Hall of Famer Trevor Hoffman melting down in the early weeks of the season and veteran LaTroy Hawkins out with an ailing shoulder, John Axford and Zach Braddock assumed significant roles in the bullpen. Originally signed as a nondrafted free  agent by the Yankees and later released by New York, Axford took over as closer and converted 24-of-27 save opportunities, obliterating the franchise rookie record of 15 saves set by Doug Henry in 1991. Braddock, a former starter who blossomed when he converted to relief in 2009, destroyed lefthanders but was more than just a specialist, recording 15 holds.

Jonathan Lucroy began the season in Double-A but was catching in Milwaukee by early June after Gregg Zaun tore the labrum in his shoulder. Lucroy eventually emerged as the Brewers' No. 1 catcher, moving ahead of fellow rookie George Kottaras. Lorenzo Cain made the most of an opportunity for regular playing time in the final two months. He batted .306 and made several spectacular catches in center field.

September marked the much-anticipated major league debuts of first-round picks Mark Rogers and Jeremy Jeffress. Rogers missed two full seasons recovering from a pair of shoulder surgeries, while Jeffress drew two minor league suspensions for marijuana use. Both showed power stuff in Milwaukee, making cases for expanded roles this season.

Besides the influx of rookies, the Brewers got nice seasons out of core veterans Ryan Braun, Prince Fielder, Corey Hart and Rickie Weeks. Additionally, Casey McGehee proved that his 2009 breakout was no fluke by driving in a team-high 104 runs.

But a lack of pitching once again sabotaged Milwaukee, which won 77 games en route to its second consecutive third-place finish in the National League Central. Yovani Gallardo and Randy Wolf were the only reliable starters, and Axford and Braddock were the lone bright spots in the bullpen as the Brewers finished 14th in the league in runs allowed. Their seemingly perennial pitching shortcomings prompted Milwaukee to trade its best prospect in December.

MORRIS FOSTOFF

Shortstop Alcides Escobar led a procession of Brewers prospects to reach the majors

TOP 30 PROSPECTS

1. Jake Odorizzi, rhp	16. Logan Schafer, of
2. Mark Rogers, rhp	17. Hunter Morris, 1b/3b
3. Jeremy Jeffress, rhp	18. Eric Arnett, rhp
4. Cody Scarpetta, rhp	19. Andre Lamontagne, rhp
5. Wily Peralta, rhp	20. Cody Hawn, 1b
6. Scooter Gennett, 2b/ss	21. Yadiel Rivera, ss
7. Kentrail Davis, of	22. Cameron Garfield, c
8. Tyler Thornburg, rhp	23. Tyler Roberts, c
9. Eric Farris, 2b	24. D'Vontrey Richardson, of
10. Jimmy Nelson, rhp	25. Mike McClendon, rhp
11. Kyle Heckathorn, rhp	26. Brandon Kintzler, rhp
12. Amaury Rivas, rhp	27. Nick Bucci, rhp
13. Matt Miller, rhp	28. Maverick Lasker, rhp
14. Erik Komatsu, of	29. Lee Haydel, of
15. Caleb Gindl, of	30. Austin Ross, rhp

The Brewers sent sweet-swinging Brett Lawrie, their 2008 first-round choice, to the Blue Jays for Shaun Marcum, who will slot behind Gallardo at the front of their rotation. More help is needed, however.

Milwaukee missed out on an opportunity to add another quality arm when it failed to sign first-round pick Dylan Covey, through no fault of its own. The 14th overall pick, Covey learned he had Type 1 diabetes just days before the Aug. 16 signing deadline. He ultimately decided it would be easier to adjust to his condition while attending the University of San Diego, near his home.

General Manager: Doug Melvin. **Farm Director:** Reid Nichols. **Scouting Director:** Bruce Seid.

Class	Team	League	W	L	PCT	Finish*	Manager
Majors	Milwaukee Brewers	National	77	85	.475	11th (16)	Ken Macha
Triple-A	Nashville Sounds	Pacific Coast	77	67	.535	5th (16)	Don Money
Double-A	Huntsville Stars	Southern	67	73	.479	6th (10)	Mike Guerrero
High A	Brevard County Manatees	Florida State	64	75	.460	10th (12)	Bob Miscik
Low A	Wisconsin Timber Rattlers	Midwest	58	80	.420	14th (16)	Jeff Isom
Rookie	Helena Brewers	Pioneer	41	34	.547	†3rd (8)	Joe Ayrault
Rookie	AZL Brewers	Arizona	34	22	.607	†2nd (12)	Tony Diggs
Overall 2010 Minor League Record			341	351	.493	17th (30)	

*Finish in overall standings (No. of teams in league). †League champion.

LAST YEAR'S TOP 30

Player, Pos.		Status
1.	Alcides Escobar, ss	Majors
2.	Brett Lawrie, 2b	(Blue Jays)
3.	Mat Gamel, 3b	Majors
4.	Eric Arnett, rhp	No. 18
5.	Jonathan Lucroy, c	Majors
6.	Kentrail Davis, of	No. 7
7.	Zach Braddock, lhp	Majors
8.	Lorenzo Cain, of	Majors
9.	Jake Odorizzi, rhp	No. 1
10.	Kyle Heckathorn, rhp	No. 11
11.	Mark Rogers, rhp	No. 2
12.	Logan Schafer, of	No. 16
13.	Cody Scarpetta, rhp	No. 4
14.	Wily Peralta, rhp	No. 5
15.	Angel Salome, c	Dropped out
16.	Amaury Rivas, rhp	No. 12
17.	Caleb Gindl, of	No. 15
18.	D'Vontrey Richardson, of	No. 24
19.	Eric Farris, 2b	No. 9
20.	Taylor Green, 1b/3b	Dropped out
21.	Jeremy Jeffress, rhp	No. 3
22.	Del Howell, lhp	Dropped out
23.	John Axford, rhp	Majors
24.	Josh Butler, rhp	Dropped out
25.	Alex Periard, rhp	Dropped out
26.	Evan Anundsen, rhp	Dropped out
27.	Brooks Hall, rhp	Dropped out
28.	Max Walla, of	Dropped out
29.	Nick Bucci, rhp	No. 27
30.	Maverick Lasker, rhp	No. 28

BEST TOOLS

Best Hitter for Average	Erik Komatsu
Best Power Hitter	Hunter Morris
Best Strike-Zone Discipline	Erik Komatsu
Fastest Baserunner	Lee Haydel
Best Athlete	D'Vontrey Richardson
Best Fastball	Jeremy Jeffress
Best Curveball	Cody Scarpetta
Best Slider	Robert Hinton
Best Changeup	Amaury Rivas
Best Control	Hiram Burgos
Best Defensive Catcher	Martin Maldonado
Best Defensive Infielder	Yadiel Rivera
Best Infield Arm	Zelous Wheeler
Best Defensive Outfielder	Logan Schafer
Best Outfield Arm	D'Vontrey Richardson

PROJECTED 2014 LINEUP

Catcher	Jonathan Lucroy
First Base	Prince Fielder
Second Base	Rickie Weeks
Third Base	Casey McGehee
Shortstop	Alcides Escobar
Left Field	Ryan Braun
Center Field	Lorenzo Cain
Right Field	Corey Hart
No. 1 Starter	Yovani Gallardo
No. 2 Starter	Jake Odorizzi
No. 3 Starter	Mark Rogers
No. 4 Starter	Shaun Marcum
No. 5 Starter	Cody Scarpetta
Closer	Jeremy Jeffress

TOP PROSPECTS OF THE DECADE

Year	Player, Pos.	2010 Org.
2001	Ben Sheets, rhp	Athletics
2002	Nick Neugebauer, rhp	Out of baseball
2003	Brad Nelson, 1b	Mariners
2004	Rickie Weeks, 2b	Brewers
2005	Rickie Weeks, 2b	Brewers
2006	Prince Fielder, 1b	Brewers
2007	Yovani Gallado, rhp	Brewers
2008	Matt LaPorta, of	Indians
2009	Alcides Escobar, ss	Brewers
2010	Alcides Escobar, ss	Brewers

TOP DRAFT PICKS OF THE DECADE

Year	Player, Pos.	2010 Org.
2001	Mike Jones, rhp	Brewers
2002	Prince Fielder, 1b	Brewers
2003	Rickie Weeks, 2b	Brewers
2004	Mark Rogers, rhp	Brewers
2005	Ryan Braun, 3b	Brewers
2006	Jeremy Jeffress, rhp	Brewers
2007	Matt LaPorta, of	Indians
2008	Brett Lawrie, c/3b	Brewers
2009	Eric Arnett, rhp	Brewers
2010	*Dylan Covey, rhp	U. of San Diego

*Did not sign.

LARGEST BONUSES IN CLUB HISTORY

Rickie Weeks, 2003	$3,600,000
Ben Sheets, 1999	$2,450,000
Ryan Braun, 2005	$2,450,000
Prince Fielder, 2002	$2,400,000
Mark Rogers, 2004	$2,200,000

MILWAUKEE BREWERS

TOP 2011 ROOKIE: Jeremy Jeffress, rhp. His overpowering fastball and his mentality seem to fit best in the bullpen, and he took off after moving there last year.

BREAKOUT PROSPECT: Erik Komatsu, of. The Brewers' 2010 minor league player of the year bounced back from injuries to hit .323 in high Class A.

SLEEPER: Dan Merklinger, lhp. With an above-average curveball, poise and command, Merklinger claimed a spot on the 40-man roster.

SOURCE OF TOP 30 TALENT

Homegrown	29	Acquired	1
College	14	Trades	0
Junior college	2	Rule 5 draft	0
High school	11	Independent leagues	1
Draft-and-follow	0	Free agents/waivers	0
Nondrafted free agents	0		
International	2		

LF
Kentrail Davis (7)
Caleb Gindl (15)
Khris Davis
Chuck Caufield
Brock Kjeldgaard

CF
Erik Komatsu (14)
Logan Schafer (16)
D'Vontrey Richardson (24)
Lee Haydel (29)
Kenny Allison

RF
Brendan Katin
Max Walla
Johnny Dishon

3B
Taylor Green
Cutter Dykstra
Sergio Miranda
Greg Hopkins

SS
Yadiel Rivera (21)
Zelous Wheeler
Josh Prince
Michael Marseco

2B
Scooter Gennett (6)
Eric Farris (9)
Shea Vucinich

1B
Hunter Morris (17)
Cody Hawn (20)
Sean Halton
Chris Dennis
Michael Walker

C
Cameron Garfield (22)
Tyler Roberts (23)
Martin Maldonado
Austin Stockfisch
Rafael Neda

RHP

RHSP	RHRP
Jake Odorizzi (1)	Jeremy Jeffress (3)
Mark Rogers (2)	Andre Lamontagne (19)
Cody Scarpetta (4)	Mike McClendon (25)
Wily Peralta (5)	Brandon Kintzler (26)
Tyler Thornburg (8)	Justin James
Jimmy Nelson (10)	Chris Smith
Kyle Heckathorn (11)	Robert Hinton
Amaury Rivas (12)	Pat Egan
Matt Miller (13)	Tim Dillard
Eric Arnett (18)	Donovan Hand
Nick Bucci (27)	Corey Frerichs
Maverick Lasker (28)	Mark Willinsky
Austin Ross (30)	Trey Watten
Michael Fiers	Jim Henderson
Joel Pierce	
Evan Anundsen	
Josh Butler	
Marco Estrada	
Alex Periard	
Michael White	

LHP

LHSP	LHRP
Dan Merklinger	Jon Pokorny
Chuck Lofgren	Brian Garman
Chris Cody	Lucas Luetge
Del Howell	Dan Meadows
Efrain Nieves	Mike Ramlow
Chase Wright	Evan Frederickson
	Thomas Keeling

DRAFT ANALYSIS

2010

BEST PURE HITTER: 1B Cody Hawn (6) has a compact swing and got better as he healed from a left shoulder sprain that hampered him early in the college season. He hit .308/.407/.542 with 13 homers in his pro debut.

BEST POWER HITTER: Hawn has power, but fellow Southeastern Conference 1B Hunter Morris (4) has more ability to loft the ball, as well as excellent strength. Some scouts like Morris' pure hitting ability more than his power, as he lacks premium bat speed.

FASTEST RUNNER: 2B/C Kevin Berard (22) and OFs Kenny Allison (39) and Johnny Dishon (42) are all plus runners. Allison runs better under way and had the best pro debut of the trio, batting .299/.350/.403 with 16 steals at two Rookie-level stops.

BEST DEFENSIVE PLAYER: Lean and athletic, SS Yadiel Rivera (9) plays with savvy and grace thanks to smooth footwork and a fine arm.

BEST FASTBALL: Milwaukee went after velocity and got it in 5-foot-11 Tyler Thornburg (3), who elicits Tim Lincecum comparisons with his height and delivery. He hits 98 mph in short stints and sat at 93-95 mph as a pro. RHP Jimmy Nelson (2) pitches at 92-93 and reaches 96 with his heater, which features boring action in on righthanders. RHP Matt Miller (5) has touched 97 and works at 91-95.

BEST SECONDARY PITCH: Nelson's slider and Thornburg's changeup show flashes of becoming plus pitches. LHP Brian Garman (17) has a hard slider that reaches the mid-80s.

BEST PRO DEBUT: Rookie-level Helena won the Pioneer League title with contributions from several draftees. Hawn powered the lineup; Miller (7-2, 4.06) led the league in wins; RHP Austin Ross (8) had a 52-6 K-BB ratio; Garman (3-1, 0.90, 9 SV) was untouchable as the closer.

BEST ATHLETE: Allison's explosiveness gives him a slight edge over Berard.

MOST INTRIGUING BACKGROUND: Unsigned OF/LHP Chad Jones (50) had first-round tools and helped Louisiana State to the 2009 College World Series championship but turned his focus to football. The New York Giants drafted him as a safety in the third round, but a June car accident nearly ended his NFL career before it started. He's rehabilitating to try to come back to play football.

CLOSEST TO THE MAJORS: The Brewers sent Morris to the Arizona Fall League, though he'll need extra development time if they follow through on plans to convert him to a third baseman. Thornburg could blow past him if he commands the strike zone and settles in as a reliever.

BEST LATE-ROUND PICK: Allison reminds Milwaukee a bit of Lorenzo Cain with his tools and center-field profile. Garman has an 89-91 mph fastball, a plus slider and also could move quickly.

THE ONE WHO GOT AWAY: The Brewers were moving toward a deal with RHP Dylan Covey (1) until he learned shortly before the signing deadline that he had Type 1 diabetes. Covey decided to attend San Diego so he could manage his condition while close to home.

ASSESSMENT: Not signing Covey was a blow, and Milwaukee's total of $2.4 million in bonus spending is the lowest in baseball over the last three drafts. The Brewers still found some intriguing arms in Nelson and Thornburg, and hope to hit on a lower pick to take some of the sting out of Covey's absence.

2009

RHP Eric Arnett (1) was a disaster in his first full pro season, and OF Kentrail Davis (1s) and RHP Kyle Heckathorn (1s) didn't quite live up to their lofty draft status either. 2B/SS Scooter Gennett (16) was a pleasant surprise, hitting .309/.354/.463 in low Class A.

GRADE: C

2008

2B Brett Lawrie (1) was the system's top prospect until he was traded for Shaun Marcum, which allowed RHP Jake Odorizzi (1s) to rise to No. 1. Milwaukee reached for LHP Evan Frederickson (1s), who has a career 5.47 ERA in the lower minors.

GRADE: B+

2007

1B Matt LaPorta (1) hasn't hit as expected, but the Brewers used him as the centerpiece of the C.C. Sabathia trade that spurred a 2008 playoff berth. C Jonathan Lucroy (3) claimed a big league starting job last summer. RHP Cody Scarpetta (11) has outperformed several higher draft picks in the system.

GRADE: C+

2006

RHP Jeremy Jeffress (1) has one of the best fastballs in the minors and seems to have found his niche in the bullpen. Since-traded OF Cole Gillespie (3) and RHP Mike McClendon (10) also have reached the majors.

GRADE: C

Draft analysis by John Manuel (2010) and Jim Callis (2006-09). Numbers in parentheses indicate draft rounds.

JAKE ODORIZZI, RHP

Born: March 27, 1990. **Bats:** R. **Throws:** R.
Height: 6-2. **Weight:** 185. **Drafted:** HS—
Highland, Ill., 2008 (1st round supplemental).
Signed by: Harvey Kuenn Jr.

BILL MITCHELL

The Brewers invested several early-round picks in pitchers in the 2008 draft, and went 1-for-5. Evan Frederickson (supplemental first round), Seth Lintz (second) and Cody Adams (second) all had ERAs of 5.93 or higher in 2010, and Josh Romanski (fourth) was released before throwing a pitch in pro ball. The lone success story from that crop is Odorizzi, who became the system's top prospect when Milwaukee traded second baseman Brett Lawrie to the Blue Jays for Shaun Marcum in December. Scouts first noticed Odorizzi because of his athleticism, which he put to good use as a pitcher, shortstop and all-league wide receiver at Highland (Ill.) High. When his fastball rose to the low 90s during his senior season, some clubs rated him as the top prep pitcher available. After drafting him 32nd overall and signing him for $1.06 million, the Brewers handled Odorizzi with care. He spent his first two pro seasons in Rookie ball, throwing a total of 68 innings. They turned him loose at low Class A Wisconsin last year, and he responded by leading the Midwest League in strikeouts per nine innings (10.1) and throwing the first eight innings of a combined no-hitter in his second-to-last start. Milwaukee named him its minor league pitcher of the year.

Two scouts who saw Odorizzi pitch at Wisconsin described him as a lesser version of Zack Greinke. Odorizzi's excellent athleticism results in a clean delivery that he repeats easily, allowing him to fill the strike zone. He consistently commands a fastball that ranges from 89-95 mph and seems even quicker because he throws with such ease. He maintains his velocity deep into games, and his fastball also features good sinking and boring action that makes it difficult to lift. Odorizzi's fastball is so effective that he has been able to thrive without a secondary pitch that presently grades as plus. He's working on two different breaking balls. Scouts like his curveball better, saying it could develop into an above-average second pitch, and his slider is really more of a cutter. He shows some feel for a changeup, though he sometimes tips it off by slowing his arm speed. Odorizzi fields his position well, though he has to do a better job of holding runners after surrendering 16 steals in 20 attempts last year. He's built for durability and though he pitched nearly twice as many innings in 2010 as he had totaled the previous two seasons, he got stronger in the second half. He's extremely poised and confident on the mound.

Though the Brewers constantly are seeking starting pitching, they won't rush Odorizzi, who will pitch this season at age 21. He still needs innings to refine his secondary pitches and his command, but his athleticism and feel for pitching should allow him to develop into a No. 2 or 3 starter in time. He'll begin 2011 at high Class A Brevard County, where pitchers usually flourish, and could find himself in Double-A Huntsville before the year out.

SCOUTING GRADES

Fastball: 65. **Command/**
Curveball: 60. **Control:** 60.
Changeup: 55. **Delivery:** 70.

Based on 20-80 scouting scale, where 50 represents major league average, and future projection rather than present tools.

Year	Club (League)	Class	W	L	ERA	G	GS	CG	SV	IP	H	HR	BB	SO	G/AWHIP	AVG
2008	Brewers (AZL)	R	1	2	3.48	11	4	0	0	21	18	2	9	19	-- 1.31	.220
2009	Helena (PIO)	R	1	4	4.40	12	10	0	0	47	55	3	9	43	1.09 1.36	.296
2010	Wisconsin (MWL)	LoA	7	3	3.43	23	20	0	1	121	99	7	40	135	1.12 1.15	.220
Minor League Totals			9	9	3.68	46	34	0	1	188	172	12	58	197	1.11 1.22	.240

2 MARK ROGERS, RHP

Born: Jan. 30, 1986. **B-T:** R-R. **Ht.:** 6-2. **Wt.:** 225. **Drafted:** HS—Mount Ararat, Maine, 2004 (1st round). **Signed by:** Tony Blengino.

Rogers missed the entire 2007 and 2008 seasons while recovering from a pair of shoulder surgeries, making it unlikely he would fulfill the expectations that came when he was drafted fifth overall and signed for $2.2 million in 2004. But he has stayed healthy the last two years and regained his stuff. He showed such determination in his comeback that the Brewers rewarded him with an unexpected September callup. Once again, Rogers regularly operates in the mid-90s and touches 97 at times. He throws both two-seamers and four-seamers, generating a lot of life on his fastball. His command has improved from earlier in his pro career, but it's still erratic. He issues too many walks and runs up high pitch counts quickly. When he throws his 12-to-6 curveball for strikes, he can be devastating. He also has a hard slider with good bite, but his changeup remains below average. Now that Rogers has proven he can stay on the mound, Milwaukee must decided whether he can be consistent enough with his command and keep his pitch counts low enough to remain a starter. The Brewers need rotation help more than relievers, and may have him open 2011 as a starter at Triple-A Nashville to make some more refinements.

Year	Club (League)	Class	W	L	ERA	G	GS	CG	SV	IP	H	HR	BB	SO	G/A	WHIP	AVG
2004	Brewers (AZL)	R	0	3	4.72	9	6	0	0	27	30	0	14	35	—	1.65	.294
2005	West Virginia (SAL)	LoA	2	9	5.11	25	20	0	1	99	87	11	70	109	—	1.59	.238
2006	Brevard County (FSL)	HiA	1	2	5.07	16	16	0	0	71	68	6	53	96	—	1.70	.253
	Brewers (AZL)	R	0	0	2.25	3	3	0	0	4	5	0	2	5	—	1.75	.294
2007	Did not play—Injured																
2008	Did not play—Injured																
2009	Brevard County (FSL)	HiA	1	3	1.67	23	22	0	0	65	46	2	29	67	1.55	1.16	.201
2010	Nashville (PCL)	AAA	0	0	2.08	1	1	0	0	4	3	0	3	3	1.50	1.38	.188
	Huntsville (SL)	AA	6	8	3.71	24	24	0	0	112	86	3	69	111	2.33	1.39	.210
	Milwaukee (NL)	MAJ	0	0	1.80	4	2	0	0	10	2	0	3	11	1.29	0.50	.067
Major League Totals			0	0	1.80	4	2	0	0	10	2	0	3	11	1.29	0.50	.067
Minor League Totals			10	25	4.02	101	92	0	1	381	325	22	240	426	1.96	1.48	.231

3 JEREMY JEFFRESS, RHP

Born: Sept. 21, 1987. **B-T:** R-R. **Ht.:** 6-1. **Wt.:** 185. **Drafted:** HS—South Boston, Va., 2006. (1st round). **Signed by:** Tim McIlvaine.

Many eyebrows were raised when Milwaukee placed Jeffress on the 40-man roster last June, five months before necessary. After two suspensions for marijuana use in the minors, the 16th overall pick in the 2006 draft was one strike away from a lifetime ban. Players on the 40-man roster can be tested but not suspended for recreational drugs, and the Brewers didn't want to lose the most electric arm in the system. They moved him to the bullpen to help him maintain a daily focus, and his performance on and off the mound earned him a September callup. Jeffress regularly pitches in the mid-90s with his fastball and hit triple digits at the Rising Stars Game in the Arizona Fall League after the season. His heater doesn't have much movement but he throws it with such an easy delivery that he blows it by hitters before they realize what happened. He also has a big-breaking curveball that he struggles to throw for strikes but is devastating when he does. He never mastered a changeup and won't need one as a reliever. Many scouts have projected Jeffress as a closer from the day he was drafted, and his success out of the bullpen did nothing to dispel those thoughts. Assuming Milwaukee opts to keep him in relief, he has a good chance to make their Opening Day roster.

Year	Club (League)	Class	W	L	ERA	G	GS	CG	SV	IP	H	HR	BB	SO	G/A	WHIP	AVG
2006	Brewers (AZL)	R	2	5	5.88	13	4	0	0	34	30	0	25	37	—	1.63	.227
2007	West Virginia (SAL)	LoA	9	5	3.13	18	18	0	0	86	62	8	44	95	—	1.23	.201
2008	Brevard County (FSL)	HiA	4	6	4.08	15	14	1	0	79	65	5	41	102	—	1.34	.226
	Huntsville (SL)	AA	2	1	5.52	4	4	0	0	15	17	2	11	13	—	1.91	.298
2009	Huntsville (SL)	AA	1	3	7.57	8	8	0	0	27	26	1	33	34	1.69	2.16	.255
	Brevard County (FSL)	HiA	2	1	2.18	6	5	1	0	33	16	2	22	36	2.33	1.15	.145
2010	Wisconsin (MWL)	LoA	0	0	0.00	5	0	0	0	8	0	0	3	14	2.00	0.38	.000
	Brevard County (FSL)	HiA	0	0	5.40	8	0	0	1	10	10	0	7	14	3.67	1.70	.244
	Huntsville (SL)	AA	1	1	1.26	11	0	0	3	14	8	0	2	15	6.67	0.70	.160
	Milwaukee (NL)	MAJ	1	0	2.70	10	0	0	0	10	8	0	6	8	1.63	1.40	.229
Major League Totals			1	0	2.70	10	0	0	0	10	8	0	6	8	1.63	1.40	.229
Minor League Totals			21	22	3.99	88	53	2	4	307	234	18	188	360	2.47	1.38	.211

4 CODY SCARPETTA, RHP

Born: Aug. 25, 1988. **B-T:** R-R. **Ht.:** 6-3. **Wt.:** 242. **Drafted:** HS—Guilford, Ill., 2007 (11th round). **Signed by:** Harvey Kuenn Jr.

Scarpetta, whose father Dan was a 1982 third-round pick by the Brewers, dropped in the 2007 draft because of a torn flexor tendon in his right index finger. He had surgery before the draft and signed for $325,000 as an 11th-rounder, but that deal was voided when he needed a second operation. He re-signed for $125,000, but to keep his rights Milwaukee had to place him on its 40-man roster. Scarpetta's fastball ranges from 90-94 mph, and he backs it up with the best curveball in the system. His improved changeup gives him a dependable third pitch. He has enough stuff to start, but his command is a work in progress. Scarpetta had a tendency to freeze his front hip and land too hard in his delivery, affecting his ability to locate his pitches. Brevard County pitching coach Fred Dabney worked with him last season to smooth out his lower half, and his mechanical improvements helped his command. Because Scarpetta went on the 40-man roster so early, the Brewers will use their final minor league option on him in 2011. They'll try to advance him as far as possible, probably starting him in Double-A and trying to get him to Triple-A by the end of the season. He's a potential No. 3 starter, but not there yet.

Year	Club (League)	Class	W	L	ERA	G	GS	CG	SV	IP	H	HR	BB	SO	G/A	WHIP	AVG
2008	Brewers (AZL)	R	1	0	0.57	6	5	0	0	16	8	0	8	27	—	1.02	.154
	Helena (PIO)	R	1	0	3.48	6	3	0	0	21	18	2	8	31	—	1.26	.237
2009	Wisconsin (MWL)	LoA	4	11	3.43	26	18	0	0	105	83	5	55	116	1.14	1.31	.217
	Huntsville (SL)	AA	0	0	5.40	1	1	0	0	5	5	1	1	1	2.50	1.20	.263
2010	Brevard County (FSL)	HiA	7	12	3.87	27	27	1	0	128	120	4	67	142	1.04	1.46	.247
Minor League Totals			13	23	3.51	66	54	1	0	274	234	12	139	317	1.11	1.36	.230

5 WILY PERALTA, RHP

Born: May 8, 1989. **B-T:** R-R. **Ht.:** 6-2. **Wt.:** 225. **Signed:** Dominican Republic, 2005. **Signed by:** Fausto Sosa Pena/Fernando Arango.

Peralta has made steady progress since missing the entire 2007 season following Tommy John surgery. After never pitching more than 104 innings in a season and totaling just 176 in his first four years as a pro, he worked a career-high 147 frames in 2010 and held his own after reaching Double-A. Milwaukee added him to its 40-man roster in November. Peralta already has three dependable pitches in place, starting with a 92-94 mph fastball that touches 96. He throws his fastball with little effort, though the pitch lacks life and doesn't induce a lot of swings and misses. Both of his secondary pitches—a low-80s slider with good tilt and a changeup—are average to slightly above-average. He simply needs to hone his pitches and command them on a more consistent basis. Peralta has a simple, repeatable delivery and a strong body, ingredients for becoming a workhorse starter. He's a focused worker with a confident demeanor. With his maturity and work ethic, the Brewers think Peralta isn't far from pitching in the majors. He'll return to Double-A to begin 2011, with a good chance for a midseason promotion. He could join Milwaukee's rotation by the end of 2012.

Year	Club (League)	Class	W	L	ERA	G	GS	CG	SV	IP	H	HR	BB	SO	G/A	WHIP	AVG
2006	Brewers (AZL)	R	2	5	6.63	14	6	0	0	38	51	5	20	28	—	1.87	.319
2007	Did not play—Injured																
2008	Helena (PIO)	R	1	1	3.07	15	2	0	2	29	23	4	8	36	—	1.06	.209
	West Virginia (SAL)	LoA	0	1	10.80	2	2	0	0	5	6	0	3	3	—	1.80	.316
2009	Wisconsin (MWL)	LoA	4	4	3.47	27	15	0	1	104	91	5	46	118	1.15	1.32	.235
2010	Brevard County (FSL)	HiA	6	3	3.86	19	17	0	0	105	102	5	40	75	1.74	1.35	.253
	Huntsville (SL)	AA	2	3	3.61	8	8	0	0	42	43	5	24	29	1.90	1.58	.269
Minor League Totals			15	17	4.06	85	50	0	3	323	316	24	141	289	1.51	1.41	.255

6 SCOOTER GENNETT, 2B/SS

Born: May 1, 1990. **B-T:** L-R. **Ht.:** 5-9. **Wt.:** 165. **Drafted:** HS—Sarasota, Fla., 2009 (16th round). **Signed by:** Tim McIlvaine.

Gennett had a polished bat for a prep middle infielder, but his commitment to Florida State caused him to slip to the 16th round of the 2009 draft. After he signed for $260,000, the Brewers planned to send him to Rookie ball last summer. But he performed so well in minor league camp last spring that he earned an assignment to the Midwest League, where he finished seventh in hitting (.309) and earned postseason all-star honors. He may look like a bat boy, but Gennett is an advanced hitter with surprising pop, as evidenced by his 52 extra-base hits in his pro debut. He has an open stance and the ball jumps off his bat. Sometimes he gets too long with his swing, leading to strikeouts, and he could use some more plate discipline. He has average speed that plays up on the bases because he has good instincts. A shortstop in high school, Gennett moved to second base as a pro and has average defensive tools. He led MWL second baseman with 21 errors in 107 games, but he should get smoother with more experience. The best-case scenario for Gennett is that he keeps hitting and proves he can stay at second base. At worst, he profiles as a gritty, offensive-minded utility man. He'll advance to high Class A in 2011.

Year	Club (League)	Class	AVG	G	AB	R	H	2B	3B	HR	RBI	BB	SO	SB	CS	OBP	SLG
2010	Wisconsin (MWL)	LoA	.309	118	482	87	149	39	4	9	55	31	91	14	4	.354	.463
Minor League Totals			.309	118	482	87	149	39	4	9	55	31	91	14	4	.354	.463

7 KENTRAIL DAVIS, OF

Born: June 29, 1988. **B-T:** L-R. **Ht.:** 5-9. **Wt.:** 195. **Drafted:** Tennessee, 2009 (1st round supplemental). **Signed by:** Joe Mason.

He entered 2009 as one of the best college hitters available in the draft, but a rough season and his extra leverage as a sophomore-eligible player allowed Davis to last until the 39th overall pick. Signed for $1.2 million, he went to high Class A last April for his pro debut. He had hamstring problems and didn't hit, prompting a demotion to Wisconsin, where he flourished. Davis has a short swing with plenty of bat speed and solid plate discipline. He should hit for average, but scouts aren't sold that he has the power desired on an outfield corner. He got too pull-conscious when he struggled last year, and did a better job of using the whole field in low Class A. He has plus speed, though his hamstring issues forced him to shut down his running game for most of 2010. Despite allowed Davis lacks the instincts to play center field. He played in center at Brevard County and in right at Wisconsin, but he has a fringy arm and probably will wind up in left. He plays with confidence. Davis will get another chance to conquer high Class A in 2011 and could reach Double-A by the end of the season. His bat is calling card, but he has to work on his outfield play and keep his legs healthy.

Year	Club (League)	Class	AVG	G	AB	R	H	2B	3B	HR	RBI	BB	SO	SB	CS	OBP	SLG
2010	Brevard County (FSL)	HiA	.244	33	123	20	30	2	5	0	17	17	28	8	2	.380	.341
	Wisconsin (MWL)	LoA	.335	64	245	44	82	26	5	3	46	31	36	3	1	.421	.518
Minor League Totals			.304	97	368	64	112	28	10	3	63	48	64	11	3	.407	.459

8 TYLER THORNBURG, RHP

Born: Sept. 29, 1988. **B-T:** R-R. **Ht.:** 5-11. **Wt.:** 185. **Drafted:** Charleston Southern, 2010 (3rd round). **Signed by:** Ryan Robinson.

Thornburg has drawn comparisons to Tim Lincecum for his height and his delivery. He impressed scouts as a closer in the Cape Cod League in the summer of 2009, then continued to throw well last spring while pulling double duty as a starter and outfielder at Charleston Southern. After signing for $351,900 as a third-round pick, he was hampered by an oblique strain in his pro debut but still had 38 strikeouts in 23 innings. Thornburg's fastball sits at 93-95 mph and tops out at 98, though it doesn't feature much life. Some scouts think his power curveball is his best pitch. He flashed an improved changeup in pro ball, so he may have the requisite three pitches to remain a starter. He'll need to improve his command, however. His aggressive nature on the mound would serve him well if the Brewers decide to make him a reliever. As a potential closer, Thornburg might offer more upside coming out of the bullpen. Milwaukee will continue to develop him as a starter for now, giving him time to work on his changeup and command. He'll probably begin his first full pro season in low Class A, but he could make a push for Brevard County with a strong spring.

Year	Club (League)	Class	W	L	ERA	G	GS	CG	SV	IP	H	HR	BB	SO	G/AWHIP	AVG
2010	Helena (PIO)	R	1	0	1.93	9	6	0	1	23	15	2	11	38	1.55 1.11	.179
Minor League Totals			1	0	1.93	9	6	0	1	23	15	2	11	38	1.55 1.11	.179

9 ERIC FARRIS, 2B

Born: March 3, 1986. **B-T:** R-R. **Ht.:** 5-10. **Wt.:** 170. **Drafted:** Loyola Marymount, 2007 (4th round). **Signed by:** Corey Rodriguez.

After Farris hit .298 and stole 70 bases at Brevard County in 2009, the Brewers jumped him all the way to Nashville last year, in part to allow since-traded Brett Lawrie to play in Double-A. Farris hit .288 in April before hurting his right knee in a collision at the plate. He missed two months and his speed and quickness were diminished when he returned, though he did look better in the Arizona Fall League, where he batted .351. Farris put the ball in play with a consistent, easy stroke and then makes things happen on the bases. He's not a blazer, but he has plus speed and excellent instincts on the bases. He doesn't contribute much offensively besides singles and steals, because he doesn't walk a lot and has little power. His skill at bunting enhances his ability to get on base. Farris is a major league-ready defender who committed just four errors in 66 games last year. He has solid range, soft hands and a fringy arm. Milwaukee loves his competitiveness. Some scouts believe Farris projects as a utility player, but the Brewers believe his instincts and drive can put him over the top as an everyday second baseman. They placed him on the 40-man roster in November. The trade of Lawrie to the Blue Jays removed one obstacle, but Rickie Weeks still blocks him in Milwaukee.

Year	Club (League)	Class	AVG	G	AB	R	H	2B	3B	HR	RBI	BB	SO	SB	CS	OBP	SLG
2007	Helena (PIO)	R	.326	63	239	34	78	16	2	1	34	16	22	21	5	.369	.423
2008	West Virginia (SAL)	LoA	.293	103	454	73	133	21	4	3	54	24	50	32	10	.332	.377
2009	Brevard County (FSL)	HiA	.298	124	473	68	141	18	1	7	49	29	46	70	6	.341	.385
2010	Brewers (AZL)	R	.250	10	32	5	8	5	0	1	9	1	3	1	0	.257	.500
	Nashville (PCL)	AAA	.274	60	230	28	63	9	1	2	15	9	25	14	2	.311	.348
Minor League Totals			.296	360	1428	208	423	69	8	14	161	79	146	138	23	.336	.385

10 JIMMY NELSON, RHP

Born: June 5, 1989. **B-T:** R-R. **Ht.:** 6-6. **Wt.:** 245. **Drafted:** Alabama, 2010 (2nd round). **Signed by:** Joe Mason.

The Brewers have focused on drafting big-bodied, hard-throwing pitchers in recent years, and Nelson fits the bill. A second-round pick, he became their top signee from the 2010 draft when first-rounder Dylan Covey was diagnosed with diabetes and opted to attend college. After landing him for $570,600, Milwaukee used Nelson strictly as a reliever because he had pitched 110 innings at Alabama in the spring, his first extended stint as a starter. Nelson can hit 96 mph with his fastball, but he has learned that he's more effective when he throws a two-seamer in the low 90s with heavy sink. He complements his fastball with a hard 84-86 mph slider that will give him a second plus pitch if he gains more consistency. He occasionally mixes in a slow curveball to keep hitters guessing. His changeup is below-average and needs work. Nelson loses his release point at times and becomes inconsistent with his control. He sometimes lands hard on a stiff front leg and must clean up his mechanics. If he does, he has the body to be a workhorse. While some teams projected Nelson as a closer, the Brewers believe he can be a middle-of-the-rotation starter. They'll turn him loose in low Class A this year.

Year	Club (League)	Class	W	L	ERA	G	GS	CG	SV	IP	H	HR	BB	SO	G/A	WHIP	AVG
2010	Helena (PIO)	R	2	0	3.71	12	0	0	3	27	30	2	13	33	2.38	1.61	.268
Minor League Totals			2	0	3.71	12	0	0	3	27	30	2	13	33	2.38	1.61	.268

11 KYLE HECKATHORN, RHP

Born: June 17, 1988. **B-T:** R-R. **Ht.:** 6-6. **Wt.:** 235. **Drafted:** Kennesaw State, 2009 (1st round supplemental). **Signed by:** Ryan Robinson.

Scouts sometimes consider Heckathorn more of a thrower who just rears back and fires fastballs in the 90-94 mph range. In shorter stints at Kennesaw State, he threw harder, into the upper 90s. His first full season was a strong success, as he led the organization with a 2.98 ERA and got 2.02 groundouts for every airout. He is a full-effort, big-bodied, non-athletic pitcher who sometimes struggles with arm action and release points. Heckathorn uses his tall frame to throw downhill and does a good job of keeping the ball in the park (three homers in 124 innings in 2010) with his best pitch a sinker. Throwing from a three-quarter delivery, he was not as consistent with a slider in the mid-to-high 80s. His changeup is effective at times, and he commands it better than his fastball, but Heckathorn doesn't repeat his delivery as much as needed. The Brewers had him work on smoothing out his lower half as the season progressed and he became more efficient with his pitches. He competes on the mound and is a real bulldog in his approach to pitching, but Heckathorn projects as a reliever because his fastball command is below-average. Milwaukee moved him up to Brevard County last summer and he held his own over eight starts. He'll probably return to high Class A in 2011, and the Brewers plan to keep him in a starting role for now.

Year	Club (League)	Class	W	L	ERA	G	GS	CG	SV	IP	H	HR	BB	SO	G/A	WHIP	AVG
2009	Helena (PIO)	R	0	1	6.04	6	5	0	0	22	30	4	4	15	2.19	1.52	.326
2010	Wisconsin (MWL)	LoA	6	6	2.96	17	13	1	0	85	82	2	23	67	2.18	1.24	.246
	Brevard County (FSL)	HiA	4	0	3.00	8	8	1	0	39	40	1	10	23	1.73	1.28	.265
Minor League Totals			10	7	3.44	31	26	2	0	146	152	7	37	105	2.05	1.29	.264

12 AMAURY RIVAS, RHP

Born: Dec. 20, 1985. **B-T:** R-R. **Ht.:** 6-2. **Wt.:** 204. **Signed:** Dominican Republic, 2005. **Signed by:** Fernando Arango/Fausto Sosa Pena.

Rivas' individual pitches don't blow hitters or scouts away. He throws his fastball mostly in the low 90s and his slider is average at best. His fastball can reach 95 mph, but straightens out with more velocity and has more boring life and sink at lesser speeds. Rivas does have a quality changeup and developed a feel for that pitch at a young age. More than anything else, Rivas knows how to pitch and how to set up hitters, and he understands the importance of location and working both sides of the plate. He pitches to contact and doesn't hurt himself with too many walks. In short, he has shown good polish and no after-effects from having Tommy John surgery in December 2006. Some scouts believe Rivas eventually will evolve into a relief pitcher at the big league level but the Brewers don't see it that way for the organization's 2009 minor league pitcher of the year. They like his knack for making pitches and the way he attacks hitters with aggressiveness on the mound, and believe he will rise to the majors as a starter. Rivas likely will begin the 2011 season in the rotation at Triple-A with the possibility he could see action in Milwaukee at some point in the season.

Year	Club (League)	Class	W	L	ERA	G	GS	CG	SV	IP	H	HR	BB	SO	G/A	WHIP	AVG
2005	Brewers (AZL)	R	2	3	6.91	14	6	0	0	42	56	1	16	34	—	1.73	.326
2006	Brewers (AZL)	R	1	0	6.43	4	2	0	0	14	17	1	3	12	—	1.43	.293
	Helena (PIO)	R	5	4	3.02	10	10	0	0	54	48	6	16	36	—	1.19	.236
2007	Brewers (AZL)	R	0	0	3.12	6	6	0	0	9	3	1	4	10	—	0.81	.107
2008	West Virginia (SAL)	LoA	8	3	3.50	19	15	0	0	90	83	11	32	70	—	1.28	.239
	Brevard County (FSL)	HiA	1	2	4.20	7	6	0	0	30	35	2	11	20	—	1.53	.294
2009	Brevard County (FSL)	HiA	13	7	2.98	26	23	0	0	133	109	11	43	123	1.29	1.14	.220
2010	Huntsville (SL)	AA	11	6	3.37	25	25	2	0	142	130	7	55	114	1.61	1.31	.253
Minor League Totals			41	25	3.67	111	93	2	0	513	481	40	180	419	1.45	1.29	.248

13 MATT MILLER, RHP

Born: Jan. 30, 1989. **B-T:** R-R. **Ht.:** 6-6. **Wt.:** 230. **Drafted:** Michigan, 2010 (5th round). **Signed by:** Mike Farrell.

Miller slipped down the draft boards of many teams after he pitched poorly during his junior season at Michigan and was removed from the rotation. He threw his fastball at 92-94 mph but it was straight for the most part, and he had trouble throwing his slider for strikes. After signing him for $157,500 in the fifth round last June, the Brewers liked just about everything they saw from him at Rookie-level Helena. Miller led the Pioneer League with seven victories and held opponents to a .244 batting average. After pitching 64 innings for Michigan in the spring, he maintained the velocity on his fastball as a pro, touching 97 mph at times, and was more consistent with his slider and changeup. Miller even mixed in a decent curveball at times. He was still throwing the ball well when Helena advanced to the playoffs and won the league crown. The coaching staff loved Miller's makeup and willingness to try coaching suggestions. With an above-average fastball and slider, and decent changeup, he projects as a middle-of-the-rotation starter in the majors. After a strong pro debut, Miller could jump to high Class A to begin the 2011 season.

Year	Club (League)	Class	W	L	ERA	G	GS	CG	SV	IP	H	HR	BB	SO	G/A	WHIP	AVG
2010	Helena (PIO)	R	7	2	4.06	14	14	0	0	71	63	7	28	53	1.63	1.28	.244
Minor League Totals			7	2	4.06	14	14	0	0	71	63	7	28	53	1.63	1.28	.244

14 ERIK KOMATSU, OF

Born: Oct. 1, 1987. **B-T:** L-L. **Ht.:** 5-10. **Wt.:** 190. **Drafted:** Cal State Fullerton, 2008 (8th round). **Signed by:** Josh Belovsky.

It seemed like Komatsu came out of nowhere to challenge for the high Class A Florida State League batting title in 2010, but that's because he missed most of the previous season with a variety of injuries. He was limited to 26 games in 2009 by a concussion and wrist and hamstring injuries. Finally healthy again, Komatsu was able to show the hitting skills that scouts liked when he played for Cal State Fullerton. With a short, quick stroke and tremendous plate discipline, he posted a .413 on-base percentage in high Class A. Komatsu has some pop in his diminutive frame but focused on hitting line drives to all fields at pitcher-friendly Brevard County, finishing with 31 doubles. He also is a slightly above-average runner and threat to steal a base anytime he is on base. Komatsu also showed versatility in the outfield, making 73 starts in center, 30 in right and 22 in left. With not enough power to project as a corner outfielder in the majors, Komatsu must continue to show he is a viable center fielder. For his overall play, attitude and adaptability to coaching, the Brewers named him their minor league player of the year for 2010. He probably will begin next season in Double-A and profiles best as a fourth outfielder at the big league level.

Year	Club (League)	Class	AVG	G	AB	R	H	2B	3B	HR	RBI	BB	SO	SB	CS	OBP	SLG
2008	Helena (PIO)	R	.321	68	277	61	89	19	4	11	47	30	42	8	4	.394	.538
2009	Brewers (AZL)	R	.308	5	13	1	4	0	0	0	3	2	2	0	0	.353	.308

	Class	AVG	G	AB	R	H	2B	3B	HR	RBI	BB	SO	SB	CS	OBP	SLG
Wisconsin (MWL)	LoA	.242	21	66	6	16	2	0	1	5	8	14	0	2	.342	.318
2010 Brevard County (FSL) HiA		.323	130	486	90	157	31	6	5	63	68	61	28	9	.413	.442
Minor League Totals		.316	224	842	158	266	52	10	17	118	108	119	36	15	.400	.462

15 CALEB GINDL, OF

Born: Aug. 31, 1988. **B-T:** L-L. **Ht.:** 5-9. **Wt.:** 185. **Drafted:** HS—Milton, Fla., 2007 (5th round). **Signed by:** Doug Reynolds.

Playing Double-A at age 21 last season, Gindl struggled more at the plate than in past seasons. He saw more breaking balls and didn't hit for as much power in the past. Still, it's Gindl's offense that has scouts projecting him as a big leaguer at some point, though his squatty build and average home run power make it difficult to see him as an everyday corner outfielder. He has a compact stroke and usually displays a good eye at the plate, proving tough to strike out and driving the ball in the gaps regularly to pile up doubles. Though a below-average runner, he shows good instincts and aggressiveness on the basepaths. Gindl is an average defender at best with average arm strength, and he's best suited for left field. The Brewers threw another challenge at him at midseason by asking him to play center field. Gindl worked hard at getting good jumps on the ball to compensate for his lack of speed. He is a grinder who shows up every day to play and Milwaukee loves the way he competes. Gindl was assigned to the Arizona Fall League as an injury replacement and rediscovered his power stroke there while swinging a hot bat. He'll get a shot to make the Triple-A roster in the spring.

Year	Club (League)	Class	AVG	G	AB	R	H	2B	3B	HR	RBI	BB	SO	SB	CS	OBP	SLG
2007	Helena (PIO)	R	.372	55	207	40	77	22	3	5	42	20	38	4	4	.420	.580
2008	West Virginia (SAL)	LoA	.307	137	508	86	156	38	4	13	81	63	144	14	5	.388	.474
2009	Brevard County (FSL) HiA		.277	112	394	61	109	15	3	17	71	57	92	18	4	.363	.459
2010	Huntsville (SL)	AA	.272	128	463	61	126	33	1	9	60	55	78	10	5	.352	.406
Minor League Totals			.298	432	1572	248	468	108	11	44	254	195	352	46	18	.375	.464

16 LOGAN SCHAFER, OF

Born: Sept. 8, 1986. **B-T:** L-L. **Ht.:** 6-1. **Wt.:** 175. **Drafted:** Cal Poly, 2008 (3rd round). **Signed by:** Corey Rodriguez.

The Brewers had high hopes for Schafer after he won the Florida State League batting title in 2009 and earned the organization's minor league player of the year award. But, in essence, his 2010 season was over before it began. Schafer suffered a groin injury in minor league minicamp the day before he was to report to his first big league spring training and missed the first half of the season as the injury morphed into a sports hernia. When finally activated, he played in only seven games before fouling a pitch off his right foot and breaking it. Milwaukee sent Schafer to the Arizona Fall League with hopes of making up some lost at-bats but continued discomfort in his foot nixed a regular assignment and landed him on the taxi squad. When healthy, Schafer is an athletic center fielder with good range, solid instincts in the field and an average, accurate arm. At the plate, he flashes some gap power on occasion but basically focuses on making contact and hitting singles. He shows poise and maturity and understands how to play the game. His lost season probably means Schafer will begin 2011 in Double-A, which was supposed to be his assignment a year ago. At 24, he already has a lot of making up to do.

Year	Club (League)	Class	AVG	G	AB	R	H	2B	3B	HR	RBI	BB	SO	SB	CS	OBP	SLG
2008	Helena (PIO)	R	.240	8	25	4	6	0	1	2	8	5	4	1	0	.355	.560
	West Virginia (SAL)	LoA	.276	43	181	25	50	13	2	0	20	8	42	3	8	.306	.370
2009	Brevard County (FSL) HiA		.313	113	457	76	143	31	6	6	58	38	53	16	8	.369	.446
	Huntsville (SL)	AA	.217	7	23	4	5	0	1	0	0	4	3	1	0	.379	.304
2010	Brevard County (FSL) HiA		.174	7	23	7	4	2	0	0	1	4	6	0	0	.286	.261
Minor League Totals			.293	178	709	116	208	46	10	8	87	59	108	21	16	.350	.420

17 HUNTER MORRIS, 1B/3B

Born: Oct. 7, 1988. **B-T:** L-R. **Ht.:** 6-4. **Wt.:** 205. **Drafted:** Auburn, 2010 (4th round). **Signed by:** Joe Mason.

Drafted in the second round out of high school in 2007 by the Red Sox, Morris opted not to sign and instead accepted a scholarship to Auburn. He was a freshman All-American but his production fell off dramatically as a sophomore. Morris responded by getting in the best shape of his life, stunning scouts with a 6.75-second time in the 60-yard dash. Still, he was unable to improve his draft stock from three years before and was taken in the fourth round by the Brewers last June, signing for a $218,700 bonus. Morris has good power but gets too aggressive at times and doesn't draw many walks. Some scouts have questioned his pure bat speed and grade his hitting ability ahead of his power. Morris, who played some left field at Wisconsin, has improved but remains a below-average defender at first base and needs improvement in his footwork and range. Accordingly, the decision was made in instructional league and later in the Arizona Fall League to convert him to a third baseman. Morris showed a strong enough arm to handle the position and was working diligently to improve his footwork. He is a dedicated worker, takes instruction well and shows mental toughness on the field. Morris probably will begin

2011 in high Class A.

Year	Club (League)	Class	AVG	G	AB	R	H	2B	3B	HR	RBI	BB	SO	SB	CS	OBP	SLG
2010	Wisconsin (MWL)	LoA	.251	71	291	38	73	19	4	9	44	20	58	7	2	.306	.436
Minor League Totals			.251	71	291	38	73	19	4	9	44	20	58	7	2	.306	.436

18 ERIC ARNETT, RHP

Born: Jan. 25, 1988. **B-T:** R-R. **Ht.:** 6-6. **Wt.:** 220. **Drafted:** Indiana, 2009 (1st round). **Signed by:** Mike Farrell.

The Brewers had reason to be more than a bit nervous about Arnett's performance in 2010. No first-round draft pick taken out of a major college program should get tattooed in low Class A the way he did. Signed for $1.197 million the year before, Arnett pitched so poorly that he was demoted for a period to the Rookie-level Arizona League, where he continued to get roughed up. For whatever reason, Arnett didn't show the consistent 91-94 mph fastball he had in his junior year at Indiana. Instead, he sat mostly at 87-90 mph and peaked at 92. When he fell behind in the count, he threw hittable fastballs that resulted in an alarming number of home runs. He ranked fourth in the Midwest League with 14 homers allowed despite his demotion. He gave in to hitters too often when he could not consistently command his often-flat slider and offspeed pitches consistently. Though he had problems repeating his herky-jerky delivery—his slow tempo didn't help—Arnett never complained of arm problems, making the slippage of his stuff more puzzling. Understandably, his confidence took a severe hit, and Milwaukee's hopes of moving him quickly through the system were dashed. Now, they have to wonder if Arnett's big junior season at Indiana was a fluke or if he merely stopped trusting his stuff. In the meantime, a major red flag has been raised.

Year	Club (League)	Class	W	L	ERA	G	GS	CG	SV	IP	H	HR	BB	SO	G/AWHIP	AVG
2009	Helena (PIO)	R	0	4	4.41	14	9	0	0	35	33	1	21	35	2.14 1.56	.228
2010	Wisconsin (MWL)	LoA	1	9	6.70	20	16	0	1	85	98	14	39	60	1.47 1.62	.282
	Brewers (AZL)	R	2	0	7.31	5	1	0	1	16	20	1	7	19	2.86 1.69	.313
Minor League Totals			3	13	6.18	39	26	0	2	135	151	16	67	114	1.72 1.61	.272

19 ANDRE LAMONTAGNE, RHP

Born: March 24, 1986. **B-T:** R-R. **Ht.:** 6-5. **Wt.:** 208. **Drafted:** Oral Roberts, 2009 (11th round). **Signed by:** Tim Collinsworth.

As the 2010 season began, there was no talk about Lamontagne being one of the Brewers' better pitching prospects. An older sign out of college, he had a so-so pro debut in 2009 and was assigned to bullpen duty in high Class A at the outset of last season. Relief duty agreed with Lamontagne, whose fastball jumped from the 89-91 mph when he was drafted to 93-95 mph in 2010. He also began using a curveball that he had dropped in college, which kept hitters off his fastball and cutter. Lamontagne showed he could impact games out of the pen and pitched well enough to earn a promotion to high Class A. After another promotion to Double-A, he returned to starting and his stuff held up deep enough into games to show promise in that role. He also pitched out of the bullpen for Team USA in the Pan Am qualifying tournament after the season. With a long, lean pitcher's body, Lamontagne throws easily on a downhill plane and commands the bottom half of the strike zone. He smoothed out his delivery to look less mechanical on the mound, making his fastball jump even more on hitters. Lamontagne has the stuff to be a starter but could prove to be a reliable late-inning reliever in the major leagues. He probably will start the 2011 season in Triple-A.

Year	Club (League)	Class	W	L	ERA	G	GS	CG	SV	IP	H	HR	BB	SO	G/AWHIP	AVG
2009	Helena (PIO)	R	2	4	4.54	13	4	0	1	36	35	2	11	17	1.75 1.29	.250
2010	Wisconsin (MWL)	LoA	2	2	2.36	16	0	0	5	27	21	0	14	26	1.72 1.31	.219
	Brevard County (FSL)	HiA	1	1	2.35	11	0	0	3	15	10	1	6	14	1.00 1.04	.185
	Huntsville (SL)	AA	4	3	3.63	13	7	0	1	45	35	4	24	39	2.50 1.32	.217
Minor League Totals			9	10	3.46	53	11	0	10	122	101	7	55	96	1.84 1.28	.224

20 CODY HAWN, 1B

Born: Aug. 11, 1988. **B-T:** L-R. **Ht.:** 6-1. **Wt.:** 205. **Drafted:** Tennessee, 2010 (6th round). **Signed by:** Joe Mason.

The Brewers originally drafted Hawn out of a Knoxville high school in the 23rd round in 2007. He didn't sign and spent a year mashing at Walters (Tenn.) JC, getting drafted in 2008 by the Athletics (41st round). He then transferred to Tennessee and hit .364 with 22 home runs as a sophomore. But he got off to a slow start as a junior due to a sprained left shoulder and never put it all together, finishing at .327/.441/.593, and Milwaukee was able to sign him in 2010 for $125,000 as a sixth-rounder. An offensive player who has power to all fields, Hawn ranked third in the Pioneer League in homers and helped carry Helena to the league championship. In the decisive game against Ogden, Hawn pounded two homers and drove in eight runs. He has very strong hands and upper-body strength. Though not a classic first baseman in stature and without good range, he gets by through hard work and making the routine plays. He shows patience at the plate but sometimes gets a bit long with his swing and becomes strikeout-prone. Hawn shows an advanced knowledge of what pitchers are trying to do with him, uses the whole field and displays a knack for driving in runs. His bat will take him through the system. He has well-below-average speed. His makeup and leadership skills also impressed the Brewers, who could jump him to high Class A for 2011.

Year	Club (League)	Class	AVG	G	AB	R	H	2B	3B	HR	RBI	BB	SO	SB	CS	OBP	SLG
2010	Helena (PIO)	R	.308	65	253	36	78	20	0	13	61	35	58	0	0	.407	.542
Minor League Totals			.308	65	253	36	78	20	0	13	61	35	58	0	0	.407	.542

21 YADIEL RIVERA, SS

Born: May 1, 1992. **B-T:** R-R. **Ht.:** 6-3. **Wt.:** 178. **Drafted:** HS—Caguas, P.R., 2010 (9th round). **Signed by:** Charlie Sullivan.

Rivera didn't hit a lick in his debut in the Arizona League, looking completely overmatched at the plate for the most part. He showed little strength and had the bat knocked out of his hands at times. Rivera showed no ability to recognize and hit off-speed pitches, revealing his inexperience. But he was playing at age 18 and the Brewers believe his offense will improve as he matures and fills out a projectable frame. Defensively, Rivera showed plenty of promise despite his 12 errors in 49 games. Very athletic, he is a true shortstop with great range and silky smooth movements in the field. He picks up instruction immediately and puts suggestions into action. With long strides, Rivera could develop into a basestealer. His arm is average but could improve as he becomes stronger and learns to set his feet and throw. How much improvement Rivera makes in terms of plate discipline and strength will determine where he begins the 2011 season. Milwaukee believes he has a high ceiling because of his already-solid instincts in the field and because his hand-eye coordination makes them confident he'll get better with the bat.

Year	Club (League)	Class	AVG	G	AB	R	H	2B	3B	HR	RBI	BB	SO	SB	CS	OBP	SLG
2010	Brewers (AZL)	R	.209	49	206	22	43	8	1	0	23	9	72	6	2	.243	.257
Minor League Totals			.209	49	206	22	43	8	1	0	23	9	72	6	2	.243	.257

22 CAMERON GARFIELD, C

Born: May 23, 1991. **B-T:** R-R. **Ht.:** 6-1. **Wt.:** 195. **Drafted:** HS—Murrieta, Calif., 2009 (2nd round). **Signed by:** Josh Belovsky.

If Garfield looked overmatched at times in 2010 in low Class A, that was to be expected. He began the season at age 18 and had only 59 games of Rookie ball experience under his belt. He really struggled offensively, having difficulty getting on base consistently and showing little power. Garfield does have some pop in his bat, however, and the Brewers believe his power will develop with physical maturity, more at-bats and the understanding that he must use his hands more. He probably won't hit for a high average but should be able to hold his own enough at the position. Defensively, Garfield improved as the season progressed in both receiving and blocking balls. Opponents ran wild on Wisconsin's pitchers last season, and while Garfield displayed a strong arm, his erratic footwork cost him time and accuracy. Runners were able to steal 140 bases (in 173 attempts, an 81 percent success rate) in just 101 games. Milwaukee likes the leadership skills he shows behind the plate and thinks he will continue to improve in all areas of the game. He has a good head on his shoulders and understands what he must do to improve. Despite his young age, Garfield will move up to high Class A this year.

Year	Club (League)	Class	AVG	G	AB	R	H	2B	3B	HR	RBI	BB	SO	SB	CS	OBP	SLG
2009	Helena (PIO)	R	.248	59	218	26	54	11	0	4	21	10	61	3	4	.299	.353
2010	Wisconsin (MWL)	LoA	.245	102	384	41	94	19	0	3	46	22	74	2	4	.287	.318
Minor League Totals			.246	161	602	67	148	30	0	7	67	32	135	5	8	.291	.331

23 TYLER ROBERTS, C

Born: Oct. 25, 1990. **B-T:** R-R. **Ht.:** 6-0. **Wt.:** 226. **Drafted:** HS—Gray, Ga., 2009 (10th round). **Signed by:** Ryan Robinson.

After playing 29 games in the Arizona League in 2009, Roberts was sent back to that circuit and impressed scouts with his dramatic improvement. Still a teenager, he projects to be a regular catcher in the majors who can contribute offensively and defensively. Slightly ahead as an offensive player, Roberts showed improved pop from his first season. He displayed good plate discipline and the ability to put the ball in play when necessary. Roberts has worked hard on strength and conditioning, firming up what was a somewhat soft body, and benefited greatly from working with catching instructor Charlie Greene. His arm is average to a tick above, but with improved footwork he should be able to control the running game. He threw out 32 percent of basestealers last year. Very raw coming out of the draft, Roberts made a big leap in calling games in his second pro season and showed he understood how to set up hitters. The pro coaching was invaluable because Roberts said most of the catching nuances he picked up in high school came from watching Atlanta Braves games on TV growing up in Georgia. He held up well catching in the heat in Arizona and should only get better with experience and maturity.

Nicknamed "Country" because of his rural upbringing, Roberts impressed the coaching staff with his character and willingness to work. He should get his first full-season test in 2011, one step behind Cameron Garfield on the organization depth chart.

Year	Club (League)	Class	AVG	G	AB	R	H	2B	3B	HR	RBI	BB	SO	SB	CS	OBP	SLG
2009	Brewers (AZL)	R	.292	24	72	11	21	1	1	1	8	13	19	2	0	.407	.375
	Helena (PIO)	R	.125	3	8	0	1	0	0	0	1	0	3	0	0	.125	.125
2010	Brewers (AZL)	R	.288	42	156	30	45	17	0	6	23	15	30	0	0	.354	.513
	Helena (PIO)	R	.000	1	3	0	0	0	0	0	0	1	1	0	0	.250	.000
Minor League Totals			.280	70	239	41	67	18	1	7	32	29	53	2	0	.363	.452

24 D'VONTREY RICHARDSON, OF

Born: July 30, 1988. **B-T:** R-R. **Ht.:** 6-2. **Wt.:** 215. **Drafted:** Florida State, 2009 (5th round). **Signed by:** Ryan Robinson.

Richardson was primarily a football player in college, showing tremendous speed as a quarterback. He was preparing to make the transition to defensive back when the Brewers drafted him and convinced him to commit to baseball with a $400,000 signing bonus spread over multiple years under baseball's provision for two-sport athletes. As might be expected for an athlete with limited baseball experience—he'd received 210 at-bats in two seasons for Florida State in baseball—he was very raw and signed too late to play pro ball in 2009. Nevertheless, Milwaukee had Richardson skip Rookie ball and assigned him to low Class A last season. Depending on what night you saw him, he either looked impressive or lost. His inexperience at facing breaking balls resulted in a high strikeout total (164 in 522 at-bats) and his lack of instincts in tracking balls in the outfield also showed at times. Big and athletic, Richardson's 70 speed on the 20-80 scale was negated at times by a lack of savvy on the bases. Basically, what the Brewers have is a raw player with tremendous tools who is still learning how to play baseball. Richardson does display solid power when he makes contact and has the range to play center field, with the plus arm for right. He has a long way to go and may never reach his lofty ceiling, but Milwaukee will be patient.

Year	Club (League)	Class	AVG	G	AB	R	H	2B	3B	HR	RBI	BB	SO	SB	CS	OBP	SLG
2010	Wisconsin (MWL)	LoA	.243	132	522	78	127	28	8	7	51	58	164	17	15	.331	.368
Minor League Totals			.243	132	522	78	127	28	8	7	51	58	164	17	15	.331	.368

25 MIKE MCCLENDON, RHP

Born: April 3, 1985. **B-T:** R-R. **Ht.:** 6-5. **Wt.:** 215. **Drafted:** Seminole (Fla.) CC, 2006 (10th round). **Signed by:** Charlie Aliano.

Undrafted out of high school, McClendon boosted his stock during two years at Seminole CC. But the real break came early in the 2008 season when the Brewers shifted the tall righthander from a starting role to relief work. McClendon flourished in that role and soared through the system, resulting in an unexpected callup to Milwaukee last August. He debuted with three perfect innings in Colorado and went on to impress the major league staff with his effective work out of the pen. McClendon's 88-92 mph fastball that he sneaks past hitters with a repeatable, simple delivery. He also disrupts hitters' timing by speeding up his delivery to the plate at times, resulting in claims of "quick pitching" by opponents. His primary out pitch is a sinker that results in ground ball after ground ball, but McClendon also mixes in a palm ball, slider and curve. He shows good command of all of his pitches and an understanding of how to set up hitters and keep them off-balance. The Brewers sent him to the Arizona Fall League to continue to hone his repertoire. The tremendous progress McClendon made in 2010 guarantees he will be given a shot to make Milwaukee's bullpen in the spring.

Year	Club (League)	Class	W	L	ERA	G	GS	CG	SV	IP	H	HR	BB	SO	G/AWHIP	AVG
2006	Helena (PIO)	R	3	2	4.23	18	4	0	0	45	54	4	8	34	— 1.39	.297
2007	West Virginia (SAL)	LoA	5	2	2.87	11	11	0	0	63	46	6	12	47	— 0.93	.198
	Brevard County (FSL)	HiA	5	6	4.23	16	14	2	1	89	108	6	19	46	— 1.42	.293
2008	Brevard County (FSL)	HiA	7	6	4.19	46	5	0	10	88	103	6	15	61	— 1.34	.287
2009	Huntsville (SL)	AA	4	3	3.30	41	2	0	3	85	86	4	20	57	1.41 1.25	.268
2010	Huntsville (SL)	AA	1	1	0.61	7	0	0	0	15	7	0	1	15	3.50 0.55	.143
	Nashville (PCL)	AAA	4	3	2.44	25	3	0	2	55	53	1	14	44	2.08 1.21	.259
	Milwaukee (NL)	MAJ	2	0	3.00	17	0	0	0	21	15	2	7	21	1.31 1.05	.195
Major League Totals			2	0	3.00	17	0	0	0	21	15	2	7	21	1.31 1.05	.195
Minor League Totals			29	23	3.50	164	39	2	16	439	457	27	89	304	1.71 1.24	.266

26 BRANDON KINTZLER, RHP

Born: Aug. 1, 1984. **B-T:** R-R. **Ht.:** 6-1. **Wt.:** 180. **Drafted:** Dixie State (Utah) JC, 2004 (40th round). **Signed by:** Anup Sinha (Padres).

Kintzler was discovered by Brewers scout Tim Collinsworth at the independent American Association all-star game in 2009. He was throwing his fastball in the mid-90s with good command and the Brewers figured it was an arm worth taking a shot on, and they were right. Kintzler spent the rest of that season at Double-A and quickly moved through the top levels of the system last year, resulting in a September callup. Kintzler was a starter earlier in his minor league career but his velocity jumped dramatically after moving to the bullpen. He also has a sharp-breaking slider that he commands consistently. He works the bottom of the strike zone well but doesn't have a reliable offspeed pitch. Kintzler has a somewhat deceptive delivery that makes his fastball get on hitters even quicker. His smallish frame has not worked against him to this point. Kintzler often was used as a closer in the minors but projects as a middle reliever and perhaps a set-up man in the majors. Milwaukee sent him to the Arizona Fall League to continue working against advanced hitters and he will be given an opportunity to win a spot in their bullpen in the spring.

Year	Club (League)	Class	W	L	ERA	G	GS	CG	SV	IP	H	HR	BB	SO	G/A	WHIP	AVG
2004	Padres (AZL)	R	3	2	2.38	21	0	0	6	34	36	0	9	38	—	1.32	.277
	Eugene (NWL)	SS	0	0	0.00	3	0	0	3	3	3	0	0	4	—	1.00	.250
2005	Padres (AZL)	R	2	0	4.09	8	0	0	1	11	15	2	4	17	—	1.73	.306
	Eugene (NWL)	SS	0	0	0.00	3	0	0	0	3	3	0	0	1	—	0.90	.273
	Fort Wayne (MWL)	LoA	1	2	3.09	19	0	0	0	23	20	2	7	19	—	1.16	.230
2006	Did Not Play																
2007	Winnipeg (NOR)	IND	5	2	4.07	29	8	0	1	77	78	8	13	41	—	1.18	.258
2008	Winnipeg (NOR)	IND	7	6	4.65	20	19	0	0	112	139	8	36	73	—	1.56	.304
2009	St. Paul (A-A)	IND	8	3	2.79	14	11	1	0	81	89	3	24	46	—	1.40	.277
	Huntsville (SL)	AA	1	2	4.54	9	6	0	0	36	41	5	9	32	1.40	1.40	.285
2010	Huntsville (SL)	AA	1	0	0.40	20	0	0	10	22	11	0	1	23	2.08	0.54	.141
	Nashville (PCL)	AAA	3	0	2.36	22	0	0	6	27	19	1	6	21	3.91	0.94	.196
	Milwaukee (NL)	MAJ	0	1	7.36	7	0	0	0	7	10	2	4	9	12.00	1.91	.357
Major League Totals			0	1	7.36	7	0	0	0	7	10	2	4	9	12.00	1.91	.357
Minor League Totals			11	6	2.71	105	6	0	26	159	148	10	36	155	2.07	1.15	.243

27 NICK BUCCI, RHP

Born: Aug. 16, 1990. **B-T:** R-R. **Ht.:** 6-2. **Wt.:** 180. **Drafted:** HS—Sarnia, Ont., 2008 (18th round). **Signed by:** Jay Lapp.

Bucci was a raw pitcher with limited experience when the Brewers drafted him out of Canada. He pitched little in 2008 but opened some eyes in the Pioneer League the next season by ranking high in several categories. Milwaukee loves his aggressive approach and fierce competitiveness on the mound, traits he's displayed for Canada's national team in the 2009 World Cup (helping lead Canada to its best-ever bronze medal) and the 2010 Pan Am qualifier. He attacks hitters with a fastball that sits at 89-92 mph and touches 93, and he isn't afraid to pitch inside and knock hitters off the plate. Bucci shows hitters his curveball to keep them off his fastball and mixes in an improving changeup that he will throw in any count. He has good balance and extension with his delivery but struggles with fastball command at times, leading to high pitch counts and too many walks. But opponents batted only .220 off him last season, so he is tough to beat when he throws strikes. Challenged in instructional league to do a better job of pitching down in the strike zone, Bucci showed improvement that had impressed the Brewers' staff. He pitched most of the season at 19 and has a good pitcher's frame and athleticism on the mound. Bucci should continue to develop because he is one of the hardest workers in the system. He should start 2011 in high Class A.

Year	Club (League)	Class	W	L	ERA	G	GS	CG	SV	IP	H	HR	BB	SO	G/A	WHIP	AVG
2008	Brewers (AZL)	R	0	3	7.36	5	4	0	0	11	12	2	2	14	—	1.27	.273
2009	Huntsville (SL)	AA	1	0	6.75	3	0	0	0	4	3	2	2	3	0.50	1.25	.231
	Helena (PIO)	R	6	3	4.41	13	12	0	0	69	59	7	21	66	1.82	1.15	.231
2010	Wisconsin (MWL)	LoA	6	7	3.51	26	20	0	1	121	96	12	68	100	1.01	1.36	.220
Minor League Totals			13	13	4.08	47	36	0	1	205	170	23	93	183	1.22	1.28	.227

28 MAVERICK LASKER, RHP

Born: Feb. 17, 1990. **B-T:** R-R. **Ht.:** 6-2. **Wt.:** 190. **Drafted:** HS—Phoenix, 2008 (5th round). **Signed by:** Kevin Clouser.

After he strained his back shortly after signing in 2008, the Brewers eased Lasker into professional ball by having him spend the entire 2009 season in the Arizona League. He quickly raised eyebrows there with his aggressive style on the mound, pounding the strike zone and pitching to contact. Lasker gets ahead of hitters with an 88-92 mph fastball with good movement. Milwaukee believes his velocity will improve as his projectable frame fills out. He spikes his curve at times and is prone to wild pitches (18 in 2010) and must improve his command of that pitch. Lasker improved in that area toward season's end and continued to improve his changeup. He adds a short slider, and at his best, he has four average pitches working. As one scout put it, he figured some things out toward the end of last season. He isn't overpowering and fits more of a back-of-the-rotation profile. One thing the Brewers are sure of is that Lasker won't sell himself short because he has a tremendous work ethic and makeup. He'll advance to high Class A to begin the 2011 season.

Year	Club (League)	Class	W	L	ERA	G	GS	CG	SV	IP	H	HR	BB	SO	G/AWHIP	AVG
2008	Did Not Play—Injured															
2009	Brewers (AZL)	R	5	1	3.26	13	1	0	0	47	43	2	9	39	1.55 1.11	.246
	Wisconsin (MWL)	LoA	1	1	5.00	2	2	0	0	9	9	0	5	4	0.33 1.56	.257
2010	Wisconsin (MWL)	LoA	7	5	4.61	23	17	0	0	105	106	3	35	70	0.85 1.34	.259
Minor League Totals			13	7	4.24	38	20	0	0	161	158	5	49	113	0.95 1.28	.255

29 LEE HAYDEL, OF

Born: July 15, 1987. **B-T:** L-R. **Ht.:** 5-11. **Wt.:** 175. **Drafted:** Delgado (La.) CC, D/F 2006 (19th round). **Signed by:** Joe Mason.

Haydel still has the tools of a center fielder—in particular, plus-plus speed—but because of a glut of players at that position throughout the organization, he played left field most of the time in Double-A last year. That was a waste of his ball-chasing skills and Haydel has no power to speak of, so it's difficult to project him as a left fielder in the major leagues. Haydel has made steady improvement in his overall approach to hitting, though he still strikes out too often and doesn't walk enough to take full advantage of his speed. He gets on fastballs with a quick stroke but still struggles with off-speed stuff. Haydel has responded to coaching and is learning to hit more balls on the ground instead of useless fly balls. The switch to left field forced him to learn how to take better routes to balls and he continues to work on his defense. He will have to play the Brett Butler game to get to the majors: slash the ball, bunt for hits and use his speed in all facets of the game. At this point, he projects as an extra outfielder at best unless he improves his plate discipline and starts getting on base more consistently. He probably will begin the 2011 season in Triple-A.

Year	Club (League)	Class	AVG	G	AB	R	H	2B	3B	HR	RBI	BB	SO	SB	CS	OBP	SLG
2007	Helena (PIO)	R	.276	62	254	42	70	12	5	0	20	12	44	12	5	.311	.362
2008	West Virginia (SAL)	LoA	.295	131	522	68	154	21	8	0	50	32	107	34	17	.337	.366
2009	Brevard County (FSL)	HiA	.275	124	491	66	135	16	5	2	50	17	110	39	10	.302	.340
2010	Huntsville (SL)	AA	.285	127	452	61	129	18	7	0	36	35	97	22	6	.337	.356
Minor League Totals			.284	444	1719	237	488	67	25	2	156	96	358	107	38	.323	.355

30 AUSTIN ROSS, RHP

Born: Aug. 12, 1988. **B-T:** R-R. **Ht.:** 6-2. **Wt.:** 190. **Drafted:** Louisiana State, 2010 (8th round). **Signed by:** Jeremy Booth.

The Brewers think they got a steal in the eighth round of the 2010 draft by grabbing Ross for $100,000. He had an impressive pro debut, posting a 52-6 K-BB ratio in 47 innings. His fastball sat mostly in the low 90s but he located it well with a repeatable clean delivery. Ross throws a consistent slider but his below-average changeup was not effective against lefties, making him profile as a relief pitcher in the majors. If Ross is able to perfect a changeup, however, he could persuade Milwaukee to keep him in a starting role. Because he throws so many strikes, he gives up a lot of hits. The coaching staff loved Ross' pitchability and how he conducted himself with poise and confidence on the mound. Because he pounds the strike zone with mostly consistent location, Ross should make quick work of Class A in 2011, but his ceiling will be limited until he improves his changeup.

Year	Club (League)	Class	W	L	ERA	G	GS	CG	SV	IP	H	HR	BB	SO	G/AWHIP	AVG
2010	Helena (PIO)	R	2	1	2.70	10	5	0	0	47	43	1	6	52	1.62 1.05	.246
Minor League Totals			2	1	2.70	10	5	0	0	47	43	1	6	52	1.62 1.05	.246

Minnesota Twins

BY JOHN MANUEL

The American League Division Series almost obscured an otherwise storybook 2010 season for the Twins. Minnesota opened Target Field and played home games outdoors for the first time since 1981. The ballpark drew rave reviews and attracted 3.22 million fans, third-best in the AL. The expected infusion of revenue helped the Twins lock up franchise icon Joe Mauer with an eight-year, $184 million contract in March.

That was general manager Bill Smith's biggest task last offseason, but he also made other moves that helped the club defend its AL Central title, its sixth in  the last decade. Jim Thome may have been the biggest free-agent bargain of the year, hitting 25 homers after signing for just $1 million. Rookie Danny Valencia filled their third-base hole. Closer Joe Nathan had Tommy John surgery in March, but Smith built an excellent bullpen anyway, adding Matt Capps (for catching prospect Wilson Ramos) and Brian Fuentes (for minor league righthander Loek Van Mil) during the summer to fortify it.

The Twins seemed ready for October, but that's when their magical season turned sour. They lost eight of their last 10 regular-season games before getting swept in the Division Series by the Yankees. New York has beaten Minnesota in four Division Series meetings since 2003, winning 12 of 14 games.

While the Twins ranked third in the AL in runs allowed and fifth in runs scored, they didn't pitch or hit well against the Yankees, and lacked the athleticism to pressure New York's defense like the Rangers did in the AL Championship Series. Though they haven't won a postseason series since 2002, the Twins' window of opportunity remains open as long as they have Mauer and his solid supporting cast. Justin Morneau's concussion—he was hurt in July and never returned to the field—is cause for concern.

Despite trading Johan Santana for pennies on the dollar to the Mets in January 2008, Minnesota has retained a solid rotation. Francisco Liriano re-emerged as an ace in 2010, his second year removed from Tommy John surgery, with homegrown products Scott Baker, Nick Blackburn, Brian Duensing and Kevin Slowey all reaching double digits in wins. The Twins believe their last two first-round picks, righties Kyle Gibson and Alex Wimmers, are at least as good and consider Gibson more of a front-of-the-rotation fit.

Minnesota has maintained its focus on scouting and player development, even though it didn't pay an

Danny Valencia had a boffo rookie year in Minnesota, filling the Twins' third-base hole

TOP 30 PROSPECTS

1. Kyle Gibson, rhp	16. Manuel Soliman, rhp
2. Aaron Hicks, of	17. Jorge Polanco, ss/2b
3. Miguel Sano, 3b/ss	18. Chris Parmelee, 1b/of
4. Joe Benson, of	19. Niko Goodrum, ss/2b
5. Ben Revere, of	20. Daniel Santana, ss/2b
6. Liam Hendriks, rhp	21. Eddie Rosario, of
7. Alex Wimmers, rhp	22. Dakota Watts, rhp
8. Adrian Salcedo, rhp	23. Pat Dean, lhp
9. Oswaldo Arcia, of	24. Trevor Plouffe, ss
10. Carlos Gutierrez, rhp	25. B.J. Hermsen, rhp
11. Max Kepler, of	26. Bruce Pugh, rhp
12. Rene Tosoni, of	27. Tom Stuifbergen, rhp
13. David Bromberg, rhp	28. Anthony Slama, rhp
14. Angel Morales, of	29. Scott Diamond, lhp
15. Billy Bullock, rhp	30. Brian Dozier, inf

above-slot bonus to a single draftee in 2010. While sticking to its draft principles of polished pitchers and athletic position players, the Twins have revitalized their Latin American scouting, spending big on the likes of Dominican infielder Miguel Sano while also developing better depth of Latin prospects.

While the Twins have prospects throughout their system, top affiliates New Britain and Rochester combined for just 93 victories. The rosters of both clubs still must provide low-cost reinforcements, as the big league club may have to replace six free-agent pitchers, including 17-game winner Carl Pavano and several relievers.

General Manager: Bill Smith. **Farm Director:** Jim Rantz. **Scouting Director:** Deron Johnson.

Class	Team	League	W	L	PCT	Finish*	Manager
Majors	Minnesota Twins	American	94	68	.580	3rd (14)	Ron Gardenhire
Triple-A	Rochester Red Wings	International	49	95	.340	14th (14)	Tom Nieto
Double-A	New Britain Rock Cats	Eastern	44	98	.310	12th (12)	Jeff Smith
High A	Fort Myers Miracle	Florida State	64	74	.464	10th (12)	Jake Mauer
Low A	Beloit Snappers	Midwest	71	65	.522	7th (16)	Nelson Prada
Rookie	Elizabethton Twins	Appalachian	41	25	.621	2nd (10)	Ray Smith
Rookie	GCL Twins	Gulf Coast	29	31	.483	10th (15)	Chris Heintz/Ramon Borrego
Overall 2010 Minor League Record			298	388	.434	30th (30)	

*Finish in overall standings (No. of teams in league). †League champion.

LAST YEAR'S TOP 30

Player, Pos.		Status
1.	Aaron Hicks, of	No. 2
2.	Wilson Ramos, c	(Nationals)
3.	Kyle Gibson, rhp	No. 1
4.	Miguel Sano, ss/3b	No. 3
5.	Ben Revere, of	No. 5
6.	Danny Valencia, 3b	Majors
7.	Carlos Gutierrez, rhp	No. 10
8.	Angel Morales, of	No. 14
9.	David Bromberg, rhp	No. 13
10.	Max Kepler, of	No. 11
11.	Adrian Salcedo, rhp	No. 8
12.	Rene Tosoni, of	No. 12
13.	Joe Benson, of	No. 4
14.	Chris Parmelee, 1b/of	No. 18
15.	Billy Bullock, rhp	No. 15
16.	Tyler Robertson, lhp	Dropped out
17.	Alex Burnett, rhp	Majors
18.	Oswaldo Arcia, of	No. 9
19.	Anthony Slama, rhp	No. 28
20.	Jeff Manship, rhp	Majors
21.	B.J. Hermsen, rhp	No. 25
22.	Deolis Guerra, rhp	Dropped out
23.	Estarlin de los Santos, ss/2b	Dropped out
24.	Trevor Plouffe, ss	No. 24
25.	Daniel Santana, ss	No. 20
26.	Matt Bashore, lhp	Dropped out
27.	Jose Morales, c	Majors
28.	Ben Tootle, rhp	Dropped out
29.	Loek Van Mil, rhp	(Angels)
30.	James Beresford, ss	Dropped out

BEST TOOLS

Best Hitter for Average	Ben Revere
Best Power Hitter	Miguel Sano
Best Strike-Zone Discipline	Aaron Hicks
Fastest Baserunner	Ben Revere
Best Athlete	Joe Benson
Best Fastball	Dakota Watts
Best Curveball	David Bromberg
Best Slider	Kyle Gibson
Best Changeup	Kyle Gibson
Best Control	Liam Hendriks
Best Defensive Catcher	Danny Lehmann
Best Defensive Infielder	Jorge Polanco
Best Infield Arm	Niko Goodrum
Best Defensive Outfielder	Aaron Hicks
Best Outfield Arm	Aaron Hicks

PROJECTED 2014 LINEUP

Catcher	Joe Mauer
First Base	Miguel Sano
Second Base	Alexi Casilla
Third Base	Danny Valencia
Shortstop	Jorge Polanco
Left Field	Delmon Young
Center Field	Denard Span
Right Field	Aaron Hicks
Designated Hitter	Justin Morneau
No. 1 Starter	Francisco Liriano
No. 2 Starter	Kyle Gibson
No. 3 Starter	Liam Hendriks
No. 4 Starter	Alex Wimmers
No. 5 Starter	Brian Duensing
Closer	Carlos Gutierrez

TOP PROSPECTS OF THE DECADE

Year	Player, Pos.	2010 Org.
2001	Adam Johnson, rhp	Out of baseball
2002	Joe Mauer, c	Twins
2003	Joe Mauer, c	Twins
2004	Joe Mauer, c	Twins
2005	Joe Mauer, c	Twins
2006	Francisco Liriano, lhp	Twins
2007	Matt Garza, rhp	Rays
2008	Nick Blackburn, rhp	Twins
2009	Aaron Hicks, of	Twins
2010	Aaron Hicks, of	Twins

TOP DRAFT PICKS OF THE DECADE

Year	Player, Pos.	2010 Org.
2001	Joe Mauer, c	Twins
2002	Denard Span, of	Twins
2003	Matt Moses, 3b	Out of baseball
2004	Trevor Plouffe, ss	Twins
2005	Matt Garza, rhp	Rays
2006	Chris Parmelee, of/1b	Twins
2007	Ben Revere, of	Twins
2008	Aaron Hicks, of	Twins
2009	Kyle Gibson, rhp	Twins
2010	Alex Wimmers, rhp	Twins

LARGEST BONUSES IN CLUB HISTORY

Joe Mauer, 2001	$5,150,000
Miguel Sano, 2009	$3,150,000
B.J. Garbe, 1999	$2,750,000
Adam Johnson, 2000	$2,500,000
Ryan Mills, 1998	$2,000,000

MINNESOTA TWINS

TOP 2011 ROOKIE: Kyle Gibson, rhp. Minnesota's top prospect should break into the rotation after getting some time in Triple-A.

BREAKOUT PROSPECT: Eddie Rosario, of. The Twins knew the 2010 fourth-round could hit, and they also like his polish and well-rounded tools.

SLEEPER: Dallas Gallant, rhp. A 23rd-round pick who signed for $122,500 last August, he's a hard-throwing reliever who could zip through the system.

SOURCE OF TOP 30 TALENT			
Homegrown	29	Acquired	1
College	7	Trades	0
Junior college	1	Rule 5 draft	1
High school	9	Independent leagues	0
Draft-and-follow	3	Free agents/waivers	0
Nondrafted free agents	0		
International	9		

LF
Rene Tosoni (12)
Luke Hughes
Danny Ortiz
Steve Liddle
Nate Roberts
Matej Hejma

CF
Aaron Hicks (2)
Ben Revere (5)
Max Kepler (11)
Eddie Rosario (21)
J.D. Williams
Brandon Roberts

RF
Joe Benson (4)
Oswaldo Arcia (9)
Angel Morales (14)

3B
Miguel Sano (3)
Reggie Williams

SS
Jorge Polanco (17)
Niko Goodrum (19)
Daniel Santana (20)
Trevor Plouffe (24)
James Beresford
Estarlin de los Santos
Jonatan Ynojoso

2B
Brian Dozier (30)
Derek McCallum

1B
Chris Parmelee (18)
Lance Ray
Danny Rams
Rory Rhodes

C
Chris Herrmann
Danny Lehmann
Kyle Knudson
Kelly Cross

RHP

RHSP	RHRP
Kyle Gibson (1)	Carlos Gutierrez (10)
Liam Hendriks (6)	Billy Bullock (15)
Alex Wimmers (7)	Dakota Watts (22)
Adrian Salcedo (8)	Bruce Pugh (26)
David Bromberg (13)	Anthony Slama (28)
Manuel Soliman (16)	Dallas Gallant
B.J. Hermsen (25)	Rob Delaney
Tom Stuifbergen (27)	Kane Holbrooks
Bobby Lanigan	Matt Hauser
Deolis Guerra	Kyle Waldrop
Eric Hacker	Shooter Hunt
Brad Stillings	Brett Jacobson
Michael Tonkin	
Ben Tootle	
Michael McCardell	
Blayne Weller	
A.J. Achter	

LHP

LHSP	LHRP
Pat Dean (23)	Tyler Robertson
Scott Diamond (29)	Edgar Ibarra
Dan Osterbrock	Logan Darnell
Matt Bashore	Matthew Tone
Martire Garcia	Andrei Labonov
	Clint Dempster

BONUSES: $3.5 MILLION

BEST PURE HITTER: Minnesota found three hitters it likes in OFs Nate Roberts (5), who has a solid, strong swing; Eddie Rosario (4), an athletic, potential five-tool player with a polished approach; and smooth-swinging Lance Ray (8), who may be more of a first baseman eventually and reminds them of ex-big leaguer Mike Aldrete.

BEST POWER HITTER: Rosario has average power. Eventually, SS Niko Goodrum (2), who has the highest ceiling of Minnesota's draftees, could surpass him. His father stands 6-foot-4 and 275 pounds, so the 6-foot-3, 180-pound Goodrum could wind up a big, fast-twitch athlete with huge power.

FASTEST RUNNER: 2B J.D. Williams (10), who probably will wind up in the outfield, should cover plenty of ground with his 6.5-second speed in the 60-yard dash.

BEST DEFENSIVE PLAYER: Rosario has a solid arm and all-around ability in center field.

BEST FASTBALL: RHP Matt Hauser (7) touched 95 mph at times while striking out 17, walking three and allowing just one earned run in 16 innings between Rookie-level Elizabethton and low Class A Beloit.

BEST SECONDARY PITCH: RHP Alex Wimmers (1) has excellent arm speed on his changeup, which could be a true plus pitch if it gains a bit more movement. RHP Dallas Gallant (23) slumped in the spring but pitched well in the Cape Cod League the last two summers, with his hard breaking ball returning to form.

BEST PRO DEBUT: Wimmers pitched four gems in high Class A, giving up just six hits and striking out 23 in 16 innings. Rosario tired at season's end but still hit .294/.343/.438 with five homers and 22 steals in 27 tries to earn a spot on the Rookie-level Gulf Coast League all-star team.

BEST ATHLETE: Williams and Goodrum are the best athletes the Twins have drafted since 2008 first-rounder Aaron Hicks. Goodrum has size, speed and plus-plus arm strength.

MOST INTRIGUING BACKGROUND: Williams' brother Reggie was picked four spots behind him by the Cardinals, and their father Reggie spent parts of four seasons in the majors. Unsigned SS Dillon Moyer (22) is the son of ageless Jamie Moyer, while OF Brandon Henderson (27) is a cousin of former Red Sox playoff hero Dave Henderson.

CLOSEST TO THE MAJORS: Wimmers.

BEST LATE-ROUND PICK: Gallant, who has a chance to move quickly.

THE ONE WHO GOT AWAY: The Twins and Braves were the only two teams that didn't go above slot to sign any of their picks. Minnesota liked both sweet-swinging 1B Tyler Kuresa (11) and quick-armed RHP DeAndre Smelter (14), who was set on attending Georgia Tech. The Twins even sent their area scout to Hawaii to follow Kuresa in the Hawaii Collegiate League but couldn't sway him from attending Oregon.

ASSESSMENT: Wimmers is a tailor-made draft pick for the Twins, as is polished LHP Pat Dean (3). Goodrum and Rosario bring the kind of upside the Twins got internationally in 2009.

2009

BONUSES: $4.7 MILLION

RHP Kyle Gibson (1) wouldn't have lasted 22 picks if he didn't come down with a stress fracture in his forearm right before the draft, and he looked like a steal when healthy in 2010. He and RHP Billy Bullock (2) could help the big league pitching staff as soon as this year. LHP Matt Bashore (1s) missed all of last season following Tommy John surgery.

GRADE: B+

2008

BONUSES: $7.3 MILLION

OF Aaron Hicks (1) has legitimate five-tool potential. RHP Carlos Gutierrez (1) is a groundball machine who's nearly ready for the Minnesota bullpen, though RHP Shooter Hunt (1s) has completely lost the strike zone. SS Tyler Ladendorf (2) helped yield Orlando Cabrera in a mid-2009 trade.

GRADE: B+

2007

BONUSES: $2.2 MILLION

OF Ben Revere (1) is one of the more shocking first-round picks in recent memory, but he has hit .328 in the minors and reached the majors in September. OF Angel Morales (3) has power and speed, though he's still figuring out his swing.

GRADE: C+

2006

BONUSES: $3.9 MILLION

3B Danny Valencia (19) hit .311 as a rookie last year, and the Twins got two other late-round big leaguers in RHPs Jeff Manship (14) and Anthony Slama (39). OF Joe Benson (2) had a breakout year in 2010, while 1B/OF Chris Parmelee (1) continues to be slow to develop.

GRADE: C+

Draft analysis by John Manuel (2010) and Jim Callis (2006-09). Numbers in parentheses indicate draft rounds.

KYLE GIBSON, RHP

Born: Oct. 23, 1987. **Bats:** R. **Throws:** R.
Height: 6-6. **Weight:** 210. **Drafted:** Missouri,
2009 (1st round). **Signed by:** J.R. DiMercurio/
Mike Ruth.

KEN BABBITT

Gibson has the ceiling, pedigree and performance of a No. 1 prospect. He ranked No. 100 on BA's list of 2006 draft prospects out of an Indiana high school before starring for three seasons at Missouri, first in the bullpen, then in the rotation. He also starred in the Cape Cod League and with Team USA, putting him in line to go in the top 10 picks of the 2009 draft. His junior season, however, ended on a down note when his velocity dropped into the mid-80s in his final start a week before the draft. He was diagnosed with a stress fracture in his forearm, causing him fall to the Twins at the No. 22 overall pick. Gibson signed for an above-slot $1.85 million bonus in August, then proved he was healthy during instructional league. He reinforced that point with a productive pro debut 2010, leading the system with 152 innings and 126 strikeouts while finishing the year at Triple-A Rochester.

The Twins have produced a bevy of pitchers in recent years who thrive on their knack for throwing quality strikes with solid but not outstanding arsenals. Gibson has similar pitch-making ability to Kevin Slowey, Nick Blackburn and former ace Brad Radke—and he has better stuff. Gibson's tall, lean frame wore down a bit toward the end of last season, but he usually showed average fastball velocity, ranging from 86-92 mph. He generally throws a two-seamer that's more notable for his command of the pitch and its excellent life than for its velocity. He can make it run, sink or cut, and has become more aggressive and confident with his fastball as a pro. He works off the fastball more now than he did as an amateur, but Gibson's secondary pitches remain his primary weapons for getting swings and misses. His slider is a plus offering that helps him generate plenty of groundballs—2.77 groundouts for every airout in 2010—and some scouts project it as a future 70 pitch on the 20-80 scale. His changeup at times equals his slider as a present plus pitch, with similar sink to his two-seamer. His command, control and makeup all enhance his total package. His ability to induce groundouts and his knack for finding a little extra velocity when needed make him adept at controlling damage and avoiding big innings. Added strength, staying healthy and a slight lack of deception (his delivery is very clean) are the only items he needs to address.

Gibson did everything the Twins could have asked last season, including staying positive while pitching for bad teams. In 2011, he likely will be asked to pitch in the major league rotation at some point, especially if Minnesota loses free agent Carl Pavano. Gibson should get a nonroster invitation to big league spring camp, though he'll probably open the season back in Triple-A and be first in line for a promotion. The Twins see him as a future No. 2 starter on a playoff club—he'd need more fastball to qualify as a true ace—and even more skeptical scouts outside the organization see him as no worse than a No. 3.

SCOUTING GRADES

Fastball: 55. **Command/**
Slider: 70. **Control:** 60.
Changeup: 60. **Delivery:** 60.

*Based on 20-80 scouting scale, where
50 represents major league average, and
future projection rather than present tools.*

Year	Club (League)	Class	W	L	ERA	G	GS	CG	SV	IP	H	HR	BB	SO	G/A	WHIP	AVG
2010	Fort Myers (FSL)	HiA	4	1	1.87	7	7	1	0	43	33	2	12	40	6.00	1.04	.213
	New Britain (EL)	AA	7	5	3.68	16	16	1	0	93	91	5	22	77	2.39	1.22	.259
	Rochester (IL)	AAA	0	0	1.72	3	3	0	0	16	12	0	5	9	1.69	1.09	.214
Minor League Totals			11	6	2.96	26	26	2	0	152	136	7	39	126	2.77	1.15	.242

2 AARON HICKS, OF

GEORGE PETRO

Born: Oct. 2, 1989. **B-T:** B-R. **Ht.:** 6-2. **Wt.:** 178. **Drafted:** HS—Long Beach, 2008 (1st round). **Signed by:** John Leavitt.

Hicks ranked No. 1 on this list in each of his first two years after signing for $1.78 million as the 14th overall pick in the 2008 draft. He also ranked first on our low Class A Midwest League list in 2009, but the Twins sent him back to Beloit last season. He got off to a 1-for-30 start before regaining his footing. Hicks remains all tooled up. As a hitter, his best asset is his patience, though at times he's too passive. He has above-average raw power from his natural right side but still has work to do from the left side, where he has more of a slap approach. His above-average speed plays better in center field than it does on the bases. He has improved his route-running and reads and projects as a possible Gold Glover as he adds more polish. Some teams liked him more as a pitcher coming out of high school, thanks to his athleticism and a fastball that reached 97 mph at times, and he retains excellent arm strength, his best present tool. Hicks could hone his swing and become a five-tool center fielder with 20-25 home run power who bats in the middle of a lineup. He also may wind up more as tablesetter, along the lines of Denard Span but with better defensive ability. He'll finally move up to high Class A Fort Myers in 2011.

Year	Club (League)	Class	AVG	G	AB	R	H	2B	3B	HR	RBI	BB	SO	SB	CS	OBP	SLG
2008	Twins (GCL)	R	.318	45	173	32	55	10	4	4	27	28	32	12	2	.409	.491
2009	Beloit (MWL)	LoA	.251	67	251	43	63	15	3	4	29	40	55	10	8	.353	.382
2010	Beloit (MWL)	LoA	.279	115	423	86	118	27	6	8	49	88	112	21	11	.401	.428
Minor League Totals			.279	227	847	161	236	52	13	16	105	156	199	43	21	.388	.427

3 MIGUEL SANO, 3B/SS

Born: May 11, 1993. **B-T:** R-R. **Ht.:** 6-3. **Wt.:** 230. **Signed:** Dominican Republic, 2009. **Signed by:** Fred Guerrero.

The Twins have dedicated more time, energy and money to signing players out of the Dominican Republic in recent years, and Sano is the crown jewel of those efforts. They spent $3.15 million on him in 2009 after sweating out a thorough MLB investigation into his age. Sano already has grown significantly since the Twins signed him, from 195 to 230 pounds. He has prodigious tools to go with his size, starting with ferocious raw power. The strength, bat speed, swing path and leverage are all there for him to hit 30 homers once he refines his approach and learns to recognize pitches. Like many young hitters, he sometimes struggles with spin, but he also shows encouraging opposite-field power. Though he split time between shortstop and third base in his 2010 pro debut, his range fits much better at the hot corner, where he shows solid hands and feet and plenty of arm strength. He projects as a below-average runner. Sano's future is tied up with how big he gets. If he doesn't grow much more, he should be able to hold down third base or an outfield corner. Even if he outgrows those spots, he could have enough bat for first base. Headed for Rookie-level Elizabethton in 2011, he has the higher ceiling among Twins farmhands.

Year	Club (League)	Class	AVG	G	AB	R	H	2B	3B	HR	RBI	BB	SO	SB	CS	OBP	SLG
2010	Twins (DSL)	R	.344	20	64	11	22	2	1	3	10	14	17	2	1	.463	.547
	Twins (GCL)	R	.291	41	148	23	43	14	0	4	19	10	43	2	2	.338	.466
Minor League Totals			.307	61	212	34	65	16	1	7	29	24	60	4	3	.379	.491

4 JOE BENSON, OF

RODGER WOOD

Born: March 5, 1988. **B-T:** R-R. **Ht.:** 6-1. **Wt.:** 211. **Drafted:** HS—Joliet, Ill., 2006 (2nd round). **Signed by:** Billy Milos.

Signed away from a Purdue football scholarship for a $575,000 bonus, Benson showed flashes of talent in his first four pro seasons. He also struggled with strikeouts and his own aggressiveness, which at times landed him on the disabled list. He had his best season in 2010, shaking off a mid-May demotion to earn his way back to Double-A New Britain a month later and lead the system with 27 homers. Benson still has five-tool ability, though he likely will never be more than an average hitter. His other tools all rate as 60s or 70s on the 20-80 scouting scale. His raw power would be the best in the system if not for Miguel Sano, and his speed ranks right behind Ben Revere's. Benson has fast hands and excellent strength, though he must trust his hands and let balls travel deeper in order to make more consistent contact. He needs to do a better job of identifying and laying off breaking balls. He has center-field range to go with a right-field arm. Scouts who saw Benson in the second half and in the Arizona Fall League were impressed by his offensive progress, as were the Twins, who added him to the 40-man roster. He'll advance to Triple-A in 2011 and could replace free-agent-to-be Michael Cuddyer in right field in 2012.

MINNESOTA TWINS

Year	Club (League)	Class	AVG	G	AB	R	H	2B	3B	HR	RBI	BB	SO	SB	CS	OBP	SLG
2006	Twins (GCL)	R	.260	52	196	30	51	11	5	5	28	21	41	9	10	.335	.444
	Beloit (MWL)	LoA	.263	8	19	2	5	0	0	0	1	0	6	1	0	.263	.263
2007	Beloit (MWL)	LoA	.255	122	432	73	110	18	8	5	38	49	124	18	16	.347	.368
2008	Beloit (MWL)	LoA	.248	69	254	39	63	16	3	4	27	24	73	17	11	.326	.382
2009	Twins (GCL)	R	.200	2	5	1	1	0	0	0	0	2	0	1	1	.429	.200
	Fort Myers (FSL)	HiA	.285	80	263	46	75	10	3	5	29	46	74	14	7	.414	.403
2010	Fort Myers (FSL)	HiA	.294	21	85	16	25	11	1	4	13	8	21	5	0	.375	.588
	New Britain (EL)	AA	.251	102	374	65	94	20	7	23	49	39	115	14	9	.336	.527
Minor League Totals			.260	456	1628	272	424	86	27	46	185	189	454	79	54	.352	.431

5 BEN REVERE, OF

Born: May 3, 1988. **B-T:** L-R. **Ht.:** 5-9. **Wt.:** 178. **Drafted:** HS—Lexington, Ky., 2007 (1st round). **Signed by:** Billy Corrigan.

Revere's $750,000 bonus remains the lowest for a healthy first-rounder since 1997. The Twins took him because he was the top player on their board, not to save money, and he has justified the decision by batting .328 in the minors. He played in the 2010 Futures Game and reached the big leagues for the first time in September after an errant pitch broke his jaw a month earlier. Revere's raw speed and quickness are as good as any Minnesota farmhand, and his speed is the most playable. He outruns his mistakes in center field and runs the bases with abandon, though he still can become a more efficient basestealer. Revere also is the system's best hitter, making contact easily and showing good feel for the barrel. While the Twins once projected him to have average power, they no longer have that conviction and he'll have to fend off power stuff inside. He has improved in terms of bunting and drawing walks, understanding that his focus is getting on base. His well below-average arm is his biggest weakness. The Twins see Revere as a potential top-of-the-order catalyst with Brett Gardner upside—a singles hitter who draws walks and steals bases. Minnesota's outfield is too crowded for him to jump to the majors full-time in 2011, so he'll get regular playing time in Triple-A.

Year	Club (League)	Class	AVG	G	AB	R	H	2B	3B	HR	RBI	BB	SO	SB	CS	OBP	SLG
2007	Twins (GCL)	R	.325	50	191	46	62	6	10	0	29	13	20	21	9	.388	.461
2008	Beloit (MWL)	LoA	.379	83	340	51	129	17	10	1	43	27	31	44	13	.433	.497
2009	Fort Myers (FSL)	HiA	.311	121	466	75	145	13	4	2	48	40	34	45	17	.372	.369
2010	New Britain (EL)	AA	.305	94	361	44	110	10	4	1	23	32	41	36	13	.371	.363
	Minnesota (AL)	MAJ	.179	13	28	1	5	0	0	0	2	2	5	0	1	.233	.179
Major League Totals			.179	13	28	1	5	0	0	0	2	2	5	0	1	.233	.179
Minor League Totals			.328	348	1358	216	446	46	28	4	143	112	126	146	52	.389	.412

6 LIAM HENDRIKS, RHP

Born: Feb. 10, 1989. **B-T:** R-R. **Ht.:** 6-1. **Wt.:** 201. **Signed:** Australia, 2007. **Signed by:** Howard Norsetter.

Hendriks' father played in Australian Rules Football and Hendriks also played the sport before the Twins signed him for $170,000 in 2007. He almost immediately had knee surgery (his second), then missed all of 2008 and half of 2009 following back surgery. He stayed healthy enough to make a run at the minor league ERA title last season, though an appendectomy in July knocked him out of the Futures Game. Hendriks repeats his compact, efficient delivery and pumps four quality pitches for strikes. He has good sinking life on his fastball, which sat at 86-91 mph early in the season but jumped to 90-93 mph when he returned from the appendectomy. His slider is tight and has late break, and some scouts consider it his best pitch. Others prefer his changeup, and his curveball—his best pitch prior to the back surgery—isn't far behind. He also throws a cutter at times. Hendriks has true command and a knack for making pitches, keeping the ball in the ballpark. Scouts in and out of the organization laud his makeup. Hendriks pitched in Australia's resurgent winter league in the offseason, getting useful extra work. He's ticketed for Double-A in 2011 and could become the best product of the Twins' extensive Australian scouting efforts.

Year	Club (League)	Class	W	L	ERA	G	GS	CG	SV	IP	H	HR	BB	SO	G/A	WHIP	AVG
2007	Twins (GCL)	R	4	2	2.05	10	10	0	0	44	41	2	11	52	—	1.18	.241
2008	Did not play—Injured																
2009	Elizabethton (APP)	R	2	0	3.71	3	3	0	0	17	19	0	1	13	1.57	1.18	.271
	Beloit (MWL)	LoA	3	5	3.51	11	11	0	0	67	73	3	15	62	2.16	1.32	.278
2010	Beloit (MWL)	LoA	2	1	1.32	6	6	0	0	34	16	0	4	39	1.52	0.59	.138
	Fort Myers (FSL)	HiA	6	3	1.93	13	12	1	0	75	63	2	8	66	1.70	0.95	.225
Minor League Totals			17	11	2.44	43	42	1	0	236	212	7	39	232	1.80	1.06	.236

RODGER WOOD

7 ALEX WIMMERS, RHP

RODGER WOOD

Born: Sept. 28, 1990. **B-T:** L-R. **Ht.:** 6-2. **Wt.:** 195. **Drafted:** Ohio State, 2010 (1st round). **Signed by:** Jay Weitzel.

Wimmers set the school record for career batting average (.457) at Cincinnati's Moeller High, the alma mater of Buddy Bell, Ken Griffey Jr. and Barry Larkin. He was strictly a pitcher in college, becoming Ohio State's ace and going 18-2 in his final two seasons. A hamstring strain limited him late last spring, but he still went 21st overall in the draft and pitched well in his brief pro debut —including five no-hit innings in his third start—after signing for $1.332 million. Wimmers fits the Twins' pitching model well, throwing strikes with three pitches that have a chance to be average or better. His best pitch is a changeup that's a tick above average now and projects as plus once he adds some life to it. He has excellent arm speed on the changeup, which is usually straight but has some sink at times. His lively fastball sits at 88-92 mph and reaches 94 at times. He needs to refine his fastball command, something Minnesota has a good track record of teaching. He's athletic and should improve his ability to repeat his delivery and throw consistent strikes. His curve gives him a third solid pitch. Wimmers isn't as polished as Kyle Gibson and doesn't have the same upside, but he could be an innings-eating No. 3 starter if his fastball command improves. Despite his late-season dominance in high Class A, he's likely to start 2011 back there.

Year	Club (League)	Class	W	L	ERA	G	GS	CG	SV	IP	H	HR	BB	SO	G/A	WHIP	AVG
2010	Fort Myers (FSL)	HiA	2	0	0.57	4	4	0	0	16	6	0	5	23	1.00	0.70	.113
Minor League Totals			2	0	0.57	4	4	0	0	16	6	0	5	23	1.00	0.70	.113

8 ADRIAN SALCEDO, RHP

Born: Feb. 5, 1991. **B-T:** R-R. **Ht.:** 6-4. **Wt.:** 175. **Signed:** Dominican Republic, 2007. **Signed by:** Fred Guerrero.

Salcedo emerged on the prospect scene by posting a 1.46 ERA and 58-3 K-BB ratio in the Rookie-level Gulf Coast League in 2009. His ability and injuries at Fort Myers prompted the Twins to move him from extended spring training to high Class A last May. He got hit hard but regrouped and showed more trust in his secondary pitches when sent to Elizabethton, his originally planned destination. Long and thin, Salcedo has room to grow physically but is mature mentally. He's the system's hardest worker, establishing that reputation even as a teenager. His 90-93 mph fastball features late action, as does his changeup. He throws both a slider and a curveball, with his slurvy slider reaching the low 80s. It can get a little big, and Salcedo must focus on either tightening his slider or committing to more of a true curveball. He has excellent movement on all of his pitches, yet manages to throw them for strikes. Thanks to his sound delivery and excellent athleticism, he projects to have at least average command. The Twins usually move pitchers slowly, but Salcedo's stuff, feel and dedication could put him on the fast track. He's slated to start 2011 in low Class A.

Year	Club (League)	Class	W	L	ERA	G	GS	CG	SV	IP	H	HR	BB	SO	G/A	WHIP	AVG
2008	Twins (DSL)	R	4	4	1.65	12	12	0	0	65	47	1	8	50	—	0.84	.198
2009	Twins (GCL)	R	3	2	1.46	11	10	0	0	62	60	1	3	58	2.15	1.02	.241
2010	Fort Myers (FSL)	HiA	1	3	6.26	6	6	0	0	27	42	3	8	16	2.00	1.83	.378
	Elizabethton (APP)	R	4	3	3.27	16	8	0	1	66	55	3	10	65	1.77	0.98	.230
Minor League Totals			12	12	2.66	45	36	0	1	220	204	8	29	189	1.96	1.06	.244

9 OSWALDO ARCIA, OF

Born: May 9, 1991. **B-T:** L-R. **Ht.:** 6-0. **Wt.:** 215. **Signed:** Venezuela, 2007. **Signed by:** Jose Leon.

The Twins have international outfield depth in their farm system. A Venezuelan, Arcia pushed himself past German teenager Max Kepler, Puerto Rican toolshed Angel Morales and solid Canadian Rene Tosoni in 2010. He led the Rookie-level Appalachian League in nine categories, including batting (.375), on-base percentage (.424) and slugging (.672) while winning MVP honors. Arcia has has good plate coverage and a sound, strong swing, giving him present hitting and power-hitting ability. He already hits balls to all fields with some authority, though he'll need to make more consistent contact. He got plenty of experience against offspeed pitches last season, getting a steady diet of them after getting off to a fast start. Previously a switch-hitter, he has batted solely lefthanded since leaving the Rookie-level Dominican Summer League two years ago. Arcia has played a lot of center field and is a solid runner, but he projects better at a corner spot. Though his average arm could allow him to fit in right field, he may be better suited for left. Arcia earns comparisons to Bobby Abreu for his stance, hitting ability and body, though he lacks Abreu's trademark plate discipline. He'll be challenged to keep putting up Nintendo numbers at Beloit in 2011, when he'll play in cold weather for the first time.

Year	Club (League)	Class	AVG	G	AB	R	H	2B	3B	HR	RBI	BB	SO	SB	CS	OBP	SLG
2008	Twins (DSL)	R	.293	61	229	38	67	12	4	4	36	16	27	8	7	.343	.432
2009	Twins (GCL)	R	.275	44	167	20	46	11	2	5	24	15	18	8	0	.337	.455
2010	Elizabethton (APP)	R	.375	64	259	47	97	21	7	14	51	19	67	4	4	.424	.672
Minor League Totals			.321	169	655	105	210	44	13	23	111	50	112	20	11	.373	.533

10 CARLOS GUTIERREZ, RHP

Born: Sept. 22, 1986. **B-T:** L-R. **Ht.:** 6-3. **Wt.:** 210. **Drafted:** Miami, 2008 (1st round). **Signed by:** Hector Otero.

Gutierrez recoved from Tommy John surgery in 2007 to go 27th overall in the 2008 draft, signing for $1.29 million after serving as the closer on Miami's College World Series team. The Twins used him as a starter in 2009 and for the first half of 2010 before returning him to the bullpen after he struggled in Double-A. They signed his brother David, also a righthander, as an 18th-rounder in June. Gutierrez has a power sinker that has earned him Derek Lowe comparisons, though he throws harder, reaching 97 mph at times. His sinker was much more effective once he moved to the bullpen, getting 4.4 groundouts for every airout, compared to a 2.6 ratio as a starter. His slider is better than his changeup, though it's more of an average pitch than a true weapon. He needs to command it better against lefthanders and throw more strikes in general. He's a solid athlete who repeats his delivery. As soon as Gutierrez can throw consistent strikes with his sinker, he'll join Minnesota's bullpen. Free agency could leave several openings in the Twins' relief corps, giving him an outside chance to open 2011 in the big leagues. It's more likely that he'll begin the season in Triple-A.

Year	Club (League)	Class	W	L	ERA	G	GS	CG	SV	IP	H	HR	BB	SO	G/A	WHIP	AVG
2008	Fort Myers (FSL)	HiA	3	1	2.10	16	0	0	1	26	23	0	7	19	—	1.17	.240
2009	Fort Myers (FSL)	HiA	2	3	1.32	11	10	0	0	55	37	1	22	33	4.48	1.08	.192
	New Britain (EL)	AA	1	3	6.19	22	6	0	0	52	62	6	24	32	2.73	1.64	.300
2010	New Britain (EL)	AA	5	8	4.57	32	16	0	2	122	136	7	50	81	3.52	1.52	.291
	Rochester (IL)	AAA	0	0	2.25	2	0	0	0	4	5	0	2	6	1.50	1.75	.333
Minor League Totals			11	15	3.93	83	32	0	3	259	263	14	105	171	3.45	1.42	.269

11 MAX KEPLER, OF

Born: Feb. 10, 1993. **B-T:** L-L. **Ht.:** 6-4. **Wt.:** 180. **Signed:** Germany, 2009. **Signed by:** Mike Radcliff.

In addition to Miguel Sano, the Twins made another big international splash in 2009, giving Kepler the largest bonus ever for a European position player at $800,000. He's from Berlin and the son of ballet dancers, with his father being Polish, his mother American. Scouts often describe him as balletic or graceful, because they like the joke and because he's an athletic, coordinated big man. His athleticism allowed Kepler to step in as a 17-year-old from Europe and hold his own in the Gulf Coast League last year while also earning his diploma at South Fort Myers (Fla.) High, across Plantation Road from the Twins' complex. His maturity helped make it work as well. Minnesota signed him for his impressive tools, particularly at the plate. He has a gap approach and an easy, low-maintenance swing that belies his age and experience. He has solid strength but has to learn to handle better pitching and how to loft the ball to develop above-average power. It's tricky projecting power on any 17-year-old, moreso one from Germany. Kepler has the range, speed and fringy arm strength to profile as an average defender in center field. He's raw in many baseball skills, such as running the bases and hitting the cutoff man. The Twins are as patient as any organization and Kepler has the makeup to grind through the low minors. He'll need it, as he'll advance one step at a time and play at Elizabethton in 2011.

Year	Club (League)	Class	AVG	G	AB	R	H	2B	3B	HR	RBI	BB	SO	SB	CS	OBP	SLG
2010	Twins (GCL)	R	.286	37	140	15	40	6	1	0	11	13	27	6	1	.346	.343
Minor League Totals			.286	37	140	15	40	6	1	0	11	13	27	6	1	.346	.343

12 RENE TOSONI, OF

Born: July 2, 1986. **B-T:** L-R. **Ht.:** 6-0. **Wt.:** 195. **Drafted:** Chipola (Fla.) JC, D/F 2005 (36th round). **Signed by:** Jim Ridley.

Tosoni had a huge 2009, hitting a career-high 15 homers in Double-A, winning MVP honors at the Futures Game after delivering the game-winning hit and leading Canada to a third-place finish at the World Cup. Last season was the opposite. He injured his right shoulder during spring training, then tried to play through it. He lasted through the first week of June, playing all but eight games at DH, before having surgery to repair his labrum. Despite his lost year and their outfield depth, the Twins placed him on the 40-man roster this offseason to protect him from the Rule 5 draft. Even with a bad shoulder, Tosoni was one of New Britain's best hitters, and his pure swing remains his best attribute. He's a solid athlete with enough strength to shoot line drives to the gaps and develop average home run power. He has average speed and is a capable center fielder when healthy, though not good enough to profile as an everyday player there. He has an average arm and has good defensive instincts. On a perennial playoff team, like Minnesota is now, he profiles best as an extra outfielder rather than as a regular. If healthy, Tosoni will advance to Triple-A this year.

Year	Club (League)	Class	AVG	G	AB	R	H	2B	3B	HR	RBI	BB	SO	SB	CS	OBP	SLG
2006	Did not play—Restricted																
2007	Elizabethton (APP)	R	.301	63	236	58	71	13	4	3	31	32	48	13	4	.407	.428
	Beloit (MWL)	LoA	.273	2	11	1	3	1	0	0	1	0	2	0	0	.273	.364
2008	Twins (GCL)	R	.667	2	6	3	4	0	0	1	3	0	1	0	0	.667	1.167
	Fort Myers (FSL)	HiA	.300	42	140	27	42	7	3	1	19	21	30	3	5	.408	.414
2009	New Britain (EL)	AA	.271	122	425	64	115	25	4	15	71	45	98	8	8	.360	.454
2010	New Britain (EL)	AA	.270	52	185	22	50	8	4	4	24	25	52	3	1	.369	.422
Minor League Totals			.284	283	1003	175	285	54	15	24	149	123	231	27	18	.381	.440

13 DAVID BROMBERG, RHP

Born: Sept. 14, 1987. **B-T:** R-R. **Ht.:** 6-5. **Wt.:** 241. **Drafted:** Santa Ana (Calif.) JC, D/F 2005 (32nd round). **Signed by:** Dan Cox.

The Twins drafted Bromberg in the 32nd round out of high school in 2005, even though he pushed 275 pounds, and signed him for $40,000 as a draft-and-follow the next spring, Since then, he has won three league strikeout crowns, reached Triple-A and earned a spot on the 40-man roster. Bromberg quietly had a solid 2010 season despite pitching on two awful teams, logging his third consecutive season with at least 150 innings. Strong and durable, he got better as the season wore on at maintaining his velocity and filling the strike the zone. Bromberg's solid-average curveball rates as the best in the organization. He can throw it for strikes or use it as a chase pitch when he's ahead in the count. More advanced hitters haven't chased it as much as lower-level batters did, which accounts for his declining strikeout rate since he led the minors in whiffs in 2008. Bromberg has enough fastball, touching 94-95 at times, to work up in the zone to set up his curve. He has an 86-92 mph two-seamer to induce early-count contact, as well as an average changeup that he used to hold lefthanders to a .229 average last season. Bromberg's elbow gets low in his delivery, causing his stuff to flatten out at times and costing him command, but he has become more consistent in maintaining his delivery. He projects as a back-of-the-rotation innings-eater and should start 2011 anchoring Rochester's rotation along with Kyle Gibson.

Year	Club (League)	Class	W	L	ERA	G	GS	CG	SV	IP	H	HR	BB	SO	G/A	WHIP	AVG
2006	Twins (GCL)	R	3	3	2.66	10	10	2	0	51	42	2	18	31	—	1.18	.230
2007	Elizabethton (APP)	R	9	0	2.78	13	11	0	0	58	45	4	32	81	—	1.32	.211
2008	Beloit (MWL)	LoA	9	10	4.44	27	27	0	0	150	149	10	54	177	—	1.35	.262
2009	Fort Myers (FSL)	HiA	13	4	2.70	27	26	1	0	153	125	6	63	148	0.78	1.23	.224
2010	New Britain (EL)	AA	5	5	3.62	17	17	0	0	99	105	4	35	65	0.73	1.41	.273
	Rochester (IL)	AAA	1	4	3.98	9	9	0	0	52	47	9	13	47	0.76	1.15	.234
Minor League Totals			40	26	3.45	103	100	3	0	564	513	35	215	549	0.76	1.29	.243

14 ANGEL MORALES, OF

Born: Nov. 24, 1989. **B-T:** R-R. **Ht.:** 6-1. **Wt.:** 195. **Drafted:** HS—Caguas, P.R., 2007 (3rd round). **Signed by:** Hector Otero.

The Twins have drafted an outfielder from Puerto Rico early in three of the last four drafts, starting with Morales in the third round in 2007. He still has the highest ceiling of the group, which also includes Danny Ortiz (fourth round, 2008) and Eddie Rosario (fourth, 2010), but Morales hasn't made tremendous progress in four pro seasons. As a right fielder with power and speed, his tools compare to those of Joe Benson. Morales isn't quite as explosive an athlete as Benson, though, and he continues to produce plenty of empty swings as he moves up the ladder. He still struggles with pitch recognition and offspeed stuff. He hasn't smoothed out his two-part swing, which leaves him with some holes he can't close. If he learns to trust his hands and stay back on breaking balls, Morales could take off as a hitter, because he has plenty of bat speed and raw power. The Twins weren't concerned that he hit just five homers in 2010, as he spent the majority of his season in the larger parks of the high Class A Florida State League. His speed and arm are plus tools, and his arm is as accurate as it is strong. He doesn't get the most out of his physical ability because his instincts are lacking and he's too aggressive. Minnesota will be patient with Morales, giving him a chance to add polish and sending him back to Fort Myers to start 2011.

Year	Club (League)	Class	AVG	G	AB	R	H	2B	3B	HR	RBI	BB	SO	SB	CS	OBP	SLG
2007	Twins (GCL)	R	.256	38	121	18	31	6	3	2	15	12	44	11	5	.357	.405
2008	Elizabethton (APP)	R	.301	54	183	33	55	12	1	15	28	26	72	7	2	.413	.623
2009	Beloit (MWL)	LoA	.266	115	376	63	100	22	5	13	62	30	104	19	6	.329	.455
2010	Beloit (MWL)	LoA	.289	60	211	34	61	13	7	4	36	24	65	18	7	.381	.474
	Fort Myers (FSL)	HiA	.272	73	261	35	71	11	3	1	19	28	75	11	5	.347	.349
Minor League Totals			.276	340	1152	183	318	64	19	35	160	120	360	66	25	.360	.456

15 BILLY BULLOCK, RHP

Born: Feb. 27, 1988. **B-T:** R-R. **Ht.:** 6-6. **Wt.:** 225. **Drafted:** Florida, 2009 (2nd round). **Signed by:** Billy Corrigan.

With their bullpen in flux, the Twins have internal options if they can't find help on the free-agent market. They include Bullock, who has one of the system's better arms and reached Double-A in 2010, his first full pro season. Despite pitching on poor teams, he ranked 11th in the minors with 27 saves, and his 105 strikeouts placed fourth among minor league relievers who didn't start a game. Bullock's velocity took a dive during instructional league in 2009, but he bumped his fastball back to 92-94 mph last year, touching 95 regularly. He drives his fastball downhill and has some armside run when he's at his best. Bullock lacked the fastball command and feel for pitching to succeed as a starter in college, which is when he moved to the bullpen, and his command remains an issue. His slider has its moments where it's a low-80s pitch with depth and power, though it can get slurvy at times. He also throws a changeup on occasion. Bullock isn't efficient and can give up some big innings, but he has the short memory and repertoire required for late-inning work. He could factor into Minnesota's mix in 2011, though he'll have to improve his command to be the club's future closer.

Year	Club (League)	Class	W	L	ERA	G	GS	CG	SV	IP	H	HR	BB	SO	G/A	WHIP	AVG
2009	Elizabethton (APP)	R	1	0	1.23	7	0	0	3	7	3	0	1	10	1.17	0.55	.125
	Beloit (MWL)	LoA	3	0	2.73	26	0	0	8	26	25	0	12	35	0.54	1.41	.253
2010	Fort Myers (FSL)	HiA	0	4	3.62	28	0	0	14	37	39	2	19	45	2.24	1.55	.281
	New Britain (EL)	AA	2	4	3.44	30	0	0	13	37	34	3	24	60	1.24	1.58	.239
Minor League Totals			6	8	3.18	91	0	0	38	108	101	5	56	150	1.19	1.46	.250

16 MANUEL SOLIMAN, RHP

Born: Aug. 11, 1989. **B-T:** R-R. **Ht.:** 6-2. **Wt.:** 195. **Signed:** Dominican Republic, 2007. **Signed by:** Fred Guerrero.

The Twins signed Soliman as a third baseman, but it clearly wasn't working out. He hit just .199/.318/.288 and committed 37 errors in two seasons in the Rookie-level Dominican Summer League. Minnesota decided to try Soliman on the mound, and he has become one of their hardest-throwing starting pitching prospects in short order. He'll have to be protected on the 40-man roster after the 2011 season, so he could get pushed a bit faster than the average Twins prospect, and he has the raw stuff to make it work. Soliman sits at 90-93 mph with his fastball and hits 94. He could find more velocity if he becomes more consistent with his arm slot and release point, as he tends to drop down and get on the side of the ball. When he keeps his hand behind the ball, he gets good late life on his fastball, which can be heavy in the bottom of the strike zone at its best. He throws a power slider that sits in the mid-80s, though it lacks depth when he gets on the side of it. He also has surprising feel for a changeup for someone so new to pitching. Soliman throws strikes but doesn't have the command potential of most of Minnesota pitching prospects. He'll have to get more consistent with his tempo and delivery to throw more quality strikes against better opponents. Soliman has intriguing upside in a system that could use some strong-armed starters. He's likely to start 2011 in Beloit, with a good chance to finish the year in Fort Myers.

Year	Club (League)	Class	W	L	ERA	G	GS	CG	SV	IP	H	HR	BB	SO	G/A	WHIP	AVG
2009	Twins (DSL)	R	6	2	2.15	14	14	0	0	71	66	0	20	55	1.17	1.21	.244
2010	Elizabethton (APP)	R	5	2	3.48	12	12	0	0	65	47	5	21	74	0.88	1.05	.201
Minor League Totals			11	4	2.79	26	26	0	0	136	113	5	41	129	1.04	1.14	.224

Year	Club (League)	Class	AVG	G	AB	R	H	2B	3B	HR	RBI	BB	SO	SB	CS	OBP	SLG
2007	Twins (DSL)	R	.189	63	201	22	38	4	0	4	16	26	46	5	3	.305	.269
2008	Twins (DSL)	R	.211	58	185	26	39	11	2	1	26	30	39	2	1	.332	.308
Minor League Totals			.199	121	386	48	77	15	2	5	42	56	85	7	4	.318	.288

17 JORGE POLANCO, SS/2B

Born: July 5, 1993. **B-T:** B-R. **Ht.:** 5-11. **Wt.:** 165. **Signed:** Dominican Republic, 2009. **Signed by:** Fred Guerrero.

The Twins have linked Polanco and Miguel Sano, signing them as part of their 2009 international class and sending them to the Dominican Summer League to start 2010. They came to the U.S. together on July 4, debuted the next day (Polanco's 17th birthday) and spent the rest of the season in the Gulf Coast League. Polanco split time at shortstop and second base there with 2010 second-round pick Niko Goodrum. Polanco has top-shelf defensive tools at shortstop, with his actions, range, hands and arm strength all rating above average. His bat isn't as advanced as his glove, and he realizes he'll have to play small ball to contribute offensively. A switch-hitter, he focuses on making contact and has the makings of good plate discipline. He needs to add strength but won't ever provide much power. Polanco is more quick than fast and won't be a big basestealing threat, though he has plus speed under way. He has impressed Minnesota with his work ethic and leadership qualities. Polanco's bat will dictate whether he's a future regular or a utility player, but his glove and makeup should get him to the majors. He's slated to join Sano at Elizabethton in 2011.

Year	Club (League)	Class	AVG	G	AB	R	H	2B	3B	HR	RBI	BB	SO	SB	CS	OBP	SLG
2010	Twins (DSL)	R	.250	18	60	5	15	2	0	0	7	6	9	1	3	.309	.283
	Twins (GCL)	R	.223	34	103	12	23	5	0	1	12	12	9	2	4	.299	.301
Minor League Totals			.233	52	163	17	38	7	0	1	19	18	18	3	7	.303	.294

18 CHRIS PARMELEE, 1B/OF

Born: Feb. 24, 1988. **B-T:** L-L. **Ht.:** 6-1. **Wt.:** 222. **Drafted:** HS—Chino Hills, Calif., 2006 (1st round). **Signed by:** John Leavitt.

Parmelee finally reached Double-A in 2010, his fourth full season since signing for $1.5 million as the 20th overall pick in the 2006 draft. He hit just .186 in the first six weeks, prompting a monthlong demotion to high Class A. Rene Tosoni's shoulder injury opened an outfield spot back in New Britain, and Parmelee took advantage of his second chance, batting .304 the rest of the way. Parmelee was drafted high for his line-drive swing and power potential, and his stroke remains pretty. He's short to the ball and uses the whole field while controlling the strike zone with a mature approach. Though he hit just eight homers in 2010, the Twins know he has plus raw power and had him focus on cutting down his strikeouts in the second half. He struck out 29 times in his first 102 at-bats in Double-A, then just 41 times in his 309 at-bats after rejoining New Britain. With a thick, unathletic body and below-average arm, Parmelee has moved down the defensive spectrum to first base, with occasional stops on the outfield corners. He has improved around the bag at first and isn't a liability there anymore. For Parmelee to be an impact player, he'll have to keep making contact while hitting for more power. While he batted .339 in the Arizona Fall League, he didn't homer in 109 at-bats. Parmelee did enough last year to get a 40-man roster spot, and he could earn a job in Triple-A with a strong spring.

Year	Club (League)	Class	AVG	G	AB	R	H	2B	3B	HR	RBI	BB	SO	SB	CS	OBP	SLG
2006	Twins (GCL)	R	.279	45	154	29	43	7	4	8	32	23	47	3	3	.369	.532
	Beloit (MWL)	LoA	.227	11	22	2	5	1	0	0	2	5	9	0	2	.370	.273
2007	Beloit (MWL)	LoA	.239	128	447	56	107	23	5	15	70	46	137	8	4	.313	.414
2008	Beloit (MWL)	LoA	.239	69	226	41	54	10	3	14	49	52	83	3	1	.385	.496
2009	Fort Myers (FSL)	HiA	.258	123	422	61	109	27	1	16	73	65	109	2	2	.359	.441
2010	Fort Myers (FSL)	HiA	.338	22	80	9	27	2	1	2	17	13	11	0	1	.430	.463
	New Britain (EL)	AA	.275	111	411	51	113	25	2	6	44	43	70	3	2	.341	.389
Minor League Totals			.260	509	1762	249	458	95	16	61	287	247	466	19	15	.352	.436

19 NIKO GOODRUM, SS/2B

Born: Feb. 28, 1992. **B-T:** B-R. **Ht.:** 6-3. **Wt.:** 180. **Drafted:** HS—Fayetteville, Ga., 2010 (2nd round). **Signed by:** Jack Powell.

The Twins' international spending spree in 2009 focused on athletes in part because the domestic draft was short in that regard. They wanted to get back to more athletes in the 2010 draft, and the long, lean Goodrum was part of that focus. Minnesota drafted him 71st overall and signed him away from a Kennesaw State commitment with a slot bonus of $514,800. He emerged from the scrum of Georgia's amazing high school talent last year, and his plus-plus arm may have been the best in the state. Goodrum is raw at the plate, where he switch-hits and has some holes because of his long arms, and in the field, where he lacks classic infield actions. Goodrum generates leverage and raw power in his swing, and he's an above-average runner, especially under way. He has good hands and there's some thought he could wind up at third base eventually. However, some with the Twins believe he has enough athletic ability and the requisite work ethic to stick at shortstop, unless he gets too big. He has the frame to get much bigger and heavier—his father is a solid 6-foot-4 and 275 pounds—and could wind up as a right fielder with big power and arm strength. As one club official put it, "Whichever way the body goes, if he gets just a little bigger or a lot bigger, it will be a great body." The Twins will take it slow with Goodrum, who could wind up back in the Gulf Coast League or move up to Elizabethton this season.

Year	Club (League)	Class	AVG	G	AB	R	H	2B	3B	HR	RBI	BB	SO	SB	CS	OBP	SLG
2010	Twins (GCL)	R	.161	36	118	10	19	4	0	0	5	9	34	4	2	.219	.195
Minor League Totals			.161	36	118	10	19	4	0	0	5	9	34	4	2	.219	.195

20 DANIEL SANTANA, SS/2B

Born: Nov. 7, 1990. **B-T:** B-R. **Ht.:** 5-11. **Wt.:** 160. **Signed:** Dominican Republic, 2007. **Signed by:** Fred Guerrero.

While Miguel Sano and Jorge Polanco attracted more attention as big-money Dominican Republic signees in 2009, Santana was at the vanguard of the Twins' renewed efforts in the baseball hotbed. He signed in December 2007, soon after turning 17. Santana's bat may take a while to develop, but the Twins showed faith in him by jumping him to low Class A last May as they shuffled the system's middle infielders, and the dominoes left Beloit an infielder short. Santana wasn't ready for the colder weather or the level of competition but has the tools to play there in 2011. He'll need to polish up his hitting skills and become more aware of game situations on both sides of the ball. Santana is one of the organization's better runners, earning 70 grades on the 20-80 scouting scale, and has the first-step quickness to play either middle-infield spot. His plus arm, actions and footwork should make him a good defender at shortstop with experience, and scouts like how his hands work. Those hands also give him some pop at the plate, and Santana hit four homers in his month at Elizabethton last summer. His biggest problem offensively is his aggressiveness, as he often hacks at the first fastball he sees, rarely draws walks and gets himself out too often. He also needs more maturity, as Santana's inconsistent effort earns criticism inside and outside the organization. He'll be young for the Midwest League when he returns there as a 20-year-old this season.

Year	Club (League)	Class	AVG	G	AB	R	H	2B	3B	HR	RBI	BB	SO	SB	CS	OBP	SLG
2008	Twins (DSL)	R	.274	51	190	37	52	6	10	1	27	20	38	15	4	.343	.426
2009	Twins (GCL)	R	.265	44	170	30	45	7	5	3	25	8	27	12	1	.302	.418
2010	Elizabethton (APP)	R	.264	30	140	23	37	8	1	4	16	3	30	5	4	.285	.421
	Beloit (MWL)	LoA	.238	40	130	14	31	4	3	0	11	7	40	10	4	.289	.315
Minor League Totals			.262	165	630	104	165	25	19	8	79	38	135	42	13	.308	.400

21 EDDIE ROSARIO, OF

Born: Sept. 28, 1991. **B-T:** L-R. **Ht.:** 6-0. **Wt.:** 170. **Drafted:** HS—Guayama, P.R., 2010 (4th round). **Signed by:** Hector Otero.

Rosario was the highest-drafted player out of Puerto Rico in 2010, signing with Minnesota for $200,000 in the fourth round. He immediately started tearing up the Gulf Coast League, with three hits and a home run in his first start. His hitting success in the GCL wasn't unexpected, because scouts rated him as Puerto Rico's top amateur hitter heading into the draft. He has a short swing and a polished, professional approach at the plate, which along with his batting stance attract comparisons to Bobby Abreu. Rosario has average power and his other tools came a bit better than advertised, and he's not just a high-contact, high-average hitter. While most scouts who saw him as an amateur projected him as a right fielder with a plus throwing arm, the Twins see him sticking in center field. He has a tick above-average speed and has good instincts, helping his quickness play up in the outfield and on the bases. He succeeded in his first 17 steal attempts as a pro before wearing down and slowing down a bit late in the summer. Rosario will have to make adjustments at higher levels to get better at hitting lefthanders, but it's nothing he can't handle with experience. His polish could allow him to skip past Elizabethton and reach Beloit sometime in his first full pro season.

Year	Club (League)	Class	AVG	G	AB	R	H	2B	3B	HR	RBI	BB	SO	SB	CS	OBP	SLG
2010	Twins (GCL)	R	.294	51	194	34	57	9	2	5	26	16	28	22	5	.343	.438
Minor League Totals			.294	51	194	34	57	9	2	5	26	16	28	22	5	.343	.438

22 DAKOTA WATTS, RHP

Born: Nov. 16, 1987. **B-T:** R-R. **Ht.:** 6-5. **Wt.:** 210. **Drafted:** Cal State Stanislaus, 2009 (16th round). **Signed by:** Elliot Strankman.

Watts pitched at three California schools in his college years, at Feather River JC, San Joaquin Delta JC and NCAA Division II Cal State Stanislaus. The Twins had an eye on him the whole time, both when scouting director Deron Johnson was their West Coast crosschecker, then when he ran his second draft in 2009. Minnesota signed him for $15,000 as a 16th-round pick. Johnson saw Watts throw 93-95 mph as an amateur, and he continues to sit in that range as a pro while touching as high as 99. He has the best raw arm strength in the system and used it to reach Double-A in his first full season. Watts showed excellent durability throughout 2010, working with quality velocity even in back-to-back outings. His fastball has some armside run and he likes to elevate it for strikeouts. He also has a power curveball that comes in at around 80 mph with tight spin and good depth, allowing him to change hitters' eye levels. Watts' stiff front leg and herky-jerky delivery cost him command and extension out front. The Twins have several vacancies in their bullpen, and Watts has the arm to force himself into the picture. More than likely, he'll return to New Britain to open 2011.

Year	Club (League)	Class	W	L	ERA	G	GS	CG	SV	IP	H	HR	BB	SO	G/A	WHIP	AVG
2009	Twins (GCL)	R	0	0	0.00	6	0	0	4	9	1	0	3	10	2.40	0.43	.034
	Fort Myers (FSL)	HiA	0	2	14.85	5	0	0	0	7	10	0	10	6	0.86	3.00	.370
	Elizabethton (APP)	R	2	0	2.70	11	0	0	1	13	9	0	12	12	1.45	1.58	.196
2010	Beloit (MWL)	LoA	2	1	2.31	30	0	0	2	47	31	2	30	55	2.15	1.31	.193
	Fort Myers (FSL)	HiA	4	2	3.19	17	0	0	6	31	26	2	12	29	2.05	1.23	.228
	New Britain (EL)	AA	0	0	12.27	2	0	0	0	4	4	0	2	5	0.67	1.64	.267
Minor League Totals			8	5	3.50	71	0	0	13	111	81	4	69	117	1.85	1.36	.207

23 PAT DEAN, LHP

Born: May 25, 1989. **B-T:** L-L. **Ht.:** 6-1. **Wt.:** 175. **Drafted:** Boston College, 2010 (3rd round). **Signed by:** John Wilson.

The Twins have had success drafting and developing college lefthanders, getting big league production from Glen Perkins and Brian Duensing. They hope Dean can be next in line after signing him for $319,500 as a third-round pick last June. He somewhat resembles Perkins physically, though he's not quite as stocky. Perkins had more fastball velocity when he signed, but Dean has a four-pitch repertoire and a similar ceiling as a No. 4 starter. His compact delivery helps him throw quality strikes regularly, and he has a feel for the strike zone with all four of his pitches. Minnesota didn't push him in his pro debut because he had a strained elbow in the spring, but he had just one walk in 29 pro innings. Dean commands his fastball, which tops out at 93 but sits at 87-91 mph when he's at his best. He's not afraid to pitch inside with his fastball, which sets up his solid changeup on the outer half. The Twins like his ability to spin a breaking ball, and he throws both a slider and a curveball. His curve has true 12-to-6 break, while his slider has some depth but acts more like a cutter. He carved up younger hitters in his debut, constantly getting ahead in counts, and has the polish to move quickly. He could push for a spot in high Class A to start his first full pro season.

Year	Club (League)	Class	W	L	ERA	G	GS	CG	SV	IP	H	HR	BB	SO	G/A	WHIP	AVG
2010	Twins (GCL)	R	0	0	0.00	4	0	0	0	5	3	0	0	5	1.25	0.60	.176
	Elizabethton (APP)	R	2	2	2.59	5	5	0	0	24	17	3	1	32	1.11	0.74	.198
Minor League Totals			2	2	2.15	9	5	0	0	29	20	3	1	37	1.14	0.72	.194

24 TREVOR PLOUFFE, SS

Born: June 15, 1986. **B-T:** R-R. **Ht.:** 6-2. **Wt.:** 200. **Drafted:** HS—Northridge, Calif., 2004 (1st round). **Signed by:** Bill Mele.

The 20th overall pick in the 2004 draft and recipient of a $1.5 million bonus, Plouffe methodically has put himself into position to contribute in Minnesota and made his big league debut in 2010, getting two hits against the Brewers in his first game on May 21. He struggled for the most part, however, and spent most of his time in Minnesota as a pinch-runner and defensive replacement. Plouffe remains much the same player he's been since he was drafted. His best tool remains his strong arm, and he has become more consistent defensively as he has learned to take fewer chances with it. He doesn't have more than average range, but his arm allows him to make plays in the hole. Plouffe's hands are steady in the field and give him surprising power at the plate. He has earned comparisons over the years to Greg Gagne, Khalil Greene and J.J. Hardy for his average power and overly aggressive approach at the plate. He's a solid athlete and fringe-average runner. He could fit on Minnesota's bench for 2011, but the Twins' bid for Japanese infielder Tsuyoshi Nishioka shows they aren't comfortable with Plouffe as Hardy's replacement. If he doesn't stick in Minnesota in 2011, Plouffe likely is out of the organization's future plans.

Year	Club (League)	Class	AVG	G	AB	R	H	2B	3B	HR	RBI	BB	SO	SB	CS	OBP	SLG
2004	Elizabethton (APP)	R	.283	60	237	29	67	7	2	4	28	19	34	2	1	.340	.380
2005	Beloit (MWL)	LoA	.223	127	466	58	104	18	0	13	60	50	78	8	4	.300	.345
2006	Fort Myers (FSL)	HiA	.246	125	455	60	112	26	4	4	45	58	93	8	5	.333	.347
2007	New Britain (EL)	AA	.274	126	497	75	136	37	2	9	50	38	89	12	7	.326	.410
2008	New Britain (EL)	AA	.269	58	227	32	61	17	3	3	21	16	43	4	2	.325	.410
	Rochester (IL)	AAA	.256	66	250	34	64	17	3	6	39	14	47	1	1	.292	.420
2009	Rochester (IL)	AAA	.260	118	430	53	112	23	5	10	60	34	68	3	6	.313	.407
2010	Rochester (IL)	AAA	.244	102	402	53	98	22	4	15	49	27	90	5	5	.300	.430
	Minnesota (AL)	MAJ	.146	22	41	7	6	1	0	2	6	0	14	0	0	.143	.317
Major League Totals			.146	22	41	7	6	1	0	2	6	0	14	0	0	.143	.317
Minor League Totals			.254	782	2964	394	754	167	23	64	352	256	542	43	31	.316	.391

25 B.J. HERMSEN, RHP

Born: Dec. 1, 1989. **B-T:** R-R. **Ht.:** 6-5. **Wt.:** 240. **Drafted:** HS—Manchester, Iowa, 2008 (6th round). **Signed by:** Mark Wilson.

The Twins planned on having Hermsen spending 2010 in Elizabethon, but injuries at Beloit gave him the opportunity to make 12 starts in low Class A. He flirted with a no-hitter June 17, getting four outs away before settling for a one-hit shutout at Cedar Rapids. That game was only an hour from Hermsen's home, and he had plenty of friends and family in attendance. Perhaps he was amped up, because he had his best fastball of the year, sitting at 90-92 mph. The near no-no improved Hermsen's record to 4-1, 3.43, but he lost his last five starts at Beloit and was bumped back down to Elizabethton. He doesn't really have no-hit stuff, as he pitches to contact and presently doesn't have a plus pitch. Instead, he throws strikes with a four-pitch mix, highlighted by a two-seam fastball that sits at 86-89 mph. With his loose arm and easy delivery, he should develop more fastball velocity down the line. He has a big, durable body and profiles as a durable innings-eater, working off his sinking fastball and slider, which can reach the low 80s but lacks depth. Hermsen's curveball shows more promise but lacks power in the low 70s, and he also has some feel for his changeup. If he adds velocity to his fastball and curve, he'll fit perfectly into Minnesota's pitching mold with his projected durability and feel for the strike zone. Hermsen is ready to return to low Class A for a full season in 2011.

Year	Club (League)	Class	W	L	ERA	G	GS	CG	SV	IP	H	HR	BB	SO	G/A	WHIP	AVG
2009	Twins (GCL)	R	6	2	1.35	10	10	1	0	53	32	0	4	42	1.90	0.68	.171
2010	Beloit (MWL)	LoA	4	6	5.00	12	12	1	0	72	85	6	15	46	1.21	1.39	.295
	Elizabethton (APP)	R	2	2	3.32	8	6	0	0	38	39	2	4	39	1.96	1.13	.257
Minor League Totals			12	10	3.42	30	28	2	0	163	156	8	23	127	1.54	1.10	.249

26 BRUCE PUGH, RHP

Born: July 18, 1988. **B-T:** R-R. **Ht.:** 6-3. **Wt.:** 176. **Drafted:** Hillsborough (Fla.) CC, 2008 (19th round). **Signed by:** Billy Corrigan.

Pugh wasn't a highly-touted amateur. He went to high school in the Baltimore area, then attended Louisburg (N.C.) JC before transferring to higher-profile Hillsborough (Fla.) CC as a sophomore. The Twins spotted him at Hillsborough in 2008 and selected him in the 19th round, signing him for $150,000. He since has emerged as one of their liveliest arms. Pugh has unorthodox mechanics that make his pitches hard to pick up. He throws across his body and from a low three-quarters slot, delivering fastballs that sit at 91-95 mph. At times, his slider can be a swing-and-miss pitch with some depth. His changeup is just fair but plays up because of his deception and the fact that hitters have to cheat to catch up to his fastball. While Pugh's mechanics make him tough on hitters, they're tough to repeat, and his low-elbow delivery causes his fastball and slider to flatten out on occasion. He walked 4.6 batters per nine innings in 2010, too many to stay in the rotation long-term. He has yet to fill out his wiry frame and could use some more strength and stamina. He has enough athleticism to improve his control a bit, and he fields his position well. Pugh's lack of fastball command probably relegates him to a future bullpen role, but he'll continue to start in Double-A this year.

Year	Club (League)	Class	W	L	ERA	G	GS	CG	SV	IP	H	HR	BB	SO	G/A	WHIP	AVG
2008	Twins (GCL)	R	1	2	3.20	13	0	0	2	25	18	1	17	26	—	1.38	.202
2009	Beloit (MWL)	LoA	4	5	2.86	35	8	0	0	85	71	4	47	99	0.89	1.39	.228
2010	Fort Myers (FSL)	HiA	7	10	4.03	20	19	0	0	103	81	10	48	106	0.83	1.26	.215
	New Britain (EL)	AA	0	2	15.43	2	2	0	0	7	15	2	8	4	0.27	3.29	.429
Minor League Totals			12	19	3.85	70	29	0	2	220	185	17	120	235	0.82	1.39	.228

27 TOM STUIFBERGEN, RHP

Born: Sept. 26, 1988. **B-T:** R-R. **Ht.:** 6-3. **Wt.:** 256. **Signed:** The Netherlands, 2006. **Signed by:** Andy Johnson.

Stuifbergen is trying to beat Max Kepler to the majors to become the first big league product of the Twins' European scouting efforts. A Netherlands native, Stuifbergen has become his homeland's go-to pitcher in international baseball, tossing four scoreless innings against the Dominican Republic in a memorable 2009 World Baseball Classic victory and matching up with Cuba in October's Intercontinental Cup. Stuifbergen thrived when healthy as he jumped to full-season ball for the first time in 2010, but he missed six weeks at midseason with an elbow strain and didn't pitch as well in the second half after his return. At his best, he has a feel for pitching that belies the stereotypes of European players. He adds and subtracts from his fastball, touching 93 at times after lulling hitters to sleep with a mid-80s sinker. Stuifbergen learned his curveball from the patron saint of Dutch baseball, Bert Blyleven, and at times it's a plus pitch. So is his changeup, a solid-average offering. Stuifbergen needs to show he can stay healthy, and his 260-pound frame could use firming up. Despite his size, he repeats his easy delivery and pounds the strike zone. He projects to have average big league command, if not a tick above. The Twins would like to see better maturity in terms of his fitness as well as mound demeanor, but a healthy Stuifbergen could jump on the fast track in 2011, starting with a stint in high Class A.

Year	Club (League)	Class	W	L	ERA	G	GS	CG	SV	IP	H	HR	BB	SO	G/A	WHIP	AVG
2007	Twins (GCL)	R	0	0	2.19	7	0	0	0	12	6	0	3	9	—	0.73	.140
2008	Did not play—Injured																
2009	Elizabethton (APP)	R	5	2	3.28	13	13	1	0	80	79	4	6	69	2.45	1.07	.257
	Fort Myers (FSL)	HiA	0	0	10.13	1	1	0	0	3	5	0	1	3	3.00	2.25	.385
2010	Beloit (MWL)	LoA	6	4	2.98	19	17	0	0	94	99	5	23	88	1.40	1.30	.273
Minor League Totals			11	6	3.15	40	31	1	0	188	189	9	33	169	1.83	1.18	.261

28 ANTHONY SLAMA, RHP

Born: Jan. 6, 1984. **B-T:** R-R. **Ht.:** 6-3. **Wt.:** 204. **Drafted:** San Diego, D/F 2006 (39th round). **Signed by:** John Leavitt.

Slama had a big year in 2010, becoming the lowest-drafted pitcher (39th round) ever to appear in the Futures Game, which was played in Anaheim, virtually down the street from his family's Orange County home. Then he earned his first major league callup, making his debut with two strikeouts in a scoreless inning against the Indians. He stuck around the majors for about two weeks before going back to Triple-A, and he wasn't as effective after his return. The Twins already have gotten a fine return on their $4,000 investment in Slama, whom they signed as a fifth-year senior draft-and-follow in June 2007. He has some deception, especially with his front arm and fairly easy delivery, that helps his average stuff play up. He relies mostly on an 88-92 mph fastball that can touch 94 and a high-70s slurve, with a changeup mixed in from time to time. He works on missing down when he does miss and generally does that, having allowed just 10 homers in 249 minor league innings. Slama tries to study hitters and their swings so he can pitch to their weaknesses. He has dominated with that approach in the minors, with a 1.95 career ERA, but scouts remain skeptical that he'll succeed in the majors. He may need better command to make his average pitches work against big league hitters. Minnesota has opportunities available in its 2011 bullpen, and Slama will get his chance to earn a middle-relief spot.

Year	Club (League)	Class	W	L	ERA	G	GS	CG	SV	IP	H	HR	BB	SO	G/A	WHIP	AVG
2007	Elizabethton (APP)	R	0	0	2.45	6	0	0	4	7	2	0	1	10	—	0.41	.091
	Beloit (MWL)	LoA	1	1	1.48	21	0	0	10	24	15	0	9	39	—	0.99	.172
2008	Fort Myers (FSL)	HiA	4	1	1.01	51	0	0	25	71	43	0	24	110	—	0.94	.173
2009	New Britain (EL)	AA	4	2	2.48	51	0	0	25	65	46	5	32	93	0.74	1.19	.201
	Rochester (IL)	AAA	0	2	3.45	11	0	0	4	16	11	0	8	19	1.23	1.21	.212
2010	Minnesota (AL)	MAJ	0	1	7.71	5	0	0	0	5	6	1	5	5	0.50	2.36	.300
	Rochester (IL)	AAA	2	2	2.20	54	0	0	17	65	41	5	32	74	1.30	1.12	.178
Major League Totals			0	1	7.71	5	0	0	0	5	6	1	5	5	1.30	2.36	.300
Minor League Totals			11	8	1.95	194	0	0	85	249	158	10	106	345	1.02	1.06	.182

29 SCOTT DIAMOND, LHP

Born: July 30, 1986. **B-T:** L-L. **Ht.:** 6-3. **Wt.:** 210. **Signed:** Binghamton, NDFA, 2007). **Signed by:** Paul Faulk/Lonnie Goldberg (Braves).

The Braves are so deep in pitching that they club couldn't find room to protect Diamond on their 40-man roster after he went from a nondrafted free agent to Triple-A in three pro seasons. As was the case with another Atlanta NDFA success, Brandon Beachy, Diamond signed with the Braves after starring in a summer college league. He earned a $50,000 bonus after going 6-2, 2.55 in the Coastal Plain League in 2007. The Twins had scouted Diamond as an amateur, and also saw him pitch for Canada during the 2009 World Baseball Classic and 2010 Pan Am Qualifier. Those reports convinced Minnesota to take him in the major league Rule 5 draft at the 2010 Winter Meetings. Diamond throws four pitches, using a high arm slot to work up and down in the strike zone. He throws downhill and has a curveball that's a plus pitch at its best. Diamond drives his 86-91 mph fastball down through the strike zone and allowed just six homers in 159 innings last year. His slider and changeup have their moments, helping him keep righthanders off balance. While Diamond throws strikes, he lacks premium command, and his ceiling is as a fourth or fifth starter. He's more likely to fill a long-relief or lefty-specialist role if he makes Minnesota's 25-man roster in 2011. If he fails, the Twins have to put him through waivers and offer him back to the Braves before they could send him to the minors.

Year	Club (League)	Class	W	L	ERA	G	GS	CG	SV	IP	H	HR	BB	SO	G/A	WHIP	AVG
2008	Rome (SAL)	LoA	3	1	3.08	9	9	0	0	53	47	2	11	38	--	1.10	.240
	Myrtle Beach (CAR)	HiA	12	2	2.79	17	15	1	0	100	95	6	28	85	--	1.23	.245
2009	Mississippi (SL)	AA	5	10	3.50	23	23	0	0	131	152	5	53	111	1.76	1.56	.294
2010	Mississippi (SL)	AA	4	6	3.52	17	17	0	0	102	113	4	39	90	2.42	1.49	.288
	Gwinnett (IL)	AAA	4	1	3.36	10	10	1	0	56	53	2	15	33	1.86	1.21	.260
Minor League Totals			28	20	3.28	76	74	2	0	442	460	19	146	357	1.97	1.37	.271

30 BRIAN DOZIER, INF

Born: May 15, 1987. **B-T:** R-R. **Ht.:** 5-11. **Wt.:** 190. **Drafted:** Southern Mississippi, 2009 (8th round). **Signed by:** Earl Winn.

Dozier had one of the best careers in Southern Mississippi history, batting .355 as a four-year starter. He missed the Golden Eagles' Cinderella run to the 2009 College World Series with a broken collarbone, though he pinch-hit in Omaha. He pushed his way up to high Class A in 2010, his first full season, even after missing 2009 instructional league so he could return to Southern Miss and pick up his degree. Dozier doesn't have any above-average tools but he does a lot of things well and has plenty of polish. He controls the strike zone well and has a contact-oriented, all-fields approach at the plate. He handles the bat well enough to profile as a No. 2 hitter. His biggest weakness is his lack of power, as he doesn't project to hit more than 5-10 homers annually. He has average speed, runs the bases well and plays the game intelligently. Dozier's fundamental approach to the game carries over to the defensive side, where he's good enough to handle shortstop at the lower levels but fits better at second because of his fringy arm strength. He also saw time at third base last season and in center field during instructional league. Dozier figures to jump to Double-A this year.

Year	Club (League)	Class	AVG	G	AB	R	H	2B	3B	HR	RBI	BB	SO	SB	CS	OBP	SLG
2009	Twins (GCL)	R	.286	5	14	1	4	0	0	0	0	2	1	0	0	.375	.286
	Elizabethton (APP)	R	.353	53	218	38	77	17	0	0	14	23	26	3	0	.417	.431
2010	Beloit (MWL)	LoA	.278	39	151	24	42	7	1	0	17	16	16	6	1	.347	.338
	Fort Myers (FSL)	HiA	.274	93	350	44	96	11	1	5	42	44	41	10	4	.352	.354
Minor League Totals			.299	190	733	107	219	35	2	5	73	85	84	19	5	.371	.372

New York Mets

BY MATT EDDY

Omar Minaya seemingly could do no wrong in the early part of his tenure as Mets general manager. He lured premium free agents Carlos Beltran, Pedro Martinez and Billy Wagner to Queens with rich contract offers. He parted with very little in trades for veterans Luis Castillo, Carlos Delgado and Paul LoDuca. He re-signed franchise cornerstones Jose Reyes and David Wright to club-friendly extensions that bought out arbitration years.

But the Mets seemed to unravel thread by thread after the 2006 edition advanced to within one game of the World Series. The 2007 and '08 teams endured

brutal September collapses. With a payroll of $142.2 million, second only to the crosstown Yankees, the 2009 club lost 92 times. Complete meltdown might have been averted if the farm system had been able to cover for a host of injuries at the big league level.

Some players from the farm began to matriculate to Citi Field in 2010, when a mediocre 79-win Mets team received contributions from four of its top prospects: Ike Davis, Jon Niese, Ruben Tejada and Josh Thole.

But the prospect breakthroughs proved to be too little, too late for Minaya, whose six-year reign as GM ended in October. New York went 506-466 on his watch but suffocated under the weight of diminished returns from expensive veterans and subpar farm system performance.

In late October, New York hired Sandy Alderson to replace Minaya. Alderson most recently had worked in the commissioner's office, where he investigated fraud and corruption in the Dominican Republic. He's most notable as the architect of Athletics teams that won four division titles, three pennants and one World Series from 1988-92. He served as Oakland GM for 14 years from 1983-1997 and also worked as CEO of the Padres from 2005-09.

Alderson immediately hired two associates from his A's days: J.P. Ricciardi as special assistant and Paul DePodesta as vice president of player development and amateur scouting. Both have recent GM experience. In November, the Mets hired Terry Collins as manager, partially because he served as field coordinator in 2010 and already knows the minor league personnel.

Alderson also reassigned scouting director Rudy Terrasas, who hadn't done much in five drafts to distinguish himself—though that may be a function of ownership's wish to heed MLB's slot recommendations. In his five drafts, New York spent a total of $20.6 million on bonuses, the second-lowest total in

General manager Sandy Alderson replaces Omar Minaya, who spent six years in charge

TOP 30 PROSPECTS

1. Jenrry Mejia, rhp	16. Dillon Gee, rhp
2. Wilmer Flores, ss	17. Erik Goeddel, rhp
3. Cesar Puello, of	18. Steve Matz, lhp
4. Matt Harvey, rhp	19. Zach Lutz, 3b
5. Kirk Nieuwenhuis, of	20. Robbie Shields, ss
6. Reese Havens, 2b	21. Brad Emaus, 3b/2b
7. Lucas Duda, of/1b	22. Mark Cohoon, lhp
8. Fernando Martinez, of	23. Matt den Dekker, of
9. Aderlin Rodriguez, 3b	24. Armando Rodriguez, rhp
10. Brad Holt, rhp	25. Jordany Valdespin, 2b/ss
11. Juan Urbina, lhp	26. Jefry Marte, 3b
12. Robert Carson, lhp	27. Kyle Allen, rhp
13. Jeurys Familia, rhp	28. Manny Alvarez, rhp
14. Darrell Ceciliani, of	29. Blake Forsythe, c
15. Cory Vaughn, of	30. Pedro Beato, rhp

baseball. The Mets hired Chad MacDonald, former international scouting director for the Diamondbacks, to replace Terrasas.

The Mets continued to be more aggressive internationally than in the draft in 2010, handing six-figure bonuses to Venezuelan outfielder Vicente Lupo and Dominican third baseman Elvis Sanchez, who drew positive reviews for their raw power. They join a growing contingency of Latin American prospects in the system, headlined by righthander Jenrry Mejia, shortstop Wilmer Flores and outfielder Cesar Puello—the Mets' three best prospects.

General Manager: Sandy Alderson. **Farm Director:** Adam Wogan. **Scouting Director:** Chad MacDonald.

Class	Team	League	W	L	PCT	Finish*	Manager
Majors	New York Mets	National	79	83	.488	10th (16)	Jerry Manuel
Triple-A	Buffalo Bisons	International	76	68	.528	5th (14)	Ken Oberkfell
Double-A	Binghamton Mets	Eastern	66	76	.465	t-10th (12)	Tim Teufel
High A	St. Lucie Mets	Florida State	62	76	.449	11th (12)	Edgar Alfonzo
Low A	Savannah Sand Gnats	South Atlantic	75	64	.540	t-4th (14)	Pedro Lopez
Short-season	Brooklyn Cyclones	New York-Penn	51	24	.680	1st (14)	Wally Backman
Rookie	Kingsport Mets	Appalachian	28	39	.418	9th (10)	Mike DiFelice
Rookie	GCL Mets	Gulf Coast	31	25	.554	4th (15)	Sandy Alomar
Overall 2010 Minor League Record			389	372	.511	9th (30)	

*Finish in overall standings (No. of teams in league). †League champion.

LAST YEAR'S TOP 30

Player, Pos.		Status
1.	Jenrry Mejia, rhp	No. 1
2.	Wilmer Flores, ss	No. 2
3.	Fernando Martinez, of	No. 8
4.	Ike Davis, 1b	Majors
5.	Brad Holt, rhp	No. 10
6.	Jon Niese, lhp	Majors
7.	Reese Havens, 2b	No. 6
8.	Josh Thole, c	Majors
9.	Ruben Tejada, ss/2b	Majors
10.	Juan Urbina, lhp	No. 11
11.	Steve Matz, lhp	No. 18
12.	Jefry Marte, 3b	No. 26
13.	Kirk Nieuwenhuis, of	No. 5
14.	Kyle Allen, rhp	No. 27
15.	Jeurys Familia, rhp	No. 13
16.	Robert Carson, lhp	No. 12
17.	Cesar Puello, of	No. 3
18.	Scott Moviel, rhp	Dropped out
19.	Robbie Shields, ss	No. 20
20.	Zach Dotson, lhp	Dropped out
21.	Zach Lutz, 3b/1b	No. 19
22.	Sean Ratliff, of	Dropped out
23.	Dillon Gee, rhp	No. 15
24.	Eric Niesen, lhp	Dropped out
25.	Eddie Kunz, rhp	Dropped out
26.	Josh Stinson, rhp	Dropped out
27.	Eric Beaulac, rhp	Dropped out
28.	Brant Rustich, rhp	Dropped out
29.	Tobi Stoner, rhp	Dropped out
30.	Jordany Valdespin, 2b/ss	No. 25

BEST TOOLS

Best Hitter for Average	Wilmer Flores
Best Power Hitter	Aderlin Rodriguez
Best Strike-Zone Discipline	Brad Emaus
Fastest Baserunner	ZeErika McQueen
Best Athlete	Cesar Puello
Best Fastball	Jenrry Mejia
Best Curveball	Matt Harvey
Best Slider	Jeurys Familia
Best Changeup	Dillon Gee
Best Control	Dillon Gee
Best Defensive Catcher	Kai Gronauer
Best Defensive Infielder	Wilfredo Tovar
Best Infield Arm	Wilmer Flores
Best Defensive Outfielder	Matt den Dekker
Best Outfield Arm	Cesar Puello

PROJECTED 2014 LINEUP

Catcher	Josh Thole
First Base	Ike Davis
Second Base	Reese Havens
Third Base	David Wright
Shortstop	Jose Reyes
Left Field	Wilmer Flores
Center Field	Angel Pagan
Right Field	Cesar Puello
No. 1 Starter	Johan Santana
No. 2 Starter	Jenrry Mejia
No. 3 Starter	Matt Harvey
No. 4 Starter	Mike Pelfrey
No. 5 Starter	Jon Niese
Closer	Bobby Parnell

TOP PROSPECTS OF THE DECADE

Year	Player, Pos.	2010 Org.
2001	Alex Escobar, of	Out of baseball
2002	Aaron Heilman, rhp	Diamondbacks
2003	Jose Reyes, ss	Mets
2004	Kazuo Matsui, ss	Rockies
2005	Lastings Milledge, of	Pirates
2006	Lastings Milledge, of	Pirates
2007	Mike Pelfrey, rhp	Mets
2008	Fernando Martinez, of	Mets
2009	Fernando Martinez, of	Mets
2010	Jenrry Mejia, rhp	Mets

TOP DRAFT PICKS OF THE DECADE

Year	Player, Pos.	2010 Org.
2001	Aaron Heilman, rhp	Diamondbacks
2002	Scott Kazmir, lhp	Angels
2003	Lastings Milledge, of	Pirates
2004	Philip Humber, rhp	Royals
2005	Mike Pelfrey, rhp	Mets
2006	Kevin Mulvey, rhp (2nd round)	Diamondbacks
2007	Eddie Kunz, rhp (1st round supp.)	Mets
2008	Ike Davis, 1b	Mets
2009	Steve Matz, lhp (2nd round)	Mets
2010	Matt Harvey, rhp	Mets

LARGEST BONUSES IN CLUB HISTORY

Mike Pelfrey, 2005	$3,550,000
Philip Humber, 2004	$3,000,000
Matt Harvey, 2010	$2,525,000
Scott Kazmir, 2002	$2,150,000
Lastings Milledge, 2003	$2,075,000

NEW YORK METS

TOP 2011 ROOKIE: Dillon Gee, rhp. The finesse righty proved his mettle with a 2.18 ERA in five big league starts in September.

BREAKOUT PROSPECT: Darrell Ceciliani, of. He already has a batting title to his credit, and the multitooled center fielder keeps improving with experience.

SLEEPER: Zach Dotson, lhp. He shows plus life on fastball and the ability to spin a breaking ball—but he must finish serving a 50-game suspension for testing positive for a stimulant.

SOURCE OF TOP 30 TALENT

Homegrown	27	Acquired	3
College	12	Trades	0
Junior college	2	Rule 5 draft	2
High school	3	Independent leagues	0
Draft-and-follow	0	Free agents/waivers	1
Nondrafted free agents	0		
International	10		

LF
Juan Lagares

CF
Darrell Ceciliani (14)
Matt den Dekker (23)
Jason Pridie
Pedro Zapata
Tillman Pugh

RF
Cesar Puello (3)
Kirk Nieuwenhuis (5)
Fernando Martinez (8)
Cory Vaughn (15)
Rafael Fernandez
Sean Ratliff
Javier Rodriguez

3B
Wilmer Flores (2)
Aderlin Rodriguez (9)
Zach Lutz (19)
Jefry Marte (26)
Richard Lucas
Brian Harrison

SS
Robbie Shields (20)
Wilfredo Tovar
Rylan Sandoval

2B
Reese Havens (6)
Brad Emaus (21)
Jordany Valdespin (25)
Justin Turner
Alonzo Harris

1B
Lucas Duda (7)
Stefan Welch

C
Blake Forsythe (29)
Kai Gronauer
Mike Nickeas
Juan Centeno
Albert Cordero

RHP

RHSP	RHRP
Jenrry Mejia (1)	Jeurys Familia (13)
Matt Harvey (4)	Armando Rodriguez (24)
Brad Holt (10)	Manny Alvarez (28)
Dillon Gee (16)	Pedro Beato (30)
Erik Goeddel (17)	Josh Stinson
Kyle Allen (27)	Ryan Fraser
Brandon Moore	Chad Sheppard
Akeel Morris	John Church
Scott Moviel	John Lujan
Tobi Stoner	Luis Rojas
Greg Peavey	Nick Carr
Mike Hebert	Eric Beaulac
Domingo Tapia	Brant Rustich
Dylan Owen	Eddie Kunz
Jake deGrom	Jeff Walters
	Kenny McDowall

LHP

LHSP	LHRP
Juan Urbina (11)	Jim Fuller
Robert Carson (12)	Mike Antonini
Steve Matz (18)	Eric Niesen
Mark Cohoon (22)	Adam Kolarek
Zach Dotson	Josh Edgin

DRAFT ANALYSIS

2010

BEST PURE HITTER: The Mets hope to hit on a few college seniors, including OF Matt den Dekker (5). After slumping in 2009, he rebounded last spring and kept hitting in his pro debut. He has a good two-strike approach and a line-drive swing he repeats now that he's stopped trying to sell out for power.

BEST POWER HITTER: OF Cory Vaughn (4) hit 14 home runs for short-season Brooklyn, though that's less than a third of the way to his father Greg's big league single-season high. He has strength and plenty of bat speed.

FASTEST RUNNER: OF Tillman Pugh (15) is an excellent athlete with 6.5-second speed in the 60-yard dash. He redshirted during the spring at NCAA Division II Sonoma State (Calif.).

BEST DEFENSIVE PLAYER: Den Dekker's above-average speed plays best in center field, where he has excellent instincts, great range and an average arm.

BEST FASTBALL: RHP Matt Harvey (1) sits at 91-95 mph and touches 97. New York didn't see much of him as he signed late and had to leave instructional league to attend a family funeral. RHP Erik Goeddel (24) worked at 93-94 and reached 96 mph late in the spring in short stints for UCLA. Senior sign RHP Ryan Fraser (16) operated at 92-95 mph in instructional league after working in the low 90s as a college starter.

BEST SECONDARY PITCH: Harvey throws both a slider and a curveball, and the slider has its plus moments. The Mets prefer his power curve and give it 70 grades on the 20-80 scouting scale.

BEST PRO DEBUT: Vaughn batted .307/.396/.557 and led the New York-Penn League in slugging while ranking second in homers and RBIs (56). Brooklyn teammate Fraser held opponents to a .155 average while going 3-3, 1.44 with 12 saves. Den Dekker hit .328/.388/.451, mostly in low Class A.

BEST ATHLETE: Pugh edges Vaughn and den Dekker.

MOST INTRIGUING BACKGROUND: RHP Akeel Morris (10), whose fastball has touched 94 mph, is the highest-drafted prep player from the Virgin Islands since 1988. Vaughn's dad hit 355 big league homers. Unsigned SS J.J. Franco (42) is the son of former Mets closer John, who had 424 major league saves.

CLOSEST TO THE MAJORS: Harvey should make his pro debut in high Class A.

BEST LATE-ROUND PICK: Goeddel, who signed for $350,000, and Fraser. 3B Brian Harrison (13) is athletic and swings the bat with some authority. He missed time with a knee injury last spring but slugged .538 at Brooklyn.

THE ONE WHO GOT AWAY: New York tried to sign summer follow OF Drew Martinez (23), Fraser's teammate at Memphis, but the sophomore-eligible returned to college after hitting .359 in the Cape Cod League.

ASSESSMENT: The Mets went over slot to sign Harvey and Goeddel, making them rare among draft picks in recent club history. Vaughn's fast start and senior values den Dekker and Fraser could make the class even deeper.

2009

The Mets didn't have a first-round pick, and their top two choices, LHP Steve Matz (2) and SS Robbie Shields (3), already have had Tommy John surgery. OF Darrell Ceciliani (4) won the NY-P batting title last year at .351.

GRADE: D

2008

1B Ike Davis (1) hit 19 homers as a rookie last year, and 2B Reese Havens (1) could make a similar impact if he can stay healthy. OF Kirk Nieuwenhuis (3) has exceeded expectations, but RHP Brad Holt (1s) has gone backwards.

GRADE: B+

2007

New York lacked a first-rounder and blew its top two picks on RHP Eddie Kunz (1s), who did reach the majors quickly, and LHP Nathan Vineyard (1s), who retired nearly as fast. OF/1B Lucas Duda (7) broke out with 27 homers last year, including four in the big leagues, while finesse RHP Dillon Gee (21) looked sharp in a September callup.

GRADE: C

2006

Again without a first-rounder, the Mets came up with four fringe big leaguers in RHPs Kevin Mulvey (2), Joe Smith (3) and Tobi Stoner (16) and 1B/OF Daniel Murphy (13). Mulvey and Smith were used in trades for Johan Santana and J.J. Putz.

GRADE: D

Draft analysis by John Manuel (2010) and Jim Callis (2006-09). Numbers in parentheses indicate draft rounds.

JENRRY MEJIA, RHP

Born: Oct. 11, 1989. **Bats:** R. **Throws:** R.
Height: 6-0. **Weight:** 180. **Signed:** Dominican
Republic, 2007. **Signed by:** Ramon Pena/
Ismael Cruz/Sandy Rosario.

MIKE JANES

Unlike many pro baseball players, Mejia didn't sign his first contract for love of the game. He began playing at age 15 only after seeing how lucrative the sport could be for many impoverished young Dominicans, citing Pedro Martinez's $53 million deal with the Mets as an eye-opener. Scouted by the Red Sox and Yankees, among others, Mejia struggled to get noticed because he was undersized and skinny. When the Mets offered $16,500 in April 2007 he signed on the spot—it sure beat the roughly $8 a day he made shining shoes in Santo Domingo. Mejia made a much quicker impression in his U.S. debut in 2008, when he came out firing mid-90s heat for Brooklyn. He began the 2010 season in the Mets big league bullpen, at 20 the youngest player to make an Opening Day roster. His youth and inexperience showed, prompting New York to option him to Double-A on June 20. He left his second start there with a strained shoulder and sat out a month. Upon his return in August, Mejia went on a monthlong tear to earn his way back to the New York. Back in the majors, Mejia got rocked in two starts and left his third with what eventually was diagnosed as a rhomboid strain of his shoulder blade.

Mejia adopted a reliever's mentality while working in the big league bullpen, showcasing his plus-plus fastball at the expense of his secondary pitches. He sits at a steady 94-96 mph and induces boatloads of groundballs because his ball features such late cutting action. Mejia throws a firm 86-88 mph straight changeup that behaves like a splitter and serves as a second out pitch. Scouts like his 12-to-6 downer curveball, which is a plus pitch at times at 79-81 mph. Because he struggles to repeat his release point on his curve, he tends to shy away from it. Concerns about Mejia center on his inconsistent secondary stuff and smallish build—though his strong lower half mitigates the latter somewhat. He worked just 81 innings last season and 95 in 2009, when he missed seven weeks with a strained right middle finger.

Mejia has the raw stuff to pitch at the front of a rotation, but he has yet to prove he can complete anything close to 200 innings in a season. Even if he flames out as a starter, he can be a dominating late-inning reliever with just a slight improvement to his control. The new front-office regime intends to slow down Mejia's development track and have him build innings as a starter at Triple-A Buffalo in 2011.

SCOUTING GRADES

Fastball: 70. **Command/**
Changeup: 60. **Control:** 50.
Curveball: 50. **Delivery:** 50.

Based on 20-80 scouting scale, where 50 represents major league average, and future projection rather than present tools.

Year	Club (League)	Class	W	L	ERA	G	GS	CG	SV	IP	H	HR	BB	SO	G/A	WHIP	AVG
2007	Mets (DSL)	R	2	3	2.47	14	7	0	1	44	24	0	27	47	—	1.17	.160
2008	Mets (GCL)	R	2	0	0.60	3	3	1	0	15	9	0	3	15	—	0.80	.164
	Brooklyn (NYP)	SS	3	2	3.49	11	11	0	0	57	42	4	23	52	—	1.15	.209
2009	St. Lucie (FSL)	HiA	4	1	1.97	9	9	0	0	50	41	0	16	44	2.21	1.13	.217
	Binghamton (EL)	AA	0	5	4.47	10	10	0	0	44	44	2	23	47	2.95	1.51	.263
2010	Mets (GCL)	R	0	0	3.00	1	1	0	0	3	4	0	1	3	—	1.67	.333
	St. Lucie (FSL)	HiA	0	0	0.00	1	1	0	0	4	1	0	0	7	—	0.25	.077
	Binghamton (EL)	AA	2	0	1.32	6	6	1	0	27	19	0	14	26	3.64	1.21	.200
	Buffalo (IL)	AAA	0	0	1.13	1	1	0	0	8	5	1	1	9	5.00	0.75	.200
	New York (NL)	MAJ	0	4	4.62	33	3	0	0	39	46	3	20	22	2.64	1.69	.289
Major League Totals			0	4	4.62	33	3	0	0	39	46	3	20	22	2.64	1.69	.289
Minor League Totals			13	11	2.64	56	49	2	1	252	189	7	108	250	2.92	1.18	.208

2 WILMER FLORES, SS

Born: Aug. 6, 1991. **B-T:** R-R. **Ht.:** 6-3. **Wt.:** 175. **Signed:** Venezuela, 2007. **Signed by:** Sandy Johnson/Ismael Cruz/Robert Alfonzo.

Flores began fine-tuning his skills at an academy near his home at age 13, but his parents allowed him to pursue a baseball career only upon early graduation from high school. Signed for $750,000 on his 16th birthday in 2007, he reached high Class A St. Lucie as an 18-year-old last June. Flores always has shown natural aptitude for hitting, something that can't be said for his running or fielding ability. He puts a charge into the ball with quick wrists and a loose, easy stroke. He doesn't swing and miss much, making rapid adjustments and excelling at barreling the ball and driving it to all fields when he gets extension. The results began to manifest in games last season when he smacked 50 extra-base hits, doubling his total from 2009. Flores' ability to hit for average and power will be crucial as he slides down the defensive spectrum. His hands work at shortstop, but his lack of first-step quickness and range won't allow him to play up the middle in the majors. He throws well enough to play third base, though his well below-average speed would make an outfield post an adventure. As he fills out and improves his selectivity, Flores could grow into a middle-of-the-order presence. He'll reach Double-A at some point in 2011, probably before his 20th birthday.

Year	Club (League)	Class	AVG	G	AB	R	H	2B	3B	HR	RBI	BB	SO	SB	CS	OBP	SLG
2008	Kingsport (APP)	R	.310	59	245	36	76	12	4	8	41	12	28	2	1	.352	.490
	Savannah (SAL)	LoA	.400	1	5	1	2	0	0	0	0	0	2	0	0	.400	.400
	Brooklyn (NYP)	SS	.267	8	30	3	8	1	0	0	1	1	7	0	0	.290	.300
2009	Savannah (SAL)	LoA	.264	125	488	44	129	20	2	3	36	22	72	3	3	.305	.332
2010	Savannah (SAL)	LoA	.278	66	277	30	77	18	2	7	44	23	37	2	1	.342	.433
	St. Lucie (FSL)	HiA	.300	67	277	32	83	18	1	4	40	9	40	2	4	.324	.415
Minor League Totals			.284	326	1322	146	375	69	9	22	162	67	186	9	9	.326	.399

3 CESAR PUELLO, OF

Born: April 1, 1991. **B-T:** R-R. **Ht.:** 6-2. **Wt.:** 195. **Signed:** Dominican Republic, 2007. **Signed by:** Ramon Pena/Ismael Cruz/Marciano Alvarez.

Signed for $400,000 in 2007, Puello was one of five teenage regulars in the low Class A South Atlantic League last year, batting .346 in the second half before missing the final three weeks with a strained lower back. Some scouts prefer him to Wilmer Flores because Puello has five-tool potential. Puello went on his tear after going from a deep crouch to a more upright stance, giving him a stronger load and better plate coverage on the inner half. Though he homered only once in 2010, he has as much raw power as anyone in the system, and scouts were impressed he never betrayed his all-fields approach to sell out for power. The home runs will come—potentially as many as 25 annually—because he accelerates the barrel through the hitting zone with strong wrists, generating ample backspin and carry. Puello's most evident tool is his plus speed, which he used to steal 45 bases in 55 tries last year. He has a plus arm and covers a lot of ground in right field, but grades as a merely average defender because of unfocused play and instincts lacking for center. If Puello truly does hit 20-plus homers a year, he'll be a fixture in right field for the Mets for a long time. His first taste of high Class A awaits in 2011.

Year	Club (League)	Class	AVG	G	AB	R	H	2B	3B	HR	RBI	BB	SO	SB	CS	OBP	SLG
2008	Mets (GCL)	R	.305	40	151	24	46	6	0	1	17	5	32	13	5	.350	.364
2009	Kingsport (APP)	R	.296	49	196	37	58	10	0	5	23	10	51	15	5	.373	.423
2010	Savannah (SAL)	LoA	.292	109	404	80	118	22	1	1	34	32	82	45	10	.375	.359
Minor League Totals			.296	198	751	141	222	38	1	7	74	47	165	73	20	.369	.377

4 MATT HARVEY, RHP

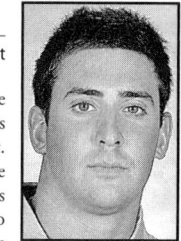

Born: March 27, 1989. **B-T:** R-R. **Ht.:** 6-4. **Wt.:** 225. **Drafted:** North Carolina, 2010 (1st round). **Signed by:** Marlin McPhail.

One of the top prep pitchers in the 2007 draft, Harvey slid to the third round because of signability and turned down the Angels to attend North Carolina. Inconsistent in his first two years, he had a strong junior season in 2010 and went seventh overall in the draft. He signed at the Aug. 16 deadline for a slightly over-slot $2.525 million. Harvey has the physicality and arm strength favored by the Mets when they select college righthanders at the top of the draft. The line traces back from Harvey to Brad Holt to Eddie Kunz to Mike Pelfrey to Philip Humber. Harvey pitches at 91-95 mph and touches 97 with his fastball, though his control wavers because his long arm action affects his release point. He throws both a slider and a curveball, but the Mets prefer that he develop the latter, a power downer that shows flashes of being a plus-plus pitch. His mid-80s slider features depth and late finish. He needs to work on his changeup after rarely using it in as an amateur. He improved the balance and tempo in his delivery through hard work in college, a testament to his improved maturity. If he maintains direction to the plate and throws strikes, Harvey has front-of-the-rotation stuff. He'll start his pro career in high Class A.

Year	Club (League)	Class	W	L	ERA	G	GS	CG	SV	IP	H	HR	BB	SO	G/AWHIP	AVG
2010	Did Not Play—Signed Late															

5 KIRK NIEUWENHUIS, OF

Born: Aug. 7, 1987. **B-T:** L-R. **Ht.:** 6-3. **Wt.:** 210. **Drafted:** Azusa Pacific (Calif.), 2008 (3rd round). **Signed by:** Fred Mazuca.

Nieuwenhuis starred as a running back in high school but opted to pursue baseball in college, leading Azusa Pacific (Calif.) to consecutive NAIA World Series and ranking as the summer Alaska League's top prospect following his sophomore year. He led the high Class A Florida State League in four categories, including extra-base hits (56) and slugging (.467), during his full-season debut in 2009. He continued to hit for power last season in Double-A, leading the Eastern League with 53 extra-base hits at the time of his August promotion to Triple-A. Nieuwenhuis' all-out approach helps sell observers on his all-around ability, which breaks down as five average to a tick below-average tools. He shows an all-fields approach that could spell a .270 average in the big leagues. He has the bat speed to hit for power, but his line-drive stroke is geared more for doubles and a ceiling of 12-15 homers. His range and instincts in center field grade as average, as does his arm, though his best speed is merely fringe-average. As an athletic, lefthanded hitter with a dollop of power and speed, Nieuwenhuis could be an ideal reserve who can cover all three outfield spots and produce at the plate. He'll begin 2011 in Triple-A and make his big league debut at some point during the season.

Year	Club (League)	Class	AVG	G	AB	R	H	2B	3B	HR	RBI	BB	SO	SB	CS	OBP	SLG
2008	Brooklyn (NYP)	SS	.277	74	285	34	79	15	5	3	29	29	70	11	7	.348	.396
2009	St. Lucie (FSL)	HiA	.274	123	482	91	132	35	5	16	71	53	118	16	4	.357	.467
	Binghamton (EL)	AA	.406	8	32	8	13	3	1	1	2	4	9	1	1	.472	.656
2010	Binghamton (EL)	AA	.289	94	394	81	114	35	2	16	60	30	93	13	7	.337	.510
	Buffalo (IL)	AAA	.225	30	120	10	27	8	1	2	17	11	39	0	0	.295	.358
Minor League Totals			.278	329	1313	224	365	96	14	38	179	127	329	41	19	.347	.459

6 REESE HAVENS, 2B

Born: Oct. 20, 1986. **B-T:** L-R. **Ht.:** 6-1. **Wt.:** 195. **Drafted:** South Carolina, 2008 (1st round). **Signed by:** Marlin McPhail.

While Ike Davis rocketed to Queens less than two years after being drafted, fellow 2008 first-rounder Havens has shifted from shortstop to second base and seen his progress stalled by a string of elbow, groin, quadriceps, hand, oblique and back injuries. He has played in 152 pro games and hit .261/.363/.467 with 26 homers and 80 walks, hinting at the type of player he could be if healthy. Havens tinkered with his swing last season, moving his hands to a higher starting position to better handle high fastballs. His quiet hitting approach and strong pitch recognition mark him as a future average hitter who will work deep counts and compile both walks and strikeouts. He's quick to the ball and can turn on the inside pitch, enough to project as a 15-20 homer threat. He'll have to make hay with the bat to profile as a big league regular, because he has a thick frame and below-average speed. His actions and hands are modest, as are his range and arm strength. He began playing second base only last season, moving from shortstop. While he won't win any Gold Gloves, Havens profiles as an offensive-oriented second baseman with power and patience. He'll begin his fourth pro season in Double-A, and could move quickly if he stays healthy.

Year	Club (League)	Class	AVG	G	AB	R	H	2B	3B	HR	RBI	BB	SO	SB	CS	OBP	SLG
2008	Brooklyn (NYP)	SS	.247	23	85	13	21	6	2	3	11	11	27	3	1	.340	.471
2009	St. Lucie (FSL)	HiA	.247	97	360	53	89	19	1	14	52	55	73	3	2	.361	.422
2010	St. Lucie (FSL)	HiA	.281	14	57	9	16	2	1	3	7	8	18	0	1	.369	.509
	Binghamton (EL)	AA	.338	18	68	12	23	2	1	6	12	6	15	0	2	.400	.662
Minor League Totals			.261	152	570	87	149	29	5	26	82	80	133	6	6	.363	.467

7 LUCAS DUDA, OF/1B

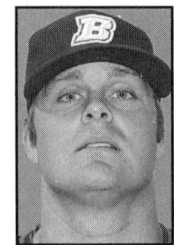

Born: Feb. 3, 1986. **B-T:** L-R. **Ht.:** 6-5. **Wt.:** 240. **Drafted:** Southern California, 2007 (7th round). **Signed by:** Steve Leavitt.

Duda went from afterthought to September callup last season, more than doubling his previous career high for homers and winning the Mets' minor league player of the year award. He recovered from a 1-for-33 start in New York to bat .314 with nine extra-base hits in his final 17 big league games. Duda always made hard contact and showed a discerning batting eye, but he began hitting more homers last season by better identifying pitches on the inner half that he could loft out of the park. He also can drive the ball to the opposite field for doubles. He doesn't strike out much for a player with his raw strength and power, and though he lacks elite bat speed, his tools suggest he could hit .275 with 15-20 homers annually. Duda's best defensive position is first base because he's a poor, lumbering runner with below-average range and arm strength in left field. With Ike Davis entrenched at first base in New York, Duda must hit to stay in the picture for playing time on an outfield corner. The presence of Jason Bay could force Duda to Triple-A to start the year. If he hits, the Mets will make room, either in right field or as a bat off the bench.

Year	Club (League)	Class	AVG	G	AB	R	H	2B	3B	HR	RBI	BB	SO	SB	CS	OBP	SLG
2007	Brooklyn (NYP)	SS	.299	67	234	32	70	20	3	4	32	34	45	3	5	.398	.462
2008	St. Lucie (FSL)	HiA	.263	133	483	58	127	26	3	11	66	66	129	2	7	.358	.398
2009	Binghamton (EL)	AA	.281	110	395	49	111	29	1	9	53	61	91	2	2	.380	.428
2010	Binghamton (EL)	AA	.286	45	161	30	46	17	0	6	34	29	27	1	0	.411	.503
	Buffalo (IL)	AAA	.314	70	264	44	83	23	2	17	53	31	57	0	0	.389	.610
	New York (NL)	MAJ	.202	29	84	11	17	6	0	4	13	6	22	0	0	.261	.417
Major League Totals			.202	29	84	11	17	6	0	4	13	6	22	0	0	.261	.417
Minor League Totals			.284	425	1537	213	437	115	9	47	238	221	349	8	14	.381	.463

8 FERNANDO MARTINEZ, OF

Born: Oct. 10, 1988. **B-T:** L-R. **Ht.:** 6-1. **Wt.:** 200. **Signed:** Dominican Republic, 2005. **Signed by:** Sandy Johnson/Rafael Bournigal/Eddie Toledo.

Martinez' signing for $1.3 million in 2005 signaled the Mets' intention to be major players on the international market, though they have given a seven-figure bonus only once since ($1.2 million for lefthander Juan Urbina in 2009). Injuries continue to define Martinez, who never has played more than 90 games in any of his five pro seasons. He looked electrifying while winning Caribbean Series MVP honors and batting .383 in big league camp in early 2010, then missed half the season with lower-back, hamstring and knee maladies. He left the Dominican League after one game with mild arthritis in his right knee. Martinez has plus power to all fields, but his pull-only approach makes him susceptible to pitches on the outer half. He has the hand-eye coordination to hit for a decent average, but he's impatient and too often gets out on his front side against offspeed stuff. Repeated injuries to his knees and hamstrings have turned Martinez into a below-average runner. He has worked to improve his range and throwing accuracy, and some scouts see his defense and arm as average tools, fit for right field. When healthy, Martinez has held his own despite being consistently younger than his competition. But unless he improves his selectivity and plate coverage, he seems destined for life as a lefthanded power bat off the bench.

Year	Club (League)	Class	AVG	G	AB	R	H	2B	3B	HR	RBI	BB	SO	SB	CS	OBP	SLG
2006	Mets (GCL)	R	.250	1	4	1	1	0	0	0	0	0	1	0	0	.250	.250
	Hagerstown (SAL)	LoA	.333	45	192	24	64	14	2	5	28	15	36	7	4	.389	.505
	St. Lucie (FSL)	HiA	.193	30	119	18	23	4	2	5	11	6	24	1	1	.254	.387
2007	Binghamton (EL)	AA	.271	60	236	32	64	11	1	4	21	20	51	3	4	.336	.377
	Mets (GCL)	R	.111	3	9	1	1	0	1	0	1	1	6	0	0	.200	.333
2008	Mets (GCL)	R	.429	4	14	2	6	1	1	0	0	0	2	0	0	.467	.643
	Binghamton (EL)	AA	.287	86	352	48	101	19	4	8	43	27	73	6	2	.340	.432
2009	Buffalo (IL)	AAA	.290	45	176	24	51	16	2	8	28	11	33	2	1	.337	.540
	New York (NL)	MAJ	.176	29	91	11	16	6	0	1	8	5	14	2	0	.242	.275
2010	St. Lucie (FSL)	HiA	.267	4	15	1	4	1	0	0	0	1	2	0	0	.313	.333
	New York (NL)	MAJ	.167	7	18	1	3	0	0	0	2	1	5	0	1	.273	.167
	Buffalo (IL)	AAA	.253	71	257	39	65	16	0	12	33	17	65	1	0	.317	.455
Major League Totals			.174	36	109	12	19	6	0	1	10	6	19	2	1	.248	.257
Minor League Totals			.277	349	1374	190	380	82	13	42	165	98	293	20	12	.334	.447

9 ADERLIN RODRIGUEZ, 3B

Born: Nov. 18, 1991. **B-T:** R-R. **Ht.:** 6-3. **Wt.:** 210. **Signed:** Dominican Republic, 2008. **Signed by:** Ismael Cruz.

After signing for $600,000 in 2008, Rodriguez missed a large chunk of his 2009 pro debut with a wrist injury. He showcased impressive hitting tools last season in the Appalachian League, finishing third in homers (13), RBIs (48) and extra-base hits (35). Rodriguez has more raw power than any player in the system and could mature into a 25-30 homer threat. His wrists are strong and quick, producing elite bat speed. With strong pitch-recognition skills and barrel awareness, he could hit for average as well. The catch is that Rodriguez is a poor runner with a thick lower half and heavy feet who may have to shift to first base. He has a strong arm and moves his feet well for his size, but his hands are hard and he simply might outgrow the hot corner. Some scouts believe Rodriguez could be playable at third if he takes care of his body and proves willing to put in the work on defense. He drew criticism in the Appy League for uneven

MARC LEVINE-NY METS

effort and lack of hustle, getting benched on at least two occasions. The Mets promoted Rodriguez to low Class A Savannah for the final week of 2010, and he'll spend this year there as a teenager. If Wilmer Flores has to play third base, he'll be an obstacle for Rodriguez in the future.

Year	Club (League)	Class	AVG	G	AB	R	H	2B	3B	HR	RBI	BB	SO	SB	CS	OBP	SLG
2009	Mets (GCL)	R	.290	17	62	5	18	3	0	1	10	9	15	1	1	.389	.387
2010	Kingsport (APP)	R	.312	61	250	44	78	22	0	13	48	15	43	3	1	.352	.556
	Savannah (SAL)	LoA	.200	8	30	3	6	1	0	1	11	6	10	0	0	.333	.333
Minor League Totals			.298	86	342	52	102	26	0	15	69	30	68	4	2	.357	.506

10 BRAD HOLT, RHP

Born: Oct. 13, 1986. **B-T:** R-R. **Ht.:** 6-4. **Wt.:** 194. **Drafted:** UNC Wilmington, 2008 (1st round supplemental). **Signed by:** Marlin McPhail.

Signed for $1.04 million as 33rd overall pick in 2008, Holt dominated in his pro debut and earned a quick promotion to Double-A the next year. He injured his ankle in his first start for Binghamton, missed three weeks and never recovered, running up a 6.62 ERA over his final 10 starts. His misadventures continued in 2010 when he hurt his right wrist in spring training, setting the stage for a season in which he allowed more baserunners per nine innings (19.6) than any minor leaguer with as many as his 95 innings. According to scouts, Holt still had plus stuff in 2010. They think his problems stemmed from a lack of focus as well as a new, overly mechanical delivery that caused his front side to open early. At his best, Holt locates his 92-94 mph four-seam fastball down in the zone, mixing in an occasional low-90s cutter. He can spin a high-70s curveball with occasional sharp bite and shows feel for a low-80s changeup with sink, but his poor command undermines both pitches. His curve often breaks too early to convince batters to commit. Holt has the stuff to profile as a No. 3 starter, but that ceiling seems impossibly tall now. He had a fine showing in instructional league and in the Arizona Fall League, giving hope he'll succeed in his third try at Double-A in 2011.

Year	Club (League)	Class	W	L	ERA	G	GS	CG	SV	IP	H	HR	BB	SO	G/AWHIP	AVG
2008	Brooklyn (NYP)	SS	5	3	1.87	14	14	0	0	72	43	3	33	96	— 1.05	.171
2009	St. Lucie (FSL)	HiA	4	1	3.12	9	9	0	0	43	34	5	13	54	0.97 1.08	.215
	Binghamton (EL)	AA	3	6	6.21	11	11	0	0	58	58	9	23	45	0.77 1.40	.270
2010	Binghamton (EL)	AA	1	5	10.20	10	9	0	0	30	43	2	23	25	0.67 2.20	.336
	St. Lucie (FSL)	HiA	2	9	7.48	14	14	0	0	65	68	4	56	62	0.61 1.91	.276
Minor League Totals			15	24	5.29	58	57	0	0	269	246	23	148	282	0.73 1.47	.246

11 JUAN URBINA, LHP

Born: May 31, 1993. **B-T:** L-L. **Ht.:** 6-2. **Wt.:** 170. **Signed:** Venezuela, 2009. **Signed by:** Sandy Johnson/ Ramon Pena/Ismael Cruz/Robert Alfonzo.

The Mets compensated for having no first-round pick in 2009 by signing Urbina for $1.2 million. New York hadn't approached that bonus figure with a foreign amateur since inking Fernando Martinez for $1.3 million in 2005. Urbina is the son of two-time all-star closer Ugueth Urbina, who is serving a 14-year prison sentence in Venezuela for two counts of attempted murder. Despite a 5.03 ERA, Juan made a promising pro debut in the Gulf Coast League last year, ranking as the circuit's top pitching prospect. He touches the low 90s now but mostly shows a fringe-average fastball at 87-88 mph. The Mets expect him to add velocity because he has plenty of room to fill out his 6-foot-2 frame and because of his loose, easy arm action. Urbina repeats his delivery well, which helps him sell the arm speed on a plus changeup that features late sink and fade. He shows precocious faith in the changeup, throwing it in any count. Urbina's slider features late downward action and two-plane break when it's right, but it's a work in progress that often sweeps more than breaks. If his fastball graduates more into the 90s and his slider comes up a grade or two, Urbina could be a rotation mainstay. He'll be 18 for all of 2011, so the Mets have time to bring him along slowly with another assignment to a short-season league.

Year	Club (League)	Class	W	L	ERA	G	GS	CG	SV	IP	H	HR	BB	SO	G/AWHIP	AVG
2010	Mets (GCL)	R	5	3	5.03	11	11	0	0	48	54	5	14	38	1.09 1.41	.284
Minor League Totals			5	3	5.03	11	11	0	0	48	54	5	14	38	1.09 1.41	.284

12 ROBERT CARSON, LHP

Born: Jan. 23, 1989. **B-T:** L-L. **Ht.:** 6-3. **Wt.:** 220. **Drafted:** HS—Hattiesburg, Miss., 2007 (14th round). **Signed by:** Benny Latino.

Carson made his full-season debut in 2009 on the same low Class A Savannah pitching staff as Jeurys Familia and Kyle Allen. He beat those two righthanders to Double-A last July, but proving his youth, Carson got hammered by Eastern League batters. Despite his poor performance, teams continued to ask the Mets about the physical lefty's availability because he ranges from 92-95 mph with his fastball and shows the potential for two average secondary pitches. Carson works off his fastball, which features tailing life and deception from a high three-quarters slot, and he holds his velocity deep into games. He locates a high-80s cutter in on righthanders, and pairs it with an average low-80s slider to induce groundballs. Some scouts throw future average grades on Carson's changeup, which he'll need to stay in the rotation. Like fellow Mets power pitching prospects Brad Holt and Familia, Carson appeared to fight his mechanics last season, and his command suffered significantly. He always will be more about power than pitchability, which prompts some to predict a move to the bullpen. Others are more bullish and see a mid-rotation starter because he has arm strength and the athleticism necessary to refine his secondary stuff. Carson will get a chance to redeem himself in Double-A to begin 2011.

Year	Club (League)	Class	W	L	ERA	G	GS	CG	SV	IP	H	HR	BB	SO	G/A	WHIP	AVG
2007	Mets (GCL)	R	1	0	5.00	4	1	0	0	9	8	1	5	9	—	1.44	.216
2008	Mets (GCL)	R	1	0	1.57	5	5	0	0	23	11	0	6	25	—	0.74	.143
	Kingsport (APP)	R	2	3	1.76	6	6	0	0	31	29	1	18	21	—	1.53	.274
2009	Savannah (SAL)	LoA	8	10	3.21	25	25	2	0	132	139	4	45	90	1.68	1.40	.270
2010	St. Lucie (FSL)	HiA	7	5	4.17	17	16	0	0	86	98	5	33	69	1.59	1.52	.287
	Binghamton (EL)	AA	1	6	8.32	10	10	0	0	49	68	7	23	30	1.64	1.87	.343
Minor League Totals			20	24	4.02	67	63	2	0	329	353	18	130	244	1.65	1.47	.277

13 JEURYS FAMILIA, RHP

Born: Oct. 10, 1989. **B-T:** R-R. **Ht.:** 6-3. **Wt.:** 185. **Signed:** Dominican Republic, 2007. **Signed by:** Ramon Pena/Ismael Cruz/Marcelino Vallejo.

Familia earned organization pitcher of the year honors in 2009 when he ranked third in the low Class A South Atlantic League in ERA (2.69) and fourth in WHIP (1.16). That same pitcher went missing in action for much of last season. Familia represented the Mets in the Futures Game despite running up a 6.38 ERA through his first 16 starts for high Class A St. Lucie. He didn't fare much better in the prospect exhibition, serving up two runs on three consecutive doubles while recording only one out. Everything fell into place for a seven-start stretch in July and August, during which Familia went 4-2, 3.38 with 58 strikeouts in 43 innings. He fought his delivery all season and finished with 5.5 walks per nine innings and 25 wild pitches. He still maintained a strong strikeout rate (10.2 per nine innings) and kept the ball on the ground, thanks mostly to plus-plus fastball velocity. Familia scatters the lower half of the zone at 94-97 mph and can sniff triple digits. He's broad-shouldered and has an ideal pitcher's frame, so he keeps his velocity deep into games. His long arm action affords the batter a long look at the ball, however. Familia buries his 86-87 mph slider as a chase pitch, but he struggles to throw it for strikes because his release point tends to wander. He'll throw an occasional average changeup with sink and fade, but it's not consistent. Even scouts outside the organization laud Familia for his work ethic, though they also foresee a shift to the bullpen in his future. He figures to spend a good portion of 2011 in Double-A as a 21-year-old.

Year	Club (League)	Class	W	L	ERA	G	GS	CG	SV	IP	H	HR	BB	SO	G/A	WHIP	AVG
2008	Mets (GCL)	R	2	2	2.79	11	11	0	0	52	46	2	13	38	—	1.14	.232
2009	Savannah (SAL)	LoA	10	6	2.69	24	23	0	0	134	109	3	46	109	1.40	1.16	.221
2010	St. Lucie (FSL)	HiA	6	9	5.58	24	24	0	0	121	117	7	74	137	1.88	1.58	.257
Minor League Totals			18	17	3.84	59	58	0	0	307	272	12	133	284	1.58	1.32	.237

14 DARRELL CECILIANI, OF

Born: June 22, 1990. **B-T:** L-L. **Ht.:** 6-1. **Wt.:** 205. **Drafted:** Columbia Basin (Wash.) CC, 2009 (4th round). **Signed by:** Jim Reeves.

Ceciliani hails from Madras, Ore., the same small town that produced Red Sox outfielder Jacoby Ellsbury. He signed with the Mets for $204,300 in 2009 as a fourth-round pick and then promptly fell on his face at Rookie-level Kingsport, batting .234 in 42 games. He made a full recovery last season with Brooklyn, hitting .351 to win the New York-Penn League batting title while also leading the league with 56 runs and 12 triples. Ceciliani is a contact-oriented, line-drive hitter who uses the whole field, which gives him a chance to be an average to plus hitter. He handles both lefthanders and righthanders, and he records his fair share of bunt hits. Ceciliani has strength in his wrists and forearms, but he's more of a gap hitter and not a big home run threat. Evaluators expect him to top out near 10 homers per season—though he did drive one ball out to right field in Brooklyn, where charging winds keep most everything in play. (Lucas Duda, Reese Havens and Kirk Nieuwenhuis hit one homer each to right field while with the Cyclones, and Ike Davis managed zero.) Ceciliani hits around the ball at times when his swing gets too big, and he'll need to improve his stolen-base success rate (just 60 percent last year in 35 attempts), but he profiles as a big league tablesetter. He's an average to a tick above-average runner who accelerates quickly and reads the ball well off the bat in center field. He has enough range to make center his permanent home, though his arm is fringe-average. A ticket to low Class A awaits.

Year	Club (League)	Class	AVG	G	AB	R	H	2B	3B	HR	RBI	BB	SO	SB	CS	OBP	SLG
2009	Kingsport (APP)	R	.234	42	158	29	37	6	0	2	13	13	31	14	2	.313	.310
2010	Brooklyn (NYP)	SS	.351	68	271	56	95	19	12	2	35	24	56	21	14	.410	.531
Minor League Totals			.308	110	429	85	132	25	12	4	48	37	87	35	16	.374	.450

15 CORY VAUGHN, OF

Born: May 1, 1989. **B-T:** R-R. **Ht.:** 6-3. **Wt.:** 225. **Drafted:** San Diego State, 2010 (4th round). **Signed by:** Fred Mazuca.

Vaughn served as batboy for the Devil Rays while his father Greg wound down his 15-year career in Tampa Bay in the early 2000s. Cory has big shoes to fill—Greg made four all-star teams, hit 30 or more homers in four seasons and finished with 355 round-trippers. Cory first met Tony Gwynn, his future coach at San Diego State, when his father played for the Padres from 1996-98. Though Vaughn's tools have been obvious since he was a teenager, he couldn't shake the feeling of promise unfulfilled in college. He had his best college season a junior last spring—.378/.454/.606 with nine homers—but still racked up strikeouts as he struggled with pitch recognition. However, scouts both inside and outside the Mets organization said that Vaughn cut down on his swing upon turning pro for $240,300 as a fourth-round pick. The results were tangible: He saw breaking balls better, used the opposite field, struck out less frequently and led the short-season New York-Penn League in slugging (.557) and OPS (.953) while ranking second with 14 homers and 56 RBIs. A physical specimen, Vaughn has prototype right-field tools. He sports above-average power and has a chance to be an average hitter, assuming his new approach holds. He's also an average runner with average range and arm strength in right field. Vaughn has Type 1 (juvenile) diabetes, which he monitors and controls with an insulin pump he wears while playing. Much like 2008 third-rounder Kirk Nieuwenhuis, Vaughn may be able to handle an assignment to high Class A for his full-season debut.

Year	Club (League)	Class	AVG	G	AB	R	H	2B	3B	HR	RBI	BB	SO	SB	CS	OBP	SLG
2010	Brooklyn (NYP)	SS	.307	72	264	45	81	14	5	14	56	34	63	12	5	.396	.557
Minor League Totals			.307	72	264	45	81	14	5	14	56	34	63	12	5	.396	.557

16 DILLON GEE, RHP

Born: April 28, 1986. **B-T:** R-R. **Ht.:** 6-1. **Wt.:** 200. **Drafted:** Texas-Arlington, 2007 (21st round). **Signed by:** Ray Corbett.

Gee made just nine starts in 2009 because he tore the labrum in his shoulder at the end of May. He opted for rest and rehab rather than surgery, and he returned strong in 2010. He led the International League with 165 strikeouts in 161 innings before making his big league debut in September. Despite a career strikeout rate of 8.0 per nine innings in the minors, Gee lacks a dominating pitch, thriving instead on command and pitch sequencing. An unheralded 21st-rounder who signed for $20,000 in 2007, he's a hard-nosed competitor who hates to come out of starts. While Gee's pitches all grade as below-average, his plus control makes them play up. He works at 87-90 mph with some sink on his fastball, though he sat more comfortably at 89-91 at the end of the season as his shoulder regained strength. Gee's low-80s, sinking changeup is probably his best pitch because he sells it with a consistent arm action. He throws a slurvy, low-70s curveball as a change-of-pace breaking ball and a short, spinning slider at 79-81 mph as a harder breaker. Like all command pitchers, Gee gets hit when he elevates his pitches or misses his spots. To that end, he allowed 23 home runs with Buffalo to rank second in the IL. Gee will have to curtail the free passes at the big league level, but his positive five-start audition last September gives him a leg up on winning New York's No. 5 starter job in 2011. He perfectly fits the description of dependable innings-eater.

Year	Club (League)	Class	W	L	ERA	G	GS	CG	SV	IP	H	HR	BB	SO	G/A	WHIP	AVG
2007	Brooklyn (NYP)	SS	3	1	2.47	14	11	0	0	62	57	1	9	56	—	1.06	.249
2008	St. Lucie (FSL)	HiA	8	6	3.25	21	21	0	0	127	117	6	19	94	—	1.07	.245
	Binghamton (EL)	AA	2	0	1.33	4	4	0	0	27	18	1	5	20	—	0.85	.194
2009	Buffalo (IL)	AAA	1	3	4.10	9	9	1	0	48	47	5	16	42	0.77	1.30	.253
2010	Buffalo (IL)	AAA	13	8	4.96	28	28	0	0	161	174	23	41	165	1.34	1.33	.275
	New York (NL)	MAJ	2	2	2.18	5	5	0	0	33	25	2	15	17	1.31	1.21	.212
Major League Totals			2	2	2.18	5	5	0	0	33	25	2	15	17	1.31	1.21	.212
Minor League Totals			27	18	3.76	76	73	1	0	426	413	36	90	377	1.16	1.18	.255

17 ERIK GOEDDEL, RHP

Born: Dec. 20, 1988. **B-T:** R-R. **Ht.:** 6-3. **Wt.:** 185. **Drafted:** UCLA, 2010 (24th round). **Signed by:** Spencer Graham.

Goeddel seemed like a certain top-three-rounds pick heading into his senior season at San Jose's Bellarmine Prep in 2007, but he had Tommy John surgery that April and missed two full years while recovering. He redshirted his first year at UCLA, returned to limited action in 2009 and then fully emerged last season as a dominant bullpen force for the Bruins as they advanced to the College World Series finals. He struck out 58 batters in 49 innings, allowing just four homers and a .232 average. A draft-eligible sophomore whose signability scared off clubs, Goeddel fell to the Mets in the 24th round and signed for $350,000, the equivalent of third-round money. New York views him as a starter, though he didn't fit in that role with UCLA because of a stacked weekend rotation that featured two potential 2011 first-rounders in Trevor Bauer and Gerrit Cole and a 2010 second-rounder in Rob Rasmussen (Marlins). Goeddel's four-seam fastball sits at 93-94 mph and touches 96 when he comes out of the bullpen, and his mid-80s slider with three-quarters tilt gives him a second plus pitch. He hasn't started a game since high school, so he'll need to dust off his changeup, which is below-average. Goeddel threw exactly one inning after signing, so the Mets will have to wait until 2011 to see what they've got. He'll be considered for assignment to a full-season club coming into spring training.

Year	Club (League)	Class	W	L	ERA	G	GS	CG	SV	IP	H	HR	BB	SO	G/AWHIP	AVG
2010	Mets (GCL)	R	0	0	0.00	1	0	0	0	1	1	0	0	1	1.00 1.00	.250
Minor League Totals			0	0	0.00	1	0	0	0	1	1	0	0	1	1.00 1.00	.250

18 STEVE MATZ, LHP

Born: May 29, 1991. **B-T:** R-L. **Ht.:** 6-2. **Wt.:** 192. **Drafted:** HS—East Setauket, N.Y., 2009 (2nd round). **Signed by:** Larry Izzo Jr.

Matz hasn't thrown an inning for the Mets since signing for $895,000 as their top pick (second round) in the 2009 draft. Like Robbie Shields, the club's third-rounder from the same draft, Matz needed Tommy John surgery. He threw well in minor league camp last spring, but stayed behind in extended spring training with a sore elbow and had reconstructive surgery in May. Before he got hurt, Matz's fastball sat at 89-91 mph and touched 94 with life to his glove side, enabling him to pitch in on the hands of righthanders. He's big and projectable, so he could work comfortably at 92-93 mph once he matures physically. He also had an average changeup with some fade and sink, as well as a curveball that showed flashes of being a plus pitch with short, down-breaking action. Matz finally should be able to make his pro debut in mid-2011, either at Brooklyn or Savannah.

Year	Club (League)	Class	W	L	ERA	G	GS	CG	SV	IP	H	HR	BB	SO	G/AWHIP	AVG
2010	Did Not Play—Injured															

19 ZACH LUTZ, 3B

Born: June 3, 1986. **B-T:** R-R. **Ht.:** 6-1. **Wt.:** 220. **Drafted:** Alvernia (Pa.), 2007 (5th round). **Signed by:** Scott Hunter.

The NCAA Division III player of the year as a senior at Alvernia (Pa.) in 2007, Lutz fractured a bone in his left foot while backhanding a ball at third base during the first inning of his first pro game. He spent the next six months on crutches and didn't reach full-season ball until 2009, when he missed more time when his ankle flared up. A stress fracture in his left foot cost him six weeks last season as well. The repeated injuries have hampered his speed and lateral movement significantly, but Lutz hasn't lost his power stroke. He cracked 17 homers in 61 games and slugged .578 in Double-A last year, showing a quick bat, strong hands and plus raw power. He uses an open stance and tries to pull the ball for power by collapsing his back side in his swing, which gets him in trouble against pitchers who can locate away. He projects as an average hitter because he has a plan at the plate and shortens his swing with two strikes. Lutz makes the routine play at third base and has an average arm, but injuries have robbed him of much of his formerly average range. He could make his way as a corner-infield extra with thunder in his bat. The Mets added him to the 40-man roster in November and he's ready for Triple-A.

Year	Club (League)	Class	AVG	G	AB	R	H	2B	3B	HR	RBI	BB	SO	SB	CS	OBP	SLG
2007	Brooklyn (NYP)	SS	.000	1	2	0	0	0	0	0	0	0	0	0	0	.000	.000
2008	Brooklyn (NYP)	SS	.333	24	72	9	24	4	0	3	12	14	12	0	2	.442	.514
2009	St. Lucie (FSL)	HiA	.284	99	356	46	101	19	2	11	62	50	72	1	1	.381	.441
	Binghamton (EL)	AA	.207	8	29	0	6	1	0	0	2	5	7	0	0	.324	.241
2010	Mets (GCL)	R	.316	5	19	2	6	1	0	1	4	1	4	0	0	.350	.526
	St. Lucie (FSL)	HiA	.000	1	4	0	0	0	0	0	0	0	2	0	0	.000	.000
	Binghamton (EL)	AA	.289	61	225	42	65	14	0	17	42	33	63	0	2	.389	.578
	Buffalo (IL)	AAA	.300	5	20	3	6	4	0	1	9	2	3	0	0	.364	.650
Minor League Totals			.286	204	727	102	208	43	2	33	131	105	163	1	5	.383	.487

20 ROBBIE SHIELDS, SS

Born: Dec. 7, 1987. **B-T:** R-R. **Ht.:** 6-1. **Wt.:** 195. **Drafted:** Florida Southern, 2009 (3rd round). **Signed by:** Tommy Jackson.

Shields settled at NCAA Division II Florida Southern when no D-I program recruited him. He started from day one for the Moccasins, and his draft stock really took flight when he hit .429 with two homers over 10 games in the Cape Cod League following his sophomore season. Shields' time on the Cape was cut short, however, when he fractured his wrist while sliding headfirst into third base, and he hasn't looked like the same player since. He had a lackluster junior year and signed with the Mets for $315,000 after going in the third round of the 2009 draft. The injury bug bit Shields one more time when he had Tommy John surgery in late October of his draft year, which helped explain his brutal pro debut. He got back on the field late last June, spending a month in Rookie ball before taking over as Savannah's everyday shortstop. A steady player with modest tools across the board, Shields has strong hands and average offensive potential. He figures to hit about .280 with gap power. He's not flashy at shortstop but makes the routine play with average range and running speed. However, many scouts pegged Shields as a future second baseman even before elbow surgery, and he hadn't fully recovered his arm strength at the conclusion of the 2010 season. The Mets say his arm played a tick above-average prior to his injury. Shields figures to begin 2011 with a club for which he can play shortstop everyday, and his assignment may hinge on the Opening Day destination for teen phenom Wilmer Flores.

Year	Club (League)	Class	AVG	G	AB	R	H	2B	3B	HR	RBI	BB	SO	SB	CS	OBP	SLG
2009	Brooklyn (NYP)	SS	.178	44	146	14	26	4	3	1	9	16	32	2	0	.273	.267
2010	Mets (GCL)	R	.244	23	82	11	20	5	0	1	7	11	10	3	1	.330	.341
	St. Lucie (FSL)	HiA	.286	2	7	0	2	0	0	0	1	1	0	1	0	.375	.286
	Savannah (SAL)	LoA	.290	39	162	26	47	10	1	5	26	10	34	4	0	.331	.457
Minor League Totals			.239	108	397	51	95	19	4	7	43	38	76	10	1	.310	.360

21 BRAD EMAUS, 3B/2B

Born: March 28, 1986. **B-T:** R-R. **Ht.:** 5-11. **Wt.:** 200. **Drafted:** Tulane, 2007 (11th round). **Signed by:** Matt Briggs (Blue Jays).

Emaus doesn't have a standout tool, but the Mets have a hole at second base and gave him a chance to fill it when they plucked him from the Blue Jays system in the major league Rule 5 draft in December. He's coming off the best season of his four-year pro career, having hit .290/.397/.476 with 15 homers and 81 walks between Double-A and Triple-A. Emaus' best skill is his ability to control the strike zone. He consistently works counts to his advantage, with the payoff of walks and doubles to the gaps. He has some home run power to his pull side and could hit as many as 15 longballs annually in the big leagues. The question with Emaus is whether he can be a big league starter at second or third base. He doesn't have ideal pop for the hot corner, where he has a decent arm and can make routine plays but is error-prone. He's more dependable at second base, though he lacks the quickness needed there. He's a well below-average runner but has good instincts on the bases. Per Rule 5 guidelines, the Mets must keep Emaus on their big league roster all season, or else put him on waivers and offer him back to Toronto.

Year	Club (League)	Class	AVG	G	AB	R	H	2B	3B	HR	RBI	BB	SO	SB	CS	OBP	SLG
2007	Auburn (NYP)	SS	.228	39	136	21	31	6	0	2	14	12	26	2	0	.298	.316
2008	Dunedin (FSL)	HiA	.302	124	473	87	143	34	3	12	71	60	56	12	4	.380	.463
2009	New Hampshire (EL)	AA	.253	137	505	67	128	28	2	10	67	59	69	10	3	.336	.376
2010	New Hampshire (EL)	AA	.272	38	136	21	37	7	0	5	26	31	19	5	0	.402	.434
	Las Vegas (PCL)	AAA	.298	87	309	58	92	25	3	10	49	50	50	8	2	.395	.495
Minor League Totals			.276	425	1559	254	431	100	8	39	227	212	220	37	9	.364	.426

22 MARK COHOON, LHP

Born: Sept. 15, 1987. **B-T:** L-L. **Ht.:** 6-2. **Wt.:** 195. **Drafted:** North Central Texas JC, 2008 (12th round). **Signed by:** Ray Corbett.

Ask any scout about Cohoon and one of the first words out of his mouth will be "pitchability." More on savvy than stuff, he has shot from Brooklyn to Binghamton in the last two seasons, going 21-7, 2.42 with nearly four times as many strikeouts (201) as walks (52). In June, Cohoon tied a South Atlantic League record when he threw three consecutive shutouts, earning a ticket straight to Double-A. He continued to throw strikes and change speeds on his three-pitch mix to good effect in the Eastern League. Cohoon pitches at 87-89 mph and can scrape 90 when he goes for strikeouts. He goes to a solid-average changeup as his second pitch, and it shows plus potential. He adds and subtracts from a soft curveball, which he'll need to tighten to have a third average pitch. Cohoon pitches to the corners of the plate, locates the ball down and knows how to read opponents' weaknesses. He keeps runners close at first base with an excellent pickoff move, and basestealers succeeded in just nine of 20 tries against him last season. Pitchers with fringy fastballs who can throw offspeed pitches for strikes usually thrive against low-level competition, so Cohoon will be tested in Triple-A in 2011. If he passes, he'll get a chance as a back-of-the-rotation starter.

Year	Club (League)	Class	W	L	ERA	G	GS	CG	SV	IP	H	HR	BB	SO	G/A	WHIP	AVG
2008	Kingsport (APP)	R	1	1	5.89	6	3	0	0	18	17	0	10	22	—	1.47	.239
	Savannah (SAL)	LoA	2	2	3.82	7	7	0	0	33	29	2	18	21	—	1.42	.242
2009	Brooklyn (NYP)	SS	9	2	2.15	14	14	2	0	92	69	4	20	70	2.21	0.97	.210
2010	Savannah (SAL)	LoA	7	1	1.30	13	13	3	0	90	68	2	17	75	1.86	0.94	.213
	Binghamton (EL)	AA	5	4	4.18	13	13	1	0	71	74	5	15	56	1.06	1.25	.272
Minor League Totals			24	10	2.78	53	50	6	0	305	257	13	80	244	1.69	1.11	.231

23 MATT DEN DEKKER, OF

Born: Aug. 10, 1987. **B-T:** L-L. **Ht.:** 6-1. **Wt.:** 205. **Drafted:** Florida, 2010 (5th round). **Signed by:** Les Parker.

On the heels of poor junior season, den Dekker turned down the Pirates as a 16th-round pick in 2009, opting to return to Florida for his senior year. He moved up 11 rounds in the draft and signed for $110,000 after a career year for the Gators, during which he batted .352/.435/.563 with 13 homers and 23 steals in 62 games. That performance helped mitigate scouts' concerns about his pitch-recognition skills and contact ability, and den Dekker continued to hit after jumping to low Class A in his pro debut. His swing can get choppy and he's not a high-contact, bat-control player, so his average may settle in the .260 range. An open batting stance this season helped him shorten his stride, though it didn't appear to aid him against lefthanders, who have tormented him since college. A physical player with strength in his swing, he can drive the ball to the alleys and to his pull side, but his power is below-average. It's on defense where den Dekker shines. He's a big league-caliber defender in center field with tremendous range and solid arm strength. He's a plus runner. The Mets intend to challenge den Dekker, a high-energy player who could have a long career as a lefty-batting extra outfielder who can defend, run and hit a bit.

Year	Club (League)	Class	AVG	G	AB	R	H	2B	3B	HR	RBI	BB	SO	SB	CS	OBP	SLG
2010	Mets (GCL)	R	.278	5	18	2	5	2	0	0	5	2	5	0	0	.350	.389
	Savannah (SAL)	LoA	.346	27	104	21	36	13	0	0	15	9	28	3	0	.404	.471
Minor League Totals			.336	32	122	23	41	15	0	0	20	11	33	3	0	.396	.459

24 ARMANDO RODRIGUEZ, RHP

Born: Jan. 28, 1988. **B-T:** R-R. **Ht.:** 6-2. **Wt.:** 185. **Signed:** Dominican Republic, 2007. **Signed by:** Ismael Cruz.

Under former general manager Omar Minaya, the Mets dedicated as many resources to Latin America as any organization. They operate two Rookie-level Dominican Summer League clubs and three domestic short-season league affiliates, and the club credits 19 international scouts in its 2010 media guide. While New York has spent liberally to acquire Latin amateurs such as Wilmer Flores, Fernando Martinez and Juan Urbina, they also have discovered a number of less-heralded talents in the Dominican Republic. In 2007 alone, the Mets signed 17-year-olds Jenrry Mejia and Jeurys Familia as well as Rodriguez and Jordany Valdespin, both in June at the relatively ripe old age of 19. Their signing age explains why both Rodriguez and Valdespin were added to the 40-man roster in November after just four seasons under contract. Rodriguez spent the better part of three seasons in short-season leagues before busting out in a big way as a 22-year-old in low Class A last year. He led the South Atlantic League with 152 strikeouts while ranking second in opponent average (.214) and third in ERA (3.08). Despite the gaudy numbers, Rodriguez is a bit of a one-trick pony. He pitches at 89-91 mph and touches 92 with his fastball, mixing in an 86-88 cutter. He's an aggressive strike-thrower who keeps the ball down. Rodriguez comes in on opposing batters and has natural deception in his drop-and-drive delivery, helping his fastball play up to average to a tick above. He tends to push his below-average slider and changeup to the plate, and they lack finish and shape. Rodriguez's fastball command could help him profile in a long-relief role, but he's going to have to prove he can get more advanced batters to swing and miss at his stuff. He's ready for high Class A this year.

Year	Club (League)	Class	W	L	ERA	G	GS	CG	SV	IP	H	HR	BB	SO	G/A	WHIP	AVG
2007	Mets (DSL)	R	2	2	3.46	11	2	0	0	26	17	1	21	29	—	1.46	.191
2008	Mets (DSL)	R	4	4	2.63	15	13	0	0	72	48	0	22	81	—	0.97	.188
2009	Kingsport (APP)	R	3	1	2.96	9	9	0	0	46	39	2	20	36	0.58	1.29	.227
	Savannah (SAL)	LoA	2	1	2.16	3	3	1	0	17	5	0	9	24	0.44	0.84	.094
2010	Savannah (SAL)	LoA	8	9	3.08	27	27	0	0	146	116	5	46	152	0.80	1.11	.214
Minor League Totals			19	17	2.94	65	54	1	0	306	225	8	118	322	0.71	1.12	.203

25 JORDANY VALDESPIN, 2B/SS

Born: Dec. 23, 1987. **B-T:** L-R. **Ht.:** 6-0. **Wt.:** 174. **Signed:** Dominican Republic, 2007. **Signed by:** Ramon Pena/Ismael Cruz/Marciano Alvarez.

Valdespin played at six different levels of the minors in 2009-10, topping out at Double-A last August. On the flip side, he bottomed out in 2009 when he landed in the Dominican Summer League as he began the rehab process from a badly sprained ankle. In both seasons, the Mets removed Valdespin from game action to cool him down after clashes with coaches and managers. Last season the organization suspended him twice for such outbursts, while in 2009 they sent him to extended spring training for two weeks. Ultimately, the Mets concluded that Valdespin's athleticism, quick lefty bat and speed would make him attractive to teams in the Rule 5 draft, so they added him to the 40-man roster in November. (They also may have recalled losing raw talents like Enrique Cruz and Jesus Flores in past Rule 5 drafts.) With a live, projectable body, Valdespin whips the bat through the zone and could hit .270 one day, but only if he tones down his aggressive approach. He has modest power for a middle infielder, though it's below-average overall. He's not an instinctive basestealer, but he's a plus runner capable of racking up 20 steals in a season. The Mets have tried Valdespin at shortstop for brief periods, but he lacks the concentration and throwing accuracy to play there on a full-time basis. He has the soft hands, average arm and quick feet necessary for second base, where he's an average defender. Valdespin's flashy, immature approach rubs a lot of observers the wrong way, but his tools are promising enough to intrigue the Mets as a potential middle-infield reserve. He'll return to Double-A in 2011.

Year	Club (League)	Class	AVG	G	AB	R	H	2B	3B	HR	RBI	BB	SO	SB	CS	OBP	SLG
2007	Mets (DSL)	R	.245	43	139	23	34	4	3	1	16	24	26	8	4	.369	.338
2008	Mets (GCL)	R	.284	34	134	23	38	6	3	3	22	7	10	9	2	.319	.440
2009	Savannah (SAL)	LoA	.322	39	152	30	49	9	3	3	18	11	32	7	2	.366	.480
	Mets (DSL)	R	.333	4	15	0	5	0	2	0	5	3	1	1	1	.421	.600
	Mets (GCL)	R	.174	6	23	0	4	0	0	0	0	1	3	1	0	.208	.174
	Brooklyn (NYP)	SS	.279	18	68	10	19	3	1	1	5	5	16	4	3	.338	.397
2010	St. Lucie (FSL)	HiA	.289	65	270	40	78	16	3	6	33	8	45	13	10	.323	.437
	Binghamton (EL)	AA	.232	28	112	8	26	8	0	0	8	2	23	4	2	.243	.304
Minor League Totals			.277	237	913	134	253	46	15	14	107	61	156	47	24	.328	.406

26 JEFRY MARTE, 3B

Born: June 21, 1991. **B-T:** R-R. **Ht.:** 6-1. **Wt.:** 187. **Signed:** Dominican Republic, 2007. **Signed by:** Ramon Pena/Ismael Cruz/Marciano Alvarez.

Marte signed for a tidy $550,000 in 2007 and hails from La Romana, the same coastal Dominican Republic city as fellow prospect Cesar Puello. Marte began and ended the 2010 season on the sidelines with a hamstring injury, but in between the down time he showed improvement across the board. He repeated low Class A, but at age 19 he still ranked as one of the South Atlantic League's youngest players. Lead-footed with slow infield actions, Marte will have to hit to make it, and his improved offensive output in last season made some scouts believers again. He improved his strikeout and walk rates and drove the ball form gap to gap with solid bat speed. One scout said Marte made as much hard contact as the college products in the SAL. He doesn't lift the ball consistently and can be pitched inside when he lengthens his swing, but the raw power is there for 15-20 homers annually. He doesn't often chase pitches outside the zone and his swing is simple enough to hit for a modest average. He's a well below-average runner. Marte led all minor leaguers with 49 errors in 2009, but he has worked hard to improve his defensive play and sports fringe-average hands, feet and range. He throws well but tends to give his first basemen a workout with errant throws. Marte will have to either improve his defensive consistency to stick at third base or hit for more power to profile at first base. He figures to spend a good portion of 2011 in high Class A.

Year	Club (League)	Class	AVG	G	AB	R	H	2B	3B	HR	RBI	BB	SO	SB	CS	OBP	SLG
2008	Mets (GCL)	R	.325	44	154	29	50	14	3	4	24	13	30	2	0	.398	.532
2009	Savannah (SAL)	LoA	.233	123	485	58	113	21	6	6	41	25	117	5	5	.279	.338
2010	Savannah (SAL)	LoA	.264	82	329	40	87	19	4	6	44	30	65	4	5	.333	.401
Minor League Totals			.258	249	968	127	250	54	13	16	109	68	212	11	10	.317	.390

27 KYLE ALLEN, RHP

Born: Feb. 12, 1990. **B-T:** R-R. **Ht.:** 6-3. **Wt.:** 195. **Drafted:** HS—Bradenton, Fla., 2008 (24th round). **Signed by:** Les Parker.

Lightning struck twice for the Mets in the 24th round of the draft. Last year, they nabbed UCLA righthander Erik Goeddel and signed him for third-round money. In 2008, they plucked Allen from the high school ranks and signed him for $150,000. A two-way star at The Pendleton School, part of the IMG Academy in Bradenton, Fla., he fell in the draft because of concerns about his maturity and his commitment to North Carolina State. On the heels of a breakout 2009 campaign, Allen regressed badly last year as his command disintegrated. A gifted athlete, he has a solid fastball at 88-92 mph and pitches downhill with sinking and tailing life. Most scouts prefer Allen's 82-84 mph changeup to his fringy slider, but both pitches need considerable tightening. He maintains balance in his delivery, but he short-arms the ball ever so slightly. Allen will require better command or improved secondary stuff to stick in the rotation, so some evaluators view him as a future reliever. Like Jeurys Familia, he may get a chance to catch his breath by repeating high Class A at the outset of 2011.

Year	Club (League)	Class	W	L	ERA	G	GS	CG	SV	IP	H	HR	BB	SO	G/AWHIP	AVG
2008	Mets (GCL)	R	1	1	2.12	11	5	0	2	34	24	1	10	45	— 1.00	.194
2009	Savannah (SAL)	LoA	9	6	3.45	25	19	0	2	125	109	8	51	111	2.17 1.28	.234
2010	St. Lucie (FSL)	HiA	6	8	5.24	21	19	0	0	101	106	6	54	53	2.06 1.58	.273
Minor League Totals			16	15	3.97	57	43	0	4	261	239	15	115	209	2.12 1.36	.244

28 MANNY ALVAREZ, RHP

Born: Dec. 18, 1985. **B-T:** R-R. **Ht.:** 5-11. **Wt.:** 200. **Signed:** Venezuela, 2004. **Signed by:** Ismael Cruz (Expos).

The Mets added Alvarez to the 40-man roster in early November, preventing him from leaving the organization as a minor league free agent. He would have generated interest from other teams after leading all minor league pure relievers in WHIP (0.85) and ranking fourth in K-BB ratio (7.0) last season. The definition of a late bloomer, Alvarez signed with the Expos in February 2004 but never made it to full-season ball in three seasons before earning his release. The Mets signed him in January 2007, in part because international scouting director Ismael Cruz knew him from their days together in the Montreal organization. Given a new lease on his career, Alvarez still languished in short-season leagues for two more seasons before graduating to full-season ball in 2009. Things began to come together for him last season when he ascended to closing games for Binghamton before finishing the year in Triple-A. Alvarez began to sit more comfortably at 91-92 mph and touch 93 with his sinker, while mixing in a cutter to give him something hard to throw to his glove side. His average slider sweeps late off the barrel of righthanders, and he'll mix in an occasional below-average changeup. With a burly build, Alvarez hides the ball well, but improved command has made the biggest difference. He doesn't project as a bullpen anchor, but he now throws enough strikes with conviction to fit in middle relief. He'll probably begin 2011 back in Buffalo.

Year	Club (League)	Class	W	L	ERA	G	GS	CG	SV	IP	H	HR	BB	SO	G/AWHIP	AVG
2004	Expos (DSL)	R	3	1	2.48	7	6	0	0	33	30	0	8	21	— 1.16	.238
2005	Did Not Play—Injured															
2006	Nationals (GCL)	R	2	3	2.79	14	0	0	0	19	14	1	8	15	— 1.14	.203
2007	Mets (VSL)	R	1	4	4.29	13	11	0	0	57	56	1	25	42	— 1.43	.257
2008	Kingsport (APP)	R	0	4	6.59	17	0	0	3	27	43	4	6	14	— 1.79	.352
2009	St. Lucie (FSL)	HiA	4	3	5.09	35	0	0	9	46	58	4	24	32	1.14 1.78	.305
2010	St. Lucie (FSL)	HiA	3	1	0.00	18	0	0	9	26	12	0	4	24	1.25 0.62	.148
	Binghamton (EL)	AA	3	1	2.87	34	0	0	8	47	35	5	6	57	0.65 0.87	.203
	Buffalo (IL)	AAA	0	2	6.00	4	0	0	0	6	8	1	2	3	0.56 1.67	.333
Minor League Totals			16	19	3.69	142	17	0	29	261	256	16	83	208	0.94 1.30	.255

29 BLAKE FORSYTHE, C

Born: July 31, 1989. **B-T:** R-R. **Ht.:** 6-2. **Wt.:** 220. **Drafted:** Tennessee, 2010 (3rd round). **Signed by:** Erwin Bryant.

Forsythe hit .347 and slugged 15 home runs as a Tennessee sophomore but suffered an apparent case of draftitis last spring, again smacking 15 homers but hitting just .286 with 54 strikeouts in 55 games. The Mets selected Forsythe in the third round and signed him for $392,400, but he didn't turn too many heads with a lifeless pro debut. Like his brother Logan, a second-base prospect with the Padres, Blake possesses strong plate discipline. He compiled a .450 on-base percentage in his last two college seasons, though his batting eye deserted him in his first taste of pro ball. He works deep counts but likes to take huge cuts and may never hit much more than .250. He has above-average power from left field to right-center, and could hit 20 homers per season. New York will accept his strikeouts if that power materializes. Forsythe throws well and nabbed 33 percent of pro basestealers. Some scouts slap above-average grades on his receiving, while others assess it as fringy. Like most catchers, he's not a runner. Forsythe has two plus tools in his power and his arm strength, which could make him a decent starter or quality backup if his receiving and game-calling are up to the task. He'll start his first full pro season in low Class A.

Year	Club (League)	Class	AVG	G	AB	R	H	2B	3B	HR	RBI	BB	SO	SB	CS	OBP	SLG
2010	Mets (GCL)	R	.200	3	10	0	2	0	0	0	0	1	2	0	0	.273	.200
	Brooklyn (NYP)	SS	.238	30	101	14	24	5	1	3	8	11	41	1	1	.310	.396
Minor League Totals			.234	33	111	14	26	5	1	3	8	12	43	1	1	.307	.378

30 PEDRO BEATO, RHP

Born: Oct. 27, 1986. **B-T:** R-R. **Ht.:** 6-6. **Wt.:** 220. **Drafted:** St. Petersburg (Fla.) JC, 2006 (1st round supplemental). **Signed by:** Nick Presto (Orioles).

The Mets took Beato out of a Brooklyn high school in the 17th round of the 2005 draft, and then controlled his rights when he attended St. Petersburg (Fla.) JC. But New York couldn't get him signed under the now-defunct draft-and-follow process, and the Orioles made him the 32nd overall pick in 2006, signing him for $1 million. The Mets finally got their man in December, when they took Beato in the second round of the major league Rule 5 draft. He had floundered as a starter in his first four years as a pro, but flourished when he moved to the bullpen in Double-A in 2010. Beato has an ideal pitcher's frame, and his fastball ranges from 86-93 mph with sink and tail. He has thrown a variety of other pitches during his career, though none of them has developed into a reliable second offering. The best is probably his changeup, which shows good sink. He throws a curveball and slider but they often morph into a slurvy breaking pitch. He has a lot of effort in his delivery, which costs him command, though he has improved his control and was able to throw strikes and generate groundballs out of the bullpen. Beato doesn't have back-of-the-bullpen stuff but should be a reliable middle reliever. To hold onto him, New York will have to keep him on its major league roster throughout 2011. He can't be sent to the minors without clearing waivers or being offered back to the Orioles.

Year	Club (League)	Class	W	L	ERA	G	GS	CG	SV	IP	H	HR	BB	SO	G/AWHIP	AVG
2006	Aberdeen (NYP)	SS	3	2	3.63	14	10	0	0	57	47	6	23	52	— 1.23	.222
2007	Delmarva (SAL)	LoA	7	8	4.05	27	27	0	0	142	139	10	59	106	— 1.39	.256
2008	Orioles (GCL)	R	0	0	2.53	2	2	0	0	11	10	1	1	3	— 1.03	.244
	Frederick (CAR)	HiA	4	10	5.85	19	19	0	0	97	119	11	33	51	— 1.57	.306
2009	Frederick (CAR)	HiA	5	7	4.53	20	20	1	0	105	125	12	40	70	1.08 1.57	.297
	Bowie (EL)	AA	1	3	4.50	6	5	0	0	32	33	6	7	18	1.03 1.25	.268
2010	Bowie (EL)	AA	4	0	2.11	43	0	0	16	60	49	4	19	50	1.28 1.14	.225
Minor League Totals			24	30	4.21	131	83	1	16	504	522	50	182	350	1.13 1.40	.268

New York Yankees

BY JOHN MANUEL

CLIFF WELCH

With many franchises, the success of the Yankees farm system in 2010 would have been the story of the organization's year.

New York had breakthrough after breakthrough in the minors, with power-armed righthanders Dellin Betances and Andrew Brackman having their best seasons and second-tier prospects such as third baseman Brandon Laird, righty Ivan Nova and infielder Eduardo Nunez turning strong performances at upper levels. The top three affiliates reached the playoffs, with high Class A Tampa winning the Florida State League title.

But that's not what grabs headlines in New York.

The Yankees won 95 games, led the planet in runs scored and once again dominated the Twins in the American League Division Series, but the season was viewed as a disappointment because they fell short of repeating as World Series champions. Not only did they lose to the Rangers in the AL Championships Series, but they were clearly the inferior team, getting outscored 31-6 in their losses.

Counting the playoffs, New York split its last 68 games after July 31. For glass-half-empty Yankee fans, there were plenty of negatives, from the death of owner George Steinbrenner and former public-address voice Bob Sheppard to empty seats at ALCS games to the impending free agency of franchise icon Derek Jeter.

Jeter did return, albeit after a contentious negotiation, as did fellow free agents Joe Girardi and Mariano Rivera. New York has done a nice job of mixing in productive homegrown youngsters to go with the veterans—Robinson Cano had an MVP-caliber season, Phil Hughes won 18 games in his first full season as a starter and Brett Gardner ranked in the AL top 10 in on-base percentage, stolen bases and assists—yet the club still needs changes.

The Yankees' modest defense and lack of athleticism was exposed during the regular season by the Rays, who beat them out for the AL East division title, and in the playoffs by the Rangers. A.J. Burnett and Javier Vazquez flopped badly and Andy Pettitte is contemplating retirement, making starting pitching an offseason priority. The Yankees, who have had MLB's highest payroll in each of the last 12 seasons, nevertheless lost out on their top free-agent target when Cliff Lee signed with the Phillies.

However, the Yankees could use their farm system to improve their big league club. They have the talent and depth to put together tempting trade packages, with three attractive catchers (Jesus Montero, Gary

Catcher Jesus Montero should be Derek Jeter's teammate in 2011 in New York

TOP 30 PROSPECTS

1. Jesus Montero, c	16. David Phelps, rhp
2. Gary Sanchez, c	17. Graham Stoneburner, rhp
3. Dellin Betances, rhp	18. D.J. Mitchell, rhp
4. Manny Banuelos, lhp	19. Melky Mesa, of
5. Andrew Brackman, rhp	20. Corban Joseph, 2b
6. Austin Romine, c	21. Cito Culver, ss
7. Hector Noesi, rhp	22. David Adams, 2b
8. Eduardo Nunez, ss/3b	23. Bryan Mitchell, rhp
9. Slade Heathcott, of	24. Jose Ramirez, rhp
10. Brandon Laird, 3b	25. Angelo Gumbs, ss
11. Brett Marshall, rhp	26. Jeremy Bleich, lhp
12. Adam Warren, rhp	27. Daniel Brewer, of
13. Ivan Nova, rhp	28. Tommy Kahnle, rhp
14. J.R. Murphy, c	29. Chase Whitley, rhp
15. Mason Williams, of	30. Pat Venditte, rhp/lhp

Sanchez, Austin Romine), plenty of up-the-middle talent (Nunez, outfielder Slade Heathcott and 2010 draftees Cito Culver and Mason Williams) and a bevy of righthanded pitchers (Betances, Brackman, Hector Noesi, Nova). The system's only significant shortages appear to be corner bats and lefthanded pitching, where Manny Banuelos stands out significantly.

New York also appears inclined to try to build its bench from within. Laird and Nunez could be multipositional reserves in 2011, which would let the Yankees stretch their $200 million budget, if such a thing can be said.

General Manager: Brian Cashman. **Farm Director:** Pat Roessler. **Scouting Director:** Damon Oppenheimer.

Class	Team	League	W	L	PCT	Finish*	Manager
Majors	New York Yankees	American	95	67	.586	2nd (14)	Joe Girardi
Triple-A	Scranton/W-B Yankees	International	87	56	.608	2nd (14)	Dave Miley
Double-A	Trenton Thunder	Eastern	83	59	.585	1st (12)	Tony Franklin
High A	Tampa Yankees	Florida State	78	57	.578	†1st (12)	Torre Tyson
Low A	Charleston RiverDogs	South Atlantic	65	74	.468	t-9th (14)	Greg Colbrunn
Short-season	Staten Island Yankees	New York-Penn	34	40	.459	t-10th (14)	Jody Reed/Josh Paul
Rookie	GCL Yankees	Gulf Coast	24	32	.429	t-12th (15)	Tom Slater
Overall 2010 Minor League Record			371	318	.538	3rd (30)	

*Finish in overall standings (No. of teams in league). †League champion.

LAST YEAR'S TOP 30

Player, Pos.		Status
1.	Jesus Montero, c	No. 1
2.	Austin Romine, c	No. 6
3.	Arodys Vizcaino, rhp	(Braves)
4.	Slade Heathcott, of	No. 9
5.	Zach McAllister, rhp	(Indians)
6.	Manny Banuelos, lhp	No. 4
7.	Gary Sanchez, c	No. 2
8.	J.R. Murphy, c	No. 14
9.	Jeremy Bleich, lhp	No. 26
10.	Andrew Brackman, rhp	No. 5
11.	Bryan Mitchell, rhp	No. 23
12.	Mike Dunn, lhp	(Braves)
13.	Corban Joseph, 2b/3b	No. 20
14.	Eduardo Nunez, ss	No. 8
15.	Mark Melancon, rhp	(Astros)
16.	Ivan Nova, rhp	No. 13
17.	D.J. Mitchell, rhp	No. 18
18.	Melky Mesa, of	No. 19
19.	Kelvin DeLeon, of	Dropped out
20.	Jose Ramirez, rhp	No. 24
21.	Graham Stoneburner, rhp	No. 17
22.	David Adams, 2b/3b	No. 22
23.	Caleb Cotham, rhp	Dropped out
24.	Hector Noesi, rhp	No. 7
25.	David Phelps, rhp	No. 16
26.	Adam Warren, rhp	No. 12
27.	Kevin Russo, 2b/3b	Dropped out
28.	Dellin Betances, rhp	No. 3
29.	Jairo Heredia, rhp	Dropped out
30.	Jaime Hoffmann, of	(Dodgers)

BEST TOOLS

Best Hitter for Average	Jesus Montero
Best Power Hitter	Jesus Montero
Best Strike-Zone Discipline	David Adams
Fastest Baserunner	Mason Williams
Best Athlete	Melky Mesa
Best Fastball	Dellin Betances
Best Curveball	Andrew Brackman
Best Slider	David Phelps
Best Changeup	Manny Banuelos
Best Control	Hector Noesi
Best Defensive Catcher	Austin Romine
Best Defensive Infielder	Eduardo Nunez
Best Infield Arm	Eduardo Nunez
Best Defensive Outfielder	Slade Heathcott
Best Outfield Arm	Melky Mesa

PROJECTED 2014 LINEUP

Catcher	Gary Sanchez
First Base	Mark Teixeira
Second Base	Robinson Cano
Third Base	Alex Rodriguez
Shortstop	Eduardo Nunez
Left Field	Brett Gardner
Center Field	Slade Heathcott
Right Field	Curtis Granderson
Designated Hitter	Jesus Montero
No. 1 Starter	C.C. Sabathia
No. 2 Starter	Phil Hughes
No. 3 Starter	Dellin Betances
No. 4 Starter	Manny Banuelos
No. 5 Starter	Hector Noesi
Closer	Andrew Brackman

TOP PROSPECTS OF THE DECADE

Year	Player, Pos.	2010 Org.
2001	Nick Johnson, 1b	Yankees
2002	Drew Henson, 3b	Out of baseball
2003	Jose Contreras, rhp	Phillies
2004	Dioner Navarro, c	Rays
2005	Eric Duncan, 3b	Braves
2006	Phil Hughes, rhp	Yankees
2007	Phil Hughes, rhp	Yankees
2008	Joba Chamberlain, rhp	Yankees
2009	Austin Jackson, of	Tigers
2010	Jesus Montero, c	Yankees

TOP DRAFT PICKS OF THE DECADE

Year	Player, Pos.	2010 Org.
2001	John-Ford Griffin, of	Newark (Atlantic)
2002	Brandon Weeden, rhp (2nd)	Out of baseball
2003	Eric Duncan, 3b	Braves
2004	Phil Hughes, rhp	Yankees
2005	C.J. Henry, ss	Out of baseball
2006	Ian Kennedy, rhp	Diamondbacks
2007	Andrew Brackman, rhp	Yankees
2008	*Gerrit Cole, rhp	UCLA
2009	Slade Heathcott, of	Yankees
2010	Cito Culver, ss	Yankees

*Did not sign.

LARGEST BONUSES IN CLUB HISTORY

Hideki Irabu, 1997	$8,500,000
Jose Contreras, 2002	$6,000,000
Andrew Brackman, 2007	$3,350,000
Gary Sanchez, 2009	$3,000,000
Willy Mo Pena, 1999	$2,440,000

NEW YORK YANKEES

TOP 2011 ROOKIE: Jesus Montero, c. He'll finally get some big league at-bats, either at catcher or DH.

BREAKOUT PROSPECT: Brett Marshall, rhp. He's back up to 97 mph after returning from Tommy John surgery and has a better feel for pitching.

SLEEPER: Ramon Flores, of/1b. After leading the Gulf Coast League with a .436 on-base percentage, he'll play in low Class A at age 19.

SOURCE OF TOP 30 TALENT			
Homegrown	30	Acquired	0
College	11	Trades	0
Junior college	1	Rule 5 draft	0
High school	10	Independent leagues	0
Draft-and-follow	0	Free agents/waivers	0
Nondrafted free agents	0		
International	8		

LF
Ramon Flores
Ben Gamel
Colin Curtis
Cody Johnson

CF
Slade Heathcott (9)
Mason Williams (15)
Eduardo Sosa
Kevin Russo
Wilmer Romero

RF
Melky Mesa (19)
Daniel Brewer (27)
Kelvin DeLeon
Abraham Almonte
Jake Anderson
Greg Golson

3B
Brandon Laird (10)
J.R. Murphy (14)
Kevin Russo
Rob Segedin
Fu Lin-Kuo

SS
Eduardo Nunez (8)
Cito Culver (21)
Kelvin Castro
Christopher Tamarez

2B
Corban Joseph (20)
David Adams (22)
Angelo Gumbs (25)
Reegie Corona
Jose Pirela

1B
Bradley Suttle
Jorge Vazquez
Rob Lyerly
Tyler Austin
Kyle Roller

C
Jesus Montero (1)
Gary Sanchez (2)
Austin Romine (6)
Kyle Higashioka

RHP

RHSP	RHRP
Dellin Betances (3)	D.J. Mitchell (18)
Andrew Brackman (5)	Tommy Kahnle (28)
Hector Noesi (7)	Chase Whitley (29)
Brett Marshall (11)	Romulo Sanchez
Adam Warren (12)	Daniel Turpen
Ivan Nova (13)	Craig Heyer
David Phelps (16)	Ryan Pope
Graham Stoneburner (17)	Conor Mullee
Bryan Mitchell (23)	Zack Varce
Jose Ramirez (24)	Daniel Burawa
Rafael DePaula	Zach Nuding
Jairo Heredia	
Gabe Encinas	
Taylor Morton	
Scott Allen	
Christofer Cabrera	
Caleb Cotham	
Brett Gerritse	
Sean Black	
Michael O'Brien	

LHP

LHSP	LHRP
Manny Banuelos (4)	Robert Fish
Jeremy Bleich (26)	Steve Garrison
Josh Romanski	Nick Turley
Evan Rutckyj	
Shaffer Hall	

RHP/LHP
Pat Venditte (30)

2010

BEST PURE HITTER: OF Ben Gamel (10) does everything easy as a hitter, with a simple, low-maintenance swing and great balance. His bat is his best tool and he has no glaring weakness.

BEST POWER HITTER: In a draft centered on athletes, the Yankees took no true sluggers other than 1B Kyle Roller (8). 3B Rob Segedin (3) has as much raw power as Roller, though he doesn't have a feel for lofting the ball yet.

FASTEST RUNNER: OF Mason Williams (4) got the largest bonus of any New York draftee ($1.45 million), thanks to his athleticism and 70 speed on the 20-80 scouting scale.

BEST DEFENSIVE PLAYER: Cito Culver (1) went 32nd overall because of his ability to play shortstop. He has good hands, range and natural instincts, and he always seems to get good hops with his feel and footwork.

BEST FASTBALL: RHP Tommy Kahnle (5) can hit 98 mph out of the bullpen and sat at 93-95 mph as a college starter last spring. Raw RHP Connor Mullee (24) has similar arm strength and a better pitcher's body at 6-foot-3 and 185 pounds.

BEST SECONDARY PITCH: RHP Chase Whitley (15) has a plus changeup. If his slider develops, he'll have a shot to start.

BEST PRO DEBUT: Whitley tied for second in the short-season New York-Penn League with 15 saves and finished his season in the high Class A Florida State League playoffs, going 4-2, 1.27 overall with 45 strikeouts in 35 innings. Culver didn't post gaudy numbers (.251/.325/.330) but reached the NY-P as a 17-year-old in August. RHP Zach Varce (11) used a solid fastball/slider combination to lead the NY-P with 74 strikeouts in 71 innings.

BEST ATHLETE: SS Angelo Gumbs (2) has strength, quickness and a lightning-fast bat. He may be athletic enough to stay in the infield, with center field his fallback position.

MOST INTRIGUING BACKGROUND: Gamel's brother Mat is in the majors with the Brewers. Unsigned Michael O'Neill (42) is the nephew of former Yankees outfielder Paul. Unsigned C Matt Rice (50), the last player drafted, was a Rhodes Scholar candidate.

CLOSEST TO THE MAJORS: Kahnle and Whitley should move quickest as relievers, with Whitley taking an early lead by finishing his debut in high Class A.

BEST LATE-ROUND PICK: Whitley and Mullee, who was mostly a shortstop in college. Mullee is raw and will have to develop his secondary stuff, but his arm strength is undeniable.

THE ONE WHO GOT AWAY: The Yankees made a late run at RHP Josh Dezse (28), a Columbus, Ohio, native who couldn't be swayed from his Ohio State commitment. He touched 95 mph late in the summer.

ASSESSMENT: This is a high-risk/high-reward class with up-the-middle athletes such as Culver, Gumbs and Williams. With strong pitching at the top of the farm system, the Yankees gambled on prep talent, so it will take time to see if it pans out.

2009

OF Slade Heathcott (1) and C J.R. Murphy (2) will need time to develop, but RHP Adam Warren (4) finished his first pro season in Double-A. RHPs Graham Stoneburner (14) and Bryan Mitchell (16), who signed for a combined $1.475 million, also show promise.

GRADE: C+

2008

The Yankees failed to sign two of their top three choices, RHPs Gerrit Cole (1), a possible No. 1 overall pick in 2011, and Scott Bittle (2). The other, LHP Jeremy Bleich (1s), had labrum surgery last year. Yet this crop still has depth, led by RHPs Brett Marshall (6) and David Phelps (14).

GRADE: C+

2007

RHP Andrew Brackman (1) finally is starting to show why New York gave him a big league contract potentially worth $13 million. C Austin Romine (2) could be Jorge Posada's successor. 3B Brandon Laird (27) was the Double-A Eastern League's 2010 MVP.

GRADE: B

2006

This draft has produced seven big leaguers, most notably RHPs Ian Kennedy (1), Joba Chamberlain (1s) and David Robertson (17). RHPs Kennedy, Zach McAllister (3), Mark Melancon (9) and Daniel McCutchen (13) helped acquire Lance Berkman, Curtis Granderson, Damaso Marte, Xavier Nady and Kerry Wood in trades.

GRADE: B+

Draft analysis by John Manuel (2010) and Jim Callis (2006-09).
Numbers in parentheses indicate draft rounds.

JESUS MONTERO, C

Born: Nov. 28, 1989. **Bats:** R. **Throws:** R.
Height.: 6-4. **Weight.:** 230. **Signed:** Venezuela,
2006. **Signed by:** Carlos Rios/Ricardo Finol.

MIKE JANES

The top international talent in the summer of 2006, Montero has lived up to the hype and his $1.65 million bonus. He played in the 2008 and 2009 Futures Games but didn't earn a spot in the 2010 contest because of a poor first half. In his first shot at Triple-A, he batted just .214 through June 6, but rallied to hit .351 with 14 homers in 44 second-half games and ranked in the top five in the International League in doubles (34), extra-base hits (58) and total bases (234). Montero nearly became a Mariner in July, when the Yankees thought they had worked out a deal in which he'd be the centerpiece of a package for Cliff Lee. But Seattle wound up opting for Justin Smoak and three prospects from the Rangers when New York wouldn't include infielder Eduardo Nunez or righthander Ivan Nova.

Montero may be the best all-around hitter in the minors, capable of hitting .300 with 30-plus homers annually. He doesn't have typical hitting mechanics, as he doesn't always have a smooth swing and can be a bit of a front-foot hitter, but his strength and hand-eye coordination help him overcome that. He has well above-average power, particularly to the opposite field, making him well-suited for Yankee Stadium. Some club officials compare him to their greatest recent development success story, Robinson Cano, for his handsy swing and natural feel for hitting. Cano became an MVP-caliber hitter when he improved his game preparation and batting-practice routine, and Montero could use more discipline in those areas as well. He tinkers with his stance, and could use a more professional approach to BP. Scouts rarely criticize his hitting tools, though, focusing more on his work as a catcher. Montero has worked hard to become a passable defender, improving his fitness and flexibility, but will have to keep working to remain behind the plate. He generally earns below-average grades for his catch-and-throw skills, and he led the IL with 15 passed balls while throwing out just 23 percent of basestealers. He has above-average arm strength but a slow transfer and inconsistent accuracy on his throws, which tend to sink. He's a well below-average runner and needs to keep up his conditioning to avoid being a baseclogger.

The Yankees' willingness to trade Montero was more a reflection of their desire to obtain Lee and the catching depth in the system than any reflection on him. He doesn't have anything left to prove in the minors as a hitter, and his defense doesn't look so bad when coupled with his offense or when compared to that of 39-year-old Jorge Posada. GM Brian Cashman has said Montero will get the chance to earn a spot on New York's 2011 roster. Now that he has experienced failure and learned how to respond to it, he should be able to earn a job as at least a part-timer at catcher and DH in 2011. The best-case scenario is that he develops into the second coming of Mike Piazza, and Montero has enough bat for first base (where he'd be blocked by Mark Teixeira) or DH if he can't stick at catcher.

SCOUTING GRADES

Batting: 70.   **Defense:** 40.
Power: 70.   **Arm:** 50.
Speed: 25.

Based on 20-80 scouting scale, where 50 represents major league average, and future projection rather than present tools.

Year	Club (League)	Class	AVG	G	AB	R	H	2B	3B	HR	RBI	BB	SO	SB	CS	OBP	SLG
2007	Yankees (GCL)	R	.280	33	107	13	30	6	0	3	19	12	18	0	0	.366	.421
2008	Charleston, SC (SAL)	LoA	.326	132	525	86	171	34	1	17	87	37	83	2	1	.376	.491
2009	Tampa (FSL)	HiA	.356	48	180	26	64	15	1	8	37	14	26	0	0	.406	.583
	Trenton (EL)	AA	.317	44	167	19	53	10	0	9	33	14	21	0	0	.370	.539
2010	Scranton/W-B (IL)	AAA	.289	123	453	66	131	34	3	21	75	46	91	0	0	.353	.517
Minor League Totals			.314	380	1432	210	449	99	5	58	251	123	239	2	1	.371	.511

2 GARY SANCHEZ, C

Born: Dec. 2, 1992. **B-T:** R-R. **Ht.:** 6-2. **Wt.:** 195. **Signed:** Dominican Republic, 2009. **Signed by:** Raymon Sanchez/Victor Mata.

The Yankees gave Sanchez the largest bonus they've ever given to a teenager, $3 million at the start of international signing period in July 2009. He backed up his scouting reports in his 2010 pro debut, homering three times in his first seven games and ranking as the No. 1 prospect in the Rookie-level Gulf Coast League. Sanchez has a higher ceiling than anyone in the organization, including Jesus Montero. Outside of his below-average speed, he has above-average tools across the board. He already has plus raw power and should add more as he adds mature strength to his youthful but solid frame. He has a good swing path and the bat speed to catch up to good fastballs, as well as a sound approach for a teenager. His offensive game requires polish that will come with at-bats, but he has no significant holes. He flashes the lateral movement, soft hands and strong arm to be a plus defender, though he's not consistent yet. He threw out 26 percent of basestealers in his debut. Sanchez's biggest issue is maintaining his motivation in the midst of $3 million and plenty of accolades. He'll have to keep working hard to reach his potential, and he'll move up to low Class A Charleston in 2011.

Year	Club (League)	Class	AVG	G	AB	R	H	2B	3B	HR	RBI	BB	SO	SB	CS	OBP	SLG
2010	Yankees (GCL)	R	.353	31	119	25	42	11	0	6	36	11	28	1	1	.419	.597
	Staten Island (NYP)	SS	.278	16	54	8	15	2	0	2	7	3	16	1	1	.333	.426
Minor League Totals			.329	47	173	33	57	13	0	8	43	14	44	2	2	.393	.543

3 DELLIN BETANCES, RHP

Born: March 23, 1988. **B-T:** R-R. **Ht.:** 6-8. **Wt.:** 245. **Drafted:** HS—New York, 2006 (8th round). **Signed by:** Cesar Presbott/Brian Barber.

The Yankees signed Betances, a New Yorker, away from Vanderbilt for a $1 million bonus in 2006. He developed slower than hoped, then had surgery to reinforce an elbow ligament in 2009. He returned to the mound last June, throwing 96-97 in his first start and wrapping up the season in the Double-A Eastern League playoffs. Ther performance earned him a 40-man roster spot. Betances' fastball usually sits at 92-96, and he uses his size to throw it downhill. He throws strikes with his heater, but fastball command remains his biggest issue to work on. His curveball is a sharp, power downer that some scouts rate as a 70 on the 20-80 scale, giving him two plus-plus pitches. His changeup draws mixed reviews but is at least fringe average, and some club officials predict it will become a plus pitch. Betances' delivery tends to get out of line to the plate, wasting energy and costing him command, but his stuff is good enough that he can thrive with just solid control. He's not a great athlete and doesn't excel at fielding his position or holding runners. If Betances can build on the progress he made last season, he'll be a frontline starter for New York, possibly as soon as 2012. If he regresses a bit, he still could wind up in the mix to eventually replace Mariano Rivera as the Yankees' closer.

Year	Club (League)	Class	W	L	ERA	G	GS	CG	SV	IP	H	HR	BB	SO	G/AWHIP	AVG
2006	Yankees (GCL)	R	0	1	1.16	7	7	0	0	23	14	1	7	27	— 0.90	.173
2007	Staten Island (NYP)	SS	1	2	3.60	6	6	0	0	25	24	0	17	29	— 1.64	.255
2008	Yankees (GCL)	R	0	1	8.53	3	2	0	0	6	13	0	3	6	— 2.53	.406
	Charleston (SAL)	LoA	9	4	3.67	22	22	0	0	115	87	9	59	135	— 1.27	.208
2009	Tampa (FSL)	HiA	2	5	5.48	11	11	0	0	44	48	2	27	44	1.00 1.69	.277
2010	Tampa (FSL)	HiA	8	1	1.77	14	14	0	0	71	43	1	19	88	1.05 0.87	.169
	Trenton (EL)	AA	0	0	3.77	3	3	0	0	14	10	3	3	20	0.46 0.91	.200
Minor League Totals			20	14	3.39	66	65	0	0	300	239	16	135	349	0.96 1.25	.217

4 MANNY BANUELOS, LHP

Born: March 13, 1991. **B-T:** L-L. **Ht.:** 5-10. **Wt.:** 155. **Signed:** Mexico, 2008. **Signed by:** Lee Sigman.

Part of a quartet of Mexican players the Yankees signed as a group for $450,000 in 2008, Banuelos excelled in Class A as an 18-year-old in 2009. His 2010 season was delayed when he needed an appendectomy during spring training, but he pitched well after returning in June and made up for lost time in the Arizona Fall League, where he was the circuit's youngest pitcher. Banuelos has a quick arm, natural arm strength and sound mechanics. The ball comes out of his hand easy and he has surprising velocity for a little lefthander, sitting at 90-94 mph with his fastball and touching 95. He has excellent fastball control, even with his improved velocity, and projects to have true big league command. His changeup and curveball can be plus pitches, though they often aren't working at the same time. His changeup is more consistent and has better action, with late fade and sink at its best. Banuelos has the poise and composure to move quickly, and now he has frontline stuff. He's the best lefthander in the system by a mile. He'll spend 2011 at Double-A Trenton and must prove he can hold up after never throwing more than seven innings in a game or 108 in a season.

Year	Club (League)	Class	W	L	ERA	G	GS	CG	SV	IP	H	HR	BB	SO	G/A	WHIP	AVG
2008	Yankees (GCL)	R	4	1	2.57	12	3	0	0	42	32	3	13	37	—	1.07	.208
2009	Charleston (SAL)	LoA	9	5	2.67	25	19	0	0	108	88	4	28	104	1.00	1.07	.219
	Tampa (FSL)	HiA	0	0	0.00	1	0	0	0	1	0	0	0	2	—	0.00	.000
2010	Yankees (GCL)	R	0	0	1.80	2	2	0	0	5	1	0	3	6	2.50	0.80	.063
	Tampa (FSL)	HiA	0	3	2.23	10	10	0	0	44	38	1	14	62	1.40	1.17	.230
	Trenton (EL)	AA	0	1	3.52	3	3	0	0	15	15	2	8	17	2.00	1.50	.273
Minor League Totals			13	10	2.59	53	37	0	0	216	174	10	66	228	1.16	1.11	.219

5 ANDREW BRACKMAN, RHP

Born: Dec. 4, 1985. **B-T:** R-R. **Ht.:** 6-10. **Wt.:** 240. **Drafted:** North Carolina State, 2007 (1st round). **Signed by:** Steve Swail.

A basketball and baseball player at North Carolina State, Brackman signed a stunning major league contract in 2007 that included a $3.35 million bonus, $4.55 million in guaranteed money and $13 million in potential total value. His development has been slowed by Tommy John surgery shortly after he signed, an appendectomy in 2008 and wildness in 2009. He got off to a poor start in 2010 as well before his delivery clicked after a promotion to Double-A. Brackman has good athleticism to go with his size, and he started to coordinate the moving parts of his delivery in 2010. When he did, he found the bottom of the strike zone more with his fastball, which jumped from 88-92 mph to 93-95 mph. His best pitch is a well above-average curveball with which he can vary the size, shape and velocity (72-81 mph). Brackman has added a nascent slider that shows potential and scrapes the upper 80s. He lacks confidence in his changeup and needs to pitch with more aggressiveness, considering his power stuff. For some scouts, Brackman's whole is less than the sum of his parts, earning comparisons to A.J. Burnett and Kyle Farnsworth. He just completed his second full pro season as a pitcher, however, and tantalized with his rapid improvement in 2010 and likely will get his first big league callup in 2011, probably as a reliever.

Year	Club (League)	Class	W	L	ERA	G	GS	CG	SV	IP	H	HR	BB	SO	G/A	WHIP	AVG
2009	Charleston (SAL)	LoA	2	12	5.91	29	19	0	0	107	106	8	76	103	1.58	1.71	.266
2010	Tampa (FSL)	HiA	5	4	5.10	12	12	0	0	60	67	5	9	56	1.95	1.27	.278
	Trenton (EL)	AA	5	7	3.01	15	14	0	0	81	77	3	30	70	1.80	1.33	.252
Minor League Totals			12	23	4.77	56	45	0	0	247	250	16	115	229	1.73	1.48	.265

6 AUSTIN ROMINE, C

Born: Nov. 22, 1988. **B-T:** R-R. **Ht.:** 6-1. **Wt.:** 185. **Drafted:** HS—Lake Forest, Calif., 2007 (2nd round). **Signed by:** David Keith.

Romine has two big leaguers in his family—father Kevin and brother Andrew, a shortstop who went 1-for-11 for the Angels in 2010—and more upside than either of them. Austin played in the Futures Game and caught a career-high 106 games (counting playoffs) last season, appearing to wear down in the second half. While Jesus Montero has more star potential with his bat, Romine is a more well-rounded player. He employs a high leg kick, and when he gets his timing right, he has solid power to the opposite field. He's still learning to pull the ball with more authority, but he should have average power to go with fringe-average hitting ability. He's a bit undisciplined at the plate. Romine has solid athleticism and runs well for a catcher. He still has some rough edges to polish up as a receiver but has good hands. He has plus arm strength but isn't consistently accurate, and threw out just 23 percent of basestealers in 2010. He needs to get stronger to handle the rigors of catching over a full season. After playing in the Arizona Fall League, Romine is headed to Triple-A Scranton/Wilkes-Barre in 2011. He may become trade bait if Montero establishes himself as Jorge Posada's successor in New York.

Year	Club (League)	Class	AVG	G	AB	R	H	2B	3B	HR	RBI	BB	SO	SB	CS	OBP	SLG
2007	Yankees (GCL)	R	.500	1	2	2	1	1	0	0	1	1	1	0	0	.667	1.000
2008	Charleston (SAL)	LoA	.300	104	407	66	122	24	1	10	49	25	56	3	0	.344	.437
2009	Tampa (FSL)	HiA	.276	118	442	61	122	28	3	13	72	29	78	11	5	.322	.441
2010	Trenton (EL)	AA	.268	115	455	61	122	31	0	10	69	37	94	2	0	.324	.402
Minor League Totals			.281	338	1306	190	367	84	4	33	191	92	229	16	5	.330	.427

7 HECTOR NOESI, RHP

Born: Jan. 26, 1987. **B-T:** R-R. **Ht.:** 6-2. **Wt.:** 174. **Signed:** Dominican Republic, 2004. **Signed by:** Victor Mata.

Noesi had a solid 2009 season, earning a spot on New York's 40-man roster after missing parts of the previous two years following Tommy John surgery. He was even better last season, appearing in the Futures Game and leading Yankees farmhands with 153 strikeouts while reaching Triple-A for the first time. Noesi has the best command in the system, with just 43 walks in 277 innings over the last two seasons. He has a fluid, easy delivery and gets good extension out front, repeating his release point. He pounds the zone with an 89-93 mph fastball, reaching as high as 96. His maintains his velocity deep into games, and his fastball has some run and tail. Noesi's No. 2 pitch is a changeup with similar action, though he doesn't quite command it like his fastball. His curveball and slider remain below-average offerings, but he flashes the ability to spin the ball. He's athletic and fields his position well. Noesi lacks the breaking ball to pitch near the front of a rotation, but his fastball command should allow him to be a No. 4 or 5 starter for the Yankees if needed. He might help New York more as trade bait. If he's still a Yankee in 2011, he'll return to Scranton.

Year	Club (League)	Class	W	L	ERA	G	GS	CG	SV	IP	H	HR	BB	SO	G/A	WHIP	AVG
2005	Yankees1 (DSL)	R	5	3	1.60	13	10	0	0	51	34	2	8	36	—	0.83	.178
2006	Yankees (GCL)	R	0	0	1.29	5	0	0	1	7	5	0	1	11	—	0.86	.192
2007	Charleston (SAL)	LoA	1	1	4.50	5	5	0	0	20	25	2	8	11	—	1.65	.309
2008	Yankees (GCL)	R	2	1	3.65	9	2	0	0	25	23	2	3	24	—	1.05	.253
	Staten Island (NYP)	SS	1	1	3.00	5	5	0	0	24	20	5	7	31	—	1.13	.227
2009	Charleston (SAL)	LoA	3	4	2.38	17	11	0	0	76	62	3	11	78	0.97	0.96	.218
	Tampa (FSL)	HiA	3	0	3.92	9	9	0	0	41	34	3	4	40	0.69	0.92	.224
2010	Tampa (FSL)	HiA	5	2	2.72	8	8	0	0	43	35	3	6	53	1.30	0.95	.212
	Trenton (EL)	AA	8	4	3.10	17	16	2	0	99	90	7	18	86	0.74	1.09	.243
	Scranton/W-B (IL)	AAA	1	1	4.82	3	3	1	0	19	23	1	4	14	1.29	1.45	.311
Minor League Totals			29	17	2.97	91	69	3	1	404	351	28	70	384	0.88	1.04	.230

8 EDUARDO NUNEZ, SS/3B

Born: June 15, 1987. **B-T:** R-R. **Ht.:** 6-0. **Wt.:** 155. **Signed:** Dominican Republic, 2004. **Signed by:** Victor Mata.

Nunez went five years between appearances on our Yankees Top 10, ranking No. 6 after his first season in the United States in 2005 before struggling for the next three years. When he began maturing and working harder late in the 2008 season, his tools started to play on the diamond. He got his first big league callup in 2010, including a spot on the postseason roster after Mark Teixeira went down with a hamstring injury. Nunez profiles well at shortstop. His best tool remains his plus-plus arm that allows him to make highlight plays from the hole, though he tends to rely on it too much, which can lead to passivity and errors. He has improved his footwork and plays with more confidence at short, where he's an above-average defender. Nunez's plus speed is his next-best tool, and he should steal 20 bases annually. His speed and ability to make contact should allow him to hit for a solid average, though he lacks selectivity and has fringy power. Nunez also saw time at second and third base in 2010, and he worked out in the outfield in instructional league. The Yankees see him in the Chone Figgins mold as a utility player, though he was in line to take over had Derek Jeter departed as a free agent.

Year	Club (League)	Class	AVG	G	AB	R	H	2B	3B	HR	RBI	BB	SO	SB	CS	OBP	SLG
2004	Yankees1 (DSL)	R	.215	57	191	29	41	9	5	3	20	27	41	16	6	.324	.361
2005	Staten Island (NYP)	SS	.313	73	281	37	88	11	6	3	46	20	43	6	3	.365	.427
2006	Tampa (FSL)	HiA	.184	37	147	17	27	5	3	4	26	8	28	6	1	.223	.340
	Charleston (SAL)	LoA	.227	90	344	36	78	11	3	2	40	23	48	16	5	.278	.294
2007	Charleston (SAL)	LoA	.238	91	328	36	78	10	2	1	28	25	42	20	8	.293	.290
	Tampa (FSL)	HiA	.285	30	123	16	35	5	0	1	13	7	18	9	0	.336	.350
2008	Tampa (FSL)	HiA	.271	94	373	45	101	18	3	6	42	19	48	14	10	.305	.383
2009	Trenton (EL)	AA	.322	123	497	70	160	26	1	9	55	22	63	19	7	.349	.433
2010	Scranton/W-B (IL)	AAA	.289	118	464	55	134	25	3	4	50	32	60	23	5	.340	.381
	New York (AL)	MAJ	.280	30	50	12	14	1	0	1	7	3	2	5	0	.321	.360
Major League Totals			.280	30	50	12	14	1	0	1	7	3	2	5	0	.321	.360
Minor League Totals			.270	713	2748	341	742	120	26	33	320	183	391	129	45	.319	.369

9 SLADE HEATHCOTT, OF

Born: Sept. 28, 1990. **B-T:** L-L. **Ht.:** 6-1. **Wt.:** 190. **Drafted:** HS—Texarkana, Texas, 2009 (1st round). **Signed by:** Mark Batchko/Tim Kelly.

While some clubs had concerns about Heathcott's health and makeup, the Yankees drafted him 29th overall in 2009 and signed him for $2.2 million. He started 2010 in extended spring training before heading in June to Charleston, where he impressed scouts and managers with his high-energy approach. He physically resembles Brett Gardner and has some similarities to New York's left fielder, but Heathcott should develop more power and has a stronger arm. He generates bat speed and has improved his swing path, but he doesn't have a lot of loft in his stroke. Some in the organization believe he injured his left shoulder trying too hard to adjust his swing to hit for power, and he required postseason surgery on the labrum in his left (throwing) shoulder, which the club considers minor. Like many young hitters, he needs to be more selective at the plate. Heathcott has plus speed and excellent range in center field, where he shows off a plus-plus arm. He was clocked at 94 mph as a high school pitcher. He's an aggressive fielder and runner who has decent instincts that should improve with experience. Thanks to his surgery, Heathcott may get a late start in 2011, but it's not a long-term concern. He should push his way to high Class A Tampa at some point during the year.

Year	Club (League)	Class	AVG	G	AB	R	H	2B	3B	HR	RBI	BB	SO	SB	CS	OBP	SLG
2009	Yankees (GCL)	R	.100	3	10	0	1	0	0	0	0	1	2	0	0	.182	.100
2010	Charleston (SAL)	LoA	.258	76	298	48	77	16	3	2	30	42	101	15	10	.359	.352
Minor League Totals			.253	79	308	48	78	16	3	2	30	43	103	15	10	.354	.344

10 BRANDON LAIRD, 3B

Born: Sept. 11, 1987. **B-T:** R-R. **Ht.:** 6-1. **Wt.:** 215. **Drafted:** Cypress (Calif.) JC, 2007 (27th round). **Signed by:** Dave Keith.

The younger brother of big league catcher Gerald Laird, Brandon signed for $120,000 as a 27th-round pick out of Cypress (Calif.) JC in 2007. He broke into pro ball as a third baseman, played primarily at first base in 2008, then returned to the hot corner the last two years. He won Eastern League MVP honors in 2010 despite spending August in Triple-A. Laird has a track record of hitting in the minors. He has good pitch recognition and feel for the barrel, which should enable him to produce for average as well as power. He has strong hands, solid bat speed and nice leverage in his swing. His aggressiveness got the best of him at Triple-A, and he needs to prove he can adjust against better pitching. Scouts used to question his glove and athletic ability, but Laird keeps answering their doubts. He has become an average defender at third, with subpar range but good hands and a strong arm. He's a below-average runner. The Yankees worked Laird on the outfield corners in the Arizona Fall League, and increased versatility would help his chances of eventually sticking in New York. He profiles as a third baseman in the Kevin Kouzmanoff mode, and with Alex Rodriguez ahead of him, Laird could become trade fodder. Added to the 40-man roster, he'll return to Scranton in 2011.

Year	Club (League)	Class	AVG	G	AB	R	H	2B	3B	HR	RBI	BB	SO	SB	CS	OBP	SLG
2007	Yankees (GCL)	R	.339	45	168	27	57	14	1	8	29	6	26	0	0	.367	.577
2008	Charleston (SAL)	LoA	.273	122	454	71	124	31	1	23	86	40	86	1	0	.334	.498
2009	Tampa (FSL)	HiA	.266	124	451	53	120	20	4	13	75	39	75	1	1	.329	.415
2010	Trenton (EL)	AA	.291	107	409	73	119	22	2	23	90	38	84	2	2	.355	.523
	Scranton/W-B (IL)	AAA	.246	31	122	13	30	6	0	2	12	4	27	0	0	.268	.344
Minor League Totals			.281	429	1604	237	450	93	8	69	292	127	298	4	3	.337	.478

11 BRETT MARSHALL, RHP

Born: March 22, 1990. **B-T:** R-R. **Ht.:** 6-1. **Wt.:** 195. **Drafted:** HS—Baytown, Texas, 2008 (6th round). **Signed by:** Steve Boros.

As another talented pitcher who bounced back well from elbow surgery, Marshall ranked with Dellin Betances and Andrew Brackman among the Yankees' feel-good stories in 2010. Like Brackman, he had full-blown Tommy John surgery, and like Betances, he impressed with his work ethic and competitiveness in returning from his elbow operation. A sixth-round pick, Marshall got the largest signing bonus of the New York's 2008 draft class at $850,000, thanks to his power arm. His fastball reached 96 mph at times before his surgery, and he boasted to club officials he'd throw 100 mph one day. That kind of velocity hasn't materialized yet, but Marshall has regained his mid-90s velocity on his four-seam fastball, touching 97. However, he no longer relies on his four-seamer, instead working off a two-seamer that ranges from 89-94 mph. Yankees senior vice president of baseball operations Mark Newman compares its life and movement to a hard slider thrown by a lefthander. Marshall gained more confidence in his two-seamer as the season wore on, allowing two earned runs in his final 36 innings in low Class A. He finished the season helping Tampa win the Florida State League championship. Marshall came to the Yankees with a slider and still throws it, though the organization prefers curveballs. He tried throwing a curve in 2009 before he got hurt, but he has gone back to the slider. It flashes above-average potential when he doesn't get around it. His average changeup joins his two-seamer in helping him combat lefthanders, and it's more consistent than his slider. Like Betances and Manny Banuelos, Marshall has significant upside but needs to prove he can pitch a full season. He figures to start 2011 back in high Class A.

Year	Club (League)	Class	W	L	ERA	G	GS	CG	SV	IP	H	HR	BB	SO	G/AWHIP		AVG
2008	Yankees (GCL)	R	0	0	0.00	3	3	0	0	6	2	0	2	8	—	0.67	.087
2009	Charleston (SAL)	LoA	3	6	5.56	17	17	0	0	87	98	7	37	60	1.28	1.55	.290
2010	Yankees (GCL)	R	0	0	2.25	2	1	0	0	8	6	0	4	8	1.29	1.25	.194
	Charleston (SAL)	LoA	4	2	2.50	13	13	1	0	72	52	2	22	56	1.76	1.03	.199
	Tampa (FSL)	HiA	0	0	4.50	1	1	0	0	4	5	0	0	6	1.50	1.25	.294
Minor League Totals			7	8	3.96	36	35	1	0	177	163	9	65	138	1.46	1.29	.243

12 ADAM WARREN, RHP

Born: Aug. 25, 1987. **B-T:** R-R. **Ht.:** 6-1. **Wt.:** 200. **Drafted:** North Carolina, 2009 (4th round). **Signed by:** Scott Lovekamp.

North Carolina signed Warren as a fairly high-profile recruit, a surprise considering his father played football as a punter at rival North Carolina State. He went 31-4 in his three seasons with the Tar Heels, getting a bit better each year, and his rate of improvement has accelerated since he signed as a fourth-round pick in 2009. He finished his first full season in Double-A, racking up 18 strikeouts in 11 innings in the Eastern League playoffs. The Yankees saw dividends from small tweaks they made in his delivery, incorporating more of a hip turn, using his legs more and quickening his tempo. Being a bit less robotic helped Warren push his fastball velocity to 90-94 mph with a high of 96, and also gave him more deception. His fastball has late life and he commands it well. It can be a swing-and-miss pitch in the strike zone at its best, as evidenced when he set a Trenton franchise record with 15 strikeouts (11 on fastballs) in seven innings in mid-August. Warren also throws a curveball and a cutter/slider. Scouts prefer the latter, as it helps him get groundballs, but don't love either breaking ball. He also throws a changeup, but it's fringe-average at best. Warren's fastball is his meal ticket, but he'll go as far as his secondary stuff takes him. He's headed back to Double-A to start 2011.

Year	Club (League)	Class	W	L	ERA	G	GS	CG	SV	IP	H	HR	BB	SO	G/AWHIP		AVG
2009	Staten Island (NYP)	SS	4	2	1.43	12	12	0	0	57	49	1	10	50	2.90	1.04	.236
2010	Tampa (FSL)	HiA	7	5	2.22	15	15	1	0	81	72	2	17	67	2.93	1.10	.235
	Trenton (EL)	AA	4	2	3.15	10	10	0	0	54	49	2	16	59	1.70	1.20	.232
Minor League Totals			15	9	2.25	37	37	1	0	192	170	5	43	176	2.52	1.11	.234

13 IVAN NOVA, RHP

Born: Jan. 12, 1987. **B-T:** R-R. **Ht.:** 6-4. **Wt.:** 210. **Signed:** Dominican Republic, 2004. **Signed by:** Victor Mata/Carlos Rios.

Nova made it to the major leagues in his seventh season as a pro after signing for $80,000 in 2004. In between he slogged his way through the low minors, was lost to the Padres in the 2008 Rule 5 draft, then returned to the Yankees. Since coming back in the spring of 2009, he has taken off and really broke out in 2010, his best minor league season. Nova's fastball once sat at 89-93 mph and now operates at 92-94 mph since he has grown into his body. At times, he reaches 97 mph with his four-seamer, and some club officials like the idea of putting him in a middle-relief role, where his fastball could sit in the upper 90s more regularly. However, Nova's three-pitch mix gives him a chance to start, and he competed well as New York's fifth starter in August and September. His changeup is his most reliable secondary pitch. His 80 mph curveball still lacks consistency but has upside, as one scout said it can range from a 30 to a 60 on the 20-80 scouting scale. He also has messed around with a slider that lacks depth and is closer to a cutter. Nova's long arm action makes it hard for him to repeat his release point, costing him command and pitch efficiency and leading to inconsistency with his curve. MLB has investigated allegations that Nova and Wilkin de la Rosa injected each other with B-12 shots while teammates at Trenton in 2009, but any findings haven't been made public. Nova is a good trade piece or insurance if the Yankees can't add enough starting pitching in the offseason. Otherwise he could get a shot in a long-relief or swingman role.

Year	Club (League)	Class	W	L	ERA	G	GS	CG	SV	IP	H	HR	BB	SO	G/AWHIP		AVG
2005	Yankees1 (DSL)	R	0	1	2.29	11	7	0	0	39	29	2	11	38	—	1.02	.200
2006	Yankees (GCL)	R	3	0	2.72	10	5	0	1	43	36	5	7	36	—	1.00	.229
2007	Charleston (SAL)	LoA	6	8	4.98	21	21	0	0	99	121	8	31	54	—	1.53	.306
2008	Tampa (FSL)	HiA	8	13	4.36	26	24	0	0	149	168	6	46	109	—	1.44	.294
2009	Trenton (EL)	AA	5	4	2.36	12	12	0	0	72	65	3	31	47	2.47	1.33	.244
	Scranton/W-B (IL)	AAA	1	4	5.10	12	12	1	0	67	72	4	28	43	1.21	1.49	.285
2010	Scranton/W-B (IL)	AAA	12	3	2.86	23	23	0	0	145	135	10	48	115	1.95	1.26	.250
	New York (AL)	MAJ	1	2	4.50	10	7	0	0	42	44	4	17	26	1.73	1.45	.268
Major League Totals			1	2	4.50	10	7	0	0	42	44	4	17	26	1.73	1.45	.268
Minor League Totals			35	33	3.70	115	104	1	1	615	626	38	202	442	1.83	1.35	.269

14 J.R. MURPHY, C

Born: May 13, 1991. **B-T:** R-R. **Ht.:** 5-10. **Wt.:** 170. **Drafted:** HS—Bradenton, Fla., 2009 (2nd round). **Signed by:** Jeff Deardorff/Brian Barber.

The Yankees loved Murphy's bat, so they drafted him in the second round in 2009 and signed him away from a Miami commitment for $1.25 million. He started last season in extended spring training before moving up to low Class A in May. Murphy shared Charleston's catching duties with 2008 draftee Kyle Higashioka, and the two presented a stark contrast. While Higashioka's glove is ahead of his offense, Murphy lags behind defensively, to the point where he may not be a catcher much longer. He worked extensively at third base and the outfield corners in New York's instructional league minicamp in September, and Murphy has the bat to move to less-demanding defensive positions. He has a professional approach and good balance and rhythm. He shows above-average barrel awareness for his age and has above-average pull power potential. He should be able to hit the ball to all fields with authority as he gains experience and work himself into more hitter's counts. Murphy has many issues defensively, starting with slow feet and modest athleticism that led to 11 errors and 13 passed balls in just 53 games behind the plate last year. He has an average arm and threw out just 23 percent of basestealers in 2010. With his arm strength and fringe-average speed, he should be a capable defender in left field if he can't handle third base. Murphy has significant offensive upside, though some scouts question just how much power will develop unless he gets more physical. He may repeat low Class A this year but has the bat to move more quickly.

Year	Club (League)	Class	AVG	G	AB	R	H	2B	3B	HR	RBI	BB	SO	SB	CS	OBP	SLG
2009	Yankees (GCL)	R	.333	9	33	4	11	2	0	1	7	3	8	0	0	.405	.485
2010	Charleston (SAL)	LoA	.255	87	330	46	84	15	2	7	54	36	64	4	5	.327	.376
Minor League Totals			.262	96	363	50	95	17	2	8	61	39	72	4	5	.334	.386

15 MASON WILLIAMS, OF

Born: Aug. 21, 1991. **B-T:** L-R. **Ht.:** 6-0. **Wt.:** 150. **Drafted:** HS—Winter Garden, Fla., 2010 (4th round). **Signed by:** Jeff Deardorff.

Williams wasn't the Yankees top pick in 2010, but he did earn the largest bonus of their draft crop, getting $1.45 million in the fourth round. He had a big spring, pitching, hitting and running West Orange High (Winter Garden, Fla.) to a state 6-A finals berth in Florida's largest classification. His athleticism first attracted New York's attention, and his improvement offensively over the summer with the Midland (Ohio) Redskins alos aided his cause. He earned all-tournament honors while helping Midland repeat as Connie Mack World Series champion. One of his teammates was Shane Rowland, the son of Yankees international scouting director Donnie Rowland. Williams' ability to sting the ball to the opposite field convinced New York he has impact offensive potential. He has good swing fundamentals and makes consistent contact. He's a plus-plus runner and has above-average arm strength, so it's easy to project Williams being an asset in center field as well. His thin, wiry frame elicits Doug Glanville comparisons, though club officials see more electricity and athleticism from Williams. He'll likely begin 2011 in extended spring training because he's still a bit raw in all phases of the game.

Year	Club (League)	Class	AVG	G	AB	R	H	2B	3B	HR	RBI	BB	SO	SB	CS	OBP	SLG
2010	Yankees (GCL)	R	.222	5	18	0	4	0	0	0	0	1	4	1	2	.263	.222
Minor League Totals			.222	5	18	0	4	0	0	0	0	1	4	1	2	.263	.222

16 DAVID PHELPS, RHP

Born: Oct. 9, 1986. **B-T:** R-R. **Ht.:** 6-3. **Wt.:** 185. **Drafted:** Notre Dame, 2008 (14th round). **Signed by:** Mike Gibbons.

The Yankees fast-tracked several of their college pitchers in 2010, Phelps among them. While Adam Warren is the better prospect, Phelps had just as strong of a season, if not better, and finished the year in Triple-A. He ranked second in the system in both innings (159) and strikeouts (141). Like Warren, Phelps has taken off while tightening his mechanics, helping him get more extension and better repeat his release point. A 14th-rounder who signed for $150,000, he pitches off his fastball and throws consistent strikes with it. He pitches at 91-92 mph but can reach back and hit 95 when needed. His fastball can flatten out and he doesn't always pitch downhill like he needs to, but he stays away from home runs, giving up just 20 in 382 pro innings. Phelps' best secondary pitch is his solid curveball, which saw its average velocity jump from 74 to 78 mph last season. It's tight and short with 11-to-5 break, though it doesn't quite have the depth to be a plus pitch.His changeup is fringy, and he also throws a slider that lacks depth but arrives at 82-86 mph. Phelps pitches with an arrogance that helps his stuff play up. He's another good trade piece who'll head back to Scranton for 2011. He has put himself in position for a big league callup if he repeats his 2010 success.

Year	Club (League)	Class	W	L	ERA	G	GS	CG	SV	IP	H	HR	BB	SO	G/AWHIP	AVG
2008	Staten Island (NYP)	SS	8	2	2.72	15	15	0	0	73	67	4	18	52	— 1.17	.245
2009	Charleston (SAL)	LoA	10	3	2.80	19	19	0	0	113	117	9	25	90	1.41 1.26	.272
	Tampa (FSL)	HiA	3	1	1.17	7	7	0	0	38	34	1	6	32	1.66 1.04	.234

Year	Club (League)	Class	W	L	ERA	G	GS	CG	SV	IP	H	HR	BB	SO	G/A	WHIP	AVG
2010	Trenton (EL)	AA	6	0	2.04	14	14	0	0	88	63	2	23	84	1.43	0.97	.199
	Scranton/W-B (IL)	AAA	4	2	3.07	12	11	0	0	70	76	4	13	57	1.17	1.27	.274
Minor League Totals			31	8	2.50	67	66	0	0	382	357	20	85	315	1.38	1.16	.248

17 GRAHAM STONEBURNER, RHP

Born: Sept. 29, 1987. **B-T:** R-R. **Ht.:** 6-1. **Wt.:** 190. **Drafted:** Clemson, 2009 (14th round). **Signed by:** Scott Lovekamp.

Stoneburner, whose older brother Davis reached Triple-A with the Rangers as an infielder last year, pitched at Clemson with fellow Yankees farmhand D.J. Mitchell. After Stoneburner fell to the 14th round in 2009 as a draft-eligible sophomore, New York gave him a $675,000 bonus despite a spotty college track record and a long medical history that included a cracked back vertebra in high school and a torn knee ligament at Clemson. He rewarded the Yankees by leading the system with a 2.41 ERA in his first full pro season. He had more success as a reliever than as a starter in college, and despite his strong debut—when he worked exclusively as a starter—most scouts consider him a better fit in the bullpen down the line. His arm stroke gets long in the back, and while it lends him some deception, it also makes it tough for him to throw more than an average breaking ball consistently as a starter. Stoneburner's athletic ability and quick arm are both assets, and New York senior vice president of baseball operations Mark Newman compares the sink on his two-seamer to that of big leaguer Jake Westbrook, a former Yankees farmhand. Stoneburner's fastball sits at 90-91 mph and tops out at 94 when he starts. His velocity figures to hover around 94 if he comes out of the bullpen, and one pro scout compared Stoneburner to Yankee reliever David Robertson. He also throws a slider and a changeup that's still in development. If he shows enough aptitude with three pitches in spring training, he'll likely stay in the rotation for another year. He could begin 2011 in Double-A.

Year	Club (League)	Class	W	L	ERA	G	GS	CG	SV	IP	H	HR	BB	SO	G/A	WHIP	AVG
2009	Staten Island (NYP)	SS	0	0	0.00	1	0	0	0	1	1	0	0	2	0.00	1.00	.250
2010	Charleston (SAL)	LoA	1	3	2.08	7	7	0	0	39	27	2	10	44	2.67	0.95	.194
	Tampa (FSL)	HiA	8	5	2.53	19	19	1	0	103	80	4	24	93	1.70	1.01	.214
Minor League Totals			9	8	2.39	27	26	1	0	143	108	6	34	139	1.86	0.99	.209

18 D.J. MITCHELL, RHP

Born: May 13, 1987. **B-T:** R-R. **Ht.:** 6-2. **Wt.:** 165. **Drafted:** Clemson, 2008 (10th round). **Signed by:** Scott Lovekamp.

Mitchell made the conversion from outfielder to pitcher at Clemson, but pro scouts still liken his thin, wiry frame to that of a position player. While he's long and lean, he has held up well over two pro seasons, throwing 291 innings and finishing last year in the Triple-A rotation. Signed for $450,000 as a 10th-round pick in 2008, Mitchell stands out for his solid command, quick arm and good tempo, all of which help the life on his two-seam fastball play well. He sits at 88-91 mph and touches 93 with his fastball, and he got 2.0 groundouts for every airout last year. As one scout put it, "His fastball moves a ton when he stays on top of it." Mitchell's slider and curveball have occasional bite, but his three-quarters arm slot may not lend itself to a consistent breaker. His sinking changeup might be his best secondary pitch, grading out as average. He's athletic but inexperienced at nuances of pitching such as holding runners and fielding his position. While Mitchell's four-pitch mix helps him profile as a back-end starter, he has more impact potential as a middle reliever for New York. He'll likely be part of a stout Scranton rotation that also should include Hector Noesi, Adam Warren and David Phelps in 2011.

Year	Club (League)	Class	W	L	ERA	G	GS	CG	SV	IP	H	HR	BB	SO	G/A	WHIP	AVG
2009	Charleston (SAL)	LoA	4	1	1.95	6	6	0	0	37	31	1	6	42	2.21	1.00	.228
	Tampa (FSL)	HiA	8	6	2.87	19	18	1	0	103	93	1	38	83	3.13	1.27	.245
2010	Trenton (EL)	AA	11	4	4.06	23	22	0	0	133	128	11	57	96	2.33	1.39	.254
	Scranton/W-B (IL)	AAA	2	0	3.57	3	3	0	0	18	19	0	7	16	1.19	1.47	.271
Minor League Totals			25	11	3.34	51	49	1	0	291	271	13	108	237	2.46	1.30	.249

19 MELKY MESA, OF

Born: Jan. 31, 1987. **B-T:** R-R. **Ht.:** 6-1. **Wt.:** 165. **Signed:** Dominican Republic, 2003. **Signed by:** Victor Mata/Carlos Rios.

His physical appearance and batting stance resemble Alfonso Soriano's, so Mesa inevitably gets compared to the former Yankees second baseman. Mesa remains one of the organization's top athletes and would be a five-tool player if scouts thought he'd ever be an average hitter. New York is willing to wait to see if his bat develops and added him to the 40-man roster in November. Mesa earned MVP honors in the Florida State League in 2010 as Tampa's everyday center fielder, primarily hitting fourth and fifth in the lineup. A pitch smashed into his wrist on Aug. 28 and forced him to miss the last 10 days of the FSL regular season and the playoffs, but he still finished second in the league in homers (19) and slugging (.475). Mesa has a loose, handsy swing and easy power that comes with a flick of the wrist. His problems stem from being overly aggressive at the plate, though he did cut his strikeout rate from 34 percent of his at-bats in 2009 to 29 percent last year. His speed and arm both grade out as plus tools as well, and he's an above-average right fielder with enough ability to fill in as a center fielder. Mesa's contact issues likely will limit his productivity at upper levels, and 2011 will be a crucial test for him in Double-A.

Year	Club (League)	Class	AVG	G	AB	R	H	2B	3B	HR	RBI	BB	SO	SB	CS	OBP	SLG
2004	Yankees2 (DSL)	R	.146	49	144	13	21	5	0	3	10	12	67	2	2	.279	.243
2005	Yankees1 (DSL)	R	.304	8	23	3	7	2	0	2	6	3	7	1	0	.407	.652
2006	Yankees (GCL)	R	.207	40	145	20	30	7	2	3	22	11	45	3	3	.266	.345
2007	Yankees (GCL)	R	.235	49	153	27	36	10	2	3	13	9	55	5	3	.293	.386
2008	Staten Island (NYP)	SS	.221	46	122	19	27	5	2	7	23	4	38	4	1	.252	.467
2009	Charleston (SAL)	LoA	.225	133	497	76	112	24	7	20	74	51	168	18	6	.309	.423
2010	Tampa (FSL)	HiA	.260	121	446	81	116	21	9	19	74	44	129	31	9	.338	.475
Minor League Totals			.228	446	1530	239	349	74	22	57	222	134	509	64	24	.306	.417

20 CORBAN JOSEPH, 2B

Born: Oct. 28, 1988. **B-T:** L-R. **Ht.:** 6-0. **Wt.:** 168. **Drafted:** HS—Franklin, Tenn., 2008 (4th round). **Signed by:** D.J. Svihlik.

Joseph's brother Caleb catches in the Orioles system, and while Caleb is two years older, Corban caught up to him, finishing 2010 in the Eastern League with him. Once Jesus Montero graduates to the majors, Joseph could succeed him as the system's best pure hitter, thanks to a smooth, loose swing that's short and quick to the ball. He's one of the more patient hitters in the system, and his 58 walks ranked second among Yankees farmhands in 2010. Joseph's other tools lag behind his hitting, and he'll have to improve his power to become a possible everyday player in New York. He needs to get stronger and he'll need to adjust the load in his swing, which adds some strength to his stroke without providing enough pop. Some scouts question whether he'll be able to fix his load. Defensively, Joseph is just adequate at second base, and his average arm strength is better than his fringy hands and footwork. He could learn from fellow Yankees second-base prospect David Adams on how to turn the double play. Joseph has played some third base, where he might be better defensively but is less of a fit with the bat. He figures to return to Double-A for a full season.

Year	Club (League)	Class	AVG	G	AB	R	H	2B	3B	HR	RBI	BB	SO	SB	CS	OBP	SLG
2008	Yankees (GCL)	R	.277	49	159	25	44	15	2	2	18	20	24	2	5	.359	.434
2009	Charleston (SAL)	LoA	.300	100	380	39	114	17	8	4	57	49	61	8	5	.381	.418
2010	Tampa (FSL)	HiA	.302	98	381	52	115	27	3	6	52	43	74	5	8	.378	.436
	Trenton (EL)	AA	.216	31	111	11	24	6	4	0	13	15	33	1	0	.305	.342
Minor League Totals			.288	278	1031	127	297	65	17	12	140	127	192	16	18	.368	.419

21 CITO CULVER, SS

Born: Aug. 26. 1992. **B-T:** B-R. **Ht.:** 6-0. **Wt.:** 185. **Drafted:** HS—Rochester, N.Y., 2010 (1st round). **Signed by:** Matt Hyde.

The Yankees surprised many in the industry by taking Culver in the first round of the 2010 draft, as his bat had other clubs considering him more of a third-round talent. He overcame a difficult home life to become a first-rounder. His father Christopher Sr. broke into the family home in March 2008 and set fire to it, and is currently imprisoned after being found guilty of arson and burglary. Before signing him for $954,000, New York saw plenty of Culver as an amateur between showcases, travel ball and the spring, and came away confident in his makeup and defensive tools. He has good hands, range and natural instincts. Thanks to his feel and footwork, he never seems to get a bad hop. His best present tool is his arm, which is at least plus if not a tick better, and he hit 94 mph as a pitcher. One of the 2010 draft's youngest players, Culver also switch-hits, which added to the Yankees' interest. He has some looseness in his hands and feel for the barrel from both sides. Scouts believe he'll have to quiet some pre-swing movement to improve his timing at the plate—he struck out 51 times in 203 pro at-bats—and he doesn't project to have even average power at this stage. Some scouts were concerned by his relatively thick lower half, but Culver lost weight after signing and trimmed up a bit by fall minicamp. He's a slightly above-average runner but not a big basestealing threat. After an encouraging debut, Culver will start 2011 in low Class A.

Year	Club (League)	Class	AVG	G	AB	R	H	2B	3B	HR	RBI	BB	SO	SB	CS	OBP	SLG
2010	Yankees (GCL)	R	.269	41	160	21	43	7	1	2	18	13	41	6	3	.320	.363
	Staten Island (NYP)	SS	.186	15	43	2	8	1	0	0	0	8	10	1	1	.340	.209
Minor League Totals			.251	56	203	23	51	8	1	2	18	21	51	7	4	.325	.330

22 DAVID ADAMS, 2B

Born: May 15, 1987. **B-T:** R-R. **Ht.:** 6-2. **Wt.:** 205. **Drafted:** Virginia, 2008 (3rd round). **Signed by:** Scott Lovekamp.

Adams had an eventful 2010 to say the least. He got off to a fast start in Double-A before injuring his right ankle while sliding into second base in late May. Initially diagnosed with a high ankle sprain, he found out in late July that he had a broken bone at the joint where the foot meets the ankle. A ligament had detached and pulled some bone off with it, and he had to have the foot immobilized, ending his season. In between, Adams was involved in the Yankees' bid to acquire Cliff Lee from the Mariners. Seattle cited his injury as one reason it pulled out of a deal that would have included Jesus Montero in favor of a trade with the Rangers. Adams was an attractive trade piece because he has good power for a middle infielder. He drives the balls to the gaps and could hit 15 homers on an annual basis. He doesn't stride in his swing but has enough strength to stay balanced and drive the ball. Some scouts think his modest bat speed could compromise his power at higher levels. With the exception of his plus arm, Adams' other tools are all average or fringy. His arm helps him excel at turning the double play, but his range is limited at second base, which is why he has played some third base in the past. He does have good hands, which helped him go 36 games without an error last year. Adams has to get healthy and regain the agility he had before he got hurt. His spring performance and Corban Joseph's presence will determine whether Adams starts 2011 in Scranton or back in Trenton.

Year	Club (League)	Class	AVG	G	AB	R	H	2B	3B	HR	RBI	BB	SO	SB	CS	OBP	SLG
2008	Staten Island (NYP)	SS	.257	67	257	45	66	19	2	4	31	32	57	8	2	.350	.393
2009	Charleston (SAL)	LoA	.290	67	259	32	75	23	2	0	34	35	49	8	4	.385	.394
	Tampa (FSL)	HiA	.281	65	231	37	65	17	6	7	41	26	39	3	4	.360	.498
2010	Trenton (EL)	AA	.309	39	152	31	47	15	3	3	32	18	31	5	2	.393	.507
Minor League Totals			.281	238	899	145	253	74	13	14	138	111	176	24	12	.370	.439

23 BRYAN MITCHELL, RHP

Born: April 19, 1991. **B-T:** L-R. **Ht.:** 6-2. **Wt.:** 175. **Drafted:** HS—Hamlet, N.C., 2009 (16th round). **Signed by:** Scott Lovekamp.

Mitchell was set to follow in Adam Warren's footsteps and pitch at North Carolina before New York stepped in and signed him in August 2009 for $800,000. Ties between the Yankees and Tar Heels are fairly strong—the team played exhibition games there in the late 1970s, and the entrance to Boshamer Stadium is the Steinbrenner Family Courtyard. When Mitchell had some initial reservations about signing and a bout of homesickness, New York got some help from Warren, who showed him around the team's Tampa complex. Mitchell is raw and needs some maturity, but there's no question about his stuff. His fastball sat at 90-91 mph when he signed, but he has a quick arm and already has hit some 94s and 95s as a pro. His curveball, which features a modified spike grip, at times is a hammer with power and bite, and it potentially could rank among the system's best. Mitchell has to learn to harness his stuff and didn't excel at throwing strikes during his pro debut last summer. He got a late start at short-season Staten Island and may return there in 2011 if he can't earn a spot in Charleston's rotation.

Year	Club (League)	Class	W	L	ERA	G	GS	CG	SV	IP	H	HR	BB	SO	G/AWHIP	AVG
2010	Yankees (GCL)	R	2	1	3.67	10	9	0	0	42	28	2	22	36	1.21 1.20	.190
	Staten Island (NYP)	SS	0	1	6.75	1	1	0	0	4	7	0	1	3	1.00 2.00	.368
Minor League Totals			2	2	3.94	11	10	0	0	46	35	2	23	39	1.19 1.27	.211

24 JOSE RAMIREZ, RHP

Born: Jan. 21, 1990. **B-T:** R-R. **Ht.:** 6-1. **Wt.:** 155. **Signed:** Dominican Republic, 2007. **Signed by:** Victor Mata.

As a Dominican righthander with a slender body and a potential power arm, Ramirez has a lot of similiarities to Hector Noesi. Ramirez opened 2010 in Charleston's rotation and missed only one turn through the middle of August, when the Yankees decided to shut him down. He wore down in the final month, with his fastball dipping to as low as the mid-80s. When he's at his best, his heater sits at 90-92 mph and touches 95. His changeup is an average pitch that could develop into a plus offering in the future. His slider shows proper rotation but lacks depth. Ramirez keeps the ball down and excels at limiting big innings, giving up just three homers in 115 innings last year. He has bouts of wildness (his 20 wild pitches ranked second in the South Atlantic League last year) and may not ever have true command. Scouts like his loose arm and projectable body while lamenting his longer arm action and sloppy delivery, which cause him to waste energy and get offline to the plate. He throws strikes to his arm side but hasn't shown he can command his fastball on the other side of the plate, limiting his options. Ramirez needs innings and experience to improve his feel for pitching, as well as strength to hold up better over the course of a full season. Only 20, he'll advance to high Class A with a good spring training.

Year	Club (League)	Class	W	L	ERA	G	GS	CG	SV	IP	H	HR	BB	SO	G/AWHIP	AVG
2008	Yankees 2 (DSL)	R	0	3	4.15	12	10	0	0	39	35	2	18	39	— 1.36	.238
2009	Yankees (GCL)	R	6	0	1.48	11	10	0	0	61	33	5	16	53	1.24 0.80	.159
	Tampa (FSL)	HiA	0	0	0.00	1	0	0	0	3	1	0	0	2	0.75 0.33	.100
2010	Charleston (SAL)	LoA	6	5	3.60	22	21	0	0	115	106	3	42	105	1.11 1.29	.239
Minor League Totals			12	8	3.06	46	41	0	0	218	175	10	76	199	1.14 1.15	.217

25 ANGELO GUMBS, SS

Born: Oct. 13, 1992. **B-T:** R-R. **Ht.:** 6-0. **Wt.:** 175. **Drafted:** HS—Torrance, Calif., 2010 (2nd round). **Signed by:** Dave Keith.

New York wanted athletes in the 2010 draft and also focused on younger players. Gumbs didn't turn 18 until mid-October, and he played young after signing for $750,000 as a second-rounder. Scouts who saw the Yankees' fall minicamp thought Gumbs was more raw than Cito Culver even though he was exposed to better competition in southern California compared to what Culver saw in upstate New York. Gumbs has plenty of ability, though, and plays with energy and enthusiasm. His best tool is his bat speed, and he catches up to good fastballs. As he learns to trust his hands, he should be able to make adjustments to offspeed stuff. Gumbs has plus speed, getting down the line from the right side of the plate in less than 4.2 seconds, and above-average arm strength. He played shortstop in high school, for the Urban Youth Academy in Compton, Calif., and in his brief six-game pro debut, and the Yankees intend to keep him in the infield. He likely won't stay at shortstop, though, and some scouts doubt that his footwork, long arm stroke and actions are good enough for him to remain in the infield at all. He profiles fine in center field if needed, and he'll get plenty of time to develop. Gumbs likely will start 2011 in extended spring training and could head back to the Gulf Coast League, which would be fine at his age. He's a long-term project, and New York can afford the luxury of patience.

Year	Club (League)	Class	AVG	G	AB	R	H	2B	3B	HR	RBI	BB	SO	SB	CS	OBP	SLG
2010	Yankees (GCL)	R	.192	7	26	1	5	1	0	0	0	1	3	3	0	.222	.231
Minor League Totals			.192	7	26	1	5	1	0	0	0	1	3	3	0	.222	.231

26 JEREMY BLEICH, LHP

Born: June 18, 1987. **B-T:** L-L. **Ht.:** 6-2. **Wt.:** 185. **Drafted:** Stanford, 2008 (1st round supplemental). **Signed by:** Mike Thurman.

The Yankees are usually aggressive in the draft, but they had trouble getting their top picks under contract in 2008. First-rounder Gerrit Cole opted to attend UCLA and second-rounder Scott Bittle failed his physical, leaving supplemental first-rounder Bleich as the only one of their first three choices to sign. After reaching Double-A in his first full pro season, he was passed by fellow 2008 draftees Brett Marshall, David Phelps and D.J. Mitchell last year. Bleich didn't throw well to start the 2010 season. He had shown a surprising 90-92 mph fastball that peaked at 94 in 2009, but pitched in the upper 80s early last year. He had his usual solid-average curveball and changeup, but his good control was missing. Bleich had elbow issues in his draft year that resulted in him accepting a below-slot $700,000 bonus, and his shoulder was the reason for his troubles in 2010. He had surgery to repair a torn labrum in late May and missed the rest of the season. New York really won't know what it has until spring training, when Bleich starts readying for 2011. He's not expected to pitch meaningful innings until the second half of the season.

Year	Club (League)	Class	W	L	ERA	G	GS	CG	SV	IP	H	HR	BB	SO	G/AWHIP	AVG
2008	Staten Island (NYP)	SS	0	0	6.00	1	1	0	0	3	2	1	0	4	— 0.67	.182
2009	Tampa (FSL)	HiA	6	4	3.40	14	14	0	0	79	79	4	22	56	1.44 1.27	.257
	Trenton (EL)	AA	3	6	6.65	13	13	0	0	65	84	6	34	60	1.61 1.82	.318
2010	Trenton (EL)	AA	3	2	4.79	8	8	0	0	41	35	2	28	26	2.18 1.52	.236
Minor League Totals			12	12	4.87	36	36	0	0	189	200	13	84	146	1.64 1.51	.274

27 DANIEL BREWER, OF

Born: June 19, 1987. **B-T:** R-R. **Ht.:** 6-0. **Wt.:** 185. **Drafted:** Bradley, 2008 (8th round). **Signed by:** Steve Lemke.

Brewer first gained attention in the Central Illinois Collegiate League (now known as the Prospect League) in 2006, when Baseball America ranked him the summer circuit's No. 7 prospect, one behind fellow current Yankees farmhand Pat Venditte. After three all-Missouri Valley Conference selections at three different positions and a strong Cape Cod League showing in 2007, Brewer went in the eighth round of the 2008 draft and started grinding his way through the minors. He has played all three outfield positions and seen brief action at first and third base, getting the most time in right field. He doesn't have typical corner-outfield power and wasn't considered much of a prospect until 2010, when a July injury to Austin Krum gave Brewer a three-week audition in center field in Double-A. He passed the test offensively and defensively. Playing with more confidence and showing the ability to make adjustments, Brewer hit .320 after July 1, including the Eastern League playoffs. Brewer earns solid grades across the board from scouts, with his hitting ability his best attribute. He has big, strong hands and good bat speed. His instincts help him in all phases of the game, enabling him to get the job done in center field and to steal 61 bases in 80 pro attempts despite just average speed. He lacks a carrying tool, but his aggressiveness, instincts and consistent production could get him to the majors. Brewer is a fourth outfielder at best for the Yankees but could be a second-division regular elsewhere. He's headed for Triple-A in 2011.

Year	Club (League)	Class	AVG	G	AB	R	H	2B	3B	HR	RBI	BB	SO	SB	CS	OBP	SLG
2008	Staten Island (NYP)	SS	.296	66	230	29	68	19	1	3	40	21	65	10	1	.372	.426

2009	Charleston (SAL)	LoA	.323	58	201	38	65	18	3	2	25	33	49	9	5	.429	.473
	Tampa (FSL)	HiA	.290	59	224	32	65	7	3	4	29	22	46	13	3	.359	.402
2010	Trenton (EL)	AA	.270	136	508	83	137	34	3	10	84	53	117	29	10	.346	.407
Minor League Totals			.288	319	1163	182	335	78	10	19	178	129	277	61	19	.368	.421

28 TOMMY KAHNLE, RHP

Born: Aug. 7, 1989. **B-T:** R-R. **Ht.:** 6-1. **Wt.:** 220. **Drafted:** Lynn (Fla.), 2010 (5th round). **Signed by:** Jeff Deardorff.

Kahnle entered 2010 season as the draft's top NCAA Division II prospect. While Southern Arkansas' Hayden Simpson passed him and went in the first round to the Cubs, Kahnle's draft stock held steady despite a 2-7, 5.06 season at Lynn (Fla.). He signed for $150,000 as a fifth-round pick. Kahnle helped pitch Lynn to a 2009 national title, earning MVP honors at the D-II College World Series after saving the championship game and pitching a total of 12 scoreless innings. The Yankees saw him throw well as a reliever in the Cape Cod League that summer and as a starter at Lynn last spring. Working out of the rotation, Kahnle showed a 93-95 mph fastball but lacked the feel for pitching or command needed to get through the order more than twice. He shifted to the bullpen full-time as a pro and pushed his fastball up to 96-98. His slider has its moments, and New York will let him keep it rather than trying to switch him to a curveball. He had a decent changeup as a starter but won't need it nearly as much as a reliever. Kahnle will shoot through the minors if he throws strikes, something that would be easier if he keeps his stocky body in shape. He could open his first full pro season in high Class A.

Year	Club (League)	Class	W	L	ERA	G	GS	CG	SV	IP	H	HR	BB	SO	G/AWHIP	AVG
2010	Staten Island (NYP)	SS	0	0	0.56	11	0	0	3	16	3	0	5	25	0.77 0.50	.061
Minor League Totals			0	0	0.56	11	0	0	3	16	3	0	5	25	0.77 0.50	.061

29 CHASE WHITLEY, RHP

Born: June 14, 1989. **B-T:** R-R. **Ht.:** 6-4. **Wt.:** 220. **Drafted:** Troy, 2010 (15th round). **Signed by:** D.J. Svihlik.

The 2011 season will be the first time Whitley concentrates solely on pitching. He was a three-sport star in high school before playing only baseball at Southern Union (Ala.) JC and Troy. Hitting was his focus for much of his college career, and he led Troy in both hitting (.364) and saves (seven) as a junior last spring. Signed for $68,000 as a 15th-round pick, Whitley finished his pro debut in high Class A, helping Tampa win the Florida State League championship. He resembles former Yankees farmhand T.J. Beam physically but has better stuff and a better future. His fastball sat at 88-92 mph in college, and New York hopes its velocity will jump now that he's a full-time pitcher. His plus changeup is his best pitch, but the Yankees had him shelve it late in the summer so he could develop his fastball and slider. His slider improved, and he could work as a starter if it continues to get better. Whitley has more upside than the average 15th-round pick and should move quickly if New York keeps him in the bullpen. He could finish his first full pro season in Double-A.

Year	Club (League)	Class	W	L	ERA	G	GS	CG	SV	IP	H	HR	BB	SO	G/AWHIP	AVG
2010	Staten Island (NYP)	SS	4	2	1.31	28	0	0	15	34	18	0	15	44	2.00 0.96	.157
	Tampa (FSL)	HiA	0	0	3.00	2	0	0	0	3	1	1	0	6	2.00 0.33	.100
Minor League Totals			4	2	1.45	30	0	0	15	37	19	1	15	50	2.00 0.91	.152

30 PAT VENDITTE, RHP/LHP

Born: June 30, 1985. **B-T:** R-B. **Ht.:** 6-1. **Wt.:** 180. **Drafted:** Creighton, 2008 (20th round). **Signed by:** Steve Lemke.

Venditte's ability to pitch effectively with both arms made him an All-American at Creighton and has allowed him to reach Double-A since signing for $10,000 as a 20th-round pick. He has been even more effective in pro ball than he was in college, going 10-4, 1.70 with 51 saves and 218 strikeouts in 175 innings. Venditte erases platoon advantages for hitters. He has more arm strength as a righthander, sitting in the upper 80s and scraping 90 mph with his fastball. He varies his arm angle and challenges hitters with three pitches, throwing strikes with his curveball and changeup. Venditte showed improvement as a lefthander in 2010, improving his fastball and tightening his slider. His velocity as a lefthander still is a concern, as his fastball operates in the lower 80s and his slider sits around 70 mph. The Yankees haven't considered Venditte a priority, but he has proven himself at every level and earned his first promotion to Double-A in 2010. He figures to return there in 2011, his first extended test at higher levels.

Year	Club (League)	Class	W	L	ERA	G	GS	CG	SV	IP	H	HR	BB	SO	G/AWHIP	AVG
2008	Staten Island (NYP)	SS	1	0	0.83	30	0	0	23	33	13	2	10	42	— 0.70	.117
2009	Charleston (SAL)	LoA	2	2	1.47	28	0	0	20	31	24	1	2	40	1.38 0.85	.212
	Tampa (FSL)	HiA	2	0	2.21	21	0	0	2	37	37	1	9	47	0.62 1.25	.261
2010	Tampa (FSL)	HiA	4	1	1.73	41	0	0	6	73	49	2	14	85	0.81 0.87	.187
	Trenton (EL)	AA	1	1	9.00	2	0	0	0	2	4	0	1	4	— 2.50	.400
Minor League Totals			10	4	1.70	122	0	0	51	175	127	6	36	218	0.87 0.93	.199

Oakland Athletics

BY JIM SHONERD

The Athletics offered their fans some reasons for hope in 2010. The club finished at 81-81 for its first non-losing season since 2006 and managed to beat out the struggling Angels for second place in the American League West.

But in other ways the season was more of the same, as Oakland failed to make the playoffs for the fourth straight season and relied heavily on its pitching staff to try to carry an underpowered offense.

The A's led the AL with a 3.58 ERA and had the league's youngest pitching staff, with Ben Sheets the only regular rotation member older than 26. Brett Anderson continued to dominate when he wasn't battling elbow issues, and all-star Trevor Cahill and Gio Gonzalez blossomed in their second full big league seasons.

The highlight of Oakland's year came on May 9, when Dallas Braden threw a perfect game against the Rays. The bullpen was solid, too, with Andrew Bailey posting a 1.47 ERA and 25 saves while fighting through ribcage and elbow problems.

While the A's have the pitching to return to contention, their offense continues to hold them back. Oakland ranked 11th in the AL in scoring and 13th in homers. Hope that the farm system would bolster the lineup turned out to be in vain.

The A's lost one of their top offensive prospects in January, when outfielder Grant Desme decided to leave baseball and enter the priesthood. He recorded the only 30-30 season in the minors in 2009, then won the Arizona Fall League home run title and MVP award before retiring.

First baseman/outfielder Chris Carter and outfielder Michael Taylor were supposed to be on the verge of contributing in Oakland after tearing up the minors in 2009, but both struggled in Triple-A. Outfielder Sean Doolittle hasn't played since May 2009 and continues to recover from two surgeries on his left knee.

The A's difficulties in developing hitters have led to more aggressive spending in the draft. They went over slot to sign shortstop Grant Green ($2.75 million) and catcher Max Stassi ($1.5 million) in 2009, and again to land outfielder Michael Choice ($2 million), shortstop Yordy Cabrera ($1.25 million), outfielder Aaron Shipman ($500,000) and third baseman Chad Lewis ($300,000) in 2010.

Oakland also has been more active than ever on the international market, in spite of a potentially epic

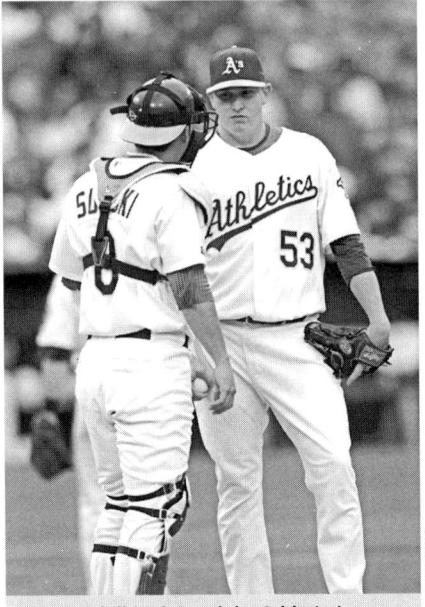

Trevor Cahill (right) and the Athletics' young pitching staff led the AL in team ERA in 2010

TOP 30 PROSPECTS

1. Grant Green, ss	16. Renato Nunez, 3b
2. Chris Carter, 1b/of	17. Sean Doolittle, of/1b
3. Michael Choice, of	18. Chad Lewis, 3b
4. Tyson Ross, rhp	19. Jonathan Joseph, rhp
5. Jemile Weeks, 2b	20. Pedro Figueroa, lhp
6. Max Stassi, c	21. Eric Sogard, inf
7. Aaron Shipman, of	22. Danny Farquhar, rhp
8. Yordy Cabrera, ss	23. Trystan Magnuson, rhp
9. Ian Krol, lhp	24. Steve Parker, 3b
10. Michael Taylor, of	25. Michael Ynoa, rhp
11. Corey Brown, of	26. Ryan Ortiz, c
12. Josh Donaldson, c	27. Matt Thomson, rhp
13. Fautino de los Santos, rhp	28. Rashun Dixon, of
14. Clay Mortensen, rhp	29. Tony Thompson, 3b
15. Adrian Cardenas, 2b/3b	30. Conner Crumbliss, 2b/of

failure. Righthander Michael Ynoa, who received a franchise- and Latin American-record $4.25 million bonus in 2008, had Tommy John surgery last summer and has pitched a total of nine innings since signing. Undaunted, the A's signed Venezuelan third baseman Renato Nunez for $2.2 million in July. In November, they bid a reported $19.1 million for the rights to Japanese righthander Hisashi Iwakuma.

Iwakuma would have ranked No. 1 on this list had he come to terms with Oakland, but negotiations broke down and he returned to the Rakuten Golden Eagles. The A's recouped the posting fee.

General Manager: Billy Beane. **Farm Director:** Keith Lieppman. **Scouting Director:** Eric Kubota.

Class	Team	League	W	L	PCT	Finish*	Manager
Majors	Oakland Athletics	American	81	81	.500	t-8th (14)	Bob Geren
Triple-A	Sacramento River Cats	Pacific Coast	79	65	.549	4th (16)	Tony DeFrancesco
Double-A	Midland RockHounds	Texas	70	70	.500	4th (8)	Darren Bush
High A	Stockton Ports	California	74	66	.529	5th (10)	Steve Scarsone
Low A	Kane County Cougars	Midwest	71	67	.514	9th (16)	Aaron Nieckula
Short-season	Vancouver Canadians	Northwest	42	34	.553	4th (8)	Rick Magnante
Rookie	AZL Athletics	Arizona	30	26	.536	6th (12)	Marcus Jensen
Overall 2010 Minor League Record			366	328	.527	6th (30)	

*Finish in overall standings (No. of teams in league). †League champion.
Low Class A affiliate changes to Burlington (Midwest), short-season affiliate changes to Vermont (New York-Penn) in 2011.

LAST YEAR'S TOP 30

Player, Pos.		Status
1.	Chris Carter, of/1b	No. 2
2.	Brett Wallace, 3b/1b	(Astros)
3.	Grant Green, ss	No. 1
4.	Max Stassi, c	No. 6
5.	Pedro Figueroa, lhp	No. 20
6.	Tyron Ross, rhp	No. 4
7.	Jemile Weeks, 2b	No. 5
8.	Grant Desme, of	(Retired)
9.	Adrian Cardenas, inf	No. 15
10.	Sean Doolittle, of	No. 17
11.	Michael Ynoa, rhp	No. 25
12.	Corey Brown, of	No. 11
13.	Henry Rodriguez, rhp	Majors
14.	Josh Donaldson, c/3b	No. 12
15.	Clayton Mortensen, rhp	No. 14
16.	Ian Krol, lhp	No. 9
17.	Fautino de los Santos, rhp	No. 13
18.	Tommy Everidge, 1b/3b	Dropped out
19.	Arnold Leon, rhp	Dropped out
20.	Justin Souza, rhp	Dropped out
21.	Ryan Ortiz, c	No. 26
22.	Connor Hoehn, rhp	Dropped out
23.	Jonathan Joseph, rhp	No. 19
24.	Julio Ramos, lhp	Dropped out
25.	Andrew Carignan, rhp	Dropped out
26.	Bobby Cassevah, rhp	(Angels)
27.	Justin Marks, lhp	(Royals)
28.	Tyreace House, of	Dropped out
29.	Josh Leyland, c	Dropped out
30.	Brett Hunter, rhp	Dropped out

BEST TOOLS

Best Hitter for Average	Grant Green
Best Power Hitter	Chris Carter
Best Strike-Zone Discipline	Conner Crumbliss
Fastest Baserunner	Tyreace House
Best Athlete	Aaron Shipman
Best Fastball	Fautino de los Santos
Best Curveball	Ian Krol
Best Slider	Tyson Ross
Best Changeup	Clay Mortensen
Best Control	Ian Krol
Best Defensive Catcher	Max Stassi
Best Defensive Infielder	Tyler Ladendorf
Best Infield Arm	Yordy Cabrera
Best Defensive Outfielder	Tyreace House
Best Outfield Arm	Jeremy Barfield

PROJECTED 2014 LINEUP

Catcher	Max Stassi
First Base	Daric Barton
Second Base	Jemile Weeks
Third Base	Yordy Cabrera
Shortstop	Grant Green
Left Field	David DeJesus
Center Field	Aaron Shipman
Right Field	Michael Choice
Designated Hitter	Chris Carter
No. 1 Starter	Brett Anderson
No. 2 Starter	Trevor Cahill
No. 3 Starter	Gio Gonzalez
No. 4 Starter	Tyson Ross
No. 5 Starter	Ian Krol
Closer	Andrew Bailey

TOP PROSPECTS OF THE DECADE

Year	Player, Pos.	2010 Org.
2001	Jose Ortiz, 2b	Fukuoka (Japan)
2002	Carlos Pena, 1b	Rays
2003	Rich Harden, rhp	Rangers
2004	Bobby Crosby, ss	Diamondbacks
2005	Nick Swisher, of	Yankees
2006	Daric Barton, 1b	Athletics
2007	Travis Buck, of	Athletics
2008	Daric Barton, 1b	Athletics
2009	Brett Anderson, lhp	Athletics
2010	Chris Carter, 1b/of	Athletics

TOP DRAFT PICKS OF THE DECADE

Year	Player, Pos.	2010 Org.
2001	Bobby Crosby, ss	Diamondbacks
2002	Nick Swisher, of	Yankees
2003	Brad Sullivan, rhp	Out of baseball
2004	Landon Powell, c	Athletics
2005	Cliff Pennington, ss	Athletics
2006	Trevor Cahill, rhp (2nd round)	Athletics
2007	James Simmons, rhp	Athletics
2008	Jemile Weeks, 2b	Athletics
2009	Grant Green, ss	Athletics
2010	Michael Choice, of	Athletics

LARGEST BONUSES IN CLUB HISTORY

Michael Ynoa, 2008	$4,250,000
Mark Mulder, 1998	$3,200,000
Grant Green, 2009	$2,750,000
Renato Nunez, 2010	$2,200,000
Michael Choice, 2010	$2,000,000

OAKLAND ATHLETICS

TOP 2011 ROOKIE: Chris Carter, 1b/of. After a 0-for-33 start to his big league career, he went 13-for-37 (.351) with three homers, and Oakland could sorely use his power.

BREAKOUT PROSPECT: Jonathan Joseph, rhp. He's starting to gain consistency with a fastball that reaches 95 mph and a curveball with 12-to-6 break.

SOURCE OF TOP 30 TALENT			
Homegrown	21	Acquired	9
College	12	Trades	9
Junior college	0	Rule 5 draft	0
High school	6	Independent leagues	0
Draft-and-follow	0	Free agents/waivers	0
Nondrafted free agents	0		
International	3		

SLEEPER: Omar Duran, lhp. He recovered from elbow problems in 2009 to run his fastball up to 95 mph in the Rookie-level Arizona League last summer.

LF
Michael Choice (3)
Corey Brown (11)
Rashun Dixon (28)
Matt Sulentic
Royce Consigli
Josh Whitaker

CF
Aaron Shipman (7)
Vicmal de la Cruz
Jermaine Mitchell
Tyreace House
Myrio Richard
Jordan Tripp

RF
Michael Taylor (10)
Jeremy Barfield

3B
Yordy Cabrera (8)
Renato Nunez (16)
Chad Lewis (18)
Steve Parker (24)

SS
Grant Green (1)
Wilfredo Solano
Josh Horton
Jason Christian
Dusty Coleman
Wade Kirkland

2B
Jemile Weeks (5)
Adrian Cardenas (15)
Eric Sogard (21)
Conner Crumbliss (30)
Steve Tolleson
Corey WImberly
Tyler Ladendorf
Zhi Fang Pan
Ryan Pineda

1B
Chris Carter (2)
Sean Doolittle (17)
Tony Thompson (29)
Shane Peterson
A.J. Kirby-Jones
Mike Spina

C
Max Stassi (6)
Josh Donaldson (12)
Ryan Ortiz (26)
Argenis Raga
Josh Leyland
John Nester

RHP

RHSP	RHRP
Tyson Ross (4)	Fautino de los Santos (13)
Clay Mortensen (14)	Danny Farquhar (22)
Jonathan Joseph (19)	Trystan Magnuson (23)
Michael Ynoa (25)	Justin Souza
Matt Thomson (27)	Paul Smyth
Tyler Vail	A.J. Griffin
Blake Hassebrock	Connor Hoehn
Dan Straily	Andrew Carignan
Rob Gilliam	Justin Murray
Travis Banwart	Jared Lansford
Arnold Leon	Brett Hunter
James Simmons	Joe Bateman
Nathan Long	Josh Lansford
	Ken Smalley
	J.C. Menna
	Josh Bowman
	Robin Rosario

LHP

LHSP	LHRP
Ian Krol (9)	Brad Kilby
Pedro Figueroa (20)	Lance Sewell
Omar Duran	Jake Brown
Ben Hornbeck	
Anthony Capra	
Julio Ramos	
Anvioris Ramirez	

2010

BEST PURE HITTER: OF Michael Choice's (1) most obvious tool is his power, but the Athletics think he has the bat speed and discipline to hit for average as well. Sweet-swinging OF Aaron Shipman (3) might have more pure hitting ability in the long run.

BEST POWER HITTER: Choice has power to all fields and 30-homer potential. He set a Texas-Arlington career record with 34 homers, then hit seven in a month at short-season Vancouver. SS Yordy Cabrera (2), 3B Tony Thompson (6) and 1B A.J. Kirby-Jones (9) all pack a lot of power.

FASTEST RUNNER: Shipman has plus-plus speed, and OFs Jordan Tripp (7) and Josh Whitaker (25) come close to matching him.

BEST DEFENSIVE PLAYER: C John Nester (39) is a good receiver with a strong, accurate arm and a quick release. Shipman's center-field defense needs more polish, but he has above-average range and arm strength.

BEST FASTBALL: RHP Blake Hassebrock (8) sits at 92-94 mph and has more projection remaining than most college pitchers. RHP Tyler Vail (5), who currently throws 90-93 mph, may pass him in time. RHP Matt Thomson's (12) velocity spiked after he signed, peaking at 95 mph. Cabrera touched the mid-90s as a high school pitcher, but the A's envision him as a position player.

BEST SECONDARY PITCH: RHP A.J. Griffin's (13) changeup is an out pitch.

BEST PRO DEBUT: Thomson reached high Class A while going 4-2, 1.94 with 71 strikeouts in 51 innings. Kirby-Jones made the short-season Northwest League all-star team after hitting .259/.414/.466 with 14 homers and a league-high 61 walks. Griffin also earned NWL all-star recognition after topping the league with 15 saves.

BEST ATHLETE: Shipman. Besides his power, Choice also has plus speed once he gets going and Oakland will try to keep him in center field.

MOST INTRIGUING BACKGROUND: Unsigned 3B Bobby Geren's (36) father Bob manages the A's and played in the big leagues. Cabrera's dad Basilio manages in the Tigers system. LHP Ryan Hughes' (10) father Ernie was an offensive lineman on Notre Dame's 1977 national championship team and played five years in the NFL.

CLOSEST TO THE MAJORS: Choice will get the opportunity to begin his first full pro season in high Class A. Griffin, who sets up his changeup with an 88-92 mph fastball, will be on the fast track as a reliever.

BEST LATE-ROUND PICK: Thomson, who got

pushed to the bullpen on a talented University of San Diego staff. Oakland also has hopes for RHP J.C. Menna (14) and Hughes, who are raw but own plus fastballs, and offensive-minded 2B Ryan Pineda (28).

THE ONE WHO GOT AWAY: 3B Scott Woodward (15) has the on-base skills the A's covet, along with speed and athleticism. He broke his foot while starring in the Cape Cod League and returned to Coastal Carolina.

ASSESSMENT: The A's haven't had much recent success in developing their own position players, something they hope will change with the over-slot signings of Choice, Cabrera, Shipman and 3B Chad Lewis (4).

2009

Three big-money signees, SS Grant Green (1), C Max Stassi (4) and LHP Ian Krol (7), all had promising first full pro seasons. LHP Justin Marks (3) helped yield David DeJesus in a November trade.

GRADE: B

2008

RHP Tyson Ross (2) surprisingly made Oakland's Opening Day bullpen last year, but his future is as a starter. 2B Jemile Weeks (1) and RHP Brett Hunter (7) have struggled to stay healthy after receiving seven-figure bonuses.

GRADE: C+

2007

OF Grant Desme (2) entered the priesthood after a 30-30 season in 2009. RHP James Simmons (1) and OF/1B Sean Doolittle (1s) were injured and also didn't play last year. OF Corey Brown (1s) is carrying this crop by himself after RHP Sam Demel (3) was traded to the Diamondbacks for Conor Jackson last June.

GRADE: D

2006

Without a first-round pick, the A's still were able to grab RHPs Trevor Cahill (2) and Andrew Bailey (6), both of whom made the American League all-star team last year. Signing RHP Mike Leake (7), who became the eighth overall pick in the 2009 draft and went straight to the majors, would have been a nice bonus.

GRADE: A

Draft analysis by Jim Callis. Numbers in parentheses indicate draft rounds.

GRANT GREEN, SS

Born: Sept. 27, 1987. **Bats:** R. **Throws:** R.
Height: 6-3. **Weight:** 180. **Drafted:** Southern
California, 2009 (1st round). **Signed by:** J.T.
Stotts.

LARRY GOREN

Green's profile as a prospect has taken a 180-degree turn since he came out of Canyon High in Anaheim in 2006. Scouts at the time praised his defensive ability at shortstop but questioned his bat, and he stayed on the board until the Padres took him in the 14th round. He opted to attend Southern California, where he became known as an offensive-minded player who might not stick at shortstop. He hit .390 as a sophomore and .374 as a junior, sandwiched around a .340 performance in the Cape Cod League in the summer of 2008. Green ranked as the top prospect on the Cape and drew comparisons to former Long Beach State star Evan Longoria. A slow start and a disappointing home run total (four) in his junior season, combined with his asking price, caused him to slide slightly in the 2009 draft, but the Athletics still made him the 13th overall pick and the first shortstop taken. He signed at the Aug. 17 deadline for $2.75 million. He played five games at high Class A Stockton in August 2009 and returned there last season, ranking second in the California League in hits (174) and fifth in slugging percentage (.520). He delivered an RBI single in the Futures Game in his hometown and joined Double-A Midland for its playoff run.

Green's bat has rarely slowed down since he was a college freshman. He has a smooth stroke with outstanding wrist actions. His swing is geared to use the opposite field and he stays inside the ball extremely well, driving balls to right-center field. The A's have worked with him to pull balls with more authority, and he has at least average power that could improve as he learns to incorporate his legs more in his swing. His strikeout totals were a bit high last year, but he still received praise for his feel for hitting and ability to get the barrel through the zone. As he moves up, he'll need to take more pitches and chase fewer out of the strike zone. There are more questions about his defensive future. Tall and lanky, he has average speed but needs to improve his first-step quickness, though his intelligence as a defender and feel for getting in the right positions help compensate. He struggles at times making routine plays and led Cal League shortstops in errors by a fairly wide margin, committing 37 while no one else had more than 27. His range and arm strength are fringy for the position, and even with a quick release he has difficulty getting carry on his throws and making them from deep in the hole. The A's hope his arm can be solid-average with the right footwork. If he has to change positions, he probably has to go to second base because he wouldn't have the arm strength for third base either.

Green's bat would have the most value at shortstop, and the A's will certainly give him every chance to stay there. Regardless of where he plays, his bat is what will get him to the major leagues. After getting a taste of Double-A in September, he'll return there to open 2011 and should be on track to get to the majors sometime the following year.

SCOUTING GRADES

Batting: 60. **Defense:** 45.
Power: 55. **Arm:** 45.
Speed: 55.

Based on 20-80 scouting scale, where 50 represents major league average, and future projection rather than present tools.

Year	Club (League)	Class	AVG	G	AB	R	H	2B	3B	HR	RBI	BB	SO	SB	CS	OBP	SLG
2009	Stockton (CAL)	HiA	.316	5	19	2	6	1	0	0	3	1	5	1	0	.350	.368
2010	Stockton (CAL)	HiA	.318	131	548	107	174	39	6	20	87	38	117	9	5	.363	.520
Minor League Totals			.317	136	567	109	180	40	6	20	90	39	122	10	5	.363	.515

2 CHRIS CARTER, 1B/OF

Born: Dec. 18, 1986. **B-T:** R-R. **Ht.:** 6-5. **Wt.:** 230. **Drafted:** HS—Las Vegas, 2005 (15th round). **Signed by:** George Kachigian/Joe Butler (White Sox).

Carter was No. 1 on this list a year ago and the A's hoped he could make an impact by season's end. Unfortunately, his first impression was a 0-for-33 streak to begin his big league career. Before that, Carter had rallied from a slow start at Triple-A Sacramento to bat .319/.421/.637 in the second half. Carter's power always will be his carrying tool. His wrists are exceptionally strong and he has lightning-quick bat speed. He has a short, easy swing capable of hitting balls out of any park in any direction. His power comes with the tradeoff of strikeouts, and his inability to recognize breaking pitches was exploited regularly in 2010. He always has been willing to take his walks, but Oakland tinkered with his approach and emphasized selectivity, which led to him being too passive at times. Carter has below-average speed and range, which limits him to first base and left field. He has enough athleticism and arm strength to play passable defense in left, but first remains his most likely long-term option. With Daric Barton at first base in Oakland, left field and DH are Carter's avenues to making a big league impact in 2011. The A's desperately need his power in their lineup.

Year	Club (League)	Class	AVG	G	AB	R	H	2B	3B	HR	RBI	BB	SO	SB	CS	OBP	SLG
2005	Bristol (APP)	R	.283	65	233	33	66	17	0	10	37	17	64	2	1	.350	.485
2006	Kannapolis (SAL)	LoA	.130	13	46	4	6	3	0	1	5	5	17	0	0	.231	.261
	Great Falls (PIO)	R	.299	69	251	37	75	21	1	15	59	34	70	4	4	.398	.570
2007	Kannapolis (SAL)	LoA	.291	126	467	84	136	27	3	25	93	67	112	3	2	.383	.522
2008	Stockton (CAL)	HiA	.259	137	506	101	131	32	4	39	104	77	156	4	0	.361	.569
2009	Midland (TL)	AA	.337	125	490	108	165	41	2	24	101	82	119	13	5	.435	.576
	Sacramento (PCL)	AAA	.259	13	54	7	14	2	0	4	14	3	14	0	1	.293	.519
2010	Sacramento (PCL)	AAA	.258	125	465	92	120	29	2	31	94	73	138	1	1	.365	.529
	Oakland (AL)	MAJ	.186	24	70	8	13	1	0	3	7	7	21	1	0	.256	.329
Major League Totals			.186	24	70	8	13	1	0	3	7	7	21	1	0	.256	.329
Minor League Totals			.284	673	2512	466	713	172	12	149	507	358	690	27	14	.380	.540

3 MICHAEL CHOICE, OF

Born: Nov. 10, 1989. **B-T:** R-R. **Ht.:** 6-0. **Wt.:** 215. **Drafted:** Texas-Arlington, 2010 (1st round). **Signed by:** Armann Brown.

After batting .413 as a sophomore, Choice hit .383 as a junior in 2010 to win the Southland Conference batting title. He also led NCAA Division I with 76 walks and set Texas-Arlington's career home run record with 34. He passed Hunter Pence as the highest-drafted player in school history when the A's took him 10th overall, and he signed for a slightly over-slot $2 million in late July. Choice generates plenty of leverage and bat speed, giving him raw power that rates a 70 on the 20-80 scouting scale. Oakland believes he can hit for a solid average as well, but his swing is unorthodox with a lot of moving parts. Scouts worry about his swing plane and believe he could be prone to high strikeout totals. Choice played center field in his pro debut and has enough speed to possibly stick there for the time being. He needs to clean up his routes on fly balls and probably will end up on a corner in the long run, with his arm strength fitting better in left field than right. Choice's swing has worked thus far, so the A's aren't going to touch it yet. He could be in for a big offensive year as he heads to the hitter-friendly California League to start his first full season.

Year	Club (League)	Class	AVG	G	AB	R	H	2B	3B	HR	RBI	BB	SO	SB	CS	OBP	SLG
2010	Athletics (AZL)	R	.000	3	7	1	0	0	0	0	0	2	2	0	0	.222	.000
	Vancouver (NWL)	SS	.284	27	102	20	29	10	2	7	26	15	43	6	1	.388	.627
Minor League Totals			.266	30	109	21	29	10	2	7	26	17	45	6	1	.377	.587

4 TYSON ROSS, RHP

Born: April 22, 1987. **B-T:** R-R. **Ht.:** 6-5. **Wt.:** 215. **Drafted:** California, 2008 (2nd round). **Signed by:** Jermaine Clark.

One of the biggest surprises of last spring, Ross made Oakland's Opening Day roster despite having made just nine starts above high Class A. He predictably had his struggles but wasn't overwhelmed in his trial by fire before being sent down in July. He was shut down in August with a sprained ligament in his elbow. Ross features two above-average pitches in his fastball and slider. The fastball usually sits in the low to mid-90s and touched 98 mph late in the season in Triple-A. He uses the sink on his heater to get plenty of groundouts. However, major league hitters exposed his inconsistent fastball command. Ross' 83-84 mph slider is the best in the system. He also throws a cutter with promise and a changeup that improved last season even though he didn't use it much as a big league reliever. The short stride and upright finish to his delivery lead to durability concerns, and he missed time with mild shoulder and biceps woes in his first two pro seasons. The A's expect Ross to be ready for spring training, but scouts continue to worry about his health. He can reach his ceiling as a No. 2 starter if he can improve his command. He'll compete for Oakland's fifth-starter job in spring training.

Year	Club (League)	Class	W	L	ERA	G	GS	CG	SV	IP	H	HR	BB	SO	G/AWHIP	AVG
2008	Kane County (MWL)	LoA	0	1	4.66	6	4	0	0	19	16	1	5	16	— 1.09	.219
2009	Stockton (CAL)	HiA	5	6	4.17	18	18	0	0	86	78	10	33	82	1.70 1.29	.237
	Midland (TL)	AA	5	4	3.96	9	9	1	0	50	40	3	20	31	2.87 1.20	.225
2010	Oakland (AL)	MAJ	1	4	5.49	26	2	0	1	39	39	4	20	32	2.52 1.50	.271
	Sacramento (PCL)	AAA	2	1	3.55	6	6	0	0	25	22	1	13	30	4.25 1.38	.253
Major League Totals			1	4	5.49	26	2	0	1	39	39	4	20	32	2.52 1.50	.271
Minor League Totals			12	12	4.08	39	37	1	0	181	156	15	71	159	2.25 1.25	.234

5 JEMILE WEEKS, 2B

Born: Jan. 26, 1987. **B-T:** B-R. **Ht.:** 5-9. **Wt.:** 170. **Drafted:** Miami, 2008 (1st round). **Signed by:** Trevor Schaffer.

Weeks (the 12th pick in 2008) and his brother Rickie (second in 2003) are the eighth pair of siblings to be drafted in the first round. Jemile, who signed for $1.91 million, has been unable to stay healthy as a pro, with repeated hip and leg injuries preventing him from playing a full season. Hip soreness knocked him out for two months during the 2010 regular season and again during the Texas League playoffs. When healthy, Weeks shows promising tools. He has a quick, explosive swing and can do damage from both sides of the plate. His strength and outstanding bat speed give him the capability to hit for more power than his body type would suggest. He's a good situational hitter who hangs in against tough pitches and rarely gets fooled. Weeks has above-average athleticism and speed, though the injuries have diminished his ability to steal bases. He's not the smoothest second baseman, but he has worked hard to improve his throwing and double-play pivot. Weeks draws some Ray Durham comparisons and has the potential to be a top-of-the-order catalyst. The A's expect him to be ready for spring training and advance to Triple-A in 2011. If he can avoid the disabled list, he could make his big league debut by the end of the year.

Year	Club (League)	Class	AVG	G	AB	R	H	2B	3B	HR	RBI	BB	SO	SB	CS	OBP	SLG
2008	Kane County (MWL)	LoA	.297	19	74	11	22	3	1	1	8	13	12	6	2	.422	.405
2009	Stockton (CAL)	HiA	.299	50	201	29	60	9	2	7	31	26	40	5	1	.385	.468
	Midland (TL)	AA	.238	30	105	10	25	5	0	2	13	10	16	4	0	.303	.343
2010	Athletics (AZL)	R	.306	10	36	9	11	2	1	0	1	7	4	5	1	.432	.417
	Midland (TL)	AA	.267	67	273	43	73	14	7	3	33	28	37	11	6	.335	.403
Minor League Totals			.277	176	689	102	191	33	11	13	86	84	109	31	10	.360	.414

6 MAX STASSI, C

Born: March 15, 1991. **B-T:** R-R. **Ht.:** 5-10. **Wt.:** 190. **Drafted:** HS—Yuba City, Calif., 2009 (4th round). **Signed by:** Jermaine Clark.

Stassi set a fourth-round record (since broken by the Nationals' A.J. Cole) when he signed for $1.5 million in 2009. He has strong baseball bloodlines, as his great-great uncle Myril Hoag played for the Yankees in the 1930s, his father Jim played in the minors and was his high school coach and his older brother Brock is entering his senior season at Nevada. Stassi's swing is compact, and he has the bat speed and strength in his forearms and wrists to hit for at least average power. He shows the ability to work counts and use the middle of the field, but also gets pull-happy and has trouble laying off high fastballs at times. Scouts worry about his open stance and how frequently he swings and misses. Nagging shoulder problems hampered his throwing in 2010, though Stassi did erase 34 percent of basestealers. He has soft hands and good agility behind the plate, and the A's praised how he took charge of the low Class A Kane County pitching staff as a teenager. He's a below-average runner. Stassi has the tools to develop into a solid all-around catcher. After Oakland gave him instructional league off so he could recover from the long grind of the season, he'll report to high Class A in 2011 and should put up bigger numbers in the California League.

Year	Club (League)	Class	AVG	G	AB	R	H	2B	3B	HR	RBI	BB	SO	SB	CS	OBP	SLG
2009	Athletics (AZL)	R	.000	1	1	0	0	0	0	0	0	1	1	0	0	.500	.000
	Vancouver (NWL)	SS	.286	13	49	3	14	4	0	0	8	2	11	0	0	.340	.367
2010	Kane County (MWL)	LoA	.229	110	411	54	94	21	1	13	51	45	141	3	3	.310	.380
Minor League Totals			.234	124	461	57	108	25	1	13	59	48	153	3	3	.314	.377

7 AARON SHIPMAN, OF

BILL MITCHELL

Born: Jan. 27, 1992. **B-T:** L-L. **Ht.:** 6-1. **Wt.:** 185. **Drafted:** HS—Quitman, Ga., 2010 (3rd round). **Signed by:** Matt Ranson.

Shipman didn't get as much exposure as other top Georgia high school prospects because he never played for the Atlanta-based East Cobb juggernaut. He would have been the biggest recruit in Mercer baseball history, but his stock soared as the 2010 draft approached. The A's drafted him in the third round and signed him at the Aug. 16 deadline for $500,000. His father Robert played briefly in the minors and coached him in high school, and his brother Robert is a sophomore outfielder at St. Petersburg (Fla.) JC. Shipman has the potential for four plus tools, with power his lone shortcoming. He has a short, slashing swing that produces consistent hard contact. He still has to learn to stay back better on pitches, but he has shown a nice aptitude for making adjustments. He could develop some power as he matures physically, but it's not going to be a focus of his game. Shipman has plus-plus speed and the chance to be an impact defender in center field, where he has above-average range and arm strength. Shipman projects as a dynamic leadoff man and ballhawking center fielder. He'll need some time to develop though, and he'll likely begin his first full professional season in extended spring training before heading to Oakland's new short-season Vermont affiliate.

Year	Club (League)	Class	AVG	G	AB	R	H	2B	3B	HR	RBI	BB	SO	SB	CS	OBP	SLG
2010	Athletics (AZL)	R	.118	4	17	2	2	0	0	0	2	0	6	3	0	.118	.118
Minor League Totals			.118	4	17	2	2	0	0	0	2	0	6	3	0	.118	.118

8 YORDY CABRERA, SS

BRIAN FLEMING

Born: Sept. 3, 1990. **B-T:** R-R. **Ht.:** 6-4. **Wt.:** 200. **Drafted:** HS—Lakeland, Fla., 2010 (2nd round). **Signed by:** Trevor Schaffer.

The son of Tigers minor league manager Basilio Cabrera, Yordy moved to United States from the Dominican Republic when he was 14. The oldest high school player drafted in the 2010 draft class at nearly 20, he signed at the deadline for $1.25 million as the 60th overall pick. Though he was a well regarded pitching prospect who could fire mid-90s fastballs, he and the A's view him as an everyday player. Cabrera has a physical frame and produces excellent raw power. He has some lift in his swing, so he'll have to adjust to get down to the ball and hit it more on a line if he's going to succeed against good pitching. He's an average runner. He'll get a chance to start his career at shortstop, and though he has good hands and is athletic for his size, he may be too big to stay there. Wherever he plays on the diamond, he'll have plenty of arm strength. Oakland loves his attitude and work ethic. If Cabrera's bat comes along, he'll have no trouble profiling as a third baseman if he can't stick at shortstop. His bat could be put to the test right away, as he's the most likely of the A's premium 2010 high school picks to start his first full pro season at their new low Class A Burlington affiliate.

Year	Club (League)	Class	AVG	G	AB	R	H	2B	3B	HR	RBI	BB	SO	SB	CS	OBP	SLG
2010	Did Not Play—Signed Late																

9 IAN KROL, LHP

Born: May 9, 1991. **B-T:** L-L. **Ht.:** 6-1. **Wt.:** 180. **Drafted:** HS—Naperville, Ill., 2009 (7th round). **Signed by:** Kevin Mello.

Krol slipped to the seventh round in 2009 after being suspended from his high school team for being found in the presence of alcohol, violating the school's athletic code of conduct for the second time. The A's signed him for $925,000 and he excelled in a return to his home turf in 2010. While at Kane County, he lived at his home 30 minutes away and led the Midwest League in ERA (2.65) and baserunners per nine innings (9.4). Krol's fastball sits at 88-89 mph and tops out at 91, but he locates it well and complements it with two potential plus pitches. He spins a quality 11-to-5 curveball that's a swing-and-miss pitch when it's on. He has learned to trust his changeup, which he didn't need much in high school. He throws it with good arm speed and it comes in at 78-81 mph with some sinking and tailing action. Krol repeats his delivery well and has an advanced feel for pitching, helping his stuff play up. Despite his big 2010, Krol's ceiling doesn't look any higher than that of a No. 3 or 4 starter as he lacks projection in his frame. He could move quickly through the minors for a high school pick, however, and will return to high Class A after finishing last season there at age 19.

Year	Club (League)	Class	W	L	ERA	G	GS	CG	SV	IP	H	HR	BB	SO	G/AWHIP	AVG
2009	Athletics (AZL)	R	0	0	0.00	1	1	0	0	1	0	0	0	0	2.00 0.00	.000
	Vancouver (NWL)	SS	0	1	8.10	3	1	0	0	3	6	0	1	4	0.50 2.10	.375
2010	Kane County (MWL)	LoA	9	4	2.65	24	23	0	0	119	98	5	19	91	1.44 0.99	.223
	Stockton (CAL)	HiA	1	0	3.66	4	4	0	0	20	18	3	9	20	1.40 1.37	.247
Minor League Totals			10	5	2.90	32	29	0	0	143	122	8	29	115	1.40 1.06	.229

10 MICHAEL TAYLOR, OF

Born: Dec. 19, 1985. **B-T:** R-R. **Ht.:** 6-6. **Wt.:** 260. **Drafted:** Stanford, 2007 (5th round). **Signed by:** Joey Davis (Phillies).

Taylor hit .312/.383/.515 in three years in the Phillies system, but Domonic Brown's emergence made him expendable and Philadelphia included him in its trade for Roy Halladay in December 2009. The Blue Jays promptly flipped Taylor to the A's for Brett Wallace. Shoulder problems cut short his winter season in Mexico and may have contributed to a slow start in Triple-A, and he never really got going. A physical specimen, Taylor still hit balls out to all fields during batting practice but rarely carried that power over into games in 2010. Scouts wondered where his bat speed had gone, and he had issues with a dead start in his swing. Oakland worked to shorten his stroke and improve his angle to the ball. He did get praise for his ability to control the strike zone and handle breaking pitches, but his production was still disappointing. Taylor has average speed and takes good routes, so he can play center field in a pinch. His strong, accurate arm works well in right field. Taylor's physical tools are still readily apparent, and the A's hope last season was simply an aberration. Their November trade for David DeJesus will make it harder for Taylor to break into the big league outfield in 2011. He's been added to Oakland's 40-man roster, but he still has to prove himself in Triple-A anyway.

Year	Club (League)	Class	AVG	G	AB	R	H	2B	3B	HR	RBI	BB	SO	SB	CS	OBP	SLG
2007	Williamsport (NYP)	SS	.227	66	233	30	53	14	0	6	33	23	53	8	2	.300	.365
2008	Lakewood (SAL)	LoA	.361	67	249	40	90	12	3	10	50	31	43	10	3	.441	.554
	Clearwater (FSL)	HiA	.329	65	243	36	80	27	1	9	38	19	46	5	6	.380	.560
2009	Reading (EL)	AA	.333	86	318	59	106	22	4	15	65	35	51	18	4	.408	.569
	Lehigh Valley (IL)	AAA	.282	30	110	15	31	6	1	5	19	13	19	3	1	.359	.491
2010	Sacramento (PCL)	AAA	.272	127	464	79	126	26	6	6	78	51	92	16	5	.348	.392
Minor League Totals			.301	441	1617	259	486	107	15	51	283	172	304	60	21	.373	.480

11 COREY BROWN, OF

Born: Nov. 26, 1985. **B-T:** L-L. **Ht.:** 6-1. **Wt.:** 205. **Drafted:** Oklahoma State, 2007 (1st round supplemental). **Signed by:** Blake Davis.

Brown attracted interest from college football programs as a wide receiver coming out of high school, but he chose to play baseball full-time at Oklahoma State and signed for $544,500 as the 59th overall pick in 2007. He struggled out of the gate in Triple-A last season but recovered after a demotion to have his most productive stretch yet in Double-A. A .267 career hitter entering 2010, Brown finished third in the Texas League batting race (.320) and ranked second in on-base percentage (.415). Brown has always tantalized the A's with his physical tools, and he began to show a more mature approach last season. He shortened his stroke last year, began using the opposite field more consistently and developed a better two-strike gameplan. He has a smooth swing with leverage that generates power to all fields, and he hit three homers in seven games in his brief return to Sacramento at the end of the season. Strikeouts remain an issue, and he has a tendency to pull off balls against lefthanders. Brown has solid speed that serves him well on the bases, and he's an intelligent runner. His good reads and routes give him a chance to stick in center field, and his strong arm would play in right. Added to the 40-man roster after the season, he'll try to keep up his momentum when he returns for another go-around with Sacramento in 2011. He could force his way into Oakland's crowded outfield picture by the end of the season if he handles Triple-A pitching.

Year	Club (League)	Class	AVG	G	AB	R	H	2B	3B	HR	RBI	BB	SO	SB	CS	OBP	SLG
2007	Vancouver (NWL)	SS	.268	59	213	31	57	18	4	11	48	37	77	5	3	.379	.545
2008	Kane County (MWL)	LoA	.270	85	300	44	81	18	2	14	49	41	96	12	0	.359	.483
	Stockton (CAL)	HiA	.260	49	196	34	51	9	0	16	34	17	72	4	1	.322	.551
2009	Midland (TL)	AA	.268	66	250	46	67	20	4	9	43	27	69	5	2	.349	.488
2010	Midland (TL)	AA	.320	90	331	63	106	14	8	10	49	52	93	19	1	.415	.502
	Sacramento (PCL)	AAA	.193	41	135	21	26	4	3	5	20	11	36	3	1	.253	.378
Minor League Totals			.272	390	1425	239	388	83	21	65	243	185	443	48	8	.359	.497

12 JOSH DONALDSON, C

Born: Dec. 8, 1985. **B-T:** R-R. **Ht.:** 6-0. **Wt.:** 215. **Drafted:** Auburn, 2007 (1st round supplemental). **Signed by:** Bob Rossi (Cubs).

Donaldson steadily climbed through the A's system since arriving with Sean Gallagher, Matt Murton and Eric Patterson in a July 2008 trade that sent Rich Harden to the Cubs. He made his big league debut last April and homered in his second big league game, though the rest of his time in Oakland wasn't as productive. The 48th overall pick in 2007 and recipient of a $652,500 bonus, Donaldson moved from third base to catcher in his sophomore season at Auburn, so his bat has always been ahead of his defense. He has fine raw power for a catcher and his 19 homers last year were a career high. He has good feel for the strike zone but needs to have a better approach and tone down his aggressiveness if he's going to hit for average. He tends to press and gets himself out in front on pitches. When he's going well, he lets the ball travel deep and hits to all fields. Donaldson is an agile defender behind the dish and has also dabbled at both corner infield spots as a pro. He needs to clean up his receiving and his transfer on his throws, but he has a strong arm and erased 39 percent of basestealers in 2010. He's a below-average runner but quicker than most backstops. Donaldson's power is tantalizing, but his hitting and defense need further polish at Sacramento before he can push for an regular role in Oakland.

Year	Club (League)	Class	AVG	G	AB	R	H	2B	3B	HR	RBI	BB	SO	SB	CS	OBP	SLG
2007	Cubs (AZL)	R	.182	4	11	1	2	2	0	0	0	2	4	0	1	.308	.364
	Boise (NWL)	SS	.346	49	162	37	56	11	2	9	35	37	34	6	2	.470	.605
2008	Peoria (MWL)	LoA	.217	63	235	27	51	13	0	6	23	17	41	7	1	.276	.349
	Stockton (CAL)	HiA	.330	47	188	37	62	13	2	9	39	17	29	0	2	.391	.564
2009	Midland (TL)	AA	.270	124	455	67	123	37	1	9	91	80	92	7	2	.379	.415
2010	Sacramento (PCL)	AAA	.238	86	294	52	70	14	1	18	67	45	79	3	1	.336	.476
	Oakland (AL)	MAJ	.156	14	32	1	5	1	0	1	4	2	12	0	0	.206	.281
Major League Totals			.156	14	32	1	5	1	0	1	4	2	12	0	0	.206	.281
Minor League Totals			.271	373	1345	221	364	90	6	51	255	198	279	23	9	.366	.460

13 FAUTINO DE LOS SANTOS, RHP

Born: Feb. 15, 1986. **B-T:** R-R. **Ht.:** 6-2. **Wt.:** 220. **Signed:** Dominican Republic, 2005. **Signed by:** Denny Gonzalez (White Sox).

De los Santos electrified a national audience at the 2007 Futures Game, hitting 97 mph on the radar gun in San Francisco. It was one of many highlights during a breakout season in which he went 10-5, 2.65 at two Class A stops in the White Sox system, but he scarcely has been heard from since. Chicago shipped him to Oakland after the 2007 season, along with Gio Gonzalez and Ryan Sweeney, to obtain Nick Swisher. De los Santos made just five appearances with his new organization before breaking down and needing Tommy John surgery. An unusually long recovery period meant he didn't get back to the mound full-time until 2010, and the A's moved him to the bullpen in light of his health problems. De los Santos had used four pitches as a starter but reinvented himself as a two-pitch reliever, relying on his fastball and slider. His lively heater sits in the mid-90s and can top out at 99 mph. His slider looks major league-caliber at times, but it's inconsistent and needs to be tightened up. He has trouble staying on line to the plate during his delivery, hurting his command and making his slider flatten out. De los Santos has the potential to be an impact reliever if he can refine his command. He'll likely return to Double-A to open 2011.

Year	Club (League)	Class	W	L	ERA	G	GS	CG	SV	IP	H	HR	BB	SO	G/AWHIP	AVG
2006	White Sox (DSL)	R	3	3	1.86	10	9	0	0	48	44	0	10	61	— 1.12	.232
2007	Kannapolis (SAL)	LoA	9	4	2.40	21	15	0	0	98	49	5	36	121	— 0.87	.148
	Winston-Salem (CAR)	HiA	1	1	3.65	5	5	0	0	25	20	3	7	32	— 1.09	.220
2008	Stockton (CAL)	HiA	2	2	5.87	5	5	0	0	23	29	3	11	26	— 1.74	.309
2009	Athletics (AZL)	R	0	1	3.86	7	7	0	0	12	12	0	4	16	1.50 1.37	.279
2010	Stockton (CAL)	HiA	1	0	2.30	12	0	0	1	16	13	0	3	22	1.44 1.02	.224
	Midland (TL)	AA	1	5	6.54	25	0	0	0	32	31	1	16	51	1.47 1.48	.250
Minor League Totals			17	16	3.31	85	41	0	1	253	198	12	87	329	1.47 1.13	.212

14 CLAY MORTENSEN, RHP

Born: April 10, 1985. **B-T:** R-R. **Ht.:** 6-4. **Wt.:** 180. **Drafted:** Gonzaga, 2007 (1st round supplemental). **Signed by:** Jay North (Cardinals).

A supplemental first-round pick who signed for $650,000 in 2007, Mortensen came to the A's along with Brett Wallace and outfield prospect Shane Peterson in the Matt Holliday trade with the Cardinals in mid-2009. Mortensen started out 10-2, 3.57 before the Pacific Coast League all-star break in 2010 before tiring down the stretch, and his .258 opponent average was fourth-lowest among PCL starters. He doesn't blow batters away, but Mortensen can mix four pitches and gets plenty of groundballs. His primary weapon is an 89-90 mph fastball with sink and run, and he can locate it to both sides of the plate. His changeup is the best of his secondary pitches, as he gets great arm action on it and it breaks down and away from lefthanders. He has a solid 83-84 mph slider and started using a high-70s curveball last year as well, though its main function is to just give hitters a different look. Mortensen has a little deception in his delivery, but he also tends to rush, causing his pitches to flatten out. When he's on, he's aggressive and pounds the strike zone. Mortensen has the ingredients to become a dependable back-of-the-rotation starter and little left to prove in Triple-A. But Oakland's rotation already is crowded with young arms, so he'll have to force his way into the mix this spring.

Year	Club (League)	Class	W	L	ERA	G	GS	CG	SV	IP	H	HR	BB	SO	G/AWHIP	AVG
2007	Batavia (NYP)	SS	1	1	1.77	6	4	0	0	20	13	0	11	23	— 1.18	.188
	Quad Cities (MWL)	LoA	0	2	3.12	10	10	0	0	40	44	2	8	45	— 1.29	.275
2008	Springfield (TL)	AA	3	4	4.22	11	11	0	0	60	59	6	22	48	— 1.36	.257
	Memphis (PCL)	AAA	5	6	5.51	15	14	0	0	80	87	12	42	57	— 1.61	.281
2009	Memphis (PCL)	AAA	7	6	4.37	17	17	1	0	105	103	11	34	82	1.83 1.30	.259

	St. Louis (NL)	MAJ	0	0	6.00	1	0	0	0	3	5	1	1	2	1.33	2.00	.417
	Sacramento (PCL)	AAA	2	2	4.45	6	6	0	0	32	40	2	14	18	1.47	1.67	.310
	Oakland (AL)	MAJ	2	4	7.81	6	6	0	0	28	37	5	12	11	1.69	1.77	.319
2010	Sacramento (PCL)	AAA	13	6	4.25	26	26	0	0	165	161	20	53	112	2.42	1.29	.258
	Oakland (AL)	MAJ	0	0	4.50	1	1	0	0	6	6	1	2	7	0.80	1.33	.250
Major League Totals			2	4	7.12	8	7	0	0	37	48	7	15	20	1.53	1.72	.316
Minor League Totals			31	27	4.29	91	88	1	0	503	507	53	184	385	2.06	1.37	.264

15 ADRIAN CARDENAS, 2B/3B

Born: Oct. 10, 1987. **B-T:** L-R. **Ht.:** 6-0. **Wt.:** 205. **Drafted:** HS—Miami, 2006 (1st round supplemental). **Signed by:** Miguel Machado (Phillies).

Cardenas was Baseball America's High School Player of the Year in 2006, en route to being taken 37th overall by the Phillies and signing for $925,000. Philadelphia packaged him with Josh Outman and outfield prospect Matt Spencer to acquire Joe Blanton from the A's in July 2008. Cardenas carried a .299 average as pro into 2010, but a thumb injury during spring training cost him most of April and he hit just .228/.285/.281 in Triple-A before being demoted in early June. He righted himself in his third stint with Midland, got back to Sacramento in August and finished strong. Cardenas has a disciplined, all-fields approach and a fluid, effortless swing. He's an intelligent hitter who can pick up on how pitchers are attacking him and make adjustments quickly. While he has a knack for getting the barrel on the ball, Cardenas shows little more than gap power, making him a poor offensive fit for third base. His bat profiles better at second base, but he's a below-average runner whose quickness, range and footwork around the bag are all subpar. He saw time at both positions in 2010, and his arm is playable in either spot. The A's added him to the 40-man roster after the season and will give him another chance to prove himself in Triple-A. He's starting to look more like a utilityman than an everyday player.

Year	Club (League)	Class	AVG	G	AB	R	H	2B	3B	HR	RBI	BB	SO	SB	CS	OBP	SLG
2006	Phillies (GCL)	R	.318	41	154	22	49	5	4	2	21	17	28	13	3	.384	.442
2007	Lakewood (SAL)	LoA	.295	127	499	70	147	30	2	9	79	47	80	20	7	.354	.417
2008	Clearwater (FSL)	HiA	.307	68	261	44	80	11	6	4	23	28	42	16	0	.371	.441
	Stockton (CAL)	HiA	.278	15	72	11	20	1	0	1	10	1	14	1	0	.297	.333
	Midland (TL)	AA	.279	26	86	12	24	4	0	0	7	15	10	0	1	.392	.326
2009	Midland (TL)	AA	.326	79	325	56	106	26	2	3	55	38	44	5	4	.392	.446
	Sacramento (PCL)	AAA	.251	51	183	23	46	15	2	1	24	17	29	3	2	.317	.372
2010	Sacramento (PCL)	AAA	.267	58	210	30	56	8	1	1	21	17	28	2	2	.320	.329
	Midland (TL)	AA	.345	51	194	36	67	15	0	3	32	33	23	4	6	.436	.469
Minor League Totals			.300	516	1984	304	595	115	17	24	272	213	298	64	25	.366	.411

16 RENATO NUNEZ, 3B

Born: April 4, 1994. **B-T:** R-R. **Ht.:** 6-1. **Wt.:** 175. **Signed:** Venezuela, 2010. **Signed by:** Julio Franco.

The A's have been aggressive on the international amateur market in recent years, with Nunez their latest prize after signing for $2.2 million last July 2. He attracted attention for his performance with the Venezuelan squad at the World Youth Championship in Taiwan in August 2009, when he hit .333/.385/.583 in seven games, but Oakland had scouted him for three years. The A's are buying into Nunez's bat, which shows plenty of promise. He has a balanced, fluid swing, giving him outstanding bat control and the ability to get the barrel on the ball consistently. His swing has leverage and he has plus raw power for his age. That power should come into play in games as he matures physically. International scouts doubted Nunez's ability to stick at third base long term, but Oakland will allow him to play his way off the position. He has the arm for the hot corner, but his hands, agility and footwork all need improvement if he's going to remain there. He has a long ways to go, but Nunez could become one of Oakland's best hitting prospects. He'll probably make his pro debut in the Rookie-level Dominican Summer League in 2011, with his U.S. debut planned for the following year.

Year	Club (League)	Class	AVG	G	AB	R	H	2B	3B	HR	RBI	BB	SO	SB	CS	OBP	SLG
2010	Did Not Play—Signed 2011 Contract																

17 SEAN DOOLITTLE, OF/1B

Born: Sept. 26, 1986. **B-T:** L-L. **Ht.:** 6-3. **Wt.:** 190. **Drafted:** Virginia, 2007 (1st round supplemental). **Signed by:** Neil Avent.

A 2007 sandwich pick who signed for $742,500, Doolittle quickly hit his way to Triple-A but hasn't played since May 2009. He fought tendinitis in both knees that year, with his left knee eventually requiring surgery. That operation and subsequent physical therapy didn't get him back to full strength, and after a setback in his rehab, he had a second operation in August 2010. When healthy, Doolittle was one of the organization's top hitting prospects. He has a quick, easy swing with an all-fields approach. He added strength and weight after coming out of college, though he has just average power. He was a two-way player at Virginia and the A's moved him to right field to utilize his arm strength, but his knee problems may preclude him playing the outfield. He was already a below-average runner before the surgeries. The good news is that he's a plus defender at first base. The A's showed their belief in Doolittle's bat by adding him to the 40-man roster after the season. Barring another setback, he'll resume his career at Sacramento this year.

Year	Club (League)	Class	AVG	G	AB	R	H	2B	3B	HR	RBI	BB	SO	SB	CS	OBP	SLG
2007	Vancouver (NWL)	SS	.283	13	46	6	13	3	0	0	4	9	10	0	0	.421	.348
	Kane County (MWL)	LoA	.233	55	193	23	45	10	0	4	29	24	40	1	0	.320	.347
2008	Stockton (CAL)	HiA	.305	86	334	64	102	25	3	18	61	46	99	7	3	.385	.560
	Midland (TL)	AA	.254	51	201	25	51	15	0	4	30	17	54	1	1	.311	.388
2009	Sacramento (PCL)	AAA	.267	28	105	17	28	5	1	4	14	15	23	0	1	.364	.448
2010	Did Not Play—Injured																
Minor League Totals			.272	233	879	135	239	58	4	30	138	111	226	9	5	.354	.449

18 CHAD LEWIS, 3B

Born: Dec. 10, 1991. **B-T:** R-R. **Ht.:** 6-3. **Wt.:** 205. **Drafted:** HS—Huntington Beach, Calif., 2010 (4th round). **Signed by:** Eric Martins.

Lewis attended the same high school, Marina High in Huntington Beach, Calif., as Oakland first baseman Daric Barton. Lewis played basketball at Marina for two years before giving up the sport as a junior to focus on baseball. He was a standout on the showcase circuit, and the A's signed him away from a San Diego State commitment for an above-slot $300,000 bonus as their fourth-round pick in 2010. Big and strong, Lewis is a physical specimen and certainly looks the part of a power-hitting third baseman. He has a quick bat and his swing generates the leverage to hit for power. He'll need to get better at recognizing breaking pitches, and his stroke needs smoothing out. Lewis has good hands and a strong arm, though his defense is a work in progress and he'll have to get better at making plays to his backhand side. While he's not a bad athlete, he's a below-average runner with limited range. Oakland lauds Lewis' makeup and expect him to put in the work to improve offensively and defensively. He has all the raw elements to be a prototypical third baseman, though he'll require a good bit of polish. He should open his first season in extended spring training before joining Vermont in June.

Year	Club (League)	Class	AVG	G	AB	R	H	2B	3B	HR	RBI	BB	SO	SB	CS	OBP	SLG
2010	Did Not Play—Signed Late																

19 JONATHAN JOSEPH, RHP

Born: May 17, 1988. **B-T:** R-R. **Ht.:** 6-1. **Wt.:** 180. **Signed:** Dominican Republic, 2006. **Signed by:** Amaurys Reyes.

After four years in short-season leagues, Joseph stumbled out of the gate in his first look at low Class A last season. He had a 4.67 ERA for Kane County before he was demoted to short-season Vancouver in June. He righted the ship in his second tour there, and continued to pitch well when he returned to Kane County in August. Joseph has a sleek, athletic frame and can unleash fastballs in the low 90s, touching 95 mph. His curveball is a tight 12-to-6 downer that's a plus pitch when it's on. His changeup shows promise, as he throws it with good arm speed and it has some depth. When Joseph gets in trouble, it's usually the result of command. He has a strike-thrower's mentality and tries to attack the zone, but he spins off in his delivery and has trouble repeating it, affecting his ability to locate his pitches. He's still getting a feel for pitching and learning the best ways to utilize his arsenal. Joseph has the potential to be a mid-rotation starter, but he's 22 and hasn't proven much in a full-season league. He'll get that chance when he moves up to high Class A in 2011.

Year	Club (League)	Class	W	L	ERA	G	GS	CG	SV	IP	H	HR	BB	SO	G/AWHIP	AVG
2006	Athletics1 (DSL)	R	4	1	3.53	11	8	0	0	43	43	4	18	36	— 1.41	.259
2007	Athletics1 (DSL)	R	1	0	1.23	2	1	0	0	7	3	0	3	5	— 0.82	.120
	Athletics (AZL)	R	1	3	7.62	16	1	0	2	39	55	4	13	38	— 1.74	.327
2008	Athletics 2 (DSL)	R	1	1	4.50	3	2	0	0	10	9	0	4	13	— 1.30	.231
	Athletics (AZL)	R	1	1	4.56	16	0	0	4	24	30	1	11	37	— 1.73	.300
2009	Vancouver (NWL)	SS	0	2	4.94	16	8	0	0	55	65	4	25	35	1.32 1.65	.300
2010	Kane County (MWL)	LoA	2	5	3.33	14	9	0	0	54	49	2	26	55	1.00 1.39	.241
	Vancouver (NWL)	SS	1	1	2.68	8	8	0	0	40	37	0	14	35	0.80 1.26	.240
Minor League Totals			11	14	4.30	86	37	0	6	272	291	15	114	254	1.05 1.49	.271

20 PEDRO FIGUEROA, LHP

Born: Nov. 23, 1985. **B-T:** L-L. **Ht.:** 6-1. **Wt.:** 205. **Signed:** Dominican Republic, 2003. **Signed by:** Juan Carlos de la Cruz.

Figueroa was the A's minor league pitcher of the year and ranked as their best pitching prospect following his breakout 2009 season, which amazingly was his first in full-season ball after five years as a pro. His 2010 got off to a good start, but he struggled in May and was shut down in June. Doctors diagnosed a ligament tear in his elbow that required Tommy John surgery. Figueroa's development already had been slow, but Oakland was encouraged by the progress he was making. His plus fastball was sitting at 92-95 mph and touching 96. He complemented the heater with a mid-80s slider with tilt, plus a solid changeup that he was throwing regularly. Some scouts worried that he tipped off his changeup by slowing his arm down when he threw it. Figueroa's biggest problem has been fastball command, as he tends to miss up in the zone too often. The A's still believe he can be a frontline starter. They hope he can get back on the mound by midseason, so that he can get in some innings and head into instructional league with an eye toward hitting the ground running in 2012—when he'll be 26.

Year	Club (League)	Class	W	L	ERA	G	GS	CG	SV	IP	H	HR	BB	SO	G/A	WHIP	AVG
2004	Athletics2 (DSL)	R	2	2	2.90	15	2	0	1	50	52	3	11	40	—	1.27	.261
2005	Athletics2 (DSL)	R	3	0	2.27	13	3	0	1	36	29	0	12	25	—	1.15	.215
2006	Athletics1 (DSL)	R	1	0	4.50	1	1	0	0	6	5	1	1	1	—	1.00	.227
	Athletics (AZL)	R	1	6	6.07	13	8	0	0	43	59	4	11	27	—	1.63	.321
2007	Vancouver (NWL)	SS	2	2	4.30	17	7	0	1	44	41	2	31	35	—	1.64	.252
2008	Vancouver (NWL)	SS	2	5	3.93	15	15	0	0	69	62	3	32	77	—	1.37	.238
2009	Kane County (MWL)	LoA	10	2	3.23	16	16	0	0	86	89	6	31	78	1.45	1.39	.267
	Stockton (CAL)	HiA	3	4	3.56	11	11	0	0	66	62	3	35	67	1.12	1.48	.251
2010	Midland (TL)	AA	1	6	5.30	13	13	0	0	71	84	6	29	57	1.62	1.58	.295
Minor League Totals			25	27	3.96	114	76	0	3	470	483	28	193	407	1.39	1.44	.264

21 ERIC SOGARD, INF

Born: May 22, 1986. **B-T:** L-R. **Ht.:** 5-10. **Wt.:** 185. **Drafted:** Arizona State, 2007 (2nd round). **Signed by:** Dave Lottsfeldt (Padres).

Jed Hoyer's first trade as Padres general manager sent Sogard and Kevin Kouzmanoff to Oakland for Aaron Cunningham and Scott Hairston in January 2010. A's scouts liked Sogard when they saw him in Double-A the year before, considering him the toughest out in the Texas League. He doesn't have flashy tools, but he's a baseball rat who has always hit. Sogard has a short swing and a quick bat, allowing him to let the ball travel deep and to foul off tough pitches. He sprays line drives all over the field, though he hits too many balls in the air considering he has no more than gap power. He consistently walks as much as he strikes out, and he ranked fourth in the Triple-A Pacific Coast League with 65 free passes last year. He's an average runner who had been considered a defensive liability, but Oakland was pleasantly surprised by his work in the field last year. His .979 fielding percentage as a second baseman was the best of his career, and he also improved his ability to turn double plays. His arm strength is fringy but good enough for second base. The A's gave him his first extended action at shortstop and third base as a pro, improving his profile as a utilityman with a useful bat. After making his big league debut last September, Sogard will head to spring training with a chance to earn a roster spot in Oakland.

Year	Club (League)	Class	AVG	G	AB	R	H	2B	3B	HR	RBI	BB	SO	SB	CS	OBP	SLG
2007	Portland (PCL)	AAA	.000	1	3	0	0	0	0	0	0	0	3	0	0	.250	.000
	Eugene (NWL)	SS	.256	31	125	20	32	9	0	2	18	19	16	4	2	.354	.376
	Fort Wayne (MWL)	LoA	.253	22	83	7	21	2	0	2	15	6	13	2	2	.308	.349
2008	Lake Elsinore (CAL)	HiA	.308	133	536	97	165	42	3	10	87	79	62	16	7	.394	.453
2009	San Antonio (TL)	AA	.293	117	457	79	134	25	3	6	51	58	47	10	6	.370	.400
2010	Sacramento (PCL)	AAA	.300	137	514	82	154	28	6	5	65	75	68	14	9	.391	.407
	Oakland (AL)	MAJ	.429	4	7	0	3	0	0	0	0	2	1	0	1	.556	.429
Major League Totals			.429	4	7	0	3	0	0	0	0	2	1	0	1	.556	.429
Minor League Totals			.295	441	1718	285	506	106	12	25	236	237	209	46	26	.380	.414

22 DANNY FARQUHAR, RHP

Born: Feb. 17, 1987. **B-T:** R-R. **Ht.:** 5-11. **Wt.:** 180. **Drafted:** Louisiana-Lafayette, 2008 (10th round). **Signed by:** Rob St. Julien (Blue Jays).

After the A's acquired David DeJesus from the Royals in November, they decided Rajai Davis was expendable and sent him to the Blue Jays for Trystan Magnuson and Farquhar, teammates in the Double-A New Hampshire bullpen last season. Farquhar had a difficult junior year as a starter for Louisiana-Lafayette in 2008, so Toronto immediately moved him to the bullpen when he entered pro ball. He has taken to the role, limiting pro hitters to a .186 average while striking out 184 in 172 innings. Farquhar's defining characteristic is his use of two different arm angles. He gets more velocity on his fastball when he uses a high three-quarters arm slot, working at 92-94 mph and touching 96. He gets more sink on his 88-92 mph two-seamer, which he throws with more of a sidearm motion. The slider he throws from the lower arm slot can be a bit sweepy but is his best secondary offering. He also will use an early-count curveball from the higher angle. Farquhar's movement, velocity and ability to give hitters different looks make him difficult to square up, especially for righthanders, who hit .156 against him in 2010. He has trouble throwing consistent strikes, though, a problem he'll have to iron out to earn a role in the majors. He'll open his first season in the A's organization in Triple-A.

Year	Club (League)	Class	W	L	ERA	G	GS	CG	SV	IP	H	HR	BB	SO	G/A	WHIP	AVG
2008	Auburn (NYP)	SS	2	2	2.39	12	0	0	0	26	20	1	6	27	—	0.99	.215
	Lansing (MWL)	LoA	0	0	0.00	3	0	0	0	6	0	0	2	4	—	0.33	.000
2009	Dunedin (FSL)	HiA	1	0	0.53	17	0	0	7	17	10	0	11	23	1.70	1.24	.164
	New Hampshire (EL)	AA	1	4	2.36	37	0	0	15	46	31	1	30	51	1.33	1.34	.193
2010	New Hampshire (EL)	AA	4	3	3.52	53	0	0	17	77	50	7	42	79	1.89	1.20	.189
Minor League Totals			8	9	2.62	122	0	0	39	172	111	9	91	184	1.65	1.18	.186

23 TRYSTAN MAGNUSON, RHP

Born: June 6, 1985. **B-T:** L-R. **Ht.:** 6-7. **Wt.:** 210. **Drafted:** Louisville, 2007 (1st round supplemental). **Signed by:** Steve Miller (Blue Jays).

Magnuson, whose late uncle Keith was an NHL defenseman for 11 seasons, went to Louisville on an academic scholarship for mechanical engineering and walked on to the baseball team. He became the Cardinals' closer as a redshirt senior and helped them reach the 2007 College World Series. The Blue Jays signed him for $462,500 as a sandwich pick in that year's draft, then dealt him to the A's along with Danny Farquhar in November for Rajai Davis. Toronto tried Magnuson out as a starter in his pro debut, but that experiment flopped and he has been much more comfortable since moving back to the bullpen in 2009. He challenges hitters with his 92-94 mph sinker, with his 6-foot-7 frame giving him deception and excellent downhill plane. He also throws a slider that's a plus pitch at times, as well as a splitter that he uses as an offspeed pitch. The latter has some sink but still needs work. Magnuson led Double-A Eastern League relievers by walking just 1.2 batters per nine innings in 2010, and and his fastball and strike-throwing ability alone should get him to the big leagues. To be more than a middle reliever, however, he'll need one of his secondary pitches to take a step forward. Added to Oakland's 40-man roster after the trade, Magnuson will join Farquhar, his teammate in the New Hampshire bullpen last year, in Sacramento this season.

Year	Club (League)	Class	W	L	ERA	G	GS	CG	SV	IP	H	HR	BB	SO	G/A	WHIP	AVG
2008	Lansing (MWL)	LoA	0	9	5.40	24	24	0	0	82	91	6	35	49	—	1.54	.282
2009	Dunedin (FSL)	HiA	4	1	2.77	38	0	0	1	62	56	2	27	45	1.24	1.35	.248
	New Hampshire (EL)	AA	1	0	0.00	5	0	0	0	10	4	0	1	7	2.29	0.50	.118
2010	New Hampshire (EL)	AA	3	0	2.58	46	0	0	5	73	70	1	10	63	1.42	1.09	.256
Minor League Totals			8	10	3.53	113	24	0	6	227	221	9	73	164	1.38	1.30	.258

24 STEVE PARKER, 3B

Born: Sept. 3, 1987. **B-T:** L-R. **Ht.:** 6-2. **Wt.:** 200. **Drafted:** Brigham Young, 2009 (5th round). **Signed by:** Jeremy Schied.

Parker shared Mountain West Conference freshman of the year honors in 2007 with Stephen Strasburg. While he didn't go on to be the No. 1 overall pick in 2009 like Strasburg did, Parker had a productive career with Brigham Young and went in the fifth round of the draft. In his first full pro season last year, he led the system with 98 RBIs and ranked second in the California League with 84 walks. Parker has a swing that's efficient and short to the ball, and he has shown more power than scouts projected when he came out of college. He hit 25 homers in three years at BYU, then went deep 21 times for Stockton, and the A's think he can continue to hit 20 homers a season as he advances. He doesn't sell out for power, either, using an easy swing and showing a good feel for hitting. His defense is another story, as his 33 errors were the most of any Cal League third baseman. He has a funky arm action and his arm strength is just adequate. He's not agile and could have to move to left field, but he's also a below-average runner. Parker will move up to Double-A in 2011, and he'll go as far as his bat takes him.

Year	Club (League)	Class	AVG	G	AB	R	H	2B	3B	HR	RBI	BB	SO	SB	CS	OBP	SLG
2009	Athletics (AZL)	R	.214	3	14	2	3	2	0	0	2	1	6	0	0	.267	.357
	Kane County (MWL)	LoA	.244	70	254	27	62	11	2	5	39	25	55	1	4	.312	.362
2010	Stockton (CAL)	HiA	.296	139	524	102	155	38	5	21	98	84	105	3	1	.392	.508
Minor League Totals			.278	212	792	131	220	51	7	26	139	110	166	4	5	.366	.458

25 MICHAEL YNOA, RHP

Born: Sept. 24, 1991. **B-T:** R-R. **Ht.:** 6-7. **Wt.:** 210. **Signed:** Dominican Republic, 2008. **Signed by:** Raymond Abreu.

Ynoa was the top prospect on the 2008 international free agent market, and the A's paid a club-record $4.25 million bonus to sign him, the largest ever given to a Latin American amateur free agent. The club has seen no return on its investment so far. Elbow tendinitis prevented Ynoa from making his pro debut in 2009. He finally got on the mound last year in the Rookie-level Arizona League but pitched just nine innings before getting shut down again. He went through several rest and rehab cycles before eventually having Tommy John surgery in August. During his brief time on the mound, Ynoa had shown what all the excitement was about. His fastball had life and sat at 92-95 mph, and he complemented it with a sharp, late-breaking curveball and a changeup with depth. He has a smooth, effortless delivery that wouldn't seem to create arm problems. Because his surgery was performed so late in the year, Ynoa isn't expected to pitch at all during the 2011 regular season, though he could be back in the fall. He's nearly fluent in English now, so that should help lessen his learning curve once he does get back to pitching in games in 2012.

Year	Club (League)	Class	W	L	ERA	G	GS	CG	SV	IP	H	HR	BB	SO	G/AWHIP	AVG
2009	Did Not Play—Injured															
2010	Athletics (AZL)	R	0	1	5.00	3	3	0	0	9	6	1	4	11	1.50 1.11	.188
Minor League Totals			0	1	5.00	3	3	0	0	9	6	1	4	11	1.50 1.11	.187

26 RYAN ORTIZ, C

Born: Sept. 29, 1987. **B-T:** R-R. **Ht.:** 6-3. **Wt.:** 195. **Drafted:** Oregon State, 2009 (6th round). **Signed by:** Jim Coffman.

The A's would have preferred for Ortiz to open his first full season in low Class A last year, but Max Stassi's presence in Kane County necessitated bumping Ortiz up a level. Oakland kept the pressure off him by not having him play every day for Stockton, and the plan seemed to work well as he hit .302 through the end of June. He batted just .202 in July, though, and was bothered by nagging right shoulder soreness, which led to him getting shut down and having surgery in August. Ortiz has an outstanding feel for hitting and a natural swing. He stays behind the ball using an up-the-middle approach, and he has learned to drive balls to the opposite field. He won't hit for a lot of power, but he had shown improvement in that regard before getting hurt. Ortiz moves well behind the plate and is an above-average receiver. He has an average arm and threw out 32 percent of basestealers in 2010, thanks largely to improved footwork. The question now is how well his arm will bounce back from the surgery. He's a below-average runner. The A's would like Ortiz to get to Double-A in 2011, but that will depend on how quickly he returns to health. They won't force the issue, and he could begin the year in extended spring training.

Year	Club (League)	Class	AVG	G	AB	R	H	2B	3B	HR	RBI	BB	SO	SB	CS	OBP	SLG
2009	Vancouver (NWL)	SS	.258	48	151	25	39	12	1	4	24	26	29	3	0	.388	.430
2010	Stockton (CAL)	HiA	.277	58	188	35	52	12	1	8	35	36	47	1	0	.394	.479
Minor League Totals			.268	106	339	60	91	24	2	12	59	62	76	4	0	.391	.457

27 MATT THOMSON, RHP

Born: March 22, 1988. **B-T:** R-R. **Ht.:** 6-4. **Wt.:** 195. **Drafted:** San Diego, 2010 (12th round). **Signed by:** Eric Martins.

Thomson went back and forth between starting and relieving in his first two years at San Diego before working as a reliever last spring and putting up a 3.38 ERA in 43 innings. After signing him for a bargain $7,500 as a 12th-round pick, the A's moved him back to the rotation during his pro debut, and he responded nicely. His fastball, which sat in the high 80s in the spring, began operating in the low 90s and touching 95 mph. His heater jumps on hitters, and he's able to command it to both sides of the strike zone. Thomson complements his fastball with a pair of solid pitches in his slurvy slider and changeup. He has limited experience with the changeup and is still developing a feel for it. Thomson has a simple delivery that he repeats well, enhancing his command. He's not afraid of contact and comes right after hitters. Thomson acquitted himself well in a spot start in high Class A at the end of the summer, striking out 10 over five shutout innings, and he could return there to open his first full pro season. More likely, he'll begin 2011 in low Class A.

Year	Club (League)	Class	W	L	ERA	G	GS	CG	SV	IP	H	HR	BB	SO	G/AWHIP	AVG
2010	Vancouver (NWL)	SS	3	2	2.15	12	9	0	0	46	35	0	8	61	1.00 0.93	.202
	Stockton (CAL)	HiA	1	0	0.00	1	1	0	0	5	2	0	2	10	0.33 0.80	.125
Minor League Totals			4	2	1.94	13	10	0	0	51	37	0	10	71	0.95 0.92	.196

28 RASHUN DIXON, OF

Born: Aug. 27, 1990. **B-T:** R-R. **Ht.:** 6-2. **Wt.:** 210. **Drafted:** HS—Terry, Miss., 2008 (10th round). **Signed by:** Kelcey Mucker.

Dixon passed up the chance to play college football with his older brother Anthony at Mississippi State to sign with the A's for $600,000 as a 10th-round pick out of high school. Anthony has gone on to become a running back with the NFL's San Francisco 49ers, and Rashun will try to join him across the bay. Like many former football players who turn to baseball as pros, Dixon had a big learning curve in order get a feel for the game, simply because he hadn't played much baseball. His physical tools are impressive. He has loose wrists and a nice, easy stroke at the plate, though he swings and misses much too much. When he reached full-season ball in 2010, his third year as a pro, he showed an improved sense of the strike zone and did a better job of fighting off tough pitches. His bat speed gives him considerable power potential, but he hasn't fully harnessed it and tends to get overaggressive. His football background shows through on defense, as Dixon is a natural athlete who goes and gets balls in the outfield. A catcher in high school, he played all three outfield positions last year, with his fringy speed and arm fitting best in left field. Dixon is still a project but his tools are hard to ignore. Oakland hopes he'll continue making strides as he moves up to high Class A in 2011.

Year	Club (League)	Class	AVG	G	AB	R	H	2B	3B	HR	RBI	BB	SO	SB	CS	OBP	SLG
2008	Athletics (AZL)	R	.263	45	179	32	47	3	10	8	42	18	68	5	2	.328	.525
2009	Vancouver (NWL)	SS	.214	57	196	25	42	7	0	2	16	23	73	6	4	.300	.281
2010	Kane County (MWL)	LoA	.275	119	444	69	122	18	3	8	54	58	135	9	7	.371	.383
Minor League Totals			.258	221	819	126	211	28	13	18	112	99	276	20	13	.345	.389

29 TONY THOMPSON, 3B

Born: Dec. 19, 1988. **B-T:** R-R. **Ht.:** 6-4. **Wt.:** 220. **Drafted:** Kansas, 2010 (6th round). **Signed by:** Yancy Ayres.

Thompson became the Big 12 Conference's first-ever triple crown winner in 2009, batting .389 with 21 homers and 82 RBIs as a sophomore. He wasn't able to duplicate that success as a junior after he fouled a ball off his left kneecap in a February practice, resulting in a hairline fracture and knocking him out of Kansas' first 19 games. After a tough start, he recovered to hit .338 for the Jayhawks, though he had just six homers. Oakland grabbed him in the sixth round and signed him for $125,000. While he managed just three homers in his pro debut, Thompson's power remains his carrying tool. He has leverage in his swing and though he utilizes a gap-to-gap approach, most of his power is geared to his pull side. His swing will need adjustments if he's going to hit for average, particularly at higher levels, because it tends to get long and he needs to stay through the ball better. Thompson has a strong arm that's suited for third base, but his speed, range and agility are all below average. He led short-season Northwest League third basemen with 21 errors last summer, and most scouts think he'll eventually have to move to first base. The best-case scenario is that Thompson fits the profile of a power-hitting third baseman, but he'll have to answer significant questions about whether he can hit for average and stay at the hot corner when he begin his first full pro season in high Class A.

Year	Club (League)	Class	AVG	G	AB	R	H	2B	3B	HR	RBI	BB	SO	SB	CS	OBP	SLG
2010	Vancouver (NWL)	SS	.246	62	236	30	58	11	0	3	21	23	43	1	1	.321	.331
Minor League Totals			.246	62	236	30	58	11	0	3	21	23	43	1	1	.321	.331

30 CONNER CRUMBLISS, 2B/OF

Born: April 19, 1987. **B-T:** R-L. **Ht.:** 5-8. **Wt.:** 175. **Drafted:** Emporia State (Kan.), 2009 (28th round). **Signed by:** Yancy Ayres.

Crumbliss led Emporia State to the 2009 NCAA Division II national title game, hitting .397 as a senior and leaving as the program's all-time leader in hits, doubles and runs. Signed for $1,500 as a 28th-round pick, he led the minors with 126 walks and the low Class A Midwest League with 95 runs in his first full pro season. Crumbliss is a grinder who consistently puts together good at-bats. He has a tremendous batting eye and a short swing that allows him to let balls travel deep in the zone. He can wait until the last instant and still get around and foul tough pitches off. He's also a capable bunter. He's not going to contribute much offensively beyond his on-base ability, however. He's undersized and offers little power, and while he's an instinctive runner, he has average speed and won't be a basestealing threat. An outfielder in college, Crumbliss has moved to second base as a pro, and that's where he profiles best. He's a steady defender with fringy range and an average arm, and he does a solid job of turning double plays. While Crumbliss doesn't have the flashiest tools, he could help as a utilityman and has the work ethic to get to the big leagues. He'll move up to high Class A in 2011.

Year	Club (League)	Class	AVG	G	AB	R	H	2B	3B	HR	RBI	BB	SO	SB	CS	OBP	SLG
2009	Vancouver (NWL)	SS	.293	57	205	40	60	9	4	2	25	49	28	11	2	.425	.405
	Kane County (MWL)	LoA	.280	14	50	11	14	4	1	0	3	11	9	2	1	.438	.400
2010	Kane County (MWL)	LoA	.271	134	491	95	133	30	2	5	56	126	92	24	8	.421	.371
Minor League Totals			.277	205	746	146	207	43	7	7	84	186	129	37	11	.423	.382

Philadelphia Phillies

BY MATTHEW FORMAN

For a team that has lost more games than any other in major league history, the Phillies are in heady territory. Though they fell short of their third straight National League pennant in 2010, it would be hard to argue that this isn't the best era in franchise history.

Philadelphia finished with the best record in the majors for the first time in franchise history, winning its fourth consecutive NL East title despite injuries to Ryan Howard, Jimmy Rollins and Chase Utley. The Phillies looked on track to reach a third consecutive World Series before tripping up against the Giants in the NL Championship Series.

Long-pursued trade target Roy Halladay finally came over from the Blue Jays in an offseason deal that cost the Phillies three of their top prospects in righthander Kyle Drabek, catcher Travis d'Arnaud and outfielder Michael Taylor. Halladay won Baseball America's Major League Player of the Year award, finishing 21-10, 2.44 with a perfect game in May, then adding a no-hitter of the Reds his playoff debut.

The Halladay trade continued the Phillies' recent habit of sending away prospects for elite pitching help, which continued when they went out and got Roy Oswalt from the Astros in July, in exchange for J.A. Happ and minor leaguers Anthony Gose and Jonathan Villar. Deals for Joe Blanton in 2008, Cliff Lee in 2009 and Halladay and Oswalt in 2010 sent away a significant amount of young talent, but accomplished the goal of keeping the team on top while its nucleus of everyday players is at its peak.

Philadelphia tried to recoup some young talent by trading Lee to Mariners after acquiring Halladay, but righthanders Phillippe Aumont and J.C. Ramirez and outfielder Tyson Gillies all had forgettable seasons. The Phillies then stunned the baseball world in December by beating out the Rangers and Yankees to sign Lee as a free agent, guaranteeing him $120 million over the next five seasons.

The one player the Phillies have refused to deal is outfielder Domonic Brown, No. 1 on this list for the last three years. There isn't much upper-level depth behind Brown, but the system does have young talent with upside. Low Class A Lakewood has won back-to-back South Atlantic League titles. After Brown, the next six prospects on this list all played there in 2010.

Assuming he takes over from departed free agent Jayson Werth as the everyday right fielder in 2011, Brown will be the first homegrown position player to join the Philadelphia lineup since Howard in 2005.

The Phillies have traded prospects for studs such as BA Player of the Year Roy Halladay

TOP 30 PROSPECTS

1. Domonic Brown, of	**16.** Tyson Gillies, of
2. Jonathan Singleton, 1b/of	**17.** J.C. Ramirez, rhp
3. Brody Colvin, rhp	**18.** Jon Pettibone, rhp
4. Jarred Cosart, rhp	**19.** Cesar Hernandez, 2b
5. Trevor May, rhp	**20.** Freddy Galvis, ss
6. Sebastian Valle, c	**21.** Perci Garner, rhp
7. Jiwan James, of	**22.** Harold Garcia, 2b
8. Jesse Biddle, lhp	**23.** Josh Zeid, rhp
9. Domingo Santana, of	**24.** Austin Hyatt, rhp
10. Aaron Altherr, of	**25.** Julio Rodriguez, rhp
11. Vance Worley, rhp	**26.** Matt Rizzotti, 1b
12. Antonio Bastardo, lhp	**27.** Leandro Castro, of
13. Scott Mathieson, rhp	**28.** Kelly Dugan, of
14. Phillippe Aumont, rhp	**29.** Kevin Walter, rhp
15. Justin DeFratus, rhp	**30.** Cameron Rupp, c

The organization hopes he's the beginning of a wave of youngsters who will reinvigorate an aging team. The 2010 lineup was by far the oldest in the league, with an average age of 31.9 years.

Whether because of age or the growing payroll, general manager Ruben Amaro Jr. may have to tweak his approach going forward. For now, the Phillies have become a model of consistency: a major league core of stars signed for the foreseeable future, with a commitment to player development. If the current group can keep winning for another year or two, the talent in the lower minors should arrive just in time.

General Manager: Ruben Amaro. **Farm Director:** Steve Noworyta. **Scouting Director:** Marti Wolever.

Class	Team	League	W	L	PCT	Finish*	Manager
Majors	Philadelphia Phillies	National	97	65	.599	1st (16)	Charlie Manuel
Triple-A	Lehigh Valley IronPigs	International	58	86	.403	13th (14)	Dave Huppert
Double-A	Reading Phillies	Eastern	69	72	.489	8th (12)	Steve Roadcap
High A	Clearwater Threshers	Florida State	67	72	.482	8th (12)	Dusty Wathan
Low A	Lakewood BlueClaws	South Atlantic	84	55	.604	†1st (14)	Mark Parent
Short-season	Williamsport Crosscutters	New York-Penn	43	33	.566	4th (14)	Chris Truby
Rookie	GCL Phillies	Gulf Coast	32	24	.571	†3rd (15)	Rolando de Armas
Overall 2010 Minor League Record			353	342	.508	12th (30)	

*Finish in overall standings (No. of teams in league). †League champion.

LAST YEAR'S TOP 30

Player, Pos.		Status
1.	Domonic Brown, of	No. 1
2.	Kyle Drabek, rhp	(Blue Jays)
3.	Michael Taylor, of	(Athletics)
4.	Travis d'Arnaud, c	(Blue Jays)
5.	Trevor May, rhp	No. 5
6.	Anthony Gose, of	(Blue Jays)
7.	Sebastian Valle, c	No. 6
8.	Jarred Cosart, rhp	No. 4
9.	Antonio Bastardo, lhp	No. 12
10.	Domingo Santana, of	No. 9
11.	Jiwan James, of	No. 7
12.	Brody Colvin, rhp	No. 3
13.	Freddy Galvis, ss	No. 20
14.	Kyrell Hudson, of	Dropped out
15.	Scott Mathieson, rhp	No. 13
16.	Mike Stutes, rhp	Dropped out
17.	Yohan Flande, lhp	(Released)
18.	Vance Worley, rhp	No. 11
19.	Heitor Correa, rhp	Dropped out
20.	Jonathan Singleton, 1b	No. 2
21.	Joe Savery, lhp	Dropped out
22.	Jonathan Villar, ss	(Astros)
23.	Mike Cisco, rhp	Dropped out
24.	B.J. Rosenberg, rhp	Dropped out
25.	Leandro Castro, of	No. 27
26.	Edgar Garcia, rhp	Dropped out
27.	Kelly Dugan, of	No. 28
28.	Matt Way, lhp	Dropped out
29.	Justin DeFratus, rhp	No. 15
30.	Zach Collier, of	Dropped out

BEST TOOLS

Best Hitter for Average	Domonic Brown
Best Power Hitter	Jonathan Singleton
Best Strike-Zone Discipline	Jonathan Singleton
Fastest Baserunner	Jiwan James
Best Athlete	Jiwan James
Best Fastball	Jarred Cosart
Best Curveball	Phillippe Aumont
Best Slider	Josh Zeid
Best Changeup	Austin Hyatt
Best Control	Justin DeFratus
Best Defensive Catcher	Tuffy Gosewisch
Best Defensive Infielder	Freddy Galvis
Best Infield Arm	Freddy Galvis
Best Defensive Outfielder	Jiwan James
Best Outfield Arm	Domonic Brown

PROJECTED 2014 LINEUP

Catcher	Sebastian Valle
First Base	Ryan Howard
Second Base	Chase Utley
Third Base	Placido Polanco
Shortstop	Jimmy Rollins
Left Field	Jonathan Singleton
Center Field	Shane Victorino
Right Field	Domonic Brown
No. 1 Starter	Roy Halladay
No. 2 Starter	Cliff Lee
No. 3 Starter	Cole Hamels
No. 4 Starter	Roy Oswalt
No. 5 Starter	Brody Colvin
Closer	Ryan Madson

TOP PROSPECTS OF THE DECADE

Year	Player, Pos.	2010 Org.
2001	Jimmy Rollins, ss	Phillies
2002	Marlon Byrd, of	Cubs
2003	Gavin Floyd, rhp	White Sox
2004	Cole Hamels, lhp	Phillies
2005	Ryan Howard, 1b	Phillies
2006	Cole Hamels, lhp	Phillies
2007	Carlos Carrasco, rhp	Indians
2008	Carlos Carrasco, rhp	Indians
2009	Domonic Brown, of	Phillies
2010	Domonic Brown, of	Phillies

TOP DRAFT PICKS OF THE DECADE

Year	Player, Pos.	2010 Org.
2001	Gavin Floyd, rhp	White Sox
2002	Cole Hamels, lhp	Phillies
2003	Tim Moss, 2b (3rd round)	Out of baseball
2004	Greg Golson, of	Yankees
2005	Mike Costanzo, 3b (2nd round)	Reds
2006	Kyle Drabek, rhp	Blue Jays
2007	Joe Savery, lhp	Phillies
2008	Anthony Hewitt, 3b/of	Phillies
2009	Kelly Dugan, of (2nd round)	Phillies
2010	Jesse Biddle, lhp	Phillies

LARGEST BONUSES IN CLUB HISTORY

Gavin Floyd, 2001	$4,200,000
Pat Burrell, 1998	$3,150,000
Brett Myers, 1999	$2,050,000
Cole Hamels, 2002	$2,000,000
Chase Utley, 2000	$1,780,000

PHILADELPHIA PHILLIES

TOP 2011 ROOKIE: Domonic Brown, of. One of the game's elite prospects, he'll take over for Jayson Werth in right field.

BREAKOUT PROSPECT: Jon Pettibone, rhp. Lesser known than the Phillies' top minor league arms, he produces 92-94 mph fastballs with ease.

SLEEPER: Colby Shreve, rhp. He had Tommy John surgery shortly after signing in 2008, but finally made his pro debut last year and showed a low-90s fastball and promising secondary pitches.

SOURCE OF TOP 30 TALENT

Homegrown	27	Acquired	3
College	6	Trades	3
Junior college	1	Rule 5 draft	0
High school	13	Independent leagues	0
Draft-and-follow	0	Free agents/waivers	0
Nondrafted free agents	0		
International	7		

LF
Jonathan Singleton (2)
Leandro Castro (27)
Kelly Dugan (28)
Miguel Alvarez
John Mayberry Jr.
Zach Collier

CF
Jiwan James (7)
Tyson Gillies (16)
Gauntlett Eldemire
D'Arby Myers
Kyrell Hudson

RF
Domonic Brown (1)
Domingo Santana (9)
Aaron Altherr (10)
Brian Pointer
Anthony Hewitt

3B
Carlos Rivero
Adam Buschini

SS
Freddy Galvis (20)
Troy Hanzawa
Stephen Malcolm

2B
Cesar Hernandez (19)
Harold Garcia (22)
Michael Martinez
Jeremy Barnes

1B
Matt Rizzotti (26)
Cody Overbeck
Joe Savery

C
Sebastian Valle (6)
Cameron Rupp (30)
Tim Kennelly

RHP

RHSP	RHRP
Brody Colvin (3)	Scott Mathieson (13)
Jarred Cosart (4)	Phillippe Aumont (14)
Trevor May (5)	Justin DeFratus (15)
Vance Worley (11)	Josh Zeid (23)
J.C. Ramirez (17)	Michael Schwimer
Jon Pettibone (18)	Mike Stutes
Perci Garner (21)	Drew Carpenter
Austin Hyatt (24)	B.J. Rosenberg
Julio Rodriguez (25)	Mike Cisco
Kevin Walter (29)	Jordan Ellis
Colby Shreve	Mike Nesseth
Drew Naylor	Eric Pettis
Heitor Correa	
David Buchanan	
Jonathan Musser	

LHP

LHSP	LHRP
Jesse Biddle (8)	Antonio Bastardo (12)
Matt Way	Sergio Escalona
Nick Hernandez	Jacob Diekman
Bryan Morgado	
Mario Hollands	

2010

BEST PURE HITTER: Philadelphia didn't focus on bats in this draft but went above slot recommendations late to sign OF Brian Pointer (28) for $350,000. He has a smooth swing, solid bat speed and a quiet approach at the plate.

BEST POWER HITTER: C Cameron Rupp (3) has a strong, durable frame that serves him well behind the plate and as a power hitter.

FASTEST RUNNER: OF Gauntlett Eldemire (6) is a classic Phillies pick as a fairly raw athlete with upside. He's a plus runner.

BEST DEFENSIVE PLAYER: Rupp has sound catch-and-throw stills and fills a need in the lower levels of the system, after Philadelphia traded away catching in the last couple of seasons. Eldemire still needs some polish, but his speed fits in center field.

BEST FASTBALL: LHP Jesse Biddle (1) has easy velocity, as his arm works well and he has a smooth delivery. He runs his fastball up to 94 mph, with more to come. RHPs Perci Garner (2) and David Buchanan (7) and LHP Bryan Morgado (4) are college arms who need polish but can reach the mid-90s.

BEST SECONDARY PITCH: Garner throws a tight curveball around 80 mph.

BEST PRO DEBUT: RHP Eric Pettis (35) went 8-0, 1.37 with seven saves while starting and relieving at short-season Batavia. He has a three-pitch mix and throws a lot of strikes.

BEST ATHLETE: Eldemire has plus raw power and speed. He's not as raw as a high schooler but is less refined than a typical college position player.

MOST INTRIGUING BACKGROUND: Garner played quarterback at Ball State before focusing on baseball. RHP Jake Smith (15) could rate as this draft's best defensive player at third base, but his slow bat, low-90s fastball and feel for pitching (he was the closer at Alabama) prompted the Phillies to move him to the mound in instructional league. RHP Jake Borup (23) spent two seasons on a Mormon mission before helping pitch Arizona State to the 2010 College World Series. Eldemire is Gauntlett Eldemire III. His great-grandparents were of Jamaican and German descent and named their son Gauntlett because of the problems he would face due to his mixed heritage.

CLOSEST TO THE MAJORS: Rupp or Pettis.

BEST LATE-ROUND PICK: Pointer or RHP Kevin Walter (20), who had an up-and-down spring but flashes low-90s velocity and two interesting breaking balls.

THE ONE WHO GOT AWAY: RHP Scott Frazier (5) spurned a seven-figure offer and opted to attend Pepperdine. When he didn't sign, Philadelphia spent $1 million combined on Walter, Pointer and RHP Jonathan Musser (21).

ASSESSMENT: The Phillies have had success in recent years polishing up pitchers similar to Garner, Morgado and Buchanan, and raw athletes like Eldemire. Biddle, on the other hand, is advanced for a high school pitcher.

2009

Philadelphia didn't have a first-round pick but found two first-round talents in RHP Brody Colvin (7) and 1B/OF Jonathan Singleton (8). Kelly Dugan (2), the team's top choice, and Aaron Altherr (9) add to the system's impressive outfield depth.

GRADE: B+

2008

OFs Anthony Hewitt (1) and Zach Collier (1s) have been disappointments, though that hasn't mattered. OF Anthony Gose (2) and RHP Jason Knapp (2) were key parts of deals for Roy Oswalt and Cliff Lee. RHP Vance Worley (3) already has contributed in the majors, while RHPs Trevor May (4) and Jarred Cosart (38) have huge upside. Keep an eye on RHP Jon Pettibone (3s), too.

GRADE: B+

2007

Stop us if this sounds familiar: disappointment in the first round (1B/LHP Joe Savery), lots of trade fodder (C Travis d'Arnaud, 1s, and OF Michael Taylor, 5, were part of the Roy Halladay deal) and a savvy late-round choice (OF Jiwan James, 22). RHP Brian Schlitter (16) reached the big leagues with the Cubs after getting traded for Scott Eyre.

GRADE: B

2006

This draft may produce two stars in RHP Kyle Drabek (1), who headlined the Halladay trade, and OF Domonic Brown (20). 2B/3B Adrian Cardenas (1s) and 2B/SS Jason Donald (3) were used in deals for Joe Blanton and Lee. RHP Drew Carpenter (2) has surfaced briefly in the majors.

GRADE: A

Draft analysis by John Manuel (2010) and Jim Callis (2006-09). Numbers in parentheses indicate draft rounds.

DOMONIC BROWN, OF

Born: Sept. 3, 1987. **Bats:** L. **Throws:** L.
Height: 6-5. **Weight:** 200. **Drafted:** HS—
Stone Mountain, Ga., 2006 (20th round).
Signed by: Chip Lawrence.

PROSPECT 1

DAVID SCHOFIELD

A football and baseball star in high school, Brown had the opportunity to play wide receiver and outfield for Miami. Prior to his senior season, he switched high schools from Pasco (Dade City, Fla.) to Redan (Stone Mountain, Ga.) because of a messy custody dispute between his mother and father, but he still dominated the competition—in both sports—in two of the nation's most heavily scouted areas. Scouts kept their distance because Brown was raw and had lofty bonus demands, but area scout Chip Lawrence tracked Brown closely and persuaded the Phillies to take a flier on him in the 20th round of the 2006 draft. The team's top scouts evaluated Brown during the summer before signing him away from the Hurricanes for $200,000. He broke out by winning the Hawaii Winter Baseball batting title (.386) after the 2008 season, and has ranked among the game's top prospects ever since. Brown played in the Futures Game and set career highs in most offensive categories in 2010. He played sparingly after a July promotion to Philadelphia, though he made the postseason roster.

Brown is the prototype of the high-risk, high-reward players the Phillies like to take. He is a physical specimen, with a lean, lithe and powerful frame that draws comparisons to a young Barry Bonds and Darryl Strawberry. He has five-tool ability, with his bat getting the most attention. Brown creates incredible bat speed with his whip-like, uppercut swing and has eliminated previous questions about his power. He developed a good eye for the strike zone in the minors, though he was overly aggressive during his first stint in the big leagues. For a player with such long arms, he has a relatively short stroke with few holes. Assuming he eliminates a tendency to open his front side too early in his swing, he could hit .300 with 20-25 homers annually once he gets established in Philadelphia. He has above-average speed and the strongest outfield arm in the system.

The unknown with Brown is how skilled a defender he can be in right field, as he needs to improve his route-running and footwork.

With the departure of free agent Jayson Werth, Brown is set to take over as the Phillies' everyday right fielder in 2011. Manager Charlie Manuel likes to break in youngsters slowly, so Brown could start the year platooning with Ben Francisco or even get a little more time at Triple-A Lehigh Valley. He's a future all-star, but he's not a finished product.

SCOUTING GRADES

Batting: 65. **Defense:** 55.
Power: 60. **Arm:** 70.
Speed: 60.

Based on 20-80 scouting scale, where 50 represents major league average, and future projection rather than present tools.

Year	Club (League)	Class	AVG	G	AB	R	H	2B	3B	HR	RBI	BB	SO	SB	CS	OBP	SLG
2006	Phillies (GCL)	R	.214	34	117	13	25	3	0	1	7	12	30	13	3	.292	.265
2007	Clearwater (FSL)	HiA	.444	3	9	2	4	1	0	1	7	2	0	0	0	.545	.889
	Williamsport (NYP)	SS	.295	74	285	43	84	11	5	3	32	27	49	14	7	.356	.400
2008	Lakewood (SAL)	LoA	.291	114	444	77	129	23	3	9	54	64	72	22	7	.382	.417
2009	Phillies (GCL)	R	.500	3	10	4	5	0	2	0	1	1	1	0	1	.583	.900
	Clearwater (FSL)	HiA	.303	66	238	41	72	12	3	11	44	34	48	15	8	.386	.517
	Reading (EL)	AA	.279	37	147	20	41	9	4	3	20	14	37	8	1	.346	.456
2010	Reading (EL)	AA	.318	65	236	50	75	16	3	15	47	29	51	12	6	.391	.602
	Lehigh Valley (IL)	AAA	.346	28	107	15	37	6	1	5	21	8	23	5	1	.390	.561
	Philadelphia (NL)	MAJ	.210	35	62	8	13	3	0	2	13	5	24	2	1	.257	.355
Major League Totals			.210	35	62	8	13	3	0	2	13	5	24	2	1	.257	.355
Minor League Totals			.296	424	1593	265	472	81	21	48	232	191	311	89	34	.373	.464

2 JONATHAN SINGLETON, 1B/OF

Born: Sept. 18, 1991. **B-T:** L-L. **Ht.:** 6-2. **Wt.:** 215. **Drafted:** HS—Long Beach, 2009 (8th round). **Signed by:** Demetrius Pittman.

Singleton impressed on the showcase circuit in 2008, but his summer performance didn't carry over into his senior year, when he pressed and hit .321 with just four home runs. The Phillies still saw him as an advanced high school hitter and signed him for $200,000 as an eighth-rounder. The youngest regular in the low Class A South Atlantic League last year, he rated as the circuit's top prospect and ranked third in on-base percentage (.393) and fourth in slugging (.479) at age 18. Singleton has uncanny balance and rhythm at the plate, as well as solid pitch recognition. His swing is simple and compact, and the strength in his hands, wrists and forearms gives him easy plus raw power. As with most young hitters, his swing can get long at times. He's not as athletic as his father Herb, a former quarterback at Oregon, but Singleton is light on his feet. He has a solid-average arm. With Ryan Howard signed through 2016, Singleton will have to find a different position to crack Philadelphia's lineup. He started working out in left field in July and continued in instructional league, showing enough promise that he'll play there at high Class A Clearwater in 2011. He could be ready for the big leagues in 2013.

Year	Club (League)	Class	AVG	G	AB	R	H	2B	3B	HR	RBI	BB	SO	SB	CS	OBP	SLG
2009	Phillies (GCL)	R	.290	31	100	12	29	9	0	2	12	18	13	1	0	.395	.440
2010	Lakewood (SAL)	LoA	.290	104	376	64	109	25	2	14	77	62	74	9	7	.393	.479
Minor League Totals			.290	135	476	76	138	34	2	16	89	80	87	10	7	.394	.471

3 BRODY COLVIN, RHP

Born: Aug. 14, 1990. **B-T:** R-R. **Ht.:** 6-4. **Wt.:** 195. **Drafted:** HS—Lafayette, La., 2009 (7th round). **Signed by:** Mike Stauffer.

Though Colvin was considered a sandwich-round talent coming out of high school, his Louisiana State commitment scared teams off. Area scout Mike Stauffer did a good job getting to know Colvin, however, and the Phillies drafted him in the seventh round and signed him for $900,000, by far the most they spent on a 2009 draft pick. He had an 8.40 ERA after seven outings last year, then posted a 2.00 ERA in his final 20 starts, adding velocity along the way. Scouts love Colvin's live arm and strong frame. His fastball sits at 92-94 mph and he can reach back for 97 when needed. He shows signs of two above-average secondary offerings, an upper-70s curveball and an 83-85 mph changeup. His competitiveness helps him maximize his stuff. Philadelphia worked to clean up Colvin's delivery, but it still needs some refinement. He throws across his body from a high three-quarters arm slot and sometimes gets on the side of his curveball. Some scouts have questioned Colvin's makeup—he was arrested on three misdemeanor charges last February—but the Phillies aren't concerned. Colvin has No. 2 starter potential and took a giant step in his first full pro season. He'll open the 2011 season in high Class A but could finish it at Double-A Reading.

Year	Club (League)	Class	W	L	ERA	G	GS	CG	SV	IP	H	HR	BB	SO	G/A	WHIP	AVG
2009	Phillies (GCL)	R	0	0	0.00	1	0	0	0	2	0	0	1	2	3.00	0.50	.000
2010	Lakewood (SAL)	LoA	6	8	3.39	27	27	0	0	138	138	7	42	120	1.40	1.30	.258
Minor League Totals			6	8	3.34	28	27	0	0	140	138	7	43	122	1.41	1.29	.256

4 JARRED COSART, RHP

Born: May 25, 1990. **B-T:** R-R. **Ht.:** 6-3. **Wt.:** 180. **Drafted:** HS—League City, Texas, 2008 (38th round). **Signed by:** Steve Cohen.

Negotiations between Cosart's father Joe and Phillies brass went down to the wire during an American Legion game that ended less than an hour before the 2008 signing deadline, with the team prying Cosart away from a Missouri commitment for a $550,000 bonus in the 38th round. A talented two-way player, he broke Clear Creek High's batting average record (.506) previously set by Jay Buhner. Shoulder and back pain delayed his pro debut in 2009, and a tender elbow shut him down in mid-2010 and kept him out of the Futures Game. Cosart is tall and lean, and scouts regard his arm as one of the most electric in the minor leagues. His fastball sits at 94-98 mph, usually at the top end of that range, with good life. His 77-79 mph curveball is a solid-average pitch, while his low-80s changeup is a work in progress. His command is advanced for his age and lively stuff. The biggest concern with Cosart is his health, though his arm action and delivery raise no red flags. His maturity and work ethic have also been called into question. Cosart pitched without pain in instructional league and should be able to begin the 2011 season in high Class A. He has the potential to become a No. 1 starter or closer—if he can stay healthy.

Year	Club (League)	Class	W	L	ERA	G	GS	CG	SV	IP	H	HR	BB	SO	G/A	WHIP	AVG
2009	Phillies (GCL)	R	2	2	2.22	7	5	0	0	24	12	0	7	25	0.84	0.78	.143
2010	Lakewood (SAL)	LoA	7	3	3.79	14	14	1	0	71	60	3	16	77	2.07	1.07	.224
Minor League Totals			9	5	3.39	21	19	1	0	96	72	3	23	102	1.61	0.99	.205

5 TREVOR MAY, RHP

Born: Sept. 23, 1989. **B-T:** R-R. **Ht.:** 6-5. **Wt.:** 215. **Drafted:** HS—Kelso, Wash., 2008 (4th round). **Signed by:** Dave Ryles.

May rated as Washington state's top prospect in the 2008 draft before signing for $375,000 as a fourth-round pick. He has been part of Lakewood's back-to-back South Atlantic League titles, allowing just one run in four playoff starts. He wasn't supposed to be in low Class A last year, but when his mechanics and control got out of whack, May got demoted at midseason at the suggestion of senior adviser and former general manager Pat Gillick. Scouts love to project on May's sturdy 6-foot-5 frame. His best pitch is his 91-95 mph fastball, which has heavy life and great angle. His high three-quarters arm slot also produces armside run. May's 76-79 mph curveball could become a plus pitch as it gains consistency. His changeup sits at 81-84 mph and has similar promise. The Phillies have worked to simplify May's delivery, which he struggles to repeat. He often flies open with his front side and drops his elbow on offspeed pitches. He also has a tendency to fall in love with strikeouts and overthrow. May got back on track in the second half, setting the stage to take another crack at high Class A in 2011. A potential No. 2 or 3 starter, he'll pitch alongside Brody Colvin and Jarred Cosart on what should be a loaded Clearwater staff.

Year	Club (League)	Class	W	L	ERA	G	GS	CG	SV	IP	H	HR	BB	SO	G/A	WHIP	AVG
2008	Phillies (GCL)	R	1	1	3.75	5	2	0	0	12	11	0	7	11	—	1.50	.256
2009	Lakewood (SAL)	LoA	4	1	2.56	15	15	0	0	77	58	3	43	95	0.77	1.31	.211
2010	Clearwater (FSL)	HiA	5	5	5.01	16	14	0	0	70	53	7	61	90	0.83	1.63	.212
	Lakewood (SAL)	LoA	7	3	2.91	11	11	0	0	65	51	3	20	92	0.89	1.09	.214
Minor League Totals			17	10	3.49	47	42	0	0	224	173	13	131	288	0.82	1.36	.215

6 SEBASTIAN VALLE, C

Born: July 24, 1990. **B-T:** R-R. **Ht.:** 6-1. **Wt.:** 170. **Signed:** Mexico, 2006. **Signed by:** Sal Agostinelli.

Phillies international supervisor Sal Agostinelli runs a budget-minded department that signed Valle for $30,000 out of Mexico in 2006. Since struggling at Lakewood to start 2009, Valle has taken bigger strides than any other player in the system. He was named short-season Williamsport's MVP that summer and impressed in the Mexican Pacific League that winter, then conquered low Class A last season. Valle has the tools to hit for power and play good defense. He employs a high leg kick to keep his weight back, and his strong wrists that generate pure bat speed. He must work on making more contact and showing more discipline, as he gets pull-happy and is a free swinger. He looks overmatched at times against premium pitching. Valle's arm strength and release improved in the second half of 2010, and he threw out 33 percent of basestealers last season. His receiving skills also are also solid. He moves well behind the plate, though he's a below-average runner. The Phillies had enough confidence in Valle to include backstops Lou Marson and Travis d'Arnaud in trades for Cliff Lee and Roy Halladay. With Carlos Ruiz entrenched in Philadelphia, Valle doesn't have to be rushed. He'll manage Clearwater's deep pitching staff in 2011.

Year	Club (League)	Class	AVG	G	AB	R	H	2B	3B	HR	RBI	BB	SO	SB	CS	OBP	SLG
2007	Phillies (DSL)	R	.284	54	176	29	50	13	1	2	25	29	26	4	4	.398	.403
2008	Phillies (GCL)	R	.281	48	167	27	47	15	0	2	18	12	31	0	0	.341	.407
2009	Williamsport (NYP)	SS	.307	50	192	25	59	15	5	6	40	10	41	0	0	.335	.531
	Lakewood (SAL)	LoA	.223	45	157	16	35	12	1	1	15	16	37	1	2	.313	.331
2010	Lakewood (SAL)	LoA	.255	117	447	51	114	28	1	16	74	27	101	3	2	.298	.430
Minor League Totals			.268	314	1139	148	305	83	8	27	172	94	236	8	8	.329	.426

7 JIWAN JAMES, OF

Born: April 11, 1989. **B-T:** B-R. **Ht.:** 6-4. **Wt.:** 195. **Drafted:** HS—Williston, Fla., 2007 (22nd round). **Signed by:** Chip Lawrence.

James was an all-state football, basketball and baseball player in high school before turning pro for $150,000 in the 22nd round. He was signed by the same scout, Chip Lawrence, who wouldn't quit on Domonic Brown. James spent his first two years in pro ball as a pitcher until he came down with a stress reaction in his forearm, at which point he moved to the outfield in 2009. He put together a 24-game hitting streak last summer in his first taste of full-season ball. An incredible athlete, James draws comparisons to Brown with his long, lean frame. A switch-hitter, James is much better from his natural left side. From the right side, he's more defensive and slaps at the ball. James doesn't use his lower half in his swing and he has poor pitch recognition. He's not going to hit many homers, but he should be able to collect extra-base hits with his plus-plus speed. Defensively, James has incredible range and gets good reads off the bat. Combine that with his solid-average arm, and he has the potential to be a top-notch centerfielder. The Phillies also love his makeup. It's hard to ignore James' four-tool package, but how much he hits will determine how far he goes. He'll advance to high Class A Clearwater in 2011.

Year	Club (League)	Class	W	L	ERA	G	GS	CG	SV	IP	H	HR	BB	SO	G/A	WHIP	AVG
2007	Phillies (GCL)	R	0	4	7.71	9	8	0	0	33	45	7	15	14	—	1.84	.321
2008	Did Not Play—Injured																
Minor League Totals			0	4	7.71	9	8	0	0	33	45	7	15	14	—	1.84	.321

Year	Club (League)	Class	AVG	G	AB	R	H	2B	3B	HR	RBI	BB	SO	SB	CS	OBP	SLG
2009	Williamsport (NYP)	SS	.264	30	121	15	32	4	3	1	13	11	22	7	4	.336	.372
2010	Lakewood (SAL)	LoA	.270	133	556	85	150	26	6	5	64	35	132	33	20	.321	.365
Minor League Totals			.269	163	677	100	182	30	9	6	77	46	154	40	24	.323	.366

8 JESSE BIDDLE, LHP

Born: Oct. 22, 1991. **B-T:** L-L. **Ht.:** 6-4. **Wt.:** 225. **Drafted:** HS—Philadelphia, 2010 (1st round). **Signed by:** Eric Valent.

Biddle didn't pitch much as a junior at Germantown Friends School in Philadelphia, but he emerged on the summer circuit. No one followed him more closely last spring than his hometown Phillies, who scouted every one of his starts. After Philadelphia selected him 27th overall and signed him away from an Oregon commitment for $1.16 million, he reached Williamsport during a successful pro debut. Biddle is a projectable lefty whose frame evokes Clayton Kershaw's. Biddle's fastball easily sits at 91-94 mph with armside run, and he could add more velocity with time. Biddle's 77-81 mph changeup shows flashes of being a plus pitch. He throws a low-70s curveball, which is in its nascent stages, and scouts are encouraged by his ability to spin the ball. During the spring, he flashed a slider that some scouts thought had more potential than his curve. More than anything, the Phillies rave about Biddle's makeup and competitiveness. He'll have to smooth out his delivery, which features a small head jerk. He'll also need to improve his fastball command and be more consistent with his offspeed pitches. Biddle has frontline-starter potential, and some scouts compare him to Brian Matusz. He'll spend his first full pro season in low Class A.

Year	Club (League)	Class	W	L	ERA	G	GS	CG	SV	IP	H	HR	BB	SO	G/A	WHIP	AVG
2010	Phillies (GCL)	R	3	1	4.32	9	9	1	0	33	35	2	9	41	1.00	1.32	.263
	Williamsport (NYP)	SS	1	0	2.61	3	3	0	0	10	5	0	11	9	1.10	1.55	.152
Minor League Totals			4	1	3.92	12	12	1	0	44	40	2	20	50	1.03	1.37	.241

9 DOMINGO SANTANA, OF

Born: Aug. 5, 1992. **B-T:** R-R. **Ht.:** 6-5. **Wt.:** 200. **Signed:** Dominican Republic, 2008. **Signed by:** Sal Agostinelli.

The Phillies don't often give six-figure bonuses to international prospects, but they signed Santana for $330,000 in 2008. Born in the Bahamas and signed out of the Dominican Republic, he wasn't ready to handle low Class A pitching last year as a 17-year-old. His numbers picked up when he went to Williamsport in June, though his inexperience still showed. All the pieces are there for Santana to be the player Philadelphia hopes he can be—a power-hitter who plays above-average defense on an outfield corner. He's athletic and physically imposing. Fundamentally sound at the plate, he has a natural load and incredible raw power. He works the center of the field well and doesn't get pull-happy. He'll have to do a better job of recognizing pitches, as he struggles with hard stuff inside and breaking balls away. He has the plus speed and arm strength to be a quality right fielder, though he needs more game repetition to improve defensively. When scouts fall in love with his upside and tools, Santana summons Vladimir Guerrero comparisons, but he's still very raw and a lot has to go right for him to reach his ceiling. The Phillies don't want him to get in over his head again, so he'll have to earn a return to Lakewood in spring training.

Year	Club (League)	Class	AVG	G	AB	R	H	2B	3B	HR	RBI	BB	SO	SB	CS	OBP	SLG
2009	Phillies (GCL)	R	.288	37	118	17	34	6	1	6	28	15	44	3	1	.388	.508
2010	Lakewood (SAL)	LoA	.182	49	165	27	30	10	0	3	16	29	76	5	6	.322	.297
	Williamsport (NYP)	SS	.237	54	186	28	44	9	0	5	20	23	73	4	4	.336	.366
Minor League Totals			.230	140	469	72	108	25	1	14	64	67	193	12	11	.344	.377

10 AARON ALTHERR, OF

Born: Jan. 14, 1991. **B-T:** R-R. **Ht.:** 6-5. **Wt.:** 190. **Drafted:** HS—Avondale, Ariz., 2009 (9th round). **Signed by:** Brad Holland.

Altherr is yet another toolsy Phillies prospect, and no player in the system improved his stock more last year. Born in Germany, he was better known in high school for his basketball talent. He hit .446 as a senior in 2009 while starring as a shortstop and a pitcher, showing enough to earn a $150,000 bonus as a ninth-round pick. He began 2010 in extended spring training before repeating the Rookie-level Gulf Coast League, where he made enough progress to merit a promotion to Williamsport. For such a big, young hitter, Altherr takes a relatively short path to the ball, allowing him to make consistent hard contact. His lanky, fast-twitch frame doesn't produce many home runs now, but he should have at least average power once he fills out. Currently an average runner, he could develop plus speed once he gets more body control. Altherr is still raw and needs more time in the outfield, where he can play all three positions now but profiles best in a corner. His arm strength significantly improved last year and now grades as average. The Phillies have plenty of projectable outfield prospects, but only Brown has a higher all-around upside than Altherr. Like Brown did, Altherr will open his third professional season at Lakewood as a breakout candidate.

Year	Club (League)	Class	AVG	G	AB	R	H	2B	3B	HR	RBI	BB	SO	SB	CS	OBP	SLG
2009	Phillies (GCL)	R	.214	28	84	10	18	3	0	1	11	8	15	6	1	.283	.286
2010	Phillies (GCL)	R	.304	27	115	12	35	6	1	1	15	3	22	10	3	.331	.400
	Williamsport (NYP)	SS	.287	28	94	11	27	7	3	0	10	8	13	2	3	.350	.426
Minor League Totals			.273	83	293	33	80	16	4	2	36	19	50	18	7	.323	.375

11 VANCE WORLEY, RHP

Born: Sept 25, 1987. **B-T:** R-R. **Ht.:** 6-2. **Wt.:** 230. **Drafted:** Long Beach State, 2008 (3rd round). **Signed by:** Tim Kissner.

The Phillies drafted Worley in the 20th round out of high school in Sacramento in 2005 but didn't sign him until they took him in the third round after he spent three years at Long Beach State. He made huge strides in 2010 after losing weight and adding core strength, allowing him to maintain velocity deeper into games. The payoff came with a pair of big league callups. Worley's fastball sits at 88-92 mph and touches 94. His 81-84 mph slider is a solid-average offering, though some scouts think his curveball is a better breaking ball. His changeup is also an average pitch, though he sometimes slows his arm speed when he throws it. He's competitive and is a strike-thrower who likes to work ahead in the count. He has a jerky delivery that gives him deception, though he throws across his body. Worley profiles as a back-of-the-rotation starter and will get a chance to contend for the fifth starter's role in Philadelphia in 2011. With no plus pitch and his reliance on command, he may be best suited for a middle-relief role in the long term.

Year	Club (League)	Class	W	L	ERA	G	GS	CG	SV	IP	H	HR	BB	SO	G/A	WHIP	AVG
2008	Williamsport (NYP)	SS	0	0	1.13	2	2	0	0	8	3	0	1	8	—	0.50	.120
	Lakewood (SAL)	LoA	3	2	2.66	11	11	0	0	61	58	4	7	53	—	1.07	.247
2009	Reading (EL)	AA	7	12	5.34	27	27	0	0	153	163	17	49	100	0.96	1.38	.275
2010	Reading (EL)	AA	9	4	3.20	19	19	1	0	113	114	9	36	83	1.21	1.33	.264
	Lehigh Valley (IL)	AAA	1	3	3.77	8	8	0	0	45	46	3	10	36	2.00	1.24	.264
	Philadelphia (NL)	MAJ	1	1	1.38	5	2	0	0	13	8	1	4	12	1.36	0.92	.178
Major League Totals			1	1	1.38	5	2	0	0	13	8	1	4	12	1.36	0.92	.178
Minor League Totals			20	21	4.00	67	67	1	0	380	384	33	103	280	1.14	1.28	.263

12 ANTONIO BASTARDO, LHP

Born: Sept. 21, 1985. **B-T:** R-L. **Ht.:** 5-11. **Wt.:** 195. **Signed:** Dominican Republic, 2005. **Signed by:** Sal Agostinelli.

Bastardo moved quickly through the system and made his big league debut in 2009, just four years after signing out of the Dominican Republic. He ascended through the system as a starter but now profiles as a reliever, mostly because he has struggled to stay healthy. He battled shoulder injuries in 2008 and '09 and missed time last year with an elbow strain. He still showed enough for the Phillies to include him on their postseason roster in each of the last two years. Bastardo's fastball ticks up a notch out of the bullpen, sitting at 92-95 mph. He has worked on improving his 82-84 mph slider, which lacks consistency but has decent tilt. He also throws a solid-average changeup in the mid-80s, though he doesn't use it as much in relief. Bastardo struggles with command at times, which may limit him to a left-on-left specialist role. With the expected departure of free agent J.C. Romero and several other key relievers, Bastardo figures to have a bullpen job in Philadelphia in 2011.

Year	Club (League)	Class	W	L	ERA	G	GS	CG	SV	IP	H	HR	BB	SO	G/A	WHIP	AVG
2005	Phillies (DSL)	R	2	2	2.13	11	5	0	1	38	22	0	22	63	—	1.16	.162
2006	Phillies (GCL)	R	1	2	3.91	9	2	0	0	23	20	1	14	27	—	1.48	.220
2007	Lakewood (SAL)	LoA	9	0	1.87	15	15	0	0	92	63	3	42	98	—	1.15	.189

Year	Club (League)	Class	W	L	ERA	G	GS	CG	SV	IP	H	HR	BB	SO	G/A	WHIP	AVG
	Clearwater (FSL)	HiA	1	0	7.20	1	1	0	0	5	5	0	3	12	—	1.60	.250
2008	Clearwater (FSL)	HiA	2	0	1.17	5	5	0	0	31	20	2	10	47	—	0.98	.183
	Reading (EL)	AA	2	5	3.76	14	14	0	0	67	56	13	37	62	—	1.39	.223
2009	Lehigh Valley (IL)	AAA	1	0	2.08	2	2	0	0	13	11	1	3	12	0.73	1.08	.234
	Phillies (GCL)	R	0	0	0.00	3	2	0	0	4	2	0	2	3	0.50	0.92	.133
	Clearwater (FSL)	HiA	0	0	27.00	1	0	0	0	1	4	0	0	2	2.00	4.00	.800
	Reading (EL)	AA	2	2	1.75	11	5	0	3	36	22	1	7	41	0.94	0.81	.179
	Philadelphia (NL)	MAJ	2	3	6.46	6	5	0	0	24	26	4	9	19	0.46	1.48	.274
2010	Clearwater (FSL)	HiA	0	0	0.00	3	0	0	0	3	3	0	0	6	2.00	1.00	.250
	Lehigh Valley (IL)	AAA	1	1	2.08	20	0	0	3	17	12	0	6	27	1.09	1.04	.190
	Philadelphia (NL)	MAJ	2	0	4.34	25	0	0	0	19	19	1	9	26	0.47	1.50	.253
Major League Totals			4	3	5.53	31	5	0	0	42	45	5	18	45	0.47	1.49	.265
Minor League Totals			21	12	2.48	95	51	0	7	330	240	21	146	398	0.91	1.17	.199

13 SCOTT MATHIESON, RHP

Born: Feb. 27, 1984. **B-T:** R-R. **Ht.:** 6-3. **Wt.:** 190. **Drafted:** HS—Aldergrove, B.C., 2002 (17th round). **Signed by:** Tim Kissner.

It has been a long road for Mathieson, but he once again appears ready to make an impact for the Phillies. He has established himself as an organization favorite in his nine seasons as a pro, and he made his major league debut in June 2006, when he was a starter who ranked among the system's top prospects. He has battled injuries trying to make it back since. Mathieson had two Tommy John surgeries and an ulnar nerve relocation in a three-year period, but he has been healthy since the beginning of 2009. He racked up 26 saves in Triple-A last year and made two cameo appearances in the majors. Philadelphia made him a reliever because of his injuries and because his secondary stuff never developed as hoped. There's no doubting his arm strength, as he still produces a mid- to high-90s fastball. His heater tends to flatten out, so the Phillies brought in Hall of Famer Bruce Sutter to teach Mathieson a splitter. His low-80s slider is an average pitch. When he struggles, it's usually because he can't command his pitches and leaves them up in the zone. His power arm gives Mathieson a ceiling as a set-up man or closer, and he'll compete for one of several bullpen openings in Philadelphia during spring training.

Year	Club (League)	Class	W	L	ERA	G	GS	CG	SV	IP	H	HR	BB	SO	G/A	WHIP	AVG
2002	Phillies (GCL)	R	0	2	5.40	7	2	0	0	17	24	0	6	14	—	1.80	.338
2003	Phillies (GCL)	R	2	7	5.52	11	11	0	0	59	59	5	13	51	—	1.23	.247
	Batavia (NYP)	SS	0	0	0.00	2	0	0	1	6	0	0	0	7	—	0.00	.000
2004	Lakewood (SAL)	LoA	8	9	4.32	25	25	1	0	131	130	7	50	112	—	1.37	.260
2005	Clearwater (FSL)	HiA	3	8	4.14	23	23	1	0	122	111	17	34	118	—	1.19	.241
2006	Reading (EL)	AA	7	2	3.21	14	14	0	0	93	73	8	29	99	—	1.10	.221
	Scranton/W-B (IL)	AAA	3	1	3.93	5	5	0	0	34	26	2	10	36	—	1.05	.208
	Philadelphia (NL)	MAJ	1	4	7.47	9	8	0	0	37	48	8	16	28	—	1.71	.312
2007	Phillies (GCL)	R	0	0	0.00	2	2	0	0	2	0	0	1	3	—	0.50	.000
	Clearwater (FSL)	HiA	0	0	4.50	3	2	0	0	4	3	0	3	5	—	1.50	.214
	Reading (EL)	AA	0	0	9.00	2	0	0	0	2	3	1	2	1	—	2.50	.333
2008	Did Not Play—Injured																
2009	Phillies (GCL)	R	2	0	0.00	4	0	0	0	6	3	0	2	8	0.57	0.83	.130
	Clearwater (FSL)	HiA	0	0	0.00	5	0	0	1	7	4	0	3	9	1.00	1.00	.167
	Reading (EL)	AA	2	0	1.40	13	0	0	1	19	10	1	7	17	0.58	0.88	.149
2010	Lehigh Valley (IL)	AAA	3	6	2.80	54	0	0	26	64	49	8	24	83	0.98	1.13	.212
	Philadelphia (NL)	MAJ	0	0	10.80	2	0	0	0	2	5	0	2	1	1.00	4.20	.556
Major League Totals			1	4	7.62	11	8	0	0	39	53	8	18	29	1.00	1.82	.325
Minor League Totals			30	35	3.82	170	84	2	29	566	495	49	184	563	0.83	1.20	.234

14 PHILLIPPE AUMONT, RHP

Born: Jan. 7, 1989. **B-T:** L-R. **Ht.:** 6-7. **Wt.:** 255. **Drafted:** HS—Gatineau, Quebec, 2007 (1st round). **Signed by:** Wayne Norton (Mariners).

The 11th overall pick in the 2007 draft by the Mariners, Aumont signed for $1.9 million. Philadelphia liked what it saw from him in the Arizona Fall League after the 2009 season and made him the centerpiece of the trade that sent Cliff Lee to Seattle that December. The Phillies also acquired outfielder Tyson Gillies and righthander J.C. Ramirez in the deal, and none of their three pickups dazzled in their first season with their new organization. Aumont had spent 2009 as a reliever and had pitched just 18 innings in Double-A, but Philadelphia sent him back to that level as a starter. That combination didn't work out well, and Aumont was demoted and returned to the bullpen in June. The Phillies are now committed to keeping him as a reliever. Aumont's go-to pitch is his heavy sinker that sits at 90-94 mph, and he should get to the big leagues on that alone. His four-seam fastball has been clocked up to 97 mph. His curveball has sharp, biting break and is a plus pitch at times, though it's inconsistent. He also throws a below-average changeup, but he won't need it much while working out of the bullpen. Aumont has a methodical delivery that's stiff and uncoordinated, and it causes him to struggle with his command. He'll go back to Reading in 2011 as a reliever, and he could move quickly if he does a better job of locating his pitches. He has closer potential if everything comes together.

Year	Club (League)	Class	W	L	ERA	G	GS	CG	SV	IP	H	HR	BB	SO	G/A	WHIP	AVG
2008	Wisconsin (MWL)	LoA	4	4	2.75	15	8	0	2	56	46	4	19	50	—	1.17	.224
2009	High Desert (CAL)	HiA	1	2	3.24	29	0	0	12	33	24	3	12	35	1.30	1.08	.195
	West Tenn (SL)	AA	1	4	5.09	15	0	0	4	18	21	1	11	24	1.55	1.81	.292
2010	Reading (EL)	AA	1	6	7.43	11	11	0	0	50	55	4	38	38	1.24	1.87	.284
	Clearwater (FSL)	HiA	2	5	4.48	16	10	1	1	72	74	6	42	77	1.27	1.60	.270
Minor League Totals			9	21	4.57	86	29	1	19	229	220	18	122	224	1.29	1.50	.253

15 JUSTIN DEFRATUS, RHP

Born: Oct. 21, 1987. **B-T:** B-R. **Ht.:** 6-4. **Wt.:** 215. **Drafted:** Ventura (Calif.) JC, 2007 (11th round). **Signed by:** Tim Kissner.

When the Phillies scouted DeFratus as an amateur, his Ventura (Calif.) JC club didn't have a full-time pitching coach. That explains why he came into pro ball so raw and unrefined. He has added strength to his frame and benefited from a daily routine, and he now has the best control in the system. Though he worked as a starter in the second half of 2009, DeFratus pitched exclusively out of the bullpen last year, including a stint as Team USA's closer in the Pan Am qualifying tournament in Puerto Rico. Relieving seems to suit him. His 92-95 mph fastball seems even harder because of his physically imposing frame, and he turned heads by hitting 98 in the high Class A Florida State League all-star game last summer. His heater can get straight at times, so he has worked to add late movement. His slider is occasionally a plus pitch and has continued to improve, though he needs to be more consistent with it. Scouts commend DeFratus' ability to work out of tough situations, noting his fearless determination. After getting added to the 40-man roster in November, he'll likely open 2010 in Triple-A, but he has an outside shot of making the big league team in spring training.

Year	Club (League)	Class	W	L	ERA	G	GS	CG	SV	IP	H	HR	BB	SO	G/A	WHIP	AVG
2007	Phillies (GCL)	R	2	3	4.30	10	8	0	0	46	51	1	3	34	—	1.17	.273
2008	Williamsport (NYP)	SS	6	5	3.67	14	14	1	0	83	87	1	25	74	—	1.34	.260
2009	Lakewood (SAL)	LoA	5	6	3.19	36	12	0	3	110	108	3	16	101	1.82	1.13	.258
2010	Clearwater (FSL)	HiA	2	0	1.79	29	0	0	15	40	31	1	11	43	1.54	1.04	.215
	Reading (EL)	AA	1	0	2.19	20	0	0	6	25	17	2	5	28	1.59	0.89	.195
Minor League Totals			16	14	3.22	109	34	1	24	304	294	8	60	280	1.72	1.16	.251

16 TYSON GILLIES, OF

Born: Oct. 31, 1988. **B-T:** L-R. **Ht.:** 6-2. **Wt.:** 195. **Drafted:** Iowa Western CC, D/F 2006 (25th round). **Signed by:** Wayne Norton (Mariners).

One of three players acquired from the Mariners in the Cliff Lee trade after the 2009 season, Gillies is also one of three Canadians on this Top 30 list. He first drew the notice of scouts in the British Columbia Premier Baseball League, which also spawned Ryan Dempster and Justin Morneau. Gillies didn't get real widespread attention until the 2009 Futures Game, when he stole two bases and got to first base in 3.4 seconds on a bunt. The Phillies had high expectations for him in 2010, but a lingering hamstring injury limited him to 28 games. He also ran into off-the-field problems, getting arrested in August on charges of cocaine possession in Clearwater, Fla. When prosecutors examined the evidence against him, they dropped the case. None of what happened in 2010 has changed Philadelphia's opinion of Gillies, who has been noted for his high character and makeup. He was born with hearing impairments in both ears and is legally deaf, though he's an adept lip reader. Gillies has a quick, strong swing and uses a slap-and-run approach in order to take advantage of his plus-plus speed. He still needs to cut down on his strikeouts and improve his basestealing proficiency, but he had good feel for the strike zone and profiles as a potential leadoff hitter. Though he's not known for it, he also has average raw power. With well above-average range and a strong arm, he has the tools to be an exceptional defender in center field. Outside of Domonic Brown, Gillies is closer to the big leagues than any of the Phillies' outfield prospects. He'll look to rebound when he returns to Double-A this year.

Year	Club (League)	Class	AVG	G	AB	R	H	2B	3B	HR	RBI	BB	SO	SB	CS	OBP	SLG
2007	Mariners (AZL)	R	.221	35	86	20	19	3	2	0	6	6	23	9	6	.337	.302
	Everett (NWL)	SS	.625	4	8	3	5	0	0	0	2	0	1	2	0	.625	.625
2008	High Desert (CAL)	HiA	.233	11	30	4	7	0	1	0	1	1	6	1	1	.281	.300
	Everett (NWL)	SS	.313	61	192	36	60	6	5	2	22	35	46	24	7	.439	.427
2009	High Desert (CAL)	HiA	.341	124	498	104	170	17	14	9	42	60	81	44	19	.430	.486
2010	Reading (EL)	AA	.238	26	105	15	25	2	1	2	6	5	24	2	2	.286	.333
	Phillies (GCL)	R	.500	2	2	3	1	0	0	0	0	1	2	0	0	.750	.500
Minor League Totals			.312	263	921	185	287	28	23	13	80	109	181	82	35	.406	.434

17 J.C. RAMIREZ, RHP

Born: Aug. 16, 1988. **B-T:** R-R. **Ht.:** 6-3. **Wt.:** 225. **Signed:** Nicaragua, 2005. **Signed by:** Luis Molina/Nemesio Porras (Mariners).

Assistant general manager Benny Looper spent 22 years in the Mariners front office before joining the Phillies in 2009, and the club relied on his insights when it traded Cliff Lee to Seattle that December. Of the three prospects Philadelphia received, Ramirez flew the most under the radar. He pitched his way to Double-A last year, topping 140 innings for the second straight season. Ramirez has the chance to have two plus pitches in his fastball and slider. His heater sits at 92-94 mph with sink, and he touches 98 at times. He has worked to locate his fastball better, but in general he has spotty command. While his slider does have upside, it still gets sweepy and slurvy at times. His changeup is very much a work in progress. Big, strong and durable, Ramirez pitched through a hip injury in 2010 that required offseason surgery to repair a torn labrum. He'll open 2010 in Reading, trying to improve his secondary offerings and add polish. He projects as a possible No. 3 starter, though he might fit better as a power reliever.

Year	Club (League)	Class	W	L	ERA	G	GS	CG	SV	IP	H	HR	BB	SO	G/A	WHIP	AVG
2006	Mariners (VSL)	R	5	1	1.66	14	13	1	0	65	43	0	35	56	—	1.20	.191
2007	Everett (NWL)	SS	3	7	4.30	15	15	0	0	75	61	3	43	73	—	1.38	.211
2008	Wisconsin (MWL)	LoA	6	9	4.14	25	22	0	0	124	112	9	38	113	—	1.21	.239
2009	High Desert (CAL)	HiA	8	10	5.12	28	27	1	0	142	153	18	53	111	1.15	1.45	.276
2010	Clearwater (FSL)	HiA	4	3	4.06	11	11	0	0	64	63	2	17	55	0.68	1.24	.259
	Reading (EL)	AA	3	4	5.45	13	13	1	0	78	89	11	24	60	0.89	1.45	.291
Minor League Totals			29	34	4.30	106	101	3	0	549	521	43	210	468	0.96	1.33	.250

18 JON PETTIBONE, RHP

Born: July 19, 1990. **B-T:** L-R. **Ht.:** 6-5. **Wt.:** 200. **Drafted:** HS—Anaheim, 2008 (3rd round). **Signed by:** Darrell Conner.

Though he doesn't have the same name recognition as Lakewood's other pitching prospects last year, Pettibone was drafted higher than Brody Colvin and Jarred Cosart. Philadelphia selected Pettibone in the third round in 2008 and signed him away from a commitment to Southern California for $500,000. Unlike Colvin and Cosart, he succeeds more with polish than power. The son of former big league pitcher Jay Pettibone, Jon has such an advanced feel for pitching that the Phillies already have introduced a two-seam fastball and slider to him, something they usually don't do until much later in the development process. He responded by posting a 2.37 ERA in his final two months in low Class A last year. Pettibone's operates at 92-94 mph with his fastball, maintaining his velocity deep into games. His arm action produces easy velocity and late life. He also has good arm speed on his solid-average changeup, which could develop into a plus pitch. He throws his short slider in the low to mid-80s, and his curveball in the upper 70s. Both breaking pitches have shown flashes of promise but have a ways to go. Pettibone's smooth, repeatable delivery gives him good command, though there's a concern that he's around the plate too much. He projects as a mid-rotation starter and will advance to high Class A in 2011.

Year	Club (League)	Class	W	L	ERA	G	GS	CG	SV	IP	H	HR	BB	SO	G/A	WHIP	AVG
2008	Phillies (GCL)	R	0	1	0.00	1	1	0	0	1	3	0	1	0	—	4.00	.600
2009	Williamsport (NYP)	SS	2	4	5.35	9	8	0	0	35	37	0	16	36	1.88	1.50	.261
2010	Lakewood (SAL)	LoA	8	6	3.49	24	23	1	0	131	114	10	41	84	1.80	1.18	.237
Minor League Totals			10	11	3.86	34	32	1	0	168	154	10	58	120	1.82	1.26	.245

19 CESAR HERNANDEZ, 2B

Born: May 23, 1990. **B-T:** B-R. **Ht.:** 5-10. **Wt.:** 166. **Signed:** Venezuela, 2006. **Signed by:** Sal Agostinelli.

Signed the same year as fellow Venezuelan infielder Freddy Galvis, Hernandez hasn't moved as quickly but has a better chance to make an impact with his bat. Hernandez has impressed scouts in instructional league for the last two years and looks primed for a breakout season. A switch-hitter, he handles the bat better from the left side and hits for more pop from his natural right side. He's a slap hitter who squares up the ball well and uses the entire field. He has plus speed and good savvy on the basepaths. Hernandez made his biggest strides in 2010 with his defense, and he plays above his solid range and arm strength because of his instincts. He spent most of his time at second base for Williamsport last season, and that's where the Phillies think he will stay. Some scouts, however, think he looks more natural at shortstop. He has a tendency to bend at his waist and not at his knees on grounders, and he needs to add strength to his medium-size frame. Hernandez made it onto the 40-man roster without ever playing in a full-season league, something that will change when he advances to Lakewood in 2011.

Year	Club (League)	Class	AVG	G	AB	R	H	2B	3B	HR	RBI	BB	SO	SB	CS	OBP	SLG
2007	Phillies (VSL)	R	.276	54	181	32	50	7	8	2	21	11	30	6	4	.328	.436
2008	Phillies (VSL)	R	.315	60	197	31	62	7	6	1	24	33	22	19	7	.412	.426
2009	Phillies (GCL)	R	.267	41	150	21	40	5	1	0	18	17	20	13	5	.351	.313
2010	Williamsport (NYP)	SS	.325	65	255	36	83	13	2	0	23	26	27	32	6	.390	.392
Minor League Totals			.300	220	783	120	235	32	17	3	86	87	99	70	22	.374	.396

20 FREDDY GALVIS, SS

Born: Nov. 14, 1989. **B-T:** B-R. **Ht.:** 5-9. **Wt.:** 170. **Signed:** Venezuela, 2006 **Signed by:** Sal Agostinelli.

The Phillies have been fans of Galvis for a long time, dating to when he was just 14 years old in Venezuela. They signed him two years later for $90,000, and he since has worked his way to Double-A. Galvis always has stood out with his incredible ability in the field. He might be the best defensive shortstop in the minor leagues, and Philadelphia think he could be an above-average defender in the majors right now. He has plus range and arm strength to go with excellent hands and keen instincts. Galvis won't be a top-flight offensive player, but he won't have to be because of his defense. What he does need to be is an average offensive player, and that's in question. He's a switch-hitter with good hand-eye coordination and the ability to make contact, but he has to get stronger to have a chance against major league pitching. He has improved at bunting and moving runners, and he profiles as a bottom-of-the-order hitter. He's an average runner. Added to the 40-man roster after the season, Galvis will return to Reading in 2011. It will be an important year in determining whether he can be an everyday major league player because Jimmy Rollins has dealt with injuries the last few seasons and has one year remaining on his contract.

Year	Club (League)	Class	AVG	G	AB	R	H	2B	3B	HR	RBI	BB	SO	SB	CS	OBP	SLG
2007	Williamsport (NYP)	SS	.203	38	143	20	29	5	1	0	7	10	20	9	4	.255	.252
2008	Lakewood (SAL)	LoA	.238	127	458	59	109	12	1	3	42	39	58	14	7	.300	.288
2009	Phillies (GCL)	R	.276	7	29	6	8	1	0	0	0	1	4	1	1	.300	.310
	Clearwater (FSL)	HiA	.247	63	251	29	62	8	2	1	15	10	43	6	3	.280	.307
	Reading (EL)	AA	.197	16	61	6	12	0	0	1	5	2	7	0	1	.222	.246
2010	Reading (EL)	AA	.233	138	502	58	117	16	4	5	48	30	89	15	4	.276	.311
Minor League Totals			.233	389	1444	178	337	42	8	10	117	92	221	45	20	.281	.294

21 PERCI GARNER, RHP

Born: Dec. 13, 1988. **B-T:** R-R. **Ht.:** 6-3. **Wt.:** 225. **Drafted:** Ball State, 2010 (2nd round). **Signed by:** Nate Dion.

Garner was a two-time all state quarterback at Dover (Ohio) High, passing for 8,800 yards and 86 touchdowns during his career before heading to Ball State with the intention of playing football. But he didn't get on the field as the third-string quarterback in two seasons of college football, so he turned his focus to baseball. He dropped football altogether after ranking as the best pitching prospect in the Great Lakes League in the summer of 2009. Garner began last spring in Ball State's bullpen before quickly moving into the rotation and up draft boards. Some clubs considered him a first-round talent, but the Phillies nabbed him in the second round and signed him for $470,700. He pitched just four innings before Philadelphia shut him down for precautionary reasons with a tender arm. Garner is new to pitching and has a lot to learn, but he has two major league-quality pitches right now. His fastball sits at 90-94 mph and touches 96, and he backs it up with a tight curveball that comes in around 80 mph. His changeup is in its nascent stages, and he tends to overthrow it. Garner is a good athlete, though some scouts thought he was a bit stiff because of his husky frame. The Phillies are working to smooth out his delivery, and he'll struggle with control and command until he feels comfortable with it. Garner will pitch as a starter for in low Class A this year to build up his innings, though he might fit better in a bullpen role in the long run.

Year	Club (League)	Class	W	L	ERA	G	GS	CG	SV	IP	H	HR	BB	SO	G/A	WHIP	AVG
2010	Williamsport (NYP)	SS	0	2	18.00	2	2	0	0	4	8	1	1	1	2.67	2.25	.400
Minor League Totals			0	2	18.00	2	2	0	0	4	8	1	1	1	2.67	2.25	.400

22 HAROLD GARCIA, 2B

Born: Oct. 25, 1986. **B-T:** B-R. **Ht.:** 5-11. **Wt.:** 164. **Signed:** Venezuela, 2004. **Signed by:** Jesus Mendez.

Garcia was in his fourth season as a pro before he reached a full-season league, but he has made much more rapid progress in the last two years. He opened 2010 in high Class A, where he broke a 59-year-old Florida State League record by hitting in 37 consecutive games, and he continued raking after getting promoted. A switch-hitter with average speed, Garcia has proven his ability at the plate. He has solid gap power and sprays the ball to all fields from both sides of the plate. He plays with lots of energy and takes the game seriously, and the Phillies say he's the best worker in the system. Garcia is a solid defender at second base, with an average arm and decent hands, and he has the athleticism to play several other positions. Philadelphia played him at every position but pitcher, catcher and center field during instructional league. Second base will be his primary position, giving him the best shot of being an everyday player, but more realistically he profiles as a utilityman with good pop. Slated to open 2011 in Double-A after claiming a spot on the 40-man roster, Garcia could help the major league team soon.

Year	Club (League)	Class	AVG	G	AB	R	H	2B	3B	HR	RBI	BB	SO	SB	CS	OBP	SLG
2005	Phillies (VSL)	R	.226	23	62	11	14	5	1	0	2	7	15	4	2	.342	.339
2006	Phillies (VSL)	R	.273	44	99	21	27	5	2	2	13	20	20	4	4	.450	.424
2007	Phillies (VSL)	R	.296	49	169	35	50	10	1	2	28	12	26	9	2	.383	.402
2008	Clearwater (FSL)	HiA	.000	2	2	0	0	0	0	0	0	0	2	0	0	.333	.000
	Phillies (GCL)	R	.299	50	174	35	52	12	5	5	21	20	32	17	2	.402	.511
2009	Lakewood (SAL)	LoA	.291	118	444	64	129	21	5	8	55	29	100	42	12	.350	.414
2010	Clearwater (FSL)	HiA	.335	46	179	27	60	13	3	3	32	12	37	17	6	.397	.492
	Reading (EL)	AA	.281	55	231	27	65	9	2	5	32	15	57	12	5	.340	.403
Minor League Totals			.292	387	1360	220	397	75	19	25	183	115	289	105	33	.374	.430

23 JOSH ZEID, RHP

Born: March 24, 1987. **B-T:** R-R. **Ht.:** 6-5. **Wt.:** 210. **Drafted:** Tulane, 2009 (10th round). **Signed by:** Mike Stauffer.

Zeid ranked as one of the top high school pitchers in the 2005 draft class, but he went undrafted because of his commitment to Vanderbilt. His prospect status took a huge hit after he turned in two unimpressive seasons with the Commodores, but he rebounded after transferring to Tulane. In his final college start, Zeid helped his cause by pitching seven shutout innings in the Conference USA tournament. The Phillies took him in the 10th round of the 2009 draft as a senior sign and inked him for $10,000. Zeid split last season between the Lakewood rotation and bullpen, where his fastball sat at 92-94 mph when starting and a few ticks higher in relief. He touched 97 on the final pitch of a four-inning, no-hit save in the South Atlantic League championship game. He also throws an above-average slider and a solid changeup. Zeid works downhill and throws strikes, though he'll occasionally drop his arm angle and leave the ball up in the zone. Scouts note his intelligence and competitive makeup. Zeid was old for low Class A at 23 last year, so Philadelphia will try to accelerate his timetable. After pitching in the Arizona Fall League, he could make the jump to Double-A. He'll probably work as a starter to keep getting innings, though he would fit best in a bullpen role down the line.

Year	Club (League)	Class	W	L	ERA	G	GS	CG	SV	IP	H	HR	BB	SO	G/A	WHIP	AVG
2009	Williamsport (NYP)	SS	8	5	2.94	15	15	0	0	80	64	1	20	72	1.17	1.05	.217
2010	Lakewood (SAL)	LoA	8	4	2.93	43	12	0	8	107	95	7	27	111	1.20	1.14	.238
Minor League Totals			16	9	2.94	58	27	0	8	187	159	8	47	183	1.19	1.10	.229

24 AUSTIN HYATT, RHP

Born: May 23, 1986. **B-T:** R-R. **Ht.:** 6-2. **Wt.:** 180. **Drafted:** Alabama, 2009 (15th round). **Signed by:** Mike Stauffer.

Hyatt was drafted in the 23rd round out of a suburban Atlanta high school by his hometown Braves in 2004, but he opted to attend Alabama instead. He didn't get picked again until the Phillies made him a 15th-round choice as a fifth-year senior in 2009, but he has moved quickly since signing for $2,500. In 2010, his first full pro season, he was named the Florida State League's most valuable pitcher before finishing the year in Double-A. Hyatt relies on command rather than plus stuff. His fastball sits at 88-92 mph with decent late life. His best pitch is his changeup, which gets so much late tumble and fade that it resembles a curveball or forkball. He also throws a short slider in the low 80s, a pitch that grades as average. Hyatt will need to keep throwing and improving his slider so he can do a better job of getting righthanders out. He made enough progress with it in 2010 that Philadelphia believes he can stay in the rotation. He'll join J.C. Ramirez at the front of Reading's rotation in 2011.

Year	Club (League)	Class	W	L	ERA	G	GS	CG	SV	IP	H	HR	BB	SO	G/A	WHIP	AVG
2009	Williamsport (NYP)	SS	3	0	0.66	17	5	0	6	54	26	1	12	81	0.52	0.70	.141
	Lakewood (SAL)	LoA	0	0	7.71	1	1	0	0	5	5	0	2	8	0.67	1.50	.278
2010	Clearwater (FSL)	HiA	11	5	3.04	23	21	0	0	124	100	5	35	156	1.04	1.09	.220
	Reading (EL)	AA	1	0	4.91	4	4	0	0	22	21	4	9	25	0.67	1.36	.247
Minor League Totals			15	5	2.72	45	31	0	6	205	152	10	58	270	0.83	1.02	.205

25 JULIO RODRIGUEZ, RHP

Born: Aug. 29, 1990. **B-T:** R-R. **Ht.:** 6-4. **Wt.:** 195. **Drafted:** HS—Gurabo, P.R., 2008 (8th round). **Signed by:** Chip Lawrence.

Rodriguez spent the majority of 2010 in low Class A, where he struck out 90 in 56 innings, but his stuff isn't as nasty as his numbers might indicate. He has a fringe-average fastball, sitting at 86-89 mph and peaking at 93, but it plays better because of Rodriguez's size. Tall with long limbs, he has a loose arm motion and gets solid extension in front of his body, which creates good plane on his pitches. He also has room for more projection in his lanky frame. Rodriguez throws two different breaking balls, a rolling curveball and a slider. The curve offers more upside, though he'll have to tighten it up to get hitters at higher levels to bite. He also throws an average changeup. Rodriguez's delivery is a little herky-jerky, which creates deception. He does a good job of repeating his mechanics and steadily has improved his command. He still can get under his fastball and leave it up in the zone at times. Rodriguez probably is headed back to Lakewood in 2011 because Clearwater's rotation is crowded, though he could earn a midseason promotion.

Year	Club (League)	Class	W	L	ERA	G	GS	CG	SV	IP	H	HR	BB	SO	G/A	WHIP	AVG
2008	Phillies (GCL)	R	0	1	12.19	7	0	0	0	10	18	3	6	8	—	2.32	.383
2009	Phillies (GCL)	R	1	2	3.08	11	8	0	0	50	36	6	14	56	0.65	1.01	.197
2010	Lakewood (SAL)	LoA	5	1	1.44	13	7	0	0	56	32	2	22	90	0.95	0.96	.160
	Williamsport (NYP)	SS	2	2	2.65	7	5	0	0	34	25	2	15	36	1.44	1.18	.200
Minor League Totals			8	6	2.99	38	20	0	0	150	111	13	57	190	0.91	1.12	.200

26 MATT RIZZOTTI, 1B

Born: Dec. 24, 1985. **B-T:** L-L. **Ht.:** 6-5. **Wt.:** 235. **Drafted:** Manhattan, 2007 (6th round). **Signed by:** Sal Agostinelli.

Rizzotti made a splash as a sophomore at Manhattan when he hit a homer off Joba Chamberlain to upset Nebraska in an NCAA regional playoff game in 2006. The Phillies took him in the sixth round of the following year's draft. Rizzotti was solid but uninspiring in his first two full pro seasons, but he rededicated himself to the game last offseason. He hired a personal trainer, lost 30 pounds and got in the best shape of his life. He blossomed in 2010, advancing from high Class A to Triple-A while ranking third in the minors with a .430 on-base percentage. Rizzotti is a patient hitter with plus raw power, though he has shown a vulnerability to premium velocity on the inner half of the plate. He has more of a line-drive than a power approach and can hit the ball to all fields. Rizzotti's value lies totally with his bat. Even though he improved his condition, he's a well below-average athlete and runner and a fringy defender at first base. Ticketed for Triple-A in 2011 after being added to the 40-man roster, Rizzotti is blocked by Ryan Howard in Philadelphia. He looks like he'll wind up as trade bait or a lefty bat off the bench.

Year	Club (League)	Class	AVG	G	AB	R	H	2B	3B	HR	RBI	BB	SO	SB	CS	OBP	SLG
2007	Williamsport (NYP)	SS	.260	63	215	26	56	19	1	2	27	30	63	0	1	.355	.386
2008	Phillies (GCL)	R	.538	4	13	1	7	1	1	0	6	4	3	0	0	.611	.769
	Lakewood (SAL)	LoA	.268	102	365	49	98	25	2	10	49	65	97	1	1	.380	.430
2009	Clearwater (FSL)	HiA	.263	101	350	44	92	26	1	13	58	48	91	0	0	.351	.454
2010	Clearwater (FSL)	HiA	.358	31	109	18	39	8	1	1	10	13	22	0	0	.426	.477
	Reading (EL)	AA	.361	77	266	48	96	25	0	16	62	40	56	1	1	.452	.635
	Lehigh Valley (IL)	AAA	.200	17	45	0	9	3	0	0	4	6	14	0	0	.308	.267
Minor League Totals			.291	395	1363	186	397	107	6	42	216	206	346	2	3	.386	.471

27 LEANDRO CASTRO, OF

Born: June 15, 1989. **B-T:** R-R. **Ht.:** 5-11. **Wt.:** 175. **Signed:** Dominican Republic, 2007. **Signed by:** Sal Agostinelli.

Unlike the other outfielders in the Phillies system, who all seem to be toolsy prospects who offer lots of projectability, Castro has made himself known for one thing: his ability to hit. He collected 46 extra-base hits last year in the South Atlantic League, a tough hitter's environment. He has strong wrists and forearms, which help produce plus bat speed, though he also has a pronounced arm bar in his swing. He has above-average raw power, but he often swings out of his shoes and struggles to recognize offspeed pitches. None of Castro's other tools grades out better than average. He's a decent outfielder, though he fits best in left field because he doesn't get great reads off the bat and his arm is average. He's a plus runner now, though he will probably slow down as he matures physically. Castro is overly aggressive and sometimes wild with everything he does. As he moves up, he'll have to play more under control. Castro will advance to high Class A in 2011, and he'll go as far as his bat takes him.

Year	Club (League)	Class	AVG	G	AB	R	H	2B	3B	HR	RBI	BB	SO	SB	CS	OBP	SLG
2007	Phillies (DSL)	R	.278	59	223	41	62	3	5	6	37	26	39	24	9	.362	.417
2008	Phillies (GCL)	R	.298	44	161	25	48	9	1	3	19	4	25	9	4	.317	.422
2009	Lakewood (SAL)	LoA	.152	22	66	9	10	4	0	0	6	5	15	2	1	.230	.212
	Williamsport (NYP)	SS	.316	66	256	48	81	19	5	7	43	13	49	18	9	.351	.512
2010	Lakewood (SAL)	LoA	.257	124	502	78	129	27	9	10	81	34	92	22	13	.305	.406
Minor League Totals			.273	315	1208	201	330	62	20	26	186	82	220	75	36	.323	.422

28 KELLY DUGAN, OF

Born: Sept. 18, 1990. **B-T:** B-R. **Ht.:** 6-3. **Wt.:** 195. **Drafted:** HS—Sherman Oaks, Calif., 2009 (2nd round). **Signed by:** Shane Bowers.

Dugan is the son of actor, director and producer Dennis Dugan, who has worked with Adam Sandler on several comedies, including sports films "Happy Gilmore" and "The Benchwarmers." The Phillies made Kelly their first pick (second round) in 2009, after they lost their first-rounder for signing free agent Raul Ibanez. Dugan impressed in a predraft workout at Citizens Bank Park, and the Phillies plucked him from a Pepperdine commitment for $485,000. He began last year in extended spring training and played in only 28 regular-season games after he sustained a lower leg contusion that became infected. A switch-hitter, Dugan is slightly better from his natural left side. His swing has gotten longer since signing, and he has added a slight bat wrap. He also has gotten bigger and stronger, giving him above-average raw power from both sides. He has average arm strength and speed, giving the tools to be a solid defender in left field. Philadelphia commends Dugan's makeup, but he can be hard on himself at times and needs to do a better job of dealing with failure. He profiles as a corner outfielder, though the Phillies also have worked him out at first base, his high school position. He'll move to low Class A in 2011.

Year	Club (League)	Class	AVG	G	AB	R	H	2B	3B	HR	RBI	BB	SO	SB	CS	OBP	SLG
2009	Phillies (GCL)	R	.233	45	150	18	35	8	1	0	8	12	30	9	5	.297	.300
2010	Williamsport (NYP)	SS	.250	19	60	6	15	6	0	0	4	5	17	0	0	.343	.350
	Phillies (GCL)	R	.576	9	33	12	19	4	1	1	4	4	4	2	2	.650	.848
Minor League Totals			.284	73	243	36	69	18	2	1	16	21	51	11	7	.360	.387

29 KEVIN WALTER, RHP

Born: May 1, 1992. **B-T:** R-R. **Ht.:** 6-5. **Wt.:** 215. **Drafted:** HS—Westminster, Colo., 2010 (20th round). **Signed by:** Brad Holland.

High school pitchers from Colorado, from Roy Halladay and Brad Lidge to Luke Hochevar and David Aardsma, have a track record of adding velocity as they grow into their bodies, and the Phillies hope the same will happen with Walter, who has a monster 6-foot-5, 215-pound frame. They picked him in the 20th round of last year's draft and pried him away from a Boston College commitment just before the signing deadline for $350,000. Philadelphia loves Walter's arm speed and projection, which should boost his fastball velocity from its present 88-90 mph. He already has touched 93 on occasion with sink. He threw both a curveball and slider in high school, and scouts think the mid-70s curveball should be a better offering down the line. The Phillies will work to teach him a changeup. Because of his size, Walter has difficulty repeating his delivery, but he has solid mechanics and control. Philadelphia likely will keep him in extended spring training before sending him to Williamsport in June.

Year	Club (League)	Class	W	L	ERA	G	GS	CG	SV	IP	H	HR	BB	SO	G/A	WHIP	AVG
2010	Phillies (GCL)	R	0	0	4.50	1	0	0	0	2	1	0	0	0	5.00	0.50	.143
Minor League Totals			0	0	4.50	1	0	0	0	2	1	0	0	0	5.00	0.50	.143

30 CAMERON RUPP, C

Born: Sept. 28, 1988. **B-T:** R-R. **Ht.:** 6-1. **Wt.:** 240. **Drafted:** Texas, 2010 (3rd round). **Signed by:** Steve Cohen.

Rupp caught nearly every game in his three years at Texas, managing the staff and calling pitches for a Longhorns team that went to the College World Series finals in 2009. Based on his durability, power and arm strength, he received first-round buzz, but the Phillies got him in the third round last June and signed him for $287,000. Rupp has unquestioned strength that generates raw power, but scouts question how much contact he'll make. His swing isn't pretty, as he has a noticeable arm bar and an awkward weight transfer that produces a lot of strikeouts. Behind the plate, Rupp has above-average arm strength, but he needs to improve his footwork. He threw out just 15 percent of basestealers during his pro debut. He is an average receiver, but he'll need to keep his body under control because he lacks athleticism. He's a well below-average runner. Rupp will spend his first full pro season in low Class A.

Year	Club (League)	Class	AVG	G	AB	R	H	2B	3B	HR	RBI	BB	SO	SB	CS	OBP	SLG
2010	Williamsport (NYP)	SS	.218	55	193	20	42	16	0	5	28	25	51	0	0	.318	.378
Minor League Totals			.218	55	193	20	42	16	0	5	28	25	51	0	0	.318	.378

Pittsburgh Pirates

BY DEJAN KOVACEVIC

The Pirates' management team is aiming for a "flood" of talent in the system, to borrow general manager Neal Huntington's oft-used term. The organization currently has a wave of hitting that has just crested over the top, a wave of pitching coming from the bottom and a whole lot of question marks in between.

Pittsburgh went 57-105 in 2010, the third-highest loss total in the franchise's 124 years and one described by team president Frank Coonelly as an "embarrassment to the city." Few who witnessed the franchise's 18th straight losing season would argue, given that the Pirates ranked last or next-to-last in the majors in scoring, runs allowed and defensive efficiency.

Manager John Russell was fired despite having another year left on his contract, while Huntington was allowed to stay for the same term. Coonelly said he remained supportive of Huntington's work in building up the farm system despite misses among the team's many veteran-for-prospect trades.

In Pittsburgh last year, those efforts were reflected in the promising rookie showings of Pedro Alvarez (No. 2 overall pick in 2008), Jose Tabata (trade acquisition) and Neil Walker (first-round pick in 2004). With Andrew McCutchen continuing to shine after a strong rookie performance in 2009, the Pirates have the most promising top four in their lineup in a generation. All four players are 25 or younger.

While Pittsburgh's 2010 Opening Day payroll of $35 million was the lowest in the majors, the club once again spent significant money at the amateur level. Coonelly helped enforce the informal slotting system when he worked for MLB, but in his three years as president, the Pirates have led all of baseball by spending $30.7 million on draft bonuses.

That includes $11.9 million in 2010, a franchise record and just $27,000 shy of the all-time draft mark the Nationals set last summer. Pittsburgh gave No. 2 overall pick Jameson Taillon $6.5 million, the second-largest bonus in draft history, and paid second-rounder Stetson Allie $2.25 million. The Pirates also signed Mexican righthander Luis Heredia for $2.6 million, shattering the team's previous international record of $400,000 given to Venezuelan outfielder Exicardo Cayonez in 2008.

Those three pitchers add top-end quality to an already-encouraging quantity of pitching in the system. Double-A Altoona won the Eastern League title behind a prospect-filled rotation of Bryan Morris,

Pedro Alvarez's solid rookie debut helped soften another losing season in Pittsburgh

TOP 30 PROSPECTS

1. Jameson Taillon, rhp	16. Victor Black, rhp
2. Tony Sanchez, c	17. Nate Baker, lhp
3. Stetson Allie, rhp	18. Zack Dodson, lhp
4. Starling Marte, of	19. Ramon Aguero, rhp
5. Luis Heredia, rhp	20. Alex Presley, of
6. Bryan Morris, rhp	21. Quincy Latimore, of
7. Rudy Owens, lhp	22. Jordy Mercer, inf
8. Jeff Locke, lhp	23. Mel Rojas Jr., of
9. Zack Von Rosenberg, rhp	24. Josh Rodriguez, ss/2b
10. Chase d'Arnaud, ss/2b	25. Robbie Grossman, of
11. Andrew Lambo, of	26. Daniel Moskos, lhp
12. Diego Moreno, rhp	27. Pedro Ciriaco, ss
13. Colton Cain, lhp	28. Aaron Pribanic, rhp
14. Gorkys Hernandez, of	29. Matt Hague, 1b
15. Justin Wilson, lhp	30. Josh Harrison, 3b/2b

Rudy Owens, Jeff Locke and Justin Wilson. Scouts outside the organization aren't nearly as excited about the collection of arms. Some say it isn't as talented as the group that brought Zach Duke, Tom Gorzelanny and Paul Maholm to Pittsburgh a few years ago.

Of greater concern was a spate of injuries in 2010. Catcher Tony Sanchez and center fielder Starling Marte missed two months each. Several other players missed long stretches, including center fielder Gorkys Hernandez and pitchers Victor Black, Colton Cain and Quinton Miller.

General Manager: Neal Huntington. **Farm Director:** Kyle Stark. **Scouting Director:** Greg Smith.

Class	Team	League	W	L	PCT	Finish*	Manager
Majors	Pittsburgh Pirates	National	57	105	.352	16th (16)	John Russell
Triple-A	Indianapolis Indians	International	71	73	.493	8th (14)	Frank Kremblas
Double-A	Altoona Curve	Eastern	82	60	.577	†2nd (12)	Matt Walbeck
High A	Bradenton Marauders	Florida State	76	62	.551	3rd (12)	P.J. Forbes
Low A	West Virginia Power	South Atlantic	65	74	.468	t-9th (14)	Gary Green
Short-season	State College Spikes	New York-Penn	33	42	.440	12th (14)	Gary Robinson
Rookie	GCL Pirates	Gulf Coast	29	30	.492	9th (15)	Tom Prince
Overall 2010 Minor League Record			356	341	.511	10th (30)	

*Finish in overall standings (No. of teams in league). †League champion.

LAST YEAR'S TOP 30

Player, Pos.		Status
1.	Pedro Alvarez, 3b	Majors
2.	Jose Tabata, of	Majors
3.	Tony Sanchez, c	No. 2
4.	Brad Lincoln, rhp	Majors
5.	Chase d'Arnaud, ss/2b	No. 10
6.	Starling Marte, of	No. 4
7.	Tim Alderson, rhp	Dropped out
8.	Zack Von Rosenberg, rhp	No. 9
9.	Rudy Owens, lhp	No. 7
10.	Gorkys Hernandez, of	No. 14
11.	Colton Cain, lhp	No. 13
12.	Victor Black, rhp	No. 16
13.	Jeff Locke, lhp	No. 8
14.	Quinton Miller, rhp	Dropped out
15.	Bryan Morris, rhp	No. 6
16.	John Raynor, of	(Marlins)
17.	Ramon Aguero, rhp	No. 19
18.	Robbie Grossman, of	No. 25
19.	Hunter Strickland, rhp	Dropped out
20.	Jarek Cunningham, 3b/ss	Dropped out
21.	Daniel McCutchen, rhp	Majors
22.	Jordy Mercer, ss/3b	No. 22
23.	Evan Chambers, of	Dropped out
24.	Donnie Veal, lhp	Dropped out
25.	Brett Lorin, rhp	Dropped out
26.	Neil Walker, 2b	Majors
27.	Brock Holt, ss/2b	Dropped out
28.	Brian Friday, ss	Dropped out
29.	Josh Harrison, of/2b/3b	No. 30
30.	Daniel Moskos, lhp	No. 26

BEST TOOLS

Best Hitter for Average	Tony Sanchez
Best Power Hitter	Quincy Latimore
Best Strike-Zone Discipline	Matt Hague
Fastest Baserunner	Justin Bencsko
Best Athlete	Starling Marte
Best Fastball	Jameson Taillon
Best Curveball	Jameson Taillon
Best Slider	Stetson Allie
Best Changeup	Jeff Locke
Best Control	Rudy Owens
Best Defensive Catcher	Tony Sanchez
Best Defensive Infielder	Argenis Diaz
Best Infield Arm	Jordy Mercer
Best Defensive Outfielder	Gorkys Hernandez
Best Outfield Arm	Starling Marte

PROJECTED 2014 LINEUP

Catcher	Tony Sanchez
First Base	Andrew Lambo
Second Base	Neil Walker
Third Base	Pedro Alvarez
Shortstop	Chase d'Arnaud
Left Field	Andrew McCutchen
Center Field	Starling Marte
Right Field	Jose Tabata
No. 1 Starter	Jameson Taillon
No. 2 Starter	James McDonald
No. 3 Starter	Luis Heredia
No. 4 Starter	Bryan Morris
No. 5 Starter	Rudy Owens
Closer	Stetson Allie

TOP PROSPECTS OF THE DECADE

Year	Player, Pos.	2010 Org.
2001	J.R. House, c	Mets
2002	J.R. House, c	Mets
2003	John Van Benschoten, rhp	Yankees
2004	John Van Benschoten, rhp	Yankees
2005	Zach Duke, lhp	Pirates
2006	Neil Walker, c	Pirates
2007	Andrew McCutchen, of	Pirates
2008	Andrew McCutchen, of	Pirates
2009	Pedro Alvarez, 3b	Pirates
2010	Pedro Alvarez, 3b	Pirates

TOP DRAFT PICKS OF THE DECADE

Year	Player, Pos.	2010 Org.
2001	John Van Benschoten, rhp	Yankees
2002	Bryan Bullington, rhp	Royals
2003	Paul Maholm, lhp	Pirates
2004	Neil Walker, c	Pirates
2005	Andrew McCutchen, of	Pirates
2006	Brad Lincoln, rhp	Pirates
2007	Daniel Moskos, lhp	Pirates
2008	Pedro Alvarez, 3b	Pirates
2009	Tony Sanchez, c	Pirates
2010	Jameson Taillon, rhp	Pirates

LARGEST BONUSES IN CLUB HISTORY

Jameson Taillon, 2010	$6,500,000
Pedro Alvarez, 2008	$6,000,000
Bryan Bullington, 2002	$4,000,000
Brad Lincoln, 2006	$2,750,000
Luis Heredia, 2010	$2,600,000

PITTSBURGH PIRATES

TOP 2011 ROOKIE: Rudy Owens, lhp. His poise, command and improved stuff point to a pivotal role later in the summer.

BREAKOUT PROSPECT: Victor Black, rhp. The 2009 sandwich pick was derailed by injuries last season, but he has the fastball and slider to move quickly as a reliever.

SLEEPER: Evan Chambers, of. He has plenty of tools and a Kirby Puckett build, but he needs to be more aggressive at the plate.

SOURCE OF TOP 30 TALENT

Homegrown	22	Acquired	8
College	9	Trades	7
Junior college	1	Rule 5 draft	1
High school	7	Independent leagues	0
Draft-and-follow	1	Free agents/waivers	0
Nondrafted free agents	0		
International	4		

LF
Andrew Lambo (11)
Alex Presley (20)
Quincy Latimore (21)
Robbie Grossman (25)
Rogelio Noris

CF
Starling Marte (4)
Gorkys Hernandez (14)
Mel Rojas Jr. (23)
Exicardo Cayonez
Justin Bencsko

RF
Evan Chambers
Adalberto Santos
Willy Garcia
Wes Freeman
Dan Grovatt

3B
Jeremy Farrell
Elevys Gonzalez
Eric Avila

SS
Chase d'Arnaud (10)
Jordy Mercer (22)
Pedro Ciriaco (27)
Brock Holt
Drew Maggi
Yhonathan Barrios
Jodaneli Carvajal
Dilson Herrera
Brian Friday

2B
Josh Rodriguez (24)
Josh Harrison (30)
Jarek Cunningham
Gift Ngoepe
Jim Negrych
Shelby Ford

1B
Matt Hague (29)
Matt Curry
Aaron Baker
Calvin Anderson
Jared Lakind

C
Tony Sanchez (2)
Eric Fryer
Ramon Cabrera
Jairo Marquez

RHP

RHSP	RHRP
Jameson Taillon (1)	Diego Moreno (12)
Stetson Allie (3)	Victor Black (16)
Luis Heredia (5)	Ramon Aguero (19)
Bryan Morris (6)	Chris Leroux
Zack Von Rosenberg (9)	Cesar Valdez
Aaron Pribanic (28)	Anthony Claggett
Phillip Irwin	Jason Townsend
Nick Kingham	Brooks Pounders
Quinton Miller	Casey Erickson
Mike Crotta	Brandon Cumpton
Jared Hughes	Brian Leach
Trent Stevenson	Mike Dubee
Tyler Waldron	Kevin Decker
Tim Alderson	Tom Boleska
Brett Lorin	Casey Sadler
Hunter Strickland	
Kyle McPherson	
Ryan Hafner	
Vincent Payne	
Jeff Inman	

LHP

LHSP	LHRP
Rudy Owens (7)	Daniel Moskos (26)
Jeff Locke (8)	Tony Watson
Colton Cain (13)	Zac Fuesser
Justin Wilson (15)	Tyler Cox
Nate Baker (17)	Jhonathan Ramos
Zack Dodson (18)	Eliecer Navarro
Joe Martinez	Rinku Singh

DRAFT ANALYSIS

2010

BEST PURE HITTER: In a draft class dominated by pitching, OF Adalberto Santos (22) has the steadiest bat. He hit .520 and was the national junior college batting leader in 2008, then was Oregon State's top hitter for two seasons.

BEST POWER HITTER: 1B Matt Curry (16) has a short, powerful stroke and the patience to work himself into counts where he can unleash his above-average power. He led short-season State College with seven home runs.

FASTEST RUNNER: OF Justin Bencsko (20) plays to his plus-plus speed, using a contact approach at the plate and showing good range in center field.

BEST DEFENSIVE PLAYER: While not quite a burner like Bencsko, OF Mel Rojas Jr. (3) has slightly above-average speed and a plus arm. Pittsburgh believes he can play center, and if not, he'll be a fine right fielder.

BEST FASTBALL: The Pirates drafted the two hardest throwers in the high school ranks in RHPs Jameson Taillon (1) and Stetson Allie (2). Taillon has touched 99 in the past and pitched at 93-97 mph in high school. Allie may throw 98-99 mph more frequently but doesn't have the same polish.

BEST SECONDARY PITCH: Taillon's curveball earns the "hammer" tag with mid-80s power and good depth. Allie's slider registers in the upper 80s at times.

BEST PRO DEBUT: Santos (.319/.406/.479, 17 SB) and Curry (.299/.421/.477) were State College's best hitters. Projectable RHP Vincent Payne (12) finished up with the Spikes as a 19-year-old after going 2-2, 2.43 in 37 innings in the Rookie-level Gulf Coast League.

BEST ATHLETE: Some clubs, including Pittsburgh, viewed Rojas as a five-tool talent. Allie was a legitimate two-way threat as a power-hitting third baseman. Versatile SS Drew Maggi (15) has good quickness and all-around skills.

MOST INTRIGUING BACKGROUND: Rojas' father Mel spent parts of 10 seasons in the majors, mostly with the Expos. Allie's father Dan is a former scout who was his high school coach. Santos was on the 2001 Bronx Little League team made infamous by his former New Mexico JC teammate, Danny Almonte.

CLOSEST TO THE MAJORS: Taillon is a special case for a high school pitcher, with electric stuff and an idea of what he's doing on the mound. His $6.5 million signing bonus was the largest ever for a high school player.

BEST LATE-ROUND PICK: The Pirates went over slot for Maggi, RHP Ryan Hafner (17) and 1B Jared

Lakind (23), but loose-armed RHP Jason Townsend (31) has impressed the club most, running his fastball up to 96 mph during his debut.

THE ONE WHO GOT AWAY: Pittsburgh went after some tough signs in the first 10 rounds and was unable to sign RHPs Jason Hursh (6, now at Oklahoma State), Austin Kubitza (7, Rice), Dace Kime (8, Louisville) and Zach Weiss (10, UCLA). RHP Connor Sadzeck (45), an Illinois prep product, showed a mid-90s fastball in the fall at Angelina (Texas) JC.

ASSESSMENT: Taillon and Allie had the two best arms in the entire draft, and the Pirates' crop will be judged by how their $8.75 investment in those two plays out. They took nine righthanders in the first 10 rounds, with Rojas the lone exception.

2009

A broken jaw is the only thing that has slowed C Tony Sanchez (1) since he was a surprise No. 4 overall pick. Pittsburgh gave hefty bonuses to RHPs Victor Black (1s) and Zack Von Rosenberg (6) and LHPs Zack Dodson (4) and Colton Cain (8), and they're all coming along slowly.

GRADE: C+

2008

3B Pedro Alvarez (1) hit 16 homers as a rookie last year. SS/2B Chase d'Arnaud (4) and LHP Justin Wilson (5) could join him in the majors soon. Signing RHP Tanner Scheppers (2) would have been nice, but he wasn't fully healthy.

GRADE: A

2007

Pittsburgh won't ever live down passing on Matt Wieters to take LHP Daniel Moskos (1) with the No. 4 overall choice. Worse yet, Moskos is the only player in this class who appears on this Top 30 list.

GRADE: F

2006

RHP Brad Lincoln (1) bombed in the big leagues last year, so draft-and-follow LHP Rudy Owens (28) might wind up being the best player from this effort. 3B Lonnie Chisenhall (11) didn't sign and eventually became a first-round pick and the Indians' top prospect.

GRADE: D

Draft analysis by John Manuel (2010) and Jim Callis (2006-09). Numbers in parentheses indicate draft rounds.

JAMESON TAILLON, RHP

Born: Nov. 18, 1991. **Bats:** R. **Throws:** R.
Height: 6-5. **Weight:** 223. **Drafted:** HS—
The Woodlands, Texas, 2010 (1st round).
Signed by: Trevor Haley.

PROSPECT 1

MIKE JANES

Taillon entered 2010 as the highest-upside pitching prospect in the draft and cemented that status with a dominating season at The Woodlands (Texas) High. He went 8-1, 1.78 with 114 strikeouts in 62 innings, including a 19-strikeout no-hitter and a 13-strikeout playoff win in his final start. The Pirates took Taillon with the No. 2 overall pick, and their scouts liked him better than No. 1 choice Bryce Harper. After a long but amicable negotiation, he agreed to a $6.5 million bonus—the second-largest in draft history—on the evening of the Aug. 16 deadline. Pittsburgh sent him and second-rounder Stetson Allie, another high school righthander with electric stuff, to short-season State College to observe the Spikes. Taillon's first pro work off a mound came during instructional league in October,

Scouts compare Taillon to Josh Beckett at the same stage of his career. The two Texans had similar stuff, but Taillon has a classic pitcher's body and is markedly bigger, with room to fill out. His fastball, which is heavy and comes with explosive movement, sits at 93-97 mph and touches 99. His mid-80s hammer curveball is just as devastating, and the consensus among scouts was that he had the two best pitches in the draft (with Allie not far behind). Taillon's curve opens on the same plane as his fastball, making it that much tougher to hit. He also has a hard slider that looked nearly as good as his curve during instructional league. Both breaking balls have late bite and depth, with the curve being a little bigger and the slider shorter with more tilt. He'll need to develop a changeup. He has flashed a decent one in the past, but the rest of his repertoire rendered it moot at the amateur level. Taillon's delivery, mostly from a three-quarters arm slot, is a work in progress. He throws his fastball with the ease of someone playing catch, but good command of all pitches will come only after he consistently trusts his natural strength rather than trying to do too much. He also has plenty of moving parts, including a trademark dip in his back shoulder, though he also has the athleticism to make it all work. Any mechani-

cal issues are minor—Pittsburgh simply wants to allow him to locate the ball down in the zone with plane—and he should develop into a solid strike-thrower. The Pirates quickly have become enamored with Taillon's intangibles. Though he still could be a little meaner on the mound—think, again, of a young Beckett—he has exemplary makeup. He had no trouble assimilating into pro ball and soaking up teaching in instructional league.

Taillon is projected as the franchise's first ace since Doug Drabek in the early 1990s, but Pittsburgh pledges to bring him along slowly. Then again, he's so gifted that his talent may dictate otherwise. He'll likely make his pro debut at low Class A West Virginia, where he'll pitch out of the rotation with a highly conservative inning count. His focus will be almost entirely on building up his durability and learning the professional game, so a midseason promotion appears unlikely.

SCOUTING GRADES

Fastball: 70.   **Command/**
Curveball: 70.   **Control:** 60.
Slider: 65.   **Delivery:** 60.

Based on 20-80 scouting scale, where 50 represents major league average, and future projection rather than present tools.

Year	Club (League)	Class	W	L	ERA	G	GS	CG	SV	IP	H	HR	BB	SO	G/A	WHIP	AVG
2010	Did Not Play—Signed Late																

2 TONY SANCHEZ, C

Born: May 20, 1988. **B-T:** R-R. **Ht.:** 6-0. **Wt.:** 220. **Drafted:** Boston College, 2009 (1st round). **Signed by:** Chris Kline.

Sanchez was a surprise pick at No. 4 overall in the 2009 draft, but he has demonstrated advanced defense and surprisingly consistent offense since signing for $2.5 million. His first full pro season ended in late June when a fastball from the Mets' Brad Holt struck him in the face. Sanchez's jaw was broken and he lost 20 pounds while recovering, but he returned for a full, productive Arizona Fall League showing. Sanchez is exceptional at blocking pitches, thanks to quick reflexes and sound technique. His arm strength grades as a 55-60 on the 20-80 scouting scale and he has a quick exchange. He threw out only 15 percent of basestealers in 2010, but that owed to a sore shoulder early in the season. He's still learning to call games, something he didn't do in high school or at Boston College. At the plate, Sanchez has shown mature recognition of the strike zone and how pitchers are trying to work him. He has some gap power and should be able to reach double digits in homers, though his strength will remain hitting to all fields for good average. His running is below-average, as with most catchers. His leadership traits are universally lauded. Sanchez will open this season with Double-A Altoona and remains on target for a big league arrival in 2012. He has the potential to become Pittsburgh's first Gold Glove catcher since Mike LaValliere in 1987.

Year	Club (League)	Class	AVG	G	AB	R	H	2B	3B	HR	RBI	BB	SO	SB	CS	OBP	SLG
2009	State College (NYP)	SS	.308	4	13	2	4	1	0	0	1	1	2	0	0	.357	.385
	West Virginia (SAL)	LoA	.316	41	155	29	49	15	1	7	46	21	34	1	0	.415	.561
	Lynchburg (CAR)	HiA	.200	3	10	2	2	2	0	0	1	1	4	0	0	.385	.400
2010	Bradenton (FSL)	HiA	.314	59	207	31	65	17	0	4	35	28	41	2	1	.416	.454
Minor League Totals			.312	107	385	64	120	35	1	11	83	51	81	3	1	.413	.494

3 STETSON ALLIE, RHP

Born: March 13, 1991. **B-T:** R-R. **Ht.:** 6-4. **Wt.:** 225. **Drafted:** HS—Lakewood, Ohio, 2010 (2nd round). **Signed by:** Brian Tracy.

The Pirates were pleasantly surprised Allie lasted 52 picks in the 2010 draft despite having a live arm to rival Jameson Taillon's. They went well above slot to sign him for $2.25 million in the second round. He didn't pitch last summer after signing but looked good during instructional league. His father Dan is a former scout who was his coach at St. Edward High (Lakewood, Ohio). Some teams were scared off by Allie's lack of command, but his pure stuff is undeniable. He threw 98-99 mph fastballs as the draft approached, and also displayed an 88-89 mph slider. The source of his power is his big, strong, physical frame, as well as an aggressive mentality that leads to explosiveness in the delivery. He'll need something to slow down opponents' bats, which is why Pittsburgh began stressing a changeup in instructional league. While his stuff is in Taillon's class, Allie doesn't have the same polish. He also was a prospect as a third baseman with plus power and a strong arm, but he realized in 2010 that his future was on the mound. Though it's easier to project Allie as a closer, the Pirates hope he can become a starter and he'll begin 2011 in the West Virginia rotation. That role will give him the innings to work on his changeup and make the transition from thrower to pitcher.

Year	Club (League)	Class	W	L	ERA	G	GS	CG	SV	IP	H	HR	BB	SO	G/A	WHIP	AVG
2010	Did Not Play—Signed Late																

4 STARLING MARTE, OF

Born: Oct. 9, 1988. **B-T:** R-R. **Ht.:** 6-2. **Wt.:** 179. **Signed:** Dominican Republic, 2007. **Signed by:** Rene Gayo/Josue Herrera.

Signed for a relatively low $85,000, Marte has shown five-tool potential since coming to the United States in 2009, becoming the franchise's most anticipated Latin American prospect since Jose Guillen. Marte was in a 1-for-18 slump last May when he was diagnosed with a broken hamate bone in his left hand. Surgery cost him two months but he quickly returned to form afterward. One club official unflinchingly calls Marte the best player in the system. He stands out most with his plus-plus speed, particularly in center field, where he also has an above-average arm. Some scouts believe he could play defensively in Pittsburgh right now. His basestealing isn't polished, but he'll be dangerous once he masters reads and jumps. At the plate, Marte drives the ball from gap to gap. He has hit just five homers in two seasons in the United States, but he has the strength and swing path to hit 15-20 annually. The Pirates want him to focus on his on-base skills, because he doesn't control the strike zone or square up many breaking balls. Marte's advanced defense will accelerate his rise, as will his intelligence and ambition. But his strike-zone discipline will have to keep pace. Ticketed for Double-A in 2011, he could push Andrew McCutchen to an outfield corner when he arrives in Pittsburgh within a couple of years.

PITTSBURGH PIRATES

Year	Club (League)	Class	AVG	G	AB	R	H	2B	3B	HR	RBI	BB	SO	SB	CS	OBP	SLG
2007	Pirates (DSL)	R	.220	45	132	27	29	4	1	1	11	10	29	16	2	.307	.288
2008	Pirates (DSL)	R	.296	65	257	53	76	10	2	9	44	16	53	20	8	.367	.455
2009	Pirates (GCL)	R	.000	2	7	1	0	0	0	0	0	0	1	0	0	.000	.000
	West Virginia (SAL)	LoA	.312	54	221	41	69	9	5	3	34	12	55	24	7	.377	.439
	Lynchburg (CAR)	HiA	1.000	1	2	0	2	0	0	0	1	0	0	0	0	1.000	1.000
2010	Pirates (GCL)	R	.346	8	26	6	9	3	0	2	5	1	6	4	1	.393	.692
	Bradenton (FSL)	HiA	.315	60	222	41	70	16	5	0	33	12	59	22	8	.386	.432
Minor League Totals			.294	235	867	169	255	42	13	15	128	51	203	86	26	.364	.424

5 LUIS HEREDIA, RHP

Born: Aug. 9, 1994. **B-T:** R-R. **Ht.:** 6-6. **Wt.:** 185. **Signed:** Mexico, 2010. **Signed by:** Rene Gayo/Jesus Valdez.

Signing Heredia for a $2.6 million bonus in August was a landmark deal for the Pirates, who never had spent more than $400,000 on an international amateur. It also was the culmination of years of intense scouting by Rene Gayo and Jesus Valdez, who forged a close relationship with Heredia and fended off more than a dozen other interested teams. Heredia doesn't have one singularly superb trait, aside from doing so much so well with such size at his age. His frame, coordination and delivery are highly advanced, and he has excelled against older competition all his life. That makes his ceiling hard to define. Heredia's fastball sits at 92-93 mph, peaking at 95 mph with some cut inward on righthanders. Moreover, the velocity comes with minimal effort, as the ball appears to explode from his hand. He has a plus curveball on which he leans heavily, perhaps too much. He also demonstrates good velocity, if precious little polish, on a slider and changeup. Because Heredia was limited to pitching in weekly exhibitions for most of the past year, Pittsburgh kept him off the mound until instructional league in October, then sent him to its Dominican academy for more work. He impressed management enough with his poise that he may pitch in the Rookie-level Gulf Coast League in 2011.

Year	Club (League)	Class	W	L	ERA	G	GS	CG	SV	IP	H	HR	BB	SO	G/A	WHIP	AVG
2010	Did Not Play—Signed 2011 Contract																

6 BRYAN MORRIS, RHP

Born: March 28, 1987. **B-T:** L-R. **Ht.:** 6-3. **Wt.:** 210. **Drafted:** Motlow State (Tenn.) CC, 2006 (1st round). **Signed by:** Marty Lamb (Dodgers).

A Dodgers first-round pick in 2006, Morris had the highest ceiling of the four prospects the Pirates acquired in the otherwise disastrous Jason Bay trade two years later. He had Tommy John surgery in 2007, biceps tendinitis in 2008, then foot surgery and a week-long suspension for berating an umpire in 2009. He rebounded in a big way last year, pitching in the Futures Game and helping Altoona win the Eastern League championship. Morris has the stuff of a frontline starter. He has a 92-94 mph fastball that has hit 96 mph when he has worked in relief. His curveball has a powerful downward arc, and he mixes it well with his fastball, which has some cutting life. He throws an average slider with late downward break. He has a changeup, too, but he shows little feel for it. Scouts love Morris' intensity, especially given his injury history, though some want to see him tone down his delivery a bit before fully believing he can hold up as a starter. Pittsburgh moved him to the bullpen late in the summer, primarily to limit his innings but also to address minor mechanical issues. Morris will start 2011 at Triple-A Indianapolis with the chance to make his big league debut later in the season. If he can stay healthy, he still might salvage something out of the Bay deal.

Year	Club (League)	Class	W	L	ERA	G	GS	CG	SV	IP	H	HR	BB	SO	G/A	WHIP	AVG
2006	Ogden (PIO)	R	4	5	5.13	14	14	0	0	60	64	3	40	79	—	1.74	.267
2007	Did not play—Injured																
2008	Great Lakes (MWL)	LoA	2	4	3.20	17	17	1	0	82	74	5	31	72	—	1.29	.247
	Hickory (SAL)	LoA	0	2	5.02	3	3	0	0	14	17	2	12	11	—	2.02	.288
2009	Lynchburg (CAR)	HiA	4	9	5.57	15	15	0	0	73	87	2	34	32	2.21	1.67	.295
2010	Bradenton (FSL)	HiA	3	0	0.60	8	8	0	0	45	37	0	7	40	1.87	0.99	.220
	Altoona (EL)	AA	6	4	4.25	19	16	0	0	89	87	9	31	84	2.07	1.33	.258
Minor League Totals			19	24	4.00	76	73	1	0	362	366	21	155	318	2.08	1.44	.262

7 RUDY OWENS, LHP

Born: Dec. 18, 1987. **B-T:** L-L. **Ht.:** 6-3. **Wt.:** 215. **Drafted:** Chandler-Gilbert (Ariz.) CC, D/F 2006 (28th round). **Signed by:** Ted Williams.

Signed for $390,000 as a draft-and-follow, Owens posted a 5.06 ERA in his first two pro seasons but has been named Pirates minor league pitcher of the year in each of the last two. In 2010, he led the Eastern League in ERA (2.46) and fewest baserunners per nine innings (9.1). He grew stronger as the season progressed, giving up just six runs and four walks in his final eight starts. Owens grew stronger as the season progressed in another way, too, as his fastball went from 87-90 to 90-93 mph down the stretch. The extra velocity highly encouraged the Pirates, who proclaimed that his soft-tossing-lefty tag no longer applied. His fastball command is solid—occasionally, it's excellent—and the pitch has some late run. His secondary offerings, a slurvy breaking ball and a changeup, are no better than average pitches but he locates them well. Owens' pinpoint control comes from easily repeating his delivery, and the way he uses it to pick apart hitters' weaknesses is reminiscent of a young Zach Duke. How well Owens retains his added velocity will determine if he's a mid-rotation starter or more of a back-end option. He'll begin 2011 in Triple-A and could reach Pittsburgh by the end of the season.

Year	Club (League)	Class	W	L	ERA	G	GS	CG	SV	IP	H	HR	BB	SO	G/A	WHIP	AVG
2007	Pirates (GCL)	R	1	4	5.32	6	4	0	0	22	20	1	8	17	—	1.27	.238
2008	State College (NYP)	SS	3	6	4.97	15	13	0	0	58	63	2	13	45	—	1.31	.269
2009	West Virginia (SAL)	LoA	10	1	1.70	19	19	0	0	101	71	8	15	91	0.71	0.85	.197
	Lynchburg (CAR)	HiA	1	1	3.86	6	6	0	0	23	29	3	2	22	0.96	1.33	.305
2010	Altoona (EL)	AA	12	6	2.46	26	26	0	0	150	124	11	23	132	1.43	0.98	.226
Minor League Totals			27	18	2.92	72	68	0	0	354	307	25	61	307	1.07	1.04	.232

8 JEFF LOCKE, LHP

Born: Nov. 20, 1987. **B-T:** L-L. **Ht.:** 6-2. **Wt.:** 175. **Drafted:** HS—Conway, N.H., 2006 (2nd round). **Signed by:** Lonnie Goldberg (Braves).

Locke looks like he'll be the best of the three players acquired in the 2009 Nate McLouth trade with the Braves, surpassing Charlie Morton and outfield prospect Gorkys Hernandez. After getting hit hard upon his arrival, Locke has settled down to become one of the system's most consistent starters. He easily handled a midseason promotion to Double-A last year, and he recorded a 1.54 ERA in two playoff starts for Eastern League champion Altoona. Locke came from Atlanta with a 91-94 mph fastball, but he now mostly sits at 90 mph and peaks at 92. His fastball is still effective, however, because it has running life and comes with some deception. Filling out his skinny frame could restore some velocity, though his narrow shoulders suggest that he won't add much more strength. Locke also uses a slurvy curveball and a changeup, both of which are average. He has a slight build and a herky-jerky delivery with good finish out front. He may not have a plus pitch, but he consistently throws strikes and keeps the ball down in the zone. Unless he regains his former fastball, Locke may not be more than a No. 4 starter. He'll return to Altoona in 2011, with the chance for another midseason promotion.

Year	Club (League)	Class	W	L	ERA	G	GS	CG	SV	IP	H	HR	BB	SO	G/A	WHIP	AVG
2006	Braves (GCL)	R	4	3	4.22	10	5	0	0	32	38	4	5	38	—	1.34	.299
2007	Danville (APP)	R	7	1	2.66	13	11	0	1	61	48	2	8	74	—	0.92	.213
2008	Rome (SAL)	LoA	5	12	4.06	25	24	1	0	140	150	6	38	113	—	1.35	.269
2009	Myrtle Beach (CAR)	HiA	1	4	5.52	10	10	0	0	46	47	1	26	43	1.63	1.60	.272
	Lynchburg (CAR)	HiA	4	4	4.08	17	17	0	0	82	98	4	18	56	1.29	1.42	.305
2010	Bradenton (FSL)	HiA	9	3	3.54	17	17	0	0	86	82	6	14	83	1.41	1.11	.248
	Altoona (EL)	AA	3	2	3.59	10	10	0	0	58	57	5	12	56	1.25	1.20	.257
Minor League Totals			33	29	3.89	102	94	1	1	504	520	28	121	463	1.37	1.27	.266

9 ZACK VON ROSENBERG, RHP

Born: Sept. 24, 1990. **B-T:** R-R. **Ht.:** 6-5. **Wt.:** 205. **Drafted:** HS—Zachary, La., 2009 (6th round). **Signed by:** Jerome Cochran.

Von Rosenberg won four state championship games in four years at two Louisiana high schools, showing top-two-rounds talent. But his commitment to Louisiana State caused him to slide until the sixth round of the 2009 draft, and it cost the Pirates a $1.2 million bonus. After signing late and pitching just one pro inning that summer, he opened 2010 in extended spring training before reporting to State College. Kept on tight pitch counts, he recovered from a slow start to post a 0.96 ERA in his final six outings. Von Rosenberg offers an advanced feel for pitching and a wiry, projectable frame that portends improved stuff in the future. His fastball currently ranges from 87-91 mph and he's able to locate it to both sides of the plate. His changeup took a big step forward last summer, showing nice spin and deception. His curveball has 11-to-5 break at times, though it also can get loopy. A good athlete who was an all-state pitcher in high school, he has a loose, easy arm action. Pittsburgh will continue to handle Von Rosenberg with care, though he'll make his full-season debut at West Virginia in 2011. If he can get stronger and add some more power to his pitches, he could become a No. 3 starter and possibly more.

Year	Club (League)	Class	W	L	ERA	G	GS	CG	SV	IP	H	HR	BB	SO	G/A	WHIP	AVG
2009	Pirates (GCL)	R	0	0	0.00	1	1	0	0	1	0	0	0	1	1.00	0.00	.000
2010	State College (NYP)	SS	1	6	3.20	13	13	0	0	59	60	4	13	39	1.24	1.24	.267
Minor League Totals			1	6	3.15	14	14	0	0	60	60	4	13	40	1.24	1.22	.263

10 CHASE D'ARNAUD, SS/2B

Born: Jan. 21, 1987. **B-T:** R-R. **Ht.:** 6-1. **Wt.:** 180. **Drafted:** Pepperdine, 2008 (4th round). **Signed by:** Rick Allen.

After cruising through his first two pro seasons, d'Arnaud hit the wall hard in Double-A last year. He batted .209 in the first two months and some dubious defense got him moved from shortstop to second base in August. Still, he showed some flashes, including a 19-game on-base streak in June, a grand slam in the Eastern League all-star game and three homers in the playoffs. His brother Travis plays in the Blue Jays system and is one of the game's top catching prospects. D'Arnaud's best tools are his plus speed and arm strength, and he covers a good amount of ground at shortstop. But he made 28 errors in 115 games at short last year, in part because he didn't maintain his focus. His offensive ceiling is as a No. 2 hitter, but he'll have to make adjustments to reach it. D'Arnaud guesses and strikes out too often. He's most effective when he doesn't try to do too much, keeps his hands inside the ball and uses the opposite field. He has some strength but below-average power, mostly because he hasn't learned to turn on pitches. Despite his struggles, the Pirates still believe d'Arnaud can be an everyday shortstop. He'll have to rebound in 2011, or a utility role will be in his future. He could return to Double-A to start the season.

Year	Club (League)	Class	AVG	G	AB	R	H	2B	3B	HR	RBI	BB	SO	SB	CS	OBP	SLG
2008	State College (NYP)	SS	.286	43	168	26	48	10	5	1	21	11	30	14	2	.333	.423
2009	West Virginia (SAL)	LoA	.291	62	213	32	62	14	3	3	31	30	31	17	3	.394	.427
	Lynchburg (CAR)	HiA	.295	54	210	45	62	19	4	4	26	30	41	14	5	.402	.481
2010	Altoona (EL)	AA	.247	132	530	91	131	33	9	6	48	56	102	33	7	.331	.377
Minor League Totals			.270	291	1121	194	303	76	21	14	126	127	204	78	17	.357	.413

11 ANDREW LAMBO, OF

Born: Aug. 11, 1988. **B-T:** L-L. **Ht.:** 6-3. **Wt.:** 190. **Drafted:** HS—Newbury Park, Calif., 2007 (4th round). **Signed by:** Chuck Crim (Dodgers).

It was another head-scratcher of a year for Lambo, who only two years ago was regarded as the Dodgers' top prospect. He continued to show promise at the plate, but he also was suspended for 50 games on May 1 for a second positive test of a "drug of abuse" under the minor league drug treatment and prevention program. As a high school sophomore he was caught smoking marijuana, and this instance also involved a recreational drug. The Pirates acquired Lambo and James McDonald at last year's trade deadline in the deal that sent Octavio Dotel to the Dodgers, adamant they had done due diligence on Lambo's makeup. Some scouts are put off by what they see as a cocky attitude, but the Pirates' view is that it is a simple case of immaturity and that Lambo has shown progress in growing out of it. Lambo is a pure hitter, and the ball jumps off his bat. He squares the ball and can hit to all fields. He remains a gap-to-gap hitter at this point, but more power is there. A reduced leg lift implemented by the Pirates has led to better swings and selectivity, and he's already got a good eye for pitches and the strike zone. Good fastballs can beat him over the inner half. He is a below-average athlete and runner but shows good anticipation in the outfield, so he should be fine in left field. His arm is slightly below-average. Lambo's season was disrupted by a sprained right shoulder in mid-August, but he came back strong in the Arizona Fall League, so he could move up to Triple-A in 2011.

Year	Club (League)	Class	AVG	G	AB	R	H	2B	3B	HR	RBI	BB	SO	SB	CS	OBP	SLG
2007	Dodgers (GCL)	R	.343	54	181	38	62	15	1	5	32	29	34	1	2	.440	.519
2008	Great Lakes (MWL)	LoA	.288	123	472	58	136	33	2	15	79	41	110	5	2	.346	.462
	Jacksonville (SL)	AA	.389	8	36	7	14	2	1	3	12	2	9	0	0	.421	.750
2009	Chattanooga (SL)	AA	.256	130	492	70	126	39	1	11	61	39	95	4	3	.311	.407
2010	Chattanooga (SL)	AA	.271	47	181	26	49	11	2	4	25	15	39	1	1	.325	.420
	Altoona (EL)	AA	.275	26	91	12	25	1	0	2	10	9	30	0	0	.353	.352
Minor League Totals			.284	388	1453	211	412	101	7	40	219	135	317	11	8	.346	.445

12 DIEGO MORENO, RHP

Born: July 21, 1986. **B-T:** R-R. **Ht.:** 6-0. **Wt.:** 216. **Signed:** Venezuela, 2006. **Signed by:** Rene Gayo/ Rodolfo Petit.

Moreno missed a month of games with a strained right rotator cuff, beginning in late May, and then on July 18 the Pirates suspended him for unprofessional conduct after an incident during a game in Altoona. Team officials never offered specifics, but all concerned were adamant that it was not a reflection on Moreno's general character. Moreno was the hardest thrower of anyone who played in the system in 2010, averaging 95 mph on the fastball and peaking at 98. The heater is mostly true but comes with a little natural sink. He uses a wipeout slider at 87-88 mph to keep hitters from sitting on the fastball. He also has a changeup used solely for balance. Command always has come easily, but the delivery is maximum-effort. Despite a stocky build, he shows good athleticism. His most striking physical trait is the exceptional length of his arms. Moreno dominated hitters in high Class A, but Double-A opponents took advantage of inconsistent velocity and fastballs left up in the zone. Scouts see him as a back-end bullpen type in the majors, though not a shutdown closer because he lacks a dominant second pitch.

Year	Club (League)	Class	W	L	ERA	G	GS	CG	SV	IP	H	HR	BB	SO	G/A	WHIP	AVG
2007	Pirates (VSL)	R	1	0	2.42	13	0	0	2	22	17	1	5	16	—	0.99	.213
2008	Pirates (VSL)	R	3	1	0.87	7	6	0	0	31	21	0	4	21	—	0.81	.186
2009	State College (NYP)	SS	0	0	1.80	2	0	0	0	5	4	1	1	4	4.00	1.00	.222
	West Virginia (SAL)	LoA	1	3	2.60	18	0	0	5	45	29	3	14	57	0.88	0.96	.182
2010	Bradenton (FSL)	HiA	4	1	1.17	28	0	0	1	38	14	3	5	57	1.00	0.50	.105
	Altoona (EL)	AA	0	0	7.04	7	0	0	2	8	10	1	3	12	0.67	1.70	.313
Minor League Totals			9	5	2.05	75	6	0	10	149	95	9	32	167	0.99	0.85	.178

13 COLTON CAIN, LHP

Born: Feb. 5, 1991. **B-T:** L-L. **Ht.:** 6-3. **Wt.:** 237. **Drafted:** HS—Waxahachie, Texas, 2009 (8th round). **Signed by:** Mike Leuzinger.

Signed to an eighth-round record $1.15 million bonus in 2009, Cain had back surgery last winter and spent much of 2010 rehabilitating what the Pirates called a minor issue. He did get back on the field by the end of June, and management was impressed with his intense work ethic and delighted that his stuff bounced back to near-peak form. His ERA is deceiving because he limited opponents to a .197 average, including .163 against lefthanded hitters. Cain's fastball tops out at 93 mph, with expected room for improvement there, and sits at 88-91. It plays up thanks to deception in his delivery and his ability to command it down in the zone. Hitters seldom had clean swings on it. The secondary pitches are a work in progress but show enough that they could be legitimate weapons. The first is a slurvy 2-to-8 breaking ball, and the other a fringy changeup. His command of the fastball is good, but he'll clearly need to improve the secondary pitches. Cain makes the most of a workhorse frame, but scouts see him as too upright in his delivery. He needs to get more comfortable with his mechanics and polish his repertoire in order to remain a starter. He should start 2011 in West Virginia's rotation.

Year	Club (League)	Class	W	L	ERA	G	GS	CG	SV	IP	H	HR	BB	SO	G/A	WHIP	AVG
2010	Pirates (GCL)	R	0	1	3.77	4	4	0	0	14	12	1	5	15	0.42	1.19	.214
	State College (NYP)	SS	1	1	5.03	11	9	0	0	34	23	2	14	32	0.62	1.09	.189
Minor League Totals			1	2	4.66	15	13	0	0	48	35	3	19	47	0.56	1.12	.197

14 GORKYS HERNANDEZ, OF

Born: Sept. 7, 1987. **B-T:** R-R. **Ht.:** 6-0. **Wt.:** 180. **Signed:** Venezuela, 2005. **Signed by:** Ramon Pena (Tigers).

Hernandez ranked as one of the top prospects in the Tigers organization when he went to the Braves in a trade for Edgar Renteria in October 2007, and he moved again when Pittsburgh traded Nate McLouth to Atlanta in June 2009. He has not shown the form with the Pirates that helped him capture a Gulf Coast League batting title in his first season and a low Class A Midwest League MVP title in his next. His best attributes are his speed and defense, and even scouts who have soured on Hernandez concede that he has few flaws in center field. He covers enough ground to play shallow, makes catches over his head look easy, glides from gap to gap and has a strong, accurate arm. He has plus speed and stole 17 bases in 20 attempts last year. A modest surge at the plate—.291 in June, .325 in July—raised hopes, but only 12 of those 57 hits were for extra bases. He broke his right ring finger in a bunt attempt on July 25, ending his season. Although he added about 10 pounds to his frame, Hernandez still lacks strength at the plate and often is late to the ball. He often looks hesitant to swing. Many of his hits never left the infield, and he offers little power. Scouts see him as young enough to improve, but he needs to get going. Depending on his spring, he could return for a third tour in Double-A.

Year	Club (League)	Class	AVG	G	AB	R	H	2B	3B	HR	RBI	BB	SO	SB	CS	OBP	SLG
2005	Tigers (DSL)	R	.265	63	211	44	56	10	0	4	19	30	38	10	10	.377	.370
2006	Tigers (GCL)	R	.327	50	205	41	67	9	2	5	23	10	27	20	4	.356	.463
2007	West Michigan (MWL)	LoA	.293	124	481	84	141	25	5	4	50	36	69	54	11	.344	.391

Year	Club (League)	Class	AVG	G	AB	R	H	2B	3B	HR	RBI	BB	SO	SB	CS	OBP	SLG
2008	Myrtle Beach (CAR)	HiA	.264	100	406	75	107	23	6	5	42	48	79	20	4	.348	.387
2009	Mississippi (SL)	AA	.316	52	212	33	67	11	2	0	19	15	54	10	8	.361	.387
	Altoona (EL)	AA	.262	86	344	45	90	14	2	3	31	24	76	9	8	.312	.340
2010	Altoona (EL)	AA	.266	92	368	45	98	11	4	2	26	33	95	17	3	.333	.334
Minor League Totals			.281	567	2227	367	626	103	21	23	210	196	438	140	48	.344	.377

15 JUSTIN WILSON, LHP

Born: Aug. 18, 1987. **B-T:** L-L. **Ht.:** 6-2. **Wt.:** 219. **Drafted:** Fresno State, 2008 (5th round). **Signed by:** Sean Campbell.

Wilson was drafted with the reputation as a big-game pitcher, having won the decisive game of the 2008 College World Series for Fresno State. He added to that in 2010 by being named MVP of the Eastern League playoffs as Altoona won the title. He went 2-0, 0.00 in starting Game Three in each of the Curve's series victories and threw a total of 13 shutout innings. Wilson's fastball peaks at 95 mph and fluctuates from 87-93, and it comes with a sneakiness that brings swings and misses. He has a long way to go to improve fastball command, and needs to work on the consistency of his velocity. His delivery is a little rough, with a slight hook in the back, and he has a tendency to shift on the rubber depending whether the batter is lefthanded or righthanded. He has a big-breaking curve and a changeup that comes with some life and promise. Although Wilson's strikeout total and opponent average ranked second in the EL last season, the Pirates might send him back to Altoona to work on his command, rather than have him get beat up by Triple-A hitters.

Year	Club (League)	Class	W	L	ERA	G	GS	CG	SV	IP	H	HR	BB	SO	G/A	WHIP	AVG
2009	Lynchburg (CAR)	HiA	6	8	4.50	26	26	0	0	116	118	14	55	94	1.37	1.49	.262
2010	Altoona (EL)	AA	11	8	3.09	27	26	0	0	143	109	4	71	134	1.83	1.26	.215
Minor League Totals			17	16	3.72	53	52	0	0	259	227	18	126	228	1.59	1.36	.237

16 VICTOR BLACK, RHP

Born: May 23, 1988. **B-T:** R-R. **Ht.:** 6-4. **Wt.:** 200. **Drafted:** Dallas Baptist, 2009 (first round supplemental). **Signed by:** Mike Leuzinger.

When the Pirates paid Black $717,000 as a supplemental pick in 2009, the view was that his hard stuff might translate best to late-inning relief. Organization officials feel even more strongly about it after he was set back significantly by missing almost all of 2010 due to various issues with his right shoulder and biceps, and he is expected to move from starting to relief in 2011. His big frame and big arm could allow him to move quickly through the system out of the bullpen. When healthy, Black's fastball tops out at 96 mph and sits at 92-94. It comes from his big, powerful frame and is delivered from a high three-quarters slot, keeping it somewhat straight. His only other fully developed pitch is a dynamic slider, one with good tilt. He abandoned his curveball in 2008, and his changeup will require more work, which will require more innings. Black did not pitch competitively after May 22, but he was healthy for instructional league activity in October, so the Pirates expect him to handle a full workload this season. Keeping him in the bullpen will also allow them to more tightly control his workload, and he'll probably go to high Class A Bradenton to begin working in his new role.

Year	Club (League)	Class	W	L	ERA	G	GS	CG	SV	IP	H	HR	BB	SO	G/A	WHIP	AVG
2009	State College (NYP)	SS	1	2	3.45	13	7	0	1	31	26	0	15	33	1.26	1.31	.213
2010	West Virginia (SAL)	LoA	0	0	9.64	2	2	0	0	5	3	1	5	8	0.50	1.71	.176
Minor League Totals			1	2	4.25	15	9	0	1	36	29	1	20	41	1.16	1.36	.209

17 NATE BAKER, LHP

Born: Dec. 27, 1987. **B-T:** L-L. **Ht.:** 6-3. **Wt.:** 207. **Drafted:** Mississippi, 2009 (5th round). **Signed by:** Darren Mazeroski.

Baker's father Tim was drafted by the Red Sox, and his grandfather, Chuck Daniel, played for the Tigers. He worked mostly in relief at Mississippi, and the knock against him was that the fastball was fine, but the secondary stuff lagged. He turned that around in his first full season, ramping up the fastball to 90-92 mph, as well as dramatically improving his slider and changeup. His overhand delivery gives him a downhill plane, and he gets some sink on the ball. His slider still projects as no better than an average pitch, and the changeup remains too firm, but both have come a long way in a short period, and that has Pirates officials encouraged. Baker has displayed good control, thanks in part to a tight delivery, and he goes right after hitters. He has not gotten many strikeouts or groundouts, and one of those two factors likely will need to improve for him to find his way through the higher levels. He began the year with West Virginia and held opponents to a .210 average, then fared well once promoted to high Class A, though his opponent average and walk rate both went up. He probably will start 2011 back in Bradenton.

Year	Club (League)	Class	W	L	ERA	G	GS	CG	SV	IP	H	HR	BB	SO	G/A	WHIP	AVG
2009	State College (NYP)	SS	0	0	1.69	6	1	0	0	16	11	0	2	9	0.58	0.81	.193
2010	West Virginia (SAL)	LoA	6	5	2.99	16	16	0	0	87	68	3	20	63	1.35	1.01	.210
	Bradenton (FSL)	HiA	2	3	3.02	9	9	0	0	45	42	6	17	31	1.14	1.32	.258
Minor League Totals			8	8	2.86	31	26	0	0	148	121	9	39	103	1.16	1.08	.222

18 ZACK DODSON, LHP

Born: July 23, 1990. **B-T:** L-L. **Ht.:** 6-2. **Wt.:** 192. **Drafted:** HS—Castroville, Texas, 2009 (4th round). **Signed by:** Trevor Haley.

Dodson was Baylor's top recruit in 2009, and many scouts expected him to get to school because of his reported seven-figure asking price. He likely would have been a two-way player in college and is a good athlete who swings a lefthanded bat, but the Pirates took him in the fourth round and were able to sign him for $600,000. Not much about his numbers jumped out in his first real action, particularly given the contact he gave up and occasional lack of control. But his stuff shows signs of being able to grow into much more. He throws a consistent 88-92 mph fastball, and it comes out of his hand easily enough that scouts think more is there. Hitters seldom squared up on his heat. His delivery, arm action and athleticism also contribute to his projection, through he does need some effort to generate velocity with his three-quarters delivery. The timing and compact nature of the delivery need occasional maintenance, but that is to be expected of someone so young. Dodson also shows a promising curveball with 12-to-6 movement, as well as a fringy changeup. He will remain in a starting role and will move into full-season ball at West Virginia.

Year	Club (League)	Class	W	L	ERA	G	GS	CG	SV	IP	H	HR	BB	SO	G/A	WHIP	AVG
2009	Pirates (GCL)	R	0	0	0.00	1	0	0	0	1	0	0	0	1	—	0.00	.000
2010	State College (NYP)	SS	2	6	4.84	15	13	0	0	58	57	2	27	41	0.87	1.46	.265
Minor League Totals			2	6	4.76	16	13	0	0	59	57	2	27	42	0.90	1.43	.261

19 RAMON AGUERO, RHP

Born: Dec. 21, 1984. **B-T:** R-R. **Ht.:** 6-4. **Wt.:** 195. **Signed:** Dominican Republic, 2005. **Signed by:** Rene Gayo/Josue Herrera.

When the Pirates signed Aguero, he was known as Samuel Vasquez and was 39 months younger. But when he came to the United States in 2008, officials discovered that he used a false birth certificate. He was on thin ice after a poor 2008 season, but he bounced back after moving into a full-time relief role. Aguero has the stuff, notably a fastball that peaks at 98 mph with some sink, to make a quick ascent to Pittsburgh. He raised significant questions about his health—and toughness—in 2010, when he was twice shut down with elbow ailments that proved to be false alarms and was limited to 25 appearances for the season. Doctors didn't find ligament damage in either case, including an arthrogram in early September. That is not the progress the Pirates hoped for when they added Aguero to the 40-man in the winter of 2009. The stuff is too good to ignore, though. His fastball sits consistently at 95-97 mph, but he has a hard time maintaining velocity. He has an average changeup to keep lefthanders honest, and his slider is still a work in progress but has potential. Aguero probably will have to prove himself anew in Altoona, and he'll be old for Double-A.

Year	Club (League)	Class	W	L	ERA	G	GS	CG	SV	IP	H	HR	BB	SO	G/A	WHIP	AVG
2006	Pirates (DSL)	R	1	1	3.41	8	4	0	0	29	28	1	9	19	—	1.28	.259
2007	Pirates (DSL)	R	5	2	2.26	16	13	1	0	76	64	5	22	81	—	1.14	.222
2008	State College (NYP)	SS	1	10	6.75	15	10	0	0	49	64	4	22	35	—	1.74	.308
2009	West Virginia (SAL)	LoA	1	2	4.71	20	3	0	0	50	58	5	16	40	1.44	1.49	.294
	Lynchburg (CAR)	HiA	1	0	2.49	11	0	0	0	22	20	1	9	22	1.41	1.34	.241
	Altoona (EL)	AA	0	2	2.84	8	0	0	4	13	8	0	6	13	0.71	1.11	.182
2010	Bradenton (FSL)	HiA	0	0	1.69	8	0	0	1	11	10	0	3	8	2.00	1.22	.256
	Altoona (EL)	AA	2	5	8.68	17	0	0	2	19	27	1	14	17	1.53	2.20	.333
Minor League Totals			11	22	4.14	103	30	1	7	267	279	16	101	235	1.39	1.42	.266

20 ALEX PRESLEY, OF

Born: July 25, 1985. **B-T:** L-L. **Ht.:** 5-10. **Wt.:** 185. **Drafted:** Mississippi, 2006 (8th round). **Signed by:** Darren Mazeroski.

Presley was no more than an organizational afterthought following a 2009 when he repeated high Class A and didn't show much improvement, but he astoundingly ended up the Pirates' minor league player of the year for 2010 and spent the final month of the season in Pittsburgh. He opened with Altoona and led the Eastern League with a .350 average before being promoted to Triple-A on June 25. His total of 166 hits between the two stops ranked 15th in the minors, and was the fifth-highest mark in the Pirates system since 1995. Presley showed occasional pop, but his sudden success came because he has made the transition to more of a little-man's game, going to a shorter swing and shooting the ball the other way. His fielding is a tick below-average, with a raw feel to his break on fly balls, and he has a below-average arm. He has plus speed, which brought many infield singles, and his baserunning is as raw as the defense, and not just in the area of stolen bases. The Pirates liked what they saw during his month in Pittsburgh, and one evaluator said he looked overmatched in only one of his 23 at-bats. Presley will come to spring training under consideration for reserve outfield duty in the big leagues.

Year	Club (League)	Class	AVG	G	AB	R	H	2B	3B	HR	RBI	BB	SO	SB	CS	OBP	SLG
2006	Williamsport (NYP)	SS	.260	61	223	26	58	7	8	3	23	17	55	3	3	.313	.404
2007	Hickory (SAL)	LoA	.293	121	495	79	145	22	8	11	63	45	108	18	10	.348	.436
2008	Lynchburg (CAR)	HiA	.258	82	287	39	74	15	1	6	35	29	50	13	6	.325	.380
2009	Lynchburg (CAR)	HiA	.257	115	417	51	107	17	11	4	37	30	87	9	5	.305	.379
2010	Altoona (EL)	AA	.350	67	246	42	86	13	7	6	47	19	33	5	1	.399	.533
	Indianapolis (IL)	AAA	.294	69	272	44	80	15	6	6	38	22	42	8	7	.349	.460
	Pittsburgh (NL)	MAJ	.261	19	23	2	6	1	0	0	0	1	8	1	1	.292	.304
Major League Totals			.261	19	23	2	6	1	0	0	0	1	8	1	1	.292	.304
Minor League Totals			.284	515	1940	281	550	89	41	36	243	162	375	56	32	.338	.427

21 QUINCY LATIMORE, OF

Born: Feb. 3, 1989. **B-T:** R-R. **Ht.:** 5-11. **Wt.:** 192. **Drafted:** HS—Apex, N.C., 2007 (4th round). **Signed by:** Greg Schilz.

Latimore has been a favorite of some in the Pirates front office since his draft year, partly because of a fiery competitiveness but mostly because of what they see as legitimate power. He lacks the size for huge home run numbers, but his quick wrists and aggressive swing—bordering on violent—on a Ron Gant frame could translate to 20 home runs a season, according to some scouts. But he'll need to get more consistent with the bat for that to count at higher levels. His walk total has remained consistently too low, and he often hacks at offspeed pitches well outside the zone. Instructors have urged him to slow the game down, as he did when posting a .942 OPS during a sizzling August. That prompted optimism because he more than held his own in high Class A at age 21. He loves to hit and covers the plate well, hitting to all fields, so if he gets more selective he should hit for a decent average. Latimore has average speed, though not enough to mature into a basestealing threat. His arm is slightly above-average, but his overall defense is suspect and will force him to remain in left field. He could move up to Double-A this season, but the Pirates might also prefer to see him work on patience by repeating high Class A.

Year	Club (League)	Class	AVG	G	AB	R	H	2B	3B	HR	RBI	BB	SO	SB	CS	OBP	SLG
2007	Pirates (GCL)	R	.257	45	171	29	44	9	2	3	17	16	25	13	4	.352	.386
2008	State College (NYP)	SS	.244	59	221	25	54	14	5	3	20	13	53	6	4	.285	.394
2009	West Virginia (SAL)	LoA	.251	118	479	63	120	24	10	11	70	23	116	3	3	.295	.411
2010	Bradenton (FSL)	HiA	.266	134	518	84	138	31	2	19	100	30	136	11	1	.323	.444
Minor League Totals			.256	356	1389	201	356	78	19	36	207	82	330	33	12	.312	.418

22 JORDY MERCER, INF

Born: Aug. 27, 1986. **B-T:** R-R. **Ht.:** 6-3. **Wt.:** 196. **Drafted:** Oklahoma State, 2008 (3rd round). **Signed by:** Matt Bimeal.

If not for Alex Presley, Mercer might have been the most pleasant surprise in the organizaiton in 2010, wrestling the starting shortstop job from more touted prospect Chase d'Arnaud at Altoona and later belting three playoff home runs—matching his regular season total—for the Eastern League champions. He was an all-Big 12 Conference player at three different positions during his college career: shortstop, utility and pitcher. So it's not surprising that he has played some third base and second base, as well as shortstop. He has performed better at short, in large part because of slow reaction time at other positions. He has a strong arm, smooth actions and catches what comes to him, making up for limited range. Offensively, Mercer has improved steadily but will never be a spectacular run producer. His pitch recognition has gotten better, and he can drive the ball gap to gap, but the better arms in the minors continue to eat him up inside. He has the ingredients to adjust but must find consistency. His speed is slightly above-average, as are his overall instincts for the game. Depending on how things shake out above him, Mercer could open the season back at Altoona, though he'll likely see Triple-A at some point.

Year	Club (League)	Class	AVG	G	AB	R	H	2B	3B	HR	RBI	BB	SO	SB	CS	OBP	SLG
2008	State College (NYP)	SS	.250	6	24	5	6	1	1	1	2	1	3	1	0	.280	.500
	Hickory (SAL)	LoA	.250	50	192	21	48	7	0	4	18	12	44	4	3	.300	.349
2009	Lynchburg (CAR)	HiA	.255	131	513	64	131	36	4	10	83	41	93	10	6	.314	.400
2010	Altoona (EL)	AA	.282	126	485	67	137	31	2	3	65	31	69	7	1	.329	.373
Minor League Totals			.265	313	1214	157	322	75	7	18	168	85	209	22	10	.317	.383

23 MEL ROJAS JR., OF

Born: May 24, 1990. **B-T:** B-R. **Ht.:** 6-3. **Wt.:** 200. **Drafted:** Wabash Valley (Ill.) CC, 2010 (3rd round). **Signed by:** Anthony Wycklendt.

Rojas was the only player the Pirates picked in the first 10 rounds of the 2010 draft who was not a right-handed pitcher, and he came not only with the potential to be an everyday center fielder but also with major league lineage. He is the son of the former reliever of the same name. He turned down offers to sign out of the Dominican Republic to attend Wabash Valley (Ill.) CC, redshirting his freshman year. After he led all national juco players with 61 steals in 64 attempts last spring, Pittsburgh drafted him in the third round and signed him for $423,900. Rojas has slightly above-average speed and good arm strength, and the Pirates are confident that he can stay in center. The bat is a much harder read. He has a fairly flat swing, which could help him keep the ball on the ground, though it does not bode well for power or even line-drive contact. He does not barrel balls consistently and often looks defensive at the plate, but a generally sound approach brought respectable strike-out/walk numbers. The swing will take work, but the Pirates appreciate the raw tools enough that the pieces could add up. Some see him as a five-tool potential, though with no true plus tool, but others see him as a tweener who won't be able to remain in center and may not hit enough for a corner. He should be able to open 2011 in the West Virginia outfield.

Year	Club (League)	Class	AVG	G	AB	R	H	2B	3B	HR	RBI	BB	SO	SB	CS	OBP	SLG
2010	State College (NYP)	SS	.207	43	164	19	34	7	0	0	14	21	42	7	3	.309	.250
Minor League Totals			.207	43	164	19	34	7	0	0	14	21	42	7	3	.309	.250

24 JOSH RODRIGUEZ, SS/2B

Born: Dec. 18, 1984. **B-T:** R-R. **Ht.:** 6-0. **Wt.:** 185. **Drafted:** Rice, 2006 (5th round). **Signed by:** Les Pajari (Indians).

The Indians made Rodriguez a fifth-round pick coming out of Rice in 2006, when current Pirates general manager Neal Huntington was still with Cleveland. Some scouts saw 2010 as his breakthrough year, as he maintained his Double-A production into Triple-A and helped Columbus win the International League title. He was old for starting the season in Double-A, but that came after missing half of 2009 with a strained right hamstring. When the Indians did not protect Rodriguez on their 40-man roster, the Pirates made him the first pick in the Rule 5 draft at the Winter Meetings. Rodriguez shows good patience at the plate, and he has a chance to be a solid bat for a middle infielder. He has a tendency to hit the ball in the air but offers little more than gap power, and good fastballs occasionally overmatch him. The Pirates will try him at shortstop, but his .947 career fielding percentage there should bring skepticism. His arm is slightly above-average, and his range and glove are adequate, but consistency is lacking and he gets inconsistent reads off the bat. In general, his upside appears to be as a utility player, and that's how the Pirates plan to use him on their major league roster, including possible outfield duty. If he doesn't stick in the big leagues, he'll have to pass through waivers and be offered back to Cleveland.

Year	Club (League)	Class	AVG	G	AB	R	H	2B	3B	HR	RBI	BB	SO	SB	CS	OBP	SLG
2006	Mahoning Valley (NYP)	SS	.268	45	157	26	42	11	4	4	24	14	33	2	0	.337	.465
2007	Kinston (CAR)	HiA	.262	133	493	84	129	20	9	20	82	68	95	21	8	.351	.460
2008	Akron (EL)	AA	.241	137	532	75	128	22	10	7	49	77	122	12	6	.335	.359
2009	Akron (EL)	AA	.295	33	105	18	31	4	0	0	12	23	30	2	3	.426	.333
2010	Akron (EL)	AA	.317	21	63	11	20	7	0	1	11	11	10	0	2	.405	.476
	Columbus (IL)	AAA	.293	86	317	49	93	23	1	12	46	40	75	6	2	.372	.486
Minor League Totals			.266	455	1667	263	443	87	24	44	224	233	365	43	21	.356	.426

25 ROBBIE GROSSMAN, OF

Born: Sept. 16, 1989. **B-T:** B-L. **Ht.:** 6-0. **Wt.:** 195. **Drafted:** HS—Cypress, Texas, 2008 (6th round). **Signed by:** Mike Leuzinger.

Was Grossman's second full season a disappointment or not? That's the question the Pirates were asking themselves, and there were no easy answers. On one hand, he survived what the team felt was an aggressive placement in high Class A at age 20, and he was a mainstay for a Bradenton team that made the playoffs despite a rash of injuries. On the other, he struck out too often, stole only 15 of 23 bases and showed little offensive versatility when other things failed, notably bunting for a hit. Pittsburgh signed Grossman away from a Texas scholarship in 2008, giving him a $1 million bonus and viewing him as a top-of-the-order threat. But he has not produced enough with the bat so far. He's a switch-hitter who makes better contact from the right side and swings and misses a lot from the left. He has raw power, including gap to gap, from both sides of the plate. But his selectivity needs to improve, as he often dug two-strike holes for himself. He has enough speed to play center field at least on occasion, but the Pirates have used him mostly in left, which is a better fit not only for his above-average speed (PNC Park's left field is huge) but also for a below-average arm. Some scouts think he should rework or scrap his lefthanded swing, and worry that he has no premium tool that can carry him to the big leagues. Grossman will probably repeat high Class A in an effort to get his bat going.

Year	Club (League)	Class	AVG	G	AB	R	H	2B	3B	HR	RBI	BB	SO	SB	CS	OBP	SLG
2008	Pirates (GCL)	R	.188	5	16	3	3	1	0	0	1	4	7	1	0	.381	.250
2009	West Virginia (SAL)	LoA	.266	116	451	83	120	21	2	5	42	75	164	35	12	.373	.355
2010	Bradenton (FSL)	HiA	.245	125	470	84	115	29	3	4	50	66	118	15	8	.344	.345
Minor League Totals			.254	246	937	170	238	51	5	9	93	145	289	51	20	.359	.348

26 DANIEL MOSKOS, LHP

Born: April 28, 1986. **B-T:** R-L. **Ht.:** 6-1. **Wt.:** 203. **Drafted:** Clemson, 2007 (1st round). **Signed by:** Greg Schilz.

Moskos likely never will live down the controversy that surrounded his selection as the fourth overall pick in 2007, just ahead of Matt Wieters going to Baltimore, or live up to his $2.475 million bonus. He appeared to be carving his own path in 2010 until hitting a wall with his midseason promotion to Triple-A. Moskos dominated Double-A batters, allowing a .179 opponent average, and nailed down 21 of 22 saves, plus a 5-for-5 showing in the playoffs for Eastern League champion Altoona. His June 25 promotion to Triple-A went poorly, though, with a 10.38 ERA and .351 opponent average. Some scouts thought he developed a case of the yips, and when he was sent back to Double-A in August he immediately found his footing again. Moskos has a 92-95 mph fastball and a plus slider that he can throw for strikes consistently, and a sinking splitter that he uses as a changeup. His delivery comes with excruciating effort, including an extra hip turn, and he is not a very flexible athlete. His command has improved and should be average. Added to the 40-man roster in November, Moskos' next step will be a second try in the Indianapolis bullpen.

Year	Club (League)	Class	W	L	ERA	G	GS	CG	SV	IP	H	HR	BB	SO	G/A	WHIP	AVG
2007	Pirates (GCL)	R	0	0	0.00	2	0	0	0	3	4	0	0	3	—	1.33	.333
	State College (NYP)	SS	0	0	4.26	11	0	0	1	13	19	1	6	13	—	1.97	.328
2008	Lynchburg (CAR)	HiA	7	7	5.95	29	20	0	0	110	124	8	43	78	—	1.51	.284
2009	Altoona (EL)	AA	11	10	3.74	27	25	1	0	149	159	11	58	77	2.10	1.46	.279
2010	Altoona (EL)	AA	3	1	1.52	37	0	0	21	41	26	0	16	43	2.00	1.02	.179
	Indianapolis (IL)	AAA	0	5	10.38	19	0	0	1	17	26	3	20	18	1.38	2.65	.351
Minor League Totals			21	23	4.53	125	45	1	23	334	358	23	143	232	2.02	1.50	.277

27 PEDRO CIRIACO, SS

Born: Sept. 27, 1985. **B-T:** R-R. **Ht.:** 6-0. **Wt.:** 165. **Signed:** Dominican Republic, 2003. **Signed by:** Junior Noboa (Diamondbacks).

Ciriaco was acquired in a trade with Arizona last July that also brought in Chris Snyder and $3 million for D.J. Carrasco, Ryan Church and Bobby Crosby. Ciriaco finally reached the majors in his eighth pro season when Pittsburgh made him a September callup. He showed enough in his brief time in the Pirates' hands to convince management that he could push everyday shortstop Ronny Cedeno at some point in 2011, after more time in Triple-A. Ciriaco long had tools ranked among the best in the Diamondbacks system, most notably his plus speed, smooth glove and strong arm. But just as with Arizona, he will need to prove himself with the bat in order to become a starter. He has shown poor pitch selection—two walks in 132 plate appearances after the trade—and his spindly frame offers little hope for power. There is occasional lively contact, and the Pirates were stressing for him to find a way to make that more consistent. The primary adjustments were creating a smooth, consistent load, and getting his head in position to see the ball better. Ciriaco has the defensive tools to contribute in the big leagues, and if he can hit he could find an everyday role. He'll open 2011 at Indianapolis and try to prove he's ready.

Year	Club (League)	Class	AVG	G	AB	R	H	2B	3B	HR	RBI	BB	SO	SB	CS	OBP	SLG
2003	Diamondbacks (DSL)	R	.231	57	221	40	51	10	2	0	16	16	34	14	8	.290	.294
2004	Diamondbacks (DSL)	R	.349	67	252	45	88	11	4	1	18	19	33	29	17	.401	.437
2005	Missoula (PIO)	R	.240	69	254	28	61	9	4	2	31	7	50	7	2	.264	.331
2006	South Bend (MWL)	LoA	.264	128	550	77	145	15	5	2	32	32	96	19	8	.308	.320
2007	Visalia (CAL)	HiA	.251	119	463	61	116	14	5	3	39	20	81	20	11	.286	.322
2008	Visalia (CAL)	HiA	.310	124	520	85	161	26	5	5	61	18	89	40	9	.333	.408
2009	Mobile (SL)	AA	.296	121	469	56	139	15	3	4	54	16	71	38	10	.319	.367
2010	Reno (PCL)	AAA	.259	87	355	44	92	15	7	6	51	10	53	14	3	.278	.392
	Indianapolis (IL)	AAA	.281	32	121	19	34	9	1	0	6	2	21	5	1	.288	.372
	Pittsburgh (NL)	MAJ	.500	8	6	3	3	1	1	0	1	0	3	0	0	.500	1.000
Major League Totals			.500	8	6	3	3	1	1	0	1	0	3	0	0	.500	1.000
Minor League Totals			.277	804	3205	455	887	124	36	23	308	140	528	186	69	.309	.359

28 AARON PRIBANIC, RHP

Born: Sept. 1, 1986. **B-T:** R-R. **Ht.:** 6-4. **Wt.:** 213. **Drafted:** Nebraska, 2008 (3rd round). **Signed by:** Phil Geisler (Mariners).

The Pirates got Pribanic as part of the five-player package they received in the 2009 trade-deadline deal that sent Jack Wilson and Ian Snell to the Mariners. The organization is generally reluctant to allow sinkerballers to lean on their best pitch at the lower levels, insisting that all prospects first demonstrate superior four-seam command. Pribanic's sinker was too good to stifle, though, and he was allowed to strut it. He has consistently maintained at least a two-to-one groundout-to-airout ratio in the minors. His pure stuff is fairly ordinary. His fastball sits at 87-92 mph, peaks at 94 and comes with solid command. His old-school sinker, as one scout described it, comes from a fluid delivery, and it arrives with a heavy sink. To continue advancing, however,

Pribanic will have to get his secondary pitches into better shape. He has used both a curveball and slider, and both are sloppy, and he has shown little feel for a changeup and struggles to throw it for strikes. His delivery also makes the ball easy for hitters to see. He pitched in relief in the Arizona League, but he will remain a starter for now, likely with Altoona in 2011.

Year	Club (League)	Class	W	L	ERA	G	GS	CG	SV	IP	H	HR	BB	SO	G/A	WHIP	AVG
2008	Mariners (AZL)	R	1	2	15.43	3	1	0	0	5	8	0	5	5	—	2.79	.364
2009	Clinton (MWL)	LoA	7	6	3.21	17	17	0	0	87	76	1	26	54	2.74	1.17	.231
	West Virginia (SAL)	LoA	4	2	2.15	7	6	0	0	38	32	5	5	18	2.60	0.98	.230
2010	Bradenton (FSL)	HiA	7	6	3.33	27	27	0	0	154	157	9	33	71	2.13	1.23	.263
Minor League Totals			19	16	3.34	54	51	0	0	283	273	15	69	148	2.36	1.21	.251

29 MATT HAGUE, 1B

Born: Aug. 20, 1985. **B-T:** R-R. **Ht.:** 6-3. **Wt.:** 225. **Drafted:** Oklahoma State, 2008 (9th round). **Signed by:** Matt Bimeal.

Hague, an inexpensive senior selection who signed for $25,000 in 2008, spent three seasons at Washington and was an 11th-round pick of the Indians in 2007. But he planned to transfer to Clemson before ending up at Oklahoma State in 2008. He was old for Double-A last season, but he showed enough genuine upside with the bat to retain prospect status. His strikeouts and walks nearly matched, and nine of his 15 home runs came in the final two months. The bat path is short, he stays inside the ball, and he's big and strong enough to produce consistent power. He is not a one-dimensional hitter, and he has the ability to go gap-to-gap and to find a way to make contact even when it appears he might be beaten. He struck out just once every 9.27, plate appearances, the fourth-best figure in the Eastern League. His other tools are unremarkable. He has decent hands at first base but below-average range, as well as a strong arm that mostly goes unnoticed at his position. His speed is below-average. Hague probably will open 2011 as the first baseman at Indianapolis, and he'll need to keep hitting, given his age.

Year	Club (League)	Class	AVG	G	AB	R	H	2B	3B	HR	RBI	BB	SO	SB	CS	OBP	SLG
2008	State College (NYP)	SS	.333	7	27	6	9	3	0	0	3	3	5	0	0	.400	.444
	Hickory (SAL)	LoA	.321	57	215	25	69	14	0	6	29	20	28	1	0	.384	.470
2009	Lynchburg (CAR)	HiA	.293	122	454	52	133	30	0	8	50	40	67	3	2	.356	.412
2010	Altoona (EL)	AA	.295	135	509	90	150	30	0	15	86	61	62	3	6	.375	.442
Minor League Totals			.300	321	1205	173	361	77	0	29	168	124	162	7	8	.370	.436

30 JOSH HARRISON, 3B/2B

Born: July 8, 1987. **B-T:** R-R. **Ht.:** 5-8. **Wt.:** 188. **Drafted:** Cincinnati, 2008 (6th round). **Signed by:** Lukas McKnight (Cubs).

It can be tempting for evaluators to write off Harrison, who is too small to hit for power, too slow to play a small man's game, too limited defensively to play shortstop, too impatient to draw walks. But all he does is hit, hit and hit. He batted .300 last year in Double-A, was the toughest player in the Eastern League to strike out (once per 11.3 plate appearances) and owns a career .306 average as a pro. During Altoona's run to the EL championship, he homered three times to nearly match his regular season total. Harrison has thickened his frame since the Pirates acquired him, Jose Ascanio and Kevin Hart from the Cubs as part of the disastrous Tom Gorzelanny/John Grabow trade in 2009. He has a balanced approach, fine control of the strike zone and makes good adjustments from at-bat to at-bat. The question with Harrison is what he can contribute beyond batting average and where he can play on the diamond. His defensive tools are fringy, leaving second base and the outfield corners as his best options. Scouts are mostly confounded by Harrison, seeing him as capable of hitting .270-.280 in the big leagues—no small feat—but limited in so many other areas. He continued to hit in the Arizona Fall League after the season, batting .330, and will try to prove himself at the Triple-A level in 2011.

Year	Club (League)	Class	AVG	G	AB	R	H	2B	3B	HR	RBI	BB	SO	SB	CS	OBP	SLG
2008	Boise (NWL)	SS	.351	33	114	27	40	11	2	1	25	23	12	12	6	.462	.509
	Peoria (MWL)	LoA	.262	31	122	15	32	4	1	1	4	3	11	6	2	.286	.336
2009	Peoria (MWL)	LoA	.337	79	303	51	102	17	7	4	33	16	25	16	9	.377	.479
	Daytona (FSL)	HiA	.286	18	70	10	20	3	1	1	9	6	7	10	1	.351	.400
	Lynchburg (CAR)	HiA	.270	34	141	15	38	8	1	1	13	1	19	4	1	.289	.362
2010	Altoona (EL)	AA	.300	135	520	74	156	33	3	4	75	32	52	19	7	.345	.398
Minor League Totals			.306	330	1270	192	388	76	15	12	159	81	126	67	26	.353	.417

St. Louis Cardinals

BY DERRICK GOOLD

Lefthander Jaime Garcia went 13-8, 2.70 with 132 strikeouts in 163 innings as a rookie

For a team that wants and needs to be more reliant on its farm system to produce talent, the Cardinals exited 2010 humbled and aware they had to make changes. They started near the top.

St. Louis contended for much of the season and sat in first place in August after a series sweep of the Reds. But the team's stars—sluggers Albert Pujols and Matt Holliday and righthanders Chris Carpenter and Adam Wainwright—didn't get enough help from complementary players and the team wilted down the stretch.

After the season, St. Louis reorganized the minor league side of its front office, promoting John Vuch  to farm director and reducing the responsibilities of vice president Jeff Luhnow, who had multitasked as director of both scouting and player development. The club positioned the move as a way to let Luhnow and others focus on specific responsibilities, and general manager John Mozeliak said it didn't represent a dramatic change in philosophy. But this was more than moving furniture in the executive offices.

Further shuffling reassigned two of Mozeliak's lieutenants, Gary LaRocque and Matt Slater, from the pro side to amateur and minor league overview positions. There was also an undercurrent to the moves that had its genesis in fissures between the major league and minor league staffs that dated back before GM Walt Jocketty's firing in 2007. The promotion of Vuch, a respected Cardinals lifer, and greater inclusion of pitching coach Dave Duncan in minor league decision-making are significant strides for internal unity.

Colby Rasmus, Jaime Garcia and Mitchell Boggs—all products of the 2005 draft—are significant parts of St. Louis' future. But after their graduations and recent trades to get players such as Holliday, the farm system is thin on talent. As the Cardinals learned at the 2010 trade deadline, when they had to use major league outfielder Ryan Ludwick to swing a deal, their system is viewed as a collection of contributors and role players but thin on high-end talent.

To turn that situation around, St. Louis added a standout college hitter (Zack Cox) and a high-ceiling high school arm (Tyrell Jenkins) in the 2010 draft. The team also added its first headline-grabbing international signing (Carlos Martinez) in recent years.

The charge now for Vuch and the restructured development staff is to mold the new talent into the next wave of prospects. The Cardinals plan a less aggressive approach to promotion and named Mark DeJohn as field coordinator after leaving the position vacant for

TOP 30 PROSPECTS

1. Shelby Miller, rhp
2. Zack Cox, 3b
3. Carlos Martinez, rhp
4. Tyrell Jenkins, rhp
5. Allen Craig, of/1b
6. Lance Lynn, rhp
7. Eduardo Sanchez, rhp
8. Seth Blair, rhp
9. Jordan Swagerty, rhp
10. Joe Kelly, rhp
11. Matt Carpenter, 3b
12. Daniel Descalso, 2b/3b
13. John Gast, lhp
14. Fernando Salas, rhp
15. Adam Reifer, rhp
16. Maikel Cleto, rhp
17. Adron Chambers, of
18. David Kopp, rhp
19. P.J. Walters, rhp
20. Francisco Samuel, rhp
21. Pete Kozma, ss
22. Blake King, rhp
23. Mark Hamilton, 1b
24. Oscar Taveras, of
25. Tony Cruz, c
26. Bryan Anderson, c
27. Adam Ottavino, rhp
28. Daryl Jones, of
29. Steven Hill, c
30. Ryan Jackson, ss

three seasons. They also hope to establish more standardized instruction from the top down, with members of the major league staff, such as Duncan, getting the influence they have sought.

Interestingly, all of the changes came in the wake of a successful season on the field for the organization's minor league affiliates, which finished 431-237, the best winning percentage in baseball (.569). Triple-A Memphis reached the Pacific Coast League finals a year after winning the league championship, and Rookie-level Johnson City won the Appalachian League title for the first time since 1976.

MORRIS FOSTOFF

General Manager: John Mozeliak. **Farm Director:** John Vuch. **Scouting Director:** Jeff Luhnow.

Class	Team	League	W	L	PCT	Finish*	Manager
Majors	St. Louis Cardinals	National	86	76	.531	6th (16)	Tony LaRussa
Triple-A	Memphis Redbirds	Pacific Coast	82	62	.569	t-1st (16)	Chris Maloney
Double-A	Springfield Cardinals	Texas	76	64	.543	2nd (8)	Ron Warner
High A	Palm Beach Cardinals	Florida State	75	65	.536	5th (12)	Luis Aguayo
Low A	Quad Cities River Bandits	Midwest	83	55	.601	2nd (16)	Johnny Rodriguez
Short-season	Batavia Muckdogs	New York-Penn	45	29	.608	2nd (14)	Dann Bilardello
Rookie	Johnson City Cardinals	Appalachian	42	24	.636	†1st (10)	Mike Shildt
Rookie	GCL Cardinals	Gulf Coast	28	28	.500	8th (15)	Steve Turco
Overall 2010 Minor League Record			431	327	.569	1st (30)	

*Finish in overall standings (No. of teams in league). †League champion.

LAST YEAR'S TOP 30

Player, Pos.		Status
1.	Shelby Miller, rhp	No. 1
2.	Jaime Garcia, lhp	Majors
3.	Lance Lynn, rhp	No. 6
4.	Daryl Jones, of	No. 28
5.	David Freese, 3b/1b	Majors
6.	Eduardo Sanchez, rhp	No. 7
7.	Allen Craig, of/1b/3b	No. 5
8.	Blake Hawksworth, rhp	(Dodgers)
9.	Daniel Descalso, 2b	No. 12
10.	Robert Stock, c	Dropped out
11.	Adam Ottavino, rhp	No. 27
12.	Francisco Samuel, rhp	No. 20
13.	Jon Jay, of	Majors
14.	Tyler Greene, ss/3b	Majors
15.	Pete Kozma, ss	No. 21
16.	Adam Reifer, rhp	No. 15
17.	Richard Castillo, rhp	Dropped out
18.	Tyler Henley, of	Dropped out
19.	Bryan Anderson, c	No. 26
20.	Sam Freeman, lhp	Dropped out
21.	Joe Kelly, rhp	No. 10
22.	Scott Bittle, rhp	Dropped out
23.	P.J. Walters, rhp	No. 19
24.	Steven Hill, c/of/1b	No. 29
25.	Ryan Jackson, ss	No. 30
26.	Mark Hamilton, 1b	No. 23
27.	Yunier Castillo, ss	Dropped out
28.	Ben Jukich, lhp	(Free agent)
29.	Trey Hearne, rhp	(Released)
30.	Cesar Valera, ss	Dropped out

BEST TOOLS

Best Hitter for Average	Zack Cox
Best Power Hitter	Allen Craig
Best Strike-Zone Discipline	Daniel Descalso
Fastest Baserunner	Reggie Williams Jr.
Best Athlete	Tyrell Jenkins
Best Fastball	Shelby Miller
Best Curveball	Jordan Swagerty
Best Slider	Blake King
Best Changeup	P.J. Walters
Best Control	Scott McGregor
Best Defensive Catcher	Tony Cruz
Best Defensive Infielder	Ryan Jackson
Best Infield Arm	Pete Kozma
Best Defensive Outfielder	Shane Robinson
Best Outfield Arm	Tommy Pham

PROJECTED 2014 LINEUP

Catcher	Yadier Molina
First Base	Albert Pujols
Second Base	Skip Schumaker
Third Base	Zack Cox
Shortstop	Pete Kozma
Left Field	Matt Holliday
Center Field	Colby Rasmus
Right Field	Allen Craig
No. 1 Starter	Adam Wainwright
No. 2 Starter	Shelby Miller
No. 3 Starter	Jaime Garcia
No. 4 Starter	Carlos Martinez
No. 5 Starter	Tyrell Jenkins
Closer	Mitchell Boggs

TOP PROSPECTS OF THE DECADE

Year	Player, Pos.	2010 Org.
2001	Bud Smith, lhp	Out of baseball
2002	Jimmy Journell, rhp	Out of baseball
2003	Dan Haren, rhp	Angels
2004	Blake Hawksworth, rhp	Cardinals
2005	Anthony Reyes, rhp	Indians
2006	Anthony Reyes, rhp	Indians
2007	Colby Rasmus, of	Cardinals
2008	Colby Rasmus, of	Cardinals
2009	Colby Rasmus, of	Cardinals
2010	Shelby Miller, rhp	Cardinals

TOP DRAFT PICKS OF THE DECADE

Year	Player, Pos.	2010 Org.
2001	Justin Pope, rhp	Out of baseball
2002	Calvin Hayes, ss (3rd round)	Out of baseball
2003	Daric Barton, 1b	Athletics
2004	Chris Lambert, rhp	Out of baseball
2005	Colby Rasmus, of	Cardinals
2006	Adam Ottavino, rhp	Cardinals
2007	Pete Kozma, ss	Cardinals
2008	Brett Wallace, 1b	Astros
2009	Shelby Miller, rhp	Cardinals
2010	Zack Cox, 3b	Cardinals

LARGEST BONUSES IN CLUB HISTORY

J.D. Drew, 1998	$3,000,000
Shelby Miller, 2009	$2,875,000
Rick Ankiel, 1997	$2,500,000
Chad Hutchinson, 1998	$2,300,000
Zack Cox, 2010	$2,000,000

ST. LOUIS CARDINALS

TOP 2011 ROOKIE: Allen Craig, of. When given the chance to play, he always has produced for power.

BREAKOUT PROSPECT: John Gast, lhp. If the improved command he showed in his pro debut is for real, he'll move quickly at a position of need for the Cardinals.

SLEEPER: Kevin Thomas, rhp. He posted a 2.27 ERA in high Class A last year, thanks to his low-90s sinker.

SOURCE OF TOP 30 TALENT

Homegrown	29	Acquired	1
College	16	Trades	1
Junior college	2	Rule 5 draft	0
High school	5	Independent leagues	0
Draft-and-follow	1	Free agents/waivers	0
Nondrafted free agents	0		
International	5		

LF
Daryl Jones (28)
Amaury Cazana
D'Marcus Ingram
Virgil Hill
Aaron Luna
Corderious Dodd

CF
Adron Chambers (17)
Oscar Taveras (24)
Tommy Pham
Nick Longmire
Shane Robinson
Reggie Williams Jr.

RF
Allen Craig (5)
Tyler Henley
Michael Swinson
Ryde Rodriguez
Alex Castellanos

3B
Zack Cox (2)
Matt Carpenter (11)
Robert de la Cruz
Niko Vasquez
Jonathan Rodriguez

SS
Pete Kozma (21)
Ryan Jackson (30)
Yunier Castillo
Cesar Valera
Sam Tuivailala

2B
Daniel Descalso (12)
Jason Stidham
Starlin Rodriguez
Jermaine Curtis

1B
Mark Hamilton (23)
Matt Adams
Xavier Scruggs
Curt Smith

C
Tony Cruz (25)
Bryan Anderson (26)
Steven Hill (29)
Robert Stock
Cody Stanley

RHP

RHSP	RHRP
Shelby Miller (1)	Eduardo Sanchez (7)
Carlos Martinez (3)	Jordan Swagerty (9)
Tyrell Jenkins (4)	Fernando Salas (14)
Lance Lynn (6)	Adam Reifer (15)
Seth Blair (8)	Maikel Cleto (16)
Joe Kelly (10)	Francisco Samuel (20)
David Kopp (18)	Blake King (22)
P.J. Walters (19)	Pete Parise
Adam Ottavino (27)	Scott Bittle
Kevin Thomas	Chuck Fick
Scott McGregor	Boone Whiting
Trevor Rosenthal	Chase Reid
Scott Gorgen	
Bryan Augenstein	
Scott Schneider	
Josh Lucas	

LHP

LHSP	LHRP
John Gast (13)	Sam Freeman
Daniel Bibona	Tyler Norrick
Tyler Lyons	Nick Greenwood
Nick Additon	Manuel de la Cruz
Ryan Copeland	Ryan Kulik
Ben Freeman	
Hector Hernandez	
Anthony Ferrara	

2010   BONUSES: $6.7 MILLION

BEST PURE HITTER: 3B Zack Cox (1) went 25th overall because of his hitting ability. He led the Southeastern Conference and set an Arkansas record with a .429 batting average last spring.

BEST POWER HITTER: The Cardinals believe Cox will develop at least average major league power. Prep OFs Anthony Bryant (16) and Corderious Dodd (17) were drafted for their plus raw power. 1B Phil Cerreto (40) surprised St. Louis with his pop, slugging seven homers while hitting .425/.460/.758 for Rookie-level Appalachian League champion Johnson City.

FASTEST RUNNER: OF Reggie Williams Jr. (10) remains raw in some phases but has plus-plus speed.

BEST DEFENSIVE PLAYER: 2B/SS Greg Garcia (7) has the soft hands, lateral quickness and infield actions to stay in the middle infield, and his arm is playable at shortstop. OF Steven Ramos (22) was a workout find who could become an above-average defender in center field.

BEST FASTBALL: RHPs Seth Blair (1s) and Jordan Swagerty (2), former Arizona State teammates, both sit at 92-94 mph and reach 96. Swagerty has more life on his fastball, while Blair maintains his velocity as a starter. RHP Tyrell Jenkins' (1s) fastball is a tick behind those two right now, but his athleticism and project-ability make it likely he'll surpass them in time.

BEST SECONDARY PITCH: The Cardinals considered Swagerty's curveball the best in the draft, for its shape and break and for his feel for it. He and RHP Chase Reid (41) have the two best curves in the system.

BEST PRO DEBUT: LHP John Gast (6) went 6-0, 1.54 with 36 strikeouts in 35 innings at short-season Batavia, where Reid led New York-Penn League relievers with a .151 opponent average. Also at Batavia, OF Nick Longmire (5) batted .287/.372/.483 with seven triples and nine homers. Cerreto and C Cody Stanley (4) helped pace Johnson City's offense, with Stanley hitting .321/.380/.498.

BEST ATHLETE: Jenkins was a Baylor quarterback recruit. The Cardinals saw him hit 94 mph after running at a track meet before the game.

MOST INTRIGUING BACKGROUND: RHP Drew Benes (35) is the son of 1988 No. 1 overall pick and former Cardinals starter Andy Benes. He posted a 1.52 ERA at Johnson City. Williams' father Reggie spent parts of four seasons in the majors, and his brother J.D. signed as the Twins' 10th-round pick this season.

CLOSEST TO THE MAJORS: Cox got a major league contract and an Arizona Fall League assignment. Swagerty, who also went to the AFL, should beat him to the big leagues if he remains a reliever.

BEST LATE-ROUND PICK: Reid reminds St. Louis of former farmhand Luke Gregorsen, whom they traded to the Padres. Ramos is also intriguing.

THE ONE WHO GOT AWAY: The Cardinals put a full-court press on OF Austin Wilson (12), one of the best athletes in the draft, but still weren't able to sway him from a Stanford commitment.

ASSESSMENT: Cox and Swagerty give this class two solid big league bets. Jenkins' athleticism makes him an excellent gamble, and Blair and Gast could make this group exceptional if they pan out.

2009   BONUSES: $5.4 MILLION

RHP Shelby Miller (1) made exciting progress in his first full pro season and looks like a future ace. RHP Joe Kelly (3) can reach 100 mph with his fastball, and 3B Matt Carpenter (13) hit .316/.412/.487 in Double-A last year.

GRADE: B+

2008   BONUSES: $5.5 MILLION

St. Louis traded 1B Brett Wallace (1) and OF Shane Peterson (2) to get Matt Holliday from the Athletics. Three trades later, Wallace is starting for the Astros. RHP Lance Lynn (1s) should crack the big league rotation at some point in 2011.

GRADE: C+

2007   BONUSES: $4.6 MILLION

SS Pete Kozma (1) hasn't lit up minor league pitching so far. The Cardinals did sign four major leaguers, though RHPs Clayton Mortensen (1s) and Jess Todd (2), 2B/3B Daniel Descalso and C Steven Hill (13) haven't made much of an impact. Mortensen and Todd were used in deals for Holliday and Mark DeRosa.

GRADE: C

2006   BONUSES: $5.3 MILLION

St. Louis deal its two best choices, RHPs Chris Perez (1s) and Luke Gregerson (28), to get DeRosa and Khalil Greene. Perez is now the Indians' closer, while Gregerson set a big league record with 40 holds for the Padres in 2010. OF/1B Allen Craig (8) could work his way into the Cardinals' lineup this year. RHPs Adam Ottavino (1) and P.J. Walters (11), OFs Jon Jay (2) and Shane Robinson (5) and 1B Mark Hamilton (2s) all have seen time in the majors.

GRADE: C+

Draft analysis by John Manuel (2010) and Jim Callis (2006-09). Numbers in parentheses indicate draft rounds.

SHELBY
MILLER, RHP

Born: Oct.10, 1990. **Bats:** R. **Throws:** R.
Height: 6-3. **Weight:** 195. **Drafted:** HS—
Brownwood, Texas, 2009 (1st round). **Signed
by:** Ralph Garr Jr.

One of the Cardinals' representatives in the 2010 Futures Game, Miller validated his place in the organization not only with the sum of his season, but with his lone playoff start. Age 19 at the time, he promised a shutout before taking the mound—and delivered. Miller struck out five of the first six batters he faced, finished with a career-high 13 whiffs, hit 95 mph in his final inning and pitched seven scoreless innings to get low Class A Quad Cities a victory. "We saw him rise to the challenge," pitching coordinator Dyar Miller said, "in a way you can't predict." St. Louis broke from tradition to draft Miller in 2009. The 19th overall pick, he was the first prep pitcher taken in the top five rounds by the Cardinals since 2005, and the first selected in the first round by them since 1991. They did so knowing that he would command an above-slot bonus, eventually signing him for $2.875 million. St. Louis projected him as a potential No. 1 starter and thought he was mature beyond his years. As his pre-playoff pronouncement indicated, Miller embraces the lofty expectations. He turned down a Texas A&M scholarship to pursue pro ball, and he quickly made an impression on the major league staff. Though Miller had pitched just three innings in his 2009 pro debut, pitching coach Dave Duncan kept him in big league camp in March, actively seeking Grapefruit League innings for the unflappable teen to see what he could do against major leaguers. (He froze Duncan's son Chris with a changeup in one opportunity.) By the time Miller started the season, he already was considered the most talented young gun the Cardinals have had since Rick Ankiel.

Miller earned his spurs as a true Texas gunslinger—a legacy he not only relishes, but invokes—by overpowering the Midwest League with his fastball. Quad Cities coaches claim he went at least his first five starts without giving up a hit on his explosive fastball, which sits at 94 mph and can regularly touch 98 mph. Some scouts see his heater as major league-ready right now. His brawny frame and simple delivery hint at sustained and perhaps improved velocity in the future. For most of June, the Cardinals pulled Miller out of the rotation and had him throw a series of bullpens designed to manage his workload and give him a laboratory to improve his secondary pitches. He emerged from that hiatus with more faith in a tighter 12-to-6 curveball and more command of what could become a plus changeup with deception and sink. Miller's fastball hops partially because of the ease of his delivery, and he needs only to refine the consistency of his mechanics to improve his command of his pitches. He combines an aggressive disposition with a cucumber-cool poise.

Further improvement of his secondary pitches will speed Miller's ascent. He'll get another nonroster invitation to big league spring training, where his performance will determine his next stop. The Cardinals are open to Miller reaching Double-A Springfield's rotation in 2011, possibly starting the season there. He could reach St. Louis by the end of 2012.

SCOUTING GRADES

Fastball: 70. **Command/**
Curveball: 60. **Control:** 60.
Changeup: 60. **Delivery:** 65.

*Based on 20-80 scouting scale, where
50 represents major league average, and
future projection rather than present tools.*

Year	Club (League)	Class	W	L	ERA	G	GS	CG	SV	IP	H	HR	BB	SO	G/A	WHIP	AVG
2009	Quad Cities (MWL)	LoA	0	0	6.00	2	2	0	0	3	5	0	2	2	2.50	2.33	.357
2010	Quad Cities (MWL)	LoA	7	5	3.62	24	24	0	0	104	97	7	33	140	1.00	1.25	.243
Minor League Totals			7	5	3.69	26	26	0	0	107	102	7	35	142	1.00	1.28	.247

2 ZACK COX, 3B

Born: May 9, 1989. **B-T:** L-R. **Ht.:** 6-0. **Wt.:** 215. **Drafted:** Arkansas, 2010 (1st round). **Signed by:** Jay Catalano.

Cox was the best pure hitter in the 2010 draft, but his $6 million asking price and extra leverage as a draft-eligible sophomore allowed him to slip to the Cardinals at No. 25 overall. He signed a $3.2 million major league contract at the Aug. 16 deadline. St. Louis threw him into the Arizona Fall League after only four pro games, and he batted a respectable .262/.333/.446. Cox's balanced and refined swing enabled him to set an Arkansas record with a .429 average last spring. He modified his approach after being too home run-conscious as a freshman, flattening and shortening his stroke and using the opposite field more. Some scouts question how much pop he'll have, but he's a gifted hitter with strength and strike-zone awareness, so he should have at least average power. Cox has the arm strength and instincts for third base, though some evaluators think his actions are better suited for second base. He has fringy speed and quickness, but he has the work ethic to improve his defense. The Cardinals will keep Cox at third base until he shows he needs to move. He may begin 2011 in low Class A, but he should get to St. Louis well before his contract forces the issue.

Year	Club (League)	Class	AVG	G	AB	R	H	2B	3B	HR	RBI	BB	SO	SB	CS	OBP	SLG
2010	Cardinals (GCL)	R	.400	4	15	0	6	1	0	0	1	1	3	0	0	.471	.467
Minor League Totals			.400	4	15	0	6	1	0	0	1	1	3	0	0	.471	.467

3 CARLOS MARTINEZ, RHP

Born: Sept. 21, 1991. **B-T:** R-R. **Ht.:** 6-0. **Wt.:** 165. **Signed:** Dominican Republic, 2010. **Signed by:** Juan Mercado.

Then known as Carlos Matias, Martinez agreed to a $160,000 bonus with the Red Sox in 2009 but failed to pass a MLB investigation and was suspended for a year. His velocity soared while he was off limits, and the Cardinals offered him $1.5 million last June. While he went through another investigation, he was able to pitch for St. Louis' Rookie-level Dominican Summer League affiliate. After confirming his true identity, MLB signed off on the deal in October. With an athletic frame and a whippy arm, Martinez consistently unleashes 96-99 mph fastballs in short stints. His fastball has a hard, natural cutting action that has some calling it an 80 pitch on the 20-80 scouting scale. He complements the pitch with a sinking 86-87 mph changeup and a sharp curveball. He has a sinker that sits at 92-93, but his command of the pitch is spotty. Martinez will come to the Cardinals' campus in Jupiter, Fla., early this spring so some coaches and officials can see him first hand for the first time. He'll be assigned to a U.S. affiliate, possibly a full-season club if his performance merits it. His rise could mirror Shelby Miller's, and St. Louis is eager to see if he can surpass Miller's debut.

Year	Club (League)	Class	W	L	ERA	G	GS	CG	SV	IP	H	HR	BB	SO	G/A	WHIP	AVG
2010	DSL Cardinals	R	3	2	0.76	12	12	1	0	59	28	1	14	78	1.20	0.71	.144
Minor League Totals			3	2	0.76	12	12	1	0	59	28	1	14	78	1.20	0.71	.144

4 TYRELL JENKINS, RHP

Born: July 20, 1992. **B-T:** R-R. **Ht.:** 6-4. **Wt.:** 180. **Drafted:** HS—Henderson, Texas, 2010 (1st round supplemental). **Signed by:** Ralph Garr Jr.

Billed as the most athletic pitcher available in the 2010 draft, Jenkins turned down a football scholarship to play quarterback at Baylor to sign with St. Louis for $1.3 million, almost twice the recommended bonus for the No. 50 overall slot. He also lettered in basketball and ran a 49-second quarter-mile in a relay race—sans training. The Cardinals saw Jenkins run a sprint in a track meet, then race to the diamond and throw low-90s fastballs. In his first pro inning, he retired the side on six pitches, inducing a strikeout and two weak groundouts. Jenkins has a loose, quick delivery that fires fastballs consistently at 92-93 mph and as hard as 95. His athleticism allows him to repeat his smooth mechanics, maintain his velocity deep into games and throw strikes. As he adds strength to his frame, his velocity could climb. He has a curveball with a tight spin and projectability and he's comfortable with a slider and changeup. However, he's relatively inexperienced on the mound and will need time to develop. Jenkins' aptitude as a starting pitcher should rise as he gains experience. The Cardinals may start him in extended spring training to soak up instruction before moving him into the rotation at short-season Batavia or Quad Cities.

Year	Club (League)	Class	W	L	ERA	G	GS	CG	SV	IP	H	HR	BB	SO	G/A	WHIP	AVG
2010	Johnson City (APP)	R	0	0	0.00	2	2	0	0	3	2	0	2	2	1.33	1.33	.200
Minor League Totals			0	0	0.00	2	2	0	0	3	2	0	2	2	1.33	1.33	.200

5 ALLEN CRAIG, OF/1B

Born: July 18, 1984. **B-T:** R-R. **Ht.:** 6-2. **Wt.:** 210. **Drafted:** California, 2006 (8th round). **Signed by:** Dane Walker.

Craig put himself in the Cardinals' plans with a breakout 2009 season in which he hit .322/.374/.547 at Triple-A Memphis. He made the Opening Day roster last April as a reserve, but he found it difficult to adjust to scattered playing time. Shipped back to Memphis after going 1-for-19, he found his swing and drove in 81 runs in 83 games before carrying that success to St. Louis at the end of the season. A seasoned hitter, Craig has improved his feel for the strike zone and his ability to turn on pitches. He has power to all fields and is learning the areas of the zone where he can drive pitches. When he gets regular playing time, he has shown a knack for making in-game adjustments. Craig continues to work out at third base, but he lacks range and arm strength, and the major league staff sees him as an outfielder. He has playable range on the corners and a decent arm for left field. He's a below-average runner. The Cardinals are on the lookout for a run-producing hitter like Craig. He may begin the 2011 season in a right-field platoon with Jon Jay.

Year	Club (League)	Class	AVG	G	AB	R	H	2B	3B	HR	RBI	BB	SO	SB	CS	OBP	SLG
2006	State College (NYP)	SS	.257	48	175	21	45	13	0	4	29	13	28	0	0	.325	.400
2007	Palm Beach (FSL)	HiA	.312	112	423	77	132	25	2	21	77	35	79	8	3	.370	.530
	Springfield (TL)	AA	.292	7	24	5	7	2	0	3	3	1	6	0	0	.320	.750
2008	Springfield (TL)	AA	.304	129	506	84	154	30	0	22	85	48	87	2	1	.373	.494
2009	Memphis (PCL)	AAA	.322	126	472	78	152	26	1	26	83	37	95	3	0	.374	.547
2010	Memphis (PCL)	AAA	.320	83	306	57	98	24	2	14	81	34	59	1	0	.389	.549
	St. Louis (NL)	MAJ	.246	44	114	12	28	7	0	4	18	9	26	0	1	.298	.412
Major League Totals			.246	44	114	12	28	7	0	4	18	9	26	0	1	.298	.412
Minor League Totals			.308	505	1906	322	588	120	5	90	358	168	354	14	4	.370	.518

6 LANCE LYNN, RHP

Born: May 12, 1987. **B-T:** R-R. **Ht.:** 6-2. **Wt.:** 250. **Drafted:** Mississippi, 2008 (1st round supplement). **Signed by:** Jay Catalano.

A sandwich pick in 2008 and St. Louis' minor league pitcher of the year in 2009, Lynn lacked his usual consistency last season. He punctuated his up-and-down year by striking out 16 batters in a Pacific Coast League playoff game, setting a Memphis franchise record for any contest. He got the 16 whiffs in a 20-batter stretch, overpowering most with a fastball that routinely hit 95 mph. Lynn remains the prototypical Cardinals draft pick—a durable and predictable college pitcher who can be relied on to gobble innings at the back of a big league rotation. His velocity markedly increased in 2010, as he went from using a 90-92 mph sinker to a mid-90s four-seamer. He took to working high in the strike zone, an approach that won't play well in the majors. To shift his crosshairs down, St. Louis is working with his mechanics so that he's throwing downhill more. His curveball also improved last year, though he continues to work on his changeup. Lynn did his best pitching at the end of 2010, setting the stage for him to compete for a big league job this spring. He has a ceiling of a No. 3 starter.

Year	Club (League)	Class	W	L	ERA	G	GS	CG	SV	IP	H	HR	BB	SO	G/A	WHIP	AVG
2008	Batavia (NYP)	SS	1	0	0.96	6	4	0	0	19	12	0	4	22	—	0.86	.179
	Quad Cities (MWL)	LoA	0	1	2.25	2	2	0	0	8	8	2	2	7	—	1.25	.258
2009	Palm Beach (FSL)	HiA	0	0	2.30	5	2	0	0	16	16	0	3	17	1.80	1.21	.276
	Springfield (TL)	AA	11	4	2.92	22	22	0	0	126	117	5	51	98	1.10	1.33	.251
	Memphis (PCL)	AAA	0	0	2.70	1	1	0	0	7	5	0	3	9	1.20	1.20	.200
2010	Memphis (PCL)	AAA	13	10	4.77	29	29	0	0	164	164	21	62	141	1.15	1.38	.259
Minor League Totals			25	15	3.66	65	60	0	0	339	322	28	125	294	1.15	1.32	.252

7 EDUARDO SANCHEZ, RHP

Born: Feb.16, 1989. **B-T:** R-R. **Ht.:** 5-11. **Wt.:** 155. **Signed:** Venezuela, 2005. **Signed by:** Enrique Brito.

With little fanfare, Sanchez breezed through his three batters in the 2010 Futures Game, getting three routine groundballs on a series of 96-97 mph fastballs. It was a familiar script. Unheralded when signed out of Venezuela, the slight reliever began a meteoric rise in 2009 and continued his ascension last year, succeeding as a closer in Double-A and a set-up man in Triple-A. The engine behind Sanchez's fastball, which sits at 95-97 mph and threatens to hit 100, is an agile and consistent delivery. He has enough command and movement with his fastball to keep it down in the zone, and he gets most of his outs on grounders and strikeouts. Sanchez's slider has good depth and terrorizes righthanders, who hit .157 against him in 2010. Control troubles surfaced at times in 2009, but he did a better job throwing strikes last year. Durability remains his biggest concern, as his small frame leaves some scouts wondering how his stuff will hold up at the major league level. Added to the 40-man roster in November, Sanchez will come to big league camp but probably open 2011 closing games at Memphis. He has a steady pulse in save situations, which will enhance his chances of sneaking into St. Louis' crowded righthanded relief picture.

Year	Club (League)	Class	W	L	ERA	G	GS	CG	SV	IP	H	HR	BB	SO	G/A	WHIP	AVG
2006	Cardinals (VSL)	R	1	2	8.71	19	2	0	0	31	47	3	24	38	—	2.29	.351
2007	Cardinals (GCL)	R	0	1	1.50	7	0	0	3	6	2	0	6	7	—	1.33	.100
	Johnson City (APP)	R	2	1	1.17	12	0	0	5	15	8	0	3	22	—	0.72	.154
2008	Quad Cities (MWL)	LoA	5	1	2.86	24	5	0	1	57	40	1	25	55	—	1.15	.209
2009	Palm Beach (FSL)	HiA	0	1	1.44	19	0	0	3	25	12	2	5	26	1.42	0.68	.146
	Springfield (TL)	AA	2	0	2.70	41	0	0	10	50	32	4	20	56	1.78	1.04	.187
2010	Springfield (TL)	AA	1	1	3.12	24	0	0	11	26	22	2	8	27	2.91	1.15	.232
	Memphis (PCL)	AAA	0	0	1.67	26	0	0	3	27	19	2	12	31	2.23	1.15	.200
Minor League Totals			11	7	3.19	172	7	0	36	237	182	14	103	262	2.23	1.93	.217

8 SETH BLAIR, RHP

Born: March 3, 1989. **B-T:** R-R. **Ht.:** 6-2. **Wt.:** 185. **Drafted:** Arizona State, 2010 (1st round supplemental). **Signed by:** Aaron Krawiec.

It's hard to imagine St. Louis going through a draft without taking a pitcher like Blair. He displayed start-to-start reliability in a top conference and Cape Cod League success, two traits the Cardinals value. After a 12-1, 3.64 All-America junior season at Arizona State, Blair went 46th overall in the 2010 draft and signed for $751,500. Blair flashes electric stuff. He touched 98 mph in his first start last spring, and his fastball usually operates at 92-94 and tops out at 96. His heater has good life and some sink. His curveball projects as a possible plus pitch, and he's working on both a changeup and cutter. He slashed his walk rate in 2010 but still floats too many pitches out of the strike zone. Cleaning up his mechanics would improve his control and make him more economical. After throwing 106 innings in the spring, Blair took a break and didn't sign until late July, so St. Louis elected not to push his arm back into game action. He spent time at Batavia, throwing on the side and getting acclimated to pro ball, and will make his debut this spring in Class A. The Cardinals will develop him as a starter, but if he can't refine a third pitch and his command, he could become a late-inning reliever.

Year	Club (League)	Class	W	L	ERA	G	GS	CG	SV	IP	H	HR	BB	SO	G/A	WHIP	AVG
2010	Did Not Play—Signed Late																

9 JORDAN SWAGERTY, RHP

Born: July 14, 1989. **B-T:** S-R. **Ht.:** 6-2. **Wt.:** 175. **Drafted:** Arizona State, 2010 (2nd round). **Signed by:** Aaron Krawiec.

Swagerty starred as both a pitcher and catcher in high school and saw action at both positions at Arizona State. Selected 29 picks after Sun Devils teammate Seth Blair last June, he used his leverage as a draft-eligible sophomore to get an above-slot $625,000 bonus in the second round. Swagerty signed too late to pitch in the minors, but did make four Arizona Fall League appearances. The Cardinals graded Swagerty's curveball as the best in the 2010 draft. He throws it in the mid-80s with both vertical and horizontal break, and it's becoming more of a hybrid pitch that he calls a slider. He relies heavily on his breaking ball, and also pounds the strike zone with a 92-94 mph fastball that peaks at 96. He'll add in an occasional changeup. He has a hitch in his delivery that adds deception, though that funkiness and his lack of size lead to concerns about his durability. He relished pitching the late innings as Arizona State's closer. As evidenced by his AFL assignment, Swagerty could move swiftly. However, St. Louis may use him as a starter in 2011 to give him innings to work on his changeup and enhance his stamina. He may open his first full pro season in the Quad Cities rotation, but his future is still as a set-up man or closer.

Year	Club (League)	Class	W	L	ERA	G	GS	CG	SV	IP	H	HR	BB	SO	G/A	WHIP	AVG
2010	Did Not Play—Signed Late																

10 JOE KELLY, RHP

Born: June 9, 1988. **B-T:** R-R. **Ht.:** 6-1. **Wt.:** 165. **Drafted:** UC Riverside, 2009 (3rd round). **Signed by:** Jeff Ishii.

Kelly set a UC Riverside record with 24 career saves, but the Cardinals made him a starter at the beginning of his first full pro season in 2010. It was meant to be a temporary assignment, giving him innings to improve his secondary pitches, but the results could prolong it. Kelly made adjustments with his delivery and showed enough command with his curveball to spend the entire year in Quad Cities' piggyback rotation. Kelly has an electric fastball, ranging from 93-99 mph last year, and he has touched 100 mph as a reliever. When he gets on top of the ball, he creates good sink to go along with raw velocity, and he can run his fastball in on righthanders. He throws two breaking balls, with his slider a better pitch but his curve featuring more command. Both have the potential to be above-average offerings, and his changeup has moments of effectiveness. Further improving his command will be key to Kelly's development, and his long arm action and wiry frame have some wondering if he can handle a starter's workload. When he's at his best, he generates more groundballs than strikeouts. Kelly has closer upside and will advance to high Class A Palm Beach this year.

Year	Club (League)	Class	W	L	ERA	G	GS	CG	SV	IP	H	HR	BB	SO	G/A	WHIP	AVG
2009	Batavia (NYP)	SS	2	3	4.75	16	2	0	1	30	33	0	11	30	2.47	1.45	.273
2010	Quad Cities (MWL)	LoA	6	8	4.62	26	18	0	1	103	103	3	45	92	3.97	1.43	.265
Minor League Totals			8	11	4.65	42	20	0	2	134	136	3	56	122	3.51	1.44	.267

11 MATT CARPENTER, 3B

Born: Nov. 26, 1985. **B-T:** L-R. **Ht.:** 6-3. **Wt.:** 200. **Drafted:** Texas Christian, 2009 (13th round). **Signed by:** Aaron Krawiec.

A fifth-year senior who signed for $1,000 as a 13th-round pick in 2009, Carpenter led St. Louis farmhands with a .418 on-base percentage in 2010. With his smooth lefthanded swing and feel for the strike zone, Carpenter has the tools to hit for a high average and get on base at a high clip. Some scouts question whether he has the power required for third base. He swings from a standstill, and the Cardinals have encouraged him to work on developing a weight shift and increasing his strength so he can have more pop. All 12 of his homers at Springfield came in a 58-game burst. Carpenter has good instincts at third, but his range and arm are merely adequate. He's a below-average runner but will steal a base if the opposition forgets about him. Caught between incumbent big leaguer David Freese and 2010 first-rounder Zack Cox, Carpenter has a small window of opportunity. He'll advance to Triple-A this season.

Year	Club (League)	Class	AVG	G	AB	R	H	2B	3B	HR	RBI	BB	SO	SB	CS	OBP	SLG
2009	Batavia (NYP)	SS	.469	9	32	9	15	3	0	0	3	4	2	0	1	.541	.563
	Quad Cities (MWL)	LoA	.295	29	105	11	31	6	2	0	10	17	13	2	0	.405	.390
	Palm Beach (FSL)	HiA	.219	32	114	13	25	6	1	2	9	10	24	1	0	.286	.342
2010	Palm Beach (FSL)	HiA	.283	28	99	17	28	5	2	1	16	26	14	0	1	.441	.404
	Springfield (TL)	AA	.316	105	396	76	125	26	3	12	53	64	88	11	2	.412	.487
Minor League Totals			.300	203	746	126	224	46	8	15	91	121	141	14	4	.403	.444

12 DANIEL DESCALSO, 2B/3B

Born: Oct. 19, 1986. **B-T:** L-R. **Ht.:** 5-10. **Wt.:** 190. **Drafted:** UC Davis, 2007 (3rd round). **Signed by:** Jay North.

It didn't take long for Descalso's nickname to follow him from the minor leagues to the majors. "We call him Dirty Dan," manager Tony LaRussa said a few days after his September callup. The grass-stained infielder proved his worth quickly as he took to starting at third, despite not playing the position in years. Such versatility has improved Descalso's stock, as he has become a lefthanded-hitting option with good instincts and a stout arm at two infield positions. He won a gold medal with Team USA in the 2009 World Cup, and he carried that momentum into spring, when LaRussa found reasons to play him late in exhibition games. Descalso has a quick, level swing that gives him gap power and good strike-zone coverage. He has a keen eye, and his pop has improved (32 doubles in 2010), and if he can grow into a little more power he can win an expanded role at second, where the Cardinals are looking to upgrade offensively.

Year	Club (League)	Class	AVG	G	AB	R	H	2B	3B	HR	RBI	BB	SO	SB	CS	OBP	SLG
2007	Batavia (NYP)	SS	.268	66	250	29	67	7	5	0	31	26	37	12	3	.346	.336
2008	Palm Beach (FSL)	HiA	.243	115	403	57	98	24	2	8	50	33	53	7	7	.313	.372
	Springfield (TL)	AA	.351	9	37	6	13	1	1	0	4	3	2	1	1	.405	.432
2009	Springfield (TL)	AA	.323	73	288	46	93	26	5	8	51	31	41	0	1	.396	.531
	Memphis (PCL)	AAA	.253	46	150	23	38	4	0	2	17	16	21	3	0	.327	.320
2010	Memphis (PCL)	AAA	.282	116	468	86	132	32	3	9	71	47	48	8	4	.350	.421
	St. Louis (NL)	MAJ	.265	11	34	6	9	2	0	0	4	2	6	1	0	.324	.324
Major League Totals			.265	11	34	6	9	2	0	0	4	2	6	1	0	.324	.324
Minor League Totals			.276	425	1596	247	441	94	16	27	224	156	202	31	16	.347	.406

13 JOHN GAST, LHP

Born: Feb. 16, 1989. **B-T:** L-L. **Ht.:** 6-1. **Wt.:** 195. **Drafted:** Florida State, 2010 (6th round). **Signed by:** Mike Elias.

The Rangers made Gast a fifth-round pick coming out of high school in Florida in 2007, even though he needed Tommy John surgery. He had a 1.18 ERA with 85 strikeouts in 58 innings as a high school senior but couldn't find that same form in college, compiling a 4.96 ERA in 123 career innings. He came back quickly in a relief role and helped the Seminoles reach the College World Series as a freshman, and flashed his best stuff again early in his junior season, but he wore down as the spring went on and slid to the sixth round. He came back strong after signing with the Cardinals for $140,000, going 6-0, 1.54 for Batavia. Gast has poise on the mound and a mature delivery with deception that adds to his 92-93 mph fastball. He plays off that with a hard curveball that can generate swings and misses, and a changeup that shows flashes of being a plus pitch. He showed great control in Batavia, in contrast to his college career, and command will remain a focus for him. In postseason meetings, several minor league coaches listed Gast alongside Tyrell Jenkins and Shelby Miller as the top arms in the organization. With his level of experience, Gast will get a shot to jump to the Palm Beach rotation.

Year	Club (League)	Class	W	L	ERA	G	GS	CG	SV	IP	H	HR	BB	SO	G/A	WHIP	AVG
2010	Batavia (NYP)	SS	6	0	1.54	8	6	0	0	35	27	1	8	36	2.00	1.00	.227
Minor League Totals			6	0	1.54	8	6	0	0	35	27	1	8	36	2.00	1.00	.227

14 FERNANDO SALAS, RHP

Born: May 30, 1985. **B-T:** R-R. **Ht.:** 6-2. **Wt.:** 200. **Signed:** Mexico, 2007. **Signed by:** Chuck Fick.

Salas served as a human yo-yo during 2010, popping up seven different times for cameo relief appearances with the major league club after making his debut in May. His poise no matter the situation won him almost as many fans as his signature command. The Cardinals signed Salas out of the Mexican League in 2007 with the promise of giving him a shot to be a starter in high Class A. He struggled and was returned to his Mexican team but got a second shot in 2008, this time in relief. He blossomed in the role and earned a spot in the 2008 Futures Game after a solid turn as the Double-A closer. In 2010, Salas returned to the ninth inning, working with with a low-90s fastball and a tight slider. He's able to use both pitches to tickle the edges of the strike zone, and he maintains his velocity while working with movement on his fastball. He rarely uses a changeup. Salas allowed one run in his first 10 major league innings, and he displayed a better ability to recover when behind the count. He'll settle into a permanent spot in the major league bullpen.

Year	Club (League)	Class	W	L	ERA	G	GS	CG	SV	IP	H	HR	BB	SO	G/A	WHIP	AVG
2005	Saltillo (MEX)	AAA	0	0	2.08	14	1	0	0	17	21	1	10	12	—	1.79	.304
2006	Saltillo (MEX)	AAA	8	2	3.02	29	1	0	0	48	40	5	20	38	—	1.26	.231
2007	Palm Beach (FSL)	HiA	2	3	5.26	16	4	0	0	39	39	12	10	25	—	1.25	.260
	Saltillo (MEX)	AAA	0	0	6.75	3	0	0	0	3	5	1	2	2	—	2.63	.417
2008	Springfield (TL)	AA	7	3	3.65	60	0	0	25	74	65	12	16	100	—	1.09	.236
2009	Memphis (PCL)	AAA	3	2	3.67	24	0	0	0	27	22	4	10	24	0.44	1.19	.220
	Cardinals (GCL)	R	0	0	0.00	1	0	0	0	1	0	0	0	1	1.00	0.00	.000
	Springfield (TL)	AA	1	0	3.18	10	0	0	0	11	10	0	2	7	0.59	1.06	.244
2010	Memphis (PCL)	AAA	1	0	3.79	34	0	0	19	36	26	2	9	44	1.33	0.98	.208
	St. Louis (NL)	MAJ	0	0	3.52	27	0	0	0	31	28	4	15	29	0.69	1.40	.241
Major League Totals			0	0	3.52	27	0	0	0	31	28	4	15	29	0.69	1.40	.241
Minor League Totals			22	10	3.69	191	6	0	44	256	228	37	79	253	0.69	1.74	.233

15 ADAM REIFER, RHP

Born: June 3, 1986. **B-T:** R-R. **Ht.:** 6-2. **Wt.:** 195. **Drafted:** UC Riverside, 2007 (11th round). **Signed by:** Jeff Ishii.

Reifer came out of college with a reputation for throwing hard but fighting to stay healthy, and over time he has learned that dialing back his velocity helps. He can throw pure gas, but he has dialed back his fastball a bit, dropping from 98 mph heat to a 93-96 range that offers him more command and supports his aggressive approach. His ball cuts more than it sinks, especially to lefthanded hitters, and he comes right after hitters. Reifer has a slider that at times can be a plus-plus pitch, and with better command last year he was able to get ahead in counts and deploy it more consistently as a put-away pitch. He has worked on a splitter that could be a plus pitch if he gets consistent with it. His strikeout-walk ratio jumped from 2.0 in 2009 to 3.3 in 2010. A compact delivery helps, and while command was key to his promotion to Triple-A, so was health. Reifer battled bone spurs and elbow tendinitis as a junior in college, and lingering durability questions have dissipated after his workload the last two seasons. He'll battle for the closer job in Memphis after being added to the 40-man roster for the first time.

Year	Club (League)	Class	W	L	ERA	G	GS	CG	SV	IP	H	HR	BB	SO	G/A	WHIP	AVG
2007	Did Not Play—Injured																
2008	Batavia (NYP)	SS	2	1	2.97	32	0	0	22	30	18	2	15	41	—	1.09	.162
2009	Palm Beach (FSL)	HiA	4	7	4.47	54	0	0	21	48	51	2	24	50	0.98	1.55	.270
2010	Springfield (TL)	AA	3	1	3.00	51	0	0	17	54	53	2	15	52	1.25	1.26	.252

Memphis (PCL)	AAA	1	0	0.00	1	0	0	0	1	0	0	1	0	2.00	1.00	.000
Minor League Totals		10	9	3.50	138	0	0	60	134	122	6	55	143	1.12	1.32	.238

16 MAIKEL CLETO, RHP

Born: May 1, 1989. **B-T:** R-R. **Ht.:** 6-3. **Wt.:** 234. **Signed:** Dominican Republic, 2006. **Signed by:** Ramon Pena (Mets).

After signing Ryan Theriot to take over at shortstop, the Cardinals sent Brendan Ryan to the Mariners for Cleto. It was Cleto's second trade in two years, as he came to the Mariners from the Mets as part of the 12-player, three-team trade that sent J.J. Putz to New York and Franklin Gutierrez to Seattle from Cleveland. Cleto has a live arm, but his below-average control and lack of command prevent him from getting the most out of his stuff. His fastball sits at 94-98 mph and touches 100 with explosive life. He can blow his heater by hitters, but focuses on velocity at the expense of throwing quality strikes. Overthrowing causes him to fall off the mound toward first base and miss to that side of the plate. The Mariners tried to point Cleto more to the plate with his delivery, having him focus on maintaining a rhythm and getting better extension out front. His curveball and changeup are both below-average pitches but show flashes of being at least average. His curve has tight downward action, almost like a slider. Cleto made progress with his delivery and maturity in the Arizona Fall League, but his future role is likely as a power arm in the bullpen. He may continue to start in Double-A this year so he can get more innings to work on his deficiencies.

Year	Club (League)	Class	W	L	ERA	G	GS	CG	SV	IP	H	HR	BB	SO	G/A	WHIP	AVG
2007	Mets (GCL)	R	1	2	5.03	11	4	0	1	34	34	2	25	28	—	1.74	.270
2008	Savannah (SAL)	LoA	5	11	4.25	25	22	1	0	136	140	8	34	81	—	1.28	.268
	St. Lucie (FSL)	HiA	0	1	9.00	1	1	0	0	5	5	1	2	1	—	1.40	.278
2009	Mariners (AZL)	R	0	1	13.50	1	0	0	0	1	3	0	1	1	—	6.00	.500
	Clinton (MWL)	LoA	0	3	5.33	8	8	0	0	25	35	4	11	24	1.27	1.82	.321
2010	High Desert (CAL)	HiA	4	9	6.16	23	21	0	0	102	125	10	44	83	1.35	1.65	.305
Minor League Totals			10	27	5.17	69	56	1	1	303	342	25	117	218	1.34	1.51	.287

17 ADRON CHAMBERS, OF

Born: Oct 8, 1986. **B-T:** L-L. **Ht.:** 5-10. **Wt.:** 185. **Drafted:** Pensacola (Fla.) JC, 2007 (38th round). **Signed by:** Steve Turco.

A former college football player trying to reinvent himself as a baseball player, Chambers got a call in junior college that if he could get to Memphis in 24 hours, he would work out in front of the Cardinals. He hopped on a bus, and got off just in time to go straight from Greyhound to the 60-yard dash and batting practice. His athleticism was enough to get him drafted with the 1,153rd overall pick in 2007 and he signed for $40,000. The Cardinals described him as agile and speedy, a cornerback in the outfield, and raw with lots of baseball to learn. Three years of cramming later, Chambers has started to translate his tools into performance and grabbed a spot on the 40-man roster. In 2009, he led the high Class A Florida State League with 16 triples, and last season he earned a taste of Triple-A. Chambers' best tool remains his above-average speed, allowing him to hold down center field even as he's improving his routes and reads out there. He should be a basestealing threat as his instincts improve. He played quarterback and pitched in high school, so he has a plus arm. He's a leadoff type who has improved his approach but still is learning to shorten his stroke and take contact over power. He holds his own against righthanded pitchers but can bail out against lefthanders. One scout said last season that Chambers has already proven productive enough to be a fourth outfielder. Securing a starting job in Triple-A will reveal if he could be more.

Year	Club (League)	Class	AVG	G	AB	R	H	2B	3B	HR	RBI	BB	SO	SB	CS	OBP	SLG
2007	Johnson City (APP)	R	.279	36	111	16	31	7	1	0	10	10	21	6	5	.362	.360
2008	Quad Cities (MWL)	LoA	.238	95	336	56	80	13	7	3	25	33	66	13	8	.322	.345
2009	Palm Beach (FSL)	HiA	.283	122	448	66	127	17	16	1	46	47	96	21	12	.370	.400
2010	Springfield (TL)	AA	.282	75	252	52	71	9	5	5	27	31	50	8	4	.376	.417
	Memphis (PCL)	AAA	.290	37	69	11	20	0	1	1	8	9	18	6	1	.390	.362
Minor League Totals			.271	365	1216	201	329	46	30	10	116	130	251	54	30	.359	.382

18 DAVID KOPP, RHP

Born: Oct. 22, 1985. **B-T:** R-R. **Ht.:** 6-3. **Wt.:** 205. **Drafted:** Clemson, 2007 (2nd round). **Signed by:** Mike Shildt.

The strong-armed Kopp came out of a stacked Clemson rotation in 2007 that featured four high-round prospects. Health held him back in his first couple of years in the organization. He missed part of the 2008 season with significant shoulder soreness, a condition that flared again in 2009 and cut him off at 90 innings. In 2010, the stat that sang out more than the groundballs and velocity was his 26 starts. He didn't miss a turn in the rotation and made the Double-A Texas League's postseason all-star team. Kopp has a two-seam fastball that he throws at 93 mph with biting sink. Look no further than the two groundouts he got for every flyout. He mixes in a slider that's becoming a swing-and-miss pitch, and a four-seam fastball at 95-96 mph. Kopp went 0-5, 8.63 in a five-game stint in Triple-A, reinforcing his need to develop a changeup. His sinker is good enough to lean on, especially if he conditions his mechanics for a consistent release point. Added to the 40-man roster after the season, Kopp will get a crack at the Memphis rotation in 2011. He reminds people of Mitchell Boggs, another college pitcher with good sink who climbed the ranks as a starter and then emerged in the majors as a strong-armed reliever.

Year	Club (League)	Class	W	L	ERA	G	GS	CG	SV	IP	H	HR	BB	SO	G/A	WHIP	AVG
2007	Batavia (NYP)	SS	0	1	0.00	2	2	0	0	4	3	0	3	3	—	1.50	.200
2008	Palm Beach (FSL)	HiA	1	3	3.76	10	6	0	1	38	38	1	15	30	—	1.38	.262
	Cardinals (GCL)	R	0	0	4.91	2	2	0	0	4	2	0	0	2	—	0.55	.154
2009	Palm Beach (FSL)	HiA	5	3	3.12	15	13	0	0	69	67	3	26	58	1.75	1.34	.262
	Springfield (TL)	AA	1	1	6.43	5	5	0	0	21	29	3	11	6	1.41	1.90	.337
2010	Springfield (TL)	AA	12	4	3.05	21	21	1	0	121	126	9	39	78	1.75	1.36	.279
	Memphis (PCL)	AAA	0	5	8.63	5	5	0	0	24	38	4	11	12	2.17	2.04	.365
Minor League Totals			19	17	3.87	60	54	1	1	281	303	20	105	189	1.75	1.45	.283

19 P.J. WALTERS, RHP

Born: May 3, 1985. **B-T:** R-R. **Ht.:** 6-4. **Wt.:** 200. **Drafted:** South Alabama, 2006 (11th round). **Signed by:** Scott Nichols.

Walters' season started with tragedy when his daughter, born 14 weeks premature, died of related complications in April. The club gave him as much time as he needed with his wife, but he ultimately found solace in his job. Walters bookended his season with five shutout innings in his first start and seven shutout innings in his final start in the majors. He's durable and has an easy, relaxed delivery. Coupled with his plus changeup, it helps him mess with hitters' timing and mask average velocity. In Triple-A, Walters was able to live outside the zone, getting hitters to swing at pitches they couldn't reach. He found major leaguers weren't so easily tempted. Working with an 87-90 mph fastball and his changeup at 77-79 mph, he was able to locate the edges of the strike zone with better consistency in 2010. He throws a two-seam changeup, one that veers in and down on righthanders. He has an effective slider to reach the other side of the plate. While still prone to homers (17 in 139 innings last year), Walters has strikeout and groundball rates that hint at the long relief/swingman role he's suited for in the majors.

Year	Club (League)	Class	W	L	ERA	G	GS	CG	SV	IP	H	HR	BB	SO	G/A	WHIP	AVG
2006	State College (NYP)	SS	2	1	3.56	26	0	0	8	30	29	1	9	31	—	1.25	.242
2007	Quad Cities (MWL)	LoA	6	1	2.62	17	10	0	1	69	59	2	12	73	—	1.03	.229
	Palm Beach (FSL)	HiA	3	1	2.67	5	5	0	0	34	29	2	6	37	—	1.04	.225
	Springfield (TL)	AA	3	4	2.37	8	8	1	0	49	42	4	15	37	—	1.16	.228
2008	Springfield (TL)	AA	1	2	3.25	6	6	0	0	36	35	5	8	34	—	1.19	.252
	Memphis (PCL)	AAA	9	4	4.87	23	23	0	0	122	123	17	62	122	—	1.52	.266
2009	Memphis (PCL)	AAA	8	10	4.54	21	20	2	0	121	128	6	44	113	1.43	1.42	.271
	St. Louis (NL)	MAJ	0	0	9.56	8	1	0	0	16	21	6	9	14	1.62	1.88	.304
2010	Memphis (PCL)	AAA	8	5	3.81	19	18	0	0	109	106	12	30	106	0.88	1.25	.254
	St. Louis (NL)	MAJ	2	0	6.00	7	3	0	0	30	32	5	10	22	1.00	1.40	.276
Major League Totals			2	0	7.24	15	4	0	0	46	53	11	19	36	1.00	1.57	.286
Minor League Totals			40	28	3.81	125	90	3	9	570	551	49	186	553	1.14	1.29	.252

20 FRANCISCO SAMUEL, RHP

Born: Dec. 20, 1986. **B-T:** R-R. **Ht.:** 6-2. **Wt.:** 185. **Signed:** Dominican Republic, 2006. **Signed by:** Rene Rojas.

Even as he inches toward the majors, Samuel remains an untamed talent. He has a live arm but hasn't been able to consistently show the command necessary for success at the higher levels. Reed-thin with an easy and explosive delivery, Samuel throws a fastball that regularly hums at 98 mph and can touch triple digits. It's when he has to throw a strike that his velocity plummets, as he works in the low 90s to assure he'll find the strike zone. He also throws a high-80s slider that he also struggles to harness. In each of the last three years, Samuel has allowed more walks than hits. His wildness was most pronounced in Triple-A, where he walked 18 batters in 12 innings in the final month of the 2010 season. He has the pure stuff to be a closer and hitters can't make consistent contact against him, but it won't matter if he can't throw strikes. He'll probably open 2011 back in Memphis.

Year	Club (League)	Class	W	L	ERA	G	GS	CG	SV	IP	H	HR	BB	SO	G/A	WHIP	AVG
2006	Cardinals (DSL)	R	1	3	7.56	11	4	0	0	17	24	0	19	17	—	2.58	.364
2007	Cardinals (GCL)	R	0	4	9.53	13	6	0	0	34	43	2	35	40	—	2.29	.309
2008	Quad Cities (MWL)	LoA	2	0	1.23	5	0	0	1	7	4	0	5	9	—	1.23	.154
	Palm Beach (FSL)	HiA	4	6	3.04	54	0	0	29	56	39	3	48	85	—	1.54	.196
2009	Springfield (TL)	AA	4	5	5.66	52	0	0	22	48	36	2	46	59	1.58	1.72	.208
2010	Palm Beach (FSL)	HiA	0	0	0.00	3	0	0	1	3	1	0	1	6	—	0.67	.111
	Springfield (TL)	AA	2	0	3.63	22	0	0	6	22	18	3	16	27	1.50	1.52	.217
	Memphis (PCL)	AAA	1	0	4.63	13	0	0	0	12	8	0	18	10	1.56	2.23	.190
Minor League Totals			13	17	5.20	173	10	0	59	199	173	10	188	253	1.61	1.81	.235

21 PETE KOZMA, SS

Born: April 11, 1988. **B-T:** R-R. **Ht.:** 6-0. **Wt.:** 170. **Drafted:** HS—Owasso, Okla., 2007 (1st round). **Signed by:** Steve Gossett.

Kozma was first held to inflated standards when the Cardinals took him over pitcher Rick Porcello in the 2007 draft, giving him a $1.395 million bonus as the 17th overall pick. Then expectations were probably tamped too low when he was called a utility player. The truth is somewhere in between. After a repeat of Double-A and .269/.329/.433 performance in the Arizona Fall League, Kozma earned a spot on the 40-man roster in November. He has no true plus tool, but the only real deficiency in his game is power, which shouldn't be a huge issue as a middle infielder. He has a short stroke and makes contact, though he hasn't made adjustments to Double-A pitching and struggles against pitches low in the strike zone. He does have a little bit of pop, including 43 extra-base hits in 2010. Kozma is generally a surehanded defender with good instincts who makes all the routine plays, but he committed 34 errors last year. Some scouts thought he looked worse in his second time around in the Texas League, and that he was down after not moving up to Triple-A. Twenty-two of his errors came in the first half as he played himself into bad hops and poor throwing positions, flaws that he corrected late in the season. He has a solid, accurate arm and is an average runner. Depending on spring training, Kozma could return for another season at Springfield, but the Cardinals hope he'll ride his second-half improvement and AFL assignment into Triple-A.

Year	Club (League)	Class	AVG	G	AB	R	H	2B	3B	HR	RBI	BB	SO	SB	CS	OBP	SLG
2007	Cardinals (GCL)	R	.154	4	13	4	2	0	0	0	0	2	2	0	0	.267	.154
	Johnson City (APP)	R	.264	30	106	16	28	8	0	2	9	12	21	3	2	.350	.396
	Batavia (NYP)	SS	.148	8	27	1	4	0	1	0	2	1	7	1	1	.179	.222
2008	Quad Cities (MWL)	LoA	.284	99	377	58	107	20	4	5	40	45	69	12	5	.363	.398
	Palm Beach (FSL)	HiA	.130	24	77	4	10	4	0	0	10	10	27	0	1	.231	.182
2009	Palm Beach (FSL)	HiA	.315	18	73	8	23	5	0	0	8	8	16	1	0	.381	.384
	Springfield (TL)	AA	.216	113	407	52	88	15	3	6	37	42	88	4	2	.288	.312
2010	Springfield (TL)	AA	.243	132	503	69	122	28	2	13	72	56	111	13	2	.318	.384
Minor League Totals			.243	428	1583	212	384	80	10	26	178	176	341	34	13	.319	.355

22 BLAKE KING, RHP

Born: April 11, 1987. **B-T:** R-R. **Ht.:** 6-1. **Wt.:** 205. **Drafted:** Eastern Oklahoma State JC, D/F 2005 (44th round). **Signed by:** Steve Gossett.

When King signed it was big news, but not because he was an endangered draft species due to the end of the draft-and-follow process. He's related to Mickey Mantle, and that baseball legacy brought a phalanx of family to his signing. King cuts the figure of a country slinger, complete with the husky frame and hard stuff. The Cardinals drafted him out of high school, and he got a year in at Eastern Oklahoma State before going pro. King has been considered one of the better relief arms in the system, but his progress has been slow because consistency and command have eluded him. His 93-94 mph fastball and a sinister slider are both plus pitches. His command of the fastball is flighty, partially because the over-the-top delivery that benefits the vanishing, downward break of his slider can cause his release point for the fastball to waver. He also throws a curveball and changeup, though both are average and inconsistent. King has the right mix of pitches, and establishing a consistent delivery and command in Triple-A will put him on the brink of the big leagues. St. Louis added him to the 40-man roster in November.

Year	Club (League)	Class	W	L	ERA	G	GS	CG	SV	IP	H	HR	BB	SO	G/A	WHIP	AVG
2006	Johnson City (APP)	R	4	3	3.02	13	13	0	0	63	37	3	29	74	—	1.05	.167
2007	Quad Cities (MWL)	LoA	2	3	5.21	19	9	0	0	57	44	3	44	62	—	1.54	.214
	Batavia (NYP)	SS	1	4	4.70	16	9	0	0	54	48	3	34	65	—	1.53	.240
2008	Quad Cities (MWL)	LoA	2	5	4.41	16	8	0	0	51	47	2	49	60	—	1.88	.251
	Palm Beach (FSL)	HiA	1	3	4.64	15	7	0	0	43	32	1	33	45	—	1.52	.218
2009	Palm Beach (FSL)	HiA	9	3	2.84	41	2	0	0	76	41	0	58	96	1.05	1.30	.160
	Springfield (TL)	AA	0	0	10.80	3	0	0	0	3	7	0	5	6	1.00	3.60	.438
2010	Springfield (TL)	AA	4	3	2.91	53	0	0	0	68	40	5	48	84	1.00	1.29	.173
Minor League Totals			23	24	3.89	176	48	0	0	414	296	17	300	492	1.03	1.44	.202

23 MARK HAMILTON, 1B

Born: July 29, 1984. **B-T:** L-L. **Ht.:** 6-4. **Wt.:** 220. **Drafted:** Tulane, 2006 (2nd round supplemental). **Signed by:** Scott Nichols.

As Memphis made a second straight run to the Pacific Coast League championship series, Hamilton provided the power. A brawny, lefthanded hitter, he slugged 18 homers in 258 at-bats with the Redbirds—his 18th clinched the division for the Redbirds—with two more in the playoffs. After a decorated college career that included All-America and Conference USA player of the year honors in 2006, Hamilton took a few years to adjust to pro ball but finally established himself as one of the best power-hitting prospects in the system. He missed parts of the 2010 season with two stays on the disabled list (hand, groin) and still set a career high for homers. His value is in his bat. Hamilton has a quick-enough swing and the leverage to damage more than just mistakes, and he knows how to work the count in his favor. He slimmed down for 2010, improving his conditioning and stamina. An experiment in the outfield proved difficult, but with experience he could be serviceable there. He's also below average at first, and the Cardinals don't expect to have an opening there for awhile anyway. Because he is so limited defensively, Hamilton isn't a natural fit for the bench and is probably best suited as a DH. He'll return to Triple-A to open the season, trying to expand his resume or swing his way through the roadblocks or into a trade.

Year	Club (League)	Class	AVG	G	AB	R	H	2B	3B	HR	RBI	BB	SO	SB	CS	OBP	SLG
2006	State College (NYP)	SS	.264	30	106	18	28	3	1	8	24	13	24	1	1	.347	.538
	Quad Cities (MWL)	LoA	.254	38	142	16	36	8	0	3	25	10	32	0	0	.307	.373
2007	Palm Beach (FSL)	HiA	.290	60	221	31	64	12	0	13	49	20	48	1	0	.348	.520
	Springfield (TL)	AA	.250	68	248	32	62	15	0	6	41	24	54	1	1	.318	.383
2008	Springfield (TL)	AA	.241	70	245	27	59	11	0	8	29	35	67	0	0	.338	.384
2009	Springfield (TL)	AA	.307	48	163	26	50	11	0	8	28	28	46	0	1	.421	.521
	Memphis (PCL)	AAA	.308	46	130	22	40	11	0	6	19	13	34	0	0	.375	.531
2010	Memphis (PCL)	AAA	.298	72	258	53	77	20	0	18	60	35	70	0	0	.389	.585
	Cardinals (GCL)	R	.296	9	27	2	8	1	0	2	2	4	9	0	0	.406	.556
	St. Louis (NL)	MAJ	.143	9	14	0	2	0	0	0	0	1	5	0	0	.200	.143
Major League Totals			.143	9	14	0	2	0	0	0	0	1	5	0	0	.200	.143
Minor League Totals			.275	441	1540	227	424	92	1	72	277	182	384	3	3	.357	.477

24 OSCAR TAVERAS, OF

Born: June 19, 1992. **B-T:** L-L. **Ht.:** 6-2. **Wt.:** 180. **Signed:** Dominican Republic, 2008. **Signed by:** Juan Mercado.

Less than two years after the Cardinals signed him as a 16-year-old athlete out of Puerto Plata, D.R., Taveras came to America and had arguably the best debut of any international signing from their recent wave. He seized the No. 2 spot in Rookie-level Johnson City's lineup with his aggressiveness and helped elevate the Cardinals to the Appalachian League title. Taveras was third in the league with a .322 average, fourth with 43 RBIs, fifth in slugging (.526), sixth in OPS (.889) and ranked as the second-best position prospect in the league. Scouts saw a teenager who played beyond his years, with a good feel for the game and bat speed that should allow him to hit at higher levels. Coaches see a five-tool type, with the solid-average arm and good range to play center if he gets more consistent with his routes. His speed is average. Taveras has a lefthanded stroke that preternaturally makes contact with the sweet spot and allows him to drive the ball to all fields. With two strikes, he limits his leg kick and adopts a streamlined swing that would work at other counts. He should make a full-season club before he turns 20.

Year	Club (League)	Class	AVG	G	AB	R	H	2B	3B	HR	RBI	BB	SO	SB	CS	OBP	SLG
2009	Cardinals (DSL)	R	.257	65	237	35	61	13	8	1	42	28	36	9	4	.338	.392
2010	Cardinals (GCL)	R	.167	7	30	1	5	1	0	0	2	1	5	1	0	.194	.200
	Johnson City (APP)	R	.322	53	211	39	68	13	3	8	43	12	41	8	5	.362	.526
Minor League Totals			.280	125	478	75	134	27	11	9	87	41	82	18	9	.340	.439

25 TONY CRUZ, C

Born: Aug. 18, 1986. **B-T:** R-R. **Ht.:** 5-11. **Wt.:** 205. **Drafted:** Palm Beach (Fla.) CC, 2007 (26th round). **Signed by:** Charlie Gonzalez.

Cruz had a reliable glove and intriguing bat to speed through the lower levels of the system as a third baseman, but moving to catcher propelled him into prospect status and earned him a spot on the 40-man roster. A couple of years learning the position culminated in a breakthrough season in 2010, one that ended in the Arizona Fall League, where he hit .342/.393/.500 in 76 at-bats. Cruz played in the Cardinals' spring-training backyard in Palm Beach, Fla., and already looked like a 26th-round bargain when he consistently hit at four levels after the draft, but there were doubts that his bat would profile at third. His ascent slowed so that he could take a crash course on catching. Cruz has developed nimble footwork behind the plate, good receiving skills and a feel for calling a game. He has a strong, accurate arm, and good mechanics enhance his timing. He threw out 53 percent of basestealers last season. Cruz was trusted enough that he started at catcher in the Triple-A playoffs. Despite his power spike in Arizona, he always has been a hitter for average more than power. This season he worked on going the other way so that he could handle pitches on the outer third and climb back toward .300. He's a well below-average runner. Cruz as a hitter looks better now that he's catching, and he'll continue his climb at Triple-A this season.

Year	Club (League)	Class	AVG	G	AB	R	H	2B	3B	HR	RBI	BB	SO	SB	CS	OBP	SLG
2007	Cardinals (GCL)	R	.375	7	32	8	12	5	0	0	4	1	7	1	0	.382	.531
	Johnson City (APP)	R	.280	6	25	2	7	2	0	2	2	2	2	1	0	.333	.600
	Batavia (NYP)	SS	.375	4	16	2	6	1	0	0	4	0	5	0	0	.412	.438
	Quad Cities (MWL)	LoA	.282	49	195	26	55	10	1	5	34	17	25	3	1	.338	.421
2008	Palm Beach (FSL)	HiA	.279	89	351	41	98	22	3	8	58	19	50	3	0	.316	.427
2009	Springfield (TL)	AA	.220	110	404	44	89	25	2	10	48	34	85	1	0	.281	.366
2010	Palm Beach (FSL)	HiA	.282	46	181	21	51	16	1	1	25	19	33	0	2	.348	.398
	Springfield (TL)	AA	.289	40	149	26	43	10	0	6	20	17	30	0	0	.363	.477
	Memphis (PCL)	AAA	.214	4	14	2	3	0	0	1	1	1	1	0	0	.267	.429
Minor League Totals			.266	355	1367	172	364	91	7	33	196	110	238	9	3	.321	.416

26 BRYAN ANDERSON, C

Born: Dec. 16, 1986. **B-T:** L-R. **Ht.:** 6-1. **Wt.:** 200. **Drafted:** HS—Simi Valley, Calif., 2005 (4th round). **Signed by:** Jay North.

Any hesitance the major league staff may have had about turning over one of its pitchers to Anderson dissipated when the lefthanded-hitting catcher gained an advocate in Gold Glove winner Mike Matheny. Matheny has tutored Anderson for a couple of years, trying to mold him into the fundamentals-first catcher the Cardinals insist on. Big league trust is the best gauge, and confirming his turnaround, a starter who once said he was uncomfortable throwing to him acknowledged Anderson's improvement in handling, if not calling, a game. Anderson doesn't snatch at pitches as much as he used to, is now average at blocking balls, and his footwork behind the plate has improved to make his throwing mechanics less awkward. Anderson's level, balanced swing remains his best asset. A .294 hitter in the minors, he hit .375 as a pinch-hitter in the majors, and his power took a step forward last year though it's below average. Still just 24, Anderson is ready to battle for major league time. But while Jason LaRue retired and defensive specialist Matt Pagnozzi was released, the Cardinals signed Gerald Laird as the backup to Yadier Molina. Anderson will battle for a bench role and if not will head back to Triple-A.

Year	Club (League)	Class	AVG	G	AB	R	H	2B	3B	HR	RBI	BB	SO	SB	CS	OBP	SLG
2005	Johnson City (APP)	R	.331	51	154	28	51	8	1	6	36	15	29	6	1	.383	.513
2006	Quad Cities (MWL)	LoA	.302	109	381	50	115	29	3	3	51	42	66	2	6	.377	.417
2007	Springfield (TL)	AA	.298	103	389	51	116	15	1	6	53	32	77	0	1	.350	.388
2008	Springfield (TL)	AA	.388	19	80	12	31	5	0	2	14	4	12	0	0	.412	.525
	Memphis (PCL)	AAA	.281	73	235	27	66	13	2	2	27	32	46	2	0	.367	.379
2009	Memphis (PCL)	AAA	.245	53	163	22	40	7	3	4	11	10	42	1	0	.293	.399
	Cardinals (GCL)	R	.313	5	16	3	5	0	0	1	2	4	4	1	0	.450	.500
2010	Memphis (PCL)	AAA	.270	82	270	39	73	12	0	12	42	27	54	0	0	.341	.448
	St. Louis (NL)	MAJ	.281	15	32	1	9	2	0	0	4	1	7	0	0	.314	.344
Major League Totals			.281	15	32	1	9	2	0	0	4	1	7	0	0	.314	.344
Minor League Totals			.294	495	1688	232	497	89	10	36	236	166	330	12	8	.359	.423

27 ADAM OTTAVINO, RHP

Born: Nov. 22, 1985. **B-T:** L-R. **Ht.:** 6-5. **Wt.:** 215. **Drafted:** Northeastern, 2006 (1st round). **Signed by:** Kobe Perez.

The Cardinals announced in July that Ottavino would need surgery to repair a torn labrum in his right shoulder—which came as news to him. The strong-armed righthander had been pitching through discomfort in his shoulder for awhile, and he lobbied the Cardinals to give non-surgical treatment a try. After an extended rest he was activated—but not used—for the final weekend of the season, and the Cardinals outrighted him off the 40-man roster in November. The injury interrupted a season when Ottavino had taken a significant step forward. No longer sabotaged by a Quixotic search for mechanics, he pitched well in the Memphis rotation. He has become comfortable with a two-seam fastball that hums in the low 90s, and he can still crank his four-seam fastball in the mid- to high 90s. His sinking changeup has become an effective weapon, and his command has improved with a consistent, easier delivery. His slurvy breaking ball lags behind his other pitches. The condition of Ottavino's shoulder will loom over his every throw early this season, but if he's healthy he could get a big league opportunity. He intrigued pitching coach Dave Duncan enough last spring that he shifted briefly to relief, and while the organization still views him as a starter long-term, he could serve an apprentice role in the major league bullpen at some point in 2010, the same path used to groom Adam Wainwright.

Year	Club (League)	Class	W	L	ERA	G	GS	CG	SV	IP	H	HR	BB	SO	G/A	WHIP	AVG
2006	State College (NYP)	SS	2	2	3.14	6	6	0	0	29	23	1	13	26	—	1.26	.211
	Quad Cities (MWL)	LoA	2	3	3.44	8	8	0	0	37	28	3	19	38	—	1.28	.211
2007	Palm Beach (FSL)	HiA	12	8	3.08	27	27	1	0	143	130	10	63	128	—	1.35	.239
2008	Springfield (TL)	AA	3	7	5.23	24	24	1	0	115	133	16	52	96	—	1.60	.291
2009	Memphis (PCL)	AAA	7	12	4.75	27	27	0	0	144	141	12	82	119	1.14	1.55	.261
2010	Memphis (PCL)	AAA	5	3	3.97	9	9	0	0	48	43	5	12	43	1.90	1.15	.239
	St. Louis (NL)	MAJ	0	2	8.46	5	3	0	0	22	37	5	9	12	1.29	2.06	.370
Major League Totals			0	2	8.46	5	3	0	0	22	37	5	9	12	1.29	2.06	.370
Minor League Totals			31	35	4.14	101	101	2	0	516	498	47	241	450	1.27	1.43	.254

28 DARYL JONES, OF

Born: June 25, 1987. **B-T:** L-L. **Ht.:** 5-11. **Wt.:** 180. **Drafted:** HS—Spring, Texas, 2005 (3rd round). **Signed by:** Joe Almaraz.

Almost universally considered within the organization as the Cardinals' best position prospect after 2009, Jones has seen his star recede as suddenly as it soared. A loose collection of plus tools coming out of high school, Jones rewarded the organization's patience with a breakout 2008. He showed a feel for the strike zone and developed a sense for exploiting his above-average speed, and a jolt of confidence mixed with better baseball instincts combined for a .909 OPS at Double-A. He represented the Cardinals in the Futures Game in 2009, but an erosion of his game already had begun because of injury. He had tendinitis in both knees, and that sapped his best skill. Healthy for 2010, he still struggled to play to his tools. Jones hit .194/.315/.274 in April, went 2-for-6 on steal attempts in May, and other Cards farmhands gained ground. Jones moved to left field, and he seemed tentative at the plate. He has the legs to handle center, while his arm profiles for left, and where he fits for the Cardinals has never been murkier. He has played passively the last couple of seasons, and his ability to make contact has worked against him as he puts too many pitchers' pitches in play with weak swings. His power is below average. His speed and eye are equalizers, but he'll have to regain confidence in his game before the Cardinals can do the same.

Year	Club (League)	Class	AVG	G	AB	R	H	2B	3B	HR	RBI	BB	SO	SB	CS	OBP	SLG
2005	Johnson City (APP)	R	.209	61	182	36	38	6	1	2	10	15	41	10	4	.311	.286
2006	Johnson City (APP)	R	.265	20	68	15	18	3	1	3	13	8	8	3	0	.367	.471
	Quad Cities (MWL)	LoA	.235	26	81	15	19	5	1	1	7	6	23	2	2	.308	.358
2007	Quad Cities (MWL)	LoA	.217	127	419	71	91	15	3	4	31	41	94	22	12	.304	.296
2008	Palm Beach (FSL)	HiA	.326	87	307	43	100	11	7	7	35	33	67	18	5	.406	.476
	Springfield (TL)	AA	.290	36	124	19	36	6	1	6	14	22	30	6	1	.409	.500
2009	Springfield (TL)	AA	.279	80	294	50	82	14	3	3	29	33	65	7	4	.360	.378
2010	Springfield (TL)	AA	.244	121	451	67	110	17	6	8	48	52	95	15	9	.335	.361
Minor League Totals			.256	558	1926	316	494	77	23	34	187	210	423	83	37	.346	.373

29 STEVEN HILL, C

Born: March 14, 1985. **B-T:** R-R. **Ht.:** 5-11. **Wt.:** 200. **Drafted:** Stephen F. Austin State, 2007 (13th round). **Signed by:** Joe Almaraz.

In a pinch for a backup catcher because of injuries at the higher levels, the Cardinals promoted Hill in August and saw what keeps him moving through the system. On a 1-0 pitch in his only game, Hill launched an opposite-field home run for his first major league hit. It was one of 25 homers the slugger hit in 2010, and it confirmed what the Cardinals already knew: the bat plays. Finding a place where Hill can get in the lineup is the quest. Stocky and strong, he has a short, swift, power-packed swing that bruises mistakes and can drive the ball to all fields. He isn't a great hitter for average and doesn't shore up his approach with two strikes. Hill got ample playing time at catcher, though he remains clunky at what really is his third position. He has difficulty blocking balls, and despite arm strength he's inconsistent under fire. He erased 34 percent of basestealers last season. Limited range at third makes him a better option at first, and he has taken some reps in the outfield, but he's a well below-average runner. Hill projects as a power bat off the bench, and his fringe ability at a variety of positions, especially moonlighting at catcher, makes that more of a possibility. He'll battle for a major league bench job in spring training.

Year	Club (League)	Class	AVG	G	AB	R	H	2B	3B	HR	RBI	BB	SO	SB	CS	OBP	SLG
2007	Batavia (NYP)	SS	.436	10	39	4	17	5	1	1	11	5	5	0	0	.511	.692
	Quad Cities (MWL)	LoA	.303	62	261	38	79	15	0	11	44	9	58	1	1	.330	.487
2008	Palm Beach (FSL)	HiA	.285	46	172	28	49	11	2	9	34	15	42	0	0	.339	.529
	Springfield (TL)	AA	.303	26	99	13	30	3	1	5	9	3	31	0	0	.330	.505
	Cardinals (GCL)	R	.313	4	16	4	5	1	0	3	5	0	7	0	0	.313	.938
2009	Springfield (TL)	AA	.282	120	464	62	131	26	2	19	64	36	106	1	2	.333	.470
2010	Springfield (TL)	AA	.280	93	361	60	101	27	1	22	86	38	90	1	0	.352	.543
	St. Louis (NL)	MAJ	.333	1	3	1	1	0	0	1	1	0	1	0	0	.333	1.333
	Memphis (PCL)	AAA	.176	9	34	2	6	1	0	2	6	3	10	0	0	.263	.382
Major League Totals			.333	1	3	1	1	0	0	1	1	0	1	0	0	.333	1.333
Minor League Totals			.289	370	1446	211	418	89	7	72	259	109	349	3	3	.341	.510

30 RYAN JACKSON, SS

Born: May 10, 1988. **B-T:** R-R. **Ht.:** 6-3. **Wt.:** 180. **Drafted:** Miami, 2009 (5th round). **Signed by:** Charlie Gonzalez.

Jackson validated his reputation as the best defensive shortstop in the college ranks in 2009 with a slick turn through his first pro season. He's nimble, with a strong arm, and his manager described him as having "educated feet," a high baseball IQ and those soft, bad-hop hands. He had six errors in his final 41 games. Jackson isn't the fleetest infielder, but his instincts, first-step accuracy and confidence to improvise give him a faster look in the field. The big issue will be whether his bat measures up. Jackson closed the year on a seven-game hitting streak that improved his average to .291 in high Class A. He has good discipline, average ability to make contact, and shows an understanding that his value is in getting on base. Strength is a concern. Jackson loses weight rapidly and has to work to maintain his strength through a full season. He's been called a throwback infielder, and his glove is good enough to keep him in the lineup as he refines a playable swing. A return to Palm Beach as the starting shortstop is likely, with a move to Double-A coming when that position opens or Jackson's play forces it.

Year	Club (League)	Class	AVG	G	AB	R	H	2B	3B	HR	RBI	BB	SO	SB	CS	OBP	SLG
2009	Batavia (NYP)	SS	.216	67	245	29	53	4	1	0	14	29	37	4	3	.297	.241
2010	Quad Cities (MWL)	LoA	.272	84	302	47	82	13	2	2	27	48	63	6	7	.366	.348
	Palm Beach (FSL)	HiA	.291	41	148	14	43	10	1	1	8	11	21	3	2	.342	.392
Minor League Totals			.256	192	695	90	178	27	4	3	49	88	121	13	12	.337	.319

San Diego Padres

BY MATT EDDY

A drian Gonzalez anchored the Padres lineup from 2006 through 2010, producing at a rate on par with any hitter in the National League this side of Albert Pujols.

Despite Gonzalez's contributions, San Diego finished in the bottom half of the NL in scoring in all five seasons, finishing as high as ninth in 2007 but plummeting to the bottom in the subsequent two seasons. The Padres won the NL West in Gonzalez's first season in San Diego, finished well out of the money in two other years, and missed the playoffs by one excruciating game in the other two seasons.

With one of those near-misses fresh in mind, the organization made the difficult decision to trade Gonzalez, a San Diego native in the final year of his contract. The Red Sox long had been viewed as natural trading partners because so many Boston expatriates populate the San Diego front office, from general manager Jed Hoyer to assistant GM Jason McLeod to vice president of baseball operations Josh Byrnes. The two sides ultimately consummated a deal in December that sent Gonzalez to Boston for righthander Casey Kelly, first baseman Anthony Rizzo, center fielder Reymond Fuentes and veteran Eric Patterson.

Kelly and Rizzo finished 2010 in Double-A and ranked as Boston's best pitching and hitting prospect at the time of the trade. McLeod drafted them and Fuentes in his former role as Red Sox scouting director, taking Kelly and Fuentes with first-round picks in 2008 and '09.

The Padres are seeking to put together enough offense to back up their consistently good pitching, which carried them to the top of the NL West for the better part of 2010. San Diego roared to a 76-49 start and held a 6½-game division lead on Aug. 25. The Padres lost 10 games in a row, scoring a grand total of 23 runs, to allow the Giants back into the race. San Francisco moved into first place on Sept. 10 and went on to win the division and the World Series.

San Diego's Bud Black still earned NL manager of the year honors because his team's performance defied all reasonable expectations. Led by Mat Latos, the young pitching staff allowed the fewest runs in the major leagues.

In an effort to find some hitting, San Diego used its pitching excess to execute three trades in 2010. At the trade deadline, the Padres swapped Nick Greenwood to the Cardinals and Corey Kluber to the Indians in

Mat Latos emerged as one of the game's dominant young arms, going 14-10, 2.92

LARRY GOREN

TOP 30 PROSPECTS

1. Casey Kelly, rhp	**16.** Edinson Rincon, 3b
2. Anthony Rizzo, 1b	**17.** Juan Oramas, lhp
3. Simon Castro, rhp	**18.** Rymer Liriano, of
4. Reymond Fuentes, of	**19.** Jose DePaula, lhp
5. Matt Lollis, rhp	**20.** Keyvius Sampson, rhp
6. Cory Luebke, lhp	**21.** Zach Cates, rhp
7. Jaff Decker, of	**22.** Anthony Bass, rhp
8. Donavan Tate, of	**23.** Adys Portillo, rhp
9. Drew Cumberland, ss/2b	**24.** Everett Williams, of
10. Jason Hagerty, c	**25.** Johnny Barbato, rhp
11. Jedd Gyorko, 3b	**26.** Jerry Sullivan, rhp
12. James Darnell, 3b	**27.** George Kontos, rhp
13. Logan Forsythe, 2b	**28.** Jeudy Valdez, 2b/ss
14. Blake Tekotte, of	**29.** Nick Schmidt, lhp
15. Jeremy Hefner, rhp	**30.** Brad Brach, rhp

a three-team deal that netted Ryan Ludwick, and sent Wynn Pelzer to the Orioles for Miguel Tejada. In November, they parted with Edward Mujica and Ryan Webb to acquire Cameron Maybin from the Marlins.

The Padres had to look outside the organization for offense because their farm system doesn't look up to the task. San Diego used 10 first-round or supplemental first-round picks on position players from 2006-09, and not one projects as a surefire big league regular. Outfielder Donavan Tate, the No. 3 overall pick in 2009, has struggled to stay healthy since signing for a club-record $6.25 million.

General Manager: Jed Hoyer. **Farm Director:** Randy Smith. **Scouting Director:** Jaron Madison.

Class	Team	League	W	L	PCT	Finish*	Manager
Majors	San Diego Padres	National	90	72	.556	5th (16)	Bud Black
Triple-A	Portland Beavers	Pacific Coast	59	85	.410	15th (16)	Terry Kennedy
Double-A	San Antonio Missions	Texas	68	72	.486	6th (8)	Doug Dascenzo
High A	Lake Elsinore Storm	California	81	59	.579	1st (10)	Carlos Lezcano
Low A	Fort Wayne TinCaps	Midwest	77	63	.550	5th (16)	Jose Flores
Short-season	Eugene Emeralds	Northwest	32	44	.421	6th (8)	Greg Riddoch
Rookie	AZL Padres	Arizona	20	35	.364	12th (12)	Ivan Cruz
Overall 2010 Minor League Record			337	358	.485	t-23rd (30)	

*Finish in overall standings (No. of teams in league). †League champion.
*Triple-A affiliate is moving to Tucson (Pacific Coast) in 2011.

LAST YEAR'S TOP 30

Player, Pos.		Status
1.	Donavan Tate, of	No. 8
2.	Simon Castro, rhp	No. 3
3.	James Darnell, 3b	No. 12
4.	Jaff Decker, of	No. 7
5.	Logan Forsythe, 3b	No. 13
6.	Cory Luebke, lhp	No. 6
7.	Wynn Pelzer, rhp	(Orioles)
8.	Everett Williams, of	No. 24
9.	Edinson Rincon, 3b	No. 16
10.	Aaron Poreda, lhp	Dropped out
11.	Drew Cumberland, ss	No. 9
12.	Keyvius Sampson, rhp	No. 20
13.	Adys Portillo, rhp	No. 23
14.	Rymer Liriano, of	No. 18
15.	Lance Zawadzki, ss/3b	(Royals)
16.	Kellen Kulbacki, of	Dropped out
17.	Blake Tekotte, of	No. 14
18.	Jeremy Hefner, rhp	No. 15
19.	Jerry Sullivan, rhp	No. 26
20.	Craig Italiano, rhp	Dropped out
21.	Chad Huffman, of/1b	(Indians)
22.	Jorge Reyes, rhp	Dropped out
23.	Cedric Hunter, of	Dropped out
24.	Ryan Webb, rhp	(Marlins)
25.	Luis Durango, of	Dropped out
26.	Cesar Ramos, lhp	Dropped out
27.	Matt Antonelli, 2b	(Nationals)
28.	Dexter Carter, rhp	Dropped out
29.	Matt Clark, 1b	Dropped out
30.	Cole Figueroa, ss/2b	Dropped out

BEST TOOLS

Best Hitter for Average	Drew Cumberland
Best Power Hitter	Anthony Rizzo
Best Strike-Zone Discipline	Logan Forsythe
Fastest Baserunner	Luis Durango
Best Athlete	Donavan Tate
Best Fastball	Eugenio Reyes
Best Curveball	Casey Kelly
Best Slider	Simon Castro
Best Changeup	Josh Spence
Best Control	Anthony Bass
Best Defensive Catcher	Luis Martinez
Best Defensive Infielder	Beamer Weems
Best Infield Arm	Edinson Rincon
Best Defensive Outfielder	Rico Noel
Best Outfield Arm	Rymer Liriano

PROJECTED 2014 LINEUP

Catcher	Jason Hagerty
First Base	Anthony Rizzo
Second Base	Drew Cumberland
Third Base	Chase Headley
Shortstop	Everth Cabrera
Left Field	Jaff Decker
Center Field	Reymond Fuentes
Right Field	Will Venable
No. 1 Starter	Mat Latos
No. 2 Starter	Casey Kelly
No. 3 Starter	Simon Castro
No. 4 Starter	Cory Luebke
No. 5 Starter	Clayton Richard
Closer	Heath Bell

TOP PROSPECTS OF THE DECADE

Year	Player, Pos.	2010 Org.
2001	Sean Burroughs, 3b	Out of baseball
2002	Sean Burroughs, 3b	Out of baseball
2003	Xavier Nady, of	Cubs
2004	Josh Barfield, 2b	Padres
2005	Josh Barfield, 2b	Padres
2006	Cesar Carrillo, rhp	Astros
2007	Cedric Hunter, of	Padres
2008	Chase Headley, 3b	Padres
2009	Kyle Blanks, 1b	Padres
2010	Donavan Tate, of	Padres

TOP DRAFT PICKS OF THE DECADE

Year	Player, Pos.	2010 Org.
2001	Jake Gautreau, 2b	Out of baseball
2002	Khalil Greene, ss	Out of baseball
2003	Tim Stauffer, rhp	Padres
2004	Matt Bush, ss	Rays
2005	Cesar Carrillo, rhp	Astros
2006	Matt Antonelli, 3b	Padres
2007	Nick Schmidt, lhp	Padres
2008	Allan Dykstra, 1b	Padres
2009	Donavan Tate, of	Padres
2010	*Karsten Whitson, rhp	University of Florida

*Did not sign.

LARGEST BONUSES IN CLUB HISTORY

Donavan Tate, 2009	$6,250,000
Matt Bush, 2004	$3,150,000
Mark Phillips, 2000	$2,200,000
Sean Burroughs, 1998	$2,100,000
Adys Portillo, 2008	$2,000,000

SAN DIEGO PADRES

TOP 2011 ROOKIE: Cory Luebke, lhp. He'll be 26 years old and his ceiling isn't huge, but he has the stuff to thrive in spacious Petco Park.

BREAKOUT PROSPECT: Jose DePaula, lhp. Recovered from a stress fracture in his elbow, he shows a promising three-pitch mix.

SLEEPER: Eugenio Reyes, rhp. He touches 97 mph and reminds some scouts of Simon Castro at the same age (20)—with the ugly ERA (5.89) to match.

SOURCE OF TOP 30 TALENT

Homegrown	26	Acquired	4
College	11	Trades	3
Junior college	2	Rule 5 draft	1
High school	6	Independent leagues	0
Draft-and-follow	0	Free agents/waivers	0
Nondrafted free agents	0		
International	7		

LF
Jaff Decker (7)
Edinson Rincon (16)
Luis Domoromo
Dan Robertson
Kellen Kulbacki
Houston Slemp

CF
Reymond Fuentes (4)
Donavan Tate (8)
Blake Tekotte (14)
Everett Williams (24)
Luis Durango
Cedric Hunter
Rico Noel
Edwin Moreno

RF
Rymer Liriano (18)
Mike Baxter
Sawyer Carroll
Jose Dore
Corey Adamson

3B
Jedd Gyorko (11)
James Darnell (12)
Vince Belnome
Duanel Jones

SS
Jeudy Valdez (28)
Jonathan Galvez
Beamer Weems
Brian Guinn

2B
Drew Cumberland (9)
Logan Forsythe (13)
Cole Figueroa
Chris Bisson

1B
Anthony Rizzo (2)
Matt Clark
Nate Freiman
Cody Decker
Allan Dykstra

C
Jason Hagerty (10)
Luis Martinez
Robert Lara
Emmanuel Quiles
Tommy Medica

RHP

RHSP	RHRP
Casey Kelly (1)	George Kontos (27)
Simon Castro (3)	Brad Brach (30)
Matt Lollis (5)	Evan Scribner
Jeremy Hefner (15)	Brandon Gomes
Keyvius Sampson (20)	Miles Mikolas
Zach Cates (21)	Alexis Lara
Anthony Bass (22)	Bryan Oland
Adys Portillo (23)	Aaron Breit
Johnny Barbato (25)	Robert Poutier
Jerry Sullivan (26)	Matt Buschmann
Eugenio Reyes	Chris Franklin
Jorge Reyes	
Dexter Carter	
Erik Davis	
Tyler Norwood	

LHP

LHSP	LHRP
Cory Luebke (6)	Cesar Ramos
Juan Oramas (17)	Aaron Poreda
Jose DePaula (19)	Colt Hynes
Nick Schmidt (29)	Rob Musgrave
Josh Spence	
Nate Culp	
Michael Watt	

2010
BONUSES: $4.3 MILLION

BEST PURE HITTER: One of the top-rated bats in the draft, 3B Jedd Gyorko (2) has the swing, approach and discipline to hit for a high average. He batted .302/.372/.444 in his pro debut between short-season Eugene and low Class A Fort Wayne.

BEST POWER HITTER: OF Jose Dore's (8) strong wrists give him above-average raw power. He also has a plus-plus arm in right field.

FASTEST RUNNER: The Padres grabbed three well above-average runners in 2B Chris Bisson (4), OF Rico Noel (5) and SS Brian Guinn (11). Noel's speed plays best on the diamond. He led NCAA Division I in steals in each of the last two seasons, and swiped 17 bases in 44 pro games.

BEST DEFENSIVE PLAYER: Not only can Noel steal bases almost at will, but he can run down most balls in center field. He has a solid arm, too.

BEST FASTBALL: RHP Zach Cates (3) sits at 92-94 mph and peaks at 96. Signed for $765,000, he was primarily a catcher as a Northeast Texas CC freshman in 2009. RHP Johnny Barbato (6), who cost $1.4 million, works at 89-92 but touches 94-95.

BEST SECONDARY PITCH: Cates' changeup can be as devastating as his fastball. LHP Josh Spence's (9) slider is the best breaking ball in this group, and he also has superlative command. Barbato's curveball projects as a potential plus pitch.

BEST PRO DEBUT: Gyorko, who also had 17 doubles and seven home runs in his 268 at-bats.

BEST ATHLETE: Bisson. In addition to his speed, he has some pop (though he gets too power-conscious at times) and fine infield actions.

MOST INTRIGUING BACKGROUND: 1B Connor Powers' (21) father John, an offensive lineman, was a seventh-round pick by the New York Giants in the 1981 NFL draft. C Rocky Gale's (24) dad Paul is the head coach at Corban (Ore.) and an area scout for the Astros. Unsigned 3B Jacoby Almaraz' (28) father Johnny is the Braves' director of international operations.

CLOSEST TO THE MAJORS: Gyorko will begin his first full season in high Class A and could finish the year in Double-A.

BEST LATE-ROUND PICK: Guinn, an athletic switch-hitter who could be a steal if he hits enough. RHP Tyler Norwood (19) has an intriguing 89-93 mph sinker.

THE ONE WHO GOT AWAY: The Padres believed they had a predraft deal to sign RHP Karsten Whitson (1) for slot money, but his asking price rose to $2.7 million. He took his plus fastball and slider to Florida after turning down $2.1 million. They offered nearly as much to RHP A.J. Vanegas (7) but couldn't divert him from Stanford. San Diego also made a run at 1B Sean Dwyer (15), who has a lot of offensive upside, only to lose him to Florida Gulf Coast.

ASSESSMENT: Not signing their first-round pick Whitson was a blow, but the Padres still think they got value out of their draft. The organization valued Gyorko and Cates as first/sandwich-round talents and stockpiled some speed.

2009
BONUSES: $9.1 MILLION

The good news is that RHP Matt Lollis (15) has quickly blossomed into the top prospect from this crop. The bad news is that he passed OFs Donavan Tate (1) and Everett Williams (2) and RHP Keyvious Sampson (4), who cost a combined $7.6 million.

GRADE: C

2008
BONUSES: $5.4 MILLION

The Padres whiffed on 1B Allan Dykstra (1) and rue not signing 2B Jason Kipnis (4), but they still found several of their best position prospects in OF Jaff Decker (1s), 2B Logan Forsythe (1s), 3B James Darnell (2) and OF Blake Tekotte (3).

GRADE: C+

2007
BONUSES: $5.9 MILLION

San Diego didn't make the most of having six picks before the second round, with only SS/2B Drew Cumberland (1s) and LHP Cory Luebke (1s) looking like keepers. RHP Wynn Pelzer (9) brought back Miguel Tejada in a trade last summer. Unsigned SS Christian Colon (10) went on to become the No. 4 overall pick in 2010.

GRADE: C+

2006
BONUSES: $6.3 MILLION

Draft-and-follow RHP Mat Latos (11) has become the Padres' ace, and LHP Wade LeBlanc (2) has contributed to the rotation as well. 3B David Freese (9) is a semiregular in St. Louis after getting traded for Jim Edmonds. 2B Matt Antonelli (1) and OF/1B Chad Huffman (2) have played in the majors but are no longer with the organization.

GRADE: A

Draft analysis by Jim Callis. Numbers in parentheses indicate draft rounds.

CASEY KELLY, RHP

Born: Oct. 4, 1989. **Bats:** R. **Throws:** R.
Height: 6-3. **Weight:** 210. **Drafted:** HS—
Sarasota, Fla., 2008 (1st round). **Signed by:**
Anthony Turco (Red Sox).

PROSPECT 1

KEN BABITT

Kelly was one of the top two-way players in the 2008 draft coming out of high school, but his high asking price and scholarship to play quarterback at Tennessee made him available to the Red Sox with the 30th overall pick. They viewed him as the most polished high school arm in the draft and signed him for $3 million, a franchise record for a draftee. The son of former big league catcher Pat Kelly, Casey preferred playing every day to pitching, and Boston agreed to let him make his debut at shortstop. He didn't pitch professionally until 2009, then switched back to shortstop after appearing in the Futures Game. But after Kelly hit .219 in two pro seasons and .171 in the '09 Arizona Fall League, he agreed that his future was on the mound. The Red Sox assigned him to Double-A last year, where at 20 he was the youngest starting pitcher in the Eastern League. Boston shut him down as a precaution when he strained a lat muscle in early August. In December, the Red Sox traded Kelly to the Padres as the centerpiece of a four-player package for Adrian Gonzalez.

Boston attributed Kelly's struggles in 2010 to him having to learn how to harness an increase in velocity and make his mechanics work as his frame started to mature. His fastball now ranges from 89-93 mph and peaks at 96. He showed the ability to consistently locate his fastball on both corners with sink in 2009 but didn't command it as well in 2010. With his fluid, athletic delivery, Kelly should regain that skill once he fully grows into his body. A cracked nail on the middle finger of his right hand also dogged him all season and affected his command. While his fastball isn't a true swing-and-miss offering, his above-average 83-84 mph changeup often is—though he became over-reliant on it last year. Batters tend to swing right over the top of the change because he delivers it with the same arm speed and slot as his fastball. His curveball is a power breaking ball at times, and more of an average pitch that he just gets over for strikes at others. Kelly has an advanced feel for pitching, though he needs to trust his stuff and challenge hitters more rather than trying to live on the corners.

The Padres envision Kelly becoming a frontline starter with three possible plus pitches and above-average command. He should reach Triple-A Tucson at some point in 2011, perhaps even to start the season, and his big league ETA is 2012.

SCOUTING GRADES

Fastball: 60. **Command/**
Curveball: 60. **Control:** 65.
Changeup: 60. **Delivery:** 65.

Based on 20-80 scouting scale, where 50 represents major league average, and future projection rather than present tools.

Year	Club (League)	Class	W	L	ERA	G	GS	CG	SV	IP	H	HR	BB	SO	G/A	WHIP	AVG
2009	Salem (CAR)	HiA	1	4	3.09	8	8	0	0	47	33	4	7	35	1.33	0.86	.196
	Greenville (SAL)	LoA	6	1	1.12	9	9	0	0	48	32	0	9	39	1.94	0.85	.184
2010	Portland (EL)	AA	3	5	5.31	21	21	0	0	95	118	10	35	81	1.54	1.61	.307
Minor League Totals			10	10	3.69	38	38	0	0	190	183	14	51	155	1.58	1.23	.252

Year	Club (League)	Class	AVG	G	AB	R	H	2B	3B	HR	RBI	BB	SO	SB	CS	OBP	SLG
2008	Red Sox (GCL)	R	.173	27	98	10	17	5	0	1	9	6	34	1	0	.229	.255
	Lowell (NYP)	SS	.344	9	32	5	11	5	1	0	4	0	8	0	1	.344	.563
2009	Red Sox (GCL)	R	.214	8	28	4	6	1	0	2	6	3	10	1	0	.290	.464
	Greenville (SAL)	LoA	.224	32	134	18	30	7	1	1	10	16	39	0	1	.305	.313
Minor League Totals			.219	76	292	37	64	18	2	4	29	25	91	2	2	.282	.336

2 ANTHONY RIZZO, 1B

RODGER WOOD

Born: Aug. 8, 1989. **B-T:** L-L. **Ht.:** 6-3. **Wt.:** 220. **Drafted:** HS—Parkland, Fla., 2007 (6th round). **Signed by:** Laz Gutierrez (Red Sox).

Rizzo was hitting .373 in low Class A in April 2008 when he was diagnosed with limited stage classical Hodgkin's lymphoma. After missing the rest of that season to get treatment, he has been cancer-free. He established himself as the best offensive prospect in the Red Sox system prior to his inclusion in Adrian Gonzalez trade. Rizzo generates plus power with strength and leverage. He drives the ball well to the opposite field and last season began pulling pitches for home runs. With his willingness to use the entire field and his patience, he should hit for a solid average and draw some walks, though he needs to refine his two-strike approach. He also must make adjustments against lefthanders after hitting .217/.290/.380 against them in 2010. Managers rated him the best defensive first baseman in the Eastern League, as he has smooth actions and does a good job of picking throws out of the dirt. He can get nonchalant in the field, however, which led to 15 errors last season. He's a below-average runner but moves well for his size. With Gonzalez out of the picture in San Diego, Rizzo projects as the organization's first baseman of the future. He'll spend much of 2011 in Triple-A and could push for a big league job the following season.

Year	Club (League)	Class	AVG	G	AB	R	H	2B	3B	HR	RBI	BB	SO	SB	CS	OBP	SLG
2007	Red Sox (GCL)	R	.286	6	21	6	6	0	0	1	3	1	2	0	0	.375	.429
2008	Greenville (SAL)	LoA	.373	21	83	9	31	6	0	0	11	3	15	0	0	.402	.446
2009	Greenville (SAL)	LoA	.298	64	245	40	73	21	0	9	42	25	60	2	1	.365	.494
	Salem (CAR)	HiA	.295	55	200	23	59	16	0	3	24	25	39	2	0	.371	.420
2010	Salem (CAR)	HiA	.248	29	117	26	29	12	0	5	20	16	32	3	0	.333	.479
	Portland (EL)	AA	.263	107	414	66	109	30	0	20	80	45	100	7	1	.334	.481
Minor League Totals			.284	282	1080	170	307	85	0	38	180	115	248	14	2	.354	.469

3 SIMON CASTRO, RHP

Born: April 9, 1988. **B-T:** R-R. **Ht.:** 6-5. **Wt.:** 210. **Signed:** Dominican Republic, 2006. **Signed by:** Randy Smith/Felix Francisco.

Castro led the low Class A Midwest League with 157 strikeouts in 2009, so the Padres felt comfortable jumping him to Double-A San Antonio last season. He was up to the challenge, topping the Texas League in WHIP (1.10) and opponent average (.223) while ranking second in ERA (2.92). He also started for the World Team at the Futures Game, allowing two runs in an inning of work. Big and durable, Castro has an ideal pitcher's build that has been likened to that of a young Jose Contreras. He sits at 91-93 mph and tops out near 95 with tailing action and occasional late sink. He relies on his 82-84 mph slider as a second pitch, and it features three-quarters break when he catches it right. He wears out the bottom of the zone with both pitches. Castro shows a feel for a sinking changeup that has average potential, though it still needs refinement. He has a long arm swing in the back of his delivery, but he repeats his mechanics well and throws strikes. Newly added to the 40-man roster, Castro is on track to begin 2011 in Triple-A and could be ready for a second-half promotion to San Diego. He profiles as a mid-rotation starter, but some scouts view his ultimate ceiling as a No. 2, which he could reach with improved command.

Year	Club (League)	Class	W	L	ERA	G	GS	CG	SV	IP	H	HR	BB	SO	G/A	WHIP	AVG
2006	Padres (DSL)	R	1	3	4.63	12	12	0	0	47	40	2	21	58	—	1.31	.219
2007	Padres (AZL)	R	2	6	6.22	14	12	0	0	51	61	4	30	55	—	1.80	.298
2008	Eugene (NWL)	SS	2	3	3.99	15	15	0	0	65	54	3	29	64	—	1.27	.223
2009	Fort Wayne (MWL)	LoA	10	6	3.33	28	27	1	0	140	118	9	37	157	0.81	1.10	.226
2010	San Antonio (TL)	AA	7	6	2.92	24	23	0	0	130	107	8	36	107	1.35	1.10	.223
	Portland (PCL)	AAA	0	1	7.84	2	2	0	0	10	16	1	6	6	1.18	2.13	.333
Minor League Totals			22	25	3.88	95	91	1	0	443	396	27	159	447	1.04	1.25	.236

4 REYMOND FUENTES, OF

RODGER WOOD

Born: Feb. 12, 1991. **B-T:** L-L. **Ht.:** 6-0. **Wt.:** 170. **Drafted:** HS—Manati, P.R., 2009 (1st round). **Signed by:** Edgar Perez (Red Sox).

The Red Sox made Fuentes the sixth Puerto Rican ever drafted in the first round, and the first since the Blue Jays' Miguel Negron in 2000, when they selected him 28th overall in 2009. Signed for $1.134 million, he held his own in low Class A at age 19 last season. He came to San Diego in the Adrian Gonzalez trade in December. Fuentes ranks among the best athletes in the system. His plus-plus speed gives him impact potential in center field and on the bases, where he stole 42 bases in 47 attempts in 2010. Managers rated Fuentes as the best defensive outfielder in the South Atlantic League, though he relies more on raw speed now to cover for mistakes. He enhances his quickness by getting great jumps on balls, and he compensates for a below-average arm by charging balls and making accurate throws. Fuentes has a line-drive stroke, and his bat speed portends some future pop once he adds some much-needed strength. He's still learning the strike zone but made positive adjustments in the second half of 2010. Though Fuentes may need four or five seasons in the minors, his upside makes him worth the wait. He has similar tools to Jacoby Ellsbury, and he's a more advanced hitter at the same stage and should become a better defender. Fuentes will spend 2011 at high Class A Lake Elsinore.

Year	Club (League)	Class	AVG	G	AB	R	H	2B	3B	HR	RBI	BB	SO	SB	CS	OBP	SLG
2009	Red Sox (GCL)	R	.290	40	145	16	42	6	2	1	14	7	24	9	5	.331	.379
2010	Greenville (SAL)	LoA	.270	104	374	59	101	15	5	5	41	25	87	42	5	.328	.377
Minor League Totals			.276	144	519	75	143	21	7	6	55	32	111	51	10	.329	.378

5 MATT LOLLIS, RHP

Born: Sept. 11, 1990. **B-T:** R-R. **Ht.:** 6-7. **Wt.:** 280. **Drafted:** Riverside (Calif.) CC, 2009 (15th round). **Signed by:** Pete DeYoung.

The Padres doled out a club-record $9.1 million in draft bonuses in 2009, and so far the player from that crop who has made the biggest impression is a relatively unknown 15th-rounder who signed for $100,000. Lollis started 2010 at short-season Eugene, allowed 10 earned runs in nine starts for low Class A Fort Wayne after a promotion and finished the year with a strong playoff start for Lake Elsinore. Lollis throws four pitches, with his high three-quarters arm slot affording him good plane on a 92-93 mph fastball that peaks at 95. San Diego typically asks pitchers to focus on one breaking ball, but it has allowed him to throw both a hard slider and a knuckle-curve that features 12-to-6 break. He still is building confidence in his changeup, a distant fourth pitch in his repertoire. Nicknamed "Big Country" because of his gigantic frame, Lollis nonetheless shows surprising athleticism and a nuanced feel for his craft, which allow him to fill the strike zone with ease. He has quick feet, belying his size, but he'll have to monitor his conditioning carefully so his body doesn't get out of control. Lollis has mid-rotation potential if his changeup develops. He'll begin the 2011 season back in high Class A.

Year	Club (League)	Class	W	L	ERA	G	GS	CG	SV	IP	H	HR	BB	SO	G/A	WHIP	AVG
2009	Padres (AZL)	R	0	0	5.19	6	0	0	0	9	11	1	2	7	2.17	1.50	.297
2010	Eugene (NWL)	SS	2	2	2.86	6	6	0	0	35	21	0	8	24	1.35	0.84	.175
	Fort Wayne (MWL)	LoA	5	2	1.66	9	9	0	0	54	47	3	13	45	1.10	1.10	.234
Minor League Totals			7	4	2.40	21	15	0	0	98	79	4	23	76	1.27	1.04	.221

6 CORY LUEBKE, LHP

Born: March 4, 1985. **B-T:** R-L. **Ht.:** 6-4. **Wt.:** 215. **Drafted:** Ohio State, 2007 (1st round supplemental). **Signed by:** Jeff Stewart.

Luebke broke out in 2009, a season that culminated with him starting Team USA's gold-medal game victory against Cuba at the World Cup. He got a late start in 2010 after straining his oblique in spring training, but he breezed through Double-A and Triple-A upon his return in late May, paving the way for a September callup to San Diego. Luebke throws three pitches for strikes, competes well and has the low-maintenance delivery that stems from solid athleticism. He locates his fastball to both sides of the plate, sitting at 88-90 mph and touching 92 with tailing action. His best attribute may be the downhill plane he generates on his heater. Luebke's out pitch a slurvy slider that often shows three-quarters rotation and rates as a tick above-average. He has made progress with his fading changeup, but he throws it in the same low-80s range as his breaking ball, so the Padres would like to see him soften the changeup further. Luebke has all the ingredients to pitch in the middle of a big league rotation, which San Diego entrusted him to do in the thick of the National League West race last September. He pitched well, positioning himself as a leading candidate for a rotation spot in 2011.

Year	Club (League)	Class	W	L	ERA	G	GS	CG	SV	IP	H	HR	BB	SO	G/A	WHIP	AVG
2007	Eugene (NWL)	SS	3	0	1.46	8	3	0	0	25	18	2	2	26	—	0.81	.194
	Fort Wayne (MWL)	LoA	1	2	3.33	5	5	0	0	27	29	2	5	30	—	1.26	.269
	Lake Elsinore (CAL)	HiA	1	1	7.71	2	1	0	0	7	10	1	1	5	—	1.57	.357
2008	Lake Elsinore (CAL)	HiA	3	6	6.84	17	15	0	0	72	97	8	23	60	—	1.66	.323
	Fort Wayne (MWL)	LoA	3	3	2.89	10	10	0	0	56	52	6	9	40	—	1.09	.265
2009	Lake Elsinore (CAL)	HiA	8	2	2.34	14	14	1	0	88	73	3	17	80	1.87	1.02	.227
	San Antonio (TL)	AA	3	2	3.70	9	9	0	0	41	38	3	15	32	0.78	1.28	.241
2010	San Antonio (TL)	AA	5	1	2.40	10	8	1	0	56	41	2	12	44	1.04	0.94	.200
	Portland (PCL)	AAA	5	0	2.97	9	9	0	0	58	42	6	17	44	1.09	1.02	.201
	San Diego (NL)	MAJ	1	1	4.08	4	3	0	0	18	17	3	6	18	1.33	1.30	.246
Major League Totals			1	1	4.08	4	3	0	0	18	17	3	6	18	1.33	1.30	.246
Minor League Totals			32	17	3.49	84	74	2	0	431	400	33	101	361	1.22	1.16	.247

7 JAFF DECKER, OF

Born: Feb. 23, 1990. **B-T:** L-L. **Ht.:** 5-10. **Wt.:** 190. **Drafted:** HS—Peoria, Ariz., 2008 (1st round supplemental). **Signed by:** Dave Lottsfeldt.

Decker won Rookie-level Arizona League MVP honors after signing for $892,000 as a sandwich pick in 2008, then encored by leading the Midwest League in OPS (.956) as a teenager in 2009. He logged just 79 games last year, sitting out until mid-May with a hamstring injury and then missing the last three weeks after an errant pitch broke his right hand. Decker has a compact, powerful stroke when he doesn't try to force the issue. He pressed in the first half of 2010, batting .195 with an uncharacteristic 8-41 BB-K ratio, but his bat came alive in the second half, when he hit .305/.439/.616 with 14 homers. His hand-eye coordination and strike-zone awareness give him a chance to hit for average, and he uses his hips and shoulders well to generate power to all fields. Decker's lack of athleticism is still an issue, but he got in better shape last year and improved his speed, though it's still below-average. He never will be more than playable on an outfield corner, but he throws well enough to handle right field. The new Padres regime concedes that Decker's bat will play bigger than it initially expected, a belief reinforced by his recent dedication to conditioning. He's on track for a promotion to Double-A and a potential big league starting gig at some point in 2012.

Year	Club (League)	Class	AVG	G	AB	R	H	2B	3B	HR	RBI	BB	SO	SB	CS	OBP	SLG
2008	Padres (AZL)	R	.352	49	159	51	56	11	2	5	34	55	36	9	1	.523	.541
	Eugene (NWL)	SS	.200	3	10	2	2	0	0	0	0	2	5	0	0	.333	.200
2009	Fort Wayne (MWL)	LoA	.299	104	358	78	107	25	2	16	64	85	92	10	6	.442	.514
2010	Lake Elsinore (CAL)	HiA	.262	79	290	53	76	14	2	17	58	47	80	5	4	.374	.500
Minor League Totals			.295	235	817	184	241	50	6	38	156	189	213	24	11	.435	.510

8 DONAVAN TATE, OF

Born: Sept. 27, 1990. **B-T:** R-R. **Ht.:** 6-3. **Wt.:** 203. **Drafted:** HS—Cartersville, Ga., 2009 (1st round). **Signed by:** Ash Lawson.

Tate signed for $6.25 million as the 2009 draft's No. 3 overall choice, setting a bonus standard for high school position players and Padres picks, but he has been beset by injuries and illnesses since. He had sports hernia surgery and a broken jaw in 2009, then contended with concussion-like symptoms (from a beaning) and a tweaked shoulder (after diving for a ball) in extended spring training last year. He didn't make a full-season club and played in just 25 games in the Arizona League as he battled a stomach virus. Tate's athleticism is obvious, but he hasn't played enough to properly showcase his talent. His plus raw power was his most evident tool in 2010. He runs very well and ranges gracefully to both gaps in center field. His arm grades as above-average. Tate did nothing to allay concerns about his feel for hitting in the AZL, where he struck out in nearly half of his at-bats with a swing that loops through the hitting zone. He tends to tilt his shoulders forward when he loads, which pushes his back elbow up and sets his stroke off kilter. Tate won MVP honors at the Padres' instructional league program, and San Diego hope he'll use that as a stepping stone to low Class A in 2011. His ceiling remains high, but he's not even the best center-field prospect in the system after Reymond Fuentes arrived in the Adrian Gonzalez trade.

Year	Club (League)	Class	AVG	G	AB	R	H	2B	3B	HR	RBI	BB	SO	SB	CS	OBP	SLG
2010	Padres (AZL)	R	.222	25	90	19	20	5	0	2	10	15	41	7	1	.336	.344
Minor League Totals			.222	25	90	19	20	5	0	2	10	15	41	7	1	.336	.344

9 DREW CUMBERLAND, SS/2B

Born: Jan. 13, 1989. **B-T:** L-R. **Ht.:** 5-10. **Wt.:** 175. **Drafted:** HS—Pace, Fla., 2007 (1st round supplemental). **Signed by:** Bob Filotei.

Cumberland ranked fourth in the minors in batting (.365) when he was promoted to Double-A last June. Fifteen games into his time with San Antonio, he slid into a railing and sustained a deep laceration to his left knee, ending his year. He still has yet to play in more than 77 games in a season while dealing with oblique, finger and hand injuries. Cumberland has three future above-average tools in his ability to hit, run and defend, though he has virtually no power and his arm is inaccurate. His short, quick lefthanded stroke could make him a .290 hitter in the big leagues because he makes contact so easily. With improved plate discipline, he would profile as an effective leadoff hitter. To that end, San Diego challenged him to bunt more and steal more frequently last season, and he stole a career-high 21 bases. Cumberland features soft hands and plus range at shortstop, but he profiles better at second base because his throws tend to sail on him—the result of excessive sideways rotation—when he makes plays from the hole. All of Cumberland's injuries have resulted from all-out play, and the Padres certainly don't want to discourage that behavior. They regard him as a potential regular at the keystone, but for now he'll head back to Double-A as a shortstop.

Year	Club (League)	Class	AVG	G	AB	R	H	2B	3B	HR	RBI	BB	SO	SB	CS	OBP	SLG
2007	Padres (AZL)	R	.318	21	85	16	27	2	1	0	7	7	9	6	1	.389	.365
	Eugene (NWL)	SS	.333	4	18	6	6	1	0	0	0	2	2	0	0	.429	.389
2008	Fort Wayne (MWL)	LoA	.286	53	206	29	59	8	1	1	17	17	24	16	4	.348	.350
	Padres (AZL)	R	.500	3	10	3	5	1	2	0	2	0	1	0	0	.500	1.000
2009	Fort Wayne (MWL)	LoA	.293	77	290	57	85	18	5	2	40	40	36	19	3	.386	.410
2010	Lake Elsinore (CAL)	HiA	.365	60	249	63	91	15	4	7	35	15	34	20	9	.404	.542
	San Antonio (TL)	AA	.278	15	54	5	15	3	0	0	6	1	11	1	2	.298	.333
Minor League Totals			.316	233	912	179	288	48	13	10	107	82	117	62	19	.380	.430

10 JASON HAGERTY, C

Born: Sept. 13, 1987. **B-T:** B-R. **Ht.:** 6-3. **Wt.:** 224. **Drafted:** Miami, 2009 (5th round). **Signed by:** Rob Sidwell.

Hagerty's 2009 pro debut barely registered, as he hit just .225/.335/.399 at Eugene. Part of the problem was that he had to get reacclimated to catching after playing primarily first base during his last two years at Miami in deference to Yasmani Grandal, the 12th overall pick in the 2010 draft. Hagerty improved as much as any Padres farmhand last year, ranking second in the Midwest League in on-base percentage (.424) and third in throwing out basestealers (34 percent). Hagerty has above-average raw power from both sides of the plate, works counts effectively and shows enough athleticism to believe the strides he made last year are sustainable. He may not make enough contact to hit better than .260, and his below-average speed won't help him leg out any hits. Hagerty improved his defense during the course of last season and now projects as an average catcher at the major league level. He has solid arm strength and a smooth transfer to go with natural leadership skills. He could stand to soften his hands while receiving and blocking. Hagerty did everything possible in 2010 to position himself as San Diego's catcher of the future. He'll begin this season in high Class A, with a chance to move quickly to Double-A if he continues to hit.

Year	Club (League)	Class	AVG	G	AB	R	H	2B	3B	HR	RBI	BB	SO	SB	CS	OBP	SLG
2009	Eugene (NWL)	SS	.225	47	173	34	39	12	0	6	26	26	47	0	0	.335	.399
	Portland (PCL)	AAA	.133	5	15	3	2	1	0	0	1	2	4	0	0	.235	.200
2010	Fort Wayne (MWL)	LoA	.302	122	431	74	130	35	3	14	74	88	104	2	1	.423	.494
Minor League Totals			.276	174	619	111	171	48	3	20	101	116	155	2	1	.395	.460

11 JEDD GYORKO, 3B

Born: Sept. 23, 1988. **B-T:** R-R. **Ht.:** 5-10. **Wt.:** 215. **Drafted:** West Virginia, 2010 (2nd round). **Signed by:** Andrew Salvo.

Gyorko played shortstop for West Virginia, but the Padres harbored no illusion of keeping him there as a pro. He shifted to third base after signing for $614,700 as the draft's 59th pick and went on to rank as the short-season Northwest League's No. 3 prospect. Gyorko is unquestionably a bat-first prospect, though he made a smooth transition from short to the hot corner and projects to stay there. He's built more like a catcher than a middle infielder, so he's not a great runner. He's quick enough—especially to his left—while his hands are soft enough and his arm is strong enough to play third base at an average level. Gyorko is geared to hit for average with a short stroke, good balance and an all-fields approach, and some scouts grade his hit tool as high as 65 on the 20-80 scale—or a .290 hitter. He generates plus bat speed despite wrapping his bat before unleashing his swing. That might cap his home run total at 12-15 annually, a tick below-average for a corner player. Scouts have compared Gyorko to Brett Wallace as a bad-bodied college hitter who projects to hit for a average with more gap power than pure home run juice—the type of hitter geared for Petco Park. First he'll have a chance to conquer the high Class A California League in 2011.

Year	Club (League)	Class	AVG	G	AB	R	H	2B	3B	HR	RBI	BB	SO	SB	CS	OBP	SLG
2010	Eugene (NWL)	SS	.330	26	106	16	35	6	0	5	18	9	26	1	1	.383	.528
	Fort Wayne (MWL)	LoA	.284	42	162	19	46	11	0	2	23	19	31	1	0	.366	.389
Minor League Totals			.302	68	268	35	81	17	0	7	41	28	57	2	1	.372	.444

12 JAMES DARNELL, 3B

Born: Jan. 19, 1987. **B-T:** R-R. **Ht.:** 6-2. **Wt.:** 195. **Drafted:** South Carolina, 2008 (2nd round). **Signed by:** Anthony Byrd.

Darnell didn't handle the jump to Double-A, at least at the outset. One season after ranking ninth in the minors with a .424 on-base percentage, he hit just .215 with little power in the first half of the season. He developed a cyst in his right hand, missed five weeks in May and June, and didn't recover his stroke until August, when he batted .349/.432/.547 with 13 extra-base hits and 23 RBIs. Darnell's simple swing and discerning batting eye should allow him to hit for average, while his strength and bat speed suggest at least average power. His work ethic is unquestioned, but San Antonio's pitcher-friendly ballpark muted his production. Reviews of his defense were less positive. Darnell led all TL third basemen with 24 errors, mostly of the throwing variety, and he struggled for the second straight season with footwork and accuracy. His arm is strong, but the majority of Darnell's miscues (31 of 54 in the past two years) have come on throws. He's an average runner who has shown little aptitude for stealing bases. While he might not stick at third base, Darnell has at least average tools across the board and could settle in right field. The Padres would like to see him unleash more aggression when he gets ahead in the count as he faces Triple-A pitchers in 2011.

Year	Club (League)	Class	AVG	G	AB	R	H	2B	3B	HR	RBI	BB	SO	SB	CS	OBP	SLG
2008	Eugene (NWL)	SS	.373	16	67	9	25	6	1	2	15	11	12	1	1	.462	.582
2009	Fort Wayne (MWL)	LoA	.329	66	222	40	73	17	2	7	38	57	51	5	5	.468	.518
	Lake Elsinore (CAL)	HiA	.294	60	235	40	69	18	2	13	43	30	38	3	1	.377	.553
2010	Fort Wayne (MWL)	LoA	.360	7	25	5	9	4	0	1	8	5	4	0	0	.500	.640
	San Antonio (TL)	AA	.265	101	373	46	99	21	1	10	50	44	64	2	0	.348	.408
Minor League Totals			.298	250	922	140	275	66	6	33	154	147	169	11	7	.399	.490

13 LOGAN FORSYTHE, 2B

Born: Jan. 14, 1987. **B-T:** R-R. **Ht.:** 6-1. **Wt.:** 205. **Drafted:** Arkansas, 2008 (1st round supplemental). **Signed by:** Lane Decker.

Forsythe ranked second in the minors with 102 walks in 2009, and he might have approached that total again last year had he not missed five weeks early in the season. He still managed to lead the Texas League with 75 walks. Forsythe broke his right hand in late April after he punched a bat rack in frustration, but in San Antonio's suppressive Wolff Stadium, he had much to be frustrated about. He batted just .189/.300/.245 in 55 home games. The Padres shifted Forsythe from third base to the keystone to free up an organizational logjam, allowing James Darnell to play third in Double-A, Vince Belnome to play there in high Class A and Edinson Rincon to man the position in low Class A. Despite leading TL second basemen with 15 errors, Forsythe showed plenty of range and a strong arm. He played all over the infield as an amateur, and his line-drive stroke profiles best at second base. With a quick bat and discerning eye, he ought to hit for a modest average. The ball carries off Forsythe's bat, though he has just gap power that could translate into 12-15 home runs in the big leagues. He's a below-average runner, but San Diego encouraged him to run more frequently and he stole a career-high 17 bases. Forsythe will contend with Drew Cumberland to be the organization's second baseman of the future, and he'll have a head start on him when he begins 2011 in Triple-A.

Year	Club (League)	Class	AVG	G	AB	R	H	2B	3B	HR	RBI	BB	SO	SB	CS	OBP	SLG
2008	Eugene (NWL)	SS	.333	3	9	2	3	1	0	0	0	1	3	0	0	.455	.444
	Padres (AZL)	R	.231	9	26	2	6	0	0	0	0	5	8	0	0	.429	.231
2009	Lake Elsinore (CAL)	HiA	.322	66	236	46	76	13	3	8	30	61	48	6	2	.472	.504
	San Antonio (TL)	AA	.279	66	244	37	68	9	3	3	31	41	63	5	0	.384	.377
2010	San Antonio (TL)	AA	.253	107	392	66	99	22	1	3	38	75	95	17	5	.377	.337
Minor League Totals			.278	251	907	153	252	45	7	14	99	183	217	28	7	.407	.389

14 BLAKE TEKOTTE, OF

Born: May 24, 1987. **B-T:** L-R. **Ht.:** 5-11. **Wt.:** 175. **Drafted:** Miami, 2008 (3rd round). **Signed by:** Rob Sidwell.

Tekotte spent his first full season in low Class A, overcoming a slow start by shortening his bat path and showing better pitch selection. He played at two levels in 2010 and reached Double-A at the end of June. Despite profiling as a top-of-the-order hitter, he has surprising power and finished third in the organization with 18 home runs. He also stole 28 bases and incorporated the bunt in his repertoire, as the Padres stressed keeping the ball on the ground and using his above-average speed. Along with his running speed, Tekotte's best asset is his plus range in center field, where he reads the ball well off the bat and glides to the ball. His bat might be a bit short for regular play, but he can drive a fastball and take a walk. Tekotte hit .252 against lefthanders in 2010, but he slugged just .384 and generally looks uncomfortable when facing southpaws. Still, he's got the goods to stick around as a reserve outfielder: lefty bat, defensive chops, speed and some power. He may get a chance to tune up at Double-A early in 2011 before making his Triple-A debut.

Year	Club (League)	Class	AVG	G	AB	R	H	2B	3B	HR	RBI	BB	SO	SB	CS	OBP	SLG
2008	Eugene (NWL)	SS	.285	47	193	43	55	15	0	6	29	27	45	7	4	.379	.456
2009	Fort Wayne (MWL)	LoA	.258	134	530	83	137	24	5	13	56	68	97	30	12	.345	.396
2010	Lake Elsinore (CAL)	HiA	.310	59	203	41	63	17	1	8	27	36	46	22	8	.419	.522
	San Antonio (TL)	AA	.250	67	268	44	67	8	7	10	37	26	63	6	9	.324	.444
Minor League Totals			.270	307	1194	211	322	64	13	37	149	157	251	65	33	.359	.438

15 JEREMY HEFNER, RHP

Born: March 11, 1986. **B-T:** R-R. **Ht.:** 6-4. **Wt.:** 215. **Drafted:** Oral Roberts, 2007 (5th round). **Signed by:** Lane Decker.

For the third consecutive season, Hefner flew under the prospect radar as a durable starter with a firm strikeout rate and strong control. He ranked third in the Midwest League with 144 strikeouts in 2008, then fourth in the California League with 142 whiffs in '09 and fourth again last season with 115 in the Texas League. Hefner served as No. 2 starter to Simon Castro at San Antonio, while finishing first in the TL in innings (168), second in WHIP (1.23) and third in ERA (2.95). After pitching in the high 80s previously, Hefner sat more comfortably at 90-91 mph last season, throwing downhill with sinking and tailing action and topping out near 93. He works fast and moves the ball in and out, while his long limbs provide deception in his delivery. Hefner dusted off a curveball for the 2009 season, a move that paid off last season as it showed improved break and definition. He has a feel for an average changeup and controls the running game—10 of 16 basestealers (63 percent) were thrown out on his watch last season. Hefner has no true out pitch, but three average offerings and a feel for the strike zone make him ideally suited to fit in the back of a rotation. Added to the 40-man roster in November, he'll move to Triple-A in 2011.

Year	Club (League)	Class	W	L	ERA	G	GS	CG	SV	IP	H	HR	BB	SO	G/A	WHIP	AVG
2007	Eugene (NWL)	SS	2	5	3.90	17	11	0	0	62	51	3	20	74	—	1.14	.221
2008	Fort Wayne (MWL)	LoA	10	5	3.33	29	24	0	0	140	117	12	41	144	—	1.13	.228
	Lake Elsinore (CAL)	HiA	0	0	3.60	1	1	0	0	5	3	0	2	6	—	1.00	.167
2009	Lake Elsinore (CAL)	HiA	14	9	4.12	27	27	0	0	151	165	13	38	142	0.93	1.35	.284
	Portland (PCL)	AAA	0	0	3.38	1	1	0	0	5	7	0	2	5	0.83	1.69	.318
2010	San Antonio (TL)	AA	11	8	2.95	28	28	2	0	168	156	11	51	115	0.91	1.23	.254
Minor League Totals			37	27	3.51	103	92	2	0	531	499	39	154	486	0.92	1.23	.252

16 EDINSON RINCON, 3B

Born: Aug. 11, 1990. **B-T:** R-R. **Ht.:** 6-1. **Wt.:** 216. **Signed:** Dominican Republic, 2007. **Signed by:** Randy Smith/Felix Francisco.

Making his full-season debut at Fort Wayne last season, Rincon started slowly before finding his stroke at midseason and batting .302/.359/.462 with six homers in June and July. Rincon's season represented a step back from his breakout campaign in 2009, when he ranked as the No. 2 prospect in the Northwest League. Nearly all his value lies in his bat. Rincon squares up all types of pitches and shows enough bat speed for scouts to slap average grades on his potential to hit for average and power. He stays back well on offspeed stuff and earns high marks for his plate discipline. Rincon drives the ball well to right-center field, but when he went against his natural swing and tried to pull the ball for power, he fell into the habit of upper-cutting the ball. Despite plus arm strength, Rincon has a slow release and his defensive actions are rough at the hot corner. He's a bottom-of-the-scale runner who gets caught in-between on hops frequently, and he led Midwest League third basemen with 36 errors in just 106 games. Rincon faces a probable shift to the corner outfield or first base down the line, so further offensive improvement is imperative. He'll head to high Class A in 2011.

Year	Club (League)	Class	AVG	G	AB	R	H	2B	3B	HR	RBI	BB	SO	SB	CS	OBP	SLG
2007	Padres (DSL)	R	.295	33	122	14	36	7	0	2	15	17	26	2	1	.383	.402
	Padres (AZL)	R	.178	15	45	6	8	1	0	0	0	7	11	0	0	.302	.200
2008	Padres (AZL)	R	.308	23	65	8	20	1	1	0	19	14	18	0	0	.429	.354
2009	Eugene (NWL)	SS	.300	70	267	47	80	18	3	7	47	46	60	5	0	.415	.468
2010	Fort Wayne (MWL)	LoA	.250	132	511	72	128	35	1	13	69	44	95	1	2	.315	.399
Minor League Totals			.269	273	1010	147	272	62	5	22	150	128	210	8	3	.359	.406

17 JUAN ORAMAS, LHP

Born: May 11, 1990. **B-T:** L-L. **Ht.:** 5-10. **Wt.:** 215. **Signed:** Mexico, 2006. **Signed by:** Robert Rowley.

The Padres signed the 16-year-old Oramas following the 2006 season, but he spent his first two seasons in the Rookie-level Dominican Summer League and another in the Mexican League prior to making his U.S. debut last year. San Diego loaned the stocky lefty to Mexico City in 2009 to challenge him with an assignment at high altitude and in a competitive environment where the average player was 29 years old. Oramas passed with flying colors, finishing second in the Mexican League ERA race (2.31), fourth in strikeouts (89) and first in opponent average (.219). San Diego deemed him ready for high Class A coming out of spring training, and sent him there when a rotation spot opened at the beginning of May. In his fourth start for Lake Elsinore, he came within two outs of pitching the third perfect game in the California League's 69-year history. Oramas throws three pitches for strikes and benefits from natural deception in his delivery and late life to his fastball. He sits at 89-91 mph and touches plus at 94, though he tends to throw uphill and would benefit from better extension and plane to his delivery. His average curveball features biting, downward action, while his changeup shows average potential. The Padres backed off Oramas' workload in the second half of the season because he threw a combined 157 innings in 2009 between the Mexican League, the Mexican Pacific League and Caribbean Series. San Diego allotted just

50 innings for him this winter. Oramas works hard, picks things up quickly and could continue to climb to the big leagues at a rapid pace. Expect him to start in Double-A.

Year	Club (League)	Class	W	L	ERA	G	GS	CG	SV	IP	H	HR	BB	SO	G/A	WHIP	AVG
2007	Padres (DSL)	R	2	3	3.81	16	5	0	0	54	39	1	20	63	—	1.09	.196
2008	Padres (DSL)	R	3	2	1.02	19	5	0	3	53	23	0	24	70	—	0.89	.125
2009	Mexico City (MEX)	AAA	9	1	2.31	25	14	0	0	90	72	4	44	89	0.91	1.29	—
2010	Fort Wayne (MWL)	LoA	0	1	1.20	5	0	0	0	15	9	0	3	25	0.40	0.80	.176
	Lake Elsinore (CAL)	HiA	7	3	3.00	24	21	0	0	84	64	10	26	90	0.62	1.07	.209
Minor League Totals			21	10	2.49	89	45	0	3	296	207	15	117	337	0.75	1.09	.182

18 RYMER LIRIANO, OF

Born: June 20, 1991. **B-T:** R-R. **Ht.:** 6-0. **Wt.:** 219. **Signed:** Dominican Republic, 2007. **Signed by:** Felix Francisco/Randy Smith.

The Padres view Liriano almost as a Dominican version of Donavan Tate. He's a boom-or-bust prospect with huge raw tools, the type of player who puts on a monstrous batting practice but doesn't yet carry that power into games. Liriano signed for $350,000 in 2007 and has wowed observers everywhere he has played. Lake Elsinore manager Carlos Lezcano watched Liriano play for just two weeks at the end of the season and already has begun lobbying the front office for a return engagement. He homered just three times in 441 at-bats between three levels in 2010 because his pitch recognition needs work. Pitchers with velocity or a breaking ball could get him to go outside his hitting zone. He probably never will hit for much of an average, but he offsets that limitation with the potential to one day hit 25-30 home runs. He's a quick-twitch athlete with strength who can drive the ball out to any part of the park. Liriano receives average to above-average grades for his speed and arm, leaving open the possibility of a future in center field, though he figures to fill out and settle in right. He stole 31 bases in 2010 and led the Northwest League with six triples, but he'll need to hone his baserunning instincts after being gunned down 13 times. Liriano works hard and has a prototype right fielder's tools. He'll return to low Class A to begin 2011, though an in-season promotion is possible.

Year	Club (League)	Class	AVG	G	AB	R	H	2B	3B	HR	RBI	BB	SO	SB	CS	OBP	SLG
2008	Padres (DSL)	R	.198	67	232	34	46	13	1	9	37	28	106	9	5	.296	.379
2009	Padres (AZL)	R	.350	50	197	44	69	8	1	8	44	15	52	14	5	.398	.523
2010	Fort Wayne (MWL)	LoA	.191	50	188	21	36	11	1	2	20	10	54	11	6	.234	.293
	Eugene (NWL)	SS	.271	53	203	35	55	13	6	0	12	17	53	17	7	.335	.394
	Lake Elsinore (CAL)	HiA	.220	14	50	3	11	2	0	1	6	5	12	3	0	.291	.320
Minor League Totals			.249	234	870	137	217	47	9	20	119	75	277	54	23	.315	.393

19 JOSE DePAULA, LHP

Born: March 4, 1990. **B-T:** L-L. **Ht.:** 6-1. **Wt.:** 195. **Signed:** Dominican Republic, 2006. **Signed by:** Felix Francisco.

The Padres have brought DePaula along slowly, but if 2010 was any indication, the lefty won't be anonymous for much longer. He missed all but two games in 2009 as he dealt with a stress fracture in his left elbow, but he hit the ground running when he joined Fort Wayne late last May. Scouts called him the best pitcher on the staff. Long and lean, DePaula throws downhill at 88-91 mph and tops out near 93 with riding life. His low-80s breaking ball features tight rotation and plus lateral break at times. Midwest League lefties hit just .196 (18-for-92) against him, with two extra-base hits and 26 strikeouts. He mixes in a promising 80-mph changeup that shows average potential. For a young pitcher with strikeout stuff, DePaula throws plenty of strikes and stands to improve on his command as he continues to learn and refine his delivery. His fastball/breaking ball combo could make him deadly as a reliever, but with the chance for three average or better pitches he could fit at the back of a big league rotation. San Diego kept DePaula on a strict pitch limit last season, but he may have a longer leash when he moves to high Class A in 2011.

Year	Club (League)	Class	W	L	ERA	G	GS	CG	SV	IP	H	HR	BB	SO	G/A	WHIP	AVG
2007	Padres (DSL)	R	2	5	2.44	14	13	0	0	66	52	0	21	78	—	1.10	.208
2008	Padres (AZL)	R	4	3	3.57	13	13	0	0	53	61	2	9	56	—	1.32	.288
2009	Eugene (NWL)	SS	1	0	2.79	2	2	0	0	10	9	0	2	10	2.00	1.14	.243
2010	Fort Wayne (MWL)	LoA	8	5	3.27	20	14	0	0	85	71	7	20	69	1.04	1.07	.222
Minor League Totals			15	13	3.07	49	42	0	0	214	193	9	52	213	1.10	1.14	.236

20 KEYVIUS SAMPSON, RHP

Born: Jan. 6, 1991. **B-T:** R-R. **Ht.:** 6-0. **Wt.:** 185. **Drafted:** HS—Ocala, Fla., 2009 (4th round). **Signed by:** Rob Sidwell.

Prior to the 2009 draft, the Padres hadn't signed a high school righthander out of the top 10 rounds since eighth-round pick David Pauley in 2001. They signed two that year: Sampson (fourth round) and James Needy (sixth). They selected Sampson only after he and his agent softened bonus demands on the second day of the draft, and they signed him for $600,000. He showcased one of the most electric arms in the Northwest League in 2010. Like teammate Adys Portillo, Sampson paired mid-90s heat with inconsistent secondary stuff. His arm action is long in back but quick out front and the ball jumps out of his hand at 90-93 mph, touching 95 with life. He throws strikes but scatters the zone and lacks command, a common affliction for teenage hurlers. Sampson's breaking ball come and goes, featuring depth and bite one time and then arriving soft and slurvy the next when he gets around the pitch. He trusts his average changeup, and most scouts preferred it to his breaking ball. Sampson is athletic and has shown he can spin the ball, so he's a potential three-pitch starter down the road. That assumes good health, which was seldom the case in 2010. He pitched with a tear in the labrum of his right shoulder, which caused him to alter his delivery and develop elbow soreness. According to the Padres, he left instructional league with a clean bill of health, ready to compete for a rotation spot in low Class A this season.

Year	Club (League)	Class	W	L	ERA	G	GS	CG	SV	IP	H	HR	BB	SO	G/A	WHIP	AVG
2009	Padres (AZL)	R	0	0	3.00	2	1	0	0	3	1	0	0	3	0.50	0.33	.111
	Eugene (NWL)	SS	0	0	3.60	2	1	0	0	5	3	0	3	5	2.33	1.20	.176
2010	Eugene (NWL)	SS	3	3	3.56	10	10	0	0	43	35	4	17	58	1.52	1.21	.226
Minor League Totals			3	3	3.53	14	12	0	0	51	39	4	20	66	1.47	1.16	.215

21 ZACH CATES, RHP

Born: Dec. 17, 1988. **B-T:** R-R. **Ht.:** 6-3. **Wt.:** 200. **Drafted:** Northeast Texas CC, 2010 (3rd round). **Signed by:** Jeff Curtis.

Cates went undrafted out of Conway (Ark.) High and again after his freshman year at Northeast Texas CC, where he started out as a two-way player. He gave up catching as a sophomore and moved full-time to the mound, where he generated significant buzz leading up to the 2010 draft by showing two strong pitches and by striking out 92 batters in 69 innings. The Padres selected him 91st overall and came to terms just before the signing deadline for $765,000, more than double the slot recommendation. Cates pitches at 92-94 mph and touched 96 in instructional league. His arm action is clean, but his delivery is rudimentary and needs smoothing out. He's narrow-waisted with room to fill out and potentially add velocity. Cates shows feel for a fading Vulcan changeup that he sells with good arm speed. His curveball has farther to go but could become average in the future if thrown with more power. Even if the breaking ball doesn't develop, Cates could profile as a set-up reliever with just average command of a quality fastball and changeup. He'll be 22 this season, so he could be destined for low Class A if he pitches well in spring training.

Year	Club (League)	Class	W	L	ERA	G	GS	CG	SV	IP	H	HR	BB	SO	G/A	WHIP	AVG
2010	Did Not Play—Signed Late																

22 ANTHONY BASS, RHP

Born: Nov. 1, 1987. **B-T:** R-R. **Ht.:** 6-2. **Wt.:** 190. **Drafted:** Wayne State (Mich.), 2008 (5th round). **Signed by:** Jeff Stewart.

Bass struck out 19 batters in a game for Trenton (Mich.) High to break J.J. Putz's school record. The Padres installed Bass as closer for short-season Eugene to keep his innings in check after signing him in 2008, but the organization has developed him as a starter in two seasons since. He led the high Class A California League in four categories last year: ERA (3.13), WHIP (1.09), opponent average (.248) and walks per nine innings (1.4). Despite the terrific year, he ultimately might fit best as a reliever because his velocity peaks at 95-96 mph in shorter stints and because his secondary stuff gets mixed reviews. He's also slightly built and has earned a reputation as a tenacious competitor who attacks batters and doesn't leave a lot in reserve. Bass delivers pitches from a high three-quarters slot, and his 90-92 mph fastball is fairly straight. He has gone away from a curveball in favor of a low- to mid-80s slider/cutter and a sinking changeup that flashes above-average potential. He works up in the zone frequently, but opposing batters at the Class A level didn't seem to see the ball well. Bass has a plus fastball, throws strikes, competes well and has improved his secondary stuff, attributes that could spell a future in late-inning relief or as a back-end starter. He'll open 2011 in the Double-A rotation.

Year	Club (League)	Class	W	L	ERA	G	GS	CG	SV	IP	H	HR	BB	SO	G/A	WHIP	AVG
2008	Eugene (NWL)	SS	2	2	2.10	25	0	0	7	34	25	3	14	41	—	1.14	.197
2009	Fort Wayne (MWL)	LoA	9	3	2.19	18	18	0	0	90	79	5	25	69	1.29	1.15	.235
	Lake Elsinore (CAL)	HiA	3	0	3.51	10	8	0	0	33	33	3	14	20	1.52	1.41	.266
2010	Lake Elsinore (CAL)	HiA	8	7	3.13	27	27	0	0	132	124	9	20	109	1.60	1.09	.248
	Portland (PCL)	AAA	0	1	7.94	1	1	0	0	6	7	1	3	3	1.80	1.76	.333
Minor League Totals			22	13	2.86	81	54	0	7	296	268	21	76	242	1.48	1.16	.242

23 ADYS PORTILLO, RHP

Born: Dec. 21, 1991. **B-T:** R-R. **Ht.:** 6-2. **Wt.:** 222. **Signed:** Venezuela, 2008. **Signed by:** Yfrain Linares/Felix Feliz/Randy Smith.

Portillo touched 93 mph as a 16-year-old amateur, sparking a bidding war that the Padres ultimately won with a $2 million bonus. The early returns have been mixed, as Portillo has spent two years in short-season ball, going 3-15, 4.94 with 5.3 walks per nine innings and limited feel for his secondary pitches. On the plus side, he has gained velocity since signing and now pitches anywhere from 90-96 mph, primarily in the lower register with late life. Portillo's fastball could be a well above-average pitch, and he used it to good effect in the Northwest League in 2010, finishing fourth in strikeouts per nine innings (9.0) and fifth in opponent average (.241). Development of his secondary stuff is slowed by a stiff arm action and wrist wrap, which also results in poor command. Portillo threw a soft, loopy curveball during the season, so San Diego introduced him to a slider during instructional league. His changeup is ahead of his breaking ball, but it's also below-average. Portillo's maturity took a step forward in 2010, as he sped up his tempo and learned to dwell less often on bad pitches. He's athletic and fields his potion well. With a reliable second pitch, Portillo could grow into a shutdown reliever, but the potential for more exists if he can master three pitches and align that with better command. He's ready to tackle full-season ball in 2011.

Year	Club (League)	Class	W	L	ERA	G	GS	CG	SV	IP	H	HR	BB	SO	G/A	WHIP	AVG
2009	Padres (AZL)	R	1	9	5.13	13	12	0	0	53	67	2	28	44	1.42	1.80	.321
2010	Eugene (NWL)	SS	2	6	4.79	14	14	0	0	62	55	2	40	62	1.68	1.53	.241
	Fort Wayne (MWL)	LoA	0	0	4.50	1	0	0	0	2	2	1	1	1	1.00	1.50	.286
Minor League Totals			3	15	4.94	28	26	0	0	117	124	5	69	107	1.53	1.65	.279

24 EVERETT WILLIAMS, OF

Born: Oct. 1, 1990. **B-T:** L-R. **Ht.:** 5-10. **Wt.:** 205. **Drafted:** HS—Austin, Texas, 2009 (2nd round). **Signed by:** Tim Holt.

The Padres were elated when Williams fell to them in the second round of the 2009 draft, but the early returns on his bat were less than expected. A poor season in the Midwest League is not exactly a death knell for a 19-year-old with Williams' strength and athleticism, and an optimist could point to his potential for five average tools with a chance to hit a bit better than that. He has strong bat speed from the left side, but he showed a late trigger in 2010 and seemed to hit everything to the opposite field. He swung and missed a lot, too, as he tended to pull off the ball and cede the middle and outer portion of the plate. When he's going well, Williams' natural swing path produces more doubles power, with the potential for 10-12 home runs. He's an average runner, but he plays an uninspired center field and has no better than average range. His arm plays better than initially thought, and he could land in right field if his defense slips any further. Williams can shake his tweener profile with improved defensive play (to stick in center) or better power output (for a corner). He'll have to tone down his aggressive, pull-happy approach and focus on using the middle of the field and let the power come naturally. Williams could be destined for a do-over in low Class A.

Year	Club (League)	Class	AVG	G	AB	R	H	2B	3B	HR	RBI	BB	SO	SB	CS	OBP	SLG
2009	Padres (AZL)	R	.389	4	18	1	7	2	1	0	6	1	7	2	1	.421	.611
	Eugene (NWL)	SS	.200	6	25	1	5	2	0	1	3	4	11	0	0	.310	.400
2010	Fort Wayne (MWL)	LoA	.244	107	390	53	95	25	5	5	59	51	131	10	5	.333	.372
Minor League Totals			.247	117	433	55	107	29	6	6	68	56	149	12	6	.335	.383

25 JOHNNY BARBATO, RHP

Born: July 11, 1992. **B-T:** R-R. **Ht.:** 6-2. **Wt.:** 185. **Drafted:** HS—Miami, 2010 (6th round). **Signed by:** Rob Sidwell/Bob Filotei.

Barbato went just 2-4 as a senior at Miami's Varela High, but his 1.79 ERA indicated his pitching skill more than his record, which was more a function of playing for an uncompetitive 6-A team. He declined to transfer to a private school because his father served as Varela's head coach. Like fellow Sunshine State prep righthander Karsten Whitson, the Padres' first-round pick at ninth overall, Barbato had committed to Florida. Whitson declined to sign and honored his commitment with the Gators, but Barbato signed at the deadline for $1.4 million, a bonus amount that nearly doubled that of any other San Diego 2010 pick. He pumps 89-92 mph fastballs and touches 95, and scouts love his loose arm and sound, repeatable delivery. San Diego slaps a present average grade on his low-70s downer curveball and sees his changeup as a future average pitch. With size, projection and a potentially well-rounded repertoire, Barbato profiles as a big league starter. He signed at age 17, so look for him begin the 2011 season in extended spring training before an assignment to short-season ball.

Year	Club (League)	Class	W	L	ERA	G	GS	CG	SV	IP	H	HR	BB	SO	G/A	WHIP	AVG
2010	Did Not Play—Signed Late																

26 JERRY SULLIVAN, RHP

Born: Jan. 18, 1988. **B-T:** R-R. **Ht.:** 6-4. **Wt.:** 220. **Drafted:** Oral Roberts, 2009 (3rd round). **Signed by:** Lane Decker.

Sullivan had Tommy John surgery as a high school senior, but he rebounded to lead Oral Roberts to three consecutive Summit League championships, earning all-conference honors each year. The Padres signed him quickly for $430,200 as a third-round pick and placed him on the same track as college righthanders Jeremy Hefner (2007 draft) and Anthony Bass (2008), who all spent most or all of their first full seasons in the Midwest League. Sullivan combined impressive arm strength with a feel for the strike zone—he ranked fifth in the MWL with 2.2 walks per nine innings. He pitches at 91-93 mph and tops out at 94-95 in shorter stints, with occasional cutting action and life. He comes from a high three-quarters arm slot and cuts off his delivery, which affects his command. Sullivan throws a future average slider at 82-84 mph, but he needs more separation on his changeup, which falls in the same velocity range as his breaking ball. A plus athlete, Sullivan takes charge of the running game—8 of 15 basestealers (53 percent) to test him were thrown out in 2010. He has the size and potentially the three-pitch mix to profile as a back-of-the-rotation starter, but if the changeup does not improve, look for him to make his way to the bullpen. He fits the organization's profile for a reliever at Petco Park, and he'll head to high Class A in 2011.

Year	Club (League)	Class	W	L	ERA	G	GS	CG	SV	IP	H	HR	BB	SO	G/A	WHIP	AVG
2009	Eugene (NWL)	SS	5	3	4.02	16	9	0	0	54	44	5	27	58	1.23	1.32	.219
2010	Fort Wayne (MWL)	LoA	7	4	4.03	27	26	0	0	116	119	9	29	92	1.28	1.28	.264
Minor League Totals			12	7	4.03	43	35	0	0	170	163	14	56	150	1.26	1.29	.250

27 GEORGE KONTOS, RHP

Born: June 12, 1985. **B-T:** R-R. **Ht.:** 6-3. **Wt.:** 215. **Drafted:** Northwestern, 2006 (5th round). **Signed by:** Steve Lemke (Yankees).

The Padres considered selecting Kontos from the Yankees in the 2009 Rule 5 draft, but opted not to take a flier on the Tommy John surgery alumnus. He had the procedure in July 2009 and did not return to action until mid-June 2010, whereupon New York shifted him to the bullpen. Kontos shook off the rust in making 24 regular-season appearances and then 10 more in the Arizona Fall League, where he got rocked for 21 runs on 21 hits in 13 innings. San Diego trusted its scouting reports and made Kontos the 11th pick in the 2010 Rule 5 draft. They must keep him on the active roster all season or else place him on waivers and offer him back to the Yankees. Given the club's recent track record with Rule 5 picks, the prognosis seems positive. In recent years, the Padres have carried Everth Cabrera and Luis Perdomo (2009), Carlos Guevara (2008) and Kevin Cameron (2007), though they ultimately had to make a trade to retain Guevara. Kontos sits at 88-90 mph with life, and while he has been up to 93 at times, he had not recovered his peak, pre-surgery velocity. His tick above-average slider makes life difficult for righthanders, who went 21-for-93 (.226) against him in the 2010 regular season. Kontos lacks feel for a changeup, and his delivery doesn't allow him to throw consistent strikes, so he's a reliever for the long haul. San Diego views him as a good fit for Petco Park with his average fastball and quality slider.

Year	Club (League)	Class	W	L	ERA	G	GS	CG	SV	IP	H	HR	BB	SO	G/A	WHIP	AVG
2006	Staten Island (NYP)	SS	7	3	2.64	14	14	0	0	78	64	3	19	82	—	1.06	.227
2007	Tampa (FSL)	HiA	4	6	4.02	19	17	0	0	94	95	15	30	101	—	1.33	.260
2008	Trenton (EL)	AA	6	11	3.68	27	27	0	0	152	134	14	57	152	—	1.26	.239
2009	Trenton (EL)	AA	1	1	2.66	4	4	0	0	20	19	0	9	24	0.71	1.38	.235
	Scranton/W-B (IL)	AAA	3	4	3.35	9	9	1	0	51	44	6	21	39	0.93	1.27	.229
2010	Tampa (FSL)	HiA	0	1	2.61	5	2	0	0	10	7	0	3	8	1.22	0.97	.194
	Trenton (EL)	AA	0	2	3.38	17	0	0	0	32	30	2	11	28	1.29	1.28	.254
	Scranton/W-B (IL)	AAA	0	1	10.13	2	0	0	0	3	5	1	1	2	—	2.25	.385
Minor League Totals			21	29	3.47	97	73	1	0	440	398	41	151	436	1.03	1.25	.242

28 JEUDY VALDEZ, 2B/SS

Born: May 5, 1989. **B-T:** R-R. **Ht.:** 5-10. **Wt.:** 183. **Signed:** Dominican Republic, 2005. **Signed by:** Felix Francisco.

Valdez hasn't advanced past low Class A in five pro seasons, but the Padres believe he turned a corner in 2010. They added him to the 40-man roster in November, something they did not do for Nick Schmidt, Kellen Kulbacki and Mitch Canham, three of the top 57 picks in the 2007 draft. Valdez has tantalized with loud raw tools at every stop, but he hit just .238/.297/.360 in two seasons in the Midwest League at ages 20 and 21. He missed a large chunk of the 2009 season with a broken wrist, but showed few ill effects last season in establishing career highs with 10 home runs, 34 doubles and 34 stolen bases. Valdez has lightning in his wrists and whips the bat through the zone with good extension, lending hope that he can top out near 15 home runs at his peak. He drives the ball well to right-center field, so his power could be average overall. He can hit premium velocity, but his pitch recognition skills are rudimentary and he gets out in front even against ordinary offspeed stuff. Learning to lay off the breaking ball would do wonders for his average, but as it is he's a below-average hitter. Valdez's abil-

Valdez's ability to run, field and throw all rate as above-average. He's quick and nimble around the bag, with soft hands and more than enough arm for shortstop, where San Diego intends to play him in 2011 as he heads to high Class A.

Year	Club (League)	Class	AVG	G	AB	R	H	2B	3B	HR	RBI	BB	SO	SB	CS	OBP	SLG
2006	Padres (DSL)	R	.238	47	168	29	40	7	2	0	10	15	44	12	6	.319	.304
2007	Padres (AZL)	R	.281	47	192	31	54	7	4	3	30	15	44	11	3	.346	.406
2008	Eugene (NWL)	SS	.227	59	216	35	49	10	2	5	22	18	64	3	4	.293	.361
2009	Fort Wayne (MWL)	LoA	.212	49	193	25	41	11	2	1	14	17	51	11	3	.283	.306
	Padres (AZL)	R	.318	12	44	8	14	3	2	0	6	6	10	3	2	.400	.477
2010	Fort Wayne (MWL)	LoA	.247	132	527	81	130	34	3	10	76	43	115	34	14	.302	.380
Minor League Totals			.245	346	1340	209	328	72	15	19	158	114	328	74	32	.310	.363

29 NICK SCHMIDT, LHP

Born: Oct. 10, 1985. **B-T:** L-L. **Ht.:** 6-5. **Wt.:** 245. **Drafted:** Arkansas, 2007 (1st round). **Signed by:** Lane Decker.

Schmidt required Tommy John surgery just seven innings into his pro career, adding to a string of snakebit Padres first-round picks that includes Tim Stauffer, Matt Bush, Cesar Carrillo, Matt Antonelli, Allan Dykstra, Donavan Tate and unsigned 2010 pick Karsten Whitson. Schmidt signed for $1.26 million in 2007 and then missed the entire 2008 campaign. He has not compiled 100 innings in either of his previous two seasons, hasn't yet reached Double-A and doesn't throw quite as hard as he did at Arkansas. As a pro starter he ranges from 85-88 mph, sitting more comfortably at 90-93 in short stints. He throws across his body, which hides the ball from opposing batters and makes his riding fastball play up to average. Schmidt has two average secondary offerings in a late-breaking, low-70s curveball and a deceptive changeup in the low 80s. His pitches all have separation, which coupled with steadier velocity could make him vicious as a reliever. Schmidt is so physical and throws so many strikes, though, that San Diego will continue to develop him as a potential back-of-the-rotation starter. He'll get his first taste of Double-A in 2011.

Year	Club (League)	Class	W	L	ERA	G	GS	CG	SV	IP	H	HR	BB	SO	G/A	WHIP	AVG
2007	Fort Wayne (MWL)	LoA	0	1	6.43	3	1	0	0	7	8	0	6	6	—	2.00	.286
2008	Did Not Play—Injured																
2009	Fort Wayne (MWL)	LoA	4	0	2.79	13	11	0	0	52	38	0	23	59	1.07	1.18	.195
	Lake Elsinore (CAL)	HiA	2	8	7.88	11	11	0	0	48	68	7	27	27	0.81	1.98	.349
2010	Lake Elsinore (CAL)	HiA	6	9	4.35	24	24	0	0	97	94	4	43	87	1.02	1.41	.257
Minor League Totals			12	18	4.85	51	47	0	0	204	208	11	99	179	0.97	1.50	.265

30 BRAD BRACH, RHP

Born: April 12, 1986. **B-T:** R-R. **Ht.:** 6-6. **Wt.:** 210. **Drafted:** Monmouth, 2008 (42nd round). **Signed by:** Jim Bretz.

A nondescript starter for Monmouth for four years, Brach signed for $1,000 as a 42nd-round pick in 2008. Installed as closer for the Padres' Arizona League club in his debut, Brach embarked on an incredible three-year run during which he's saved 78 of 83 opportunities, while pitching a 1.90 ERA and a ridiculous 7-to-1 strikeout-to-walk ratio. Brach set a California League record with 41 saves in 2010, while also placing second among relievers in opponent average (.207) and fourth in strikeouts per nine innings (10.1). He's done it all using almost exclusively a 92-94 mph fastball with tailing action. Fearless, Brach works quickly and attacks the bottom half of the strike zone. His velocity has climbed steadily each season, up from the high 80s in 2009 to a peak of 96 mph last season. Brach has no real go-to secondary pitch. He shows a good splitter in bullpen sessions, but his slider is generic. At 24, Brach was considerably older than the average Cal League player last season, and he didn't exactly overpower batters in the Arizona Fall League, striking out just four over 13 innings. He'll be tested in Double-A in 2011.

Year	Club (League)	Class	W	L	ERA	G	GS	CG	SV	IP	H	HR	BB	SO	G/A	WHIP	AVG
2008	Padres (AZL)	R	1	1	2.01	17	0	0	4	22	21	0	5	33	—	1.16	.250
2009	Fort Wayne (MWL)	LoA	3	3	1.27	60	0	0	33	64	36	1	11	82	0.71	0.74	.164
2010	Lake Elsinore (CAL)	HiA	5	2	2.47	62	0	0	41	66	50	6	11	74	1.19	0.93	.207

San Francisco Giants

BY ANDY BAGGARLY

The Giants couldn't win a World Series during the Barry Bonds era. They couldn't get it done with names like Mays, McCovey and Marichal, either. Yet there was a magic within their starless ranks in 2010.

As unbelievable as the story might be, the Giants really did win the first World Series in the franchise's 53 seasons in San Francisco. They're still cleaning up the ticker tape from the parade down Market Street, which drew almost a million people.

For all the talk of misfits, castoffs, rally thongs and black beards, the Giants won the National  League West and charged through three postseason series because their homegrown pitching staff was deeper and better than every opponent they faced. Tim Lincecum, Matt Cain and Madison Bumgarner—all first-round picks—remained solid to the end, and Jonathan Sanchez was just as good in his first two playoff starts before fading down the stretch. The bullpen was dominant, led by Brian Wilson, whom the organization shrewdly took as a 24th-round pick in 2003 knowing he'd just had Tommy John surgery.

Guiding these golden arms was Buster Posey, who became the first rookie backstop to hit in the middle of the order for a World Series winner since Yogi Berra in 1947. Posey won the NL rookie of the year award, San Francisco's first recipient since John Montefusco in 1975. That's a pretty good reflection on scouting director John Barr, who made Posey his first pick for the franchise in 2008, and a big reason why the Giants were Baseball America's Organization of the Year.

San Francisco stood in fourth place at the all-star break and made over its Opening Day lineup during the summer. Only Aubrey Huff and Juan Uribe remained everyday players from beginning to end. From Pat Burrell to Cody Ross to Andres Torres, there weren't enough Cinderella slippers to go around.

The title was an affirmation for Brian Sabean, the longest-tenured general manager in the game, who refused to break up his rotation to get offensive help. In a champagne-soaked clubhouse after the clinching win against the Rangers, Sabean resisted wagging his finger at critics of his insular management style and his scouting-heavy evaluation methods. Instead, he said he was happy for the club's longtime employees, folks behind the scenes and long-suffering fans in the Bay Area.

Now San Francisco looks ahead to defending in 2011, confident in a rotation that is under club control through 2012 but aware the lineup needs work.

BILL NICHOLS

Madison Bumgarner went from first-round pick to World Series hero in three years

TOP 30 PROSPECTS

1. Brandon Belt, 1b/of	**16.** Mike Kickham, lhp
2. Zack Wheeler, rhp	**17.** Conor Gillaspie, 3b
3. Gary Brown, of	**18.** Chuckie Jones, of
4. Francisco Peguero, of	**19.** Heath Hembree, rhp
5. Ehire Adrianza, ss	**20.** Jake Dunning, rhp
6. Brandon Crawford, ss	**21.** Jorge Bucardo, rhp
7. Thomas Neal, of	**22.** Jason Stoffel, rhp
8. Charlie Culberson, 2b	**23.** Nick Noonan, 2b
9. Eric Surkamp, lhp	**24.** Juan Perez, of
10. Tommy Joseph, c/1b	**25.** Ryan Verdugo, lhp
11. Rafael Rodriguez, of	**26.** Ydwin Villegas, ss
12. Jarrett Parker, of	**27.** Darren Ford, of
13. Jose Casilla, rhp	**28.** Johnny Monell, c
14. Roger Kieschnick, of	**29.** Henry Sosa, rhp
15. Chris Dominguez, 3b	**30.** Clayton Tanner, lhp

Sabean received the green light to take the payroll over $100 million for the first time, which should give him enough money to cover raises to his nine arbitration-eligible players, and the team re-signed Burrell and Huff and replaced Uribe with Miguel Tejada.

In Posey and Bumgarner, the Giants graduated most of their elite minor league talent, and the system is light on starting pitching. They do have first baseman Brandon Belt on the cusp of the majors, and they're eager to see how quickly their top two 2010 draft picks, college outfielders Gary Brown and Jarrett Parker, can move through the system.

General Manager: Brian Sabean. **Farm Director:** Fred Stanley. **Scouting Director:** John Barr.

Class	Team	League	W	L	PCT	Finish*	Manager
Majors	San Francisco Giants	National	92	70	.568	†2nd (16)	Bruce Bochy
Triple-A	Fresno Grizzlies	Pacific Coast	75	69	.521	6th (16)	Steve Decker
Double-A	Richmond Flying Squirrels	Eastern	68	73	.482	9th (12)	Andy Skeels
High A	San Jose Giants	California	76	64	.543	†3rd (10)	Brian Harper
Low A	Augusta GreenJackets	South Atlantic	79	59	.572	2nd (14)	Dave Machemer
Short-season	Salem-Keizer Volcanoes	Northwest	31	45	.408	7th (8)	Tom Trebelhorn
Rookie	AZL Giants	Arizona	34	20	.630	1st (12)	Mike Goff
Overall 2010 Minor League Record			363	330	.524	7th (30)	

*Finish in overall standings (No. of teams in league). †League champion.

LAST YEAR'S TOP 30

Player, Pos.		Status
1.	Buster Posey, c	Majors
2.	Madison Bumgarner, lhp	Majors
3.	Zack Wheeler, rhp	No. 2
4.	Thomas Neal, of	No. 7
5.	Dan Runzler, lhp	Majors
6.	Tommy Joseph, c	No. 10
7.	Roger Kieschnick, of	No. 14
8.	Ehire Adrianza, ss	No. 5
9.	Brandon Crawford, ss	No. 6
10.	Francisco Peguero, of	No. 4
11.	Nick Noonan, 2b	No. 23
12.	Rafael Rodriguez, of	No. 11
13.	Darren Ford, of	No. 27
14.	Waldis Joaquin, rhp	Dropped out
15.	Jason Stoffel, rhp	No. 22
16.	Henry Sosa, rhp	No. 29
17.	Conor Gillaspie, 3b	No. 17
18.	Chris Dominguez, 3b	No. 15
19.	Eric Surkamp, lhp	No. 9
20.	Steve Johnson, rhp	(Orioles)
21.	Brett Pill, 1b	Dropped out
22.	Johnny Monell, c	No. 28
23.	Clayton Tanner, lhp	No. 30
24.	Matt Graham, rhp	Dropped out
25.	Mike McBryde, of	Dropped out
26.	Craig Clark, lhp	Dropped out
27.	Jose Casilla, rhp	No. 13
28.	Aaron King, lhp	Dropped out
29.	Brock Bond, 2b	Dropped out
30.	Angel Villalona, 1b	(Restricted list)

BEST TOOLS

Best Hitter for Average	Brandon Belt
Best Power Hitter	Chris Dominguez
Best Strike-Zone Discipline	Brandon Belt
Fastest Baserunner	Gary Brown
Best Athlete	Francisco Peguero
Best Fastball	Zack Wheeler
Best Curveball	Eric Surkamp
Best Slider	Jose Casilla
Best Changeup	Eric Surkamp
Best Control	Eric Surkamp
Best Defensive Catcher	Jackson Williams
Best Defensive Infielder	Ehire Adrianza
Best Infield Arm	Chris Dominguez
Best Defensive Outfielder	Gary Brown
Best Outfield Arm	Francisco Peguero

PROJECTED 2014 LINEUP

Catcher	Buster Posey
First Base	Brandon Belt
Second Base	Brandon Crawford
Third Base	Pablo Sandoval
Shortstop	Ehire Adrianza
Left Field	Thomas Neal
Center Field	Gary Brown
Right Field	Francisco Peguero
No. 1 Starter	Tim Lincecum
No. 2 Starter	Matt Cain
No. 3 Starter	Madison Bumgarner
No. 4 Starter	Jonathan Sanchez
No. 5 Starter	Zack Wheeler
Closer	Brian Wilson

TOP PROSPECTS OF THE DECADE

Year	Player, Pos.	2010 Org.
2001	Jerome Williams, rhp	Out of baseball
2002	Jerome Williams, rhp	Out of baseball
2003	Jesse Foppert, rhp	Out of baseball
2004	Merkin Valdez, rhp	Blue Jays
2005	Matt Cain, rhp	Giants
2006	Matt Cain, rhp	Giants
2007	Tim Lincecum, rhp	Giants
2008	Angel Villalona, 3b/1b	Giants
2009	Madison Bumgarner, lhp	Giants
2010	Buster Posey, c	Giants

TOP DRAFT PICKS OF THE DECADE

Year	Player, Pos.	2010 Org.
2001	Brad Hennessey, rhp	Twins
2002	Matt Cain, rhp	Giants
2003	David Aardsma, rhp	Mariners
2004	Eddy Martinez-Esteve, of (2nd round)	Giants
2005	Ben Copeland, of (4th round)	Giants
2006	Tim Lincecum, rhp	Giants
2007	Madison Bumgarner, lhp	Giants
2008	Buster Posey, c	Giants
2009	Zack Wheeler, rhp	Giants
2010	Gary Brown, of	Giants

LARGEST BONUSES IN CLUB HISTORY

Buster Posey, 2008	$6,200,000
Zack Wheeler, 2009	$3,300,000
Rafael Rodriguez, 2008	$2,550,000
Angel Villalona, 2006	$2,100,000
Tim Lincecum, 2006	$2,025,000

SAN FRANCISCO GIANTS

TOP 2011 ROOKIE: Brandon Belt, 1b/of. He might not make the Opening Day roster, but neither did Buster Posey—and that didn't stop Posey from becoming National League rookie of the year.

BREAKOUT PROSPECT: Mike Kickham, lhp. Kickham has a low-90s fastball and two breaking balls that are murder on lefthanders, so he could move quickly if developed as a reliever.

SLEEPER: Armando Paniagua, rhp. He flashed a 94-mph fastball in his U.S. debut last summer.

SOURCE OF TOP 30 TALENT

Homegrown	29	Acquired	1
College	13	Trades	1
Junior college	2	Rule 5 draft	0
High school	6	Independent leagues	0
Draft-and-follow	1	Free agents/waivers	0
Nondrafted free agents	0		
International	7		

LF
Thomas Neal (7)
Nick Liles
Wendell Fairley
James Simmons

CF
Gary Brown (3)
Jarrett Parker (12)
Chuckie Jones (18)
Juan Perez (24)
Darren Ford (27)
Chris Lofton

RF
Francisco Peguero (4)
Rafael Rodriguez (11)
Roger Kieschnick (14)
Ben Copeland
Ryan Lollis

3B
Chris Dominguez (15)
Conor Gillaspie (17)
Jose Flores
Ryan Rohlinger

SS
Ehire Adrianza (5)
Brandon Crawford (6)
Ydwin Villegas (26)
Carter Jurica

2B
Charlie Culberson (8)
Nick Noonan (23)
Brock Bond
Ryan Cavan

1B
Brandon Belt (1)
Brett Pill
Luke Anders

C
Tommy Joseph (10)
Johnny Monell (28)
Hector Sanchez
Dan Burkhart
Jackson Williams
Drew Biery
Joe Staley

RHP

RHSP	RHRP
Zack Wheeler (2)	Jose Casilla (13)
Jake Dunning (20)	Heath Hembree (19)
Jorge Bucardo (21)	Jason Stoffel (22)
Michael Main	Henry Sosa (29)
Seth Rosin	Armando Paniagua
Daryl Maday	Steve Edlefsen
Matthew Graham	Waldis Joaquin
Austin Fleet	Jose Valdez
David Mixon	Kendry Flores
Justin Fitzgerald	Jacob Dunnington
Brandon Allen	Reinier Roibal
Chris Heston	Craig Whitaker
	Edwin Quirarte
	Stephen Harrold
	Brett Bochy

LHP

LHSP	LHRP
Eric Surkamp (9)	Ryan Verdugo (25)
Mike Kickham (16)	Aaron King
Clayton Tanner (30)	David Quinowski
Chris Gloor	
Edwin Escobar	

2010

BEST PURE HITTER: The Giants believe in OF Gary Brown (1), who gained confidence in his hitting ability with a .310 showing in the Cape Cod League in 2009. He's a slasher with gap power who could use more patience.

BEST POWER HITTER: Just 17 when drafted, 6-foot-3, 235-pound OF Chuckie Jones (7) has big tools, topped off by his power. He has present strength and generates good bat speed while showing the aptitude to make adjustments.

FASTEST RUNNER: Brown was one of the draft's better runners, turning in top-of-the-scale times in getting to first base in less than 4.0 seconds from the right side.

BEST DEFENSIVE PLAYER: Brown's speed and average arm strength should make him a plus-plus center fielder with more experience. He spent parts of his first two seasons at Cal State Fullerton in the infield.

BEST FASTBALL: Scouting director John Barr saw RHP Heath Hembree (5) hit 99 mph, and Hembree sits at 94-97 range. He has a clean arm and ideal pitcher's body at 6-foot-4 and 205 pounds.

BEST SECONDARY PITCH: LHP Mike Kickham (6) got an above-slot $410,000 bonus thanks in part to being a lefty who can run his fastball up to 94 mph. But it's his breaking stuff that stands out the most, as he throws both a plus slider and a hard slurve. RHP Stephen Harrold (12) flashes a plus slider and locates it well.

BEST PRO DEBUT: A college senior, RHP Austin Fleet (16) predictably dominated the Rookie-level Arizona League, ranking fourth in strikeouts (65) while going 6-3, 2.65 in 51 innings. Jones hit .279/.360/.461 in the AZL with a team-best five homers.

BEST ATHLETE: Brown stands out, but OF Chris Lofton (9) also merits mention. Lofton batted .268/.350/.343 with 15 steals for short-season Salem-Keizer, a pleasant surprise considering he hit just .331 with one homer at the Division II juco level.

MOST INTRIGUING BACKGROUND: Lofton had planned to transfer to Alabama-Birmingham to play football as a cornerback. RHP Brett Bochy (20), son of big league manager Bruce, is a legitimate prospect who had a low-90s fastball and solid slider before having Tommy John surgery in early April.

CLOSEST TO THE MAJORS: Brown should race to San Francisco as he gets some distance from the broken finger that ended his college season early. He was rusty after signing but could break out in 2011.

BEST LATE-ROUND PICK: Harrold, whose fastball sits at 90-92 mph, and Fleet are two intriguing college arms.

THE ONE WHO GOT AWAY: The Giants really liked OF/1B Austin Southall (19) for his lefthanded bat and power potential. Originally committed to Louisiana State, he wound up at Chipola (Fla.) JC.

ASSESSMENT: The Giants intended to get more athletic, leading them to select Brown, OF Jarrett Parker (2) and SS Carter Jurica (3) with their first three picks. Then they found their usual stash of power arms and might have hit on a sleeper in the toolsy Jones.

2009

RHP Zack Wheeler (1) and C/1B Tommy Joseph (2) got off to slow starts as pros, but unheralded 1B/OF Brandon Belt (5) led the minors in hitting last year and could force his way to San Francisco in early 2011. 3B Chris Dominguez (3) has big-time power.

GRADE: B+

2008

All C Buster Posey (1) did as rookie last year was rally the Giants to a division title and lead them to a World Series championship. OF Roger Kieschnick (3), SS Brandon Crawford (4) and LHP Eric Surkamp (6) rank among the system's best prospects.

GRADE: A

2007

LHP Madison Bumgarner (1) was another key component of San Francisco's championship run. San Francisco whiffed on two other first-rounders, RHP Tim Alderson (1) and OF Wendell Fairley (1), but was able to use Alderson in a trade for Freddy Sanchez. 2B Charlie Culberson (1s) had a breakout 2010, while LHP Dan Runzler (9) raced to the big league bullpen.

GRADE: A

2006

As strange as it seems that four teams passed on Posey, it's even harder to fathom that nine clubs didn't take RHP Tim Lincecum (1), a two-time Cy Young Award winner. 2Bs Emmanuel Burriss (1s) and Matt Downs (36), 3B Ryan Rohlinger (6) and SS Brian Bocock (9) have made it to the majors, albeit with little impact.

GRADE: A

Draft analysis by John Manuel (2010) and Jim Callis (2006-09). Numbers in parentheses indicate draft rounds.

BRANDON BELT, 1B/OF

Born: April 20, 1988. **Bats:** L. **Throws:** L.
Height: 6-5. **Weight:** 210. **Drafted:** Texas, 2009
(5th round). **Signed by:** Todd Thomas.

PROSPECT 1

BILL MITCHELL

Belt first drew the attention of scouts as a pitcher at Hudson High (Lufkin, Texas), showing an 88-93 mph fastball from the left side and a solid feel for throwing strikes. The Red Sox drafted him in the 11th round in 2006 but couldn't sign him, as he opted instead to attend San Jacinto (Texas) JC. He had more success as a hitter than a pitcher at San Jac, and turned down another 11th-round offer (this one from the Braves) in 2007 to attend Texas as a full-time first baseman. He had a closed stance and an armsy swing that served him well with a metal bat (.961 OPS as a junior), but scouts weren't sold on his approach. Longtime Giants crosschecker Doug Mapson urged his team to take a fifth-round gamble on Belt in 2009 because of his athleticism and knowledge of the strike zone, a move that has paid off bigger than anyone could have forecasted. He held out all summer before agreeing to a slightly over-slot $200,000 bonus, signing too late to make his pro debut. In instructional league following the 2009 season, Belt made rapid progress after coaches had him try an upright, open stance. "All we did was square him up and give him some direction back toward the middle," San Francisco farm director Fred Stanley said. "Just kind of freed him up so his hips and hands can work . . . and my goodness." Belt exploded in 2010, dominating on three levels. He batted .352/.455/.620 while moving from high Class A San Jose to Triple-A Fresno, leading the minors in hitting and OPS while ranking second in on-base percentage. He continued to batter pitchers in the Arizona Fall League, where he hit .372/.427/.616.

Belt combines tremendous plate discipline with an up-the-middle approach that serves him well against lefthanders and righthanders alike. He makes adjustments from pitch to pitch—something almost unheard of for a first-year pro—and enjoys the mental side of hitting. His power is through the middle of the field, and he should be good for at least 20 homers a year. His ability to make consistent hard contact could provide the Giants a lefthanded version of Buster Posey in the very near future. Belt is built like a beanpole but has no glaring weaknesses. He runs well for his size, has average speed and is a smart baserunner. He has plus range and hands at first base, where he could contend for Gold Gloves. His athleticism also led to a trial on the outfield corners late last season, and he performed well. He understands where to position himself has enough arm strength for right field. His intelligence and aptitude are off the charts.

Belt's pro debut was so overwhelmingly successful that Giants GM Brian Sabean was willing to consider handing him an everyday job on Opening Day, knowing he might have a young Luis Gonzalez or Larry Walker on his hands. More likely, Belt will start 2011 in Triple-A with San Francisco hoping he'll force a promotion, much like Posey did last May.

SCOUTING GRADES

Batting: 65. **Defense:** 70.
Power: 55. **Arm:** 60.
Speed: 50.

Based on 20-80 scouting scale, where 50 represents major league average, and future projection rather than present tools.

Year	Club (League)	Class	AVG	G	AB	R	H	2B	3B	HR	RBI	BB	SO	SB	CS	OBP	SLG
2010	San Jose (CAL)	HiA	.383	77	269	62	103	28	4	10	62	58	50	18	7	.492	.628
	Richmond (EL)	AA	.337	46	175	26	59	11	6	9	40	22	34	2	1	.413	.623
	Fresno (PCL)	AAA	.229	13	48	11	11	4	0	4	10	13	15	2	0	.393	.563
Minor League Totals			.352	136	492	99	173	43	10	23	112	93	99	22	8	.455	.620

2 ZACK WHEELER, RHP

Born: May 30, 1990. **B-T:** R-R. **Ht.:** 6-4. **Wt.:** 185. **Drafted:** HS—Dallas, Ga., 2009 (1st round). **Signed by:** Sean O'Connor.

The Giants made Wheeler the sixth overall pick in the 2009 draft—the highest they've taken a pitcher since selecting Jason Grilli at No. 4 in 1997—and signed him for $3.3 million. It was a bad omen when he recorded only one out in his pro debut in April, as a persistent cracked-fingernail issue derailed his season. He did post a 3.27 ERA in his final five starts. With his size, broad shoulders and loose arm action, Wheeler has plenty of projection remaining. His cracked nail was a blessing in disguise because it forced him to take time out to work on smoothing out his mechanics. He got on a more direct line to the plate and cut down the effort in his delivery, allowing him to command the bottom of the strike zone much better. Wheeler threw an easy 94-97 mph fastball during instructional league with improved location. His changeup became functional toward the end of the season, and his breaking ball became tighter and more consistent. He can throw an overhand curveball but has had more success with a slurve. He did a lot of maturing on the mound in his first pro season and learned he can't strike out the world. Wheeler remains an elite arm with room to grow. After a promising instructional league, he'll move up to high Class A if he competes well in spring training.

Year	Club (League)	Class	W	L	ERA	G	GS	CG	SV	IP	H	HR	BB	SO	G/A	WHIP	AVG
2010	Augusta (SAL)	LoA	3	3	3.99	21	13	0	0	59	47	0	38	70	3.17	1.45	.218
Minor League Totals			3	3	3.99	21	13	0	0	59	47	0	38	70	3.17	1.45	.218

3 GARY BROWN, OF

Born: Sept. 28, 1988. **B-T:** R-R. **Ht.:** 6-0. **Wt.:** 185. **Drafted:** Cal State Fullerton, 2010 (1st round). **Signed by:** Brad Cameron.

Brown was leading the Big West Conference with a .438 average and .695 slugging percentage last spring when he broke his left middle finger on a slide in mid-May, ending his season. Drafted 24th overall and signed for $1.45 million in August, he looked rusty in his brief pro debut. Brown is a self-described hellraiser who raises plenty of it with his blazing speed. He was clocked at 3.69 seconds to first base on a bunt last spring at Cal State Fullerton—from the right side of the plate. He showed he can hit with wood bats with a .310 average in the summer Cape Cod League in 2009 and projects as an above-average hitter, though he has some lower-body movement in his swing that could hamper him. Brown has exceptionally quick hands that allow him to turn on pitches and give him gap power. He doesn't draw as many walks as he should to take full advantage of his speed. He's a potential Gold Glove center fielder whose fly-catching skills should prove valuable in the large prairies of the National League West. His arm is nothing special, but his throws are accurate. Brown may begin his first full pro season in high Class A. The Giants need a long-term center fielder, and he might not require more than two years in the minors.

Year	Club (League)	Class	AVG	G	AB	R	H	2B	3B	HR	RBI	BB	SO	SB	CS	OBP	SLG
2010	Giants (AZL)	R	.182	6	22	6	4	1	0	0	0	4	5	2	0	.333	.227
	Salem-Keizer (NWL)	SS	.136	6	22	2	3	0	1	0	2	2	7	0	1	.259	.227
Minor League Totals			.159	12	44	8	7	1	1	0	2	6	12	2	1	.296	.227

4 FRANCISCO PEGUERO, OF

Born: June 1, 1988. **B-T:** R-R. **Ht.:** 5-11. **Wt.:** 186. **Signed:** Dominican Republic, 2006. **Signed by:** Pablo Peguero.

Peguero concluded 2009 by winning MVP honors in the high Class A California League playoffs, and he helped San Jose win another title in 2010. After a slow start, he batted .372 in the second half and .350 in the postseason. He also led the league with 16 triples, provided quality outfield defense and appeared in the Futures Game. Peguero has the best blend of power and speed in the system, and he might be the most energetic player too. In some ways, he's reminiscent of a more compact Vladimir Guerrero. Peguero has terrific plate coverage that suits his aggressive style, and has learned to turn on pitches in hitters' counts. His lack of patience hasn't worked against him yet, but he'll have to lay off better breaking pitches as he moves up the ranks. Peguero has easy plus speed but still has a lot to learn on the basepaths after getting caught stealing 22 times in 2010. His speed, excellent instincts and well above-average arm make him a long-term option in either center or right field. He played winter ball in his native Dominican, which should be good preparation for making the jump to Double-A Richmond in 2011. With Gary Brown now in the organization, Peguero's future in San Francisco figures to come in right field.

Year	Club (League)	Class	AVG	G	AB	R	H	2B	3B	HR	RBI	BB	SO	SB	CS	OBP	SLG
2006	Giants (DSL)	R	.275	56	182	24	50	10	3	4	16	6	37	3	2	.307	.429

2007	Giants (DSL)	R	.294	69	235	51	69	12	2	1	17	15	39	25	5	.341	.374
2008	Augusta (SAL)	LoA	.261	50	180	23	47	2	4	2	15	12	43	15	1	.309	.350
	Salem-Keizer (NWL)	SS	.307	50	202	33	62	11	4	2	28	9	43	10	3	.349	.431
2009	Salem-Keizer (NWL)	SS	.394	17	71	14	28	3	1	0	12	3	9	7	0	.421	.465
	Augusta (SAL)	LoA	.340	58	238	28	81	12	4	1	34	5	39	15	5	.359	.437
2010	San Jose (CAL)	HiA	.329	122	510	78	168	19	16	10	77	18	88	40	22	.358	.488
Minor League Totals			.312	422	1618	251	505	69	34	20	199	68	298	115	38	.346	.434

5 EHIRE ADRIANZA, SS

Born: Aug. 21, 1989. **B-T:** B-R. **Ht.:** 6-0. **Wt.:** 168. **Signed:** Venezuela, 2006. **Signed by:** Ciro Villalobos.

The Giants almost traded Adrianza to the Mariners in a July 31 deadline deal that would've netted David Aardsma. When talks fells through, San Francisco was happy to hold onto the premium playmaker. He barely said a word in his first big league camp last spring, but he made a statement whenever he took infield practice. Cal League managers almost unanimously rated Adrianza as the best defensive shortstop in the league last year. He has plus range to both sides, a lightning-quick transfer and an accurate arm, even while throwing on the run. He doesn't rush and makes everything look easy in the field. He made just 16 errors in 121 games last season, none after July 31. A switch-hitter, Adrianza hasn't impressed with the bat thus far. His swing gets long and he can be too pull-conscious despite his lack of power. He does have some plate discipline and should improve as a hitter as he gains strength. While not a burner, he's a smart baserunner and makes the most of his excellent first-step quickness. With Brandon Crawford in the system, the Giants don't need to rush Adrianza. Added to the 40-man roster in November, he'll move up the ranks as his bat allows, moving to Double-A this year and potentially arriving in San Francisco in 2012.

Year	Club (League)	Class	AVG	G	AB	R	H	2B	3B	HR	RBI	BB	SO	SB	CS	OBP	SLG
2006	Giants (DSL)	R	.156	44	122	17	19	2	1	0	7	24	31	3	2	.311	.189
2007	Giants (DSL)	R	.241	66	249	44	60	17	2	0	30	41	31	23	6	.351	.325
2008	Fresno (PCL)	AAA	.500	2	6	2	3	1	0	0	0	2	1	0	0	.625	.667
	Giants (AZL)	R	.255	15	55	13	14	4	0	1	6	7	4	0	1	.349	.382
	Salem-Keizer (NWL)	SS	.400	1	5	3	2	0	0	0	0	0	1	0	0	.400	.400
2009	Augusta (SAL)	LoA	.258	117	388	54	100	15	3	2	46	42	66	7	1	.333	.327
2010	San Jose (CAL)	HiA	.256	124	445	70	114	22	5	3	35	47	87	33	15	.333	.348
Minor League Totals			.246	369	1270	203	312	61	11	6	124	163	221	66	25	.337	.325

6 BRANDON CRAWFORD, SS

Born: Jan. 21, 1987. **B-T:** L-R. **Ht.:** 6-2. **Wt.:** 211. **Drafted:** UCLA, 2008 (4th round). **Signed by:** Michael Kendall.

A Bay Area native who grew up a Giants fan, Crawford has the tools to star at shortstop but continues to be plagued by inconsistency at the plate. He has hit just .250/.313/.369 in parts of two seasons in Double-A. Breaking his right hand last July, when he was hit by a liner during batting practice, didn't help. He returned to help San Jose win the California League playoffs, hitting two crucial homers in the finals. Crawford's athleticism and awareness make him a potential Gold Glove shortstop, though he's not as gifted as Ehire Adrianza. He makes plays with plus range, a solid arm and smart positioning. Crawford opens eyes with his opposite-field power, but has yet to show he'll make enough consistent contact to be a big league regular. Coaches worked with him in instructional league to eliminate his leg kick and give him a different timing mechanism, hoping to improve his balance and keep his head on the ball longer. He has solid speed and good instincts but won't be a prolific basestealer. The Giants kept Crawford in big league camp longer than they kept Buster Posey, hoping it would help him be ready to take over as their shortstop in 2011 after Edgar Renteria's contract expired. Crawford's bat isn't ready to make that leap, and he'll probably open the season in Triple-A instead.

Year	Club (League)	Class	AVG	G	AB	R	H	2B	3B	HR	RBI	BB	SO	SB	CS	OBP	SLG
2008	Giants (AZL)	R	.429	4	14	3	6	1	1	0	3	0	3	0	1	.429	.643
	Salem-Keizer (NWL)	SS	.000	1	2	0	0	0	0	0	0	0	0	0	0	.000	.000
2009	San Jose (CAL)	HiA	.371	25	105	21	39	2	2	6	17	10	32	2	4	.445	.600
	Connecticut (EL)	AA	.258	108	392	38	101	26	2	4	31	20	100	11	7	.294	.365
2010	Richmond (EL)	AA	.241	79	291	43	70	12	3	7	22	39	77	4	1	.337	.375
	San Jose (CAL)	HiA	.167	5	18	4	3	1	0	0	1	2	5	0	0	.250	.222
Minor League Totals			.266	222	822	109	219	42	8	17	74	71	217	17	13	.330	.399

7 THOMAS NEAL, OF

Born: Aug. 17, 1987. **B-T:** R-R. **Ht.:** 6-2. **Wt.:** 225. **Drafted:** Riverside (Calif.) CC, D/F 2005 (36th round). **Signed by:** Lee Carballo.

A $220,000 draft-and-follow signee out of Riverside (Calif.) CC, Neal dislocated his throwing shoulder in 2007 and missed nearly 12 months. He broke out in 2009, hitting .337/.431/.579 and leading the California League in on-base percentage, then turned in a solid season in Double-A last year to earn a spot on the 40-man roster. As a youth, he played on a San Diego-area travel team that included Stephen Strasburg, Mike Leake and Giants manager Bruce Bochy's son Brett. Neal is more athletic than most 6-foot-2, 225-pounders. His combination of power, arm strength and surprising ability to cover ground in either outfield corner draws comparisons to Jermaine Dye. But Neal needed time to figure out Double-A pitchers, who worked him with sinkers down and in, followed by sliders away. He has the bat speed to handle quality fastballs but gets a little overeager in RBI situations. While a below-average runner, he's opportunistic on the bases and coaches love his hustle. By the end of the season, Neal learned to take a consistent plan into every at-bat, something he can build on in Triple-A in 2011. There's a good chance he'll be introduced to the big leagues at some point this year, with the chance to establish himself as an everyday player in 2012.

Year	Club (League)	Class	AVG	G	AB	R	H	2B	3B	HR	RBI	BB	SO	SB	CS	OBP	SLG
2006	Salem-Keizer (NWL)	SS	.250	50	176	26	44	6	2	4	20	7	44	1	3	.289	.375
2007	Giants (AZL)	R	.308	10	39	7	12	3	0	1	4	5	7	0	0	.413	.462
2008	Augusta (SAL)	LoA	.276	117	428	69	118	25	1	15	81	48	103	3	4	.359	.444
2009	San Jose (CAL)	HiA	.337	129	475	102	160	41	4	22	90	65	98	3	0	.431	.579
2010	Richmond (EL)	AA	.291	136	525	69	153	40	1	12	69	46	94	11	5	.359	.440
Minor League Totals			.296	442	1643	273	487	115	8	54	264	171	346	18	12	.375	.475

8 CHARLIE CULBERSON, 2B

Born: April 10, 1989. **B-T:** R-R. **Ht.:** 6-1. **Wt.:** 191. **Drafted:** HS—Calhoun, Ga., 2007 (1st round supplemental). **Signed by:** Sean O'Connor.

A surprise supplemental first-round pick in 2007, Culberson played close to home for two seasons at low Class A Augusta but couldn't enjoy the experience. He hit a combined .241/.299/.311 and missed a month in 2008 when he broke his hand punching a paper-towel dispenser. He has never lacked for bat speed, and his hard-nosed attitude helped him re-establish himself as a prospect with a strong 2010 season in high Class A. He has excellent bloodlines: His father Charles was a Giants minor league outfielder, his grandfather Leon played in the majors, and he's also related to the Sislers (Hall of Famer George, former all-star Dick and big leaguer Dave). Culberson has a powerful swing and strong hands to go along with fast-twitch athleticism. Though he's an aggressive hitter who doesn't walk much, his improved plate discipline and pitch recognition skills keyed the progress he made last year. He has average power and solid speed. Drafted as a shortstop, Culberson moved to third base in 2009 and second base last year. His strong arm and quick release make him an asset on double plays. Culberson showed his breakout was no fluke by batting .366/.394/.591 in the Arizona Fall League. He has caught up to fellow 2007 sandwich pick and second baseman Nick Noonan, and the Giants will have to find at-bats for both in Double-A this year.

Year	Club (League)	Class	AVG	G	AB	R	H	2B	3B	HR	RBI	BB	SO	SB	CS	OBP	SLG
2007	Giants (AZL)	R	.286	46	161	32	46	8	5	1	16	19	38	19	1	.374	.416
2008	Augusta (SAL)	LoA	.234	81	282	31	66	11	2	3	27	18	57	6	6	.290	.319
2009	Augusta (SAL)	LoA	.246	132	509	71	125	19	3	2	36	33	110	15	4	.303	.306
2010	San Jose (CAL)	HiA	.290	128	503	80	146	28	4	16	71	33	99	25	7	.340	.457
Minor League Totals			.263	387	1455	214	383	66	14	22	150	103	304	65	18	.322	.373

9 ERIC SURKAMP, LHP

Born: July 16, 1987. **B-T:** L-L. **Ht.:** 6-5. **Wt.:** 220. **Drafted:** North Carolina State, 2008 (6th round). **Signed by:** Pat Portugal.

Surkamp was on his way to leading Giants minor leaguers in strikeouts for the second consecutive season and was within a week of being promoted to Double-A when he partially dislocated his hip while fielding a ground ball in mid-July. He had surgery to tighten the labrum in his hip and should be 100 percent for spring training. He's a product of Cincinnati's famed Moeller High, whose alumni include Buddy Bell, Ken Griffey Jr. and Barry Larkin. Surkamp's fastball sits in the upper 80s, but he gets good sink on it and throws it to both sides of the plate from a three-quarters delivery that adds deception. Coaches believe he can throw harder, both because of his size and the fact that he didn't use his fastball much in college. His curveball and changeup are both plus pitches and he commands his entire arsenal, generating plenty of swings and misses. He also has toyed with a cut fastball to give him another weapon against righthanders. San

Francisco is aggressive with starting pitchers who throw strikes and has a limited inventory of them in the system, so expect Surkamp to move quickly if healthy. He could put up gaudy numbers this year in the Double-A Eastern League, a pitcher's paradise compared to the Cal League.

Year	Club (League)	Class	W	L	ERA	G	GS	CG	SV	IP	H	HR	BB	SO	G/A	WHIP	AVG
2008	Giants (AZL)	R	0	0	2.70	2	0	0	0	3	3	0	0	7	—	0.90	.231
	Salem-Keizer (NWL)	SS	0	2	6.43	5	4	0	0	14	20	1	5	16	—	1.79	.351
2009	Augusta (SAL)	LoA	11	5	3.30	23	23	2	0	131	129	6	39	169	1.09	1.28	.257
2010	San Jose (CAL)	HiA	4	2	3.11	17	17	1	0	101	79	5	22	108	0.99	1.00	.218
Minor League Totals			15	9	3.39	47	44	3	0	250	231	12	66	300	1.04	1.19	.247

10 TOMMY JOSEPH, C/1B

Born: July 16, 1991. **B-T:** R-R. **Ht.:** 6-1. **Wt.:** 210. **Drafted:** HS—Scottsdale, Ariz., 2009 (2nd round). **Signed by:** Chuck Hensley.

Joseph was one of the best power-hitting high school prospects in the 2009 draft and boosted his value by moving behind the plate as a senior. He attended a literal school of hard knocks in his pro debut last year, sustaining a concussion in late May and taking a beating from a barrage of foul tips behind the plate. The Giants don't put much stock in his disappointing numbers because they knew he was nicked up and one of the youngest players in the low Class A South Atlantic League. Joseph arrived straight from high school with a short, direct swing that should lead to plenty of hard contact in time. He generates consistent backspin in batting practice and competes well against quality fastballs. He lacks a consistent approach, though, and his strikeout numbers were indicative of that. Joseph's power is his only plus tool. He has a stocky build, poor speed and defensive limitations. He has a lot of work to do as a catcher after allowing 19 passed balls and 52 steals in 65 games last year. He does have solid arm strength. Joseph started 10 games at first base last year and has the power to play there. That seems like an automatic move with Buster Posey in San Francisco, but the Giants plan to continue developing Joseph as a catcher this year in high Class A.

Year	Club (League)	Class	AVG	G	AB	R	H	2B	3B	HR	RBI	BB	SO	SB	CS	OBP	SLG
2010	Augusta (SAL)	LoA	.236	117	436	46	103	22	1	16	68	26	116	0	0	.290	.401
Minor League Totals			.236	117	436	46	103	22	1	16	68	26	116	0	0	.290	.401

11 RAFAEL RODRIGUEZ, OF

Born: July 13, 1992. **B-T:** R-R. **Ht.:** 6-5. **Wt.:** 200. **Signed:** Dominican Republic, 2008. **Signed by:** Felix Peguero/Pablo Peguero.

Club officials felt Rodriguez could compete as a 17-year-old in the short-season Northwest League, but he struggled with a bad back and was overmatched by recent college draftees while hitting just .163 in 12 games. So the gifted teenager returned to Arizona, and he regained some confidence while finishing out the season in Rookie ball. It will be a challenge for Rodriguez to cover his huge strike zone against pro pitching, but if he reaches his potential, he could be a physical force and plus outfielder in the Dave Winfield mold. His $2.55 million bonus remains a club record for an international player. Rodriguez gained strength in his first full year in the United States and began to trust his ability, but he got caught in between pitches often. He made the biggest improvement in the outfield, where he learned to position himself better and improved on his throwing accuracy. He has a strong arm suitable for right field. He is a long strider who times out faster than he looks, especially when he gets moving on an extra-base hit. He's expected to make his full-season debut in low Class A this year.

Year	Club (League)	Class	AVG	G	AB	R	H	2B	3B	HR	RBI	BB	SO	SB	CS	OBP	SLG
2009	Giants (AZL)	R	.299	35	127	25	38	8	0	0	19	16	23	5	4	.392	.362
2010	Salem-Keizer (NWL)	SS	.163	12	43	3	7	0	1	0	4	3	12	1	0	.250	.209
	Giants (AZL)	R	.301	32	123	20	37	6	0	2	14	5	23	4	2	.323	.398
Minor League Totals			.280	79	293	48	82	14	1	2	37	24	58	10	6	.343	.355

12 JARRETT PARKER, OF

Born: Jan. 1, 1989. **B-T:** L-L. **Ht.:** 6-3. **Wt.:** 190. **Drafted:** Virginia, 2010 (2nd round). **Signed by:** John DiCarlo.

Parker's lean, athletic frame is ideal for a major league outfield prospect and he has a nice blend of running ability, some power potential and plus defensive skills in center field. He put on 20 pounds before his sophomore year and his home runs jumped from zero to 16, turning him into one of the top draft-eligible college hitters in the country. He also led Virgnia to the College World Series in the process. But he hit .188 in the Cape Cod League, and an inconsistent junior season allowed him to fall to the Giants in the second round last June. He signed for an over-slot $700,000 bonus as the 74th overall pick. Parker projects to hit at or near the top of the order, but he must develop better on-base skills because some scouts don't believe he'll hit for average. He had contact issues in college with 177 strikeouts in 656 at-bats, and he'll need to shorten up his long-armed swing if he wants to cut down on strikeouts. His arm is fringe-average but playable in center field, where he otherwise projects to be a solid defender at a premium position. He should start out at Augusta in 2011.

Year	Club (League)	Class	AVG	G	AB	R	H	2B	3B	HR	RBI	BB	SO	SB	CS	OBP	SLG
2010	Did Not Play—Signed Late																

13 JOSE CASILLA, RHP

Born: May 21, 1989. **B-T:** R-R. **Ht.:** 6-1. **Wt.:** 180. **Signed:** Dominican Republic, 2006. **Signed by:** Pablo Peguero.

Casilla's older brother Santiago won a World Series ring with the Giants while finally establishing himself as a valuable short reliever after parts of six seasons with the Athletics. The younger Casilla also had an impressive season and claimed a spot on the 40-man roster. He posted a 1.16 ERA in 46 games in low Class A, used mainly in the closer role, and didn't allow a home run. He doesn't quite have his brother's upper-90s velocity and his fastball is harder some days than others, but his two-seamer makes him a ground-ball machine. He posted a 2.53 groundout/airout ratio last year and induced nine double plays, and at times it sits at 90-93 mph. He throws an average to plus slider that he tends to overuse, and at times he mixes in a slower-breaking curve. He is less consistent from the stretch and must work harder to control opposing runners. He tends to snap his head during his delivery when he overthrows, a flaw he worked hard to address. The younger Casilla received his own postseason experience when San Francisco promoted him to high Class A for the Cal League playoffs. He might be a year or two away from figuring it out, but his command and ability to pitch for a strikeout should allow him to move up through the system.

Year	Club (League)	Class	W	L	ERA	G	GS	CG	SV	IP	H	HR	BB	SO	G/A	WHIP	AVG
2006	Giants (DSL)	R	1	0	2.00	2	2	0	0	9	8	1	4	11	—	1.33	.235
2007	Giants (DSL)	R	6	3	3.76	16	14	0	0	69	58	0	22	58	—	1.15	.223
2008	Giants (AZL)	R	3	1	1.59	6	5	0	0	23	19	1	1	19	—	0.88	.216
	Salem-Keizer (NWL)	SS	0	0	2.70	2	0	0	0	3	4	0	1	4	—	1.50	.308
2009	Salem-Keizer (NWL)	SS	1	1	1.67	25	0	0	12	27	22	0	9	31	2.77	1.15	.210
2010	Augusta (SAL)	LoA	4	1	1.16	46	0	0	14	54	40	0	17	41	2.53	1.05	.214
Minor League Totals			15	6	2.33	97	21	0	26	186	151	2	54	164	2.60	1.10	.220

14 ROGER KIESCHNICK, OF

Born: Jan. 21, 1987. **B-T:** L-R. **Ht.:** 6-3. **Wt.:** 229. **Drafted:** Texas Tech, 2008 (3rd round). **Signed by:** Todd Thomas.

The Giants had high hopes for Kieschnick after his terrific 2009 season in high Class A, which included a farm system-leading 23 home runs. But he was one of several hitting prospects who got off to a slow start in the bad weather of the Double-A Eastern League last year, and it soon became a wasted year for the big kid from Texas. Back spasms sapped his power and he finally spoke up after a horrendous 0-for-34 streak in late May. His stay on the disabled list lasted three weeks, and he wasn't much better when he returned in June. He finally shut it down for good in early July. Eventually, doctors diagnosed a stress fracture in his back, and he worked all winter to rehab the injury. Not only did Kieschnick miss out on valuable development time, but he also couldn't take early batting practice or work on shortening up his swing. When healthy, Kieschnick is an exciting prospect with strength, fast hands and pull power. An above-average runner for his size, he's a plus defender with a plus arm in right field. He plays the game hard. A healthy Kieschnick should return to Double-A.

Year	Club (League)	Class	AVG	G	AB	R	H	2B	3B	HR	RBI	BB	SO	SB	CS	OBP	SLG
2009	San Jose (CAL)	HiA	.296	131	517	86	153	37	8	23	110	36	130	9	1	.345	.532
2010	Richmond (EL)	AA	.251	60	223	21	56	8	3	4	23	18	55	2	3	.305	.368
Minor League Totals			.282	191	740	107	209	45	11	27	133	54	185	11	4	.333	.482

15 CHRIS DOMINGUEZ, 3B

Born: Nov. 22, 1986. **B-T:** R-R. **Ht.:** 6-4. **Wt.:** 240. **Drafted:** Louisville, 2009 (3rd round). **Signed by:** Kevin Christman.

After helping lead Louisville to the 2007 College World Series, Dominguez finished a fine college career in 2009 with 61 home runs, second all-time at Louisville, and a school-record 218 RBIs. He arrived with an uppercut swing that suited him in college but led to a lot of strikeouts and didn't put him in position to handle breaking balls. He made changes last year and competed better against offspeed stuff, but still struck out once per 4.2 at-bats in low Class A. He also hit 21 home runs—second to Brandon Belt in the system—and led the South Atlantic League with 101 RBIs. Dominguez led the league in games played and at-bats, too, and maintained his energy level over the hot summer despite his stocky build. Dominguez is an average runner and isn't blessed with tremendous range at third base, but he can play two steps deeper because his arm strength is off the charts. A rival league manager called it the strongest arm he's ever seen from a minor league third baseman. He makes errors when he rushes things, though. Dominguez, who failed to sign with the Rockies in 2008 as a fifth-round pick, was a bit old for low Class A and will need to make progress quickly. Learning to lay off the high fastball will be among the keys to establishing himself as a future major leaguer. He'll try to make adjustments in 2011, perhaps with a jump to Double-A.

Year	Club (League)	Class	AVG	G	AB	R	H	2B	3B	HR	RBI	BB	SO	SB	CS	OBP	SLG
2009	Giants (AZL)	R	.306	9	36	8	11	2	0	2	8	3	9	1	0	.375	.528
	Salem-Keizer (NWL)	SS	.254	47	181	31	46	5	1	9	32	9	57	11	2	.298	.442
2010	Augusta (SAL)	LoA	.272	137	559	85	152	32	4	21	101	35	133	14	7	.326	.456
Minor League Totals			.269	193	776	124	209	39	5	32	141	47	199	26	9	.322	.456

16 MIKE KICKHAM, LHP

Born: Dec. 12, 1988. **B-T:** L-L. **Ht.:** 6-4. **Wt.:** 210. **Drafted:** Missouri State, 2010 (6th round). **Signed by:** Hugh Walker.

Kickham was a draft-eligible sophomore from a Missouri State program that has produced several well-regarded pitching prospects in recent years, as well as several big leaguers such as Shaun Marcum and Brad Ziegler. The Giants gave him an above-slot $410,000 to sign as a sixth-rounder and believe they might have gotten one of the steals of the 2010 draft. Pitching coordinator Bert Bradley already knew Kickham's repertoire, having watched him compete against his son at Southern Illinois. He's a physical lefty who throws his fastball consistently in the 90s, touching 94 mph, and commands a plus slider that has good, sweeping action. He further confounds lefty hitters with a hard breaking ball that he can drop under their hands. Kickham will change arm angles and showed a good feel for setting up hitters during instructional league—all traits that indicate he could move quickly. He also can throw a decent changeup, giving him a starter's repertoire. Kickham had thrown from a slide step in college and didn't fully load, so coaches worked with him to see if he could boost his velocity. Although he could be murder on lefties as a reliever, San Francisco doesn't have much lefthanded inventory among their starters and so he's likely to get stretched out. Kickham has a twin brother, Dan, who was taken by the Rockies in the 27th round but didn't sign.

Year	Club (League)	Class	W	L	ERA	G	GS	CG	SV	IP	H	HR	BB	SO	G/A	WHIP	AVG
2010	Giants (AZL)	R	0	0	11.57	3	0	0	0	2	4	0	2	3	—	2.57	.400
Minor League Totals			0	0	11.57	3	0	0	0	2	4	0	2	3	—	2.57	.400

17 CONOR GILLASPIE, 3B

Born: July 18, 1987. **B-T:** L-R. **Ht.:** 6-1. **Wt.:** 201. **Drafted:** Wichita State, 2008 (1st round supplemental). **Signed by:** Hugh Walker.

Gillaspie is one of the best contact men in the system whose only plus tool is his ability to hit fastballs. He's a smart hitter with great eye-hand coordination, and he successfully made adjustments after falling into a team-wide slump to start the season in Double-A. Then he continued his momentum in the Arizona Fall League while showing a bit more power, tying with the Blue Jays' Adam Loewen for the league lead with five homers. While Gillaspie doesn't take many walks, he works deep counts and isn't afraid to hit with two strikes. He did a better job fighting off hard stuff inside and learned not to be surprised to see breaking balls in hitters' counts as he boosted his final average to .287. Gillaspie has good gap power and likes to be aggressive when he splits the outfielders, as his eight triples will attest. He's a below-average defender at third base but put in a lot of effort on improving his footwork, and his 17 errors were 10 fewer than the previous year in high Class A. While he's focused on third base, Gillaspie profiles as more of a utility type, so don't be surprised if he's asked to work at second base and left field in the near future. He's an average runner. Gillaspie is on the 40-man roster and was a September callup in 2008—a tradeout benefit because he signed for slot money. Perhaps this is the year Gillaspie gets a legitimate callup.

Year	Club (League)	Class	AVG	G	AB	R	H	2B	3B	HR	RBI	BB	SO	SB	CS	OBP	SLG
2008	Giants (AZL)	R	.273	6	22	2	6	3	0	0	7	3	1	0	1	.360	.409
	Salem-Keizer (NWL)	SS	.268	18	71	4	19	4	0	0	8	9	13	2	0	.350	.324
	San Francisco (NL)	MAJ	.200	8	5	1	1	0	0	0	0	2	0	0	0	.429	.200
2009	San Jose (CAL)	HiA	.286	126	469	62	134	31	2	4	67	55	68	2	3	.364	.386
2010	Richmond (EL)	AA	.287	132	491	57	141	25	8	8	67	37	67	0	4	.335	.420
Major League Totals			.200	8	5	1	1	0	0	0	0	2	0	0	0	.429	.200
Minor League Totals			.285	282	1053	125	300	63	10	12	149	104	149	4	8	.349	.398

18 CHUCKIE JONES, OF

Born: July 28, 1992. **B-T:** R-R. **Ht.:** 6-3. **Wt.:** 235. **Drafted:** HS—Boonville, Mo., 2010 (7th round). **Signed by:** Hugh Walker.

Jones was a high school quarterback and basketball player, but baseball was his best sport. He was Missouri's high school athlete of the year, and the Cardinals already had called to say they were planning to take him in the seventh round before the Giants swooped in one pick earlier. Jones had committed to Maple Woods (Mo.) CC, following his role model, Albert Pujols, but was eager to start his career. He signed quickly and then showed the ultra-athleticism that made him a three-sport standout in high school. Competing mostly before his 18th birthday, he posted a .461 slugging percentage in 46 games in the Rookie-level Arizona League, amassing five homers, four triples and seven doubles among his 46 hits. He has good bat speed to go with his present strength. Jones didn't bother to cut down his swing with two strikes, fanning 61 times in 165 at-bats. But he also drew a team-high 20 walks, indicating he has some plate discipline. Despite his tender age, Jones is built like an NFL linebacker with above-average throwing and running ability. He'll probably outgrow center field, but scouting director John Barr assumed the same thing about Matt Kemp when he was with the Dodgers. He has enough arm strength to make right field a possibility.

Year	Club (League)	Class	AVG	G	AB	R	H	2B	3B	HR	RBI	BB	SO	SB	CS	OBP	SLG
2010	Giants (AZL)	R	.279	46	165	25	46	7	4	5	17	20	61	6	2	.360	.461
Minor League Totals			.279	46	165	25	46	7	4	5	17	20	61	6	2	.360	.461

19 HEATH HEMBREE, RHP

Born: Jan. 13, 1989. **B-T:** R-R. **Ht.:** 6-4. **Wt.:** 205. **Drafted:** College of Charleston, 2010 (5th round). **Signed by:** Jeremy Cleveland.

Hembree was a draft curiosity as a seldom-used closer at the College of Charleston, with rumors in the scouting community that he could hit 100 mph. But he also walked 18 in 29 innings and he didn't have much track record, and he missed his senior year of high school with a torn ACL he sustained in a football game. He pitched only one inning as a college freshman at South Carolina before getting in a year of work in junior college and then at Charleston. Hembree signed relatively quickly and the Giants got right to work, giving him a simple guide move with his front arm that allowed him to repeat his otherwise clean delivery and stay on line to the plate. To call Hembree a quick learner would be an understatement. In 11 relief innings in the Arizona League, he struck out 22 and didn't walk a batter while working from 94-99 mph with his fastball and mixing in a power slider. San Francisco forced him to throw 90 percent changeups in instructional league and it wasn't deemed a wasted effort. He doesn't have a pitch to combat lefthanders, though some think his power repertoire and big hands make him an excellent future candidate for a splitter. Hembree profiles as a premium closer or set-up man, with the potential to move fast as a reliever.

Year	Club (League)	Class	W	L	ERA	G	GS	CG	SV	IP	H	HR	BB	SO	G/A	WHIP	AVG
2010	Giants (AZL)	R	0	0	0.82	12	0	0	3	11	9	0	0	22	1.50	0.82	.220
Minor League Totals			0	0	0.82	12	0	0	3	11	9	0	0	22	1.50	0.82	.220

20 JAKE DUNNING, RHP

Born: Aug. 12, 1988. **B-T:** R-R. **Ht.:** 6-4. **Wt.:** 188. **Drafted:** Indiana, 2009 (33rd round). **Signed by:** Kevin Christman.

A starting shortstop and occasional relief pitcher at Indiana, Dunning hit .227 in Rookie ball before he bought into a full mound conversion. The Giants did the same thing a decade ago with former all-star closer Joe Nathan, who like Dunning is tall, and coaches were thrilled when Dunning showed much better feel and touch at a similar stage. Dunning quickly was able to show command of a curveball, slider and changeup while his fastball consistently hit 94-95 mph. All could be solid-average pitches or better. His slider has good tilt, and his changeup fades away from lefty hitters. He's just learning how to compete on the mound and take the same demeanor out there every time. But his delivery is under control, he is confident and he is committed to his current career path. It's a bonus that he fields his position well, too. Dunning's grasp of four pitches should warrant his development as a starter, but San Francisco might have him work out of the bullpen this season as the organization tries to avoid overtaxing a fresh arm.

Year	Club (League)	Class	AVG	G	AB	R	H	2B	3B	HR	RBI	BB	SO	SB	CS	OBP	SLG
2009	Giants (AZL)	R	.227	22	88	11	20	3	2	0	11	1	19	3	2	.244	.307
Minor League Totals			.227	22	88	11	20	3	2	0	11	1	19	3	2	.244	.307

Year	Club (League)	Class	W	L	ERA	G	GS	CG	SV	IP	H	HR	BB	SO	G/A	WHIP	AVG
2009	Giants (AZL)	R	0	0	9.00	1	0	0	0	1	2	0	1	2	0.00	3.00	.400
2010	Salem-Keizer (NWL)	SS	1	0	2.95	18	0	0	2	37	30	2	8	46	2.22	1.04	.221
Minor League Totals			1	0	3.11	19	0	0	2	38	32	2	9	48	2.11	1.09	.227

21 JORGE BUCARDO, RHP

Born: Oct. 18, 1989. **B-T:** R-R. **Ht.:** 6-1. **Wt.:** 155. **Signed:** Nicaragua, 2006 **Signed by:** Pablo Peguero.

Bucardo is so slender that he could sleep in the barrel of a shotgun, according to farm director Fred Stanley. Club officials were curious how durable he would prove to be in his first full season, and Bucardo was a pleasant surprise, not only with the way he maintained his stuff but also with how he competed on two levels. He led the South Atlantic League in opponent average (.208) and ranked second in ERA (2.21). His lack of strength might have caught up to him in nine unimpressive late-season appearances in high Class A, but it's notable that he threw over 150 innings before his 21st birthday. Bucardo is wiry strong, and his stuff plays as a starter or reliever.

He throws from several arm angles while touching 94 mph, but mostly pitching in the 88-90 range, and gets ground balls with an effective sinker. His slider is average and his changeup is haphazard, but he has a good idea of when to use it. Bucardo is a good athlete who springs off the mound when fielding his position. His older brother Wilber is also in the Giants system, but hasn't developed along the same lines.

Year	Club (League)	Class	W	L	ERA	G	GS	CG	SV	IP	H	HR	BB	SO	G/A	WHIP	AVG
2007	Giants (DSL)	R	7	2	1.35	12	11	0	0	60	45	3	7	39	—	0.87	.200
2008	Giants (AZL)	R	3	1	3.68	11	11	1	0	51	51	4	15	51	—	1.29	.259
2009	Salem-Keizer (NWL)	SS	6	3	2.64	15	15	0	0	82	65	3	21	64	2.41	1.05	.229
2010	Augusta (SAL)	LoA	9	4	2.21	19	18	1	0	114	83	3	31	95	2.51	1.00	.203
	San Jose (CAL)	HiA	2	2	4.42	8	7	0	0	39	46	3	19	26	2.43	1.68	.297
Minor League Totals			27	12	2.63	65	62	2	0	346	290	16	93	275	2.46	1.11	.228

22 JASON STOFFEL, RHP

Born: Sept. 15 1988. **B-T:** R-R. **Ht.:** 6-2. **Wt.:** 220. **Drafted:** Arizona, 2009 (4th round). **Signed by:** Chuck Hensley.

The Giants hoped to see a little more polish from Stoffel, who was Arizona's all-time saves leader and served as closer in a Wildcats bullpen that included Ryan Perry and Daniel Schlereth, a pair of first-rounders from the 2008 draft. Stoffel recorded 25 saves in 29 chances in high Class A, but had trouble controlling his tempo and ran into control problems when he'd overthrow, causing him to get underneath the ball. Stoffel ended the year with a huge control positive, though, when he threw three scoreless innings in a deciding Game Five in the California League playoffs as San Jose won an 11-inning thriller at Rancho Cucamonga. Stoffel struck out the final hitter with the tying run at third base—his eighth strikeout in 20 batters faced during the postseason. Stoffel throws his fastball at 88-93 mph, at times reaching the mid-90s, and has a true power slider that can sits in upper 70s and touches 80 mph. He can turn it into a hard slurve at times. He worked on a changeup on the side but didn't have the confidence to use it in games. His future depends on his ability to locate his fastball down and to both sides of the plate—something he's shown the ability to do when he's composed on the mound.

Year	Club (League)	Class	W	L	ERA	G	GS	CG	SV	IP	H	HR	BB	SO	G/A	WHIP	AVG
2009	Giants (AZL)	R	0	0	1.86	9	0	0	2	10	8	0	0	6	1.88	0.83	.211
	Salem-Keizer (NWL)	SS	1	0	0.00	8	0	0	2	10	6	0	1	13	3.50	0.68	.158
2010	San Jose (CAL)	HiA	2	4	4.80	52	0	0	25	51	55	4	24	66	2.04	1.56	.276
Minor League Totals			3	4	3.69	69	0	0	29	71	69	4	25	85	2.16	1.33	.251

23 NICK NOONAN, 2B

Born: May 4, 1989. **B-T:** L-R. **Ht.:** 6-0. **Wt.:** 185. **Drafted:** HS—San Diego, 2007 (1st round supplemental). **Signed by:** Ray Krawczyk.

The Giants fast-tracked Noonan after he lit up the AZL in his pro debut three years ago, even though there were signs his offensive approach needed work and he wasn't ready to make the jump. Sure enough, Noonan came upon a speed bump in Double-A, struggling to hit anything but singles and missing more than 40 games with a recurring hamstring injury. Despite gifted hand-eye coordination and a knack for hitting with runners on base in the past, Noonan had trouble competing against Double-A pitching. He was off-balance and lunged at pitches, leading him to accept an overhauled approach in instructional league. Coaches had him put more weight on his back leg, firm up his front side and get his hands on a shorter path to the ball. According to Richmond manager Andy Skeels, Noonan started driving the ball, staying back against lefties and generating better bat speed—looking more like the lefthanded hitter who drew comparisons to Robin Ventura when San Francisco drafted him. Noonan hasn't added much strength to his rangy frame. He's an average defender and runner whose bat is his ticket to advancement, so he'll have to reestablish his value with a return trip to Double-A.

Year	Club (League)	Class	AVG	G	AB	R	H	2B	3B	HR	RBI	BB	SO	SB	CS	OBP	SLG
2007	Giants (AZL)	R	.316	52	206	33	65	11	4	3	40	12	20	18	3	.357	.451
2008	Augusta (SAL)	LoA	.279	119	499	79	139	27	7	9	68	24	98	29	4	.315	.415
2009	San Jose (CAL)	HiA	.259	124	459	82	119	26	8	7	64	48	97	9	5	.330	.397
2010	Richmond (EL)	AA	.237	101	372	43	88	12	2	3	26	22	74	7	3	.280	.304
Minor League Totals			.268	396	1536	237	411	76	21	22	198	105	289	63	15	.317	.387

24 JUAN PEREZ, OF

Born: Nov. 13, 1986. **B-T:** R-R. **Ht.:** 5-11. **Wt.:** 185. **Drafted:** Western Oklahoma State JC, 2008 (13th round). **Signed by:** Todd Thomas.

Perez earned his prospect stripes a little later than most. But then again, he has a better story to tell. The Dominican native moved to the United States in 2001 and wasn't drafted out of high school in the Bronx, so he apprenticed for his father's plumbing company and played in an amateur men's league. After facing all those ex-pros, Perez was well prepared when he got an opportunity to play at Western Oklahoma JC. He set Division II national juco records with 37 homers and 102 RBIs in 2008, which got him drafted in the 13th round by San

Francisco. Perez packs a lot of punch in a small body, and his ability to play second base in addition to all three outfield spots gives him multiple avenues to advance. He was so good in center field that the Giants moved a better prospect, Francisco Peguero, to right field. He's an above-average runner and thrower who could hit for average and power. He showed that power in the Carolina League-California League all-star game, earning MVP honors with a homer and a double. Breaking balls at times gave Perez problems in high Class A, and he doesn't have premium bat speed to catch up to the best fastballs. He'll have to become more efficient on the bases after he was caught stealing (15) almost as often as he succeeded. Special assistant Felipe Alou said his tools conjure Craig Biggio, but Perez needs to boost his walk rate and turn some of his fly balls into line drives.

Year	Club (League)	Class	AVG	G	AB	R	H	2B	3B	HR	RBI	BB	SO	SB	CS	OBP	SLG
2009	Augusta (SAL)	LoA	.244	123	447	56	109	29	3	9	54	23	101	18	4	.283	.383
2010	San Jose (CAL)	HiA	.298	131	551	83	164	37	10	13	63	31	116	17	15	.337	.472
Minor League Totals			.274	254	998	139	273	66	13	22	117	54	217	35	19	.313	.432

25 RYAN VERDUGO, LHP

Born: April 10, 1987. **B-T:** L-L. **Ht.:** 6-0. **Wt.:** 195. **Drafted:** Louisiana State, 2008 (9th round). **Signed by:** Andrew Jefferson.

Verdugo won a Mr. Baseball award in Washington and was drafted in 2005 (43rd round) by the Phillies even though he had just had Tommy John surgery. He opted to go to Skagit Valley (Wash.) JC instead, where he pitched a no-hitter and reestablished himself on draft boards. The Giants took a flier on him in the 47th round of the 2007 draft, even though they knew he had committed to Louisiana State. Verdugo fulfilled that commitment, and after he had a strong year as a starting pitcher, San Francisco spent another pick on him. They saw a pitcher with easy arm action whose 92 mph fastball seemed to jump out of his hand. Verdugo is a deceptive lefty whose stuff consistently misses bats. Working in relief, he fanned 94 in 63 innings between Augusta and San Jose, right in line with his pro average of 13.4 strikeouts per nine innings. His changeup is his best offspeed pitch and shows flashes of being above-average. If Verdugo can tighten up his slider, he could get a chance to start again. Verdugo remains a minus command pitcher who posted a 2.45 ERA while starting and throwing three- and four-inning stints in the Arizona Fall League, but didn't work many clean innings (37 baserunners in 22 innings). If he can start to fill up the strike zone, he will advance quickly.

Year	Club (League)	Class	W	L	ERA	G	GS	CG	SV	IP	H	HR	BB	SO	G/A	WHIP	AVG
2008	Giants (AZL)	R	1	0	2.08	8	0	0	2	13	9	0	6	19	—	1.15	.200
	Salem-Keizer (NWL)	SS	0	0	4.50	1	0	0	0	2	1	1	1	3	—	1.00	.167
2009	Giants (AZL)	R	0	0	0.00	2	0	0	0	3	0	0	0	6	0.50	0.00	.000
	Augusta (SAL)	LoA	4	0	1.39	21	0	0	0	32	19	0	19	45	1.14	1.18	.170
2010	Augusta (SAL)	LoA	4	1	2.25	22	0	0	1	32	26	0	14	50	1.05	1.25	.226
	San Jose (CAL)	HiA	4	0	1.47	22	1	0	0	31	15	3	19	44	1.21	1.11	.149
Minor League Totals			13	1	1.75	76	1	0	3	113	70	4	59	167	1.11	1.14	.180

26 YDWIN VILLEGAS, SS

Born: Sept. 1, 1990. **B-T:** B-R. **Ht.:** 5-10. **Wt.:** 165. **Signed:** Venezuela, 2008. **Signed by:** Ciro Villalobos.

San Francisco still has to dream a bit on Villegas, who wasn't strong enough for a full-season assignment and hit just .189/.215/.242 in low Class A last year. He began the season in extended spring training and went up to Augusta to replace Sharlon Schoop and wound up a semi-regular thanks to his glove. Villegas' defensive skills and playmaking abilities at shortstop rival Ehire Adrianza and Brandon Crawford. In instructional league, Villegas moved to second base to form an acrobatic double-play combination with Adrianza that had coaches slapping their foreheads in amazement. Villegas played much looser after reporting to the Giants' winter instructional camp in the Dominican Republic after the season, running better and swinging the bat with more authority. Villegas is from the same area (Carabobo) in Venezuela as Pablo Sandoval, but San Francisco doesn't have him on the Panda's calorie counter. Villegas needs to gain weight and prove he's durable enough to play a full season, to say nothing of the strides he must make with his switch-hitting approach. For now, he has enough youth, projection and premium defensive tools to warrant attention. He's expected to make a repeat visit to Augusta in 2011.

Year	Club (League)	Class	AVG	G	AB	R	H	2B	3B	HR	RBI	BB	SO	SB	CS	OBP	SLG
2008	Giants (DSL)	R	.219	67	219	40	48	7	1	0	25	40	36	13	7	.348	.260
2009	Giants (AZL)	R	.302	40	159	28	48	6	1	0	21	9	21	12	3	.345	.352
	Salem-Keizer (NWL)	SS	.375	3	8	1	3	0	0	0	2	1	2	0	0	.444	.375
2010	Augusta (SAL)	LoA	.189	79	264	20	50	9	1	1	24	9	55	1	2	.215	.242
Minor League Totals			.229	189	650	89	149	22	3	1	72	59	114	26	12	.298	.277

27 DARREN FORD, OF

Born: Oct. 1, 1985. **B-T:** R-R. **Ht.:** 5-9. **Wt.:** 192. **Drafted:** Chipola (Fla.) JC, D/F 2004 (18th round). **Signed by:** Tony Blengino (Brewers).

Ford was acquired along with lefthander Steve Hammond in a July 2008 trade that sent Ray Durham to the Brewers. Ford's eventful 2010 season began with an eye-opening spring training that included an electric 11-for-22 performance that won him the clubhouse award for best rookie in camp. He made a memorable major league debut as a pinch-runner Sept. 1, sprinting madly around the bases on a wild pitch and error to score the winning run against the Rockies. Ford wasn't on the playoff roster, but he enjoyed a front-row seat for the Giants' run to a World Series title. His season wasn't all good news, though. In July, Ford surrendered to authorities in New Jersey after investigators suspected he made up a story over the winter about being robbed at gunpoint while making a bank deposit from his offseason job at a car dealership. The charges were a distraction for the hyper-fast leadoff hitter—he earns 80 speed grades on the 20-80 scale from some scouts—as he struck out too much and threw away at-bats against tougher Double-A pitching. His choppy swing precludes him from driving the ball consistently, and he hits too many groundballs. Ford was in the process of resolving his legal situation over the winter. If he can avoid distractions and develop a consistent righthanded swing, his blinding speed and tremendous range in center field make him an option as a reserve outfielder.

Year	Club (League)	Class	AVG	G	AB	R	H	2B	3B	HR	RBI	BB	SO	SB	CS	OBP	SLG
2005	Helena (PIO)	R	.271	61	236	57	64	4	3	1	24	33	70	18	4	.365	.326
2006	West Virginia (SAL)	LoA	.283	125	491	93	139	24	3	7	54	56	133	69	15	.361	.387
2007	West Virginia (SAL)	LoA	.335	51	224	48	75	15	4	5	33	23	56	31	10	.398	.504
	Brevard County (FSL)	HiA	.231	72	273	46	63	7	1	4	27	35	67	36	6	.317	.308
2008	Brevard County (FSL)	HiA	.230	91	343	57	79	13	3	2	27	46	88	48	11	.322	.303
	San Jose (CAL)	HiA	.219	38	128	21	28	4	1	0	7	23	42	14	1	.346	.266
2009	San Jose (CAL)	HiA	.300	101	380	81	114	17	9	9	50	49	97	35	12	.386	.463
2010	Richmond (EL)	AA	.251	113	463	64	116	20	9	5	40	39	106	37	15	.315	.365
	San Francisco (NL)	MAJ	—	7	0	1	0	0	0	0	0	0	0	2	1	—	—
Major League Totals			—	7	0	1	0	0	0	0	0	0	0	2	1	—	—
Minor League Totals			.267	652	2538	467	678	104	33	33	262	304	659	288	74	.349	.373

28 JOHNNY MONELL, C

Born: March 27, 1986. **B-T:** L-R. **Ht.:** 5-11. **Wt.:** 216. **Drafted:** Seminole (Fla.) CC, 2007 (30th round). **Signed by:** Glenn Tufts.

A Bronx native, Monell is the son of a well-traveled former minor leaguer, also named Johnny, who played for 17 seasons on three continents. The younger Monell grew up soft-tossing with the likes of Jim Thome in winter ball in Puerto Rico and has lefthanded power of his own. He didn't disappoint in his first exposure to the Cal League and hit 19 home runs in the regular season, then connected for three more for San Jose in the championship series to win playoff MVP honors. He's more slugger than hitter and was being exposed by older competition in the Puerto Rican League over the winter. Monell was old for high Class A and his receiving skills remain raw. Pitchers generally like throwing to him, though, and he used his solid arm to throw out 29 percent of basestealers last year. Monell has a bulldog attitude that makes him a good competitor and teammate and he shows some ability as a game-caller. His arm is slightly above-average and he runs well for a catcher, hitting four triples and stealing 12 bases in 15 attempts. He remains an interesting platoon candidate if he can polish up his defensive skills. At his age, though, he can't afford to repeat any levels, so a move up to Double-A is in the offing.

Year	Club (League)	Class	AVG	G	AB	R	H	2B	3B	HR	RBI	BB	SO	SB	CS	OBP	SLG
2007	Giants (AZL)	R	.240	28	75	11	18	3	1	3	19	15	16	3	4	.376	.427
2008	Giants (AZL)	R	.405	11	42	13	17	7	0	1	10	4	5	3	0	.479	.643
	Salem-Keizer (NWL)	SS	.267	43	161	21	43	17	0	5	25	11	36	1	2	.330	.466
2009	Augusta (SAL)	LoA	.273	91	293	46	80	21	0	8	44	33	45	4	1	.355	.427
2010	San Jose (CAL)	HiA	.273	115	421	66	115	25	4	19	70	48	105	12	3	.350	.487
	Fresno (PCL)	AAA	.200	5	15	0	3	1	1	0	1	2	4	0	0	.294	.400
Minor League Totals			.274	293	1007	157	276	74	6	36	169	113	211	23	10	.355	.467

29 HENRY SOSA, RHP

Born: July 28, 1985. **B-T:** R-R. **Ht.:** 6-1. **Wt.:** 202. **Signed:** Dominican Republic, 2004. **Signed by:** Rick Ragazzo/Pablo Peguero.

After a few injury-marred seasons that included knee surgery and a strained muscle in his upper back, Sosa came out blazing in spring training, throwing consistently in the mid-90s while keeping a spotless 0.00 ERA in 10 appearances covering 12 innings. It looked like he'd be the first reliever called upon when the Giants needed a fresh arm in April or May. But Sosa's season in Triple-A didn't go as planned and San Francisco still seemed confused about whether he fits best as a starter or reliever. Sosa hit a low point in late May, when he was suspended two games for fighting a teammate. He took a step back with command and got punished by Triple-A hitters when he elevated the ball. He had trouble establishing his secondary pitches because he tends to push his changeup and his breaking balls (he throws both a curve and a slider) are fringy. San Francisco hoped Sosa would have matured into a better competitor by now, as he's starting to get a bit old to maintain his prospect status. He remains one of the more electric arms in the system, though, warranting a continuing look.

Year	Club (League)	Class	W	L	ERA	G	GS	CG	SV	IP	H	HR	BB	SO	G/A	WHIP	AVG
2004	Giants (DSL)	R	0	5	5.30	13	7	0	0	36	40	2	19	25	—	1.65	.282
2005	Giants (DSL)	R	5	6	3.58	13	12	0	0	55	53	4	8	46	—	1.10	.250
2006	Giants (AZL)	R	2	1	3.90	9	6	0	0	32	20	3	12	41	—	0.99	.177
2007	Augusta (SAL)	LoA	6	0	0.73	13	10	0	1	62	30	2	25	61	—	0.89	.144
	San Jose (CAL)	HiA	5	5	4.38	14	14	0	0	64	66	8	36	78	—	1.60	.262
2008	San Jose (CAL)	HiA	3	4	4.31	12	12	0	0	56	62	6	18	58	—	1.42	.283
	Augusta (SAL)	LoA	0	0	0.00	2	0	0	0	1	1	0	2	0	—	2.25	.250
2009	Connecticut (EL)	AA	6	0	2.36	14	14	0	0	72	61	4	25	44	0.59	1.19	.231
2010	Fresno (PCL)	AAA	7	8	4.07	36	14	0	0	115	113	20	55	83	0.87	1.46	.256
Minor League Totals			34	29	3.48	126	89	0	1	494	446	49	200	436	0.74	1.31	.240

30 CLAYTON TANNER, LHP

Born: Dec. 5, 1987. **B-T:** R-L. **Ht.:** 6-2. **Wt.:** 211. **Drafted:** HS—Concord, Calif., 2006 (3rd round). **Signed by:** Keith Snider.

Tanner's ability to miss bats has trended in the wrong direction since the Giants grabbed him out of a northern California high school, but he's an intelligent command pitcher who is usually around the plate and impresses on nights when he has three pitches working. Tanner had a strained oblique in May, missing two starts, but strung together enough solid starts in June to be named an Eastern League all-star replacement for Daryl Maday, who was promoted to Triple-A. Tanner's season high for strikeouts was just six, and he pitches to contact. He'll need finer control to live up to his back-of-the-rotation ceiling. He induces ground balls with a sinking fastball and changeup and changes speeds well. At times he gets good, downward tilt on his low-80s slider, and at others it's more of a groundball pitch than a swing-and-miss offering. His slider helps him neutralize lefthanders, who hit just .180 against him, and he could have a future as a lefty specialist if needed. Tanner is always studying opposing hitters for weaknesses or looking for a new wrinkle to exploit. San Francisco added him to its 40-man roster in November, and he should move up to Fresno in 2011.

Year	Club (League)	Class	W	L	ERA	G	GS	CG	SV	IP	H	HR	BB	SO	G/A	WHIP	AVG
2006	Salem-Keizer (NWL)	SS	2	2	3.46	13	0	0	1	26	17	1	8	25	—	0.96	.183
2007	Augusta (SAL)	LoA	12	8	3.59	27	23	1	0	135	147	5	44	104	—	1.41	.282
2008	San Jose (CAL)	HiA	10	8	3.69	24	24	0	0	117	124	1	39	84	—	1.39	.274
2009	San Jose (CAL)	HiA	12	6	3.17	26	23	0	0	139	132	18	42	121	1.46	1.25	.254
2010	Richmond (EL)	AA	9	9	3.68	27	27	0	0	149	150	10	64	79	1.93	1.44	.265
Minor League Totals			45	33	3.53	117	97	1	1	567	570	35	197	413	1.69	1.35	.265

Seattle Mariners

BY **CONOR GLASSEY**

The Mariners' 2010 season was arguably the worst in franchise history.

The franchise debuted in 1977 and didn't post its first winning season until 1990, so there were certainly plenty of lean years. But 2010 was much more disappointing because even the most pessimistic fans in Seattle couldn't have seen it coming.

The Mariners went 85-77 in 2009, their first season under general manager Jack Zduriencik, and optimism reigned only one year after they became the first team with a $100 million payroll to lose more than 100 games. When Zduriencik signed free agent Chone Figgins and traded for Cliff Lee last offseason, many analysts picked Seattle to win the American League West.

But everything went wrong for the Mariners. Local writers reported that franchise icon Ken Griffey Jr. was caught napping in the clubhouse when he was needed for pinch-hitting duty during a game in May, and he retired in June after batting .184/.250/.204 in 98 at-bats. Figgins started slowly and never got on track and he got into a dugout fight with manager Don Wakamatsu in July. Wakamatsu and three big league coaches were fired in early August.

The Mariners lost 100 games for the fifth time in franchise history. While Ichiro Suzuki became the first player ever to record 10 straight 200-hit seasons, Seattle scored just 513 runs, the lowest full-season total for an AL team since the introduction of the designated hitter. Righthander Felix Hernandez won the Cy Young Award, yet went 13-12 because he was saddled with poor run support and a shaky bullpen.

By July it was obvious the Mariners would need to trade Lee, who was headed toward free agency, but even that ended up backfiring. The Mariners shipped Lee and Mark Lowe to the Rangers for first baseman Justin Smoak, righthanders Blake Beavan and Josh Lueke, and second baseman Matt Lawson.

Lueke was charged with rape and sodomy in a May 2008 incident and served 42 days in jail before reaching a plea deal for lesser charges—false imprisonment with violence—that included three years felony probation. His past was common knowledge within the industry, but Zduriencik contended he hadn't known the extent of Lueke's legal troubles. The Mariners, who have worked with groups opposing violence toward women, drew fire for acquiring Lueke, and director of pro scouting Carmen Fusco took the fall when he was fired in September. The franchise took

LARRY GOREN

Acquired at the trade deadline, Justin Smoak is part of the Mariners promising young core

TOP 30 PROSPECTS

1. Dustin Ackley, 2b	**16.** Carlos Triunfel, ss
2. Michael Pineda, rhp	**17.** Blake Beavan, rhp
3. Nick Franklin, ss/2b	**18.** Matt Mangini, 3b/1b
4. Taijuan Walker, rhp	**19.** Esteilon Peguero, ss
5. Guillermo Pimentel, of	**20.** Phillips Castillo, of
6. Mauricio Robles, lhp	**21.** Stephen Pryor, rhp
7. Johermyn Chavez, of	**22.** James Jones, of
8. Marcus Littlewood, ss	**23.** Jordan Shipers, lhp
9. Kyle Seager, inf	**24.** Josh Fields, rhp
10. Dan Cortes, rhp	**25.** Carlos Peguero, of
11. Greg Halman, of	**26.** Tom Wilhelmsen, rhp
12. Josh Lueke, rhp	**27.** Steve Baron, c
13. Alex Liddi, 3b/1b	**28.** Erasmo Ramirez, rhp
14. Ramon Morla, 3b	**29.** Mickey Wiswall, 1b/3b
15. Rich Poythress, 1b/3b	**30.** Yoervis Medina, rhp

another hit Nov. 10, when Hall of Fame broadcaster Dave Niehaus died of a heart attack.

The Mariners do have hope for the future. Hernandez is the best pitcher in baseball, and Ichiro shows no signs of slowing down. Smoak and second baseman Dustin Ackley, the system's No. 1 prospect, should help rejuvenate the lineup in the next couple of years, and righthander Michael Pineda eventually should slot in right behind Hernandez in the rotation.

Seattle may not be able to contend under new manager Eric Wedge in 2011, but the season can't be as disheartening as the one that preceded it.

General Manager: Jack Zduriencik. **Farm Director:** Pedro Grifol. **Scouting Director:** Tom McNamara.

Class	Team	League	W	L	PCT	Finish*	Manager
Majors	Seattle Mariners	American	61	101	.377	14th (14)	D. Wakamatsu/D. Brown
Triple-A	Tacoma Rainiers	Pacific Coast	74	69	.517	†7th (16)	D. Brown/J. Castro
Double-A	West Tenn Diamond Jaxx	Southern	73	66	.525	4th (10)	Tim Laker
High A	High Desert Mavericks	California	75	65	.536	4th (10)	J. Horner/D. Garner
Low A	Clinton LumberKings	Midwest	74	65	.532	6th (16)	John Tamargo
Short-season	Everett AquaSox	Northwest	49	26	.645	†1st (8)	Jose Moreno
Rookie	Pulaski Mariners	Appalachian	37	28	.569	3rd (10)	Eddie Menchaca
Rookie	AZL Mariners	Arizona	20	36	.357	11th (12)	Jesus Azuaje
Overall 2010 Minor League Record			402	356	.530	5th (30)	

*Finish in overall standings (No. of teams in league). †League champion.
*Double-A affiliate will be known as Jackson in 2011.

LAST YEAR'S TOP 30

Player, Pos.		Status
1.	Dustin Ackley, of/1b	No. 1
2.	Michael Saunders, of	Majors
3.	Adam Moore, c	Majors
4.	Phillippe Aumont, rhp	(Phillies)
5.	Alex Liddi, 3b	No. 13
6.	Carlos Triunfel, ss/2b	No. 16
7.	Michael Pineda, rhp	No. 2
8.	Tyson Gillies, of	(Phillies)
9.	Nick Franklin, ss	No. 3
10.	Greg Halman, of	No. 11
11.	Danny Cortes, rhp	No. 10
12.	Mario Martinez, 3b/1b	Dropped out
13.	Mauricio Robles, lhp	No. 6
14.	Nick Hill, lhp	Dropped out
15.	Ezequiel Carrera, of	(Indians)
16.	Josh Fields, rhp	No. 24
17.	Steven Hensley, rhp	Dropped out
18.	J.C. Ramirez, rhp	(Phillies)
19.	Matt Tuiasosopo, 3b/2b	Majors
20.	James Jones, of	No. 22
21.	Dennis Raben, 1b	Dropped out
22.	Julio Morban, of	Dropped out
23.	Mike Carp, 1b	Dropped out
24.	Gabriel Noriega, ss	Dropped out
25.	Steve Baron, c	No. 27
26.	Kanekoa Texeira, rhp	(Royals)
27.	Ricky Orta, rhp	(Rays)
28.	Rich Poythress, 1b	No. 15
29.	Guillermo Pimentel, of	No. 5
30.	Kyle Seager, 2b/3b	No. 9

BEST TOOLS

Best Hitter for Average	Dustin Ackley
Best Power Hitter	Johermyn Chavez
Best Strike-Zone Discipline	Dustin Ackley
Fastest Baserunner	Dustin Ackley
Best Athlete	Greg Halman
Best Fastball	Michael Pineda
Best Curveball	Josh Fields
Best Slider	Michael Pineda
Best Changeup	Mauricio Robles
Best Control	Erasmo Ramirez
Best Defensive Catcher	Steve Baron
Best Defensive Infielder	Gabriel Noriega
Best Infield Arm	Carlos Triunfel
Best Defensive Outfielder	Matt Cerione
Best Outfield Arm	Johermyn Chavez

PROJECTED 2014 LINEUP

Catcher	Adam Moore
First Base	Justin Smoak
Second Base	Dustin Ackley
Third Base	Chone Figgins
Shortstop	Nick Franklin
Left Field	Guillermo Pimentel
Center Field	Franklin Gutierrez
Right Field	Michael Saunders
Designated Hitter	Ichiro Suzuki
No. 1 Starter	Felix Hernandez
No. 2 Starter	Michael Pineda
No. 3 Starter	Taijuan Walker
No. 4 Starter	Mauricio Robles
No. 5 Starter	Blake Beavan
Closer	Dan Cortes

TOP PROSPECTS OF THE DECADE

Year	Player, Pos.	2010 Org.
2001	Ryan Anderson, lhp	Out of baseball
2002	Ryan Anderson, lhp	Out of baseball
2003	Rafael Soriano, rhp	Rays
2004	Felix Hernandez, rhp	Mariners
2005	Felix Hernandez, rhp	Mariners
2006	Jeff Clement, c	Pirates
2007	Adam Jones, of	Orioles
2008	Jeff Clement, c	Pirates
2009	Greg Halman, of	Mariners
2010	Dustin Ackley, of/1b	Mariners

TOP DRAFT PICKS OF THE DECADE

Year	Player, Pos.	2010 Org.
2001	Michael Garciaparra, ss (1st round supp.)	Astros
2002	*John Mayberry Jr., of	Phillies
2003	Adam Jones, ss (1st round supp.)	Orioles
2004	Matt Tuiasosopo, ss (3rd round)	Mariners
2005	Jeff Clement, c	Pirates
2006	Brandon Morrow, rhp	Blue Jays
2007	Phillippe Aumont, rhp	Phillies
2008	Josh Fields, rhp	Mariners
2009	Dustin Ackley, of/1b	Mariners
2010	Taijuan Walker, rhp (1st round supp.)	Mariners

*Did not sign.

LARGEST BONUSES IN CLUB HISTORY

Dustin Ackley, 2009	$6,000,000
Ichiro Suzuki, 2000	$5,000,000
Jeff Clement, 2005	$3,400,000
Esteilon Peguero, 2010	$2,900,000
Brandon Morrow, 2006	$2,450,000

MINOR LEAGUE DEPTH CHART

SEATTLE MARINERS

TOP 2011 ROOKIE: Dustin Ackley, 2b. It's not likely he starts the year in Seattle, but his bat should make an immediate impact once he gets there.

BREAKOUT PROSPECT: Ramon Morla, 3b. After leading the Rookie-level Appalachian League with 17 homers in 2010, he's ready to make the jump to full-season ball.

SLEEPER: Stephen Landazuri, rhp. The 22nd-rounder sat 91-93 in the instructional league with a three-pitch mix and projection remaining in his body.

SOURCE OF TOP 30 TALENT

Homegrown	24	Acquired	6
College	8	Trades	5
Junior college	0	Rule 5 draft	0
High school	5	Independent leagues	0
Draft-and-follow	0	Free agents/waivers	1
Nondrafted free agents	0		
International	11		

LF
Guillermo Pimentel (5)
Julio Morban
Jake Shaffer
Reggie Lawson

CF
Denny Almonte
Matt Cerione
Danny Carroll

RF
Johermyn Chavez (7)
Greg Halman (11)
Phillips Castillo (20)
James Jones (22)
Carlos Peguero (25)
Jabari Blash
Michael Wilson
Alexy Palma
Alfredo Morales
Kevin Rivers

3B
Alex Liddi (13)
Ramon Morla (14)
Carlos Triunfel (16)
Matt Mangini (18)
Mario Martinez
Nate Tenbrink
Vinnie Catricala
Kevin Mailloux

SS
Nick Franklin (3)
Marcus Littlewood (8)
Gabriel Noriega
Yordyn Calderon
Bryan Brito

2B
Dustin Ackley (1)
Kyle Seager (9)
Esteilon Peguero (19)
Matt Lawson
Jorge Agudelo

1B
Rich Poythress (15)
Mickey Wiswall (29)
Ji-Man Choi
Dennis Raben
Mike Carp
Stefen Romero
Jharmidy DeJesus

C
Steve Baron (28)
Christian Carmichael
Trevor Coleman
Larry Gonzalez

RHP

RHSP	RHRP
Michael Pineda (2)	Dan Cortes (10)
Taijuan Walker (4)	Josh Lueke (12)
Blake Beavan (17)	Stephen Pryor (21)
Erasmo Ramirez (28)	Josh Fields (24)
Yoervis Medina (30)	Tom Wilhelmsen (26)
Steven Hensley	Anthony Varvaro
Richard Vargas	Tyler Burgoon
Chaz Roe	Jose Flores
Tyler Blandford	Forrest Snow
Stephen Landazuri	Jarrett Grube
Jose Campos	Fray Martinez
George Mieses	Seon Gi Kim
Brandon Maurer	Ben Versnik
Andrew Carraway	
Luke Taylor	
Stephen Kohlscheen	
Jose Torres	
Charles Kaalekahi	
Tim Boyce	

LHP

LHSP	LHRP
Mauricio Robles (6)	Edward Paredes
Jordan Shipers (23)	Brian Moran
Jimmy Gillheeney	Nick Hill
Jon Hesketh	Chris Seddon
Anthony Vasquez	Jason Markovitz
Luis Pina	Nick Czyz
Anthony Fernandez	Bobby LaFromboise
Edlando Seco	
Brandol Perez	

BEST PURE HITTER: 1B/3B Mickey Wiswall (7) hit just .301 with metal bats at Boston College in the spring, then matched that average in low Class A.

BEST POWER HITTER: Wiswall. He hit nine homers in two minor league stops and ranks second all-time at BC in single-season (19) and career (37) longballs.

FASTEST RUNNER: OF Jabari Blash (8) has plus speed once he gets going, though he isn't a big bas-estealing threat.

BEST DEFENSIVE PLAYER: While some scouts believe Marcus Littlewood (2) lacks the range to stay at shortstop, Seattle thinks he covers enough ground and rate his hands, arm, actions and instincts all as above-average.

BEST FASTBALL: RHP Stephen Pryor (5) operates at 94-97 mph. He touches 98 mph, as does ultra-athletic RHP Taijuan Walker (1s), the club's top pick.

BEST SECONDARY PITCH: LHP Jason Markovitz (13) gets by with a high-80s fastball because he has a quality curveball. Walker flashes a 12-to-6 hammer, while RHP Tyler Burgoon (10) attacks hitters with his slider.

BEST PRO DEBUT: RHP Forrest Snow (36) had a 0.60 ERA, nine saves and 55 strikeouts in 45 innings between two stops. Pryor posted a 2.04 ERA and fanned 55 in 35 innings while reaching low Class A. RHP Tim Boyce (44) was a Rookie-level Appalachian League all-star and led the circuit in wins, going 9-3, 2.98 with 55 strikeouts in 57 innings. He throws 90-92 mph.

BEST ATHLETE: Walker averaged 21 points and 15 rebounds a game as a senior basketball forward and could have played college hoops. Blash, who has raw power and arm strength to go with his speed, is the most athletic of the Mariners' position players.

MOST INTRIGUING BACKGROUND: Unsigned RHP David Holman's (50) father Brian came within one out of throwing a perfect game for Seattle in 1990. Unsigned OF Colton Keough's (49) dad Matt also pitched in the majors, and his mother Jeana is a former Playboy Playmate and cast member of "The Real Housewives of Orange County." RHP Stephen Kohlscheen's (45) father Brian is the Midwest cross-checker for the Phillies. RHP Ben Versnik's (38) dad Ron was a center drafted by the United States Football League's Chicago Blitz.

CLOSEST TO THE MAJORS: Flamethrowing relievers like Pryor often move quickly.

BEST LATE-ROUND PICK: LHP Jordan Shipers (16), who signed for $800,000, has an 89-92 mph fastball and the makings of possible plus pitches in his slider and changeup. Both Snow and Kohlscheen touched the mid-90s after signing.

THE ONE WHO GOT AWAY: RHP Ryne Stanek (3), who has an easy 91-96 mph fastball, could blossom into a first-round pick after heading to Arkansas. Seattle still is negotiating with LHP James Paxton (4), whose stuff was down this spring after he declined to sign with the Blue Jays as a sandwich pick in 2009.

ASSESSMENT: Not having a first-round pick because of free-agent signings hurt the Mariners, as did failing to sign Stanek. They tried to compensate by doling out $2.5 million in bonuses to Walker, Littlewood and Shipers.

2009   BONUSES: $10.9 MILLION

2B Dustin Ackley (1) and SS/2B Nick Franklin (1) quickly became the system's top position prospects, with Ackley reaching Triple-A and Franklin leading the low Class A Midwest League in homers during their first full pro seasons. 1B/3B Rich Poythress (2) led the minors with 130 RBIs, while INF Kyle Seager (3) topped the minors with 192 hits.

GRADE: A

2008   BONUSES: $4.3 MILLION

RHP Josh Fields (1) and 1B Dennis Raben (2) have been plagued by injuries, so the Mariners may not get much out of this group. They did use RHPs Aaron Pribanic (3) and Brett Lorin (5) in a five-player package to trade for Ian Snell and Jack Wilson.

GRADE: D

2007   BONUSES: $4.5 MILLION

RHP Phillippe Aumont's (1) stock is dropping, but Seattle got value out of him when they stole Cliff Lee from the Phillies in a one-sided trade. 3B/1B Matt Mangini (1s) and RHP Shawn Kelley (13) have reached the majors.

GRADE: D

2006   BONUSES: $4.8 MILLION

The Mariners did well taking RHPs Brandon Morrow (1) and Chris Tillman (2) to start their draft, but gave both away in ill-advised trades for Brandon League and Erik Bedard. C Adam Moore (6) and RHPs Doug Fister (7) and Kam Mickolio (18) also have seen big league action.

GRADE: B+

Draft analysis by Jim Callis. Numbers in parentheses indicate draft rounds.

DUSTIN ACKLEY, 2B

Born: Feb. 26, 1988. **Bats:** L. **Throws:** R.
Height: 6-1. **Weight:** 185. **Drafted:** North
Carolina, 2009 (1st round). **Signed by:** Rob
Mummau.

PROSPECT 1

JOHN WILLIAMSON

Undrafted out of high school, Ackley starred as a first baseman at North Carolina. He hit .412 in three years with the Tar Heels and led them to three College World Series, where he set a record with 28 hits in 15 games. The consensus No. 2 player in the 2009 draft behind Stephen Strasburg, he went second overall and signed at the Aug. 17 deadline for a big league contract that included a $6 million bonus and $7.5 million in guaranteed money. He entered pro ball as a center fielder in the Arizona Fall League, but the Mariners decided to try him at second base in his 2010 debut. He got off to a rocky start at Double-A West Tenn, batting .139 through May 3, but he hit .301 in the next two months. Ackley finished the year by destroying the Arizona Fall League, hitting .424/.581/.758, setting a league record for on-base percentage and winning MVP honors.

Scouts regarded Ackley as one of the most polished hitters to come out of the draft in years. He's extremely patient at the plate, recognizes pitches well and isn't afraid to wait for the pitch he wants or to hit with two strikes. He can sometimes pull off pitches, but he gets his bat on plane with the ball extremely quickly and his barrel stays in the hitting zone for a long time. His picturesque swing and uncanny hand-eye coordination produce excellent plate coverage. Ackley is mostly a gap hitter now, but he can drive the ball to all fields and occasionally shows nice loft. He sometimes hits off his front foot too much, but Seattle is confident he'll develop at least 15-homer power as he adds strength to his unimposing frame. Getting stronger also will help him fight fatigue over the long season. He looked worn down even while tearing up the AFL, but to his credit he always hustles and never gives away at-bats. Ackley has 65 speed on the 20-80 scouting scale, and the Mariners want him to make better use of it on the basepaths after stealing just 10 bases in 13 attempts in 2010. He played shortstop in high school, but the move to second base wasn't easy. Rough at first, he worked diligently and improved his footwork, range and hands, especially on backhanding balls to his right. He learned how to read and anticipate hops, as well as the need for throwing from different arm angles. He hurt his arm pitching as a high school senior and had Tommy John surgery in 2008, but it's average now. While he may never be an asset at second base, he's a good athlete and could handle any of three outfield positions. He also could be a plus defender at first base. Ackley's father, John, spent seven seasons as a catcher in the Red Sox organization and Dustin has a professional approach and a strong work ethic.

Ackley is nearly ready for the big leagues. Seattle traded Jose Lopez to the Rockies in December, opening a spot in the lineup. It also would make sense for the Mariners to give Ackley some more Triple-A time to further refine his defense and delay his arbitration and free-agency eligibility for an extra year.

SCOUTING GRADES

Batting: 70.   **Defense:** 50.
Power: 45.   **Arm:** 50.
Speed: 65.

Based on 20-80 scouting scale, where 50 represents major league average, and future projection rather than present tools.

Year	Club (League)	Class	AVG	G	AB	R	H	2B	3B	HR	RBI	BB	SO	SB	CS	OBP	SLG
2010	West Tenn (SL)	AA	.263	82	289	42	76	21	4	2	28	55	41	8	2	.389	.384
	Tacoma (PCL)	AAA	.274	52	212	37	58	12	4	5	23	20	38	2	1	.338	.439
Minor League Totals			.267	134	501	79	134	33	8	7	51	75	79	10	3	.368	.407

2 MICHAEL PINEDA, RHP

Born: Jan. 18, 1989. **B-T:** R-R. **Ht.:** 6-5. **Wt.:** 250. **Signed:** Dominican Republic, 2005. **Signed by:** Patrick Guerrero/Franklin Taveras.

Pineda has had little trouble with minor league hitters, posting a 2.49 ERA and 396 strikeouts in 404 innings. After elbow soreness limited him to 47 innings in 2009, he returned healthy last season and reached Triple-A at age 21. Pineda has the size, stuff and control to pitch at the top of a rotation. He throws a crisp fastball that sits at 93-97 mph and gets as high as 101 with explosive life and occasional heavy sink. He tightened and added more tilt to his quality slider this year, though he can still get under it occasionally, causing it to flatten out. He also did a better job of selling his upper-80s changeup with the same arm speed as his fastball, keeping it down and getting hitters to chase it. Pineda throws all three pitches from the same three-quarter arm slot. With his velocity, high-effort delivery and unusual arm action, it's surprising how well he throws strikes. While he has good control, his command could be sharpened. Pineda is on the 40-man roster and will challenge for a rotation spot in Seattle in 2011. He eventually should become the No. 2 starter behind Felix Hernandez, but he shouldn't be expected to be that guy right out of the gate.

Year	Club (League)	Class	W	L	ERA	G	GS	CG	SV	IP	H	HR	BB	SO	G/A	WHIP	AVG
2006	Mariners (DSL)	R	2	1	0.44	8	3	0	0	20	14	0	7	14	—	1.03	.189
2007	Mariners (DSL)	R	6	1	2.29	15	12	0	0	59	70	2	11	48	—	1.37	.286
2008	Wisconsin (MWL)	LoA	8	6	1.95	26	21	1	0	138	109	7	35	128	—	1.04	.216
2009	Mariners (AZL)	R	0	0	0.00	2	2	0	0	3	2	0	0	4	3.00	0.67	.200
	High Desert (CAL)	HiA	4	2	2.84	10	8	0	0	44	29	3	6	48	1.65	0.79	.190
2010	West Tenn (SL)	AA	8	1	2.22	13	13	0	0	77	67	1	17	78	1.19	1.09	.228
	Tacoma (PCL)	AAA	3	3	4.76	12	12	0	0	62	54	9	17	76	1.24	1.14	.227
Minor League Totals			31	14	2.49	86	71	1	0	404	345	22	93	396	1.32	1.08	.227

3 NICK FRANKLIN, SS/2B

Born: March 2, 1991. **B-T:** B-R. **Ht.:** 6-1. **Wt.:** 175. **Drafted:** HS—Altamonte Springs, Fla., 2009 (1st round). **Signed by:** Chuck Carlson.

The 27th overall pick and recipient of a $1.28 million bonus in 2009, Franklin surprisingly launched 23 homers in his first full pro season, breaking Dick Kenworthy's 49-year-old franchise record in the process. Franklin gets everything out of his 175-pound frame with above-average bat speed, nice whip in his barrel and good leverage. He swings hard, which inevitably leads to some strikeouts, but he has the hand-eye coordination to get away with it. Though his stroke can get a little long, he drives the ball hard to all fields. He can get too aggressive at the plate at times. A switch-hitter, he was more effective batting lefthanded in 2010 (.953 OPS, compared to .494 righthanded) but his swing is similar from both sides. An average runner, he has good instincts and was one of only three minor leaguers to hit 20 homers and steal 20 bases last season. Franklin has solid actions and range at shortstop, though some scouts think his fringy arm will make him a second baseman. The Mariners promoted Franklin to Double-A for the Southern League playoffs and may let him stay there in 2011. He has the ability and maturity to handle the jump.

Year	Club (League)	Class	AVG	G	AB	R	H	2B	3B	HR	RBI	BB	SO	SB	CS	OBP	SLG
2009	Mariners (AZL)	R	.302	10	43	6	13	2	0	1	4	1	6	0	0	.318	.419
	Everett (NWL)	SS	.400	6	20	4	8	2	1	0	2	1	2	1	0	.429	.600
2010	Clinton (MWL)	LoA	.281	129	513	89	144	22	7	23	65	50	123	25	10	.351	.485
	West Tenn (SL)	AA	.667	1	3	3	2	0	0	0	0	1	1	0	0	.750	.667
Minor League Totals			.288	146	579	102	167	26	8	24	71	53	132	26	10	.354	.485

4 TAIJUAN WALKER, RHP

Born: Aug. 13, 1992. **B-T:** R-R. **Ht.:** 6-5. **Wt.:** 195. **Drafted:** HS—Yucaipa, Calif., 2010 (1st round supplemental). **Signed by:** John Ramey.

Walker was known more as a shortstop and basketball forward prior to 2010. He averaged 21 points and 15 rebounds per game as a high school senior, with his dunking ability earning him the nickname "Sky Walker." He focused more on pitching last spring and worked his way into the supplemental first round, signing quickly for $800,000. Walker is both a work in progress and a tremendously gifted athlete. His fastball ranged from 91-95 mph in high school, and after he was shut down in his pro debut with shoulder stiffness, he returned in instructional league to sit at 95 and top out at 98 with heavy sink. His 12-to-6 curveball shows flashes of being a plus pitch, though he focused more on honing his changeup during instructional league. Walker's athleticism helps him repeat his delivery, but he still needs to smooth out his mechanics and improve his command. He's still learning the intricacies of pitching, such as pitch selection, fielding the position, holding runners and between-starts preparation. Because Walker is relatively new to pitching, the Mariners won't rush him. He could start 2011 in extended spring training, though his electric arm and competitive drive could prompt an assignment to low Class A.

Year	Club (League)	Class	W	L	ERA	G	GS	CG	SV	IP	H	HR	BB	SO	G/A	WHIP	AVG
2010	Mariners (AZL)	R	1	1	1.29	4	0	0	0	7	2	0	3	9	1.75	0.71	.087
Minor League Totals			1	1	1.29	4	0	0	0	7	2	0	3	9	1.75	0.71	.087

5 GUILLERMO PIMENTEL, OF

Born: Oct. 5, 1992. **B-T:** L-L. **Ht.:** 6-1. **Wt.:** 180. **Signed:** Dominican Republic, 2009. **Signed by:** Patrick Guerrero/Bob Engle/Luis Scheker.

Pimentel spurned the Rangers to sign with the Mariners for $2 million in July 2009 and made his pro debut last summer. He shook off a slow start to bat .293/.318/.537 in August and rank as the Rookie-level Arizona League's No. 1 prospect. Pimentel has five-tool potential, attracting the most attention with his light-tower power. He has the bat speed and strength in his hands to launch balls 450 feet from home plate. He has a mechanically sound swing and routinely stays through the ball with nice extension. He's overly aggressive at this point, as evidenced by his 58-5 K-BB ratio, and geared to hit fastballs. He's going to have to develop more discipline and learn to stay back on offspeed pitches as he advances through the minors. Pimentel has average raw speed but doesn't make the best use of it yet on the basepaths or in left field. He has an average arm that could become plus with some mechanical tweaks, such as using his lower half more. He's a good teammate but needs to understand failure is a part of the game and not be too hard on himself. Pimentel will likely spend the first part of the year in extended spring training before joining Rookie-level Pulaski in June. He could arrive in Seattle at some point in 2014.

Year	Club (League)	Class	AVG	G	AB	R	H	2B	3B	HR	RBI	BB	SO	SB	CS	OBP	SLG
2010	Mariners (AZL)	R	.250	51	184	20	46	7	6	6	31	5	58	5	1	.276	.451
Minor League Totals			.250	51	184	20	46	7	6	6	31	5	58	5	1	.276	.451

6 MAURICIO ROBLES, LHP

Born: March 5, 1989. **B-T:** L-L. **Ht.:** 5-10. **Wt.:** 205. **Signed:** Venezuela, 2006. **Signed by:** German Robles (Tigers).

The Mariners snagged Robles and Luke French from the Tigers at the 2009 trade deadline in exchange for Jarrod Washburn. Washburn bombed in Detroit and Robles is now one of Seattle's best prospects, ranking fourth in the Southern League in strikeouts (120) and opponent average (.239) in 2010. Robles doesn't cast an imposing figure, but he has a lot of strength in his 5-foot-10 frame. He has an aggressive delivery and a fastball that sits at 91-93 mph and touches 95 deep into games. Because of his youth, strength and willingness to pitch off his fastball, scouts believe he will still add more velocity. He has the best changeup in the system, a potential plus pitch with good fade. He controls it better than his curveball, which flashes tight rotation but is still inconsistent. He needs to work on throwing strikes more frequently. Scouts think the problem is more mental than mechanical, as he sometimes tries to blow his fastball by hitters instead of trusting his other pitches. After joining Tacoma for a successful Pacific Coast League playoff run at the end of 2010, Robles will return to Triple-A. Robles was added to the Mariners' 40-man roster. He has the stuff to pitch in the middle of a big league rotation and could make his Seattle debut later in the season.

Year	Club (League)	Class	W	L	ERA	G	GS	CG	SV	IP	H	HR	BB	SO	G/A	WHIP	AVG
2006	Tigers/Marlins (VSL)	R	0	1	3.38	14	0	0	0	16	17	0	16	20	—	2.06	.279
2007	Tigers (VSL)	R	3	6	3.26	14	14	0	0	69	60	4	27	83	—	1.26	.237
2008	West Michigan (MWL)	LoA	5	3	2.66	23	16	0	0	91	54	2	54	79	—	1.18	.176
2009	West Michigan (MWL)	LoA	4	4	4.63	11	11	0	0	56	45	6	27	71	0.94	1.28	.221
	Lakeland (FSL)	HiA	4	2	3.60	7	7	0	0	35	34	3	14	40	0.91	1.37	.256
	High Desert (CAL)	HiA	3	2	2.78	7	6	0	0	32	23	1	19	34	2.11	1.30	.202
2010	West Tenn (SL)	AA	6	6	4.11	22	22	0	0	114	102	10	51	120	0.96	1.34	.239
	Tacoma (PCL)	AAA	3	1	3.54	5	5	0	0	28	19	2	20	34	0.83	1.39	.188
Minor League Totals			28	25	3.54	103	81	0	0	442	354	28	228	481	1.03	1.32	.221

7 JOHERMYN CHAVEZ, OF

Born: Jan. 26, 1989. **B-T:** R-R. **Ht.:** 6-3. **Wt.:** 220. **Signed:** Venezuela, 2005. **Signed by:** Rafael Moncada (Blue Jays).

The Mariners regret swapping Brandon Morrow for Brandon League in December 2009, but at least they got Chavez in the deal with the Blue Jays. He ranked second in the high Class A California League with 32 homers in 2010, though 23 of those longballs came in the friendly confines of High Desert. He continued to hit well in the Venezuelan League during the winter. The ball jumps off Chavez's bat and he has power to all fields. He worked with minor league hitting coaches Tommy Cruz and Jose Castro on his swing in 2010, eliminating a loop and a tendency to chop down on the ball. The changes allowed him to start turning on inside pitches and tap into his above-average raw power. He does strike out a lot, and he must continue to work on his pitch recognition and strike-zone awareness, though he showed improvement in that regard this year. Chavez is a below-average runner but moves well in right field. He fits nicely in right because he has well-above-average arm strength. Though he's a streaky player, he's level-headed and handles his ups and downs well. Added to Seattle's 40-man roster in November, Chavez will spend 2011 in Double-A. The Mariners are well-stocked in the outfield, so he'll have to keep producing to get a big league opportunity.

Year	Club (League)	Class	AVG	G	AB	R	H	2B	3B	HR	RBI	BB	SO	SB	CS	OBP	SLG
2006	Pulaski (APP)	R	.276	36	105	19	29	9	0	0	18	9	23	1	2	.371	.362
2007	Blue Jays (GCL)	R	.301	50	176	29	53	12	2	6	21	20	50	7	2	.389	.494
2008	Lansing (MWL)	LoA	.211	115	402	40	85	20	2	7	39	25	128	9	5	.272	.323
2009	Lansing (MWL)	LoA	.283	134	508	87	144	22	6	21	89	40	137	10	6	.346	.474
2010	High Desert (CAL)	HiA	.315	136	534	109	168	30	7	32	96	52	131	6	9	.387	.577
Minor League Totals			.278	471	1725	284	479	93	17	66	263	146	469	33	24	.348	.466

8 MARCUS LITTLEWOOD, SS

Born: March 18, 1992. **B-T:** B-R. **Ht.:** 6-3. **Wt.:** 200. **Drafted:** HS—St. George, Utah, 2010 (2nd round). **Signed by:** Chris Pelekoudas.

Littlewood won a gold medal with the U.S. 16-and-under national team at the 2008 Pan American Youth Games and played for the 18-and-under squad last summer after Seattle drafted him in the second round. The Mariners bought him away from a San Diego commitment for $900,000—the largest draft bonus it paid out in 2010. His father Mike played briefly in the Brewers system and is the head baseball coach at Dixie State (Utah). Littlewood's natural hitting ability and tireless work ethic allowed him to pick up switch-hitting while in high school. He has a simple swing that looks similar from either side of the plate, though he has more strength from his natural right side. With his advanced approach and understanding of the strike zone, he should hit for a solid average. He's more of a line-drive/doubles hitter than a slugger, though he could hit 10-15 homers per year. A below-average runner, Littlewood doesn't have ideal range for a shortstop. He makes up for it with fluid action, a strong arm and a knack for being in the right place. With his baseball upbringing and Team USA experience, Littlewood is prepared to start his pro career in a full-season league. He'll take over for Nick Franklin as Clinton's everyday shortstop in 2011.

Year	Club (League)	Class	AVG	G	AB	R	H	2B	3B	HR	RBI	BB	SO	SB	CS	OBP	SLG
2010	Did Not Play—Signed Late																

9 KYLE SEAGER, INF

Born: Nov. 3, 1987. **B-T:** L-R. **Ht.:** 5-10. **Wt.:** 175. **Drafted:** North Carolina, 2009 (3rd round). **Signed by:** Rob Mummau.

Along with Dustin Ackley and lefthander Brian Moran, Seager was one of three players the Mariners drafted from North Carolina in the first seven rounds of the 2009 draft. In his first full pro season, Seager led the minor leagues with 192 hits—the most in the minors since Joe Thurston recorded 196 in 2002. Seager's best tool is his hitting ability, and he projects to bat around .280 in the big leagues. He shows good balance with a compact swing and his bat stays in the hitting zone for a long while. While he hit 14 homers in 2010, he's more of a line-drive hitter who will spray doubles from gap to gap. He's a below-average runner who needs to improve his instincts on the bases. Like he did in college, Seager has split his time as a pro between second and third base, and he also saw action at shortstop last season. His range isn't suited for the middle infield, but he handles routine plays and shows good quickness when turning the double play. With questionable range and top prospects Dustin Ackley and Nick Franklin ahead of him at second base and shortstop, Seager profiles best as a utility player. If he continues to hit in Double-A in 2011, he could be a valuable contributor for the Mariners in the near future.

SEATTLE MARINERS

Year	Club (League)	Class	AVG	G	AB	R	H	2B	3B	HR	RBI	BB	SO	SB	CS	OBP	SLG
2009	Mariners (AZL)	R	.000	1	3	0	0	0	0	0	0	0	1	0	0	.000	.000
	Clinton (MWL)	LoA	.275	41	153	17	42	8	0	1	22	22	20	4	2	.360	.346
	High Desert (CAL)	HiA	.000	2	5	1	0	0	0	0	0	0	0	0	0	.000	.000
2010	High Desert (CAL)	HiA	.345	135	557	126	192	40	3	14	74	71	94	13	12	.419	.503
Minor League Totals			.326	179	718	144	234	48	3	15	96	93	115	17	14	.402	.464

10 DAN CORTES, RHP

Born: March 4, 1987. **B-T:** R-R. **Ht.:** 6-6. **Wt.:** 215. **Drafted:** HS—Pomona, Calif., 2005 (7th round). **Signed by:** Dan Ontiveros (White Sox).

Acquired by the Royals from the White Sox in a 2006 trade for Mike MacDougal, Cortes established himself as Kansas City's top pitching prospect entering 2009. But after he was arrested for public intoxication that July, the Royals sent him and lefthander Derrick Saito to the Mariners for Yuniesky Betancourt. He took off after Seattle moved him to the bullpen in mid-2010 and ended the year in the big leagues. Relieving suits Cortes and his fastball, which rose from 94-97 mph to a consistent 96-98 and regularly touched triple digits. The pitch explodes out of his hand and comes in on a sharp downhill plane thanks to his height and high three-quarters arm slot. His hammer 12-to-6 curveball and sharp slider give him a pair of power breaking pitches, but he throws more strikes with the slider. He mostly scrapped his changeup in his new role, but can still pull one out of his back pocket to keep hitters off-balance. His biggest weakness is his below-average control and command. Cortes' brief but impressive major league stint has him in line to make the Mariners' Opening Day bullpen.

Year	Club (League)	Class	W	L	ERA	G	GS	CG	SV	IP	H	HR	BB	SO	G/A	WHIP	AVG
2005	Bristol (APP)	R	1	4	5.17	15	7	0	0	38	44	2	13	38	—	1.49	.289
2006	Kannapolis (SAL)	LoA	3	9	4.01	20	19	0	0	108	109	6	38	96	—	1.37	.260
	Burlington (MWL)	LoA	1	2	6.69	7	7	0	0	35	40	7	17	30	—	1.63	.284
2007	Wilmington (CAR)	HiA	8	8	3.07	24	24	0	0	123	102	7	45	120	—	1.20	.226
2008	NW Arkansas (TL)	AA	10	4	3.78	23	23	0	0	117	103	13	55	109	—	1.35	.241
2009	NW Arkansas (TL)	AA	6	6	3.92	16	15	0	0	80	77	3	50	57	1.16	1.58	.258
	West Tenn (SL)	AA	1	5	4.94	10	10	0	0	55	51	4	35	55	1.10	1.57	.248
2010	West Tenn (SL)	AA	6	4	5.27	25	16	0	1	84	77	4	53	85	1.70	1.55	.239
	Tacoma (PCL)	AAA	1	2	4.97	9	0	0	1	13	13	1	4	13	1.71	1.34	.277
	Seattle (AL)	MAJ	0	1	3.38	4	0	0	0	5	3	0	3	6	0.38	1.13	.158
Major League Totals			0	1	3.38	4	0	0	0	5	3	0	3	6	0.38	1.13	.158
Minor League Totals			37	44	4.25	149	121	0	2	652	616	47	310	603	1.32	1.42	.250

11 GREG HALMAN, OF

Born: Aug. 26, 1987. **B-T:** R-R. **Ht.:** 6-4. **Wt.:** 190. **Signed:** Netherlands, 2004. **Signed by:** Wayne Norton/Bob Engle/Peer Van Dalen.

Halman spent the majority of the 2010 in Triple-A, continuing to show well-above-average raw power and a propensity for striking out. He finished second in the Pacific Coast League with 33 homers and led the league with 169 whiffs. He made his major league debut in a September callup, during which he whiffed 11 times in 29 at-bats. Halman worked on his approach at the plate, becoming less pull-happy and setting a career high in walks (37), but still had the third-worst strikeout rate among minor league qualifiers at 36 percent. The No. 1 prospect on this list two years ago, Halman is a gifted athlete who can hit the ball out of any part of the park. But opponents don't fear his power because they know his swing can get long and has lots of holes. He'll swing through fastballs in on his hands or chase soft stuff off the plate. Halman is an average runner who shows good range in the outfield, though not quite enough for center field. He has a strong arm. The Mariners would like to see him be more aggressive on the basepaths and less aggressive at the plate. If he can make strides in that area, he could be an everyday player in the Preston Wilson mold. If he doesn't, he could languish in Triple-A. Halman will head back to Tacoma and continue to refine his approach at the plate.

Year	Club (League)	Class	AVG	G	AB	R	H	2B	3B	HR	RBI	BB	SO	SB	CS	OBP	SLG
2005	Mariners (AZL)	R	.258	26	89	17	23	2	3	3	11	10	19	1	3	.350	.449
2006	Everett (NWL)	SS	.259	28	116	19	30	6	4	5	15	3	32	10	4	.295	.509
2007	Wisconsin (MWL)	LoA	.182	52	187	26	34	5	0	4	15	8	77	15	7	.234	.273
	Everett (NWL)	SS	.307	62	238	37	73	19	1	16	37	21	85	16	8	.371	.597
2008	High Desert (CAL)	HiA	.268	67	257	52	69	15	3	19	53	16	76	23	1	.320	.572
	West Tenn (SL)	AA	.277	61	235	43	65	14	2	10	30	16	66	8	6	.332	.481
2009	Mariners (AZL)	R	.182	3	11	1	2	0	1	0	2	2	8	0	0	.308	.364
	West Tenn (SL)	AA	.210	121	457	64	96	17	2	25	72	29	183	9	7	.278	.420
2010	Tacoma (PCL)	AAA	.243	112	424	82	103	21	4	33	80	37	169	15	4	.310	.545
	Seattle (AL)	MAJ	.138	9	29	1	4	1	0	0	3	1	11	1	0	.167	.172
Major League Totals			.138	9	29	1	4	1	0	0	3	1	11	1	0	.167	.172
Minor League Totals			.246	532	2014	341	495	99	20	115	315	142	715	97	40	.308	.486

12 JOSH LUEKE, RHP

Born: Dec. 5, 1984. **B-T:** R-R. **Ht.:** 6-5. **Wt.:** 220. **Drafted:** Northern Kentucky, 2007 (16th round). **Signed by:** Mark Gigler (Rangers).

Seattle acquired Lueke as part of the package they received from the Rangers in the Cliff Lee trade in July, but his arrival quickly turned into a media firestorm. Lueke was charged with rape and sodomy in a May 2008 incident and served 42 days in jail before reaching a plea agreement to a lesser charge of false imprisonment with violence. Mariners officials claimed they weren't aware of the charges when they made the deal, though his past was common knowledge within the industry. From a pure talent standpoint, Lueke has all the tools for success. He has a quick arm, and his fastball sits between 94-98 mph and comes at hitters from a steep downhill angle. He mixes in a splitter that falls off the table, a slider that's also a plus pitch and an occasional changeup. Lueke has the power arsenal to get out both lefthanders and righthanders, and he attacks the strike zone with a closer's mentality. Lueke is ready to pitch in a major league bullpen, but the Mariners will have to decide if they want that to happen in Seattle. They added him to their 40-man roster in November.

Year	Club (League)	Class	W	L	ERA	G	GS	CG	SV	IP	H	HR	BB	SO	G/A	WHIP	AVG
2007	Spokane (NWL)	SS	0	0	0.00	2	0	0	0	3	2	0	0	6	—	0.75	.200
	Clinton (MWL)	LoA	0	3	3.34	20	0	0	6	35	29	4	10	31	—	1.11	.225
2008	Clinton (MWL)	LoA	1	1	2.61	8	0	0	2	10	10	0	2	12	—	1.16	.244
	Bakersfield (CAL)	HiA	2	6	5.03	35	0	0	1	59	65	6	16	72	—	1.37	.270
2009	Bakersfield (CAL)	HiA	0	1	1.17	4	0	0	1	8	5	0	1	11	0.83	0.78	.179
2010	Hickory (SAL)	LoA	2	1	0.46	17	0	0	10	20	12	0	5	36	4.00	0.86	.167
	Frisco (TL)	AA	1	1	3.86	15	0	0	2	19	18	2	5	26	1.25	1.23	.254
	West Tenn (SL)	AA	1	0	0.00	6	0	0	3	7	4	0	0	14	1.00	0.55	.148
	Tacoma (PCL)	AAA	1	0	2.08	12	0	0	2	17	14	0	5	18	0.67	1.10	.215
Minor League Totals			8	13	3.19	119	0	0	27	178	159	12	44	226	1.19	1.14	.232

13 ALEX LIDDI, 3B/1B

Born: Aug. 14, 1988. **B-T:** R-R. **Ht.:** 6-4. **Wt.:** 200. **Signed:** Italy, 2005. **Signed by:** Wayne Norton/Mario Mazzotti.

When Liddi took the field in 2006, he became the first Italian position player to play Organized Baseball in the United States. He broke out by leading the minors with a .345 average and winning the California League MVP award in 2009. He encored by hitting well in Double-A last year at age 21, earning a spot on the 40-man roster. Liddi has a pro body and strength in his swing. He has good bat speed with power to all fields, though his swing can get long at times. He hits fastballs well and is still working to remedy his trouble recognizing breaking balls out of the pitcher's hand, which led to his 145 strikeouts in 2010. Developing pitch recognition comes largely through experience, and Liddi did his part by getting extra at-bats in the Venezuelan League this winter. He has soft hands and above-average arm strength at third base, but he's a well-below-average runner and doesn't have good range or footwork around the bag. He also tries to be too flashy—all factors that contributed to him leading Southern League third basemen with 27 errors last season. He also saw some action at first base, where he's a better fit. Liddi will move up to Triple-A and spend most of his time at the hot corner in 2011. He'll also play some first base and DH to give Matt Mangini some time at third base.

Year	Club (League)	Class	AVG	G	AB	R	H	2B	3B	HR	RBI	BB	SO	SB	CS	OBP	SLG
2006	Mariners (AZL)	R	.313	47	182	31	57	13	6	3	25	12	48	9	2	.355	.500
	Wisconsin (MWL)	LoA	.184	11	38	4	7	1	0	0	2	1	8	0	1	.200	.211
2007	Wisconsin (MWL)	LoA	.240	113	400	41	96	28	3	8	52	36	123	5	4	.308	.385
2008	Wisconsin (MWL)	LoA	.244	125	447	65	109	26	4	6	53	42	115	17	5	.313	.360
2009	High Desert (CAL)	HiA	.345	129	493	97	170	44	5	23	104	53	122	10	6	.411	.594
2010	West Tenn (SL)	AA	.281	134	502	78	141	37	8	15	92	50	145	5	7	.353	.476
Minor League Totals			.281	559	2062	316	580	149	26	55	328	194	561	46	25	.347	.459

14 RAMON MORLA, 3B

Born: Nov. 20, 1989. **B-T:** R-R. **Ht.:** 6-1. **Wt.:** 175. **Signed:** Dominican Republic, 2006. **Signed by:** Patrick Guerrero.

No Mariners farmhand took a bigger leap forward in 2010 than Morla. Signed out of the Dominican Republic in 2006, he made his U.S. debut three years later, when a broken hand limited him to 102 at-bats. Fully healthy in 2010, he led the Rookie-level Appalachian League with 17 homers while finishing second in batting (.323), hits (81) and RBIs (49). Morla has five-tool potential but stands out mostly for his bat. He has simple swing mechanics and exceptional balance at the plate, though his stroke can get too big at times. He has strength in his wrists and above-average bat speed, so the ball really jumps off his bat. He can drive the ball out to all fields and hit several homers to straightaway center last year. He's also an above-average runner with good athleticism. Morla played shortstop before moving to third base full-time in 2010. He has good range and agility, along with a strong but erratic arm. Most of his 21 errors last season came on throws. He also shows strong leadership skills, frequently going to the mound to settle down Pulaski pitchers when they got rattled. Morla's development path could speed up if he handles his first full-season assignment in Clinton with aplomb in 2011.

Year	Club (League)	Class	AVG	G	AB	R	H	2B	3B	HR	RBI	BB	SO	SB	CS	OBP	SLG
2007	Mariners (DSL)	R	.233	34	116	23	27	7	0	2	13	18	35	4	7	.364	.345
2008	Mariners (DSL)	R	.256	55	164	34	42	7	1	2	17	28	38	7	4	.399	.348
2009	Mariners (AZL)	R	.294	28	102	20	30	2	1	2	12	6	29	4	2	.345	.392
2010	Pulaski (APP)	R	.323	62	251	60	81	17	2	17	49	15	65	13	4	.364	.610
Minor League Totals			.284	179	633	137	180	33	4	23	91	67	167	28	17	.371	.458

15 RICH POYTHRESS, 1B/3B

Born: Aug. 11, 1987. **B-T:** R-R. **Ht.:** 6-4. **Wt.:** 235. **Drafted:** Georgia, 2009 (2nd round). **Signed by:** Garrett Ball.

The Mariners were looking for a power bat when they drafted Poythress in the second round of the 2009 draft, so they're hoping his first full season wasn't just a High Desert mirage. After breaking Gordon Beckham's Georgia school record with 86 RBIs in his draft year, he led the minors with 130 in his first full pro season. He also ranked second in the California League in slugging (.580) and third in homers (31), and he did it all while remaking his approach. Poythress employed more of an inside-out swing in the first half of the season, then pulled the ball a lot more after the all-star break. His swing is built more for line drives than homers, but he has the strength to hit balls out to the opposite field. If he can pull the ball consistently, he can be a legitimate masher. He puts together quality at-bats and shows the ability to make quick adjustments, though his swing can get long and he'll need to prove he can get around on quality fastballs. Poythress has an average arm and played a handful of games at third base last season, but his hands are stiff and he doesn't have the range to play there regularly. He's an acceptable defender at first base, though a bottom-of-the-scale runner. All Cal League numbers have to be taken with a grain of salt, particularly those at High Desert, so Double-A will be a great litmus test for Poythress in 2011.

Year	Club (League)	Class	AVG	G	AB	R	H	2B	3B	HR	RBI	BB	SO	SB	CS	OBP	SLG
2009	Mariners (AZL)	R	.300	6	20	4	6	0	0	1	6	5	6	0	0	.462	.450
	West Tenn (SL)	AA	.230	26	87	11	20	2	0	1	9	15	24	1	0	.337	.287
2010	High Desert (CAL)	HiA	.315	123	476	88	150	33	0	31	130	52	100	3	2	.381	.580
Minor League Totals			.302	155	583	103	176	35	0	33	145	72	130	4	2	.377	.532

16 CARLOS TRIUNFEL, SS

Born: Feb. 27, 1990. **B-T:** R-R. **Ht.:** 5-11. **Wt.:** 200. **Signed:** Dominican Republic, 2006. **Signed by:** Bob Engle/Patrick Guerrero.

Signed for $1.3 million in 2006, Triunfel created buzz by reaching high Class A the next year as a 17-year-old. But his development has stalled, as he played in only 11 games in 2009 after breaking the fibula and tearing ankle ligaments in his left leg in a gruesome baserunning collision.

The Mariners were just happy to see him play a full season in Double-A last year, but he put up the worst numbers of his pro career. The tools are in place for Triunfel to be a successful hitter. He has a good swing and the strength to hit for average power as well. He has exceptional hand-eye coordination, which actually gets him into trouble because he can put his bat on nearly any pitch. He gets overanxious and too often swings at bad pitches, making weak contact. He also had too much of an inside-out approach, so Seattle is trying to teach him to be more patient and to pull the ball more, as well as improving his recognition of offspeed pitches. The Mariners still are playing Triunfel at shortstop, but he's a below-average runner and lacks the range for the position. He has improved his fundamentals and toned down a glove flip that led to errors, but he still plays back on balls too much and loves showing off his cannon arm. His arm strength is good enough for a move to third base, which could happen soon but also would place greater demands on his bat. Triunfel wears his emotions on his sleeve and needs to stay more even-keeled. He has always received the benefit of the doubt because of his age and raw tools, but he's getting to the point where he needs to produce. He will still be just 21 years old when he repeats Double-A in 2011.

Year	Club (League)	Class	AVG	G	AB	R	H	2B	3B	HR	RBI	BB	SO	SB	CS	OBP	SLG
2007	Wisconsin (MWL)	LoA	.309	43	152	18	47	8	2	0	14	5	23	4	8	.342	.388
	Mariners (AZL)	R	.273	3	11	1	3	0	0	0	3	0	1	0	0	.231	.273
	High Desert (CAL)	HiA	.288	50	208	32	60	10	2	0	22	12	31	3	4	.333	.356
2008	High Desert (CAL)	HiA	.287	108	436	75	125	20	4	8	49	30	52	30	9	.336	.406
2009	Mariners (AZL)	R	.250	4	16	0	4	1	0	0	4	0	2	1	0	.250	.313
	West Tenn (SL)	AA	.231	7	26	2	6	1	0	0	4	1	2	0	0	.286	.269
2010	West Tenn (SL)	AA	.257	129	470	51	121	12	1	7	42	13	54	2	8	.286	.332
Minor League Totals			.277	344	1319	179	366	52	9	15	138	61	165	40	29	.316	.365

17 BLAKE BEAVAN, RHP

Born: Jan. 17, 1989. **B-T:** R-R. **Ht.:** 6-7. **Wt.:** 250. **Drafted:** HS—Irving, Texas, 2007 (1st round). **Signed by:** Jay Eddings (Rangers).

Justin Smoak headlined the package the Mariners received in the Cliff Lee trade with the Rangers last July, but Seattle also received pitching prospects Beavan and Josh Lueke along with minor league second baseman/outfielder Matt Lawson. Baseball America's 2006 Youth Player of the Year, Beavan went 17th overall in the 2007 draft and signed for $1,497,500. He flashed 95-96 mph heat as an amateur, but once he started pitching every five days as a pro, his fastball settled into the 90-92 mph range. His fastball is still effective because it has good sink and he pounds the lower half of the strike zone with a smooth, repeatable delivery. He had the lowest walk rate (1.1 per nine innings) of any Double-A or Triple-A starter in 2010. Beavan's slider is his best secondary pitch, featuring good tilt and occasional late bite. He also mixes in a changeup that projects to be an average pitch. Beavan needs to work on staying on top of the ball to give his fastball better angle and his secondary pitches better depth. He's a good athlete for his size with strong competitive makeup. While Beavan doesn't blow scouts away with overpowering stuff, his ability to throw strikes and his workhorse build suggest he could be an innings eater as a No. 4 starter.

Year	Club (League)	Class	W	L	ERA	G	GS	CG	SV	IP	H	HR	BB	SO	G/A	WHIP	AVG
2008	Clinton (MWL)	LoA	10	6	2.37	23	23	0	0	122	105	12	20	73	—	1.03	.234
2009	Bakersfield (CAL)	HiA	5	4	4.30	12	12	1	0	73	75	6	16	51	1.54	1.24	.264
	Frisco (TL)	AA	4	4	4.01	15	15	0	0	90	113	4	13	34	1.04	1.41	.309
2010	Frisco (TL)	AA	10	5	2.78	17	17	0	0	110	100	6	12	68	1.37	1.02	.242
	West Tenn (SL)	AA	2	1	5.00	3	3	0	0	18	18	1	1	11	1.24	1.06	.277
	Tacoma (PCL)	AAA	2	2	6.47	7	7	0	0	40	56	6	8	22	1.29	1.59	.331
Minor League Totals			33	22	3.58	77	77	1	0	453	467	35	70	259	1.27	1.19	.267

18 MATT MANGINI, 3B/1B

Born: Dec. 21, 1985. **B-T:** L-R. **Ht.:** 6-4. **Wt.:** 232. **Drafted:** Oklahoma State, 2007 (1st round supplemental). **Signed by:** Dan Wright.

Three years after the Mariners drafted him 52nd overall and signed him for $603,000 in 2007, Mangini finally hit as hoped. He made his major league debut in September, starting 10 of Seattle's final 11 games. Mangini has a professional approach at the plate with quiet hands, and he has a good feel for hitting. Mostly a gap-to-gap hitter in the past, he tapped into some power last year and could have average pop. He's a below-average runner but moves well for his size. Mangini's hands work well defensively, though he doesn't have great footwork or range at third base. He has a solid arm but too often just flips the ball across the diamond to get the out. While he also has seen action at first base, he lacks the bat to profile as a regular at that position. He brings a blue-collar work ethic to the game and always has a positive attitude. Mangini hasn't hit well against lefthanders and ultimately profiles as a corner utility player and lefty bat off the bench, similar to a player the Mariners had a few years ago, Greg Dobbs.

Year	Club (League)	Class	AVG	G	AB	R	H	2B	3B	HR	RBI	BB	SO	SB	CS	OBP	SLG
2007	Everett (NWL)	SS	.291	22	79	12	23	4	0	2	9	13	18	3	0	.398	.418
	Mariners (AZL)	R	.000	2	6	0	0	0	0	0	0	2	1	0	0	.250	.000
	High Desert (CAL)	HiA	.226	17	62	7	14	1	2	2	8	6	21	1	0	.304	.403
2008	High Desert (CAL)	HiA	.265	52	181	26	48	12	0	6	25	23	52	3	1	.376	.431
	West Tenn (SL)	AA	.202	69	238	22	48	5	0	2	25	12	64	0	1	.247	.248
2009	West Tenn (SL)	AA	.273	124	422	48	115	18	5	12	67	38	92	10	2	.339	.424
2010	Tacoma (PCL)	AAA	.313	117	447	73	140	31	4	18	63	26	96	3	0	.352	.521
	Seattle (AL)	MAJ	.211	11	38	2	8	0	0	0	1	2	13	0	0	.250	.211
Major League Totals			.211	11	38	2	8	0	0	0	1	2	13	0	0	.250	.211
Minor League Totals			.270	403	1435	188	388	71	11	42	197	120	344	20	4	.335	.423

19 ESTEILON PEGUERO, SS

Born: Nov. 3, 1993. **B-T:** R-R. **Ht.:** 6-1. **Wt.:** 185. **Signed:** Dominican Republic, 2010. **Signed by:** Franklin Taveras Jr./Patrick Guerrero.

Peguero worked with trainer Enrique Soto in the Dominican Republic and other teams expected him to sign with the Rangers after Texas signed Colombian catcher Jorge Alfaro (another Soto client) for $1.3 million, as well as Soto's son Lee, a 25-year-old third baseman released by the Blue Jays. But the Mariners remained interested—and have one of Soto's sons (second baseman George) in their system as well. Seattle signed Peguero for $2.9 million in December, giving him the largest bonus in the 2010 international amateur class. The Mariners also landed Dominican outfielder Phillips Castillo earlier, giving them the top two amateur hitters on the international market last year. Peguero's bat is his carrying tool and he has shown the ability to hit in game situations against live pitching. He has advanced bat speed, good pitch recognition for his age and a sound stroke. He does have a late trigger to his swing, which can give him problems against good fastballs, especially ones on the inner half of the strike zone. But once he gets his hands going, he's able to whip his bat through the zone with excellent finish. He doesn't show the same raw pop that Castillo does, but Peguero drives balls into the gaps and should grow into more power down the road. He has a physical frame and almost certainly will have to move off shortstop, probably to second base because his arm isn't strong enough for third base. He's an average runner and some scouts believe he could become a solid defender in time. Because Peguero signed so late, he may spend 2011 in the Dominican Summer League before making his U.S. debut in 2012, though he's talented enough to accelerate that timetable.

Year	Club (League)	Class	W	L	ERA	G	GS	CG	SV	IP	H	HR	BB	SO	G/A	WHIP	AVG
2010	Did Not Play—Signed 2011 Contract																

20 PHILLIPS CASTILLO, OF

Born: Feb 2, 1994. **B-T:** R-R. **Ht.:** 6-2. **Wt.:** 190. **Signed:** Dominican Republic, 2010. **Signed by:** Patrick Guerrero/Franklin Taveras Jr./Bob Engle.

The Mariners spent just $4 million on their 2010 draft but made up for it by shelling out $5.1 million for a pair of talented Dominican hitters. They signed Castillo for $2.2 million in July, a club record for an international amateur until shortstop Esteilon Peguero inked for $2.9 million in December. As with any Latin American teenager, Castillo's game is raw, but he stands out for his impressive build and potential at the plate. He was already 6-foot-2 and 190 pounds as a 16-year-old, with great strength for his age and physical projection remaining. Castillo swings hard, showing above-average raw power. The ball explodes off his bat, thanks to his quick hands and excellent barrel whip. He shows the ability to handle breaking balls and can crush pitches down in the zone. He does have a small hitch in his swing that will need to be ironed out, but the tools are there for him to be an impact hitter. Castillo has average speed but may lose a step as he fills out, so he'll be limited to an outfield corner. He has the plus arm strength to play in right field and needs work on defensive fundamentals. Castillo has strong makeup and could follow the same path Guillermo Pimentel took in his first full season with the Mariners, starting in extended spring training before heading to the Arizona League.

Year	Club (League)	Class	W	L	ERA	G	GS	CG	SV	IP	H	HR	BB	SO	G/A	WHIP	AVG
2010	Did Not Play—Signed 2011 Contract																

21 STEPHEN PRYOR, RHP

Born: July 23, 1989. **B-T:** R-R. **Ht.:** 6-6. **Wt.:** 225. **Drafted:** Tennessee Tech, 2010 (5th round). **Signed by:** Alvin Rittman.

Pryor transferred from Cleveland State (Tenn.) CC to Tennessee Tech before his junior year in 2010, making a name for himself when he touched 98 mph in a game against Red Sox sandwich pick Bryce Brentz and Middle Tennessee State. Mariners scouting director Tom McNamara was in attendance, and one inning was all he needed to see to pop Pryor in the fifth round and sign him for $153,000. Pryor's fastball typically sits at 94-97 mph, and he used it to strike out 75 in 41 innings for the Golden Eagles and then 55 in 35 pro innings. He alternated between throwing a curveball and a slider this spring and is back to using a curve now. His breaking ball can get caught in between and exhibit slurvy movement, but it's a power pitch either way. Pryor has a physical body with tree trunks for legs. Despite his large frame, he shows good body control, but his delivery is a little unorthodox with a pause at his balance point as he turns his back to the hitters. He could add even more life to his fastball if he smoothes out some of the rough edges in his delivery. As a power-armed college reliever, Pryor could move quickly through the minors. He could reach Double-A in his first full pro season and challenge for a spot in the big league bullpen in 2012.

Year	Club (League)	Class	W	L	ERA	G	GS	CG	SV	IP	H	HR	BB	SO	G/A	WHIP	AVG
2010	Everett (NWL)	SS	0	0	0.49	11	0	0	4	18	7	0	7	26	0.71	0.76	.119
	Clinton (MWL)	LoA	0	2	3.71	12	0	0	1	17	17	0	6	29	1.57	1.35	.250
Minor League Totals			0	2	2.04	23	0	0	5	35	24	0	13	55	1.00	1.05	.189

22 JAMES JONES, OF

Born: Sept. 24, 1988. **B-T:** L-L. **Ht.:** 6-4. **Wt.:** 195. **Drafted:** Long Island, 2009 (4th round). **Signed by:** David May.

Because he had a fastball he could dial up to 95 mph, many teams preferred Jones as a lefthanded pitcher when he played both ways at Long Island. The Mariners liked him better as a position player and have kept him in the outfield since drafting him in the fourth round in 2009. After a solid pro debut, he got out of the gate slowly in low Class A last year, batting .205/.319/.364 in the first half. To his credit, he never let his struggles get in his head and got better as the season wore on. Following the all-star break, he hit .321/.387/.487. Jones works pitchers and has some snap in his loose swing, but he doesn't recognize breaking balls well and swings through a lot of pitches. His stride is long and he often gets out on his front foot too early. The Mariners will be patient with him as a hitter, knowing he's more raw than most college position players because he was a two-way player from the Northeast. Jones has a wiry build with good athleticism. He plays right field with ease, showing well-above-average arm strength. His fringe-average speed precludes him from playing center field, so he'll have to show he can hit enough to be an everyday player on an outfield corner. If not, he'll always have the fallback option of returning to the mound. Jones will play in high Class A this year.

Year	Club (League)	Class	AVG	G	AB	R	H	2B	3B	HR	RBI	BB	SO	SB	CS	OBP	SLG
2009	Everett (NWL)	SS	.311	45	164	28	51	12	2	3	24	19	40	0	3	.392	.463
2010	Clinton (MWL)	LoA	.269	132	491	87	132	24	10	12	65	62	122	24	10	.356	.432
Minor League Totals			.279	177	655	115	183	36	12	15	89	81	162	24	13	.365	.440

23 JORDAN SHIPERS, LHP

Born: June 27, 1991. **B-T:** L-L. **Ht.:** 6-0. **Wt.:** 170. **Drafted:** HS—Bethany, Mo., 2010 (16th round). **Signed by:** Alvin Rittman.

Shipers enticed scouts with his performance at the World Wood Bat Championships in Jupiter, Fla., during the fall of 2009. But he was tough to follow last spring because South Harrison High (Bethany, Mo.) is so small that it doesn't have a baseball team. He and his mother drove four hours each way to Iowa to play in a spring wood-bat league so scouts could see him pitch. After graduating, he also pitched against older competition in the California Collegiate League. His diligence paid off, as the Mariners drafted Shipers in the 16th round and paid him $800,000 in August after it became clear they weren't going to sign third-rounder Ryne Stanek. Following his summer performance, Seattle viewed Shipers as a second-round talent. He's a little undersized, but he's a quick-twitch athlete who can run a 6.6-second 60-yard dash. He has a compact, aggressive delivery and good body control, producing the potential for three average or better pitches. Shipers sits at 89-92 mph and can touch 94 with his fastball, which could wind up being his third-best pitch. His slider has sharp break and hard tilt, and his advanced changeup drops like a splitter when it's on. Because he hasn't had much experience, Shipers is raw as a pitcher and still needs to learn fundamentals such as setting up hitters, holding runners and fielding his position. He'll also need to learn how to pitch every fifth day and go deeper into games. Shipers may stay in extended spring training to address those areas before joining Pulaski or short-season Everett in June.

Year	Club (League)	Class	W	L	ERA	G	GS	CG	SV	IP	H	HR	BB	SO	G/A	WHIP	AVG
2010	Did Not Play—Signed Late																

24 JOSH FIELDS, RHP

Born: Aug. 19, 1985. **B-T:** R-R. **Ht.:** 6-0. **Wt.:** 185. **Drafted:** Georgia, 2008 (1st round). **Signed by:** Chuck Carlson.

The Mariners' first-round pick in 2008, Fields has pitched just 62 pro innings since signing for $1.75 million. He didn't agree to terms until February 2009, and has been sidelined by a dead arm, a strained oblique and a strained forearm muscle as a pro. When at his best, Fields has a 92-95 mph fastball, though he worked mostly at 90-93 in the Arizona Fall League this offseason. His 12-to-6 curveball plummets with tight rotation and good depth, and he has made improvements with his changeup. Fields has a quick tempo and aggressive mechanics. He nearly jumps off the mound and tilts his body out of the way of his over-the-top arm slot. His dynamic delivery is what gives Fields above-average stuff, but there's a lot of moving parts and he struggles to throw strikes consistently, especially with his secondary pitches. His stuff loses some life after an inning of work, but he could be a useful middle reliever if he can tighten up his control. Seattle hopes he'll have his first fully healthy year in pro ball in 2011, when he'll advance to Triple-A and possibly the big leagues.

Year	Club (League)	Class	W	L	ERA	G	GS	CG	SV	IP	H	HR	BB	SO	G/A	WHIP	AVG
2009	West Tenn (SL)	AA	2	2	6.48	31	0	0	1	33	33	2	22	36	1.07	1.65	.254
2010	West Tenn (SL)	AA	1	1	3.14	21	0	0	6	29	19	0	18	28	1.50	1.29	.190
Minor League Totals			3	3	4.94	52	0	0	7	62	52	2	40	64	1.25	1.48	.226

25 CARLOS PEGUERO, OF

Born: Feb. 22, 1987. **B-T:** L-L. **Ht.:** 6-5. **Wt.:** 247. **Signed:** Dominican Republic, 2005. **Signed by:** Bob Engle/Patrick Guerrero.

Peguero always has had big power and even bigger strikeout rates. He got off to a blistering start in 2010, hitting nine home runs in April, but he didn't adjust after pitchers altered their approach. Over the final four months, he batted just .227/.317/.399. He led all of Double-A with 178 strikeouts this season, and only two minor leaguers had more whiffs. Peguero chases bad pitches, which gets him frustrated, so he'll compound his problems by swinging harder in his next at-bat. He doesn't recognize breaking balls well and always will strike out a lot. However, scouts believe he has closed some holes in his swing and is hitting balls harder when he does make contact. He also struggles against lefthanders, and his offensive weaknesses will limit him to being a platoon player at best. Peguero is a freakish athlete for a 6-foot-5, 247-pounder, surprisingly possessing plus speed. He did a nice job last season of sharpening up his routes in the outfield and he could be an average defender on an outfield corner. His above-average arm plays well in right field. Peguero presents an interesting package of tools, but his shortcomings are just as glaring. Added to the 40-man roster in November, he'll move up to

Triple-A in 2011.

Year	Club (League)	Class	AVG	G	AB	R	H	2B	3B	HR	RBI	BB	SO	SB	CS	OBP	SLG
2005	Mariners (DSL)	R	.251	59	179	31	45	8	4	6	30	22	66	1	3	.337	.441
2006	Mariners (AZL)	R	.313	34	134	27	42	10	7	7	30	13	49	3	2	.380	.649
	Everett (NWL)	SS	.204	25	93	7	19	4	1	2	9	2	34	0	2	.221	.333
2007	Wisconsin (MWL)	LoA	.263	79	297	35	78	21	6	9	50	16	97	4	3	.315	.465
2008	High Desert (CAL)	HiA	.299	92	371	47	111	25	3	12	74	10	96	6	4	.317	.480
2009	High Desert (CAL)	HiA	.271	126	491	92	133	21	14	31	98	42	172	3	4	.335	.560
2010	West Tenn (SL)	AA	.254	130	488	86	124	23	5	23	73	56	178	7	9	.340	.463
Minor League Totals			.269	545	2053	325	552	112	40	90	364	161	692	24	27	.329	.494

26 TOM WILHELMSEN, RHP

Born: Dec. 16, 1983. **B-T:** R-R. **Ht.:** 6-6. **Wt.:** 200. **Drafted:** HS—Tucson, 2002 (7th round). **Signed by:** Brian Johnson (Brewers).

Wilhelmsen may have the most interesting backstory in the minor leagues. A seventh-round pick by then-Brewers scouting director Jack Zduriencik in 2002, he pitched only one year in the minors after signing for $250,000. He missed all of 2004 after Milwaukee suspended him twice for testing positive for marijuana use, then walked away from the game. He spent the next three years backpacking around the world and bartending in Tucson. Wilhelmsen got the itch to pitch again, joining the Tucson club in the independent Golden League in 2009. Now the general manager of the Mariners, Zduriencik gave Wilhelmsen a second chance by signing him to a minor league contract in 2010. He showed enough in 74 innings in the low minors and in an Arizona Fall League stint to claim a spot on the 40-man roster. Wilhelmsen throws his fastball at 91-93 mph, topping out at 96. He gets good downhill angle on the pitch and commands it well, but it doesn't have a lot of movement. His best offering is a hard 12-to-6 curveball that he throws in the upper 70s with sharp break and good depth. He also mixes in a changeup with fade and sink. The three-pitch mix and his clean delivery give him what he needs to continue as a starter, but Seattle had him relieve in the AFL to limit his innings and that may have been a glimpse of things to come. His advanced age and power curve make him a candidate to be fast-tracked if the Mariners make him a full-time reliever in 2010.

Year	Club (League)	Class	W	L	ERA	G	GS	CG	SV	IP	H	HR	BB	SO	G/A	WHIP	AVG
2003	Brewers (AZL)	R	0	1	4.50	2	2	0	0	4	5	0	4	4	—	2.25	—
	Beloit (MWL)	LoA	5	5	2.76	15	15	1	0	88	78	6	27	63	—	1.19	—
2004	Did Not Play—Suspended																
2005	Did Not Play—Retired																
2006	Did Not Play—Retired																
2007	Did Not Play—Retired																
2008	Did Not Play—Retired																
2009	Tucson (Golden)	Ind	0	0	6.17	11	0	0	2	12	15	1	4	13	—	1.63	—
2010	Mariners (AZL)	R	0	0	0.60	5	3	0	0	15	4	0	2	22	1.20	0.40	.078
	Everett (NWL)	SS	1	0	3.68	3	3	0	0	15	14	1	2	14	0.92	1.09	.255
	Clinton (MWL)	LoA	6	1	2.23	7	6	1	0	44	33	1	15	37	1.02	1.08	.198
Minor League Totals			12	7	2.55	32	29	2	0	166	134	8	50	140	1.03	1.11	.216

27 STEVE BARON, C

Born: Dec. 17, 1990. **B-T:** R-R. **Ht.:** 6-0. **Wt.:** 195. **Drafted:** HS—Miami, 2009 (1st round supplemental). **Signed by:** Mike Tosar.

The Mariners signed Baron away from a Duke commitment for $980,000 as a sandwich pick in 2009, largely on the strength of his defense. He hasn't disappointed in that regard, though he already has raised questions as to whether he can hit enough to be a major league regular. Baron is exceptionally polished behind the plate. With his soft hands, strong and accurate arm and agility, he's years ahead of most high school catchers. He blocks balls very well and has a quick transfer on throws down to second base, throwing out 47 percent of basestealers last year. Whether a pitcher is throwing 88 or 98 mph, it looks the same going into Baron's mitt. He's tough behind the plate and working to become a more vocal leader. Baron's catch-and-throw skills are good enough to get him to the big leagues, but he needs a lot of work offensively. He was overmatched in low Class A last year, necessitating a midseason demotion to Everett. He has the strength and hand-eye coordination to produce offensively, but his swing gets too loopy and long. Baron also has some stiffness and chops down on the ball too much, diminishing his average raw power. Seattle wants him to level his swing and incorporate his lower half more. He runs well for a catcher. Baron hit better after his demotion, which the Mariners hope he can use as a stepping stone to a more productive year when he returns to Clinton in 2011.

Year	Club (League)	Class	AVG	G	AB	R	H	2B	3B	HR	RBI	BB	SO	SB	CS	OBP	SLG
2009	Pulaski (APP)	R	.179	30	106	12	19	6	0	2	13	7	38	0	0	.241	.292
2010	Clinton (MWL)	LoA	.182	45	154	10	28	3	0	1	14	10	47	1	1	.229	.221
	Everett (NWL)	SS	.253	53	198	18	50	12	2	3	22	6	60	1	0	.282	.379
Minor League Totals			.212	128	458	40	97	21	2	6	49	23	145	2	1	.254	.306

28 ERASMO RAMIREZ, RHP

Born: May 2, 1990. **B-T:** R-R. **Ht.:** 5-11. **Wt.:** 180. **Signed:** Nicaragua, 2007. **Signed by:** Bob Engle/ Ubaldo Heredia.

Ramirez won the pitching triple crown in the Rookie-level Venezuelan Summer League in 2009, going 11-1, 0.51 with 80 strikeouts in 88 innings. That performance earned him Seattle's minor league pitcher of the year award and a jump to low Class A when he made his U.S. debut last season. He ranked second in the Midwest League in K-BB ratio (5.6) and fifth in ERA (2.97). Ramirez commands the strike zone with his 89-92 mph fastball and can dial it up to 94. He has incredible feel for a changeup that is already a major league average pitch and should continue to improve. His slider has the makings of becoming an average pitch, though it's a little short right now. Ramirez has a stocky, maxed-out frame with a thick lower half, so he's unlikely to add more velocity. But if his secondary stuff improves as projected, he could become a back-of-the-rotation option. On the fast track, he'll move to high Class A before his 21st birthday.

Year	Club (League)	Class	W	L	ERA	G	GS	CG	SV	IP	H	HR	BB	SO	G/A	WHIP	AVG
2008	Mariners (VSL)	R	4	1	2.86	13	11	1	0	63	67	2	9	46	—	1.21	.276
2009	Mariners (VSL)	R	11	1	0.51	14	13	0	0	88	54	1	5	80	3.45	0.67	.174
2010	Clinton (MWL)	LoA	10	4	2.97	26	23	1	1	152	142	13	21	117	1.94	1.07	.248
Minor League Totals			25	6	2.23	53	47	2	1	303	263	16	35	243	2.37	0.98	.234

29 MICKEY WISWALL, 1B/3B

Born: Nov. 25, 1988. **B-T:** L-R. **Ht.:** 6-1. **Wt.:** 200. **Drafted:** Boston College, 2010 (7th round). **Signed by:** Brian Nichols.

The Mariners were ecstatic to land Wiswall in the seventh round of the 2010 draft. He first stood out to Seattle scouting director Tom McNamara as a sophomore in 2009, when McNamara watched an entire North Carolina-Boston College series while scouting future Mariners Dustin Ackley and Kyle Seager. Wiswall hit well in the Cape Cod League that summer, but some scouts soured on him when he started slowly as a junior last spring. He finished strongly, hitting 19 homers for BC before signing for $150,000.

Wiswall has a muscular build and compact swing with good leverage, and the ball jumps off his bat. He hangs in well against lefthanders and can hit to the opposite field with authority, leading the Mariners to believe he'll hit for solid average and power. Wiswall played both infield corners in college and during his pro debut. He's not agile and lacks a quick first step, but he has soft hands and average arm strength. Though he has a blue-collar work ethic, it's probably a stretch to project him playing third base on an everyday basis in the big leagues. His lefthanded power is suited for Safeco Field, but he profiles best as a utility player on the infield and outfield corners. He'll likely spend his first full pro season in high Class A.

Year	Club (League)	Class	AVG	G	AB	R	H	2B	3B	HR	RBI	BB	SO	SB	CS	OBP	SLG
2010	Everett (NWL)	SS	.271	12	48	7	13	3	0	5	17	2	16	0	0	.327	.646
	Clinton (MWL)	LoA	.301	33	136	13	41	14	0	4	18	6	29	1	0	.331	.493
Minor League Totals			.293	45	184	20	54	17	0	9	35	8	45	1	0	.330	.533

30 YOERVIS MEDINA, RHP

Born: July 27, 1988. **B-T:** R-R. **Ht.:** 6-3. **Wt.:** 210. **Signed:** Venezuela, 2005. **Signed by:** Bob Engle/Pedro Avila.

After spending four seasons in the Venezuelan Summer League, Medina finally made his U.S. debut in 2010. He pitched well in the lower minors, won an emergency start in Triple-A and was rewarded with a spot on Seattle's 40-man roster at the end of the season. Nicknamed "El Caballo," Medina is a workhorse at 6-foot-3 and 210 pounds. He showed one of the best breaking balls in the short-season Northwest League, a sharp curveball that generates a lot of swings and misses and projects as a plus pitch. He sets up his curve with a 90-91 mph fastball that gets up to 94. He mixes in a splitter as a chase pitch, as well as a changeup to keep hitters off-balance. Mechanically, Medina is working to better incorporate his strong lower half into his delivery. His command and control also need improvement. With his relatively advanced age, sharp breaking ball and competitive nature, the Mariners could challenge Medina with a promotion to high Class A at some point in 2011.

Year	Club (League)	Class	W	L	ERA	G	GS	CG	SV	IP	H	HR	BB	SO	G/A	WHIP	AVG
2006	Mariners (VSL)	R	3	4	3.60	17	4	0	1	50	56	3	14	22	—	1.40	.293
2007	Mariners (VSL)	R	4	2	3.42	16	6	1	2	50	64	1	19	36	—	1.66	.320
2008	Mariners (VSL)	R	4	3	1.79	17	1	0	5	40	32	1	12	36	—	1.09	.213
2009	Mariners (VSL)	R	3	4	2.65	15	13	0	1	68	46	1	23	62	2.22	1.01	.192
2010	Everett (NWL)	SS	3	2	4.20	8	8	0	0	41	49	4	15	48	1.54	1.57	.297
	Tacoma (PCL)	AAA	1	0	0.00	1	1	0	0	6	3	0	4	4	0.33	1.24	.158
	Clinton (MWL)	LoA	5	0	2.50	6	6	0	0	36	30	3	12	42	1.19	1.17	.221
Minor League Totals			23	15	2.97	80	39	1	9	291	280	13	99	250	1.61	1.30	.255

Tampa Bay Rays

BY BILL BALLEW

The Rays were left with a feeling of missed opportunity when the Rangers eliminated them in the American League Division Series. After winning the AL East on the final day of the regular season, Tampa Bay looked like a good bet to make the World Series, only to falter against Texas by losing all three games played at Tropicana Field. While manager Joe Maddon assured the masses that he expects his team to contend again in 2011, that will require productivity from several new and most likely inexperienced contributors.

The reality is that the Rays took some huge free-agent losses during the offseason, including four-time all-star Carl Crawford, franchise career home run leader Carlos Pena and top set-up man Joaquin Benoit. AL saves leader Rafael Soriano was expected to depart, and the club was shopping veterans Jason Bartlett and Matt Garza in an effort to further lower payroll.

Tampa Bay's 2010 Opening Day payroll of $72.8 million ranked just 21st in the majors but also represented a franchise record. The Rays, who have won 277 games and made the playoffs twice in the last three years, would like to reduce their salary expenditures to $60 million while remaining competitive. A farm system that has produced as much talent as any in recent years may make that goal possible.

Solid drafts and a commitment to developing talent in Latin America have stocked the Rays with players ready to contribute. Righthander Jeremy Hellickson, the 2010 Minor League Player of the Year, and out-fielder Desmond Jennings have had to wait patiently, receiving only brief callups to the majors in 2010 when they would have been regulars for most other teams.

Hellickson and Jennings are two examples of how no team is more methodical in developing prospects than the Rays. While other clubs promote players at the first hint of success at lower levels of the minors, full-season stints at every step are the rule rather than the exception for Tampa Bay. Lefthander Matt Moore, who led the minors in strikeouts for the second straight year, spent all of 2010 in high Class A even though it was his fourth pro season and even while he torched the Florida State League in the second half.

The Rays also take their time developing talent because they focus on signing young players. The first nine players on this list entered pro ball as teenagers, and Tampa Bay spent four of its six picks in the first three rounds of the 2010 draft on high schoolers. The

Tampa Bay will have to move on without Carl Crawford after he signed with the Red Sox

CLIFF WELCH

TOP 30 PROSPECTS

1. Jeremy Hellickson, rhp	16. Alex Cobb, rhp
2. Matt Moore, lhp	17. Luke Bailey, c
3. Desmond Jennings, of	18. Yoel Araujo, of
4. Jake McGee, lhp	19. Joe Cruz, rhp
5. Josh Sale, of	20. Zach Quate, rhp
6. Alex Torres, lhp	21. Todd Glaesmann, of
7. Alex Colome, rhp	22. Derek Dietrich, ss
8. Justin O'Conner, c	23. Ryan Brett, 2b
9. Drew Vettleson, of	24. Scott Shuman, rhp
10. Jake Thompson, rhp	25. Wilking Rodriguez, rhp
11. Enny Romero, lhp	26. Kevin Kiermaier, of
12. Nick Barnese, rhp	27. Hector Guevara, 2b
13. Ty Morrison, of	28. Leslie Anderson, of/1b
14. Braulio Lara, lhp	29. Kyle Lobstein, lhp
15. Tim Beckham, ss	30. Stephen Vogt, c/of/1b

Rays also signed 16-year-old Dominican outfielder Yoel Araujo for $800,000, a franchise record for an international amateur.

The Rays are efficient at producing players who fit Maddon's desire for a roster full of versatile athletes. The creative skipper maximizes matchups to keep certain players from being exposed over lengthy stints, resulting in 132 different lineups and eight Rays who played at least three defensive positions in 2010. Many of those multi-tasking abilities can be honed in the minor leagues, which should continue to be the lifeblood of baseball's most overachieving franchise.

General Manager: Andrew Friedman. Farm Director: Mitch Lukevics. Scouting Director: R.J. Harrison.

Class	Team	League	W	L	PCT	Finish*	Manager
Majors	Tampa Bay Rays	American	96	66	.593	1st (14)	Joe Maddon
Triple-A	Durham Bulls	International	88	55	.615	1st (14)	Charlie Montoyo
Double-A	Montgomery Biscuits	Southern	72	66	.522	5th (10)	Billy Gardner
High A	Charlotte Stone Crabs	Florida State	80	59	.576	2nd (12)	Jim Morrison
Low A	Bowling Green Hot Rods	Midwest	61	78	.439	12th (16)	Brady Williams
Short-season	Hudson Valley Renegades	New York-Penn	39	36	.520	5th (14)	Jared Sandberg
Rookie	Princeton Rays	Appalachian	33	35	.485	6th (10)	Michael Johns
Rookie	GCL Rays	Gulf Coast	34	26	.567	2nd (15)	Joe Alvarez
Overall 2010 Minor League Record			407	355	.534	4th (30)	

*Finish in overall standings (No. of teams in league). †League champion.

LAST YEAR'S TOP 30

Player, Pos.		Status
1.	Desmond Jennings, of	No. 3
2.	Jeremy Hellickson, rhp	No. 1
3.	Wade Davis, rhp	Majors
4.	Matt Moore, lhp	No. 2
5.	Reid Brignac, ss	Majors
6.	Tim Beckham, ss	No. 15
7.	Alex Colome, rhp	No. 7
8.	Jake McGee, lhp	No. 4
9.	Alex Torres, lhp	No. 6
10.	Nick Barnese, rhp	No. 12
11.	Kyle Lobstein, lhp	No. 29
12.	Luke Bailey, c	No. 17
13.	Joe Cruz, rhp	No. 19
14.	Ty Morrison, of	No. 13
15.	Fernando Perez, of	Dropped out
16.	Todd Glaesmann, of	No. 21
17.	Wilking Rodriguez, rhp	No. 25
18.	Shawn O'Malley, ss	Dropped out
19.	Jeff Malm, 1b	Dropped out
20.	Albert Suarez, rhp	Dropped out
21.	Alex Cobb, rhp	No. 16
22.	Cody Rogers, of	Dropped out
23.	David Newmann, lhp	Dropped out
24.	Matt Sweeney, 3b	Dropped out
25.	Jason McEachern, rhp	Dropped out
26.	Frank de los Santos, lhp	Dropped out
27.	Aneury Rodriguez, rhp	(Astros)
28.	Matt Gorgen, rhp	(Cardinals)
29.	Jake Jefferies, c	Dropped out
30.	Kevin James, lhp	Dropped out

BEST TOOLS

Best Hitter for Average	Drew Vettleson
Best Power Hitter	Josh Sale
Best Strike-Zone Discipline	Desmond Jennings
Fastest Baserunner	Desmond Jennings
Best Athlete	Desmond Jennings
Best Fastball	Matt Moore
Best Curveball	Matt Moore
Best Slider	Alex Torres
Best Changeup	Jeremy Hellickson
Best Control	Jeremy Hellickson
Best Defensive Catcher	Nevin Ashley
Best Defensive Infielder	Shawn O'Malley
Best Infield Arm	Tim Beckham
Best Defensive Outfielder	Desmond Jennings
Best Outfield Arm	Todd Glaesmann

PROJECTED 2014 LINEUP

Catcher	John Jaso
First Base	Ben Zobrist
Second Base	Sean Rodriguez
Third Base	Evan Longoria
Shortstop	Reid Brignac
Left Field	Drew Vettleson
Center Field	Desmond Jennings
Right Field	B.J. Upton
Designated Hitter	Josh Sale
No. 1 Starter	David Price
No. 2 Starter	Jeremy Hellickson
No. 3 Starter	Matt Moore
No. 4 Starter	Jeff Niemann
No. 5 Starter	Wade Davis
Closer	Jake McGee

TOP PROSPECTS OF THE DECADE

Year	Player, Pos.	2010 Org.
2001	Josh Hamilton, of	Rangers
2002	Josh Hamilton, of	Rangers
2003	Rocco Baldelli, of	Rays
2004	B.J. Upton, ss	Rays
2005	Delmon Young, of	Twins
2006	Delmon Young, of	Twins
2007	Delmon Young, of	Twins
2008	Evan Longoria, 3b	Rays
2009	David Price, lhp	Rays
2010	Desmond Jennings, of	Rays

TOP DRAFT PICKS OF THE DECADE

Year	Player, Pos.	2010 Org.
2001	Dewon Brazelton, rhp	Kansas City (Northern)
2002	B.J. Upton, ss	Rays
2003	Delmon Young, of	Twins
2004	Jeff Niemann, rhp	Rays
2005	Wade Townsend, rhp	Laredo (United)
2006	Evan Longoria, 3b	Rays
2007	David Price, lhp	Rays
2008	Tim Beckham, ss	Rays
2009	*LeVon Washington, of	Indians
2010	Josh Sale, of	Rays

*Did not sign.

LARGEST BONUSES IN CLUB HISTORY

Matt White, 1996	$10,200,000
Rolando Arrojo, 1997	$7,000,000
Tim Beckham, 2008	$6,150,000
David Price, 2007	$5,600,000
B.J. Upton, 2002	$4,600,000

TAMPA BAY RAYS

TOP 2011 ROOKIE: Jeremy Hellickson, rhp. Baseball America's 2010 Minor League Player of the Year is expected to force his way into the Rays' talented rotation.

BREAKOUT PROSPECT: Kevin Kiermaier, of. The former Division II Junior College World Series MVP has all-around tools and was a steal as a 31st-round pick.

SOURCE OF TOP 30 TALENT			
Homegrown	29	**Acquired**	**1**
College	5	Trades	1
Junior college	3	Rule 5 draft	0
High school	14	Independent leagues	0
Draft-and-follow	0	Free agents/waivers	0
Nondrafted free agents	0		
International	7		

SLEEPER: Isaias Velasquez, of. Picked up in a trade with the Indians in 2009, he started to blossom after moving from third base to center field last season.

LF
Josh Sale (5)
Henry Wrigley
Justin Ruggiano

CF
Desmond Jennings (3)
Ty Morrison (13)
Yoel Araujo (18)
Isaias Velazquez
Cody Rogers
Deshun Dixon
Craige Lyerly

RF
Drew Vettleson (9)
Todd Glaesmann (21)
Kevin Kiermaier (26)
Reid Fronk

3B
Tim Beckham (15)
Derek Dietrich (22)
Matt Sweeney
Cesar Perez
Russ Canzler

SS
Leonardo Reginatto
Shawn O'Malley
Juniel Querecuto

2B
Ryan Brett (23)
Hector Guevara (27)
Elliot Johnson
Tyler Bortnick
Nick Schwaner
Robby Price

1B
Leslie Anderson (28)
Jeff Malm
Travis Flores
Phil Wunderlich
Joe Ruiz
Mike Sheridan

C
Justin O'Conner (8)
Luke Bailey (17)
Stephen Vogt (30)
Jake DePew
Nevin Ashley
Mayo Acosta
Jake Jeffries
Jose Lobaton

RHP

RHSP
Jeremy Hellickson (1)
Alex Colome (7)
Jake Thompson (10)
Nick Barnese (12)
Alex Cobb (16)
Joe Cruz (19)
Wilking Rodriguez (25)
Jason McEachern
Ian Kendall
Jesse Hahn
Albert Suarez
Wilmer Almonte
Shane Dyer
Andrew Bellatti

RHRP
Zach Quate (20)
Scott Shuman (24)
Chris Andujar
Merrill Kelly
Austin Hubbard
Dane de la Rosa
Matt Bush

LHP

LHSP
Matt Moore (2)
Alex Torres (6)
Enny Romero (11)
Braulio Lara (14)
Kyle Lobstein (29)
David Newmann
Frank de los Santos
Kevin James
Brandon Henderson

LHRP
Jake McGee (4)
Sergio Espinosa
Josh Satow
Cesar Cabral

2010

BEST PURE HITTER: OFs Josh Sale (1) and Drew Vettleson (1s), both Washington high school products, were two of the best prep hitters in the draft.

BEST POWER HITTER: Sale and C Justin O'Conner (1) have well-above-average power, and O'Conner shares the Indiana high school record with 51 career homers. The Rays didn't stop there. 1B Travis Flores (11) won the 2010 Power Showcase, an international home run derby for high schoolers, with his longest blast traveling 471 feet. Vettleson and SS Derek Dietrich (2) also have good pop.

FASTEST RUNNER: OF Craige Lyerly's (19) plus-plus speed helped him reach base safely in his last 88 games at NCAA Division II Catawba (N.C.).

BEST DEFENSIVE PLAYER: C Jake DePew (9) has advanced receiving skills and an average arm. O'Conner is new to catching but has a well-above-average arm that delivers 1.8-second pop times. He also threw 93-95 mph as a high school pitcher.

BEST FASTBALL: RHP Jake Thompson (2) works at 92-94 mph and touched 97 during the summer and in instructional league. RHP Jesse Hahn (6) had similar velocity before having Tommy John surgery in July. RHP Ian Kendall (5) is a high schooler with little projection remaining, but he throws 91-95 mph.

BEST SECONDARY PITCH: Thompson has taken off since picking up a mid-80s slider during the spring at Long Beach State, and he also has a good changeup. Hahn had a power curve before he got hurt.

BEST PRO DEBUT: Thompson went 4-1, 1.06 and ranked as the top pitching prospect in the short-season New York-Penn League. Scrappy 2B Robby Price (13) hit .294, stole 13 bases and led the NY-P with a .437 on-base percentage. RHP Austin Hubbard (14) commanded his slider well enough to post a 0.39 ERA and 12 saves in the NY-P.

BEST ATHLETE: LHP Justin Woodall (26) won a national football championship as a starting safety at Alabama. He signed with the Rays after hitting 94 mph during a tryout—despite not having pitched in four years. OFs Deshun Dixon (10) and Kevin Kiermaier (31) both have plus speed, solid arms and gap power.

MOST INTRIGUING BACKGROUND: While Vettleson's bat is his ticket, he has received more notoriety for his switch-pitching ability. Dietrich is the grandson of former big leaguer Steve Demeter. LHP Jimmy Patterson (18) is the grandson of former Pacific Coast League president Bill Cutler.

CLOSEST TO THE MAJORS: Thompson.

BEST LATE-ROUND PICK: Flores or Kiermaier.

THE ONE WHO GOT AWAY: The Rays made significant offers to RHP Austin Wood (4), a hard thrower who starred in the Cape Cod League, and OF Michael Lorenzen (7), who has five-tool potential. But Wood transferred from St. Petersburg (Fla.) JC to Southern California, and Lorenzen opted to attend Cal State Fullerton.

ASSESSMENT: The Rays didn't set out to sign position players with five of their six picks in the first three rounds, but doing so restored some balance to a pitching-heavy farm system. If Hahn regains his stuff, he's great value for a sixth-rounder.

2009

The Rays failed to sign their top two picks, OF LeVon Washington (1) and SS Kenny Diekroeger (2). The did go over slot to sign OF Todd Glaesmann (3), C Luke Bailey (4), 1B Jeff Malm (5) and LHP Kevin James (9)—none of whom has gotten off to a fast start in pro ball.

GRADE: D

2008

Tampa Bay spent the No. 1 overall pick on SS Tim Beckham (1), who's still young but hasn't lived up to his billing. They also invested in the projectability of LHP Kyle Lobstein (2) and OF Ty Morrison (4), who will need time to develop.

GRADE: C

2007

LHP David Price (1), the No. 1 overall pick, makes this draft all by himself, and the Rays got another frontline lefty in Matt Moore (8). RHPs Nick Barnese (3) and Joe Cruz (30) add more pitching depth.

GRADE: A

2006

3B Evan Longoria (1) almost immediately achieved superstardom. OF Desmond Jennings (10) looks like the leadoff man Tampa Bay has sought. RHP Josh Butler (2) made it to the majors after getting dealt to the Brewers.

GRADE: A

Draft analysis by Jim Callis. Numbers in parentheses indicate draft rounds.

JEREMY
HELLICKSON, RHP

Born: April 8, 1987. **Bats:** R. **Throws:** R.
Height: 6-1. **Weight:** 185. **Drafted:** HS—
Des Moines, 2005 (4th round). **Signed by:**
Tom Couston.

CARL KLINE

A high school pitcher from Iowa, Hellickson was brought along slowly after the Rays drafted him in the fourth round and signed him away from a Louisiana State scholarship for $500,000 in 2005. He didn't reach full-season ball until his third year as a pro and spent parts of two seasons each at Double-A Montgomery and Triple-A Durham. He led Rays farmhands with a 2.96 ERA and 163 strikeouts in 2008, then starred in the International League playoffs and earned MVP honors in the Triple-A national championship game in 2009. With no openings in Tampa Bay's rotation, "Hellboy" returned to Durham in 2010. He led the IL in ERA (2.45) and strikeouts per nine innings (9.4). He also was pacing the IL in wins and strikeouts when the Rays called him up in August. Hellickson turned in four quality starts in as many tries, then helped out in a bullpen role in September.

Hellickson throws four pitches for strikes and does a great job of getting ahead in the count with outstanding fastball command. He keeps his four-seam fastball down in the zone, sitting at 91-92 mph and touching 95. His best pitch is a low-80s changeup, which he has added depth to over the past two years, giving him a formidable weapon against lefthanders. He also throws a solid curveball with tight spin for strikes early in the count. Hellickson added two-seam and cut fastballs to his repertoire in 2010, which helped his four-seamer play up. In the past, scouts worried about the lack of movement on his four-seamer, but those worries have been alleviated by the life on his new fastballs. He throws all of his pitches from the same arm angle, which creates good deception. Hellickson also repeats his clean delivery with impres-

sive consistency, with his lone problem a tendency to get too straight up and down on occasion.

Hellickson has proven at every step that he's as good as advertised. He made the most of his opportunities during his encore in Durham, which made him a better pitcher once he finally received the call to Tampa Bay. The Rays' rotation remains crowded, but Hellickson showed during the second half of 2010 that he's ready. Though he'll likely serve as a fourth or fifth starter as a rookie, Hellickson should become Tampa Bay's No. 2 or 3 starter in the not-too-distant future.

SCOUTING GRADES

Fastball: 60.   **Command/**
Curveball: 55.   **Control:** 65.
Changeup: 70.   **Delivery:** 65.

*Based on 20-80 scouting scale, where
50 represents major league average, and
future projection rather than present tools.*

Year	Club (League)	Class	W	L	ERA	G	GS	CG	SV	IP	H	HR	BB	SO	G/A	WHIP	AVG
2005	Princeton (APP)	R	0	0	6.00	4	0	0	0	6	6	1	1	11	—	1.17	.240
2006	Hudson Valley (NYP)	SS	4	3	2.43	15	14	0	0	78	55	3	16	96	—	0.91	.193
2007	Columbus (SAL)	LoA	13	3	2.67	21	21	1	0	111	87	7	34	106	—	1.09	.214
2008	Vero Beach (FSL)	HiA	7	1	2.00	14	14	0	0	77	64	7	5	83	—	0.90	.224
	Montgomery (SL)	AA	4	4	3.94	13	13	0	0	75	84	15	15	79	—	1.31	.292
2009	Montgomery (SL)	AA	3	1	2.38	11	11	0	0	57	41	4	14	62	0.62	0.97	.198
	Durham (IL)	AAA	6	1	2.51	9	9	0	0	57	31	4	15	70	0.96	0.80	.157
2010	Durham (IL)	AAA	12	3	2.45	21	21	0	0	118	103	5	35	123	0.98	1.17	.238
	Charlotte (FSL)	HiA	0	0	21.60	1	0	0	0	2	4	0	2	4	0.00	3.60	.444
	Tampa Bay (AL)	MAJ	4	0	3.47	10	4	0	0	36	32	5	8	33	0.74	1.10	.232
Major League Totals			4	0	3.47	10	4	0	0	36	32	5	8	33	0.74	1.10	.232
Minor League Totals			49	16	2.71	109	103	1	0	580	475	46	137	634	0.86	1.05	.222

2 MATT MOORE, LHP

Born: June 18, 1989. **B-T:** L-L. **Ht.:** 6-2. **Wt.:** 200. **Drafted:** HS—Moriarty, N.M., 2007 (8th round). **Signed by:** Jack Powell.

Moore has led the minors in strikeouts in each of the past two seasons. He battled his control at the beginning of 2010, going 0-7, 6.63 in his first 11 starts, then got back on track and allowed just 14 earned runs in his final 15 starts. Rated as the top prospect in the high Class A Florida State League, he finished with 208 strikeouts, the most in the minors since Clint Nageotte had 214 in 2002. Moore has an electric arm with hard, late life on his 92-96 mph fastball. He has an easy arm action and uses the same stroke to throw a late-breaking curveball that dives on hitters. His changeup also has the makings of a plus pitch, though he needs to throw it more often. The Rays loved how Moore responded to adversity. With the help of Charlotte pitching coach Neil Allen, he changed his grip to put his thumb more under the ball, enabling him to keep his pitches down in the zone. Though he quieted his delivery during the second half, his mechanics still got out of sync on occasion. His command needs refinement, though his wildness also can keep hitters off balance. Moore will open 2011 as a 21-year-old in Double-A. While he requires some fine-tuning, he has the potential to be a top-of-the-rotation starter in the major leagues.

Year	Club (League)	Class	W	L	ERA	G	GS	CG	SV	IP	H	HR	BB	SO	G/A	WHIP	AVG
2007	Princeton (APP)	R	0	0	2.66	8	3	0	0	20	12	1	16	29	—	1.38	.160
2008	Princeton (APP)	R	2	2	1.66	12	12	0	0	54	30	0	19	77	—	0.90	.154
2009	Bowling Green (SAL)	LoA	8	5	3.15	26	26	0	0	123	86	6	70	176	1.34	1.27	.195
2010	Charlotte (FSL)	HiA	6	11	3.36	26	26	0	0	145	109	7	61	208	1.27	1.18	.210
Minor League Totals			16	18	2.97	72	67	0	0	342	237	14	166	490	1.30	1.18	.193

3 DESMOND JENNINGS, OF

Born: Oct. 30, 1986. **B-T:** R-R. **Ht.:** 6-2. **Wt.:** 180. **Drafted:** Itawamba (Miss.) CC, 2006 (10th round). **Signed by:** Rickey Drexler.

Jennings looked ready for Tampa Bay after a banner 2009 that saw him win the Double-A Southern League MVP award and help Durham to the International League title and Triple-A National Championship. But the Rays didn't have an everyday job for him, so he returned to Durham. Though he had a wrist injury that limited his productivity early in 2010, managers rated him the IL's best baserunner, top defensive outfielder and most exciting player. A former junior college all-America wide receiver, Jennings is a pure athlete with three above-average tools. He has plus-plus speed and ranked second in the IL with 37 steals in 41 attempts. He covers center field from gap to gap, gets to balls quickly by taking the right routes and shows average arm strength. With his speed and disciplined approach, he should hit for a high average and get on base at a good clip. While the wrist injury affected his power, Jennings drives the ball well and could hit 15 homers per year. He needs to take greater advantage of his speed by putting the ball on the ground more often. All signs point to Jennings replacing departed free agent Carl Crawford in Tampa Bay's outfield. He eventually should become the Rays' leadoff hitter and center fielder.

Year	Club (League)	Class	AVG	G	AB	R	H	2B	3B	HR	RBI	BB	SO	SB	CS	OBP	SLG
2006	Princeton (APP)	R	.277	56	213	48	59	10	1	4	20	22	39	32	5	.360	.390
2007	Columbus (SAL)	LoA	.315	99	387	75	122	21	5	9	37	45	53	45	15	.401	.465
2008	Vero Beach (FSL)	HiA	.259	24	85	17	22	5	1	2	6	14	16	5	2	.360	.412
2009	Montgomery (SL)	AA	.316	100	383	69	121	25	8	8	45	48	52	37	5	.395	.486
	Durham (IL)	AAA	.325	32	114	23	37	6	2	3	17	19	15	15	2	.419	.491
2010	Durham (IL)	AAA	.278	109	399	82	111	25	6	3	36	47	67	37	4	.362	.393
	Tampa Bay (AL)	MAJ	.190	17	21	5	4	1	1	0	2	2	4	2	2	.292	.333
Major League Totals			.190	17	21	5	4	1	1	0	2	2	4	2	2	.292	.333
Minor League Totals			.299	420	1581	314	472	92	23	29	161	195	242	171	33	.384	.441

4 JAKE McGEE, LHP

Born: Aug. 6, 1986. **B-T:** L-L. **Ht.:** 6-3. **Wt.:** 230. **Drafted:** HS—Sparks, Nev., 2004 (5th round). **Signed by:** Fred Repke.

McGee was one of the top lefty pitching prospects in the minors when he blew out his elbow and had Tommy John surgery in June 2008. After working his way back to the mound for 30 innings in 2009, McGee climbed two levels last season and made his major league debut in September. McGee hasn't shown any negative effects from reconstructive elbow surgery. He generates tremendous late action on his fastball, which jumped to 92-95 mph and peaked at 97 when he moved to the bullpen at midseason. His breaking ball is a power curve that becomes slurvy when he gets under it. His changeup has the potential to be at least an average pitch. Command and consistency were issues prior to his injury, but he has shown better feel for all of his offerings since his return. A starter in 128 of his first 129 games as a pro, McGee was very effective as a reliever after reaching Triple-A. With the Rays' bullpen expected to undergo a complete overhaul in 2011, he should claim a regular role and could emerge as a closer in the near future.

Year	Club (League)	Class	W	L	ERA	G	GS	CG	SV	IP	H	HR	BB	SO	G/A	WHIP	AVG
2004	Princeton (APP)	R	4	1	3.97	12	12	0	0	57	49	5	25	53	—	1.31	.244
2005	Hudson Valley (NYP)	SS	5	4	3.64	15	14	0	0	77	64	4	23	89	—	1.13	.226
2006	SW Michigan (MWL)	LoA	7	9	2.96	26	26	0	0	134	103	7	65	171	—	1.25	.211
2007	Vero Beach (FSL)	HiA	5	4	2.93	21	21	0	0	117	86	8	39	145	—	1.07	.203
	Montgomery (SL)	AA	3	2	4.24	5	5	0	0	23	19	2	13	30	—	1.37	.224
2008	Montgomery (SL)	AA	6	4	3.94	15	15	0	0	78	65	6	37	65	—	1.31	.230
2009	Rays (GCL)	R	0	2	3.52	5	5	0	0	8	5	0	3	14	1.25	1.04	.172
	Charlotte (FSL)	HiA	0	2	6.45	11	11	0	0	22	26	2	9	26	1.67	1.57	.299
2010	Montgomery (SL)	AA	3	7	3.57	19	19	0	0	88	81	3	33	100	1.04	1.29	.245
	Durham (IL)	AAA	1	1	0.52	11	1	0	1	17	9	0	3	27	1.56	0.69	.148
	Tampa Bay (AL)	MAJ	0	0	1.80	8	0	0	0	5	2	0	3	6	1.67	1.00	.118
Major League Totals			0	0	1.80	8	0	0	0	5	2	0	3	6	1.67	1.00	.118
Minor League Totals			34	36	3.45	140	129	0	1	621	507	37	250	720	1.20	1.22	.223

5 JOSH SALE, OF

Born: July 5, 1991. **B-T:** L-R. **Ht.:** 6-0. **Wt.:** 215. **Drafted:** HS—Seattle, 2010 (1st round). **Signed by:** Paul Kirsch.

Sale had a single-digit handicap in golf, though he swung righthanded. The first player in the history of the Area Code Games to hit for the cycle, Sale was one of the best high school hitters available in the 2010 draft. A Gonzaga recruit, he went 17th overall and signed for $1.62 million at the Aug. 16 deadline. He saw his first pro action in instructional league. The top prep power hitter in the 2010 draft, Sale projects as a significant run producer and a corner outfielder. He generates incredible bat speed and shows a great feel for the strike zone while employing a patient approach. He has good present strength, which makes sense considering his father was a competitive natural powerlifter. He also has impressive hand-eye coordination, though he does have a few flaws in his swing, including a high back elbow and an early stride. He has the makeup and work ethic to make adjustments, and he should be able to do so without compromising his power. His speed, defensive ability and arm strength are all fringy, so while he works hard, he'll probably wind up in left field. Sale's offensive prowess gives him the potential to move quickly, though the Rays rarely rush high school signees. Because he signed late, he'll likely make his pro debut at Rookie-level Princeton in June.

Year	Club (League)	Class	AVG	G	AB	R	H	2B	3B	HR	RBI	BB	SO	SB	CS	OBP	SLG
2010	Did not play—Signed late																

6 ALEX TORRES, LHP

Born: Dec. 8, 1987. **B-T:** L-L. **Ht.:** 5-10. **Wt.:** 160. **Signed:** Venezuela, 2005. **Signed by:** Carlos Porte (Angels).

Torres may turn out to be the most valuable of the three players the Rays received from the Angels for Scott Kazmir in August 2009. Acquired along with Sean Rodriguez and third-base prospect Matt Sweeney, Torres appeared in the Futures Game and led the Southern League with 150 strikeouts in his first full season in Tampa Bay's system. Torres has a strong lower half that helps him produce lively stuff. His low-90s fastball has outstanding movement, and his changeup is just as effective. His feel for his curveball comes and goes, though it gives him a third plus pitch when he throws it for strikes. He throws across his body and almost falls over his front side—and those mechanics are a blessing and a curse. His delivery generates velocity and life but also creates problems with his control and high pitch counts. He led the SL in walks (70) as well as strikeouts. Scouts laud his competitiveness. Torres has the makings of three above-average pitches but remains a work in progress because of his inability to repeat his mechanics consistently. He could emerge as a No. 2 or 3 starter in the big leagues if he fine-tunes his control, or he could be a set-up man if he doesn't. He'll pitch in the Rays' Triple-A rotation in 2011.

Year	Club (League)	Class	W	L	ERA	G	GS	CG	SV	IP	H	HR	BB	SO	G/A	WHIP	AVG
2005	Angels (DSL)	R	4	2	1.52	9	9	1	0	53	23	2	23	87	—	0.86	.122
2006	Angels (AZL)	R	2	5	4.29	14	9	0	1	50	42	1	36	47	—	1.55	.235
2007	Angels (AZL)	R	1	0	4.76	4	0	0	0	6	4	0	8	3	—	2.12	.190
2008	Angels (AZL)	R	4	0	1.54	4	4	0	0	23	11	1	10	24	—	0.90	.153
	R. Cucamonga (CAL)	HiA	3	2	3.91	10	10	0	0	53	52	1	29	62	—	1.53	.264
2009	R. Cucamonga (CAL)	HiA	10	3	2.74	21	19	0	0	121	93	4	63	124	2.66	1.29	.217
	Arkansas (TL)	AA	3	1	2.77	5	5	0	0	26	23	0	17	25	1.58	1.54	.245
	Montgomery (SL)	AA	0	2	3.12	2	2	0	0	9	7	1	5	7	3.75	1.38	.219
2010	Montgomery (SL)	AA	11	6	3.47	27	27	0	0	143	136	9	70	150	1.90	1.44	.256
Minor League Totals			38	21	3.08	96	85	1	1	484	391	19	261	529	2.19	1.35	.224

7 ALEX COLOME, RHP

Born: Dec. 31, 1988. **B-T:** R-R. **Ht.:** 6-2. **Wt.:** 185. **Signed:** Dominican Republic, 2007. **Signed by:** Eddy Toledo.

Colome spent three years in Rookie and short-season leagues before advancing to low Class A Bowling Green in 2010. The nephew of former Rays reliever Jesus Colome, he faded in the second half but did impress with eight strikeouts in a four-inning start for Charlotte in September. Colome's live arm rivals that of anyone in the system. His 91-93 mph fastball touches 96 and features natural sink as well as armside run. He also throws a tight 11-to-5 curveball that has the makings of a plus pitch. He has improved the consistency of his changeup and used it frequently last season to retire lefthanders. Colome tends to overthrow at times, and his control and command can be erratic. He has learned to use the inner half of the plate by challenging hitters with his fastball, and he has shown some promise in backdooring his curve for strikes. Though Colome remains a raw prospect, he has the upside of a frontline starter. He has succeeded thus far simply by overpowering hitters, though he'll have to adopt a more polished approach when he returns to high Class A for a full season in 2011.

Year	Club (League)	Class	W	L	ERA	G	GS	CG	SV	IP	H	HR	BB	SO	G/A	WHIP	AVG
2007	Devil Rays (DSL)	R	1	6	2.97	14	11	0	0	39	30	1	31	50	—	1.55	.208
2008	Princeton (APP)	R	0	5	6.80	12	11	0	0	46	50	5	26	52	—	1.64	.272
2009	Hudson Valley (NYP)	SS	7	4	1.66	15	15	2	0	76	46	0	32	94	1.57	1.03	.174
2010	Bowling Green (SAL)	LoA	6	6	3.95	22	22	1	0	114	98	14	45	118	1.12	1.25	—
	Charlotte (FSL)	HiA	0	0	2.25	1	1	0	0	4	5	0	0	8	0.50	1.25	.333
Minor League Totals			14	21	3.64	64	60	3	0	280	229	20	134	322	1.26	1.30	.223

8 JUSTIN O'CONNER, C

Born: March 31, 1992. **B-T:** R-R. **Ht.:** 6-0. **Wt.:** 190. **Drafted:** HS—Muncie, Ind., 2010 (1st round). **Signed by:** James Bonnici.

O'Conner was a top prospect as a slugging third baseman and strong-armed righthander before moving behind the plate as a high school senior. He emerged as the top prep catcher in the 2010 draft, tying the Indiana high school record with 51 career homers. The Rays drafted him 31st overall and signed him away from an Arkansas commitment for $1.025 million. Though he struggled at the plate in his pro debut, O'Conner's well-above-average raw power still was evident. He has tremendous bat speed and can drive the ball to all fields, though he gets pull-happy during games. He doesn't project as a high-average hitter and may need to shorten his swing to make more consistent contact. O'Conner has plus-plus arm strength and has posted pop times as low as 1.8 seconds. He has quick feet and moves well behind the plate but is still working on the nuances of catching, such as maintaining consistent mechanics, calling games and working with pitchers. He's a below-average runner but not bad for a catcher. By selecting O'Conner, Luke Bailey and Jake DePew in consecutive drafts, the Rays have built impressive catching depth in the lower minors. They can give O'Conner time to develop, likely sending him to Princeton in 2011.

Year	Club (League)	Class	AVG	G	AB	R	H	2B	3B	HR	RBI	BB	SO	SB	CS	OBP	SLG
2010	Rays (GCL)	R	.211	48	161	18	34	13	0	3	29	18	46	1	0	.301	.348
Minor League Totals			.211	48	161	18	34	13	0	3	29	18	46	1	0	.301	.348

9 DREW VETTLESON, OF

Born: July 19, 1991. **B-T:** L-R. **Ht.:** 6-0. **Wt.:** 185. **Drafted:** HS—Silverdale, Wash., 2010 (1st round supplemental). **Signed by:** Paul Kirsch.

Vettleson attracted attention for his switch-pitching ability in high school, and while some scouts liked him on the mound, he drew more notice as one of the purest prep hitters in the 2010 draft. He worked out occasionally with fellow Washington outfielder and Rays draft pick Josh Sale. A supplemental first-round pick, Vettleson signed at the deadline for $845,000. A shortstop/center fielder/pitcher in high school, Vettleson profiles as a corner outfielder with the ability to hit for power and average. He has a quiet approach from the left side of the plate, with good patience and pitch recognition. He's short to the ball and drives pitches from gap to gap, though at times his swing features a stiff lead arm, which could create issues against good fastballs. His speed is a tick below-average, but he has great instincts on the bases and in the field. He has enough arm strength to play in right field. Vettleson didn't face top competition in high school—though he performed well on the summer showcase circuit—and signed too late to make his pro debut. Because his only pro experience has come in instructional league, he'll probably start 2011 in extended spring training before reporting to Princeton in mid-June.

Year	Club (League)	Class	AVG	G	AB	R	H	2B	3B	HR	RBI	BB	SO	SB	CS	OBP	SLG
2010	Did Not Play—Signed Late																

10 JAKE THOMPSON, RHP

MIKE JANES

Born: Aug. 8, 1989. **B-T:** R-R. **Ht.:** 6-3. **Wt.:** 225. **Drafted:** Long Beach State, 2010 (2nd round). **Signed by:** Robbie Moen.

After earning his GED diploma and enrolling early in college, Thompson became a weekend starter as a freshman before experiencing an inconsistent career at Long Beach State. Expected to be the 49ers' ace in 2010, he went 5-4, 5.16 in 14 starts before signing for $555,000 as a second-round pick. In his pro debut, he ranked as the short-season New York-Penn League's top pitching prospect before throwing 11 scoreless innings in high Class A. Thompson has the stuff, frame and mound presence to eat up innings in the middle of a big league rotation. His fastball usually sits at 92-94 mph and touched 97 during his debut. He picked up a mid-80s slider during the spring at Long Beach State, and it showed more consistency and peaked in the upper-80s in pro ball. His changeup can be a plus pitch at times, though it gets too firm on occasion. Hudson Valley pitching coach Jack Giese worked extensively with Thompson to improve his slider and mechanics. He no longer flies open or rushes his delivery, which led to improved command. Given his experience and pro debut, Thompson could move quicker than the average Rays farmhand. He figures to open his first full season by returning to high Class A.

Year	Club (League)	Class	W	L	ERA	G	GS	CG	SV	IP	H	HR	BB	SO	G/A	WHIP	AVG
2010	Hudson Valley (NYP)	SS	2	1	1.35	10	7	0	0	40	28	0	6	33	1.26	0.85	.200
	Charlotte (FSL)	HiA	2	0	0.00	2	2	0	0	11	2	0	2	6	1.36	0.36	.059
Minor League Totals			4	1	1.06	12	9	0	0	51	30	0	8	39	1.28	0.75	.172

11 ENNY ROMERO, LHP

Born: Jan. 24, 1991. **B-T:** L-L. **Ht.:** 6-3. **Wt.:** 165. **Signed:** Dominican Republic, 2008. **Signed by:** Eddy Toledo.

Romero is one of the big early finds in the Rays' recent emphasis on Latin America. In 2010, he rated as the No. 2 prospect in the Appalachian League, pacing the Rookie-level circuit with a 1.95 ERA while ranking second with a 0.94 WHIP, third with 9.4 strikeouts per nine innings and fourth with a .204 opponent average. In addition to his statistical success, he also displayed projectability that could lead to bigger things in the future. Romero throws two plus pitches: a 92-96 mph four-seam fastball with armside run and an overhand curveball with a 12-to-6 break and tight, quick spin. His changeup improved considerably over the course of the summer, showing added softness and some late fade. Romero does an excellent job of mixing his pitches and keeping them down in the strike zone. His maturity on the mound exceeds his age, as he has a good overall feel for pitching as well as the ability to attack hitters and exploit their weaknesses. A fast worker, he should continue to improve as he adds strength to his lanky frame. With a ceiling as high as any young pitcher in the Rays farm system, Romero should open the 2011 season in low Class A.

Year	Club (League)	Class	W	L	ERA	G	GS	CG	SV	IP	H	HR	BB	SO	G/A	WHIP	AVG
2008	Rays (DSL)	R	1	0	2.76	10	0	0	0	16	11	0	8	20	—	1.16	.175
2009	Rays (GCL)	R	2	4	4.81	11	4	0	0	39	38	2	21	33	1.05	1.50	.255
2010	Princeton (APP)	R	4	1	1.95	13	13	0	0	69	51	2	14	72	1.95	0.94	.204
	Hudson Valley (NYP)	SS	1	0	1.80	1	1	0	0	5	1	0	5	4	4.50	1.20	.071
Minor League Totals			8	5	2.91	35	18	0	0	130	101	4	48	129	1.60	1.15	.212

12 NICK BARNESE, RHP

Born: Jan. 11, 1989. **B-T:** R-R. **Ht.:** 6-2. **Wt.:** 170. **Drafted:** HS—Simi Valley, Calif., 2007 (3rd round). **Signed by:** Robbie Moen.

Barnese has yet to turn in a healthy full season in pro ball, as he has battled tenderness in the back of his shoulder in each of the past two seasons. He missed the first two months of 2009 in low Class A, then the most of the final month last season in high Class A. However, he did throw a career-high 122 innings in 2010 and maintained the steady effectiveness he has shown throughout his career. Barnese generates quick arm action from an over-the-head delivery. His fastball resides in the low 90s and can touch 94 mph. His changeup has good depth and shows signs of developing into an above-average pitch, yet its consistency continues to lag. Besides staying healthy, Barnese needs to improve his slider and do a better job of pitching down in the strike zone. Commanding the fastball, particularly on the inner half of the plate, will also improve the quality of his other pitches. A potential No. 3 starter, Barnese has posted a career 2.80 ERA while being handled carefully by the Rays. They hope he'll be able to handle a full season of starts in Double-A this year.

BaseballAmerica.com

Year	Club (League)	Class	W	L	ERA	G	GS	CG	SV	IP	H	HR	BB	SO	G/A	WHIP	AVG
2007	Princeton (APP)	R	2	2	3.22	9	8	0	0	36	30	1	4	37	—	0.94	.216
2008	Hudson Valley (NYP)	SS	5	3	2.45	13	13	0	0	66	52	1	24	84	—	1.15	.212
2009	Bowling Green (SAL)	LoA	6	5	2.53	15	15	0	0	75	56	3	25	62	1.44	1.08	.202
2010	Charlotte (FSL)	HiA	8	4	3.02	21	20	1	0	122	114	5	26	100	1.44	1.14	.246
Minor League Totals			21	14	2.80	58	56	1	0	299	252	10	79	283	1.44	1.11	.224

13 TY MORRISON, OF

Born: July 22, 1990. **B-T:** L-R. **Ht.:** 6-2. **Wt.:** 170. **Drafted:** HS—Tigard, Ore., 2008 (4th round). **Signed by:** Paul Kirsch.

One of the best athletes in the system, Morrison signed for an above-slot $500,000 as a fourth-round pick in 2008. He used his plus speed to rank fourth in the minors in steals (58 in 68 tries) and eighth in triples (13) in his first taste of full-season ball last year, recovering from a slow start in which he batted .129 in April. Morrison has good bat speed with a solid swing and path through the strike zone. He can pull inside pitches, yet his lack of physical strength limits his ability to drive the ball with consistency. Given his youth and broad shoulders, he has the room to add considerable strength, which would make him a more dynamic offensive presence. He also needs to become more patient and make more consistent contact, which would allow him to get on base and use his speed more often. Morrison gets good jumps in center field but could use some work on his routes. His arm is below-average, though he does make accurate throws to the right bases. After flying under the radar in his first three pro seasons, he could be poised for a breakout 2011 season in high Class A.

Year	Club (League)	Class	AVG	G	AB	R	H	2B	3B	HR	RBI	BB	SO	SB	CS	OBP	SLG
2008	Princeton (APP)	R	.265	10	34	2	9	0	0	0	1	2	12	3	1	.297	.265
2009	Princeton (APP)	R	.271	59	225	34	61	9	2	3	18	27	61	20	5	.365	.369
2010	Bowling Green (SAL)	LoA	.250	131	452	65	113	21	13	6	56	43	133	58	10	.324	.394
Minor League Totals			.257	200	711	101	183	30	15	9	75	72	206	81	16	.336	.380

14 BRAULIO LARA, LHP

Born: Dec. 20, 1988. **B-T:** L-L. **Ht.:** 6-1. **Wt.:** 180. **Signed:** Dominican Republic, 2008. **Signed by:** Junior Ramirez.

After leading his Dominican Summer League teams in strikeouts in 2008 and 2009, Lara made a smooth transition to the Appalachian League last year. He led the league in opponent average (.200), ranked second behind teammate Enny Romero in ERA (2.18) and tied for fourth in wins (six). Lara does a good job of jamming hitters on both sides of the plate with a 92-96 mph fastball that seems to jump on them. He has an easy, smooth delivery and throws both a two-seam and four-seam fastball. He made steady progress last summer with his curveball and changeup, with scouts believing both pitches have a chance to become average or better. While Lara has a live arm, he struggles with his control, particularly with his secondary pitches. In the past, he would lose confidence when he couldn't find the strike zone, but he made significant strides with his maturity in 2010. He's still working on the feel of his pitches and maintaining his focus from start to finish, yet should be ready to graduate to the full-season ranks at Bowling Green in 2011.

Year	Club (League)	Class	W	L	ERA	G	GS	CG	SV	IP	H	HR	BB	SO	G/A	WHIP	AVG
2008	Rays (DSL)	R	2	2	3.97	17	3	0	0	34	28	1	21	39	—	1.44	.220
2009	Rays (DSL)	R	5	3	3.58	13	8	1	0	55	52	2	21	58	1.04	1.32	.242
2010	Princeton (APP)	R	6	4	2.18	13	13	1	0	66	49	2	25	58	1.78	1.12	.200
Minor League Totals			13	9	3.07	43	24	2	0	155	129	5	67	155	141	1.26	.220

15 TIM BECKHAM, SS

Born: Jan. 27, 1990. **B-T:** R-R. **Ht.:** 6-0. **Wt.:** 190. **Drafted:** HS—Griffin, Ga., 2008 (1st round). **Signed by:** Milt Hill.

After seeing Beckham in action in 2010, multiple scouts said it would be impossible to know by watching him that he was the No. 1 overall pick and the recipient of a then-record $6.15 million bonus in 2008. Though that may be harsh, his former ceiling as an all-around shortstop no longer appears realistic. He's still young and spent last year in high Class A at age 20, producing mixed results. A minor wrist injury slowed him early in the season and he hit just .212 in the first half. He rebounded to bat .285 after the all-star break, but he also went homerless as his slugging percentage declined to .352 from .370 in the first half. Beckham still has plus bat speed and the strength in his hands and wrists to eventually hit for above-average power, but he also swings through too many high-80s fastballs. Beckham was in better shape last year, yet is a fringe-average runner at best. He has more than enough arm to play shortstop and cut his errors from 43 in 2009 to 25 last year, but his hands aren't soft and he doesn't have the athleticism to remain at the position. Third base is a better option, though it will place greater demands on his bat. The Rays will remain patient with Beckham, and manager Joe Maddon has said he likes Beckham's overall ability and approach to the game. He should make the move up to Double-A in 2011.

Year	Club (League)	Class	AVG	G	AB	R	H	2B	3B	HR	RBI	BB	SO	SB	CS	OBP	SLG
2008	Princeton (APP)	R	.243	46	177	30	43	12	0	2	14	13	43	5	1	.297	.345
	Hudson Valley (NYP)	SS	.333	2	6	5	2	1	0	0	0	2	1	1	0	.556	.500
2009	Bowling Green (SAL)	LoA	.275	125	491	58	135	33	4	5	63	34	116	13	10	.328	.389
2010	Charlotte (FSL)	HiA	.256	123	465	68	119	23	5	5	57	62	119	22	14	.346	.359
Minor League Totals			.263	296	1139	161	299	69	9	12	134	111	279	41	25	.332	.371

16 ALEX COBB, RHP

Born: Oct. 7, 1987. **B-T:** R-R. **Ht.:** 6-1. **Wt.:** 180. **Drafted:** HS—Vero Beach, Fla., 2006 (4th round). **Signed by:** Kevin Elfering.

Because he doesn't have spectacular stuff, Cobb doesn't attract much attention, yet he continues to achieve solid results. He has lowered his ERA in each of his five pro seasons, ranking fourth in the Southern League (2.71) last year while topping the circuit with 9.6 strikeouts per nine innings. The Rays added him to the 40-man roster in the offseason. Cobb's fastball resides in the low 90s with some sinking action, and he pitches off it well by mixing it with his above-average changeup. His fastball command can be erratic, one reason lefthanders hit .293 off him last year (compared to righties batting .230), but he throws strikes and has a good idea of how to set up hitters. His breaking balls, a high-70s curveball and a low-80s slider, show some promise on occasion. His curveball is more effective than his slider at this point, though he'll still need to refine one or both to succeed in the majors. Following a stint in the International League playoffs and Arizona Fall League, he's ready for a full season in Triple-A. His big league future could be as a set-up man, though he'll remain a starter for the foreseeable future.

Year	Club (League)	Class	W	L	ERA	G	GS	CG	SV	IP	H	HR	BB	SO	G/A	WHIP	AVG
2006	Princeton (APP)	R	0	0	5.19	6	1	0	0	9	9	3	3	8	—	1.38	.265
2007	Hudson Valley (NYP)	SS	5	6	3.54	16	16	0	0	81	78	4	31	62	—	1.34	.259
2008	Columbus (SAL)	LoA	9	7	3.29	25	25	0	0	140	113	16	35	97	—	1.06	.224
2009	Charlotte (FSL)	HiA	8	5	3.03	24	23	0	0	125	116	6	31	107	1.58	1.18	.249
2010	Montgomery (SL)	AA	7	5	2.71	23	22	0	0	120	120	7	35	128	1.99	1.30	.262
Minor League Totals			29	23	3.15	94	87	0	0	474	436	36	135	402	1.74	1.20	.247

17 LUKE BAILEY, C

Born: March 11, 1991. **B-T:** R-R. **Ht.:** 6-0. **Wt.:** 198. **Drafted:** HS—LaGrange, Ga., 2009 (4th round). **Signed by:** Milt Hill.

The Tommy John surgery Bailey had late in his senior season of high school not only prevented him from playing pro ball in 2009, it also limited his development in the early stages of his 2010 pro debut. Considered the top prep catching prospect in his draft class before he got hurt, he fell to the fourth round but signed with Tampa Bay for supplemental first-round money ($750,000). When he returned to action last season, Bailey showed above-average power but struggled with his ability to control the strike zone. He tended to become pull-happy after striking out early in games and needs to do a better job of incorporating his solid power to all fields. Bailey had more success defensively, as his plus arm strength returned and he threw out 31 percent of basestealers. He has soft hands and moves well behind the plate, doing a laudable job of blocking balls. He runs surprisingly well for a catcher. The Rays believe Bailey made more strides than anyone in the organization late in the season and through instructional league, which they attribute to making some necessary adjustments as well as trusting his elbow again. Tampa Bay hasn't had much success developing catchers—John Jaso's 2010 season notwithstanding—but has made significant investments in high school backstops Bailey, Justin O'Conner and Jake DePew in the last two drafts. At least one of them will need to move to low Class A next year, and Bailey is the most likely candidate.

Year	Club (League)	Class	AVG	G	AB	R	H	2B	3B	HR	RBI	BB	SO	SB	CS	OBP	SLG
2010	Rays (GCL)	R	.182	42	137	18	25	8	0	5	14	17	47	0	0	.298	.350
Minor League Totals			.182	42	137	18	25	8	0	5	14	17	47	0	0	.298	.350

18 YOEL ARAUJO, OF

Born: Dec. 3, 1993. **B-T:** R-R. **Ht.:** 6-3. **Wt.:** 190. **Signed:** Dominican Republic, 2010. **Signed by:** Danny Santana.

Tampa Bay made its biggest move yet in Latin America by signing Araujo for $800,000, the largest bonus in franchise history for an international amateur player. He's wiry and gangly as a 16-year-old, and the Rays believe he has the ability to develop into a five-tool outfielder. Unlike most young Dominicans, Araujo already has a solid approach at the plate and the ability to drive the ball from gap to gap. Though his hitting mechanics are still raw, he gets good extension on his swing and should continue to add strength in order to hit for significant power at higher levels. With strong hands and quick wrists, he has shown the ability to handle power pitching and should continue to improve in that area. Araujo is a plus runner with the ability to cover center field from gap to gap. His arm strength is average. With his maturing body and solid skill set, Araujo has some of the highest upside in the system. Tampa Bay will be patient with his development, which will start in the Dominican

Summer League in 2011.

Year	Club (League)	Class	AVG	G	AB	R	H	2B	3B	HR	RBI	BB	SO	SB	CS	OBP	SLG
2010	Did Not Play—Signed 2011 Contract																

19 JOE CRUZ, RHP

Born: July 20, 1988. **B-T:** R-R. **Ht.:** 6-4. **Wt.:** 190. **Drafted:** East Los Angeles JC, 2007 (30th round). **Signed by:** Robbie Moen.

The Rays had believed for a while that Cruz was on the verge of putting together a breakthrough season. It finally happened in 2010, when his hard work paid off with him leading the Florida State League with 13 wins and posting a career-low 2.85 ERA. Cruz's best pitch is his fastball, which sits around 92 mph and tops out at 95. He started last season without a decent breaking ball, but put in time with Charlotte pitching coach Neil Allen to develop a slurvy curveball that he can throw for strikes at any time in the count. The bender has a huge, high break on occasion, clocking as slow as 73 mph. He also has a fringy changeup. Cruz has become more adept at adding and subtracting from all of his offerings in order to keep hitters off balance. Lanky with a long arm action, he uses his ideal pitcher's frame to his advantage by throwing on a sharp downhill plane. He has thrown strikes throughout his pro career. He's still experimenting with all of his pitches, but he mainly needs to maintain his consistency against more experienced hitters at higher levels. A potential fourth or fifth starter if he solidifies his repertoire, Cruz will move up to Double-A in 2011.

Year	Club (League)	Class	W	L	ERA	G	GS	CG	SV	IP	H	HR	BB	SO	G/A	WHIP	AVG
2007	Princeton (APP)	R	2	0	0.00	3	0	0	0	9	5	0	3	13	—	0.89	.161
2008	Princeton (APP)	R	1	3	3.17	13	13	0	0	54	61	5	14	62	—	1.39	.270
2009	Bowling Green (SAL)	LoA	5	8	4.04	21	21	0	0	98	110	5	26	99	1.26	1.39	.284
2010	Charlotte (FSL)	HiA	13	6	2.85	25	25	1	0	142	137	6	39	131	1.72	1.24	.258
Minor League Totals			21	17	3.21	62	59	1	0	303	313	16	82	305	1.51	1.30	.266

20 ZACH QUATE, RHP

Born: Sept. 12, 1987. **B-T:** R-R. **Ht.:** 6-1. **Wt.:** 200. **Drafted:** Appalachian State, 2009 (14th round). **Signed by:** Brad Matthews.

Quate has been nothing short of dominant since signing for $7,500 as a 14th-round pick in 2009. He surrendered only one earned run while going a perfect 13-for-13 in save opportunities in his pro debut, then jumped to high Class A and earned Florida State League all-star honors last year. Quate mixes a hard slider with a 90-91 mph fastball. Hitters have a difficult time laying off the slider because it emerges from the same slot as his fastball. He back-doors his slider most of the time, and all of his pitches are at the knees or below, forcing hitters to hit the ball on the ground. He has outstanding mound presence and the mentality to close games. His greatest need at this point is to pitch inside more consistently. Scouts say he reminds them of Anthony Slama, another unheralded draft pick who made it to the majors as a reliever. Quate will advance to Double-A in 2011, and Tampa Bay won't be far off if he continues to overmatch hitters.

Year	Club (League)	Class	W	L	ERA	G	GS	CG	SV	IP	H	HR	BB	SO	G/A	WHIP	AVG
2009	Hudson Valley (NYP)	SS	1	0	0.35	18	0	0	13	26	15	0	4	34	1.21	0.73	.170
2010	Charlotte (FSL)	HiA	2	2	1.49	49	0	0	25	72	51	2	18	90	1.16	0.95	.199
Minor League Totals			3	2	1.19	67	0	0	38	98	66	2	22	124	1.18	0.89	.192

21 TODD GLAESMANN, OF

Born: Oct. 24, 1990. **B-T:** R-R. **Ht.:** 6-4. **Wt.:** 220. **Drafted:** HS—Waco, Texas, 2009 (3rd round). **Signed by:** Pat Murphy.

With the Rays failing to sign first-rounder LeVon Washington and second-rounder Kenny Diekroeger, Glaesmann became the highest-drafted player to join the club out of the 2009 draft. He played briefly that summer after signing for $930,000, then flashed five-tool potential in 2010. Glaesmann has a body built for power, showing excellent strength, plus bat speed and long limbs that generate leverage. He has more of a line-drive swing than one built for home runs, and the Rays hope he maintains that approach while making the necessary adjustments to hit for better average. His swing gets long, causing him to miss fastballs on occasion, and he tends to chase breaking balls down and away. Glaesmann has played center field but looks more natural in right. He has plus arm strength and speed, though he's still learning the nuances of basestealing. Glaesmann is raw in many ways but his tools give him a high ceiling. He'll move up to low Class A in 2011.

Year	Club (League)	Class	AVG	G	AB	R	H	2B	3B	HR	RBI	BB	SO	SB	CS	OBP	SLG
2009	Rays (GCL)	R	.278	5	18	1	5	1	0	0	2	0	3	1	0	.278	.333
2010	Princeton (APP)	R	.233	62	236	41	55	17	5	4	24	13	70	13	6	.297	.398
Minor League Totals			.236	67	254	42	60	18	5	4	26	13	73	14	6	.296	.394

22 DEREK DIETRICH, SS

Born: July 18, 1989. **B-T:** L-R. **Ht.:** 6-1. **Wt.:** 200. **Drafted:** Georgia Tech, 2010 (2nd round). **Signed by:** Milt Hill.

Dietrich was the Astros' top pick (third round) in the 2007 draft but chose to attend Georgia Tech rather than accept Houston's slot-money offer of $270,000. Three years later, he went one round higher and signed for $457,200. Dietrich, who hit 17 homers for the Yellow Jackets last spring, stands out most with his power. He has good physical strength and drives the ball consistently from the left side of the plate. He needs to focus on hitting line drives and let his power come naturally instead of adding loft to his swing, which gets him into trouble at times. Though he played shortstop in his pro debut, Dietrich lacks the range and fast-twitch athleticism to play the position much longer. He's a below-average runner with soft hands and a strong arm, so he probably will fit better at third base than at second or short. Some Rays officials believe he could become a versatile defender who plays a variety of positions, including left field. Dietrich holds promise but isn't expected to develop into a game-changer at the major league level. The grandson of former big leaguer Steve Demeter, he'll open his first full season in low Class A.

Year	Club (League)	Class	AVG	G	AB	R	H	2B	3B	HR	RBI	BB	SO	SB	CS	OBP	SLG
2010	Hudson Valley (NYP)	SS	.279	45	179	33	50	12	2	3	20	11	42	2	2	.340	.419
Minor League Totals			.279	45	179	33	50	12	2	3	20	11	42	2	2	.340	.419

23 RYAN BRETT, 2B

Born: Oct. 9, 1991. **B-T:** R-R. **Ht.:** 5-9. **Wt.:** 180. **Drafted:** HS—Burien, Wash., 2010 (3rd round). **Signed by:** Paul Kirsch.

Brett was the third of Tampa Bay's three premium picks from the state of Washington in the 2010 draft, going two rounds after first-rounders Josh Sale and Drew Vettleson. Signed for $341,100, he had a fine pro debut and consistently brought a high-intensity approach to the ballpark every day. Though he's just 5-foot-9, Brett is an offensive-minded player with plenty of bat speed. His quick, short stroke and solid knowledge of the strike zone produces line drives to all fields and should enable him to hit for average. A plus runner, he does a good job of keeping the ball on the ground to enhance his chances of getting on base. His basestealing skills are a work in progress, but he projects to swipe 20 or more bases annually. He needs to improve his bunting skills in order to take better advantage of his speed and become more of a top-of-the-lineup hitter. Defensively, Brett is rough around the edges. His hands aren't particularly soft and his actions are choppy at second base. Scouts believe a move to center field could be in his future, given his speed, potential range and average arm strength. With his athleticism and drive, Brett has the makings of what the Rays consider an ideal major leaguer. He's expected to open 2011 in Princeton but could get a shot at the full-season ranks at Bowling Green.

Year	Club (League)	Class	AVG	G	AB	R	H	2B	3B	HR	RBI	BB	SO	SB	CS	OBP	SLG
2010	Rays (GCL)	R	.303	27	89	8	27	5	2	0	9	8	17	12	3	.364	.404
Minor League Totals			.303	27	89	8	27	5	2	0	9	8	17	12	3	.364	.404

24 SCOTT SHUMAN, RHP

Born: March 28, 1988. **B-T:** R-R. **Ht.:** 6-3. **Wt.:** 205. **Drafted:** Auburn, 2009 (19th round). **Signed by:** Milt Hill.

After a strong freshman year at Auburn, Shuman posted a 6.07 ERA as a sophomore and a 7.90 ERA as a junior. Scouts questioned his competitive makeup and he dropped to the 19th round of the 2009 draft, signing for $25,000. He has exceeded expectations so far, averaging 13.4 strikeouts per nine innings in his first two pro seasons and leading Midwest League relievers by averaging 13.9 last season. Shuman's fastball sits at 92-95 mph and can run as high as 98. He mixes it with a hard 84-mph slider with good tilt. Both pitches display some natural sink, and when he's throwing them both for strikes, he can be untouchable. On two occasions last year, he had two-inning outings where he whiffed six hitters. Shuman's control still deserts him at times and will determine his future success. If he can throw strikes consistently, he could move quickly. He'll start 2011 in high Class A but it's not out of the question that he could reach Tampa Bay at some point in 2012 if all goes well.

Year	Club (League)	Class	W	L	ERA	G	GS	CG	SV	IP	H	HR	BB	SO	G/A	WHIP	AVG
2009	Princeton (APP)	R	0	0	0.82	10	0	0	3	22	18	0	9	29	2.36	1.23	.222
2010	Bowling Green (SAL)	LoA	4	5	3.01	46	0	0	14	72	50	5	38	111	1.31	1.23	—
	Charlotte (FSL)	HiA	0	0	0.00	1	0	0	0	2	0	0	2	3	3.00	0.86	.000
Minor League Totals			4	5	2.44	57	0	0	17	96	68	5	49	143	1.56	1.22	.198

25 WILKING RODRIGUEZ, RHP

Born: March 2, 1990. **B-T:** R-R. **Ht.:** 6-1. **Wt.:** 160. **Signed:** Venezuela, 2007. **Signed by:** Ronnie Blanco.

Rodriguez's 5-16 record in the United States isn't reflective of his potential. He has a live arm that delivers 89-95 mph fastballs with natural tail and cutting action on occasion. He backs it up with an average 76-78 mph curveball that he tends to rely on too often. His curve shows flashes of being a plus offering when he generates tight spin and late bite. Rodriguez's changeup has shown promise on the side and during warmups, but he has been reluctant to use it during games and must develop it in order to remain in the rotation. He's not especially tall and relies on a drop-and-drive delivery to work down in the strike zone. He throws strikes but gets hit when he leaves his pitches up. Rodriguez needs to get stronger after fading down the stretch in 2010. He pitched a career-high 106 innings but went 0-7, 4.84 in his final 11 starts. His next challenge will come in high Class A this year.

Year	Club (League)	Class	W	L	ERA	G	GS	CG	SV	IP	H	HR	BB	SO	G/A	WHIP	AVG
2007	Devil Rays/Reds (VSL)	R	3	2	1.95	17	0	0	2	32	23	1	14	28	—	1.14	.200
2008	Rays (VSL)	R	0	1	3.71	10	8	0	0	27	26	3	6	29	—	1.20	.260
2009	Princeton (APP)	R	1	6	3.21	13	13	0	0	56	44	5	12	52	1.24	1.00	.213
2010	Bowling Green (SAL)	LoA	4	10	4.23	22	19	0	0	106	109	11	28	93	1.09	1.29	—
Minor League Totals			8	19	3.58	62	40	0	2	221	202	20	60	202	1.14	1.18	.242

26 KEVIN KIERMAIER, OF

Born: Oct. 24, 1990. **B-T:** L-R. **Ht.:** 6-1. **Wt.:** 200. **Drafted:** Parkland (Ill.) JC, 2010 (31st round). **Signed by:** Tom Couston.

Kiermaier set several school records at Parkland (Ill.) JC and was named MVP of the Division II Junior College World Series in 2009, when he set a tournament record with 12 RBIs as the Cobras won the national championship. His commitment to Purdue for 2011 led teams to believe he'd be difficult to sign, but the Rays landed him almost immediately for $75,000 after drafting him in the 31st round in June. Displaying solid athleticism and all-around skills after turning pro, he attracted raves during a strong pro debut and also throughout instructional league. His instincts and work ethic are impressive as well. Kiermaier has a quick, short swing that allows him to stay on the ball well. He uses the entire field and has some present gap power. Once he learns to turn on inside pitches more consistently, he could develop average home run pop. He has plus speed and stole 17 bases in 22 attempts during his debut, but he still is learning how to read pitchers and steal bases. He has the tools to be a quality right fielder, with good range and a solid, accurate arm. Kiermaier will advance to low Class A this year and could prove to be one of the biggest late-round steals from the 2010 draft.

Year	Club (League)	Class	AVG	G	AB	R	H	2B	3B	HR	RBI	BB	SO	SB	CS	OBP	SLG
2010	Princeton (APP)	R	.303	57	218	44	66	8	7	2	16	24	54	17	5	.380	.431
Minor League Totals			.303	57	218	44	66	8	7	2	16	24	54	17	5	.380	.431

27 HECTOR GUEVARA, 2B

Born: Oct. 7, 1991. **B-T:** R-R. **Ht.:** 5-11. **Wt.:** 170. **Signed:** Venezuela, 2008. **Signed by:** Ronnie Blanco.

Guevara was the MVP of the Rays' Rookie-level Venezuelan Summer League club in 2009 before bypassing the Rookie-level Gulf Coast League and reporting to Princeton for his U.S. debut last year. Despite being the youngest starting position player in the Appalachian League, he handled the leap with relative ease, just as he did a move from shortstop to second base. Guevara makes good contact with his patient approach. He has average speed and could develop power to match, potentially fitting into the No. 2 slot in a lineup. Guevara has good, soft hands and a decent arm that's fine at second base but was fringy at shortstop. His feet work well and he does an excellent job of turning double plays. He has a strong desire to succeed and is a quintessential baseball rat, making the sum of his game greater than the individual parts. A promotion to high Class A is next on his agenda.

Year	Club (League)	Class	AVG	G	AB	R	H	2B	3B	HR	RBI	BB	SO	SB	CS	OBP	SLG
2009	Rays (VSL)	R	.330	54	206	29	68	14	2	8	36	16	21	6	5	.374	.534
2010	Princeton (APP)	R	.251	64	223	24	56	13	3	2	26	15	31	9	3	.308	.363
Minor League Totals			.289	118	429	53	124	27	5	10	62	31	52	15	8	.340	.445

28 LESLIE ANDERSON, OF/1B

Born: March 20, 1982. **B-T:** L-L. **Ht.:** 6-1. **Wt.:** 205. **Signed:** Cuba, 2010. **Signed by:** Eddy Toledo.

A career .320 hitter in Cuba's major league, Anderson played in the 2006 and 2009 World Baseball Classic. When Cuba's national team subsequently dropped him, he defected in 2009 and signed a four-year, $1.725 million contact with the Rays last April. He began his U.S. career in high Class A and reached Triple-A by the end of the season. He lived up to his reputation as a high-average hitter in his pro debut, batting a combined .302. He does a good job of squaring the ball on the barrel despite an unconventional setup and approach. He has good size and a smooth lefthanded swing, but he doesn't project to hit more than 15 homers annually at the major league level. While he makes contact, he doesn't draw many walks. Tampa Bay had Anderson split time between left field and first base in 2010, but he's shaky in the outfield and can't play there in the majors. His below-average speed and range aren't liabilities at first base, where he won the equivalent of a Gold Glove while in Cuba. He has a strong arm for the position. Anderson continued his development in the Arizona Fall League, where he won the Rising Stars Game with a ninth-inning homer. With Carlos Pena leaving as a free agent, Anderson could get a chance to make the Rays in spring training. If he doesn't, he'll return to Durham to start 2011.

Year	Club (League)	Class	AVG	G	AB	R	H	2B	3B	HR	RBI	BB	SO	SB	CS	OBP	SLG
2010	Charlotte (FSL)	HiA	.262	21	84	13	22	3	0	3	11	4	6	0	1	.303	.405
	Montgomery (SL)	AA	.304	48	181	24	55	11	1	6	25	18	28	3	1	.382	.475
	Durham (IL)	AAA	.328	30	122	14	40	5	0	2	13	5	20	0	0	.359	.418
Minor League Totals			.302	99	387	51	117	19	1	11	49	27	54	3	2	.359	.442

29 KYLE LOBSTEIN, LHP

Born: Aug. 12, 1989. **B-T:** L-L. **Ht.:** 6-3. **Wt.:** 200. **Drafted:** HS—Flagstaff, Ariz., 2008 (2nd round). **Signed by:** Jason Durocher.

The Rays gave Lobstein $1.5 million as a second-round pick in 2008 because they liked his feel for pitching and projected that he would add to a fastball that dipped to 87-88 mph during his high school senior season. Though he's athletic and his body has room to add more strength, Lobstein's heater hasn't improved. His fastball has good angle, some deception and late movement, but it sat at 86-87 mph and didn't feature much sink in 2010. Tampa Bay still looks at his maturing frame and easy delivery and thinks he'll gain some more velocity, but several scouts outside the organization disagree. Lobstein has good command, particularly for a young lefty. His high-70s curveball shows a sharp break at times, and he also demonstrates some aptitude for throwing a changeup. The Rays should have a better idea of what the future holds for Lobstein after he spends 2011 in high Class A.

Year	Club (League)	Class	W	L	ERA	G	GS	CG	SV	IP	H	HR	BB	SO	G/A	WHIP	AVG
2009	Hudson Valley (NYP)	SS	3	5	2.58	14	14	0	0	73	55	4	23	74	1.23	1.06	.204
2010	Bowling Green (SAL)	LoA	9	8	4.14	27	27	1	0	148	140	14	54	128	0.73	1.31	—
Minor League Totals			12	13	3.62	41	41	1	0	221	195	18	77	202	0.88	1.23	.236

30 STEPHEN VOGT, C/OF/1B

Born: Nov. 1, 1984. **B-T:** L-R. **Ht.:** 6-3. **Wt.:** 215. **Drafted:** Azusa Pacific (Calif.), 2007 (12th round). **Signed by:** Jake Wilson.

At 26, Vogt is old for a prospect, particularly for the Rays. But his ability to put the bat on the ball and his ability to play multiple positions has placed him on the organization's radar. A career .448 hitter in four seasons at Azusa Pacific (Calif.), an NAIA school, Vogt signed for $6,000 as a 12th-round pick in 2007. After batting .294 in his first two pro seasons, he tore his rotator cuff in April 2009 and missed most of the season. He rebounded last year to lead the Florida State league in hitting (.345) and slugging (.511). Vogt uses the entire field and rarely wastes an at-bat. He has no trouble hanging in against lefthanders, batting .377 against them in 2010, though his modest power may preclude him from becoming a big league regular. Though his pure speed grades as below-average, Vogt has some athleticism and arm strength. He saw action at catcher, the outfield corners and first base last year. Behind the plate, he calls a good game and works well with pitchers. He threw out 31 percent of basestealers in 2010, but his exchange and pop times— which hovered between 1.95 and 2.0 seconds last year—need improvement. His range and arm are solid in left field. Vogt earns high marks for makeup as well, winning the organization's Erik Walker community champion award, given annually to the Rays minor leaguer who best displays teamwork, sportsmanship and community involvement. His Double-A performance in 2011 will give a better indication of his long-term value, and he could emerge as a valuable reserve in Tampa Bay as soon as 2012.

Year	Club (League)	Class	AVG	G	AB	R	H	2B	3B	HR	RBI	BB	SO	SB	CS	OBP	SLG
2007	Hudson Valley (NYP)	SS	.300	70	240	40	72	8	0	4	48	31	31	6	1	.371	.383
2008	Columbus (SAL)	LoA	.291	113	392	57	114	22	3	6	54	47	48	6	1	.368	.408
2009	Charlotte (FSL)	HiA	.171	10	35	0	6	2	0	0	3	2	4	0	1	.216	.229
2010	Charlotte (FSL)	HiA	.345	106	368	56	127	31	3	8	47	31	46	3	1	.399	.511
Minor League Totals			.308	299	1035	153	319	63	6	18	152	111	129	15	4	.375	.433

Texas Rangers

BY AARON FITT

Shortly after Jon Daniels became the youngest general manager in baseball history following the 2005 season, the Rangers fully committed to building a winner through their farm system. They restocked the organization through trades and the draft, and they poured resources into their Latin American operations.

After sinking to 28th in Baseball America's farm system rankings before the 2007 season, Texas rose to No. 1 just two years later. And in 2010, its plan reached fruition.

Led by young stars such as American League MVP  Josh Hamilton, AL rookie of the year Neftali Feliz, Elvis Andrus and Nelson Cruz—trade acquisitions all—the Rangers cruised to 90 wins, their best season and first AL West title since 1999. The farm system, which has sent key players such as Julio Borbon, Derek Holland, Tommy Hunter and Mitch Moreland to Texas in recent years, also provided trade bait for reinforcements. The Rangers had the depth to swing a blockbuster trade for Cliff Lee, plus smaller deals for Jorge Cantu, Cristian Guzman and Bengie Molina.

Texas won a playoff series for the first time in franchise history, beating the Rays in the Division Series before vanquishing the Yankees in the AL Championship Series. Though the Rangers lost the World Series in five games to the Giants, their season was an overwhelming success—on and off the field.

Now the franchise should find financial stability as well, after concluding a drawn-out process to replace former owner Tom Hicks, whose financial problems dragged the team into bankruptcy. Major League Baseball had to prop up the team's finances for a couple of years as Hicks' holdings went into bankruptcy—and in fact made a multimillion-dollar loan in May to keep the club going until the ownership situation could be resolved—but now has given way to a group led by team president Nolan Ryan and Pennsylvania attorney Chuck Greenberg.

The new owners inherit a team poised to win for years. Most of its best players are in their 20s, and the team will have more financial flexibility than it did in the final years under Hicks. While the farm system has been depleted by graduations and trades, it still has elite prospects in lefthander Martin Perez, shortstop Jurickson Profar and righty Tanner Scheppers.

The talent remains deep at the lower levels of the minors. Having four of the first 49 picks in the 2010

MORRIS FOSTOFF

Neftali Feliz won the AL rookie of the year award after anchoring the Rangers' bullpen

TOP 30 PROSPECTS

1. Martin Perez, lhp	16. Kellin Deglan, c
2. Jurickson Profar, ss	17. Jorge Alfaro, c
3. Tanner Scheppers, rhp	18. Justin Grimm, rhp
4. Robbie Erlin, lhp	19. Robbie Ross, lhp
5. Engel Beltre, of	20. Miguel Velazquez, of
6. Michael Kirkman, lhp	21. Luke Jackson, rhp
7. Mike Olt, 3b	22. Joe Wieland, rhp
8. Luis Sardinas, ss	23. Fabio Castillo, rhp
9. Jake Skole, of	24. Barret Loux, rhp
10. Miguel de los Santos, lhp	25. Jared Hoying, of
11. David Perez, rhp	26. Jose Felix, c
12. Christian Villanueva, 3b	27. Neil Ramirez, rhp
13. Roman Mendez, rhp	28. Cody Buckel, rhp
14. Wilmer Font, rhp	29. Josh Richmond, of
15. Leury Garcia, ss	30. Jacob Brigham, rhp

draft helped replenish the cupboard with outfielder Jake Skole, catcher Kellin Deglan, righthander Luke Jackson and third baseman Mike Olt. Another wave of exciting Latin American talent is on the way, led by Profar and Venezuelan shortstop Luis Sardinas.

The Rangers also took steps to improve their stock of catchers, after what had been regarded as an area of strength became a weakness when Jarrod Saltalamacchia, Taylor Teagarden and Max Ramirez didn't pan out. They not only drafted Deglan but also signed 16-year-old Colombian Jorge Alfaro for $1.3 million.

ORGANIZATION OVERVIEW

General Manager: Jon Daniels. **Farm Director:** Scott Servais. **Scouting Director:** Kip Fagg.

Class	Team	League	W	L	PCT	Finish*	Manager
Majors	Texas Rangers	American	90	72	.556	†4th (14)	Ron Washington
Triple-A	Oklahoma City RedHawks	Pacific Coast	73	70	.510	8th (16)	Bobby Jones
Double-A	Frisco RoughRiders	Texas	72	67	.518	3rd (8)	Steve Buechele
High A	Bakersfield Blaze	California	67	73	.479	8th (10)	Bill Haselman
Low A	Hickory Crawdads	South Atlantic	75	64	.540	t-4th (14)	Bill Richardson
Short-season	Spokane Indians	Northwest	43	33	.566	t-2nd (8)	Tim Hulett
Rookie	AZL Rangers	Arizona	31	24	.564	t-3rd (12)	Jayce Tingler
Overall 2010 Minor League Record			361	331	.522	8th (30)	

*Finish in overall standings (No. of teams in league). †League champion.
Triple-A affiliate changes to Round Rock (Pacific Coast), high Class A affiliate changes to Myrtle Beach (Carolina) in 2011.

LAST YEAR'S TOP 30

Player, Pos.	Status
1. Neftali Feliz, rhp	Majors
2. Justin Smoak, 1b	(Mariners)
3. Martin Perez, lhp	No. 1
4. Tanner Scheppers, rhp	No. 3
5. Jurickson Profar, ss	No. 2
6. Kasey Kiker, lhp	Dropped out
7. Robbie Ross, lhp	No. 19
8. Mitch Moreland, of/1b	Majors
9. Danny Gutierrez, rhp	Dropped out
10. Wilmer Font, rhp	No. 14
11. Max Ramirez, c	Dropped out
12. Joe Wieland, rhp	No. 22
13. Luis Sardinas, ss	No. 8
14. Engel Beltre, of	No. 5
15. Leury Garcia, ss	No. 15
16. Michael Kirkman, lhp	No. 6
17. Blake Beavan, rhp	(Mariners)
18. Tommy Mendonca, 3b	Dropped out
19. Guillermo Moscoso, rhp	Dropped out
20. Omar Poveda, rhp	(Marlins)
21. Michael Main, rhp	(Giants)
22. Miguel Velazquez, of	No. 20
23. Pedro Strop, rhp	Dropped out
24. Neil Ramirez, rhp	No. 27
25. Jake Brigham, rhp	No. 30
26. Tomas Telis, c	Dropped out
27. Wilfredo Boscan, rhp	Dropped out
28. Craig Gentry, of	Dropped out
29. Andrew Doyle, rhp	Dropped out
30. Richard Alvarez, rhp	Dropped out

BEST TOOLS

Best Hitter for Average	Jurickson Profar
Best Power Hitter	Mike Olt
Best Strike-Zone Discipline	Chris McGuiness
Fastest Baserunner	Leury Garcia
Best Athlete	Jordan Akins
Best Fastball	Tanner Scheppers
Best Curveball	Tanner Scheppers
Best Slider	Michael Kirkman
Best Changeup	Miguel de los Santos
Best Control	Robbie Erlin
Best Defensive Catcher	Jose Felix
Best Defensive Infielder	Jurickson Profar
Best Infield Arm	Leury Garcia
Best Defensive Outfielder	Engel Beltre
Best Outfield Arm	Engel Beltre

PROJECTED 2014 LINEUP

Catcher	Kellin Deglan
First Base	Mitch Moreland
Second Base	Jurickson Profar
Third Base	Mike Olt
Shortstop	Elvis Andrus
Left Field	Nelson Cruz
Center Field	Josh Hamilton
Right Field	Engel Beltre
Designated Hitter	Ian Kinsler
No. 1 Starter	Martin Perez
No. 2 Starter	Tanner Scheppers
No. 3 Starter	Robbie Erlin
No. 4 Starter	C.J. Wilson
No. 5 Starter	Derek Holland
Closer	Neftali Feliz

TOP PROSPECTS OF THE DECADE

Year	Player, Pos.	2010 Org.
2001	Carlos Pena, 1b	Rays
2002	Hank Blalock, 3b	Rays
2003	Mark Teixeira, 3b	Yankees
2004	Adrian Gonzalez, 1b	Padres
2005	Thomas Diamond, rhp	Cubs
2006	Edinson Volquez, rhp	Reds
2007	John Danks, lhp	White Sox
2008	Elvis Andrus, ss	Rangers
2009	Neftali Feliz, rhp	Rangers
2010	Neftali Feliz, rhp	Rangers

TOP DRAFT PICKS OF THE DECADE

Year	Player, Pos.	2010 Org.
2001	Mark Teixeira, 3b	Yankees
2002	Drew Meyer, ss	Angels
2003	John Danks, lhp	White Sox
2004	Thomas Diamond, rhp	Cubs
2005	John Mayberry Jr., of	Phillies
2006	Kasey Kiker, lhp	Rangers
2007	Blake Beavan, rhp	Mariners
2008	Justin Smoak, 1b	Mariners
2009	*Matt Purke, lhp	Texas Christian
2010	Jake Skole, of	Rangers

*Did not sign.

LARGEST BONUSES IN CLUB HISTORY

Mark Teixeira, 2001	$4,500,000
Justin Smoak, 2008	$3,500,000
John Danks, 2003	$2,100,000
Vincent Sinisi, 2003	$2,070,000
Thomas Diamond, 2004	$2,025,000

TEXAS RANGERS

TOP 2011 ROOKIE: Tanner Scheppers, rhp. He could help as a reliever immediately but Texas is committed to making him a starter, which could delay his arrival in the majors.

BREAKOUT PROSPECT: David Perez, rhp. With his advanced feel for an intriguing three-pitch repertoire, he looks like the next blue-chip prospect out of the Rangers' prolific Latin American machine.

SLEEPER: Hanser Alberto, ss. He won the Rookie-level Dominican Summer League batting title with a .358 average at age 17 last summer.

SOURCE OF TOP 30 TALENT

Homegrown	28	Acquired	2
College	4	Trades	2
Junior college	0	Rule 5 draft	0
High school	11	Independent leagues	0
Independent/drafted	1	Free agents/waivers	0
Drafted free agents	1		
International	11		

LF
Jared Hoying (25)
Joey Butler
Mike Bianucci

CF
Engel Beltre (5)
Jake Skole (9)
Teodoro Martinez
Craig Gentry
David Paisano
Ryan Strausborger
Braxton Lane

RF
Miguel Velazquez (20)
Josh Richmond (29)
Jordan Akins
Ruben Sierra Jr.
Jared Prince
Guillermo Pimentel

3B
Mike Olt (7)
Christian Villanueva (12)
Tommy Mendonca

SS
Jurickson Profar (2)
Luis Sardinas (8)
Leury Garcia (15)
Hanser Alberto
Jonathan Roof
Nick Urbanus

2B
Drew Robinson
Odubel Herrera
Santiago Chirino
Marcus Lemon

1B
Chris McGuiness
Clark Murphy
Chad Tracy
Andrew Clark

C
Kellin Deglan (16)
Jorge Alfaro (17)
Jose Felix (26)
Tomas Telis
Brett Nicholas

RHP

RHSP	RHRP
Tanner Scheppers (3)	Fabio Castillo (23)
David Perez (11)	Jacob Brigham (30)
Roman Mendez (13)	Yoshinori Tateyama
Wilmer Font (14)	Carlos Melo
Justin Grimm (18)	Ovispo de los Santos
Luke Jackson (21)	Pedro Strop
Joe Wieland (22)	Cody Eppley
Barret Loux (24)	Joe Van Meter
Neil Ramirez (27)	Mark Hamburger
Cody Buckel (28)	Omar Beltre
Matt Thompson	Ryan Tucker
Eric Hurley	Guillermo Moscoso
Nick Tepesch	Braden Tullis
Santo Perez	Zach Osborne
Wilfredo Boscan	Colby Killian
Richard Alvarez	Kennil Gomez
Shawn Blackwell	Carlos Pimentel
Steve McKinnon	
Danny Gutierrez	
Nick McBride	
Andrew Doyle	
Trevor Hurley	
Mason Tobin	

LHP

LHSP	LHRP
Martin Perez (1)	Jimmy Reyes
Robbie Erlin (4)	Corey Young
Michael Kirkman (6)	Zach Phillips
Miguel de los Santos (10)	Tim Murphy
Robbie Ross (19)	Ben Snyder
Chris Hanna	
Chad Bell	
Kasey Kiker	
Victor Payano	

2010

BEST PURE HITTER: SS/2B/OF Drew Robinson (4) used a loose lefthanded swing and strong hands to bat .286/.406/.357 in the Rookie-level Arizona League.

BEST POWER HITTER: 3B Mike Olt (1s), who owns the single-season (23) and career (44) home run records at Connecticut, smacked nine longballs at short-season Spokane. OFs Jake Skole (1) and Jared Hoying (10) and C Kellin Deglan (1) also have promising power.

FASTEST RUNNER: OF Ryan Strausborger (16) has a quicker first step, while OF Jordan Akins (3) is faster under way. They're both 65 runners on the 20-80 scouting scale. Strausborger stole 62 bases in 71 attempts between Indiana State and pro ball in 2010.

BEST DEFENSIVE PLAYER: Skole and Deglan have the potential to be solid or better defenders at up-the-middle positions, and Olt is similarly gifted at third base.

BEST FASTBALL: RHP Justin Grimm (5) can't always command his fastball, but he can throw it at 92-96 mph. RHP Luke Jackson (1s) could pass him in time and already touches 96 on occasion.

BEST SECONDARY PITCH: RHP Cody Buckel's (2) curveball, and he also has a promising changeup. RHP Nick Tepesch (14) has the best slider in this group.

BEST PRO DEBUT: Hoying won Northwest League MVP honors by batting .325/.378/.543 with 10 homers and 20 steals at Spokane. LHP Chris Hanna (11) commands and hides his fringy stuff well, which is how he posted a 0.94 ERA and a 40-4 K-BB ratio in 29 innings in the AZL.

BEST ATHLETE: Skole gave up a football scholarship to play defensive back at Georgia Tech. Fellow Georgia prep product Akins is a fast-twitch athlete.

MOST INTRIGUING BACKGROUND: OF Kendall Radcliffe (25) is the great nephew of Ted "Double Duty" Radcliffe, one of the best two-way players in Negro Leagues history. Unsigned 3B Garrett Buechele's (18) father Steve played in the majors and manages the Rangers' Double-A Frisco affiliate. SS/2B Jonathan Roof's (8) dad Gene and uncle Phil also played in the big leagues, and his brothers Eric and Shawn play in the Tigers system.

CLOSEST TO THE MAJORS: Olt, the only college player among Texas' seven picks in the first four rounds. LHP Jimmy Reyes (7) has the solid stuff to move fast in a relief role.

BEST LATE-ROUND PICK: Hoying has average speed and plus arm strength to go with his bat. OF Josh Richmond (12) and Tepesch had the physical talent to go in the first five rounds, but Richmond missed much of the spring with a hand injury and Tepesch was inconsistent.

THE ONE WHO GOT AWAY: Stanford-bound OF Brian Ragira (30) is a solid athlete with enough power potential to blossom into a first-rounder in 2013. RHP Trae Davis (29), who went to Baylor, has a 91-94 mph fastball and good feel for pitching.

ASSESSMENT: New scouting director Kip Fagg had three extra picks to play with, and the Rangers found the money to sign all of them. Texas loaded up on projectable high schoolers early and took some intriguing collegians in later rounds.

2009

RHP Tanner Scheppers (1s) is already on the verge of helping the big league club, while LHP Robbie Erlin (3) won the low Class A South Atlantic League ERA title last year. OF Riley Cooper (25) already has made the big time—as a wide receiver with the NFL's Philadelphia Eagles.

GRADE: B+

2008

1B Justin Smoak (1) was the key player in the Cliff Lee trade, without which the Rangers wouldn't have made their first-ever World Series appearance. Smoak and LHP Robbie Ross (2) took small steps back in 2010 after signing for $5.075 million, but they still could pay off on that investment.

GRADE: B

2007

OF Julio Borbon (1s), RHP Tommy Hunter (1s) and OF/1B Mitch Moreland (17) all played roles in Texas' World Series run. So did RHPs Blake Beavan (1), Michael Main (1) and Josh Lueke (16)—as trade bait in deals for Lee and Bengie Molina. Unsigned RHP Anthony Ranaudo (11) and LHP Drew Pomeranz (12) blossomed into elite college pitchers and signed for $5.2 million last summer.

GRADE: B+

2006

Then-unknown draft-and-follow LHP Derek Holland (25) is the best player from this bunch. 1B Chris Davis (5), OF Craig Gentry (10) and since-traded LHP Danny Ray Herrera (45) also have reached the majors, and there's still some hope for LHP Kasey Kiker (1).

GRADE: C+

Draft analysis by Jim Callis. Numbers in parentheses indicate draft rounds.

MARTIN PEREZ, LHP

Born: April 4, 1991. **Bats:** L. **Throws:** L.
Height: 6-0. **Weight:** 178. **Signed:** Venezuela,
2007. **Signed by:** Rafic Saab/Manny Batista/
Don Welke.

BILL MITCHELL

After signing for $580,000 in 2007, Perez rocketed through the Rangers system to reach Double-A Frisco as an 18-year-old two years later. Along the way, he was often compared to fellow Venezuelan Johan Santana and former Yankees ace Ron Guidry for his short stature, big stuff and competitiveness. But Perez tasted adversity for the first time when he made the jump from the low Class A South Atlantic League, where he ranked as the No. 1 prospect in 2009, to the Texas League for a cameo at the end of the season. He got nervous, overthrew and didn't repeat his delivery well, posting a 5.57 ERA in five starts. He returned to Frisco in 2010 and posted a 2.45 ERA in his first six starts. But Perez was erratic from May onward, and a lower back strain caused him to miss a few starts in July and August. He regained some of his old form in a dominant playoff start, then carried his momentum over to instructional league.

There aren't many lefthanders who can match Perez's potential with three pitches, not even in the major leagues. His fastball velocity has increased from the mid-80s when he signed, to 91-95 mph with good sink when he's at his best. He did sit around 89-92 for much of last summer before regaining velocity toward the end of the season. His fastball command deserted him at times, playing a major role in his disappointing season. When he got in trouble, he would try to reach back and throw harder. That caused his head to jerk, his alignment to get out of whack, his release point to vary and his control to falter. Perez does have an easy arm action with minimal effort, and his smooth delivery has always been one of his greatest assets. Filling the strike zone shouldn't be an issue if he resists the temptation to overthrow. Perez's changeup was his best secondary pitch when he signed, and Texas had him focus on throwing it early in his career so he could refine it. The changeup was his go-to pitch in 2010, a plus offering with sink and fade. He throws it with good arm speed and deception. He also flashes a quality curveball with sharp 1-to-7 break, though he showed less feel for it last season than he did in 2009, when he could add and subtract from it at will, varying it from 68-81 mph. He worried about curveball velocity at the expense of command too often in 2010. He needs to do a better job throwing it for strikes early in counts and burying it once he gets ahead of hitters. Some scouts worry that his small frame won't lends itself to durability, but the Rangers aren't concerned.

Texas believes that the speed bump Perez hit in 2010 will help him in the long run. He's still just 19 and is on his way to having three legitimate plus pitches and becoming a true ace. He figures to pitch at the Rangers' new Triple-A Round Rock affiliate in 2011. The Rangers still believe he has the stuff to pitch at the front of a big league rotation.

SCOUTING GRADES

Fastball: 65.   **Command/**
Curveball: 60.   **Control:** 60.
Changeup: 65.   **Delivery:** 60.

Based on 20-80 scouting scale, where 50 represents major league average, and future projection rather than present tools.

Year	Club (League)	Class	W	L	ERA	G	GS	CG	SV	IP	H	HR	BB	SO	G/A	WHIP	AVG
2008	Spokane (NWL)	SS	1	2	3.65	15	15	0	0	62	66	3	28	53	—	1.52	.274
2009	Hickory (SAL)	LoA	5	5	2.31	22	14	0	1	94	82	3	33	105	1.58	1.23	.236
	Frisco (TL)	AA	1	3	5.57	5	5	0	0	21	29	2	5	14	1.25	1.62	.326
2010	Frisco (TL)	AA	5	8	5.96	24	23	0	0	100	117	12	50	101	1.69	1.68	.290
Minor League Totals			12	18	4.17	66	57	0	1	276	294	20	116	273	1.59	1.49	.272

2 JURICKSON PROFAR, SS

Born: Feb. 20, 1993. **B-T:** B-R. **Ht.:** 6-0. **Wt.:** 170. **Signed:** Curacao, 2009. **Signed by:** Mike Daly/Chu Halabi/Jose Felomina.

Profar led Curacao to the 2004 Little League World Series championship and attracted plenty of interest on the international market as a pitcher. The Rangers raised some eyebrows when they signed him as a shortstop for $1.55 million, a franchise record for an international signee, but he ranked as the No. 1 prospect in the short-season Northwest League as a 17-year-old last summer. Still young and skinny, Profar projects as a true five-tool talent once he matures physically. A natural righthanded hitter, he has a nice line-drive stroke from both sides of the plate, though he fell off from the left side as he wore down late in 2010. He likes pitches on the outer half and tends to cut off his swing a bit, so he'll need to learn to pull the ball with more authority. He controls the strike zone well for his age, and should become a plus hitter with average power. Profar's instincts make his average speed play up on the bases and help him get friendly hops at short. His range, quickness, soft hands and strong hands give him a chance to be a plus defender at shortstop. As with his hero, Elvis Andrus, Profar's makeup sets him apart. Profar wants to get to the big leagues as quickly as Andrus did. While that's unlikely, he's moving quickly and will play at low Class A Hickory at age 18.

Year	Club (League)	Class	AVG	G	AB	R	H	2B	3B	HR	RBI	BB	SO	SB	CS	OBP	SLG
2010	Spokane (NWL)	SS	.250	63	252	42	63	19	0	4	23	28	46	8	3	.323	.373
Minor League Totals			.250	63	252	42	63	19	0	4	23	28	46	8	3	.323	.373

3 TANNER SCHEPPERS, RHP

Born: Jan. 17, 1987. **B-T:** R-R. **Ht.:** 6-4. **Wt.:** 200. **Drafted:** St. Paul (American Association), 2009 (1st round supplemental). **Signed by:** Derek Lee.

Shoulder problem caused Scheppers to miss Fresno State's 2008 College World Series championship run and knocked him from a projected top-10 choice to the second round of the draft. He resurfaced in independent ball in 2009, then signed for $1.25 million as a sandwich pick. He pitched mostly in relief last year because the Rangers wanted to limit his innings and needed bullpen reinforcements. Scheppers' four-seam fastball rarely drops below 95 mph and tops out at 98 when he pitches as a starter, and bumps triple digits when he comes out of the bullpen. Some scouts say his fastball is straight, but others say it has good riding life up in the zone. He dabbled late in the year with a low-90s sinker. Scheppers throws both an 11-to-5 curveball and a hard slider that are plus pitches at times. He has feel for a changeup but throws it too hard at 87-88 mph. He rushes his delivery when he works from the stretch, causing him to lose his release point and pitch up in the zone. Texas is committed to developing Scheppers as a starter. He has the stuff to pitch at the front of a rotation, if he can refine his command, or in the late innings as a reliever. He figures to open 2011 in Triple-A and get a taste of the big leagues at some point.

Year	Club (League)	Class	W	L	ERA	G	GS	CG	SV	IP	H	HR	BB	SO	G/A	WHIP	AVG
2010	Frisco (TL)	AA	0	0	0.82	6	0	0	2	11	3	1	0	19	0.83	0.27	.079
	Oklahoma City (PCL)	AAA	1	3	5.48	30	7	0	4	69	82	5	30	71	1.22	1.62	.297
Minor League Totals			1	3	4.84	36	7	0	6	80	85	6	30	90	1.18	1.44	.271

4 ROBBIE ERLIN, LHP

Born: Oct. 8, 1990. **B-T:** L-L. **Ht.:** 6-0. **Wt.:** 175. **Drafted:** HS—Scotts Valley, Calif., 2009 (3rd round). **Signed by:** Butch Metzger.

After signing him away from a Cal Poly commitment for $425,000 as a 2009 third-round pick, the Rangers planned for Erlin to begin 2010 in extended spring training and then begin his professional career with short-season Spokane. Instead, Erlin forced his way to low Class A Hickory with a strong spring and led the South Atlantic League in ERA (2.12) and strikeout-walk ratio (7.4) as a 19-year-old. Erlin is polished beyond his years, with outstanding command of all three of his offerings. He keeps hitters off-balance by throwing any pitch in any count and can even mix a big leg kick with a slide step to disrupt their timing. Erlin attacks all four quadrants of the strike zone with an 89-91 mph fastball, an 11-to-7 curveball that's a plus pitch at times, and a quality changeup with fade and some turnover action. He can change speeds with his curveball and changeup, which is 12-15 mph slower than his fastball. He's a fierce competitor with the best delivery in the system. Despite his lack of size, Erlin profiles as a quality big league starter because of his off-the-charts feel for pitching and his competitiveness. He'll advance to Texas' new high Class A Myrtle Beach affiliate in 2011 and could race through the minors.

Year	Club (League)	Class	W	L	ERA	G	GS	CG	SV	IP	H	HR	BB	SO	G/A	WHIP	AVG
2009	Rangers (AZL)	R	0	0	2.25	3	0	0	0	4	5	0	1	9	2.00	1.50	.294
2010	Hickory (SAL)	LoA	6	3	2.12	28	17	0	1	115	89	9	17	125	0.89	0.92	.213
Minor League Totals			6	3	2.12	31	17	0	1	119	94	9	18	134	0.90	0.94	.216

5 ENGEL BELTRE, OF

Born: Nov. 1, 1989. **B-T:** L-L. **Ht.:** 6-2. **Wt.:** 180. **Signed:** Dominican Republic, 2006. **Signed by:** Pablo Lantigua (Red Sox).

The centerpiece of the 2007 Eric Gagne trade with the Red Sox, Beltre struggled to slow the game down in his first taste of high Class A in 2009. He made big progress in his return last season, taking off after moving to the No. 3 slot in the Bakersfield lineup, where he hit .356/.402/.485. He started fast after a July promotion to Double-A, then cooled off. Beltre has an exciting package of tools, though there are varying opinions about his power potential. Some evaluators say he has plus raw power and envision him developing at least average game power, while others see him maxing out at 12-15 homers per year. He has a quick lefthanded swing and the ability to hit for average. Beltre made a concerted effort to be more patient last year, but at times he still tries to kill the ball, causing him to roll his front shoulder and not see the ball as well. Beltre has plus speed and is very aggressive on the basepaths—sometimes too aggressive. His range and instincts will make him a plus defender in center field, and his arm is both strong and accurate. The Rangers added Beltre to the 40-man roster and he will start 2011 back at Frisco as a 21-year-old. If he continues to refine his offensive approach, he could arrive in Texas sometime the following season.

Year	Club (League)	Class	AVG	G	AB	R	H	2B	3B	HR	RBI	BB	SO	SB	CS	OBP	SLG
2007	Red Sox (GCL)	R	.208	34	125	20	26	3	3	5	13	12	44	6	3	.310	.400
	Rangers (AZL)	R	.310	22	84	19	26	3	4	4	15	8	21	3	2	.388	.583
	Spokane (NWL)	SS	.211	9	38	3	8	0	0	0	1	2	10	2	1	.250	.211
2008	Clinton (MWL)	LoA	.283	130	566	87	160	26	9	8	47	15	105	31	11	.308	.403
2009	Bakersfield (CAL)	HiA	.227	84	357	44	81	13	5	3	23	17	77	17	7	.281	.317
	Rangers (AZL)	R	.300	3	10	4	3	1	1	0	0	0	3	2	0	.364	.600
	Frisco (TL)	AA	.071	4	14	1	1	1	0	0	1	0	2	1	0	.133	.143
2010	Bakersfield (CAL)	HiA	.331	68	263	38	87	11	4	5	35	11	34	10	7	.376	.460
	Frisco (TL)	AA	.254	47	181	14	46	4	4	1	14	10	24	8	2	.301	.337
Minor League Totals			.267	401	1638	230	438	62	30	26	149	75	320	80	33	.315	.389

6 MICHAEL KIRKMAN, LHP

Born: Sept. 18, 1986. **B-T:** L-L. **Ht.:** 6-4. **Wt.:** 195. **Drafted:** HS—Lake City, Fla., 2005 (5th round). **Signed by:** Guy DeMutis.

Kirkman's mechanics and confidence deserted him after he hurt his hamstring in 2006, and for two years he barely could throw a ball above 80 mph—and nowhere near the plate. Pitching coordinator Keith Comstock got him back on track, and Kirkman earned Triple-A Pacific Coast League pitcher of the year honors in 2010 before contributing to the Rangers' World Series run as a reliever. Kirkman has good size and a strong arm that generates 91-94 mph fastballs with some sink. His plus 84-85 mph slider is an out pitch that he can bury on the back foot of righthanders and get lefties to chase out of the zone. He also mixes in a mid-70s curveball and a decent changeup, though he seldom used either in relief. He has a herky-jerky delivery with some length that makes it hard for hitters to pick up the ball but also impacts his command, which can be spotty. Texas still believes Kirkman can be a big league starter, but his lack of fine command might make him a better fit in the bullpen. He should make the Opening Day roster as a reliever unless the Rangers decide to move him back to the rotation, in which case he could return to Triple-A until an opportunity arises.

Year	Club (League)	Class	W	L	ERA	G	GS	CG	SV	IP	H	HR	BB	SO	G/A	WHIP	AVG
2005	Rangers (AZL)	R	3	1	3.44	14	9	0	0	52	51	0	19	58	—	1.34	.249
2006	Clinton (MWL)	LoA	0	3	6.98	6	6	0	0	19	23	0	24	22	—	2.43	.303
	Rangers (AZL)	R	1	2	13.20	8	4	0	0	15	21	0	27	8	—	3.20	.333
2007	Spokane (NWL)	SS	1	4	7.00	9	6	0	0	27	33	2	25	24	—	2.15	.306
	Clinton (MWL)	LoA	0	1	7.43	5	2	0	0	13	17	1	12	12	—	2.17	.304
2008	Spokane (NWL)	SS	1	1	0.00	2	2	0	0	10	7	0	2	9	—	0.90	.184
	Clinton (MWL)	LoA	4	3	4.36	15	14	0	0	74	78	8	23	58	—	1.36	.269
2009	Bakersfield (CAL)	HiA	4	1	2.06	8	7	0	0	48	43	1	18	54	0.98	1.27	.244
	Frisco (TL)	AA	5	7	4.19	18	18	0	0	97	93	9	43	64	1.00	1.41	.254
2010	Oklahoma City (PCL)	AAA	13	3	3.09	24	22	0	0	131	115	8	68	130	0.92	1.40	.235
	Texas (AL)	MAJ	0	0	1.65	14	0	0	0	16	9	0	10	16	1.07	1.16	.161
Major League Totals			0	0	1.65	14	0	0	0	16	9	0	10	16	1.07	1.16	.161
Minor League Totals			32	26	4.18	109	90	0	0	487	481	29	261	439	0.96	1.52	.258

7 MIKE OLT, 3B

Born: Aug. 27, 1988. **B-T:** R-R. **Ht.:** 6-2. **Wt.:** 215. **Drafted:** Connecticut, 2010 (1st round supplemental). **Signed by:** Jay Heafner.

After setting Connecticut career records with 44 home runs and 177 RBIs and leading the Huskies to the NCAA playoffs for the first time since 1994, Olt was the fourth of Texas' four picks before the second round of the 2010 draft. He signed for $717,300 and had a strong debut in the Northwest League, where he ranked as the No. 4 prospect. Midway through last spring, Olt went to a narrower stance that he said helped him see the ball better, but he took to a wider, more balanced set-up last summer. He has good leverage and generates above-average raw power, but a hitch in his swing causes his timing to get out of whack at times. He can get pull-happy and still must improve against good breaking balls. Olt began his college career as a shortstop, and his athleticism plays very well at the hot corner. He excels at making plays on slow rollers, and he owns smooth actions, soft hands and a plus arm. He's a slightly below-average runner. Scouts and coaches constantly laud his makeup and work ethic. Olt may never be better than an average hitter, but his power potential and defensive ability give him a chance to be a valuable everyday player. He figures to start 2011 at Hickory but could reach Myrtle Beach quickly.

Year	Club (League)	Class	AVG	G	AB	R	H	2B	3B	HR	RBI	BB	SO	SB	CS	OBP	SLG
2010	Spokane (NWL)	SS	.293	69	263	57	77	16	1	9	43	40	77	6	0	.390	.464
Minor League Totals			.293	69	263	57	77	16	1	9	43	40	77	6	0	.390	.464

8 LUIS SARDINAS, SS

Born: May 16, 1993. **B-T:** B-R. **Ht.:** 6-1. **Wt.:** 150. **Signed:** Venezuela, 2009. **Signed by:** Mike Daly/Rafic Saab/Pedro Avila.

Texas invested seven-figure bonuses in two Latin American shortstops in 2009, landing Jurickson Profar and Sardinas ($1.2 million). Sardinas' 2010 pro debut was delayed when a pitch hit him on the hand in extended spring training, and he dislocated his shoulder on a swing and miss during instructional league. Sardinas is a quick-twitch athlete who reminds the Rangers of a young Tony Fernandez. He has louder raw tools than Profar but is less advanced in all phases of the game. Sardinas is a plus-plus runner with a lightning-quick first step that gives him excellent range at shortstop and the potential to be an elite basestealer. He also has above-average arm strength, but he must become more consistent defensively and avoid concentration lapses. Sardinas currently lacks strength at the plate and tries to compensate—especially as a lefthanded hitter—with his upper body in a way that gets his lower half out of sync and causes him to swing uphill. The Rangers want him to stay on top of the ball and hit it on the ground to use his speed better. He'll never hit for power, but he has the hand-eye coordination to hit for average and use the gaps. Shoulder surgery will knock Sardinas out for most of 2011, but the Rangers can wait on his talent. If he adds strength and polish, he could be a dynamic shortstop.

Year	Club (League)	Class	AVG	G	AB	R	H	2B	3B	HR	RBI	BB	SO	SB	CS	OBP	SLG
2010	Rangers (AZL)	R	.311	26	103	22	32	4	0	0	8	7	15	8	2	.363	.350
Minor League Totals			.311	26	103	22	32	4	0	0	8	7	15	8	2	.363	.350

9 JAKE SKOLE, OF

Born: Jan. 17, 1992. **B-T:** L-R. **Ht.:** 6-1. **Wt.:** 192. **Drafted:** HS—Roswell, Ga., 2010 (1st round). **Signed by:** Ryan Coe.

The younger brother of Georgia Tech slugger Matt Skole, Jake committed to the Yellow Jackets to play football and baseball. His gridiron commitment and an ankle injury depressed his draft stock until he came on late last spring. Shortly after he got two hits off Angels first-rounder Kaleb Cowart in a Georgia high school playoff game, the Rangers drafted Skole 15th overall and signed him for $1.56 million. Physical and athletic, Skole has plenty of strength but needs to use his lower half better in his swing in order to drive the ball with more authority. He projects to have average to plus power, and he could be an average or slightly better hitter from the left side. As a multisport athlete, Skole has some rough edges to polish, but Texas was pleasantly surprised by his offensive approach and strike-zone discipline. His ankle continued to hamper him a bit during his pro debut, but he has slightly above-average speed when fully healthy. The Rangers believe he has a chance to play center field, though some scouts project him as a right fielder. He has a solid-average arm. Skole will advance to low Class A to start 2011. With his football days in the rear-view mirror, he should begin to develop more quickly.

Year	Club (League)	Class	AVG	G	AB	R	H	2B	3B	HR	RBI	BB	SO	SB	CS	OBP	SLG
2010	Rangers (AZL)	R	.286	8	28	7	8	2	0	0	5	5	5	3	0	.394	.357
	Spokane (NWL)	SS	.254	57	201	29	51	9	2	2	27	23	52	6	4	.327	.348
Minor League Totals			.258	65	229	36	59	11	2	2	32	28	57	9	4	.336	.349

10 MIGUEL DE LOS SANTOS, LHP

Born: July 10, 1988. **B-T:** L-L. **Ht.:** 6-1. **Wt.:** 205. **Signed:** Dominican Republic, 2006. **Signed by:** Danilo Trancoso.

De los Santos' development was slowed by Tommy John surgery in 2007 and visa issues that kept him in the Rookie-level Dominican Summer League in 2009, but he made a splash back in the United States last season. He averaged 14.3 strikeouts per nine innings while reaching low Class A for the first time, and he fanned eight of the 15 batters he faced in the South Atlantic League playoffs. De los Santos has an exciting three-pitch mix, highlighted by the best changeup in the system, a plus-plus pitch with screwball action and two-plane depth. His fastball sits at 90-92 mph range and tops out at 94, but his fastball command comes and goes. He tends to fall in love with his heater at the expense of his other pitches. He also throws a sharp overhand curveball that rates as at least a solid-average pitch. Whether de los Santos can repeat his delivery and refine his fastball command will determine if his future is in a starting or relieving role, but he has the pure stuff to be a quality No. 3 starter. The Rangers added him to the 40-man roster this offseason. He's already 22 and has pitched just 179 innings in five pro seasons, so the Rangers will start pushing him in 2011. He'll probably open the season in high Class A.

Year	Club (League)	Class	W	L	ERA	G	GS	CG	SV	IP	H	HR	BB	SO	G/A	WHIP	AVG
2006	Rangers (DSL)	R	0	1	1.59	13	4	0	0	34	16	1	15	48	—	0.91	.136
2007	Rangers (DSL)	R	0	0	0.00	1	0	0	0	3	0	0	0	2	—	0.00	.000
	Rangers (AZL)	R	0	1	6.35	3	3	0	0	6	7	0	3	6	—	1.76	.292
2008	Rangers (AZL)	R	0	2	4.67	10	10	0	0	35	28	2	18	54	—	1.33	.217
2009	Rangers 2 (DSL)	R	1	1	1.41	22	0	0	12	32	8	0	22	70	1.08	0.94	.074
2010	Spokane (NWL)	SS	2	0	1.69	7	7	0	0	32	13	0	20	50	0.79	1.03	.116
	Hickory (SAL)	LoA	2	2	3.99	12	6	0	0	38	27	3	24	62	0.79	1.33	.199
Minor League Totals			5	7	2.81	68	30	0	12	179	99	6	102	292	0.85	1.12	.156

11 DAVID PEREZ, RHP

Born: Dec. 20, 1992. **B-T:** R-R. **Ht.:** 6-5. **Wt.:** 200. **Signed:** Dominican Republic, 2009. **Signed by:** Rodolfo Rosario.

Perez's velocity was up and down as an amateur, and the Rangers signed him for $425,000 out of the Dominican Republic in 2009 on the strength of his projectability. His stock soared during his dominating pro debut in the Dominican Summer League, as his riding fastball sat consistently at 88-93 mph and he pounded the strike zone with three pitches. He was one of the major stories of Texas' instructional league camp after running his fastball up to 95 mph in one-inning stints. Perez's mid-70s curveball has good spin, and though it's currently a below-average major league offering, it projects as a potential plus pitch once he adds some power to it. He also has good feel for a changeup, which could give him a third average-or-better offering. Perez has a loose, easy delivery and does a good job of throwing downhill. His command and feel for pitching are advanced for his age, and he emerged as a leader of the DSL Rangers staff. He needs to add 10-15 pounds to his lean frame, and when he does he could become an elite pitching prospect. The Rangers expect him to jump to Spokane in 2011, and some club officials expect to see him at Hickory by the end of the season.

Year	Club (League)	Class	W	L	ERA	G	GS	CG	SV	IP	H	HR	BB	SO	G/A	WHIP	AVG
2010	Rangers (DSL)	R	4	4	1.41	14	14	0	0	70	50	0	8	68	2.44	0.83	.201
Minor League Totals			4	4	1.41	14	14	0	0	70	50	0	8	68	2.44	0.83	.201

12 CHRISTIAN VILLANUEVA, 3B

Born: June 19, 1991. **B-T:** R-R. **Ht.:** 5-11. **Wt.:** 160. **Signed:** Mexico, 2008. **Signed by:** Bill McLaughlin/ Mike Daly.

Villanueva played in just eight games in the Dominican Summer League before a knee injury cut short his 2009 pro debut. He worked hard on his rehabilitation in the offseason and posted a breakout 2010 campaign in the Rookie-level Arizona League. Villanueva stands out most for his above-average defensive ability at third base. He has excellent body control, first-step quickness, good hands and instincts, and a plus arm. An average runner, he might be athletic enough to handle second base, but the Rangers see him growing into a Vinny Castilla-type player at third, though without as much power. Villanueva is a line-drive hitter with an up-the-middle approach and a nice, compact swing. He uses his lower half well and squares balls up consistently, and the Rangers think he'll develop average power as he matures physically. He does need to add strength and learn to drive the ball with more authority, particularly to the pull side. Villanueva has a natural feel for hitting and defending, so if his power comes as Texas hopes, he could be a solid everyday big leaguer. He's intelligent and a hard worker who could move fairly quickly. His next step is low Class A.

Year	Club (League)	Class	AVG	G	AB	R	H	2B	3B	HR	RBI	BB	SO	SB	CS	OBP	SLG
2009	Rangers 2 (DSL)	R	.208	8	24	2	5	1	0	0	3	6	5	1	0	.375	.250
2010	Rangers (AZL)	R	.314	51	188	30	59	14	1	2	35	13	42	6	2	.365	.431
Minor League Totals			.302	59	212	32	64	15	1	2	38	19	47	7	2	.367	.410

13 ROMAN MENDEZ, RHP

Born: July 25, 1990. **B-T:** R-R. **Ht.:** 6-2. **Wt.:** 191. **Signed:** Dominican Republic, 2007. **Signed by:** Luciano del Rosario (Red Sox).

The Rangers saw Mendez throw 87-88 mph in tryouts before he signed with the Red Sox for $125,000 out of the Dominican Republic in 2007. His velocity jumped over the course of two dominant seasons in Rookie ball, and Boston skipped him to low Class A to start 2010. He was hit hard but recovered in the short-season New York-Penn League before the Red Sox traded him and two other minor leaguers, first baseman Chris McGuiness and righthander Michael Thomas, to get Jarrod Saltalamacchia last July. Mendez showed electric stuff in three appearances in Spokane before tweaking his forearm throwing to first base on a bunt play. He returned to action in the Rangers' Dominican instructional league program and generated buzz with a fastball that reached 98 mph. His heater sits around 94-96 mph with explosive life. He flashed a plus slider that reached 87 mph with the Red Sox, but Texas took away that pitch and his changeup for the time being, instead getting him to focus on developing a promising hard curveball. Mendez has a tendency to break his hands late and deep and collapse prematurely on his back side in his delivery. When he's fresh, he has the arm speed to catch up, but when he starts to get fatigued he tends to miss armside and high. If he can maintain his alignment and learn to repeat his arm slot and release point, his command should improve. If it does, Mendez has frontline-starter upside—but he has a ways to go. He should get another crack at low Class A to start 2011.

Year	Club (League)	Class	W	L	ERA	G	GS	CG	SV	IP	H	HR	BB	SO	G/A	WHIP	AVG
2008	Red Sox (DSL)	R	3	1	2.65	11	11	0	0	51	43	1	16	46	—	1.16	.222
2009	Red Sox (GCL)	R	2	3	1.99	12	10	0	0	50	33	1	8	47	0.85	0.83	.184
2010	Greenville (SAL)	LoA	0	2	11.40	6	6	0	0	15	29	5	10	18	0.57	2.60	.392
	Lowell (NYP)	SS	2	3	4.36	8	8	0	0	33	31	6	19	35	1.11	1.52	.240
	Spokane (NWL)	SS	1	1	2.31	3	3	0	0	12	19	2	3	13	1.57	1.89	.373
Minor League Totals			8	10	3.59	40	38	0	0	160	155	14	56	159	0.93	1.32	.247

14 WILMER FONT, RHP

Born: May 24, 1990. **B-T:** R-R. **Ht.:** 6-4. **Wt.:** 245. **Signed:** Venezuela, 2006. **Signed by:** Manny Batista/ Andres Espinosa.

Font made his high Class A debut four days before turning 20 in May, and he showed overpowering stuff in nine starts before the Rangers shut him down with elbow soreness. He tried to rehab and started throwing again in instructional league, but the pain persisted and he wound up having Tommy John surgery. Though he'll miss the entire 2011 season, Texas protected him on its 40-man roster. When healthy, Font regularly runs his fastball up to 97-98 mph, and he holds his velocity deep into games. The pitch also has heavy life, giving it a chance to be a true 80 pitch on the 20-80 scale scouting if he can refine his command of it. His No. 2 pitch is an average changeup that has come a long way in the last year and a half, but his breaking ball remains well-below-average. He throws a curveball but lacks feel for the pitch, and he may need to scrap it in favor of a slider in the future. Font has a long, complicated delivery that could prevent him from developing the necessary command to stick as a starter. He does work around the strike zone, but he needs to do a better job getting into pitcher's counts and locating within the zone. When he returns to action—perhaps in the fall of 2011—the Rangers figure to continue developing him as a starter. He's still ahead of most pitchers his age, and his upside is tantalizing.

Year	Club (League)	Class	W	L	ERA	G	GS	CG	SV	IP	H	HR	BB	SO	G/A	WHIP	AVG
2007	Rangers (AZL)	R	2	3	4.53	14	10	0	0	46	41	2	24	61	—	1.42	.238
2008	Rangers (AZL)	R	1	0	10.38	3	0	0	0	4	1	1	1	6	—	0.46	.071
2009	Hickory (SAL)	LoA	8	3	3.49	29	24	0	0	108	93	4	59	105	0.73	1.40	.231
2010	Hickory (SAL)	LoA	4	1	5.16	7	7	0	0	30	35	3	13	33	1.24	1.62	.294
	Bakersfield (CAL)	HiA	1	2	3.86	9	9	0	0	49	38	5	32	52	0.98	1.43	.217
Minor League Totals			16	9	4.10	62	50	0	0	237	208	15	129	257	0.85	1.42	.236

15 LEURY GARCIA, SS

Born: March 18, 1991. **B-T:** B-R. **Ht.:** 5-10. **Wt.:** 160. **Signed:** Dominican Republic, 2007. **Signed by:** Jesus Ovalle.

Garcia was rushed to low Class A as an 18-year-old in 2009 because the Rangers needed to fill a hole, and he made progress offensively and mentally in his second stint at Hickory in 2010. A shoulder injury cost him six weeks in the middle of the summer, but he still finished 10th in the minor leagues with 51 steals in 62 attempts.

Garcia is at least a 70 runner on the 20-80 scouting scale, and he sometimes shows 80 speed. He's very aggressive on the basepaths and has become a better bunter, giving him another way to make use of his wheels. He also has plus-plus arm strength and range—on groundballs as well as pop-ups—giving him the ability to make spectacular plays that most shortstops can't make. He also has very good hands, but he still loses focus at times and must do a better job making routine plays. A switch-hitter, Garcia has just enough strength to get himself into trouble at the plate. He too often tries to muscle up, causing him to get out on his front foot, especially from the left side. Texas wants him to stay on top of the ball better and hit the ball in the air less. Like many young hitters, he chases breaking balls out of the zone too often. If he learns to control the strike zone and stay within himself, Garcia has the tools to be an impact big leaguer. Even if he never becomes an average hitter, he could be a quality defensive shortstop in the Cesar Izturis mold, with the added value of game-changing speed. Garcia should start 2011 at the Rangers' new high Class A Myrtle Beach affiliate.

Year	Club (League)	Class	AVG	G	AB	R	H	2B	3B	HR	RBI	BB	SO	SB	CS	OBP	SLG
2008	Rangers (AZL)	R	.209	41	129	17	27	3	3	0	14	8	40	12	3	.250	.279
2009	Hickory (SAL)	LoA	.232	83	276	28	64	6	3	1	18	18	64	19	6	.288	.286
2010	Rangers (AZL)	R	.500	6	18	5	9	2	0	0	2	4	4	4	2	.591	.611
	Hickory (SAL)	LoA	.262	89	359	57	94	5	4	3	22	23	57	47	9	.307	.323
Minor League Totals			.248	219	782	107	194	16	10	4	56	53	165	82	20	.298	.309

16 KELLIN DEGLAN, C

Born: May 3, 1992. **B-T:** L-R. **Ht.:** 6-2. **Wt.:** 195. **Drafted:** HS—Langley, B.C., 2010 (1st round). **Signed by:** Gary McGraw.

Deglan faced his share of quality competition as the catcher for Canada's junior national team, so the Rangers challenged him after drafting him 22nd overall and signing him for a below-slot $1 million last June. After a 10-game tuneup in the Arizona League, they sent him to Spokane, where he struggled mightily with the bat. Deglan has average or better lefthanded power potential down the road, but he must get stronger. He tended to get overly rigid at the plate last summer, and he must do a better job staying back on pitches, though he made progress in that regard during instructional league. Deglan's troubles came in part because he was worn down after a long year, but he still impressed with his defense and makeup. He has a strong, accurate arm that consistently generates 1.92- to 1.98-second pop times, helping him throw out 36 percent of basestealers in his pro debut. He's still learning how to handle pitchers, but he has a good idea how to call a game and he's a quick study. As he fine-tunes his setup and footwork behind the plate, he has a chance to become an above-average receiver. Deglan needs plenty of work at the plate, but he has the tools and leadership skills to be an everyday big league catcher. He could get a crack at low Class A at some point in 2011.

Year	Club (League)	Class	AVG	G	AB	R	H	2B	3B	HR	RBI	BB	SO	SB	CS	OBP	SLG
2010	Rangers (AZL)	R	.286	10	28	5	8	0	1	0	5	2	7	0	0	.355	.357
	Spokane (NWL)	SS	.159	22	82	7	13	2	0	1	4	7	21	0	0	.222	.220
Minor League Totals			.191	32	110	12	21	2	1	1	9	9	28	0	0	.256	.255

17 JORGE ALFARO, C

Born: June 11, 1993. **B-T:** R-R. **Ht.:** 6-2. **Wt.:** 200. **Signed:** Colombia, 2010. **Signed by:** Rodolfo Rosario/Don Welke.

The Rangers signed Alfaro as a 16-year-old last January for a $1.3 million bonus, the most ever given to a Colombian player. His first exposure to pro ball came in spring training, where he put too much pressure on himself and was overmatched by the level of competition. The first taste of failure was a shock to Alfaro, who went to the Rangers' Dominican complex and got off to a miserable start in the Dominican Summer League, though he hit a more respectable .254 in August. He gained some momentum with a strong showing in the Dominican instructional league. Alfaro has two premium tools in his arm strength and his raw power, and some evaluators rate both as well-above-average. A converted infielder, he had very little catching experience before signing with Texas, so he has a long way to go defensively, but his receiving and blocking skills already have made progress in his first year of pro ball. Like most 17-year-olds, he needs to get stronger, but he has flashed provocative power. Alfaro has to prove himself at the plate, but the Rangers say he hangs in there against breaking balls and insist he does have feel for hitting. He's a good athlete with average speed. Alfaro will arrive in the United States for good in 2011, and there is some talk about skipping him a level to Spokane. His ceiling is that of an all-star catcher, but it's too early to tell if he'll ever tap into his potential.

Year	Club (League)	Class	AVG	G	AB	R	H	2B	3B	HR	RBI	BB	SO	SB	CS	OBP	SLG
2010	Rangers (DSL)	R	.221	48	172	18	38	5	2	1	23	5	48	1	4	.278	.291
Minor League Totals			.221	48	172	18	38	5	2	1	23	5	48	1	4	.278	.291

18 JUSTIN GRIMM, RHP

Born: Aug. 16, 1988. **B-T:** R-R. **Ht.:** 6-4. **Wt.:** 195. **Drafted:** Georgia, 2010 (5th round). **Signed by:** Ryan Coe.

An unsigned 13th-round pick by the Red Sox out of a Virginia high school in 2007, Grimm had a disappointing college career at Georgia, posting a 5.84 career ERA in three seasons. Nevertheless, the Rangers signed him for a well-over-slot bonus of $825,000 as a fifth-round pick last summer, and he showed off one of the liveliest arms in the system during instructional league. Grimm pitches at 92-96 mph with his fastball, and his sharp overhand curveball arrives at 82-83 and gives him a second potential plus offerings. His changeup still lags behind his power pitches, but he's working on it. Grimm has an electric arm and a prototype pitcher's frame, and Texas believes he could take off with a couple of mechanical tweaks. He tended to rush through his delivery in college, often causing him to miss armside and up. He also had a head jerk in his delivery that affected his command, and the Rangers had some success calming that down in instructional league. He also did a much better job repeating his mechanics in the fall. Grimm has the arm strength, size and stuff to be at least a mid-rotation big league starter if his delivery and command continue to improve. He'll likely make his pro debut as a starter in low Class A.

Year	Club (League)	Class	W	L	ERA	G	GS	CG	SV	IP	H	HR	BB	SO	G/A	WHIP	AVG
2010	Did Not Play—Signed Late																

19 ROBBIE ROSS, LHP

Born: June 24, 1989. **B-T:** L-L. **Ht.:** 5-11. **Wt.:** 185. **Drafted:** HS—Lexington, Ky., 2008 (2nd round). **Signed by:** Jon Poloni.

Ross signed for $1.575 million as a second-round pick just before the 2008 signing deadline, then made his pro debut the following summer, when he led the Northwest League in strikeouts per nine innings (9.2). He made a successful leap to full-season ball in 2010, earning South Atlantic League all-star honors and reaching high Class A. Ross' best pitch is an 89-90 mph fastball that reaches 93 with serious life. He can cut it and sink it, but he doesn't know which way it's going, which makes him hard to catch. He flashes a good slider, but it tends to flatten out and needs some tightening. He also must become more comfortable with his changeup. His delivery is effectively funky, giving him good deception. Ross is still maturing on and off the field, but he demonstrated more focus in his bullpens and in games last season. His command made some progress as well, though it needs to improve. He also has to do a better job of keeping his body in shape. The Rangers will continue to develop him as a starter, but his frame, command and repertoire might be better suited for the bullpen. Texas has a logjam of talented arms in the lower levels of its system, so it figures to push Ross to Double-A to start 2011.

Year	Club (League)	Class	W	L	ERA	G	GS	CG	SV	IP	H	HR	BB	SO	G/A	WHIP	AVG
2009	Spokane (NWL)	SS	4	4	2.66	15	15	0	0	74	68	5	17	76	3.21	1.14	.240
2010	Hickory (SAL)	LoA	8	7	2.59	16	16	0	0	94	89	2	20	62	3.39	1.16	.245
	Bakersfield (CAL)	HiA	4	4	5.37	11	11	0	0	52	67	4	17	49	4.21	1.62	.305
Minor League Totals			16	15	3.27	42	42	0	0	220	224	11	54	187	3.48	1.26	.258

20 MIGUEL VELAZQUEZ, OF

Born: May 15, 1988. **B-T:** R-R. **Ht.:** 6-2. **Wt.:** 205. **Drafted:** HS—San Juan, P.R., 2006 (19th round). **Signed by:** Frankie Thon.

A run-in with the law torpedoed Velazquez's draft stock out of high school. He was projected to go in the top three rounds before he was involved in a shooting with his brother in March 2006. His brother shot and seriously injured their neighbor, whom they say was trying to harm their sister. After investigating the incident, the Rangers took him in the 19th round and signed him for $72,000. Velazquez had a strong pro debut but missed all of 2008 when he had to spend the year in Puerto Rico as part of three years of probation. He picked up where he left off after returning and played well at two Class A stops last season. Velazquez has average-or-better tools across the board, and when he shows up ready to play he can look like one of Texas' best prospects. But he still needs to mature, and he'll have to buy into the mechanical changes he'll have to make at the plate. Loaded with righthanded power potential, he has gotten by on his strength so far in his career. But his bat doesn't stay in the zone long enough, his timing is inconsistent and he struggles against breaking balls. An average runner, Velazquez can play all three outfield positions. He's an aggressive defender who gets good reads and does a nice job of cutting balls off in the gaps. His above-average arm is one of the best in the system. Velazquez has the physical toolset to be an everyday big league right fielder, but his makeup remains a question mark. He must show more maturity in 2011, when he figures to reach Double-A at some point.

Year	Club (League)	Class	AVG	G	AB	R	H	2B	3B	HR	RBI	BB	SO	SB	CS	OBP	SLG
2007	Rangers (AZL)	R	.330	24	94	18	31	5	2	2	21	7	27	7	1	.381	.489
2008	Did Not Play—On Restricted List																
2009	Rangers (AZL)	R	.294	9	34	7	10	0	2	1	6	4	11	1	0	.385	.500
	Spokane (NWL)	SS	.297	54	209	33	62	12	2	10	40	19	43	9	2	.359	.517
2010	Hickory (SAL)	LoA	.270	71	274	46	74	17	1	10	53	26	47	12	4	.342	.449
	Bakersfield (CAL)	HiA	.270	48	189	27	51	6	1	5	25	12	38	3	1	.333	.392
Minor League Totals			.285	206	800	131	228	40	8	28	145	68	166	32	8	.351	.460

21 LUKE JACKSON, RHP

Born: Aug. 24, 1991. **B-T:** R-R. **Ht.:** 6-2. **Wt.:** 187. **Drafted:** HS—Fort Lauderdale, 2010 (1st round supplemental). **Signed by:** Juan Alvarez.

The athletic Jackson didn't start pitching seriously until his freshman year in high school, and his fastball sat at 87-91 mph when he was a junior. His velocity jumped last spring, and the Rangers saw him at 93-96 at his best. They bought him out of a commitment to Miami with a $1.545 million bonus in the supplemental first round. Jackson flashed 93-94 mph heat in instructional league while usually working at 91-92. Jackson's electric fastball is his best pitch, and his hard breaking ball is promising, though still a work in progress. He also has some feel for a nascent changeup. Jackson still is learning to harness his pitches, and he'll need to add strength in order to improve his durability. He has the makings of a good delivery, but his mechanics can be inconsistent. Jackson is a strong competitor with plenty of intelligence and aptitude. He has loads of upside and projection but a ways to go. Texas typically holds back its high school pitchers in extended spring training and sends them to Spokane in their first full pro season, and Jackson figures to follow that model.

Year	Club (League)	Class	W	L	ERA	G	GS	CG	SV	IP	H	HR	BB	SO	G/A	WHIP	AVG
2010	Did Not Play—Signed Late																

22 JOE WIELAND, RHP

Born: Jan. 21, 1990. **B-T:** R-R. **Ht.:** 6-3. **Wt.:** 175. **Drafted:** HS—Reno, Nev., 2008 (4th round). **Signed by:** Butch Metzger.

Wieland got off to a strong start in low Class A for the second straight season in 2010, and this time he earned a midseason promotion. He was brilliant at times in the high Class A California League—on Aug. 3, he struck out 14 without issuing a walk over seven shutout innings against Visalia—but at other times he struggled to command his secondary stuff and got lit up. Wieland's quality three-pitch mix is highlighted by his hard, late-breaking overhand curveball, which is a plus pitch when it's on. He also owns an 88-92 mph fastball that bores in on lefthanders, along with an average changeup. He's polished for his age, with the ability to add and subtract velocity, to sink his fastball or elevate it, to pitch in or work away. Wieland is hungry for knowledge, works hard at his craft and is a dogged competitor on the mound. He lacks overpowering stuff and big-time projection, but he's a fairly safe bet to become a back-of-the-rotation starter in the big leagues, with a ceiling of a mid-rotation starter. Wieland likely will return to high Class A at the Rangers new Myrtle Beach affiliate to open 2011, with another midseason promotion possible.

Year	Club (League)	Class	W	L	ERA	G	GS	CG	SV	IP	H	HR	BB	SO	G/A	WHIP	AVG
2008	Rangers (AZL)	R	5	1	1.44	13	7	0	0	44	32	2	8	41	—	0.92	.200
2009	Hickory (SAL)	LoA	4	6	5.31	19	18	0	0	83	102	7	24	73	1.45	1.52	.299
2010	Hickory (SAL)	LoA	7	4	3.34	15	15	2	0	89	84	4	15	71	1.31	1.11	.251
	Bakersfield (CAL)	HiA	4	3	5.19	11	10	0	0	59	67	6	10	62	0.65	1.31	.283
Minor League Totals			20	14	4.03	58	50	2	0	275	285	19	57	247	1.15	1.25	.266

23 FABIO CASTILLO, RHP

Born: Feb. 19, 1989. **B-T:** R-R. **Ht.:** 6-3. **Wt.:** 238. **Signed:** Dominican Republic, 2005. **Signed by:** Danilo Trancoso.

Castillo burst onto the prospect landscape as an 18-year-old in 2007, when he threw 92-97 mph during his first extended action in the United States. Struggles with his mechanics, breaking ball and maturity caused his stock to drop over the next two years, and the Rangers gave up on the idea of making him a starter, converting him to the bullpen full-time in 2008. He turned a corner at Bakersfield last year, earning a late-season promotion to Frisco. Castillo's bread and butter is still his fastball, which routinely reaches 96-97 mph in relief. Texas had him scrap the curveball he once threw in favor of a high-80s slider. The pitch usually has quick, late lateral action, similar to a cutter, and when he's locked in the pitch drops straight down, the way Robb Nen's slider used to. Castillo also can throw a solid changeup, but he very seldom uses it. For years, the Rangers have been trying to get him to stay closed in his delivery, because he gets into trouble when his front leg opens up prematurely and his arm slot drops. Last year, they altered his mechanics to keep him from flying open and give him some deceptive, crossfire action. It's still not the cleanest delivery, but it works. Castillo needs to refine his secondary stuff and get a better feel for the finer points of pitching, such as fielding his position and holding runners. He'll open 2011 as a 22-year-old in Double-A, so he has time to smooth out the rough edges. The Rangers added him to their 40-man roster in November.

Year	Club (League)	Class	W	L	ERA	G	GS	CG	SV	IP	H	HR	BB	SO	G/A	WHIP	AVG
2006	Rangers (AZL)	R	0	0	0.00	1	1	0	0	3	1	0	2	4	—	1.00	.100
2006	Rangers (DSL)	R	1	4	3.46	7	6	0	0	26	21	0	12	37	—	1.27	.216
2007	Spokane (NWL)	SS	3	5	5.92	14	14	0	0	62	73	4	27	46	—	1.60	.289
2008	Clinton (MWL)	LoA	2	5	5.28	36	7	0	4	90	88	11	47	78	—	1.49	.257
2009	Hickory (SAL)	LoA	3	6	4.05	40	2	0	2	80	87	5	25	67	1.68	1.40	.269
2010	Bakersfield (CAL)	HiA	1	3	1.92	36	0	0	6	52	41	2	26	65	1.63	1.30	.219
	Frisco (TL)	AA	0	0	4.91	3	0	0	0	4	3	0	4	2	0.33	1.91	.214
Minor League Totals			10	23	4.34	137	30	0	12	317	314	22	143	299	1.58	1.44	.256

24 BARRET LOUX, RHP

Born: April 6, 1989. **B-T:** R-R. **Ht.:** 6-5. **Wt.:** 220. **Signed:** Texas A&M, 2010. **Signed by:** Randy Taylor.

Loux turned down $800,000 as a Tigers 27th-round pick out of high school to attend Texas A&M, and he showed up on campus as a flamethrower with underdeveloped secondary stuff. Bone chips in his elbow limited him to 48 innings as a sophomore, but he rebounded to go 11-2, 2.83 with 136 strikeouts in 105 innings to earn first-team All-America honors as a junior. The Diamondbacks drafted him sixth overall in 2010, in part because he agreed to a below-slot bonus of $2 million, but he failed a postdraft physical because Arizona didn't like the wear and tear on his shoulder and elbow. Declared a free agent by Major League Baseball, he started working out for clubs in September and signed with the Rangers in November for $312,000. Loux has run his fastball up to 95 mph in the past, but he worked mostly at 90-92 mph last spring and he sat at 89-91 in workouts in the fall. Texas doesn't expect him to ever regain his premium velocity, but he has the tenacity and polish to succeed with an average fastball. Throwing breaking balls hurt his elbow during his sophomore year, so he relied heavily on his changeup, which became his No. 2 pitch. He also throws a curveball and a slider, both of which are serviceable. Loux is a polished strike-thrower, so the Rangers will move him quickly and he could start his pro career in high Class A. His health remains a huge question mark. Some doctors think he'll need elbow or shoulder surgery in the near future, while Loux told Texas in the fall that he feels as good as he ever has. If he stays healthy, he could become an innings-eating workhorse in the big leagues.

Year	Club (League)	Class	W	L	ERA	G	GS	CG	SV	IP	H	HR	BB	SO	G/A	WHIP	AVG
2010	Did Not Play—Signed Late																

25 JARED HOYING, OF

Born: May 18, 1989. **B-T:** L-R. **Ht.:** 6-3. **Wt.:** 190. **Drafted:** Toledo, 2010 (10th round). **Signed by:** Roger Coryell.

Hoying hit 34 homers in three seasons at Toledo, but he ran hot and cold, posting a .284 career average with metal bats. The Rangers signed him for $85,000 as a 10th-round pick and assigned him to the Northwest League, where he won MVP honors. A mechanical adjustment proved critical to Hoying's success in his debut. In college, his swing featured no stride or even a pivot of his back foot, so he relied entirely on his lightning-quick wrists and strong upper half. He also hooked everything and had no ability to use the opposite field. Texas got him to start using his lower half, which allowed him to start using the whole field. Lanky and athletic, Hoying has plus raw power, and though his hitting mechanics will never be completely orthodox, he has the bat speed and hand-eye coordination to hit for average, too. A shortstop for most of his college career, Hoying played mostly left field at Spokane. His solid speed and slightly above-average arm give him a chance to play all three outfield spots, but he profiles best in a corner. He's still learning to play the outfield, but he has good aptitude and should be at least an average defender with more experience. Hoying's all-around ability gives him a chance to be an everyday big leaguer, assuming he continues to improve his hitting mechanics. He figures to start 2011 at Hickory but could reach Myrtle Beach quickly.

Year	Club (League)	Class	AVG	G	AB	R	H	2B	3B	HR	RBI	BB	SO	SB	CS	OBP	SLG
2010	Spokane (NWL)	SS	.325	62	243	47	79	13	5	10	51	19	70	20	9	.378	.543
Minor League Totals			.325	62	243	47	79	13	5	10	51	19	70	20	9	.378	.543

26 JOSE FELIX, C

Born: June 28, 1988. **B-T:** R-R. **Ht.:** 5-10. **Wt.:** 198. **Signed:** Mexico, 2008. **Signed by:** Mel Didier/Bill McLaughlin.

The Rangers have raved about Felix's makeup and defense since signing him out of the Mexican League in 2008. He's an outstanding receiver who has improved his footwork and throwing accuracy to the point that he erased 55 percent of basestealers last year despite just average arm strength. A high-energy player, he excels at running the game and handling pitchers. When Felix arrived in the system, he had a bad habit of double-tapping his front foot in his setup. He has worked hard to eliminate this timing mechanism, and it's nearly imperceptible now. He probably won't be an average hitter and he'll never hit for power, but he does hit some line drives and he can bunt well. He makes contact but doesn't walk very much. Felix made progress at the plate in 2010, which he capped by hitting .347/.360/.429 in 49 at-bats in the Arizona Fall League. He offers little speed and clogs up the bases. Most club officials see Felix as a backup catcher and occasional starter along the lines of Yorvit Torrealba or Henry Blanco, but he has an outside chance to become a regular. His defense and leadership skills make him a safe bet to become a big leaguer even if he doesn't hit, perhaps as soon as the second half of 2011. A promotion to Triple-A at least seems likely at some point this year.

Year	Club (League)	Class	AVG	G	AB	R	H	2B	3B	HR	RBI	BB	SO	SB	CS	OBP	SLG
2007	Quintana Roo (MEX)	AAA	.247	58	162	12	40	6	0	1	21	9	29	1	5	.284	.302
2008	Clinton (MWL)	LoA	.262	88	302	30	79	10	0	1	24	15	38	2	2	.300	.305
2009	Bakersfield (CAL)	HiA	.241	90	320	35	77	15	1	0	34	16	45	0	2	.282	.294
2010	Bakersfield (CAL)	HiA	.282	73	248	27	70	13	1	2	31	17	25	2	0	.326	.367
	Frisco (TL)	AA	.267	27	105	7	28	3	0	1	6	1	6	0	1	.274	.324
Minor League Totals			.259	336	1137	111	294	47	2	5	116	58	143	5	10	.296	.317

27 NEIL RAMIREZ, RHP

Born: May 25, 1989. **B-T:** R-R. **Ht.:** 6-3. **Wt.:** 185. **Drafted:** HS—Kempsville, Va., 2007 (1st round supplemental). **Signed by:** Russ Ardolina.

Since signing for $1 million as a sandwich pick in 2007, Ramirez has developed slowly over his first three pro seasons, but things started to click for him in 2010. A short-armer when he entered the system, he worked very hard to lengthen his arm action. That allowed him to be more consistent last year, though his timing was still off at times. He also showed more dedication to improving his conditioning, which also helped. Ramirez's fastball sits around 92-94 mph and touches 95. His overhand curveball once rated among the best in the system, but he lost some of his confidence in the pitch in 2009, partly because he was constantly falling behind in counts and was unable to use it as a chase pitch. He did a better job getting ahead of hitters last year, and his curveball benefited. At its best, it's a plus power pitch with tight 1-to-7 break, generating plenty of swings and misses. He also flashes an average changeup that he's learning to use more effectively. Long and athletic, Ramirez still has a chance to be a starter in the big leagues if he can continue to improve his command and repeat his delivery. The Rangers stress that he would have just finished his junior year at Georgia Tech if he'd gone to college, and they emphasize patience. He'll advance to high Class A in 2011 and Texas would like him to reach Double-A quickly to help replenish the upper levels of the system, which were depleted in trades last year.

Year	Club (League)	Class	W	L	ERA	G	GS	CG	SV	IP	H	HR	BB	SO	G/A	WHIP	AVG
2008	Spokane (NWL)	SS	1	2	2.66	13	13	0	0	44	25	5	29	52	—	1.23	.166
2009	Hickory (SAL)	LoA	3	6	4.75	18	14	0	0	66	58	8	41	56	0.55	1.49	.235
2010	Hickory (SAL)	LoA	10	8	4.43	28	26	1	0	140	150	14	37	142	0.78	1.33	.281
Minor League Totals			14	16	4.20	59	53	1	0	251	233	27	107	250	0.68	1.36	.250

28 CODY BUCKEL, RHP

Born: June 18, 1992. **B-T:** R-R. **Ht.:** 6-1. **Wt.:** 183. **Drafted:** HS—Simi Valley, Calif., 2010 (2nd round). **Signed by:** Todd Guggiana.

The colorful Buckel was a fledgling singer and actor before forgoing a Pepperdine commitment to sign with the Rangers for $590,000 as a second-round pick in 2010. He made four scoreless relief appearances in the Arizona League before a pulled ribcage ended his pro debut. A bit undersized, Buckel idolizes another offbeat, smallish righthander: Tim Lincecum. He doesn't have that kind of electric stuff, but his long arm action and high-effort, self-made delivery are somewhat similar to Lincecum's. For a high school draftee, Buckel has a fairly polished four-pitch mix. His fastball sits around 88-92 mph but bumps 94 at times. He also has the makings of three average or better secondary pitches in his curveball, changeup and cutter. The cerebral Buckel likes asking questions and soaking up knowledge from older pitchers. His makeup, size and repertoire remind Texas of a righthanded Robbie Erlin, though he does not have Erlin's command and feel at this stage. Durability is also a concern, as Buckel tended to lose 3-4 mph on his fastball as games progressed in high school. He profiles as a back-end starter or a middle reliever down the road. Buckel will pitch at Spokane or Hickory in 2011.

Year	Club (League)	Class	W	L	ERA	G	GS	CG	SV	IP	H	HR	BB	SO	G/A	WHIP	AVG
2010	Rangers (AZL)	R	0	0	0.00	4	0	0	0	5	2	0	1	9	2.00	0.60	.125
Minor League Totals			0	0	0.00	4	0	0	0	5	2	0	1	9	2.00	0.60	.125

29 JOSH RICHMOND, OF

Born: June 14, 1989. **B-T:** R-R. **Ht.:** 6-3. **Wt.:** 214. **Drafted:** Louisville, 2010 (12th round). **Signed by:** Derek Lee.

Richmond might have been drafted as high as the third round if injuries hadn't short-circuited his college career at Louisville. He injured his left hand when he was hit by a pitch as a junior in 2009, and he eventually had surgery the following winter. A circulation problem kept his hand from healing property, and he re-injured it diving for a ball last February, causing him to miss 41 games. After signing with the Rangers for an above-slot $195,000 bonus as a 12th-rounder, Richmond had a solid pro debut but then hurt his left thumb in instructional league. He's often banged up because he plays with reckless abandon. One club official said Richmond "plays like a chicken with his head cut off, running into walls all the time." However, his tools are tantalizing. He has good size and athleticism, though he needs to use his lower half better in order to unlock his above-average righthanded power potential. He struggles to recognize breaking balls at times, and he doesn't figure to be better than an average hitter, but he could be a physical, run-producing corner outfielder. Richmond has slightly above-average speed and a strong arm that plays very well in right field, and he can also play center. He plays hard and works hard, but he sometimes tries to do too much. Richmond will try to put together a full healthy season in 2011, starting in low Class A.

Year	Club (League)	Class	AVG	G	AB	R	H	2B	3B	HR	RBI	BB	SO	SB	CS	OBP	SLG
2010	Spokane (NWL)	SS	.297	35	118	23	35	8	1	3	19	16	23	4	3	.417	.458
Minor League Totals			.297	35	118	23	35	8	1	3	19	16	23	4	3	.417	.458

30 JACOB BRIGHAM, RHP

Born: Feb. 10, 1988. **B-T:** R-R. **Ht.:** 6-3. **Wt.:** 210. **Drafted:** HS—Ococee, Fla., 2006 (6th round). **Signed by:** Guy DeMutis.

Brigham's 2010 was a tale of two seasons. He started the year in high Class A Bakersfield and struggled, especially with the command of his overhand curveball. The Rangers sent him down to low Class A, where he turned his season around after abandoning his curveball in favor of a hard slider. Brigham's mid-80s slider acts almost like a cutter, and he showed the ability to throw it in the strike zone. His best pitch is his fastball, which ranges from 94-97 mph. He also dabbles with a splitter as a changeup but doesn't throw it often. Brigham has one of the best power arms in the organization, but he's still maturing on and off the field. Now that he's three full years removed from Tommy John surgery, Texas hopes he can turn the corner with his command and become more consistent in all facets of the game. Most club officials envision him as a late-inning reliever, but the Rangers will continue to develop him as a starter for now. They plan to challenge him with an assignment to Double-A to start 2011.

Year	Club (League)	Class	W	L	ERA	G	GS	CG	SV	IP	H	HR	BB	SO	G/A	WHIP	AVG
2006	Rangers (AZL)	R	2	6	3.70	14	11	0	0	58	54	5	19	58	—	1.25	.236
2007	Spokane (NWL)	SS	5	4	3.16	15	15	0	0	77	69	9	34	65	—	1.34	.248
2008	Did Not Play—Injured																
2009	Hickory (SAL)	LoA	2	11	5.52	25	17	0	1	90	104	10	38	81	0.94	1.58	.292
2010	Bakersfield (CAL)	HiA	1	5	6.93	11	10	0	0	49	67	5	26	39	1.00	1.89	.333
	Hickory (SAL)	LoA	6	5	3.36	14	13	2	0	83	66	5	24	67	2.93	1.08	.214
Minor League Totals			16	31	4.41	79	66	2	1	357	360	34	141	310	2.93	1.40	.262

Toronto Blue Jays

BY NATHAN RODE

A year into their new regime, the Blue Jays already were beginning to see results. Alex Anthopoulos took over as general manager in October 2009 and quickly began a much-needed rebuilding process. Toronto had been treading water as the fourth-best team in the American League East, and one of the worst farm systems in baseball wasn't going to provide nearly enough help for a quick turnaround.

Anthopoulos quickly made his mark by trading franchise icon Roy Halladay to the Phillies in December. In return, the Blue Jays received three quality prospects in righthander Kyle Drabek, outfielder  Michael Taylor (who was flipped to the Athletics for first baseman Brett Wallace) and catcher Travis d'Arnaud. That was just the first of several moves that infused young talent into the system.

Anthopoulos vowed to focus more on scouting and player development, and he made good on that promise. He doubled the size of the scouting staff and appointed Andrew Tinnish as scouting director, replacing Jon Lalonde, who was reassigned. Armed with more scouts, nine picks in the first three rounds and the go-ahead from management to spend, Tinnish and his crew had one of the best drafts in 2010.

The Blue Jays spent $11.6 million on bonuses, the third-highest amount in draft history, handing out 20 six-figure bonuses, including $2 million for first-rounder Deck McGuire and $1.5 million for fifth-rounder Dickie Joe Thon. McGuire and sandwich picks Asher Wojciechowski and Aaron Sanchez all cracked this Top 10 Prospects list.

Toronto also made a splash in the international market. In April, the Jays signed Cuban shortstop Adeiny Hechavarria to a $10 million major league contract that included a franchise-record $4 million bonus. They later landed a pair of top international amateurs from Venezuela in righthander Adonis Cardona ($2.8 million) and third baseman Gabriel Cenas ($700,000).

The Blue Jays did some more dealing at the trade deadline as well. Toronto initially tried to pry outfielder Anthony Gose from the Phillies in the Halladay trade but were rebuffed. They got a second chance when Philadelphia sent him to the Astros as part of a package for Roy Oswalt. The Jays sent Wallace to Houston for Gose, and also got younger at shortstop by swapping Alex Gonzalez to the Braves for Yunel Escobar. In December, they added another prospect when they sent Shaun Marcum to the Brewers for

Jose Bautista's 54 home runs surpassed George Bell's single-season franchise record

TOP 30 PROSPECTS

1. Kyle Drabek, rhp	16. Dickie Joe Thon, ss
2. Brett Lawrie, 2b	17. Henderson Alvarez, rhp
3. Deck McGuire, rhp	18. Kellen Sweeney, 3b
4. Anthony Gose, of	19. Adonis Cardona, rhp
5. Travis d'Arnaud, c	20. Justin Nicolino, lhp
6. Zach Stewart, rhp	21. David Cooper, 1b
7. Asher Wojciechowski, rhp	22. K.C. Hobson, 1b
8. J.P. Arencibia, c	23. Moises Sierra, of
9. Carlos Perez, c	24. Noah Syndergaard, rhp
10. Aaron Sanchez, rhp	25. Drew Hutchison, rhp
11. Jake Marisnick, of	26. Christopher Hawkins, 3b/of
12. Eric Thames, of	27. Marcus Knecht, of
13. Adeiny Hechavarria, ss	28. Gabriel Cenas, 3b
14. Griffin Murphy, lhp	29. Gustavo Pierre, ss
15. Chad Jenkins, rhp	30. Brad Mills, lhp

sweet-swinging Brett Lawrie.

At the major league level, Toronto finished fourth in the AL East for the third consecutive year. However, the Jays won 85 games (up from 75 in 2009) and received some promising glimpses of the future. Jose Bautista crushed 54 homers, leading the major leagues and erasing George Bell's franchise record of 47. The Jays topped the big leagues with 257 homers, with seven different players hitting at least 20.

The rebuilding process is only beginning in Toronto. While the Blue Jays won't return to contention overnight, 2010 was a pretty good start.

General Manager: Alex Anthopoulos. **Farm Director:** Charlie Wilson. **Scouting Director:** Andrew Tinnish.

Class	Team	League	W	L	PCT	Finish*	Manager
Majors	Toronto Blue Jays	American	85	77	.525	7th (14)	Cito Gaston
Triple-A	Las Vegas 51s	Pacific Coast	66	78	.458	12th (16)	Dan Rohn
Double-A	New Hampshire Fisher Cats	Eastern	79	62	.560	3rd (12)	Luis Rivera
High A	Dunedin Blue Jays	Florida State	72	67	.518	6th (12)	Clayton McCullough
Low A	Lansing Lugnuts	Midwest	70	69	.504	10th (16)	Sal Fasano
Short-season	Auburn Doubledays	New York-Penn	35	40	.467	9th (14)	Dennis Holmberg
Rookie	GCL Blue Jays	Gulf Coast	31	28	.525	t-5th (15)	John Schneider
Overall 2010 Minor League Record			353	344	.506	14th (30)	

*Finish in overall standings (No. of teams in league). †League champion.
Short-season affiliate changes to Vancouver (Northwest), additional Rookie affiliate in Bluefield (Appalachian) will be added in 2011.

LAST YEAR'S TOP 30

Player, Pos.		Status
1.	Zach Stewart, rhp	No. 6
2.	J.P. Arencibia, c	No. 8
3.	Chad Jenkins, rhp	No. 15
4.	David Cooper, 1b	No. 21
5.	Henderson Alvarez, rhp	No. 17
6.	Jake Marisnick, of	No. 11
7.	Josh Roenicke, rhp	Majors
8.	Brad Mills, lhp	No. 30
9.	Justin Jackson, ss	Dropped out
10.	Carlos Perez, c	No. 9
11.	Moises Sierra, of	No. 23
12.	Kevin Ahrens, 3b	Dropped out
13.	K.C. Hobson, 1b	No. 22
14.	Danny Farquhar, rhp	(Athletics)
15.	Luis Perez, lhp	Dropped out
16.	Ryan Schimpf, 2b	Dropped out
17.	Tyler Pastornicky, ss	(Braves)
18.	Eric Thames, of	No. 12
19.	Tim Collins, lhp	(Royals)
20.	Daniel Webb, rhp	Dropped out
21.	Johermyn Chavez, of	(Mariners)
22.	Trystan Magnuson, rhp	(Athletics)
23.	Brian Dopirak, 1b	(Astros)
24.	Ryan Goins, ss	Dropped out
25.	Brad Emaus, 2b	(Mets)
26.	Andrew Liebel, rhp	Dropped out
27.	John Tolisano, 2b	Dropped out
28.	Kenny Wilson, of	Dropped out
29.	Gustavo Pierre, ss	No. 29
30.	Rei Gonzalez, rhp	Dropped out

BEST TOOLS

Best Hitter for Average	Brett Lawrie
Best Power Hitter	J.P. Arencibia
Best Strike-Zone Discipline	Carlos Perez
Fastest Baserunner	Anthony Gose
Best Athlete	Jake Marisnick
Best Fastball	Zach Stewart
Best Curveball	Kyle Drabek
Best Slider	Deck McGuire
Best Changeup	Henderson Alvarez
Best Control	Drew Hutchison
Best Defensive Catcher	Travis d'Arnaud
Best Defensive Infielder	Adeiny Hechavarria
Best Infield Arm	Gustavo Pierre
Best Defensive Outfielder	Anthony Gose
Best Outfield Arm	Anthony Gose

PROJECTED 2014 LINEUP

Catcher	Travis d'Arnaud
First Base	Adam Lind
Second Base	Aaron Hill
Third Base	Jose Bautista
Shortstop	Adeiny Hechavarria
Left Field	Travis Snider
Center Field	Anthony Gose
Right Field	Brett Lawrie
Designated Hitter	J.P. Arencibia
No. 1 Starter	Kyle Drabek
No. 2 Starter	Ricky Romero
No. 3 Starter	Brandon Morrow
No. 4 Starter	Deck McGuire
No. 5 Starter	Brett Cecil
Closer	Zach Stewart

TOP PROSPECTS OF THE DECADE

Year	Player, Pos.	2010 Org.
2001	Vernon Wells, of	Blue Jays
2002	Josh Phelps, c	Bridgeport (Atlantic)
2003	Dustin McGowan, rhp	Blue Jays
2004	Alex Rios, of	White Sox
2005	Brandon League, rhp	Mariners
2006	Dustin McGowan, rhp	Blue Jays
2007	Adam Lind, of	Blue Jays
2008	Travis Snider, of	Blue Jays
2009	Travis Snider, of	Blue Jays
2010	Zach Stewart, rhp	Blue Jays

TOP DRAFT PICKS OF THE DECADE

Year	Player, Pos.	2010 Org.
2001	Gabe Gross, of	Athletics
2002	Russ Adams, ss	Mets
2003	Aaron Hill, ss	Blue Jays
2004	David Purcey, lhp	Blue Jays
2005	Ricky Romero, lhp	Blue Jays
2006	Travis Snider, of	Blue Jays
2007	Kevin Ahrens, 3b	Blue Jays
2008	David Cooper, 1b	Blue Jays
2009	Chad Jenkins, rhp	Blue Jays
2010	Deck McGuire, rhp	Blue Jays

LARGEST BONUSES IN CLUB HISTORY

Adeiny Hechavarria, 2010	$4,000,000
Adonis Cardona, 2010	$2,800,000
Ricky Romero, 2005	$2,400,000
Felipe Lopez, 1998	$2,000,000
Deck McGuire, 2010	$2,000,000

MINOR LEAGUE DEPTH CHART

TORONTO BLUE JAYS

TOP 2011 ROOKIE: Kyle Drabek, rhp. His September cameo showed that the system's top prospect is ready for a rotation spot.

BREAKOUT PROSPECT: Kellen Sweeney, 3b. He has an advanced bat for a high schooler and has made a smooth transition to the hot corner.

SLEEPER: A.J. Jimenez, c. He threw out 51 percent of basestealers in 2010, and his bat is beginning to progress.

SOURCE OF TOP 30 TALENT

Homegrown	25	Acquired	5
College	7	Trades	5
Junior college	1	Rule 5 draft	0
High school	10	Independent leagues	0
Draft-and-follow	0	Free agents/waivers	0
Nondrafted free agents	0		
International	7		

LF
Eric Thames (12)
Michael Crouse

CF
Anthony Gose (4)
Jake Marisnick (11)
Darin Mastrioanni
Kenny Wilson
Markus Brisker
Ronnie Melendez

RF
Moises Sierra (23)
Christopher Hawkins (26)
Marcus Knecht (27)
Dalton Pompey

3B
Kellen Sweeney (18)
Gabriel Cenas (28)
Kevin Ahrens

SS
Adeiny Hechavarria (13)
Dickie Joe Thon (16)
Gustavo Pierre (29)
Justin Jackson
Brandon Mims
Gary Pena

2B
Brett Lawrie (2)
Ryan Schimpf
Ryan Goins
John Tolisano
Shane Opitz
Mike McCoy

1B
David Cooper (21)
K.C. Hobson (22)
Mike McDade
Art Charles
Lance Durham

C
Travis d'Arnaud (5)
J.P. Arencibia (8)
Carlos Perez (9)
A.J. Jimenez
Brian Jeroloman
Santiago Nessy
Sean Ochinko

RHP

RHSP	RHRP
Kyle Drabek (1)	Masual Diaz
Deck McGuire (3)	Matt Daly
Zach Stewart (6)	Alan Farina
Asher Wojciechowski (7)	Milciades Santana
Aaron Sanchez (10)	Ronald Uviedo
Chad Jenkins (15)	Drew Permison
Henderson Alvarez (17)	Andrew Liebel
Adonis Cardona (19)	Steve Turnbull
Noah Syndergaard (24)	Dustin Antolin
Drew Hutchison (25)	Dayton Marze
Sam Dyson	Nestor Molina
Daniel Webb	Travis Garrett
Miles Jaye	Brian Slover
Adaric Kelly	
Joel Carreno	

LHP

LHSP	LHRP
Griffin Murphy (14)	Frank Gailey
Justin Nicolino (20)	Aaron Loup
Brad Mills (30)	Rommie Lewis
Mitchell Taylor	
Sean Nolin	
Zak Adams	
Luis Perez	
Ryan Page	

2010

BEST PURE HITTER: Scouts consider 3B Kellen Sweeney (2) a better hitter than his brother (Athletics outfielder Ryan) at the same stage of their careers. Sweeney has a quick bat and a smooth stroke, and he doubled off a 98-mph fastball from the Phillies' Jarred Cosart in instructional league.

BEST POWER HITTER: OF Marcus Knecht (3s), a Toronto native, has huge power potential and hit several balls into the second deck at Rogers Centre during a predraft workout. Sweeney, 3B Christopher Hawkins (3) and 1B Art Charles (20) all have plus raw power.

FASTEST RUNNER: SS Brandon Mims (9) and OF Ronnie Melendez (24) both are 75-80 runners on the 20-80 scouting scale.

BEST DEFENSIVE PLAYER: Sweeney had Tommy John surgery in August 2009 and played shortstop in high school, but he has taken quickly to third base.

BEST FASTBALL: RHP Asher Wojciechowski (1s) sits at 92-94 and peaks at 96. Projectable high school RHPs Aaron Sanchez (1s) and Noah Syndergaard (1s) worked at 92 and topped out at 95 in instructional league. RHP Sam Dyson (4) had Tommy John surgery after signing, but when healthy, he operates at 93-95 mph and can touch 98 with explosive life.

BEST SECONDARY PITCH: Toronto drafted several pitchers with quality breaking balls, most notably RHP Deck McGuire's (1) slider, LHP Mitchell Taylor's (7) curveball and Sanchez's curve.

BEST PRO DEBUT: RHP Drew Permison (42) racked up a 2.31 ERA, seven saves and 59 strikeouts in 39 innings with a 90-93 mph fastball.

BEST ATHLETE: Hawkins is the best all-around athlete in Toronto's draft, with average to plus tools across the board. SS Dickie Joe Thon (5), who signed for $1.5 million, has plus speed, range and arm strength to go with a loose swing and gap power.

MOST INTRIGUING BACKGROUND: Besides Sweeney, three other draftees have big league connections. Thon's father Dickie was an all-star shortstop. Unsigned RHP Gabriel Romero's (47) brother Ricky won 14 games for the Jays in 2010. 3B/2B Andy Fermin's (32) dad Felix played 10 years in the majors.

CLOSEST TO THE MAJORS: McGuire was one of the most polished college pitchers in the draft. He has a 90-94 mph fastball and throws four pitches for strikes. Wojciechowski is also on the fast track.

BEST LATE-ROUND PICK: Athletic RHP Myles Jaye (17) has a ton of projection remaining in his 6-foot-3, 175-pound frame, and he already throws 91-94 mph with good life.

THE ONE WHO GOT AWAY: Toronto went over slot for 13 different players and went after several other tough signs. The best they missed out on were LHP Logan Ehlers (8) and RHP Nick Vander Tuig (39). Ehlers, now at Nebraska, has an 89-92 mph fastball and a plus curveball. Vander Tuig, now at UCLA, flashed a low-90s fastball and plus slider before having Tommy John surgery in 2009.

ASSESSMENT: With a new general manager (Alex Anthopoulos), scouting director (Andrew Tinnish) and philosophy, the Jays set about rebuilding their system. They had nine picks in the first three rounds and went over slot to sign several others.

2009

The Blue Jays whiffed on signing LHPs James Paxton (1s) and Jake Eliopoulos (2) and RHP Jake Barrett (3). At least they salvaged something by grabbing RHP Chad Jenkins (1), OF Jake Marisnick (3) and 1B K.C. Hobson (6).

GRADE: C+

2008

Toronto sought a potent bat, and may have a better bet in finding one with OF Eric Thames (7) than 1B David Cooper (1). Steady SS Tyler Pastornicky (5) went to the Braves in a deal for Yunel Escobar.

GRADE: C

2007

With five picks before the first round, the Jays scored with C J.P. Arencibia (1) and LHP Brett Cecil (1s), found a piece of trade bait in RHP Trystan Magnuson (1s) and whiffed on 3B Kevin Ahrens (1) and SS Justin Jackson (1s). LHP Mark Rzepcynski (5) has joined Cecil in the big league rotations, while LHP Brad Mills (4) also has pitched in the majors.

GRADE: B+

2006

This draft crop depends on OF Travis Snider (1), who has been slow to get acclimated in Toronto but still has upside with the bat. The Jays sacrificed their second- and third-round picks as free-agent compensation.

GRADE: C+

Draft analysis by Jim Callis. Numbers in parentheses indicate draft rounds.

KYLE DRABEK, RHP

Born: Dec. 8, 1987. **Bats:** R. **Throws:** R.
Height.: 6-1. **Weight.:** 190. **Drafted:** HS—
The Woodlands, Texas, 2006 (1st round).
Signed by: Steve Cohen (Phillies).

PROSPECT 1

DAVID SCHOFIELD

The son of former Cy Young Award winner Doug Drabek, Kyle led The Woodland (Texas) High to a national title as a senior in 2006 by going 14-0 on the mound and belting 12 homers as a short-stop. Some teams believed he had the best pure stuff in the 2006 draft, but he lasted until the 18th overall pick because his makeup worried clubs. He had separate incidents which resulted in a public-intoxication charge (later dropped) and a single-car accident in which he struck a tree. Drabek signed for $1.55 million and had a rough pro debut, then blew out his elbow early in the 2007 season. He used his rehab time to mature, improve his conditioning and refine his delivery. He broke out in 2009, pitching in the Futures Game and reaching Double-A at age 21. His name started to come up in trade rumors as Philadelphia looked for pitching help. The Phillies balked at giving him up for Roy Halladay at the 2009 trade deadline, but pulled the trigger in mid-December, sending him to Toronto along with catcher Travis d'Arnaud and outfielder Michael Taylor. Drabek spent 2010 at Double-A New Hampshire and won Eastern League pitcher of the year honors, leading the league with 14 wins and throwing a nine-inning no-hitter on Independence Day. The Blue Jays gave him a September callup and while he didn't earn a win in three starts, he didn't allow more than three runs in any outing.

Drabek has the stuff to pitch at the front of a rotation. His curveball is his best pitch, a power offering with 12-to-6 action and low-80s velocity. It comes out of his hand at the same height as his fastball, giving it good depth and deception that produces a lot of swings and misses. He throws two- and four-seam fastballs, ranging from 90-96 mph and sitting comfortably in the low 90s. He has good life to the two-seamer, using it to induce groundouts. Toronto challenged Drabek to get better against lefthanders in 2010—they had a

.924 OPS against him the year before—and he did just that. By adding a cutter that he'd throw 10-12 times per game, he held Double-A lefties to a .227/.301/.350 line. His changeup has shown depth and sink, but he's still refining his arm speed and command with the pitch. Drabek doesn't have pinpoint command, but he throws enough strikes and locates his pitches well enough. His athleticism is an asset, allowing him to repeat his delivery, field his position and hold runners.

After his big league cameo, Drabek will have a chance to make Toronto's rotation out of spring training. The development of his cutter and changeup are critical as they give him an edge over lefties.

SCOUTING GRADES

Fastball: 65.   **Command/**
Curveball: 70.   **Control:** 50.
Cutter: 45.   **Delivery:** 50.

Based on 20-80 scouting scale, where 50 represents major league average, and future projection rather than present tools.

Year	Club (League)	Class	W	L	ERA	G	GS	CG	SV	IP	H	HR	BB	SO	G/A	WHIP	AVG
2006	Phillies (GCL)	R	1	3	7.71	6	6	0	0	23	33	2	11	14	—	1.89	.333
2007	Lakewood (SAL)	LoA	5	1	4.33	11	10	0	0	54	50	9	23	46	—	1.35	.239
2008	Phillies (GCL)	R	0	1	2.25	4	4	0	0	12	6	0	6	6	—	1.00	.150
	Williamsport (NYP)	SS	1	2	2.21	4	4	0	0	20	11	1	6	10	—	0.84	.159
2009	Clearwater (FSL)	HiA	4	1	2.48	10	9	1	0	62	49	0	19	74	0.98	1.10	.218
	Reading (EL)	AA	8	2	3.64	15	14	0	0	96	92	9	31	76	1.01	1.28	.252
2010	New Hampshire (EL)	AA	14	9	2.94	27	27	1	0	162	126	12	68	132	1.94	1.20	.215
	Toronto (AL)	MAJ	0	3	4.76	3	3	0	0	17	18	2	5	12	3.50	1.35	.295
Major League Totals			0	3	4.76	3	3	0	0	17	18	2	5	12	3.50	1.35	.295
Minor League Totals			33	19	3.41	77	74	2	0	430	367	33	164	358	1.39	1.24	.230

2 BRETT LAWRIE, 2B

Born: Jan. 18, 1990. **B-T:** R-R. **Ht.:** 5-11. **Wt.:** 200. **Drafted:** HS—Langley, B.C., 2008 (1st round). **Signed by:** Marty Lehn (Brewers).

Lawrie became the highest-drafted Canadian hitter ever when the Brewers selected him 16th overall in 2008. He agreed to try catching after signing for $1.7 million, but before he made his pro debut he asked to move to second base, which he thought would provide a quicker path to Milwaukee. A member of Canada's 2008 Olympic team and 2009 World Baseball Classic club, he led the Double-A Southern League in runs (90), hits (158), triples (16) and total bases (250) last year despite being the second-youngest regular in the circuit. The Brewers had discussed using Lawrie to find some pitching help, and in December they sent him to the Blue Jays for Shaun Marcum. Lawrie has very strong hands and a quick bat, allowing him to wait on pitches and drive the ball to all fields. He's not a prolific home run hitter but piles up extra-base hits by shooting the ball into the gaps. He needs to balance his aggressiveness with more plate discipline, however. Though he stole 30 bases in 2010, he was caught 13 times and his speed is just average. Lawrie has smoothed out some of his rough edges in the field but still must work on making his hands softer, as evidenced by the 25 errors he committed in 131 games at second base last year. He has solid arm strength but may not have the first-step quickness to remain at second, where he's now blocked by Aaron Hill in Toronto. Lawrie won't have to be a Gold Glove defender because his bat will get him to the big leagues and keep him there. If he has to move to an outfield corner, he'll still provide enough offense to profile as a quality regular. He'll spend 2010 in Triple-A.

Year	Club (League)	Class	AVG	G	AB	R	H	2B	3B	HR	RBI	BB	SO	SB	CS	OBP	SLG
2009	Wisconsin (MWL)	LoA	.274	105	372	48	102	18	5	13	65	41	70	19	11	.348	.454
	Huntsville (SL)	AA	.269	13	52	6	14	0	1	0	0	0	14	0	2	.283	.308
2010	Huntsville (SL)	AA	.285	135	554	90	158	36	16	8	63	47	118	30	13	.346	.451
Minor League Totals			.280	253	978	144	274	54	22	21	128	88	202	49	26	.343	.445

3 DECK McGUIRE, RHP

Born: June 23, 1989. **B-T:** R-R. **Ht.:** 6-6. **Wt.:** 225. **Drafted:** Georgia Tech, 2010 (1st round). **Signed by:** Eric McQueen.

A Virginia prep product, McGuire emerged as Georgia Tech's Friday starter and the Atlantic Coast Conference pitcher of the year in 2009. He followed up by winning nine games and becoming the second Yellow Jackets pitcher ever selected in the first round in 2010, going 11th overall and signing at the Aug. 16 deadline for $2 million. McGuire combines good stuff and polish. He commands a 90-94 mph fastball to both sides of the plate and complements it with three secondary offerings that he can throw for strikes. His slider is a swing-and-miss pitch, sitting at 82-85 mph with late life. He can backdoor it against righthanders and sneak it under lefties' hands. His changeup arrives at 80-84 with some fade, and he maintains good arm speed, giving the pitch plenty of deception. His curveball has tightened up since the spring—he threw it at 78-79 during instructional league, as opposed to 70-75 during the spring—and could be an average pitch. Because he's an advanced college pitcher, McGuire should move quickly. Though he signed too late to make his pro debut in 2010, the Blue Jays probably will start him out at high Class A Dunedin. His arsenal and command eventually should land him in the middle of Toronto's rotation, and he could reach the majors before the end of 2012.

Year	Club (League)	Class	W	L	ERA	G	GS	CG	SV	IP	H	HR	BB	SO	G/A	WHIP	AVG
2010	Did Not Play—Signed Late																

4 ANTHONY GOSE, OF

Born: Aug. 10, 1990. **B-T:** L-L. **Ht.:** 6-1. **Wt.:** 190. **Drafted:** HS—Bellflower, Calif., 2008 (2nd round). **Signed by:** Tim Kissner (Phillies).

Though his fastball was 97 mph in high school, Gose developed shoulder problems and didn't show much of a desire to pitch in pro ball. The Phillies refused to part with him when the Blue Jays shopped Roy Halladay in 2009. Toronto finally got him a year later, as Philadelphia included Gose in a package to get Roy Oswalt from the Astros, who immediately flipped him to the Jays for Brett Wallace. One of the fastest prospects in baseball, Gose led the minors with 76 steals in 2009 but wasn't as successful in high Class A. He's still working on reading pitchers and getting good jumps, and he got caught a minor league-high 32 times in 77 attempts. His center-field defense and arm strength give him two more plus tools, but his bat still needs to come around. He needs to cut down on his strikeouts and put the ball in play more consistently. He could develop average power, though he'll be better off putting the ball in the gaps and wreaking havoc on the bases. If Gose becomes just an average hitter, his speed and defense could make him a force. His bat is still a work in progress, so a return to high Class A is possible.

Year	Club (League)	Class	AVG	G	AB	R	H	2B	3B	HR	RBI	BB	SO	SB	CS	OBP	SLG
2008	Phillies (GCL)	R	.256	11	39	4	10	2	1	0	3	1	12	3	1	.293	.359
2009	Lakewood (SAL)	LoA	.259	131	510	72	132	24	9	2	52	35	110	76	20	.323	.353
2010	Clearwater (FSL)	HiA	.263	103	418	67	110	17	11	4	21	32	103	36	27	.325	.385
	Dunedin (FSL)	HiA	.255	27	94	21	24	3	2	3	6	13	29	9	5	.360	.426
Minor League Totals			.260	272	1061	164	276	46	23	9	82	81	254	124	53	.326	.372

5 TRAVIS D'ARNAUD, C

Born: Feb. 10, 1989. **B-T:** R-R. **Ht.:** 6-2. **Wt.:** 195. **Drafted:** HS—Lakewood, Calif., 2007 (1st round supplemental). **Signed by:** Tim Kissner (Phillies).

The 37th overall pick in 2007, d'Arnaud moved from the Phillies to the Blue Jays along with Kyle Drabek and outfield prospect Michael Taylor in the Roy Halladay trade in December 2009. In his first season in the Toronto system, d'Arnaud missed most of May with back problems that led to him getting shut down at the end of July. His older brother Chase is one of the Pirates' better position prospects. D'Arnaud has the tools to do it all at catcher. He has a quick bat and does a good job of using the whole field. His swing usually stays compact, and he should hit for a solid average with 15-20 homers per season. Defensively, he has a plus arm and threw out 30 percent of basestealers in high Class A in 2010. He sometimes rushes his throws, which affects his accuracy. He has quick feet and the athleticism and agility to stay behind the plate. He's a below-average runner, typical for a catcher. J.P. Arencibia may have had a more spectacular 2010 season, but d'Arnaud has better all-around skills. A winter of rest should resolve his back problems, though his missed time may dictate a return to high Class A to start 2011 with an opportunity to be promoted during the season.

Year	Club (League)	Class	AVG	G	AB	R	H	2B	3B	HR	RBI	BB	SO	SB	CS	OBP	SLG
2007	Phillies (GCL)	R	.241	41	141	18	34	3	0	4	20	4	23	4	2	.278	.348
2008	Williamsport (NYP)	SS	.309	48	175	21	54	13	1	4	25	18	29	1	2	.371	.463
	Lakewood (SAL)	LoA	.297	16	64	12	19	5	0	2	5	5	10	0	0	.357	.469
2009	Lakewood (SAL)	LoA	.255	126	482	71	123	38	1	13	71	41	75	8	4	.319	.419
2010	Dunedin (FSL)	HiA	.259	71	263	36	68	20	1	6	38	20	63	3	1	.315	.411
Minor League Totals			.265	302	1125	158	298	79	3	29	159	88	200	16	9	.323	.418

6 ZACH STEWART, RHP

Born: Sept. 28, 1986. **B-T:** R-R. **Ht.:** 6-2. **Wt.:** 205. **Drafted:** Texas Tech, 2008 (3rd round). **Signed by:** Jerry Flowers (Reds).

The fifth trade acquisition among the first six players on this list, Stewart came to the Blue Jays along with Edwin Encarnacion and Josh Roenicke in a mid-2009 deal that sent Scott Rolen to the Reds. Cincinnati broke him into pro ball as a reliever in 2008, started him at the beginning of 2009 and shifted him back to the bullpen shortly before the trade in an effort to keep his innings down. Toronto kept him in the rotation to finish 2009. Stewart returned to the rotation in 2010, and he pitched well in Double-A. Stewart works with two plus pitches in his fastball and slider. His fastball sits in the low 90s and routinely reaches 95-96 mph, featuring above-average sink. His mid-80s slider has depth and misses bats. The slider sits in the mid-80s and is a good swing-and-miss pitch with depth. He commands both pitches well. Stewart also developed some feel for a changeup last season, and it has the potential to become an average offering. With a third effective pitch to go with his durability, Stewart could become a mid-rotation starter. Stewart is in the mix to win a big league rotation spot in 2011. If he can't cut it as a starter, he has the stuff and makeup to become a set-up man or a closer.

Year	Club (League)	Class	W	L	ERA	G	GS	CG	SV	IP	H	HR	BB	SO	G/A	WHIP	AVG
2008	Dayton (MWL)	LoA	1	2	0.55	11	0	0	3	16	10	0	3	13	—	0.80	.175
	Sarasota (FSL)	HiA	0	2	1.62	13	0	0	2	17	16	0	11	23	—	1.62	.262
2009	Sarasota (FSL)	HiA	1	1	2.13	7	7	1	0	42	47	1	8	32	2.42	1.30	.283
	Carolina (SL)	AA	3	0	1.46	7	7	0	0	37	29	1	10	31	1.96	1.05	.218
	Louisville (IL)	AAA	0	0	0.73	9	0	0	2	12	11	0	8	16	1.22	1.54	.234
	Las Vegas (PCL)	AAA	0	0	3.38	11	0	0	0	13	18	1	6	14	2.13	1.80	.327
2010	New Hampshire (EL)	AA	8	3	3.63	26	26	0	0	136	131	13	54	106	1.64	1.36	.255
Minor League Totals			13	8	2.66	84	40	1	7	274	262	16	100	235	1.81	1.32	.254

7 ASHER WOJCIECHOWSKI, RHP

GLENN GASTON

Born: Dec. 21, 1988. **B-T:** R-R. **Ht.:** 6-4. **Wt.:** 235. **Drafted:** The Citadel, 2010 (1st round supplemental). **Signed by:** John Hendricks.

Wojciechowski benefited from a stint with Team USA in 2009, working off his fastball more often at the urging of pitching coach Mike Kennedy (Elon). His velocity increased, and he ranked second in NCAA Division I in strikeouts with 155 in 126 innings last spring. He also became the highest draft pick in the history of The Citadel, going 41st overall and signing for $815,400. The Blue Jays limited him to 12 innings in his debut to keep his workload down. After throwing his fastball more frequently and refining his mechanics, Wojciechowski now pitches at 92-94 mph and touches 96. He maintains his velocity into the late innings and controls his heater well. Before his velocity spiked, he was known for his big, durable frame and his slider. It's a hard-breaking pitch that grades out as above-average. Wojciechowski had little use for a changeup in college, but he has made some strides with it since turning pro. He has similar stuff to Zach Stewart and likewise could develop into a quality starter if he can refine his changeup. Stewart is a little more polished, but Wojciechowski has a slightly higher ceiling as a potential No. 2 starter. Even without the changeup, he could be a mid-rotation innings eater. He should start 2011 in high Class A.

Year	Club (League)	Class	W	L	ERA	G	GS	CG	SV	IP	H	HR	BB	SO	G/A	WHIP	AVG
2010	Auburn (NYP)	SS	0	0	0.75	3	3	0	0	12	6	0	4	11	1.88	0.83	.146
Minor League Totals			0	0	0.75	3	3	0	0	12	6	0	4	11	1.88	0.83	.146

8 J.P. ARENCIBIA, C

Born: Jan. 5, 1986. **B-T:** R-R. **Ht.:** 6-1. **Wt.:** 210. **Drafted:** Tennesse, 2007 (1st round). **Signed by:** Matt Briggs.

The 21st overall pick in 2007, Arencibia has hit 82 homers in three full pro seasons since signing for $1,327,500. LASIK surgery improved his night vision and helped him raise his Triple-A numbers from .236/.284/.444 in 2009 to .301/.359/.626 last season, earning him Pacific Coast League MVP honors. Called to Toronto in August, he became the first player in modern baseball history to collect four hits and two homers in his big league debut. Afterward, he went 1-for-30 with 11 strikeouts. Arencibia's carrying tool is his power to all fields, which is at least above-average and draws 70 grades on the 20-80 scale from some scouts. He overswings at times and isn't terribly disciplined at the plate, so he may not hit for a high average. His defense also is in question. He has solid arm strength but threw out just 23 percent of PCL basestealers. His receiving and blocking skills are improving, though just average at best, and he can get lackadaisical at times. He has below-average speed but isn't terrible for a catcher. John Buck made his first all-star team in 2010, but he departed as a free agent to the Marlins, leaving Arencibia as the favorite to win the catching job out of spring training in 2011.

Year	Club (League)	Class	AVG	G	AB	R	H	2B	3B	HR	RBI	BB	SO	SB	CS	OBP	SLG
2007	Auburn (NYP)	SS	.254	63	228	31	58	17	1	3	25	14	56	0	0	.309	.377
2008	Dunedin (FSL)	HiA	.315	59	248	38	78	22	0	13	62	11	46	0	0	.344	.560
	New Hampshire (EL)	AA	.282	67	262	32	74	14	0	14	43	7	55	0	0	.302	.496
2009	Las Vegas (PCL)	AAA	.236	116	466	67	110	32	1	21	75	26	114	0	1	.284	.444
2010	Las Vegas (PCL)	AAA	.301	104	412	76	124	36	1	32	85	38	85	0	0	.359	.626
	Toronto (AL)	MAJ	.143	11	35	3	5	1	0	2	4	2	11	0	0	.189	.343
Major League Totals			.143	11	35	3	5	1	0	2	4	2	11	0	0	.189	.343
Minor League Totals			.275	409	1616	244	444	121	3	83	290	96	356	0	1	.319	.507

9 CARLOS PEREZ, C

GLENN GASTON

Born: Oct. 27, 1990. **B-T:** R-R. **Ht.:** 6-0. **Wt.:** 193. **Signed:** Venezuela, 2008. **Signed by:** Rafael Moncada.

Signed out of Venezuela as a 17-year-old, Perez has been named MVP of his team in each of his first three pro seasons. He ranked as the No. 1 prospect in the short-season New York-Penn League in 2010, adding to the system's impressive depth behind the plate. Perez doesn't possess loud tools, but his fundamentals and instincts help him play above his pure physical ability. His arm is a tick above-average, and he enhances that with quick feet that allow him to get into a good throwing position. He caught 36 percent of NYP basestealers. He has soft hands, though he's still working on his receiving and blocking skills after committing 13 passed balls in 44 games. At the plate, Perez has a quiet lower half and consistently puts the bat on the ball. He has gap power now and could develop average power to the pull side. He draws his share of walks and holds a career .412 on-base percentage in 167 games. He has average speed, surprising for a catcher, and the Blue Jays insist he has the best baserunning instincts in their system. With J.P. Arencibia at the major league doorstep and Travis d'Arnaud showing plenty of potential, the Blue Jays have no problem taking it slow with Perez. He'll make his full-season league debut with low Class A Lansing at age 20.

Year	Club (League)	Class	AVG	G	AB	R	H	2B	3B	HR	RBI	BB	SO	SB	CS	OBP	SLG
2008	Blue Jays 1 (DSL)	R	.306	58	196	27	60	10	2	0	29	52	28	7	5	.459	.378
2009	Blue Jays (GCL)	R	.291	43	141	17	41	11	3	1	21	16	23	2	5	.364	.433
2010	Auburn (NYP)	SS	.298	66	235	44	70	11	8	2	41	34	41	7	3	.396	.438
Minor League Totals			.299	167	572	88	171	32	13	3	91	102	92	16	13	.412	.416

10 AARON SANCHEZ, RHP

BRIAN FLEMING

Born: July 1, 1992. **B-T:** R-R. **Ht.:** 6-4. **Wt.:** 190. **Drafted:** HS—Barstow, Calif., 2010 (1st round supplemental). **Signed by:** Blake Crosby.

Sanchez projected as a possible first-round pick after starring on the showcase circuit in the summer of 2009, and the Blue Jays were delighted to get him with the No. 34 overall choice in June. After signing for $775,000, he pitched well in 10 pro starts, though Toronto kept him on a tight pitch limit that prevented him from earning his first pro victory. Scouts love Sanchez's prototypical, projectable frame. He has long, loose limbs with wiry strength and plenty of room to add more. There's plenty of reason to think that he'll add more velocity as he fills out, and it already has started to happen. His fastball worked at 89-92 mph in the spring, sat in the low 90s during his pro debut and touched 95 during instructional league. Sanchez is able to spin a breaking ball and flashes a plus curveball. His changeup is a work in progress right now, as he throws it a little too hard, but he has shown some feel for the pitch. A wandering arm slot affected his command in high school and pro ball, so repeating his delivery will be important. Sanchez created a lot of buzz at instructs, and the Jays are excited about his potential as a frontline starter. He'll likely begin his first full pro season in low Class A.

Year	Club (League)	Class	W	L	ERA	G	GS	CG	SV	IP	H	HR	BB	SO	G/A	WHIP	AVG
2010	Blue Jays (GCL)	R	0	2	1.42	8	8	0	0	19	19	1	12	28	2.57	1.63	.271
	Auburn (NYP)	SS	0	1	4.50	2	2	0	0	6	4	0	5	9	2.67	1.50	.182
Minor League Totals			0	3	2.16	10	10	0	0	25	23	1	17	37	2.60	1.60	.250

11 JAKE MARISNICK, OF

Born: March 30, 1991. **B-T:** R-R. **Ht.:** 6-4. **Wt.:** 200. **Drafted:** HS—Riverside, Calif. 2009 (3rd round). **Signed by:** Rick Ingalls.

The Blue Jays signed just two of their first five 2009 draft picks, first-rounder Chad Jenkins and Marisnick, who agreed to a $1 million bonus at the signing deadline. One of the best athletes available in the 2009 draft, he made his pro debut last season. After performed well in the Rookie-level Gulf Coast League, Toronto gave him a taste of his 2011 assignment by jumping him to low Class A. Marisnick has five-tool potential, though concerns about his bat dropped him to the third round and continue to linger. He has improved his timing at the plate and the ball jumps off his bat when he makes contact. However, he can get too aggressive at times, and the Jays are working with him to stay tall and drive through the ball. Marisnick has a long, wiry frame with plenty of strength and raw power. His speed, range and arm are all above-average. Should he have to move from center field, he also profiles well in right. Marisnick looked overmatched at Lansing, and he'll probably spend the entire 2011 season there. His development will require patience, but the payoff could be worth it.

Year	Club (League)	Class	AVG	G	AB	R	H	2B	3B	HR	RBI	BB	SO	SB	CS	OBP	SLG
2010	Blue Jays (GCL)	R	.287	35	122	17	35	12	0	3	14	13	18	14	1	.373	.459
	Lansing (MWL)	LoA	.220	34	127	16	28	8	2	1	12	9	37	9	2	.298	.339
Minor League Totals			.253	69	249	33	63	20	2	4	26	22	55	23	3	.336	.398

12 ERIC THAMES, OF

Born: Nov. 10, 1986. **B-T:** L-R. **Ht.:** 6-0. **Wt.:** 205. **Drafted:** Pepperdine, 2008 (7th round). **Signed by:** Tim Rooney.

Thames started to soar up draft boards as a redshirt junior at Pepperdine in 2008 when he batted .407 with 13 homers, but he tore a quadriceps muscle late in the spring. The injury allowed the Blue Jays to get him in the seventh round, but it also meant they had to wait two years to really see what they had in him. Surgery delayed his pro debut until 2009, and he played in just 52 games while dealing with more quad problems. Thames headed into last offseason knowing he needed to find a way to stay healthy. He dialed back on weightlifting and started doing yoga to add flexibility. His efforts came to fruition in 2010, as he played in 130 games, led Toronto farmhands with 104 RBIs and showed the best lefthanded power in the system. Thames has excellent bat speed and plus power. He can get too aggressive, chase pitches and pile up strikeouts, but he also draws his share of walks. With average speed and arm strength, he has the tools to be an average defender in left field, but his defense still needs polish. Thames could put up huge numbers in 2011 at the hitter's haven that is Triple-A Las Vegas, and he could find himself in Toronto late in the season.

Year	Club (League)	Class	AVG	G	AB	R	H	2B	3B	HR	RBI	BB	SO	SB	CS	OBP	SLG
2009	Blue Jays (GCL)	R	.286	7	21	4	6	3	0	0	1	3	5	0	0	.360	.429
	Dunedin (FSL)	HiA	.313	52	195	33	61	15	5	3	38	21	40	1	1	.386	.487
2010	New Hampshire (EL)	AA	.288	130	496	95	143	25	6	27	104	50	121	8	5	.370	.526
Minor League Totals			.295	189	712	132	210	43	11	30	143	74	166	9	6	.374	.513

13 ADEINY HECHAVARRIA, SS

Born: April 15, 1989. **B-T:** R-R. **Ht.:** 5-11. **Wt.:** 180. **Signed:** Cuba, 2010. **Signed by:** Marco Paddy.

Hechavarria defected from Cuba in July 2009 and finalized a $10 million major league contract with the Blue Jays nine months later, getting a franchise-record $4 million bonus. He couldn't reach the Mendoza Line after Toronto sent him to high Class A, but he performed significantly better after a promotion to Double-A at the end of June. The Blue Jays credit the in-season improvement to Hechavarria adapting to culture in the United States and taking well to instruction from Fisher Cats manager Luis Rivera. Hechavarria is a live-bodied player with quick-twitch athleticism. He stands out more now as a defender, though he also has potential at the plate. His best tool is his strong, accurate arm, and he also has good actions and soft hands at shortstop. Hechavarria has bat speed and makes consistent contact but lacks upper-body strength and doesn't do much damage. He can get stronger but won't have much more than gap power. His primary concern is to get on base, and he walked just 17 times in 440 plate appearances during his pro debut. He's an above-average runner who can use his speed to beat out hits and steal a few bases. Toronto is pleased at how well he adjusted to professional baseball and a new culture. Hechavarria may need some more time in Double-A but also could see his first big league action in 2011.

Year	Club (League)	Class	AVG	G	AB	R	H	2B	3B	HR	RBI	BB	SO	SB	CS	OBP	SLG
2010	Dunedin (FSL)	HiA	.193	41	161	21	31	7	3	1	7	5	25	7	0	.217	.292
	New Hampshire (EL)	AA	.273	61	253	36	69	11	1	3	34	12	40	6	3	.305	.360
Minor League Totals			.242	102	414	57	100	18	4	4	41	17	65	13	3	.272	.333

14 GRIFFIN MURPHY, LHP

Born: Jan. 16, 1991. **B-T:** L-L. **Ht.:** 6-3. **Wt.:** 200. **Drafted:** HS—Redlands, Calif., 2010 (2nd round). **Signed by:** Dan Cox.

The overall 2010 draft class was thin in high school lefthanders. A strong spring put Murphy at the head of the class along with Phillies first-rounder Jesse Biddle, and the Blue Jays took Murphy in the second round and signed him for $800,000 at the deadline. He offers a nice combination of quality stuff and rare polish for a prep pitcher. Murphy's fastball ranges from 87-93 mph, but he sits at 89-91 and has the potential to add a little more velocity in the future. He can manipulate his fastball as he sees fit, running it to either side of the plate or sinking it down in the zone. He maintains good arm speed on his above-average changeup, which runs in the low 80s and has some fade. He also shows the ability to spin a curveball, and he'll change its shape depending on whether he's facing lefties and righties. A potential middle-of-the-rotation starter, Murphy signed too late to make his pro debut. Nevertheless, his advanced feel could allow him to start 2011 in low Class A.

Year	Club (League)	Class	W	L	ERA	G	GS	CG	SV	IP	H	HR	BB	SO	G/A	WHIP	AVG
2010	Did Not Play—Signed Late																

15 CHAD JENKINS, RHP

Born: Dec. 22, 1987. **B-T:** R-R. **Ht.:** 6-4. **Wt.:** 235. **Drafted:** Kennesaw State, 2009 (1st round). **Signed by:** Matt Briggs.

Kyle Heckathorn was supposed to be the main attraction at Kennesaw State in 2009, but scouts who came to see him were more intrigued by Jenkins, his teammate. While Heckathorn went in the supplemental first round to the Brewers, Jenkins became the No. 20 overall pick and signed for $1.359 million. He reached high Class A during a 2010 pro debut that was solid if not spectacular—which also is an apt description of his stuff. Jenkins works with a very heavy fastball that ranges from 88-94 mph. He'll throw his two-seamer in on righthanders and use a four-seamer with riding life up in the zone. His slider was inconsistent last year but has shown the makings of being a plus pitch in the past, sitting in the mid-80s with late tilt. He also has good feel for a changeup. Though he has a thick frame and some effort in his delivery, he repeats it well and throws strikes. A possible No. 3 starter, he could open 2011 in Double-A.

Year	Club (League)	Class	W	L	ERA	G	GS	CG	SV	IP	H	HR	BB	SO	G/A	WHIP	AVG
2010	Lansing (MWL)	LoA	5	4	3.63	13	13	1	0	79	87	5	13	64	1.72	1.26	.277
	Dunedin (FSL)	HiA	2	6	4.33	13	13	1	0	62	73	6	18	42	2.02	1.46	.281
Minor League Totals			7	10	3.94	26	26	2	0	142	160	11	31	106	1.85	1.35	.279

16 DICKIE JOE THON, SS

Born: Nov. 16, 1991. **B-T:** R-R. **Ht.:** 6-2. **Wt.:** 175. **Drafted:** HS—San Juan, P.R., 2010 (5th round). **Signed by:** Jorge Rivera.

Though he was the Blue Jays' 11th pick (fifth round) in the 2010 draft, Thon received the second-highest bonus at $1.5 million. He commanded such a high price because of his all-around potential and the leverage that a Rice scholarship gave him. He has the tools to follow in his father Dickie's footsteps as an all-star shortstop one day, but he'll need time to develop because he didn't focus on baseball in Puerto Rico. He also starred in basketball, track and volleyball. Thon has shown he can handle wood bats against quality pitching at high school showcase events, and he already has some gap power. As he gets stronger, Toronto believes he can become a plus hitter with plus power. His speed and range are also above-average tools. He's a solid defender with an average arm at shortstop. He'll need to gain consistency and shorten his release on his throws. After signing late, Thon likely will see some time in extended spring training before making his pro debut in mid-2011.

Year	Club (League)	Class	AVG	G	AB	R	H	2B	3B	HR	RBI	BB	SO	SB	CS	OBP	SLG
2010	Did Not Play—Signed Late																

17 HENDERSON ALVAREZ, RHP

Born: April 18, 1990. **B-T:** R-R. **Ht.:** 6-0. **Wt.:** 190. **Signed:** Venezuela, 2006. **Signed by:** Rafael Moncada.

After posting a 5.63 ERA in two years of Rookie ball, Alvarez had a breakthrough season in the 2009, leading the low Class A Midwest League in fewest walks (1.4) and homers (0.1) allowed per nine innings. Interestingly, his pure stuff improved last year but his performance didn't. After ranging from 86-94 mph the previous season, his fastball sat at 92-94 and touched 97 during the high Class A Florida State League all-star game in 2010. His changeup remained a plus pitch with splitter action. Yet despite possessing two plus pitches, Alvarez was more hittable and his strikeout rate declined. He may have gotten caught up in his newfound power and lost some feel for pitching. He throws too many strikes and doesn't try to get hitters to chase pitches enough when he's ahead in the count. His breaking ball lags well behind his other two pitches at this point. It's a hybrid of a curveball and a slider, though he'll show an average slider on occasion. If he can refine his breaking ball, he could become a No. 3 starter. With a good spring, Alvarez could open 2011 in Double-A.

Year	Club (League)	Class	W	L	ERA	G	GS	CG	SV	IP	H	HR	BB	SO	G/A	WHIP	AVG
2007	Blue Jays 1 (DSL)	R	1	2	5.61	8	7	0	0	26	36	0	8	20	—	1.71	.324
2008	Blue Jays (GCL)	R	1	4	5.63	12	11	0	0	46	63	3	6	34	—	1.49	.310
2009	Lansing (MWL)	LoA	9	6	3.47	23	23	1	0	124	121	1	19	92	1.33	1.13	.251
2010	Dunedin (FSL)	HiA	8	7	4.33	23	21	0	0	112	137	10	27	78	1.75	1.46	.300
Minor League Totals			19	19	4.29	66	62	1	0	309	357	14	60	224	1.75	1.51	.285

18 KELLEN SWEENEY, 3B

Born: Sept. 14, 1991. **B-T:** L-R. **Ht.:** 6-0. **Wt.:** 180. **Drafted:** HS—Cedar Rapids, Iowa, 2010 (2nd round). **Signed by:** Wes Penick.

The Blue Jays are extremely excited about Sweeney's polish and maturity, which should come as no surprise considering he already had some experience with pro ball before they signed him for $600,000 as a second-round pick in 2010. He's the younger brother of Athletics outfielder Ryan Sweeney, and scouts consider Kellen a better hitter at the same stage of their careers. He has a smooth, quick lefthanded stroke and a good idea of the strike zone. While he's patient and should draw plenty of walks, Toronto would like him to be more aggressive when he gets ahead in the count. He's strong and should develop at least average power. He has slightly above-average speed. A shortstop in high school, Sweeney moved to third base after signing. He has regained average arm strength since having Tommy John surgery in August 2009, and has soft hands and good footwork at the hot corner. He probably could handle second base as well. Sweeney signed early enough to spend a month in the Gulf Coast League last summer, laying the groundwork to begin 2011 in low Class A.

Year	Club (League)	Class	AVG	G	AB	R	H	2B	3B	HR	RBI	BB	SO	SB	CS	OBP	SLG
2010	Blue Jays (GCL)	R	.267	16	45	7	12	3	1	1	7	15	12	0	1	.450	.444
Minor League Totals			.267	16	45	7	12	3	1	1	7	15	12	0	1	.450	.444

19 ADONIS CARDONA, RHP

Born: Jan. 16, 1994. **B-T:** R-R. **Ht.:** 6-4. **Wt.:** 170. **Signed:** Venezuela, 2010. **Signed by:** Marco Paddy.

Cardona signed with the Blue Jays in early July for $2.8 million—the highest bonus ever given to a Venezuelan pitcher and the second-highest in franchise history. He had an ideal, projectable frame for a 16-year-old at 6-foot-4 and 170 pounds. His fastball already sits at 89-91 mph and can touch 93, giving plenty of reason to think he'll sit in the mid-90s down the road. Cardona has plenty of work to do with his secondary stuff. He has shown feel for a changeup that has some sink. It's a better pitch than his curveball, which shows depth at times but lacks consistency and grades as below-average. There's some effort in his delivery as well. Though Cardona is far from a finished product, time is on his side and his upside is significant. He'll probably make his pro debut in the Rookie-level Dominican Summer League in 2011 and not come to the United States until 2012.

Year	Club (League)	Class	W	L	ERA	G	GS	CG	SV	IP	H	HR	BB	SO	G/A	WHIP	AVG
2010	Did Not Play—Signed 2011 Contract																

20 JUSTIN NICOLINO, LHP

Born: Nov. 22, 1991. **B-T:** L-L. **Ht.:** 6-3. **Wt.:** 175. **Drafted:** HS—Orlando, 2010 (2nd round). **Signed by:** Carlos Rodriguez.

Some clubs considered Nicolino a top-three-rounds talent in the 2010 draft, but many were wary of his commitment to Virginia. The Blue Jays could afford to gamble because they had six extra draft picks as free-agent compensation, and his performance at the Florida state high school all-star games in late May convinced them to take him in the second round. He signed in August for $615,000. Nicolino's fastball ranged from 85-91 mph in the spring, but he got stronger over the summer and sat at 90 and topped out at 92 during instructional league. He also showed a firmer breaking ball—an overhand curveball in the low 80s that features average bite. His changeup is his best secondary pitch, as he throws it with excellent arm speed and gets some good fade. Nicolino has added 15 pounds in the last year and still has some room to fill out and get stronger. He should begin 2011 in extended spring training and make his pro debut during the summer.

Year	Club (League)	Class	W	L	ERA	G	GS	CG	SV	IP	H	HR	BB	SO	G/A	WHIP	AVG
2010	Did Not Play—Signed Late																

21 DAVID COOPER, 1B

Born: Feb. 12, 1987. **B-T:** L-L. **Ht.:** 6-0. **Wt.:** 200. **Drafted:** California, 2008 (1st round). **Signed by:** Chris Becerra.

Scouts regarded Cooper as one of the better pure hitters in the 2008 draft, which got him drafted 17th overall and a slightly below-slot $1.5 million bonus. He looked primed to live up to that reputation when he hit .333/.399/.502 and reached high Class A in his pro debut, but he has spent the last two years batting .257 in Double-A. The Blue Jays still like his offensive potential, however. They track hard-hit balls as a statistic and say he ranked among their minor league leaders, hitting into more than his share of bad luck. He still shows a knack for getting the barrel to the ball and uses the whole field. He has started to turn on balls with power without pulling off pitches, allowing him to double his home run output from 10 in 2009 to 20 last season. Cooper has below-average athleticism and speed and is still a work in progress as a first baseman. He spent time in instructional league to work on his conditioning, agility and footwork. Ticketed for Triple-A this year, he could find himself in the big leagues quickly if he progresses at the plate especially after Lyle Overbay signed with the Pirates as a free agent.

Year	Club (League)	Class	AVG	G	AB	R	H	2B	3B	HR	RBI	BB	SO	SB	CS	OBP	SLG
2008	Auburn (NYP)	SS	.341	21	85	10	29	10	1	2	21	10	16	0	1	.411	.553
	Lansing (MWL)	LoA	.354	24	96	15	34	10	0	2	17	10	14	0	0	.415	.521
	Dunedin (FSL)	HiA	.304	24	92	10	28	9	0	1	13	10	16	0	0	.373	.435
2009	New Hampshire (EL)	AA	.258	128	473	62	122	32	0	10	66	59	92	0	0	.340	.389
2010	New Hampshire (EL)	AA	.257	132	498	59	128	30	1	20	78	52	74	0	0	.327	.442
Minor League Totals			.274	329	1244	156	341	91	2	35	195	141	212	0	1	.348	.435

22 K.C. HOBSON, 1B

Born: Aug. 22, 1990. **B-T:** L-L. **Ht.:** 6-2. **Wt.:** 210. **Drafted:** HS—Bakersfield, Calif., 2009 (6th round). **Signed by:** Tim Rooney.

Hobson resembles his father Butch, a former big league player and manager, with his bulldog mentality, 6-foot-2 and 205-pound frame, and strong hands and forearms. Lured away from a commitment to Texas A&M with a $500,000 bonus as a sixth-round pick in 2009, he signed late that summer and made his pro debut last season. Hobson has a compact stroke and his bat stays in the hitting zone for a long time. He can go to the opposite field with authority, and he really started to sting the ball in 2010 as he learned to pull the ball more. His power hasn't quite shown up yet, but he has plenty to all fields. Because he grew up around the game, he has a good understanding of hitting mechanics and fundamentals. Though he pitched and played some outfield in high school, Hobson is a below-average runner who is limited to first base. He shows good footwork and has improved defensively since signing. He'll head to low Class A this year.

Year	Club (League)	Class	AVG	G	AB	R	H	2B	3B	HR	RBI	BB	SO	SB	CS	OBP	SLG
2010	Blue Jays (GCL)	R	.279	35	129	17	36	5	0	4	17	7	17	1	5	.316	.411
	Lansing (MWL)	LoA	.261	23	92	14	24	4	1	2	9	4	17	0	0	.286	.391
Minor League Totals			.271	58	221	31	60	9	1	6	26	11	34	1	5	.303	.403

23 MOISES SIERRA, OF

Born: Sept. 24, 1988. **B-T:** R-R. **Ht.:** 6-0. **Wt.:** 225. **Signed:** Domincan Republic, 2005. **Signed by:** Hilario Soriano.

In his first three pro seasons, Sierra hit just .241/.304/.366, but he responded well to a challenging assignment to Dunedin in 2009 and had a breakout year. He finished the season in New Hampshire and figured to return there in 2010, but he never made it. He came down with a stress fracture in his leg during spring training, which combined with a strained oblique and a hand injury limited him to just 20 games, none above high Class A. When he's on the field, Sierra shows solid all-fields power that's still developing. He makes consistent contact but doesn't draw many walks. Sierra runs well for his size but won't be a basestealing threat. He has average range in right field and a powerful arm that rates as a 70 on the 20-80 scouting scale. After playing winter ball in his native Dominican Republic to recoup some of his lost at-bats and being added to the Blue Jays' 40-man roster, he'll finally make it back to Double-A in 2011.

Year	Club (League)	Class	AVG	G	AB	R	H	2B	3B	HR	RBI	BB	SO	SB	CS	OBP	SLG
2006	Blue Jays (DSL)	R	.253	69	245	35	62	16	1	4	26	24	50	17	3	.345	.376
2007	Blue Jays (GCL)	R	.203	43	143	17	29	5	1	5	15	5	39	2	2	.248	.357
2008	Lansing (MWL)	LoA	.246	130	451	50	111	16	5	9	39	26	114	12	11	.297	.364
2009	Dunedin (FSL)	HiA	.286	110	405	56	116	24	2	5	56	34	66	10	2	.360	.393
	New Hampshire (EL)	AA	.353	8	34	1	12	1	0	1	6	1	8	0	1	.361	.471
2010	Blue Jays (GCL)	R	.265	10	34	4	9	2	0	1	3	4	8	0	0	.342	.412
	Dunedin (FSL)	HiA	.162	10	37	4	6	1	0	1	5	1	11	0	1	.175	.270
Minor League Totals			.256	380	1349	167	345	65	9	26	150	95	296	41	20	.320	.375

24 NOAH SYNDERGAARD, RHP

Born: Aug. 29, 1992. **B-T:** L-R. **Ht.:** 6-5. **Wt.:** 200. **Drafted:** HS—Mansfield, Texas, 2010 (1st round supplemental). **Signed by:** Steve Miller.

Syndergaard's stock started to soar just before the 2010 draft when he starred in the Texas 4-A playoffs, pumping low-90s fastballs and striking out 39 in his final three starts. The Blue Jays were on him earlier than anyone, thanks to area scout Steve Miller. He saw Syndergaard sit at 87-90 mph in the first few innings of a game in March, but Miller stuck around and saw him finish the contest at 92-94. With its hand forced by his postseason heroics, Toronto took him in the supplemental first round and signed him for a below-slot $600,000. He pitched just 13 innings in his first pro summer before the Jays shut him down as a precaution when his elbow bothered him, but he returned for instructional league. Syndergaard is big and athletic with a good delivery for his size. His fastball now sits at 92-93 mph and touches 95. He has an effective changeup and good shape to his curveball. His breaking ball is still a work in progress and could develop into a slider. He may open 2011 in extended spring training and head to short-season Auburn in June.

Year	Club (League)	Class	W	L	ERA	G	GS	CG	SV	IP	H	HR	BB	SO	G/A	WHIP	AVG
2010	Blue Jays (GCL)	R	0	1	2.70	5	5	0	0	13	11	0	4	6	1.67	1.13	.229
Minor League Totals			0	1	2.70	5	5	0	0	13	11	0	4	6	1.67	1.13	.229

25 DREW HUTCHISON, RHP

Born: Aug. 22, 1990. **B-T:** L-R. **Ht.:** 6-2. **Wt.:** 165. **Drafted:** HS—Lakeland, Fla., 2009 (15th round). **Signed by:** Joel Grampietro.

The Blue Jays certainly didn't want to miss out on signing pitchers James Paxton, Jake Eliopoulos and Jake Barrett after drafting them in the first three rounds in 2009. But that failure did free up the money to spend $400,000 on Hutchison, their 15th-round pick. He signed at the Aug. 17 deadline and didn't make his pro debut until 2010, which he finished by posting a 1.52 ERA in five low Class A starts. A Stetson recruit who would have been a two-way player in college, Hutchison is athletic and very polished for a high school pitcher. He works at 88-92 mph with his fastball and should be able to gain a little more velocity as he fills out. He has a pair of promising secondary pitches in his slider, which he has tightened up and now sits in the low 80s, and a changeup that he'll throw in any count. He repeats his clean delivery well and has good command. He'll return to Lansing to start 2011.

Year	Club (League)	Class	W	L	ERA	G	GS	CG	SV	IP	H	HR	BB	SO	G/A	WHIP	AVG
2010	Auburn (NYP)	SS	1	1	3.00	10	10	0	0	45	34	1	12	44	2.48	1.02	.201
	Lansing (MWL)	LoA	1	2	1.52	5	5	0	0	24	17	1	7	19	0.76	1.01	.191
Minor League Totals			2	3	2.49	15	15	0	0	69	51	2	19	63	1.56	1.02	.198

26 CHRISTOPHER HAWKINS, 3B/OF

Born: Aug. 17, 1991. **B-T:** L-R. **Ht.:** 6-2. **Wt.:** 195. **Drafted:** HS—Suwanee, Ga., 2010 (3rd round). **Signed by:** Eric McQueen.

Part of an exceptionally deep Georgia high school class of athletic position players, Hawkins declined a Tennessee scholarship to sign for $350,000 as a third-round pick in June. When he turned pro, he had an unorthodox swing that included an arm bar and had his upper body doing most of the work. He has started to smooth out his stroke and incorporate his lower half more, which helped him finish 2010 on a strong note by batting .304 in August. He still needs to shorten his swing some more, but he has a quick bat and shows plus raw power in batting practice. A shortstop in high school, Hawkins moved to third base in pro ball and also saw time in left field at the end of his pro debut. Some amateur scouts projected him as a center fielder, and he has the above-average speed and instincts to make that happen. His average arm plays up because he gets to balls quickly and has a compact release. Because he'll need some time to develop and the Blue Jays have several young third basemen and outfielders headed to low Class A, Hawkins figures to play 2011 at Auburn.

Year	Club (League)	Class	AVG	G	AB	R	H	2B	3B	HR	RBI	BB	SO	SB	CS	OBP	SLG
2010	Blue Jays (GCL)	R	.255	46	157	29	40	9	3	0	15	15	37	8	3	.324	.350
Minor League Totals			.255	46	157	29	40	9	3	0	15	15	37	8	3	.324	.350

27 MARCUS KNECHT, OF

Born: June 21, 1990. **B-T:** R-R. **Ht.:** 6-1. **Wt.:** 200. **Drafted:** Connors State (Okla.) JC, 2010 (3rd round supplemental). **Signed by:** Darin Vaughan.

After getting just 12 at-bats as a freshman for Oklahoma State, Knecht transferred to Connors State (Okla.) JC and intrigued scouts with his upside. He ranked among the national juco leaders in batting (.453) and homers (21), playing his way into the supplemental third round and earning a $250,000 bonus. The Blue Jays have a long history with Knecht, a native Canadian. He met Toronto scouting director Andrew Tinnish when he was 11 years old and began working with him on his hitting at age 14. The first thing evaluators notice about Knecht is his tremendous bat speed. He has raw power to all fields and hit several balls into the Rogers Centre's second deck during a predraft workout. He was able to handle short-season pitching in his pro debut, giving the Jays confidence that he'll hit for a solid average. Knecht's speed and arm are slightly above average, though he doesn't quite have the quickness or instincts to play in center field. He fits best in right field, where he saw most of his action during the summer. A broken foot sidelined Knecht with about a week left in the season, but he was able to return to action before the end of instructional league. He'll advance to low Class A in 2011.

Year	Club (League)	Class	AVG	G	AB	R	H	2B	3B	HR	RBI	BB	SO	SB	CS	OBP	SLG
2010	Auburn (NYP)	SS	.268	61	231	32	62	18	3	5	34	26	48	7	1	.345	.437
Minor League Totals			.268	61	231	32	62	18	3	5	34	26	48	7	1	.345	.437

28 GABRIEL CENAS, 3B

Born: Oct. 16, 1993. **B-T:** R-R. **Ht.:** 6-1. **Wt.:** 175. **Signed:** Venezuela, 2010. **Signed by:** Marco Paddy.

Under former general manager J.P. Ricciardi, the Blue Jays weren't aggressive on the international market, but that changed in their first year with Alex Anthopoulos at the helm. Toronto handed a $10 million big league deal to Cuban defector Adeiny Hechavarria and spent another $3.5 million on bonuses for Venezuelans Adonis Cardona and Cenas. In a workout for international prospects, Cenas was the only hitter who wasn't overmatched by Cardona. Signed for $700,000, Cenas is precocious in his ability to get the barrel on the ball and smoke line drives. He's still growing into his power but could develop into a 20-25 home run threat. He's a fringe-average runner who will slow down as he gets bigger and stronger. Cenas has an above-average arm and should be able to remain at third base. He'll probably begin 2011 in the Dominican Summer League.

Year	Club (League)	Class	AVG	G	AB	R	H	2B	3B	HR	RBI	BB	SO	SB	CS	OBP	SLG
2010	Did Not Play—Signed 2011 Contract																

29 GUSTAVO PIERRE, SS

Born: Dec. 28, 1991. **B-T:** R-R. **Ht.:** 6-2. **Wt.:** 183. **Signed:** Dominican Republic, 2008. **Signed by:** Miguel Bernard/Hilario Soriano.

Signed for $700,000 as a 16-year-old in 2008, Pierre is a gifted defender who ranks with Adeiny Hechavarria as the best among Blue Jays farmhands. Lean and athletic, he has good actions at shortstop and a cannon for an arm. Though he has made 43 errors in 106 pro games at shortstop, those can mostly be attributed to youth and inexperience. Pierre has plus speed to go with his defensive gifts, but he's still figuring things out with the bat. He has good bat speed and has the projectable frame to develop average or better power. He's too aggressive, however, which has led to struggles when he has faced significantly older pitchers in his two years in the United States. He has made some improvements, toning down his load and leg kick and keeping his head more still at the plate. Pierre's English is getting better, allowing him to soak up more instruction. Though he'll be just 19 in 2011, he may move up to low Class A.

Year	Club (League)	Class	AVG	G	AB	R	H	2B	3B	HR	RBI	BB	SO	SB	CS	OBP	SLG
2009	Blue Jays (GCL)	R	.259	48	174	22	45	10	4	4	22	3	45	8	5	.272	.431
2010	Auburn (NYP)	SS	.236	66	250	29	59	12	3	3	22	17	64	8	4	.283	.344
Minor League Totals			.245	114	424	51	104	22	7	7	44	20	109	16	9	.279	.380

30 BRAD MILLS, LHP

Born: March 5, 1985. **B-T:** L-L. **Ht.:** 5-11. **Wt.:** 185. **Drafted:** Arizona, 2007 (4th round). **Signed by:** Dan Cholowsky.

The Blue Jays drafted Mills in the 22nd round in 2006, but he turned them down to return to Arizona to finish his civil-engineering degree. Toronto signed him as a fourth-rounder in 2007, and he made his big league debut just two years later. He's still trying to find establish himself against top-level hitters, as his ERA has risen from 1.96 through Double-A to 4.58 in Triple-A to 7.80 in the majors. Mills depends on his feel for pitching and deception rather than pure stuff. In his brief time in Toronto, he has fallen behind in the count too often and then gotten hammered when he has been forced to come over the plate. Mills' best pitch is his changeup, which throws hitters off because he maintains good arm speed and has a herky-jerky delivery. He sets it up with a high-80s fastball that can touch 91 and an average 12-to-6 curveball. Mills will be 26 this season, and his window to crack the back of the Jays' rotation may be drawing to a close. If it closes completely, then he could be useful as a long reliever.

Year	Club (League)	Class	W	L	ERA	G	GS	CG	SV	IP	H	HR	BB	SO	G/A	WHIP	AVG
2007	Auburn (NYP)	SS	2	0	2.00	6	2	0	0	18	9	0	6	21	—	0.83	.143
2008	Lansing (MWL)	LoA	6	3	2.55	15	15	0	0	81	71	3	28	92	—	1.22	.233
	New Hampshire (EL)	AA	3	2	1.10	6	6	0	0	33	24	2	12	32	—	1.10	.205
	Dunedin (FSL)	HiA	4	0	1.35	6	6	0	0	33	25	2	12	35	—	1.11	.210
2009	Toronto (AL)	MAJ	0	1	14.09	2	2	0	0	8	14	4	6	9	0.30	2.61	.400
	Las Vegas (PCL)	AAA	2	8	4.06	14	14	1	0	84	83	6	35	72	1.16	1.40	.263
2010	Las Vegas (PCL)	AAA	8	6	4.97	20	20	0	0	112	118	15	43	100	1.01	1.43	.268
	Toronto (AL)	MAJ	1	0	5.64	7	3	0	0	22	20	2	13	18	1.14	1.48	.241
Major League Totals			1	1	7.80	9	5	0	0	30	34	6	19	27	1.14	1.77	.288
Minor League Totals			25	19	3.38	67	63	1	0	362	330	28	136	352	1.07	1.29	.243

Washington Nationals

BY AARON FITT

Stephen Strasburg electrified Nationals fans before an elbow injury ended his season

For the first time since the franchise arrived in Washington five years earlier, Nationals fans had legitimate reason to be excited in 2010. The team still finished in last place for the fifth time in six seasons since moving from Montreal, but the anticipated arrival of top prospect Stephen Strasburg infused Nationals Park with energy—and fans.

Strasburg, the No. 1 overall pick in the 2009 draft, made his major league debut on June 8. Before that, the Nationals averaged 21,560 fans a game. They drew more than 40,000 fans for each of his first two starts, and averaged 33,446 fans in his seven home outings.

Strasburg held up his end of the bargain, electrifying the baseball world with 14 strikeouts over seven innings in his debut against Pittsburgh. He continued to pitch well, going 5-3, 2.91 with 92 strikeouts in 68 innings before his rookie season ended abruptly in August when he tore an elbow ligament. He had Tommy John surgery that will sideline him for most of 2011.

The Nationals are optimistic Strasburg can regain his pre-surgery form, and they hope to pair him with another phenom before too long. Washington had the No. 1 choice for the second consecutive draft and chose 17-year-old slugger Bryce Harper. A year after giving Strasburg a draft-record $15.1 million major league contract, the Nationals handed Harper a $9.9 million big league deal, the largest ever for a position player in the draft.

For the second straight year, the Nationals set a record for bonus spending. They spent $11.51 million in 2009 and $11.93 million in 2010. In addition to Harper, they also gave over-slot deals to A.J. Cole, Sammy Solis and Robbie Ray last summer. Those three immediately ranked among the best starting pitching prospects in an organization short on impact arms.

Washington's big league staff ranked 12th in the National League in runs allowed, and among its six most regular starters, only 35-year-old Livan Hernandez posted an ERA below 4.65. The lineup provided more reason for optimism, albeit while finishing 14th in the NL in scoring. Franchise cornerstone Ryan Zimmerman put together another strong season, homegrown shortstop Ian Desmond enjoyed a solid rookie campaign and Danny Espinosa, Desmond's double-play partner of the future, reached the big leagues in September. Adam Dunn gave the Nationals another 38-homer season before leaving for the White Sox via free agency.

TOP 30 PROSPECTS

1. Bryce Harper, of	**16.** Tom Milone, lhp
2. Derek Norris, c	**17.** Adrian Sanchez, 2b/3b
3. Danny Espinosa, ss/2b	**18.** A.J. Morris, rhp
4. A.J. Cole, rhp	**19.** Michael Burgess, of
5. Wilson Ramos, c	**20.** Elvin Ramirez, rhp
6. Sammy Solis, lhp	**21.** Jeff Kobernus, 2b
7. Cole Kimball, rhp	**22.** Jason Martinson, ss
8. Eury Perez, of	**23.** Danny Rosenbaum, lhp
9. Chris Marrero, 1b	**24.** Tyler Moore, 1b
10. Brad Peacock, rhp	**25.** J.P. Ramirez, of
11. Yunesky Maya, rhp	**26.** Ryan Tatusko, rhp
12. Destin Hood, of	**27.** Brad Meyers, rhp
13. Steve Lombardozzi, 2b	**28.** Trevor Holder, rhp
14. Rick Hague, ss	**29.** Adam Carr, rhp
15. Robbie Ray, lhp	**30.** Hassan Pena, rhp

Washington made a huge move just before the Winter Meetings, signing free agent Jayson Werth for seven years and $126 million—more money than it had spent on free agents in the previous 20 years combined. General manager Mike Rizzo said the deal signaled the start of the next phase in the club's plan, when it plans to "really compete for division titles and championships."

The farm system remains thin in premium prospects, but Rizzo did pick up one of the minors' top catchers in Wilson Ramos when he traded all-star Matt Capps to the Twins in July.

General Manager: Mike Rizzo. **Farm Director:** Doug Harris. **Scouting Director:** Kris Kline.

Class	Team	League	W	L	PCT	Finish*	Manager
Majors	Washington Nationals	National	69	93	.426	14th (16)	Jim Riggleman
Triple-A	Syracuse Chiefs	International	76	67	.531	6th (14)	Trent Jewett
Double-A	Harrisburg Senators	Eastern	77	65	.542	4th (12)	Randy Knorr
High A	Potomac Nationals	Carolina	70	69	.504	†5th (8)	Gary Cathcart
Low A	Hagerstown Suns	South Atlantic	65	75	.464	12th (14)	Matthew LeCroy
Short-season	Vermont Lake Monsters	New York-Penn	36	38	.486	8th (14)	Jeff Garber
Rookie	GCL Nationals	Gulf Coast	24	32	.429	t-12th (15)	Bobby Williams
Overall 2010 Minor League Record			348	346	.501	16th (30)	

*Finish in overall standings (No. of teams in league). †League champion.
*Short-season affiliate changes to Auburn (New York-Penn) in 2011.

LAST YEAR'S TOP 30

Player, Pos.		Status
1.	Stephen Strasburg, rhp	Majors
2.	Derek Norris, c	No. 2
3.	Drew Storen, rhp	Majors
4.	Ian Desmond, ss	Majors
5.	Danny Espinosa, ss	No. 3
6.	Chris Marrero, 1b	No. 9
7.	Jeff Kobernus, 2b	No. 21
8.	Justin Maxwell, of	Majors
9.	Michael Burgess, of	No. 19
10.	Destin Hood, of	No. 12
11.	Eury Perez, of	No. 8
12.	Aaron Thompson, lhp	Dropped out
13.	J.R. Higley, of	Dropped out
14.	Brad Meyers, rhp	No. 27
15.	A.J. Morris, rhp	No. 18
16.	Brad Peacock, rhp	No. 10
17.	Juan Jaime, rhp	(Diamondbacks)
18.	Marco Estrada, rhp	(Brewers)
19.	Graham Hicks, lhp	Dropped out
20.	Luis Atilano, rhp	Majors
21.	Jack McGeary, lhp	Dropped out
22.	Roger Bernadina, of	Majors
23.	Will Atwood, lhp	Retired
24.	Atahualpa Severino, lhp	Dropped out
25.	Adrian Nieto, c	Dropped out
26.	Hassan Pena, rhp	No. 30
27.	Jeff Mandel, rhp	Dropped out
28.	Steve Lombardozzi, 2b	No. 13
29.	J.P. Ramirez, of	No. 25
30.	Danny Rosenbaum, lhp	No. 23

BEST TOOLS

Best Hitter for Average	Bryce Harper
Best Power Hitter	Bryce Harper
Best Strike-Zone Discipline	Derek Norris
Fastest Baserunner	Eury Perez
Best Athlete	Bryce Harper
Best Fastball	Cole Kimball
Best Curveball	Brad Peacock
Best Slider	A.J. Morris
Best Changeup	Josh Wilkie
Best Control	Tommy Milone
Best Defensive Catcher	Wilson Ramos
Best Defensive Infielder	Danny Espinosa
Best Infield Arm	Danny Espinosa
Best Defensive Outfielder	Eury Perez
Best Outfield Arm	Bryce Harper

PROJECTED 2014 LINEUP

Catcher	Wilson Ramos
First Base	Derek Norris
Second Base	Danny Espinosa
Third Base	Ryan Zimmerman
Shortstop	Ian Desmond
Left Field	Jayson Werth
Center Field	Eury Perez
Right Field	Bryce Harper
No. 1 Starter	Stephen Strasburg
No. 2 Starter	Jordan Zimmermann
No. 3 Starter	A.J. Cole
No. 4 Starter	Sammy Solis
No. 5 Starter	John Lannan
Closer	Drew Storen

TOP PROSPECTS OF THE DECADE

Year	Player, Pos.	2010 Org.
2001	Donnie Bridges, rhp	Out of baseball
2002	Brandon Phillips, ss	Reds
2003	Clint Everts, rhp	Blue Jays
2004	Clint Everts, rhp	Blue Jays
2005	Mike Hinckley, lhp	Blue Jays
2006	Ryan Zimmerman, 3b	Nationals
2007	Collin Balester, rhp	Nationals
2008	Chris Marrero, 1b	Nationals
2009	Jordan Zimmermann, rhp	Nationals
2010	Stephen Strasburg, rhp	Nationals

TOP DRAFT PICKS OF THE DECADE

Year	Player, Pos.	2010 Org.
2001	Josh Karp, rhp	Out of baseball
2002	Clint Everts, rhp	Blue Jays
2003	Chad Cordero, rhp	Mets
2004	Bill Bray, lhp	Reds
2005	Ryan Zimmerman, 3b	Nationals
2006	Chris Marrero, of	Nationals
2007	Ross Detwiler, lhp	Nationals
2008	*Aaron Crow, rhp	Royals
2009	Stephen Strasburg, rhp	Nationals
2010	Bryce Harper, of	Nationals

*Did not sign.

LARGEST BONUSES IN CLUB HISTORY

Stephen Strasburg, 2009	$7,500,000
Bryce Harper, 2010	$6,250,000
Ryan Zimmerman, 2006	$2,975,000
Justin Wayne, 2000	$2,950,000
Josh Karp, 2001	$2,650,000

WASHINGTON NATIONALS

TOP 2010 ROOKIE: Danny Espinosa, ss/2b. After homering six times during his September callup, he's poised to take over at second base in Washington.

BREAKOUT PROSPECT: Adrian Sanchez, 2b/3b. The switch-hitting Venezuelan is one of the best pure hitters in the system.

SLEEPER: Wade Moore, of. A 19th-round pick out of NCAA Division II Catawba (N.C.) last June, he demonstrated intriguing athleticism, arm strength and speed in his pro debut.

SOURCE OF TOP 30 TALENT			
Homegrown	27	Acquired	3
College	13	Trades	2
Junior college	3	Rule 5 draft	1
High school	7	Independent leagues	0
Draft-and-follow	1	Free agents/waivers	0
Nondrafted free agents	0		
International	3		

LF
Destin Hood (12)
J.P. Ramirez (25)
Randolph Oduber
Jeff Frazier
Kevin Keyes
Jesus Valdez

CF
Eury Perez (8)
Michael Taylor
Boomer Whiting
Chad Mozingo
Chris Curran

RF
Bryce Harper (1)
Michael Burgess (19)
Wade Moore
J.R. Higley

3B
Rick Hague (14)
Steven Souza
Stephen King

SS
Danny Espinosa (3)
Jason Martinson (22)
Chris McConnell
Francisco Soriano

2B
Steve Lombardozzi (13)
Adrian Sanchez (17)
Jeff Kobernus (21)
Blake Kelso

1B
Chris Marrero (9)
Tyler Moore (24)
Justin Bloxom

C
Derek Norris (2)
Wilson Ramos (5)
Sandy Leon
David Freitas
Cole Leonida
Roberto Perez
Adrian Nieto

RHP

RHSP	RHRP
A.J. Cole (4)	Cole Kimball (7)
Brad Peacock (10)	A.J. Morris (18)
Yunesky Maya (11)	Elvin Ramirez (20)
Ryan Tatusko (26)	Adam Carr (29)
Brad Meyers (27)	Hassan Pena (30)
Trevor Holder (28)	Josh Wilkie
Taylor Jordan	Tim Wood
Brian Broderick	Jeff Mandel
Paul Demny	Rob Wort
Tanner Roark	Neil Holland
Pedro Encarnacion	Kyle Morrison
Chris McKenzie	Mark Herrera
Adrian Alaniz	Tyler Hanks
	Dean Weaver
	Zech Zinicola
	Cameron Selik
	Aaron Barrett
	Colin Bates

LHP

LHSP	LHRP
Sammy Solis (6)	Atahualpa Severino
Robbie Ray (15)	Patrick McCoy
Tom Milone (16)	Josh Smoker
Danny Rosenbaum (23)	Aaron Thompson
Matt Grace	Chris Manno
Graham Hicks	Jack Spradlin
Bobby Hansen	Cory Van Allen
Jack McGeary	
Chad Jenkins	

2010

BEST PURE HITTER: OF Bryce Harper (1), the No. 1 overall pick, earns a lot of attention for his power, and his pure hitting ability helps bring it out. He trusts his hands, lets balls get deep and has the present strength to hit with wood. He hit .443 in the spring with wood bats at the JC of Southern Nevada.

BEST POWER HITTER: Harper is a true top-of-the-scale power prospect, with strength and the ability to backspin the ball with power to all fields. He has as much power as any player in the draft era and led all national juco players with 31 homers as a 17-year-old last spring.

FASTEST RUNNER: The Nationals didn't draft any burners. SS Blake Kelso (10) is an above-average runner. Harper flashes plus speed and can handle center field, though he'll move to right.

BEST DEFENSIVE PLAYER: Harper's bazooka arm and range should make him an above-average defender in right, but SS Jason Martinson (5) has more value as a fluid shortstop with easy arm strength and good infield actions.

BEST FASTBALL: Scouting director Kris Kline saw RHP A.J. Cole (4) touch 97 mph this spring. When Cole was on, he sat at 94 with some command and a good downhill angle. Harper's Southern Nevada teammate, RHP Tyler Hanks (17), hit 97 in the past but worked at 90-91 mph in instructional league.

BEST SECONDARY PITCH: LHP Sammy Solis (2) commands his changeup, which has some tail and good sink, and has supreme confidence in it.

BEST PRO DEBUT: SS Rick Hague (3) had a rough year defensively, both in college at Rice and after signing. But he hit .317/.385/.477 in 199 pro at-bats, mostly in low Class A. OF Randolph Oduber (32) was MVP of the Rookie-level Gulf Coast League, leading the circuit in batting (.366) and slugging (.569) while finishing second in on-base percentage (.434).

BEST ATHLETE: Harper and Martinson, who originally attended Texas State on a football scholarship as a wide receiver.

MOST INTRIGUING BACKGROUND: Harper earned his general equivalency diploma so he could pass up his last two years of high school, attend junior college and enter the draft. The Cubs drafted Harper's older brother Bryan, his teammate at Southern Nevada, in the 27th round but didn't sign him. Oduber is an Aruban who attended Western Oklahoma JC.

CLOSEST TO THE MAJORS: Solis pitched in the Arizona Fall League and could reach Double-A in his first full pro season. Harper will move exceptionally quickly for a player drafted at age 17.

BEST LATE-ROUND PICK: Washington gave LHP Robbie Ray (12) $799,000 and love his loose arm and makings of three average pitches. His fastball could be better than that, because he threw in the mid-90s on the high school showcase circuit.

THE ONE WHO GOT AWAY: RHP John Simms (39), who was the foil of No. 2 overall pick Jameson Taillon (Pirates) in high school, will push for the first round in 2013 after three seasons at Rice.

ASSESSMENT: The Nationals spent $11.9 million on draft bonuses, breaking the record of $11.5 million they set a year earlier. Washington rated Harper, Solis, Hague and Cole as top-50 talents entering the season, and was happy to land all four. Signing Ray was the final touch to a draft that the Nats provides much more than just Harper.

2009

The first team ever to have two top-10 picks, Washington turned them into their ace (RHP Stephen Strasburg, 1) and closer (RHP Drew Storen, 1) for years to come. Both reached the majors in 2010, and Strasburg was spectacular before succumbing to Tommy John surgery.

GRADE: A

2008

The Nationals failed to sign RHP Aaron Crow (1), though they turned the resulting consolation pick into Storen a year later. SS/2B Danny Espinosa (3) had a 20-20 season in the minors last summer before hitting six big league homers in September.

GRADE: C+

2007

Washington may not get much out of seven-figure investments in LHPs Ross Detwiler (1), Josh Smoker (1s) and Jack McGeary (6). But it still came away with RHP Jordan Zimmermann (2) and C Derek Norris (4), making this a solid draft.

GRADE: B+

2006

1B Chris Marrero (1) has developed more slowly than hoped, while RHP Colten Willems' (1s) mechanics disintegrated and RHP Sean Black (2) was the highest unsigned pick in the entire draft.

GRADE: D

Draft analysis by John Manuel (2010) and Jim Callis (2006-09). Numbers in parentheses indicate draft rounds.

BRYCE HARPER, OF

Born: Oct. 16, 1992. **Bats:** L. **Throws:** R.
Height: 6-3. **Weight:** 225. **Drafted:** JC of
Southern Nevada, 2010 (1st round). **Signed
by:** Mitch Sokol.

CLIFF WELCH

Harper was already established as a phenom before Sports Illustrated dubbed him "Baseball's Chosen One" on its cover in June 2009—when he had just completed sophomore year in high school and was 16 years old. Since then, he has been confronted with gargantuan expectations everywhere he has gone, yet he has managed to exceed even the loftiest projections. In the fall of 2009, Harper earned his general equivalency diploma so he could skip his final two seasons at Las Vegas High and enroll early at the JC of Southern Nevada. Playing in a wood bat conference, he destroyed the school record and led national juco players with 31 homers while hitting .443/.526/.987 with 20 steals in 24 tries. He led the Coyotes to a third-place finish at the Junior College World Series, showcasing his athleticism by playing right field, center field and third base in addition to his primary high school position of catcher. Harper was a slam-dunk choice for the Golden Spikes Award as the nation's top amateur player and the No. 1 overall pick in the draft. He signed right before the Aug. 16 deadline for a $9.9 million major league contract (the largest ever given to a position player in the draft) that included a $6.25 million bonus (the third-highest in draft history). After moving to right field full-time during instructional league, Harper faced much older competition yet again in the Arizona Fall League, where he hit .343/.410/.629 with one homer in 35 at-bats as a taxi-squad player.

Harper's raw tools are freakish. His power rates as a legitimate 80 tool on the 20-80 scouting scale. There are plenty of stories and videos of him hitting 500-foot homers, and he has the ability to easily backspin the ball over the fence to any part of the park. Harper is incredibly intense and aggressive in all phases of the game, including at the plate. Some scouts wonder if he'll hit for a high average because of his propensity to take huge swings, often with an exaggerated leg kick, and get jumpy at the plate. But at other times he shows a much quieter, more efficient swing. Those flashes, coupled with his uncanny hand-eye coordination and irreproachable work ethic, give other scouts

SCOUTING GRADES

Batting: 60. **Defense:** 60.
Power: 80. **Arm:** 80.
Speed: 55.

Based on 20-80 scouting scale, where 50 represents major league average, and future projection rather than present tools.

reason to believe he'll eventually become more selective and produce for average as well as power. Harper has shown 95 mph heat off the mound in the past, and his accurate outfield arm gives him a second 80 tool. His slightly above-average speed plays up on the basepaths because he's extremely aggressive at taking the extra base. He's still refining his routes and reads in right field, but he has the athleticism and instincts to be a plus defender there. He has impressed the Nationals by hustling to put himself in position to back up plays.

The most hyped prospect in draft history, Harper has superstar potential, and it's hard to find an evaluator who thinks he'll fall short of that ceiling. He's also incredibly advanced for an 18-year-old, and a strong spring could put him in position to jump right to high Class A Potomac to make his professional debut. He won't start any lower than low Class A Hagerstown. A realistic big league ETA for Harper is 2013—when he'll be just 20.

Year	Club (League)	Class	AVG	G	AB	R	H	2B	3B	HR	RBI	BB	SO	SB	CS	OBP	SLG
2010	Did Not Play—Signed Late																

2 DEREK NORRIS, C

Born: Feb. 14, 1989. **B-T:** R-R. **Ht.:** 6-0. **Wt.:** 210. **Drafted:** HS—Goddard, Kan., 2007 (4th round). **Signed by:** Ryan Fox.

After establishing himself as the best position-player prospect in the Nationals system in 2009, Norris broke the hamate bone in his left hand that fall. Complications from surgery caused him to miss the first month of the 2010 season, and he was hit in the head with a 95-mph fastball shortly after returning. He never really got fully healthy until the fall, when he hit .278/.403/.677 in the Arizona Fall League. Norris has a compact, efficient swing with plus power potential, and he can hit the ball to all fields. He has exceptional pitch recognition, feel for the strike zone and discipline, allowing him to lead his leagues in walks in each of the last two years. Sometimes he takes too many pitches, and Washington wants him to pounce when he gets a pitch he can drive. Considering he had little catching experience before turning pro, Norris has made major strides defensively. He still needs to improve his receiving, but he has gotten better at blocking balls in the dirt. His solid-average arm plays up because of his quick release and accuracy, allowing him to throw out 51 percent of basestealers last year. He has fringe-average speed. An offensive catcher with all-star potential, Norris will reach Double-A Harrisburg at age 22 in 2011. If his defense continues to progress, he could reach the big leagues the following year.

Year	Club (League)	Class	AVG	G	AB	R	H	2B	3B	HR	RBI	BB	SO	SB	CS	OBP	SLG
2007	Nationals (GCL)	R	.203	37	123	16	25	6	2	4	15	25	38	2	1	.344	.382
2008	Vermont (NYP)	SS	.278	70	227	42	63	12	0	10	38	63	56	11	9	.444	.463
2009	Hagerstown (SAL)	LoA	.286	126	437	78	125	30	0	23	84	90	116	6	3	.413	.513
2010	Potomac (CAR)	HiA	.235	94	298	67	70	19	0	12	49	89	94	6	3	.419	.419
Minor League Totals			.261	327	1085	203	283	67	2	49	186	267	304	25	16	.414	.462

3 DANNY ESPINOSA, SS/2B

Born: April 25, 1987. **B-T:** B-R. **Ht.:** 6-0. **Wt.:** 190. **Drafted:** Long Beach State, 2008 (3rd round). **Signed by:** Mark Baca.

Espinosa was one of three minor leaguers to hit 20 homers and steal 20 bases in 2010. He also earned a September taste of the big leagues, following in the footsteps of fellow Long Beach State shortstops Bobby Crosby, Troy Tulowitzki and Evan Longoria. The switch-hitting Espinosa has a tightly wound frame and strong, quick wrists that generate excellent bat speed. He swings hard and has solid power despite his smallish frame, but the Nationals want him to be a bit less aggressive. Harrisburg hitting coach Troy Gingrich helped him make his upper and lower halves work together more effectively in his swing. If Espinosa can continue to refine his approach and setup he could become an average hitter, thanks to his excellent hand-eye coordination and bunting skills. Espinosa's plus-plus arm plays well at shortstop, and his instincts, intelligence and hands give him a chance to be a standout at second base or solid at short. An unorthodox defender, he worked hard to improve on backhand plays this year, but he still has some work to do. He has average speed but runs the bases well. Espinosa had surgery to remove the hamate bone in his right wrist in late November but should be ready to compete for Washington's second-base job in spring training. He projects as a solid regular.

Year	Club (League)	Class	AVG	G	AB	R	H	2B	3B	HR	RBI	BB	SO	SB	CS	OBP	SLG
2008	Vermont (NYP)	SS	.328	19	64	8	21	2	0	0	4	17	17	2	2	.476	.359
2009	Potomac (CAR)	HiA	.264	133	474	90	125	31	4	18	72	74	129	29	11	.375	.460
2010	Harrisburg (EL)	AA	.262	99	386	66	101	16	4	18	54	33	94	20	8	.334	.464
	Syracuse (IL)	AAA	.295	24	95	14	28	2	1	4	15	8	22	5	3	.349	.463
	Washington (NL)	MAJ	.214	28	103	16	22	4	1	6	15	9	30	0	2	.277	.447
Major League Totals			.214	28	103	16	22	4	1	6	15	9	30	0	2	.277	.447
Minor League Totals			.270	275	1019	178	275	51	9	40	145	132	262	56	24	.365	.455

4 A.J. COLE, RHP

Born: Jan. 5, 1992. **B-T:** R-R. **Ht.:** 6-4. **Wt.:** 180. **Drafted:** HS—Oviedo, Fla., 2010 (4th round). **Signed by:** Paul Tinnell.

Regarded as a potential top-10-overall pick heading into his senior year at Oviedo (Fla.) High in 2010, Cole got off to a slow start because of the flu and bad weather. His velocity dipped to 88-93 mph early in the year, though he touched the mid-90s later in the spring. Signability concerns dropped him in the draft, and the Nationals were elated to get him in the fourth round. He signed a day before the Aug. 16 deadline for $2 million—a record for the round. Cole has an athletic, projectable frame and a loose, electric arm. He attacks the strike zone with his fastball and curveball, and his low-maintenance delivery suggests he'll have at least solid-average command. His fastball topped out at 93 mph in instructional league,

BRIAN FLEMING

but he regularly has reached 95-97 in the past. As he matures physically, his heater should be a premium pitch. Cole's 76-80 mph spike curveball has short 11-to-5 break, good rotation and depth, giving him the makings of a second plus offering. He also has feel for a changeup, though it's inconsistent. He's an intense competitor with a professional approach to preparation. Cole has frontline-starter upside and could move fairly quickly for a high school draftee. With one pro inning under his belt, he'll probably open 2011 in low Class A.

Year	Club (League)	Class	W	L	ERA	G	GS	CG	SV	IP	H	HR	BB	SO	G/A	WHIP	AVG
2010	Vermont (NYP)	SS	0	0	0.00	1	0	0	0	1	1	0	1	1	—	2.00	.333
Minor League Totals			0	0	0.00	1	0	0	0	1	1	0	1	1	—	2.00	.333

5 WILSON RAMOS, C

Born: Aug. 8, 1987. **B-T:** R-R. **Ht.:** 6-0. **Wt.:** 220. **Signed:** Venezuela, 2004. **Signed by:** Jose Leon (Twins).

Ramos had ranked as one of the Twins' best prospects since 2007, but he also found himself blocked by Joe Mauer. In need of a closer, Minnesota traded him and lefthander Joe Testa to the Nationals for all-star Matt Capps last July. Ramos spent September in Washington, then put together a solid winter in the Venezuela League. Strong and physical, Ramos stands out for his defensive skills behind the plate and his power potential. He's a good receiver with soft hands, and his plus arm helped him throw out an International League-best 50 percent of basestealers in 2010. He's still learning to call games and manage pitchers, but he has plenty of aptitude. Ramos has good loft and leverage in his swing, giving him a chance to hit for solid-average or slightly better power in time. He does get pull-happy, and he must improve his contact rate and patience at the plate. Conditioning has been an issue for Ramos in the past, and he's a well below-average runner. Ramos might never be an average hitter, but his defense and power potential still could make him a valuable everyday catcher. He should battle for time behind the plate in Washington this year.

Year	Club (League)	Class	AVG	G	AB	R	H	2B	3B	HR	RBI	BB	SO	SB	CS	OBP	SLG
2005	Twins (DSL)	R	.252	39	127	16	32	5	1	1	15	8	13	1	0	.295	.331
2006	Twins (GCL)	R	.286	46	154	18	44	12	1	3	26	12	14	4	2	.339	.435
2007	Beloit (MWL)	LoA	.291	73	292	40	85	17	1	8	42	19	61	1	1	.345	.438
2008	Fort Myers (FSL)	HiA	.288	126	452	50	130	23	2	13	78	37	103	0	1	.346	.434
2009	Twins (GCL)	R	.316	5	19	4	6	1	1	3	6	0	0	0	0	.316	.947
	New Britain (EL)	AA	.317	54	205	31	65	16	1	4	29	6	23	0	0	.341	.454
2010	Minnesota (AL)	MAJ	.296	7	27	2	8	3	0	0	1	0	3	0	0	.321	.407
	Rochester (IL)	AAA	.241	71	278	25	67	14	0	5	30	12	49	1	2	.280	.345
	Syracuse (IL)	AAA	.316	20	79	14	25	3	1	3	8	3	12	0	0	.341	.494
	Washington (NL)	MAJ	.269	15	52	3	14	4	0	1	4	2	9	0	0	.296	.404
Major League Totals			.278	22	79	5	22	7	0	1	5	2	12	0	0	.305	.405
Minor League Totals			.283	434	1606	198	454	91	7	40	234	97	275	7	6	.329	.423

6 SAMMY SOLIS, LHP

Born: Aug. 10, 1988. **B-T:** R-L. **Ht.:** 6-5. **Wt.:** 230. **Drafted:** San Diego, 2010 (2nd round). **Signed by:** Tim Reynolds.

Solis missed nearly all of 2009 because of a herniated disc in his back, but he rebounded to go 9-2, 3.42 with 92 strikeouts in 92 innings as a redshirt sophomore at San Diego last spring. The 51st overall selection in the 2010 draft, he signed two days before the Aug. 16 deadline for $1 million. He impressed against older competition in the Arizona Fall League, posting a 3.80 ERA in 24 innings. His family owns an AIDS orphanage in Africa. With a big, physical frame and an easy arm action, Solis projects as a mid-rotation workhorse. He has good command and feel for his three-pitch mix, highlighted by a plus changeup that he throws with good arm speed and deception. He pitched at 88-92 mph with late life on his fastball last spring, then sat at 91-92 in the fall and topped out at 94. Solis adds and subtracts from a knuckle-curve that ranges from 74-81 mph. It's a true downer with good depth when he stays on top of it. Some scouts think his three-quarters to low-three-quarters arm slot is better suited for a slider. A polished strike-thrower with an unflappable mound demeanor, Solis figures to jump to high Class A to start his first full pro season and could reach Double-A in the second half. He could arrive in Washington by 2012.

Year	Club (League)	Class	W	L	ERA	G	GS	CG	SV	IP	H	HR	BB	SO	G/A	WHIP	AVG
2010	Hagerstown (SAL)	LoA	0	0	0.00	2	2	0	0	4	2	0	0	3	0.80	0.50	.143
Minor League Totals			0	0	0.00	2	2	0	0	4	2	0	0	3	0.80	0.50	.143

7 COLE KIMBALL, RHP

Born: Aug. 1, 1985. **B-T:** R-R. **Ht.:** 6-3. **Wt.:** 225. **Drafted:** Centenary (N.J.), 2006 (12th round). **Signed by:** Alex Smith.

Kimball ranked as the top draft prospect in a weak New Jersey college crop in 2006 based solely on his arm strength, but he was regarded as a long-term project who needed to transform from thrower to pitcher. The Nationals used him as a starter for his first three pro seasons to get him innings, but he found a home in the bullpen in 2009 and broke out in 2010, capped by a dominant turn in the Arizona Fall League that earned him a spot on the 40-man roster. Kimball has taken off as he's learned to control his big, physical body. He has a long arm action and a high arm slot, but he has figured out how to repeat his mechanics fairly well, and he's throwing increasingly more quality strikes. Kimball attacks hitters with a heavy fastball that ranges from 93-98 mph. His 83-87 splitter is a swing-and-miss offering that ranges from average to plus-plus. Kimball has learned to throw his low-80s curveball for strikes early in counts, and it gives him a third out pitch at times. He has a fierce mound presence. Kimball will compete for a big league bullpen job out of spring training, though some seasoning at Triple-A Syracuse would do him some good. He projects as the future set-up man for Drew Storen in Washington.

Year	Club (League)	Class	W	L	ERA	G	GS	CG	SV	IP	H	HR	BB	SO	G/A	WHIP	AVG
2006	Vermont (NYP)	SS	1	4	5.82	16	5	0	0	34	43	3	24	28	—	1.97	.307
2007	Vermont (NYP)	SS	3	6	4.20	14	13	0	1	64	52	4	40	72	—	1.43	.223
2008	Hagerstown (SAL)	LoA	6	8	5.05	28	27	1	0	128	103	5	83	122	—	1.45	.226
2009	Potomac (CAR)	HiA	4	5	6.36	39	0	0	9	47	49	4	28	52	0.72	1.65	.269
2010	Potomac (CAR)	HiA	3	0	1.82	19	0	0	6	25	17	0	8	27	1.41	1.01	.210
	Harrisburg (EL)	AA	5	1	2.33	38	0	0	12	54	33	4	31	74	1.02	1.19	.171
Minor League Totals			22	24	4.50	154	45	1	28	352	297	20	214	375	0.95	1.45	.231

8 EURY PEREZ, OF

Born: May 30, 1990. **B-T:** R-R. **Ht.:** 6-0. **Wt.:** 180. **Signed:** Dominican Republic, 2007. **Signed by:** Dana Brown/Moises de la Mota.

After winning the Rookie-level Gulf Coast League batting title with a .381 average in 2009, Perez posted a .571 OPS Hagerstown in the first two months of last season. The Nationals were prepared to send him down to short-season Vermont once its season began. But after Hagerstown hitting coach Tony Tarasco and Nats minor league hitting coordinator Rick Schu worked with him on minimizing his leg kick and staying inside the ball, Perez caught fire and had an .835 OPS in the second half. Perez sticks out most with his well above-average speed, and he became a much better basestealer last year. He finished second in the minors with 64 steals and succeeded at an 83 percent rate, up from 67 percent in 2009. The Nationals challenged him to play shallower in center field and trust that his speed would allow him to catch up with balls over his head. He projects as a plus defender with an average, accurate arm. Perez isn't a power hitter, but he's strong enough to drive the ball to the gaps. He thrives when he slashes the ball to the middle of the field, and he knows how to protect with two strikes. He has become a good bunter. Perez profiles as a tablesetter with premium speed and strong defensive skills in center. He'll advance to high Class A in 2011.

Year	Club (League)	Class	AVG	G	AB	R	H	2B	3B	HR	RBI	BB	SO	SB	CS	OBP	SLG
2007	Nationals 1 (DSL)	R	.253	51	158	41	40	5	1	0	14	32	39	15	5	.399	.297
2008	Nationals 1 (DSL)	R	.324	60	213	51	69	9	2	4	44	32	36	28	6	.428	.441
2009	Nationals (GCL)	R	.381	47	181	38	69	3	5	3	24	15	20	16	8	.443	.503
2010	Hagerstown (SAL)	LoA	.299	131	438	88	131	17	5	3	42	23	74	64	13	.345	.381
Minor League Totals			.312	289	990	218	309	34	13	10	124	102	169	123	32	.391	.403

9 CHRIS MARRERO, 1B

Born: July 2, 1988. **B-T:** R-R. **Ht.:** 6-3. **Wt.:** 210. **Drafted:** HS—Opa Locka, Fla., 2006 (1st round). **Signed by:** Tony Arango.

A 2006 first-round pick who signed for $1.625 million, Marrero ranked No. 1 on this list heading into the 2008 season, during which he broke the fibula in his right leg and tore ligaments in his ankle on a slide at home plate. After recovering, he turned in a solid Double-A performance in 2010 to claim a spot on Washington's 40-man roster. His brother Christian is a first baseman in the White Sox system. Marrero's ticket always has been his plus to plus-plus raw power, but he has yet to really tap into it in games. He has some length and leverage in his swing, and he has battled—with mixed success—to stride forward rather than step in the bucket. He expanded his strike zone too often when Double-A pitchers fed him a steady diet of breaking balls early last season, but he showed more discipline in the second half. Some scouts wonder if he'll hit enough to justify an everyday job, and he remains a defensive liability at first base. The

Nationals rave about his commitment to improving his agility and footwork in 2010, though he still needs more work. He's a well below-average runner. Marrero will advance to Triple-A to start 2011. Just 22, he still has time to develop into the middle-of-the-order slugger the Nationals always hoped he'd be.

Year	Club (League)	Class	AVG	G	AB	R	H	2B	3B	HR	RBI	BB	SO	SB	CS	OBP	SLG
2006	Nationals (GCL)	R	.309	22	81	10	25	9	0	0	16	8	19	0	0	.374	.420
2007	Hagerstown (SAL)	LoA	.293	57	222	31	65	14	0	14	53	14	39	0	4	.337	.545
	Potomac (CAR)	HiA	.259	68	255	40	66	11	3	9	35	32	63	0	0	.338	.431
2008	Potomac (CAR)	HiA	.250	70	256	40	64	15	2	11	38	25	55	0	0	.325	.453
2009	Potomac (CAR)	HiA	.287	112	414	58	119	21	2	16	65	42	97	2	3	.360	.464
	Harrisburg (EL)	AA	.267	23	75	9	20	6	0	1	11	8	18	0	1	.345	.387
2010	Harrisburg (EL)	AA	.294	141	524	73	154	28	0	18	82	43	102	1	3	.350	.450
Minor League Totals			.281	493	1827	261	513	104	7	69	300	172	393	3	11	.347	.459

10 BRAD PEACOCK, RHP

Born: Feb. 2, 1988. **B-T:** R-R. **Ht.:** 6-1. **Wt.:** 175. **Drafted:** Palm Beach (Fla.) CC, D/F 2006 (41st round). **Signed by:** Tony Arango.

Primarily a shortstop in high school, Peacock has made significant strides on the mound since signing with for $110,000 as a draft-and-follow in 2007. He led Nationals farmhands with 148 strikeouts in 142 innings last season, then racked up 17 more whiffs in 12 innings as a reliever in the Arizona Fall League. Peacock always has owned a quick, loose arm, and his velocity climbed last year, when his fastball sat at 92-94 mph and regularly topped out at 96. He's a bit undersized and often has struggled to pitch downhill, so the Nationals worked to help him turn his front shoulder more and keep his head down. He made some progress but still needs to do a better job working down in the zone. Peacock's knuckle-curve is a plus offering with sharp downer action that complements his straight fastball well. He also has developed a decent changeup to use against lefties, though it still lags behind his other two offerings. Peacock fields his position and holds runners well. Peacock has the arm strength and stuff to become a mid-rotation starter in the big leagues if he can put everything together. There's some sentiment that his AFL bullpen stint was a sign of things to come, and that his frame is better suited for relief. For now, he'll return to the Harrisburg rotation.

Year	Club (League)	Class	W	L	ERA	G	GS	CG	SV	IP	H	HR	BB	SO	G/A	WHIP	AVG
2007	Nationals (GCL)	R	1	1	3.89	13	7	0	0	39	38	1	15	34	—	1.35	.242
2008	Hagerstown (SAL)	LoA	0	5	9.09	8	8	0	0	34	38	8	21	23	—	1.75	.284
	Vermont (NYP)	SS	4	7	3.12	14	14	2	0	75	67	3	27	54	—	1.25	.235
2009	Hagerstown (SAL)	LoA	5	8	4.05	19	17	0	0	100	104	10	32	77	1.41	1.36	.272
	Potomac (CAR)	HiA	3	3	4.34	8	7	0	0	48	46	4	10	27	1.07	1.17	.253
2010	Potomac (CAR)	HiA	4	9	4.44	19	18	1	0	103	109	11	25	118	1.13	1.30	.268
	Harrisburg (EL)	AA	2	2	4.66	7	7	0	0	39	33	5	22	30	1.52	1.42	.234
Minor League Totals			19	35	4.44	88	78	3	0	438	435	42	152	363	1.26	1.34	.258

11 YUNESKY MAYA, RHP

Born: Aug. 28, 1981. **B-T:** R-R. **Ht.:** 5-11. **Wt.:** 170. **Signed:** Cuba, 2010. **Signed by:** Johnny DiPuglia.

A veteran of the big stage in Cuba, Maya pitched for Cuba in the World Baseball Classic in 2006 and 2009. In the latter year, he went 13-4, 2.22 in Cuba's Serie Nacionale and led the league in wins, innings and shutouts while ranking second to Aroldis Chapman in strikeouts. Maya defected that September to the Dominican Republic, where he lived for nine months before being authorized to sign with a major league team. The Nationals inked him to a four-year, $7.4 million contact that included a $1 million bonus last July. After five tuneup appearances in the minors, he came to Washington for five starts in September. When he was younger, Maya pitched in the low 90s and topped out at 96 mph, but in 2010, working his way back into form afer a long layoff, he worked at 88-91. His fastball still can be effective at lower velocities because he can cut and sink it. Maya lacks overpowering stuff but is a polished strike-thrower who knows how to work hitters. His best pitch is an average curveball that shows flashes of being a plus pitch. He adds and subtracts from his curve, which ranges from 76-82 mph. His 83-87 mph changeup has some splitter action, and his 82-85 mph slider gives him another serviceable pitch. Maya still has to learn the nuances of American baseball, including holding runners, but he fields his position well. He has a sturdy frame and repeats his easy arm action well, giving him a very good chance to be a back-of-the-rotation workhorse in the big leagues. That's where he figures to spend all of 2011.

Year	Club (League)	Class	W	L	ERA	G	GS	CG	SV	IP	H	HR	BB	SO	G/A	WHIP	AVG
2010	Nationals (GCL)	R	0	0	1.29	2	2	0	0	7	3	0	2	5	4.33	0.71	.125
	Potomac (CAR)	HiA	0	1	13.50	1	1	0	0	4	7	1	3	4	3.00	2.50	.389
	Syracuse (IL)	AAA	1	1	0.87	2	2	0	0	10	8	0	5	9	3.00	1.26	.211
	Washington (NL)	MAJ	0	3	5.88	5	5	0	0	26	30	3	11	12	0.81	1.58	.294
Major League Totals			0	3	5.88	5	5	0	0	26	30	3	11	12	0.81	1.58	.294
Minor League Totals			1	2	3.38	5	5	0	0	21	18	1	10	18	3.40	1.31	.225

12 DESTIN HOOD, OF

Born: April 3, 1990. **B-T:** R-R. **Ht.:** 6-1. **Wt.:** 225. **Drafted:** HS—Mobile, Ala., 2008 (2nd round). **Signed by:** Eric Robinson.

The Nationals say Hood made as much progress as anybody in their system in 2010. A wide receiver who passed up an Alabama football scholarship to sign for $1.1 million as a second-round pick in 2008, he was very raw when he entered the system. He got too big and lost some of his athleticism in 2009, so he dedicated himself to toning his body in the offseason and arrived at spring training 20 pounds lighter last year. Hood has tremendous bat speed and can backspin balls to the opposite field with authority. He has a compact swing and a middle-to-away approach, but he needs to learn to unload and drive the ball in hitter's counts in order to unlock his average to plus raw power. Hood's pitch recognition improved greatly last season, and his strikeouts decreased every month from April to July. He'll still chase sliders out of the zone at times, though. Getting in better shape helped Hood improve his speed—which is back up to average—and he took dramatic steps forward defensively in the outfield. His throwing motion was stiff in the past, but he has improved his release and done a better job of incorporating his lower half. He projects as a solid left fielder with fringy arm strength. Hood is still far from a finished product, but the Nats are excited about his development. He'll advance to high Class A Potomac in 2011.

Year	Club (League)	Class	AVG	G	AB	R	H	2B	3B	HR	RBI	BB	SO	SB	CS	OBP	SLG
2008	Nationals (GCL)	R	.256	25	86	18	22	6	1	0	14	8	19	5	2	.333	.349
2009	Nationals (GCL)	R	.330	25	88	18	29	10	3	3	24	8	19	3	0	.388	.614
	Vermont (NYP)	SS	.246	38	138	12	34	4	1	2	24	11	45	2	1	.302	.333
2010	Hagerstown (SAL)	LoA	.285	129	492	56	140	30	3	5	65	33	119	5	7	.333	.388
Minor League Totals			.280	217	804	104	225	50	8	10	127	60	202	15	10	.334	.399

13 STEVE LOMBARDOZZI, 2B

Born: Sept. 20, 1988. **B-T:** B-R. **Ht.:** 6-0. **Wt.:** 170. **Drafted:** St. Petersburg (Fla.) JC, 2008 (19th round). **Signed by:** Paul Tinnell.

Lombardozzi is a quintessential baseball rat, no surprise considering his father Steve played in the big leagues and was a member of the Twins' 1987 World Series champions. Though his tools are modest, the younger Lombardozzi has hit at each minor league stop so far in his career, including Double-A in the second half of 2010 and the Arizona Fall League. He batted .293/.385/.439 for the league-champion Scottsdale Scorpions this fall and won the AFL's Dernell Stenson Sportsmanship Award. Lombardozzi makes consistent contact and has excellent bat control from both sides of the plate. He has a balanced setup and an efficient swing. He's also a disciplined hitter who works counts and simply finds ways to get on base. He has well below-average power, but he's strong enough to drive some balls into the gaps. He's a solid-average runner and is aggressive on the basepaths. A shortstop in college, Lombardozzi has taken to second base in pro ball and made just nine errors in 134 games there last year. His average range plays up because he positions himself well and reads balls nicely off the bat. His arm is fringy at best, but his hands are above-average. He's still working on his pivots around the bag and his throws from the backhand side. He filled in ably at shortstop in the AFL, showing off valuable versatility. Lombardozzi figures to reach Triple-A in 2011, and he has a chance to be an everyday second baseman or a valuable, high-energy reserve.

Year	Club (League)	Class	AVG	G	AB	R	H	2B	3B	HR	RBI	BB	SO	SB	CS	OBP	SLG
2008	Nationals (GCL)	R	.283	48	152	23	43	4	1	0	24	21	32	4	1	.371	.322
2009	Hagerstown (SAL)	LoA	.296	128	496	90	147	26	7	3	58	62	80	16	7	.375	.395
2010	Potomac (CAR)	HiA	.293	110	440	71	129	30	9	1	38	49	60	20	10	.370	.409
	Harrisburg (EL)	AA	.295	27	105	19	31	5	2	5	11	12	15	4	2	.373	.524
Minor League Totals			.293	313	1193	203	350	65	19	9	131	144	187	44	20	.373	.402

14 RICK HAGUE, SS

Born: Sept. 18, 1988. **B-T:** R-R. **Ht.:** 6-2. **Wt.:** 190. **Drafted:** Rice, 2010 (3rd round). **Signed by:** Tyler Wilt.

Hague stepped right into Rice's starting shortstop job as a freshman in 2008, and he established himself as a first-round candidate after tying for the Team USA lead with a .371 batting average the summer after his sophomore year. But he got off to a brutal start in 2010, hitting .290 with metal bats and committing 22 errors in his first 38 games. Hague did finish strong, batting .413 and committing just one error in his final 24 contests. The Nationals were pleased to land him in the third round and sign him for $430,200. Hague batted .317 in his pro debut, but he also committed 20 errors in 38 games. He's a line-drive, gap-to-gap hitter who projects as an average or slightly better hitter with fringy power. He's streaky at the plate and can fall into ruts when he tries to pull everything. His fringy speed plays up because of his good instincts on the basepaths, and he's a better runner under way. Hague's defensive issues in 2010 largely stemmed from a loss of confidence and poor technique. He had trouble throwing accurately, but he does flash an above-average arm when he plays through the ball, rather than stopping when he fields it. He lacks the range to play shortstop in the major leagues and fits best defensively at third base, where he shined for Team USA in 2009. But scouts wonder if he'll hit for enough power for the hot corner. Hague is a grinder who gets the most out of his tools, and the Nationals will leave him at shortstop until he plays his way off the position. He could advance to high Class A to start his first full pro season.

Year	Club (League)	Class	AVG	G	AB	R	H	2B	3B	HR	RBI	BB	SO	SB	CS	OBP	SLG
2010	Nationals (GCL)	R	.275	10	40	7	11	1	0	0	6	8	9	3	0	.380	.300
	Hagerstown (SAL)	LoA	.327	39	159	26	52	12	5	3	27	14	34	3	2	.386	.522
Minor League Totals			.317	49	199	33	63	13	5	3	33	22	43	6	2	.385	.477

15 ROBBIE RAY, LHP

Born: Oct. 1, 1991. **B-T:** L-L. **Ht.:** 6-2. **Wt.:** 170. **Drafted:** HS—Brentwood, Tenn., 2010 (12th round). **Signed by:** Paul Faulk.

Ray garnered early-rounds draft buzz after running his fastball into the mid-90s on the showcase circuit in 2009, but when the velocity on his fastball and breaking ball dropped last spring, so did his draft stock. Even so, he threw three no-hitters as a high school senior, including a five-inning perfect game. He slipped to the 12th round of the draft, and the Nationals signed him away from a commitment to Arkansas the day before the Aug. 16 deadline with a $799,000 bonus. He pitched one inning at Vermont, then had a solid instructional league. Ray's fastball sat at 89-91 with natural late movement in the spring, and his whippy arm action and projectable, athletic frame suggest he could have a plus heater in time. His No. 2 pitch is a quality changeup with late fade. He needs to tighten up his slurvy breaking ball, but it projects as an average pitch. Ray has good feel for pitching for his age and has a chance to be a quality mid-rotation starter down the road. He figures to begin 2011 in extended spring training, then head to the Nationals' new short-season Auburn affiliate.

Year	Club (League)	Class	W	L	ERA	G	GS	CG	SV	IP	H	HR	BB	SO	G/A	WHIP	AVG
2010	Vermont (NYP)	SS	0	0	0.00	1	0	0	0	1	0	0	0	2	—	0.00	.000
Minor League Totals			0	0	0.00	1	0	0	0	1	0	0	0	2	—	0.00	.000

16 TOM MILONE, LHP

Born: Feb. 16, 1987. **B-T:** L-L. **Ht.:** 6-1. **Wt.:** 205. **Drafted:** Southern California, 2008 (10th round). **Signed by:** Craig Kornfield.

Milone spent three seasons in Southern California's starting rotation, learning to keep the ball down as he progressed. As a result, he cut his home run total from 16 as a freshman to eight as a sophomore to four as a junior in 2008, when the Nationals signed him for $65,000 as a 10th-round pick. He lacks overpowering stuff and has had to prove himself at every level, but he has done just that, putting himself on the prospect map. Milone's below-average fastball sits at 85-87 and maxes out at 90, but it plays up because of his deception and command. He has a slow, funky delivery that disrupts batters' timing, and his ball seems to jump on them. He throws his above-average changeup, average cutter and fringy curveball with exactly the same delivery and arm action as his fastball, and he keeps opponents off balance by mixing speeds and locations. Perhaps Milone's greatest strength is his ability to read hitters and expose their weaknesses. He also excels at fielding his position and holding runners—he allowed just four steals in 10 attempts last year—and he handles the bat well for a pitcher. Milone lacks upside, but he has a good shot to be a back-of-the-rotation starter in the big leagues, perhaps as soon as 2011. He'll start the season in Triple-A.

Year	Club (League)	Class	W	L	ERA	G	GS	CG	SV	IP	H	HR	BB	SO	G/A	WHIP	AVG
2008	Vermont (NYP)	SS	1	3	4.57	6	3	0	0	22	27	4	3	22	—	1.38	.307
	Hagerstown (SAL)	LoA	0	3	2.89	7	7	0	0	37	36	0	6	27	—	1.13	.257
2009	Potomac (CAR)	HiA	12	5	2.91	27	25	0	0	151	144	9	36	106	0.95	1.19	.257
2010	Harrisburg (EL)	AA	12	5	2.85	27	27	2	0	158	161	10	23	155	1.20	1.16	.261
Minor League Totals			25	16	2.98	67	62	2	0	368	368	23	68	310	1.06	1.18	.262

17 ADRIAN SANCHEZ, 2B/3B

Born: Aug. 16, 1990. **B-T:** B-R. **Ht.:** 6-0. **Wt.:** 175. **Signed:** Venezuela, 2007. **Signed by:** Mike Rizzo/Dana Brown.

Then-assistant GM Mike Rizzo and former scouting director Dana Brown signed Sanchez and catcher Sandy Leon, a defensive stalwart, on the same trip to Venezuela in 2007. Both players have turned themselves into prospects. Sanchez spent three years in Rookie ball before breaking out in 2010, when he batted .378 in the Gulf Coast League and .317 at Hagerstown. A switch-hitter, he has a compact, line-drive swing from both sides of the plate. He uses the whole field, has decent pop to the gaps and is a good situational hitter. He has an aggressive approach and doesn't walk much, however. He's an average runner. Sanchez played every infield position except first base in 2010, and he profiles best as second base because he lacks the range for shortstop or the power potential for third. His soft hands, good actions and sound footwork around the bag should make him at least an average defender at second base, where his arm also plays well. Sanchez figures to return to low Class A to start 2011 but could earn a promotion by midseason.

Year	Club (League)	Class	AVG	G	AB	R	H	2B	3B	HR	RBI	BB	SO	SB	CS	OBP	SLG
2007	Nationals1 (DSL)	R	.269	42	145	21	39	11	1	1	19	12	25	4	3	.354	.379
2008	Nationals 1 (DSL)	R	.282	58	227	40	64	13	1	3	32	19	36	21	3	.340	.388
2009	Nationals (GCL)	R	.246	24	65	13	16	7	0	0	5	3	6	3	0	.271	.354
2010	Nationals (GCL)	R	.378	29	119	23	45	10	0	3	21	2	15	4	2	.395	.538
	Hagerstown (SAL)	LoA	.317	25	104	15	33	1	0	1	15	0	18	0	2	.330	.356
Minor League Totals			.298	178	660	112	197	42	2	8	92	36	100	32	10	.344	.405

18 A.J. MORRIS, RHP

Born: Dec. 1, 1986. **B-T:** R-R. **Ht.:** 6-2. **Wt.:** 185. **Drafted:** Kansas State, 2009 (4th round). **Signed by:** Kerrick Jackson.

Morris went from undrafted redshirt sophomore in 2008 to first-team All-American and fourth-round pick in 2009, thanks largely to improved mechanics and command. He started his first full pro season in the Potomac rotation, but the wear and tear of starting every fifth day gave him a sore arm, so the Nationals moved him to the bullpen in August. Morris' fastball played up in his new role, sitting at 93-95 mph, and his arm felt better once Washington limited him to two innings per outing. His lack of a reliable changeup probably makes him better suited for relief anyway. Morris' fastball has explosive, heavy sink and bore, helping him post a 2.16 groundout/airout ratio as a pro. He also has a solid slider with hard bite that he can throw for strikes or use as a chase pitch. He commands his fastball better than his slider, and he attacks the strike zone aggressively. The Nationals are still having him work on a changeup, but it has a ways to go. Morris could move quickly as a reliever. He'll start the season in Double-A and could reach Washington by the second half.

Year	Club (League)	Class	W	L	ERA	G	GS	CG	SV	IP	H	HR	BB	SO	G/A	WHIP	AVG
2009	Nationals (GCL)	R	0	0	0.00	2	2	0	0	5	0	0	0	4	4.00	0.00	.000
	Hagerstown (SAL)	LoA	0	4	3.82	8	8	0	0	38	44	2	8	36	1.80	1.38	.297
2010	Potomac (CAR)	HiA	5	3	3.88	23	12	0	2	72	67	4	27	61	2.40	1.31	.240
	Nationals (GCL)	R	0	0	3.21	4	4	0	0	14	9	1	1	10	1.73	0.71	.176
Minor League Totals			5	7	3.64	37	26	0	2	129	120	7	36	111	2.16	1.21	.243

19 MICHAEL BURGESS, OF

Born: Oct. 20, 1988. **B-T:** L-L. **Ht.:** 5-11. **Wt.:** 195. **Drafted:** HS—Tampa, 2007 (1st round supplemental). **Signed by:** Paul Tinnell.

A supplemental first-round pick who was once regarded among the top prospects in the system, Burgess foundered in high Class A, spending most of the last three seasons there before finally getting a promotion last August. Burgess always has possessed provocative power, but his mighty hacks result in loads of strikeouts. The Nationals asked him to try to control his swing more and use more of the field in 2010. He made a bit of progress in that regard, but he still projects to be a below-average hitter at best. His raw power ranks second only to Bryce Harper's among Washington farmhands, but scouts wonder if he'll ever make enough contact to make his pop usable. At the end of 2009, the Nationals were concerned about where Burgess' stocky build was headed, but he dedicated himself to conditioning in the offseason. His efforts helped his mobility in right field, though he's still a below-average runner. He has a strong, accurate arm, and he loves to throw. Burgess plays the game hard, and at 22 years old, he still has time to make the necessary offensive adjustments. His power and arm give him a chance to be an everyday right fielder if he can improve his feel for hitting. He'll head back to Double-A to begin 2011.

Year	Club (League)	Class	AVG	G	AB	R	H	2B	3B	HR	RBI	BB	SO	SB	CS	OBP	SLG
2007	Nationals (GCL)	R	.336	36	128	22	43	6	3	8	32	25	37	1	2	.442	.617
	Vermont (NYP)	SS	.286	19	70	10	20	1	1	3	10	10	23	1	1	.383	.457
2008	Hagerstown (SAL)	LoA	.249	112	401	60	100	26	4	18	60	46	136	5	1	.335	.469
	Potomac (CAR)	HiA	.225	19	71	12	16	3	0	6	19	9	26	0	2	.325	.521
2009	Potomac (CAR)	HiA	.235	131	480	63	113	23	2	19	71	54	135	12	8	.325	.410
2010	Potomac (CAR)	HiA	.262	101	386	57	101	21	4	12	70	47	89	5	2	.351	.430
	Harrisburg (EL)	AA	.284	21	74	11	21	5	2	6	15	10	27	0	0	.391	.649
Minor League Totals			.257	439	1610	235	414	85	16	72	277	201	473	24	16	.349	.464

20 ELVIN RAMIREZ, RHP

Born: Oct. 10, 1987. **B-T:** R-R. **Ht.:** 6-3. **Wt.:** 210. **Signed:** Dominican Republic, 2004. **Signed by:** Eddy Toledo/Rafael Bournigal (Mets).

Ramirez signed with the Mets as a 16-year-old and spent three seasons in Rookie ball, followed by two more in low Class A. New York converted him from starter to reliever in 2010, and he pitched well enough to earn a late-season promotion to Double-A. After he Mets declined to protect him on their 40-man roster, his stock climbed after he ran his fastball up to 99 mph in the Dominican Winter League. The Nationals selected him with the fifth pick in the major league Rule 5 draft. In the past, Ramirez worked at 89-94 mph with his fastball, with some scouts speculating his velocity would increase if he could lengthen his short stride in the front. He showed improved control in winter ball after averaging 4.8 walks per nine innings in six minor league seasons. Ramirez throws a changeup, curveball and slider, though none stands out as more than serviceable. He'll have to prove his progress this winter is for real, but Ramirez was worth a flier for an organization lacking in live arms. Though he has made just three appearances above Class A, he'll have to make the jump to the big leagues to remain Washington property. He can't be sent to the minors unless he clears waivers and New York declines to take him back for half his $50,000 draft price.

Year	Club (League)	Class	W	L	ERA	G	GS	CG	SV	IP	H	HR	BB	SO	G/A	WHIP	AVG
2005	Mets (DSL)	R	2	6	6.53	16	6	0	0	40	48	2	23	24	—	1.78	.284
2006	Mets (DSL)	R	0	1	2.63	11	6	0	0	27	16	0	10	28	—	0.95	.165
2007	Kingsport (APP)	R	1	4	5.52	12	12	0	0	46	52	5	29	48	—	1.77	.280
2008	Savannah (SAL)	LoA	6	7	3.67	18	18	0	0	81	81	1	36	62	—	1.44	.257
2009	Savannah (SAL)	LoA	3	7	4.09	15	15	0	0	73	73	2	39	48	1.16	1.54	.261
2010	St. Lucie (FSL)	HiA	4	3	4.17	49	0	0	0	73	56	0	43	65	1.38	1.35	.212
	Binghamton (EL)	AA	0	1	4.05	3	0	0	0	7	5	2	6	7	0.71	1.65	.208
Minor League Totals			16	29	4.36	124	57	0	0	347	331	12	186	282	1.23	1.49	.248

21 JEFF KOBERNUS, 2B

Born: June 30, 1988. **B-T:** R-R. **Ht.:** 6-2. **Wt.:** 210. **Drafted:** California, 2009 (2nd round). **Signed by:** Ryan Fox.

Kobernus hasn't been able to stay healthy since signing for $705,500 as a second-round pick in 2009. His pro debut was cut short after 10 games by an old knee injury that required surgery. He was back on the field by last spring, but he missed a month early and a month late with more nagging injuries. The Nationals think his aggressive style of play has led to some of his physical setbacks. The son of a former Athletics minor leaguer of the same name, Kobernus is a baseball rat who plays the game hard. He has a nice line-drive stroke, but Washington wants him to do a better job controlling the strike zone. He's strong enough to drive balls to the gaps but his home run power is below average at best. Kobernus is an excellent athlete with above-average speed and good baserunning instincts. His solid range, hands and arm strength give him a chance to be a good defender at second base, but he's still learning the finer points of the position after playing mostly third base in college. Kobernus has the skill set to be an everyday big league second baseman, but he must prove he can stay on the field and he needs to refine his overall game. He should start 2011 in high Class A.

Year	Club (League)	Class	AVG	G	AB	R	H	2B	3B	HR	RBI	BB	SO	SB	CS	OBP	SLG
2009	Vermont (NYP)	SS	.220	10	41	8	9	1	0	0	2	2	5	4	0	.273	.244
2010	Hagerstown (SAL)	LoA	.279	74	312	40	87	18	0	1	42	17	58	21	10	.316	.346
Minor League Totals			.272	84	353	48	96	19	0	1	44	19	63	25	10	.311	.334

22 JASON MARTINSON, SS

Born: Oct. 15, 1988. **B-T:** R-R. **Ht.:** 6-1. **Wt.:** 190. **Drafted:** Texas State, 2010 (5th round). **Signed by:** Tyler Wilt.

Martinson arrived at Texas State on a football scholarship, but he tore his hamstring on his first catch as a wide receiver and then decided to focus on baseball. After hitting .153 as a freshman, he made great strides over his next two seasons, playing his way into the fifth round of the 2010 draft and a $174,000 bonus. Wiry strong and athletic, Martinson has quick hands and should be able to drive balls into the gaps, with occasional home run pop. He must improve at recognizing breaking balls and laying off pitches out of the zone. He also needs to shorten his swing a bit and focus on using the middle of the field instead of getting pull-happy. His bat speed and hand-eye coordination give him a chance to hit for a solid average as he matures. Martinson also has the hands and actions for shortstop, but he needs to refine his footwork and become more consistent. He has above-average arm strength and throws with minimal effort. He's a slightly above-average runner. Martinson is ultra-competitive and plays the game with an edge. His upside is that of an everyday shortstop, but he has plenty of rough edges to polish before he'll be ready for the upper levels of the game. He'll advance to low Class A in 2011.

Year	Club (League)	Class	AVG	G	AB	R	H	2B	3B	HR	RBI	BB	SO	SB	CS	OBP	SLG
2010	Vermont (NYP)	SS	.241	70	253	38	61	8	6	2	36	38	74	4	2	.346	.344
Minor League Totals			.241	70	253	38	61	8	6	2	36	38	74	4	2	.346	.344

23 DANNY ROSENBAUM, LHP

Born: Oct. 10, 1987. **B-T:** R-L. **Ht.:** 6-1. **Wt.:** 210. **Drafted:** Xavier, 2009 (22nd round). **Signed by:** Alex Smith.

After helping Xavier reach its first NCAA regional—where he struck out nine in a win against Sam Houston State—Rosenbaum signed for a bargain bonus of $20,000 as a 22nd-round pick in 2009. He dominated younger competition in the Gulf Coast League in his pro debut, then proved that was no fluke by carving up Class A hitters in 2010. Rosenbaum is a polished strike-thrower and a dogged competitor. His 88-91 mph fastball plays up because he naturally cuts it, allowing him to jam righthanders. The life on his heater also helps him rack up groundouts—2.03 of them for every airout as a pro. He can throw his solid curveball for strikes or use it as a putaway pitch. The Nationals believe Rosenbaum is a solid changeup away from the big leagues. He started throwing the pitch more after his promotion to Potomac, and it has the makings of a serviceable offering. Rosenbaum repeats his mechanics well and has good command of the strike zone. He's not as tall as John Lannan, but Washington envisions him becoming a crafty innings-eating starter in the same mold. He'll head to Double-A to open 2011 and could get a taste of the big leagues by season's end.

Year	Club (League)	Class	W	L	ERA	G	GS	CG	SV	IP	H	HR	BB	SO	G/A	WHIP	AVG
2009	Nationals (GCL)	R	4	1	1.95	11	8	0	0	37	29	1	9	38	1.59	1.03	.215
2010	Hagerstown (SAL)	LoA	2	5	2.32	18	18	0	0	101	95	5	28	84	2.90	1.22	.253
	Potomac (CAR)	HiA	3	2	2.09	8	7	0	0	43	35	2	13	31	1.25	1.12	.230
Minor League Totals			9	8	2.19	37	33	0	0	181	159	8	50	153	2.03	1.15	.240

24 TYLER MOORE, 1B

Born: Jan. 30, 1987. **B-T:** R-R. **Ht.:** 6-2. **Wt.:** 185. **Drafted:** Mississippi State, 2008 (16th round). **Signed by:** Eric Robinson.

The Nationals drafted Moore in the 41st round out of high school and again in the 33rd round after his first year at Meridian (Miss.) CC. As a sophomore at Meridian, he led national juco players with 19 homers and ranked fourth in batting .472, and he followed up by hitting 14 homers at Mississippi State in 2008. The Nats drafted him for a third time that June and finally signed him for $55,000 in the 16th round. Moore led all Washington farmhands with 87 RBIs in his first full pro season, then won Carolina League MVP honors last year after topping the high Class A circuit in doubles (43), homers (31), RBIs (111), extra-base hits (77) and slugging percentage (.552). His 2010 was a tale of two very different halves, as he hit .197 with nine homers before the all-star break and .346 with 22 homers afterward. Moore is a very good fastball hitter who doesn't miss mistakes when he's locked in. Early in the year, he got too geared up when he saw a pitch to attack, causing him to dip his barrel and swing through or foul off the pitch. He was more direct to the ball in the second half. Moore has above-average power potential and can hit the ball hard from pole to pole. He still must prove that he's a good enough hitter to handle upper-level pitching, but the ball carries very well off his bat. Moore's strong arm led the Nationals to consider moving him behind the plate or to right field after drafting him, but he lacks the athleticism to play any position but first base. He might have playable mobility and hands there, but he needs to improve his pitch-to-pitch focus and his technique, and he'll never be a standout defender. He has well below-average speed. Moore's bat will have to carry him, but he at least has entered the conversation about Washington's first baseman of the future. He'll advance to Double-A in 2011.

Year	Club (League)	Class	AVG	G	AB	R	H	2B	3B	HR	RBI	BB	SO	SB	CS	OBP	SLG
2008	Vermont (NYP)	SS	.200	71	265	17	53	10	0	6	28	13	66	1	1	.239	.306
2009	Hagerstown (SAL)	LoA	.297	111	421	38	125	30	3	9	87	40	111	2	2	.363	.447
2010	Potomac (CAR)	HiA	.269	129	502	78	135	43	3	31	111	40	125	0	0	.321	.552
Minor League Totals			.263	311	1188	133	313	83	6	46	226	93	302	3	3	.319	.460

25 J.P. RAMIREZ, OF

Born: Sept. 29, 1989. **B-T:** L-L. **Ht.:** 5-10. **Wt.:** 185. **Drafted:** HS—New Braunfels, Texas, 2008 (15th round). **Signed by:** Tyler Wilt.

Ramirez grew up with a batting cage in his backyard and he loves to hit. The Nationals bought him out of a commitment to Tulane with a 15th-round-record $1 million just before the signing deadline in 2008. He struggled in 2009 but got back on track last year in low Class A, showing the offensive promise that earned him that big bonus and making significant strides on defense. Ramirez has a smooth, compact lefthanded swing and textbook hitting mechanics. He has good bat speed and average power despite his smaller frame. His bat will have to carry him through the upper levels of the system, but he must control the strike zone better and become more selective in order to reach his ceiling as an above-average hitter. Defense was a major weakness for Ramirez heading into the season, but he worked hard to improve his jumps and routes. He also must become more efficient and accurate with his throwing. He's still a below-average runner, defender and thrower, but he's getting closer to passable in left field. Ramirez will try to carry his momentum into 2011, when he's ticketed for high Class A.

Year	Club (League)	Class	AVG	G	AB	R	H	2B	3B	HR	RBI	BB	SO	SB	CS	OBP	SLG
2008	Nationals (GCL)	R	.364	5	11	2	4	0	0	0	8	4	0	0	0	.533	.364
2009	Vermont (NYP)	SS	.264	72	295	35	78	18	6	4	39	14	45	6	9	.306	.407
2010	Hagerstown (SAL)	LoA	.296	132	506	74	150	32	4	16	75	25	83	3	6	.341	.470
Minor League Totals			.286	209	812	111	232	50	10	20	122	43	128	9	15	.332	.446

26 RYAN TATUSKO, RHP

Born: March 27, 1985. **B-T:** R-R. **Ht.:** 6-5. **Wt.:** 200. **Drafted:** Indiana State, 2007 (18th round). **Signed by:** Derek Lee (Rangers).

Tatusko had Tommy John surgery as a high school senior and redshirted in 2004 at Indiana State. After a solid three-year career, he was drafted in the 18th round by the Rangers, signed for $20,000 and advanced steadily through their system. Texas traded him and righthander Tanner Roark to get Cristian Guzman from the Nationals last July. Tatusko made a positive first impression with his new organization, posting the best ERA (1.72) and strikeout rate (8.8 per nine innings) of his career over 37 innings at Harrisburg. Tatusko's 6-foot-5 frame helps him create excellent leverage. He pitched at 93-94 mph and ran his fastball up to 97 after the trade. He also showed an improved ability to throw his fastball for strikes. His secondary pitches lag behind his fastball, but his slider does have a chance to become an average offering and his changeup has some sink to it. Big and durable, Tatusko has a chance to be an innings-eating starter in the big leagues, though his lack of pinpoint command or standout secondary stuff might make him a better fit in relief at some point. He could compete for a big league job in spring training, but he's likely to start 2011 in Triple-A.

Year	Club (League)	Class	W	L	ERA	G	GS	CG	SV	IP	H	HR	BB	SO	G/A	WHIP	AVG
2007	Spokane (NWL)	SS	3	7	4.13	16	13	0	0	65	66	4	22	50	—	1.35	.262
2008	Clinton (MWL)	LoA	3	11	4.46	32	16	0	1	113	113	9	42	96	—	1.37	.256
2009	Bakersfield (CAL)	HiA	7	6	4.64	29	16	1	0	120	123	4	38	86	1.98	1.34	.265
2010	Frisco (TL)	AA	9	2	2.97	24	13	1	0	100	94	2	40	58	1.88	1.34	.254
	Harrisburg (EL)	AA	3	1	1.72	6	6	0	0	37	30	2	13	36	2.35	1.17	.222
Minor League Totals			25	27	3.89	107	64	2	1	435	426	26	155	326	1.98	1.33	.256

27 BRAD MEYERS, RHP

Born: Sept. 13, 1985. **B-T:** R-R. **Ht.:** 6-6. **Wt.:** 195. **Drafted:** Loyola Marymount, 2007 (5th round). **Signed by:** Craig Kornfield.

Durability has been a repeated question about Meyers since he turned pro as a fifth-round pick in 2007. A dead arm caused his velocity to dip into the mid-80s in 2008. He missed a few starts with a heel injury in 2009, though he led the minors with a 1.72 ERA and earned the Nationals' minor league pitcher of the year award. That December, he had left foot surgery to address a stress fracture suffered while jogging months earlier, and he didn't make his 2010 debut until May. After a dominant six-start stretch, Meyers was sidelined for the rest of the season because screws from his surgery caused problems with the bone in his foot. He had another operation in the fall, and while Washington believes his second surgery was more successful, he may not be completely healthy for the start of the 2011 season. When healthy, Meyers pounds the zone with a polished four-pitch mix. His 88-90 mph fastball bumps 92, and it plays up because of the deceptive angles created by his lanky body and high front side in his delivery. He has excellent command of his fastball and three secondary pitches: an average changeup, average slider and a short curve that he uses as a show pitch. If Meyers can stay healthy, he could be a solid back-of-the-rotation starter as soon as 2011. He's certainly ready to tackle Triple-A whenever he gets a clean bill of health.

Year	Club (League)	Class	W	L	ERA	G	GS	CG	SV	IP	H	HR	BB	SO	G/A	WHIP	AVG
2007	Nationals (GCL)	R	0	0	0.00	3	3	0	0	9	2	0	0	9	—	0.22	.067
	Hagerstown (SAL)	LoA	1	1	0.44	4	4	0	0	21	13	1	8	9	—	1.02	.178
	Potomac (CAR)	HiA	0	0	5.06	3	3	0	0	11	15	1	9	7	—	2.25	.357
2008	Hagerstown (SAL)	LoA	9	7	4.79	22	21	0	0	107	129	8	34	94	—	1.52	.299
2009	Potomac (CAR)	HiA	6	2	1.43	15	14	0	0	88	71	1	21	65	1.34	1.04	.222
	Harrisburg (EL)	AA	5	1	2.25	9	9	1	0	48	40	2	11	43	0.98	1.06	.225
2010	Harrisburg (EL)	AA	1	0	1.47	6	6	0	0	31	23	3	7	35	2.12	0.98	.205
Minor League Totals			22	11	2.72	62	60	1	0	314	293	16	90	262	1.31	1.22	.247

28 TREVOR HOLDER, RHP

Born: Jan. 8, 1987. **B-T:** R-R. **Ht.:** 6-2. **Wt.:** 185. **Drafted:** Georgia, 2009 (3rd round). **Signed by:** Eric Robinson.

After serving as the ace of Georgia's 2008 College World Series team, Holder was drafted in the 10th round, but he turned down the Marlins to return to school for his senior year. His fastball jumped from 88-92 in 2008 to 91-94 in 2009, though at the expense of movement. Washington took a senior discount and signed him for $200,000 as a third-round pick. Holder was fatigued so his stuff was down during his pro debut, and his confidence took a hit. It took the Nationals some time to build him back up, but by the second half of 2010 he was back to the competitive bulldog scouts saw during his college days. Holder is back to pitching at 88-92 mph with good sink. He complements his sinker with an average slider, an average changeup and a fringy curveball, doing a good job of throwing strikes and keeping hitters off balance. Holder lacks a plus pitch, and his upside is limited to the back of a big league rotation or a long-relief role. He'll move up to Double-A in 2011.

Year	Club (League)	Class	W	L	ERA	G	GS	CG	SV	IP	H	HR	BB	SO	G/A	WHIP	AVG
2009	Vermont (NYP)	SS	0	0	5.06	2	2	0	0	5	10	0	2	3	1.00	2.25	.476
	Hagerstown (SAL)	LoA	2	0	3.55	3	3	0	0	13	17	1	3	12	0.69	1.58	.333
	Potomac (CAR)	HiA	2	3	9.26	6	6	0	0	23	33	4	9	18	0.85	1.80	.337
2010	Hagerstown (SAL)	LoA	4	3	3.15	12	12	0	0	66	68	3	7	50	2.02	1.14	.262
	Potomac (CAR)	HiA	3	3	4.09	15	14	0	0	70	76	11	22	52	1.44	1.39	.277
Minor League Totals			11	9	4.42	38	37	0	0	177	204	19	43	135	1.42	1.39	.290

29 ADAM CARR, RHP

Born: April 1, 1984. **B-T:** R-R. **Ht.:** 6-2. **Wt.:** 220. **Drafted:** Oklahoma State, 2006 (18th round). **Signed by:** Ryan Fox.

Carr's road to Washington's 40-man roster this winter was long and winding. A power-hitting first baseman at Oklahoma State, Carr pitched just five innings in two years with the Cowboys, but Nationals area scout Ryan Fox saw him light up radar guns in fall practice and urged the club to draft him as a pitcher. Signed for $1,000 as an 18th-round pick, he posted a 1.78 ERA between Potomac and Harrisburg in his first full pro season but got hammered repeatedly during the next two years with those same two clubs. Essentially left for dead as a prospect heading into 2010, Carr showed up in spring training with a dramatically less violent and more repeatable delivery that translated into better stuff and command. His calling card is a 93-95 mph fastball that touches 96. He can use his average slider as a chase pitch, and he also learned to throw it for strikes last year. He has developed a serviceable changeup, though it's definitely his third-best option. After posting identical 2.08 ERAs in Triple-A and the Arizona Fall League, Carr looks ready to compete for a big league middle-relief job in spring training.

Year	Club (League)	Class	W	L	ERA	G	GS	CG	SV	IP	H	HR	BB	SO	G/A	WHIP	AVG
2006	Nationals (GCL)	R	1	0	3.06	10	0	0	1	18	13	1	7	19	—	1.13	.200
	Savannah (SAL)	LoA	0	0	2.25	6	0	0	0	8	8	0	4	8	—	1.50	.267
2007	Potomac (CAR)	HiA	3	1	1.81	41	0	0	10	50	30	4	38	65	—	1.37	.171
	Harrisburg (EL)	AA	1	0	1.64	7	0	0	2	11	7	1	9	13	—	1.45	.189
2008	Potomac (CAR)	HiA	3	4	6.15	21	0	0	5	26	29	3	13	31	—	1.59	.284
	Harrisburg (EL)	AA	3	4	6.95	30	0	0	11	34	39	7	22	27	—	1.81	.287
2009	Harrisburg (EL)	AA	0	1	8.71	8	0	0	0	10	16	2	9	7	1.00	2.42	.372
	Potomac (CAR)	HiA	2	6	5.82	24	11	1	1	73	84	7	34	62	0.88	1.62	.296
2010	Harrisburg (EL)	AA	6	1	3.04	36	0	0	5	50	43	2	14	48	1.39	1.13	.231
	Syracuse (IL)	AAA	0	1	2.08	17	0	0	9	22	16	1	10	19	0.83	1.20	.203
Minor League Totals			19	18	4.27	200	11	1	44	301	285	28	160	269	1.00	1.48	.251

30 HASSAN PENA, RHP

Born: March 25, 1985. **B-T:** R-R. **Ht.:** 6-2. **Wt.:** 210. **Drafted:** Palm Beach (Fla.) CC, 2006 (13th round). **Signed by:** Tony Arango.

Pena worked as a closer in Cuba before defecting. He spent a year at Palm Beach (Fla.) CC, and the Nationals signed him for $149,500 as a 13th-round pick in 2006. They tried to make him a starter, but he was plagued by shoulder soreness until he moved to the bullpen in 2009. He pitched a career-high 71 innings in 2010, then dominated in the Puerto Rican League. Pena's quality four-pitch repertoire is highlighted by a 90-94 mph fastball and an average-to-plus curveball that rates as one of the best in the system. He also throws a solid slider and changeup, though he throws the latter sparingly. Consistency is the key for Pena. He has a long arm action and his mechanics get out of whack occasionally, inhibiting his command. He could be ready to compete for a big league job some time in 2011, though he'll likely start the year in Triple-A. He profiles as a middle reliever.

Year	Club (League)	Class	W	L	ERA	G	GS	CG	SV	IP	H	HR	BB	SO	G/A	WHIP	AVG
2007	Vermont (NYP)	SS	4	5	4.25	13	13	0	0	59	55	3	33	36	—	1.48	.256
2008	Hagerstown (SAL)	LoA	2	2	2.08	6	6	0	0	26	24	0	5	24	—	1.12	.245
	Potomac (CAR)	HiA	2	2	4.15	8	8	0	0	43	42	4	24	30	—	1.52	.266
2009	Nationals (GCL)	R	0	1	2.70	2	2	0	0	7	6	0	3	3	2.20	1.35	.261
	Hagerstown (SAL)	LoA	1	0	1.13	3	3	0	0	16	8	0	4	11	0.84	0.75	.151
	Potomac (CAR)	HiA	2	1	2.39	12	2	0	0	26	16	1	12	21	1.15	1.06	.174
2010	Harrisburg (EL)	AA	2	2	4.29	48	0	0	1	71	73	5	30	64	0.91	1.44	.265
Minor League Totals			13	13	3.58	92	34	0	1	249	224	13	111	189	1.01	1.35	.245

Two prominent Japanese players were posted by their Nippon Professional Baseball teams this offseason, a system that allows teams in Major League Baseball to pay a fee to Japanese teams for exclusive negotiating rights. First, the Athletics won the rights to Rakuten Golden Eagles righthander Hisashi Iwakuma with a bid of $19.1 million. The Pacific League MVP in 2008 and a member of Japan's World Baseball Classic team in 2009, Iwakuma ultimately couldn't agree to terms after a month of negotiations with Oakland. He will return to Rakuten for the 2011 season, while the A's got their posting fee back. Had he signed, Iwakuma would have ranked No. 1 on our Oakland Top 30 Prospects list.

The Twins topped the bidding for the rights to Chiba Lotte Mariners middle infielder Tsuyoshi Nishioka at $5,329,000. He accepted a three-year, $9.25 million deal in mid-December, too late for inclusion in our Twins section of the Handbook. If he had signed earlier, Nishioka would have ranked at No. 6, between outfielder Ben Revere and righthander Liam Hendriks.

TSUYOSHI NISHIOKA, 2B/SS

BORN: July 27, 1984. **B-T:** B-R. **HT.:** 5-11. **WT.:** 175.

The Twins got decent production from middle infielders J.J. Hardy and Orlando Hudson in 2010, but both have no better than average speed and the club wanted to get quicker. As a result, Minnesota traded Hardy, let Hudson become a free agent and aggressively pursued Nishioka. After the Chiba Lotte Marines posted him, the Twins won his negotiating rights with a $5,329,000 bid and signed him to a three-year deal worth $9.25 million. He's the first Japanese player in franchise history, leaving the Diamondbacks, Marlins and Reds as the only big league clubs never to have one. Nishioka played in the inaugural World Baseball Classic in 2006, hitting two homers as Japan won the tournament, but was left off the 2009 team despite posting back-to-back .300 seasons. He had a career year in 2010, batting .346/.423/.482 and winning the Pacific League batting title. Nishioka profiles as a No. 2 hitter. A natural righthander, he learned to switch-hit as a 19-year-old at the Japanese big league level. His best attributes are his ability to make contact and play a speed-oriented game. Nishioka bunts well and has the pitch recognition and plate discipline to draw walks, though he'll have to prove that pitchers can't knock the bat out of his hands. He hit 38 home runs in his last three seasons in Japan, but some U.S. scouts grade his power as 30 on the 20-80 scale. He's not a burner, but he does have plus speed. When Bobby Valentine managed the Marines, he shifted Nishioka to shortstop, and the Twins say they're open to him competing with Alexi Casilla for the shortstop job. He's a plus runner who has enough range for shortstop, but his average arm plays better at second base. How his hitting ability translates to the States will determine whether or not he can be a regular.

2010 DRAFT

FIRST FIVE ROUNDS

Bonuses and estimated slot recommendations by Major League Baseball for the first five rounds of the 2010 draft. MLB establishes guidelines for every pick through the first five rounds, and set a $150,000 ceiling (roughly equivalent to the final choice in the fifth round) for subsequent rounds. Asterisks indicate bonuses that were part of a major league contract, and crosses signify a two-sport contract, which allows the club to spread the bonus over as many as five years.

FIRST ROUND

Pick. Team: Player, Pos.	Bonus	Slot
1. Was: Bryce Harper, of	*$6,250,000	$4,000,000
2. Pit: Jameson Taillon, rhp	$6,500,000	$3,250,000
3. Bal: Manny Machado, ss	$5,250,000	$3,000,000
4. KC: Christian Colon, ss	$2,750,000	$2,750,000
5. Cle: Drew Pomeranz, lhp	$2,650,000	$2,520,000
6. Ari: Barret Loux, rhp	Did Not Sign	$2,340,000
7. NYM: Matt Harvey, rhp	$2,525,000	$2,178,000
8. Hou: Delino DeShields, 2b	$2,150,000	$2,043,000
9. SD: Karsten Whitson, rhp	Did Not Sign	$1,962,000
10. Oak: Michael Choice, of	$2,000,000	$1,863,000
11. Tor: Deck McGuire, rhp	$2,000,000	$1,791,000
12. Cin: Yasmani Grandal, c	*$2,000,000	$1,719,000
13. CWS: Chris Sale, lhp	$1,656,000	$1,656,000
14. Mil: Dylan Covey, rhp	Did Not Sign	$1,602,000
15. Tex: Jake Skole, of	+$1,557,000	$1,557,000
16. ChC: Hayden Simpson, rhp	$1,060,000	$1,512,000
17. TB: Josh Sale, of	$1,620,000	$1,467,000
18. LAA: Kaleb Cowart, 3b/rhp	$2,300,000	$1,422,000
19. Hou: Mike Foltynewicz, rhp	$1,305,000	$1,386,000
20. Bos: Kolbrin Vitek, 2b/of	$1,359,000	$1,359,000
21. Min: Alex Wimmers, rhp	$1,332,000	$1,332,000
22. Tex: Kellin Deglan, c	$1,000,000	$1,287,000
23. Fla: Christian Yelich, of	$1,700,000	$1,260,000
24. SF: Gary Brown, of	$1,450,000	$1,242,000
25. StL: Zack Cox, 3b	*$2,000,000	$1,215,000
26. Col: Kyle Parker, of	+$1,400,000	$1,197,000
27. Phi: Jesse Biddle, lhp	$1,160,000	$1,161,000
28. LAD: Zach Lee, rhp	+$5,250,000	$1,134,000
29. LAA: Cam Bedrosian, rhp	$1,116,000	$1,116,000
30. LAA: Chevez Clarke, of	$1,089,000	$1,089,000
31. TB: Justin O'Conner, c	$1,025,000	$972,000
32. NYY: Cito Culver, ss	$954,000	$954,000

SUPPLEMENTAL FIRST ROUND

Pick. Team: Player, Pos.	Bonus	Slot
33. Hou: Mike Kvasnicka, 3b/c	$936,000	$936,000
34. Tor: Aaron Sanchez, rhp	$775,000	$918,000
35. Atl: Matt Lipka, ss	$800,000	$900,000
36. Bos: Bryce Brentz, of	$889,200	$889,200
37. LAA: Taylor Lindsey, ss	$873,000	$873,000
38. Tor: Noah Syndergaard, rhp	$600,000	$858,600
39. Bos: Anthony Ranaudo, rhp	$2,550,000	$844,200
40. LAA: Ryan Bolden, of	$829,800	$829,800
41. Tor: Asher Wojciechowski, rhp	$815,400	$815,400
42. TB: Drew Vettleson, of	$845,000	$802,800
43. Sea: Taijuan Walker, rhp	$800,000	$789,300
44. Det: Nick Castellanos, 3b	$3,450,000	$776,700
45. Tex: Luke Jackson, rhp	$1,545,000	$764,100
46. StL: Seth Blair, rhp	$751,500	$751,500
47. Col: Peter Tago, rhp	$982,500	$739,800
48. Det: Chance Ruffin, rhp	$1,150,000	$728,100
49. Tex: Mike Olt, 3b	$717,300	$717,300
50. StL: Tyrell Jenkins, rhp	+$1,300,000	$705,600

SECOND ROUND

Pick. Team: Player, Pos.	Bonus	Slot
51. Was: Sammy Solis, lhp	$1,000,000	$694,800
52. Pit: Stetson Allie, rhp	$2,250,000	$684,000
53. Atl: Todd Cunningham, of	$674,100	$674,100
54. KC: Brett Eibner, of/rhp	$1,250,000	$663,300
55. Cle: LeVon Washington, of	$1,200,000	$653,400
56. Ari: J.R. Bradley, rhp	$643,500	$643,500
57. Bos: Brandon Workman, rhp	$800,000	$634,500
58. Hou: Vincent Velasquez, rhp	$655,830	$624,600
59. SD: Jedd Gyorko, 2b	$614,700	$614,700
60. Oak: Yordy Cabrera, 3b	$1,250,000	$605,700
61. Tor: Griffin Murphy, lhp	$800,000	$596,700
62. Cin: Ryan LaMarre, of	$587,700	$587,700
63. CWS: Jacob Petricka, rhp	$540,000	$579,600
64. Mil: Jimmy Nelson, rhp	$570,600	$570,600
65. ChC: Reggie Golden, of	$720,000	$562,500
66. TB: Jake Thompson, rhp	$555,000	$555,000
67. Sea: Marcus Littlewood, ss	$900,000	$545,400
68. Det: Drew Smyly, lhp	$1,100,000	$537,300
69. Tex: Kellen Sweeney, 3b	$600,000	$530,100
70. Atl: Andrelton Simmons, rhp	$522,000	$522,000
71. Min: Niko Goodrum, ss	$514,800	$514,800
72. Tex: Cody Buckel, rhp	$590,000	$506,700
73. Fla: Rob Rasmussen, lhp	$499,500	$499,500
74. SF: Jarrett Parker, of	$700,000	$492,300
75. StL: Jordan Swaggerty, rhp	$625,000	$485,100
76. Col: Chad Bettis, rhp	$477,000	$477,900
77. Phi: Perci Garner, rhp	$470,700	$470,700
78. LAD: Ralston Cash, rhp	$463,500	$463,500
79. TB: Derek Dietrich, 3b	$457,200	$457,200
80. Tor: Justin Nicolino, rhp	$615,000	$450,000
81. LAA: Daniel Tillman, rhp	$443,700	$443,700
82. NYY: Angelo Gumbs, of	$750,000	$436,500

THIRD ROUND

Pick. Team: Player, Pos.	Bonus	Slot
83. Was: Rick Hague, ss	$430,200	$430,200
84. Pit: Mel Rojas Jr., of	$423,900	$423,900
85. Bal: Dan Klein, rhp	$499,900	$417,600
86. KC: Mike Antonio, ss	$411,000	$411,300
87. Cle: Tony Wolters, ss	$1,350,000	$405,000
88. Ari: Robby Rowland, rhp	$395,000	$398,700
89. NYM: Blake Forsythe, c	$392,400	$392,400
90. Hou: Austin Wates, 2b	$550,000	$387,000
91. SD: Zach Cates, rhp	$765,000	$380,700
92. Oak: Aaron Shipman, of	$500,000	$375,300
93. Tor: Christopher Hawkins, 3b	$350,000	$369,000
94. Cin: Devin Lohman, ss	$363,600	$363,600
95. CWS: Addison Reed, rhp	$358,200	$358,200
96. Mil: Tyler Thornburg, rhp	$351,900	$351,900
97. ChC: Micah Gibbs, c	$350,000	$346,500
98. TB: Ryan Brett, 2b	$341,100	$341,100
99. Sea: Ryne Stanek, rhp	Did Not Sign	$335,700
100. Det: Rob Brantly, c	$330,300	$330,300
101. Atl: Joe Leonard, 3b	$324,900	$324,900
102. Min: Pat Dean, lhp	$319,500	$319,500
103. Tex: Jordan Akins, of	+$350,000	$315,000
104. Fla: J.T. Realmuto, ss	+$600,000	$309,600
105. SF: Carter Jurica, ss	$304,200	$304,200

Pick. Team: Player, Pos.	Bonus	Slot
106. StL: Sam Tuivailala, ss	$299,700	$299,700
107. Col: Josh Rutledge, ss	$295,000	$295,000
108. Phi: Cameron Rupp, c	$287,000	$289,800
109. LAD: Leon Landry, of	$284,400	$284,400
110. Bos: Sean Coyle, ss	$1,300,000	$279,900
111. LAA: Wendell Soto, ss	$274,500	$274,500
112. NYY: Rob Segedin, 3b	$377,500	$270,000

SUPPLEMENTAL THIRD ROUND

Pick. Team: Player, Pos.	Bonus	Slot
113. Tor: Marcus Knecht, of	$250,000	$267,300
114. CWS: Thomas Royse, rhp	$263,500	$263,700
115. LAA: Donnie Roach, rhp	$261,000	$261,000

FOURTH ROUND

Pick. Team: Player, Pos.	Bonus	Slot
116. Was: A.J. Cole, rhp	$2,000,000	$258,300
117. Pit: Nick Kingham, rhp	$480,000	$254,700
118. Bal: Trent Mummey, of	$252,000	$252,000
119. KC: Kevin Chapman, lhp	$250,000	$250,000
120. Cle: Kyle Blair, rhp	$580,000	$245,700
121. Ari: Kevin Munson, rhp	$243,000	$243,000
122. NYM: Cory Vaughn, of	$240,300	$240,300
123. Hou: Bobby Doran, rhp	$236,700	$236,700
124. SD: Chris Bisson, 2b	$234,000	$234,000
125. Oak: Chad Lewis, 3b	$300,000	$231,300
126. Tor: Sam Dyson, rhp	$600,000	$227,700
127. Cin: Brodie Greene, 2b	$112,500	$225,000
128. CWS: Matthew Grimes, rhp	Did Not Sign	$222,300
129. Mil: Hunter Morris, 1b	$218,700	$218,700
130. ChC: Hunter Ackerman, lhp	$216,000	$216,000
131. TB: Austin Wood, rhp	Did Not Sign	$213,300
132. Sea: James Paxton, lhp	Unsigned	$209,700
133. Det: Cole Green, rhp	Did Not Sign	$207,000
134. Atl: Dave Filak, rhp	$204,300	$204,300
135. Min: Eddie Rosario, of	$200,000	$200,700
136. Tex: Drew Robinson, ss	$198,000	$198,000
137. Fla: Andrew Toles, of	Did Not Sign	$195,300
138. SF: Seth Rosin, rhp	$191,700	$191,700
139. StL: Cody Stanley, c	$189,000	$189,000
140. Col: Russell Wilson, of	$200,000	$186,300
141. Phi: Bryan Morgado, lhp	$182,700	$182,700
142. LAD: James Baldwin, of	$180,000	$180,000
143. Bos: Garin Cecchini, ss	$1,310,000	$179,100
144. LAA: Max Russell, lhp	$177,300	$177,300
145. NYY: Mason Williams, of	$1,450,000	$176,400

FIFTH ROUND

Pick. Team: Player, Pos.	Bonus	Slot
146. Was: Jason Martinson, ss	$174,000	$174,600
147. Pit: Tyler Waldron, rhp	$173,500	$173,700
148. Bal: Connor Narron, ss	$650,000	$171,900
149. KC: Jason Adam, rhp	$800,000	$171,000
150. Cle: Cole Cook, rhp	$299,000	$169,200
151. Ari: Cody Wheeler, lhp	$168,300	$168,300
152. NYM: Matt den Dekker, of	$110,000	$166,500
153. Hou: Ben Heath, c	$160,000	$165,600
154. SD: Rico Noel, of	$163,800	$163,800
155. Oak: Tyler Vail, rhp	$162,900	$162,900
156. Tor: Dickie Joe Thon, ss	$1,500,000	$161,100
157. Cin: Wes Mugarian, rhp	$198,000	$160,200
158. CWS: Andy Wilkins, 1b	$195,000	$158,400
159. Mil: Matt Miller, rhp	$157,500	$157,500
160. ChC: Matt Szczur, of	$100,000	$155,700
161. TB: Ian Kendall, rhp	$250,000	$154,800
162. Sea: Stephen Pryor, rhp	$153,000	$153,000
163. Det: Alex Burgos, lhp	$152,100	$152,100
164. Atl: Phillip Gosselin, 2b	$150,300	$150,300
165. Min: Nate Roberts, of	$149,000	$149,400
166. Tex: Justin Grimm, rhp	$825,000	$147,600
167. Fla: Robert Morey, rhp	$150,000	$146,700
168. SF: Heath Hembree, rhp	$185,000	$144,900
169. StL: Nick Longmire, of	$144,000	$144,000
170. Col: Josh Slaats, rhp	$142,200	$142,200
171. Phi: Scott Frazier, rhp	Did Not Sign	$141,300
172. LAD: Jake Lemmerman, ss	$139,500	$139,500
173. Bos: Henry Ramos, of	$138,200	$138,600
174. LAA: Jesus Valdez, rhp	Did Not Sign	$136,800
175. NYY: Tommy Kahnle, rhp	$150,000	$135,900

2009 DRAFT

Bonuses and estimated slot recommendations by Major League Baseball for the top 100 picks of the 2009 draft. MLB establishes guidelines for every pick through the first five rounds, and set a $150,000 ceiling (roughly equivalent to the final choice in the fifth round) for subsequent rounds. Asterisks indicate bonuses that were part of a major league contract, and crosses signify a two-sport contract, which allows the club to spread the bonus over as many as five years.

FIRST ROUND

Pick. Team: Player, Pos.	Bonus	Slot
1. Was: Stephen Strasburg, rhp	*$7,500,000	$4,000,000
2. Sea: Dustin Ackley, of	*$6,000,000	$3,250,000
3. SD: Donavan Tate, of	+$6,250,000	$3,000,000
4. Pit: Tony Sanchez, c	$2,500,000	$2,750,000
5. Bal: Matt Hobgood, rhp	$2,422,000	$2,520,000
6. SF: Zack Wheeler, rhp	$3,300,000	$2,340,000
7. Atl: Mike Minor, lhp	$2,420,000	$2,178,000
8. Cin: Mike Leake, rhp	$2,270,000	$2,043,000
9. Det: Jacob Turner, rhp	*$4,700,000	$1,962,000
10. Was: Drew Storen, rhp	$1,600,000	$1,863,000
11. Col: Tyler Matzek, lhp	$3,900,000	$1,791,000
12. KC: Aaron Crow, rhp	*$1,500,000	$1,719,000
13. Oak: Grant Green, ss	$2,750,000	$1,656,000
14. Tex: Matt Purke, lhp	Did Not Sign	$1,602,000
15. Cle: Alex White, rhp	$2,250,000	$1,557,000
16. Ari: Bobby Borchering, 3b	$1,800,000	$1,512,000
17. Ari: A.J. Pollock, of	$1,400,000	$1,467,000
18. Fla: Chad James, lhp	$1,700,000	$1,422,000
19. StL: Shelby Miller, rhp	+$2,875,000	$1,386,000
20. Tor: Chad Jenkins, rhp	$1,359,000	$1,359,000
21. Hou: Jiovanni Mier, ss	$1,358,000	$1,332,000
22. Min: Kyle Gibson, rhp	$1,850,000	$1,287,000
23. CWS: Jared Mitchell, of	$1,200,000	$1,260,000
24. LAA: Randal Grichuk, of	$1,242,000	$1,242,000
25. LAA: Mike Trout, of	$1,215,000	$1,215,000
26. Mil: Eric Arnett, rhp	$1,197,000	$1,197,000
27. Sea: Nick Franklin, ss	$1,280,000	$1,161,000
28. Bos: Reymond Fuentes, of	$1,134,000	$1,134,000
29. NYY: Slade Heathcott, of	$2,200,000	$1,116,000
30. TB: LeVon Washington, 2b	Did Not Sign	$1,089,000
31. ChC: Brett Jackson, of	$972,000	$972,000
32. Col: Tim Wheeler, of	$900,000	$954,000

SUPPLEMENTAL FIRST ROUND

Pick. Team: Player, Pos.	Bonus	Slot
33. Sea: Steven Baron, c	$980,000	$936,000
34. Col: Rex Brothers, lhp	$969,000	$918,000
35. Ari: Matt Davidson, 3b	$900,000	$900,000
36. LAD: Aaron Miller, lhp	$889,200	$889,200
37. Tor: James Paxton, lhp	Did Not Sign	$873,000
38. CWS: Josh Phegley, c	$858,600	$858,600
39. Mil: Kentrail Davis, of	$1,200,000	$844,200
40. LAA: Tyler Skaggs, lhp	$1,000,000	$829,800
41. Ari: Chris Owings, ss	$950,000	$815,400
42. LAA: Garrett Richards, rhp	$802,800	$802,800
43. Cin: Brad Boxberger, rhp	$857,000	$789,300
44. Tex: Tanner Scheppers, rhp	$1,250,000	$776,700
45. Ari: Mike Belfiore, lhp	$725,000	$764,100
46. Min: Matt Bashore, lhp	$751,500	$751,500
47. Mil: Kyle Heckathorn, rhp	$776,000	$739,800

Pick. Team: Player, Pos.	Bonus	Slot
48. LAA: Tyler Kehrer, lhp	$728,100	$728,100
49. Pit: Victor Black, rhp	$717,000	$717,300

SECOND ROUND

Pick. Team: Player, Pos.	Bonus	Slot
50. Was: Jeff Kobernus, 2b	$705,500	$705,600
51. Sea: Rich Poythress, 1b	$694,800	$694,800
52. SD: Everett Williams, of	$775,000	$684,000
53. Pit: Brooks Pounders, rhp	$670,000	$674,100
54. Bal: Mychal Givens, ss	$800,000	$663,300
55. SF: Tommy Joseph, c	$712,500	$653,400
56. LAD: Blake Smith, of	$643,500	$643,500
57. Cin: Billy Hamilton, ss	+$623,600	$634,500
58. Det: Andrew Oliver, lhp	$1,495,000	$624,600
59. Col: Nolan Arenado, 3b	$625,000	$614,700
60. Ari: Eric Smith, rhp	$605,700	$605,700
61. CWS: Trayce Thompson, of	$625,000	$596,700
62. Tex: Tommy Mendonca, 3b	$587,700	$587,700
63. Cle: Jason Kipnis, of	$575,000	$579,600
64. Ari: Marc Krauss, of	$550,000	$570,600
65. LAD: Garrett Gould, rhp	$900,000	$562,500
66. Fla: Bryan Berglund, rhp	$572,500	$554,400
67. StL: Robert Stock, c	$525,000	$545,400
68. Tor: Jake Eliopoulos, lhp	Did Not Sign	$537,300
69. Hou: Tanner Bushue, rhp	$530,000	$530,100
70. Min: Billy Bullock, rhp	$522,000	$522,000
71. CWS: David Holmberg, lhp	$514,000	$514,800
72. NYM: Steve Matz, lhp	$895,000	$506,700
73. Mil: Max Walla, of	$499,000	$499,500
74. Mil: Cameron Garfield, c	$492,200	$492,300
75. Phi: Kelly Dugan, of	$485,000	$485,100
76. NYY: J.R. Murphy, c	$1,250,000	$477,900
77. Bos: Alex Wilson, rhp	$470,700	$470,700
78. TB: Kenny Diekroeger, ss	Did Not Sign	$463,500
79. ChC: D.J. LeMahieu, 2b	$508,000	$457,200
80. LAA: Pat Corbin, lhp	$450,000	$450,000

THIRD ROUND

Pick. Team: Player, Pos.	Bonus	Slot
81. Was: Trevor Holder, rhp	$200,000	$443,700
82. Sea: Kyle Seager, 2b	$436,500	$436,500
83. SD: Jerry Sullivan, rhp	$430,200	$430,200
84. Pit: Evan Chambers, of	$423,900	$423,900
85. Bal: Tyler Townsend, 1b	$417,600	$417,600
86. SF: Chris Dominguez, 3b	$411,300	$411,300
87. Atl: David Hale, rhp	$405,000	$405,000
88. Cin: Donnie Joseph, lhp	$398,000	$398,700
89. Det: Wade Gaynor, 3b	$392,400	$392,400
90. Col: Ben Paulsen, 1b	$391,000	$387,000
91. KC: Wil Myers, c/3b	$2,000,000	$380,700
92. Oak: Justin Marks, lhp	$375,300	$375,300
93. Tex: Robbie Erlin, lhp	$425,000	$369,000
94. Cle: Joe Gardner, rhp	$363,000	$363,600
95. Ari: Keon Broxton, of	$358,000	$358,200
96. LAD: Brett Wallach, rhp	$351,900	$351,900
97. Fla: Marquise Cooper, of	$345,000	$346,500
98. StL: Joe Kelly, rhp	$341,000	$341,100
99. Tor: Jake Barrett, rhp	Did Not Sign	$335,700
100. Hou: Telvin Nash, of	$330,300	$330,300

SIGNING BONUSES

2008 DRAFT

Bonuses and estimated slot recommendations by Major League Baseball for the top 100 picks of the 2008 draft. Asterisk indicates the bonus was part of a major league contract, and a cross signifies a two-sport contract, allowing the club to spread the bonus over as many as five years.

FIRST ROUND

Pick. Team: Player, Pos.	Bonus	Slot
1. TB: Tim Beckham, ss	+$6,150,000	$4,000,000
2. Pit: Pedro Alvarez, 3b	*$6,000,000	$3,500,000
3. KC: Eric Hosmer, 1b	$6,000,000	$3,250,000
4. Bal: Brian Matusz, lhp	*$3,200,000	$3,000,000
5. SF: Buster Posey, c	$6,200,000	$2,800,000
6. Fla: Kyle Skipworth, c	$2,300,000	$2,600,000
7. Cin: Yonder Alonso, 1b	*$2,000,000	$2,420,000
8. CWS: Gordon Beckham, ss	$2,600,000	$2,270,000
9. Was: Aaron Crow, rhp	Did Not Sign	$2,150,000
10. Hou: Jason Castro, c	$2,070,000	$2,070,000
11. Tex: Justin Smoak, 1b	$3,500,000	$1,990,000
12. Oak: Jemile Weeks, 2b	$1,910,000	$1,910,000
13. StL: Brett Wallace, 3b/1b	$1,840,000	$1,840,000
14. Min: Aaron Hicks, of	$1,780,000	$1,780,000
15. LAD: Ethan Martin, rhp	$1,730,000	$1,730,000
16. Mil: Brett Lawrie, c/3b	$1,700,000	$1,680,000
17. Tor: David Cooper, 1b	$1,500,000	$1,630,000
18. NYM: Ike Davis, 1b	$1,575,000	$1,580,000
19. ChC: Andrew Cashner, rhp	$1,540,000	$1,540,000
20. Sea: Joshua Fields, rhp	$1,750,000	$1,510,000
21. Det: Ryan Perry, rhp	$1,480,000	$1,480,000
22. NYM: Reese Havens, ss	$1,419,000	$1,430,000
23. SD: Allan Dykstra, 1b	$1,150,000	$1,400,000
24. Phi: Anthony Hewitt, 3b	$1,380,000	$1,380,000
25. Col: Christian Friedrich, lhp	$1,350,000	$1,350,000
26. Ari: Daniel Schlereth, lhp	$1,330,000	$1,330,000
27. Min: Carlos Gutierrez, rhp	$1,290,000	$1,290,000
28. NYY: Gerrit Cole, rhp	Did Not Sign	$1,260,000
29. Cle: Lonnie Chisenhall, ss	$1,100,000	$1,240,000
30. Bos: Casey Kelly, rhp/ss	+$3,000,000	$1,210,000

SUPPLEMENTAL FIRST ROUND

Pick. Team: Player, Pos.	Bonus	Slot
31. Min: Shooter Hunt, rhp	$1,080,000	$1,080,000
32. Mil: Jake Odorizzi, rhp	$1,060,000	$1,060,000
33. NYM: Brad Holt, rhp	$1,040,000	$1,040,000
34. Phi: Zach Collier, of	$1,020,000	$1,020,000
35. Mil: Evan Frederickson, lhp	$1,010,000	$1,010,000
36. KC: Mike Montgomery, lhp	$988,000	$988,000
37. SF: Conor Gillaspie, 3b	$970,000	$970,000
38. Hou: Jordan Lyles, rhp	$930,000	$954,000
39. StL: Lance Lynn, rhp	$938,000	$938,000
40. Atl: Brett DeVall, lhp	$1,000,000	$922,000
41. ChC: Ryan Flaherty, ss	$906,000	$906,000
42. SD: Jaff Decker, of	$892,000	$892,000
43. Ari: Wade Miley, lhp	$877,000	$877,000
44. NYY: Jeremy Bleich, lhp	$700,000	$863,000
45. Bos: Bryan Price, rhp	$849,000	$849,000
46. SD: Logan Forsythe, 3b	$835,000	$835,000

SECOND ROUND

Pick. Team: Player, Pos.	Bonus	Slot
47. TB: Kyle Lobstein, lhp	$1,500,000	$822,000
48. Pit: Tanner Scheppers, rhp	Did Not Sign	$809,000
49. KC: Johnny Giavotella, 2b	$787,000	$796,000
50. Bal: Xavier Avery, of	+$900,000	$784,000
51. Phi: Anthony Gose, of	$772,000	$772,000
52. Fla: Brad Hand, lhp	$760,000	$760,000
53. Mil: Seth Lintz, rhp	$900,000	$749,000
54. Mil: Cutter Dykstra, of	$737,000	$737,000
55. Was: Destin Hood, of	+$1,100,000	$726,000
56. Hou: Jay Austin, of	$715,000	$715,000
57. Tex: Robbie Ross, lhp	$1,575,000	$705,000
58. Oak: Tyson Ross, rhp	$694,000	$694,000
59. StL: Shane Peterson, of	$683,000	$683,000
60. Min: Tyler Ladendorf, ss	$673,000	$673,000
61. LAD: Josh Lindblom, rhp	$663,000	$663,000
62. Mil: Cody Adams, rhp	$653,000	$653,000
63. Tor: Kenny Wilson, of	$644,000	$644,000
64. Atl: Tyler Stovall, lhp	$750,000	$634,000
65. ChC: Aaron Shafer, rhp	$625,000	$625,000
66. Sea: Dennis Raben, of	$616,000	$616,000
67. Det: Cody Satterwhite, rhp	$606,000	$606,000
68. NYM: Javier Rodriguez, of	$585,000	$597,000
69. SD: James Darnell, 3b	$740,000	$589,000
70. Atl: Zeke Spruill, rhp	$600,000	$580,000
71. Phi: Jason Knapp, rhp	$590,000	$572,000
72. Col: Charlie Blackmon, of	$563,000	$563,000
73. Ari: Bryan Shaw, rhp	$553,000	$553,000
74. LAA: Tyler Chatwood, rhp	$547,000	$547,000
75. NYY: Scott Bittle, rhp	Did Not Sign	$539,000
76. Cle: Trey Haley, rhp	$1,250,000	$531,000
77. Bos: Derrik Gibson, ss	$600,000	$523,000

THIRD ROUND

Pick. Team: Player, Pos.	Bonus	Slot
78. TB: Jake Jefferies, c	$515,000	$515,000
79. Pit: Jordy Mercer, ss	$508,000	$508,000
80. KC: Tyler Sample, rhp	$500,000	$500,000
81. Bal: L.J. Hoes, 2b	$490,000	$493,000
82. SF: Roger Kieschnick, of	$525,000	$485,000
83. Fla: Edgar Olmos, lhp	$478,000	$478,000
84. Cin: Zach Stewart, rhp	$450,000	$471,000
85. Bos: Stephen Fife, rhp	$464,000	$464,000
86. CWS: Brent Morel, 3b	$440,000	$457,000
87. Was: Danny Espinosa, ss	$525,000	$450,000
88. Hou: Chase Davidson, 1b	Did Not Sign	$443,000
89. Tex: Tim Murphy, lhp	$436,000	$436,000
90. Oak: Petey Paramore, c	$430,000	$430,000
91. StL: Niko Vasquez, ss	$423,000	$423,000
92. Min: Bobby Lanigan, rhp	$417,000	$417,000
93. LAD: Kyle Russell, of	$410,000	$410,000
94. Mil: Logan Schafer, of	$404,000	$404,000
95. Tor: Andrew Liebel, rhp	$340,000	$397,000
96. Atl: Craig Kimbrel, rhp	$391,000	$391,000
97. ChC: Chris Carpenter, rhp	$385,000	$385,000
98. Sea: Aaron Pribanic, rhp	$390,000	$379,000
99. Det: Scott Green, rhp	$373,000	$373,000
100. NYM: Kirk Nieuwenhuis, of	$360,000	$367,000

COLLEGE TOP 100

Rank	Player	Position	B-T	Ht.	Wt.	College	Last Drafted
1.	Anthony Rendon	3B	R-R	5-11	170	Rice	Braves 2008 (27)
2.	Gerrit Cole	RHP	R-R	6-4	215	UCLA	Yankees 2008 (1)
3.	Matt Purke	LHP	L-L	6-3	175	Texas Christian	Rangers 2009 (1)
4.	Taylor Jungmann	RHP	R-R	6-6	195	Texas	Angels 2008 (24)
5.	George Springer	OF	R-R	6-3	205	Connecticut	Twins 2008 (48)
6.	Jackie Bradley	OF	L-R	5-10	175	South Carolina	Never drafted
7.	Matt Barnes	RHP	R-R	6-3	180	Connecticut	Never drafted
8.	Sonny Gray	RHP	R-R	6-0	185	Vanderbilt	Cubs 2008 (27)
9.	John Stilson	RHP	R-R	6-4	190	Texas A&M	Twins 2009 (19)
10.	Jed Bradley	LHP	L-L	6-3	203	Georgia Tech	Never drafted
11.	Danny Hultzen	LHP	L-L	6-2	195	Virginia	D'backs 2008 (10)
12.	Trevor Bauer	RHP	R-R	6-1	175	UCLA	Never drafted
13.	Anthony Meo	RHP	R-R	6-2	190	Coastal Carolina	Nationals 2008 (43)
14.	Peter O'Brien	C	R-R	6-3	215	Bethune-Cookman	Never drafted
15.	Kolten Wong	2B	L-R	5-8	175	Hawaii	Twins 2008 (16)
16.	Tyler Anderson	LHP	L-L	6-3	195	Oregon	Never drafted
17.	Logan Verrett	RHP	R-R	6-2	180	Baylor	Never drafted
18.	Jason Esposito	3B	R-R	6-1	195	Vanderbilt	Royals 2008 (7)
19.	Alex Dickerson	OF	L-L	6-3	220	Indiana	Nationals 2008 (48)
20.	Jason Coats	OF	R-R	6-2	190	Texas Christian	Never drafted
21.	Alex Meyer	RHP	R-R	6-9	220	Kentucky	Red Sox 2008 (20)
22.	Andrew Chafin	LHP	L-L	6-2	190	Kent State	Never drafted
23.	Andrew Susac	C	R-R	6-1	200	Oregon State	Phillies 2009 (16)
24.	Tony Zych	RHP	R-R	6-3	175	Louisville	Cubs 2008 (46)
25.	Zach Cone	OF	R-R	6-2	200	Georgia	Angels 2008 (3)
26.	Austin Wood	RHP	R-R	6-4	205	Southern California	Rays 2010 (4)
27.	John Ruettiger	OF	L-L	6-2	180	Arizona State	Rangers 2008 (35)
28.	Noe Ramirez	RHP	R-R	6-3	180	Cal State Fullerton	Never drafted
29.	Adam Conley	LHP	L-L	6-3	170	Washington State	Twins 2008 (32)
30.	Ryan Wright	2B	R-R	6-1	190	Louisville	Never drafted
31.	Mikie Mahtook	OF	R-R	6-1	205	Louisiana State	Marlins 2008 (39)
32.	Levi Michael	SS	R-R	5-10	170	North Carolina	Never drafted
33.	Ricky Oropesa	1B	L-R	6-2	215	Southern California	Red Sox 2008 (24)
34.	Zack MacPhee	2B	R-R	5-9	170	Arizona State	Tigers 2008 (22)
35.	Brad Miller	SS	L-R	6-0	185	Clemson	Rangers 2008 (39)
36.	James McCann	C	R-R	6-2	185	Arkansas	White Sox 2008 (31)
37.	Harold Martinez	3B	R-R	6-3	190	Miami	Rangers 2008 (19)
38.	Zach Wilson	OF/3B	R-R	6-1	190	Arizona State	Pirates 2008 (26)
39.	Joe Panik	SS	L-R	6-1	180	St. John's	Never drafted
40.	C.J. Cron	C	R-R	6-3	230	Utah	White Sox 2008 (44)
41.	Ryan Carpenter	LHP	L-L	6-5	205	Gonzaga	Rays 2008 (21)
42.	Kyle Gaedele	OF	R-R	6-3	225	Valparaiso	Rays 2008 (32)
43.	Sam Stafford	LHP	L-L	6-3	185	Texas	Red Sox 2008 (40)
44.	Carson Smith	RHP	R-R	6-5	215	Texas State	Never drafted
45.	Matt Price	RHP	R-R	6-2	215	South Carolina	Never drafted
46.	Jack Armstrong Jr.	RHP	R-R	6-7	200	Vanderbilt	Rangers 2008 (36)
47.	Scott McGough	RHP	R-R	6-0	150	Oregon	Pirates 2008 (46)
48.	Grayson Garvin	LHP	L-L	6-5	217	Vanderbilt	Astros 2008 (45)
49.	Andrew Gagnon	RHP	R-R	6-3	190	Long Beach State	Pirates 2008 (10)
50.	Kevin Medrano	2B	L-R	6-0	150	Missouri State	Never drafted

51.	Burch Smith	RHP	R-R	6-5	195	Oklahoma	Indians 2010 (20)
52.	Dixon Anderson	RHP	R-R	6-5	225	California	Orioles 2010 (6)
53.	Nick Ahmed	SS	R-R	6-2	180	Connecticut	Never drafted
54.	B.A. Vollmuth	3B/SS	R-R	6-4	200	Southern Mississippi	Astros 2008 (32)
55.	Charlie Lowell	LHP	L-L	6-4	225	Wichita State	Texas 2008 (27)
56.	Derek Dennis	SS	R-R	6-3	170	Michigan	Rays 2009 (10)
57.	Nick Maronde	LHP	R-L	6-3	200	Florida	Athletics 2008 (43)
58.	Brett Mooneyham	LHP	L-L	6-5	235	Stanford	Padres 2008 (15)
59.	Tyler Pill	RHP/OF	L-R	6-1	180	Cal State Fullerton	Rockies 2008 (38)
60.	Sam Gaviglio	RHP	R-R	6-2	180	Oregon State	Rays 2008 (40)
61.	Navery Moore	RHP	R-R	6-1	205	Vanderbilt	Red Sox 2008 (26)
62.	Erik Johnson	RHP	R-R	6-3	210	California	Never drafted
63.	Preston Tucker	1B	L-L	6-1	205	Florida	Never drafted
64.	Steven Proscia	3B	R-R	6-2	210	Virginia	Twins 2008 (39)
65.	Aaron Westlake	1B	L-R	6-4	220	Vanderbilt	Blue Jays 2010 (22)
66.	Sean Gilmartin	LHP	L-L	6-2	190	Florida State	Padres 2008 (31)
67.	Kyle Winkler	RHP	R-R	5-10	180	Texas Christian	Brewers 2008 (37)
68.	Marcus Semien	SS	R-R	6-0	175	California	White Sox 2008 (34)
69.	Austin Nola	SS	R-R	6-2	200	Louisiana State	Rockies 2008 (48)
70.	Chris Marlowe	RHP	R-R	6-1	175	Oklahoma State	Blue Jays 2010 (21)
71.	Mark Pope	RHP	R-R	6-2	195	Georgia Tech	Braves 2008 (17)
72.	Matthew Stites	RHP	L-R	5-11	170	Missouri	Cubs 2010 (33)
73.	Matt Andriese	RHP	R-R	6-2	188	UC Riverside	Rangers 2008 (37)
74.	Andy Burns	3B	R-R	6-1	180	Arizona	Rockies 2008 (25)
75.	John Hinson	3B/2B	L-R	6-1	195	Clemson	Phillies 2010 (13)
76.	Tyler Bream	3B	R-R	6-3	205	Liberty	Never drafted
77.	Cole Green	RHP	R-R	6-1	210	Texas	Tigers 2010 (4)
78.	Anthony DeSclafani	RHP	R-R	6-2	180	Florida	Red Sox 2008 (22)
79.	Kes Carter	OF	L-L	6-1	190	Western Kentucky	Marlins 2008 (43)
80.	Michael Palazzone	RHP	R-R	6-2	190	Georgia	Indians 2010 (32)
81.	Martin Viramontes	RHP	R-R	6-4	190	Loyola Marymount	Yankees 2008 (27)
82.	Johnny Coy	1B	R-R	6-7	205	Wichita State	Phillies 2008 (7)
83.	Harold Riggins	3B/1B	R-R	6-3	230	North Carolina State	White Sox 2008 (35)
84.	Will Lamb	LHP/OF	L-L	6-5	185	Clemson	Never drafted
85.	Ian Gardeck	RHP	R-R	6-2	200	Angelina (Texas) JC	Never drafted
86.	John Hicks	C/OF	R-R	6-1	182	Virginia	Angels 2008 (31)
87.	Jake Floethe	RHP	R-R	6-3	195	Cal State Fullerton	D'backs 2010 (29)
88.	Cody Asche	3B/1B	L-R	6-1	189	Nebraska	Never drafted
89.	Nick Tropeano	RHP	R-R	6-4	205	Stony Brook	Never drafted
90.	Kyle McMyne	RHP	R-R	6-0	210	Villanova	Never drafted
91.	Joe Terry	3B/2B	L-R	6-0	200	Cal State Fullerton	White Sox 2010 (8)
92.	Taylor Featherston	SS	R-R	6-1	175	Texas Christian	Never drafted
93.	Adam Smith	SS	R-R	6-3	195	Texas A&M	D`backs 2008 (28)
94.	Ray Black	RHP	R-R	6-4	220	Pittsburgh	Never drafted
95.	Cecil Tanner	RHP	R-R	6-6	240	Georgia	Braves 2008 (36)
96.	Brooks Pinckard	RHP	L-R	6-1	195	Baylor	Cubs 2010 (18)
97.	Cohl Walla	OF	R-R	6-3	165	Texas	Never drafted
98.	Drew Martinez	OF	L-L	5-10	170	Memphis	Mets 2010 (23)
99.	Austin Dicharry	RHP	R-R	6-4	195	Texas	Never drafted
100.	Andrew Triggs	RHP	R-R	6-3	210	Southern California	Indians 2010 (24)

HIGH SCHOOL TOP 100

Rank. Player	Position	B/t	Ht.	Wt.	High School	College Commitment
1. Bubba Starling	OF/RHP	R/R	6-4	180	Gardner-Edgerton HS, Gardner, Kan.	Nebraska
2. Daniel Norris	LHP	L/L	6-3	180	Science Hill HS, Johnson City, Tenn.	Clemson
3. Archie Bradley	RHP	R/R	6-4	210	Broken Arrow (Okla.) HS	Oklahoma
4. Dillon Howard	RHP	R/R	6-2	200	Searcy (Ark.) HS	Arkansas
5. Dylan Bundy	RHP	B/R	6-1	200	Owasso (Okla.) HS	Texas
6. Josh Bell	OF	B/R	6-3	205	Jesuit College Prep, Dallas	Texas
7. Francisco Lindor	SS	S/R	5-11	175	Montverde (Fla.) Academy	Florida State
8. Blake Swihart	C	S/R	6-0	175	Cleveland HS, Rio Rancho, N.M.	Texas
9. Derek Fisher	OF	L/R	6-3	210	Cedar Crest HS, Lebanon, Pa.	Virginia
10. Brandon Nimmo	OF	L/R	6-3	185	East HS, Cheyenne, Wyo.	Arkansas
11. Jose Fernandez	RHP	R/R	6-3	215	Alonso HS, Tampa	South Florida
12. Austin Hedges	C	R/R	6-1	190	JSerra HS, San Juan Capistrano, Calif.	UCLA
13. Nicky Delmonico	C/3B	L/R	6-3	215	Farragut HS, Knoxville, Tenn.	Georgia
14. Javier Baez	3B/C	R/R	6-1	205	Arlington Country Day, Jacksonville	Uncommitted
15. Adam McCreery	LHP	L/L	6-8	200	Bonita HS, La Verne, Calif.	Arizona State
16. Robert Stephenson	RHP	R/R	6-2	185	Alhambra (Calif.) HS	Washington
17. Charlie Tilson	OF	R/R	6-0	165	New Trier HS, Winnetka, Ill.	Illinois
18. Billy Flamion	OF	L/L	6-0	160	Central Catholic HS, Modesto, Calif.	Oregon
19. Tyler Beede	RHP	R/R	6-4	200	Lawrence Academy, Groton, Mass.	Vanderbilt
20. Henry Owens	LHP	L/L	6-5	185	Edison HS, Huntington Beach, Calif.	Miami
21. Joe Ross	RHP	R/R	6-2	170	Bishop O'Dowd HS, Oakland	UCLA
22. Cody Kukuk	LHP	L/L	6-4	185	Free State HS, Lawrence, Kan.	Kansas
23. Taylor Guerrieri	RHP	R/R	6-3	180	Spring Valley HS, Columbia S.C.	South Carolina
24. Roman Quinn	OF	S/R	5-9	165	Port St. Joe (Fla.) HS	Florida State
25. Michael Kelly	RHP	R/R	6-5	195	West Boca Raton HS, Boca Raton, Fla.	Florida
26. Nick Burdi	RHP	R/R	6-3	175	South HS, Downers Grove, Ill.	Louisville
27. Tyler Goeddel	SS	R/R	6-4	170	St. Francis HS, Mountain View, Calif.	UCLA
28. Dillon Maples	RHP	R/R	6-1	175	Pinecrest HS, Southern Pines, N.C.	North Carolina
29. Jake Hager	SS	R/R	6-1	170	Sierra Vista HS, Las Vegas	Arizona State
30. Dwight Smith	OF	L/R	5-11	185	McIntosh HS, Peachtree City, Ga.	Georgia Tech
31. Phillip Evans	SS	R/R	5-10	185	La Costa Canyon HS, Carlsbad, Calif.	San Diego State
32. Bryan Brickhouse	RHP	R/R	6-1	185	The Woodlands (Texas) HS	North Carolina
33. Cameron Gallagher	C	R/R	6-3	210	Manheim Township HS, Lancaster, Pa.	East Carolina
34. Mason Hope	RHP	R/R	6-3	180	Broken Arrow (Okla.) HS	Oklahoma
35. Kevin Comer	RHP	R/R	6-4	210	Seneca HS, Tabernacle, N.J.	Vanderbilt
36. Dante Bichette	3B	R/R	6-1	215	Orangewood Christian HS, Maitland, Fla.	Georgia
37. Tyler Greene	SS	R/R	6-3	175	West Boca Raton HS, Boca Raton, Fla.	Georgia
38. Andrew Suarez	LHP	L/L	6-2	200	Columbus HS, Miami	Miami
39. Trevor Story	SS/RHP	R/R	6-0	170	Irving (Texas) HS	Louisiana State
40. Travis Harrison	3B	R/R	6-2	215	Tustin (Calif.) HS	Southern California
41. John Curtiss	RHP	R/R	6-4	190	Carroll HS, Southlake, Texas	Texas
42. Brandon Martin	SS	R/R	5-11	160	Santiago HS, Corona, Calif.	Oregon State
43. Christian Lopes	SS	R/R	6-0	185	Edison HS, Huntington Beach, Calif.	Southern California
44. Jake Cave	OF/LHP	L/L	6-1	180	Kecoughtan HS, Hampton, Va.	Louisiana State
45. Desmond Henry	OF	R/R	5-11	165	Centennial HS, Cornoa, Calif.	Uncommitted
46. Hudson Boyd	RHP	R/R	6-2	235	Bishop Verot HS, Fort Myers, Fla.	Florida
47. Brett Austin	C	R/R	6-0	192	Providence HS, Charlotte	North Carolina State
48. Johnny Eierman	SS	R/R	6-1	195	Warsaw (Mo.) HS	Louisiana State
49. Christian Montgomery	RHP	R/R	6-1	240	Lawrence Central HS, Indianapolis	Uncommitted
50. Aaron Brown	OF	L/L	6-1	205	Chatsworth (Calif.) HS	Pepperdine

51.	Danny Keller	RHP	R/R	6-4	200	Newbury Park (Calif.) HS	Cal State Northridge
52.	Julius Gaines	SS	R/R	6-0	150	Luella HS, Locust Grove, Ga.	Florida International
53.	Jorge Lopez	RHP	R/R	6-5	165	Academia la Milagrosa, Cayey, P.R.	Uncommitted
54.	Mason Robbins	OF	L/L	6-1	195	George County HS, Lucedale, Miss.	Southern Miss
55.	Austin Slater	SS	R/R	6-2	190	The Bolles School, Jacksonville, Fla.	Stanford
56.	Chris McFarland	2B	R/R	6-1	195	Lufkin (Texas) HS	Rice
57.	Michael Conforto	OF	L/R	6-1	190	Redmond (Wash.) HS	Oregon State
58.	Philip Pfeifer	LHP	L/L	6-0	190	Farragut HS, Knoxville, Tenn.	Vanderbilt
59.	Shawon Dunston	OF	L/R	6-2	162	Valley Christian HS, Cerritos, Calif.	Vanderbilt
60.	Matthew Dean	3B	R/R	6-2	190	The Colony (Texas) HS	Texas
61.	Ricardo Jacquez	RHP	R/R	5-9	155	Franklin (Texas) HS	Texas
62.	Patrick Leonard	SS	R/R	6-3	200	Creekside HS, St. Johns, Fla.	Georgia
63.	Josh Tobias	2B/OF	S/R	5-9	194	Southeast Guilford HS, Greensboro, N.C.	Florida
64.	Jerrick Suiter	RHP/C	R/R	6-3	210	Valparaiso (Ind.) HS	Texas Christian
65.	Kevin Kramer	SS	R/R	5-11	165	Turlock (Calif.) HS	UCLA
66.	Carlos Rodon	LHP	L/L	6-2	210	Holly Springs (N.C.) HS	North Carolina State
67.	Daniel Camarena	OF/LHP	L/L	6-0	195	Cathedral Catholic HS, San Diego	San Diego
68.	Dylan Davis	RHP	R/R	6-0	200	Redmond (Wash.) HS	Oregon State
69.	Cody Glenn	LHP	L/R	6-4	185	Westbury Christian HS, Houston	Louisiana State
70.	Jacob Anderson	OF	R/R	6-4	185	Chino (Calif.) HS	Pepperdine
71.	Gabriel Rosa	3B	R/R	6-4	175	Puerto Rico BB Academy HS, Gurabo, P.R.	Bethune-Cookman
72.	Thomas Robson	RHP	R/R	6-4	200	Delta (B.C.) SS	Uncommitted
73.	Larry Greene	OF/1B	L/R	6-1	231	Berrien County HS, Nashville, Ga.	Uncommitted
74.	Eric Snyder	OF	L/R	5-11	165	Edison HS, Huntington Beach, Calif.	UCLA
75.	Cole Wiper	RHP	R/R	6-3	170	Newport HS, Bellevue, Wash.	Oregon
76.	T.J. Costen	SS/OF	R/R	6-0	180	First Colonial HS, Virginia Beach	South Carolina
77.	Patrick Connaughton	RHP	R/R	6-5	190	St. John's Prep, Danvers, Mass.	Notre Dame
78.	Dillon Peters	LHP	L/L	6-0	195	Cathedral HS, Indianapolis	Texas
79.	Garrett Nuss	RHP	R/R	6-2	185	Mount Dora (Fla.) HS	Central Florida
80.	Kyle Smith	RHP	R/R	6-0	170	Santaluces Community HS, Lantana, Fla.	Florida
81.	Shon Carson	OF	S/R	5-11	180	Lake City (S.C.) HS	South Carolina
82.	Adrian Houser	RHP	R/R	6-3	200	Locust Grove (Okla.) HS	Oklahoma
83.	Ryan Meyer	RHP	R/R	6-5	192	Oviedo (Fla.) HS	Central Florida
84.	Mike Papi	OF	L/R	6-2	190	Tunkhannock (Pa.) Area HS	Virginia
85.	Benton Moss	RHP	R/R	6-2	177	Rocky Mount (N.C.) HS	North Carolina
86.	John Magliozzi	RHP	R/R	5-10	175	Dexter School, Brookline, Mass.	Florida
87.	Corey Stump	LHP	L/L	6-5	195	Lakeland (Fla.) Christian HS	Florida
88.	Taylor Nunez	RHP	R/R	6-4	175	Salmen HS, Slidell, La.	Southern Miss
89.	Elvin Soto	C	S/R	6-0	188	Xaverian HS, Brooklyn	Pittsburgh
90.	Nicholas Howard	SS	R/R	6-3	205	St. John College HS, Washington D.C.	Virginia
91.	John Norwood	OF	R/R	6-2	190	Seton Hall Prep, West Orange, N.J.	Vanderbilt
92.	Aaron Nola	RHP	R/R	6-2	170	Catholic HS, Baton Rouge	Louisiana State
93.	Daniel Mengden	C/RHP	R/R	6-1	180	Westside HS, Houston	Texas A&M
94.	Parker French	RHP	L/R	6-1	180	Dripping Springs (Texas) HS	Texas
95.	Hunter Cole	3B	R/R	6-1	185	Dorman HS, Roebuck, S.C.	Georgia
96.	John Taylor	RHP	R/R	6-4	190	Franklin County HS, Carnesville, Ga.	Georgia
97.	Dan Vogelbach	1B	L/R	6-1	240	Bishop Verot HS, Fort Myers, Fla.	Florida
98.	Kevin Matthews	LHP	L/L	6-3	195	Richmond Hill (Ga.) HS	Virginia
99.	Dante Flores	SS	L/R	5-11	160	St. John Bosco HS, Bellflower, Calif.	Southern California
100.	Dominic Jose	OF	S/R	6-3	182	Boca Raton (Fla.) Community HS	Stanford

FROM EVERY MINOR LEAGUE

As a complement to our organization prospect rankings, Baseball America also ranks prospects in each minor league at the end of their seasons. Like the organization lists, they place more weight on potential than performance and should not be regarded as all-star teams. Unlike the organization lists, which are from more of a scouting perspective, the minor league lists reflect the views of minor league managers, who give more weight to what a player does on the field now. We think both perspectives are useful, so we give you both, even though they don't always match up. For a player to qualify for a league prospect list, he must have spent at least one-third of the season in a league. Also unlike the organization lists, players can make the league lists even if they exhausted their rookie eligibility during the 2010 season.

TRIPLE-A

INTERNATIONAL LEAGUE
1. Carlos Santana, c, Columbus Clippers (Indians)
2. Jeremy Hellickson, rhp, Durham Bulls (Rays)
3. Aroldis Chapman, lhp, Louisville Bats (Reds)
4. Jesus Montero, c, Scranton/Wilkes-Barre Yankees
5. Freddie Freeman, 1b, Gwinnett Braves
6. Zach Britton, lhp, Norfolk Tides (Orioles)
7. Desmond Jennings, of, Durham Bulls (Rays)
8. Pedro Alvarez, 3b, Indianapolis Indians (Pirates)
9. Ivan Nova, rhp, Scranton/Wilkes-Barre Yankees
10. Daniel Hudson, rhp, Charlotte Knights (White Sox)
11. Brent Morel, 3b/ss, Charlotte Knights (White Sox)
12. Yonder Alonso, 1b/of, Louisville Bats (Reds)
13. Eduardo Nunez, ss/3b, Scranton/Wilkes-Barre Yankees
14. Jake Arrieta, rhp, Norfolk Tides (Orioles)
15. Brad Lincoln, rhp, Indianapolis Indians (Pirates)
16. Jose Tabata, of, Indianapolis Indians (Pirates)
17. Ryan Kalish, of, Pawtucket Red Sox
18. Wilson Ramos, c, Rochester (Twins)/Syracuse (Nationals)
19. Andy Oliver, lhp, Toledo Mud Hens (Tigers)
20. Carlos Carrasco, rhp, Columbus Clippers (Indians)

PACIFIC COAST LEAGUE
1. Buster Posey, c/1b, Fresno Grizzlies (Giants)
2. Mike Moustakas, 3b, Omaha Royals
3. Michael Pineda, rhp, Tacoma Rainiers (Mariners)
4. Madison Bumgarner, lhp, Fresno Grizzlies (Giants)
5. Dustin Ackley, 2b, Tacoma Rainiers (Mariners)
6. Logan Morrison, 1b/of, New Orleans Zephyrs (Marlins)
7. Tanner Scheppers, rhp, Oklahoma City RedHawks (Rangers)
8. J.P. Arencibia, c, Las Vegas 51s (Blue Jays)
9. Justin Smoak, 1b, Oklahoma City (Rangers)/Tacoma (Mariners)
10. Brett Wallace, 1b, Las Vegas 51s (Blue Jays)
11. Jason Castro, c, Round Rock Express (Astros)
12. Mat Gamel, 3b, Nashville Sounds (Brewers)
13. Michael Kirkman, lhp, Oklahoma City RedHawks (Rangers)
14. Chris Carter, 1b/of, Sacramento River Cats (Athletics)

15. Peter Bourjos, of, Salt Lake Bees (Angels)
16. Mitch Moreland, 1b/of, Oklahoma City RedHawks (Rangers)
17. Henry Rodriguez, rhp, Sacramento River Cats (Athletics)
18. Greg Halman, of, Tacoma Rainiers (Mariners)
19. Cory Luebke, lhp, Portland Beavers (Padres)
20. Mark Trumbo, 1b/of, Salt Lake Bees (Angels)

DOUBLE-A

EASTERN LEAGUE
1. Domonic Brown, of, Reading Phillies
2. Zach Britton, lhp, Bowie Baysox (Orioles)
3. Kyle Drabek, rhp, New Hampshire Fisher Cats (Blue Jays)
4. Brandon Belt, Richmond Flying Squirrels (Giants)
5. Andrew Brackman, Trenton Thunder (Yankees)
6. Lonnie Chisenhall, 3b, Akron Aeros (Indians)
7. Kyle Gibson, rhp, New Britain Rock Cats (Twins)
8. Alex White, rhp, Akron Aeros (Indians)
9. Jason Kipnis, 2b, Akron Aeros (Indians)
10. Casey Kelly, rhp, Portland Sea Dogs (Red Sox)
11. Brandon Laird, 3b, Trenton Thunder (Yankees)
12. Danny Espinosa, ss, Harrisburg Senators (Nationals)
13. Andy Oliver, Erie SeaWolves (Tigers)
14. Bryan Morris, rhp, Altoona Curve (Pirates)
15. Rudy Owens, lhp, Altoona Curve (Pirates)
16. Hector Noesi, rhp, Trenton Thunder (Yankees)
17. Jose Iglesias, ss, Portland Sea Dogs (Red Sox)
18. Anthony Rizzo, 1b, Portland Sea Dogs (Red Sox)
19. Kirk Nieuwenhuis, of, Binghamton Mets
20. Austin Romine, c, Trenton Thunder (Yankees)

SOUTHERN LEAGUE
1. Mike Stanton, of, Jacksonville Suns (Marlins)
2. Dustin Ackley, 2b, West Tenn Diamond Jaxx (Mariners)
3. Michael Pineda, rhp, West Tenn Diamond Jaxx (Mariners)
4. Mike Minor, lhp, Mississippi Braves
5. Brett Lawrie, 2b, Huntsville Stars (Brewers)
6. Dee Gordon, ss, Chattanooga Lookouts (Dodgers)
7. Devin Mesoraco, c, Carolina Mudcats (Reds)
8. Brett Jackson, of, Tennessee Smokies (Cubs)
9. Chris Archer, rhp, Tennessee Smokies (Cubs)
10. Matt Dominguez, 3b, Jacksonville Suns (Marlins)
11. Chris Withrow, rhp, Chattanooga Lookouts (Dodgers)
12. Alex Torres, lhp, Montgomery Biscuits (Rays)
13. Trayvon Robinson, of, Chattanooga Lookouts (Dodgers)
14. Brandon Guyer, of, Tennessee Smokies (Cubs)
15. David Sappelt, of, Carolina Mudcats (Reds)
16. Alex Liddi, 3b/1b, West Tenn Diamond Jaxx (Mariners)
17. Brandon Beachy, rhp, Mississippi Braves
18. Brent Morel, 3b, Birmingham Barons (White Sox)
19. Alex Cobb, rhp, Montgomery Biscuits (Rays)
20. Jerry Sands, of/1b, Chattanooga Lookouts (Dodgers)

TEXAS LEAGUE
1. Mike Moustakas, 3b, Northwest Arkansas Naturals (Royals)
2. Eric Hosmer, 1b, Northwest Arkansas Naturals (Royals)
3. Mike Montgomery, lhp, Northwest Arkansas Naturals (Royals)

4. Wilin Rosario, c, Tulsa Drillers (Rockies)
5. Martin Perez, lhp, Frisco Roughriders (Rangers)
6. Aaron Crow, rhp, Northwest Arkansas Naturals (Royals)
7. Jordan Lyles, rhp, Corpus Christi Hooks (Astros)
8. Simon Castro, rhp, San Antonio Missions (Padres)
9. Blake Beavan, rhp, Frisco Roughriders (Rangers)
10. Christian Friedrich, lhp, Tulsa Drillers (Rockies)
11. Cory Luebke, lhp, San Antonio Missions (Padres)
12. Jordan Walden, rhp, Arkansas Travelers (Angels)
13. James Darnell, 3b, San Antonio Missions (Padres)
14. Eduardo Sanchez, rhp, Springfield Cardinals
15. Rex Brothers, lhp, Tulsa Drillers (Rockies)
16. Louis Coleman, rhp, Northwest Arkansas Naturals (Royals)
17. Charlie Blackmon, of, Tulsa Drillers (Rockies)
18. Engel Beltre, of, Frisco Roughriders (Rangers)
19. Wynn Pelzer, rhp, San Antonio Missions (Padres)
20. Trevor Reckling, lhp, Arkansas Travelers (Angels)

HIGH CLASS A

CALIFORNIA LEAGUE
1. Mike Trout, of, Rancho Cucamonga Quakes (Angels)
2. Brandon Belt, 1b, San Jose Giants
3. Grant Green, ss, Stockton Ports (Athletics)
4. Tyler Chatwood, rhp, Rancho Cucamonga Quakes (Angels)
5. Engel Beltre, of, Bakersfield Blaze (Rangers)
6. Jonathan Villar, ss, Lancaster JetHawks (Astros)
7. Jaff Decker, of, Lake Elsinore Storm (Padres)
8. Aaron Miller, lhp, Inland Empire 66ers (Dodgers)
9. Juan Nicasio, rhp, Modesto Nuts (Rockies)
10. Pat Corbin, lhp, Rancho Cucamonga (Angels)/Visalia (Diamondbacks)
11. Francisco Peguero, of, San Jose Giants
12. Rex Brothers, lhp, Modesto Nuts (Rockies)
13. Ehire Adrianza, ss, San Jose Giants
14. Marc Krauss, of, Visalia Rawhide (Diamondbacks)
15. Ethan Martin, rhp, Inland Empire 66ers (Dodgers)
16. Kyle Russell, of, Inland Empire 66ers (Dodgers)
17. Paul Goldschmidt, 1b, Visalia Rawhide (Diamondbacks)
18. Johermyn Chavez, of, High Desert Mavericks (Mariners)
19. Eric Surkamp, lhp, San Jose Giants
20. Drew Cumberland, ss, Lake Elsinore Storm (Padres)

CAROLINA LEAGUE
1. Julio Teheran, rhp, Myrtle Beach Pelicans (Braves)
2. Eric Hosmer, 1b, Wilmington Blue Rocks (Royals)
3. John Lamb, lhp, Wilmington Blue Rocks (Royals)
4. Wil Myers, c, Wilmington Blue Rocks (Royals)
5. Devin Mesoraco, c, Lynchburg Hillcats (Reds)
6. Randall Delgado, rhp, Myrtle Beach Pelicans (Braves)
7. Chris Dwyer, lhp, Wilmington Blue Rocks (Royals)
8. Oscar Tejeda, 2b, Salem Red Sox
9. Christian Colon, ss, Wilmington Blue Rocks (Royals)
10. Jason Kipnis, 2b, Kinston Indians
11. Derek Norris, c, Potomac Nationals
12. Xavier Avery, of, Frederick Keys (Orioles)
13. Will Middlebrooks, 3b, Salem Red Sox
14. Michael Burgess, of, Potomac Nationals
15. Gregory Infante, rhp, Winston-Salem Dash (White Sox)
16. J.J. Hoover, rhp, Myrtle Beach Pelicans (Braves)
17. Ryan Lavarnway, c, Salem Red Sox
18. Tyler Moore, 1b, Potomac Nationals
19. Jordan Henry, of, Kinston Indians
20. Santos Rodriguez, lhp, Winston-Salem Dash (White Sox)

FLORIDA STATE LEAGUE
1. Matt Moore, lhp, Charlotte Stone Crabs (Rays)
2. Chris Archer, rhp, Daytona Cubs
3. Jacob Turner, rhp, Lakeland Flying Tigers
4. Dellin Betances, rhp, Tampa Yankees
5. Travis d'Arnaud, c, Dunedin Blue Jays
6. Tony Sanchez, c, Bradenton Marauders (Pirates)
7. Brett Jackson, of, Daytona Cubs
8. Anthony Gose, of, Clearwater (Phillies)/Dunedin Blue Jays
9. Trevor May, rhp, Clearwater Threshers (Phillies)
10. Wilmer Flores, ss, St. Lucie Mets
11. Adeiny Hechavarria, ss, Dunedin Blue Jays
12. Henderson Alvarez, rhp, Dunedin Blue Jays
13. Adam Warren, rhp, Tampa Yankees
14. Liam Hendriks, rhp, Fort Myers Miracle (Twins)
15. Joe Cruz, rhp, Charlotte Stone Crabs (Rays)
16. Diego Moreno, rhp, Bradenton Marauders (Pirates)
17. Francisco Martinez, 3b, Lakeland Tigers
18. Jhan Marinez, rhp, Jupiter Hammerheads (Marlins)
19. Melky Mesa, of, Tampa Yankees
20. Andrew Brackman, rhp, Tampa Yankees

LOW CLASS A

MIDWEST LEAGUE
1. Mike Trout, of, Cedar Rapids Kernels (Angels)
2. Shelby Miller, rhp, Quad Cities River Bandits (Cardinals)
3. Wil Myers, c, Burlington Bees (Royals)
4. Jacob Turner, rhp, West Michigan Whitecaps (Tigers)
5. Aaron Hicks, of, Beloit Snappers (Twins)
6. Nick Franklin, ss/2b, Clinton LumberKings (Mariners)
7. Trey McNutt, rhp, Peoria Chiefs (Cubs)
8. Jake Odorizzi, rhp, Wisconsin Timber Rattlers (Brewers)
9. Matt Davidson, 3b, South Bend Silver Hawks (Diamondbacks)
10. Tyler Skaggs, lhp, Cedar Rapids (Angels)/South Bend (Diamondbacks)
11. Allen Webster, rhp, Great Lakes Loons (Dodgers)
12. Jean Segura, 2b, Cedar Rapids Kernels (Angels)
13. Hak-Ju Lee, ss, Peoria Chiefs (Cubs)
14. Fabio Martinez, rhp, Cedar Rapids Kernels (Angels)
15. Rubby de la Rosa, rhp, Great Lakes Loons (Dodgers)
16. Alex Colome, rhp, Bowling Green Hot Rods (Rays)
17. Chris Owings, ss, South Bend Silver Hawks (Diamondbacks)
18. Jerry Sands, 1b/of, Great Lakes Loons (Dodgers)
19. Matt Lollis, rhp, Fort Wayne TinCaps (Padres)
20. Chad Jenkins, rhp, Lansing Lugnuts (Blue Jays)

SOUTH ATLANTIC LEAGUE
1. Jonathan Singleton, 1b, Lakewood BlueClaws
2. Nolan Arenado, 3b, Asheville Tourists (Rockies)
3. Tyler Matzek, lhp, Asheville Tourists (Rockies)
4. Brody Colvin, rhp, Lakewood BlueClaws (Phillies)
5. Robbie Erlin, lhp, Hickory Crawdads (Rangers)
6. Arodys Vizcaino, rhp, Rome Braves
7. Jarred Cosart, rhp, Lakewood BlueClaws (Phillies)
8. Jonathan Villar, ss, Lakewood BlueCaws (Phillies)
9. Reymond Fuentes, of, Greenville Drive (Red Sox)
10. Chad James, lhp, Greensboro Grasshoppers (Marlins)
11. Trevor May, rhp, Lakewood BlueClaws (Phillies)
12. Zack Wheeler, rhp, Augusta Greenjackets (Giants)
13. Cesar Puello, of, Savannah Sand Gnats (Mets)
14. Christian Bethancourt, c, Rome Braves
15. Robbie Ross, lhp, Hickory Crawdads (Rangers)
16. Drake Britton, lhp, Greenville Drive (Red Sox)
17. J.D. Martinez, of, Lexington Legends (Astros)
18. Slade Heathcott, of, Charleston Riverdogs (Yankees)

19. Sebastian Valle, C, Lakewood BlueClaws (Phillies)
20. Chris Dominguez, 3b, Augusta Greenjackets (Giants)

SHORT-SEASON

NEW YORK-PENN LEAGUE
1. Carlos Perez, c, Auburn Doubledays (Blue Jays)
2. Jake Thompson, rhp, Hudson Valley Renegades (Rays)
3. Cory Vaughn, of, Brooklyn Mets
4. Marcell Ozuna, of, Jamestown Jammers (Marlins)
5. Roman Mendez, rhp, Lowell Spinners (Red Sox)
6. Zack Von Rosenberg, rhp, State College Spikes (Pirates)
7. Kolbrin Vitek, 3b, Lowell Spinners (Red Sox)
8. Nick Longmire, of, Batavia Muckdogs (Cardinals)
9. Cesar Hernandez, 2b, Williamsport Crosscutters (Phillies)
10. Colton Cain, lhp, State College Spikes (Pirates)
11. Darrell Ceciliani, of, Brooklyn Mets
12. Domingo Santana, of, Williamsport Crosscutters (Phillies)
13. Bryce Brentz, of, Lowell Spinners (Red Sox)
14. Mike Kvasnicka, of/3b/c, Tri-City Valley Cats (Astros)
15. Aaron Altherr, of, Williamsport Crosscutters (Phillies)
16. Drew Hutchison, rhp, Auburn Doubledays (Blue Jays)
17. Zack Dodson, lhp, State College Spikes (Pirates)
18. Daniel Webb, rhp, Auburn Doubledays (Blue Jays)
19. Josue Carreno, rhp, Connecticut Tigers
20. Madison Younginer, rhp, Lowell Spinners (Red Sox)

NORTHWEST LEAGUE
1. Jurickson Profar, ss, Spokane Indians (Rangers)
2. Michael Choice, of, Vancouver Canadians (Athletics)
3. Jedd Gyorko, 3b, Eugene Emeralds (Padres)
4. Mike Olt, 3b, Spokane Indians (Rangers)
5. Chad Bettis, rhp, Tri-City Dust Devils (Rockies)
6. Matt Lollis, rhp, Eugene Emeralds (Padres)
7. Erik Stavert, rhp, Tri-City Dust Devils (Rockies)
8. Rymer Liriano, of, Eugene Emeralds (Padres)
9. Adys Portillo, rhp, Eugene Emeralds (Padres)
10. Miguel de los Santos, lhp, Spokane Indians (Rangers)
11. Kellin Deglan, c, Spokane Indians (Rangers)
12. Keyvius Sampson, rhp, Eugene Emeralds (Padres)
13. Jake Skole, of, Spokane Indians (Rangers)
14. Zach Walters, ss, Yakima Bears (Diamondbacks)
15. Yoervis Medina, rhp, Everett AquaSox (Mariners)
16. Jared Hoying, of, Spokane Indians (Rangers)
17. Stephen Pryor, rhp, Everett AquaSox (Mariners)
18. Josh Slaats, rhp, Tri-City Dust Devils (Rockies)
19. Rico Noel, of, Eugene Emeralds (Padres)
20. Jake Dunning, rhp, Salem-Keizer Volcanoes (Giants)

ROOKIE

APPALACHIAN LEAGUE
1. Carlos Perez, lhp, Danville Braves
2. Enny Romero, lhp, Princeton Rays
3. Oswaldo Arcia, of, Elizabethton Twins
4. Oscar Taveras, of, Johnson City Cardinals
5. Delino Deshields Jr., of, Greeneville Astros
6. Ramon Morla, 3b, Pulaski Mariners
7. Mike Foltynewicz, rhp, Greeneville Astros
8. Adrian Salcedo, rhp, Elizabethton Twins
9. Aderlin Rodriguez, 3b, Kingsport Mets
10. Manuel Soliman, rhp, Elizabethton Twins
11. Vincent Velasquez, rhp, Greeneville Astros
12. Andrelton Simmons, ss, Danville Braves
13. Braulio Lara, lhp, Princeton Rays
14. Cody Stanley, c, Johnson City Cardinals
15. Todd Glaesmann, of, Princeton Rays
16. Pat Dean, lhp, Elizabethton Twins
17. Matt Heidenreich, rhp, Bristol White Sox

18. Richard Vargas, rhp, Pulaski Mariners
19. Jacob Petricka, rhp, Bristol White Sox
20. Hector Guevara, 2b, Princeton Rays

PIONEER LEAGUE
1. Billy Hamilton, 2b/ss, Billings Mustangs (Reds)
2. Albert Campos, rhp, Casper Ghosts (Rockies)
3. Daniel Tillman, rhp, Orem Owlz (Angels)
4. Leon Landry, of, Ogden Raptors (Dodgers)
5. Yorman Rodriguez, of, Billings Mustangs (Reds)
6. Jake Lemmerman, ss, Ogden Raptors (Dodgers)
7. Mike Blanke, c, Great Falls Voyagers (White Sox)
8. Addison Reed, rhp, Great Falls Voyagers (White Sox)
9. Matt Miller, rhp, Helena Brewers
10. Will Swanner, c, Casper Ghosts (Rockies)
11. Daniel Corcino, rhp, Billings Mustangs (Reds)
12. Cristhian Adames, ss, Casper Ghosts (Rockies)
13. Garrett Gould, rhp, Ogden Raptors (Dodgers)
14. Jimmy Nelson, rhp, Helena Brewers
15. David Holmberg, lhp, Great Falls (White Sox)/Missoula (Diamondbacks)
16. Robby Rowland, rhp, Missoula Osprey (D'backs)
17. Travis Witherspoon, of, Orem Owlz (Angels)
18. Rafael Ortega, of, Casper Ghosts (Rockies)
19. Thomas Royse, rhp, Great Falls Voyagers (White Sox)
20. Kevin Eichhorn, rhp, Missoula Osprey (D'backs)

ARIZONA LEAGUE
1. Guillermo Pimentel, of, Mariners
2. Yordano Ventura, rhp, Royals
3. Robinson Yambati, rhp, Royals
4. Tyler Roberts, c, Brewers
5. Junior Arias, ss, Reds
6. Donavan Tate, of, Padres
7. Cheslor Cuthbert, 3b, Royals
8. Luis Sardinas, ss, Rangers
9. Ismael Guillon, lhp, Reds
10. James Baldwin, of, Dodgers
11. Austin Reed, rhp, Cubs
12. Jonathan Correa, rhp, Reds
13. Chuckie Jones, of, Giants
14. Christian Villanueva, 3b, Rangers
15. Carlos Melo, rhp, Rangers
16. Heath Hembree, rhp, Giants
17. Chevez Clarke, of, Angels
18. Ji-Man Choi, 1b/c, Mariners
19. Teodoro Martinez, of, Rangers
20. Ralston Cash, rhp, Dodgers

GULF COAST LEAGUE
1. Gary Sanchez, c, Yankees
2. Miguel Sano, 3b/ss, Twins
3. Justin O'Conner, c, Rays
4. Jake Marisnick, of, Blue Jays
5. Matt Lipka, ss, Braves
6. Juan Urbina, lhp, Mets
7. Jesse Biddle, lhp, Phillies
8. Aaron Altherr, of, Phillies
9. Max Kepler, of, Twins
10. Cito Culver, ss, Yankees
11. Luke Bailey, c, Rays
12. Kellen Sweeney, 3b, Blue Jays
13. Ramon Flores, 1b/of, Yankees
14. K.C. Hobson, 1b, Blue Jays
15. Bruce Rondon, rhp, Tigers
16. Keury de la Cruz, of, Red Sox
17. Christopher Hawkins, 3b, Blue Jays
18. Ryan Brett, 2b, Rays
19. Henry Ramos, of, Red Sox
20. Dixon Machado, ss, Tigers

INDEX

Darnell, James (Padres)	390
Davidson, Matt (Diamondbacks)	19
Davis, Kentrail (Brewers)	261
de la Cruz, Kelvin (Indians)	138
de la Rosa, Rubby (Dodgers)	243
de los Santos, Fautino (Athletics)	327
de los Santos, Miguel (Rangers)	454
Dean, Pat (Twins)	282
Decker, Jaff (Padres)	389
Deduno, Samuel (Rockies)	154
DeFratus, Justin (Phillies)	344
Deglan, Kellin (Rangers)	456
DeJesus Jr., Ivan (Dodgers)	247
DeLeon, Jorge (Astros)	201
Delgado, Dimasther (Braves)	41
Delgado, Randall (Braves)	35
den Dekker, Matt (Mets)	298
DePaula, Jose (Padres)	393
Descalso, Daniel (Cardinals)	374
DeShields Jr., Delino (Astros)	195
Diamond, Scott (Twins)	285
Dickerson, Corey (Rockies)	156
Dietrich, Derek (Rays)	442
Dirks, Andy (Tigers)	166
Dixon, Rashun (Athletics)	332
Dodson, Zack (Pirates)	361
Dolis, Rafael (Cubs)	85
Dominguez, Chris (Giants)	407
Dominguez, Matt (Marlins)	178
Donaldson, Josh (Athletics)	326
Doolittle, Sean (Athletics)	328
Doubront, Felix (Red Sox)	68
Dozier, Brian (Twins)	285
Drabek, Kyle (Blue Jays)	466
Duda, Lucas (Mets)	292
Duffy, Danny (Royals)	212
Dugan, Kelly (Phillies)	349
Dunn, Mike (Marlins)	182
Dunning, Jake (Giants)	409
Duran, Juan (Reds)	124
Dwyer, Chris (Royals)	213
Dyson, Jarrod (Royals)	217

E

Eaton, Adam (Diamondbacks)	29
Eibner, Brett (Royals)	214
Elbert, Scott (Dodgers)	244
Emaus, Brad (Mets)	298
Eovaldi, Nate (Dodgers)	248
Erbe, Brandon (Orioles)	60
Erlin, Robbie (Rangers)	451
Escalona, Edgmer (Rockies)	156
Escobar, Eduardo (White Sox)	100
Espinosa, Danny (Nationals)	483

F

Familia, Jeurys (Mets)	295
Farquhar, Danny (Athletics)	330
Farris, Eric (Brewers)	261
Federowicz, Tim (Red Sox)	74
Felix, Jose (Rangers)	459
Field, Thomas (Rockies)	157
Fields, Daniel (Tigers)	164
Fields, Josh (Mariners)	427
Figueroa, Pedro (Athletics)	329
Filak, David (Braves)	43
Flaherty, Ryan (Cubs)	91
Flores, Wilmer (Mets)	291
Florimon, Pedro (Orioles)	61
Flowers, Tyler (White Sox)	104
Foltynewicz, Mike (Astros)	195
Font, Wilmer (Rangers)	455

Ford, Darren (Giants)	412
Forsythe, Blake (Mets)	301
Forsythe, Logan (Padres)	391
Francisco, Juan (Reds)	117
Franklin, Nick (Mariners)	419
Frazier, Parker (Rockies)	155
Frazier, Todd (Reds)	118
Freeman, Freddie (Braves)	35
Friedrich, Christian (Rockies)	147
Fuentes, Reymond (Padres)	387
Furbush, Charlie (Tigers)	171

G

Galloway, Isaac (Marlins)	184
Galvis, Freddy (Phillies)	346
Gamboa, Eddie (Orioles)	59
Garcia, Avisail (Tigers)	165
Garcia, Harold (Phillies)	346
Garcia, Jonathan (Dodgers)	250
Garcia, Leury (Rangers)	455
Gardner, Joe (Indians)	133
Garfield, Cameron (Brewers)	266
Garner, Cole (Rockies)	154
Garner, Perci (Phillies)	346
Gast, John (Cardinals)	375
Gaynor, Wade (Tigers)	171
Gee, Dillon (Mets)	296
Gennett, Scooter (Brewers)	260
Giavotella, Johnny (Royals)	216
Gibson, Derrik (Red Sox)	72
Gibson, Kyle (Twins)	274
Gillaspie, Conor (Giants)	408
Gillies, Tyson (Phillies)	344
Gilmore, Jon (White Sox)	108
Gindl, Caleb (Brewers)	264
Givens, Mychal (Orioles)	53
Glaesmann, Todd (Rays)	441
Goeddel, Erik (Mets)	296
Golden, Reggie (Cubs)	91
Goldschmidt, Paul (Diamondbacks)	22
Gomez, Hector (Rockies)	150
Gonzalez, Miguel (White Sox)	107
Goodrum, Niko (Twins)	281
Gordon, Dee (Dodgers)	242
Gose, Anthony (Blue Jays)	467
Gosselin, Phil (Braves)	43
Gould, Garrett (Dodgers)	249
Grandal, Yasmani (Reds)	116
Green, Grant (Athletics)	322
Green, Tyler (Diamondbacks)	25
Greenwalt, Kyle (Astros)	203
Gregorius, DiDi (Reds)	121
Grichuk, Randal (Angels)	231
Grimm, Justin (Rangers)	457
Grimmett, Zachary (Astros)	205
Grossman, Robbie (Pirates)	363
Guerra, Javy (Dodgers)	251
Guevara, Hector (Rays)	443
Guillon, Ismael (Reds)	120
Gumbs, Angelo (Yankees)	315
Gutierrez, Carlos (Twins)	278
Guyer, Brandon (Cubs)	86
Gyorko, Jedd (Padres)	390

H

Ha, Jae-Hoon (Cubs)	92
Hagadone, Nick (Indians)	134
Hagerty, Jason (Padres)	390
Hague, Matt (Pirates)	365
Hague, Rick (Nationals)	487
Hale, David (Braves)	41
Halman, Greg (Mariners)	422

Hamilton, Billy (Reds)	115
Hamilton, Mark (Cardinals)	378
Hand, Brad (Marlins)	180
Harper, Bryce (Nationals)	482
Harrell, Lucas (White Sox)	104
Harrilchak, Cory (Braves)	45
Harrison, Josh (Pirates)	365
Harvey, Matt (Mets)	291
Hawn, Cody (Brewers)	265
Havens, Reese (Mets)	292
Hawkins, Christopher (Blue Jays)	475
Haydel, Lee (Brewers)	269
Hayes, Brett (Marlins)	189
Hazelbaker, Jeremy (Red Sox)	74
Heath, Ben (Astros)	202
Heathcott, Slade (Yankees)	309
Hechavarria, Adeiny (Blue Jays)	471
Heckathorn, Kyle (Brewers)	262
Hefner, Jeremy (Padres)	392
Heid, Drew (Angels)	237
Heidenreich, Matt (White Sox)	108
Hellickson, Jeremy (Rays)	434
Hellweg, Johnny (Angels)	235
Hembree, Heath (Giants)	409
Hendriks, Liam (Twins)	276
Henry, Jordan (Indians)	136
Henson, Tyler (Orioles)	58
Heredia, Luis (Pirates)	356
Hermsen, B.J. (Twins)	283
Hernandez, Cesar (Phillies)	345
Hernandez, Gorkys (Pirates)	259
Herrera, Kelvin (Royals)	220
Herrera, Rosell (Rockies)	150
Hicks, Aaron (Twins)	275
Hill, Steven (Cardinals)	381
Hobgood, Matt (Orioles)	55
Hobson, K.C. (Blue Jays)	474
Hoes, L.J. (Orioles)	51
Hoffman, Matt (Tigers)	168
Holaday, Bryan (Tigers)	169
Holder, Trevor (Nationals)	492
Holmberg, David (Diamondbacks)	26
Holt, Brad (Mets)	294
Holt, Tyler (Indians)	140
Hood, Destin (Nationals)	487
Hoover, J.J. (Braves)	38
Hosmer, Eric (Royals)	210
House, T.J. (Indians)	135
Hoying, Jared (Rangers)	459
Hutchison, Drew (Blue Jays)	475
Hyatt, Austin (Phillies)	347

I

Iglesias, Jose (Red Sox)	66
Infante, Gregori (White Sox)	100
Iorg, Cale (Tigers)	170

J

Jackson, Brett (Cubs)	83
Jackson, Jay (Cubs)	88
Jackson, Luke (Rangers)	458
Jackson, Ryan (Cardinals)	381
Jacobs, Brandon (Red Sox)	76
James, Chad (Marlins)	179
James, Jiwan (Phillies)	340
Jansen, Kenley (Dodgers)	245
Jeffress, Jeremy (Brewers)	259
Jenkins, Chad (Blue Jays)	471
Jenkins, Tyrell (Cardinals)	371
Jennings, Dan (Marlins)	184
Jennings, Desmond (Rays)	435
Jimenez, Luis (Angels)	234

Jones, Chuckie (Giants)	408	Lindsey, Taylor (Angels)	233	Mitchell, Bryan (Yankees)	315
Jones, Daryl (Cardinals)	380	Linton, Ty (Diamondbacks)	22	Mitchell, D.J. (Yankees)	313
Jones, James (Mariners)	426	Lipka, Matt (Braves)	36	Mitchell, Jared (White Sox)	99
Jones, Mycal (Braves)	41	Liriano, Rymer (Padres)	393	Monell, Johnny (Giants)	412
Jones, Nate (White Sox)	106	Littlewood, Marcus (Mariners)	421	Montero, Jesus (Yankees)	306
Joseph, Caleb (Orioles)	60	Lo, Chia-Jen (Astros)	203	Montgomery, Mike (Royals)	212
Joseph, Corban (Yankees)	314	Lobstein, Kyle (Rays)	444	Moore, Jeremy (Angels)	232
Joseph, Donnie (Reds)	119	Locke, Jeff (Pirates)	357	Moore, Matt (Rays)	435
Joseph, Jonathan (Athletics)	329	Lollis, Matt (Padres)	388	Moore, Tyler (Nationals)	491
Joseph, Tommy (Giants)	406	Lombardozzi, Steve (Nationals)	487	Morales, Angel (Twins)	279
Judy, Josh (Indians)	137	Lopez, Robinson (Cubs)	90	Morel, Brent (White Sox)	99
		Lotzkar, Kyle (Reds)	118	Moreno, Diego (Pirates)	359
K		Lough, David (Royals)	219	Morey, Robert (Marlins)	189
		Loux, Barret (Rangers)	459	Morla, Ramon (Mariners)	423
Kahnle, Tommy (Yankees)	316	Luebke, Cory (Padres)	388	Morris, A.J. (Nationals)	489
Keating, Patrick (Royals)	218	Lueke, Josh (Mariners)	423	Morris, Bryan (Pirates)	356
Kelly, Casey (Padres)	386	Lutz, Zach (Mets)	297	Morris, Hunter (Brewers)	264
Kelly, Joe (Cardinals)	373	Lyles, Jordan (Astros)	194	Morrison, Ty (Rays)	439
Kepler, Max (Twins)	278	Lynn, Lance (Cardinals)	372	Mortensen, Clay (Athletics)	327
Keuchel, Dallas (Astros)	202			Moskos, Daniel (Pirates)	364
Kickham, Mike (Giants)	408	**M**		Moustakas, Mike (Royals)	211
Kiermaier, Kevin (Rays)	443			Mummey, Trent (Orioles)	56
Kieschnick, Roger (Giants)	407	Machado, Dixon (Tigers)	172	Munson, Kevin (Diamondbacks)	23
Kimball, Cole (Nationals)	485	Machado, Manny (Orioles)	50	Murphy, Griffin (Blue Jays)	471
Kimbrel, Craig (Braves)	36	Magnuson, Trystan (Athletics)	331	Murphy, J.R. (Yankees)	311
King, Blake (Cardinals)	378	Mahoney, Joe (Orioles)	54	Myers, Wil (Royals)	211
Kintzler, Brandon (Brewers)	267	Maine, Scott (Cubs)	87		
Kipnis, Jason (Indians)	131	Mangini, Matt (Mariners)	425	**N**	
Kirkman, Michael (Rangers)	452	Marinez, Jhan (Marlins)	179		
Klein, Dan (Orioles)	52	Marisnick, Jake (Blue Jays)	470	Narron, Connor (Orioles)	56
Kluber, Corey (Indians)	139	Marrero, Chris (Nationals)	485	Nash, Telvin (Astros)	199
Knapp, Jason (Indians)	132	Marshall, Brett (Yankees)	310	Navarro, Raul (Diamondbacks)	27
Knecht, Marcus (Blue Jays)	475	Marte, Jefry (Mets)	300	Navarro, Yamaico (Red Sox)	14
Kobernus, Jeff (Nationals)	490	Marte, Starling (Pirates)	355	Neal, Thomas (Giants)	405
Koehler, Tom (Marlins)	183	Martin, Ethan (Dodgers)	246	Nelson, Chris (Rockies)	152
Kohn, Michael (Angels)	232	Martinez, Carlos (Cardinals)	371	Nelson, Cole (Tigers)	173
Komatsu, Erik (Brewers)	263	Martinez, Fabio (Angels)	229	Nelson, Jimmy (Brewers)	262
Kontos, George (Padres)	396	Martinez, Fernando (Mets)	293	Nicasio, Juan (Rockies)	149
Kopp, David (Cardinals)	376	Martinez, Francisco (Tigers)	163	Nicolino, Justin (Blue Jays)	473
Kozma, Pete (Cardinals)	378	Martinez, J.D. (Astros)	196	Nieuwenhuis, Kirk (Mets)	292
Krauss, Marc (Diamondbacks)	20	Martinez, Osvaldo (Marlins)	180	Noesi, Hector (Yankees)	308
Krol, Ian (Athletics)	325	Martinson, Jason (Nationals)	490	Noonan, Nick (Giants)	410
Kurcz, Aaron (Cubs)	92	Mateo, Marcus (Cubs)	89	Norris, Derek (Nationals)	483
Kvasnicka, Mike (Astros)	199	Mateo, Wagner (Diamondbacks)	25	Nova, Ivan (Yankees)	311
		Mathieson, Scott (Phillies)	343	Nunez, Eduardo (Yankees)	309
		Matz, Steve (Mets)	297	Nunez, Gustavo (Tigers)	170
L		Matzek, Tyler (Rockies)	146	Nunez, Jhonny (White Sox)	106
		May, Trevor (Phillies)	340	Nunez, Renato (Athletics)	328
Laird, Brandon (Yankees)	310	Maya, Yunesky (Nationals)	486		
Lake, Junior (Cubs)	92	McClendon, Mike (Brewers)	267	**O**	
LaMarre, Ryan (Reds)	118	McGee, Jake (Rays)	435		
Lamb, John (Royals)	211	McGuire, Deck (Blue Jays)	467	Oberholtzer, Brett (Braves)	38
Lambo, Andrew (Pirates)	358	McNutt, Trey (Cubs)	83	O'Conner, Justin (Rays)	437
Lamontagne, Andre (Brewers)	265	Medina, Yoervis (Mariners)	429	Odorizzi, Jake (Brewers)	258
Landry, Leon (Dodgers)	246	Mejia, Jenrry (Mets)	290	O'Gara, Joey (Marlins)	189
Lara, Braulio (Rays)	439	Mejias, Ronny (Diamondbacks)	28	Oliver, Andy (Tigers)	163
Lasker, Maverick (Brewers)	268	Melville, Tim (Royals)	215	Oliveros, Lester (Tigers)	168
Latimore, Quincy (Pirates)	362	Mendez, Roman (Rangers)	455	Olmos, Edgar (Marlins)	186
Lavarnway, Ryan (Red Sox)	72	Mercer, Jordy (Pirates)	362	Olt, Mike (Rangers)	453
Lavisky, Alex (Indians)	134	Mesa, Melky (Yankees)	313	Oramas, Juan (Padres)	392
Lawrie, Brett (Blue Jays)	467	Mesoraco, Devin (Reds)	115	Ortega, Jose (Tigers)	166
Lebron, Luis (Orioles)	58	Meyers, Brad (Nationals)	492	Ortiz, Ryan (Athletics)	332
LeCure, Sam (Reds)	123	Mickolio, Kam (Diamondbacks)	24	Ottavino, Adam (Cardinals)	380
Lee, Chen (Indians)	137	Miclat, Greg (Orioles)	60	Ovando, Ariel (Astros)	197
Lee, Hak-Ju (Cubs)	83	Middlebrooks, Will (Red Sox)	70	Owens, Rudy (Pirates)	357
Lee, Zach (Dodgers)	243	Mier, Jiovanni (Astros)	196	Owings, Chris (Diamondbacks)	19
Leesman, Charlie (White Sox)	102	Miley, Wade (Diamondbacks)	21	Ozuna, Marcell (Marlins)	181
LeMahieu, D.J. (Cubs)	87	Miller, Aaron (Dodgers)	247		
Lemmerman, Jake (Dodgers)	251	Miller, Matt (Brewers)	263	**P**	
Leonard, Joe (Braves)	43	Miller, Shelby (Cardinals)	370		
Lewis, Chad (Athletics)	329	Milligan, Adam (Braves)	42	Pacheco, Jordan (Rockies)	153
Liddi, Alex (Mariners)	423	Mills, Brad (Blue Jays)	477	Packer, Matt (Indians)	138
Lin, Che-Hsuan (Red Sox)	75	Milone, Tom (Nationals)	488	Paredes, Jimmy (Astros)	196
Linares, Juan Carlos (Red Sox)	76	Minor, Mike (Braves)	35	Parker, Jarrett (Giants)	406
Lindblom, Josh (Dodgers)	248				

Parker, Jarrod (Diamondbacks) 18
Parker, Kyle (Rockies) 148
Parker, Steve (Athletics) 331
Parmelee, Chris (Twins) 281
Pastornicky, Tyler (Braves) 39
Paulsen, Ben (Rockies) 156
Peacock, Brad (Nationals) 486
Pederson, Joc (Dodgers) 251
Peguero, Carlos (Mariners) 427
Peguero, Esteilon (Mariners) 425
Peguero, Francisco (Giants) 403
Pelzer, Wynn (Orioles) 52
Pena, Hassan (Nationals) 493
Pendleton, Lance (Astros) 205
Peralta, Wily (Brewers) 260
Perez, Carlos (Blue Jays) 469
Perez, Carlos (Braves) 38
Perez, David (Rangers) 454
Perez, Eury (Nationals) 485
Perez, Felix (Reds) 125
Perez, Juan (Giants) 410
Perez, Martin (Rangers) 450
Perez, Salvador (Royals) 216
Perio, Noah (Marlins) 188
Petersen, Bryan (Marlins) 185
Petricka, Jacob (White Sox) 101
Pettibone, Jon (Phillies) 345
Phegley, Josh (White Sox) 108
Phelps, Cord (Indians) 137
Phelps, David (Yankees) 312
Pierre, Gustavo (Blue Jays) 476
Pimentel, Elisaul (Royals) 220
Pimentel, Guillermo (Mariners) 420
Pimentel, Stolmy (Red Sox) 68
Pineda, Michael (Mariners) 419
Plouffe, Trevor (Twins) 283
Polanco, Jorge (Twins) 280
Pollock, A.J. (Diamondbacks) 20
Pomeranz, Drew (Indians) 131
Portillo, Adys (Padres) 395
Poveda, Omar (Marlins) 187
Poythress, Rich (Mariners) 424
Presley, Alex (Pirates) 361
Pribanic, Aaron (Pirates) 364
Profar, Jurickson (Rangers) 451
Pryor, Stephen (Mariners) 426
Puello, Cesar (Mets) 291
Pugh, Bruce (Twins) 284
Putnam, Zach (Indians) 136

Q

Quate, Zach (Rays) 441

R

Raley, Brooks (Cubs) 92
Ramirez, Elvin (Nationals) 490
Ramirez, Erasmo (Mariners) 429
Ramirez, J.C. (Phillies) 344
Ramirez, Jose (Yankees) 315
Ramirez, J.P. (Nationals) 491
Ramirez, Neil (Rangers) 460
Ramos, Wilson (Nationals) 484
Ranaudo, Anthony (Red Sox) 67
Rasmussen, Rob (Marlins) 182
Ray, Robbie (Nationals) 488
Realmuto, J.T. (Marlins) 184
Reckling, Trevor (Angels) 230
Reddick, Josh (Red Sox) 67
Reed, Addison (White Sox) 103
Reifer, Adam (Cardinals) 375
Revere, Ben (Twins) 276
Reyes, Elmer (Braves) 42

Reynolds, Matt (Rockies) 153
Rhee, Dae-Eun (Cubs) 93
Richards, Garrett (Angels) 229
Richardson, D'Vontrey (Brewers) 267
Richmond, Josh (Rangers) 461
Rienzo, Andre (White Sox) 107
Rincon, Edinson (Padres) 392
Riordan, Cory (Rockies) 155
Rivas, Amaury (Brewers) 263
Rivera, Yadiel (Brewers) 266
Rizzo, Anthony (Padres) 387
Rizzotti, Matt (Phillies) 348
Roach, Donn (Angels) 235
Roberts, Tyler (Brewers) 266
Robinson, Clint (Royals) 220
Robinson, Derrick (Royals) 219
Robinson, Trayvon (Dodgers) 246
Robles, Mauricio (Mariners) 420
Rodriguez, Aderlin (Mets) 293
Rodriguez, Aneury (Astros) 198
Rodriguez, Armando (Mets) 299
Rodriguez, Henry (Reds) 122
Rodriguez, Josh (Pirates) 363
Rodriguez, Julio (Phillies) 347
Rodriguez, Luigi (Indians) 139
Rodriguez, Rafael (Giants) 406
Rodriguez, Santos (White Sox) 102
Rodriguez, Wilking (Rays) 443
Rodriguez, Yorman (Reds) 116
Rogers, Mark (Brewers) 259
Rojas Jr., Mel (Pirates) 362
Romero, Enny (Rays) 438
Romine, Andrew (Angels) 232
Romine, Austin (Yankees) 308
Rondon, Bruce (Tigers) 167
Rondon, Hector (Indians) 135
Rosario, Adrian (Orioles) 61
Rosario, Eddie (Twins) 282
Rosario, Sandy (Marlins) 186
Rosario, Wilin (Rockies) 147
Rosenbaum, Danny (Nationals) 491
Ross, Austin (Brewers) 269
Ross, Robbie (Rangers) 457
Ross, Tyson (Athletics) 323
Rowland, Robby (Diamondbacks) 26
Royse, Thomas (White Sox) 104
Ruffin, Chance (Tigers) 164
Rupp, Cameron (Phillies) 349
Russell, Kyle (Dodgers) 248
Ryan, Kyle (Tigers) 172

S

Saladino, Tyler (White Sox) 106
Salas, Fernando (Cardinals) 375
Salcedo, Adrian (Twins) 277
Salcedo, Edward (Braves) 40
Sale, Chris (White Sox) 98
Sale, Josh (Rays) 436
Sampson, Keyvius (Padres) 394
Samuel, Francisco (Cardinals) 377
Sanchez, Aaron (Blue Jays) 470
Sanchez, Adrian (Nationals) 488
Sanchez, Eduardo (Cardinals) 372
Sanchez, Gary (Yankees) 307
Sanchez, Tony (Pirates) 355
Sands, Jerry (Dodgers) 244
Sano, Miguel (Twins) 275
Santana, Daniel (Twins) 281
Santana, Domingo (Phillies) 341
Sappelt, Dave (Reds) 121
Sardinas, Luis (Rangers) 453
Scahill, Rob (Rockies) 152
Scarpetta, Cody (Brewers) 260

Schafer, Logan (Brewers) 264
Schebler, Scott (Dodgers) 250
Scheppers, Tanner (Rangers) 451
Schmidt, Nick (Padres) 397
Schoop, Jonathan (Orioles) 54
Seager, Kyle (Mariners) 421
Seaton, Ross (Astros) 200
Segura, Jean (Angels) 227
Shaw, Bryan (Diamondbacks) 28
Shields, Robbie (Mets) 297
Shipers, Jordan (Mariners) 427
Shipman, Aaron (Athletics) 325
Short, Brandon (White Sox) 101
Shuck, J.B. (Astros) 200
Shuman, Scott (Rays) 442
Sierra, Moises (Blue Jays) 474
Simmons, Andrelton (Braves) 40
Simpson, Hayden (Cubs) 85
Singleton, Jonathan (Phillies) 339
Skaggs, Tyler (Diamondbacks) 19
Skipworth, Kyle (Marlins) 181
Skole, Jake (Rangers) 453
Slama, Anthony (Twins) 284
Smit, Kyle (Cubs) 90
Smith, Blake (Dodgers) 252
Smith, Eric (Diamondbacks) 23
Smolinski, Jake (Marlins) 187
Smyly, Drew (Tigers) 165
Snyder, Brandon (Orioles) 57
Spoone, Chorye (Orioles) 59
Sogard, Eric (Athletics) 330
Soliman, Manuel (Twins) 280
Solis, Sammy (Nationals) 484
Songco, Angelo (Dodgers) 252
Sosa, Henry (Giants) 413
Soto, Neftali (Reds) 123
Stassi, Max (Athletics) 324
Sterling, Felix (Indians) 135
Stewart, Zach (Blue Jays) 468
Stoffel, Jason (Giants) 410
Stoneburner, Graham (Yankees) 312
Stowell, Bryce (Indians) 136
Strieby, Ryan (Tigers) 167
Stuifbergen, Tom (Twins) 284
Sullivan, Jerry (Padres) 396
Sullivan, Richard (Braves) 45
Surkamp, Eric (Giants) 405
Swagerty, Jordan (Cardinals) 373
Swanner, Will (Rockies) 152
Sweeney, Kellen (Blue Jays) 472
Syndergaard, Noah (Blue Jays) 474
Szczur, Matt (Cubs) 85

T

Tago, Peter (Rockies) 148
Taillon, Jameson (Pirates) 354
Tanner, Clayton (Giants) 413
Tate, Donavan (Padres) 389
Tatusko, Ryan (Nationals) 492
Taveras, Oscar (Cardinals) 379
Taylor, Drew (Angels) 236
Taylor, Michael (Athletics) 326
Tazawa, Junichi (Red Sox) 75
Teheran, Julio (Braves) 34
Tejeda, Oscar (Red Sox) 70
Tekotte, Blake (Padres) 391
Thames, Eric (Blue Jays) 470
Thompson, Daryl (Reds) 124
Thompson, Jake (Rays) 438
Thompson, Tony (Athletics) 333
Thompson, Trayce (White Sox) 101
Thomson, Matt (Athletics) 332
Thon, Dickie Joe (Blue Jays) 472

Thornburg, Tyler (Brewers)	261	Villanueva, Christian (Rangers)	454	Westmoreland, Ryan (Red Sox)	77
Tillman, Daniel (Angels)	231	Villanueva, Elih (Marlins)	183	Wheeler, Ryan (Diamondbacks)	24
Todd, Jess (Indians)	140	Villar, Henry (Astros)	202	Wheeler, Tim (Rockies)	154
Torres, Alex (Rays)	436	Villar, Jonathan (Astros)	195	Wheeler, Zack (Giants)	403
Torreyes, Ronald (Reds)	122	Villarreal, Brayan (Tigers)	169	White, Alex (Indians)	131
Tosoni, Rene (Twins)	278	Villegas, Ydwin (Giants)	411	Whitley, Chase (Yankees)	317
Townsend, Tyler (Orioles)	57	Vitek, Kolbrin (Red Sox)	70	Wieland, Joe (Rangers)	458
Triunfel, Carlos (Mariners)	424	Vitters, Josh (Cubs)	84	Wilhelmsen, Tom (Mariners)	428
Trout, Mike (Angels)	226	Vizcaino, Arodys (Braves)	37	Wilk, Adam (Tigers)	172
Trumbo, Mark (Angels)	229	Vogt, Stephen (Rays)	444	Wilkins, Andy (White Sox)	105
Turner, Jacob (Tigers)	162	Von Rosenberg, Zack (Pirates)	357	Williams, Everett (Padres)	395
				Williams, Mason (Yankees)	312
				Wilson, Alex (Red Sox)	73

U

Urbina, Juan (Mets)	294			Wilson, Justin (Pirates)	360
Urshela, Giovanny (Indians)	141			Wilson, Russell (Rockies)	153

W

		Walden, Jordan (Angels)	227	Wimmers, Alex (Twins)	277
		Waldrop, Kyle (Reds)	122	Wiswall, Mickey (Mariners)	429

V

		Walker, Taijuan (Mariners)	419	Witherspoon, Travis (Angels)	234
		Walter, Kevin (Phillies)	349	Withrow, Chris (Dodgers)	243
Valaika, Chris (Reds)	119	Walters, P.J. (Cardinals)	377	Wojciechowski, Asher (Blue Jays)	469
Valdespin, Jordany (Mets)	299	Walters, Zach (Diamondbacks)	28	Wolters, Tony (Indians)	133
Valdez, Jeudy (Padres)	396	Waring, Brandon (Orioles)	58	Workman, Brandon (Red Sox)	73
Valiquette, Philippe (Reds)	125	Warren, Adam (Yankees)	311	Worley, Vance (Phillies)	342
Valle, Sebastian (Phillies)	340	Washington, LeVon (Indians)	132		
Van Mil, Loek (Angels)	237	Wates, Austin (Astros)	197		
Vasquez, Danry (Tigers)	171	Watkins, Logan (Cubs)	90		

Y

Vasquez, Luis (Dodgers)	253	Watts, Dakota (Twins)	282		
Vaughn, Cory (Mets)	296	Weathers, Casey (Rockies)	151	Yambati, Robinson (Royals)	216
Velasquez, Vince (Astros)	198	Webster, Allen (Dodgers)	244	Yelich, Christian (Marlins)	179
Velazquez, Miguel (Rangers)	457	Weeks, Jemile (Athletics)	324	Ynoa, Michael (Athletics)	331
Venditte, Pat (Yankees)	317	Weglarz, Nick (Indians)	132	Younginer, Madison (Red Sox)	75
Ventura, Yordano (Royals)	214	Weiland, Kyle (Red Sox)	73		
Verdugo, Ryan (Giants)	411	Weinhardt, Robbie (Tigers)	166		

Z

Vettleson, Drew (Rays)	437	Wells, Ben (Cubs)	91		
Viciedo, Dayan (White Sox)	99	Wells, Casper (Tigers)	169	Zeid, Josh (Phillies)	347
		Welty, Ronnie (Orioles)	57		